MATHEMATICS

for Elementary Teachers

A Balanced Approach

Second Edition

MATHEMATICS

for Elementary Teachers
A Balanced Approach

Second Edition

Eugene F. Krause
University of Michigan

D. C. Heath and Company
Lexington, Massachusetts   Toronto

Address editorial correspondence to:
D. C. Heath
125 Spring Street
Lexington, MA 02173

Acquisitions Editor: Ann Marie Jones
Developmental Editor: Philip Charles Lanza
Production Editor: Ron Hampton
Designer: Kenneth Hollman
Production Coordinator: Lisa Merrill
Text Permissions Editor: Margaret Roll

Cover Photograph: Eric S. Fordham

Acknowledgments: Figure 1.2 Used by permission Silver Burdett Company—*Mathematics for Mastery* © 1981; Figure 2.59 reprinted from *Real Math,* Level 5, by Stephen S. Willoughby et al. by permission of Open Court Publishing Company; Figures 3.56 and 7.8 from *Mathematics Today*, Level 4 Orange, © 1985 by Harcourt Brace Jovanovich, Inc. Reprinted by permission of the publisher, Figure 3.56 photo courtesy of Halley Ganges; Figures 3.73, 3.75, 6.35, 8.1, and 9.1 *Mathematics,* Level (4, 5, 7), © 1987. Reprinted by permission of D. C. Heath. Figure 5.2 from *Mathematics Today,* Level 5 Purple, © 1985 by Harcourt Brace Jovanovich, Inc. Reprinted by permission of the publisher; Figure 8.2 R. Eicholz et al., *Addison-Wesley Mathematics,* Level 5, © 1985 Addison-Wesley Publishing Co. Inc.; Figure 16.3 reprinted with permission of Scribner Educational Publishers from *Harper & Row Mathematics,* Level 3, © 1985, Photo credit © Michal Heron 1983.

Published simultaneously in Canada.

Printed in the United States of America.

International Standard Book Number: 0-669-24882-7

Library of Congress Catalog Number: 90-83094

10   9   8   7   6   5   4   3   2   1

PREFACE

It is in response to the gratifying reception of *Mathematics for Elementary Teachers: A Balanced Approach* that this second edition of the text has been prepared. Revision was guided by (1) suggestions from users of the first edition, including comments received through a detailed survey conducted by the publisher; (2) extensive notes on student reactions kept by the author during three years of continuous teaching from the first edition; (3) several in-depth reviews; and (4) recommendations from the CUPM (Committee on the Undergraduate Program in Mathematics), the NCSM (National Council of Supervisors of Mathematics), and the NCTM (National Council of Teachers of Mathematics) Because the NCTM's 1989 publication *Curriculum and Evaluation Standards for School Mathematics* had a particularly strong influence on this second edition, a few things should be noted about these *Standards*.

The NCTM *Standards* for School Mathematics

The commission that produced the *Standards* was charged with (1) defining what it will mean to be mathematically literate in the 1990s and (2) writing standards that will serve as criteria for excellence along the path toward that mathematical literacy. The *Standards* that emerged will be to the 1990s what the NCTM's *Agenda for Action* was to the 1980s—a consensus on what school mathematics ought to become. Of course, every independently thinking math educator will find specific items with which to disagree, but the general thrust of the *Standards* represents a shared vision—as evidenced by endorsement of the *Standards* by a long list of educational, scientific, and mathematical organizations including the American Mathematical Association of Two-Year Colleges, the American Mathematical Society, the American Statistical Association, the Mathematical Association of America, and the Society for Industrial and Applied Mathematics.

The curriculum section of the *Standards* is split into three subsections by grade level: K–4, 5–8, and 9–12. The recommendations in the K–4 and 5–8 subsections are of greatest relevance for prospective elementary teachers; we have listed the 13 standards for each of these two grade levels in Appendix B.

As you will see in Appendix B, standards 1 through 4 are qualitatively different from standards 5 through 13. While standards 5–13 are reasonably concrete *content* recommendations (bearing titles like "whole number computation," "measurement," "fractions and decimals," etc.), standards 1–4 (labeled "problem solving," "communication," "reasoning," and "connections"—at all three grade levels) focus more on the *style* in which the mathematics is to be presented. Standards 1–4 envision a classroom in which students use a variety of strategies and draw on a wide range of techniques to solve nonroutine problems both pure and applied; in which students describe and discuss their methods; and in which ideas are critically analyzed and then accepted, discarded, revised, or elaborated.

Our Response to the *Standards*

If the "critical thinking" experiences called for in the *Standards* are good for children, then the opportunity for analogous experiences ought to be good for prospective teachers as well. The implications for a textbook for teachers would seem to include these: (1) the exposition in the book should be so clear and reliable that the instructor can assign reading and cut back on lecturing to free up class time for discussion; (2) there should be good thought-provoking problems in every section to serve as a basis and catalyst for investigation of important mathematical concepts. Users of the first edition of this book listed these two characteristics as its strongest features. We have striven to enhance both clarity of exposition and quality of problems in this second edition. We have also followed the recommendations of the *Standards* in increasing the emphasis on several topics, as described below.

New to the Second Edition

The following topics are given increased attention. Problem solving is strengthened with 60 percent more problems in Chapter 1, additional challenging problems in each of the other chapters, and more specific references to problem-solving strategies throughout the book. Estimation, approximation, and mental arithmetic receive extra attention in both the exposition and in dozens of exercise sets. Our goal here is to develop what is referred to in the *Standards* as an "estimation mindset"—to bring students to the point where they think of estimation as a natural part of any mathematical investigation. The number of applied problems is increased to emphasize the "connections" between mathematics and the real world. The topics of statistics and geometry receive more extensive treatment. More use is made of calculators.

The most noticeable content changes in the second edition are the following. A thorough new section on simple and compound interest has been added to Chapter 8 on decimals and real numbers. Chapter 9 is devoted entirely to probability. A considerable amount of new material in statistics has been included so that statistics now constitutes a chapter by itself. In this new Chapter 10 you will find more graphical displays, new problems with up-to-date real data, discussion of *z*-scores, and a new section on sampling. Coverage of geometry has been increased substantially with many more worked examples, a more concrete approach to transformations, additional constructions, and an extensive investigation of tessellations. There are now four, instead of three, chapters devoted completely to geometry (Chapters 11–14), and large portions of two other chapters (15 and 16) are also geometric in nature.

Changes from the first edition that are not apparent from a perusal of the Contents are these. There are many more figures (over 200 more), worked examples (55 more), and exercises (about 400 more). New exercises have been added to *every* exercise set, and the number of chapter review exercises (which now include challenging as well as routine questions) has been increased by nearly 60 percent. The new exercises were designed to increase the emphasis on problem solving, estimation and mental arithmetic, real-world applications, and the use of calculators. The flowchart symbols have been changed to conform to ANSI standards. More attention has been given to educational theory and terminology. In particular, reference is made to the *Standards* in every chapter to help students see the relevance of their college course to their future careers.

Content Summary

The global organization of content in this second edition is similar to what it was in the first edition. A listing of topics can be found in the Contents, and details about the philosophy, goals, and organization of each chapter can be found in the individual chapter introductions. Here is a brief summary.

Chapter 1 is an expanded introduction to problem solving that names and illustrates the most common strategies, thus providing a conceptual framework for problem solving in subsequent chapters. The strategies of Chapter 1 are revisited throughout the remainder of the text both in the exposition and in the exercise sets, every one of which contains at least one challenging, nonroutine problem.

Chapter 2 covers the fundamental concepts of set, function, and relation that underlie, organize, and unify subsequent work in number systems, probability and statistics, geometry and measurement, algebra, and computer programming.

Chapters 3–8 cover the number systems of school mathematics from whole numbers through reals. Along with the standard topics are some topics that are not always treated: estimation, permutations and combinations, algorithms and flow charts, ratio and proportion, percent and scientific notation, and compound interest. The topic of estimation, in particular, receives heavy emphasis. Specific named estimation strategies ("front end," "clustering," "rounding," "compatible numbers") are now described in the text. And two entire sections,

Section 10.5 "Sampling" (new in this edition) and Section 13.4 "Approximation and Error," can be thought of as topics in estimation. But the main emphasis on estimation (and its close relative, mental computation) remains in the exercise sets where students are asked to estimate in literally dozens of places, in contexts ranging from arithmetic through probability and statistics, to geometry and algebra.

Chapter 9 "Probability," and **Chapter 10** "Statistics," cover the standard basic concepts of these two closely related fields as well as such recently recommended topics as simulation, stem-and-leaf and box-and-whisker plots, and inference from a sample. The exposition is arranged so that the basic ideas of probability and statistics can be investigated without first having to master the technicalities of permutations and combinations.

Chapters 11–14 are devoted to geometry although geometric representations and references permeate earlier chapters. The content in Chapters 11–14 is organized around a few major concepts and is developed and amplified in an unusually large number of exercises and problems.

Chapter 15 provides a careful, thorough, and self-contained development of algebra and coordinate geometry. Simple algebraic ideas and skills, however, are refreshed and exercised, where appropriate, beginning in Chapter 1 and continuing throughout the text. Chapter 15 should be particularly valuable to prospective upper-elementary and middle-school teachers (who lay the foundation for future work in algebra) because of its emphasis on the underlying unifying concepts and on the use of algebra in problem solving. Students who need a review of the most basic ideas of algebra might profit from covering Section 15.1 at an earlier point in the course, perhaps between Chapters 3 and 4.

Chapter 16 gives an introduction to computer programming in both BASIC and Logo. This largely self-contained chapter could be covered at almost any point in the course, depending on the instructor's views on the position of programming in the curriculum for elementary teachers.

Appendix A on Logic also deserves comment. While all mathematics instructors want their students to learn to reason logically (see Curriculum Standard 3, "Reasoning," in Appendix B), there are many opinions on how to achieve that goal. Some instructors think it best to do a fairly thorough and pure unit on logic somewhere in the course, usually early. Others prefer to develop logical concepts gradually, in context, throughout the course, and perhaps summarize the topic at the end. I have tried to accommodate both groups. Appendix A on "Logic" can be inserted into the course at a number of different points. In the body of the text there is also ad hoc discussion of logical concepts as they arise. Instructors who cover Appendix A early may think of these ad hoc remarks as useful reinforcement. Those who prefer to introduce logic gradually can view Appendix A as an organized recapitulation and extension of the logical ideas appearing throughout the text.

Flexibility of Coverage

There is more than enough material for a full year's course. A two-semester arrangement might cover Chapters 1 to 7 or 8 in the first term, and Chapters 8 or 9 to 15 or 16 in the second term. A three-quarter arrangement might cover Chapters 1 to 6, 7 to 12, and 13 to 16. Certain sections have been marked with an asterisk (*) as optional, but, of course, what is optional is a matter of one's own tastes, priorities, and time constraints. The asterisk signifies only that omission of that particular section will not adversely impact the study of subsequent sections. The full 16 chapters, including optional sections, together with Appendix A provide sufficient material for a solid three-semester course.

Features in This Edition

The following special features have been included to make the text more valuable to prospective elementary school teachers.

1. **Reproductions of Pages from Elementary Textbooks.** These are useful for showing students connections between the theory in their college course and the practice in the elementary classroom.

2. **Computer Vignettes.** Each of these twelve strategically located vignettes consists of discussion, a program (written in either BASIC or Logo), and a run. They can be used in several ways. Students who have no access to a machine can look at the printouts and appreciate the kinds of things that can be done using a computer. Students who have access to a machine, but who have no particular expertise in programming, can simply type in the programs and run them (most are interactive). Students who already know how to program in BASIC or Logo can modify or extend the programs as suggested in the accompanying discussion.

3. **Chapter Review Exercises.** As noted earlier, the review exercise sets in this edition (which can be thought of as practice tests) have been lengthened by nearly 60 percent by the addition of new nonroutine as well as routine questions. (Answers to these Review Exercises are available only in the *Instructor's Guide*.)

4. **References.** The list of related references at the end of each chapter has been updated and expanded from the first edition.

5. **Historical Sketches.** The history of mathematics is, among other things, a melancholy record of discrimination against women. Imagine how much more might have been accomplished in the field of mathematics if women had been encouraged (or even allowed!) to contribute. These historical sketches concern five famous male mathematicians and five remarkable women who became mathematicians despite the obstacles. Future teachers

might find these stories useful for encouraging young women to consider careers in mathematics.

6. **Key Concepts.** In response to suggestions from users of the first edition, a checklist of key concepts has been included at each chapter end to help structure a student's review.

7. **Critical Thinking Problems.** In each section one problem has been designated with a chambered nautilus icon (🐚) to indicate that it is particularly well-suited to fostering the step-by-step, essentially limitless growth of students' problem-solving and thinking skills. These problems are intended to trigger the critical thinking and class discussion of concepts that reformers hope will characterize mathematics classrooms in the 1990s.

8. **Calculator Exercises.** The number of exercises for which a calculator is either helpful or essential has been increased in this edition. Such exercises are marked with a calculator symbol 🖩

9. **Challenging Problems.** The traditional five-point star (★) is used to indicate problems that are particularly challenging. Most sections include at least one of these.

Supplements to the Text

Six supplements are available.

Student Activities and Study Guide. For the student there is now a *Student Activities and Study Guide,* prepared by Professor DeAnn Huinker of the University of Wisconsin at Milwaukee, in collaboration with the author of the text. This new supplement provides an array of math lab and calculator activities, along with additional examples, exercises, and selected answers. It also features an annotated bibliography of computer software. Professor Huinker brought to the writing her experience as an elementary school teacher and, more recently, as the instructor of the mathematics methods course for elementary school teachers at the University of Michigan.

Instructor's Guide. For the professor there is an *Instructor's Guide,* written by the author, with complete solutions to all text exercises. This guide now contains two sample tests for each chapter, with answer keys.

D. C. Heath Exam Computerized Testing. A computerized testing program for the IBM-PC containing a test bank of over 500 questions, each keyed by section number and level of difficulty, is available to professors who want to construct customized tests. Items may be selected randomly by chapter, based on difficulty level, and the program is able to generate multiple scrambled versions of the same exam. The program also allows instructors to import their own test items into the test bank or to edit existing items. Answers and solutions are included.

Test Item File. This is a printed file of all the test items and solutions appearing in the computerized testing program.

D. C. Heath Class **Gradebook Software.** This new grading software provides a convenient grade management program for the IBM-PC. The program allows professors to track and assess student performance, or the relative performance of sections within a multisection course, and to print out grading reports designed to the individual instructor's specifications.

Elementary School Textbooks. As an additional resource, one set of current editions of grade levels K, 2, 4, 6 and 8 of D. C. Heath's elementary school textbook series are available, upon request, to institutions making class-size adoptions. Contact your local D. C. Heath sales representative to place your request.

Acknowledgments

Many people have influenced the final form of this book. I would like to thank the reviewers of both the first and second editions for their many suggestions and constructive criticisms. They are Mary K. Alter, University of Maryland; Peter Braunfeld, University of Illinois; Robert Butner, Ohio University; Calvin C. Clifton, Clark College; Helen Coulson, California State University—Northridge; Richard Crouse, University of Delaware; Carolyn Ehr, Fort Hays State University; Richard Enstad, University of Wisconsin—Whitewater; David L. Fitzgerald, Northeastern State University; Joseph Hohman, Pennsylvania State University; Herbert A. Hollister, Bowling Green State University; Ruth Horak, Tarleton State University; Gary Ivy, Texas A&M University; Patricia Ann Jenkins, South Carolina State University; Jerry L. Johnson, Western Washington University; Richard A. Little, Baldwin–Wallace College; Carole R. Maken, Huntington Beach Union High School District; John W. McGhee, California State University—Northridge; Joyce T. Myster, Morgan State University; Dennis Parker, University of the Pacific; Sister M. Geralda Schaefer, Pan American University; Michael Schiro, Boston College; Marie E. Sejersen, State University of New York—Oneonta; Robert Shaw, University of Connecticut; Dorothy Smith, University of New Orleans; Frank A. Smith, Kent State University; Joe K. Smith, Northern Kentucky University; William W. Smith, University of North Carolina; Keith Swanson, University of Wisconsin—La Crosse; C. Ralph Verno, West Chester University; Richard G. Vinson, University of South Alabama; John Wagner, Michigan State University; Derald Walling, Texas Tech University; Bruce E. White, Lander College; and Harry L. Wolff, University of Wisconsin—Oshkosh.

I would also like to acknowledge those individuals who graciously responded to a survey conducted by D. C. Heath that helped to shape this second edition. They are Ernest E. Allen, University of Southern Colorado; Mary K. Alter, University of Maryland; Tom Bassarear, Keene State College; Elton

Beougher, Fort Hays State University; Barbara L. Boe, University of Wisconsin—Whitewater; Phyllis Chinn, Humboldt State University; Forrest Coltharp, Pittsburg State University (Kansas); Maria Cossio, La Guardia Community College; Thomas Dunion, Atlantic Union College; Laura Dyer, Lincoln Land Community College; Thomas J. Fernsler, Wilson College; Beverly J. Ferrucci, Keene State College; Marjorie Fitting, San Jose State University; Cynthia Fleck, Wright State University; Barbara Garni, Mesabi Community College; Terry Goodman, Central Missouri State University; Elizabeth D. Gray, Southeastern Louisiana University; Jeffrey Habib, University of Toledo; Robert P. Hostetler, Pennsylvania State University/Behrend College; Paul M. Jones, Valley Forge Christian College; Glen A. Just, Mount St. Clare College; Susan Kidd, University of Wisconsin—Whitewater; Donald Larsen, Buena Vista College; Betty B. Long, Appalachian State University; Richard Marks, Sonoma State University; Ralph B. McBride, Manchester College; Donald W. Miller, University of Nebraska—Lincoln; Barbara Moses, Bowling Green State University; Virginia S. Muraski, Grand Valley State University; Charles Nicewonder, University of Toledo; Andrew C. Nickolakis, Long Island University; Martha Novak, Emporia State University; Judy E. Pate, Mississippi University for Women; Sarah E. Patrick, Troy State University—Dothan; Cloyd Payne, University of Toledo; Joan Pearson, Labette Community College; John P. Pommersheim, Bowling Green State University/Firelands College; Peter Rosnick, Westfield State College; Ayse A. Sahin, University of Maryland; Anne Sanford, Blue Mountain College; Mary Scherer, University of Redlands; Charles Shull, University of North Alabama; Jean S. Simutis, Alma College; B. L. Smith, University of Ozarks; James L. Smith, Muskingum College; Nikki Lee Starkey, University of Toledo; Marta Tucker, Monmouth College; Anna Jo Turner, Augusta College; Stanley Van Steenvoort, Northwestern Oklahoma State University; Richard G. Vinson, University of South Alabama; Fred W. Warnke, Texas Southmost College; Joseph Wissmann, University of Maryland; John L. Wisthoff, Anne Arundel Community College; Harold D. Yotter, Dr. Martin Luther College; and Albert W. Zechmann, University of Nebraska—Lincoln.

Finally, I would like to express my gratitude to Ann Marie Jones, the Acquisitions Editor at D. C. Heath, for her encouragement and confidence over the last five years, and to Philip C. Lanza, the Developmental Editor at D. C. Heath, for his substantial contributions to the second edition.

Eugene F. Krause

To the Student

Congratulations on your choice of teaching as your future profession! You will occupy a position of fundamental importance in the lives of students who pass through your class. In your classroom you will be the mathematician-in-residence. Your students' future success in mathematics will depend to a large degree on your competence, confidence, and enthusiasm. Competence, of course, is the key element. Without it there can be neither confidence nor a genuine enthusiasm for the subject.

Mathematical competence, as you probably know, is not what it used to be. The elementary school mathematics curriculum is undergoing fundamental change in response to the ubiquitous presence of calculators and computers and to the increasing mathematical demands that a technological society is placing on its citizens. The central focus of elementary mathematics will no longer be on mechanical, symbol-manipulation skills such as paper-and-pencil procedures for adding, subtracting, multiplying, and dividing. Rather the emphasis will be on applying mathematics to solve nonroutine problems, understanding the mathematical concepts that underlie the symbols, and communicating and evaluating mathematical ideas in a group setting. Perhaps the most influential blueprint for the mathematics curriculum of the 1990s, the NCTM *Standards for Curriculum and Evaluation,* calls for a "conceptually oriented" K–4 curriculum and a "broad, concept-driven" 5–8 curriculum. The teacher who stands at the center of this conceptual curriculum will need a perspective and depth of understanding that does not develop automatically during the successful completion of her or his high school mathematics courses. That teacher will need to have surveyed, purposefully and thoughtfully, the entire breadth of elementary mathematics and to have identified and mastered its fundamental concepts.

This book was written with that conceptual goal in mind. That does not mean it is a difficult or abstract text or that it is unrelated to classroom practice. Quite the opposite. It is possible to explain important mathematical ideas in simple language and to illustrate key concepts with concrete examples, many of which could even be used in an elementary classroom. There is little necessity for formal deduction. I hope that you will find the exposition clear, the problems interesting, and your mathematical power increasing.

CONTENTS

*Optional section

4 THE WHOLE NUMBERS: A FORMAL APPROACH 191

5 NUMBER THEORY 245

6 THE INTEGERS 285

7   THE RATIONAL NUMBERS: FRACTIONS   333

8   DECIMALS AND REAL NUMBERS   413

9   PROBABILITY   471

16   COMPUTER PROGRAMMING   827

APPENDIX A: LOGIC   A1

APPENDIX B: STANDARDS   A23

ANSWERS TO SELECTED EXERCISES   A31

INDEX   A57

1

PROBLEM SOLVING

In 1980 the National Council of Teachers of Mathematics (NCTM) published *An Agenda for Action,* a list of recommendations for school mathematics in the ensuing decade. First on the list was this: "Problem solving must be the focus of school mathematics in the 1980s." In 1989 the NCTM followed up the *Agenda* with what promises to be an even more influential publication, *Curriculum and Evaluation Standards for School Mathematics.* In the introduction to the *Standards* we find reaffirmation of the importance attached to problem solving: "We strongly endorse the first recommendation of *An Agenda for Action.* . . ." And in the body of the *Standards* we find "problem solving" listed as the first standard *at all three grade levels:* K–4, 5–8, and 9–12.

As an elementary school teacher in the next decade, you can expect to find, in your textbooks, an increasing emphasis on the creative use of mathematics in nonroutine situations. To train children to carry out routine calculations will not be enough; you will be asked to help them develop their analytic abilities as well. This is a tall order, but an exciting and challenging one. We are all being galvanized to aim for the highest and most satisfying goal a teacher can have: to get students to *think.*

The spiritual father of today's problem-solving movement is undoubtedly George Polya (1887–1985), an outstanding mathematician and teacher whose pioneering book *How to Solve It* (1945) and subsequent writings laid the foundation for much of what is being advocated now. Polya credits René Descartes (1596–1650) and Gottfried Leibniz (1646–1716) with shaping his views, and of course no chronology of the teachers of problem solving could omit Socrates (469–399 B.C.). To paraphrase Isaac Newton (1642–1727), we all stand on the shoulders of giants.

Up until a few years ago, though, Polya's crusade was a rather lonely one. Problem solving tended to be viewed as frosting on the cake rather than the *focus* of instruction. The textbooks you studied from in school undoubtedly included intermittent nonstandard problems that might have been called "brain teasers," "challenge problems," or "extras for experts." Such problems were usually set off from the more routine exercises, and the implication was plain that no harm would be done if they were ignored. Students who were interested could puzzle over them, but no explicit instruction was given on how to attack such problems. The underlying, rather pessimistic, assumption was that problem solving was more an art than a science, and that the ability to solve problems would develop spontaneously in a gifted few as they struggled with more and more problems.

Now a more optimistic point of view is being espoused. There are specific techniques or strategies of problem solving (called "heuristics" by Polya) that can be isolated, taught, and learned. Many students, who would not have discovered the techniques on their own, can become problem solvers. The goal is to improve everyone's problem-solving ability, and the means to this end is to give students explicit instruction in the most common strategies. In the K–4 *Standards* we find endorsement of this program: "A major goal of problem-solving instruction is to enable children to develop and apply strategies. . . ." And again in the 5–8 *Standards:* "Instruction should . . . help students develop their ability to understand and apply a variety of strategies. . . ."

 **1.1** *Some Strategies*

Various individuals and groups have compiled lists of problem-solving strategies. The lists differ in length and detail, but they do seem to share a common core. If we could teach that common core of techniques, we could, perhaps, create more and better problem solvers. To be specific, Figure 1.1 gives one example of such a list from the Ohio Department of Education.

Even if everyone were to agree that this is *the* list, we would not drill on all sixteen strategies here. Instead, we will illustrate their use in a few examples. In future chapters, as we progress through the content of elementary school mathematics, you will have many opportunities to exercise the heuristics. At

> 1. Look for a pattern.
> 2. Construct a table.
> 3. Account for all possibilities.
> 4. Act it out.
> 5. Make a model.
> 6. Guess and check.
> 7. Work backwards.
> 8. Make a drawing, figure, or graph.
> 9. Select appropriate notation.
> 10. Restate the problem in your own words.
> 11. Identify wanted, given, and needed information.
> 12. Write an open sentence.
> 13. Identify a subgoal.
> 14. Solve a simpler (or similar) problem.
> 15. Change your point of view.
> 16. Check for hidden assumptions.

Figure 1.1 Sixteen problem-solving strategies.

first you might want to use the list as a source of ideas for getting started on a problem. Later on you might want to add your own successful strategies to it. It is particularly valuable for teachers to be introspective. After you have solved a problem think back about how you approached it, how you got a grip on it, and how you finished it off. Would your methods be comprehensible to children? How might you amend them to make them simpler or clearer?

Before we look at the problems, we give one disclaimer: Not all of these problems are suitable for young children; they are meant for *you*. To learn something about problem solving, it is necessary to solve some problems; and what might be a nice problem for a youngster could easily be a routine exercise for you. In Polya's words, "No teacher can impart to his students the spirit of discovery if he has not got it himself."

PROBLEM 1

Out in a pasture are lambs and ducks. A hawk flying over counts 80 heads. A field mouse in the grass counts 246 feet. How many lambs are there?

Solution

Begin with a straightforward **guess-and-check strategy.** *First guess:* No lambs, all (80) ducks. *Check:* That accounts for only 160 feet—not enough. We need more lambs. *Second guess:* All (80) lambs, no ducks. *Check:* That gives 320 feet—too many. We need fewer lambs. *Third guess:* 40 lambs and 40 ducks. *Check:* That yields 240 feet—not quite enough. *Fourth guess:* 45 lambs and 35 ducks. *Check:* That gives 250 feet—a few too many. *Fifth guess:* 43 lambs and 37 ducks. *Check:* That yields 246 feet—exactly right. *Answer:* 43 lambs.

If we **construct a table** (Table 1.1) and enter the target number 246 in it right away, the guesses become educated guesses and the procedure takes on the character of systematic *successive approximation.* ❏

Table 1.1

	Lambs	Ducks	Feet	
Guess 1	0	80	$4 \cdot 0 + 2 \cdot 80 = 160$	
Guess 3	40	40	$4 \cdot 40 + 2 \cdot 40 = 240$	
Guess 5	43	37	$4 \cdot 43 + 2 \cdot 37 = 246$	(target)
Guess 4	45	35	$4 \cdot 45 + 2 \cdot 35 = 250$	
Guess 2	80	0	$4 \cdot 80 + 2 \cdot 0 \ = 320$	

Satchel Paige, who at age 44 became the first black pitcher in the American League, said to never look back ("something might be gaining on you"); George Polya's advice is just the opposite. He said we should *always look back* at a solution to a problem; maybe it can be improved. Reconsider our guess 3. It yields 240 feet and we want 246. Thus we need 6 more feet. We reason that by trading in a duck for a lamb, we gain 2 feet; so trading in 3 ducks for 3 lambs will give us the 6 feet we need. Thus we can jump directly from guess 3 to the answer. But maybe we can get there in even fewer steps.

After guess 1 we find ourselves 86 feet short. Thus we should trade in 43 ducks for lambs. Done in two steps.

***

PROBLEM 2   What is the units digit of 7^{399}?

Solution   The strategies we use now are to **solve simpler problems** and **look for a pattern.** What makes the original problem difficult is the large power of 7, so we begin by looking at lower powers of 7.

Units digit of 7^1	$= 7$
Units digit of 7^2 = units digit of 49	$= 9$
Units digit of 7^3 = units digit of 49×7 = units digit of 343	$= 3$
Units digit of 7^4 = units digit of 343×7 = units digit of 2401	$= 1$

By this time the numbers are getting large, and we have the uneasy feeling that unless we find some shortcut, we will soon get bogged down. To find the units digit of 7^5, we don't have to compute 2401×7 exactly. We can simply observe that it is some number of the form ****7, and thus its units digit is 7. To find the units digit of 7^6, we think of multiplying $7^5 = $ ****7 by 7 to get another unspecified number, this time ending in 9. We use this important problem-solving technique (not on the Ohio list) of **ignoring irrelevancies** to construct Table 1.2.

Table 1.2

Power of 7	Units Digit
7^1	7
7^2	9
7^3	3
7^4	1
7^5	7
7^6	9
7^7	3
7^8	1
7^9	7
7^{10}	9
$\vdots$	$\vdots$

The pattern of units digits almost jumps out at us. We keep getting 7–9–3–1 over and over again. The only question that remains is: Which of 7, 9, 3, and 1 is the 399th number on the list? An easier question is: Which is the 400th? The answer is 1, since 1s occupy the 4th, 8th, 12th, . . . positions. And of course, if there is a 1 in the 400th position, then there must be a 3 in the 399th. *Answer:* 3.   ❏

problem solving Patterns

tell
show
solve
check

The dashed lines in this figure are diagonals. How many diagonals can be drawn in a 12-sided polygon?

Sometimes it is helpful to show and solve easier problems first.

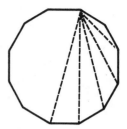

How many diagonals can be drawn in a square?

show   **solve**   Two diagonals can be drawn.

How many diagonals can be drawn in a 5-sided polygon?

show   **solve**   Five diagonals can be drawn.

SKILL CHECK

Find how many diagonals can be drawn in a 6-sided polygon.

EXERCISES

1. How many diagonals can be drawn in figure A? In figure B?

A   B

2. Copy and complete the table below. Use drawings if you need to.

sides	4	5	6	7	8	9	10	11
diagonals	2	5	?	?	?	?	?	?

3. How many diagonals can be drawn in a 12-sided polygon?

276

Figure 1.2 Problem solving in a fifth-grade textbook.

Figure 1.2 shows how the strategies of solving simpler problems, constructing a table, and looking for a pattern are illustrated in a fifth-grade textbook.

PROBLEM 3   We will call a triangle an "integral triangle" if all three of its sides have integral length in centimeters (i.e., 1 cm, 2 cm, etc.). How many different integral triangles are there whose longest side is 5 cm long?

Solution   A natural way to begin investigating this problem is to **make a drawing,** as in Figure 1.3, of one such triangle. A glance at the drawing reminds us of a geometric fact that will be important in our solution: the sum of the lengths of (any) two sides of a triangle must exceed the length of the third side. (You might have memorized this fact in words like these: "The shortest path between two points is the straight-line path.")

Now back to the enumeration problem. We will surely want our list of triangles to include the one in Figure 1.3:

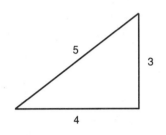

Figure 1.3

Long side 5, Medium side 4, Short side 3

Another one for the list will be

Long side 5, "Medium" side 4, "Short" side 4

Rather than continue this piecemeal list, we replace the clumsy descriptions above with more **appropriate notation,** namely 543 and 544. This economical symbolism suggests how we could set about making a **systematic list,** one that will **account for all possibilities** and include no duplications.

A reasonable organizing principle for making such a list is to always give the side lengths in decreasing (or at least nonincreasing) order. Thus the one triangle with sides of length 5, 4, and 3 will appear on the list just one time, as 543, rather than six times (as 543 and 534, and 453 and 435, and 354 and 345). Another sensible organizing principle is to exhaust all triangles with medium side 5 before moving on to triangles with medium side 4 and then 3. Thus our systematic list is

555	554	553	552	551
544	543	542	(Why not 541?)	
533	(Why not 532?)			

And the answer to the original question is that there are nine integral triangles with longest side 5 cm.   ❑

PROBLEM 4   A boatman is to transport a fox, a goose, and a sack of corn across a river. There is only room in his boat for one of the three at a time. Furthermore, if the fox and the goose are left alone together, the fox will eat the goose. And if the goose and the corn are left alone together, the goose will eat the corn. How can the boatman do the job?

Solution

For this problem one could **make a model** and **act it out,** a particularly appropriate approach for youngsters. Let a penny stand for the goose, a nickel for the fox, and a dime for the sack of corn. Line up the three coins at the north end of a table and try to slide them to the south end, subject to the two rules: (1) Only one coin can be moved at a time; (2) a copper coin and a silver coin can never be allowed to be alone together at either end of the table.

If you try playing this game, it won't be long before you solve the problem. Then you will probably find yourself in agreement with a precept of another famous problem solver, legendary football coach and winner of 323 college games, Bear Bryant: "Avoid losing before you worry about winning." Here is a solution:

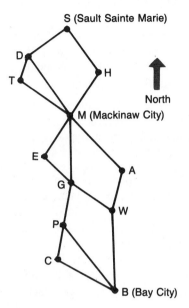

Trip south: To avoid losing, take the goose.

Trip north: To avoid going around in circles, come back empty.

Trip south: To avoid going around in circles, take something, say the corn.

Trip north: To avoid losing, you can't come back empty; and to avoid going in circles, you can't take the corn back; so take the goose back.

Trip south: To avoid losing, you can't travel empty; and to avoid going in circles, you can't take the goose; so take the fox.

Trip north: Come back empty.

Trip south: Take the goose. ❑

Figure 1.4

PROBLEM 5

The map in Figure 1.4 shows towns and highways between Bay City (B) and Sault Sainte Marie (S), Michigan. How many different routes are possible from B to S?

Solution

The first thing we need to do is **look for hidden assumptions,** for without some further conditions the question is meaningless. If, for example, routes like BWAWAWAMHS were allowed, then there would be infinitely many routes. So we disallow any route that has a leg with a southerly component. With this assumption made explicit, we have an unambiguous question and can seek an answer. Since random tracing of (permissible) routes from B to S could easily result in our missing a route or counting the same route twice, a systematic way of counting is called for.

One of the towns in Figure 1.4 stands out as special: M (Mackinaw City at the bridge). Every route from B to S must pass through M. This suggests a strategy. Think of driving from B to M in the morning, stopping for lunch, and then continuing to S in the afternoon. Clearly, there are just three afternoon routes: MTDS, MDS, MHS. And each of these three afternoon routes can be tacked onto any morning route from B to M to yield a complete route from B to S. Thus we need only figure out how many morning routes there are from B to M and then multiply by three. So we have reduced the original problem to a simpler one. In the language of the Ohio list we have **worked backwards** to **identify a subgoal.**

The subgoal of counting the morning routes from B to M can be broken down in much the same way as the original problem. First, we set aside the one morning route that passes through A. Now all of the other morning routes pass through G. There are 3 routes from B to G (before breakfast) and 2 from G to M (after breakfast), so there are 6 routes from B to M through G. Thus there are 7 morning routes in all, and $3 \cdot 7 = 21$ all-day routes. We shall expand on this connection between counting and multiplication when we investigate the *choice principle* in Chapter 3.   ❏

PROBLEM 6   The hexagon in Figure 1.5 is made of six matchsticks. By moving two and adding one, can you form two diamonds (rhombi)?

Solution   Problems of this sort seem tailor-made for the heuristic of **acting it out.** But if the first few random attempts fail, often a good idea is to sit back, **change your point of view,** and work backwards. One might reason as follows: A diamond has four sides. We have only seven matches available. Therefore, if it is possible to make two diamonds, they must share a common side. There are essentially only two ways they could do so, as shown in Figure 1.6. Transforming the hexagon of Figure 1.5 (and an extra match) into the second arrangement in Figure 1.6 is now easy. (The first arrangement requires more than the allotted number of moves.)   ❏

Figure 1.5

Figure 1.6

We have given just one solution for each problem so far. That should *not* suggest that there is only one way of doing things. Usually, quite the opposite is true. Different people look at a given problem from very different perspectives and levels of mathematical sophistication. One of the pleasures of teaching is seeing the variety of thought patterns in a class of students. We will give three quite different solutions to each of the next two problems.

PROBLEM 7   Find the sum of the first 100 odd numbers.

Solution 1   Solve simpler problems, construct a table, and look for a pattern.

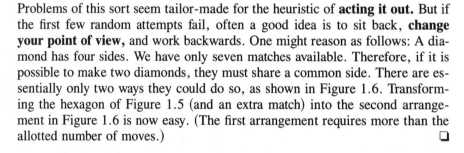

	n	Sum of First n Odd Numbers
1	1	1
$1 + 3 = 4$	2	$4 = 2^2$
$1 + 3 + 5 = 9$	3	$9 = 3^2$
$1 + 3 + 5 + 7 = 16$	4	$16 = 4^2$
	⋮	⋮
	100	$10{,}000 = 100^2$

Solution 2

$1 \rightarrow$ · · · ·

$3 \rightarrow$ · · · ·

$5 \rightarrow$ · · · ·

$7 \rightarrow$ · · · ·

Figure 1.7

Make a drawing. As is shown in Figure 1.7, $1 + 3 =$ the number of dots in a 2×2 square array (4), $1 + 3 + 5 =$ the number of dots in a 3×3 square array (9), and $1 + 3 + 5 + 7 + \cdots + 199 =$ the number of dots in a 100×100 square array, that is, $100 \times 100 = 10,000$.

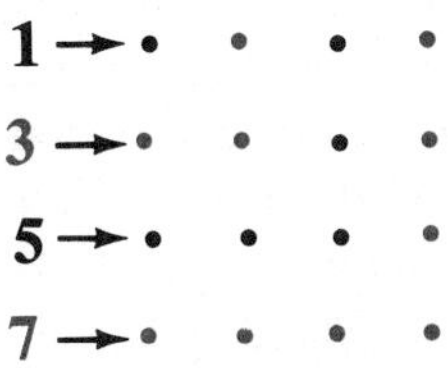

Solution 3

This method is attributed to Gauss. Write the desired sum *twice*, once in ascending and once in descending order:

$$
\begin{array}{lcccccccc}
 & 1 + & 3 + & 5 + \cdots + & 195 + & 197 + & 199 & \text{(100 terms)} \\
\text{Add} & 199 + & 197 + & 195 + \cdots + & 5 + & 3 + & 1 & \text{(100 terms)} \\
\hline
 & 200 + & 200 + & 200 + \cdots + & 200 + & 200 + & 200 & \text{(100 terms)}
\end{array}
$$

Thus the sum we seek is

$$\tfrac{1}{2}(100 \cdot 200) = 100 \cdot \tfrac{1}{2} \cdot 200 = 100 \cdot 100 = 10,000 \qquad \square$$

PROBLEM 8

In a group of 60 children there are two-thirds as many boys as girls. How many boys are there?

Solution 1

Guess and check. *First guess:* 20 boys; then 30 girls. But that makes only 50 children. *Guess again* (higher): 30 boys; then 45 girls. That makes 75 children. *Guess again* (lower). And so on.

Solution 2

Select appropriate notation and **write an open sentence.** Keeping track, as in Table 1.3, of the guesses of Solution 1 suggests this second solution. Let b stand for the number of boys.

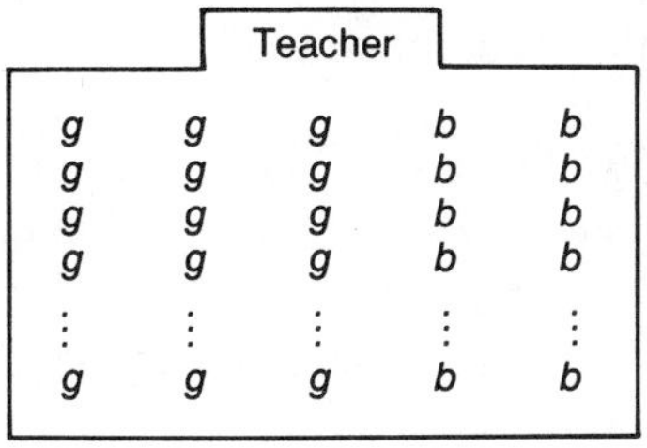

Teacher
g g g b b
g g g b b
g g g b b
g g g b b
⋮ ⋮ ⋮ ⋮ ⋮
g g g b b

Figure 1.8

Table 1.3

	Boys	Girls	Children
Guess 1	20	30	50
	b	$\frac{3}{2}b$	60 (goal)
Guess 2	30	45	75

From the table we see that the open sentence (an equation) to be solved is

$$b + \tfrac{3}{2}b = 60$$

That is, $\tfrac{5}{2}b = 60$, or $b = \tfrac{2}{5} \cdot 60 = 24$.

Solution 3

Restate the problem in your own words and make a drawing. Restating the comparison condition in the problem like this, "There are two boys for every three girls," gets rid of the fraction and calls to mind a picture of the class arranged as in Figure 1.8. Each row has 2 boys and 3 girls, the correct ratio.

Since there are 60 children in all and 5 in each row, there must be 12 rows. Twelve rows with 2 boys in each implies that there are 24 boys. ❏

The next problem is representative of a very popular genre of puzzles that you are sure to encounter in elementary school textbooks of the 1990s.

PROBLEM 9 Make 100 using each of the numbers 1, 2, 3, 4, 5, 6, 7 exactly once, and using only parentheses and the four basic arithmetic operations.

Solution A natural approach to this problem is to work backwards and establish subgoals. The large target number 100 can be broken down into smaller numbers in a variety of ways, one being $100 = 10 \times 10$, so our two subgoals are to make two 10s using the numbers 1 through 7. An easy way to make one of the 10s is $10 = 4 + 6$. Thus we have reduced the original problem to this simpler one: make 10 from 1, 2, 3, 5, 7. Since the sum $5 + 7$ overshoots the target 10 by 2, it will suffice to make 2 out of the remaining numbers 1, 2, and 3. One way to do that uses division, $2 = (1 + 3) \div 2$. We can summarize our solution schematically as follows:

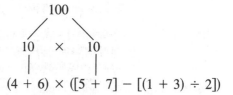

Of course there are many other solutions to this problem. ❏

In his analysis of the problem-solving process, Polya identified four stages. We have touched on them implicitly in the examples of this section. We list them explicitly now, because many people find **Polya's four-step process** to be a useful guide to refer to when presented with a nonroutine task.

1. *Understand the problem*. For example, when we looked for hidden assumptions in Problem 5 we were trying to understand exactly what was being asked.
2. *Devise a plan*. This is the heart of the process. This is where you choose a strategy or strategies appropriate to the situation.
3. *Carry out the plan*. This stage consists of doing the detail work associated with the master plan. For example, in Problem 2 the calculation of units digits to enter in the table was part of carrying out the plan.
4. *Look back*. In some situations this phase consists of testing one's proposed solution against the original problem to see if it makes sense. In other situations it can mean looking for an improvement in one's methods or for a generalization of the original problem.

The next example shows, in detail, how one might follow Polya's four steps.

PROBLEM 10   Figure 1.9 is a part of a city street map showing Molly's apartment M and the school S where she teaches. Molly always drives to work. Can she follow a different route to school every day for four weeks?

Solution   1. *Understand the problem.* If the problem is to have a solution, certain assumptions must be made. It is reasonable to assume that all the streets in Figure 1.9 are two-way streets and that Molly never goes out of her way by driving south or west. Further, we assume that Molly works a five-day week so that the question is really whether there are at least 20 different routes from M to S.

2. *Devise a plan.* Our plan will be to make a systematic list of all possible routes, and then count them. To simplify the process of listing we will denote each route by a string of 5 N's and 2 E's, where an N represents driving one block north and an E represents driving one block east.

3. *Carry out the plan.* A natural organizing principle for a list of "words" is to list them in alphabetical order. Here is the complete list (in columns):

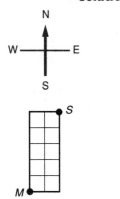

Figure 1.9

EENNNNN NEENNNN NNEENNN NNNEENN NNNNEEN NNNNNEE
ENENNNN NENENNN NNENENN NNNENEN NNNNENE
ENNENNN NENNENN NNENNEN NNNENNE
ENNNENN NENNNEN NNENNNE
ENNNNEN NENNNNE
ENNNNNE

There are 21 routes, so the answer to the original question is yes, she can drive a different route to work every day for four (work) weeks.

4. *Look back.* Our list of "words" exhibits an interesting pattern. There are 6 words that begin with an E, 5 in which the first E occurs as the second letter, 4 in which the first E occurs as the third letter, and so on down to 1. Had we noticed this pattern, we could have saved some time and calculated the sum, $6 + 5 + 4 + 3 + 2 + 1 = 21$, without completing the list of actual routes. The pattern of summing the numbers from 6 down to 1 also suggests extensions and generalizations. If Molly lived 10 blocks south (and 2 blocks west) of her school, she would have $9 + 8 + \cdots + 2$ routes available.

As an extension of this problem, we could pose more general q For example, we might ask: What if Molly lived n blocks s blocks west of her school? What if she lived 3 blocks west r What if she lived n blocks south and m blocks west? What skyscraper of the future and her place of employment building, but 2 hallways east, 5 hallways north, and 3

EXERCISE SET 1.1

1. The word *problem* was not defined.
   (a) What distinction would you make between a problem and a routine exercise?
   (b) Is finding 27 + 46 a problem for you? Would it be a problem for a kindergartner?
   (c) Is solving the equation $x^2 - 3x = 4$ a problem for you?

2. Here is an algebraic solution to Problem 1 (p. 3). Reconsider Table 1.1. If we put an "unknown" number x in the Lambs column, what expression has to go in the Ducks column? Then what expression goes in the Feet column? If we require that the number of feet be 246, what equation has to be solved?

3. This exercise is similar to Problem 2 (p. 4). What is the units digit of 8^{238}?

4. Ask and answer another question like the one in Exercise 3.

5. This exercise is similar to Problem 3 (p. 6). How many integral triangles are there whose longest side is 6 cm long?

6. How many integral triangles are there whose longest side is *at most* 5 cm long?

7. Figure 1.10 shows the first three steps of the solution to Problem 4 (p. 6) in an appropriate mathematical notation. Show that you understand the notation by completing the solution.

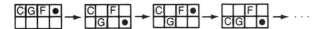

Figure 1.10

8. This exercise is similar to Problem 4 (p. 6). A 175-lb man, his 105-lb wife, and their 70-lb son want to cross a river in a boat, but the boat can hold, at most, 175 lb. Can they do it?

We solved Problem 5 (p. 7) by identifying **special elements** (M and G) and concentrating on

them. Look for special elements as you try to solve this puzzle. Insert the numbers 1 through 8 into the eight squares in Figure 1.11 in such a way that no two consecutive numbers occupy two squares having a common edge (side) or vertex (corner).

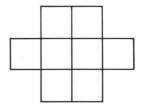

Figure 1.11

10. In Figure 1.12 how many routes are there from A to J? (Rule out any routes that have a leg with a westerly component.)

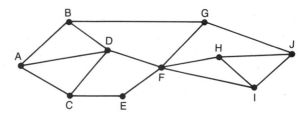

Figure 1.12

11. This exercise is similar to Problem 6 (p. 8). Move two matchsticks in Figure 1.13 so that four squares are formed. Each matchstick must be the side of some square.

Figure 1.13

12. Using six matchsticks, make four equilateral triangles, with each side being a matchstick.

13. Reconsider the three solutions to Problem 7 (p. 8). Which do you find most convincing? Which strikes you as most elegant? Which do you think would be most comprehensible to an elementary school child?

14. Find the sum of the first 100 (positive) even numbers.

15. Answer the questions of Exercise 13, but this time consider Problem 8 (p. 9).

16. There are three-fifths as many boys as girls and 12 more girls than boys. How many children in all?

17. A pile of dimes and quarters is worth $4.95. There are twice as many dimes as quarters. How many quarters?

18. Find another solution to Problem 9 (p. 10); this time begin with the factorization, $100 = 5 \times 20$.

Exercises 19–23 are all taken from NCTM problem-a-day calendars from 1985–1987. In Exercises 19–22 use the same ground rules as in Problem 9 (p. 10).

19. Make 16 using six 5s.

20. Make 3 using 2, 9, 10, and 11.

21. Make 30 using six 3s.

22. Make 7 using nine 7s.

23. Using exponentiation along with any of the basic arithmetic operations, make 1000 using 2, 3, 4, and 5.

In Exercises 24–30, look for a pattern, and supply a plausible next term for each sequence. (In Chapter 5 we will describe a formal procedure for extending certain types of sequences. There is, however, no method that applies universally.)

24. 3, 7, 11, 15, 19, _____

25. 3, 6, 12, 24, _____

26. 1, 1, 2, 3, 5, 8, 13, 21, _____

27. 1, 1, 1, 3, 5, 9, 17, 31, _____

28. 2, 3, 6, 18, 108, _____

29. $\frac{1}{5}, \frac{1}{3}, \frac{3}{7}, \frac{1}{2}, \frac{5}{9}, \frac{3}{5},$ _____

30. 2, 6, 30, 260, _____

In Exercises 31–33, use the strategies of solving simpler problems and looking for a pattern. Challenging problems are marked with a star (★).

31. How many diagonals has a convex (no indents) 15-sided polygon?

32. What is the 88th digit of the decimal for $\frac{1}{27}$?

★ 33. If today is Friday, what day of the week will it be 10^{100} days from now?

In Exercises 34–36, use the guess-and-check strategy.

34. Jane did 633 sit-ups in five days. Each day she did $1\frac{1}{2}$ times as many as the previous day. How many did she do on the first day?

35. If the digit 8 is appended to the standard numeral for a whole number, the new number represented is 8000 greater than the original number. Find the original number.

36. Every member of the legislature is on one three-person committee, one four-person committee, and one six-person committee. If there are 63 committees, how many legislators are there?

In Exercises 37–39, account for all possibilities by making a systematic list.

37. How many squares are there on a standard 8 × 8 checkerboard?

38. How many equilateral triangles are there in the design in Figure 1.14?

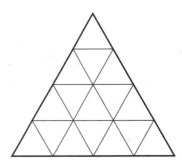

Figure 1.14

39. In how many ways can you brick a 2 × 5 wall using 1 × 2 bricks? One way is shown in Figure 1.15.

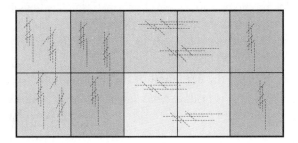

Figure 1.15

For the rest of the exercises you are on your own in choosing strategies.

40. There are 50 guests at a party. Everyone shakes hands (once) with everyone else. How many handshakes?

41. What is the maximum number of crossing points one can make by drawing 10 straight lines on a sheet of paper?

42. Put the numbers 1 through 9 in the boxes in Figure 1.16 so that every row, every column, and both diagonals have the same sum. *Hint:* What is that sum?

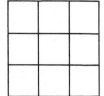

Figure 1.16

43. Write the digits 1 through 9 in order and try to insert plus signs so that the resulting sum is 99. Here, for example, is an unsuccessful attempt:
$$1 + 23 + 4 + 56 + 7 + 8 + 9 = 108$$

44. Repeat Exercise 43 with the target sum 234.

45. The standard bracketing for a 4-team single-elimination tournament with teams seeded #1 through #4 is shown in Figure 1.17. The stan-

dard bracketing for an 8-team tournament with eight seeded teams is shown in Figure 1.18. Look for a pattern and then make the standard bracketing for a 16-team tournament.

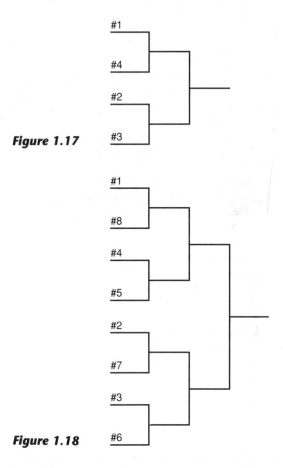

Figure 1.17

Figure 1.18

46. One thousand players are entered in a single-elimination tennis tournament (one loss and you're out). After the first round 500 survive; after the second 250 survive; then 125; then 63 (someone gets a bye); and so on. How many matches (not rounds) are played before the champion is determined?

47. A traveler wishes to stay at an inn for a week. He has no money, but he has a gold chain of seven links, and the innkeeper agrees to accept one link for each day's lodging. Each day the innkeeper

must be paid. Show that the traveler can cut only one link of his chain and still pay his daily bills.

48. Show how a traveler with a 23-link chain could pay his bill each day for 23 days by cutting just two links.

49. If it takes a clock 30 seconds to chime "six," how long does it take to chime "twelve"?

50. *The Tower of Hanoi:* In 1881 a French mathematician, E. Lucas, posed a problem that has become a classic. According to Lucas's fable, at the dawn of creation God placed 64 rings on spindle A as shown in Figure 1.19. Priests were given the task of transferring the 64 rings to spindle C, subject to the following rules:
    (i) Only one ring can be moved at a time.
    (ii) The ring being moved has to be placed on one of the other two spindles.
    (iii) A ring can never be placed on top of a smaller ring.

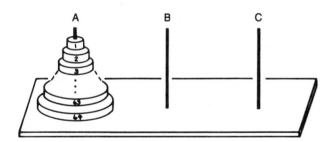

Figure 1.19

When all the rings are on spindle C, the world will end. How many moves will it take to effect the transfer?

51. Three people play a game with the understanding that the loser is to double the money of each of the other two. After three games each has lost just once and each ends up with $24. With how much money did each one start?

52. How many different hollow rectangles can you build using 100 square tiles? The two shown in Figure 1.20 are not considered to be different since they will look exactly alike if one is tipped on its side.

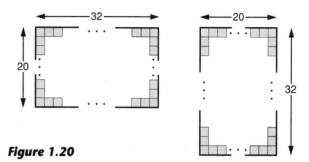

Figure 1.20

53. Show that no matter how you arrange the numbers 1 through 10 in a circle, some three adjacent numbers will have a sum greater than 16.

54. You have a glass of water and a glass of root beer. You transfer a tablespoon of the root beer into the glass of water and then a tablespoon of that mixture back into the root beer. Is there more root beer in the water or more water in the root beer?

55. Three-fifths of the class favors Jackson; the rest favor Walker. Jackson can lose three supporters to Walker and still have the majority, but if four Jackson supporters switch to Walker, then Walker supporters will become the majority. How many students are in the class?

56. The sum of the ages (whole numbers) of Mrs. Smith's four children is nine. How many possibilities are there for the ages of the children? One possibility is: a 5-year old, a 0-year old, and two 2-year olds.

57. Figure 1.21 shows a freeway and six entrance/exit points *A–F* with their corresponding mile markers. The state tourist commission wants to locate an information booth at point *P* so that the sum of the six distances from *P* to each of *A–F* is as small as possible. At which mile marker(s) should *P* be located?

Figure 1.21　　　　Mile 85

58. Statistics show that in Gotham City there are seven high-crime locations, given by points *A–G* on the road map in Figure 1.22. The police commissioner wants to build a police station at a point *P* chosen so that the sum of the seven driving distances from *P* to each of the individual high-crime points is as small as possible. Where should *P* be located?

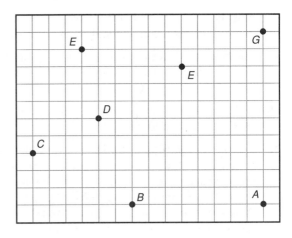

Figure 1.22

1.2   *Computers and Problem Solving*

One can often bring the power of a computer to bear on a problem that would be difficult or impossible to solve with pencil and paper. Consider the following (classical) problem.

PROBLEM 1   Mr. MacGregor wants to grow vegetables along the south side of his house. To keep out rabbits, he plans to enclose three sides with chicken wire and use his house wall as the fourth side (see Figure 1.23). For aesthetic reasons he wants the garden to be rectangular. If he has a 50-ft roll of chicken wire, what dimensions should he give his garden to maximize its area?

Solution 1   Guess and construct a table. As a first guess, make the garden 6 ft deep. The two short sides require 12 ft of wire, leaving 38 ft for the long side. The resulting rectangle has an area of 6 ft × 38 ft = 228 ft². As a second guess, make the garden 10 ft deep. The short sides require 20 ft of wire, leaving 30 ft for the long side. The resulting rectangle has an area of 10 ft × 30 ft = 300 ft², an improvement over the first guess. These first two guesses and two others are shown in Table 1.4.

It appears that in a few more clever guesses we should be able to arrive at the depth and length that maximize area. There is an alternative to being

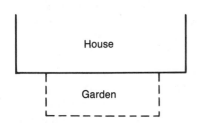

Figure 1.23

Table 1.4

Depth	Length	Area
6	38	228
10	30	300
14	22	308
18	14	252

clever, though, if one has at one's command an obedient servant who can calculate rapidly, accurately, and tirelessly. A computer is just such a servant.

Solution 2   Use a computer. Instruct the computer to compile a table like Table 1.4, but showing all of the depths: 0, 1, 2, . . . , 25. Figure 1.24 lists the instructions given to the computer (the **program**). If you have had experience with computers, you might recognize that the program is written in BASIC, one of the most common languages in which people give instructions to computers. For the moment, though, we don't want to be distracted by the technicalities of programming. Instead, we are interested in what the computer produces when this program is "run." Figure 1.25 shows the printout.

```
10    PRINT "DEPTH", "LENGTH", "AREA"
20    FOR D = 0 TO 25
30    LET L = 50 - 2 * D
40    LET A = L * D
50    PRINT D,L,A
60    NEXT D
70    END
```

Figure 1.24

As we look down the list of numbers in the AREA column, we see that area increases as depth increases from 0 to 12, then it levels off, and then it decreases as depth continues to increase from 13 to 25. The symmetry of the numbers in the AREA column suggests strongly (but does not guarantee) that the optimal dimensions for the garden are $12\frac{1}{2}$ ft deep by 25 ft long.   ❑

The next solution depends on some fairly technical algebraic skills. Do not be alarmed if you cannot follow every detail. The point we are trying to make is that there is an algebraic method for determining the *exact* optimal dimensions.

Solution 3   Use algebra. If we let x represent the depth of the garden, then its length must be $50 - 2x$. Hence its area will be $x(50 - 2x) = 50x - 2x^2$. The task is to find the value of x that maximizes the value of the expression $50x - 2x^2$. You might recall from an algebra II course a procedure for doing this, *completing the square:*

$$
\begin{aligned}
50x - 2x^2 &= -(2x^2 - 50x) \\
&= -2(x^2 - 25x) \\
&= -2[x^2 - 25x + (\tfrac{25}{2})^2] + 2(\tfrac{25}{2})^2 \\
&= \tfrac{625}{2} - 2(x - \tfrac{25}{2})^2
\end{aligned}
$$

To maximize this last expression, we need to make the subtrahend, $2(x - \frac{25}{2})^2$, as small as possible, namely 0. So choose $x = \frac{25}{2}$, and the corresponding maximum value of the expression $50x - 2x^2$ is $\frac{625}{2}$. That is, the optimal dimensions for the garden are $12\frac{1}{2}$ ft by 25 ft, and the area of that rectangle is $312\frac{1}{2}$ ft². ❑

```
]RUN
DEPTH        LENGTH          AREA
0            50              0
1            48              48
2            46              92
3            44              132
4            42              168
5            40              200
6            38              228
7            36              252
8            34              272
9            32              288
10           30              300
11           28              308
12           26              312
13           24              312
14           22              308
15           20              300
16           18              288
17           16              272
18           14              252
19           12              228
20           10              200
21           8               168
22           6               132
23           4               92
24           2               48
25           0               0
```

Figure 1.25   ❏

If you have had some calculus, then the maximizing process from Solution 3 can be simplified. (If you have not had calculus, do not worry; just skip Solution 4.)

Solution 4   Use calculus. We begin as in the algebraic solution. But now we find the x that maximizes the expression

$$50x - 2x^2$$

by *differentiating* the expression to obtain

$$50 - 4x$$

setting this *derivative* equal to zero

$$50 - 4x = 0$$

and solving for x

$$x = \frac{50}{4} = 12\frac{1}{2} \qquad \qquad \square$$

For many of you the algebraic and calculus solutions are probably unfamiliar procedures, and for elementary and middle school students they are surely inaccessible. Of the four solutions given you will probably agree that the *plan* of the computer solution is the most straightforward. Its execution, of course, is the catch. Learning how to program a computer to carry out your wishes is not a trivial matter. Chapter 16 covers the rudiments of programming in BASIC and also in Logo, another very popular language.

The point of this first example is that once one has learned to control and direct the power of a computer, one can solve problems that might otherwise be intractable. Let us consider a second optimization problem (also a classic).

PROBLEM 2 You are given a rectangular piece of cardboard of dimensions 30 cm by 40 cm. Your task is to cut away squares from the four corners, fold up the sides, and tape them to produce an open-topped box having maximum volume. See Figure 1.26. How big should the corner squares be?

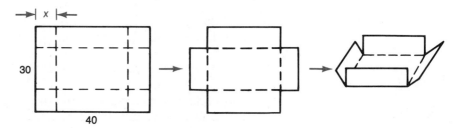

Figure 1.26

Solution 1 Use a computer. Again we want the computer to carry out the guess/make-a-table strategy for us. We want it to successively try the values 0, 1, 2, . . . , 15 for the dimension x in Figure 1.26 (why stop at 15?) and calculate the corresponding volumes. A program that does this is given in Figure 1.27. The printout appears in Figure 1.28. Apparently, the optimal side length of the corner square is somewhere between 5 and 7.

```
10    PRINT "SQUARE SIDE", "VOLUME"
20    FOR X = 0 TO 15
30    LET V = X * (30 − 2 * X) * (40 − 2 * X)
40    PRINT X,V
50    NEXT X
60    END
```

Figure 1.27

```
]RUN
SQUARE SIDE          VOLUME
0                    0
1                    1064
2                    1872
3                    2448
4                    2816
5                    3000
6                    3024
7                    2912
8                    2688
9                    2376
10                   2000
11                   1584
12                   1152
13                   728
14                   336
15                   0
```

Figure 1.28

We can get a closer approximation to the optimal value by making one small change in the program: Simply replace old line 20 by this new line 20:

$$20 \quad \text{FOR } X = 5 \text{ TO } 7 \text{ STEP } 0.1$$

A run of the revised program is shown in Figure 1.29. Evidently, the optimal side length is between 5.6 and 5.8.

To get a still better approximation, replace line 20 once again:

$$20 \quad \text{FOR } X = 5.6 \text{ TO } 5.8 \text{ STEP } 0.01$$

The printout in Figure 1.30 shows that the optimal side length is between 5.65 and 5.67. Clearly, we could continue revising line 20 to get sharper and sharper estimates of the side length of the square.

Again, there is a precise solution for this problem that uses higher mathematics (and again, don't worry if you can't follow it).

Solution 2   Use algebra and calculus. The volume of the box in Figure 1.26 is the product of its length, width, and height.

$$V = (40 - 2x)(30 - 2x)x$$

which simplifies to

$$V = 4x^3 - 140x^2 + 1200x$$

```
]RUN
SQUARE SIDE        VOLUME
5                  3000
5.1                3009.204
5.2                3016.832
5.3                3022.908
5.4                3027.456
5.5                3030.5
5.6                3032.064
5.7                3032.172
5.8                3030.848
5.9                3028.116
6                  3024
6.1                3018.524
6.2                3011.712
6.3                3003.588
6.4                2994.176
6.5                2983.5
6.6                2971.584
6.7                2958.452
6.8                2944.128
6.9                2928.636
7                  2912
```

Figure 1.29

The task is to find a value of x that maximizes V. The procedure is to calculate the derivative,

$$V' = 12x^2 - 280x + 1200$$

set it equal to zero,

$$12x^2 - 280x + 1200 = 0$$

solve for x (by the *quadratic formula*)

$$x = \frac{35 \pm 5\sqrt{13}}{3}$$

and keep the value of x that meets the restriction, $0 < x < 15$, of our problem.

$$x = \frac{35 - 5\sqrt{13}}{3} \doteq 5.65741454$$

The eight-place decimal approximation to x was found by using a calculator.

```
]RUN
SQUARE SIDE        VOLUME
5.6                3032.064
5.61               3032.13993
5.62               3032.20131
5.63               3032.24819
5.64               3032.28058
5.65               3032.2985
5.66               3032.30199
5.67               3032.29105
5.68               3032.26573
5.69               3032.22604
5.7                3032.172
5.71               3032.10364
5.72               3032.02099
5.73               3031.92407
5.74               3031.8129
5.75               3031.6875
5.76               3031.5479
5.77               3031.39413
5.78               3031.22621
5.79               3031.04416
5.8                3030.848
```

Figure 1.30   ❏

The contrast between the two solutions to the cardboard box problem is striking. The computer solution follows a simple, straightforward plan. The only mathematical prerequisite is knowing that the volume of a box is given by length times width times height. (Can you find this formula in the program of Figure 1.27?) The programming skills needed are also rather minimal. The final "answer," that side length is between 5.65 and 5.67 cm, is close enough for all practical purposes. You would need good eyes, a sharp pencil, and an even sharper knife to cut a square of cardboard having edges between 5.65 and 5.67 cm long.

The algebra/calculus solution employs a sophisticated strategy and depends on advanced mathematical techniques. It has two advantages: the elegance of the approach and the absolute accuracy of the answer it produces: $x = \frac{1}{3}(35 - 5\sqrt{13})$.

The issue of machine power versus human ingenuity received national publicity in 1976 when two mathematicians at the University of Illinois, Kenneth Appel and Wolfgang Haken, used a computer to overpower one of the most famous problems in the mathematical literature, the notorious "four-color problem." Here is a brief history of the problem.

In 1853 Francis Guthrie, a mathematics student at University College, London, conjectured that every map can be colored with four (or less) colors so that countries sharing a border receive different colors. For example, map A in Figure 1.31 requires four colors, map B can be done with three, and map C needs only two. (Do you see why?)

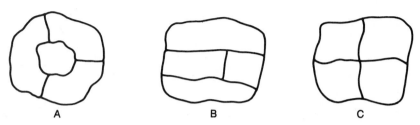

A   B   C

Figure 1.31

In 1890 P. J. Heawood proved that five colors will suffice no matter how complicated the map. For the next 85 years legions of mathematicians struggled unsuccessfully to prove that only four colors were needed, because every map that anyone was able to draw turned out to be colorable with four. In the summer of 1976 Appel and Haken finally proved Guthrie's conjecture: Four colors do suffice. Their proof reportedly runs to hundreds of pages and depends on over a thousand hours of computer calculation.

Appel and Haken's announcement drew a mixed response. Predictably, some mathematicians were delighted, but surprisingly, others greeted it rather coolly. They objected to the ponderous nature of the proof and called for an elegant new proof done on a human scale.

EXERCISE SET 1.2

1. In the program of Figure 1.24, what do you suppose the asterisks in lines 30 and 40 stand for?

2. In the cardboard box problem we determined, by computer, that the optimal side length for the corner squares is between 5.65 and 5.67. How would you revise line 20 of the program in Figure 1.27 to get a still sharper estimate?

3. Figure 1.32 shows a simple program for a computer solution of the lambs-ducks problem (p. 3). If you have access to a machine, type it in and run it.

★ 4. Revise the program in Figure 1.32 to shift the burden of scanning the table to the machine.

```
10   PRINT "LAMBS", "DUCKS", "FEET"
20   PRINT
30   FOR L = 0 TO 80
40   LET D = 80 - L
50   LET F = 4 * L + 2 * D
60   PRINT L, D, F
70   NEXT L
80   END
```

Figure 1.32

5. Figure 1.33 shows a simple program for a computer solution of Problem 7 (p. 8): finding the sum of the first 100 odd numbers.

(a) If you have access to a machine, type it in and run it. (The printout should be just the number 10,000.)
(b) Revise this program so that it finds the sum of the first 200 odd numbers.
(c) Revise it again so that it finds the sum of the first 200 (positive) even numbers.

```
10    FOR I = 1 TO 100
20    LET S = S + (2 * I - 1)
30    NEXT I
40    PRINT S
50    END
```

Figure 1.33

Before you try Exercises 6 and 7 you might want to review the conventions governing order of operations, pp. 211–212.

6. Find a natural number solution to each of the following equations. Use your calculator to carry out the guess/make-a-table strategy.
   (a) $n^3 - 7n^2 - 10n = -16$

   (b) $\dfrac{99}{1 + \dfrac{1}{1 + \dfrac{1}{n}}} = 54$

   (c) $(\sqrt{78 - 3n})^5 - n^2 = 7580$
   (d) $2^{2n} - 3^{n+1} = 59n$

7. Use your calculator to find a pair of consecutive natural numbers that bracket a solution to each of the following equations.
   (a) $x^3 + x^5 = 20{,}000$
   (b) $\dfrac{1}{x} + \dfrac{1}{x + 5} = \dfrac{1}{10}$

8. Color the map in Figure 1.34 with at most four colors.

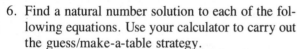

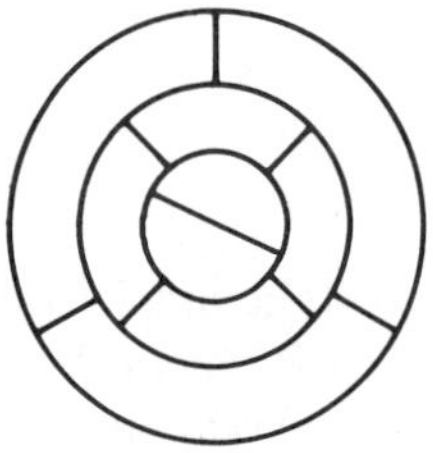

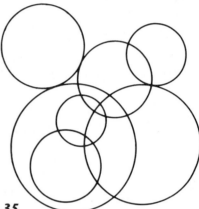

Figure 1.34

9. The map in Figure 1.35 shows 19 countries formed by seven circles.
   (a) See how few colors are needed to color it.
   (b) Draw another map using only a compass, and determine how few colors are needed to color it.
   (c) Make a conjecture and try to prove it.

Figure 1.35

10. Suppose a map is made by drawing straight lines completely across a sheet of paper, as in Figure 1.36. How many colors are needed to color such a map? Can you prove your conjecture?

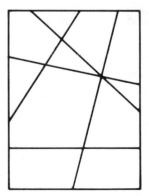

Figure 1.36

References

Arithmetic Teacher. Focus Issue—"Mathematical Thinking." vol. 32, no. 6, February 1985.

Arithmetic Teacher. Focus Issue—"Teaching Problem Solving." vol. 29, no. 6, February 1982.

Brown, S. and M. Walter. *The Art of Problem Posing*. Providence, R.I.: Janson Publications, 1989.

Charles, R. and F. Lester. *Teaching Problem Solving: What, Why, & How*. Palo Alto, Calif.: Dale Seymour Publications, 1982.

Clements, D. *Computers in Early and Primary Education*. Englewood Cliffs, N.J.: Prentice-Hall, 1985.

Immerzeel, George, *et al. Iowa Problem Solving Project Resource Decks*. Cedar Falls: University of Northern Iowa, 1978.

Krulik, S. and J. Rudnick. *A Sourcebook for Teaching Problem Solving*. Newton, Mass.: Allyn and Bacon, 1984.

Morris, J. *How to Develop Problem Solving Using a Calculator*. Reston, Va.: NCTM, 1981.

National Council of Teachers of Mathematics. *An Agenda for Action*. Reston, Va.: NCTM, 1980.

———. *Curriculum and Evaluation Standards for School Mathematics*. Reston, Va.: NCTM, 1989.

———. *1980 Yearbook: Problem Solving in School Mathematics*. Reston, Va.: NCTM, 1980.

———. *1983 Yearbook: The Agenda in Action*. Reston, Va.: NCTM, 1983.

Polya, G. *How to Solve It*. 2nd ed. Princeton: Princeton University Press, 1973.

Soifer, A. *Mathematics as Problem Solving*. Palo Alto, Calif.: Dale Seymour Publications, 1987.

Many journals in mathematics education now contain problems, as well as articles on problem solving, in nearly every issue. Here are a few of the best known such periodicals:

The Arithmetic Teacher. Reston, Va.: NCTM.

Classroom Computer Learning. Dayton, Ohio: Peter Li, Inc.

Journal of Computers in Mathematics and Science Teaching. Charlottesville, Va.: AHCE.

Journal for Research in Mathematics Education. Reston, Va.: NCTM.

Mathematics and Computer Education. Old Bethpage, NY: The MATYC Journal, Inc.

The Mathematics Teacher. Reston, Va.: NCTM.

School Science and Mathematics. Bowling Green, Ohio: Bowling Green State University.

2

STRUCTURE

Problem solving is an important aspect of mathematics, but it is not the only one. A danger of reform movements in education is that fundamental ideas are often cast aside simply because they are not new. The drafters of the National Council of Teachers of Mathematics (NCTM) *Agenda for Action* warned against this when they qualified their call for emphasis on problem solving with the following sentences: "This recommendation should not be interpreted to mean that the mathematics to be taught is solely a function of the particular mathematics needed at a given time to solve a given problem. Structural unity and interrelationships of the whole should not be sacrificed." The National Advisory Committee on Mathematical Education was even more explicit in warning that we not be "manipulated into a false choice between structure and problem solving." They advocated a "judicious combination of both elements" for every mathematics program. A similar message appears in the *Standards*, where one of the goals listed for students at the 5–8 level (Standard 4) is to "see mathematics as an integrated whole." Later (Standard 6) one finds a more emphatic reiteration: ". . . students should come to understand and appreciate mathematics as a coherent body of knowledge rather than a vast, perhaps bewildering, collection of isolated facts."

In this chapter we begin to look at "structure." Structure in mathematics is provided by broad and powerful concepts that unify and organize the subject. Such concepts are not just pleasing abstractions; they are practical necessities. Mathematics without its unifying concepts would be a hopelessly large bag of tricks. It would be like a brick skyscraper without structural steel, or a dictionary without alphabetical ordering. The two unifying concepts that we will look at are *set* and *function*. While both have long been recognized as important for organizing traditional mathematics, the function concept has emerged as particularly fundamental in the newer areas of problem solving and calculator and computer use. Quoting again from the *Standards*, where "patterns and functions" is listed among the topics meriting increased attention at the 5–8 level: "One of the central themes of mathematics is the study of patterns and functions. . . . It begins in K–4, is extended and made more central in 5–8, and reaches maturity . . . in grades 9–12."

2.1 *Sets: The Basic Concepts*

The concept of *set* is a very general and a very simple one.

> Any collection of things is a **set.**

The things can be tangible or intangible: a set of golf clubs, a set of dishes, a set of rules for how to play checkers. In certain contexts more colorful words are used to refer to collections: a *pod* of whales, a *sounder* of hogs, a *muster* of peacocks. On an election night a number of years ago, when Rockefellers were leading in elections in New York, West Virginia, and Arkansas, the news commentator Eric Sevareid remarked that we might soon be confronted by "a *wealth* of Rockefellers." In mathematical contexts, however, the word *set* is used almost exclusively.

Surrounding the basic concept of set are a number of associated concepts and notational conventions. We can bring out the most important of these by looking at one specific set in some detail. We have chosen to investigate a set of six famous men: Babbage, Bach, Beethoven, Darwin, Gauss, and Newton. We shall denote this set by *U* to indicate that, for the time being, it will be our *universal set* or *universe*.

> The set to which all participants in a discussion agree to restrict their attention is called the **universal set** or **universe** for that discussion.

Membership

The people who make up our universal set are referred to as its *members* or *elements*. The conventional shorthand way of reporting that "Gauss is a member of *U*" is to write

$$\text{Gauss} \in U$$

That is, the symbol for membership is $\in$, which can be read "is a member of," "belongs to," or "is an element of."

> The symbolic expression $a \in A$ indicates that a is a **member** of the set A.

A slash through the membership symbol indicates nonmembership. For example,

$$\text{Lenin} \notin U$$

means that Lenin is not a member of *U*.

Notation for Sets

The most common notation for sets is **roster notation.** To describe a set in this notation, we simply list the elements of the set within a pair of braces. For our example,

$$U = \{Babbage, Bach, Beethoven, Darwin, Gauss, Newton\}$$

The braces are read "the set consisting of," so the symbols above are read "U equals the set consisting of Babbage, Bach, Beethoven, Darwin, Gauss, and Newton." It may seem fastidious to insist on braces when listing a set, but this is the notation that is universally used and understood. Ordinary round parentheses will carry other meanings, as we shall soon see.

Another way of describing a set is by means of a **Venn diagram.** In its simplest form a Venn diagram for a set is just a rectangle or circle or other convenient figure, with the elements of the set listed inside. See Figure 2.1. Important variations on the basic Venn diagram will be discussed shortly.

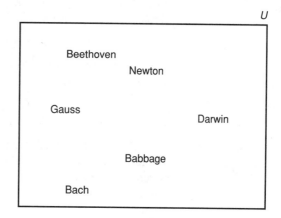

Figure 2.1

A third way of denoting certain sets is by means of **permanent symbols.** Some sets are referred to so often that we assign them special letters once and for all. In this book the most important sets and their symbols are the following:

N, the set of **natural numbers** = $\{1, 2, 3, 4, 5, \ldots\}$
W, the set of **whole numbers** = $\{0, 1, 2, 3, 4, \ldots\}$
I, the set of **integers** = $\{\ldots {}^{-}3, {}^{-}2, {}^{-}1, 0, 1, 2, 3, \ldots\}$
Q, the set of **rational numbers**
R, the set of **real numbers**

Each of these sets of numbers will be studied in detail as we progress; for now it is enough to recall only these facts about Q and R.

A rational number is one that can be expressed as a quotient of integers. Thus:

5/8	is a rational number
$\dfrac{^-9}{2}$	is a rational number
17	is a rational number, since $17 = \frac{17}{1}$
3.05	is a rational number, since $3.05 = \frac{305}{100}$

The set of real numbers contains all of the rational numbers and many other numbers as well. Two common real numbers that are not rational are $\sqrt{2}$ and π. The number $\sqrt{2}$ is the length of an edge of a square whose area is 2; see Figure 2.2(a). We shall prove that $\sqrt{2}$ is not rational in Chapter 8. The number π is the ratio of circumference to diameter in a circle; see Figure 2.2(b). Some rational numbers close to π are $\frac{22}{7}$, 3.14, and 3.1416, but no rational number is exactly equal to π.

A fourth notation for sets is **set builder notation.** It is a modification of roster notation that employs both a *variable* and an *open sentence*. A set builder description of the set of whole numbers 0 through 5 is

$$\{x \mid x \text{ is a whole number less than 6}\}$$

The vertical bar is read "such that." Thus the complete translation of the set builder notation above is

"The set of all x such that x is
a whole number less than 6."

The letter x is the variable; the defining property to the right of the vertical bar is the open sentence. A fuller discussion of variables and open sentences is given in Chapter 15 and in the Appendix A. The following examples should suffice for now.

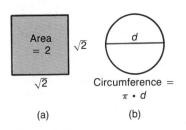

Figure 2.2

EXAMPLE 1   Make a roster for each of these sets described in set builder notation.
(a) $\{x \mid x \text{ is a whole number greater than 10}\}$
(b) $\{x \mid x \in U \text{ and } x \text{ was English}\}$, where U is our universe of six famous men.

Solution   (a) $\{11, 12, 13, 14, 15, \ldots\}$ The three dots are called an *ellipsis*, and they indicate that the listing should continue following the pattern suggested by the first few terms. This example illustrates a virtue of set builder notation: it can provide a concise, unambiguous description of a set that is too large to list completely.
(b) $\{$Babbage, Darwin, Newton$\}$ Notice that in this example, too, the universal set is mentioned explicitly in the defining property. Sometimes, the universal set is mentioned to the left of the bar, as in

$$\{x \in U \mid x \text{ was English}\}$$

(read "The set of all x in U such that x was English"). Sometimes, if the universal set is absolutely clear, it is omitted altogether:

$$\{x \mid x \text{ was English}\} \qquad \square$$

Subsets

If every member of a first set is also a member of a second set then we say the first set is a *subset* of the second set. For example, the set N of natural numbers is a subset of the set I of integers. In our universe of famous men, if we let E by the set of Englishmen, that is, $E = \{\text{Babbage, Darwin, Newton}\}$, then E is a subset of U. In shorthand,

$$E \subseteq U$$

Notice that the symbol $\subseteq$ for "is a subset of" differs from the symbol $\in$ for "is a member of."

The symbolic expression $A \subseteq B$ indicates that A is a **subset** of B; that is, every member of A is also a member of B.

A Venn diagram for E and U, Figure 2.3, shows graphically that E is a subset of U; E is inside U.

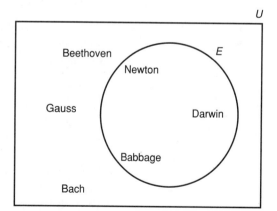

Figure 2.3

We used the property "was English" to define the subset E. Any other unambiguous property will also define a subset. For example, the property "was a mathematician (among other things)" defines the subset

$$M = \{\text{Babbage, Gauss, Newton}\}$$

The property "name ends in n" defines the subset

$$N = \{\text{Beethoven, Darwin, Newton}\}$$

These subsets are shown in Figure 2.4. Note, however, that the property "was handsome," being ambiguous, does *not* define a subset.

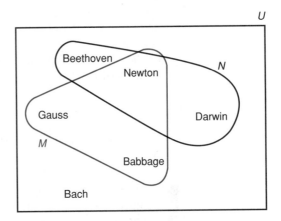

Figure 2.4

Special Subsets

Consider the property "lived to be 100." This property is certainly unambiguous, so it defines a subset of U. The fact that this subset has no members makes it easy to overlook, but it is a subset nonetheless. The set with no members is referred to as the **empty set** and is denoted either by $\{\}$ (roster notation) or by $\varnothing$ (symbol).

Consider next the property "was a biologist." The subset it defines, $\{\text{Darwin}\}$, has just one member. Still, it *is* a subset. Any set having just one member is called a **singleton.** Because some people find it difficult to conceive of a one-element set, we put singletons in the special category too.

A third type of subset is special not because it is small, like singletons or the empty set, but because it is large. Consider the unambiguous property "was a European." The subset of U that this property defines is the entire set U. That is, U is a subset of U. To remind ourselves of its peculiar character, we call U the **improper subset** of U. Every set is a subset (the improper subset) of itself. All other subsets of U are called *proper subsets*.

Set A is a **proper subset** of set B, written $A \subset B$, if every element of A is in B, but some element of B is *not* in A.

Note the difference between the proper subset symbol $\subset$ and the (arbitrary) subset symbol $\subseteq$: "$A \subseteq B$" allows the possibility that $A = B$; "$A \subset B$" excludes the possibility that $A = B$.

EXAMPLE 2

Find all subsets of the two-element set $\{a, b\}$.

Solution

All four of its subsets are special!

The empty set $\{\}$
Two singleton subsets, $\{a\}$ and $\{b\}$
The improper subset $\{a, b\}$ ❑

Equality

Let us consider one final property, "name has two syllables." From our universe of famous men, this property picks out the subset

$$T = \{\text{Babbage, Darwin, Newton}\}$$

With hindsight we observe that this set has exactly the same members as the set E of Englishmen. That is, we have two names but just one set. This is what we mean when we write

$$T = E$$

The equal sign will always signify that we are dealing with two names for one thing, whether the thing is a set, a number, a person, or anything else. For example,

$$\text{Newton} = \text{master of the British mint in 1700}$$
$$7 = \text{VII}$$
$$\tfrac{3}{8} = 0.375 = 37\tfrac{1}{2}\%$$

For sets we can relate **equality** to membership.

Set $A = $ set B if and only if every element of A is in B and every element of B is in A.

In this and in future exercise sets you will find many straightforward questions that test and sharpen your understanding of the concepts and symbols introduced in the section. You will also find some problems (in the sense of Chapter 1). Sometimes, a problem-solving strategy will be laid out for you, as in the following trio of exercises, 16–18 and in Exercises 23 and 24. At other times you will be left to your own devices. Do not be discouraged if you cannot solve every problem; you can still learn a lot by making a gallant effort. One of the world's great body builders developed his muscles by pushing against a door frame that never moved.

EXERCISE SET 2.1

1. Make a roster for each of the following sets.
   (a) The set A of all states that touch the Gulf of Mexico.
   (b) The set B of all odd numbers between 10 and 20.
   (c) The set C of all lucky numbers less than 12.
   (d) The set D of all cities in Colorado with a population over 500,000.
   (e) The set E of all cities in North Dakota with a population over 1,000,000.
   (f) The set F in the Venn diagram in Figure 2.5.
   (g) The set G in the Venn diagram in Figure 2.5.

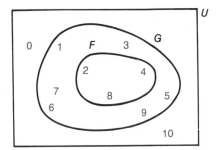

Figure 2.5

2. Make a Venn diagram showing the following three sets.
   $U = \{1, 2, 3, 4, 5, 6, 7, 8, 9, 10\}$
   A = the set of numbers in U that are less than 7
   B = the set of odd numbers in U

3. Refer to the Venn diagram in Figure 2.5 and mark the following statements true or false.
   (a) $7 \in G$ (b) $7 \notin F$
   (c) $G \subseteq F$ (d) $F \subset U$
   (e) $\varnothing \subseteq F$ (f) $F \subset F$
   (g) $G \in U$ False   (h) $0 \in \varnothing$ False
   (i) $\{5\} \in G$ (j) $G \subseteq G$

4. Using the set $U = \{1, 2, 3, \ldots, 12\}$ as universe, make rosters for the following sets that are described in set builder notation.
   (a) $\{x \mid x \in U \text{ and } x > 9\}$

   (b) $\{x \mid x \in U \text{ and } x/3 \in N\}$ $= \{3, 6, 9, 12\}$
   (c) $\{x \in U \mid 2x \in U\}$ $\{1, 2, 3, 4, 5, 6\}$
   (d) $\{x \in U \mid x^2 = 25\}$
   (e) $\{x \in U \mid x^2 > 0\}$
   (f) $\{x \in U \mid x \text{ is even and } 9 \le x\}$
   (g) $\{x \mid x \le 3 \text{ or } x > 10\}$ $\{1, 2, 3, 11, 12\}$
   (h) $\{x \mid 2x + 5 = 11\}$

5. Using the same universal set U as in Exercise 4, describe each of these sets in set builder notation. (Answers are not unique.)
   (a) $\{1, 3, 5, 7, 9, 11\}$
   (b) $\{5, 10\}$
   (c) $\{6, 7, 8, 9\}$
   (d) $\{7\}$
   (e) $\varnothing$
   (f) $\{6, 8, 10, 12\}$
   (g) $\{1, 4, 9\}$
   (h) $\{1, 2, 3, 4, 5, 6, 7, 8, 9, 10, 11, 12\}$

6. Fill in all 12 elements in the Venn diagram in Figure 2.6, which shows the set M of the months of the year and the subsets T of the 30-day months and F of the fall-term months (at your school).

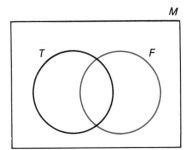

Figure 2.6

7. Refer to Exercise 6 and mark the following statements true or false.
   (a) Christmas $\in M$
   (b) December $\subseteq M$
   (c) Christmas $\in$ December
   (d) Christmas $\subset$ December
   (e) If R is the subset of all months whose names end in r, then $R = F$.

(f) If W is the subset of all winter-term months (at your school), then $W = F$.

8. Think of the United Nations as a set of countries, and each country as a set of citizens. Mark the following statements true or false.
   (a) U.S.A. $\subseteq$ U.N.
   (b) U.S.A. $\in$ U.N.
   (c) George Bush $\in$ U.S.A.
   (d) George Bush $\in$ U.N.

9. True or false?
   (a) If $A \subseteq B$ and $B \subseteq C$, then $A \subseteq C$.
   (b) If $A \in B$ and $B \in C$, then $A \in C$.
   (c) If $A \in B$ and $B \subseteq C$, then $A \subseteq C$.
   (d) If $A \in B$ and $B \subseteq C$, then $A \in C$.

10. In each of the following sentences the underlined verb has nearly the same meaning as one of the three relations $=$, $\in$, $\subseteq$. Choose the best one for each sentence.
    (a) Neil Armstrong <u>is</u> the first human to set foot on the moon.
    (b) Paul <u>is</u> Hungarian.
    (c) The New York Yankees <u>are</u> the American League champions.
    (d) Chryslers <u>are</u> economy cars.

11. Sketch a Venn diagram showing the subset relationships among the five sets of numbers N, W, I, Q, and R.

12. The diagram for Exercise 11 should have five compartments. Write one appropriate number in each compartment.

13. How many numbers are in the set $\{1, 3, 5, 7, 3\}$?

14. How many numbers are in the set $\{2^2, (7 + 1)/2, \sqrt{16}\}$?

15. Does $\{1, 3, 5\} = \{5, 1, 3\}$?

16. Given the set $S = \{a, b, c\}$. List, in roster notation, every subset of S, beginning with the zero-element subset and ending with the three-element subset. Be systematic. How many subsets in all does S have?

17. List and count all subsets of the set $T = \{a, b, c, d\}$.

18. If a set has n elements, how many subsets does it have?

19. How many proper subsets does an n-element set have?

20. How many 2-element subsets does an n-element set have?

★ 21. Burger Baron allows its customers to have any combination of the following custom options on its basic hamburger: mustard, catsup, onions, pickles, lettuce. How many different styles of hamburger are available?

★ 22. How many different (meaningful) ways are there of inserting plus signs among these digits?

$$1 \quad 2 \quad 3 \quad 4 \quad 5 \quad 6 \quad 7 \quad 8 \quad 9$$

(In Exercise 43 of Exercise Set 1.1 you were asked to insert them so that a sum of 99 would result.)

★ 23. A *partition* of a set can be thought of as a separation of that set into nonempty, nonoverlapping subsets. Two different partitions of a four-element set are shown in Figure 2.7:

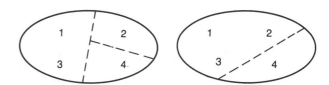

Figure 2.7

In roster notation the first partition is $\{\{1, 3\}, \{2\}, \{4\}\}$, and the second is $\{\{1, 2, 3\}, \{4\}\}$. Note that these partitions are *not* ordered. For example, $\{\{1, 3\}, \{2\}, \{4\}\} = \{\{4\}, \{1, 3\}, \{2\}\}$
Use the problem-solving strategy of making a systematic list to find how many partitions there are of a four-element set. (Perhaps you are interested in deciding how many different ability groupings are possible in a class of four children.)

★ 24. Consider some small (nonempty) sets, and compare the number of subsets having an even number of elements with the number of subsets having an odd number of elements. Make a conjecture.

2.2 *Operations on Sets*

We continue our survey of concepts associated with the basic idea of set by investigating four important operations on sets. Think of an *operation* on sets as something you do to two sets to produce another set, just as you think of an operation on numbers, such as addition or multiplication, as something you do to two numbers to produce another number.

Intersection

The *intersection* operation, which is denoted by ∩, can be illustrated by returning to our set U of famous men. Let E be the subset defined by the property "was English"; that is,

$$E = \{\text{Newton, Darwin, Babbage}\}$$

Let M be the subset defined by the property "was a mathematician"; that is,

$$M = \{\text{Gauss, Newton, Babbage}\}$$

Then the intersection of E with M, written $E \cap M$ and read "E intersect M," is the subset defined by the property "was English *and* was a mathematician." In set builder notation we write

$$E \cap M = \{x \mid x \in E \quad \text{and} \quad x \in M\}$$

To make a roster for $E \cap M$, we go through the rosters for E and M and pick out exactly those elements that appear on both lists:

$$E \cap M = \{\text{Newton, Babbage}\}$$

The intersection of two sets can be thought of as an exclusive club: two membership requirements must be met to be admitted.

The intersection of two sets is illustrated in the Venn diagram in Figure 2.8, where it appears as the overlap. In general, we have the following definition.

The **intersection** of sets A and B, written $A \cap B$, is the set of all elements that belong to both A and B.

In set builder notation we write the intersection as follows:

$$A \cap B = \{x \mid \in A \quad \text{and} \quad x \in B\}$$

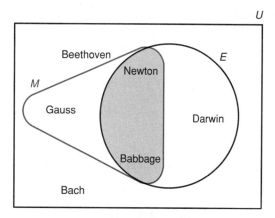

Figure 2.8 $E \cap M$ is shaded.

When there is no overlap—that is, when the intersection is empty—the sets are said to be *disjoint*.

Sets A and B are **disjoint** if and only if $A \cap B = \varnothing$.

EXAMPLE 1   Let the universal set U be $\{1, 2, 3, 4, 5, 6, 7, 8\}$, P be the subset of prime numbers $\{2, 3, 5, 7\}$, E be the subset of even numbers, and O be the subset of odd numbers. Describe each of these intersections.
(a) $P \cap O$
(b) $P \cap E$
(c) $E \cap O$
(d) $U \cap P$

Solution   (a) $P \cap O = \{3, 5, 7\}$
(b) $P \cap E = \{2\}$
(c) $E \cap O = \varnothing$ (E and O are disjoint sets.)
(d) $U \cap P = P$ ❏

EXAMPLE 2   Sketch a Venn diagram that shows the set U of Example 1; the subsets P, E, and O; and the elements 1 through 8.

Solution   First, draw the rectangle and the overlapping circles, as in Figure 2.9; then fill in the elements 1 through 8 by working from the inside out. Notice that even though there is a region for $E \cap O$, it has no elements in it. Can you explain why there are no elements outside both E and O?   ❏

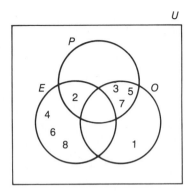

Figure 2.9

Union

Again, let *E* and *M* be the subsets of Englishmen and mathematicians, respectively. The *union* of *E* with *M*, written $E \cup M$ and read "*E* union *M*," is the subset defined by the property "was English *or* was a mathematician." In set builder notation we write

$$E \cup M = \{x \mid x \in E \ \text{ or } \ x \in M\}$$

It is not a very exclusive club: one membership card is enough to get in. Of course, people with two membership cards are admitted too:

$$E \cup M = \{\text{Newton, Darwin, Babbage, Gauss}\}$$

Again, a Venn diagram such as the one in Figure 2.10 is helpful.

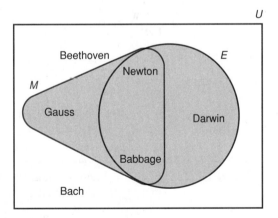

Figure 2.10 $E \cup M$ is shaded.

In general, we have the following definition.

The **union** of sets A and B, written $A \cup B$, is the set of all elements that belong to A or to B.

In set builder notation we write the union as follows:

$$A \cup B = \{x \mid x \in A \quad \text{or} \quad x \in B\}$$

Remember that in both the verbal and the symbolic definitions the key word *or* is to be interpreted in the inclusive *and/or* sense. For a further discussion of the meanings of the word *or*, see Appendix A.

EXAMPLE 3   The sets U (universe), P (primes), E (evens), and O (odds) are the same as in Example 1. Describe each union.
(a) $P \cup E$
(b) $P \cup O$
(c) $E \cup O$

Solution   A glance at Figure 2.9 gives us the answers.
(a) $P \cup E = \{2, 3, 4, 5, 6, 7, 8\}$
(b) $P \cup O = \{1, 2, 3, 5, 7\}$
(c) $E \cup O = \{1, 2, 3, 4, 5, 6, 7, 8\} = U$ ❑

Complement

The *complement* operation is deceptive. Even though it is an operation that acts on two sets, as do intersection and union, one of the two sets receives most of the attention while the other is nearly ignored. For example, the complement of the subset E of Englishmen in the universal set U of six famous men, written E' and read "E complement" or "E prime," is the subset of U defined by the property "was *not* English." From the notation E' it is not clear that E is in the limelight while U is virtually ignored. Still, if we wish to make a roster for E', we must begin with a roster for U and then cross off the members of E:

$$E' = \{\cancel{\text{Babbage}}, \text{Bach}, \text{Beethoven}, \cancel{\text{Darwin}}, \text{Gauss}, \cancel{\text{Newton}}\}$$

That is,

$$E' = \{\text{Bach, Beethoven, Gauss}\}$$

Which of the following forms of set builder notation is *least* clear?

$$E' = \{x \mid x \in U \quad \text{and} \quad x \notin E\}$$
$$E' = \{x \in U \mid x \notin E\}$$
$$E' = \{x \mid x \notin E\}$$

To locate E' on a Venn diagram, again we start with U and then remove the subset E. The result is shown in Figure 2.11.

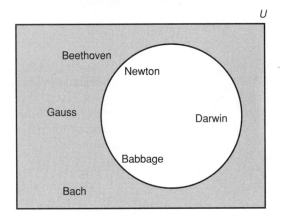

Figure 2.11 *E' is shaded.*

In general, we have the following definition.

If A is a subset of a universal set U, then the **complement** of A in U, written A' (or sometimes $\bar{A}$ or $\sim A$), is the set of all elements of U that are not elements of A.

In set builder notation we write the complement as follows:

$$A' = \{x \in U \,|\, x \notin A\}$$

In contexts where the universal set is not clear, complements need to be handled carefully. For example, let B (for big) be the infinite set

$$B = \{10, 11, 12, 13, 14, \ldots\}$$

Can we list B'? No, not until we agree on a universal set for this discussion. If the universal set is W, then

$$B' = \{0, 1, 2, 3, 4, 5, 6, 7, 8, 9\}$$

If the universal set is I, then

$$B' = \{\ldots, {}^-3, {}^-2, {}^-1, 0, 1, 2, 3, 4, 5, 6, 7, 8, 9\}$$

If the universal set is Q, then many other numbers are members of B' as well.

EXAMPLE 4   The sets U (universe), P (primes), E (evens), and O (odds) are as defined in Examples 1 and 3. Describe each complement.
(a) P'
(b) E'
(c) O'
(d) U'

Solution   Again, Figure 2.9 (repeated here) is helpful.
(a) $P' = \{1, 4, 6, 8\}$
(b) $E' = O$
(c) $O' = E$
(d) $U' = \varnothing$

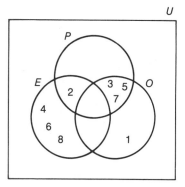

Figure 2.9

Cartesian Product

The fourth set operation, *Cartesian product,* is inherently more abstract than the first three, which admit concrete interpretation. For example, let the universal set U be a standard deck of 52 cards, let H be the subset of (13) hearts, and let F be the subset of (12) face cards. A child could be asked to physically construct the sets $H \cap F$, $H \cup F$, and H'. To produce $H \cap F$, he might go through the deck picking out all the hearts and then from these hearts pick out the three face cards. To exhibit $H \cup F$, he might go through the deck once picking out all the hearts and then go through what's left picking out the remaining face cards to add to his collection. (How many members are in $H \cup F$?) To exhibit H', he could pick out all the hearts, set them to one side, and keep what's left. The three sets $H \cap F$, $H \cup F$, and H' are all constructible subsets of the original tangible set of cards.

In contrast, the Cartesian product of H and F, written $H \times F$ and read "H cross F," does not consist of playing cards. It is not a subset of the original universal set (deck of cards). Its members are 156 abstract mathematical objects called *ordered pairs* that cannot be displayed except in a symbolic way.

Rather than attempt to list $H \times F$, we will use smaller sets to illustrate Cartesian product. Let

$$A = \{1, 2, 3, 4\} \quad \text{and} \quad B = \{1, 3, 5\}$$

Then

$$A \times B = \{(1, 1), (1, 3), (1, 5), (2, 1), (2, 3), (2, 5), (3, 1), (3, 3), (3, 5),$$
$$(4, 1), (4, 3), (4, 5)\}$$

The element $(1, 3)$ on this list is referred to as an **ordered pair** whose **first component** is 1 and whose **second component** is 3. (Parentheses are used to indicate an ordered pair.) Thus $A \times B$ consists of all possible ordered pairs (12 of them) whose first component comes from A and whose second component comes from B. Note that $(1, 3)$ and $(3, 1)$ are distinct (not equal) members of $A \times B$.

The general **equality criterion** for ordered pairs is as follows:

$$(a, b) = (c, d) \quad \text{if and only if} \quad a = c \text{ and } b = d$$

The general definition of Cartesian product is as follows:

The **Cartesian product** of set A with set B, written $A \times B$, is the set of all possible ordered pairs (a, b) for which $a \in A$ and $b \in B$.

In set builder notation we write

$$A \times B = \{(a, b) \mid a \in A \text{ and } b \in B\}$$

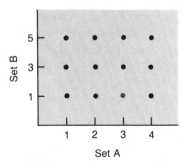

Figure 2.12 Representation of $A \times B$ by a rectangular array.

Two different geometric representations have been devised to give substance to the intangible, abstract notions of ordered pair and Cartesian product. One is a **rectangular array** of dots. The rectangular array in Figure 2.12 represents $A \times B$. Notice that the first set, A, is listed on the horizontal axis and the second set, B, is listed on the vertical axis. The red dot represents the ordered pair $(3, 1)$. Can you locate the dot that represents $(1, 3)$?

The other schematic representation is a **tree**. The tree in Figure 2.13 represents $A \times B$. Observe that there is one branch for each element of the first set A, and on every branch there is one twig for each element of the second set B. Each path down the tree represents one of the ordered pairs belonging to $A \times B$. The red path represents $(3, 1)$. Can you locate the path corresponding to $(2, 5)$?

Trees turn out to be convenient problem-solving devices in a variety of situations where multiplication is involved. We shall use them often. Venn diagrams are occasionally helpful as well.

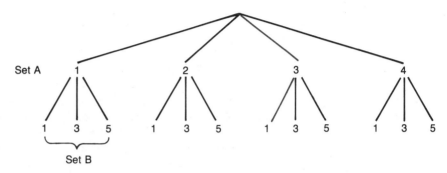

Figure 2.13 Representation of $A \times B$ by a tree.

Venn Diagrams in Problem Solving

For certain kinds of problems Venn diagrams are an appropriate scheme for displaying information. Here are two examples.

EXAMPLE 5

There are 30 sixth graders and 12 patrol persons. Eight of the patrol persons are sixth graders. A meeting of all sixth graders and patrol persons is called. How many should come to the meeting?

Solution

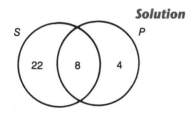

Figure 2.14

Sketch a Venn diagram, as in Figure 2.14, where S represents the set of sixth graders and P the set of patrol persons. Now, enter the number 8 in $S \cap P$ to signify that 8 children are members of both S and P. Next, enter the numbers 22 and 4 where shown. (Since 8 of the 30 elements of S are inside P, the other 22 must be outside P. Since 8 of the 12 elements of P are inside S, the other 4 must be outside.) Now add: $22 + 8 + 4 = 34$ people should come. ❑

EXAMPLE 6

In a recent survey of 200 freshmen this information was obtained:

    28 drink apple juice, buttermilk, and cocoa
    50 drink apple juice and buttermilk
    60 drink buttermilk and cocoa
    30 drink apple juice and cocoa
  100 drink buttermilk
    65 drink apple juice
  102 drink cocoa

How many drink none of the three beverages?

Solution   Let F be the universe of 200 freshmen, and let A, B, C be the subsets of apple juice, buttermilk, and cocoa drinkers, respectively. Draw the Venn diagram, and begin entering numbers from the inside out. That is, put 28 in $A \cap B \cap C$, 22 in the other part of $A \cap B$ (Why?), etc. The completed diagram is shown in Figure 2.15. The number of people who drink none of the three is

$$200 - (40 + 2 + 13 + 22 + 18 + 32 + 28) = 200 - 155 = 45 \qquad \square$$

For another application of Venn diagrams, see Appendix A.

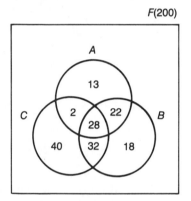

Figure 2.15

EXERCISE SET 2.2

1. Given universal set $U = \{1, 2, 3, 4, 5, 6, 7, 8, 9, 10\}$ and subsets $A = \{1, 3, 5, 7, 9\}$ and $B = \{1, 2, 3, 4\}$, list the following sets in roster notation.
   (a) $A \cap B$ (b) A' (c) $A \cup B$
   (d) $A' \cup B$ (e) $A' \cap B'$ (f) $A \cap U$
   (g) U' (h) $A \times B$ (i) $B \times B$
   (j) $\varnothing \times A$

2. Refer to Exercise 1 and fill in the numbers 1 through 10 in the Venn diagram shown in Figure 2.16.

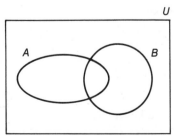

Figure 2.16

3. Make a Venn diagram showing universal set $U = \{1, 2, 3, 4, 5, 6, 7, 8, 9, 10\}$ and the following subsets:

   A: the odd numbers in U
   B: the perfect squares in U
   C: the numbers in U that divide 18 with no remainder

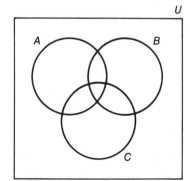

Figure 2.17

4. Make several copies of the Venn diagram in Figure 2.17, which shows a universal set U and three subsets, A, B, and C. Shade the following subsets on your Venn diagrams.
   (a) $A \cap B$ (b) $C \cup A$
   (c) B' (d) $(A \cup C) \cap B$
   (e) $A \cup (C \cap B)$ (f) $A' \cap (B \cup C)$
   (g) $B \cup B'$ (h) $(C')'$

5. The tree diagram shown in Figure 2.18 represents a Cartesian product $S \times T$. Describe the sets S and T in roster notation.

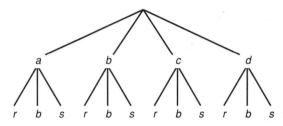

Figure 2.18

6. The rectangular array of dots in Figure 2.19 represents a Cartesian product $A \times B$. Draw a tree that represents $B \times A$.

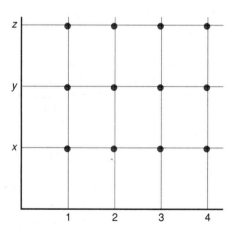

Figure 2.19

7. Given $A = \{1, 2, 3, 4, 5\}$ and $B = \{2, 4, 6\}$.
   (a) Represent $A \times B$ by a rectangular array of dots.

(b) Represent $B \times A$ by a rectangular array of dots.
(c) Represent $A \times B$ by a tree.
(d) Represent $B \times A$ by a tree.
(e) Describe $(A \times B) \cap (B \times A)$ in roster notation.

8. The diagram in Figure 2.20 shows a universal set U (the set of natural numbers 1 through 10) and one of its subsets A.
   (a) Loop and label the subset $B = \{1, 2, 5, 6\}$ of U.
   (b) Loop and label the subset C of U consisting of all numbers exactly divisible by 3.
   (c) Describe $A \cup B$ in roster notation.
   (d) Describe $B \cap C$ in roster notation.
   (e) Is it true that $(1, 2) \subset B$?
   (f) Is it true that $\{1, 2\} = (1, 2)$?
   (g) Is it true that $A \times B \subseteq U$?
   (h) How many elements has $A \times B$?
   (i) How many elements has $(A \cup B)'$?

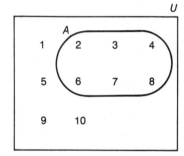

Figure 2.20

9. Four of the many subsets of your math class are these: A (artists), B (baseball fans), C (cooks), and D (dancers). Represent yourself with a dot in the appropriate region in each of the Venn diagrams in Figure 2.21. Which diagram is better for representing four subsets?

10. In the math department 20 people ride bikes to work and carry their lunches, 32 people carry their lunches, and 35 people ride bikes to work or carry their lunches. How many people ride bikes to work?

11. In a group of 100 people 70 read *Newsweek*, 60 read *Time*, and 20 read neither magazine. How many read both?

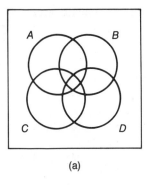
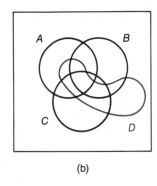

(a)   (b)

Figure 2.21

★ 12. If set A has 7 elements, set B has 8 elements, set C has 9 elements, and $A \cup B$ has 10 elements, how many nonempty subsets has $(A \cap B) \times C$? *Hint:* Use the problem-solving strategy of working backwards.

13. In a group of 100 people there are 54 smokers and 67 drinkers. What can be said about the number who both smoke and drink?

14. A public opinion survey was conducted to determine how much support the president had for his economic (E), military (M), and social (S) policies. The percents of support were EMS 8%, EM 12%, MS 11%, ES 18%, E 40%, M 40%, and S 33%.
    (a) What percent disagreed with all three policies?
    (b) What percent agreed with just one of the three policies?

15. At an election 100 voters voted on three propositions, A, B, and C:

    10 did not vote yes on any proposition
    50 voted yes on C but not A
    30 voted yes on both B and A
    20 voted yes on B but not A
    12 voted yes on all three

    How many voted yes on proposition A?

★ 16. *A three-ring circus:* We assign a weight of 12 to Figure 2.22(a) because there is one triple intersection (indicated by a 3), three doubles (indicated by 2s), and three singles (indicated by 1s). Figure 2.22(b) is assigned weight 5. Using just three rings each time, make diagrams for all weights from 3 up through 13. (Notice that the circles may be of different sizes.)

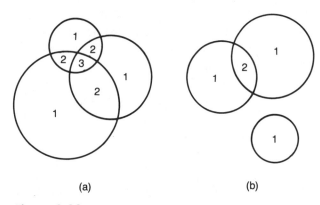

(a)   (b)

Figure 2.22

17. The intersection operation ∩ is said to be *commutative* because for any sets A and B, $A \cap B = B \cap A$.
    (a) What would it mean to say that the union operation is commutative? Is it?
    (b) What would it mean to say that the Cartesian product operation is commutative? Is it?

18. The intersection operation is said to be *associative* because for any sets A, B, and C, $(A \cap B) \cap C = A \cap (B \cap C)$, where the parentheses indicate which sets are to be intersected first.
    (a) Shade in two identical Venn diagrams (of the kind shown in Figure 2.17), one to show $(A \cap B) \cap C$ and the other to show $A \cap (B \cap C)$. Do your diagrams look alike?
    (b) What would it mean to say that the union operation is associative? Show that it is by shading two Venn diagrams as you did in part (a).

19. A universal set U is said to be an *identity element* for the intersection operation because for any subset A of U, $U \cap A = A$. What would it mean to say that the empty set $\varnothing$ is an identity element for the union operation? Is it?

20. Use (small) sets of numbers and the rectangular array representation for Cartesian product to illustrate that Cartesian product *distributes* over union; that is, $A \times (B \cup C) = (A \times B) \cup (A \times C)$.

2.3　*Functions: The Basic Concepts*

The concept of function is more subtle than the concept of set. Rather than begin with a definition, we will build up to the concept via examples.

Consider the diagram in Figure 2.23 for our set of six famous men, and the set of two letters, E and G. When presented with such a diagram, we have a natural impulse to do some matching, as indicated in Figure 2.24. What interpretations of E and G underlie the matching shown?

Next consider the pair of sets in Figure 2.25. Again, there is a natural way to match up the elements of the first set with those of the second. Sketch in the arrows. In doing so, you describe a *function*.

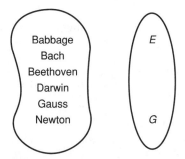

Figure 2.23

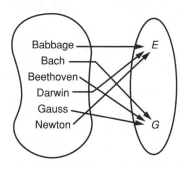

Figure 2.24

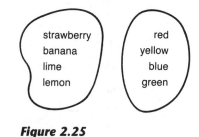

Figure 2.25

As a first approximation to a definition of function, use this:

Any time you assign to each element of a first set an element of a second set, you create a **function.**

Now consider the set of geometric figures A, B, C, and D and the set of natural numbers 1 through 12 shown in Figure 2.26. Does some function suggest itself naturally? Different people give different responses to this mathematical Rorschach test. Some see the area function a indicated in Figure 2.27. Some see the perimeter function p illustrated in Figure 2.28. Others see the function v that counts the number of vertices (corners), as shown in Figure 2.29.

These geometric examples show that to describe a function, we cannot simply list two sets and hope that everyone will see the same matching. We must

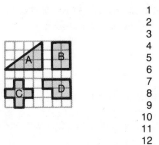

Figure 2.26

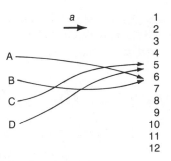

Figure 2.27

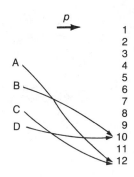

Figure 2.28

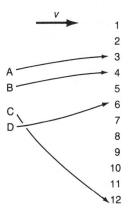

Figure 2.29

specify what the matching is. They also show that since there can be many different functions between the same two sets, it is useful to distinguish them with letter names (such as *a*, *p*, and *v*) that suggest what the matchings are.

Ways of Describing Functions

There are many ways to describe or denote functions. We shall illustrate five common ways, using as examples the area function *a* of Figure 2.27 and the multiply-by-two function M_2, which assigns to each whole number its double.

The first way is by an **arrow diagram.** In an arrow diagram the two sets are listed and arrows are drawn to show what is matched with what. An arrow diagram has already been given for the area function *a*. An incomplete arrow diagram for the function M_2 (from *W* to *W*) is given in Figure 2.30.

A second way of describing a function is by means of a **table.** In a table matching elements are listed across from each other. This is the way functions are generally described in newspapers and magazines. For example, Table 2.1 might appear in a football program to describe the approximate-weight-in-pounds function that assigns a whole number to each member of the team. Tables for our functions *a* and M_2 are given in Table 2.2.

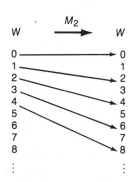

Figure 2.30

Table 2.1

Adams	212
Brown	250
Chavez	230
Drake	185
Escobar	200
⋮	⋮

Table 2.2

a		M_2	
A	6	0	0
B	6	1	2
C	5	2	4
D	5	3	6
		4	8
		⋮	⋮

A third way of describing a function is by means of a **set of ordered pairs.** Matching elements are simply paired up, as illustrated here for a and M_2:

a: $\{(A, 6), (B, 6), (C, 5), (D, 5)\}$

M_2: $\{(0, 0), (1, 2), (2, 4), (3, 6), (4, 8), \ldots\}$

Clearly, there is not much difference between the description of a function by a table and its description by a set of ordered pairs. There is *theoretical value,* however, in thinking of a function as a set of ordered pairs: From this point of view a function from a set A to a set B is just a special kind of subset of the set $A \times B$. That is, the idea of function can be thrown back on the earlier concept of Cartesian product. The practical importance of this way of thinking is that it leads naturally to the description of a function by means of a graph.

Describing a function by a **graph,** our fourth method, is probably familiar from high school. A graph of the area function a is shown in Figure 2.31. Observe that the four dots representing this function constitute a subset of the rectangular array of 48 dots representing

$$\{A, B, C, D\} \times \{1, 2, 3, \ldots, 12\}$$

The graph of M_2 in Figure 2.32 is a subset of $W \times W$.

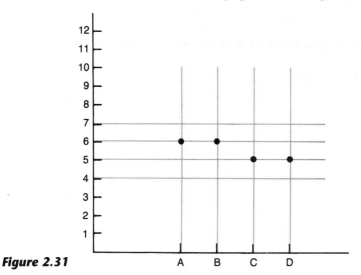

Figure 2.31

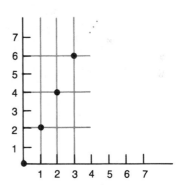

Figure 2.32

The fifth way of describing a function is by means of a **formula.** The formula for the multiply-by-two function M_2 is

$$M_2(x) = 2 \cdot x$$

which is read "M_2 of x equals 2 times x." The x can be thought of as a blank that can be filled by any whole number. For example, to determine what number is assigned to 17 by M_2, replace x by 17 and simplify:

$$M_2(17) = 2 \cdot 17 = 34$$

That is M_2 assigns to 17 the number 34.

Not every function can be described by a formula, though. In particular, our area function a cannot. If all of the geometric figures in our example had been triangles, then we could have written a formula:

$$a(x) = \tfrac{1}{2} \cdot (\text{base of } x) \cdot (\text{height of } x)$$

If they had all been rectangles or all circles, other formulas could have been used. But no single formula covers the mixture of figures in our example.

Machine Viewpoint

So far we have thought about a function as a rather passive matching of the elements of a first set with those of a second. Another way of thinking about a function, which is very helpful in many contexts, is as a *machine* that actively transforms the elements of the first set into elements of the second. From this point of view the first set is considered the **input set** and the second set, or some subset of it, the **output set.**

For example, the area function a can be thought of as a machine that accepts geometric figures as inputs and produces numbers as outputs. See Figure 2.33. Imagine a wise elf sitting inside machine a. When a geometric figure falls in, he takes some measurements, applies an appropriate area formula (if necessary), writes his result on a slip of paper, and drops it through the output chute.

The multiply-by-two function M_2 accepts whole numbers as inputs and produces (even) whole numbers as outputs. See Figure 2.34. The elf in this machine has an easy job.

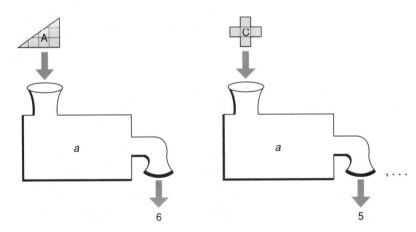

Figure 2.33

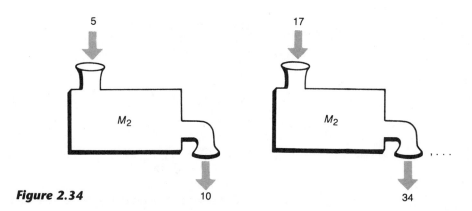

Figure 2.34

This machine viewpoint emphasizes an important property of functions. Each input into a function gives rise to exactly one output. For example, when a geometric figure is dropped in, the area machine *a* does not spew out a whole batch of numbers; instead, exactly one number drops out. We can use the following as a workable definition of function.

> A **function** is a rule that assigns to each element of one set (the input set, or **domain**) *exactly one* element of another set (the output set, or **range**).

EXAMPLE 1   Why does the arrow diagram in Figure 2.35 *not* represent a function?

Solution   The input 3 has more than one output. This example illustrates a *relation*. The concept of relation is explored in an (optional) section at the end of this chapter.   ❑

Figure 2.35

The machine viewpoint also helps to clarify the notation used when a function is described by a formula. Figure 2.36 shows how each piece of the notation can be interpreted. Some people find it helpful to remember that the *in*put is *in* the parentheses.

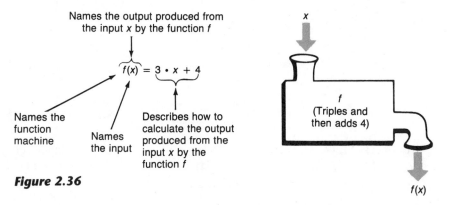

Figure 2.36

EXAMPLE 2   A function f is defined by the formula $f(x) = 15 - 2x$.
(a) $f(3) = $ ___?___
(b) $f($ ___?___ $) = 1$
(c) $f[f(4)] = $ ___?___
(d) Find c so that $f(c) = c$.

Solution   (a) $f(3) = 15 - 2 \cdot 3 = 9$
(b) $f(x) = 1 \Rightarrow 15 - 2x = 1 \Rightarrow x = 7$
(c) $f[f(4)] = f[15 - 2 \cdot 4] = f[7] = 15 - 2 \cdot 7 = 1$
(d) $f(c) = c \Rightarrow 15 - 2c = c \Rightarrow c = 5$ ❏

The view of functions as input-output machines is a very natural one in this age of the calculator and computer. To illustrate the idea for youngsters, you could hold up a calculator and go through pairs of keystrokes of the following type:

$\boxed{7}$ "I am giving the machine the input 7" (The display shows 7)

$\boxed{x^2}$ "I am waking up the elf who squares things" (The display shows the output 49)

Computer Vignette A (p. 56) provides a more complex illustration of how the computer can act as a function machine (complete with messages from the elf inside).

EXERCISE SET 2.3

In Exercises 1–5 a function is presented in one of five ways: by an arrow diagram, by a table, by a set of ordered pairs, by a graph, or by a formula. Describe that function in the other four ways.

1.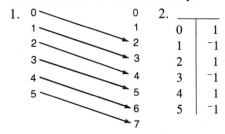

2.

0	1
1	⁻1
2	1
3	⁻1
4	1
5	⁻1

3. $\{(0, 0), (1, 1), (2, 4), (3, 9), (4, 16)\}$

4. $f(x) = x^2 - 2x$ (for $x = 0, 1, 2, 3, 4$)

5.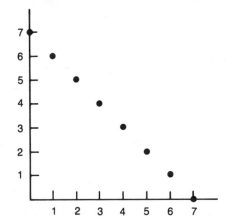

6. The input set is $\{0, 1, 2, 3, 4, 5\}$; the rule is $f(x) = x \cdot (x - 1)$. List the output set.

7. The rule is $f(x) = 3x + 2$; the output set is $\{8, 14, 20\}$. List the input set.

★ 8. How many different functions are there with input set $\{1, 2, 3, 4\}$ and output set a subset of $\{1, 2, 3\}$? *Hint:* Use the problem-solving strategies of asking easier questions and looking for a pattern.

9. Two arrow diagrams are shown in Figure 2.37. Try to discover a simple formula for each function.

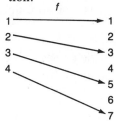 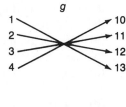

$f(x) =$ _____ $g(x) =$ _____

Figure 2.37

🐚 10. The following table was taken from the instruction manual for an electronic flash unit. Discover a formula for the (approximate) flash guide number $f(x)$ corresponding to an ASA film speed of x, and use it to predict the (approximate) flash guide number for film of ASA speed 1000.

ASA film speed x	25	64	80	100	125	160	200	400	800
Flash guide number $f(x)$	60	96	108	120	135	150	170	240	340

11. A function f is defined by the formula $f(x) = 4x - 1$.
    (a) $f(2) = $?   (b) $f(5) = $?
    (c) $f(\underline{?}) = 35$
    (d) Find c so that $f(c) = c$.

12. Figure 2.38 shows the graph of a function f with input set all real numbers between 0 and 7 and output set all real numbers between 0 and 4. Use the graph to estimate the following:
    (a) $f(1\frac{1}{2})$
    (b) The number x for which $f(x) = 1$

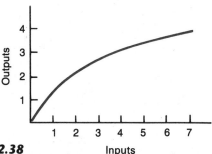

Figure 2.38

(c) $f(3) + f(4)$
(d) $f(3 + 4)$
(e) $f[f(7)]$
(f) The number x for which $f(x) = x$

13. Repeat Exercise 12, using the graph in Figure 2.39.

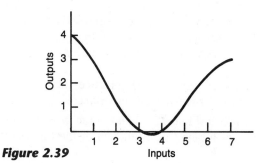

Figure 2.39

14. Which of the following do *not* describe functions?

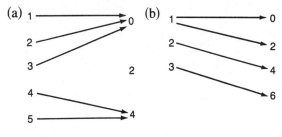

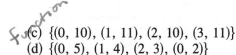
(c) $\{(0, 10), (1, 11), (2, 10), (3, 11)\}$
(d) $\{(0, 5), (1, 4), (2, 3), (0, 2)\}$

(e)

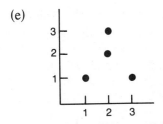

(f) $S(x) = x$'s senator, where the input set is the set of 50 states and the output set is the set of all U.S. senators.

15. If you stretch your imagination a little, you can think of a ruler as a function machine.
    (a) If it is the usual foot rule sold in dime stores, what sort of inputs could it accept? Describe its output set as carefully as you can.
    (b) Suppose it is a ruler with centimeters marked on it. Describe its output set as carefully as you can.

16. With your imagination still stretched, describe the input set and the output set of a dime store protractor viewed as a function machine.

Exercises 17–20 give some practice in reading graphs, a skill of fundamental importance.

17. The graph in Figure 2.40 shows the weight w in pounds of a rabbit as a function of the time t in

weeks since a new feeding program was instituted. Estimate the following from the graph.
(a) How much the rabbit weighed after 3 weeks
(b) How long it took the rabbit to reach a weight of 6 lb
(c) How many pounds the rabbit gained from the end of week 3 to the end of week 5
(d) How long it took for the rabbit's weight to go from 6 lb to 7 lb

18. Figure 2.41 is a graph of the population P of a town as a function of time t. Use it to estimate the following:
(a) The population in 1950
(b) The year when the population reached 3000
(c) The year when the population hit its maximum
(d) The maximum population
(e) The minimum population
(f) The change in population between 1950 and 1960
(g) The change in population between 1970 and 1980
(h) The decade of greatest population growth

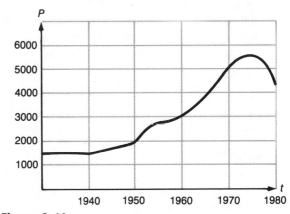

Figure 2.41

The next two exercises illustrate the usefulness of graphing two related functions on the same set of axes.

19. The red graph in Figure 2.42 shows the cost C in dollars of producing n widgets. For example, it costs over $8 to produce the first widget (heavy

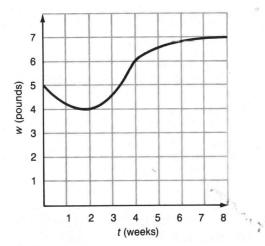

Figure 2.40

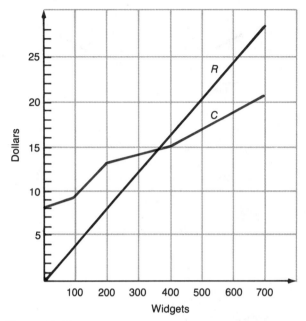

Figure 2.42

start-up costs) and $13 to produce the first 200 widgets. The black graph shows the revenue *R* in dollars from sales of *n* widgets. For example, selling the first 100 widgets brings in $4, selling the first 200 widgets brings in $8, and so on. Estimate the following from the graphs.

(a) The cost of producing (the first) 500 widgets
(b) The revenue generated by the sale of (the first) 300 widgets
(c) The profit (or loss) if 300 widgets are produced and sold
(d) The profit (or loss) if 600 widgets are produced and sold
(e) The break-even point, that is, the number of widgets one must produce and sell to have neither profit nor loss
(f) The number of widgets that must be sold to break even if 700 have already been produced
(g) The selling price of each widget
(h) The (total) cost of producing widgets 201 through 400
(i) The marginal cost of the 300th widget, that is, the difference in cost between producing 300 and producing 299

(j) The marginal cost of the 500th widget

20. Estimate the following from the graphs of cost and revenue functions shown in Figure 2.43.
(a) The cost of producing 500 widgets
(b) The revenue generated by the sale of 500 widgets
(c) The profit on 500 widgets
(d) The break-even point
(e) The marginal cost of the 500th widget
(f) The selling price of each widget

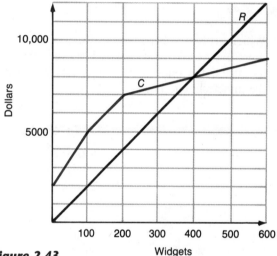

Figure 2.43

21. In Exercises 17–20 you were given graphs and asked to decipher the story each one told. In this exercise you are given a story and asked to encode it in a graph.

A motorist is driving along at 65 mph when she passes a patrol car just pulling out from behind a billboard alongside the highway. She takes her foot off the accelerator until 20 seconds later she is going 55 mph; then she holds her speed steady. After another 40 sec the patrol car whizzes past her at a high rate of speed.
(a) Represent the motorist's actions during the minute in question by a (solid) graph on the time-speed graph paper of Figure 2.44.
(b) Represent (roughly) the policeman's actions by a (dotted) graph on the same graph paper.

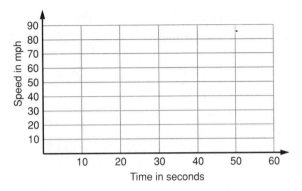

Figure 2.44

Figure 2.45

22. Which of the following graphs (Figure 2.45) best represents the changing distance between the motorist and the policeman of Exercise 21 during the minute in question?

Computer Vignette A

Manual computation of outputs of a function like

$$f(x) = 2x^3 - 5x^2 + 6x + 1$$

even for small inputs, is quite an arithmetic chore. For example, input 3 yields output

$$2 \cdot 3^3 - 5 \cdot 3^2 + 6 \cdot 3 + 1 = 2 \cdot 27 - 5 \cdot 9 + 6 \cdot 3 + 1$$
$$= 54 - 45 + 18 + 1 = 28$$

A hand calculator can save some time. On an AOS (algebraic operating system) calculator this sequence of 17 keystrokes,

$$\boxed{2}\ \boxed{\times}\ \boxed{3}\ \boxed{y^x}\ \boxed{3}\ \boxed{-}\ \boxed{5}\ \boxed{\times}\ \boxed{3}\ \boxed{x^2}\ \boxed{+}\ \boxed{6}\ \boxed{\times}\ \boxed{3}\ \boxed{+}\ \boxed{1}\ \boxed{=}$$

will produce a display of 28. To find the output produced by the input 4, though, requires another 17 keystrokes.

A great laborsaving device is the **interactive** computer program. When the program in Figure 2.46 is run, it asks you what input you want to submit. After you type it in, the computer responds immediately with the output. Then it asks you if you want to submit another input. All this is done in a matter of seconds. Thus you only have to work hard once—when you write the program. After that you can get as many input-output pairs as you please with no further effort. A sample run is shown in Figure 2.47.

Figure 2.46
```
10    PRINT "WHAT INPUT DO YOU WANT TO SUBMIT?"
20    INPUT X
30    LET Y = 2 * X ∧ 3 − 5 * X ∧ 2 + 6 * X + 1
40    PRINT "THE CORRESPONDING OUTPUT IS ";Y
50    PRINT "DO YOU WANT TO SUBMIT ANOTHER INPUT?
      IF YES TYPE '1'; IF NO, TYPE '0'."
60    INPUT A
70    IF A = 1 THEN 10
80    END
```

Figure 2.47
```
]RUN
WHAT INPUT DO YOU WANT TO SUBMIT?
?3
THE CORRESPONDING OUTPUT IS 28
DO YOU WANT TO SUBMIT ANOTHER INPUT? IF YES, TYPE '1';
IF NO, TYPE '0'.
?1
WHAT INPUT DO YOU WANT TO SUBMIT?
?8
THE CORRESPONDING OUTPUT IS 753
DO YOU WANT TO SUBMIT ANOTHER INPUT? IF YES, TYPE '1';
IF NO, TYPE '0'.
?1
WHAT INPUT DO YOU WANT TO SUBMIT?
?100
THE CORRESPONDING OUTPUT IS 1950601
DO YOU WANT TO SUBMIT ANOTHER INPUT? IF YES, TYPE '1';
IF NO, TYPE '0'.
?0
```

Remember that at this point you should *not* be worrying about the details of the program, how it was devised, or why it works as it does. Programming is the subject of Chapter 16. The purpose of this vignette, and ensuing ones, is to show what kinds of things a computer *can* do.

If you have access to a machine and have had some computing experience, type in the program and run it. Notice (line 30) that our machine uses $X \wedge 3$ for x^3. Some other machines use $X \uparrow 3$ or $X ** 3$.

Note: On some machines and for some integers X, $X \wedge 2$, and $X \wedge 3$ take on nonintegral values because the machine's internal exponentiation algorithm is not simple repeated multiplication. For example, on my machine

$$9 \wedge 2 = 81.0000001 \quad \text{and} \quad 9 \wedge 3 = 729.0000001$$

To avoid this difficulty, in line 30 replace

$$X \wedge 2 \text{ by } X * X \quad \text{and} \quad X \wedge 3 \text{ by } X * X * X$$

Sometimes, you know beforehand just which inputs you want to submit. In such cases you may be able to automate the whole process, as we did in the program of Figure 1.24, where the area function A = D(50 − 2D) was evaluated for all values of D in the input set {0, 1, 2, . . . , 25}.

2.4 *Composition of Functions; One-to-One Correspondences*

In our work with sets we studied four operations on sets. Each was a way of putting together two sets to make a third set. There are also a number of operations on functions, that is, ways of putting together two functions to make a third. Only one will be important in our work, the operation of *composition*. After we have explained what is meant by composition, we will see some occurrences of this fundamental mathematical concept: in chain computations on a calculator, in simple algebra, and in problem solving. Later in the book composition will be helpful in clarifying certain arithmetic operations on the integers and rational numbers and in defining the geometric ideas of congruence and similarity.

Composition

To compose two functions, you simply hook them up in sequence. For example, we can hook up the area function a and the multiply-by-two function M_2 of the previous section in the order, first a then M_2, and arrive at a new function, the red machine in Figure 2.48. (The informal *hookup* terminology that we have begun to employ is less forbidding than the *compose* terminology and has been used successfully with elementary school children in the Comprehensive School Mathematics Project.) The inputs for the hookup in Figure 2.48 must be geometric figures, since that's what a accepts. Its outputs will be numbers, since that's what M_2 produces. Figure 2.48 shows how the input C is transformed into the output 10 by the composite function first-a-then-M_2. Notice how the outputs of the first machine automatically become inputs for the second.

There are two things to watch out for concerning composition. One is that not just *any* pair of functions can be composed (hooked up). The outputs of the first function must be acceptable inputs for the second one. For example, if we tried to hook up M_2 with a in the order first M_2 then a, a nonoperating machine would result. See Figure 2.49.

The other danger spot is that even when two functions can be hooked up in either order, the resulting functions can be different. For example, let's hook up the multiply-by-two function M_2 and the add-three function A_3 in two different orders and see what their effect is on some input, say 7. The effects, shown in Figure 2.50 are not the same. These two hookups are different functions.

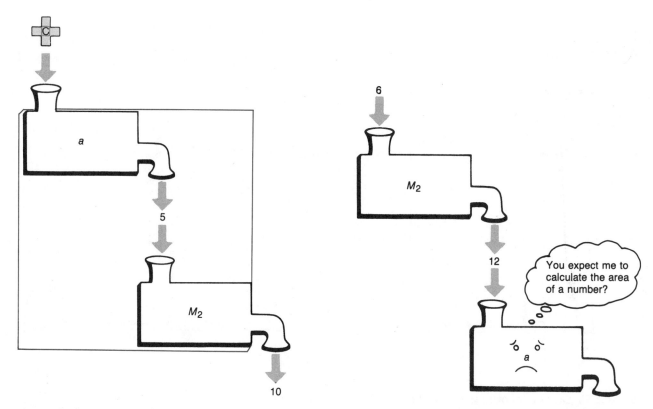

Figure 2.48 The hookup, first a then M_2.

Figure 2.49 An unhappy elf.

There are certain pairs of functions for which the order of hookup is immaterial (try A_3 and A_4, or M_2 and M_5), but usually the order of hookup makes a difference.

The composition operation is valuable because it permits one to break up a complicated process into a sequence of simple ones. This is what Henry Ford had in mind when he set up his assembly line. Another nonmathematical example of the value of hookups is in the teaching of piano. The goal is to have the student look at a note on a musical score and strike the appropriate key on the piano. Typically, this goal is attained by means of a hookup. We illustrate for the simple case of the key of C. First, the student learns to assign letters of the alphabet to printed notes. Then she learns to assign piano keys to letters of the alphabet. Finally, she hooks up these two functions, as shown in Figure 2.51, so that when she sees a printed note she automatically hits the correct key, without consciously thinking about the intervening alphabet letter. In this sense every piano player is a composer.

Complicated mathematical functions can frequently be broken down into hookups of much simpler functions. For example, the function

$$f(x) = 3 \cdot x + 4$$

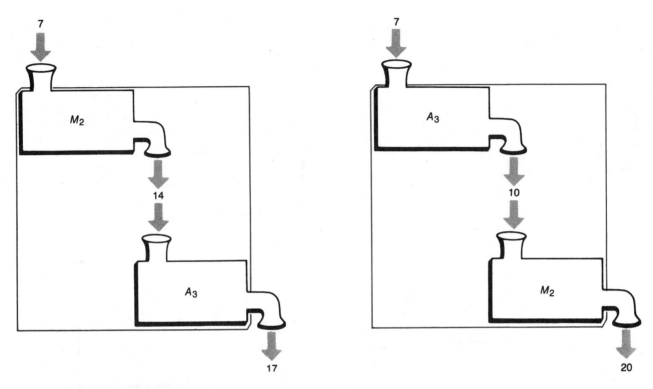

Figure 2.50 Order of hookup makes a difference.

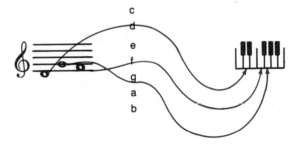

Figure 2.51

is the hookup

First M_3, then A_4

where M_3 is the multiply-by-three function and A_4 is the add-four function. As another example, the function

$$g(x) = \frac{7(x - 3) + 5}{2}$$

is the hookup

First S_3, then M_7, then A_5, then D_2

where S_3 is the subtract-three function, M_7 is the multiply-by-seven function, A_5 is the add-five function, and D_2 is the divide-by-two function.

There are several reasons why it is important to be able to decompose a function like g in the way we have. If you want to evaluate a function like g on a calculator, one way is to key in a hookup of simple functions. For example, to find $g(8)$, key in

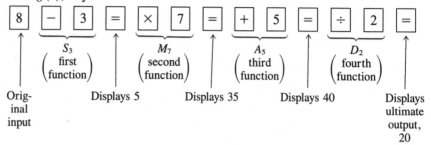

The result is $g(8) = 20$.

Another reason—and perhaps a more compelling reason for future middle or junior high school teachers—is that a conceptually simple technique for solving equations like

$$\frac{7(x - 3) + 5}{2} = 13$$

can be based on expressing the left side as a hookup. We will learn the technique shortly.

One-to-One Correspondences

There is one very special type of function that is important in all branches and at all levels of mathematics: the *one-to-one correspondence*. Informally,

A **one-to-one correspondence** between two sets is a *pairing off* of all the elements of the first set with all of the elements of the second set.

Speaking more precisely, we have the following definition:

A one-to-one correspondence from a set A to a set B is a function from A to B that has two properties:

1. Two different inputs (from A) never yield the same output (in B).
2. Every element in B is an output.

A beautiful symmetry appears in this definition if the phrase "is a function from A to B" is replaced by its two defining conditions:

1'. Two different outputs (in B) never come from the same input (from A).

2'. Every element in A is an input.

EXAMPLE 1   Which of the arrow diagrams in Figure 2.52 represent one-to-one correspondences from A to B?

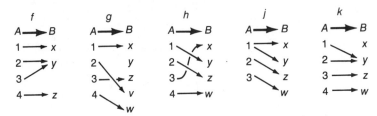

Figure 2.52

Solution   Assignment f is *not* a one-to-one correspondence from A to B because condition 1 is violated: Two different inputs (2 and 3) yield the same output (y). This function is many-to-one, not one-to-one. Note that condition (2) is satisfied, however.

Assignment g is *not* a one-to-one correspondence from A to B because condition (2) is violated: The element y in set B is not an output. It doesn't "correspond" to anything in A. Note that condition (1) is satisfied.

Assignment h *is* a one-to-one correspondence from A to B because both conditions (1) and (2) are satisfied.

Assignment j is *not* a one-to-one correspondence from A to B because it is not a function: condition (1') is violated. Note that conditions (1) and (2) are satisfied.

Assignment k is *not* a one-to-one correspondence from A to B because both conditions (1) and (2) are violated.   ❑

The following examples illustrate the important point that the property of being a one-to-one correspondence is a property of the function f *and* of the sets A and B. It is meaningless to ask if a function f is a one-to-one correspondence without specifying the sets A and B.

EXAMPLE 2   The multiply-by-two function M_2 is *not* a one-to-one correspondence from W to W (from the whole numbers to the whole numbers). But it *is* a one-to-one correspondence from W to the set E of even whole numbers. See Figure 2.53.

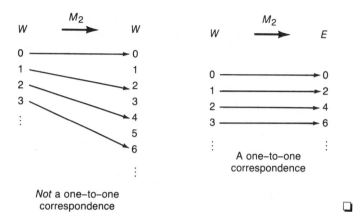

Figure 2.53

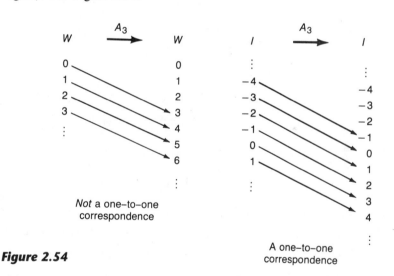

Figure 2.54

EXAMPLE 3   The add-three function A_3 is not a one-to-one correspondence from W to W. But it is a one-to-one correspondence from I to I (from the integers to the integers). See Figure 2.54.

Inverse of a One-to-One Correspondence

One reason one-to-one correspondences are so important is that they are reversible. Consider, for example, the one-to-one correspondence shown in Figure 2.55. By simply reversing the arrows, we get a one-to-one correspondence from B to A, which we write as f^{-1} and read "f inverse." See Figure 2.56.

Clearly, the hookup, f then f^{-1}, sends each element of A back to itself. In this sense f^{-1} "undoes" the effect of f.

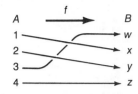

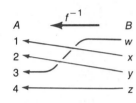

Figure 2.55

Figure 2.56

If f is a one-to-one correspondence from A to B, then the **inverse** of f, written f^{-1}, is the function from B to A that undoes the effect of f.

In symbols,

$$f^{-1}(f(a)) = a \quad \text{for all } a \in A \qquad \text{and} \qquad f(f^{-1}(b)) = b \quad \text{for all } b \in B$$

In many examples more suggestive notation is available for the inverse of a one-to-one correspondence. For example, the inverse of the one-to-one correspondence M_2 (multiply by 2) from W to E is the one-to-one correspondence D_2 (divide by 2) from E to W, and the inverse of the one-to-one correspondence A_3 (add 3) from I to I is the one-to-one correspondence S_3 (subtract 3) from I to I. In terms of machines the add-three machine is reversible, and when it is running in reverse it is a subtract-three machine, as indicated in Figure 2.57.

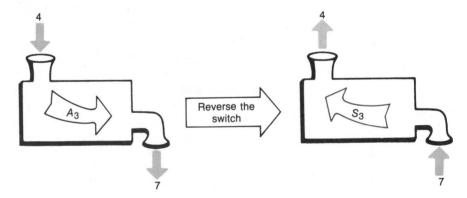

Figure 2.57

All of the simple arithmetic functions (except M_0, multiply by zero) are one-to-one correspondences from Q to Q, and their inverses are fairly obvious:

$$Q \underset{S_6}{\overset{A_6}{\rightleftarrows}} Q \quad Q \underset{A_2}{\overset{S_2}{\rightleftarrows}} Q \quad Q \underset{D_3}{\overset{M_3}{\rightleftarrows}} Q \quad Q \underset{M_8}{\overset{D_8}{\rightleftarrows}} Q$$

(Remember that Q represents the set of rational numbers.)

The functional point of view, then, provides a precise meaning for the rather vague statements

"Addition and subtraction are inverse operations"
"Multiplication and division are inverse operations"

which you have undoubtedly heard since your own elementary school days.

Hookups of the simple arithmetic functions also turn out to be one-to-one correspondences from Q to Q. (Can you see why different inputs into the hookup, first A_3, then M_2, will yield different outputs?) To find the inverse of a

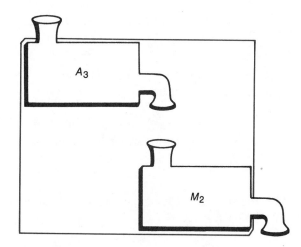

Figure 2.58

hookup such as first-A_3-then-M_2 is not difficult once you picture the machines. The hookup is shown in Figure 2.58.

If this machine is run in reverse, a number enters at the bottom, passes through M_2 in reverse (that is, D_2), passes through A_3 in reverse (that is, S_3), and emerges at the top. That is, the inverse of first-A_3-then-M_2 is first-D_2-then-S_3. Notice that besides reversing all the simple functions, one also *reverses the order in which they are hooked up*. Here is an analogy that might be helpful: When you get up in the morning, you put on your socks and then your shoes; when you reverse the process at night, you take your shoes off first and then your socks.

Figure 2.59 on page 66 is a page from a fifth-grade textbook showing the concepts of function, inverse of a function, composite function, and inverse of a composite function.

An interesting approach to equation solving can be based on the ideas of hookups and inverses.

EXAMPLE 4

Solve the equation $\dfrac{7(x - 3) + 5}{2} = 13$ by using hookups and inverses.

Solution

One can view the x as an unknown input into the machine S_3-then-M_7-then-A_5-then-D_2, which then outputs 13. Figure 2.60 illustrates how one arrives at the solution $x = 6$.

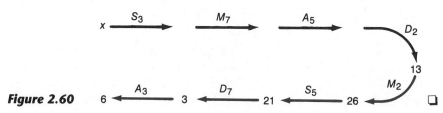

Figure 2.60

Using Inverse Functions

Suppose a number goes into a ×6 function machine and 21 comes out. What number went in?

You can use the inverse function rule to find out. $21 \div 6 = 3.5$ So the number that went in must have been 3.5.

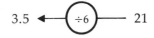

Use the inverse, if it helps you, to find the value of x in each case.

1. x —(+7)→ 8   **4.** x —(−20)→ 0

2. x —(+10)→ 5   **5.** x —(−5)→ (−10)

3. x —(×4)→ 12   **6.** x —(×0)→ 0

Look at this rule for a composite function:

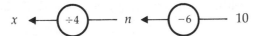

If y is 10, what is x?   You can use the inverse to find out.

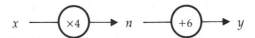

If y is 10, n is 4; and since n is 4, x is 1.

7. Copy and complete this chart.

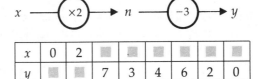

x	0		2						
y				7	3	4	6	2	0

145

Figure 2.59 Inverses and composition of functions in a fifth-grade textbook.

A whole class of mathematical puzzles can be solved by the method illustrated in Example 4, which you can think of as a formalization of the problem-solving strategy "work backwards." Here is an example of the class.

EXAMPLE 5   A merchant visited three fairs. At the first he doubled his money, then spent $25. At the second he tripled his money, then spent $15. At the third he earned $50, spent nothing, and left with $230 in his pocket. How much money did he take to the first fair?

Solution   Follow the arrows in Figure 2.61 to see that he started out with $45.

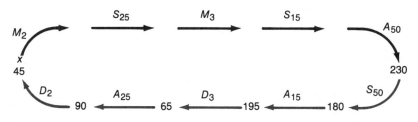

Figure 2.61 ❑

EXERCISE SET 2.4

Exercises 1–3 deal with functions M_2, C, and P described here. For C and P the unit of measure is the centimeter:

├────────┤

1 cm

M_2 (multiplication by 2): inputs are positive numbers. When fed a number, M_2 outputs twice that number.

C (for compass): inputs are positive numbers. When fed a number, C outputs a circle having that number of centimeters as radius.

P (for perimeter): inputs are geometric figures. When fed a geometric figure, P outputs its perimeter (in centimeters).

1. Fill in the missing inputs and outputs.

(a)

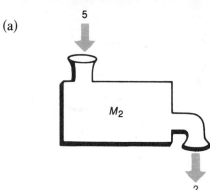

(b)

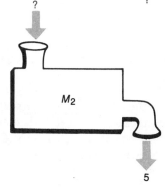

(c)

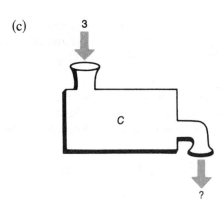

(d)

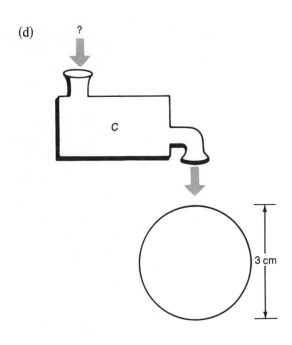

(e)

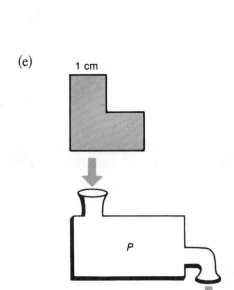

(f)

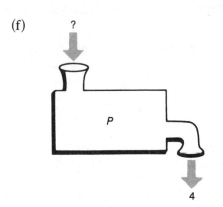

2. Which of the following hookups (compositions) make sense?
   (a) First M_2, then C (b) First C, then M_2
   (c) First C, then P (d) First P, then C
   (e) First P, then M_2 (f) First M_2, then P
   (g) First M_2, then M_2 (h) First C, then C
   (i) First P, then P

3. Fill in the missing items. (The machines have been stylized.)
   (a)

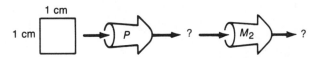

(b)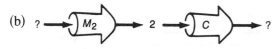

(c)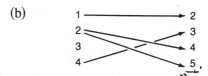

(d)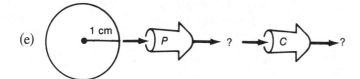

(e)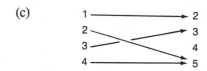

(f)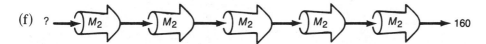

4. The clerk at the post office weighs your parcel, glances at a chart, and tells you it will cost $1.80 in postage. Identify a hookup of two functions in this situation.

5. Express each of the following functions as a hookup of simple arithmetical functions (like A_5, M_2, etc.).

(a) $\dfrac{2x - 3}{4}$

(b) $5(x - 3) + 2$

(c) $3\left(7 + \dfrac{x}{4}\right) - 5$

(d) $\dfrac{4(3 - 2x)}{5}$

6. Use a calculator and the hookups you constructed to find outputs of all four of the functions in Exercise 5 when the input is $x = 5280$.

7. Which of the following represent one-to-one correspondences from $\{1, 2, 3, 4\}$ to $\{2, 3, 4, 5\}$?

(a)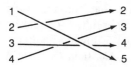

(b)

```
1 ────────→ 2
2 ──╲  ╱──→ 3
3 ──╱  ╲──→ 4
4 ────────→ 5 ˌ
```

(c)

```
1 ────────→ 2
2 ──╲  ╱──→ 3
3 ──╱  ╲──→ 4
4 ────────→ 5
```

(d)

```
1 ────────→ 2
2 ──╲  ╱──→ 3
3 ──╱  ╲──→ 4
4 ────────→ 5
```

8. Which condition of the definition of one-to-one correspondence is violated if one reverses the arrows in the following?

(a) Exercise 7(b)

(b) Exercise 7(c)

★ 9. How many one-to-one correspondences are there?

(a) From $\{1, 2, 3, 4\}$ to $\{2, 3, 4, 5\}$

(b) From $\{1, 2, 3, 4\}$ to $\{6, 7, 8\}$

(c) From $\{1, 2, 3, 4\}$ to $\{9, 10, 11, 12, 13\}$

10. Which of the following functions are one-to-one correspondences between the sets named?
    (a) S_4 from W to I
    (b) A_2 from I to I
    (c) M_2 from I to I
    (d) M_2 from Q^+ to Q^+, where Q^+ denotes the set of positive rational numbers
    (e) f from R^+ to R^+, given by the graph in Figure 2.62

![graph]

Figure 2.62

(f) g from R^+ to R^+, given by the graph in Figure 2.63

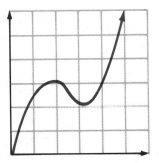

Figure 2.63

11. For each of the one-to-one correspondences in Exercise 10, describe the inverse function.

12. Find the missing input x.
    (a)

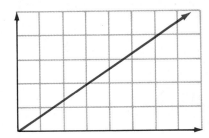

(b)

$x \rightarrow \boxed{A_4} \rightarrow \boxed{D_3} \rightarrow 4$

(c)

$x \rightarrow \boxed{S_2} \rightarrow \boxed{M_5} \rightarrow \boxed{A_3} \rightarrow 18$

(d) $x \xrightarrow{D_2} \xrightarrow{A_3} \xrightarrow{M_5} \xrightarrow{D_4} \xrightarrow{S_3} 7$

13. Solve the following equations by using hookups and inverses (the method illustrated in Example 4).
    (a) $2x - 1 = 11$
    (b) $\dfrac{6(x + 3)}{20} = 3$
    (c) $\dfrac{5(3x - 4) + 1}{8} = 7$
    (d) $\dfrac{(14 - 3x) \cdot 5}{4} = 10$

14. A function f is defined by $f(x) = \dfrac{(5 - 2x)}{3} - 4$.
    Write a formula for the inverse function: $f^{-1}(x) = \underline{\hspace{1cm}}$.

15. While three watchmen were guarding an orchard, a thief slipped in and stole some apples. On his way out he met the three watchmen, one after another, and to each in turn he gave half of the apples he had and two besides. He escaped with one apple. How many had he stolen originally?

16. A gambler lost $20 at the slot machines, doubled her money at roulette, won $50 at blackjack, spent $5 on a snack, lost $\frac{2}{3}$ of her money at bingo, tipped the hatcheck boy $2, and left with $43. What did the evening cost her?

17. I am thinking of a number. If you multiply it by 4, then add 5, then take square root, then subtract 2, then divide by 20, then take reciprocal, and finally cube, you get 64. What is my number?

18. The function that converts Celsius temperature readings to Fahrenheit (C input, F output) can be viewed as the following hookup:
    $$M_9, \text{ then } D_5, \text{ then } A_{32}$$

(a) Use this hookup to convert 20°C to Fahrenheit.

(b) Convert 95°F to Celsius.

(c) Write an equation relating C and F.

★ (d) Find a temperature for which the Celsius and Fahrenheit readings are the same.

19. Does your calculator have an inverse key $\boxed{\text{INV}}$ and a logarithm key $\boxed{\text{LOG}}$ on it? If so, carry out these sequences of keystrokes, and record the corresponding sequences of displays.

(a) $\boxed{5}$ $\boxed{\text{LOG}}$ $\boxed{\text{INV}}$ $\boxed{\text{LOG}}$

(b) $\boxed{5}$ $\boxed{\text{INV}}$ $\boxed{\text{LOG}}$ $\boxed{\text{LOG}}$

★ 20. A function f from W to I is defined as follows:

$$f(x) = \begin{cases} \dfrac{x}{2}, & \text{if } x \text{ is even} \\[2mm] -\left(\dfrac{x+1}{2}\right), & \text{if } x \text{ is odd} \end{cases}$$

Begin drawing an arrow diagram for f, and decide whether f is a one-to-one correspondence from W to I.

21. If A is a finite set and f is a one-to-one correspondence from A to B, must A and B have the same number of elements?

22. If A and B are finite sets with the same number of elements, does there exist a one-to-one correspondence from A to B?

★ 23. Suppose A is a finite set, say $A = \{1, 2, 3, 4, 5\}$, and f is a function from A to A.

(a) If f satisfies condition (1) of the definition of one-to-one correspondence, must it also satisfy condition (2)?

(b) If f satisfies condition (2) of the definition of one-to-one correspondence, must it also satisfy condition (1)?

24. Repeat Exercise 23 under the assumption that A is an infinite set, say $A = W$. If your answer to (a) or (b) is no, support it with an example.

2.5 *One-to-One Correspondences and Comparison of Sets (Optional)*

Suppose you have a set of cups and a set of spoons, and you want to find out which set has more elements. One way would be to count the cups, count the spoons, and compare the two numbers that you obtain. Another way would be to begin placing one spoon in each cup. If you run out of spoons while there are still empty cups, you conclude that there are more cups than spoons. If you have spoons left after putting one in each cup, you conclude that there are more spoons. If you finish by putting the last spoon in the last empty cup, you have set up a one-to-one correspondence between spoons and cups, and you conclude that there are equally many cups and spoons. This second way, although cumbersome, is conceptually simpler than the first.

We formalize the connection between numerosity and one-to-one correspondence in this general property of finite sets.

Two finite sets have equally many elements if and only if there is a one-to-one correspondence between them.

Here is another obvious fact about finite sets.

A finite set *cannot* be placed in one-to-one correspondence with a proper subset of itself; that is, a finite set and a proper subset *cannot* have equally many elements.

We have displayed these two apparently trivial properties because for infinite sets the situation is quite different. First of all, we need to agree on what is meant when we say that two infinite sets have "equally many" elements. The conventional definition is as follows:

Two infinite sets are said to have **equally many** elements (to be *equivalent*) if there is a one-to-one correspondence between them.

Thus the first obvious fact about finite sets becomes the definition of "equally many" for infinite sets.

The second obvious fact about finite sets is false for infinite sets.

An infinite set *can* be placed in one-to-one correspondence with a proper subset of itself; that is, an infinite set and a proper subset *can* have equally many elements.

This property has been known for a long time. For example, Galileo, in 1638, was bold enough to point out that there is a one-to-one correspondence between all of the natural numbers and the subset of perfect squares:

$$
\begin{array}{ccccccc}
1 & 2 & 3 & 4 & 5 & \cdots \\
\downarrow & \downarrow & \downarrow & \downarrow & \downarrow & \cdots \\
1 & 4 & 9 & 16 & 25 & \cdots
\end{array}
$$

That is, the set of natural numbers and the proper subset of perfect squares have equally many elements. Similarly, the one-to-one correspondence M_2 from W to E shows that there are just as many even whole numbers as whole numbers, and the one-to-one correspondence A_1 from W to N shows that there are just as many natural numbers as whole numbers.

A common misconception about infinite sets is that they are all equally large—that somehow the fact that two sets are infinite guarantees that they can be placed in one-to-one correspondence. This most assuredly is *not* the case, as Georg Cantor proved simply but elegantly a little over a hundred years ago (1874). Cantor proved the following property.

> There can be no one-to-one correspondence between the infinite set N of natural numbers and the infinite set C of real numbers between 0 and 1.

To follow his argument, we need only grant that every real number between 0 and 1 can be named by an infinite decimal.

Cantor's strategy was to show that *no* function from N to C could possibly use up every member of C. His tactics are best illustrated with a specific example. Suppose we were to present Cantor with this function from N to C:

$$1 \rightarrow .5 \quad 2 \quad 7 \quad 3 \quad 8 \quad 1 \quad \ldots$$
$$2 \rightarrow .0 \quad 7 \quad 6 \quad 0 \quad 0 \quad 0 \quad \ldots$$
$$3 \rightarrow .8 \quad 1 \quad 1 \quad 7 \quad 4 \quad 7 \quad \ldots$$
$$4 \rightarrow .3 \quad 2 \quad 5 \quad 9 \quad 6 \quad 1 \quad \ldots$$
$$5 \rightarrow .1 \quad 0 \quad 7 \quad 3 \quad 6 \quad 4 \quad \ldots$$
$$\vdots$$

He would look down the diagonal and construct, as follows, a number d between 0 and 1 not touched by our function:

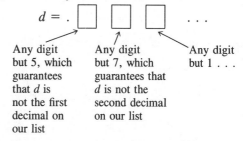

Thus the set of real numbers between 0 and 1 is definitely of a larger order of infinity than the set of natural numbers. Infinite sets do come in different sizes!

The Pigeonhole Principle

Let's go back to the cups and the spoons. Suppose there are 12 cups and 15 spoons, and a child is told to put all of the spoons into the cups. Which of the following statements *must* be true?

1. Every cup will have at least one spoon in it.
2. Three cups will have two spoons apiece.
3. No cup will be empty.
4. Some cup will have at least two spoons in it.

Georg Cantor

Grace Chisholm Young

❧ GEORG FERDINAND CANTOR (1845–1918) was born in St. Petersburg, Russia, but received his mathematical training in Berlin (Ph.D. 1867) and spent the rest of his life in Germany at the relatively obscure University of Halle. His revolutionary theory of infinite sets ignited a fire storm of controversy in the German mathematical community, and powerful enemies, notably Leopold Kronecker (1823–1891), blocked Cantor's efforts to get an appointment at either Berlin or Göttingen. Frustrated and angry at his exclusion from these two centers of intellectual activity during Germany's golden age of mathematics, Cantor suffered a nervous breakdown in 1884. Mental illness dogged him intermittently for the rest of his life. Only in his declining years did he begin to receive the recognition he deserved. David Hilbert (1862–1943), a mathematical giant at Göttingen, declared Cantor's work to be "the finest product of mathematical genius and one of the supreme achievements of purely intellectual human activity."

Grace Chisholm Young (1868–1944), the first woman to earn a German doctoral degree (Göttingen 1895) in *any* subject through the regular examination process, collaborated with her husband William to publish (1906) the first comprehensive textbook that would disseminate Cantor's set theory to the world.

Only statement (4) *has* to be true. Can you explain why each of the other statements could be false? Statement (4) is an instance of an apparently trivial, but surprisingly powerful, problem-solving device known as the **pigeonhole principle.**

If a set of objects is distributed into a set of pigeonholes, and if there are more objects than pigeonholes, then some pigeonhole will contain more than one object.

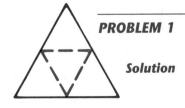

Figure 2.64

PROBLEM 1   A boy shoots five beebees into a triangular target having 2 ft sides. How close together must two of the holes be?

Solution   Divide the target into four regions, as shown in Figure 2.64. By the pigeonhole principle, at least one of these regions must have at least two beebee holes in it. But the greatest distance between two points in any one of the smaller triangles is 1 ft. *Answer:* Two holes must be within 1 ft of each other.   ❏

PROBLEM 2   At a party there are 50 people, the host and 49 of his friends. Each guest shakes hands with each of his acquaintances. Show that at least two people participate in the same number of handshakes.

Solution   Everyone knows the host, so everyone participates in at least one handshake. Since no one shakes hands with himself, everyone participates in at most 49 handshakes. Thus we can think of having 49 pigeonholes:

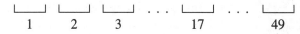

In pigeonhole 17, for instance, we put all people who participate in precisely 17 handshakes. Since there are 50 people at the party and only 49 pigeonholes, at least one pigeonhole must contain at least 2 people. Those people participate in the same number of handshakes.   ❑

EXERCISE SET 2.5

1. A crowd of students is milling about in a classroom having 40 chairs. Describe a quick way of determining how many students are in a room.

2. First, draw a (natural) arrow diagram, and then write a formula, $f(x) = $ _____ , for each of the following.
   (a) A one-to-one correspondence between $\{0, 1, 2, 3, 4\}$ and $\{16, 17, 18, 19, 20\}$
   (b) A one-to-one correspondence between the even whole numbers and the odd negative integers
   (c) A one-to-one correspondence between the set of all integers and some proper subset of the integers

3. True or false? If true, explain why; if false, give a counter-example.
   (a) If (set) A is equivalent to (set) B, then $A = B$.
   (b) If $A = B$, then A is equivalent to B.

4. Write a formula, $f(n) = $ _____ , for a function from the set of natural numbers to the set of real numbers between 0 and 1. Now find a real number between 0 and 1 that is not an output of your function. (There must be one because of Cantor's discovery.)

5. In 1888 Richard Dedekind *defined* a set to be infinite if and only if it could be put in one-to-one correspondence with a proper subset of itself. Using this definition, prove that the set of rational numbers strictly between 0 and 1 is infinite.

6. *The big hotel:* Suppose that you are the manager of an infinite hotel with one room for every natural number (see Figure 2.65), and suppose further that all of your rooms are occupied. A weary traveler arrives and asks if you can give him a room. Can you do it? Now suppose that all of your rooms are doubly occupied and every guest suddenly demands a private room. Can you accommodate them?

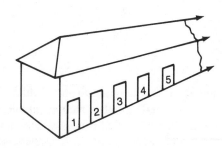

Figure 2.65

★ 7. *The big house:* In an infinite house lives a wizard. At 11:59, ten Ping-Pong balls are thrown in the side window and the wizard throws one out the front (see Figure 2.66). At 11:59$\frac{1}{2}$, ten more Ping-Pong balls are thrown in and one is thrown out; at 11:59$\frac{3}{4}$, ten more in and one more out; at 11:59$\frac{7}{8}$, ten more in and one more out; and so on. At 12:00, the door is opened and there sits the wizard with exactly seven Ping-Pong balls. How did he do it?

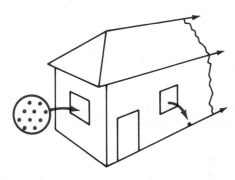

Figure 2.66

8. Cantor also showed that the set D of all *rational* numbers between 0 and 1 *can* be put in one-to-one correspondence with the set of all natural numbers N. Here is a one-to-one correspondence:

$$1 \rightarrow \tfrac{1}{2}$$
$$2 \rightarrow \tfrac{1}{3}$$
$$3 \rightarrow \tfrac{2}{3}$$
$$4 \rightarrow \tfrac{1}{4}$$
$$5 \rightarrow \tfrac{3}{4}$$
$$6 \rightarrow \tfrac{1}{5}$$
$$7 \rightarrow \tfrac{2}{5}$$
$$\cdots$$

Continue the arrow diagram to show which rationals are assigned to the natural numbers 8 through 22. Is it clear that every rational number between 0 and 1, for example, $\frac{2093}{11757}$, must appear on the list eventually?

9. Explain how Figure 2.67 shows that a 2-cm segment and a 3-cm segment have the same number of points.

Figure 2.67

10. Five darts are thrown into a 2-ft by 2-ft square target.
    (a) How close together must two of them be?
    (b) Can you arrange the five darts so that no two are closer together than your answer in part (a)?

11. Ten beebees are shot into a 1-ft by 1-ft by 1-ft triangular target.
    (a) How close together must two of the holes be?
    (b) Can you arrange the holes so that no two are closer together than your answer in part (a)?

★ 12. A set S consists of five natural numbers, the largest of which is 8 or less. Associated with each subset of S is a number, namely the sum of its elements. Show that some two subsets of S must have the same sum. *Hint:* Compare the number of subsets with the number of possible sums.

★ 13. Repeat Exercise 12 in the case where S consists of six natural numbers, the largest of which is 13 or less.

14. A pair of dice is rolled 100 times. Why must one of the possible sums come up at least 10 times?

★ 15. In the handshake problem (Problem 2, p. 75) suppose we remove the restriction that everyone knows the host. Can we still conclude that there are two people who participate in the same number of handshakes?

2.6 *Relations (Optional)*

There are many important *relations* in mathematics. The *equivalence* relation among sets that we examined in Section 2.5 is fundamental. The *is-less-than* relation and the *is-a-factor-of* relation will be crucial in our study of arithmetic; the *is-congruent-to* and *is-similar-to* relations play central roles in geometry. It is possible to understand each individual relation on an *ad hoc* basis (that is why we labeled this section "optional"), but insight is gained by studying the general concept.

Relations from One Set to Another

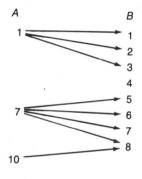

Figure 2.68

The concept of relation is a generalization of the concept of function. While a function from a set A to a set B associates with each input exactly one output, a relation can associate many outputs with a single input. For example, let $A = \{1, 7, 10\}$, let $B = \{1, 2, 3, 4, 5, 6, 7, 8\}$, and with each element a in A associate all elements b in B that differ from a by 2 or less. An arrow diagram for this relation is shown in Figure 2.68. The same relation can be represented by a graph, as shown in Figure 2.69, or by a set of eight ordered pairs that can be read either from the graph or from the arrow diagram. The formal definition of relation is stated in terms of ordered pairs.

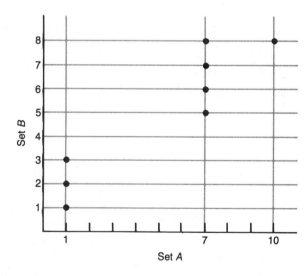

Figure 2.69

A **relation** from a set A to a set B is any subset of $A \times B$, that is, any set of ordered pairs of the form (a, b), where $a \in A$ and $b \in B$.

Relations on a Set

When the inputs and outputs for a relation come from a single set *A*, we call the relation a *relation on A* or a *relation in A*. This is not really a special case, as any relation from *A* to *B* can be thought of as a relation on *A* ∪ *B*. Each of the five important relations that we mentioned at the beginning of this section is thought of most naturally as a relation *on* a set.

EXAMPLE 1   The is-a-factor-of relation on the set {1, 2, 3, 4, 5, 6} assigns to each element of the set all elements of the set into which that element divides with remainder zero. Represent this relation by both an arrow diagram and a graph.

Solution   The arrow diagram is shown in Figure 2.70. The graph is given in Figure 2.71.

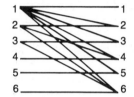

Figure 2.70

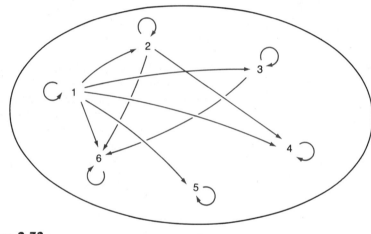

Figure 2.72   ❏

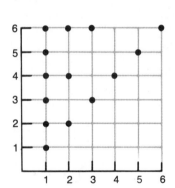

Figure 2.71

The arrow diagram representation is often modified so that each element of *A* appears just once in a Venn diagram for *A*. For example, the relation of Example 1 can be represented as shown in Figure 2.72. We shall call this representation an **arrow Venn diagram.** For a certain kind of relation the arrow Venn diagram representation is particularly revealing.

EXAMPLE 2   The set is {1, 2, 3, 4, 5}. The relation is defined as follows: *a* is related to *b* if *a* and *b* are equal or else differ by 3. Represent this relation by an arrow Venn diagram.

Solution   The arrow Venn diagram is given in Figure 2.73. Notice how the elements of the set are partitioned into (three) subsets; in the previous example, Figure 2.72, there was no such partitioning.   ❏

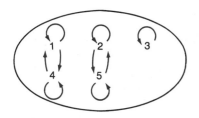

Figure 2.73

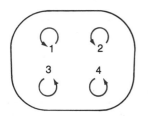

Figure 2.74

We shall look now at the important special category of relations, the so-called equivalence relations, that are associated with partitioning of sets.

Equivalence Relations

An **equivalence relation** on a set A is a relation having all three of these properties:

Reflexive Property   For every $a \in A$, a is related to itself.
Symmetric Property   If a is related to b, then b is related to a.
Transitive Property   If a is related to b and b is related to c, then a is related to c.

The most common equivalence relation is the relation of equality. Replace the phrase "is related to" by "is equal to" in the definitions of reflexivity, symmetry, and transitivity to see that equality does satisfy all three. Figure 2.74 shows an arrow Venn diagram for the equality relation on $\{1, 2, 3, 4\}$. Some of the most important relations in mathematics are equivalence relations. Here are a few examples.

EXAMPLE 3   The set is the set of triangles shown in Figure 2.75. The *congruence relation* is defined as follows: Triangle a is congruent to triangle b if a tracing of triangle a can be superimposed exactly on triangle b. Show that congruence is an equivalence relation, and draw the arrow Venn diagram.

Solution   The congruence relation is reflexive because a tracing of a triangle can certainly be superimposed exactly on the original triangle. It is symmetric because if a tracing of triangle a fits on triangle b, then a tracing of b fits on a. It is transitive because if a tracing of a fits on b and a tracing of b fits on c, then a tracing of a fits on c.

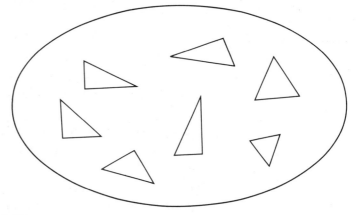

Figure 2.75

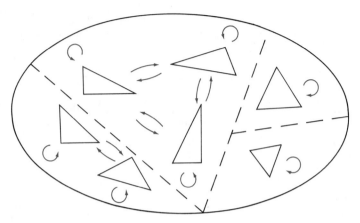

Figure 2.76

The arrow Venn diagram is shown in Figure 2.76. Notice how the reflexive property shows up as the small curved arrows (one from each element to itself), and the symmetric property shows up as two-way arrows. There is no easy graphical interpretation for transitivity. Notice also the (dashed) partitioning of the original set that this equivalence relation induces. The "pieces" of this partition are called *equivalence classes*.   ❏

EXAMPLE 4   The set is the set of sets shown in Figure 2.77. The relation called *equivalence* is defined as follows: Set *a* is *equivalent* to set *b* if there is a one-to-one correspondence from *a* to *b*. Show that *equivalence* satisfies the three defining conditions for a general equivalence relation (and hence is worthy of its name), and draw the arrow Venn diagram.

Solution   The *equivalence* relation is reflexive because for any set *a* there is a one-to-one correspondence from *a* to *a* (send each element to itself). It is symmetric be-

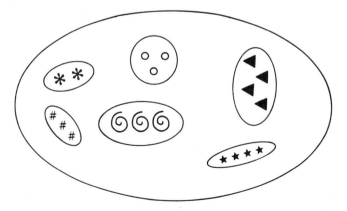

Figure 2.77

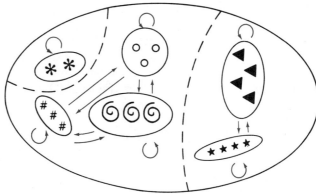

Figure 2.78

cause any one-to-one correspondence from a to b can be reversed to give a one-to-one correspondence from b to a. It is transitive because hooking up a one-to-one correspondence from a to b with a one-to-one correspondence from b to c yields a one-to-one correspondence from a to c. Thus *equivalence* really is an equivalence relation. The arrow Venn diagram is shown in Figure 2.78. Notice again the partitioning of the original set into equivalence classes.

❏

Not all important mathematical relations are equivalence relations, as the next example shows.

EXAMPLE 5   Show that the following relations on the set {1, 2, 3, 4, 5} are *not* equivalence relations.
(a) The less-than-or-equal-to relation
(b) The is-a-factor-of relation

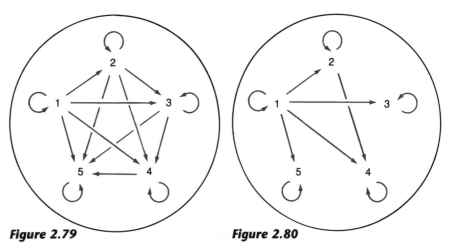

Figure 2.79   **Figure 2.80**

Solution   (a) Although reflexive and transitive, this relation is not symmetric since, for example, $3 \leq 5$ but $5 \nleq 3$. The arrow Venn diagram in Figure 2.79 has some one-way arrows and does not show a (nontrivial) partitioning.

(b) Although reflexive and transitive, this relation is not symmetric. For example, 2 is a factor of 4, but 4 is not a factor of 2. Again, the arrow Venn diagram (Figure 2.80) has some one-way arrows and does not show a partitioning.   ❏

Before stating the connection between equivalence relations and partitions, we ought to define the latter precisely.

A **partition** of a set A is a set of subsets of A, $\{A_1, A_2, A_3, \ldots\}$, such that the following conditions hold:

1. All pairs of these subsets are disjoint (the subsets are *mutually exclusive*).
2. $A_1 \cup A_2 \cup A_3 \cup \ldots = A$ (the subsets are *exhaustive*).

Right now we are interested in partitions because of their connection with equivalence relations. In the next chapter partitions will be important in their own right because of their relationship with the division operation.

The examples we have considered suggest this generalization.

Associated with any equivalence relation on a set A is a partition of the set A.

Conversely, associated with any partition of a set is an equivalence relation. For example, consider the set $A = \{1, 2, 3, 4, 5, 6, 7, 8\}$ and the partition shown by the dotted lines in Figure 2.81. Formally, the partition is

$$\{\{1, 2\}, \{3, 7\}, \{4, 5, 6\}, \{8\}\}$$

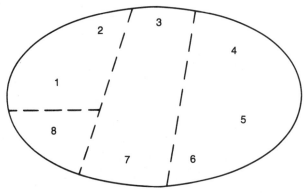

Figure 2.81

but we shall continue to refer to each of these four subsets of A as "pieces" of the partition. Let us define a relation as follows: a is related to b if a and b "belong to the same piece" of the partition. This relation clearly satisfies the three defining conditions of an equivalence relation: a and a belong to same piece; if a and b belong to same piece, then b and a belong to same piece; if a and b belong to same piece and b and c belong to same piece, then a and c belong to same piece.

EXERCISE SET 2.6

1. Let L be the set of Great Lakes {L. Erie, L. Huron, L. Michigan, L. Ontario, L. Superior}, and let S be the set of upper Great Lakes states {Minnesota, Wisconsin, Michigan}. Minnesota touches only L. Superior; Wisconsin touches L. Superior and L. Michigan; and Michigan touches all but L. Ontario. "Touches" is a relation from S to L. Represent it by both an arrow diagram and a graph. Does reversing the arrows produce a function?

2. Let F be the set of four seasons {spring, summer, fall, winter}, and let H be the set of holidays {Easter, Memorial Day, Fourth of July, Labor Day, Halloween, Thanksgiving, Christmas, New Year's Day}. Represent the natural relation from F to H by both an arrow diagram and a graph. Does reversing the arrows produce a function?

3. Represent the is-less-than relation on the set {1, 2, 3, 4, 5} by an arrow Venn diagram and by a graph. Is this relation a function?

4. A relation on {1, 2, 3, 4, 5} is defined as follows: a is related to b if $a + b = 6$. Represent this relation by an arrow Venn diagram and by a graph. Is this relation a function?

Each of the following exercises defines a relation on a set of children. For each relation, determine which of reflexivity, symmetry, and transitivity are satisfied.

5. a related to b if a and b have the same mother

6. a related to b if a and b have different mothers

7. a related to b if a is taller than b

8. a related to b if a is not taller than b

Check each of the mathematical relations in Exercises 9–13 for reflexivity, symmetry, and transitivity.

9. The subset relation $\subseteq$ on a set of sets

10. The proper-subset relation $\subset$ on a set of sets

11. The relation "has the same area" on a set of rectangles

12. The relation "has the same perimeter" on a set of rectangles

13. The relation "is within 2 of" on the set {1, 2, 3, 4, 5}

14. Figure 2.82 is the graph of a relation on {1, 2, 3, 4, 5, 6} that is *not* an equivalence relation.

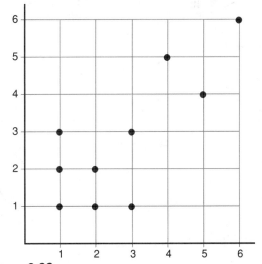

Figure 2.82

(a) Draw an arrow Venn diagram for this relation.

(b) Now draw in just enough dotted arrows so that the new relation is an equivalence relation.

(c) Add the dots to Figure 2.82 that correspond to the arrows you drew in part (b).

The term *equivalent* is widely and often loosely used in a variety of mathematical contexts. If you look hard enough, though, you can usually find an equivalence relation in the precise sense of the word, as we saw with *equivalence* of sets. The next three exercises illustrate three other familiar uses of the word.

15. Fraction a_1/a_2 is *equivalent* to fraction b_1/b_2 if $a_1 \cdot b_2 = a_2 \cdot b_1$. Fill in the relation arrows and the partition lines in the Venn diagram in Figure 2.83.

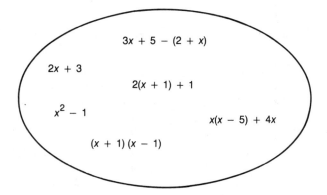

Figure 2.83

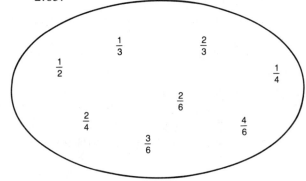

Figure 2.84

16. Two algebraic expressions involving a variable x are *equivalent* if they have the same value for every numerical replacement for x. Fill in the relation arrows and the partition lines in the Venn diagram in Figure 2.84. (You will need to recall some algebra.)

17. Two equations are *equivalent* if they have the same solution set. Fill in the relation arrows and the partition lines in the Venn diagram in Figure 2.85. (Again, you will need to recall some algebra.)

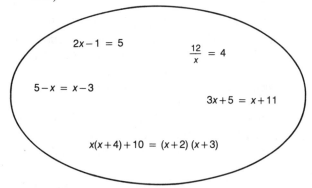

Figure 2.85

★ 18. Associated with each function is a natural partition of its domain and hence a natural equivalence relation on its domain. Describe, as a set of sets, the partition of A that you would naturally associate with the function shown in Figure 2.86.

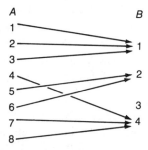

Figure 2.86

★ 19. The equivalence relation of Exercise 5 is the natural one associated with the function that assigns

to each child its mother. What functions give rise naturally to the following?
(a) The equivalence relation in Exercise 11
(b) The equivalence relation in Exercise 12

20. Another way of representing a relation on a set is by means of a *zero-one matrix*, like the one in Figure 2.87 which represents a relation on the set $\{a, b, c, d, e\}$. The 1 in row a column c signifies that a is related to c. The 0 in row d column b signifies that d is not related to b.
(a) Draw an arrow Venn diagram for the relation in Figure 2.87.
(b) Is this relation reflexive?
(c) What pattern of 1s in a zero-one matrix corresponds to reflexivity of the relation represented?
(d) Is the relation in Figure 2.87 symmetric?

	a	b	c	d	e
a	1	0	1	0	1
b	0	1	0	0	0
c	0	0	1	0	0
d	0	0	0	0	1
e	1	0	0	1	1

Figure 2.87

(e) What pattern of 1s in a zero-one matrix corresponds to symmetry of the relation represented?

Key Concepts in Chapter 2

Set
Member
Subset
Venn diagram
Intersection
Union
Cartesian product
Complement

Function
Composition
One-to-one correspondence
Inverse
Equivalent sets
*Relation
*Equivalence relation

*These concepts are taken from optional sections.

‎ Chapter 2 Review Exercises ‎

1. Given the following:
$$A = \{1, 4, 5, 9\ 10\}$$
$$A \cap B = \{5, 10\}$$
$$A \cup B = \{1, 2, 3, 4, 5, 6, 7, 8, 9, 10\}$$
make a roster for B.

2. The Venn diagram in Figure 2.88 shows a universal set $U = \{1, 2, 3, 4, 5, 6, 7, 8\}$ and three of its subsets: A, B, and C. True or false:
(a) $1 \in (A' \cap B') \cup C$
(b) $A \cap C = \varnothing$

(c) $B \subset A \cup C$
(d) $A = C$

3. Refer to the Venn diagram in Figure 2.88 and make a roster for the set $D = \{x \in C \mid x - 5 \in A\}$.

4. Given the universal set $U = \{1, 2, 3, 4, 5, 6, 7\}$ and the subsets
$C = \{x \mid x \text{ is odd}\}$ and $D = \{x \mid x \text{ is less than 4}\}$
make a roster for $(C \cup D)'$.

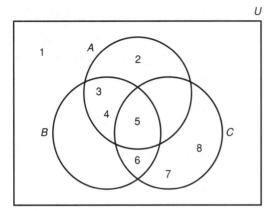

U

Figure 2.88

5. For the same sets U and C of Exercise 4, how many subsets of U have C as a subset?

6. The tree diagram in Figure 2.89 represents the Cartesian product $S \times T$. Give one ordered pair that belongs to $S \times T$ but not to $T \times S$.

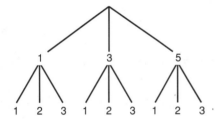

Figure 2.89

7. There are 12 elements in $E \times F$. Four of them are $(1, 6)$, $(3, 2)$, $(4, 2)$, and $(5, 5)$. List the rest.

8. If set A has 5 elements, set B has 6 elements, set C has 7 elements, and $A \cap B$ has 2 elements, how many proper subsets has $(A \cup B) \times C$?

9. Using only mathematical symbols, no words, express each of the following relationships.
   (a) The set A is a subset of the set of whole numbers.
   (b) The number 6 is a member of set A.
   (c) The set of elements that A and B have in common is nonempty.
   (d) The elements that are not in A are in B or C.

(e) The elements that are in neither C nor D are exactly the ones that are in B.

10. There are 70 people at a party. The hostess invited 44 of them, the host invited 40 of them, and 4 of them are crashers. How many received exactly one invitation?

11. One hundred people were surveyed about their participation in the three sports of golf, softball, and tennis. Ten said they played all three. Fifteen golfers and 20 tennis players said that they also played softball. Forty said they did not play softball. How many people played only softball?

12. A restaurant rating service awards one star for each of the following: good food, good service, good atmosphere. Thus every restaurant has a rating of 3 stars, 2 stars, 1 star, or 0 stars. In Tallahassee there are 50 restaurants, 5 of which have 3 stars and 2 of which have 0 stars. Of the 18 2-star restaurants, 4 have bad food and 6 have bad service. If 30 of the restaurants serve good food and 20 have good atmosphere, how many offer good service?

13. The students living in North Quad are distributed in Chemistry, English, and History courses as follows: 10 are in all three courses, 20 are in none of the three, 20 are in exactly two of the three, 17 are in English only, and of the 70 students not in English, 29 are in History and 28 are in Chemistry. How many students live in North Quad?

14. A function is described by the set of ordered pairs
$$f = \{(5, 13), (6, 16), (7, 19), (8, 22)\}$$
   (a) Draw an arrow diagram for f.
   (b) Write a formula for f: $f(x) = $ _____ .

15. The graph in Figure 2.90 shows the temperature outside Lisa's office window as a function of time in hours since she arrived at work at 8:00 A.M.
   (a) What was the temperature at 10:00 A.M.?
   (b) How long did it take for the temperature to rise from 70°F to 75°F?
   (c) At what time did the temperature begin to fall?

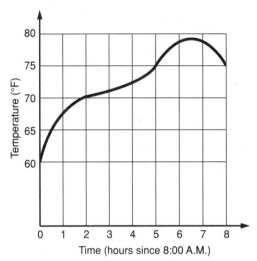

Figure 2.90

(d) During which hour did the temperature rise most rapidly?

(e) Does the graph represent a one-to-one correspondence between times (between 8:00 A.M. and 4:00 P.M.) and temperatures (between 60°F and 79°F)?

16. The graph in Figure 2.91 shows cost (C) and revenue (R) functions. Find the following:
    (a) The cost of producing 700 widgets

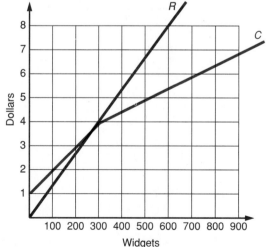

Figure 2.91

(b) The profit realized if 600 widgets are produced and sold

(c) The marginal cost of the 600th widget

(d) The number of widgets that must be produced to bring their average cost down to 1¢ apiece.

17. A function f is described by the accompanying table. Complete the following.
    (a) $f(2) =$ ___?___ .
    (b) $f($___?___$) = 4$
    (c) If g is the hookup f then f then f, $g(3) =$ ___?___ .

In	Out
1	0
2	1
3	2
4	3
5	4
6	5
⋮	⋮

18. Write down a function hookup diagram equivalent to the algebraic equation $\frac{1}{3}[11 + 4(x - 3)] = 9$. Now solve it.

19. Write an algebraic expression for the (final) output of this hookup
$$x \xrightarrow{M_3} \xrightarrow{S_5} \xrightarrow{D_2} \xrightarrow{A_4}$$

20. A function g is described by the formula
$$g(x) = \frac{3 \cdot x + 5}{2} - 1$$
    (a) Find the input that gives rise to the output 27.
    (b) Describe g^{-1} by a formula:
    $$g^{-1}(\square) = \underline{\quad\quad} .$$

21. I am thinking of a natural number. If I triple it, add three, divide by eight, square, and subtract four, I get five. What number am I thinking of?

22. A woman beginning without any money cashes her paycheck, deposits one-third of it in her savings account, spends $10 at a clothing store, spends one-fourth of what is left at the grocery

store, then buys a \$1 lottery ticket that pays her \$10 instantly. She ends up with \$33 in her purse. How much was her paycheck for?

★ 23. Write a formula for a one-to-one correspondence h from I to a proper subset of I.

★ 24. Write a formula $f(x) =$ _____ for a one-to-one correspondence from the set of all whole numbers to the proper subset of odd whole numbers greater than 100.

★ 25. The 27-member local chapter of the Flat Earth Society has a bylaw that every member must be-

long to one and only one of its four standing committees. If one of these committees has just 2 members, how small can the largest committee be?

★ 26. A relation on $\{1, 2, 3, 4, 5\}$ is defined as follows: a is related to b if $a - b$ is an odd integer.
(a) Represent this relation by an arrow Venn diagram.
(b) Which of the three defining properties of an equivalence relation does this relation satisfy?

References

National Council of Teachers of Mathematics. *29th Yearbook: Topics in Mathematics for Elementary School Teachers*. Reston, Va.: NCTM, 1964.

Papy, G. *Modern Mathematics*. Vol. 1. Translated by Frank Gorner. New York: Macmillan, 1968.

Peterson, J., and J. Hashisaki. *Theory of Arithmetic*. New York: Wiley, 1963.

Roman, S. *An Introduction to Discrete Mathematics*. 2nd ed. San Diego, Calif.: Harcourt Brace Jovanovich, 1988.

University of Maryland Mathematics Project. *Unifying Concepts and Processes in Elementary Mathematics*. Boston: Allyn and Bacon, 1978.

3

THE WHOLE NUMBERS: AN INFORMAL APPROACH

The organization of this chapter conforms to principles put forth in the K–4 *Standards:* that symbolic tasks with numbers and operations should not be emphasized until a meaningful conceptual base has been established, and that "placing computation in a problem-solving context motivates students to learn computational skills and serves as an impetus for the mastery of paper-and-pencil algorithms." Accordingly, the first objective in this chapter is to assign meanings to both the whole numbers (as represented by Hindu-Arabic numerals) and the operations of addition, multiplication, subtraction, and division (as represented by $+$, $\times$, $-$, $\div$, and $/$). These meanings can be thought of as definitions, models, or representations. Their value is in providing specific physical or schematic interpretations for whole number arithmetic.

These interpretations allow us to match arithmetic solutions to real-world problems. A variety of word problems is provided in this chapter to give you practice in translating real problems into mathematical ones. Thus our second objective in this chapter is to develop your ability to make these translations. While most of the problems involving addition and subtraction are rather straightforward, those related to multiplication and division take more thought. The challenging optional section on permutations and combinations can be thought of as an extended set of applications of multiplication and (exact) division. (Some instructors prefer to cover this self-contained section in conjunction with Section 9.4 of the probability chapter.)

Once one has analyzed a problem and decided what arithmetic operations are appropriate, an entirely different kind of question needs to be addressed: What are the efficient formal procedures for getting from the given numerical data and the appropriate operations to an answer? This question is about computational schemes, or algorithms. An *algorithm* can be thought of as a step-by-step procedure. The word comes from the name of an Arabian mathematician, Alkarismi or Al-Khowarizme, whose algebra book of 830 A.D. introduced decimal notation to the West.

Our third objective is to describe algorithms for the four operations. Modern educational theory holds that algorithms should evolve from slow, clear, understandable forms toward rapid, more mechanical ones. Students should know why an algorithm works as well as how. The interpretations of the numbers and operations that were developed in the first part of the chapter will be instrumental in explaining why the algorithms work.

The final section of the chapter concerns algorithms in general and their representation by flowcharts. The modern ideas of this section will provide continuing themes for much of the computational work in ensuing chapters.

3.1 *Pathways to Hindu-Arabic Numeration*

This section has two main purposes: to retrace briefly the stages through which children pass before they reach our (Hindu-Arabic) numeration system; to describe briefly two historical numeration systems through which mankind passed before reaching the Hindu-Arabic system. In describing these stages and systems, we will use two technical terms, *ordinal* and *cardinal,* which relate to how numbers are used.

Uses of Numbers

The most common use of the whole numbers 0, 1, 2, 3, . . . is to tell how many things are in some set. This use is referred to as **cardinal use.** When we say there are seven days in a week, we are using the whole number 7 in a cardinal sense. A second use of whole numbers is simply to name things. Social Security numbers, bank account numbers, and credit card numbers are examples of this **naming** (nominal) **use.** A third use is **ordinal use** in which a number is used to specify the position of a thing in some ordering. When a football fan brags that her team is number 5 in this week's press ratings, she is using 5 in an ordinal sense. Consider the following sentence: "In frame *seven* I got *seven* pins to go with my spare, but on the next ball I left the *seven* pin standing." The first use of seven is somewhat debatable but is probably ordinal. The second use is clearly cardinal, and the third is naming.

A word of warning about these new terms: although it is convenient to refer to ordinal and cardinal *uses* of whole numbers, it is pointless and confusing to speak of ordinal and cardinal *numbers*. Only in the study of *transfinite* numbers is there a reason for distinguishing between these two types. Thus for everyone except professional mathematicians there is just one set of whole numbers; sometimes they are used in a cardinal sense and other times in an ordinal sense.

Stages of Verbal Counting

Children's introduction to mathematics begins long before they are able to read or write the numerals 1, 2, 3, ... Counting skill develops during the preschool years and seems to progress through three identifiable stages. The first stage is simply the rote repetition of the nonsense sounds "one," "two," "three," "four," . . . in order. Parents will correct a child if he begins "two," "four," "three," "one," . . . . Thus children's first sense of the natural numbers is an ordinal one.

The second stage of counting is the stage of counting objects. When a child is asked to count a set of blocks, he is again expected to recite some of the initial number sounds in order, but now he must do more. As he makes each sound, he is expected to touch each of the blocks. In effect, he is naming the blocks with numbers, as indicated in Figure 3.1.

Figure 3.1

If we think of the pointing fingers as arrows, we see that the child is being asked to exhibit a function from a set of number sounds to a set of blocks. Furthermore, the requirements on this function are quite stringent. The function in Figure 3.2 would be criticized because it is many-to-one. The function in Figure 3.3 would be ruled out because it fails to use up the set of blocks. Clearly, what we want from the child is a one-to-one correspondence. Certainly, no one suggests using the words *one-to-one correspondence* with children, but that is what we demand of them.

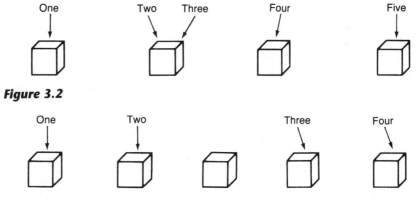

Figure 3.2

Figure 3.3

A third stage of counting is reached when we ask a child to count his blocks and tell us how many he has. Here we are interested in the *last* number he names. We don't really care what one-to-one correspondence he sets up. The two shown in Figure 3.4 are equally good. Note that when he reports that he has five blocks, he is using five in a cardinal sense.

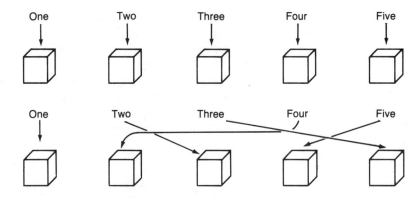

Figure 3.4

Professor Charles Brumfiel relates a revealing story about a child's use of numbers. He had given his young son five pieces of candy, which the boy had "counted," touching each piece as he said, "One, two, three four, five." Then he ate two of them. His father, sensing a chance to teach some arithmetic, said, "You had five and you ate two. How many are left?" The boy's reply was, "I didn't eat two. I ate one and three. Two, four, and five are left." The child was using numbers to name objects; the father was using them in a cardinal sense.

A good deal of the arithmetic done in the early grades is necessarily verbal. The ability to write symbols for numbers develops quite slowly. Symbols such as

$$ \text{ᒚ} \quad \text{Ɛ} \quad \text{ᒐ} $$

are not rare, even in the third and fourth grades. Verbal arithmetic can be based on counting skill. For example, a sum such as eighteen plus three can be found by counting forward three from eighteen:

   Nineteen, twenty, twenty-one

A difference like twelve minus four can be found by counting backwards

   Eleven, ten, nine, eight

A product like three times five can be found by counting by fives:

   Five, ten, fifteen

More complicated calculations, however, demand written symbols for numbers. It would be a rare person who could calculate seventy-three times fifty-nine without writing some symbols down or at least visualizing symbols for the numbers in his mind.

Historical Numeration Systems

Written symbols for numbers are called **numerals;** any logically structured set of numerals for all the counting numbers is called a **numeration system.** We have selected several numeration systems for study. Each was chosen for the light that it sheds on our own familiar Hindu-Arabic numeration system. These numeration systems can be separated into two classes: historical systems (Caveman, Egyptian, Hindu-Arabic, and Mayan) and recently fabricated systems (bases other than ten). In this section we will look briefly at the first three historical systems; in the next section we will examine recently manufactured systems and the Mayan system.

The **Caveman numerals** for the first twelve counting numbers are, in order,

| || ||| |||| ||||| |||||| ||||||| |||||||| ||||||||| |||||||||| ||||||||||| ||||||||||||

To count, in an ordinal (what's next?) sense, is a triviality. The rule of succession is this: Given a Caveman numeral, to write the next one, simply make one additional scratch. The cardinal (how many?) interpretation on each Caveman numeral is also obvious: The scratches that make up each numeral are in one-to-one correspondence with the set that the numeral counts. This property makes computation in the Caveman system very simple. We have not yet defined addition and subtraction formally, but your intuitive understandings of the operations will suffice for these examples.

EXAMPLE 1 (Addition)   There are ||||| boys and ||||||| girls. How many children are there?

Solution To solve this problem, we observe that the numeral ||||| for the number of boys gives a clear picture of how many boys there are. Similarly, the numeral for the number of girls can be thought of as an abstract picture of the actual set of girls. To form the set of children, we put the boys and girls together. The numeral for the number of children is obtained similarly by putting together the abstract pictures of the boys and the girls, as indicated in Figure 3.5.   ❏

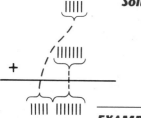

EXAMPLE 2 (Subtraction)   There are ||||||||| children and ||||| boys. How many girls are there?

Solution Once again, the numerals can be treated as abstract pictures of the actual sets of children. The subtraction is shown in Figure 3.6.   ❏

Figure 3.5

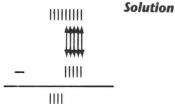

Figure 3.6

The **Egyptian** (hieroglyphic) **system** is like the Caveman system, but with abbreviations for groups of ten. The first nine numerals are unchanged:

| || ||| |||| ||||| |||||| ||||||| |||||||| |||||||||

Abbreviation begins with the numeral for ten. Think of drawing a tenth staff (that's what the Egyptians called their scratches) and then trading in those ten staffs for a single heel bone, ∩. The Egyptian numerals for the numbers ten through twenty-one are as follows:

∩ ∩| ∩|| ∩||| ∩|||| ∩||||| ∩|||||| ∩||||||| ∩|||||||| ∩||||||||| ∩∩ ∩∩|

The rule of succession is clear. To get from one numeral to the next, just draw in another staff. If that gives you nine or less staffs, you are done. If it gives you ten staffs, trade them in for one heel bone. All goes well up through ninety-nine:

∩∩∩ ∩∩∩ ∩∩∩ |||||||||

To form the next numeral, think of drawing one more staff. Now you have ten staffs, which are traded in on a heel bone. But that makes ten heel bones, and another abbreviation is appropriate. A coiled rope ℰ represents ten heel bones and is thus the Egyptian numeral for one hundred. Table 3.1 shows some selected Egyptian numerals and their Hindu-Arabic equivalents.

Table 3.1

Egyptian numeral		Hindu-Arabic numeral
Staff	|	1
Heel bone	∩	10
Coiled rope	ℰ	100
Lotus		1000
Pointing finger		10,000
Burbot fish		100,000
Astonished man		1,000,000
	⚡ ⌒⌒⌒ |||||| ℰℰ ∩ ||||	1,350,214

The Egyptian and Hindu-Arabic systems are similar in that both involve grouping by tens, tens of tens, and so forth. Notice, however, these two differences: In the Egyptian system there is no symbol for zero (if there are no thousands in a number, just don't draw any lotuses), and the order in which the individual Egyptian symbols are drawn is immaterial (both ∩|| ∩|| and ∩∩ |||| represent twenty-four).

EXAMPLE 3   Use Table 3.1 to write the following:
(a) A Hindu-Arabic numeral for ⌒ ⚡ ⚡ ⚡ ℰℰ ||||
(b) An Egyptian numeral for 1380

Solution   (a) 103,204
(b) ⚡ ℰℰℰ ∩∩∩∩∩ ∩∩∩∩   ❑

Computing in the Egyptian system is somewhat more complicated than computing in the Caveman system because the abbreviations begin to mask the cardinal interpretation of the numerals. Consider the following two questions:

1. Which number is greater, ||||||| or |||||||||||| ?
2. Which number is greater, 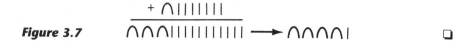 ?

Anyone can answer question 1 at a glance. Most people, however, have to pause and think before they can answer question 2.

EXAMPLE 4   (Addition)   There are ∩|||| boys and ∩||||||| girls. How many children are there?

Solution   Again, one begins by simply pushing the numerals together. But then an abbreviation must be made, as indicated in Figure 3.7. Clearly, the abbreviation step is the forerunner of the carrying or regrouping we do in our own numeration system.

$$\begin{array}{r} \cap\cap||||\ \\ +\ \cap|||||||| \end{array}$$

Figure 3.7   ∩∩∩|||||||||||| ⟶ ∩∩∩∩| ❑

EXAMPLE 5   (Subtraction)   There are ∩∩||| children and ||||||| boys. How many girls are there?

Solution   Now we do some unabbreviating, which corresponds to our own borrowing or regrouping: see Figure 3.8.

$$\begin{array}{r} \cap\cap|||\ \\ -|||||||\ \end{array} \longrightarrow \begin{array}{r} \cap||||||||||\ |||\ \\ -\qquad ||||\ |||\ \\ \hline \cap|||||| \end{array}$$

Figure 3.8   ❑

Our familiar numeration system is called the **Hindu-Arabic system** because it was developed by the Hindus and introduced to Europe by the Arabs during the Moorish occupation of Spain. The first nine numerals in the *Hindu-Arabic* system are, as we all know,

1 2 3 4 5 6 7 8 9

These one-piece numerals, together with the numeral 0, are called **digits.** Beyond nine, multidigit numerals are required. The evolution of the first few Hindu-Arabic digits can be traced back to marks like those in the Caveman system, as illustrated in Figure 3.9. Evolution of the other digits is less clear. Accounts of their development can be found in nearly any encyclopedia or history of mathematics text. (See the References at the end of this chapter, p. 189)

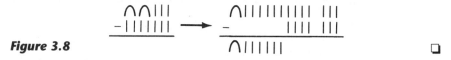

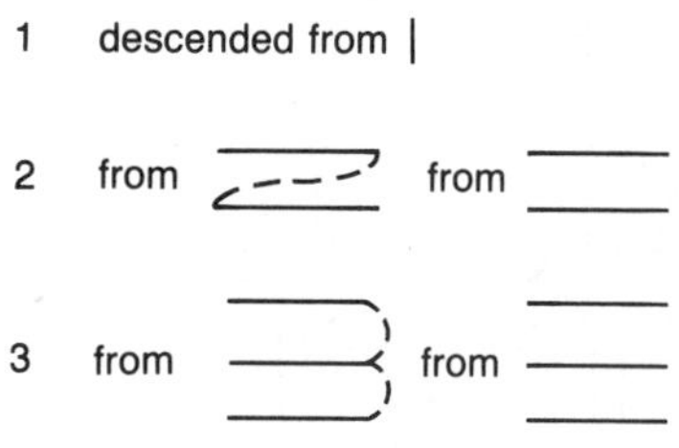

Figure 3.9

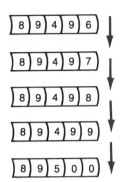

Figure 3.10

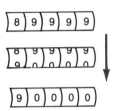

Figure 3.11

The rule of succession in the Hindu-Arabic system is surprisingly complicated to verbalize: To write the numeral following a given numeral, begin at the right. If the rightmost digit is not 9, increase it by one. If it is 9, replace it by 0 and see whether there is a digit to its left. If there is none, write a 1. If there is one and it is not 9, increase it by one. If there is one and it is 9, replace it by 0 and see whether there is a digit to its left. And so on.

Chances are that you never verbalized this rule before; yet you understand it perfectly. Here is a Hindu-Arabic numeral that in all probability you never saw before in your life:

$$27,089,499$$

Still, if asked to write the next numeral, you would do so without hesitation.

In some nonverbal way all of us have come to understand the rule of succession in the Hindu-Arabic numeration system. Probably the simplest way to explain the rule to children in our automobile culture is to ask them to visualize an odometer. Almost every child has had the experience of watching the numerals parade by, as shown in Figure 3.10, and has watched the passing of repeated nines (Figure 3.11) with special pleasure.

The cardinal interpretation of Hindu-Arabic numerals, on which computation is based, is not nearly as obvious as it is for Caveman or Egyptian numerals. To be able to look at a Hindu-Arabic numeral and see *how many* things it represents requires a thorough understanding of two prerequisite concepts, base and place value. We shall develop these thoroughly in the next section.

EXERCISE SET 3.1

1. Classify each use of a number in the following sentence as cardinal, naming, or ordinal use: "The number three batter is good old number nine, John McSwat, who has hit five home runs this year."

2. In order to form four teams, the gym teacher has her class count off: 1, 2, 3, 4, 1, 2, 3, 4, 1, 2, 3, 4, ... All of the 1s make up one team, the 2s another, and so on.
   (a) What understanding of numbers, cardinal or ordinal, must the children have in order to perform the counting off?
   (b) When the teacher says, "All threes go to the northeast corner of the gym," how is the number 3 being used?

3. A kindergartner claims he can count to 30, but when the teacher asks him to count the (12) colored leaves pinned up on the bulletin board, he fails miserably. Explain briefly the different meanings that *count* has for this child and his teacher.

4. Using function terminology, tell what, if anything, is wrong with these attempts at counting.

(a)

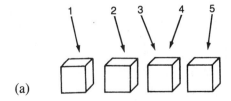

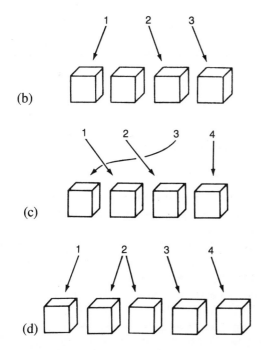

(b)

(c)

(d)

5. Find 9 + 4 by counting forward from 9. Use your fingers to keep track of how many number sounds you make.

6. Find 9 − 4 by counting backward from 9. Again, use your fingers so that you will know when to stop.

7. Find 9 × 4 by counting by fours. How will you use your fingers this time?

8. Find 28 ÷ 4 by counting to 28 by fours and keeping score on your fingers.

9. Suppose that in a newly discovered language the first few counting number sounds are

Sis, boom, bah, tra, la

and that much later in the sequence these sounds occur:

Hip, hoo, ray, fo, fum

Complete the following:
(a) Hoo + bah = fum
(b) Fo − boom = _____
(c) Fum − hip = _____

10. Write as Hindu-Arabic numerals.
(a) 𝟤𝟤𝟤∩∩∣∣∣∣ ∣∣∣   (b) 𝟤∩∩∣∣𝟤∩∣∩∩
(c) 𝟤̄∩∩

11. Write as Egyptian numerals.
(a) 5280   (b) 2085   (c) 999

12. What is the least natural number that has 25 individual symbols in its Egyptian numeral? Give your answer in Hindu-Arabic notation.

13. Use Egyptian numerals to write the following numbers:
(a) The number that comes just after

𝟤 ∣∣∣ 𝟤 ∣∣∣ 𝟤 ∣∣∣

(b) The number that comes just before 𝟤𝟤

14. Perform the following calculations within the Caveman system; that is, do not convert to Hindu-Arabic numerals. Make up a story to go with each problem.

(a)   ∣∣∣∣∣
    + ∣∣∣∣
   ―――――

(b)   ∣∣∣∣∣∣∣
    − ∣∣∣
   ―――――

15. Perform the following calculations within the Egyptian system; that is, do not convert to Hindu-Arabic numerals. Make up a story to go with each problem.

(a)   𝟤∩∩∩∣∣∣∣∣∣∣∣
    + 𝟤∩∩∩∩∩∩∣∣∣∣
   ―――――――――

(b)   𝟤𝟤∩∣∣∣
    − 𝟤∩∩∣∣∣∣
   ―――――――

★ 16. The base and place value features of the Hindu-Arabic numeration system make it a very efficient system for reporting large numbers.
(a) How many individual symbols are needed to express 999,999 in Egyptian notation?
(b) If you were to make one mark per second, how many days would it take you to write the Caveman numeral for 999,999?

(c) The earth would fit easily inside a cubical box 10,000 mi on an edge. Suppose such a box were packed tightly full of tiny cubical grains of sand, 0.01 in on an edge. How many grains of sand would be in the box?

3.2 *Numeration Systems with Base and Place Value*

The Hindu-Arabic numeration system is a marvelously economical one. By marking down just a few digits, we can represent numbers that would require huge collections of hieroglyphs of Caveman scratches. This economy is achieved through an ingenious coding system involving the concepts of *base* and *place value*. To clarify the meaning and the role of these two concepts, we will begin with a fable suggested by the creative people at the Comprehensive School Mathematics Project. The fable is entitled "The Base-Four Caramel Factory."

Before beginning the story, though, we should explain why we have chosen to begin with base four (grouping by fours) rather than base ten (grouping by tens). There are several reasons. One is that we come to understand familiar things more deeply when we compare and contrast them with unfamiliar ones. Thus for many people English grammar finally becomes clear in their first foreign language course. Our eyes are opened about American culture when we learn about other cultures in an anthropology or sociology course. You have grown up with the (base-ten) Hindu-Arabic numeration system; to deepen your understanding of it, it is important that you step back and see it in comparison with other systems.

A second purpose in working with other bases is to give you a chance to re-experience the learning of an unfamiliar system. This experience should help you to pinpoint areas where your own students might encounter difficulties.

Another reason for considering bases besides ten is that they have intrinsic value. Base two and base sixteen are fundamental in the design of computers and calculators. Base twelve survives in the packaging of items by the dozen and by the gross. Base sixty can be seen in our units of time and of angle measure.

Note: This material on bases is for your information. How much of it should be taught to youngsters, and at what age, is uncertain. During the new-math era it was a rather standard topic in the curriculum. During the back-to-basics reaction it nearly dropped out of sight.

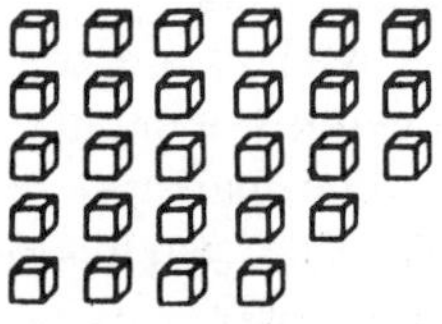

Here is the fable. Suppose you own a caramel factory but are having trouble finding good help. In fact, the people you have hired, like the rabbits in the novel *Watership Down,* are able to count only up to four. Thus when your machine spews out the caramels shown in Figure 3.12, your employees are unable

Figure 3.12

to tell you how many there are. (The rabbits would say "hrair," a word meaning "many," that they use for any number beyond four.) After some deliberation you decide that the thing to do is to package your product by fours. Any time an employee sees four caramels, he is to put them in a pack. Any time he sees four packs, he is to put them in a box. And any time he sees four boxes, he is to put them in a case. That is, your caramels are available in the quantities shown in Figure 3.13.

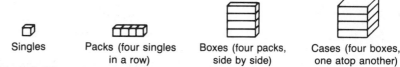

| Singles | Packs (four singles in a row) | Boxes (four packs, side by side) | Cases (four boxes, one atop another) |

Figure 3.13

Using these packaging instructions, your employees are now able to report how many caramels the machines has produced without ever having to count beyond four. The first step is to package the caramels by four, as indicated in Figure 3.14. Then the packs are boxed by fours, as shown in Figure 3.15. Now an employee can report the number of caramels as

1 box, 2 packs, and 3 singles

The word **base** is synonymous with the packaging instructions. We have called it the base-four caramel factory because the packaging instructions are by fours.

To simplify ordering, you supply your customers with order forms like the one below:

Cases	Boxes	Packs	Singles

And you request that they use only the digits 0, 1, 2, and 3 in filling them out since your employees will never send out more than three unpackaged singles, three unboxed packs, and so forth.

Your shipping clerk is quick to learn, and after filling a few such orders, he no longer has to read the entire form. Instead, he simply glances at the digits:

Cases	Boxes	Packs	Singles
2	1	3	1

Then he sends out the quantity of caramels shown in Figure 3.16. (Notice how the containers have been stylized for ease of drawing.) He knows from experience that the rightmost digit, 1, stands for singles; that the next digit, 3, stands

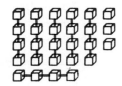

Figure 3.14

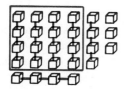

Figure 3.15

Figure 3.16

for packs; the next digit, 1, for boxes; and the next digit, 2, for cases. He has come to understand **place value:** The position (place) of a digit in a multidigit numeral determines its "value."

Let us take time out from the fable to summarize. The numerals suggested by the filled-out order forms make up the **base-four numeration system.** There are four digits in the system: 0, 1, 2, and 3. The value of each digit in a multidigit numeral is determined by its place. In the rightmost position a digit represents units (caramels); in the next position left it represents fours (packs); in the next it represents fours of fours (boxes); and so forth. The first ten numerals in the base-four system are shown in Table 3.2.

Table 3.2 Equivalent Base-Ten and Base-Four Numerals

Base-ten numerals	1	2	3	4	5	6	7	8	9	10
Base-four numerals	1_{four}	2_{four}	3_{four}	10_{four}	11_{four}	12_{four}	13_{four}	20_{four}	21_{four}	22_{four}

An easy way to make such a list is to imagine an odometer that has only the digits 0, 1, 2, 3 so that 3s act like 9s. Notice that we use the subscript "four" to distinguish base-four numerals from the usual base-ten numerals, which will ordinarily be written without the subscript "ten." We write out the word *four* rather than the numeral 4 to emphasize that in the base-four system there is no digit 4. *Caution:* Read the symbol 10_{four} as "one zero base four," *not* as "ten base four." "Ten" tells how many fingers a person has. Thus in base-four notation ten is 22_{four} (read "two two base four," *not* "twenty-two base four").

Using schematic caramel diagrams and the concepts of base and place value, we can now attach a very concrete cardinal interpretation to each base-four numeral.

EXAMPLE 1   Represent each base-four numeral by a caramel diagram.
(a) 2313_{four}
(b) 1032_{four}

Solution   (a)

Where the pack contains 4 singles, each box contains 4 packs or 4 × 4 singles, and each cube contains 4 boxes or 4 × 4 × 4 singles.

(b)

Having the cardinal interpretation of base-four numerals, it is now possible to move on to computation in that system. Again, we rely on your intuitive understanding of what it means to add and subtract. We return to the fable.

Customer A has been ordering caramels at a furious pace. In fact, two orders from her, 2013_{four} and 231_{four}, are waiting to be filled. You give the two orders to your shipping clerk and ask him to send them off in a single shipment and to tell the billing department how many were sent off. He proceeds as shown in Figure 3.17. Clearly, what the shipping clerk has done is to find, in a manipulative way, the base-four sum, $2013_{four} + 231_{four}$.

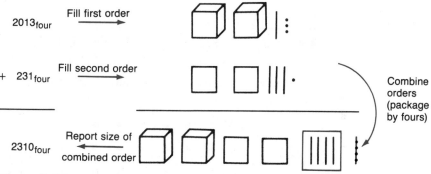

Figure 3.17

Customer B had sent in an order for 3132_{four} caramels. Now she phones and says that this is 113_{four} more than she needs. The shipping clerk handles the problem as shown in Figure 3.18. This time he has found the base-four difference, $3132_{four} - 113_{four}$.

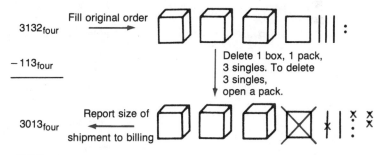

Figure 3.18

The situation for other bases is analogous to that for base four. The digits always go from 0 to one less than the base. For example, the digits in base two are 0, 1; in base three they are 0, 1, 2; and in base seven they are 0, 1, 2, 3, 4, 5, 6. If the base exceeds ten, then new digits need to be invented. For example, the digits in base twelve are

0 1 2 3 4 5 6 7 8 9 T (ten) E (eleven)

Notice that it is all right to omit subscripts from the digits of a system because, for example, 2 represents the same number whether it is viewed as a digit in the base-three system, the base-seven system, or any other system in which it makes sense (base more than two).

EXAMPLE 2   Write base-three numerals for the first thirteen natural numbers.

Solution

1_{three} 2_{three} 10_{three} 11_{three} 12_{three} 20_{three} 21_{three} 22_{three} 100_{three} 101_{three} 102_{three} 110_{three} 111_{three}
❏

EXAMPLE 3   Package the caramels shown in Figure 3.19 in base three, and write the base-three numeral for their number.

Solution   The packaging is shown in Figure 3.20. The base-three numeral is 210_{three}.

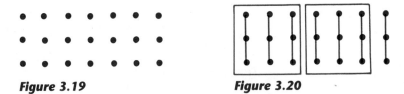

Figure 3.19   **Figure 3.20**   ❏

Addition and subtraction problems in other bases can be solved in the same manipulative way as in base four.

EXAMPLE 4   Find $235_{six} + 143_{six}$.

Solution   Keep in mind that now the packaging is by sixes, but place value is as usual. See Figure 3.21.

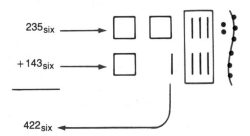

Figure 3.21   ❏

EXAMPLE 5   Find $783_{ten} - 259_{ten}$.

Solution   See Figure 3.22 and notice that one pack was opened.

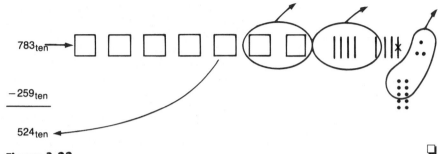

$783_{ten} \longrightarrow$

-259_{ten}

$524_{ten} \longleftarrow$

Figure 3.22

Teaching Note. If you worked with bases other than ten in junior high school or high school, you might be impatient with the manipulative techniques suggested by our caramel diagrams. You know faster ways of computing. (It won't be long before we will be describing some of these more efficient computational techniques.) But the caramel diagram stage is one that you, as a prospective teacher, should not be in a hurry to pass over. Educational psychologists feel that in mathematics, as in other areas, a child should creep before she walks.

Manipulative materials very much like our singles, packs, boxes, and cases of caramels are in widespread use in elementary schools to implant the ideas of base and place value, and to lay a solid foundation for addition and subtraction of whole numbers. The most common of these materials are called **Dienes blocks** [named after Z. P. Dienes, a contemporary math educator, although descriptions of such blocks can be found as far back as Robert Recorde's *Whetstone of Witte* (1557)]. A set of Dienes blocks is shown in Figure 3.23. Dienes blocks are also available in bases other than ten.

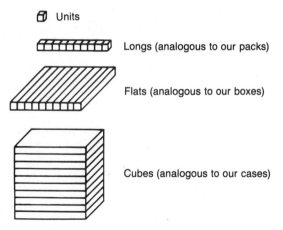

Units

Longs (analogous to our packs)

Flats (analogous to our boxes)

Cubes (analogous to our cases)

Figure 3.23

Converting Between Systems

There are occasions when you may wish to convert from a numeral in one base to an equivalent numeral (a numeral representing the same number) in another base. Converting *to* base ten is straightforward, as the following examples show.

EXAMPLE 6   Write the base-ten numeral for the following:
(a) 253_{six}
(b) $E07_{twelve}$

Solution   (a) 253_{six} represents 3 caramels, 5 packs of six, and 2 boxes of six times six. In base-ten notation that is a total of

$$2 \cdot (6 \cdot 6) + 5 \cdot (6) + 3 = 2 \cdot 36 + 5 \cdot 6 + 3 = 105$$

Answer: $253_{six} = 105_{ten}$. (Ordinarily, we follow the convention that when no base is indicated, base ten is understood. Here and in the next few examples we use the subscript ten, occasionally, for emphasis.)

(b) $E07_{twelve}$ can be written in base-ten notation as

$$11 \cdot (12 \cdot 12) + 0 \cdot 12 + 7 = 11 \cdot 144 + 7 = 1591$$

Answer: $E07_{twelve} = 1591_{ten}$.   ❏

Converting *from* base ten to another base can be done mentally when the number is small.

EXAMPLE 7   Write the base-four numeral for 13_{ten}.

Solution   Thirteen is 3 packs of four with 1 single left over. *Answer:* $13_{ten} = 31_{four}$.   ❏

When the number is large, a very elegant algorithm (step-by-step procedure) can be carried out. We will have occasion to refer to this algorithm later.

EXAMPLE 8   Write the base-five numeral for 894_{ten}.

Solution   View the task as one of packaging 894 caramels in base five.

Step 1   Divide the base-ten numeral 894 by the new base 5 and record quotient and remainder. (894 caramels have been put, by fives, into 178 packs, with 4 singles remaining. Thus the singles digit of the base-five numeral must be 4.)

$$\frac{178}{5 \overline{)894}} \quad R4$$

Step 2   Divide the previous quotient 178 by the new base 5, again recording quotient and remainder. (The 178 packs have been put, by fives, into 35 boxes, with 3 packs remaining. Thus the packs digit of the base-five numeral must be 3.)

$$
\begin{array}{r}
35 \quad \text{R3} \\
5\overline{)178} \quad \text{R4} \\
5\overline{)894}
\end{array}
$$

Step 3   Divide the previous quotient 35 by the new base 5, and record quotient and remainder. (The 35 boxes make 7 cases, with no boxes remaining. Thus the boxes digit is 0.)

$$
\begin{array}{r}
7 \quad \text{R0} \\
5\overline{)35} \quad \text{R3} \\
5\overline{)178} \quad \text{R4} \\
5\overline{)894}
\end{array}
$$

Step 4   Divide the previous quotient 7 by 5, and record quotient and remainder. (7 cases make 1 crate, with 2 cases left over. Thus the cases digit is 2.)

$$
\begin{array}{r}
1 \quad \text{R2} \\
5\overline{)7} \quad \text{R0} \\
5\overline{)35} \quad \text{R3} \\
5\overline{)178} \quad \text{R4} \\
5\overline{)894}
\end{array}
$$

Step 5   Divide the previous quotient 1 by 5, and record quotient and remainder. The new quotient 0 is a signal to cease dividing and to record the remainders in the reverse order in which they arose. (1 crate cannot fill the next larger containers, so 1 crate is left over. The crate's digit is 1.)

$$
\begin{array}{r}
0 \quad \text{R1} \\
5\overline{)1} \quad \text{R2} \\
5\overline{)7} \quad \text{R0} \\
5\overline{)35} \quad \text{R3} \\
5\overline{)178} \quad \text{R4} \\
5\overline{)894}
\end{array}
$$

$$\rightarrow 12034_{\text{five}}$$

Answer: $894_{\text{ten}} = 12034_{\text{five}}$.   ❏

EXAMPLE 9   Write the base-two numeral for 19_{ten}.

Solution

$$
\begin{array}{r}
0 \quad \text{R1} \\
2\overline{)1} \quad \text{R0} \\
2\overline{)2} \quad \text{R0} \\
2\overline{)4} \quad \text{R1} \\
2\overline{)9} \quad \text{R1} \\
2\overline{)19}
\end{array}
$$

$$\rightarrow 10011_{\text{two}} = 19_{\text{ten}}$$ ❏

One advantage of knowing how to change to and from base ten is that it gives another way of solving problems posed in an unfamiliar base. The following calculation shows how to compute $243_{\text{five}} \times 34_{\text{five}}$ by changing it to a base-ten problem, finding the product by using base-ten skills, and then expressing that product in the original base-five notation:

$$
\begin{array}{r}
243_{\text{five}} \xrightarrow{\text{Convert to base ten}} 73 \\
\times\ 34_{\text{five}} \xrightarrow{\text{Convert to base ten}} \times\ 19 \\
\hline
21022_{\text{five}} \xleftarrow{\text{Convert to base five}} 1387
\end{array}
\left.\begin{array}{l} \\ \\ \\ \end{array}\right\} \begin{array}{l} \text{A routine calculation} \\ \text{in a familiar base} \end{array}
$$

A Common Pattern in Problem Solving

The pattern of taking a difficult problem, translating it into an easier context, solving it there, and bringing the answer back, is a familiar one. We did the same thing when we solved base-four problems via caramel diagrams:

$$
\begin{array}{r}
123_{\text{four}} \rightarrow\quad \square\,||\,\vdots \\
+\quad 32_{\text{four}} \rightarrow\quad ||\,|\,\vdots \\
\hline
221_{\text{four}} \leftarrow\quad \square\square||\,\cdot
\end{array}
\left.\begin{array}{l} \\ \\ \end{array}\right\} \begin{array}{l} \text{Package} \\ \text{by fours} \end{array}
$$

You might even recall from your junior high school days how complicated multiplication problems involving "mixed numbers" were solved by converting them to easier multiplication problems involving fractions:

$$
\begin{array}{r}
3\frac{1}{3} \rightarrow\quad \frac{10}{3} \\
\times\ 2\frac{1}{2} \rightarrow\ \times\ \frac{5}{2} \\
\hline
8\frac{1}{3} \leftarrow\quad \frac{50}{6}
\end{array}
\left.\begin{array}{l} \\ \\ \end{array}\right\} \begin{array}{l} \text{Multiply numerators} \\ \text{and denominators} \end{array}
$$

Children in the elementary grades employ the same general pattern. By studying this pattern in the next two sections, we shall arrive at concrete meanings for the abstract arithmetic operations of addition and multiplication.

A Historical Note

The Hindu-Arabic numeration system—and the associated base-two, base-three, . . . systems—are not the only numeration systems to employ base, place value, and a symbol for zero. The Mayans, whose civilization flourished in Central America from Southern Mexico to Honduras between about 300 A.D. and 800 A.D., developed a numeration system with the very same features. The Mayan system was almost a base-twenty system. Instead of having 20 digits, though, they represented the numbers from 0 to 19 by a special symbol for zero and by dots and dashes representing 1 and 5 respectively.

To represent numbers greater than 19 the Mayans used place value, with a bottom-to-top hierarchy rather than a right-to-left one. Numerals at the lowest

0	⬯	5	▬	10	▬▬	15	▬▬▬
1	•	6	•/▬	11	•/▬▬	16	•/▬▬▬
2	••	7	••/▬	12	••/▬▬	17	••/▬▬▬
3	•••	8	•••/▬	13	•••/▬▬	18	•••/▬▬▬
4	••••	9	••••/▬	14	••••/▬▬	19	••••/▬▬▬

level represented units. Numerals at the next higher level represented twenties. Thus, for example,

$$\frac{\overline{••}}{\underline{\overline{•}}} = 7 \cdot 20 + 11 = 151$$

One would think that numerals at the next higher level should represent $20 \cdot 20 = 400$, and there is some indication that they did when used by the peasants. But the priests, who had defined the official Mayan year to consist of 360 days—and who left all of the written records—assigned a place value of $18 \cdot 20 = 360$ to the next level. Thus

$$\frac{\overline{••}}{\frac{\overline{•}}{\overline{••••}}} = 2 \cdot (18 \cdot 20) + 11 \cdot 20 + 19 = 959$$

and

$$\frac{\overline{•••}}{\frac{\overline{⬯}}{\overline{••}}} = 13 \cdot (18 \cdot 20) + 0 \cdot 20 + 7 = 4687$$

Place values at higher levels are shown in Table 3.3.

Table 3.3 Place Values in the Mayan System

Level	Value
⋮	⋮
4	$18 \cdot 20^3$
3	$18 \cdot 20^2$
2	$18 \cdot 20$
1	20
0	1

EXAMPLE 10   Write a Hindu-Arabic numeral equivalent to each Mayan numeral and a Mayan numeral equivalent to each Hindu-Arabic numeral.

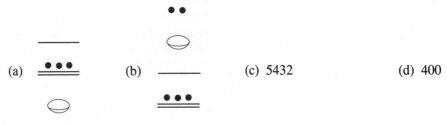

(a)   (b)   (c) 5432   (d) 400

Solution   (a) $5 \cdot (18 \cdot 20) + 13 \cdot 20 = 2060$
(b) $2 \cdot (18 \cdot 20^2) + 0 \cdot (18 \cdot 20) + 5 \cdot 20 + 13 = 14{,}513$
(c) Divide 5432 by 360 to get $5432 = 15 \cdot 360 + 32$. Then divide 32 by 20 to get $32 = 1 \cdot 20 + 12$. Thus

$$5432 = 15 \cdot (18 \cdot 20) + 1 \cdot 20 + 12 =$$

(d) Since $400 = 1 \cdot 360 + 2 \cdot 20$, $400 =$

❑

EXERCISE SET 3.2

1. Package each of these sets of caramels (base four), and then write the base-four numeral for the number of caramels.

   (a)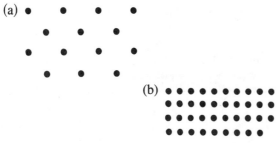

   (b)

   (c)

   (d)

2. Make a schematic drawing of singles ·, packs—, boxes ☐, and cases⬠for each base-four numeral.

   Example $1231_{four} \rightarrow$ 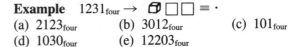 ≡ ·
   (a) 2123_{four} (b) 3012_{four} (c) 101_{four}
   (d) 1030_{four} (e) 12203_{four}

3. Solve these base-four addition problems by drawing caramels and packaging.
   (a) $213_{four} \rightarrow$ ☐☐|⦙
          $+\ 102_{four} \rightarrow$?
          $\overline{\qquad ? \leftarrow}$

(b) 121_{four}
    $+ \ 223_{four}$

4. Solve these base-four subtraction problems by drawing a diagram and taking away caramels.

(a) $233_{four} \rightarrow$
    $- \ 112_{four}$
    $?$

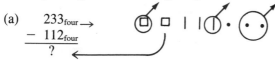

(b) 231_{four}
    $- \ 112_{four}$

(c) 2021_{four}
    $- \ 123_{four}$

5. Write out the first 25 counting numbers in base-four notation.

6. Write out the first 30 counting numbers in base-three notation.

7. Package each set of caramels in the base requested. Then write the numeral, in that base, for the number of caramels.

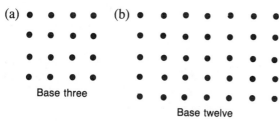

Base three

Base twelve

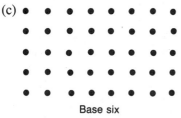

Base six

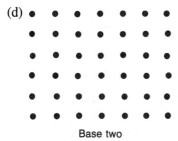

Base two

8. Archaeologists have unearthed a Weird numeration system that employs a base but no place value. They have determined that ⟩⟨⟩⟨⟩⟨⟩ must represent 31 and ⟨⟩⟩⟨⟩⟩⟨⟩⟩⟨ must represent 46.

(a) Write the Hindu-Arabic numeral for ⟨⟨⟩⟨⟨⟩⟩⟨

(b) Write the Weird numeral for 37.

9. Make a schematic drawing of singles, packs, boxes, and cases for each of the following:

(a) 371_{nine} (b) 1042_{ten}

(c) $T0E_{twelve}$ (d) 1010_{two}

10. Solve each problem by drawing a caramel diagram.

(a) 345_{six} (b) 641_{nine}
    $+ \ 413_{six}$ $- \ 228_{nine}$

(c) 1011_{two} (d) 904_{ten}
    $+ \ 101_{two}$ $- \ 678_{ten}$

11. Write the numeral that follows these numerals.

(a) 102_{four} (b) 123_{four}

(c) 30133_{four} (d) 599_{twelve}

(e) 10_{twelve} (f) 66_{seven}

12. Write the numeral that precedes these numerals.

(a) 311_{four} (b) E_{twelve}

(c) 10_{twelve} (d) 5000_{seven}

(e) 10100_{two} (f) 12_{twelve}

13. Express "two times ten is twenty" in the following bases:

(a) Base four

(b) Base five

(c) Base twenty

14. We have used schematic drawings of units (singles), longs (packs), flats (boxes), cubes (cases), . . . to represent Hindu-Arabic numerals.

(a) In what ways are the drawings (•, —, □, ⬚ , . . .) like Egyptian numerals?

(b) What complication of the Hindu-Arabic numeration system is avoided when we translate an arithmetic problem from Hindu-Arabic notation into unit-long-flat-cube notation?

15. Write a base-ten numeral for each of the following:
    (a) 1210_{four}
    (b) 1234_{five}
    (c) $20E_{twelve}$

16. Use the repeated-division algorithm to rewrite each numeral as indicated.
    (a) 150_{ten} in base-three notation
    (b) 255_{ten} in base-four notation
    (c) 1000_{ten} in base-twelve notation

17. Write 456_{seven} in base-three notation.

18. Find x in each of the following. Where no base is specified, you are to assume that the base is ten.
    (a) $2 \cdot 8^3 + 4 \cdot 8^2 + 7 \cdot 8 + 5 = 2475_x$
    (b) $3 \cdot 7^4 + 2 \cdot 7^2 + 5 \cdot 7 + 6 = x_{seven}$
    (c) $25_x + 25_x = 51_x$
    (d) $9 \cdot 9 = 74_x$
    (e) $10_B \cdot 10_B = x_B$ (where B is some unspecified base)
    (f) $100_B \cdot 23054_B = x_B$ (where B is unspecified but greater than five)
    (g) $4 \cdot 123_x = 514_x$

19. Space travelers discover a primitive civilization on a distant planet that employs a numeration system (for the natural numbers) with a base of six, but without place value. Their hierarchy of symbols begins

    $| , \triangledown , \diamondsuit , \square , . . .$

    Write their symbol for ninety-nine.

20. Solve each of these arithmetic problems by translating it into a base-ten problem, solving that problem, and then converting the answer to the original base.
    (a) 532_{seven}
        $+ 160_{seven}$
    (b) 3132_{four}
        $- 213_{four}$
    (c) 283_{nine}
        $\times 75_{nine}$
    (d) $15_{twelve} \overline{)304_{twelve}}$

21. Classify each number as even or odd.
    (a) 213_{five}
    (b) 313_{five}

★ 22. Recall (or assume if you don't recall) that
    $(-4)^0 = 1$
    $(-4)^1 = -4$
    $(-4)^2 = 16$
    $(-4)^3 = -64$
    $(-4)^4 = 256$
    Decide what number is represented by the numeral
    $$12312_{negative\ four}$$
    and express it in ordinary base-ten notation. Now write each of the following base-ten numerals as base-negative-four numerals. The only permissible digits are 0, 1, 2, and 3.
    (a) 10   (b) 50   (c) 75
    (d) 100   (e) −50

23. Suppose that a sixth grader knows how to multiply fractions and how to convert back and forth between fractions and decimals but does not know how to multiply decimals. Complete the following diagram to show how he could find the product .2 × .3 as a decimal.
    $$.2 \rightarrow \frac{2}{10}$$
    $$\times\ .3 \rightarrow \frac{3}{10}$$

24. Suppose that a seventh grader knows how to add decimals and how to convert back and forth between fractions and decimals but finds addition of fractions tiresome. Draw a diagram like the one in Exercise 23 to show how he could find
    $$\frac{3}{5} + \frac{7}{8}$$
    as a decimal. You would employ this method if you were to use a calculator. The initial conversions from fractions to decimals would be accomplished by punching
    $\boxed{3} \boxed{\div} \boxed{5}$ and $\boxed{7} \boxed{\div} \boxed{8}$

★ 25. A "magic" trick can be performed using the following four cards: The magician asks a volunteer to think of a number from 1 to 15. Let's suppose the number is 13.

A				B			
1	3	5	7	2	3	6	7
9	11	13	15	10	11	14	15

C			
4	5	6	7
12	13	14	15

D			
8	9	10	11
12	13	14	15

The volunteer replies that it appears on cards A, C, and D. Then the magician simply adds the upper-left numbers on those cards, $1 + 4 + 8$, to determine the number. To see why the trick works, express each of 1 through 15 in base-two notation. Observe that all numbers with units digit 1 appear on card A, all numbers with twos digit 1 appear on card B, all numbers with fours digit 1 appear on card C, and all numbers with eights digit 1 appear on card D. Complete the explanation.

★ 26. Write $8\frac{5}{6}$ in duodecimal notation.

27. Write the Hindu-Arabic numeral for each of the following numbers.

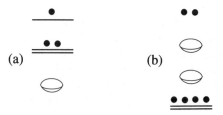

28. Write the Mayan numeral for each of the following numbers.
(a) 3660
(b) 1,000,000

Computer Vignette B

The repeated-division algorithm for changing bases is so mechanical that it lends itself readily to programming on a computer. Figure 3.24 is an interactive program that converts from base-ten to base-eight notation. Figure 3.25 is a sample run. Lines 80 and 90 are of special interest. The notation INT is for a function that is built into computers and rounds nonintegral numbers down to the next lower integer. (It leaves integers alone.) For example, if N = 93 at line 80, it is first divided by 8, yielding $11\frac{5}{8}$. Then INT rounds this result down to 11. Thus Q = 11. At line 90, $R = 93 - 11 \cdot 8 = 5$. Thus the effect of lines 80 and 90 is to find the whole number quotient (Q = 11) and remainder (R = 5) when 93 is divided by 8.

Figure 3.24

```
10    PRINT
20    PRINT "TYPE IN A WHOLE NUMBER LESS THAN A MILLION
      THAT YOU WANT EXPRESSED IN BASE-EIGHT NOTATION"
30    INPUT N
70    FOR J = 1 to 7
80    LET Q = INT (N / 8)
90    LET R = N - Q * 8
100   LET D(J) = R
110   LET N = Q
120   NEXT J
130   PRINT "THE BASE-EIGHT NUMERAL IS "; D(7); D(6);
      D(5); D(4); D(3); D(2); D(1)
140   PRINT
```

```
150   PRINT "DO YOU WANT TO STOP? 1 = YES, 0 = NO."
160   INPUT A
170   IF A = 0 THEN 10
180   END
```

Figure 3.25   ]RUN

```
TYPE IN A WHOLE NUMBER LESS THAN A MILLION THAT YOU
  WANT EXPRESSED IN BASE-EIGHT NOTATION
?93
THE BASE-EIGHT NUMERAL IS 0000135

DO YOU WANT TO STOP? 1 = YES, 0 = NO.
?0
TYPE IN A WHOLE NUMBER LESS THAN A MILLION THAT YOU
  WANT EXPRESSED IN BASE-EIGHT NOTATION
?876543
THE BASE-EIGHT NUMERAL IS 3257777

DO YOU WANT TO STOP? 1 = YES, 0 = NO.
?1
```

Even some fairly inexpensive calculators have the *built-in* capability of converting to and from base-two (binary), base-eight (octal), and base-sixteen (hexadecimal) notation. In base sixteen, the digits for ten through fifteen are A, B, C, D, E, F.

3.3   *Addition: Definitions and Applications*

If a kindergartner who knows no addition facts is asked to compute $5 + 8$, he might proceed as shown in Figure 3.26. He translates the abstract mathematical addition problem into the concrete problem of uniting two sets. His ability to count is what permits him to move back and forth between the abstract numbers and the concrete sets.

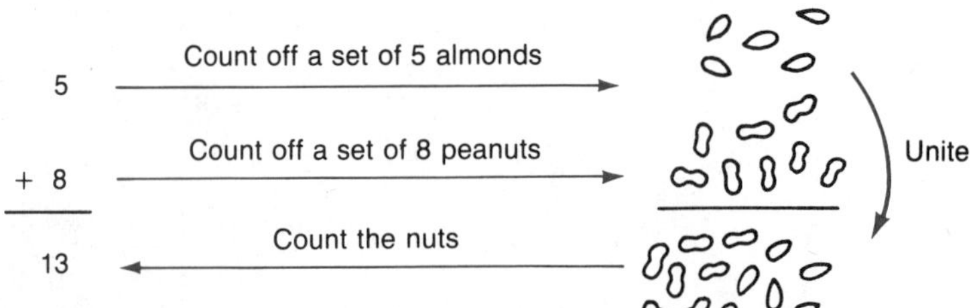

5	Count off a set of 5 almonds →	
+ 8	Count off a set of 8 peanuts →	Unite
13	← Count the nuts	

Figure 3.26

A mathematical formalization of the kindergartner's procedure can be used as a definition of addition.

Definition of Addition of Whole Numbers

Let n be the function that assigns to each (finite) set its (whole) number of elements, let a and p be arbitrary whole numbers, and let A and P be any disjoint sets such that $n(A) = a$ and $n(P) = p$. Then

$$a + p = n(A \cup P)$$

For ease of remembering we often abbreviate the definition into a single equation:

$$n(A) + n(P) = n(A \cup P) \qquad \text{for disjoint sets } A \text{ and } P$$

We verbalize the definition even more loosely:

Addition of whole numbers "corresponds" to union of disjoint sets.

The connection with union underlies the applications of addition to real problems.

Applications of Addition

A third grader makes quite a different use of the correspondence between addition and union than did the kindergartner. If asked to determine the total number of kindergartners in the (disjoint) A.M. and P.M. kindergarten classes, she does not form a union and count it. Instead, she counts each class separately and adds those numbers in the abstract mathematical way that she has mastered. See Figure 3.27.

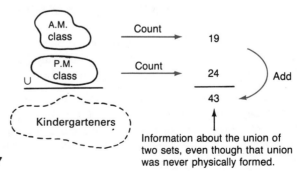

Figure 3.27

A.M. class — Count → 19
P.M. class — Count → 24
} Add
43

∪

Kindergarteners

↑
Information about the union of two sets, even though that union was never physically formed.

Symbolically, we write

$$n(K) = n(A \cup P) = n(A) + n(P) = 19 + 24 = 43$$

The third grader has applied her arithmetic to the solution of a real-world problem. The following examples illustrate some other very simple applications of the correspondence between addition of numbers and union of disjoint sets.

EXAMPLE 1   If there are 4 rams and 15 ewes, how many sheep are there?

Solution   Since the set of sheep (S) is the union of the set of rams (R) with the set of ewes (E), and since union corresponds to addition, the number of sheep is $4 + 15 = 19$. Schematically, we have

$$
\begin{array}{rcr}
R & \to & 4 \\
\underline{\cup\, E} & \to & \underline{+\ 15} \\
S & \to & 19
\end{array}
$$

Symbolically, we write

$$n(S) = n(R \cup E) = n(R) + n(E) = 4 + 15 = 19$$

The numbers 4 and 15 in the equation $4 + 15 = 19$ are called the **addends,** and 19 is called their **sum.**   ❏

EXAMPLE 2   If there are 20 sheep and 8 rams, how many ewes are there?

Solution   Schematically, we have

$$
\begin{array}{rcr}
R & \to & 8 \\
\underline{\cup\, E} & \to & \underline{+\ \boxed{?}} \\
S & \to & 20
\end{array}
$$

That is, we find the number of ewes by solving the equation $8 + \square = 20$ for the missing addend. Note that we need *not* use subtraction to solve such an equation. Guess-and-check addition will suffice. *Answer:* 12 ewes.   ❏

Further Applications: A Chart Technique

Not all addition problems are as simple as the ones considered so far. Sometimes, so many data are given that one must display them in a systematic fashion. The chart technique illustrated here is an aid in such problems.

EXAMPLE 3   In a group of 100 people, 58 are women, 30 are Republicans, and 30 are neither Republicans nor Democrats. Of the men, 14 are Republicans and 16 are Democrats. How many women are neither Republican nor Democrat?

Solution   Begin by making the chart shown in Figure 3.28, which partitions the group of 100 people into six categories, and enter the given data in appropriate boxes, as shown. (Do you see how entries below the red line represent column sums, and entries to the right of the red line represent row sums?) Now fill in the remaining boxes. The order in which the boxes are filled is not unique. In Figure 3.29 we filled in the entries in the order 40, 24, 16, 18. You might try to arrive at the answer, 18, by a different route.   ❑

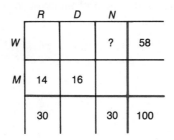

Figure 3.28   **Figure 3.29**

Abstract Properties of Addition

Having a formal definition of addition in terms of union allows one to derive a number of general properties of addition from corresponding properties of union. The following properties will be investigated thoroughly in Chapter 4.

Commutative Property of Addition. $a + b = b + a$ for all whole numbers a and b.

Derivation.   This derivation is based on the commutative property of union. Choose disjoint sets A and B having a and b elements, respectively; that is, $n(A) = a$ and $n(B) = b$. Then

$$a + b = n(A) + n(B) \qquad \text{choice of } A \text{ and } B$$
$$= n(A \cup B) \qquad \text{definition of addition}$$
$$= n(B \cup A) \qquad \text{commutative property of union}$$
$$= n(B) + n(A) \qquad \text{definition of addition}$$
$$= b + a \qquad \text{choice of } A \text{ and } B$$

Associative Property of Addition. $(a + b) + c = a + (b + c)$ for all whole numbers a, b, and c.

Additive Property of Zero.   (Zero is the Additive Identity) $a + 0 = a$ for all whole numbers a.

Deviations of these last two properties are outlined in the exercises.

Another Definition of Addition (Optional)

The definition we have given for addition of whole numbers is the standard one, but it is not the only one. The Italian mathematician Giuseppe Peano (1858–1932) gave an ingenious definition, which in terms of human development is more primitive than ours. While our definition uses the function n, which tells *how many* elements are in a set, Peano's definition uses the *successor function S*, which formalizes the earliest kind of counting, namely, the *what's next* assignment of numbers to numbers. The input-output table for S is shown below.

x	$S(x)$
0	1
1	2
2	3
3	4
4	5
5	6
6	7
7	8
⋮	⋮

Peano's *recursive definition* of addition is

$$\begin{cases} a + 0 = a \\ a + S(b) = S(a + b) \end{cases}$$

The word *recursive* suggests that to find out what is meant by, say, $4 + 2$, you should expect to circle back to this definition several times. Specifically, here is how it is done:

$4 + 2 = 4 + S(1)$	definition of S	$[S(1) = 2]$
$\quad = S(4 + 1)$	definition of $+$	[Second clause with $a = 4, b = 1$]
$\quad = S(4 + S(0))$	definition of S	$[S(0) = 1]$
$\quad = S(S(4 + 0))$	definition of $+$	[Second clause with $a = 4, b = 0$]
$\quad = S(S(4))$	definition of $+$	[First clause with $a = 4$]

Thus $4 + 2$ is the number you get by starting with 4 and applying the successor function two times in a row. That is, you start at 4 and *count forward* 2, just the way a kindergartner might!

The idea of recursion has become more and more important in modern mathematics and computer science. We will touch on it again particularly in Chapter 16.

EXERCISE SET 3.3

In solving these first six arithmetic problems, make an effort to identify sets and unions of sets.

1. How many singers are in the school choir of 9 basses, 12 tenors, 14 altos, and 17 sopranos?

2. If there are 21 cars, 3 buses, and 4 trucks in the school parking lot, how many vehicles are there?

3. Thirty-five of the 63 voters were women. How many were men?

4. Of the 21 people who showed up for the meeting, 8 had to leave early. How many stayed until the end?

5. In a class of 75 undergraduates 41 are freshmen or sophomores, and there are as many seniors as there are juniors. How many seniors are there?

6. In a class of 28 children twice as many get rides to school as take their bikes, and twice as many walk as get rides. How many get rides?

The next two exercises seem to fit the count-forward view of addition better than the unite-sets view. Solve them by counting.

7. Grandma is 68 years old. How old will she be 4 years from now?

8. Last Monday George weighed 147 lb. Since then he has gained 5 lb. How much does he weigh now?

9. A spot check of 30 trucks and 80 cars revealed that 10 cars had bad brakes and 28 trucks had good brakes. What fraction of the vehicles had good brakes?

10. One hundred people, half of whom were children, were asked if they liked licorice. Sixty said they did, including 12 of the 20 men. Sixteen of the women said they did not like licorice. How many children liked licorice?

11. An auto dealer's monthly sales of 120 vehicles included 20 new trucks, 18 new vans out of a total of 40 vans, and 35 used cars out of a total of 43 cars. How many used trucks did she sell?

12. According to a survey of 100 Democrats, 100 Republicans, and many Independents concerning the president's economic program, 54 Democrats and 32 Republicans were pro, 38 of the 144 cons were Independents, and 7 of the 20 undecideds were Democrats. How many Independents were undecided?

13. We were careful to distinguish between the abstract mathematical operation, addition of numbers, and the related, more concrete operation, union of sets. This distinction is often blurred in ordinary discourse. Replace each underlined word below by a more accurate one.

   (a) The new Plymouth offers high mileage plus low price.
   (b) Two and two is four.
   (c) Your life is the sum of your experiences.
   (d) How much mixture do you get when you add 2 cups of sugar to 10 cups of lemonade?

14. Explain how the language used in Exercise 13(d) could lead to a ridiculous answer to the question.

★ 15. Fill in missing reasons in this derivation of the associative property of addition. You can use "associative property of union" as a reason.
   Derivation Choose (pairwise) disjoint sets A, B, and C having a, b, and c elements, respectively; that is, $n(A) = a$, $n(B) = b$, and $n(C) = c$. Then

$(a + b) + c$

$= [n(A) + n(B)] + n(C)$	(a) _____
$= n(A \cup B) + n(C)$	(b) _____
$= n[(A \cup B) \cup C]$	(c) _____
$= n[A \cup (B \cup C)]$	(d) _____
$= n(A) + n(B \cup C)$	(e) _____
$= n(A) + [n(B) + n(C)]$	(f) _____
$= a + (b + c)$	(g) _____

★ 16. Fill in missing reasons in this derivation of the additive property of zero. You can use "$\varnothing$ is the identity element for union" as a reason.

Derivation   Choose a set A with a elements; that is, $n(A) = a$. Note that $n(\varnothing) = 0$ and that A and $\varnothing$ are disjoint. Then

$a + 0 = n(A) + n(\varnothing)$	(a) _____
$= n(A \cup \varnothing)$	(b) _____
$= n(A)$	(c) _____
$= a$	(d) _____

★ 17. A function f, from W to W, is defined recursively by

$$\begin{cases} f(0) = 1 \\ f(n) = n \cdot f(n - 1) & \text{for all natural numbers } n \end{cases}$$

(a) Complete this evaluation of $f(5)$:

$$f(5) = 5 \cdot f(4) \qquad \text{by clause 2 with } n = 5$$
$$= 5 \cdot 4 \cdot f(3) \quad \text{by clause 2 with } n = 4$$
$$\vdots$$

(b) What is the usual name for this function f?

★ 18. A function g, from W to W, is defined recursively by

$$\begin{cases} g(0) = 1 \\ g(n) = 2 \cdot g(n - 1) & \text{for all natural numbers } n \end{cases}$$

(a) Evaluate $g(5)$.
(b) What is the usual name for this function g?

19. A function h, from W to W, is defined recursively by

$$\begin{cases} h(0) = 0 \\ h(1) = 1 \\ h(n) = h(n - 1) + h(n - 2) & \text{for all } n \geq 2 \end{cases}$$

Fill in the outputs in this table for f:

Input	0	1	2	3	4	5	6	7
Output								

3.4 *Multiplication: Definitions and Applications*

Like addition, the abstract mathematical operation of multiplication can be related to sets and a set operation. To see exactly what the relation is, consider this problem: There are three kinds of crackers—graham, rye, and soda—and four kinds of jelly—apple, boysenberry, plum, and quince. How many cracker-and-jelly combinations are possible?

The most straightforward (though certainly not the quickest) way to solve this problem would be to exhibit, somehow, all the combinations and then count them. Perhaps one would represent the combinations by the paths down the tree shown in Figure 3.30. Or one might use the crossing points in the rectangular display in Figure 3.31. Or, getting closer to essentials, one could use the ordered pairs listed here:

$$\{(g, a), (g, b), (g, p), (g, q), (r, a), (r, b), (r, p), (r, q), (s, a),$$
$$(s, b), (s, p), (s, q)\}$$

When viewed in any of these ways, the original problem has two essential aspects. We are given two sets: a set of crackers $C = \{g, r, s\}$ and a set of jellies $J = \{a, b, p, q\}$. We are asked to find the number of elements in the Cartesian product set $C \times J$.

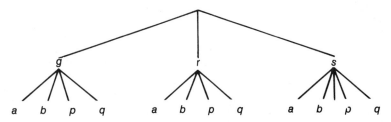

Figure 3.30

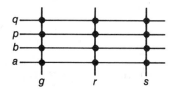

Figure 3.31

The way most adults solve this problem is to avoid entirely the tedious job of representing the Cartesian product but, instead, to count C, count J, and then multiply. That is, on the following diagram the *efficient* route from upper left to lower right is across first and then down; the conceptually simple route is down first and then across:

$$
\begin{array}{r}
C \rightarrow \quad 3 \\
\times\, J \rightarrow \cdot\ \ 4 \\
\hline
C \times J \rightarrow \quad 12
\end{array}
$$

The fact that both routes lead to the same number can be expressed in a single equation:

$$n(C \times J) = n(C) \cdot n(J)$$

Generalization of this example provides a formal mathematical definition of multiplication.

Definition of Multiplication of Whole Numbers

Let n be the function that assigns to each (finite) set its (whole) number of elements, let a and b be arbitrary whole numbers, and let A and B be any sets (disjoint or not) such that $n(A) = a$ and $n(B) = b$. Then

$$a \cdot b = n(A \times B)$$

For ease of remembering we often abbreviate the definition into a single equation:

$$n(A) \cdot n(B) = n(A \times B)$$

We verbalize it even more loosely.

Multiplication of whole numbers "corresponds" to Cartesian product of sets.

Another view of multiplication—as repeated addition—is usually presented to children first. The formal definition follows.

For any whole numbers a and b

$$a \cdot b = \underbrace{a + a + a + \cdots + a}_{b \text{ addends}}$$

with the understanding that $a \cdot 0 = 0$ and $a \cdot 1 = a$.

For example,

$$3 \cdot 4 = 3 + 3 + 3 + 3 = 12$$

The number 3 and 4 in the equation $3 \cdot 4 = 12$ are referred to as **factors,** and 12 is called their **product.**

The repeated-addition view has the virtue of being relatively easy to understand (there being no need to grapple with the operation of Cartesian product), and it does have a sound mathematical basis (as we shall see later). But eventually, the Cartesian product interpretation needs to be understood as well. As the efficient solution to the crackers-and-jelly problem suggests, the connection with Cartesian product underlies applications of multiplication to a certain class of real-world problems. As you work through this section, you will begin to get a feeling for how large and important that class is.

Applications of Multiplication

Once one recognizes that the solution to a word problem can be represented by a tree, a rectangular array, or a set of ordered pairs, then the appropriate arithmetic operation is multiplication.

EXAMPLE 1   Six telephone wires are to be strung over four poles. How many insulators are needed? (One insulator is used wherever a wire touches a pole.)

Solution   This problem can be represented very naturally by a rectangular array, the crossing points corresponding to the insulators. See Figure 3.32. Thus the indicated arithmetic operation is multiplication: $4 \cdot 6 = 24$ insulators. (Do you see how this same problem can be viewed as a repeated-addition problem involving four 6s? Six 4s?)

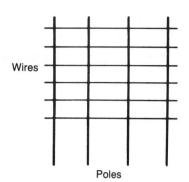

Figure 3.32

Wires

Poles

❏

EXAMPLE 2   Twenty-four people each contributed $5 to a fund. How much money was contributed?

Solution   It is easy to visualize (if not draw) a tree with 24 branches, each having 5 twigs. (Each branch is an outstretched arm offering five $1 bills.) See Figure 3.33. Thus multiplication is the appropriate operation 24 · 5 = $120.   ❏

Figure 3.33

EXAMPLE 3   How many two-letter "words" (meaningful or not, pronounceable or not) can be formed by using letters of the English alphabet?

Solution   Once we start to list them,

aa, ab, ac, . . . , az, ba, bb, . . .

it becomes clear that we are listing the Cartesian product $E \times E$, where E is the set of all English alphabet letters. To find how many "words," then, it is enough to count E and multiply this number by itself: 26 · 26 = 676.   ❏

Further Applications: Areas of Rectangles

When we are asked to find the area of a 5-cm by 3-cm rectangle, we are really being asked how many square centimeters are required to cover that rectangle. See Figure 3.34. That is, we are being asked to count a 5-by-3 rectangular array of squares. This counting task is no different from counting a rectangular array of dots (the set of squares is in one-to-one correspondence with the set of their upper right-hand vertices). As we have seen, the quickest way to count such an array of dots is to multiply 5 by 3. Thus the familiar area formula for a rectangle,

$$\text{Area} = \text{base} \times \text{height}$$

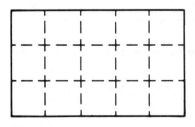

Figure 3.34

is a consequence of the Cartesian product interpretation of multiplication.

EXAMPLE 4   Find the area, in square inches, of a poster that is 2 ft 5 in high and 16 in wide.

Solution

$$\text{Base} = 16 \text{ in}$$
$$\text{Height} = 2 \text{ ft } 5 \text{ in} = 29 \text{ in}$$
$$\text{Area} = \text{base} \times \text{height} = 16 \text{ in} \times 29 \text{ in} = 464 \text{ in}^2$$

Notice how the formal multiplication of units,

$$\text{in} \times \text{in} = \text{in}^2$$

automatically produces the correct unit of area.   ❏

Further Applications: The Choice Principle

Suppose there are 6 restaurants and 2 movie theaters in town, and you have decided to go out to dinner and then a show. How many different ways can you spend the evening? The tree in Figure 3.35 shows how each of the 6 choices of a restaurant can be combined with 2 choices of a theater to yield 12 possible ways to spend the evening.

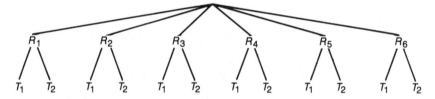

Figure 3.35

Since problems of this type arise so frequently, and since sketching trees (to determine that one is really faced with a multiplication problem) can be tedious, a verbalized rule, called the *choice principle* (or *multiplication principle,* or *fundamental counting principle*), is handy.

> ### The Choice Principle
>
> If there are F choices for how to perform a first act and S choices for how to perform a second act, then there are $F \cdot S$ choices for how to perform the two acts in succession.

EXAMPLE 5   In the closet are 5 skirts and 9 blouses. How many skirt-blouse outfits are possible?

Solution   First, choose a skirt (5 choices), and then choose a blouse (9 choices). There are $5 \cdot 9 = 45$ outfits.   ❏

The choice principle generalizes to successions of 3, 4, 5, . . . acts.

EXAMPLE 6   In the game of Clue the suspects are Mr. Green, Col. Mustard, Mrs. Peacock, Prof. Plum, Miss Scarlett, and Mrs. White. The possible murder weapons are candlestick, knife, lead pipe, revolver, rope, and wrench; the possible scenes for the crime are ballroom, billiard room, conservatory, dining room, hall, kitchen, library, lounge, and study. How many different crimes are possible? (One crime is: Mr. Green did it in the study with a knife.)

Solution   There are 6 choices for the perpetrator, 6 for the weapon, and 9 for the scene of the crime. Therefore, by the generalized choice principle there are $6 \cdot 6 \cdot 9 = 324$ possible crimes. ❑

Abstract Properties of Multiplication

Having a formal definition of multiplication in terms of Cartesian product allows one to derive general properties of multiplication from corresponding properties of Cartesian product. These properties will be examined in detail in Chapter 4.

Commutative Property of Multiplication. $a \cdot b = b \cdot a$ for all whole numbers a and b.

Derivation.   Choose any sets A and B for which $n(A) = a$ and $n(B) = b$. Then

$$
\begin{aligned}
a \cdot b &= n(A) \cdot n(B) &&\text{choice of } A \text{ and } B \\
&= n(A \times B) &&\text{definition of multiplication} \\
&= n(B \times A) &&\underline{\quad ? \quad} \\
&= n(B) \cdot n(A) &&\text{definition of multiplication} \\
&= b \cdot a &&\text{choice of } A \text{ and } B
\end{aligned}
$$

Supplying a reason at line 3 takes a little thought because the Cartesian product operation is *not* commutative; in general, $A \times B \neq B \times A$. However, $A \times B$ and $B \times A$ are in one-to-one correspondence, so they have the same number of elements. (The function from $A \times B$ to $B \times A$ that simply interchanges the components of its input ordered pairs is a one-to-one correspondence.)

Associative Property of Multiplication. $(a \cdot b) \cdot c = a \cdot (b \cdot c)$ for all whole numbers a, b, and c.

The key reason in a formal derivation of the associative property of multiplication is the observation that for any sets A, B, and C, $(A \times B) \times C$ is in one-to-one correspondence with $A \times (B \times C)$. Figure 3.36 illustrates the associative property of multiplication by showing a block of 60 sugar cubes that is cut up in two different ways: into vertical slabs and into horizontal slabs. Since the number of sugar cubes does not change, one concludes that $(3 \cdot 4) \cdot 5 = 3 \cdot (4 \cdot 5)$.

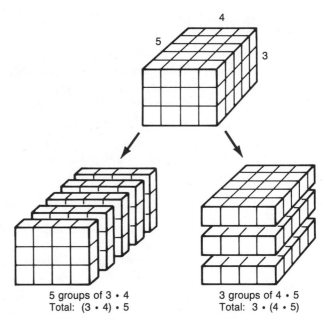

5 groups of 3 • 4   3 groups of 4 • 5
Total: (3 • 4) • 5   Total: 3 • (4 • 5)

Figure 3.36

Multiplicative Property of One. (One is the Multiplicative Identity)   For every whole number a, $a \cdot 1 = a$.

A derivation is sketched in the exercise set.

Distributive Property of Multiplication over Addition. $(a + b) \cdot c = a \cdot c + b \cdot c$ for all whole numbers a, b, and c.

The distributive property plays such a fundamental role throughout mathematics, elementary and advanced, that we explain it in two different ways. (A third derivation of it from formal properties of sets and set operations is outlined in the exercise set.) An arithmetic explanation can be based on the repeated-addition definition of multiplication and certain abstract properties of the addition operation:

$(4 + 5) \cdot 3 = (4 + 5) + (4 + 5) + (4 + 5)$ repeated addition
                                                 definition

$\qquad = (4 + 4 + 4) + (5 + 5 + 5)$ commutative and
                                                 associative properties
                                                 of addition

$\qquad = 4 \cdot 3 + 5 \cdot 3$ repeated addition
                                                   definition

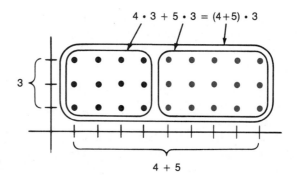

Figure 3.37

A geometric illustration that $(4 + 5) \cdot 3 = 4 \cdot 3 + 5 \cdot 3$ comes from the connection between multiplication and Cartesian product and from the rectangular array representation of Cartesian product. See Figure 3.37.

Another Definition of Multiplication (Optional)

Peano defined multiplication recursively in terms of the successor function S (see p. 116) and the previously defined addition operation:

$$\begin{cases} a \cdot 1 = a \\ a \cdot S(b) = (a \cdot b) + a \end{cases}$$

Here is how one can use the definition to find out what is meant by $4 \cdot 3$:

$$
\begin{aligned}
4 \cdot 3 &= 4 \cdot S(2) && \text{definition of } S \, [S(2) = 3] \\
&= (4 \cdot 2) + 4 && \text{definition of } \cdot \text{ [second clause with } a = 4, b = 2] \\
&= [4 \cdot S(1)] + 4 && \text{definition of } S \, [S(1) = 2] \\
&= (4 \cdot 1 + 4) + 4 && \text{definition of } \cdot \text{ [second clause with } a = 4, b = 1] \\
&= (4 + 4) + 4 && \text{definition of } \cdot \text{ [first clause with } a = 4]
\end{aligned}
$$

Thus $4 \cdot 3$ is the number you get by using 4 as an addend 3 times. Peano's definition amounts to repeated addition! This is what we meant when we said that repeated addition has a sound mathematical basis.

EXERCISE SET 3.4

1. The options available on the new Sportsmobile are as follows:

   Color: red, yellow, blue, green
   Body style: 2-door, 3-door, 4-door

   How many types of Sportsmobile are available to the customer?

2. In the cafeteria each child has to pick one main dish, one drink, and one dessert from the following menu:

   Main dishes: chicken, meat loaf, fish
   Drinks: milk, water
   Desserts: pie, cake, sherbet

How many different lunches are possible? How many different lunches are possible if the only rule is that the child can choose at most one food from each category?

3. In a certain state license numbers consist of three letters followed by five digits. How many license numbers are possible?

4. A left-right-left combination lock has the numbers 0 through 30 on it. No combination can use the same number twice in succession; that is, L17–R10–L17 is okay, but L17–R17–L10 is not. First estimate, then compute exactly how many combinations are possible.

5. Which allows more combinations, an LRL lock with 0–60 on it, or an LRLR lock with 0–30 on it?

6. To get from Salem to Round Lake, one must pass through Evansville. The only ways to get from Salem to Evansville are by car, train, or plane. The only ways to get from Evansville to Round Lake are by foot, horseback, bicycle, or canoe. How many modes of travel are there from Salem to Round Lake?

7. How many different left-to-right routes are there from A to D in Figure 3.38?

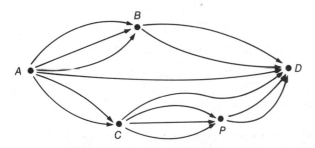

Figure 3.38

8. Once there were 12 pence in a shilling and 20 shillings in a pound. How many pence were there in a pound?

9. There are 8 furlongs in a mile and 1760 yards (yd) in a mile. How many yards are there in a furlong?

10. In Springfield there are 12 elementary schools with 8 classrooms in each, 3 junior high schools with 20 classrooms in each, and 1 high school with 54 classrooms. How many classrooms are there in Springfield?

11. Once there were two baseball leagues, each with the same number of teams, and there were 64 possible World Series matchups. How many teams were in each league?

12. Find the area, in square centimeters (cm^2), of each rectangle in Figure 3.39.

Figure 3.39

13. Guess a formula for the volume of a right rectangular prism (a box), and use it to calculate the volume of each one in Figure 3.40. Be sure to specify your unit of measure.

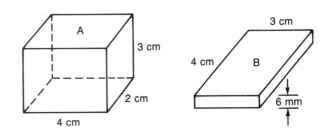

Figure 3.40

14. In the game of Clue, described in Example 6, on p. 123, which would narrow down the possibilities more drastically, clearing one suspect or ruling out one scene for the crime?

15. A sound system consists of a matched pair of speakers, a receiver, a turntable, and a tape deck. If a dealer offers 12 different matched pairs of speakers, 5 receivers, 3 turntables, and 8 tape decks, how many sound systems are possible?

16. If the dealer in Exercise 15 wants to give her customers the most choices possible, but she is willing to stock just one more model of one component, which should it be: receiver, turntable, tape deck, or matched pair of speakers?

17. A class of 25 students plans to elect a president and a vice president. How many choices are possible for these class officers? In this and the next problem you might want to use the strategy of asking easier questions.

★ 18. A class of 25 students plans to elect two student council representatives. How many different sets of representatives are possible?

19. License plates are to be done in two colors from the color wheel shown in Figure 3.41, one for the numerals and one for the background. So that there will be sufficient contrast, colors that are adjacent on the color wheel will not be used together. How many color combinations are possible?

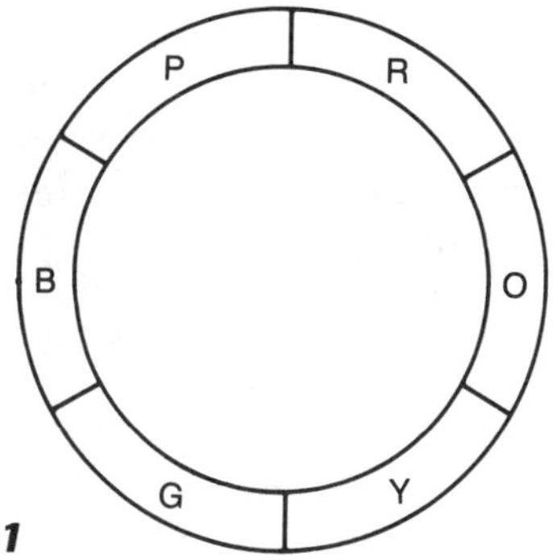

Figure 3.41

20. Four stripes are to be painted on a flagpole as shown in Figure 3.42. There is to be one stripe each of red, yellow, blue, and green. How many distinguishable flagpoles can be produced in this way?

21. Four stripes are to be painted on a stick as shown in Figure 3.43. There is to be one stripe each of red, yellow, blue, and green. How many distinguishable sticks can be produced in this way?

Figure 3.43

Figure 3.42

★ 22. Four stripes are to be painted on a circular bracelet as shown in Figure 3.44. There is to be one stripe each of red, yellow, blue, and green. How many distinguishable bracelets can be produced in this way?

Figure 3.44

23. Citizens band call signals used to consist of three letters followed by four digits. The Federal Communications Commission (FCC) claimed it used up all possibilities, and now it uses four letters followed by four digits. Do you believe the FCC?

24. A *palindrome* is a string of letters that reads the same backwards as forwards, for example "SATSTAS."
   (a) How many seven-letter palindromes are there?
   (b) How many eight-letter palindromes are there?

(c) How many five-letter palindromes are there in which no letter occurs more than twice?

25. How many ways are there of answering a five-question, multiple-choice quiz, if each question has four choices, one of which *must* be selected?

26. How many whole numbers are there between 10,000 and 100,000 whose base-ten numerals have no repeated digits?

27. Table 3.4 is a *data array* or matrix that shows the driving distances among four cities A, B, C, and D. A salesman who lives in city A wants to devise an itinerary that will take him to each of the cities B, C, D once and then back home.

Table 3.4 Mileage Chart

	A	B	C	D
A	0	60	100	80
B	60	0	150	90
C	100	150	0	100
D	80	90	100	0

(a) How many different itineraries are possible?
(b) Which one(s) will minimize his driving distance?
(c) If another city E is added to the salesman's list of stops, how many itineraries are possible?

★ 28. Supply reasons in this derivation of the multiplicative property of one: $a \cdot 1 = a$ for all whole numbers a.

Derivation   Choose set A such that $n(A) = a$. Choose any set B containing just one element. Then

$$a \cdot 1 = n(A) \cdot n(B) \qquad \text{(a)} \underline{\hspace{2cm}}$$
$$= n(A \times B) \qquad \text{(b)} \underline{\hspace{2cm}}$$
$$= n(A) \qquad \text{(c)} \underline{\hspace{2cm}}$$
$$= a \qquad \text{(d)} \underline{\hspace{2cm}}$$

★ 29. Supply reasons in this derivation of the distributive property: $(a + b) \cdot c = a \cdot c + b \cdot c$. You can use "Cartesian product distributes over union" as a reason.

Derivation   Choose disjoint sets A and B such that $n(A) = a$ and $n(B) = b$. Choose any set C such that $n(C) = c$. Then

$$(a + b) \cdot c$$
$$= [n(A) + n(B)] \cdot n(C) \qquad \text{(a)} \underline{\hspace{1.5cm}}$$
$$= n(A \cup B) \cdot n(C) \qquad \text{(b)} \underline{\hspace{1.5cm}}$$
$$= n[(A \cup B) \times C] \qquad \text{(c)} \underline{\hspace{1.5cm}}$$
$$= n[(A \times C) \cup (B \times C)] \qquad \text{(d)} \underline{\hspace{1.5cm}}$$
$$= n(A \times C) + n(B \times C) \qquad \text{(e)} \underline{\hspace{1.5cm}}$$
$$= n(A) \cdot n(C) + n(B) \cdot n(C) \qquad \text{(f)} \underline{\hspace{1.5cm}}$$
$$= a \cdot c + b \cdot c \qquad \text{(g)} \underline{\hspace{1.5cm}}$$

3.5   *Subtraction: Definitions and Applications*

Within the system of whole numbers the concepts of order and subtraction are intimately related: We can subtract 3 from 5 and get a whole number, because 3 is less than 5; we cannot subtract 9 from 5 and get a whole number, because 9 is greater than 5. Clearly, then, there must be a connection between the definitions of subtraction and of the order relation *less than*.

There are, in fact, a number of equivalent definitions of less than, and each has associated with it a definition of subtraction. We will give three such pairs, rather than just one, for the following reasons. First, each of the three views of subtraction is appropriate for a slightly different class of real-world problems. (We will look at applications once we are finished with the definitions, but you might want to glance ahead at page 131 right now.) Second, examining the three views helps us to realize that definitions are human creations; there need be no single best one. And as a teacher, you will have to be flexible enough to co-exist with whatever definitions appear in the text you are using.

Definitions

As we have seen, order is one of the first mathematical ideas a child encounters: The number 3 is less than the number 5 because 3 precedes 5 in the memorized sequence

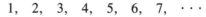

$$1, \quad 2, \quad 3, \quad 4, \quad 5, \quad 6, \quad 7, \quad \cdots$$

Put another way, 3 is less than 5 because we can begin at 3 and count forward to 5. But counting forward is a way of adding. Thus 3 is less than 5 because there is a *natural number* (nonzero whole number) solution to the equation $3 + \square = 5$. We shall generalize this observation shortly as the *missing-addend* definition of less than.

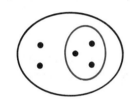

Figure 3.45

From the cardinal viewpoint there are two ways of explaining why 3 is less than 5. Here is the first way, which will soon be formalized as the *subset* definition of less than: 3 is less than 5 because there is a 5-element set having a *proper* 3-element subset, as indicated in Figure 3.45. Here is the second way, which will be called the *comparison* definition of less than: 3 is less than 5 because a 3-element set can be put in one-to-one correspondence with a *proper* subset of a 5-element set, as indicated in Figure 3.46.

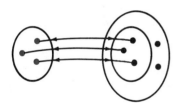

Figure 3.46

To simplify the statements of the general definitions, we adopt the usual shorthand abbreviation

$$< \text{ is read ``is less than''}$$

Missing-Addend Definition of Less-Than ($<$). $a < b$ means there is a natural number solution to the equation $a + \square = b$.

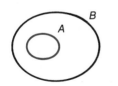

Figure 3.47

Subset Definition of Less-Than ($<$). $a < b$ means there is a set B with b elements that includes a proper subset A with a elements. See Figure 3.47.

Comparison Definition of Less-Than ($<$). $a < b$ means that if A is a set with a elements and B is a set with b elements, then A can be put in one-to-one correspondence with a proper subset of B. See Figure 3.48.

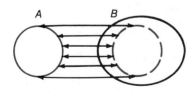

Figure 3.48

One fine point needs to be cleared up before we state the corresponding definitions of subtraction. Eventually, we want $b - a$ to be defined for any whole numbers a and b for which $a \le b$ (a is less than *or equal to* b). Let us agree that $b - b = 0$ for every b. Thus it remains to define subtraction only in the case of $a < b$.

Missing-Addend Definition of Subtraction

Given $a < b$ so that $a + \square = b$ has a natural number solution, then $b - a$ is the missing addend in the equation $a + \square = b$.

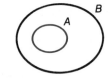

Figure 3.49

Subset, or Take-Away, Definition of Subtraction

Given $a < b$ so that there is a proper subset A of a elements in a set B of b elements, then $b - a = n(A')$, where A' is the complement of A in the (universal) set B. See Figure 3.49. (One thinks of taking away the subset A and counting the elements that remain.)

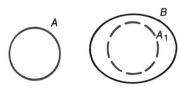

Figure 3.50

Comparison Definition of Subtraction

Given $a < b$ so that a set A with a elements is in one-to-one correspondence with a proper subset A_1 (see Figure 3.50) of a set B with b elements, then $b - a = n(A_1')$.

Terminology: The expression $b - a$ is called the **difference** of b and a, b is called the **minuend,** and a is called the **subtrahend.** The **minus sign** $(-)$ by itself denotes the function that assigns to each ordered pair (b, a), with $a < b$, the number $b - a$ (the difference).

EXAMPLE 1   Find $7 - 4$, using all three definitions.

Solution   *Missing-addend:* $7 - 4$ is the missing addend in the equation $4 + \square = 7$. By guess-and-check addition, the missing addend is 3.

Subset, or take-away: Draw a set of 7 dots, take away 4, and count the survivors (3). See Figure 3.51.

Comparison: Pair off a set of 4 objects with a subset of a set of 7 objects, and count the unpaired objects (3). See Figure 3.52.

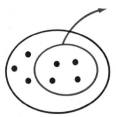   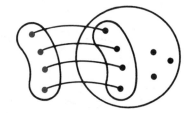

Figure 3.51   **Figure 3.52**   ❑

Applications

Having three different ways of thinking about subtraction will be helpful in solving word problems.

EXAMPLE 2   Today is the 23rd. Payday is the 30th. How many days until payday?

Solution   This is a count-forward, that is, add-on or missing-addend, situation:

$$23 + \square = 30$$

Hence the problem can be solved by subtracting: $30 - 23 = 7$.   ❏

EXAMPLE 3   There were 127 cows in a pasture. Cattle rustlers stole 42 of them. How many are left?

Solution   This is pretty clearly a take-away situation, as indicated in Figure 3.53. So the answer is found by subtracting: $127 - 42 = 85$.

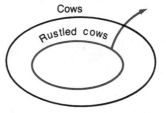

Figure 3.53   ❏

EXAMPLE 4   At the dance there are 93 boys and 77 girls. How many more boys than girls are there?

Solution   This is a comparison situation. (Pair off all of the girls with some of the boys, and count the boys without partners.) See Figure 3.54. Thus the answer is found by subtracting: $93 - 77 = 16$.

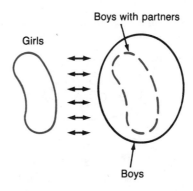

Figure 3.54   ❏

EXAMPLE 5   There are 172 children in the school, 94 of whom are boys. How many girls are there?

Solution   It is not always clear which interpretation of subtraction best fits a given problem. Some people look at this problem and see a union of disjoint sets:

$$
\begin{array}{rcl}
B \text{ (boys)} & \rightarrow & 94 \\
\cup\ G \text{ (girls)} & \rightarrow & +\ \square \\
\hline
C \text{ (children)} & \rightarrow & 172
\end{array}
$$

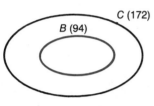

Thus they view it as a missing-addend question, which they answer by subtracting: $172 - 94 = 78$. Other people look at the same problem and visualize the boys as a subset of the children, as indicated in Figure 3.55. Thus the subset (take-away) view of subtraction fits the problem. The same computation as before yields the same answer: $172 - 94 = 78$.   ❏

Figure 3.56 shows how the three interpretations of subtraction are illustrated in a fourth-grade textbook.

Figure 3.55

EXERCISE SET 3.5

Write the subtraction problem and answer suggested by each equation.

1. $7 + \square = 10$

2. $79 + \square = 203$

3. $12 + \square = 12$

4. How might a second grader react to the equation $6 + \square = 4$?

Write a subtraction problem and answer suggested by each diagram.

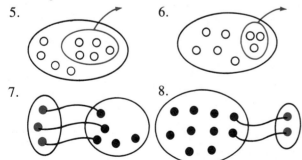

5.   6.

7.   8.

Solve the following word problems. For each one, decide which interpretation of subtraction (missing-addend, take-away, or comparison) seems to fit best. The choice is not always clear-cut.

9. Thirty students started out in chemistry, but seven dropped the class. How many finished?

10. There are 63 cars but only 45 parking places. How many cars will not be able to park?

11. There are 5 roosters in a flock of 64 chickens. How many hens are there? (There are no chicks.)

12. Fifty doctors and lawyers attended a rap session on malpractice. After ten minutes all 32 lawyers stalked out. How many doctors were at the session?

13. Joan weighed w pounds before losing d pounds while dieting. How much did she weigh after dieting?

14. There are k children on the baseball team but only g gloves. How many children will not have gloves?

PROBLEM SOLVING · STRATEGIES

Three Uses of Subtraction

Three Uses of Subtraction ⎰ to find how many are left
to find how many more are needed
⎱ to compare

Read each problem carefully.

Sarah buys 7 baseball cards. She
gives 3 cards away. How many
baseball cards are left?
Subtract to find how many are left.
4 baseball cards are left.

$$\begin{array}{r} 7 \\ -3 \\ \hline 4 \end{array}$$

Kiyoshi is saving baseball cards. He
needs 8 cards to get a prize. He has
5 cards. How many more cards does
he need?
Subtract to find how many more are needed.
He needs 3 more cards.

$$\begin{array}{r} 8 \\ -5 \\ \hline 3 \end{array}$$

Linda has 5 baseball cards. Tommy
has 3 cards. How many more cards
does Linda have?
Subtract to compare.
Linda has 2 more cards.

$$\begin{array}{r} 5 \\ -3 \\ \hline 2 \end{array}$$

Can you use subtraction to solve? Write YES or NO.

1. You have 12 cards. You lose 8 of
   them. How many cards do you
   have left?

   Read the problem carefully.

2. You want 16 cards. You have 8.
   How many more cards do you
   need?

3. You have 7 cards. Lily has 15.
   How many cards are there
   in all?

Figure 3.56 Three interpretations of subtraction in a fourth-grade textbook.

15. A shipment of n radios included m defective ones. How many good ones were there?

★ 16. It is traditional to define less-than ($<$) first, and then to define less-than-or-equal-to ($\leq$) by

  $a \leq b$ if $a < b$ or $a = b$

  That is how we did it. A case can be made for defining $\leq$ first and then defining $<$ by

  $a < b$ if $a \leq b$ and $a \neq b$

Revise the three definitions of $<$ so that they become definitions of $\leq$, and revise the three definitions of subtraction so that they apply to all a and b for which $a \leq b$, not just for which $a < b$.

 ## 3.6 *Division: Definitions and Applications*

To arrive at meanings for division it will be helpful to distinguish between "division with remainder" and "exact division."

Division with Remainder

Suppose a youngster asks what it means to "divide" 23 by 5. A specific example like the following one covers the key ideas.

EXAMPLE 1   You have 23 pennies that you want to trade in for nickels, so you separate them into groups of 5. To divide 23 by 5 means to determine how many groups of 5 you can make (4, the quotient), and how many singles are left over (3, the remainder). See Figure 3.57.

Figure 3.57   ❑

The general definition follows.

> **Set Definition of Division with Remainder**
>
> Dividing n by d corresponds to partitioning an n-element set into as many d-element subsets as possible, counting the subsets (this number is the quotient), and counting the remaining elements (this number is the remainder).

Arithmetically, we can view the finding of quotient and remainder as a repeated-subtraction process:

23	original amount
− 5	made one group
18	remain; keep grouping
− 5	made a second group
13	remain; keep grouping
− 5	made a third group
8	remain: keep grouping
− 5	made a fourth group
3	remain; no further grouping possible; quotient 4, remainder 3

A check that the calculations are correct can be made by working backwards. Two conditions must be satisfied:

Is the remainder 3 less than 5? Yes.
Does $3 + 4 \cdot 5 = 23$? Yes.

The following arithmetic definition of division depends on the fact that as long as the divisor is greater than zero, the repeated subtraction process will always terminate and produce a unique quotient and a unique remainder. This existence-uniqueness property is sometimes called the division theorem.

Division Theorem

Given any whole numbers n and d with $d \neq 0$, there exist unique whole numbers q and r that satisfy the following two properties:

1. $n = d \cdot q + r$
2. $r < d$

Notice that without the restriction $d \neq 0$, this theorem couldn't possibly be true. (How could condition 2 be satisfied?)

To divide n by d means to find the numbers q and r.

Arithmetic Definition of Division with Remainder

For any whole numbers n and d with $d \neq 0$, to divide n by d means to find the two whole numbers q and r such that

1. $n = d \cdot q + r$,
and
2. $r < d$.

Terminology: In the definition of division n is called the **dividend,** d is called the **divisor,** q is called the **quotient,** and r is called the **remainder.** Thus the two conditions in the definition of division can be restated as follows:

1. Dividend = divisor · quotient + remainder
2. Remainder < divisor

Notation: The instructions "divide 23 by 5" are sometimes given symbolically by writing $23 \div 5$. Thus the symbol $\div$ denotes a function that assigns to each ordered pair of whole numbers with nonzero second component (dividend, divisor) another ordered pair of whole numbers (quotient, remainder).

$$23 \div 5 \qquad \text{abbreviates the function notation} \qquad \div (23, 5)$$

Exact Division

The first kind of division problems to which youngsters are exposed are those in which the remainder is zero, called *exact division* because the divisor divides exactly into the dividend. In this case the two defining conditions collapse to a single condition:

$$\text{Dividend = divisor · quotient,} \qquad \text{where divisor} \neq 0$$

The condition that the remainder be less than the divisor is satisfied automatically.

Just as subtraction was related to the less-than relation, so exact division is related to the divides relation. Again, several definitions of *divides* are possible, and each leads to a definition of exact division. (And again, the payoff for grappling with multiple definitions is greater insight into word problems.) To simplify the statements of the definitions, we use the standard vertical-bar abbreviation:

$$3 \,|\, 12 \text{ is read "3 divides 12"}$$

And in all the definitions d is restricted to be a nonzero number.

Missing-Factor Definition of Divides ($|$). $d\,|\,n$ means there is a (whole number) solution to the equation $d \cdot \square = n$.

EXAMPLE 2   According to this definition $3\,|\,12$, because $3 \cdot \square = 12$ has a solution (in W).

First Set Definition of Divides ($|$). $d\,|\,n$ means that if N is a set with n elements, then N can be (completely) partitioned into d-element subsets.   ❏

EXAMPLE 3   Now $3\,|\,12$, because, as Figure 3.58 shows, a 12-element set can be completely partitioned into 3-element subsets.

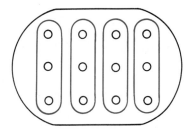

Figure 3.58

Second Set Definition of Divides ($|$). $d\,|\,n$ means that if N is a set with n elements, then N can be (completely) partitioned into d equivalent subsets.   ❏

EXAMPLE 4   This time $3\,|\,12$, because, as Figure 3.59 shows, a 12-element set can be completely partitioned into 3 equivalent subsets. Remember that sets are said to be equivalent if they can be put in one-to-one correspondence, that is, if they have the same number of elements.

The corresponding definitions of exact definition follow.

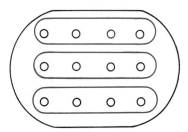

Figure 3.59   ❏

Missing-Factor Definition of Exact Division

Given $d\,|\,n$ so that $d \cdot \square = n$ has a solution, then $n\,/d$ is the missing factor in the equation $d \cdot \square = n$.

EXAMPLE 5   Find $12/3$ by the missing-factor definition.

Solution   Here $12/3$ is the missing factor in the equation $3 \cdot \square = 12$. That missing factor is 4 (perhaps by guess-and-check multiplication).   ❏

Number-of-Subsets Definition of Exact Division

Given $d\,|\,n$ so that an n-element set can be completely partitioned into d-element subsets, then n/d is the *number of* those *subsets*.

EXAMPLE 6   Find 12/3 by the number-of-subsets definition.

Solution   Draw a set of 12 dots, partition it into 3-element subsets, and count the sub- sets. See Figure 3.60.   ❏

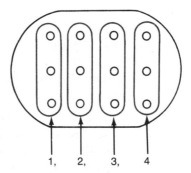

Figure 3.60   1,   2,   3,   4

> **Number-of-Elements Definition of Exact Division**
>
> Given $d \mid n$ so that an n-element set can be completely partitioned into d equiv- alent subsets, then n / d is the *number of elements* in any one of those subsets.

EXAMPLE 7   Find 12/3 by the number-of-elements definition.

Solution   Draw a set of 12 dots, partition it into 3 equivalent subsets, and count the ele- ments in any one of them. See Figure 3.61.   ❏

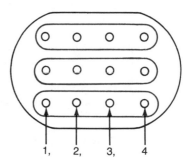

Figure 3.61   1,   2,   3,   4

More About Notation

Perhaps you noticed that we changed division symbols. For exact division we used the slash symbol, as in 12/3, rather than the dotted bar symbol, as in $12 \div 3$. We did so to make the point that, strictly speaking, we are dealing with two different functions.

One function is the division-with-remainder function, which assigns ordered pairs (q, r) to all ordered pairs (n, d), with $d \neq 0$, according to the definition $\div(n, d) = n \div d =$ the unique ordered pair (q, r) that satisfies

$$(1)\ n = d \cdot q + r \quad \text{and} \quad (2)\ r < d.$$

The second function is the exact-division function, which assigns numbers q to only very special ordered pairs (n, d) according to the definition

$$/(n, d) = n/d = \text{the missing factor in the equation } d \cdot \square = n.$$

In practice, nearly everyone uses the two notations interchangeably, and you have to decide from context whether the answer you are after is an ordered pair of numbers or a number.

It should be noted, however, that in the widely used computer programming language, *Pascal*, a careful distinction is made between the two different division operations. Exact division is represented as we have represented it, by a slash. For example, the expression 11/4 is assigned the value 2.75. To obtain the whole-number quotient and remainder in a division problem, two operations are required, DIV and MOD, respectively. For example, the expression 11 DIV 4 has value 2 and the expression 11 MOD 4 has value 3. There is even an inexpensive calculator now (the Math Explorer® from Texas Instruments) that is designed to carry out both kinds of division. A separate "integer-division" key provides the quotient-remainder output.

Division Involving Zero

Why is it that in division we always require the divisor to be nonzero? Specifically, why is a symbol like 7/0 undefined? A physical explanation that could be given to children is as follows: To divide 7 by 0 means to take 7 pennies, put them into groups of 0 until every penny is in such a group, and then count the groups. Obviously, that task is impossible. Now here is an arithmetic explanation: If 7/0 were to be defined, then it ought to behave like other quotients; that is, 7/0 should act as the missing factor in the equation $0 \cdot \square = 7$. But there is no number that multiples 0 to give 7.

But what about 0/0? The physical explanation leads to a puzzling question: How many groups of zero can you make from an original set of zero pennies? Here is the arithmetic explanation: 0/0 should act as the missing factor in the equation $0 \cdot \square = 0$. But *every* whole number satisfies this equation. We sometimes say that 0/0 is "indeterminate" in order to indicate the ambiguity.

$n/0$ is undefined for all whole numbers n.

Finally, what about cases like 0/7 where the dividend is zero but the divisor is not? Now there is no problem. We can begin with a set of 0 pennies, partition them completely into 0 groups of 7, and count the groups: 0. Arithmetically, $0/7$ is the missing factor in the multiplication equation $7 \cdot \square = 0$, and clearly 0 is that missing factor. Thus $0/7 = 0$. In general:

$0/d = 0$ for all nonzero whole numbers d.

Applications

We begin with a division-with-remainder problem.

EXAMPLE 8   Each child is to receive a dozen jelly beans. How many children will a bag of 100 jelly beans supply?

Solution   Think of partitioning the set of 100 beans into 12-element subsets. There are 8 such subsets ($8 \cdot 12 = 96$), and 4 beans are left over. *Answer:* 8 children will be supplied (and 4 jelly beans will be left over).   ❏

   The next examples illustrate the usefulness of having several intepretations for exact division.

EXAMPLE 9   A field mouse in a pasture of tall grass counts 132 cows' feet. How many cows are there?

Solution   This problem is a missing-factor multiplication problem:

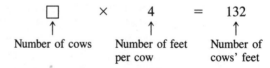

$$\square \quad \times \quad 4 \quad = \quad 132$$

Number of cows   Number of feet per cow   Number of cows' feet

By the missing-factor definition of division the answer is $132/4 = 33$.   ❏

EXAMPLE 10   How many nickels can you buy with 245 pennies?

Solution   Think of partitioning the set of 245 pennies into subsets of 5 and then counting those subsets, as indicated in Figure 3.62. This technique fits the number-of-

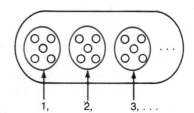

Figure 3.62   1,   2,   3, . . .

subsets interpretation of division. Thus the answer is 245/5 = 49. People in education sometimes refer to this number-of-subsets interpretation of division as the *measurement* interpretation because (here) a 245-element set is being "measured" in "units" of 5. ❏

EXAMPLE 11   Four children want to share 168 jelly beans equally. How many should each child get?

Solution   Think of partitioning the set of 168 jelly beans into 4 equivalent subsets and counting the elements in any one of them, as indicated in Figure 3.63. This procedure fits the number-of-elements interpretation of division. Thus the answer is 168/4 = 42. This number-of-elements interpretation of division is sometimes called the *partitive* interpretation to distinguish it from the measurement interpretation illustrated in Example 10. ❏

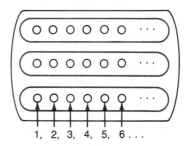

Figure 3.63

EXERCISE SET 3.6

Write the the division problem and answer suggested by each equation.

1. $6 \cdot \square = 18$

2. $13 \cdot \square = 299$

3. $17 \cdot \square = 17$

4. $6 \cdot \square + \triangle = 50$

5. $17 \cdot \square + \triangle = 100$

6. $8 \cdot \square + \triangle = 40$

7. $12 \cdot \square + \triangle = 7$

8. How might a second grader react to the equation $8 \cdot \square = 5$?

Write *two* division problems and answers suggested by each diagram. Identify each problem as a count-subsets (measurement) or a count-elements (partitive) division problem.

9.

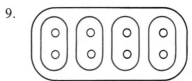

10.

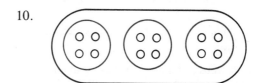

✎ 11. Figure 3.64 suggests a division-with-remainder problem. Assign numerical values to each of the following:

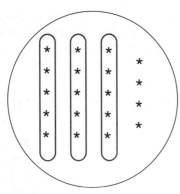

Figure 3.64

(a) dividend
(b) divisor
(c) quotient
(d) remainder

12. Ninety-five players come to the bridge club and seat themselves four to a table. How many do not get to play, and how many games can be played (simultaneously)?

13. How many quarters can you buy for 267 pennies, and how many pennies will be left?

Solve the following word problems. For each one, tell which interpretation of exact division (missing-factor, count-subsets, or count-elements) seems to fit best.

14. During a prolonged power failure a supermarket manager decides to give away 3 free eggs to each customer until his stock of 5364 eggs is exhausted. How many customers will he be able to accommodate? Estimate the answer before calculating it exactly.

15. Seventy-two first graders are to be split up evenly among 3 classrooms. How many should go in each?

16. How long is a rectangle that has area 84 cm^2 and height 7 cm?

17. A telescope lens is reported to have a diameter of 192 in. What is its diameter in feet?

18. In her will a woman leaves an estate of $65,585 to be divided equally among her c children. How much will each receive?

19. How many hours does it take to travel 180 mi at a rate of r miles per hour?

20. If a dollar is worth 3 German marks and is also worth 174 Japanese yen, how many yen is a mark worth?

21. Two hundred thirty-four children are going on a field trip. Six are to ride in each car, and the cars are to leave in three convoys. How many cars should there be in each convoy if the convoys are to be equally large?

22. Three proofreaders, each of whom can read 15 pages per hour, are to proofread a 540-page manuscript. How long will it take?

23. One thousand pennies are to be put in 50-coin rolls and divided equally among 4 children. How many rolls will each child get?

The next six exercises provide some practice in choosing appropriate operations on whole numbers.

24. Each of a cats has b fleas, and each of c dogs has d fleas. How many fleas in all?

25. On a field trip there are a buses with 1 driver, b teachers, and c children in each. How many more children than adults are there on the trip?

26. If each of a spectators is charged b dollars and the promoter keeps c dollars, then how much can each of the d performers be paid?

27. Suppose your old salary was a dollars and your old tax b dollars. Your new salary is c dollars more than the old, and your new tax is d dollars less than the old. How much is your new after-tax pay?

28. The teacher empties a bags with b gummy bears in each onto a table. She gives c to each of the d kindergartners, takes e for herself, and distributes the rest equally among the f first graders. Write an expression for the number of gummy bears each first grader receives.

29. At the fourth-grade party each boy in the class of c children supplies m mints. All of the mints are then distributed equally to the g girls in the class.

Write an expression for the number of mints each girl receives.

We saw in Example 9 how a clever field mouse could count a herd of cows: Count their feet and divide by four. This multiple-counting technique is a problem-solving strategy that will be useful in the next section. Practice it on the next two word problems.

30. Each student at Liberal High has 5 classes and 1 free period per day. During a free period the student wanders the halls or goes outside. Each teacher keeps track of the number of students in his or her classes during the day. At the end of the day the principal totals these numbers and arrives at the sum 3000. How many students were in school that day?

31. Ten people are seated around a table. Everyone clinks glasses with everyone else. How many clinks are heard?

32. A general property of exact division that will be used repeatedly in the next section is the *raising-reducing* or *cancellation* property:
$$\frac{a}{b} = \frac{a \cdot c}{b \cdot c}$$
The diagrams in Figure 3.65 show that
$$\frac{12}{3} = \frac{5 \cdot 12}{5 \cdot 3}$$

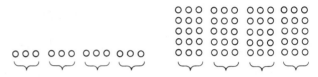

Figure 3.65

Which intepretation of (exact) division is used in both diagrams?

3.7 *Permutations and Combinations (Optional)*

Problems that ask "How many?" can sometimes be difficult to solve. We have encountered a few of them already, and we have begun to identify useful solution strategies. For example, in Exercise Set 3.6 we considered this problem:

Ten people are seated around a table. Everyone clinks glasses with everyone else. How many clinks are heard?

A quick solution, based on the strategy of *multiple counting*, is as follows: Each of 10 people clink 9 times. Ten times 9 is 90. But that product counts each clink twice. (When A and B clink, A counts that clink among her 9 and B counts the same clink among his 9.) Thus the answer is $\frac{90}{2} = 45$.

In Exercise Set 3.4 we posed this question:

In how many different ways can a red, a yellow, a blue, and a green stripe be painted on a flagpole?

The powerful *choice principle* led to a fast solution. There are 4 choices for the top stripe, 3 for the next one down, 2 for the next one down, and just 1 for the bottom stripe. *Answer:* $4 \times 3 \times 2 \times 1 = 24$ ways.

In this section we develop some formulas, based on the choice principle and the multiple-counting strategy, that will extend our ability to answer "How many?" questions. We will have to learn some new terminology and notation, but the benefit in mathematical power gained far outweighs the effort involved in mastering the new notation.

Permutations

A **permutation** of a set is an arrangement of it. For example, there are 6 permutations of the 3-element set $\{A, B, C\}$, namely, the 6 ordered triples

(A, B, C) (A, C, B) (B, A, C) (B, C, A) (C, A, B) (C, B, A)

We can see the result immediately by visualizing a tree such as the one shown in Figure 3.66.

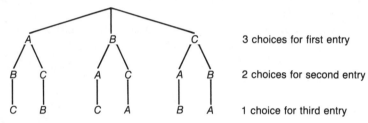

Figure 3.66

For a four-element set $\{A, B, C, D\}$, listing all the permutations (ordered 4-tuples with distinct entries) by tracing paths down a tree becomes tedious. But determining how many such 4-tuples there are remains a simple application of the choice principle:

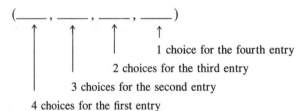

There are $4 \times 3 \times 2 \times 1$ permutations of the 4-element set. The generalization to an n-element set is immediate: There are

$$n \times (n - 1) \times (n - 2) \times \cdots \times 3 \times 2 \times 1$$

permutations of an n-element set.

EXAMPLE 1   In how many different ways can the 10 children in a nursery school class be lined up to go out for recess?

Solution   We are being asked to count the number of arrangements (permutations) of a 10-element set. There are

$$10 \times 9 \times 8 \times 7 \times 6 \times 5 \times 4 \times 3 \times 2 \times 1$$

of them. That's 3,628,800 ways! Thus if you line the children up for recess every day all year, you could go for nearly 10,000 years before having to repeat an arrangement used earlier. ❑

It's a nuisance to write the product of all the natural numbers from 10 to 1. So special **factorial notation** is used instead. This notation employs an exclamation point:

$$4! = 4 \times 3 \times 2 \times 1$$
$$10! = 10 \times 9 \times 8 \times 7 \times 6 \times 5 \times 4 \times 3 \times 2 \times 1$$
$$100! = 100 \times 99 \times 98 \times \cdots \times 3 \times 2 \times 1$$

The symbol "10!", for instance, is read "ten factorial." Of course, using factorial notation doesn't eliminate computations. If you want an answer expressed in standard Hindu-Arabic notation, you must still perform many multiplications.

EXAMPLE 2   Express each factorial in standard notation
(a) 5!
(b) 12!

Solution   (a) $5! = 5 \times 4 \times 3 \times 2 \times 1 = 20 \times 3 \times 2 = 60 \times 2 = 120$
(b) $12! = 12 \times 11 \times 10 \times 9 \times 8 \times 7 \times 6 \times 5 \times 4 \times 3 \times 2 \times 1$

One solution would be to multiply this all out as was done in part (a)—not a very inviting prospect. Another would be to recall that 10! turned out to be 3,628,800 and observe that 12! is just $12 \times 11 \times 10!$. Thus $12! = 132 \times 3,628,800$—still not a very pretty product to compute. A third solution, and probably the most attractive, would be to reach for a calculator. My machine gives the answer

$$12! = 479,001,600$$

A fourth solution would be to *estimate* the value of 12! by grouping the factors in a convenient way. For example,

$$12 \times 8 \approx 100$$
$$11 \times 9 \approx 100$$
$$10 = 10$$
$$7 \times 5 \times 3 \approx 100$$
$$6 \times 4 \times 2 = 48$$

Thus

$$12! \approx 48 \times 100 \times 100 \times 100 \times 10 = 480,000,000$$

which is not a bad estimate. ❑

We summarize our earlier generalization about permutations by using factorial notation.

There are $n! = n \times (n - 1) \times (n - 2) \times \cdots \times 3 \times 2 \times 1$ permutations of an n-element set.

EXAMPLE 3   In how many ways can the letters in the word FLORIDA be arranged?

Solution $7! = 7 \times 6 \times 5 \times 4 \times 3 \times 2 \times 1 = 5040$ ❑

Now consider this question. How many ways are there of choosing a president, a vice president, a secretary, and a treasurer from a class of 25 students? Again, order (arrangement) is important, because the following two slates of officers are certainly different, even though the same four students appear on both:

President	Vice President	Secretary	Treasurer
Alice	Bob	Charlie	Dawn
Charlie	Alice	Dawn	Bob

Abstractly, the question is: How many ordered 4-tuples, with distinct entries, can be made up from a 25-element set? The answer follows immediately from the choice principle:

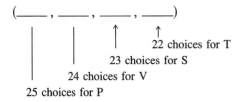

There are $25 \times 24 \times 23 \times 22 = 303{,}600$ ordered 4-tuples (slates of officers).

Since problems like this one come up frequently, a special terminology and notation has been developed to codify their solution. An ordered 4-tuple with distinct entries selected from a set of 25 elements is called a "permutation of 25 things taken 4 at a time." If you are asked to list, in decreasing order of preference, your 5 favorite states, you are being asked to write down a permutation of 50 things taken 5 at a time. Your answer might be

(Utah, Maine, Iowa, Kansas, Ohio)

But it could *not* be

(Florida, Alaska, Delaware, Kentucky, Florida)

(Why not?) The number of permutations of 50 things taken 5 at a time is, by the choice principle,

$$50 \times 49 \times 48 \times 47 \times 46 = 254{,}251{,}200$$

In general, a permutation of n things taken k at a time is an ordered k-tuple with distinct entries chosen from a set of n elements. The *number of permutations* of n things taken k at a time is denoted by P_k^n and is equal, by the choice principle, to the product of k factors beginning with n and decreasing successively by 1.

The number of permutations of n things taken k at a time is

$$P_k^n = \underbrace{n \times (n - 1) \times (n - 2) \times \cdots \times (n - k + 1)}_{k \text{ factors}}$$

EXAMPLE 4

Evaluate each symbol.
(a) P_3^{10}
(b) P_4^5
(c) P_2^{16}

Solution

(a) $P_3^{10} = 10 \times 9 \times 8 = 720$ (*Note:* The third factor $8 = 10 - 3 + 1$.)
(b) $P_4^5 = 5 \times 4 \times 3 \times 2 = 120$
(c) $P_2^{16} = 16 \times 15 = 240$ ❏

EXAMPLE 5

Four stripes of different colors are to be painted on a flagpole. There are 8 colors of paint available. How many distinct color schemes are possible?

Solution

$$P_4^8 = 8 \times 7 \times 6 \times 5 = 40 \times 42 = 1680 \qquad ❏$$

EXAMPLE 6

How many 5-letter words can be made from the letters in the word FLORIDA? The ground rules are (1) no letter can be used more than once and (2) a word doesn't have to appear in a dictionary.

Solution

$$P_5^7 = 7 \times 6 \times 5 \times 4 \times 3 = 2520 \qquad ❏$$

Combinations

How many 3-element subsets are there in the 5-element set $\{A, B, C, D, E\}$? The answer is *not* P_3^5, because now we are counting ordinary unordered subsets, not ordered triples. The number $P_3^5 = 5 \times 4 \times 3 = 60$ will be very useful in arriving at the correct answer. What we should do is apply the multiple-counting strategy: to find the number of 3-element subsets, go ahead and count all 60 ordered triples, but then divide by the number of times each 3-element subset has been counted. The 3-element subset $\{A, B, C\}$ has been counted $3! = 6$ times, because it gives rise to that many ordered triples:

$$\{A, B, C\}$$

$(A, B, C) \quad (A, C, B) \quad (B, A, C) \quad (B, C, A) \quad (C, A, B) \quad (C, B, A)$

Thus the number of 3-element subsets is

$$\frac{P_3^5}{3!} = \frac{60}{6} = 10$$

To determine how many 6-element subsets there are in a 10-element set, begin with the number of ordered 6-tuples, P_6^{10}, and then divide by the number of ordered 6-tuples that each 6-element subset gives rise to, namely, $6!$. The number of 6-element subsets is

$$\frac{P_6^{10}}{6!} = \frac{10 \times 9 \times 8 \times 7 \times 6 \times 5}{6 \times 5 \times 4 \times 3 \times 2 \times 1} = 210$$

A special terminology and notation is used with counting problems of this type. The number of 6-element subsets of a 10-element set is referred to as the number of **combinations** of 10 things taken 6 at a time, and it is denoted by the symbol C_6^{10}.* Here is the generalization.

The number of combinations of n things taken k at a time is given by

$$C_k^n = \frac{P_k^n}{k!}$$

That is, to determine the number of k-element subsets of an n-element set, begin with the number of ordered k-tuples, P_k^n, and then divide by the number of ordered k-tuples representing each such subset, namely, $k!$.

EXAMPLE 7   Evaluate each symbol.
(a) C_4^6
(b) C_7^{15}

Solution   (a) $C_4^6 = \dfrac{P_4^6}{4!} = \dfrac{6 \times 5 \times 4 \times 3}{4 \times 3 \times 2 \times 1} = 15$

(b) $C_7^{15} = \dfrac{P_7^{15}}{7!} = \dfrac{15 \times 14 \times 13 \times 12 \times 11 \times 10 \times 9}{7 \times 6 \times 5 \times 4 \times 3 \times 2 \times 1} = 6435$ ❏

---

*Some authors use $_nP_k$ and $_nC_k$ rather than P_k^n and C_k^n. A notation that is more common than either C_k^n or $_nC_k$ is $\binom{n}{k}$, but there is no analogous symbol for the number of permutations.

Canceling common factors is a helpful technique for reducing the fractions that arise in these problems.

EXAMPLE 8

A quiz consists of 13 questions. The instructions are to choose any 10 and answer these. How many different choices of the 10 are there?

Solution

$$C_{10}^{13} = \frac{P_{10}^{13}}{10!} = \frac{13 \times 12 \times 11 \times 10 \times 9 \times 8 \times 7 \times 6 \times 5 \times 4}{10 \times 9 \times 8 \times 7 \times 6 \times 5 \times 4 \times 3 \times 2 \times 1}$$

$$= \frac{13 \times 12 \times 11}{3 \times 2 \times 1} = 286$$

❏

The solution for Example 8 reveals an interesting relationship. After the obvious cancellations are made, the fraction for C_{10}^{13} reduces to

$$\frac{13 \times 12 \times 11}{3 \times 2 \times 1}$$

which is just

$$\frac{P_3^{13}}{3!} = C_3^{13}$$

That is,

$$C_{10}^{13} = C_3^{13}$$

In retrospect this relationship, which we discovered algebraically, is obvious intuitively. Clearly, there are exactly as many ways to choose 10 questions to answer as there are ways to choose 3 questions not to answer. In general:

$$C_k^n = C_{n-k}^n$$

EXAMPLE 9

The boss says that you have to work 5 days next week, and he doesn't care which 5 you choose. How many choices do you have?

Solution

$$C_5^7 = C_2^7 = \frac{7 \times 6}{2 \times 1} = 21$$

❏

EXAMPLE 10

How many 8-letter words can be made from the 8 letters in the word COLORADO?

Solution 1

If the O's were distinguishable, say O_1, O_2, O_3, then the question would be like ones we considered earlier; the answer would be 8!. But the three's O's are not distinguishable. Ignoring subscripts, there is no way to tell

DRO₁CO₂O₃LA   from   DRO₁CO₃O₂LA

Since there are 3! arrangements of the subscripted O's, it is clear that *DROCOOLA* and every other word on the list is counted 3! times in the inflated total of 8!. Thus the correct answer is

$$\frac{8!}{3!} = 8 \times 7 \times 6 \times 5 \times 4 = 6720$$

Solution 2   Build 8-letter words by beginning with 8 empty slots:

$$\underline{\hspace{1cm}}\quad\underline{\hspace{1cm}}\quad\underline{\hspace{1cm}}\quad\underline{\hspace{1cm}}\quad\underline{\hspace{1cm}}\quad\underline{\hspace{1cm}}\quad\underline{\hspace{1cm}}\quad\underline{\hspace{1cm}}$$

First, choose the 3 slots to be occupied by the O's. There are C_3^8 ways of doing this. Now count how many ways there are of arranging the other 5 letters, C, L, R, A, and D, into the 5 empty slots. There are 5! ways of doing this. Thus the total number of words is

$$C_3^8 \times 5! = \frac{8 \times 7 \times 6}{3 \times 2 \times 1} \times 5! = \frac{8!}{3!}$$

as before.   ❏

Pascal's Triangle

Angular obstructions are attached to an inclined board as shown in Figure 3.67: one at the 0 level, two at the 1 level, three at the 2 level, and so on. A small ball is released through the chute at the top of the board. Each time it hits one of the obstructions as it rolls down the board, it can go either left or right (from our vantage point). The path indicated in Figure 3.67 can represented by the symbol LRLLR. It is one of 10 paths that lead to the same point at the 5 level:

RRLLL	RLRLL	RLLRL	RLLLR	LRRLL
LRLRL	LRLLR	LLRRL	LLRLR	LLLRR

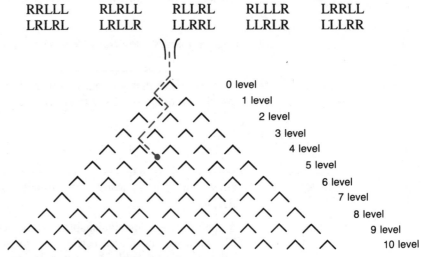

Figure 3.67 Pascal's pinball machine.

The entries in **Pascal's triangle,** Figure 3.68, represent the number of paths the ball can take to each of the points on the board. Clearly, there is just one path to the only point at the 0 level, and one path to each of the two points at the 1 level. At the 2 level there is just one path to each endpoint but two paths, LR and RL, to the middle point. Convince yourself that the numbers at the 3 level are correct.

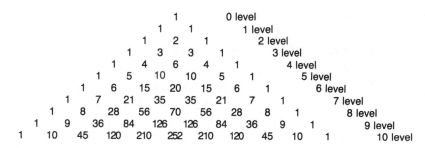

Figure 3.68 Pascal's triangle.

We introduce Pascal's triangle here because its entries are precisely the combination numbers. At the 5 level, for example, the numbers in Pascal's triangle are

$$1 \quad 5 \quad 10 \quad 10 \quad 5 \quad 1$$

which are just the combination numbers

$$C_0^5 \quad C_1^5 \quad C_2^5 \quad C_3^5 \quad C_4^5 \quad C_5^5$$

The explanation for this is not deep. The red entry 10 was found by counting all ordered 5-tuples consisting of 2 R's and 3 L's. One manufactures such 5-tuples by beginning with a blank one (__ , __ , __ , __ , __) and choosing which 2 of the positions are to be occupied by R's. There are C_2^5 ways of making that choice.

EXAMPLE 11   Use Pascal's triangle to evaluate C_4^9.

Solution   The entries at the 9 level at Pascal's triangle are

$$C_0^9 \quad C_1^9 \quad C_2^9 \quad \ldots$$

Thus C_4^9 is the fifth entry at the 9 level, namely 126. If we number the entries as we did the levels, beginning with 0 rather than 1, then C_4^9 is the 4 entry at the 9 level.   ❏

EXERCISE SET 3.7

Write the answers to Exercises 1–4 as products of natural numbers.

1. How many permutations are there of the set $\{A, B, C, D, E\}$?

2. In how many ways can 8 people stand in line at a supermarket checkout aisle?

3. How many different batting orders are possible for a softball team of 9 players?

4. A softball league has 6 teams. How many final standings are possible? (Ties are resolved by a flip of a coin.)

5. Evaluate each factorial.
   (a) 4!
   (b) 7!
   (c) 9!
   (d) 1!

6. Express the answer to each of Exercises 1–4 in factorial notation.

Write the answers to Exercises 7–12 as products of natural numbers.

7. How many ordered pairs can be made up from the 26 letters of the alphabet if no letter is used twice?

8. How many ordered triples can be made up from the digits 0, 1, 2, 3, 4, 5, 6, 7 if no digit is used twice?

9. How many ways are there of choosing a winner and a first, a second, a third, and a fourth runner-up in a competition involving 50 contestants?

10. How many 5-letter words can be made from the letters in VERMONT? The usual ground rules apply: (1) No letter can be used more than once, and (2) a "word" doesn't have to appear in anyone's dictionary.

11. How many 5-letter words can be made from the letters in IDAHO?

12. A softball team has 15 players. Only 9 can play at a time. How many different batting orders can the coach turn in to the umpire at the start of the game?

13. Express each permutation number as a product.
   (a) P_3^{10}
   (b) P_7^{10}
   (c) P_4^{100}
   (d) P_5^7
   (e) P_1^7
   (f) P_7^7
   (g) P_5^n
   (h) P_{n-5}^n

14. Evaluate each permutation number.
   (a) P_4^{10}
   (b) P_2^{40}
   (c) P_4^8
   (d) P_6^6

15. Express the answer to each of Exercises 7–12 in permutation notation.

16. First express each combination number as a quotient of products of whole numbers; then evaluate—that is, express as a whole number in standard notation.
   (a) C_2^{16}
   (b) C_3^{11}
   (c) C_6^{12}
   (d) C_1^8
   (e) C_7^9
   (f) C_{98}^{100}

In Exercises 17–20, first write the answer in combination number notation; then evaluate.

17. How many 2-element sets can be formed by using the 26 letters of our alphabet?

18. How many 3-element subsets are there of $\{0, 1, 2, 3, 4, 5, 6, 7\}$?

19. How many different 5-card poker hands can be made from a standard 52-card deck?

20. Twelve softball teams are to be split up into two 6-team leagues. In how many ways can these leagues be formed?
   Caution: Use the problem-solving strategy of asking an easier question to test whether your method of solution gives the correct result in the case of a small number of teams.

Express the answers to Exercises 21–26 in either permutation (P_k^n) or combination (C_k^n) notation, whichever is appropriate.

21. From her wardrobe of 12 pairs of shoes Ms. Adams must select 3 pairs to bring on a vacation. In how many ways can she choose them?

22. In how many ways can 10 finalists be chosen in a contest involving 80 contestants?

23. Two hundred runners are entered in a marathon. In how many ways can the first five finishing places be filled?

24. In one state-sponsored Lotto game each entrant chooses six (different) numbers from among the whole numbers 1 through 40. The order in which the numbers are chosen is immaterial. How many different sets of numbers can be chosen?

25. Seventy people attend a banquet at which five different door prizes are awarded. No one is allowed to win more than one. In how many ways can the prizes be awarded?

26. Each of 200 clergymen is asked to list, in order, the three worst of the seven deadly sins. Must two clergymen turn in the same list?

27. How many words can be made by permuting the letters in the following words?
    (a) ALABAMA   (b) GEORGIA
    (c) ILLINOIS   (d) MISSISSIPPI

28. Allowing repetitions of a letter, how many 3-letter words can be made by using the letters in the following words?
    (a) MAINE   (b) MISSISSIPPI

29. Estimate.
    (a) 8!   (b) P_5^{12}

30. Use Pascal's triangle to evaluate each of the following.
    (a) C_2^4 (b) C_5^8
    (c) C_2^2 (d) C_0^7

31. Study Pascal's triangle and decide how each interior entry can be computed from entries above it. Express your observation as an equation involving combination symbols.

★ 32. Sum the entries in each of the first few rows of Pascal's triangle. Generalize.

★ 33. One of many "shortest" taxicab routes from street corner A to street corner B is shown in Figure 3.69. How many different shortest routes are there? *Hint:* The path shown has the code name RUURURRRUURR.

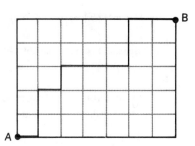

Figure 3.69   A

34. Pose and solve a three-dimensional problem analogous to Exercise 33.

★ 35. How many paths in Figure 3.70 spell out ORANGUTAN? One is shown.

```
O R A N G U T A N
R A N G U T A N
A N G U T A N
N G U T A N
G U T A N
U T A N
T A N
A N
N
```

Figure 3.70

★ 36. How many (steadily falling) paths are there from the top to the bottom of the diamond design in Figure 3.71? One is indicated.

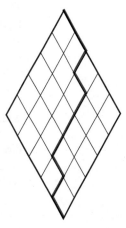

Figure 3.71

37. Complete the following explanations of why $C_0^4 = 1$.
    (a) By definition, C_0^4 represents the number of 0-element subsets there are in a 4-element set. . . .
    (b) The choices for dessert were ice cream, cake, pie, and cookies. I chose not to break my diet. . . .

38. Show that each equation is correct.
    (a) $C_3^{10} = \dfrac{10!}{3!\,7!}$ (b) $C_5^7 = \dfrac{7!}{5!\,2!}$

(c) $C_k^n = \dfrac{n!}{k!(n-k)!}$

39. If we want the generalization in Exercise 38(c) to remain true even when $k = n$, how must 0! be defined?

40. If we want the formula
$$C_k^n = \frac{P_k^n}{k!}$$
to remain true even when $k = 0$, how must P_0^n be defined?

3.8 *Algorithms for Addition and Subtraction*

Some of the most dramatic changes in emphasis advocated in the NCTM *Standards* are in the area of algorithms. In the old precalculator days, paper-and-pencil algorithms dominated the K–8 mathematics curriculum. Even today large amounts of time are devoted to their mastery—too much time in the opinion of many mathematics educators. In the K–4 *Standards* one finds calls for fundamental change: "Calculators must be accepted at the K–4 level. . . . Clearly paper-and-pencil computation cannot continue to dominate the curriculum or there will be insufficient time for children to learn other, more important mathematics. . . . Calculators should be used to solve problems that require tedious calculations." And the 5–8 *Standards* call for "abandoning the teaching of tedious calculations using paper-and-pencil algorithms in favor of exploring more mathematics."

But while the *Standards* call for less emphasis on developing mechanical skill in carrying out algorithms, they call for more attention to mental computation and estimation and to developing children's understanding of algorithms. From the K–4 *Standards:* "Both mental computation and estimation should be ongoing emphases that are integrated throughout all computational work. . . . instruction [in paper-and-pencil algorithms] should emphasize the meaningful development of these procedures, not speed of processing." The 5–8 *Standards* call for "fostering a solid understanding of, and proficiency with, simple calculations" and remind us that "a knowledge of basic facts and procedures is critical in mental arithmetic and estimation," but reiterate that tedious computations should be done on a calculator or computer.

The situation with paper-and-pencil algorithms is similar to the situation with writing. In the old days, much time and effort was spent on developing clear, legible handwriting. (Perhaps you have a grandparent with a beautiful "hand.") Then typewriters, and later word processors, came into common use and the emphasis changed. Nowadays people still learn how to write, but few develop their skill to a high level. When neatness and legibility are important, most of us turn to a machine. We can expect to see the same trend in computation. Children will still learn how to compute by hand, but most will also learn to turn to a calculator or computer when voluminous or complicated calculations need to be carried out quickly and accurately.

In this section we look at some common and some uncommon algorithms for adding and subtracting whole numbers. There are several reasons for bringing in the uncommon ones. First, they allow prospective teachers to relive the experience of learning algorithms. Second, they show that there is more than one algorithm for each operation. No single technique is best for every student or for every occasion. For instance, nonstandard algorithms offer interesting possibilities for both remedial and enrichment work. And there are situations better-served by algorithms other than the standard ones; we shall note a few. Third, nonstandard algorithms can be fun.

As you read this section, notice another thing. The algorithms are explained here, as they are in the excerpted elementary text pages, by reference to the meanings or interpretations of the symbols described in the first six sections of this chapter. Meticulous rationalization of these algorithms on the basis of abstract properties like the commutative and associative properties of addition is left to the next chapter.

Addition Algorithms

The usual **right-to-left addition algorithm** is illustrated here along with the chant that might run through your mind while using it:

$$
\begin{array}{c}
\overset{1}{787} \\
+\ 365 \\
\hline
2
\end{array}
\ \rightarrow \
\begin{array}{c}
\overset{1\ 1}{787} \\
+\ 365 \\
\hline
52
\end{array}
\ \rightarrow \
\begin{array}{c}
\overset{1\ 1\ 1}{787} \\
+\ 365 \\
\hline
152
\end{array}
\ \rightarrow \
\begin{array}{c}
787 \\
+\ 365 \\
\hline
1\,152
\end{array}
$$

"7 and 5 is 12.   "1 and 8 is 9 and 6 is   "1 and 7 is 8 and 3 is   "Write 1."
Write 2. Carry 1."   15. Write 5. Carry 1."   11. Write 1. Carry 1."

Clearly, the ability to use this algorithm efficiently presupposes a body of memorized addition facts through 9 + 9. The arrangement of the calculations in this algorithm corresponds so closely to the caramel packaging (regrouping)

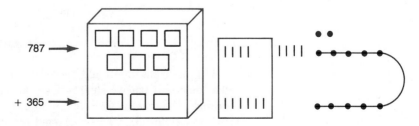

Figure 3.72

done earlier that there is little need to verbalize an explanation of why the algorithm works. Figure 3.72, tells us what to write and what to carry. Figure 3.73 shows how addition involving regrouping is explained to children in a fourth-grade text.

A **left-to-right addition algorithm** can be based on reversing the order of packaging: First put the boxes into cases; then put the packs into boxes; and then put the singles into packs. The calculation is

$$
\begin{array}{r} 787 \\ +\ 365 \\ \hline 10 \end{array}
\quad \rightarrow \quad
\begin{array}{r} 787 \\ +\ 365 \\ \hline 1\not04 \\ {\scriptstyle 1} \end{array}
\quad \rightarrow \quad
\begin{array}{r} 787 \\ +\ 365 \\ \hline 1\not0\not42 \\ {\scriptstyle 1\ 5} \end{array}
$$

"7 and 3 is 10.   "8 and 6 is 14. Write 4.   "7 and 5 is 12. Write 2.
Write 10."   Carry 1 to the hundreds.   Carry 1 to the tens. 1
    1 and 0 is 1. Write 1."   and 4 is 5. Write 5."

Obviously this algorithm would be just as easy to use as the usual one. The only difference is that carrying is done below the line rather than above.

There are times when the left-to-right addition algorithm is preferable to the right-to-left algorithm. One is when estimating. The estimation technique known as **front-end estimation** is based on *mental* left-to-right computation. In the illustration above, the initial front-end estimate of the sum is 1000. A refinement of that estimate is 1140. (A second context in which left-to-right addition is more natural than the usual algorithm is illustrated in Exercise 6.)

Another estimation technique, called **clustering,** is also related to left-to-right addition. Consider the column of numbers in Table 3.5. To estimate (roughly) the total of wages paid out to the six employees, look at only the first two digits and notice that the individuals' wages "cluster" around $11,000. Thus the total of wages is about 6 × $11,000 or $66,000.

Table 3.5

Employee	Annual wage
Cecile	$10,585
Guido	$14,040
Larry	$ 9,775
Maria	$13,100
Vivian	$11,250
Zeke	$10,845

Both the right-to-left and the left-to-right algorithm can be used with bases other than ten, but we shall restrict our attention to the usual right-to-left algorithm. The reasons for bringing in bases other than ten are the same as they were in Section 3.2: we understand familiar things better when we compare

Regrouping more than once

Sometimes you have to regroup more than once when adding. Study these examples.

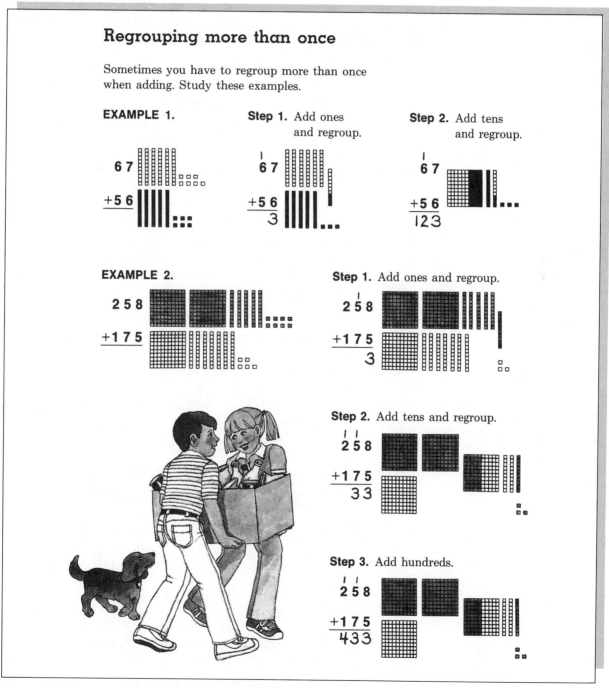

EXAMPLE 1.

$$67$$
$$+56$$

Step 1. Add ones and regroup.

$$\overset{1}{6}7$$
$$+56$$
$$\overline{3}$$

Step 2. Add tens and regroup.

$$\overset{1}{6}7$$
$$+56$$
$$\overline{123}$$

EXAMPLE 2.

$$258$$
$$+175$$

Step 1. Add ones and regroup.

$$2\overset{1}{5}8$$
$$+175$$
$$\overline{3}$$

Step 2. Add tens and regroup.

$$\overset{1}{2}\overset{1}{5}8$$
$$+175$$
$$\overline{33}$$

Step 3. Add hundreds.

$$\overset{1}{2}\overset{1}{5}8$$
$$+175$$
$$\overline{433}$$

Figure 3.73 Regrouping in addition in a fourth-grade textbook.

and contrast them with unfamiliar things, and certain bases other than ten have intrinsic importance. Again we remind you that it is not at all clear whether or when any of this material should be taught to youngsters.

Consider the problem

$$787_{nine}$$
$$+\ 365_{nine}$$

Now the addition facts are quite different. For example,

$$7 + 5 = 13_{nine} \qquad \text{(read ``one three base nine,'' \textit{not} ``thirteen'')}$$

These new addition facts can be seen by visualizing caramels, as in Figure 3.74, or by reverting to base-ten facts,

$$7 + 5 = 12_{ten} = 1 \cdot 9 + 3 = 13_{nine}$$

Figure 3.74

And they can be compiled into a table of base-nine addition facts, as in Table 3.6.

Except for these new addition facts, the calculation proceeds as before:

$$\overset{1}{7}87_{nine} \qquad \overset{1\ 1}{7}87_{nine} \qquad \overset{1\ 1}{7}87_{nine}$$
$$+\ 365_{nine} \rightarrow +\ 365_{nine} \rightarrow +\ 365_{nine}$$
$$3_{nine} \qquad\qquad 63_{nine} \qquad\qquad 1263_{nine}$$

Table 3.6 Table of Base-Nine Addition Facts

	1	2	3	4	5	6	7	8
1	2	3	4	5	6	7	8	10
2	3	4	5	6	7	8	10	11
3	4	5	6	7	8	10	11	12
4	5	6	7	8	10	11	12	13
5	6	7	8	10	11	12	13	14
6	7	8	10	11	12	13	14	15
7	8	10	11	12	13	14	15	16
8	10	11	12	13	14	15	16	17

EXAMPLE 1   Determine the missing base in this addition problem:

$$257_x + 144_x = 412_x$$

Solution The first step of the usual right-to-left algorithm tells us that 7 singles plus 4 singles yields 2 singles. Thus the other 9 singles must have been put in packs. Therefore the base is either 3 or 9. But the presence of digits beyond 2 rules out base 3. Thus the only possible base is 9.

Check: $257_{nine} + 144_{nine} = 412_{nine}$. ❑

Subtraction Algorithms

The usual **right-to-left, take-away subtraction algorithm** is

$$
\begin{array}{r} 753 \\ -\,268 \\ \hline \end{array}
\;\rightarrow\;
\begin{array}{r} 7\overset{413}{\cancel{5}\cancel{3}} \\ -\,268 \\ \hline 5 \end{array}
\;\rightarrow\;
\begin{array}{r} \overset{14}{\overset{6\,413}{\cancel{7}\cancel{5}\cancel{3}}} \\ -\,268 \\ \hline 85 \end{array}
\;\rightarrow\;
\begin{array}{r} \overset{14}{\overset{6\,413}{\cancel{7}\cancel{5}\cancel{3}}} \\ -\,268 \\ \hline 485 \end{array}
$$

"You can't take 8 from 3 so take away 1 from the tens to make the 3 a 13. 8 from 13 is 5."

"You can't take 6 from 4 so take away 1 from the hundreds to make the 4 a 14. 6 from 14 is 8."

"2 from 6 is 4"

Again, the connection with caramel diagrams is readily seen. The taking away (or borrowing) of 1 from the tens and giving 10 to the units corresponds to opening a pack to produce 10 more singles (regrouping). Taking away a 1 from the hundreds and giving 10 to the tens corresponds to opening a box to produce 10 more packs. Figure 3.75, on the next page, shows how subtraction involving regrouping is explained to children in a fourth-grade text.

To use this algorithm with a base other than ten, we must know different subtraction facts. For example, in the problem that follows, $13_{nine} - 6 = 6$. This fact can be deduced by visualizing caramels (1 pack of nine and 3 singles, take away 6), by converting to base ten mentally ($13_{nine} = 12_{ten}$) and using a base-ten subtraction fact, or by referring to a table of base-nine addition facts (look across row 6 until you find 13; then look up to the top of that column).

$$
\begin{array}{r} 513_{nine} \\ -\,256_{nine} \\ \hline \end{array}
\quad\rightarrow\quad
\begin{array}{r} 5\overset{013}{\cancel{1}\cancel{3}}_{nine} \\ -\,256_{nine} \\ \hline 6_{nine} \end{array}
\quad\rightarrow\quad
\begin{array}{r} \overset{10}{\overset{4\,\cancel{0}13}{\cancel{5}\cancel{1}\cancel{3}}}_{nine} \\ -\,256_{nine} \\ \hline 246_{nine} \end{array}
$$

A **left-to-right subtraction algorithm** can be based on taking away (borrowing) from the difference rather than from the minuend:

$$
\begin{array}{r} 5274 \\ -\,1782 \\ \hline \end{array}
\rightarrow
\begin{array}{r} 5274 \\ -\,1782 \\ \hline 4 \end{array}
\rightarrow
\begin{array}{r} \overset{12}{5\cancel{2}74} \\ -\,1782 \\ \hline \underset{3}{4\cancel{5}} \end{array}
\rightarrow
\begin{array}{r} \overset{12\,17}{5\cancel{2}\cancel{7}4} \\ -\,1782 \\ \hline \underset{3\ 4}{4\cancel{5}\cancel{9}} \end{array}
\rightarrow
\begin{array}{r} \overset{12\,17}{5\cancel{2}\cancel{7}4} \\ -\,1782 \\ \hline \underset{3\ 4}{4\cancel{5}92} \end{array}
$$

In terms of a caramel diagram: 5 cases take away 1 leaves 4; now you can't take 7 boxes away from 2, so open one of the 4 cases to get 10 more boxes; and so on.

Subtracting with regrouping

In this example, 1 ten is regrouped for 10 ones.

EXAMPLE 1.

Step 1. Not enough ones.
Regroup 1 ten for 10 ones.

Step 2. Subtract ones.
Subtract tens.

In this example, 1 hundred is regrouped for 10 tens.

EXAMPLE 2.

Step 1. Subtract ones.

Step 2. Not enough tens.
Regroup 1 hundred for 10 tens.

Step 3. Subtract tens.

Step 4. Subtract hundreds.

Figure 3.75 Regrouping in subtraction in a fourth-grade textbook.

The preceding example illustrates again the role of left-to-right computation in estimation. In subtracting left-to-right, you get good approximations to the difference right away. After one step you know that the difference is near 4000, after two steps near 3500, after three near 3490, and after four exactly 3492. If all you are interested in is an estimate of the answer, then you can stop subtracting after one or two steps. If you were to use the usual right-to-left technique, however, the only thing you would know after one step is that the units digit of the difference is 2. You would have to carry out the calculation to the very end to get any idea of the size of the difference.

EXAMPLE 2   Estimate the difference $32,851.65 - $15,607.94 to the nearest thousand dollars.

Solution   We use left-to-right subtraction and stop as soon as we have achieved the precision specified; that is, we front-end estimate the difference.

$$
\begin{array}{r}
32\ 851.65 \\
-\ 15\ 607.94 \\
\hline
17\ 2**.** \quad \rightarrow \quad \$17,000
\end{array}
$$

The final subtraction algorithm that we shall consider is called the **equal-additions algorithm.** Certain math educators consider this algorithm to be conceptually simpler than the usual algorithm and prefer it as the method taught in schools. We illustrate the equal-additions algorithm with an example.

$$
\begin{array}{ccc}
625 & 62\overset{15}{5} & 6\overset{12}{2}\overset{15}{5} \\
-\ 387 & -\ 3\overset{9}{8}7 & -\ \overset{4}{3}\overset{9}{8}7 \\
\hline
 & 8 & 238
\end{array}
$$

"You can't take 7 from 5 so give the minuend 10 changing 5 to 15. But if you give the minuend 10 then you must give the subtrahend 10 as well or you will have changed the problem. So change the 8 to a 9. Now subtract 7 from 15, getting 8, and move on to the tens place."

"You can't take 9 from 2 so give the minuend 100, changing 2 to 12, and balance this by giving the subtrahend 100, changing 3 to 4. Now subtract 9 from 12, getting 3, and subtract 4 from 6, getting 2."

The exercises that follow are directed primarily toward these specific objectives:

1. You should be able to compute sums in any base by the usual right-to-left algorithm.

2. You should be able to compute sums in base ten by the left-to-right algorithm as well.

3. You should be able to compute differences in any base by the usual right-to-left, take-away algorithm.

4. You should be able to compute differences in base ten by the left-to-right and equal-additions algorithms as well.

EXERCISE SET 3.8

1. Find each sum by using both right-to-left and left-to-right algorithms. Show all crossing out.

   (a)   285
       + 379

   (b)   648
       + 383

   (c)   4607
       + 709

   (d)   728
          563
       + 319

2. Construct tables of addition facts for these bases.
   (a) Base two   (b) Base seven   (c) Base twelve

3. Compute each sum by using the usual right-to-left algorithm.

   (a) 235_{seven}
       + 446_{seven}

   (b) 1011_{two}
       + 110_{two}

   (c) $E58_{twelve}$
       + $4T5_{twelve}$

4. Use the left-to-right algorithm to front-end approximate these sums to the nearest million.

   (a)   263,175,877
       +   94,310,654

   (b)   2,870,349,391
       + 1,365,407,857

   (c)   482,267,974
       + 315,312,287

   (d)   69,187,501
          35,119,798
       + 25,203,689

5. Use the technique of clustering to estimate:
   (a) The sum $3750 + 2974 + 3607 + 3068$
   (b) The total weight of all of the students in your math class.

6. Use left-to-right addition to find the sum of these two *repeating decimals*. Carry out your calculation to enough decimal places that you can recognize the repeating pattern in the sum.

   .494949 . . .
   + .827827 . . .

7. Compute each difference in three ways: usual right-to-left, left-to-right, and method of equal additions.

   (a)   4259
       − 1674

   (b)   6005
       − 3747

   (c)   8416
       − 2997

8. Compute each difference by using the usual right-to-left algorithm.

   (a) 4152_{seven}
       − 354_{seven}

   (b) 101101_{two}
       − 1110_{two}

   (c) 925_{twelve}
       − $1E6_{twelve}$

9. Use the left-to-right algorithm to front-end approximate these differences to the nearest million.

   (a)   75,600,000
       − 38,127,595

   (b)   328,875,194
       −   59,348,775

   (c)   87,653,907
       − 24,175,688

10. Use left-to-right subtraction to express this difference as a repeating decimal.
    .827827 . . .
    − .494949 . . .

11. Determine the missing base x.

    (a) 64_x
        + 35_x
        ──────
          132_x

    (b) 62_x
        − 35_x
        ──────
           26_x

    (c) 23_x
           32_x
        + 23_x
        ──────
          210_x

12. You ask a child to add 58 and 24. She thinks out loud: "seventy-eight, eight-two." Which of our algorithms is she using?

13. You ask a child to subtract 95 from 362. He thinks out loud: "three hundred sixty-seven, two

hundred sixty-seven." Which of our algorithms is his method closest to?

14. A palindrome is a word or phrase that reads the same forward and backward. Some examples are

POP

RADAR

MADAM I'M ADAM

ABLE WAS I ERE I SAW ELBA

A MAN A PLAN A CANAL PANAMA

According to the *Guinness Book of World Records*, the longest palindromic composition is one of 242 words by Howard Bergeson of Oregon. Number palindromes are easier to construct:

5

33

171

5225

Here is an activity that provides addition drill in a nonroutine setting: Take a 3-digit number that is not a palindrome. Reverse its digits to form a second number. Add those 2 numbers. If the sum is a palindrome, stop; if not, reverse its digits, add, and so on.

Example
$$\begin{array}{r} 315 \\ + \ 513 \\ \hline 828 \end{array}$$ palindrome in 1 step

Example
$$\begin{array}{r} 615 \\ + \ 516 \\ \hline 1131 \\ + \ 1311 \\ \hline 2442 \end{array}$$ palindrome in 2 steps

Certain 3-digit numbers require many steps before a palindrome results. For example, the number 394 requires 20 steps. Pick a 3-digit number and see how many steps it takes.

15. Here is an activity, somewhat akin to the palindrome activity, that provides subtraction drill in a nonroutine context. Pick any 4-digit number for which not all 4 digits are equal, for example, 8303. Rearrange the digits to produce the largest and smallest numbers possible, and find their difference:

$$\begin{array}{r} 8330 \\ - \ 0338 \\ \hline 7992 \end{array}$$

Now do the same thing with the digits of the difference:

$$\begin{array}{r} 9972 \\ - \ 2799 \\ \hline 7173 \end{array}$$

Repeat the procedure until you obtain a difference that appeared earlier. At that point the computations will begin to repeat:

$$\begin{array}{r} 7731 \\ - \ 1377 \\ \hline 6354 \end{array} \nearrow \begin{array}{r} 6543 \\ - \ 3456 \\ \hline 3087 \end{array} \nearrow \begin{array}{r} 8730 \\ - \ 0378 \\ \hline 8352 \end{array} \nearrow \begin{array}{r} 8532 \\ - \ 2358 \\ \hline 6174 \end{array} \nearrow \begin{array}{r} 7641 \\ - \ 1467 \\ \hline 6174 \end{array}$$

Here the computation repeats as soon as the number 6174 appears. Carry out this activity with at least two numbers of your choosing; then make a conjecture.

16. Another rather surprising subtraction activity is the following. Choose any four whole numbers, for example

17   120   56   3

Now calculate the differences between the first and second, the second and third, the third and fourth, and the fourth and first to get four more numbers:

103   64   53   14

Repeat the process with these four numbers, the next four, and so on, until a row of zeros is obtained:

39	11	39	89
28	28	50	50
0	22	0	22
22	22	22	22
0	0	0	0

It took six steps, with the four numbers chosen here, to reach a row of zeros. See if you can find a quadruple that requires more than six steps.

17. The following example suggests a subtraction algorithm having the virtue that one always subtracts the smaller digit from the larger one, but

the drawback that negative integers can arise and later need to be removed:

```
    7 0 8 1
  − 3 5 7 8
  ‾‾‾‾‾‾‾‾‾
  4⁻5 1⁻7 → 3 5 1⁻7 → 3 5 0 3
```

Use this algorithm to find the following differences.

(a)   9345   (b)   5003   (c)   8275
     − 5876   − 2657   − 3079

18. How many palindromes are there between 0 and 1000 (inclusive)? What problem-solving strategy seems appropriate?

★ 19. Given any five whole numbers, explain why some three of them will have a sum that is a multiple of 3. *Hint:* Imagine that the numbers have been expressed in base-three notation, and sort them into categories according to their units digit.

20. Here are instructions for a magic trick to amaze your friends. Pick a three-digit number, but make sure that the first and third digits differ by at least two. Reverse the digits and subtract the smaller number from the larger. Now, reverse the digits again and add. Your results is 1089. For example,

$$249 \xrightarrow{\text{Reverse}} 942 \xrightarrow{\text{Subtract}} \begin{matrix} 942 \\ -\ 249 \\ \hline 693 \end{matrix} \xrightarrow{\text{Reverse}} 396$$

$$\xrightarrow{\text{Add}} \begin{matrix} 693 \\ +\ 396 \\ \hline 1089 \end{matrix}$$

Try to show why this trick works. *Hint:* Begin with an arbitrary three-digit number *abc*.

3.9 *Algorithms for Multiplication and Division*

We will describe three algorithms each for the operations of multiplication and division. They will range from slow, safe methods to fast, risky ones, with the usual algorithms that are taught in the schools falling in the middle. The slow algorithms can be useful for remediation, the fast for enrichment.

Evolution of the Usual Multiplication Algorithm

In the elementary school algorithms for all four operations are developed over several years, beginning with calculations involving single-digit numbers and then progressing, one new complication at a time, to calculations involving multidigit numbers. For multiplication the repeated-addition interpretation is generally used to get things started. The development is illustrated in Figure 3.76.

The transition from calculations involving a single-digit multiplier, like those in Figure 3.76, to calculations involving a two-digit multiplier, say 134 × 36, is a classic illustration of the strategy of trying to break down a difficult problem into several easier problems that one already knows how to solve. Here is the general idea: Begin by splitting up the new multiplier, 36, into a sum of numbers that are easier to work with. Then invoke the distributive property to effect a corresponding split of the original product into a sum of two easier ones:

$$134 \times 36 = 134 \times (3 \times 10 + 6) = \underbrace{134 \times 3 \times 10} + \underbrace{134 \times 6}$$

This is the kind of product we already know how to find. In fact, its value is 402.

We have already mastered addition.

This is the kind of product we already know how to find. Its value is 804.

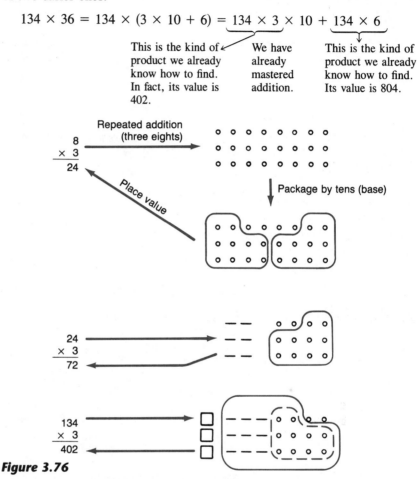

Figure 3.76

Only one small gap remains. How do we find the product 402 × 10? We all know a quick mechanical way of multiplying by 10: simply append a zero to (the Hindu-Arabic numeral for) the number being multiplied. Children can be led to this shortcut by the kind of diagram we have been using:

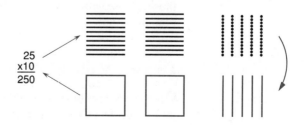

The following schematic summarizes the calculations of 134×36. The numbers 804 and 4020 are called **partial products.**

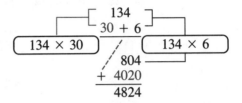

The polished arrangement of calculations that you use probably looks like the following, with or without the dotted zero:

$$
\begin{array}{r}
{\scriptstyle 1\ 1} \\
{\scriptstyle 2\ 2} \\
134 \\
\times\ \ \ 36 \\
\hline
804 \\
4020 \\
\hline
4824
\end{array}
$$

Generalization to the case of three-digit multipliers follows the same pattern.

EXAMPLE 1   Calculate 263×374 by the usual algorithm, and explain what each partial product represents.

Solution

$$
\begin{array}{r}
263 \\
\times\ 374 \\
\hline
1052 \\
18410 \\
78900 \\
\hline
98362
\end{array}
$$

represents 263×4
represents 263×70
represents 263×300

We can check the reasonableness of our calculations by estimation: Round 263 down to 250 and 374 up to 400. Since $250 \times 400 = 100{,}000$, which is close to 98,362, our calculation can't be too far off.   ❏

You may have noticed an implicit use of the associative property of multiplication in the second equation on page 165. In the next chapter we will give a thorough mathematical explanation of everything that underlies our multiplication algorithm.

Lattice Multiplication

Consider again the task of computing 263×374. If we split up *both* numbers into hundreds, tens, and units and then apply the distributive property, *nine*

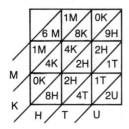

Figure 3.77

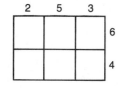

Figure 3.78

partial products will arise as each of the three addends in the first factor multiplies each of the three addends in the second factor:

$$(2 \cdot 100 + 6 \cdot 10 + 3) \times (3 \cdot 100 + 7 \cdot 10 + 4)$$

A convenient way of displaying the product 263 × 374 so that all nine partial products appear is shown in Figure 3.77, where U, T, H, K (for kilo-), and M (for myria-) represent units, tens, hundreds, thousands, and ten thousands, respectively. For example, the entry 18K in the first row and second column represents the partial product

$$6T \times 3H = 6 \times 10 \times 3 \times 100 = 18 \times 1000$$

If we now package by tens in each of the nine compartments, a very interesting pattern emerges, as indicated in Figure 3.78. All of the hundreds are found along the same diagonal from lower left to upper right. The same is true for units, tens, thousands, and ten thousands.

Thus to sum the partial products, we should sum the digits along these diagonals:

Units: 2.
Tens: 1 + 1 + 4 = 6.
Hundreds: 9 + 2 + 2 + 2 + 8 = 23. Write 3, carry 2 to the thousands.
Thousands: 2(carried) + 0 + 8 + 4 + 4 + 0 = 18. Write 8, carry 1 to the ten thousands.
Ten thousands: 1(carried) + 1 + 6 + 1 = 9.

Answer: 263 × 374 = 98,362.

Dropping the letters U, T, H, . . . gives an alternative multiplication algorithm called the **lattice** (or grating) **algorithm.**

EXAMPLE 2   Compute 253 × 64 by the lattice algorithm.

Solution   *Step 1*   Draw a partitioned rectangle with 253 across the top and 64 down the right-hand side. See Figure 3.79.

Step 2   Draw in diagonals from lower left to upper right, and fill in the multiplication facts. See Figure 3.80.

Step 3   Sum the diagonals, starting with the far right (units) diagonal. See Figure 3.81. In this example we must carry 1 from the hundreds to the thousands.   ❏

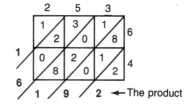

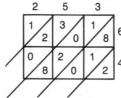

Figure 3.79

Figure 3.80   **Figure 3.81**

The drawbacks and the virtues of the lattice algorithm are apparent. It is slow; it takes a certain amount of time even to sketch the lattice. But if one is willing to sacrifice speed, the lattice algorithm is a safe, sure technique. It requires only minimal mathematical skills: One must know the multiplication facts to fill in the lattice, and one must be able to add short columns of single-digit numbers mentally.

Cross Multiplication

The third multiplication algorithm we shall study is called the **cross-** (or lightning) **multiplication algorithm.** For someone who is good at mental computation, it is faster than the usual algorithm because nothing but the answer is written down. For many people, however, it is dangerous because so much calculation has to be done in one's head.

To see what the method is and why it works, consider the product 64×79 and keep in mind the lattice representation in Figure 3.82. In cross multiplication we begin by looking for the units digit of the product. The only way to make units is by multiplying units times units: 4 times 9 is 36. Write 6. Carry 3 to the tens.

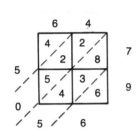

Figure 3.82

$$
\begin{array}{r}
6 \quad 4 \\
| \\
\times \quad 7 \quad 9 \\
\hline
6 \\
\scriptstyle 3
\end{array}
$$

Next, we look for tens. There are two ways to make tens, tens times units and units times tens: 6 times 9 is 54; 4 times 7 is 28; $54 + 28 + 3$(carried) = 85. Write 5. Carry 8 to the hundreds.

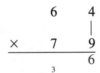

Next, we look for hundreds. The only way to make hundreds in this problem is to multiply tens times tens: 6 times 7 is 42; $42 + 8$(carried) = 50. Write 50.

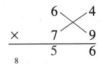

Answer: $64 \times 79 = 5056$.

Check by estimation: Round 64 down to 60 and 79 up to 80. Now $60 \times 80 = 4800$, which is close to 5056.

EXAMPLE 3   Compute 73×86 by the cross-multiplication algorithm.

Solution   This time let us estimate first: $70 \times 90 = 6300$. Now use the algorithm

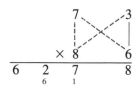

$6 \cdot 3 = 18.$ Write 8. Carry 1.
$1 + 6 \cdot 7 + 8 \cdot 3 = 67.$ Write 7.
Carry 6. $6 + 8 \cdot 7 = 62.$ Write 62.

❑

EXAMPLE 4   (For experts only)   Find 473×256 by cross multiplication.

Solution   One way to get units: 6×3.
Two ways to get tens: 6×7 and 5×3.
Three ways to get hundreds: 6×4, 5×7, and 2×3.
Two ways to get thousands: 5×4 and 2×7.
One way to get ten thousands: 2×4.

The calculation, with carried numbers showing, should look like this:

$$
\begin{array}{r}
473 \\
\times\ 256 \\
\hline
121088 \\
{\scriptstyle 4\,7\,5\,1}
\end{array}
$$

❑

Multiplication in Other Bases

Which multiplication algorithm would be the best one to use if you were asked to work a list of multiplication exercises in base eight? Your answer is probably, "the safe, slow lattice algorithm." To apply it, you need to know the base-eight multiplication facts, and you have to be able to find sums of single-digit, base-eight numbers. If the exercise list is a long one, you may wish to begin by constructing a table of base-eight multiplication facts. Calculating its entries may involve visualizing caramels, as in Figure 3.83. Or it may involve converting to and from base ten:

$$5_{\text{eight}} \times 7_{\text{eight}} \rightarrow 5 \times 7 = 35 = 4 \times 8 + 3 \rightarrow 43_{\text{eight}}$$

Recalling that multiplication is commutative cuts the work of filling in the multiplication table (Table 3.7) nearly in half.

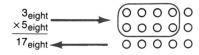

3_{eight}
$\times 5_{\text{eight}}$
17_{eight}

Figure 3.83

Table 3.7 Table of Base-Eight Multiplication Facts

	1	2	3	4	5	6	7
1	1	2	3	4	5	6	7
2	2	4	6	10	12	14	16
3	3	6	11	14	17	22	25
4	4	10	14	20	24	30	34
5	5	12	17	24	31	36	43
6	6	14	22	30	36	44	52
7	7	16	25	34	43	52	61

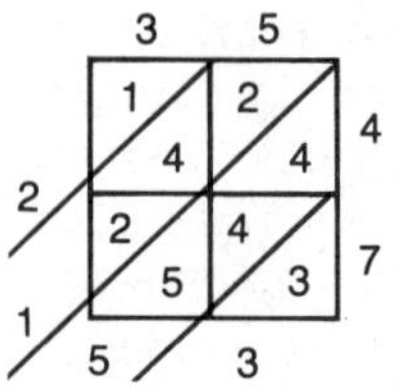

EXAMPLE 5   Compute $35_{eight} \times 47_{eight}$ by the lattice algorithm.

Solution   Sketch the lattice and fill it in with base-eight multiplication facts. Then as you add down the diagonals, think of packaging by eights. See Figure 3.84.   ❏

Figure 3.84

EXAMPLE 6   Compute $35_{eight} \times 47_{eight}$ by the usual algorithm.

Solution   Again, the base-eight multiplication facts are needed, but now the burden of mental arithmetic is heavier:

$$\begin{array}{r} \overset{2}{\overset{4}{}} \\ 35_{eight} \\ \times \quad 47_{eight} \\ \hline 313_{eight} \\ 1640_{eight} \\ \hline 2153_{eight} \end{array}$$

❏

Before leaving multiplication and moving to division, we mention a peculiar multiplication algorithm that is quite unlike the three we have studied in detail. It is called the **Russian peasant** (or halving-doubling) **algorithm.** We illustrate it with the problem 37×65. Write 37 and 65 next to each other. Here we have put 37 on the left, but we could have put 65 on the left. Then successively halve 37 and double 65. When halving results in a fraction, round it down:

$$\begin{array}{rr} 37 & 65 \\ 18\tfrac{1}{2} \rightarrow 18 & 130 \\ 9 & 260 \\ 4\tfrac{1}{2} \rightarrow 4 & 520 \\ 2 & 1040 \\ 1 & 2080 \end{array}$$

Now strike out each line that has an even number in the left-hand column, and add the surviving members of the right-hand column:

$$\begin{array}{rr} 37 & 65 \\ \cancel{18} & \cancel{130} \\ 9 & 260 \\ \cancel{4} & \cancel{520} \\ \cancel{2} & \cancel{1040} \\ 1 & 2080 \\ \hline & 2405 \end{array}$$

This sum is the desired product: $37 \times 65 = 2405$. Exercises 11 and 12 suggest why this algorithm works.

Division Algorithms

The three division algorithms we shall consider stand in a direct evolutionary line. The first one, sometimes called the scaffolding algorithm, is slow but conceptually simple. It is not much more than a guess-and-check method. Many people feel that this method is the way children should be introduced to division. As the guesses improve, scaffolding evolves into usual long division. For some students in some situations long division is streamlined further to short division.

Scaffolding

Consider the division problem

$$7\overline{)5281}$$

What we are being asked to do here is find out how many 7s can be taken away from 5281, and what, if anything, will remain. So we begin taking away 7s in a piecemeal, experimental way. Suppose we start by taking away 50 sevens. That accounts for 350 and leaves 4931:

$$
\begin{array}{r}
50 \\
7\overline{)5281} \\
-350 \\
\hline
4931
\end{array}
$$

Obviously, we could have proceeded more boldly, so suppose we take away 500 more 7s. That accounts for 3500 more but still leaves 1431:

$$
\begin{array}{r}
500 \\
50 \\
7\overline{)5281} \\
-350 \\
\hline
4931 \\
-3500 \\
\hline
1431
\end{array}
$$

May our next guess is 200. Taking away 200 more 7s leaves 31:

$$
\begin{array}{r}
200 \\
500 \\
50 \\
7\overline{)5281} \\
-350 \\
\hline
4931 \\
-3500 \\
\hline
1431 \\
-1400 \\
\hline
31
\end{array}
$$

Now we see that we should take away 4 more 7s, which will leave just 3:

$$
\begin{array}{r}
4 \\
200 \\
500 \\
50 \\
\hline
7)\overline{5281} \\
-\ 350 \\
\hline
4931 \\
-\ 3500 \\
\hline
1431 \\
-\ 1400 \\
\hline
31 \\
-\ 28 \\
\hline
3
\end{array}
$$

Thus the quotient is $50 + 500 + 200 + 4 = 754$ and the remainder is 3:

$$5281 - 754 \cdot 7 = 3$$

Or in the customary format of

$$\text{Dividend} = \text{divisor} \times \text{quotient} + \text{remainder}$$

we write

$$5281 = 7 \times 754 + 3$$

The method we have just illustrated is called **scaffolding.**

Long Division

An intermediate evolutionary stage between scaffolding and usual long division might look like this:

$$
\begin{array}{r}
4 \\
50 \\
700 \\
\hline
7)\overline{5281} \\
4900 \\
\hline
381 \\
350 \\
\hline
31 \\
28 \\
\hline
3
\end{array}
$$

By this stage the child has discovered, or has been instructed, how to make better guesses by examining the first few digits of the dividend and of subsequent differences. The usual **long division** algorithm abbreviates this calculation by dropping out many zeros and by bringing down only those digits that affect the next guess:

$$
\begin{array}{r}
754 \\
7\overline{)5281} \\
49 \\
\hline
38 \\
35 \\
\hline
31 \\
28 \\
\hline
3
\end{array}
$$

Short Division

Usual long division—that is, the arrangement of calculations just illustrated—is what most of today's schools aim for as a final division algorithm. Not too many years ago, though, students were expected to move on to a still more abbreviated algorithm known as **short division.** In short division all multiplication and subtraction was to be done mentally. The use of superscripts was tolerated as a kind of crutch, but it was hoped that eventually they would disappear from the scene too.

Long Division   *Short Division*

$$
\begin{array}{r}
754 \\
7\overline{)5281} \\
49 \\
\hline
38 \\
35 \\
\hline
31 \\
28 \\
\hline
3
\end{array}
\qquad
\begin{array}{r}
7\ 5\ 4\ \text{R}3 \\
7\overline{)52\ {}^{3}8\ {}^{3}1}
\end{array}
$$

Summary

The various pencil-and-paper division algorithms illustrate again the balance one tries to strike between tedious, accurate techniques and fast, dangerous ones. Students of different abilities can be expected to stop at different points on the evolutionary path we have sketched. The idea of forcing everyone along to short division was probably a poor one. In the case of two-digit and three-digit divisors short division was never demanded; long division was. At present, many people are willing to retreat a bit further, namely, to require that all students be able to use long division in the case of one-digit divisors, but to settle for scaffolding when the divisor has two or more digits.

The division algorithms also illustrate the important point that algorithms tend to *pyramid*. In order to divide, one first needs to know how to multiply and subtract. And of course, to multiply, one must be able to add. We will study the pyramiding of algorithms more closely in the next section.

You have been introduced to six main algorithms in this section. You have also used some of them in bases other than ten. The exercises that follow are directed primarily toward the objectives suggested by Table 3.8.

Table 3.8

Algorithm	Bases other than ten	Base ten, all numbers	Base ten, small numbers
Lattice multiplication	✓	✓	✓
Usual multiplication		✓	✓
Cross multiplication			✓
Scaffolding division	✓	✓	✓
Long division		✓	✓
Short division			✓

EXERCISE SET 3.9

1. Compute each product by using both the lattice and the usual multiplication algorithms.

   (a)   65   (b)   243   (c)   378   (d)   208
       $\times$ 43 $\times$ 53 $\times$ 126 $\times$ 375

2. Compute each product by cross multiplication.

   (a)   65   (b)   78   ★ (c)   327
       $\times$ 43 $\times$ 94 $\times$ 648

3. Construct tables of multiplication facts for these bases.

   (a) Base seven   (b) Base two

4. Compute each product by using the lattice algorithm.

   (a) 35_{seven} (b) 1101_{two}
       $\times$ 24_{seven} $\times$ 110_{two}

5. Estimate product by rounding the factors.

   (a)   65   (b)   78   (c)   212   (d)   782
       $\times$ 48 $\times$ 94 $\times$ 385 $\times$ 52

6. Estimate these products by rounding the two-digit factor to the nearest ten (that is, multiple of

ten) and the three-digit factor to the nearest fifty (that is, multiple of fifty).

   (a)   345   (b)   870   (c)   160   (d)   210
       $\times$ 22 $\times$ 19 $\times$ 78 $\times$ 41

7. Use the digits, 2, 3, 5, and 8 to form two two-digit numbers whose product is as large as possible.

8. Find the product of these two "polynomials" using a cross-multiplication algorithm:
   $$(3x^2 + 2x + 5)$$
   $$\cdot \ (\ x^2 + 4x + 6)$$

9. The multiplication calculation below has been begun using the cross-multiplication algorithm. Find A and B and complete the calculation.

   $$\begin{array}{r} 47 \\ \times \ AB \\ \hline \square\square 8\,1 \end{array}$$

10. Compute 85×47 in two different ways, using the Russian peasant algorithm.

11. Historical evidence shows that the ancient Egyptians did multiplication problems by a clever system of successive doubling. For example, to compute 19×35 by the Egyptian method, one begins by doubling 35 several times:

$1 \times 35 = 35$

$2 \times 35 = 70$

$4 \times 35 = 140$

$8 \times 35 = 280$

$16 \times 35 = 560$

Then one notes that

$19 \times 35 = 16 \times 35 + 2 \times 35 + 1 \times 35$

Thus the product 19×35 is just the sum

$560 + 70 + 35 = 665$

(a) Compute 21×44 by the Egyptian method.

(b) Compute 44×21 by the Egyptian method.

12. Compute 19×35 by the Russian peasant method (halving 19 and doubling 35 as first step), and compare your calculations with the Egyptian method in Exercise 11.

13. Here is a trick you can use to help children learn their 9s facts. Number your fingers from 1 to 10 beginning with your right thumb and ending with your left thumb. See Figure 3.85. Now hold up your hands to the class, palms toward yourself. To find 9×4, bend down finger number 4. Students will see 3 fingers to the left and 6 to the right. *Answer:* 36. Try the trick for 9×8, 9×5, ...

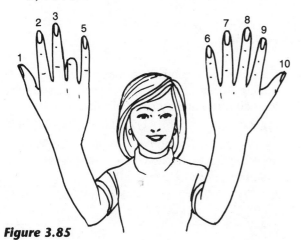

Figure 3.85

14. Here is another finger multiplication technique that can be used to find the product of any two numbers between 5 and 10. We illustrate it for the product 6×8. Mentally subtract 5 from the first number and hold up that many fingers on one hand. Mentally subtract 5 from the second number and hold up that many fingers on the other hand. See Figure 3.86. Add the up fingers to get the tens digit of the product:

$1 + 3 = 4$

Multiply the down fingers to get the units digit of the product:

$4 \times 2 = 8$

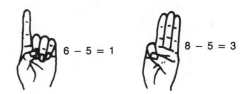

Figure 3.86

Answer: $6 \times 8 = 48$. Use this technique to calculate the following products.

(a) 7×8 (b) 6×9 (c) 6×7

(d) 7×10 (e) 5×8 (f) 10×10

(g) 4×7 (h) $6\frac{1}{2} \times 8$

15. Over the years teachers have devised countless games and activities to take some of the pain out of memorizing multiplication facts. Here is one such geometrical activity. We illustrate it for the 6s facts ($6 \cdot 0 = 0$, $6 \cdot 1 = 6$, $6 \cdot 2 = 12$, $6 \cdot 3 = 18$, . . . , $6 \cdot 10 = 60$).

Begin with a circle with ten equally spaced points on it numbered 0, 1, 2, . . . , 9. (How would you locate such points?) See Figure 3.87. Now start with your pencil at the units digit of $6 \cdot 0$ (namely 0). First move in a straight line to the units digit of $6 \cdot 1$ (namely 6), then to the units digit of $6 \cdot 2$ (namely 2), and so forth, until you end at the units digit of $6 \cdot 10$ (namely 0). See Figure 3.88. The resulting drawing is a star, as shown in Figure 3.89 (traced twice).

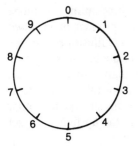

Figure 3.87

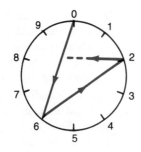

Figure 3.88

Figure 3.89

Carry out the activity just described to get a design for the following:
(a) The 2s facts (use Figure 3.90)
(b) The 3s facts (use Figure 3.91)

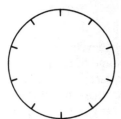

Figure 3.90

Figure 3.91

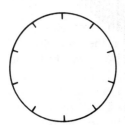

Figure 3.92

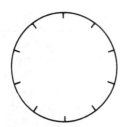

Figure 3.93

(c) The 4s facts (use Figure 3.92)
(d) The 5s facts (use Figure 3.93)
(e) The 9s facts (use Figure 3.94)

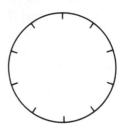

Figure 3.94

16. Use your table of base-seven multiplication facts from Exercise 3 to make star designs for the base-seven multiplication facts. Use Figure 3.95, parts a and b.

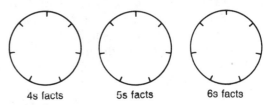

    1s facts   2s facts   3s facts

Figure 3.95a

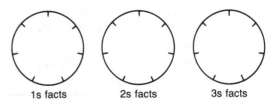

    4s facts   5s facts   6s facts

Figure 3.95b

17. Compute each quotient in three ways: by scaffolding (make an effort to be a bad guesser), by long division, and by short division.

    (a) $7\overline{)59829}$ (b) $11\overline{)91817}$ (c) $12\overline{)5436}$

18. Carry out long division only as far as necessary to approximate each quotient to the nearest thousand (multiple of a thousand).

    (a) $27\overline{)92502}$ (b) $65\overline{)2762565}$ (c) $268\overline{)6425032}$

19. Find each quotient by scaffolding.

    (a) $4_{\text{seven}}\overline{)132_{\text{seven}}}$ (b) $47_{\text{eight}}\overline{)1042_{\text{eight}}}$

20. When 100 is divided by x, a quotient of $y \neq 1$ and a remainder of 9 result. Find x and y.

21. Dividing a certain whole number by 44 yields a quotient of 3 and a remainder one-fifth as large as the original number. What was the original number?

22. In a division problem, the dividend is 155, the remainder is 12, and the quotient is not 1. What is the divisor?

23. Determine the missing base in each division problem.

$$\text{(a)}\ \ 23_x \overline{)1440_x} \quad \begin{array}{l} 41_x \ \ \text{R: } 13_x \end{array}$$

$$\text{(b)}\ \ 33_x \overline{)1332_x} \quad \begin{array}{l} 33_x \ \ \text{R: } 1_x \end{array}$$

24. The usual way to estimate a quotient is to replace the dividend and divisor by a "compatible" pair of nearby numbers. For example, $614 \div 87 \approx 630 \div 90 = 7$. Estimate each quotient.
    (a) $400 \div 17$ (b) $371 \div 23$
    (c) $10,000 \div 216$ (d) $149,546 \div 1824$

25. Use a calculator to find the whole number quotient and remainder for each part of Exercise 24.

3.10 *Algorithms and Flowcharts*

Educators may debate about the level of proficiency to aim for with paper-and-pencil algorithms, but all parties agree that in this computer age the general concept of algorithm (a step-by-step procedure) deserves more attention than ever before. To arrive at this general concept we shall consider three of the many algorithms that you know.

EXAMPLE 1   The algorithm for expressing a number in percent notation is suggested by the following examples:

$$.137 \rightarrow 13.7\%$$
$$2.7 \rightarrow 2.70 \rightarrow 270\%$$
$$12 \rightarrow 12.00 \rightarrow 1200\%$$
$$\tfrac{3}{8} \rightarrow .375 \rightarrow 37.5\%$$
$$\pi \rightarrow 3.14159 \ldots \rightarrow 314.159 \ldots \%$$

The basic idea is to move a decimal point two places to the right, but for certain numbers a preliminary step is needed. We will describe this algorithm more explicitly a little later. ❑

EXAMPLE 2   The algorithm for testing whether a number is divisible by 3 is suggested by these examples:

$$132 \rightarrow 1 + 3 + 2 = 6 \quad \text{yes}$$
$$233 \rightarrow 2 + 3 + 3 = 8 \quad \text{no}$$
$$5286 \rightarrow 5 + 2 + 8 + 6 = 21 \rightarrow 2 + 1 = 3 \quad \text{yes}$$
$$637598 \rightarrow 6 + 3 + 7 + 5 + 9 + 8 = 38 \rightarrow 3 + 8$$
$$= 11 \rightarrow 1 + 1 = 2 \quad \text{no}$$
$$24_{\text{six}} \rightarrow 16 \rightarrow 1 + 6 = 7 \quad \text{no}$$

The basic idea is to sum the digits and see if a 3, 6, or 9 results. For certain numbers the summing process may have to be repeated several times to arrive at a single-digit sum. And it is crucial that the original number be expressed in base-ten notation. ❏

EXAMPLE 3   The algorithm for converting from base-ten to base-five notation is suggested by the following diagram.

$$
\begin{array}{rl}
0 & \text{R3} \\
\overline{3} & \text{R1} \\
\overline{16} & \text{R3} \\
\overline{83} & \text{R4} \\
5\overline{)419} & \rightarrow 3134_{\text{five}} = 419_{\text{ten}}
\end{array}
$$
❏

Most of the algorithms that you know have become routine by working through many examples. To explain them to someone else, as we have recalled the preceding three to you, we ordinarily use illustrative examples. There is, however, a more explicit way of describing an algorithm and that is by a **flowchart.** We will look at flowcharts from a nontechnical point of view, as is done in many current elementary, junior high, and high school texts. These nontechnical flowcharts are a halfway step between the informal way we communicate algorithms to people and the formal way we communicate them to machines (by computer programs).

Flowcharts

Consider this algorithm for making a thick chocolate malt:

1. Assemble these ingredients: milk, malt powder, chocolate ice cream.
2. Put a cup of milk in a mixer.
3. Put a tablespoon of malt powder in the mixer.
4. Put a scoop of ice cream in the mixer.
5. Turn on the mixer for one minute.
6. Turn off the mixer.
7. Does a spoon stand up in the malt? If no, go back to step 4. If yes, go on to step 8.
8. You now have a thick chocolate malt.

This step-by-step procedure can be described schematically by an arrangement of variously shaped boxes, as shown in Figure 3.96. The shapes of the boxes are those prescribed by the American National Standards Institute (ANSI) for flowcharts. The **start** and **stop** ("terminal") boxes are oval. The **input** box is a parallelogram. It gives the ingredients. The **operation** (or "process") boxes are

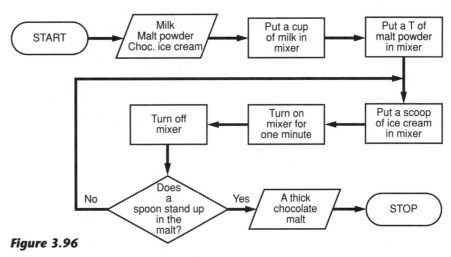

Figure 3.96

rectangular. They contain instructions that tell the user of the chart what to do. A **decision** box, represented by a diamond (rhombus) shape, always contains a question that can be answered yes or no. A flowchart always branches at a decision box. The branch one follows out of the box depends on the answer to the question. The **output** box, which describes the finished product, is a parallelogram like the input box.

Two other important features of flowcharts are illustrated by the chocolate malt example. One is the concept of **subroutine.** A subroutine can be thought of as an assumed capability of the user. In our flowchart we assumed that the user is capable of measuring out a tablespoon of malt powder, measuring out a cup of milk, turning a mixer on and off, and so forth. Every flowchart assumes certain capabilities of the user. In writing a flowchart, one must keep in mind who will use it, and one must be careful not to assume skills that the user doesn't have.

The other important feature that many, but not all, flowcharts exhibit is a **loop.** In our example a loop is initiated every time the question in the decision box is answered no. The user of this flowchart may run around that loop six or seven times before a yes answer puts him on a different branch.

Now let us return to our three original mathematical algorithms and describe them by flowcharts.

EXAMPLE 4 The flowchart for expressing a number in percent notation is shown in Figure 3.97. Notice the sophisticated subroutine "Express it as a decimal." This is a fine flowchart for an eighth grader to use, but it would be useless in the hands of a third grader.

After one devises a flowchart, a good practice is to see whether it works by sending through an input or two. Here is the itinerary of the input $\boxed{3/5}$.

$$\tfrac{3}{5} \to .6 \to \text{No} \to .60 \to \text{Yes} \to 60 \to 60\%$$

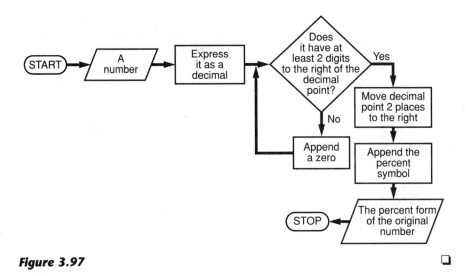

Figure 3.97   ❏

EXAMPLE 5   The flowchart for testing a number for divisibility by 3 is shown in Figure 3.98. On what subroutines does this algorithm depend? The itinerary of the input $\boxed{315_{\text{six}}}$ is as follows:

$315_{\text{six}} \rightarrow 119 \rightarrow \text{No} \rightarrow 11 \rightarrow \text{No}$

$\rightarrow 2 \rightarrow \text{Yes} \rightarrow \text{No} \rightarrow 315_{\text{six}}$ is not divisible by 3

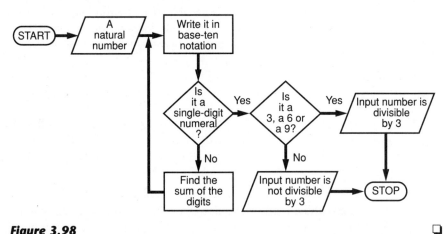

Figure 3.98   ❏

EXAMPLE 6   The flowchart for converting from base-ten to base-five notation is shown in Figure 3.99. Test this flowchart with the input $\boxed{508}$. What capabilities are assumed of the user?

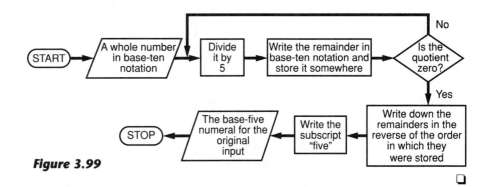

Figure 3.99

EXERCISE SET 3.10

1. Classify each of the following boxes as an input, an output, an operation, a decision, or a start or stop box.

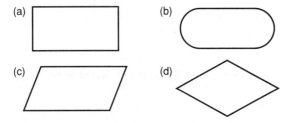

2. Instructions for preparing cake batter follow. Make a flowchart for this algorithm.
   1. Ingredients: cake mix, egg, water.
   2. Put cake mix in bowl.
   3. Put egg in bowl.
   4. Put 2 cups water in bowl.
   5. Beat what's in bowl for 4 minutes.
   6. Batter is ready.

3. Instructions for baking a cake (beginning with prepared batter) follow. Make a flowchart.
   1. Ingredients: batter, grease, flour.
   2. Turn on oven to 350°.
   3. Grease a cake pan.
   4. Flour the cake pan.
   5. Pour batter in cake pan.
   6. Put pan in oven.
   7. Bake for 35 minutes.

8. Remove pan from oven.
9. Poke toothpick into center of cake.
10. Does toothpick come out clean? If yes, go to step 13. If no, go to step 11.
11. Put cake in oven.
12. Bake for 2 minutes. Return to step 8.
13. Turn off oven.
14. A finished cake.

4. In recipes one often finds the instructions "salt to taste." Show how this instruction would be handled in a flowchart.

5. Make a flowchart for this step-by-step procedure for finding the area of a rectangle.
   1. Materials: rectangle, ruler.
   2. Measure one side.
   3. Measure an adjacent side.
   4. Multiply your two measurements.
   5. The area of the rectangle.

   What capabilities are assumed of the user of this flowchart? Write a brief formula that summarizes this flowchart.

6. Make a flowchart for averaging two whole numbers. What capabilities are assumed of the user?

   Trace the input $\boxed{27, 40}$ through your flowchart.

7. Arrange this mixed-up collection of boxes into a flowchart for making a cheese sandwich (with plenty of cheese).

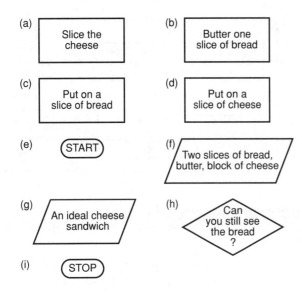

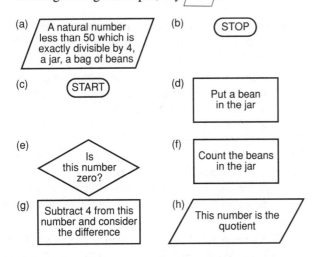

8. Arrange the following boxes into a flowchart for finding quotients when certain small natural numbers are divided by 4. Test your flowchart by sending through an input, say ⌹ 12 ⌹ .

9. Put the following into appropriately shaped boxes, and arrange them into a flowchart for an algorithm for rounding a whole number (of two or more digits) to the nearest multiple of ten. (In

ambiguous cases, such as 375, *nearest* means next higher, that is, 380.) Test your chart by inputting one number that should round up and another that should round down.
(a) Replace units digit by zero.
(b) Drop units digit.
(c) Consider units digit.
(d) Start.
(e) Append a zero.
(f) A whole number expressed by a base-ten numeral.
(g) Stop.
(h) The approximation to the nearest multiple of ten.
(i) Is it less than 5?
(j) Write the next base-ten numeral.

10. With reference to the algorithm in Exercise 9, suppose now that in ambiguous cases *nearest* means next lower, for example, 375 → 370. Revise the flowchart accordingly.

11. The algorithm in Exercise 9 is *numeration-dependent:* Inputs are represented by base-ten numerals; one considers a specific digit in the numeral, drops digits, replaces digits, appends zero. There are also *numeration-independent* algorithms for rounding to the nearest multiple of ten. Arrange the following into a flowchart for such an algorithm. (We are again using the "when in doubt, round up" convention of Exercise 9.)
(a) Multiply by 10.
(b) Divide by 10 (getting whole number quotient and remainder).
(c) Multiply quotient by 10.
(d) A whole number.
(e) Stop.
(f) Add 1 to the quotient.
(g) Is remainder less than 5?
(h) Start.
(i) The approximation to the nearest multiple of 10.

12. Review the flowchart in Exercise 11 so that it describes an algorithm for rounding whole numbers

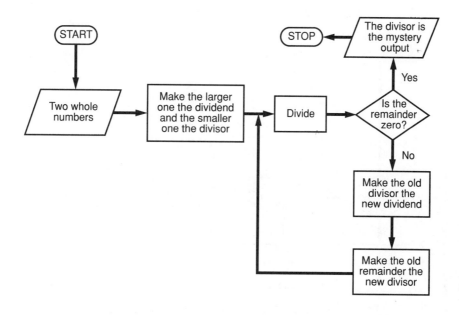

Figure 3.100

to the nearest multiple of one hundred. (Again, use the "when in doubt, round up" convention.)

13. Put the following phrases into appropriately shaped boxes and arrange them into a flowchart that tells how to proceed from any base-ten (Hindu-Arabic) numeral to the next one. (This procedure was a subroutine in Exercise 9.)
    (a) A base-ten numeral
    (b) Replace its rightmost digit by the next higher digit.
    (c) The next base-ten numeral
    (d) Start.
    (e) Does it have any terminal 9s?
    (f) Write a 1 at the left of the terminal 0s.
    (g) Replace this digit by the next higher digit.
    (h) Is there a digit to the left of the terminal 0s?
    (i) Stop.
    (j) Replace all terminal 9s by 0s.

14. Consider the following instructions:
    1. Start with any natural number.
    2. If it is even, divide it by 2. If it is odd, triple it and add 1.
    3. Now take the resulting number. If it is 1, stop. Otherwise, return to step 2.
    For example, if we start with 6, we get the following pattern:
    $6 \rightarrow 3 \rightarrow 10 \rightarrow 5 \rightarrow 16 \rightarrow 8 \rightarrow 4 \rightarrow 2 \rightarrow 1$
    Organize these instructions into a flowchart. (For every input number that has ever been tried, a 1 eventually resulted, but no one has been able to prove that this will always happen.)

15. Figure 3.100 is a flowchart for an algorithm that is very important in arithmetic and algebra.
    (a) Send the input $\boxed{252, 420}$ through the flowchart, and find the mystery output.
    (b) Repeat for the input $\boxed{117, 140}$.

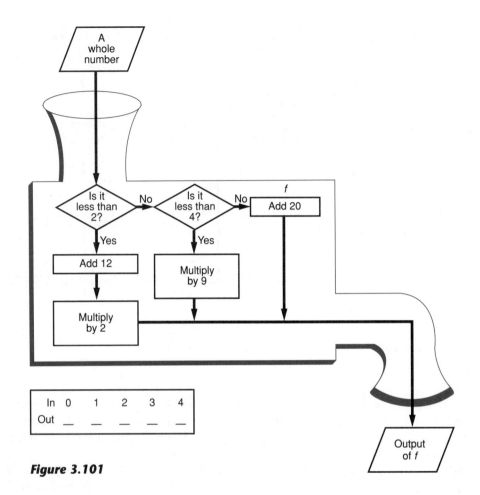

Figure 3.101

16. A flowchart ultimately acts as an input-output machine, that is, as a *function*. Complete the input-output tables for the functions *f* and *g* that are described by flowcharts. (As is sometimes done, we have omitted the start and stop symbols.)
    (a) Use the flowchart in Figure 3.101.
    (b) Use the flowchart in Figure 3.102 (p. 185).

17. Draw appropriately shaped boxes around the steps in the flowchart in Figure 3.103. Now:
    (a) Find the output produced by input 29.
    (b) Find *all* the inputs that yield the output 11.

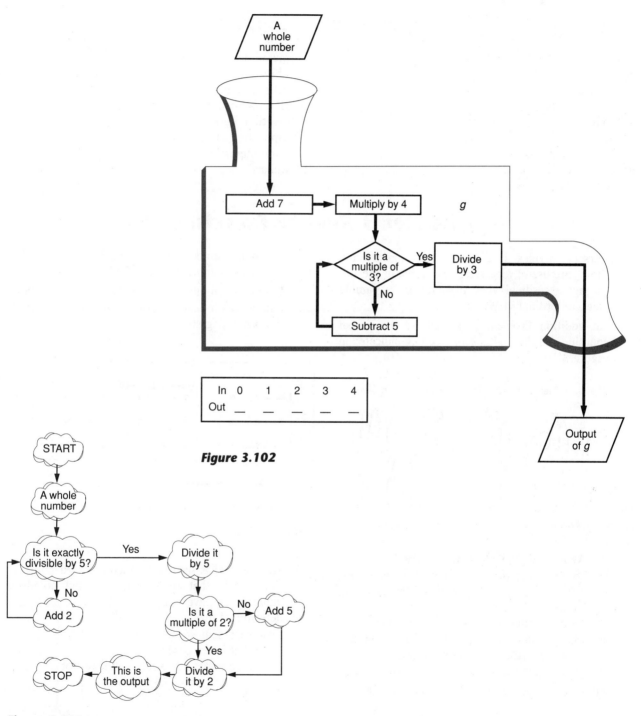

Figure 3.102

Figure 3.103

Key Concepts in Chapter 3

Numeration system
Base
Place value
Addition and union
Multiplication and Cartesian product
Choice principle
Subtraction and less than
Exact division and divides
Division with remainder

Permutations
Combinations
Pascal's triangle
Addition algorithms
Subtraction algorithms
Multiplication algorithms
Division algorithms
Flowchart

✺ *Chapter 3 Review Exercises* ✺

1. Nursery rhymes like "One, two, buckle my show" are useful for developing which of the following: a cardinal view of numbers, a naming view, an ordinal view?

2. An addition problem is solved by the verbal counting and the digital scorekeeping indicated in Figure 3.104.

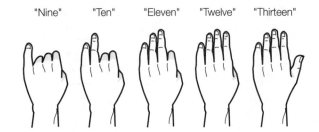

Figure 3.104

  (a) Write down the problem, and answer.
  (b) To carry out the verbal counting, one must have _____ understanding of the counting numbers.
  (c) To determine, from the digital scoreboard, when to stop, one must have _____ understanding of the counting numbers.

3. I am thinking of a numeration system with base and (usual) place value. The digits in the system are
  0, 1, 2, 3, 4, 5, 6, 7, 8, 9, T, E, ∗, · · · , ☾, ☼

  (a) What number follows 3 ∗ 5E ☼ ?
  (b) What number precedes 20E ☼ 0?

4. Report the number of caramels in Figure 3.105 in a numeration system whose base is appropriate to the packaging shown.

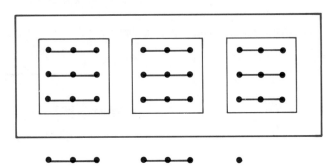

Figure 3.105

5. Archaeologists have unearthed a Weird numeration system that employs a base, but no place value. They have determined that  must represent 86.
  (a) What is the base?
  (b) Write the Hindu-Arabic numeral for

  ⌐ ⌐ ⌐ ⌐ ℒ ♢ ℒ ⌐ ⌐

  (c) Write the Weird numeral for 101.

6. In Figure 3.106 each caramel diagram represents an arithmetic problem and its answer. Write each problem and answer (three numerals with base, one arithmetic operation, and one equal sign).
    (a)

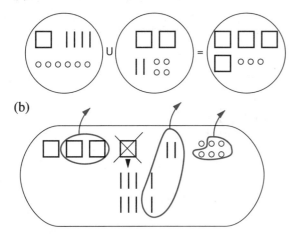

    (b)

Figure 3.106

7. Write the base-four numeral for $E3_{twelve}$.

8. Find the base-three numeral that represents $213_{four} + 10010_{two}$.

9. An auto dealer has three sizes of cars on his lot—compact, medium-sized, and luxury—each of which he categorizes as new, used, or demonstrator. Among his total of 200 cars he has 4 luxury demonstrators, 90 compacts including 36 used and 48 new ones, a total of 15 demonstrators, and a total of 75 medium-sized cars of which there are exactly as many used as new. If he has a total of 100 new cars, how many used luxury cars does he have?

10. The 150 guests at a wedding reception are sorted into three mutually exclusive categories: "family," "friends," and "other." Fifteen of the guests were children, of whom 10 were family. All 17 of the people in the "other" category were adults—and, in that category, women outnumbered men by 3. If 6 of the 60 men present were family, and family totaled 23 people, how many women friends were present?

11. Sets A, B, and C have 4, 5, and 6 elements, respectively. Furthermore, A and B have no elements in common.
    (a) How many elements has $(A \cup B) \times C$?
    (b) How many elements has $(A \times C) \cup (B \times C)$?

12. Suppose there are six traffic lights between home and work, and suppose that each time you make the trip, you record the pattern of colors of the lights that you meet. For example, the pattern GGRRGY indicates that on that trip you hit two greens followed by two reds followed by a green and lastly a yellow. How many different color patterns are possible?

13. This is Omar Khayyam's prescription for paradise:
    "A Book of Verses underneath the Bough,
    A Jug of Wine, A Loaf of Bread—and Thou . . ."
    (a) If Omar had 5 different books of verses, 8 different jugs of wine, 3 different loaves of bread, and 4 girlfriends, how many kinds of paradise were available to him?
    (b) Suppose Omar could obtain three more items (for example, two more girlfriends and one more book of verses). Which three should he choose in order to increase his number of paradises most dramatically?

14. The motor vehicle department wants to choose a color combination for next year's license plates. There are 7 light and 9 dark colors of paint available. It is all right to have light numerals on a dark background or dark numerals on a light background, but light on light or dark on dark are not permissible. How many choices for a color combination are there?

15. Classify each problem as one of the three types: missing addend, take away, or comparison. Then solve it.
    (a) There are 22 students but only 14 textbooks. How many students will be without books?
    (b) Of the 14 textbooks 9 are new. How many are used?

16. A delivery truck loaded with 24 identical refrigerators and a 200 lb driver weighs in at the truck scale at 10,000 lb. After dropping off six of the re-

frigerators it weighs in again, this time at 8500 lb. What does the truck weigh empty?

17. A big box of 1008 red, yellow, and green jelly beans contain equally many of each of the three colors. The favorite red ones are to be put in little bags by sixes, the green into other little bags by sevens, and the unpopular yellow ones into still other little bags by eights. How many little bags will be needed?

18. A teacher collects a cents from each of her b students and contributes c cents of her own. All of the money is spent on gum balls for a party. On the day of the party d students are absent. The gum balls are distributed e per student, and the teacher is left with f. How much did each gum ball cost?

★ 19. Evaluate each of the following.
    (a) 4!   (b) P_4^6 (c) C_4^6

★ 20. Express the answer to the following question by using a permutation or combination symbol, whichever is appropriate. In a horse race all that matters is which horses finish first, second, and third. How many different finishes are possible when 12 horses race?

21. Use left-to-right algorithms to approximate the sum and the difference to the nearest million. Show all crossing out.

    (a)   76,295,287   (b)   405,753,238
           83,246,439   − 168,406,754
         + 64,037,856

22. Calculate $50,047 - 26,583$ by the equal-additions algorithm. Show all crossing out and all superscripts.

23. Carry out the digit-reversal/addition activity on 213_{four} *within the base-four numeration system* until a palindrome results.

24. Compute $403_{five} \times 214_{five}$ in base five, using the lattice algorithm.

25. A student has begun calculating 594×368 by the cross-multiplication algorithm. Complete the calculation, showing all numbers "carried."

$$
\begin{array}{r}
5\ 9\ 4 \\
\times\ 3\ 6\ 8 \\
\hline
\square\square\square\square\ 9\ 2 \\
\square\ \square\ \square\ 9\ \ 3
\end{array}
$$
the product
the numbers carried

26. Fill in the missing numbers in this (scaffolding) division of 238 by 9. Conclude that the quotient is _____ and the remainder is _____ .

$$
\begin{array}{r}
\square \\
5 \\
1\ 0 \\
1\ 0 \\
9\overline{)2\ 3\ 8} \\
\square\square \\
\square\square\square \\
\square\square \\
\square\square \\
\square\square \\
\square\square \\
\square \\
\square
\end{array}
$$

27. Determine the missing base (x) and the missing tens digit (Y) of the quotient.

$$
\begin{array}{r}
Y\,3_x\ \ R1_x \\
12_x\overline{)332_x}
\end{array}
$$

28. Put the letters (a) through (i) into appropriately shaped boxes and arrange them into a flowchart that describes an algorithm for converting from base-ten to base-twelve notation.
    (a) Divide it by twelve.
    (b) Attach the subscript "twelve."
    (c) A whole number in base-ten notation.
    (d) Stop.
    (e) Is the quotient zero?
    (f) Write down the remainders in reverse order of storage.
    (g) Start.
    (h) Write the remainder as a base-twelve digit and store it.
    (i) The base-twelve numeral for the original number.

29. Put the letters (a)–(f) into appropriately shaped boxes and arrange them into a flowchart for the palindrome addition-drill activity.
    (a) Consider the sum.
    (b) A whole number in base-ten notation.
    (c) Start.
    (d) Add it to the number having the same digits but in reverse order.
    (e) Stop.
    (f) Is it a palindrome?

References

Arithmetic Teacher. Focus Issue—"Manipulatives." vol. 33, no. 6, February 1986.

Arithmetic Teacher. Focus Issue—"Early Childhood Mathematics." vol. 35, no. 6, February 1988.

Eves, H. *An Introduction to the History of Mathematics*. 4th ed. New York: Holt, Rinehart and Winston, 1976.

Flegg, G. *Numbers: Their History and Meaning*. London: André Deutsch Limited, 1983.

Jacobs, H. *Mathematics, A Human Endeavor*. 2nd ed. New York: Freeman, 1982.

National Council of Teachers of Mathematics. *29th Yearbook: Topics in Mathematics for Elementary School Teachers*. Reston, Va.: NCTM, 1964.

———.*1975 Yearbook: Mathematics Learning in Early Childhood*. Reston, Va.: NCTM, 1975.

———. *1978 Yearbook: Developing Computational Skills*. Reston, Va.: NCTM, 1978.

———. *1986 Yearbook: Estimation and Mental Computation*. Reston, Va.: NCTM, 1986.

Reys, R. *et al. Keystrokes: Calculator Activities for Young Students: Addition and Subtraction, Multiplication and Division*. Palo Alto, Calif.: Creative Publications, 1980.

Smith, D. and L. Karpinski. *The Hindu-Arabic Numerals*. Boston: Ginn, 1911.

Suydam, M. and D. Dessart. *Classroom Ideas from Research on Computational Skills*. Reston, Va.: NCTM, 1976.

THE WHOLE NUMBERS: A FORMAL APPROACH

This is the second chapter on whole numbers. The point of view is entirely different from what it was in Chapter 3 and should round out and deepen your understanding.

In Chapter 3 we were interested in attaching interpretations to numbers and operations. The whole numbers, via base and place value numeration, were represented concretely by caramel diagrams. The arithmetic operations of addition, multiplication, subtraction, and division were associated with the more tangible operations of union, Cartesian product, complement, and equipartitioning. The pairing of arithmetic concepts with external referents opened the way for application of arithmetic to real-world problems. Of course, to carry out the purely arithmetic computations, we had to develop efficient procedures, or algorithms. Initial forms of the algorithms were explained in terms of the interpretations of the numbers and operations. Later, we concentrated on mechanical proficiency and ignored the external referents.

In this chapter we will study whole number arithmetic as a self-contained mathematical system. There will be no external referents. The whole numbers will be thought of only as elements of an abstract set, the operations of addition and multiplication as abstract binary operations. Meaning will be given to these numbers and operations only by describing, through a specific list of assumptions, how they interact with each other. These assumptions, of course, will be plausible ones, most of them having been encountered in the previous chapter as consequences of the interpretations. But in this chapter plausibility will not be our concern. In fact, we shall studiously ignore everything external to the mathematical system. In zoological terms, we shall take the specimen called the whole number system into our laboratory and dissect it to determine its skeletal structure.

There are several reasons why an elementary school teacher should see such an analysis of the whole number system. One reason is that the system is basically simple. All of whole number arithmetic depends ultimately on only a small number of general principles. While many people are shown the underlying principles of geometry in their high school course, few get a corresponding picture of the situation in arithmetic. Another reason is that the successively more complicated systems of integers, rational numbers, and real numbers are structurally very similar to the whole numbers. In fact, by adding one or two bones at a time to the skeleton of the whole number system we will get the skeletons of the integers, the rationals, and the real numbers. A third reason is that the idea of mathematical system sheds light on topics beyond the number systems of arithmetic. For instance, we shall have occasion to study some geometric systems later on.

Note: Most of the work in this chapter is directed toward deepening your own mathematical understanding. This material could not be presented to elementary school children in anything like the form in which you will see it here. In fact, much of this material is probably inappropriate in *any* form before the middle school years. The drafters of the 5–8 curriculum *Standards* do, however, emphasize the importance of understanding mathematical structure in their standard on number systems and number theory: "The central theme of this standard is the underlying structure of mathematics. . . . Without an understanding of number systems and number theory, mathematics is a mysterious collection of facts. With such an understanding, mathematics is seen as a beautiful, cohesive whole."

4.1 *Mathematical Systems and Binary Operations*

There is no single answer to the question "What is a mathematical system?" Mathematical systems come in all degrees of complexity. The simplest definition, and the one we will use for the time being, follows.

A **mathematical system** is a set, together with one or more binary operations on it.

The archetypical mathematical system is the set of whole numbers together with the binary operations of addition and multiplication. For our definition of mathematical system to make sense, of course, a definition of binary operation is required.

Binary Operations

We can arrive at a definition of binary operation by thinking about addition and multiplication of whole numbers. Loosely speaking, both are ways of combining two elements of W to get another element of W. They can also be thought of as machines that accept (ordered) pairs of whole numbers as inputs and yield whole numbers as outputs, as illustrated in Figure 4.1. Thus techni-

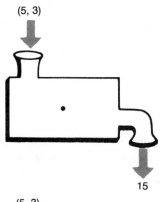

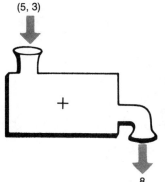

Figure 4.1

cally, addition and multiplication are functions from $W \times W$ to W. But instead of using function notation, like

$$+ ((5, 3)) = 8 \qquad \cdot ((5, 3)) = 15$$

we use a modification of it, *infix notation,* in which the function symbol stands between the first and second members of the input pair

$$5 + 3 = 8 \qquad 5 \cdot 3 = 15$$

In general, then, the definitions are as follows.

Informal

A **binary operation** on a set S is a way of combining two elements of S to get another element of S.

Formal

A **binary operation** on a set S is a function from $S \times S$ to S. If $*$ denotes this function and if (a, b) is an input for $*$, then the corresponding output is written $a * b$ rather than $* ((a, b))$.

Let us consider some specific examples of this general concept.

EXAMPLE 1 The set is N, the natural numbers. An exponentiation operation $\wedge$ is defined by

$$m \wedge n = m^n$$

For instance,

$$2 \wedge 3 = 2^3 = 8 \qquad 5 \wedge 2 = 5^2 = 25 \qquad 3 \wedge 3 = 3^3 = 27$$

Is $\wedge$ a binary operation on N?

Solution Yes, it is, because $\wedge$ acts on ordered pairs of natural numbers and produces numbers that are still in N. In short, $\wedge$ is a function from $N \times N$ to N. See Figure 4.2.

The symbol $\wedge$ is a commonly used computer notation for exponentiation. You can pronounce it "hat." ❑

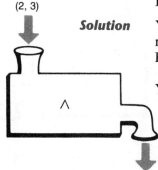

Figure 4.2

EXAMPLE 2   The set is N. A maximization operation ⓜ is defined by

$$p \; ⓜ \; r = \text{maximum of } p \text{ and } r$$

For instance,

$$3 \; ⓜ \; 7 = 7 \qquad 5 \; ⓜ \; 2 = 5 \qquad 3 \; ⓜ \; 3 = 3$$

Is ⓜ a binary operation on N?

Solution   Yes, it is, because ⓜ accepts ordered pairs of natural numbers as inputs and produces natural numbers as outputs. In short, ⓜ is a function from $N \times N$ to N. See Figure 4.3.

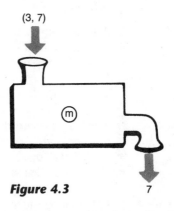

Figure 4.3

EXAMPLE 3   The set is W. Is subtraction a binary operation on W?

Solution   No, it is not, because some of the outputs are not in W, as indicated in Figure 4.4. That is, $-$ is not a function from $W \times W$ to W. Subtraction is, however, a binary operation on the set I of all integers, $\{\ldots, {}^-3, {}^-2, {}^-1, 0, 1, 2, 3, \ldots\}$.

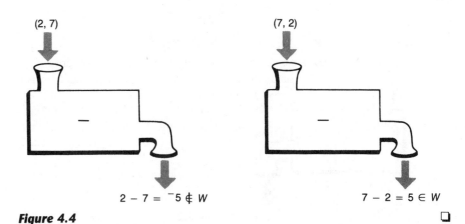

Figure 4.4

EXAMPLE 4 The set is W. The squaring operation ⓢⓠ is defined as usual. Is ⓢⓠ a binary operation on W?

Solution No, it is not. This time the outputs are all right (whole numbers), but the inputs are wrong. They are whole numbers rather than ordered pairs of whole numbers; ⓢⓠ is a function from W to W rather than from $W \times W$ to W. See Figure 4.5. Some people refer to ⓢⓠ as a **unary operation** on W because of its single-number inputs.

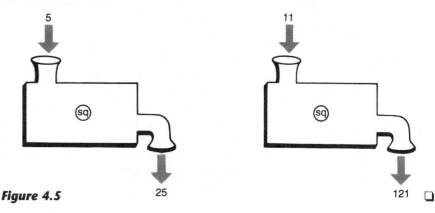

Figure 4.5

EXAMPLE 5 The set is $\{0, 1, 2, 3, 4, 5, 6\}$, which we denote by I_7 and represent geometrically by seven evenly spaced hours on a seven clock, as shown in Figure 4.6. The operation, written $+_7$ and called **seven-clock addition,** is suggested by the following examples:

$3 +_7 5 = 1$ because on this clock 5 hours after 3 o'clock is 1 o'clock

$6 +_7 4 = 3$ because if you start at 6 and move (clockwise) 4 hours, you will end up at 3

To find $a +_7 b$ arithmetically, compute their ordinary whole number sum; then if the sum is more than 6, subtract 7 from it:

$$6 +_7 4 \rightarrow 10 - 7 \rightarrow 3$$

Is $+_7$ a binary operation on I_7?

Solution Yes, it is. Given any pair of numbers from $\{0, 1, 2, 3, 4, 5, 6\}$, the operation $+_7$ assigns to them a number in this same set.

Figure 4.6

EXAMPLE 6 The set is again $I_7 = \{0, 1, 2, 3, 4, 5, 6\}$. The operation, written $\cdot_7$ and called **seven-clock multiplication,** can be viewed as repeated seven-clock addition:

$$2 \cdot_7 5 = 5 +_7 5 = 3$$
$$3 \cdot_7 6 = 6 +_7 6 +_7 6 = 5 +_7 6 = 4$$

The quickest way to find $a \cdot_7 b$, though, is to compute the ordinary whole number product and then subtract as many 7s as necessary to bring it into the 0-to-6 range:

$$2 \cdot_7 5 \rightarrow 10 - 7 \rightarrow 3$$
$$3 \cdot_7 6 \rightarrow 18 - 14 \rightarrow 4$$

Is $\cdot_7$ a binary operation on I_7?

Solution   Yes, it is. It is a way of combining two elements from I_7, which yields another element of I_7. ❏

The mathematical system consisting of the set $I_7 = \{0, 1, 2, 3, 4, 5, 6\}$ and the two binary operations $+_7$ and $\cdot_7$ is called **seven-clock arithmetic,** or sometimes the *system of integers modulo seven*. This system is very much like the usual number systems in surprisingly many ways, yet it is quite unlike them in a few others. Just as bases other than ten helped to deepen our understanding of the standard numeration system, and as nonstandard algorithms put the conventional ones in perspective, so seven-clock arithmetic will provide us with thought-provoking comparisons and contrasts as we study the usual number systems.

Closure

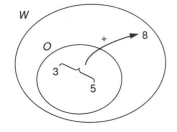

Figure 4.7

Consider again the binary operation $+$ on the set W of all whole numbers. Is $+$ also a binary operation on the subset E of even whole numbers? Yes, it is, because the sum of two even numbers is even. We say that the subset E of W is *closed* with respect to addition, or E is closed under addition. The word *closed* should suggest that you cannot escape from E by adding. Is $+$ also a binary operation on the subset O of odd whole numbers? No, it is not, because the sum of two odd numbers is not in O. The subset O of W is not closed with respect to addition; it is possible to escape from O by adding. See Figure 4.7. Here is a formal definition.

Given a binary operation $*$ on a set S, and given a subset $T \subseteq S$; T is **closed** with respect to $*$, means that for every t_1 and t_2 in T, $t_1 * t_2$ is also in T.

Note: The set S itself is, by definition, closed under any binary operation on S.

EXAMPLE 7   As before, E and O stand for the subsets of even and odd whole numbers, respectively. Is E closed under multiplication? Is O closed under multiplication?

Solution   Set E is closed under multiplication since even times even is even. Set O is also closed under multiplication because odd times odd is odd. ❏

EXAMPLE 8   Is O closed under the exponentiation operation $\wedge$ on W?

Solution   Yes, it is. For example,

$$7 \wedge 3 = 7^3 = 7 \cdot 7 \cdot 7 \qquad \text{which is odd}$$

$$5 \wedge 9 = 5^9 = 5 \cdot 5 \cdot 5 \cdot 5 \cdot 5 \cdot 5 \cdot 5 \cdot 5 \cdot 5 \qquad \text{which is odd} \qquad ❑$$

EXAMPLE 9   Is $\{0, 1\}$ closed under the addition operation on W?

Solution   No, it is not. Four sums need to be checked: $0 + 0, 0 + 1, 1 + 0,$ and $1 + 1$. The first three are in $\{0, 1\}$, but the fourth is not. It is possible to escape from $\{0, 1\}$ by adding. ❑

EXAMPLE 10   Is $\{0, 1\}$ closed under the multiplication operation on W?

Solution   Yes, it is. This time all four possible products are in $\{0, 1\}$. ❑

Terminology: Most college texts define "binary operation on a set" the way we did. Thus in most college texts the statement "Addition is a binary operation on W" implies that W is closed under addition. In many precollege texts the concept of binary operation is defined loosely or not at all, and the fact that addition is a binary operation on W is stated as follows and referred to as the *closure property for addition of whole numbers:* "For any whole numbers a and b, $a + b$ is a unique whole number."

Cayley Tables

A binary operation on a set can be described by means of a **Cayley table** [named for the English mathematician Arthur Cayley (1821–1895), one of the fathers of modern abstract algebra]. For example, the Cayley table for the binary operation $\cdot$ on the set $\{^-1, 1\}$ is given in Figure 4.8.

The familiar table of multiplication facts is just one small corner of the infinite Cayley table for the binary operation $\cdot$ on the set N, as indicated in Figure 4.9. In the exercises you will be asked to fill in some Cayley tables.

$\cdot$	1	-1
1	1	-1
-1	-1	1

Figure 4.8

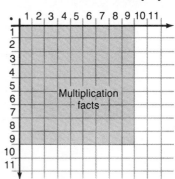

Figure 4.9

EXERCISE SET 4.1

1. Two very common types of hand-held calculators are the AOS (algebraic operating system) and RPN (reverse Polish notation). In the former one finds $3 + 5$ by punching the keys

   ⟨3⟩⟨+⟩⟨5⟩⟨=⟩

   In the latter one punches

   ⟨3⟩⟨enter⟩⟨5⟩⟨+⟩

   Relate these two types to the two notations, function and infix, for binary operations.

2. An operation $*$ is defined as follows:
   $$a * b = a + 2 \cdot b \qquad (\text{or } \square * \triangle = \square + 2 \cdot \triangle$$
   $$\text{if you prefer})$$
   For example,
   $$3 * 5 = 3 + 2 \cdot 5 = 13$$
   (a) Compute $2 * 4$, $0 * 3$, $5 * 5$.
   (b) Is $*$ a binary operation on W?

3. The averaging operation ⓐ is defined by
   $$x \, ⓐ \, y = \frac{x + y}{2}$$
   (a) Compute $5 \, ⓐ \, 9$, $2 \, ⓐ \, 3$, $\frac{2}{3} \, ⓐ \, \frac{1}{4}$.
   (b) Is ⓐ a binary operation on W?
   (c) Is ⓐ a binary operation on Q (the rational numbers)?

★ 4. Let $S = \{a, b\}$ and let T be the set of all four subsets of S; that is,
   $$T = \{\varnothing, \{a\}, \{b\}, S\}$$
   Which of the following operations are binary operations on T?
   (a) $\cup$ (union)
   (b) $\cap$ (intersection)
   (c) $'$ (complement)
   (d) $\times$ (Cartesian product)
   (e) $\triangle$ (defined by $A \triangle B = $ the set of all elements that are in A or B but not both)

5. Multiplication is a binary operation on the set R of all real numbers. Which of the following subsets of R are closed under multiplication?
   (a) N
   (b) $\{^-1, 1\}$
   (c) $\{1\}$
   (d) $\{1, 3, 5, 7, 9, 11, \ldots\}$
   (e) All rational numbers except 0
   (f) $\{7, 14, 21, 28, 35, \ldots\}$

6. Which of the six sets in Exercise 5 are closed under the following operations?
   (a) Addition   (b) Subtraction   (c) Division

7. Which of the following subsets of N are closed under the exponentiation operation $\wedge$?
   (a) $\{2, 4, 6, 8, \ldots\}$ (b) $\{1, 2, 3, 4, 5\}$
   (c) $\{6, 7, 8, 9, 10, 11, \ldots\}$ (d) $\{1\}$
   (e) $\{5, 17, 93\}$

8. Which of the five sets in Exercise 7 are closed under the max operation ⓜ?

9. Consider the subset $\{0, 2, 4, 6\}$ of I_7.
   (a) Is it closed under $+_7$?
   (b) Is it closed under $\cdot_7$?

10. Fill in the empty boxes in the flowchart in Figure 4.10 for seven-clock addition.

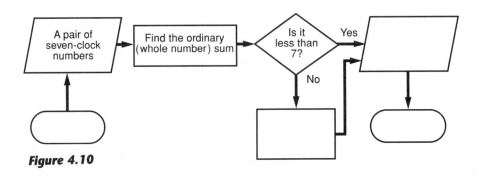

Figure 4.10

11. Make a flowchart for seven-clock multiplication.

12. Fill in the Cayley tables for the binary operations $+_7$ and $\cdot_7$ on the set of seven-clock numbers $I_7 = \{0, 1, 2, 3, 4, 5, 6\}$. .

   (a)   (b)

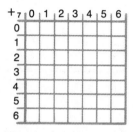 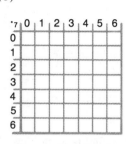

13. List the smallest subset of $\{0, 1, 2, 3, 4, 5, 6\}$ with each property:
   (a) Contains 2 and is closed under seven-clock multiplication
   (b) Contains 2 and is closed under seven-clock addition

14. Make a Cayley table for the max operation ⓜ on the set $\{1, 2, 3, 4\}$.

15. Make a Cayley table for the set T and the binary operation $\cup$ of Exercise 4(a).

🐚 16. How many different binary operations can be defined on these sets? (*Hint:* Think in terms of Cayley tables.)
   (a) A 2-element set
   (b) A 3-element set
   (c) An n-element set

17. The max operation can be used to define a function that is very important in arithmetic and in higher mathematics. Here is the definition:
$$f(x) = \max(x, \,^-x)$$
Find $f(7)$, $f(^-5)$, and $f(0)$. Do you know the usual name for this function?

 ## 4.2 *Properties of Equality*

The substitution and RST properties that will be described in this section are general consequences of our use of the equal sign, and apply to *all* mathematical systems.

Substitution

In dealing with a set of tangible objects, such as people, there is no need to worry about the ideas of equality and substitution. Anyone can see whether he is talking to two people or to one. But once the actual people are represented by labels, the situation becomes less clear. Do "John" and "Jack" both name the same person? If they do, we write

John = Jack

and we freely substitute either of these labels for the other in any statement about the person bearing those labels. For example, if the statement

John drives a school bus

is true, then

Jack drives a school bus

is true also. In general the **substitution principle** can be stated as follows.

If $a = b$ (so that "a" and "b" are two labels for a single thing), then "a" and "b" can be used interchangeably in any statement about the thing that they name.

EXAMPLE 1 $\left.\begin{array}{l} \text{Dwight Eisenhower} = \text{Ike} \\ \text{Ike was the 34th president} \end{array}\right\}$ $\Rightarrow$ Dwight Eisenhower was the 34th president

The two-shafted arrow is read "implies." ❑

EXAMPLE 2 $\left.\begin{array}{l} a = b \\ a \text{ is high in protein} \end{array}\right\}$ $\Rightarrow$ b is high in protein ❑

In each of the mathematical systems that we shall study, the set will consist of intangible objects. For example, in the whole number system the set is

$$W = \{0, 1, 2, 3, \ldots\}$$

Since no one ever has or ever will see or touch a whole number, we are forced to work with symbols (numerals) for the objects (numbers), and thus we constantly use the substitution principle. A very simple sort of substitution is illustrated by this example:

$\left.\begin{array}{l} 8 = 13_{\text{five}} \\ 8 \text{ is an even number} \end{array}\right\}$ $\Rightarrow$ 13_{five} is an even number

This substitution is legitimate because evenness is a property of numbers, and just one number underlies the two labels 8 and 13_{five}. A situation in which substitution is *not* legitimate is this:

$\left.\begin{array}{l} 8 = 13_{\text{five}} \\ 8 \text{ is a single-digit number} \end{array}\right\}$ $\not\Rightarrow$ 13_{five} is a single-digit number

The reason substitution is not permissible here is that single-digitness is not a property of numbers; it is a property of numerals (labels).

Binary Operations and Substitution

When the substitution principle is applied to inputs for binary operations, fundamental algebraic principles result. Here is an example of one of these principles:

$$13 = 10 + 3 \quad \Rightarrow \quad 13 + 5 = (10 + 3) + 5$$

To see that this is a version of the substitution principle, we can rewrite the example slightly:

$\left.\begin{array}{l} 13 = 10 + 3 \\ 13 + 5 = 13 + 5 \end{array}\right\}$ $\Rightarrow$ $13 + 5 = (10 + 3) + 5$

Now it is clear that we started out with a true statement about numbers, $13 + 5 = 13 + 5$, and then substituted $10 + 3$ for the second occurrence of 13 in that statement.

This version of the substitution principle is referred to as the **addition property of equality** (APE). Its general symbolic form is

$$a = b \implies a + c = b + c$$

which can be read as follows:

If $a = b$, then $a + c = b + c$.

It is often verbalized colloquially as well:

"You can add the same number to both sides of an equation."

This last statement is a useful mnemonic, but you should realize that, literally, it says nothing: The word *can* has no mathematical or logical content.

The corresponding **multiplication property of equality** (MPE) is symbolized

$$a = b \implies a \cdot c = b \cdot c$$

and is read as follows:

If $a = b$, then $a \cdot c = b \cdot c$.

It is colloquialized as

"You can multiply both sides of an equation by the same number."

Again, the equation $a \cdot c = b \cdot c$ can be thought of as having arisen from the obviously true equation $a \cdot c = a \cdot c$ by substitution of b for the second occurrence of a.

The addition and multiplication properties of equality underlie conventional equation-solving techniques, as the following examples illustrate. A thorough treatment of equations, their solution, and their applications is given in Chapter 15.

EXAMPLE 3

$$x - 3 = 6$$
$$\Downarrow \qquad \text{by addition property of equality}$$
$$x - 3 + 3 = 6 + 3$$
$$\Downarrow \qquad \text{by properties of integers yet to be described}$$
$$x = 9$$

What has been shown is that *if* $x - 3 = 6$, *then* $x = 9$. That is, the only possible solution is $x = 9$. It is still necessary to check that, in fact, 9 is a solution. Does $9 - 3 = 6$? Yes. ❏

EXAMPLE 4 $\frac{1}{3}x = 6$

⇓   by multiplication property of equality

$3 \cdot \frac{1}{3}x = 3 \cdot 6$

⇓   by properties of rational numbers yet to be described

$x = 18$

That is, if $\frac{1}{3}x = 6$, then $x = 18$. *Check:* $\frac{1}{3} \cdot 18 = 6$.   ❑

Clearly, the addition and multiplication properties of equality that are associated so closely with the usual number systems are special cases of a more general principle (also a consequence of the substitution principle) that asserts that if $*$ is any binary operation on any set S, and if a, b, and c are any elements of S such that $a = b$, then $a * c = b * c$.

EXAMPLE 5 $x +_7 5 = 4 \ \Rightarrow \ (x +_7 5) +_7 2 = 4 +_7 2$

(Can you see any particular reason for the choice of 2 as the number to be added to both sides?)   ❑

EXAMPLE 6 $5 \cdot_7 x = 4 \ \Rightarrow \ 3 \cdot_7 (5 \cdot_7 x) = 3 \cdot_7 4$

(Why choose 3?)   ❑

EXAMPLE 7 $10 + 3 = 13 \ \Rightarrow \ 2 \wedge (10 + 3) = 2 \wedge 13$ ❑

The RST Properties

A few other simple properties that are closely related to the ideas of equality and substitution bear brief mention here. These are the reflexive, symmetric, and transitive properties of equality—known familiarly as the RST properties. If you covered the optional section on relations in Chapter 2, you recognize these as the defining properties of an equivalence relation. We have used all of these properties tacitly already.

The **reflexive property** is simple, so a few examples will make its meaning clear:

$$4 = 4 \qquad 13 + 5 = 13 + 5 \qquad a \cdot c = a \cdot c$$

Loosely speaking, anything is equal to itself. In symbols:

$$a = a$$

You might like to think of this property as an agreement that, locally, symbols will be used unambiguously. That is, if the symbol "a" appears twice in a single exercise or paragraph, then in both occurrences it designates the same thing.

The **symmetric property** asserts the following:

> If $a = b$, then $b = a$.

That is, equations can be read from left to right or from right to left. For instance, the symmetric property allows us to rewrite the equation $9 = 2x + 3$ as $2x + 3 = 9$.

The **transitive property** asserts the following:

> If $a = b$ and $b = c$, then $a = c$.

This property justifies the use of chains of equal signs, as in

$$2^3 = 2 \cdot 2 \cdot 2 = 8$$

That is, from $2^3 = 2 \cdot 2 \cdot 2$ and $2 \cdot 2 \cdot 2 = 8$, we may infer that $2^3 = 8$.

In view of our agreement that the equal sign stands between labels for a single object, all three of the RST properties are obviously true.

EXERCISE SET 4.2

1. Use the substitution principle to draw a conclusion from these premises.

   (a) $\left.\begin{array}{l} x = 3t \\ y = 5 - x \end{array}\right\}$ (b) $\left.\begin{array}{l} x = t + 1 \\ y < 2 + 3x \end{array}\right\}$

   (c) $\left.\begin{array}{l} y = 2 - x \\ y \neq x^2 \end{array}\right\}$

2. Make the substitutions called for and then compute each product mentally.

   (a) $\frac{100}{4}$ for 25 in the product 25×240

   (b) 9×4 for 36 in 36×225

   (c) $2 \times 2 \times 2$ for 8 in 185×8

   (d) $20 + 3$ for 23 and $20 - 3$ for 17 in 23×17

3. When Amy hears the statement, "Joe has three letters," she pictures a boy walking to a mailbox with three envelopes in his hand. When Kim hears the same statement she thinks of the conso-

nant J and the two vowels O and E. Suppose now that "Joseph" is substituted for "Joe" in the statement.

   (a) Is the meaning still the same for Amy?

   (b) Is the meaning still the same for Kim?

4. What is wrong with each substitution?

   (a) $\left.\begin{array}{l} \frac{5}{8} = \frac{15}{24} \\ \frac{5}{8} \text{ is in lowest terms} \end{array}\right\} \Rightarrow \begin{array}{l} \frac{15}{24} \text{ is in lowest} \\ \text{terms} \end{array}$

   (b) $\left.\begin{array}{l} \frac{1}{3} = 0.3333 \ldots \\ 0.3333 \ldots \text{ is a} \\ \text{repeating} \\ \text{decimal} \end{array}\right\} \Rightarrow \begin{array}{l} \frac{1}{3} \text{ is a repeating} \\ \text{decimal} \end{array}$

5. A student refers to the square in Figure 4.11 and presents you with the following paradox: "Since

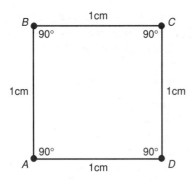

Figure 4.11

$\overline{AB} = \overline{BC}$ and $\overline{AB}$ is perpendicular to $\overline{AD}$, it follows, by the substitution principle, that $\overline{BC}$ is perpendicular to $\overline{AD}$." How do you respond?

6. Solve these equations by using the additive and/or the multiplicative property of equality; that is, solve by adding the same number to both sides or multiplying both sides by the same number. Remember to check.
   (a) $x - 4 = 7$
   (b) $x - 5 = 0$
   (c) $\frac{1}{4}x = 6$
   (d) $\frac{1}{2}x - 5 = 7$
   (e) $\frac{1}{2}(x - 5) = 7$
   (f) $x +_7 5 = 4$
   (g) $x +_7 3 = 0$
   (h) $2 \cdot_7 x = 5$
   (i) $5 \cdot_7 x +_7 4 = 1$
   (j) $5 \cdot_7 (x +_7 4) = 1$

7. Suppose that $a = b$ and $b = c$ and $c = d$. Use the transitive property of equality to show that $a = d$. Generalize this result.

8. Both the symmetric and transitive properties of equality can be viewed as special cases of substitution.
   (a) Explain how this substitution diagram yields the symmetric property:
   $$\left. \begin{array}{l} a = b \\ a = a \end{array} \right\} \Rightarrow b = a$$
   (b) Draw a substitution diagram that yields the transitive property.

9. In some computer programming languages like BASIC the equal sign has a very different meaning than the mathematical one we have agreed upon here. For example, line 115 of the program in Figure 4.20 later in the chapter is

$$\text{LET} \quad R = R + 1$$

This line is an instruction to the computer to replace the number that is currently stored in memory location R by the number that is one larger. For our mathematical (not computer) meaning of $=$, what numbers R satisfy the equation $R = R + 1$?

 ### 4.3 *Fundamental Structural Properties of the Whole Number System*

The mathematical system called the whole number system consists of a set

$$W = \{0, 1, 2, 3, \cdots\}$$

and two binary operations on W:

$$+ \quad \text{and} \quad \cdot$$

It shares with every other mathematical system the properties of equality studied in the previous section, namely, substitution (and its special cases APE and MPE) and the RST properties. Henceforth we will refer to these universal properties of mathematical systems as **logical properties.**

Now we want to investigate some further properties of the whole number system that may or may not be true in other mathematical systems. We will call these **structural properties.** There are nine structural properties in all: four that refer to addition, four analogous ones that refer to multiplication, and one that relates addition and multiplication. In this section we will look at the seven that are most familiar; in the next section we will consider the other two.

The Associative Properties

Addition, being a binary operation, acts on pairs of numbers. How, then, can we add three numbers such as 8, 2, and 3? Technically, we cannot feed the ordered triple (8, 2, 3) into the addition machine. It is the wrong kind of input. Figure 4.12 shows two different ways of handling the problem. The **associative property of addition** says that it makes no difference which way addition is done:

$$(8 + 2) + 3 = 8 + (2 + 3)$$

More generally:

$$(a + b) + c = a + (b + c)$$

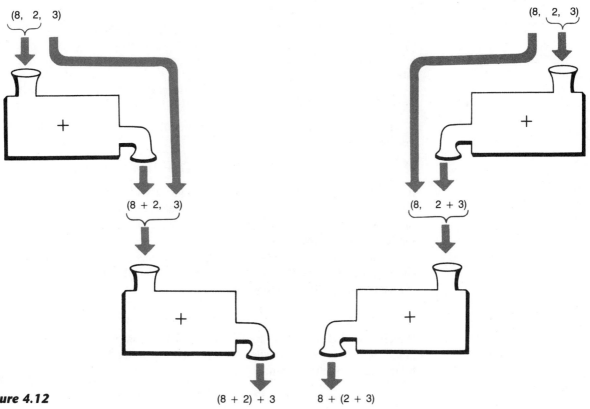

Figure 4.12

for any whole numbers a, b, and c. Recall that the parentheses in an expression such as $8 + (2 + 3)$ indicate which numbers are to be operated on first.

The associative property of addition, like most of the structural properties of W, is so "obvious" that it is not easy to see exactly what it does and does not say. Observe that in the equation

$$(8 + 2) + 3 = 8 + (2 + 3)$$

the order of the three numbers is the same on both sides—only the grouping has been changed. A useful mnemonic is this: The middleman, 2, can associate with either endman, 8 or 3, as illustrated in Figure 4.13.

Figure 4.13

Very young children make use of the associative property of addition (not by name, of course) when they learn their addition facts. A child who finds $8 + 5$ by thinking "Take 2 from the 5 and put it with the 8" is computing mentally as follows:

$$8 + 5 = 8 + (2 + 3) = (8 + 2) + 3 = \cdots$$

The associative property applies to sums of more than three terms as well. For instance,

$$[7 + (3 + 8)] + 9 = (7 + 3) + (8 + 9)$$

In general, parentheses can be moved about at will in an addition expression without affecting the sum. Consequently, parentheses are usually omitted entirely in addition expressions. Readers are then free to group the terms according to their own preferences.

The **associative property of multiplication** has the same form as the associative property of addition; only the operation is different. An example of the associative property of multiplication is

$$(6 \cdot 4) \cdot 5 = 6 \cdot (4 \cdot 5)$$

Which side of the equation do you find easier to compute? Children make implicit use of this property when they calculate a product such as $4 \cdot 7$ by doubling 7 and doubling again:

$$4 \cdot 7 = (2 \cdot 2) \cdot 7 = 2 \cdot (2 \cdot 7) = \cdots$$

The general form of the associative property of multiplication for three factors is as follows:

$$(a \cdot b) \cdot c = a \cdot (b \cdot c)$$

Again, this property generalizes to products of any number of factors. Thus there is no ambiguity in writing a product with no parentheses at all

$$7 \cdot 4 \cdot 5 \cdot 5$$

All possible insertions of parentheses will lead to the same result.

To appreciate the significance of the associative properties for the whole number system it is useful to inquire if other mathematical systems have this property. Consider first the mathematical system consisting of the set of natural numbers N and the exponentiation operation $\wedge$. Is $\wedge$ associative? That is, is it true that

$$(a \wedge b) \wedge c = a \wedge (b \wedge c)$$

for all natural numbers a, b, and c? Let's test this equation for a specific triple of natural numbers, say $a = 2$, $b = 3$, and $c = 4$:

$$(2 \wedge 3) \wedge 4 = 8 \wedge 4 = 4096$$

$$2 \wedge (3 \wedge 4) = 2 \wedge 81 = \text{a number larger than 1 septillion}$$

Thus the exponentiation operation is *not* associative; the location of the parentheses is critical.

Consider next the mathematical system consisting of the set N and the maximization operation ⓜ. Is ⓜ associative? Again, we begin by investigating a specific triple of numbers:

$$(3 \text{ ⓜ } 7) \text{ ⓜ } 5 \overset{?}{=} 3 \text{ ⓜ } (7 \text{ ⓜ } 5)$$

$$\| \qquad\qquad \|$$

$$7 \text{ ⓜ } 5 \qquad\qquad 3 \text{ ⓜ } 7$$

$$\| \qquad\qquad \|$$

$$7 \qquad\qquad 7$$

The fact that

$$(3 \text{ ⓜ } 7) \text{ ⓜ } 5 = 3 \text{ ⓜ } (7 \text{ ⓜ } 5)$$

does not, by itself, prove that

$$(a \text{ ⓜ } b) \text{ ⓜ } c = a \text{ ⓜ } (b \text{ ⓜ } c)$$

for all possible triples of natural numbers. It does, however, suggest rather clearly that no matter where the parentheses are inserted,

$$a \text{ ⓜ } b \text{ ⓜ } c = \text{the largest of } a, b, \text{ and } c$$

that is, ⓜ is associative.

Finally, consider the mathematical system consisting of the set $I = \{\ldots,$ $^-3, \,^-2, \,^-1, 0, 1, 2, 3, \ldots\}$ of integers and the subtraction operation. Is subtraction associative? Try a specific triple:

$$(5 - 2) - 1 \overset{?}{=} 5 - (2 - 1)$$
$$\|\qquad\qquad\qquad\|$$
$$3 - 1 \qquad\qquad 5 - 1$$
$$\|\qquad\qquad\qquad\|$$
$$2 \qquad\qquad\quad 4$$

No, subtraction is not associative.

We have seen that some binary operations are associative and others are not. The fact that both $+$ and $\cdot$ are associative operations on W can thus be expected to have significant consequences.

The Commutative Properties

The **commutative property of addition** states the following:

$$a + b = b + a$$

for all whole numbers a and b. In particular,

$$2 + 19 = 19 + 2$$

Young children, who add by counting, probably prefer the calculation on the right-hand side. It is easier to start at 19 and count forward 2—"twenty, twenty-one"—than it is to start at 2 and count forward 19. How one learns to match the word *commutative* with the order reversal property, $a + b = b + a$, is not clear. It might be helpful to think of how a commuter train looks in the morning:

and how that same train looks at night:

Like the associative property of addition, the commutative property generalizes to sums of any number of terms. One can freely rearrange the terms in an addition expression without affecting the sum.

The **commutative property of multiplication** states the following:

$$a \cdot b = b \cdot a$$

for all whole numbers a and b. The main value of this property to children is that it cuts the job of learning multiplication facts nearly in half. If one has already learned that $3 \cdot 8 = 24$, then there is no need to struggle with $8 \cdot 3$.

Like the associative property of multiplication, the commutative property generalizes to products of more than two factors.

Now to our other mathematical systems. Is $\wedge$ a commutative operation on N? No, it is not, because

$$2 \wedge 3 = 2^3 = 8$$

whereas

$$3 \wedge 2 = 3^2 = 9$$

Is (m) a commutative operation on N? Yes, clearly it is. Is $-$ a a commutative operation on I? No, it is not, because

$$5 - 8 = {}^-3$$

whereas

$$8 - 5 = 3$$

The Identity Element Properties

Adding 0 to a whole number is a little like adding turpentine to paint: It leaves the other addend unchanged. Thus

$$6 + 0 = 6 \qquad 0 + 13 = 13 \qquad 0 + 1 = 1$$

We say that 0 is the **identity element for the addition operation,** and we refer to the following property as the **additive property of zero.**

$$a + 0 = a \qquad \text{and} \qquad 0 + a = a$$

The multiplication operation also has an identity element, namely 1:

$$6 \cdot 1 = 6 \qquad 1 \cdot 13 = 13 \qquad 0 \cdot 1 = 0$$

Multiplying by 1 leaves the other factor unchanged. In general:

$$a \cdot 1 = a \qquad \text{and} \qquad 1 \cdot a = a$$

for any whole number a. We call this property the **multiplicative property of one,** and we refer to 1 as the **identity element for multiplication.**

Does $\wedge$ have an identity element in N? The equations

$$7 \wedge 1 = 7^1 = 7 \qquad 31 \wedge 1 = 31^1 = 31$$

seem to suggest that 1 is an identity. It is when it appears on the right, but when it appears on the left, it certainly does not leave the other number alone:

$$1 \wedge 7 = 1 \neq 7 \qquad 1 \wedge 31 = 1 \neq 31$$

Thus 1 is not an identity element for ∧. It is not hard to convince oneself that there is no number that is an identity for ∧.

Does ⓜ have an identity element in N? Yes, it does. The equations

$$1 \text{ ⓜ } 4 = 4 \qquad 13 \text{ ⓜ } 1 = 13$$

show clearly that 1 is the identity element for ⓜ.

Does the subtraction operation, $-$, have an identity element in I? No, it does not. Although 0 acts like an identity element on the right, it does not act like one on the left.

The Distributive Property

So far the properties of the whole number system have come in pairs, one for addition and a corresponding one for multiplication. The distributive property is the exception. It stands alone and relates addition and multiplication. An example of the distributive property is

$$4 \cdot (12 + 5) = 4 \cdot 12 + 4 \cdot 5$$

The factor 4 is "distributed" to both terms of the sum. Here is an abstract formulation of the simplest version of the **distributive property.**

$$a \cdot (b + c) = a \cdot b + a \cdot c \quad \text{and} \quad (a + b) \cdot c = a \cdot c + b \cdot c$$

A few of the many generalizations of this basic property are

$$a \cdot (b + c + d) = a \cdot b + a \cdot c + a \cdot d$$

$$(a + b) \cdot (c + d) = a \cdot c + a \cdot d + b \cdot c + b \cdot d$$

You probably recall how the distributive property underlies the common multiplication algorithms:

$$237 \cdot 58 = (200 + 30 + 7) \cdot (50 + 8)$$

$$= 200 \cdot 50 + 30 \cdot 50 + 7 \cdot 50 + 200 \cdot 8 + 30 \cdot 8 + 7 \cdot 8$$

$$= \cdots$$

Technically, we should say that "multiplication distributes over addition," because if we reverse the roles of $+$ and $\cdot$, we get something false:

$$a \cdot (b + c) = a \cdot b + a \cdot c \qquad \text{true}$$

$$a + (b \cdot c) = (a + b) \cdot (a + c) \qquad \text{false}$$

Addition is not distributive over multiplication.

Is exponentiation distributive over maximization? That is,

$$a \wedge (b \text{ ⓜ } c) \stackrel{?}{=} (a \wedge b) \text{ ⓜ } (a \text{ ⓜ } c)$$

Let's test this equation with some specific numbers, say $a = 3$, $b = 4$, and $c = 2$:

$$3 \wedge (4 \text{ⓜ} 2) = 3 \wedge 4 = 81$$

$$(3 \wedge 4) \text{ⓜ} (3 \wedge 2) = 81 \text{ⓜ} 9 = 81$$

Thus

$$3 \wedge (4 \text{ⓜ} 2) = (3 \wedge 4) \text{ⓜ} (3 \wedge 2)$$

One instance of distributivity does not, of course, prove that the property holds in general, but it does provide some evidence in that direction. Can you give a convincing argument why

$$a \wedge (b \text{ⓜ} c) = (a \wedge b) \text{ⓜ} (a \wedge c)$$

for every choice of values for a, b, and c?

Is maximization distributive over exponentiation? That is,

$$a \text{ⓜ} (b \wedge c) \stackrel{?}{=} (a \text{ⓜ} b) \wedge (a \text{ⓜ} c)$$

Let's test again with $a = 3$, $b = 4$, and $c = 2$:

$$3 \text{ⓜ} (4 \wedge 2) = 3 \text{ⓜ} 16 = 16$$

$$(3 \text{ⓜ} 4) \wedge (3 \text{ⓜ} 2) = 4 \wedge 3 = 64$$

Thus maximization is definitely not distributive over exponentiation. A single *counterexample* is enough to establish that fact incontrovertibly.

Order of Operations

We mentioned that when parentheses appear in an expression, they say, "Do this first." For example, in the expression

$$(7 + 5) \cdot 4$$

they tell us to first add 7 and 5, then multiply the resulting number by 4. When no parentheses appear in an expression, there are two conventions that govern the order of operations. Until now, we have left these conventions unspoken, but you probably followed them unconsciously by force of habit.

The first might be called the **hierarchy convention:** In the absence of parentheses operations at a higher level in the following hierarchy are performed before operations at a lower level:

Hierarchy of Operations

Exponentiation
Multiplication and Division
Addition and Subtraction

EXAMPLE 1   Simplify.
(a) $60 - 4 \cdot 2^3$
(b) $(5 + 3)^2 \div 16$

Solution   (a) $60 - 4 \cdot 2^3 = 60 - 4 \cdot 8$ exponentiation is done first
$= 60 - 32$ then multiplication
$= 28$ then subtraction
(b) $(5 + 3)^2 \div 16 = 8^2 \div 16$ parentheses say, "Do this first"
$= 64 \div 16 \Big\}$ exponentiation precedes division
$= 4 \quad \Big\}$ ❏

The second convention is the **left-to-right convention:** In the absence of parentheses, if two operations at the same hierarchical level appear in an expression, they are to be performed in left-to-right order.

EXAMPLE 2   Simplify.
(a) $12 - 8 + 3 - (5 + 1)$
(b) $24 \div 4 \cdot 2$

Solution   (a) $12 - 8 + 3 - (5 + 1) = 12 - 8 + 3 - 6$ parentheses say, "Do
this first"
$= 4 + 3 - 6 \Big]$ additions and sub-
$= 7 - 6 \Big\}$ tractions are done
$= 1 \quad \Big]$ left to right

(b) Since there are no parentheses and since multiplication and division are at the same hierarchical level, they are performed in left-to-right order:

$$24 \div 4 \cdot 2 = 6 \cdot 2$$
$$= 12$$

Note: Since not everyone is fully conversant with the left-to-right convention, a good practice is to insert a pair of (superfluous) parentheses to remove all doubt about what order of operations is intended: $(24 \div 4) \cdot 2$.   ❏

If you have an AOS (algebraic operating system) calculator, then the two order-of-operations conventions we have just described are built in.

EXAMPLE 3   Evaluate the following expression first by hand and then by using an AOS calculator: $5 + 6 \div 2 \cdot 3 - 4 \cdot 2 - 5$.

Solution   By hand,

$$5 + 6 \div 2 \cdot 3 - 4 \cdot 2 - 5 = 5 + 3 \cdot 3 - 4 \cdot 2 - 5$$
$$= 5 + 9 - 8 - 5$$

$$= 14 - 8 - 5$$
$$= 6 - 5$$
$$= 1$$

By calculator, perform these keystrokes in order:

$$\boxed{5}\boxed{+}\boxed{6}\boxed{\div}\boxed{2}\boxed{\times}\boxed{3}\boxed{-}\boxed{4}\boxed{\times}\boxed{2}\boxed{-}\boxed{5}\boxed{=}$$ ❑

EXERCISE SET 4.3

1. Each of the following is an instance of one of the seven structural properties of the whole number system investigated so far. Identify the property.
   (a) $(3 \cdot 4) \cdot 12 = 3 \cdot (4 \cdot 12)$
   (b) $5 + 19 = 19 + 5$
   (c) $5 \cdot 19 = 19 \cdot 5$
   (d) $12 \cdot 1 = 12$
   (e) $7 + (3 + 5) = (7 + 3) + 5$
   (f) $(3 + x) \cdot 9 = 3 \cdot 9 + x \cdot 9$
   (g) $1 \cdot 0 = 0$
   (h) $1 + 0 = 1$
   (i) $9 \cdot 7 = 7 \cdot 9$
   (j) $3 \cdot 5 + 8 = 5 \cdot 3 + 8$
   (k) $3 + (6 + 3) = (6 + 3) + 3$
   (l) $6(x + 12) = 6(12 + x)$
   (m) $4 \cdot (3x) = (4 \cdot 3)x$
   (n) $5 + (5 + 5) = (5 + 5) + 5$
   (o) $(12x + 3) + 0 = 12x + 3$
   (p) $(5 + x) \cdot 4 = 4 \cdot (5 + x)$

2. The associative and commutative properties justify regrouping and rearranging terms in a sum or factors in a product. Compute each of the following mentally by first choosing a particularly convenient arrangement and grouping. (There may be several equally good ways.)
   Example
   $$8 + 6 + 2 + 4 = (8 + 2) + (6 + 4)$$
   $$= 10 + 10 = 20$$
   (a) $7 + 6 + 4 + 3$
   (b) $1 + 8 + 9 + 2 + 7$
   (c) $1 + 2 + 3 + 4 + 5 + 6 + 7 + 8 + 9$
   (d) $1 + 2 + 3 + 4 + \cdots + 97 + 98 + 99$
   (e) $2 \cdot 9 \cdot 5$
   (f) $2 \cdot 9 \cdot 3 \cdot 5$

   (g) $5 \cdot 5 \cdot 8 \cdot 6$
   (h) $6 \cdot 5 \cdot 4 \cdot 3 \cdot 2 \cdot 1$
   (i) $15 \cdot 8 \cdot 3 \cdot 0 \cdot 2 \cdot 6$

3. Ann Marie earns \$2 per hour for baby-sitting. Last week she sat for 3 hours on Friday and 5 on Saturday. Find the total amount of money she earned in two different ways. Which structural property do your solutions illustrate?

4. In the song "The Twelve Days of Christmas," how many gifts are given? (Imagine, at least, a systematic list.)

5. Use the three words *big dog show* to illustrate that concatenation (linking together) of English expressions is a nonassociative operation. Use the two words *dog show* to illustrate its noncommutativity.

6. The binary operation $*$ on W is defined by
   $$a * b = a + 2b$$
   (a) Compute $(2 * 3) * 4$ and $2 * (3 * 4)$.
   (b) Is $*$ associative?
   (c) Compute $3 * 4$ and $4 * 3$.
   (d) Is $*$ commutative?
   (e) Compute $5 * 0$ and $0 * 7$.
   (f) Is 0 an identity element for $*$?

7. The averaging operation a defined by
   $$x \, ⓐ \, y = \frac{x + y}{2}$$
   is a binary operation on Q.
   (a) Is ⓐ associative?
   (b) Is ⓐ commutative?
   (c) Is 0 an identity element for ⓐ?
   (d) Is any number an identity with respect to ⓐ?

8. Which of these structural properties are true in the system of seven-clock arithmetic, $[I_7, +_7, \cdot_7]$?
   Give an illustration for each one.

Associative prop. of $+_7$	Associative prop. of $\cdot_7$
Commutative prop. of $+_7$	Commutative prop. of $\cdot_7$
Additive prop. of 0	Multiplicative prop. of 1

$\cdot_7$ Distributes over $+_7$

9. Evaluate each expression using the conventions governing the order of operations.
   (a) $21 \div 3 + 4$
   (b) $21 \div (3 + 4)$
   (c) $40 - (3 \cdot 5 - 8)$
   (d) $40 - 3 \cdot 5 - 8$
   (e) $10 - 3 + 6 - 1$
   (f) $4 \cdot 12 \div 2 \cdot 3$
   (g) $6^2 \div 2 \cdot (5 \cdot 4 - 11)$
   (h) $[(3 + 4)^2 - 5 \cdot 2] \div 3 + 10$

10. Sometimes, grouping is indicated by the position of numerals in an expression rather than by parentheses. For example,
    $$2^{3+4} \quad \text{means} \quad 2^{(3+4)}$$
    and
    $$\frac{13 - 1}{7 - 3} \quad \text{means} \quad (13 - 1) \div (7 - 3)$$
    Evaluate.
    (a) $(2^{3+4} - 8) \div 10$
    (b) $\dfrac{12 \cdot (5 - 2)}{2 \cdot 4 + 1}$

11. Give the sequence of keystrokes you would use to evaluate each expression. (If your calculator has parentheses buttons, evaluate each expression twice, once with and once without parentheses.)
    (a) $[3 + 5(9 - 3)/2]/6$
    (b) $[(9 - 1)/2 + 5]/[2 + 1]$

12. Interesting analogies are suggested by the following observations:
    1. Multiplication is repeated addition; for example,
       $$4 \cdot 3 = 4 + 4 + 4$$

2. Exponentiation is repeated multiplication; for example,
   $$4 \wedge 3 = 4 \cdot 4 \cdot 4$$
   Define a new operation ★ to be "repeated exponentiation" and compute $4 ★ 3$.

13. Suppose that $*$ is a commutative binary operation on the set $S = \{a, b, c\}$, and suppose that c is the identity element for $*$.
    (a) Fill in the missing entries in the Cayley table in Figure 4.14.

$*$	a	b	c
a	a		
b	c	a	
c			

Figure 4.14

    (b) Does $(a * a) * b = a * (a * b)$?

★ 14. How many different commutative binary operations can be defined on the following sets? *Hint:* Refer to Exercise 16 in Exercise set 4.1.
    (a) A 2-element set
    (b) A 3-element set
    (c) An n-element set

★ 15. How many binary operations are there on the set $\{i, a, b, c\}$ that have i as an identity element?

★ 16. How many of the binary operations in Exercise 15 are commutative?

★ 17. In advanced mathematics courses numbers are attached to certain "infinite sums." For example, the number 1 is attached to
    $$\frac{1}{2} + \frac{1}{4} + \frac{1}{8} + \cdots$$
    because the "partial sums"
    $$\frac{1}{2}, \frac{1}{2} + \frac{1}{4}, \frac{1}{2} + \frac{1}{4} + \frac{1}{8}, \cdots$$
    "approach" 1. An infinite sum like
    $$1 + {}^-1 + 1 + {}^-1 + 1 + {}^-1 + \cdots$$
    on the other hand, is assigned no number, since the partial sums
    $$1, 1 + {}^-1, 1 + {}^-1 + 1, \cdots$$
    approach no single number but oscillate between two numbers. Insert parentheses in the infinite

sum of 1s and ⁻1s so that the partial sums approach the following numbers.
(a) 0
(b) 1
Conclude that there is no associative property for arbitrary infinite sums.

4.4 *Two More Structural Properties: Logical Consequences*

Two more structural properties are needed to describe the whole number system. These *cancellation* properties are more technical than the seven discussed in the previous section, and are included here only for the sake of mathematical completeness. They are rarely mentioned in the precollege curriculum. Perhaps the reason the two cancellation properties are the most difficult of the nine structural properties is that, unlike the first seven, they are of the if-then form.

The Cancellation Properties

The **cancellation property of addition** asserts the following:

If $b + a = c + a$, then $b = c$.

This statement is just the addition property of equality with the "if" and "then" clauses reversed; that is, the cancellation property of addition is the **converse** of the addition property of equality. (See Appendix A for a fuller discussion of converse.)

Loosely speaking, the cancellation property of addition says that we can subtract the same whole number from both sides of an equation. At this point, of course, subtraction has not been defined. We have only two binary operations on W, addition and multiplication. Later when we work with the set of integers, the cancellation property of addition will be subsumed under the addition property of equality: To subtract 3 from both sides of an equation, we will instead add ⁻3 to both sides.

EXAMPLE 1   Assuming that $8 = 5 + 3$, use the cancellation property of addition to solve the equation $x + 3 = 8$.

Solution
$$x + 3 = 8$$
$$\Downarrow \qquad \text{substitution}$$
$$x + 3 = 5 + 3$$
$$\Downarrow \qquad \text{cancellation property of addition}$$
$$x = 5$$

❏

In our theoretical development of whole number arithmetic, the very definition of subtraction will depend on the cancellation property of addition. (See Exercises 6 and 8.)

The corresponding **cancellation property of multiplication** has a restriction. You are not permitted to cancel a common factor 0. If you could, you could "prove" many wonderful things, among them that $1 = 2$:

$$(?) \quad 0 = 0 \;\Rightarrow\; 0 \cdot 1 = 0 \cdot 2 \;\Rightarrow\; 1 = 2 \quad (\text{no!})$$

↑
Canceling 0s

The general statement follows.

> If $a \cdot b = a \cdot c$ and if $a \neq 0$, then $b = c$.

The importance of this property is that it allows us to divide before the division operation is defined. Also, it underlies the very definition of (exact) division in the same way that the cancellation property of addition underlies subtraction. (See Exercise 7 and 9.)

EXAMPLE 2   Assuming that $15 = 3 \cdot 5$, use the cancellation property of multiplication to solve the equation $3x = 15$.

Solution

$$3 \cdot x = 15$$
$$\Downarrow \qquad \text{substitution}$$
$$3 \cdot x = 3 \cdot 5$$
$$\Downarrow \qquad \text{cancellation property of multiplication}$$
$$x = 5 \qquad\qquad\qquad ❏$$

When we study the system of rational numbers, the cancellation property of multiplication will be subsumed under the multiplication property of equality: To divide both sides of an equation by 3, we will instead multiply both sides by $\frac{1}{3}$.

The Multiplicative Properties of Zero

At this point we have identified 11 basic properties of the whole number system:

LOGICAL PROPERTIES

Substitution	RST of equality

STRUCTURAL PROPERTIES

Associative property of addition	Associative property of multiplication
Commutative property of addition	Commutative property of multiplication
Additive property of 0	Multiplicative property of 1
Cancellation property of addition	Cancellation property of multiplication

Distributive property

We will assume that these 11 properties are true and see what consequences flow from them.

This approach should be familiar to you from your high school geometry course. There you accepted as true a list of properties of the following sort:

Through any two points there is exactly one line.
Through any three noncollinear points there is exactly one plane.

You called these properties *axioms* or *postulates*. Then you went on to *deduce* other properties from them and called those properties *theorems*. In a similar way, we can think of the 11 properties as some axioms for whole number arithmetic. Now we want to see what theorems follow from them.

Theorem 1   Any whole number times zero equals zero. In symbols,

$$a \cdot 0 = 0$$

Proof.   The word *proof* is a sign that what follows is a logical deduction of the theorem from the (assumed) axioms. A proof normally consists of a chain of *statements,* each supported by a *reason*. In this proof, don't worry about how we arrived at the chain of statements. Do convince yourself that the given reasons adequately justify the statements.

Statements	*Reasons*
1. $a + 0 = a$	additive property of 0
2. $a = a \cdot 1$	multiplicative property of 1
3. $a \cdot 1 = a \cdot (1 + 0)$	additive property of 0 (and substitution)
4. $a \cdot (1 + 0) = a \cdot 1 + a \cdot 0$	distributive property
5. $a \cdot 1 + a \cdot 0 = a + a \cdot 0$	multiplicative property of 1 (and substitution)

6. Thus $a + 0 = a + a \cdot 0$ transitive property of equality (applied to statements 1–5)

7. Thus $0 = a \cdot 0$ cancellation property of addition

8. Thus $a \cdot 0 = 0$ symmetric property of equality

Q.E.D.

(The initials Q.E.D. stand for the Latin *quod erat demonstrandum,* meaning "which was to be proved," and indicate that the proof has been completed.)

Often the proof of a theorem does not lend itself to the statement-reason format. In such cases the train of logical thought is indicated in paragraph form. The following proof is of this type. Its logical structure is not simple, so again you should not be too concerned about the construction of the proof. You should, however, examine the reasoning critically, line by line, to convince yourself that it is sound.

Theorem 2   The only way a product can be zero is for one or both factors to be zero. In symbols,

$$a \cdot b = 0 \ \Rightarrow \ a = 0 \ \ or \ \ b = 0$$

Proof.   To prove the implication, we temporarily assume that $a \cdot b = 0$. That is, we add $a \cdot b = 0$ to our collection of true things (11 axioms and Theorem 1). Now we try to deduce, from the augmented collection, that $a = 0$ or $b = 0$. The argument goes like this. Either

$$a = 0 \quad \text{or} \quad a \neq 0$$

In the first case, $a = 0$, it is certainly true that

$$a = 0 \quad \text{or} \quad b = 0$$

In the second case, $a \neq 0$, we observe that

$a \cdot b = 0$ assumption

$a \cdot 0 = 0$ Theorem 1

and thus

$a \cdot b = a \cdot 0$ transitive property of equality (or substitution)

But now, since $a \neq 0$, we can invoke the cancellation property of multiplication to get

$$b = 0$$

from which it again follows that

$$a = 0 \quad \text{or} \quad b = 0$$ Q.E.D.

Theorems 1 and 2 will be referred to collectively as the **multiplicative properties of zero.** In symbols:

$$a \cdot b = 0 \iff a = 0 \quad \text{or} \quad b = 0$$

The left-to-right implication is Theorem 2; the right-to-left implication follows from Theorem 1. The double arrow symbol $\iff$ is often read "if and only if."

EXERCISE SET 4.4

1. Fill in each box with a number to make the implication true.
   (a) If $x + 5 = 9 + 5$, then $x = \square$.
   (b) If $9 \cdot x = 9 \cdot 13$, then $x = \square$.
   (c) $2x + 3 = 12 + 3 \Rightarrow 2x = \square$.
   (d) $4x = \boxed{4} \cdot 11 \Rightarrow x = 11$.

2. Show that the equation $2x + 3 = 2 \cdot 5 + 3$ has solution set $\{5\}$ by showing:
   (a) If $x = 5$, then $2x + 3 = 2 \cdot 5 + 3$.
   (b) If $2x + 3 = 2 \cdot 5 + 3$, then $x = 5$.

3. Solve each equation by inspection, keeping in mind the nine structural properties of W.
   (a) $17x = 17 \cdot 3$ (b) $5 + x = 5 + 11$
   (c) $(9 + x) + 4 = 9 + 4$
   (d) $9x + 4 = 9 + 4$
   (e) $5 \cdot x \cdot 8 = 3 \cdot 5 \cdot 7 \cdot 8$
   (f) $3x = 5x$

4. Show that the equation $x \cdot x = 7 \cdot x$ has solution set $\{0, 7\}$ by showing the following:
   (a) If $x = 0$ or $x = 7$, then $x \cdot x = 7 \cdot x$.
   (b) If $x \cdot x = 7 \cdot x$, then $x = 0$ or $x = 7$.

5. Use the multiplicative properties of zero to find all solutions (in W) to each of the following equations.
   (a) $3 \cdot x = 0$ $x = 0$ (b) $5 \cdot x \cdot 7 \cdot 0 = 0$ infinite solut.
   (c) $3 + 0 \cdot x = 7$ No solution   (d) $x(x - 1)(x - 5) = 0$ $x = 0$

6. Prove that the equation $x + b = a$, where a and b are whole numbers, can have no more than one solution in W. *Hint:* Suppose x_1 and x_2 are solutions. Then $x_1 + b = a$ and $x_2 + b = a$. Thus. . .

7. Prove that the equation $b \cdot x = a$, where a and b are whole numbers and $b \neq 0$, can have no more than one solution in W.

8. Exercise 6 justifies the missing-addend definition of subtraction of whole numbers: $a - b =$ *the whole number solution to the equation* $x + b = a$, *if there is one.* Use this definition to find the following:
   (a) $12 - 4$ (b) $4 - 4$ (c) $7 - 0$

9. Exercise 7 justifies the missing-factor definition of exact division of whole numbers: $a/b =$ *the whole number solution to the equation* $b \cdot x = a$, *if there is one.* Use this definition to find the following:
   (a) $12/4$ (b) $4/4$ (c) $7/1$

The cancellation properties of both addition and multiplication are true in seven-clock arithmetic, as the following two exercises suggest.

10. Fill in missing reasons in the proof of this instance of the cancellation property of addition:
    If $x +_7 3 = 5 +_7 3$, then $x = 5$

Statements	Reasons
$x +_7 3 = 5 +_7 3$	given
$(x +_7 3) +_7 4$	
$\quad = (5 +_7 3) +_7 4$	(a) *add it. prop. of equality*
$x +_7 (3 +_7 4)$	
$\quad = 5 +_7 (3 +_7 4)$	(b) *assoc. prop*
$x +_7 0 = 5 +_7 0$	definition of $+_7$
$x = 5$	(c) *additive prop. of 0*

11. Fill in missing reasons in the proof of this instance of the cancellation property of multiplication:

If $x \cdot_7 4 = 5 \cdot_7 4$, then $x = 5$

Statements		Reasons
$x \cdot_7 4 = 5 \cdot_7 4$	(a)	*given*
$(x \cdot_7 4) \cdot_7 2$ $= (5 \cdot_7 4) \cdot_7 2$	(b)	*mult. prop.*
$x \cdot_7 (4 \cdot_7 2)$ $= 5 \cdot_7 (4 \cdot_7 2)$	(c)	*assoc. prop of $\cdot_7$*
$x \cdot_7 1 = 5 \cdot_7 1$	(d)	*multiplication fact*
$x = 5$	(e)	*identity prop*

12. Using Exercise 10 as a model, write a statement-reason proof that if $x +_7 6 = 5 +_7 6$, then $x = 5$.

13. Using Exercise 11 as a model, write a statement-reason proof that if $3 \cdot_7 x = 3 \cdot_7 4$, then $x = 4$.

14. Because seven-clock arithmetic satisfies the two cancellation properties, we can define (unambiguously) seven-clock subtraction and division, just as we did whole-number subtraction and division, in terms of missing addends and missing factors respectively. Think in terms of missing addends and factors to assign a seven-clock value to each of these expressions:

    (a) $5 - 3$ (b) $2 - 6$
    (c) $2/5$ (d) $4/3$

15. A binary operation $*$ is defined on W by
    $a * b = 2a + 3b$
    Prove that "$*$ has the cancellation property."
    (You will first have to state what the phrase in quotation marks means.)

16. Find the flaw in this "proof" that $1 = 2$.
    $$a = b$$
    $$ab = b^2$$
    $$ab - a^2 = b^2 - a^2$$
    $$a(b - a) = (b + a)(b - a)$$
    $$a = b + a$$
    $$a = a + a$$
    $$1a = 2a$$
    $$1 = 2$$

17. We have assumed that the set W of whole numbers is closed under multiplication. Explain why the subset N of natural numbers is also closed under multiplication.

★ 18. Decide what is meant by six-clock arithmetic; that is, define I_6, $+_6$, and $\cdot_6$. Investigate the multiplicative properties of zero in six-clock arithmetic. Investigate the cancellation law of multiplication in six-clock arithmetic.

4.5   *Numeration-Related Properties of the Whole Number System; Algorithms Revisited*

The nine structural properties that we just finished describing are fundamental truths about the whole number system. They remain valid no matter how one represents the whole numbers—by Caveman scratches, by Egyptian hieroglyphics, or by base-seventeen numerals. In this section we will supplement these abstract properties with four more concrete properties that are specifically related to our base-ten numeration system. From a theoretical point of view these numeration-related properties are of lesser importance, but from a computational standpoint they are essential. They play a fundamental role in the common algorithms of whole-number arithmetic, as we shall see.

Elementary Addition and Multiplication Facts

Deduction of the multiplicative properties of zero from the two logical and nine structural properties of the whole number system is an impressive feat. But after such a triumph, we have to admit that we cannot prove

$$1 + 1 = 2$$

That is, although our assumptions tell us something about $=$, $+$, and 1, they tell us nothing about the squiggle, 2. And our present point of view is to refuse to use any information that is not explicitly written down.

One way to get around this and similar problems is to define 2 to be $1 + 1$, 3 to be $2 + 1$, 4 to be $3 + 1$, and so on. A taste of this approach is given in Exercises 1 and 2, but its tedium becomes clear when we realize that $1 + 1 = 2$, $2 + 2 = 4$, and $2 \cdot 2 = 4$ are only a few of the many arithmetic facts that we eventually want in our collection of true things. So we take a different approach.

We simply *assume* all of the **elementary addition facts** up through $9 + 9 = 18$ (see Figure 4.15). And we *assume* all of the **elementary multiplication facts** up through $9 \times 9 = 81$ (see Figure 4.16).

Notice that we have incorporated into our list of assumptions exactly the same facts that youngsters are expected to commit to memory. These facts provide complete information about single-digit numerals. Soon we shall list two further assumptions that give meaning to multidigit numerals, but before we do, let us make some observations about the elementary addition and multiplication facts.

+	1	2	3	4	5	6	7	8	9
1	2	3	4	5	6	7	8	9	10
2	3	4	5	6	7	8	9	10	11
3	4	5	6	7	8	9	10	11	12
4	5	6	7	8	9	10	11	12	13
5	6	7	8	9	10	11	12	13	14
6	7	8	9	10	11	12	13	14	15
7	8	9	10	11	12	13	14	15	16
8	9	10	11	12	13	14	15	16	17
9	10	11	12	13	14	15	16	17	18

Figure 4.15 Elementary addition facts.

•	1	2	3	4	5	6	7	8	9
1	1	2	3	4	5	6	7	8	9
2	2	4	6	8	10	12	14	16	18
3	3	6	9	12	15	18	21	24	27
4	4	8	12	16	20	24	28	32	36
5	5	10	15	20	25	30	35	40	45
6	6	12	18	24	30	36	42	48	54
7	7	14	21	28	35	42	49	56	63
8	8	16	24	32	40	48	56	64	72
9	9	18	27	36	45	54	63	72	81

Figure 4.16 Elementary multiplication facts.

First, these facts are clearly numeration-related properties. They describe how certain small whole numbers behave when dressed in base-ten, Hindu-Arabic clothing. In another base, say base six, the "fact"

$$3 + 4 = 7$$

is nonsensical, and the "fact"

$$3 \cdot 4 = 12$$

is false.

Second, much of what is in the tables is superfluous. Certainly, the first row and first column of multiplication facts are already implied by the multiplicative property of 1. And, of course, everything above the upper-left–to–lower-right diagonal in each table is excess baggage because of the commutative properties.

Third, there is more information in these tables than meets the eye, although they seem to tell us only how single-digit numbers add and multiply. In fact, when used in combination with the structural properties, they give us information about certain multidigit numbers too. For example, we learn that $5 + 12 = 17$ as follows:

$$
\begin{aligned}
5 + 12 &= 5 + (3 + 9) & &\text{elementary addition fact (and substitution)}\\
&= (5 + 3) + 9 & &\text{associative property of addition}\\
&= 8 + 9 & &\text{elementary addition fact (and substitution)}\\
&= 17 & &\text{elementary addition fact}
\end{aligned}
$$

Similarly, we can deduce that $4 \cdot 18 = 72$:

$$4 \cdot 18 \stackrel{?}{=} 4 \cdot (2 \cdot 9) \stackrel{?}{=} (4 \cdot 2) \cdot 9 \stackrel{?}{=} 8 \cdot 9 \stackrel{?}{=} 72$$

and that $15 + 12 = 27$:

$$15 + 12 \stackrel{?}{=} 3 \cdot 5 + 3 \cdot 4 \stackrel{?}{=} 3 \cdot (5 + 4) \stackrel{?}{=} 3 \cdot 9 \stackrel{?}{=} 27$$

There seems to be much buried treasure in the tables.

Expanded Form and Exponents

Is the sum $14 + 9$ buried somewhere in the tables? A little reflection tells us that it couldn't be. We know (intuitively) that 23 is the sum we are looking for. But we also know that 23 is not in the addition table, since the largest entry there is 18; and 23 is not in the multiplication table, since it is not the product of numbers less than 10. Thus there is no way we can find information about 23. We are in the same situation we were in with 2 before the tables of facts gave it meaning.

One procedure for finding out about 23 is to expand it into tens and units:

$$23 = 2 \cdot 10 + 3$$

To justify such a move, we need to add another assumption to our list, an assumption that formalizes the caramel diagram interpretation that we attached to Hindu-Arabic numerals in the preceding chapter. We call it **expanded form,** and its application is illustrated in the following examples:

$$14 = 1 \cdot 10 + 4$$
$$270 = 2 \cdot 10^2 + 7 \cdot 10 + 0$$
$$50{,}137 = 5 \cdot 10^4 + 0 \cdot 10^3 + 1 \cdot 10^2 + 3 \cdot 10 + 7$$
$$6 \cdot 10^3 + 1 \cdot 10^2 + 0 \cdot 10 + 8 = 6108$$

Notice from the examples that we have adopted these two rather arbitrary conventions: (1) We attach all digits that appear in a numeral, *including zeros,* to appropriate powers of ten; (2) we write 10 rather than 10^1.

One loose end remains to be tied up. Strictly speaking, it is meaningless to say that

$$270 = 2 \cdot 10^2 + 7 \cdot 10 + 0$$

until we have declared what is meant by the superscript 2 on the 10. Let us review the definition, terminology, and one property of the exponentiation operation.

Here is the definition.

For any whole number a and any natural number n,

$$a^n = \underbrace{a \cdot a \cdot a \cdot \ \cdots \ \cdot a}_{n \text{ factors}}$$

For example,

$$10^2 = 10 \cdot 10$$
$$5^3 = 5 \cdot 5 \cdot 5$$
$$3^5 = 3 \cdot 3 \cdot 3 \cdot 3 \cdot 3$$

The expression a^n is read "a to the nth *power*"; a is called the **base,** and n the **exponent.** Thus the exponent tells how many times to list the base as a factor.

The one property that will be needed in this chapter is suggested by the following example:

$$5^3 \cdot 5^4 = \underbrace{(5 \cdot 5 \cdot 5)}_{3} \cdot \underbrace{(5 \cdot 5 \cdot 5 \cdot 5)}_{4} = \underbrace{5 \cdot 5 \cdot 5 \cdot 5 \cdot 5 \cdot 5 \cdot 5}_{7} = 5^7$$

In general:

For any whole number a and any natural numbers m and n,

$$a^m \cdot a^n = a^{m+n}$$

In words: To multiply two powers having the same base, retain the base and add the exponents. We will group this property together with the preceding definition under the single heading **exponents.**

In summary, then, we have added four numeration-related properties to our original list of two logical and nine structural properties:

LOGICAL PROPERTIES

Substitution	RST of equality

STRUCTURAL PROPERTIES

Associative property of addition	Associative property of multiplication
Commutative property of addition	Commutative property of multiplication
Additive property of 0	Multiplicative property of 1
Cancellation property of addition	Cancellation property of multiplication

Distributive property

NUMERATION-RELATED PROPERTIES

Elementary Addition Facts
Elementary Multiplication Facts
Expanded Form
Exponents

These 15 properties are enough to allow us to calculate sums and products of arbitrary whole numbers, as we shall demonstrate now. Before we begin, though, remember that the purpose here is to clarify, in your own mind, the role of the basic properties. This material is *not* anything you would try to teach to children. Algorithms are explained to children as we explained them in Chapter 3.

Calculating Sums

Let us begin by considering an addition problem say $285 + 167$. Our calculation will actually be a statement-reason *proof* that $285 + 167 = 452$. The reasons will all be chosen from the list of 15 properties. To keep the proof manageable, we will cite just one main reason at each step; the reasons "substitution" and "associative property of addition" will often be suppressed.

Here is some advice: Don't worry yet about how to arrive at the statements; concentrate first on simply supplying reasons for the given statements. A good way to give yourself practice in recognizing the 15 properties in context is to cover the reason column with a sheet of paper and see whether you can fill it

Figure 4.17

in. Sometimes, deciding on a reason is difficult because the change from one line to the next is buried in the middle of a complicated expression. It's like trying to decide how the two pictures in Figure 4.17 differ. So look at the two arithmetic expressions, determine how they differ, and then give the reason that asserts that two expressions, differing in that way, are equal.

$285 + 167$

$= 2 \cdot 10^2 + 8 \cdot 10 + 5 + 1 \cdot 10^2 + 6 \cdot 10 + 7$ expanded form

$= 2 \cdot 10^2 + 1 \cdot 10^2 + 8 \cdot 10 + 6 \cdot 10 + 5 + 7$ commutative property of addition

$= 2 \cdot 10^2 + 1 \cdot 10^2 + 8 \cdot 10 + 6 \cdot 10 + 12$ elementary addition fact

$= 2 \cdot 10^2 + 1 \cdot 10^2 + 8 \cdot 10 + 6 \cdot 10 + 1 \cdot 10 + 2$ expanded form

$= 2 \cdot 10^2 + 1 \cdot 10^2 + (8 + 6 + 1) \cdot 10 + 2$ distributive property

$= 2 \cdot 10^2 + 1 \cdot 10^2 + (8 + 7) \cdot 10 + 2$ elementary addition fact

$= 2 \cdot 10^2 + 1 \cdot 10^2 + 15 \cdot 10 + 2$ elementary addition fact

$= 2 \cdot 10^2 + 1 \cdot 10^2 + (1 \cdot 10 + 5) \cdot 10 + 2$ expanded form

$= 2 \cdot 10^2 + 1 \cdot 10^2 + 1 \cdot 10 \cdot 10 + 5 \cdot 10 + 2$ distributive property

$= 2 \cdot 10^2 + 1 \cdot 10^2 + 1 \cdot 10^2 + 5 \cdot 10 + 2$ exponents

$= (2 + 1 + 1) \cdot 10^2 + 5 \cdot 10 + 2$ distributive property

$= (2 + 2) \cdot 10^2 + 5 \cdot 10 + 2$ elementary addition fact

$= 4 \cdot 10^2 + 5 \cdot 10 + 2$ elementary addition fact

$= 452$ expanded form

A similar analysis can be carried out for any other sum of whole numbers. In summary:

> The sum of any two whole numbers can be calculated by using only the 15 basic properties of the whole number system.

The arrangement of the steps in the calculation is not unique. The sequence we chose was suggested by the usual right-to-left algorithm: step 2 corresponds to writing 167 below 285 so that units are together, tens are together, and hundreds are together; steps 3–5 correspond to finding the sum of the units (12), writing the 2 and carrying the 1 to the tens column; steps 6–11 correspond to finding the sum of the tens (15), writing the 5, and carrying 1 to the hundreds column; the remaining steps correspond to adding the hundreds.

Calculating Products

We now illustrate the corresponding result about multiplication.

The product of any two whole numbers can be calculated by using only the 15 basic properties of the whole number system.

For multiplication, though, the situation is complicated. To attack straightforwardly an arbitrarily chosen product such as $539 \cdot 286$, the way we did the sum $285 + 167$, would require *several pages* of steps. We need to be more subtle. Our strategy will be to establish two simpler preliminary results and then combine them to get the general result about multiplication. This technique should be reminiscent of the way we developed the standard multiplication algorithm in the previous chapter.

Preliminary Result 1. The product of a single-digit whole number and an arbitrary whole number can be calculated by using only the 15 basic properties.

Consideration of the specific product $9 \cdot 286$ should be convincing evidence of the truth of preliminary result 1:

$$
\begin{array}{ll}
9 \cdot 286 = 9 \cdot (2 \cdot 10^2 + 8 \cdot 10 + 6) & \text{expanded form} \\[4pt]
\quad = 9 \cdot 2 \cdot 10^2 + 9 \cdot 8 \cdot 10 + 9 \cdot 6 & \text{distributive property} \\[4pt]
\quad = 9 \cdot 2 \cdot 10^2 + 9 \cdot 8 \cdot 10 + 54 & \text{elementary} \\
& \quad \text{multiplication fact} \\[4pt]
\quad = 9 \cdot 2 \cdot 10^2 + 9 \cdot 8 \cdot 10 + 5 \cdot 10 + 4 & \text{expanded form} \\[4pt]
\quad = 9 \cdot 2 \cdot 10^2 + (9 \cdot 8 + 5) \cdot 10 + 4 & \text{distributive property} \\[4pt]
\quad = 9 \cdot 2 \cdot 10^2 + (72 + 5) \cdot 10 + 4 & \text{elementary} \\
& \quad \text{multiplication fact} \\[4pt]
\quad = 9 \cdot 2 \cdot 10^2 + 77 \cdot 10 + 4 & \text{previously established} \\
& \quad \text{result about sums} \\[4pt]
\quad = 9 \cdot 2 \cdot 10^2 + (7 \cdot 10 + 7) \cdot 10 + 4 & \text{expanded form} \\[4pt]
\quad = 9 \cdot 2 \cdot 10^2 + 7 \cdot 10 \cdot 10 + 7 \cdot 10 + 4 & \text{distributive property} \\[4pt]
\quad = 9 \cdot 2 \cdot 10^2 + 7 \cdot 10^2 + 7 \cdot 10 + 4 & \text{exponents} \\[4pt]
\quad = (9 \cdot 2 + 7) \cdot 10^2 + 7 \cdot 10 + 4 & \text{distributive property} \\[4pt]
\quad = (18 + 7) \cdot 10^2 + 7 \cdot 10 + 4 & \text{elementary} \\
& \quad \text{multiplication fact} \\[4pt]
\quad = 25 \cdot 10^2 + 7 \cdot 10 + 4 & \text{previously established} \\
& \quad \text{result about sums} \\[4pt]
\quad = (2 \cdot 10 + 5) \cdot 10^2 + 7 \cdot 10 + 4 & \text{expanded form} \\[4pt]
\quad = 2 \cdot 10 \cdot 10^2 + 5 \cdot 10^2 + 7 \cdot 10 + 4 & \text{distributive property}
\end{array}
$$

$$= 2 \cdot 10^3 + 5 \cdot 10^2 + 7 \cdot 10 + 4 \qquad \text{exponents}$$
$$= 2574 \qquad \text{expanded form}$$

As before, the sequence of steps was suggested by the words one chants in computing the product

$$\begin{array}{r} 286 \\ \times 9 \\ \hline \end{array}$$

by the usual algorithm.

The second preliminary result describes the effect on its numeral of multiplying a whole number by a power of ten.

Preliminary Result 2. The effect of multiplying a whole number by 10 (by 10^2, by 10^3, . . .) is to append a zero (2 zeros, 3 zeros, . . .) to its (base-ten) numeral.

Again, consideration of a specific product, here $858 \cdot 10$, suggests the general truth of preliminary result 2.

$$858 \cdot 10 = (8 \cdot 10^2 + 5 \cdot 10 + 8) \cdot 10 \qquad \text{expanded form}$$
$$= 8 \cdot 10^2 \cdot 10 + 5 \cdot 10 \cdot 10 + 8 \cdot 10 \qquad \text{distributive property}$$
$$= 8 \cdot 10^3 + 5 \cdot 10^2 + 8 \cdot 10 \qquad \text{exponents}$$
$$= 8 \cdot 10^3 + 5 \cdot 10^2 + 8 \cdot 10 + 0 \qquad \text{additive property of 0}$$
$$= 8580 \qquad \text{expanded form}$$

See Exercise 24 for an example of multiplication by 10^2.

Now we are ready to put the two preliminary results together to establish the general result about multiplying two arbitrary whole numbers. We consider the original product $539 \cdot 286$:

$$539 \cdot 286 = (5 \cdot 10^2 + 3 \cdot 10 + 9) \cdot 286 \qquad \text{expanded form}$$
$$= 5 \cdot 10^2 \cdot 286 + 3 \cdot 10 \cdot 286 + 9 \cdot 286 \qquad \text{distributive property}$$
$$= 5 \cdot 286 \cdot 10^2 + 3 \cdot 286 \cdot 10 + 9 \cdot 286 \qquad \text{commutative property of multiplication}$$
$$= 1430 \cdot 10^2 + 858 \cdot 10 + 2574 \qquad \text{preliminary result 1 used three times}$$
$$= 143{,}000 + 8580 + 2574 \qquad \text{preliminary result 2 used twice}$$
$$= 154{,}154 \qquad \text{previously established result about sums}$$

After disposing of $529 \cdot 286$ you should not find it hard to believe that the product of *any* two whole numbers can be computed by using only the 15 basic properties.

1. In this exercise assume only the two logical properties, the nine structural properties, and the following definitions:

   $2 = 1 + 1$ $3 = 2 + 1$ $4 = 3 + 1$

   Do *not* assume any elementary addition or multiplication facts.

   (a) Supply reasons in this proof that $2 + 2 = 4$.

   $2 + 2 = 2 + (1 + 1)$ _____

   $= (2 + 1) + 1$ _____

   $= 3 + 1$ _____

   $= 4$ _____

   [handwritten annotations: 1b. 2·2=4 fact def. / 2(1+1)= given / 2·1+2·1 DP / 2+2 mult. Ident. / 4 (part a) / ?]

   (b) Write a statement-reason proof, as in part (a), that $2 \cdot 2 = 4$.

2. Using the same ground rules as in Exercise 1 and the additional definitions $5 = 4 + 1$ and $6 = 5 + 1$, prove the following:

   (a) $3 + 2 = 5$ (*Hint:* Try the strategy of working backwards.)

   (b) $3 + 3 = 6$

   (c) $3 \cdot 2 = 6$

3. Use only logical and structural properties of the whole number system and the tables of addition and multiplication facts to find the following. Do *not* use expanded form. Show your work. (You are really being asked to create short statement-reason proofs for six simple theorems of arithmetic.) Again, the problem-solving strategy of working backwards should prove helpful.

   (a) $14 + 3$ (b) $7 + 7$ (c) $7 \cdot 4$
   (d) $3 \cdot 24$ (e) $18 + 30$ (f) $72 + 9$

4. How many elementary facts do our youngsters have to memorize? How many would they need to learn if we switched to base four? To base twelve?

5. Make the following false statement into a true one by changing the position of just one digit:
   $101 - 102 = 1$.

6. Write in expanded form.

   (a) 4175   (b) 16,079
   (c) 100,090   (d) 271,828,459

7. Express as a multidigit numeral.

   (a) $4 \cdot 10^2 + 6 \cdot 10 + 8$
   (b) $9 \cdot 10^4 + 3 \cdot 10^3 + 0 \cdot 10^2 + 0 \cdot 10 + 5$
   (c) $7 \cdot 10^5 + 2 \cdot 10^2 + 8$
   (d) $5 \cdot 10 + 8 \cdot 10^4 + 7 + 9 \cdot 10^3 + 2 \cdot 10^2$

8. Write as a product of repeated factors.

   (a) 6^3 (b) 3^6 (c) 10^3 (d) 2^1

9. Write each product in exponential notation.

   (a) $10 \cdot 10 \cdot 10 \cdot 10$ (b) $3 \cdot 3 \cdot 3 \cdot 3$
   (c) $4 \cdot 4 \cdot 4$ (d) $0 \cdot 0 \cdot 0 \cdot 0 \cdot 0 \cdot 0 \cdot 0$

10. Fill in the missing exponents

    (a) $10^2 \cdot 10^5 = 10^\square$ (b) $10^4 \cdot 10^9 = 10^\square$
    (c) $10^m \cdot 10^3 = 10^\square$ (d) $10^6 \cdot 10^n = 10^\square$
    (e) $10^m \cdot 10^n = 10^\square$ (f) $10^7 \cdot 10^\square = 10^{11}$
    (g) $10^7 \cdot 10^\square = 10^8$ (h) $10^7 \cdot 10^\square = 10^7$

11. Assign a meaning to the symbol 10^0 and defend your choice.

12. Find all *integer* solutions to the equation
    $(x - 1)^{x+2} = 1$

13. Fill in missing exponents. *Hint:* First rewrite each exponential expression as a repeated product.

    (a) $(5^3)^4 = 5^\square$ (b) $(5^6)^2 = 5^\square$
    (c) $(5^3)^n = 5^\square$ (d) $(5^m)^n = 5^\square$

14. Supply reasons in this short proof that $100 = 10 \cdot 10$. Suppress substitution and associativity.

    $100 = 1 \cdot 10^2 + 0 \cdot 10 + 0$ _____

    $= 1 \cdot 10^2 + 0 \cdot 10$ _____

    $= 1 \cdot 10^2 + 0$ _____

    $= 1 \cdot 10^2$ _____

    $= 10^2$ _____

    $= 10 \cdot 10$ _____

15. Supply one main reason at each step in the following deduction that $36 + 17 = 53$.

    $36 + 17 = 3 \cdot 10 + 6 + 1 \cdot 10 + 7$ _____

    $= 3 \cdot 10 + 1 \cdot 10 + 6 + 7$ _____

    $= 3 \cdot 10 + 1 \cdot 10 + 13$ _____

    $= 3 \cdot 10 + 1 \cdot 10 + 1 \cdot 10 + 3$ _____

$$= (3 + 1 + 1) \cdot 10 + 3 \qquad \underline{\hspace{1cm}}$$
$$= (4 + 1) \cdot 10 + 3 \qquad \underline{\hspace{1cm}}$$
$$= 5 \cdot 10 + 3 \qquad \underline{\hspace{1cm}}$$
$$= 53 \qquad \underline{\hspace{1cm}}$$

16. Supply one main reason at each step in this proof that $12 \cdot 11 = 132$.

$$12 \cdot 11 = 12 \cdot (1 \cdot 10 + 1) \qquad \textit{expanded}$$
$$= 12 \cdot 1 \cdot 10 + 12 \cdot 1 \qquad \textit{distributive}$$
$$= 12 \cdot 10 + 12 \qquad \textit{identity}$$
$$= (1 \cdot 10 + 2) \cdot 10 + (1 \cdot 10 + 2) \qquad \textit{expanded}$$
$$= 1 \cdot 10 \cdot 10 + 2 \cdot 10 + 1 \cdot 10 + 2 \qquad \textit{distr.}$$
$$= 1 \cdot 10 \cdot 10 + (2 + 1) \cdot 10 + 2 \qquad \textit{''}$$
$$= 1 \cdot 10 \cdot 10 + 3 \cdot 10 + 2 \qquad \textit{fact}$$
$$= 1 \cdot 10^2 + 3 \cdot 10 + 2 \qquad \textit{exponent}$$
$$= 132 \qquad \textit{expanded}$$

17. Supply one main reason at each step in this proof that
$$(x + 3) \cdot (x + 4) = x^2 + 7 \cdot x + 12$$
$$\text{(for any } x \in W)$$

$$(x + 3) \cdot (x + 4) = (x + 3) \cdot x + (x + 3) \cdot 4 \qquad \textit{distributive}$$
$$= x \cdot x + 3 \cdot x + x \cdot 4 + 3 \cdot 4 \qquad \textit{''}$$
$$= x \cdot x + 3 \cdot x + x \cdot 4 + 12 \qquad \textit{x fact}$$
$$= x \cdot x + 3 \cdot x + 4 \cdot x + 12 \qquad \textit{commutative mult.}$$
$$= x \cdot x + (3 + 4) \cdot x + 12 \qquad \textit{distributive}$$
$$= x \cdot x + 7 \cdot x + 12 \qquad \textit{add fact}$$
$$= x^2 + 7 \cdot x + 12 \qquad \textit{expanded form}$$

18. Prove as in Exercise 17 (statements and reasons) that
$$(x + 5) \cdot (x + 5) = x^2 + 10 \cdot x + 25$$

19. Which structural property guarantees that no number can appear twice in the same row of the table of multiplication facts? *Hint:* What are the entries in row a column b and row a column c respectively?

20. Supply a reason (justification) for each step.
$$64 + 59 = 6 \cdot 10 + 4 + 5 \cdot 10 + 9 \qquad \textit{expanded}$$
$$= 6 \cdot 10 + 5 \cdot 10 + 4 + 9 \qquad \textit{commutative of add}$$
$$= 6 \cdot 10 + 5 \cdot 10 + 13 \qquad \textit{add. fact}$$
$$= 6 \cdot 10 + 5 \cdot 10 + 1 \cdot 10 + 3 \qquad \textit{expanded form}$$
$$= (6 + 5 + 1) \cdot 10 + 3 \qquad \textit{distri.}$$
$$= (6 + 6) \cdot 10 + 3 \qquad \textit{add. fact}$$
$$= 12 \cdot 10 + 3 \qquad \textit{''}$$
$$= (1 \cdot 10 + 2) \cdot 10 + 3 \qquad \textit{expanded}$$
$$= 1 \cdot 10 \cdot 10 + 2 \cdot 10 + 3 \qquad \textit{distributive}$$
$$= 1 \cdot 10^2 + 2 \cdot 10 + 3 \qquad \textit{expanded}$$
$$= 123 \qquad \textit{expanded (contracted)}$$

21. Write out, as in Exercise 20, a step-by-step calculation (with reasons) of $85 + 76$. The usual right-to-left algorithm can serve as a guide to the order of the steps.

22. Supply a reason for each step:
$$3 \cdot 749 = 3 \cdot (7 \cdot 10^2 + 4 \cdot 10 + 9) \qquad \textit{expanded}$$
$$= 3 \cdot 7 \cdot 10^2 + 3 \cdot 4 \cdot 10 + 3 \cdot 9 \qquad \textit{distr.}$$
$$= 3 \cdot 7 \cdot 10^2 + 3 \cdot 4 \cdot 10 + 27 \qquad \textit{x fact}$$
$$= 3 \cdot 7 \cdot 10^2 + 3 \cdot 4 \cdot 10 + 2 \cdot 10 + 7 \qquad \textit{expanded}$$
$$= 3 \cdot 7 \cdot 10^2 + (3 \cdot 4 + 2) \cdot 10 + 7 \qquad \textit{distr.}$$
$$= 3 \cdot 7 \cdot 10^2 + (12 + 2) \cdot 10 + 7 \qquad \textit{x fact}$$
$$= 3 \cdot 7 \cdot 10^2 + 14 \cdot 10 + 7 \qquad \textit{previously}$$
$$= 3 \cdot 7 \cdot 10^2 + (1 \cdot 10 + 4) \cdot 10 + 7 \qquad \textit{expanded}$$
$$= 3 \cdot 7 \cdot 10^2 + 1 \cdot 10 \cdot 10 + 4 \cdot 10 + 7 \qquad \textit{distrib.}$$

$= 3 \cdot 7 \cdot 10^2 + 1 \cdot 10^2 + 4 \cdot 10 + 7$ *exponents*

$= (3 \cdot 7 + 1) \cdot 10^2 + 4 \cdot 10 + 7$ *distributive*

$= (21 + 1) \cdot 10^2 + 4 \cdot 10 + 7$ *× fact*

$= 22 \cdot 10^2 + 4 \cdot 10 + 7$ *previously*

$= (2 \cdot 10 + 2) \cdot 10^2 + 4 \cdot 10 + 7$ *expanded*

$= 2 \cdot 10 \cdot 10^2 + 2 \cdot 10^2 + 4 \cdot 10 + 7$ *distributive*

$= 2 \cdot 10^3 + 2 \cdot 10^2 + 4 \cdot 10 + 7$ *exponents*

$= 2247$ *expanded form*

23. Write out, as in Exercise 22, a step-by-step calculation (with reasons) of $9 \cdot 68$. The usual multiplication algorithm can serve as a guide to the order of the steps.

24. Supply reasons in the following calculation, which illustrates the effect of multiplying by ten to the second power.

$5073 \cdot 10^2 = (5 \cdot 10^3 + 0 \cdot 10^2 + 7 \cdot 10 + 3) \cdot 10^2$ *expanded*

$= 5 \cdot 10^3 \cdot 10^2 + 0 \cdot 10^2 \cdot 10^2 + 7 \cdot 10 \cdot 10^2 + 3 \cdot 10^2$ *distr.*

$= 5 \cdot 10^5 + 0 \cdot 10^4 + 7 \cdot 10^3 + 3 \cdot 10^2$ *exponents*

$= 5 \cdot 10^5 + 0 \cdot 10^4 + 7 \cdot 10^3 + 3 \cdot 10^2 + 0$ *add. prop. of zero*

$= 5 \cdot 10^5 + 0 \cdot 10^4 + 7 \cdot 10^3 + 3 \cdot 10^2 + 0 \cdot 10$ *mult. prop of zero*

$= 5 \cdot 10^5 + 0 \cdot 10^4 + 7 \cdot 10^3 + 3 \cdot 10^2 + 0 \cdot 10 + 0$ *additive prop of zero*

$= 507,300$ *expanded*

25. Given that $749 \cdot 3 = 2247$, $749 \cdot 5 = 3745$, and $749 \cdot 2 = 1498$, supply reasons in this calculation:

$749 \cdot 352 = 749 \cdot (3 \cdot 10^2 + 5 \cdot 10 + 2)$ *expanded form*

$= 749 \cdot 3 \cdot 10^2 + 749 \cdot 5 \cdot 10 + 749 \cdot 2$ *distributive prop-*

$= 2247 \cdot 10^2 + 3745 \cdot 10 + 1498$ *given*

$= 224,700 + 37,450 + 1498$ *expanded form*

$= 224,700 + 38,948$

$= 263,648$ *prev. est.*

26. Given that $68 \cdot 9 = 612$ and $68 \cdot 4 = 272$, write out, as in Exercise 25, a step-by-step calculation (with reasons) of $68 \cdot 94$.

★ 27. In seven-clock arithmetic exponential notation means what you might expect. For example, 5^3 means $5 \cdot_7 5 \cdot_7 5$. Thus $5^3 = 4 \cdot_7 5 = 6$. Compute 5^{6122} in seven-clock arithmetic.

★ 28. Perhaps you recall (Exercise 50, Section 1.1) that the Tower of Hanoi problem requires $2^{64} - 1$ moves. Estimate how many digits the base-ten numeral for 2^{64} has. *Hint:* $2^{10} = 1024$, which is approximately 10^3.

★ 29. In Problem 2, Section 1.1, we considered the number 7^{399}. Show that, when expressed as a base-ten numeral, 7^{400} has at least 337 digits. *Hint:* $7^5 > 2^4 \cdot 10^3$.

Computer Vignette C

Computers can be programmed to provide practice on any number of topics. Figure 4.18 is a program that drills the user on five of the more difficult multiplication facts. Figure 4.19 shows a typical run. Do you see where the numbers in line 150 appear in the printout?

Figure 4.18

```
10    READ X, Y
20    LET C = X * Y
30    IF C = 0 THEN 160
40    PRINT "WHAT IS THE PRODUCT OF ";X;" AND ";Y
50    INPUT F
60    IF F = C THEN 120
70    PRINT "THAT'S NOT IT. TRY AGAIN."
80    INPUT S
90    IF S = C THEN 120
100   PRINT "THAT'S STILL NOT IT. THE CORRECT ANSWER
      IS "; C
110   GOTO 130
120   PRINT "VERY GOOD"
130   PRINT
140   GOTO 10
150   DATA 9,7,8,6,6,7,6,9,8,9,1,0
160   PRINT "THAT'S ENOUGH DRILL FOR NOW."
170   END
```

Figure 4.19

```
]RUN
WHAT IS THE PRODUCT OF 9 AND 7
?72
THAT'S NOT IT. TRY AGAIN.
?63
VERY GOOD

WHAT IS THE PRODUCT OF 8 AND 6
?48
VERY GOOD

WHAT IS THE PRODUCT OF 6 AND 7
?36
THAT'S NOT IT. TRY AGAIN.
?49
THAT'S STILL NOT IT. THE CORRECT ANSWER IS 42

WHAT IS THE PRODUCT OF 6 AND 9
?54
VERY GOOD

WHAT IS THE PRODUCT OF 8 AND 9
?72
VERY GOOD

THAT'S ENOUGH DRILL FOR NOW.
```

You might like to amend this program so that it keeps score on how well the student does. If so, type in the program just as it is, and then type in the additional lines of Figure 4.20 at the bottom.

Figure 4.20

```
60    IF F = C THEN 115
115   LET R = R + 1
165   PRINT "YOU GOT ";R;" CORRECT OUT OF 5"
```

When the program is run, the computer will automatically read line 115 between lines 110 and 120, and read line 165 between lines 160 and 170. Furthermore, it will automatically expunge the original line 60 as soon as you type in the new line 60.

 ## 4.6   *Order in the Whole Number System*

In our formal development of the whole number system to this point, we have considered only the two primitive binary operations, addition and multiplication. To bring subtraction and division into the picture, we first need to incorporate into our mathematical system the order relation *less than* and its basic properties. The order relation, of course, is important for reasons besides its connection with subtraction and division; we will consider inequalities and their solution in Chapters 6, 7 and 15.

There are at least three ways to introduce the order relation: by simply postulating its existence and its fundamental properties; by defining it algebraically in terms of the addition operation; or by defining it geometrically. We shall look at all three approaches and then return to the topics of subtraction and division.

Less Than as an Undefined Relation

If you covered (optional) Section 2.6, then you know what a relation on W is. (Formally, it is a subset of $W \times W$, but you may prefer to visualize an arrow diagram or an arrow Venn diagram.) We include the (undefined) relation $<$ with the (undefined) set W and the (undefined) binary operations $+$ and $\cdot$ as the basic elements of the mathematical system that we call the whole number system:

$$[W, +, \cdot, <]$$

Then we adjoin to the 15 assumptions we have already made some other assumptions that describe how $<$ behaves both alone and in combination with the binary operations.

Two plausible assumptions to make about the behavior of the less-than relation are the *trichotomy* and *transitivity* properties.

Trichotomy Property

For any whole numbers a and b, exactly one of the following is true:

$$a < b \qquad a = b \qquad b < a$$

Transitivity Property

For any whole numbers a, b, and c, if $a < b$ and $b < c$, then $a < c$.

An assumption relating $<$ to $+$, that is quite similar to the addition property of equality, is the following:

Addition Property of Less Than

If $a < b$, then $a + c < b + c$.

Colloquially,

"You can add the same number to both sides of an inequality."

The corresponding assumption relating $<$ to $\cdot$ follows.

Multiplication Property of Less Than

If $a < b$ and $c \neq 0$, then $a \cdot c < b \cdot c$.

Colloquially,

"You can multiply both sides of an inequality by the same natural number."

These latter two assumptions will play fundamental roles in the solution of inequalities.

Algebraic Definition of Less Than

We can define $<$ as follows:

Algebraic Definition of Less Than ($<$)

$a < b$ means that there is a natural number solution to the equation $a + \square = b$.

Thus you can view the string of symbols

$$5 < 8$$

as mathematical shorthand for the statement

There is a natural number solution to the equation $5 + \square = 8$.

Since this latter statement is true ($5 + \boxed{3} = 8$ and 3 is a natural number), it follows that $5 < 8$ is true.

EXAMPLE 1   Show that $9 < 13$.

Solution   By an elementary addition fact $9 + \boxed{4} = 13$, and 4 is a natural number.   ❑

Now that less than has been defined, we should try to *prove* the four basic properties that we had to *assume* about the undefined relation. Unfortunately, we cannot do so without first adding two more assumptions to our basic 15. The first is the trichotomy property: for any whole numbers a and b, exactly one of $a < b$, $a = b$, or $b < a$ is true. The second is the assumption that the sum of two natural numbers (nonzero whole numbers) is again a natural number. Thus we add these two *order-related* properties to our list of assumptions, bringing the number to 17. Shortly, we shall complete the list by adding a third order-related property.

ORDER-RELATED PROPERTIES

Trichotomy
N is closed with respect to $+$

We shall now *prove* the transitivity property of less than from these 17 assumptions. (In the exercises are proofs of the addition and multiplication properties of less than.) We begin by assuming that $a < b$ and $b < c$. We want to prove that $a < c$. The proof is similar to solving a maze (see Figure 4.21) and can be thought of as a refinement of the problem-solving strategy of working backwards. We know where to go in (with $a < b$ and $b < c$) and we know

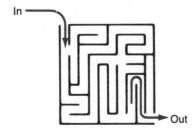

Figure 4.21

where to come out (with $a < c$). We also know that the second and the second-to-last steps must surely involve the definition of $<$:

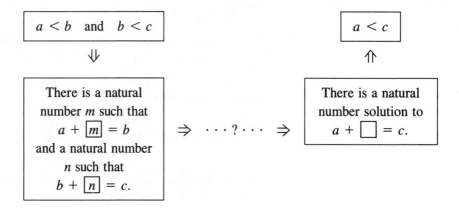

$a < b$ and $b < c$

$\Downarrow$

There is a natural number m such that
$$a + \boxed{m} = b$$
and a natural number n such that
$$b + \boxed{n} = c.$$

$\Rightarrow \quad \cdots ? \cdots \quad \Rightarrow$

$a < c$

$\Uparrow$

There is a natural number solution to
$$a + \square = c.$$

The problem is to fill in the intermediate steps. A little reflection suggests how to get from the equations

$$a + m = b$$
$$b + n = c$$

to a solution to the equation

$$a + \square = c$$

The deduction proceeds as follows:

$$a + m = b$$
$$b + n = c$$

$\Downarrow$ substituting $a + m$ for b in the second equation

$$(a + m) + n = c$$

$\Downarrow$ associative property of addition

$$a + (m + n) = c$$

$\Downarrow$

$a + \square = c$ has a solution in N namely $m + n$, which is in N since both m and n are and we assumed that N is closed with respect to $+$

Geometric Definition of Less Than

The algebraic definition of less than, while theoretically satisfying, is inappropriate for the elementary school. Children have a firm, intuitive grasp of the less-than relation and experience no difficulty in deciding which of two given whole numbers is the smaller. If one decides that a definition of less than is necessary, then recourse is usually had to the number line:

> **Geometric Definition of Less Than** ($<$)
>
> $a < b$ means a is left of b on the number line.

This definition is, of course, too loose for theoretical purposes, because the notion of "left of" is ambiguous. (Although it may appear that 3 is left of 5 on the number line in Figure 4.22, that's not the way it will look if you rotate your book through 90° or 180°.) Still the geometric viewpoint is useful. If we translate $<$ as "is left of," then the trichotomy and transitivity properties are obvious. The addition and multiplication properties of less than will also become obvious once we give a geometric interpretation to $+$ and to $\cdot$ the way we have to $<$.

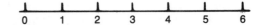

Figure 4.22

Before considering geometric interpretations of $+$ and $\cdot$, let us recall that each number on the number line has a *dual* geometric reference. On the one hand, the number 3 on the number line labels a point. On the other hand, it gives the length of the segment from the origin to that point, where the unit of measure is the segment from 0 to 1. See Figure 4.23.

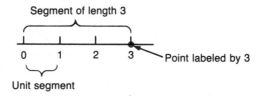

Figure 4.23

A geometric interpretation of addition is suggested by the following examples:

$4 + 3$; start at point 4 and *slide* right 3 units (Figure 4.24)

$2 + 5$; start at point 2 and slide right 5 units (Figure 4.25)

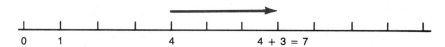

Figure 4.24

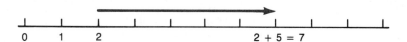

Figure 4.25

Under this interpretation the addition property of less than,

$$\text{If } a < b, \text{ then } a + c < b + c$$

is clear, because both slides are of length c units. See Figure 4.26.

Figure 4.26

A geometric interpretation of multiplication is suggested by these examples:

$2 \cdot 4$: *stretch* to twice its original length the segment from 0 to 4 (Figure 4.27)

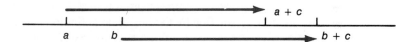

Figure 4.27

$3 \cdot 2$: stretch to three times its original length the segment from 0 to 2 (Figure 4.28)

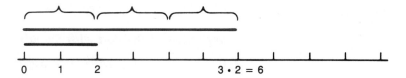

Figure 4.28

Under this interpretation the multiplication property of less than,

$$\text{If } a < b \text{ and } c \neq 0, \text{ then } a \cdot c < b \cdot c$$

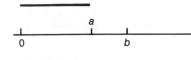

Figure 4.29

is also clear, because both the segment from 0 to a and the segment from 0 to b are being subjected to the same stretch factor. See Figure 4.29.

Subtraction and Division

The formal definitions of subtraction and division are exactly those of the previous chapter, but now we look at them a little more critically.

Missing-Addend Definition of Subtraction

If $a \leq b$, then $b - a$ is the missing addend in the equation $a + \square = b$.

Before we can accept this definition, we need to establish the *existence* and the *uniqueness* of a whole number solution to the equation. Existence is guaranteed by the condition $a \leq b$. For if $a < b$, then there is a natural number solution by the algebraic definition of $<$. And if $a = b$, then the whole number 0 is a solution. Uniqueness is guaranteed by the cancellation property of addition. For if x_1 and x_2 are solutions, then $a + x_1 = b$ and $a + x_2 = b$. Hence $a + x_1 = a + x_2$, from which $x_1 = x_2$ follows.

For (exact) division we use the following definition.

Missing-Factor Definition of Exact Division

If $d \neq 0$ and $d \mid n$, then n/d is the missing factor in the equation $d \cdot \square = n$.

Again, we need to establish the existence and uniqueness of a solution to the equation before the definition makes sense. Existence is guaranteed by the condition $d \mid n$, because that is precisely how the vertical-bar symbol was defined. Uniqueness is guaranteed by the cancellation property of multiplication and the restriction that $d \neq 0$. For if x_1 and x_2 are solutions, then $d \cdot x_1 = n$ and $d \cdot x_2 = n$. Hence $d \cdot x_1 = d \cdot x_2$, from which $x_1 = x_2$ follows.

The remaining question concerns division with a remainder. We use the definition of the previous chapter.

Definition of Division with Remainder

If $d \neq 0$, $n \div d$ is the ordered pair (q, r) satisfying (1) $n = dq + r$ and (2) $r < d$.

Again, we are confronted by the existence-uniqueness question. How do we know that there is an ordered pair satisfying conditions 1 and 2? And if there is such an ordered pair, how do we know that there is not another one that also satisfies 1 and 2? To establish existence and uniqueness requires a rather complex argument (which we shall omit) that is based on the following final, eminently plausible assumption about the order relation, known as the **well-ordering property:**

> Any nonempty subset of whole numbers has a least (first) element.

To clarify what is meant by least, or first, consider the following example.

EXAMPLE 2   Determine the least element in each of these subsets of W.
(a) {7, 4, 10, 3, 11}
(b) $\{n \in W \mid n \text{ is odd}\}$
(c) $\{n \in W \mid n^2 > 100\}$

Solution   (a) 3
(b) 1
(c) 11   ❏

Thus our final list of fundamental properties of the whole-number system, with the numbers expressed by Hindu-Arabic numerals, is as follows:

LOGICAL PROPERTIES

Substitution	RST of equality

STRUCTURAL PROPERTIES

Associative property of addition	Associative property of multiplication
Commutative property of addition	Commutative property of multiplication
Additive property of 0	Multiplicative property of 1
Cancellation property of addition	Cancellation property of multiplication

Distributive property

NUMERATION-RELATED PROPERTIES

Elementary Addition Facts
Elementary Multiplication Facts
Expanded Form
Exponents

ORDER-RELATED PROPERTIES

Trichotomy
N is closed under $+$
W is well ordered by $<$

EXERCISE SET 4.6

1. Using the algebraic definition of $<$, explain the following statements.
   (a) $3 < 8$
   (b) $12 < 39$
   (c) $n < n + 1$ (for any $n \in W$)
   (d) $n < 2n$ (for any $n \in N$)

2. Fill in missing reasons in this proof of the addition property of less than, which is based on the full set of assumptions about W (logical, structural, numeration-related, and order-related) and the algebraic definition of $<$. Given $a < b$, we want to prove that $a + c < b + c$.
   (a) $a < b$ _____?_____
   (b) There is a natural number n
       such that $a + \boxed{n} = b$ _____?_____
   (c) $a + n + c = b + c$ _____?_____
   (d) $a + c + n = b + c$ _____?_____
   (e) There is a natural number solution to
       $a + c + \Box = b + c$ (What is it?) _____?_____
   (f) $a + c < b + c$ _____?_____

3. Fill in missing reasons in the following proof of the multiplication property of less than. Given $a < b$ and $c \neq 0$, we want to prove that $a \cdot c < b \cdot c$.
   (a) $a < b$ _____?_____
   (b) There is a natural number n
       such that $a + \boxed{n} = b$ _____?_____
   (c) $(a + n) \cdot c = b \cdot c$ _____?_____
   (d) $a \cdot c + n \cdot c = b \cdot c$ _____?_____
   (e) There is a natural number solution to
       $a \cdot c + \Box = b \cdot c$ (What is it?) _____?_____
   (f) $a \cdot c < b \cdot c$ _____?_____

4. The divides-exactly-into relation (denoted by $|$) bears certain similarities to the is-less-than relation (denoted by $<$).
   (a) Is this trichotomy property true? For any whole numbers a and b exactly one of $a|b$, $a = b$, $b|a$ holds.
   (b) Is this transitive property true? If $a|b$ and $b|c$, then $a|c$.
   (c) Formulate an addition property of $|$ and decide whether it is true.
   (d) Formulate a multiplication property of $|$ and decide whether it is true.

5. Let us agree that a whole number a is "close to" a whole number b if the difference between them is less than ten. Let us also agree to symbolize "a is close to b" by "$a \sim b$."
   (a) Which, if any, of the RST properties does the relation $\sim$ have?
   (b) Does $\sim$ have an addition property analogous to those of $=$ and $<$?
   (c) Does $\sim$ have a multiplication property analogous to those of $=$ and $<$?

6. Each number line diagram represents an addition fact. Write the fact.
   (a)
   (b)

7. Draw a number line diagram to represent the following.
   (a) $5 + 3$ (b) $3 + 5$

8. Each number line diagram represents a multiplication fact. Write the fact.

   (a)

   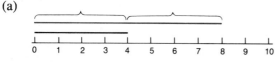

   (b)

   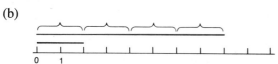

9. Decide, on the basis of your understanding of the number line, whether each of the following is true (a, b, and c are whole numbers).
   (a) If $a + c < b + c$, then $a < b$.
   (b) If $a \cdot c < b \cdot c$ and $c \neq 0$, then $a < b$.
   (c) If $a < b$ and $c < d$, then $a + c < b + d$.
   (d) If $a < b$ and $c < d$, then $a \cdot c < b \cdot d$.

10. Suppose you have decided to impose the usual less-than relation on the numbers of seven-clock arithmetic. For example, $2 < 6$ and $4 < 5$. Which of the following properties are true?
    (a) Trichotomy
    (b) Transitivity
    (c) Addition property of less than
    (d) Multiplication property of less than

11. Is there a least odd integer? Does your answer contradict the well-ordering property?

12. Is there a least positive rational number? Does your answer contradict the well-ordering property?

13. Does every nonempty set of whole numbers have a greatest element?

14. Complete these definitions of $\div$ and $<$.
    (a) When asked to divide 200 by 13 we are really being asked to find two whole numbers q and r such that (i) _____ and (ii) _____ .
    (b) When we say that $5 < n$, we are asserting the existence of a whole number k such that (i) _____ and (ii) _____ .

★ 15. Use the missing-addend definition of subtraction to prove that multiplication distributes over subtraction: that is, $c(b - a) = cb - ca$ for all a, b, c such that $a \leq b$.

★ 16. Use the missing-factor definition of exact division to prove the rule for raising and reducing fractions:
$$\frac{bc}{ac} = \frac{b}{a}$$
for all a, b, c such that $a \neq 0$, $c \neq 0$, and $a \mid b$.

17. In this exercise, think of all the relations as being defined on the set N of natural numbers. The less-than relation $<$ is defined in terms of the addition operation $+$ as follows:
$a < b$ if there is a natural number n so that
$a + n = b$
The divides relation $\mid$ is defined in terms of the multiplication operation $\cdot$ as follows:
$a \mid b$ if there is a natural number n so that
$a \cdot n = b$
    (a) Define a relation $\uparrow$ analogously in terms of the exponentiation operation $\wedge$:
    $a \uparrow b$ if . . .
    (b) Is it true that $2 \uparrow 32$?
    (c) Is it true that $5 \uparrow 10$?
    (d) Is $\uparrow$ a transitive relation?

★ 18. This is a continuation of Exercise 17, and again pattern recognition and extension is the task. Subtraction ($-$) is defined on N as follows:
If $a < b$, then $b - a$ is the solution to
$a + \square = b$
Exact division ($/$) is defined on N as follows:
If $a \mid b$, then b/a is the solution to $a \cdot \square = b$
    (a) By analogy define a new operation $*$ on N that is related to $\uparrow$:
    If $a \mid b$, then $b * a$ · · ·
    (b) Compute $32 * 2$.
    (c) Compute $1000 * 10$.
    (d) Have you ever encountered this operation before?

Key Concepts in Chapter 4

Mathematical system
Binary operation
Closure
Seven-clock arithmetic
Cayley table
Substitution
Properties of equality
Associativity

Commutativity
Identity element
Distributivity
Order of operations
Cancellation
Expanded form
Exponent
Properties of less-than

❧ Chapter 4 Review Exercises ❧

1. Find the following numbers, where $\wedge$ and ⓜ are the exponentiation and maximization operations, respectively.
   (a) $2 \wedge (3 \text{ ⓜ } 4)$
   (b) $(2 \wedge 3) \text{ ⓜ } 4$

2. Does the maximization operation ⓜ on the set of natural numbers satisfy the cancellation property?

3. A binary operation min, denoted by $\star$, can be defined on N much as max was. For example,
   $$3 \star 10 = 3 \qquad 8 \star 5 = 5 \qquad 4 \star 4 = 4$$
   (a) Is $\star$ a commutative operation on N? Yes
   (b) Is $\star$ an associative operation on N? Yes
   (c) Does $\star$ have a neutral element in N? If so, what is it? $(a \star 1) = a$
   (d) Is $\{5, 10\}$ closed with respect to $\star$? Yes
   (e) Is multiplication distributive over $\star$? Yes

4. Two binary operations $*$ and $\square$ are defined on W by
   $$m \square n = m + n + 1 \qquad m * n = mn + m + n$$
   Does $*$ distribute over $\square$?

5. Figure 4.30 is the Cayley table for a binary operation $*$ on a 3-element set $\{a, b, c\}$.

$*$	a	b	c
a	b	a	c
b	a	b	c
c	a	c	b

   Figure 4.30

   (a) Is $*$ commutative?
   (b) Does $*$ have an identity element?
   (c) Is $\{a, c\}$ closed under $*$?
   (d) Find an ordered triple that shows $*$ is not associative.
   (e) Name the mathematical principle that justifies the statement: "Since $b * c = c$, it follows that $(b * c) * a = c * a$."

6. Exhibit a two-element subset of $\{0, 1, 2, 3, 4, 5, 6\}$ that is closed under seven-clock multiplication.

7. Is the set of even natural numbers closed under these operations?
   (a) Addition
   (b) Subtraction
   (c) Multiplication
   (d) Division

8. Use the substitution principle to draw a conclusion from these assumptions:
   $$\begin{cases} y > 2 + 6x \\ y = x^2 + 11 \end{cases}$$

9. Transform the given expression according to the property cited. Do no more (and no less) than is justified by the given property (and perhaps substitution).
   (a) $(3 \cdot 4) \cdot (1 \cdot 5 + 6) = $ _____ by the multiplicative property of 1
   (b) $(3 \cdot 4) \cdot (1 \cdot 5 + 6) = $ _____ by the commutative property of addition
   (c) $(3 \cdot 4) \cdot (1 \cdot 5 + 6) = $ _____ by the associative property of multiplication

(d) $(3 \cdot 4) \cdot (1 \cdot 5 + 6) =$ _____ by the distributive property

10. Name the mathematical principle that justifies each of the following inferences.
    (a) If $3x - 4 = 8$, then $3x - 4 + 4 = 8 + 4$.
    (b) If $x + 2 = 3y + 4$ and $3y + 4 = 5$, then $x + 2 = 5$.
    (c) If $4 \cdot x + 3 = y + 3$, then $4 \cdot x = y$.
    (d) If $x + 2 < y + 1$, then $3(x + 2) < 3(y + 1)$.
    (e) If $x + 3y = 5$ and $x = 2$, then $2 + 3y = 5$.

11. Which, if any, of the RST properties are enjoyed by the perpendicularity relation $\perp$ among lines?

12. Supply one main reason at each step in this proof that
    $(x + 2) \cdot (x + 5) = x^2 + 7 \cdot x + 10$
    for any $x \in W$
    $(x + 2) \cdot (x + 5)$
    $= (x + 2) \cdot x + (x + 2) \cdot 5$ _____
    $= x \cdot x + 2 \cdot x + x \cdot 5 + 2 \cdot 5$ _____
    $= x \cdot x + 2 \cdot x + x \cdot 5 + 10$ _____
    $= x \cdot x + 2 \cdot x + 5 \cdot x + 10$ _____
    $= x \cdot x + (2 + 5) \cdot x + 10$ _____
    $= x \cdot x + 7 \cdot x + 10$ _____
    $= x^2 + 7 \cdot x + 10$ _____

13. Fill in the blanks to make a proof that $17 \cdot 10 = 170$.
    $17 \cdot 10 =$ _____ expanded form
    $=$ _____ distributive property
    $=$ _____ exponents
    $=$ _____ additive property of 0
    $=$ _____ expanded form

14. Suppose that in addition to the nine structural properties of the whole number system, you also know these (and only these) arithmetic facts:
    A: $2 \cdot 4 = 8$
    B: $3 = 2 + 1$
    C: $4 = 3 + 1$
    D: $8 + 3 = 11$
    E: $12 = 11 + 1$
    Write a statement-reason proof that $3 \cdot 4 = 12$. Each reason must be a structural property or one of the arithmetic facts A–E. (What problem-solving strategy should prove helpful?)

15. (a) If $x = y$, does it follow that $0 \cdot x = 0 \cdot y$?
    (b) If $0 \cdot x = 0 \cdot y$, does it follow that $x = y$?

16. Evaluate.
    (a) $20 - 6 \div 2 \cdot 3 \div 1 + 5 \cdot 2$
    (b) $[5^2 - (5 + 2)] \div 3 \cdot 2 + 1$

17. Put the letters (a)–(g) into appropriately shaped boxes and arrange them into a flowchart for calculating products in seven-clock arithmetic.
    (a) The seven-clock product
    (b) Is it greater than six?
    (c) Stop.
    (d) Find a difference by subtracting 7 in the usual (whole number) way.
    (e) A pair of seven-clock numbers
    (f) Start.
    (g) Find their usual (whole number) product.

18. Solve $5 \cdot_7 x +_7 4 = 3$.

19. In seven-clock arithmetic exponential notation means what you might expect. For example, 5^3 means $5 \cdot_7 5 \cdot_7 5$. Find 5^{100} in seven-clock arithmetic. (What will your strategy be?)

20. By direct application of the algebraic definition of less than, two inequalities can be inferred from the equation $4 + 3 = 7$. Write them.

21. Suppose you have decided to impose the usual less-than relation on the numbers 0, 1, 2, 3, 4, 5, 6 of seven-clock arithmetic.
    (a) Give an example to show that the addition property of less-than is not true.
    (b) Give an example to show that the multiplication property of less-than is not true.

22. Which structural property of the whole number system guarantees the uniqueness of the missing addend in $7 + \square = 12$?

23. Which structural property of the whole-number system guarantees that (no matter what value is given to a) the equation $3 \cdot \square = a$ cannot have more than one solution?

24. Each statement below is an instance of some general property. Name the general property.

(a) If $x + 3 = y + 3$, then $x = y$.

(b) If $x = y$, then $x + 3 = y + 3$.

(c) If $x + 3 = y + 3$, then $y + 3 = x + 3$.

(d) If $x + 3 = y$, then $2 \wedge (x + 3) = 2 \wedge y$.

(e) If $(x + 3) \cdot y = 0$, then $x + 3 = 0$ or $y = 0$.

References

Arithmetic Teacher. Focus Issue—"Calculators." vol. 34, no. 6, February 1987.

Dodge, C. *Numbers and Mathematics*. 2nd ed. Boston: Prindle, Weber & Schmidt, 1975.

National Council of Teachers of Mathematics. *29th Yearbook: Topics in Mathematics for Elementary School Teachers*. Reston, Va.: NCTM, 1964.

Webber, G., and J. Brown. *Basic Concepts of Mathematics*. Reading, Mass.: Addison-Wesley, 1963.

NUMBER THEORY

Before moving on from the whole number system, we pause to consider a few topics from the area of mathematics known as *number theory*. There are several reasons for doing so. One very practical reason is that the basic ideas of number theory, which we are about to look at, are firmly entrenched in the elementary school curriculum. Another is that some of the most common types of calculations with fractions depend on these ideas. A perhaps less practical, but no less important, reason is that elementary number theory is an intriguing subject and a rich source of problems.

We cover the major topics of elementary number theory informally in the first two sections. In the third section we extend the coverage in a more formal way. In the fourth section we consider some enrichment topics.

Number theory is one of the oldest branches of mathematics, going back to the ancient Greeks. Some of the old questions in number theory are so simple a child can understand them. Yet many of them have defied the best mathematical minds for centuries and remain unanswered to this day. Probably the most famous of these questions is known as Fermat's last theorem, after Pierre de Fermat (1601–1665), a lawyer by trade but possibly the greatest amateur mathematician of all time.

It has been known since ancient times (at least 1600 B.C.) that the Pythagorean equation

$$\triangle^2 + \square^2 = \hexagon^2$$

has solutions in W. For example,

$$\triangle{3}^2 + \boxed{4}^2 = \langle 5 \rangle^2$$
$$\triangle{5}^2 + \boxed{12}^2 = \langle 13 \rangle^2$$

Leonhard Euler, who lived a hundred years after Fermat, proved that the equation

$$\triangle^3 + \square^3 = \hexagon^3$$

has *no* (nonzero) solutions in W. Fermat himself proved that the equation

$$\triangle^4 + \square^4 = \hexagon^4$$

245

has *no* (nonzero) solutions in *W*. But then Fermat went on to claim that he had proved that

$$\triangle^{\,n} + \square^{\,n} = \hexagon^{\,n}$$

has no (nonzero) solutions in *W* *no matter what* value is chosen for *n* (as long as *n* > 2). This assertion is known as **Fermat's last theorem.** Fermat's claim to a proof is contained in one of the most famous sentences in all of mathematical literature, which he wrote in the margin of one of his books on Diophantine equations: ". . . I have assuredly found an admirable proof of this, but the margin is too narrow to contain it." In 1987 the mathematical world was stunned by the announcement of a proof of Fermat's theorem, but within a few months the argument was shown to be incomplete. To this day, more than three hundred fifty years after Fermat's claim, no one has been able to either prove or disprove Fermat's last theorem.

We will consider a few other famous problems after we review some basic definitions.

 ## 5.1   *Factors, Multiples, and Primes*

We have seen that the missing-factor definition of (exact) division depends on the divides relation. That same relation is fundamental in number theory where other terminology is often used. Instead of saying that 3 divides 12, we often say that 3 is a *factor* of 12. Both expressions mean the same thing: that there is a whole number solution (namely 4) to the equation $3 \cdot \square = 12$. We also say that 12 is a *multiple* of 3, or 12 is *divisible* by 3. Here is the old definition in the new terminology.

> If *a* and *b* are whole numbers, then *a* is a **factor** of *b* (or *a* **divides** *b*, written $a \mid b$) if there is a whole number *c* such that $a \cdot c = b$. If *a* is a factor of *b*, then we also say that *b* is a **multiple** of *a* (or *b* is **divisible** by *a*).

EXAMPLE 1   Decide which of the following statements are true.
(a) 8 is a factor of 24.
(b) 7 divides 35.
(c) 30 is a multiple of 4.
(d) 42 is divisible by 6.
(e) $0 \mid 3$.
(f) 0 is a multiple of 3.
(g) 1 is a factor of *n* for every whole number *n*.

Solution   (a) True, since $8 \cdot \boxed{3} = 24$.
(b) True, since $7 \cdot \boxed{5} = 35$.

(c) False, since $4 \cdot \boxed{} = 30$ has no whole number solution.

(d) True, since $6 \cdot \boxed{7} = 42$.

(e) False, since $0 \cdot \boxed{} = 3$ has no whole number solution.

(f) True, since $3 \cdot \boxed{0} = 0$.

(g) True, since $1 \cdot \boxed{n} = n$ by the multiplicative property of 1. ❏

Throughout the field of number theory it is important to be able to determine if one whole number is a factor of another. One way, of course, is with a calculator, where it takes only seconds to decide that 37 is a factor of 15,281. Simply divide 15,281 by 37 on the machine, and observe that the quotient is a whole number (413). If a calculator is not handy, one can resort to paper-and-pencil division, not a particularly easy task when the divisor is large like 37. For certain very small divisors there are *divisibility tests,* which can be faster than a calculator. Here, for example, are three such tests that are undoubtedly familiar to you. In Section 5.3 we will look into *why* these and some less familiar tests work. A number expressed by a base-ten numeral is

divisible by 2 if and only if its units digit is 0, 2, 4, 6, or 8.
divisible by 3 if and only if the sum of its digits is divisible by 3.
divisible by 5 if and only if its units digit is 0 or 5.

EXAMPLE 2 List all the factors of 30.

Solution Notice that the factors come in pairs:

1 is a factor; it is paired with 30.
2 is a factor; it is paired with 15.
3 is a factor; it is paired with 10.
5 is a factor; it is paired with 6.

Notice also that in each pair one number is less than $\sqrt{30}$ (a number between 5 and 6 whose square is 30) and the other is greater than $\sqrt{30}$. (Do you see why both could not be less than $\sqrt{30}$ or both greater than $\sqrt{30}$?) Since 4 is not a factor, we have found all factors (1, 2, 3, and 5) less than $\sqrt{30}$. And since we have paired each with its companion over $\sqrt{30}$, our list is complete: {1, 2, 3, 5, 6, 10, 15, 30}. (The topic of square root is covered in Chapter 8.) ❏

EXAMPLE 3 List all the factors of 36.

Solution This time, since 36 is a *perfect square*, one factor, 6, is its own partner:

$$\{1, \quad 2, \quad 3, \quad 4, \quad 6, \quad 9, \quad 12, \quad 18, \quad 36\}$$ ❏

The whole numbers other than 0 and 1 are separated into two categories according to the scarcity of their factors.

A **prime number** is a natural number other than 1 whose only factors are 1 and itself. The nonprime natural numbers other than 1 are called **composite numbers**.

The first few prime numbers are, 2, 3, 5, 7, 11, 13, 17, ...

The Greek mathematician and astronomer Eratosthenes (ca. 276–194 B.C.) devised an algorithm, now known as the sieve of Eratosthenes, that in principle allows us to find, in order, as many primes as we please. Suppose for example, that we want to find all the prime numbers less than 50. Begin by listing all the candidates, circle the 2, and cross off all subsequent multiples of it, since none of them can be prime:

$$
\begin{array}{cccccccccc}
② & 3 & \cancel{4} & 5 & \cancel{6} & 7 & \cancel{8} & 9 & \cancel{10} \\
11 & \cancel{12} & 13 & \cancel{14} & 15 & \cancel{16} & 17 & \cancel{18} & 19 & \cancel{20} \\
21 & \cancel{22} & 23 & \cancel{24} & 25 & \cancel{26} & 27 & \cancel{28} & 29 & \cancel{30} \\
31 & \cancel{32} & 33 & \cancel{34} & 35 & \cancel{36} & 37 & \cancel{38} & 39 & \cancel{40} \\
41 & \cancel{42} & 43 & \cancel{44} & 45 & \cancel{46} & 47 & \cancel{48} & 49
\end{array}
$$

Now, circle the first surviving number, 3, and cross off all subsequent multiples of it (some will have been removed already):

$$
\begin{array}{ccccc}
② & ③ & 5 & 7 & \cancel{9} \\
11 & 13 & \cancel{15} & 17 & 19 \\
\cancel{21} & 23 & 25 & \cancel{27} & 29 \\
31 & \cancel{33} & 35 & 37 & \cancel{39} \\
41 & 43 & \cancel{45} & 47 & 49
\end{array}
$$

Now, circle the first surviving number, 5, and cross off all multiples of it:

$$
\begin{array}{ccccc}
② & ③ & ⑤ & 7 & \\
11 & 13 & & 17 & 19 \\
& 23 & \cancel{25} & & 29 \\
31 & & \cancel{35} & 37 & \\
41 & 43 & & 47 & 49
\end{array}
$$

Finally, circle the first surviving number, 7, and cross off all subsequent multiples of it:

$$
\begin{array}{ccccc}
② & ③ & ⑤ & ⑦ & \\
11 & 13 & & 17 & 19 \\
& 23 & & & 29 \\
31 & & & 37 & \\
41 & 43 & & 47 & \cancel{49}
\end{array}
$$

At this point every number that remains is prime. The reason is this: Since no multiples of 2, 3, 5, or 7 survive (uncircled), the only way that a number on this list could fail to be prime is if it were a product of primes greater than 7. But if two numbers are greater than 7, then their product is greater than 49 and hence off the end of our list. The generalization follows:

If n is not a multiple of p for some prime number p such that $p^2 \le n$, then n is prime.

Here is an equivalent statement of this theorem.

A composite number n always has a prime factor $p \le \sqrt{n}$.

EXAMPLE 4	Show that 229 is a prime number.
Solution	We need only check that 229 is not divisible by the primes 2, 3, 5, 7, 11, and 13, because the next prime is 17, and $17^2 = 289$, which exceeds 229. By calculator, by pencil and paper, or by mental divisibility tests, none of 2, 3, 5, 7, 11, or 13 divides exactly into 229. Thus 229 is prime. ❑

Even though Eratosthenes' algorithm permits us to generate as many primes as we please, we cannot hope to ever get a complete list. The Greek mathematician Euclid (ca. 300 B.C.) is credited with being the first person to prove that we cannot.

There are infinitely many prime numbers

We will trace his proof in Section 5.3.

Now that we have reviewed the concept of prime, we can state a second famous old question, known as the **Goldbach conjecture.** Christian Goldbach (1690–1764) asserted the following:

Every even number greater than 4 is the sum of two odd primes.

Evidence for this conjecture is abundant:

$$6 = 3 + 3 \qquad 8 = 5 + 3 \qquad 10 = 7 + 3 \qquad 12 = 7 + 5 \qquad \ldots$$

But no one has proved it true in general or come up with a counterexample to show it false.

A third interesting question concerns Fermat's quest for a function that outputs only primes. Fermat noted that the function

$$F(n) = 2^{(2^n)} + 1$$

yields primes for inputs, 1, 2, 3, and 4; namely,

$$F(1) = 2^{(2^1)} + 1 = 2^2 + 1 = 5$$
$$F(2) = 2^{(2^2)} + 1 = 2^4 + 1 = 17$$
$$F(3) = 2^{(2^3)} + 1 = 2^8 + 1 = 257$$
$$F(4) = 2^{(2^4)} + 1 = 2^{16} + 1 = 65,537$$

He thought perhaps F would always yield primes, although—and this is historically important—he never claimed to have proven that it would. In 1732 Euler showed that

$$F(5) = 4,294,967,297$$

is not prime by factoring it into

$$641 \times 6,700,417$$

The search for a function that will always output primes still goes on.

Another famous mathematician, Carl Friedrich Gauss (1777–1855), also contributed to number theory. Gauss is credited with giving the first rigorous proof of the following theorem, called the **fundamental theorem of arithmetic.**

Except for the order in which they are written, every whole number greater than 1 is uniquely expressible as a product of primes.

A systematic way of arriving at the prime factorization of a number is to begin with the smallest prime, 2, and factor it out as many times as possible; then move to the next prime, 3, and do the same; then 5; and so on.

EXAMPLE 5	Factor 360 into a product of primes.

Solution

$$360 = 2 \times 180$$
$$= 2 \times 2 \times 90$$
$$= 2 \times 2 \times 2 \times 45$$
$$= 2 \times 2 \times 2 \times 3 \times 15$$
$$= 2 \times 2 \times 2 \times 3 \times 3 \times 5$$
$$= 2^3 \times 3^2 \times 5$$

❏

Carl Friedrich Gauss

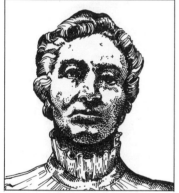

Sophie Germain

≥ **CARL FRIEDRICH GAUSS** (1777–1855), Archimedes (ca. 287–212 B.C.), and Isaac Newton (1642–1727) are considered by many to be the three greatest mathematicians of all time. Gauss was born in Brunswick, Germany, the only child of uneducated parents. His father, a sometimes stone mason, disparaged formal education, but his mother encouraged the boy, who showed his prodigious powers early by teaching himself to read and do arithmetic before entering elementary school. As an undergraduate at Göttingen, Gauss worked alone because his mathematics professor could not understand him. His doctoral dissertation, the first convincing proof of the *fundamental theorem of algebra,* was also written independently and was so spectacular that it earned him the doctoral degree, in absentia and without examination, from the University of Helmstädt in 1801. In 1804, Gauss returned to the University of Göttingen as director of its observatory. There he remained for the rest of his life, never once leaving Germany, even as a traveler. His enormous contributions to astronomy, electricity, magnetism, and optics made even more remarkable his command of all fields of mathematics. He is known as the "last complete mathematician" and was called by his contemporaries the "Prince of Mathematicians." During Gauss's tenure, Göttingen became an international mecca for mathematicians and remained so until the 1930s.

A curious story concerns the connection between Gauss and one of the earliest female mathematicians, Sophie Germain (1776–1831). Denied entrance to French and German universities because of her sex, Sophie Germain exchanged mathematical correspondence with Gauss under the pseudonym M. LeBlanc. Eventually, Gauss found out that M. LeBlanc was, in fact, a woman and recommended that the University of Göttingen award her an honorary doctor's degree. Tragically, Sophie Germain died before she could meet Gauss or receive the degree.

Another way to determine prime factorization is to fill in a **factor tree** like the one in Figure 5.1. In this method there is more freedom of choice of factors at the early stages, but eventually, by the fundamental theorem, one must end

Figure 5.1

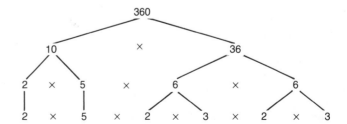

up with the same factorization. For 360, one finishes with three 2s, two 3s, and one 5 (in some order). Factor trees are popular devices in elementary school textbooks, as Figure 5.2 shows.

Prime Factors

A composite number can be shown as the product of **prime factors**.
A **factor tree** can help you find prime factors.

Step 1 Find a pair of factors for the number.

Step 2 If both factors are not prime, continue until all are prime.

Write 18 as a product of prime factors.   Write 24 as a product of prime factors.

$$18 = 2 \times 3 \times 3 \qquad 24 = 2 \times 3 \times 2 \times 2$$

All the factors are prime.

Practice • Complete the factor trees.

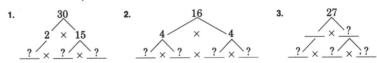

Write the number as a product of prime factors. Use a factor tree.

4. 8   **5.** 15   **6.** 28   **7.** 20   **8.** 40   **9.** 42

158

Figure 5.2 Factor trees in a fifth-grade textbook.

EXERCISE SET 5.1

1. Determine whether each statement is true or false.
   - (a) 12 is a factor of 6.
   - (b) 9 is a factor of 27.
   - (c) 3 is a factor of 3.
   - (d) 3 | 15.
   - (e) 5 is a multiple of 20.
   - (f) 18 is a multiple of 9.
   - (g) 17 is a multiple of 1.
   - (h) 10 is divisible by 20.
   - (i) $2^3 \cdot 5$ is a factor of $2^4 \cdot 3^2 \cdot 5$.
   - (j) $2 \cdot 3^2 \cdot 5^3$ is a multiple of $2^2 \cdot 3 \cdot 5$.

2. List all factors of each of the following numbers.
   - (a) 18
   - (b) 36
   - (c) $2 \cdot 3 \cdot 5 \cdot 7$ (Leave each number on your list in factored form.)
   - (d) $3 \cdot 5^2$
   - (e) 407   (*Hint:* One of the factors is 37.)

★ 3. Decide *how many* factors $2^5 \cdot 3^2 \cdot 5^4 \cdot 7$ has. Do not list them.

4. The task is to find how many factors 10! has.
   - (a) George decides to use the strategy of asking easier questions, recording the answers in a table, looking for a pattern in the table, and extending the pattern. Carry out George's plan.

Factorials	1! = 1	2! = 2	3! = 3	4! = 24	5! = ?	⋯
Number of factors	1	2	4	?	?	⋯

   - (b) Amanda decides to express 10! as a product of powers of prime numbers, and then use the technique she remembers from Exercise 3 (above). Carry out Amanda's plan.

★ 5. *An old standard:* A school has 100 students and 100 lockers. The 1st student opens all of the lockers. The 2nd student closes lockers 2, 4, 6, . . . , 100. The 3rd student changes the state of lockers 3, 6, 9, . . . , 99. (That is, he closes any of these lockers that were open and opens those that were closed.) The 4th student changes the state of lockers 4, 8, 12, . . . , 100. And so forth. Which lockers are open after the 100th student has passed by?

6. A child has 48 cubical blocks. How many different rectangular shapes can he make by using all the blocks? The two sketched in Figure 5.3 have the same shape since they are congruent (superimposable).

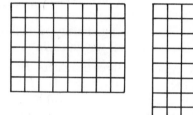

Figure 5.3

7. Pose and solve a 3-dimensional analog of Exercise 6.

8. Each of A, B, and C is a nonempty set; A and C are equivalent; and B has less elements than A. If $(A \times B) \cup C$ has 77 elements, how many elements does B have?

9. Complete the factor trees.
   - (a)

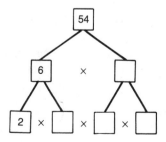

(b)

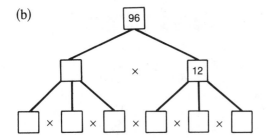

21	22	23	24	25	26	27	28	29	30
31	32	33	34	35	36	37	38	39	40
41	42	43	44	45	46	47	48	49	50
51	52	53	54	55	56	57	58	59	60
61	62	63	64	65	66	67	68	69	70
71	72	73	74	75	76	77	78	79	80
81	82	83	84	85	86	87	88	89	90
91	92	93	94	95	96	97	98	99	100

(a) Use the sieve of Eratosthenes to find all the prime numbers less than 100.

(b) Were any composite numbers left after you finished crossing off the multiples of 7?

(c) What is the smallest composite number that is not a multiple of 2, 3, 5, or 7?

★ 10. *A modern classic:* A host has three daughters. He tells a guest that the product of their ages is 72 and the sum of their ages is the house number. The guest rushes out to see the house number, comes back, and says that he needs to know more. The host says that the oldest daughter likes strawberry pudding. How old are they?
Hint: The problem-solving strategy of making a systematic list is a natural way to begin.

★ 11. *A variation:* A host has three daughters. He tells a guest that the sum of their ages is 13 and the product of their ages is the (nonzero) house number. The guest rushes out to see the house number, comes back, and says that he needs to know more. The host says that the oldest daughter likes strawberry pudding. How old are they?

12. Express each of the following as a product of primes.
(a) 42
(b) 63
(c) 64
(d) 100
(e) 1000
(f) 180
(g) 126
(h) 1001
(i) $30 \cdot 40$
(j) $12 \cdot 15 \cdot 17$
(k) 24^3
(l) 12^5

★ 13. How many 0s occur at the end of the Hindu-Arabic numeral for $100 \cdot 99 \cdot 98 \cdot 97 \cdot \cdot \cdot \cdot \cdot 4 \cdot 3 \cdot 2 \cdot 1$?

14. Is every even number greater than 4 *uniquely* expressible as a *sum* of two primes?

15. Here is a list of all natural numbers from 2 to 100:

	2	3	4	5	6	7	8	9	10
11	12	13	14	15	16	17	18	19	20

16. To prove that 167 is a prime number, it suffices to check that no prime number less than _____ is a factor of it. Do so.

17. If you wanted to prove that Fermat's number, $F(4) = 65,537$, is prime, it would suffice to check that no prime less than _____ is a factor of it.

18. The prime numbers 2 and 3 are consecutive primes. Are there any other pairs of consecutive primes?

19. The prime numbers 17 and 19 are called *twin primes* because they differ by 2. Find some other twin primes on your list of primes less than 100.

★ 20. The prime numbers 3, 5, 7 are triplet primes. Are there any other triplet primes? *Hint:* Imagine that each of the natural numbers n, $n + 2$, and $n + 4$ is expressed in base-three notation. Conclude that one of them must be a multiple of 3.

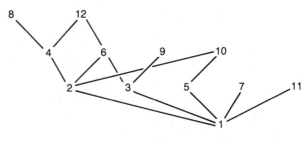

Figure 5.4

21. In Figure 5.4 the numbers 1 through 12 are arranged in a *lattice* that shows which numbers are factors of which.
    (a) How can you tell, by looking at the lattice, that 3 is a factor of 6? That 6 is not a factor of 3? That 3 is a factor of 12? That 3 is not a factor of 8?
    (b) Use the lattice to find the set of all factors of 12.
    (c) Where are the prime numbers in this lattice?
    (d) Extend the lattice so that all of the numbers 1 through 18 are included.
    (e) How can you tell, by looking at the lattice, that 2 is a factor of both 8 and 12? Find the "greatest common factor" of 8 and 12.
    (f) How can you tell, by looking at the lattice, that 12 is a multiple of both 2 and 3? Find the "least common multiple" of 2 and 3.

22. The function $f(n) = n^2 - n + 41$ outputs primes for each of the inputs 1, 2, 3, . . . , 40.
    (a) Find $f(1), f(2), f(3), f(4)$, and $f(5)$.
    (b) Show that $f(41)$ is not prime.
    (c) Show that $f(42)$ is composite.

★ 23. Show that if $f(n) = an^2 + bn + c$, where a, b, and c are natural numbers and $c > 1$, then there is a natural number n for which $f(n)$ is composite.

24. Convince yourself that this trick works; then explain why: "Take a three-digit number with all digits the same. Divide it by the sum of its digits. Your answer is 37."

5.2 Greatest Common Factor and Least Common Multiple

In the previous section we considered factors and multiples of a *single* number. Now we shall investigate common factors and common multiples of a *pair* of numbers.

Greatest Common Factor

The greatest common factor of two numbers is exactly what the words say.

The **greatest common factor** of a and b, written GCF(a, b), is the largest number that is a factor of both a and b.

Many college texts use the term *greatest common divisor* and the initials GCD. At the elementary level, though, the initials CD suggest too strongly "common denominator"—and, of course, there is no such thing as a greatest common denominator. That is why we prefer GCF. In the exercises you will see several kinds of problems whose solutions depend on finding the GCF of two numbers. Perhaps the main reason the concept of GCF appears in the elementary grades, however, is its relation to reducing fractions to lowest terms. If you are given a fraction like $\frac{30}{45}$, and if you spot that 15 is the GCF of its numerator and denominator, then you can reduce it to lowest terms in one step:

$$\frac{30}{45} = \frac{2 \cdot \cancel{15}}{3 \cdot \cancel{15}} = \frac{2}{3}$$

We shall consider three methods for finding the GCF of two numbers a and b. The first is the method suggested by the definition.

> **Definition Method for Finding the GCF**
>
> 1. List all factors of a and list all factors of b.
> 2. Consider the numbers that appear on both lists.
> 3. The greatest number is the GCF.

EXAMPLE 1 Find the following.
(a) GCF(30, 45)
(b) GCF(252, 420)

Solution (a) The factors of 30 are $\{1, 2, 3, 5, 6, 10, 15, 30\}$. The factors of 45 are $\{1, 3, 5, 9, 15, 45\}$. The common factors are $\{1, 3, 5, 15\}$. The greatest common factor is 15.

(b) The factors of 252 are

$$\{1, 2, 3, 4, 6, 7, 9, 12, 14, 18, 21, 28, 36, 42, 63, 84, 126, 252\}$$

The factors of 420 are

$$\{1, 2, 3, 4, 5, 6, 7, 10, 12, 14, 15, 20,$$
$$21, 28, 30, 35, 42, 60, 70, 84, 105, 140, 260, 420\}$$

Thus the common factors are

$$\{1, 2, 3, 4, 6, 7, 12, 14, 21, 28, 42, 84\}$$

So

$$\text{GCF}(252, 420) = 84 \qquad ❏$$

Clearly, the definition method is ponderous even for moderately large numbers like 252 and 420.

Our second method of finding the GCF is based on prime factorization and is reasonably efficient for moderately large numbers. We illustrate it with examples before formalizing.

EXAMPLE 2 Use the prime factorization method to find the following.
(a) GCF(30, 45)
(b) GCF(252, 420)

Solution   (a) Factor both 30 and 45 into products of primes:

$$30 = 2 \cdot 3 \cdot 5$$
$$\qquad\qquad | \quad |$$
$$45 = 3 \cdot 3 \cdot 5$$

Notice that $3 \cdot 5$ is a common factor of 30 and 45, and that no larger number is a factor of both.

(b) Factor both 252 and 420 into products of primes:

$$252 = 2 \cdot 126 = 2 \cdot 2 \cdot 63 = 2 \cdot 2 \cdot 9 \cdot 7 = \quad 2 \cdot 2 \cdot 3 \cdot 3 \cdot 7$$
$$\qquad\qquad\qquad\qquad\qquad\qquad\qquad\qquad | \quad | \quad | \qquad |$$
$$420 = 2 \cdot 210 = 2 \cdot 2 \cdot 105 = 2 \cdot 2 \cdot 3 \cdot 35 = 2 \cdot 2 \cdot 3 \cdot 5 \cdot 7$$
$$\text{GCF}(252, 420) = 2 \cdot 2 \cdot 3 \cdot 7 = 84$$ ❏

To reveal a pattern in the prime factorization procedure, we use exponential notation, including zero exponents:

$$252 = 2^2 \cdot 3^2 \cdot 5^0 \cdot 7^1$$
$$420 = 2^2 \cdot 3^1 \cdot 5^1 \cdot 7^1$$

The GCF now appears as the product of the *lowest* powers of the distinct primes:

$$\text{GCF}(252, 420) = 2^2 \cdot 3^1 \cdot 5^0 \cdot 7^1$$

Here is the generalization.

Prime Factorization Method for Finding the GCF

1. Express a and b as products of powers of primes. Include zero exponents if necessary so that the same primes appear in the representations of both a and b.

2. The product of the *lowest* powers of all the distinct primes is the GCF.

EXAMPLE 3   Use the prime factorization method to determine the GCF of the following numbers, which have been expressed as products of powers of primes:

$$a = 2^3 \cdot 3 \cdot 5^4 \cdot 11 \qquad b = 2 \cdot 3 \cdot 7^2 \cdot 11^3$$

Solution   Rewrite a and b using exponents 0 and 1, as needed, so that exactly the same primes appear in both factorizations:

$$a = 2^3 \cdot 3^1 \cdot 5^4 \cdot 7^0 \cdot 11^1$$
$$b = 2^1 \cdot 3^1 \cdot 5^0 \cdot 7^2 \cdot 11^3$$

Now, collect the lowest powers:

$$\text{GCF}(a, b) = 2^1 \cdot 3^1 \cdot 5^0 \cdot 7^0 \cdot 11^1 = 66 \qquad \square$$

This example illustrates the effectiveness of the prime factorization algorithm on even very large numbers, providing they have already been factored into primes. The catch is that factoring a large number into a product of primes is generally tedious. Consider, for example, the task of finding the GCF of 6050 and 12,199. An enormous amount of time would be required to determine the prime factorizations

$$6050 = 2 \cdot 5^2 \cdot 11^2 \qquad \text{and} \qquad 12{,}199 = 11 \cdot 1109$$

before one could draw the conclusion that

$$\text{GCF}\,(6050, 12{,}199) = 11$$

For large numbers there is a third algorithm for finding the GCF that is much more efficient than the prime factorization algorithm. It is called the **Euclidean algorithm,** and you met its flowchart in Exercise 15 of Section 3.10. To review briefly, it is a successive division algorithm in which old divisors become new dividends and old remainders become new divisors. It stops when a remainder of zero occurs, and its output, the GCF, is the last divisor.

EXAMPLE 4   Use the Euclidean algorithm to find the following.
(a) GCF(252, 420)
(b) GCF(6050, 12,199)

Solution

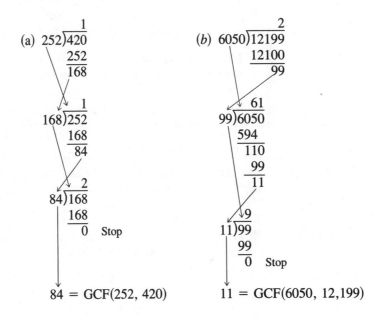

$$84 = \text{GCF}(252, 420) \qquad\qquad 11 = \text{GCF}(6050, 12{,}199) \qquad \square$$

For now you should be content to understand *how* to run the Euclidean algorithm. In the next section we will look at *why* it works.

Least Common Multiple

The least common multiple of two numbers is, again, just what the words say, except that nonzero is assumed.

The **least common multiple** of a and b, written LCM(a, b), is the smallest nonzero number that is a multiple of both a and b.

Although we shall see a variety of applications in the exercises, the main use of the LCM concept in the elementary grades is in adding and subtracting fractions with different denominators. If you are given a sum like

$$\tfrac{7}{30} + \tfrac{8}{45}$$

to compute, and if you can spot that 90 is the LCM of the two denominators, then you have the found the "least common denominator" and can finish up the problem as follows:

$$\tfrac{7}{30} + \tfrac{8}{45} = \tfrac{21}{90} + \tfrac{16}{90} = \tfrac{37}{90}$$

As in the case of the GCF, there are three methods of finding the LCM. The definition method follows.

Definition Method for Finding the LCM

1. Begin listing nonzero multiples of a, and begin listing nonzero multiples of b.
2. Consider the numbers that appear on both lists.
3. The first (smallest) number is the LCM.

EXAMPLE 5   Use the definition method to find LCM(30, 45).

Solution   The first several nonzero multiples of 30 are

$$30, 60, 90, 120, 150, 180, 210, 240, 270, 300, \ldots$$

The first several nonzero multiples of 45 are

$$45, 90, 135, 180, 225, 270, 315, \ldots$$

The common multiples are

$$90, 180, 270, \ldots$$

The least common multiple is 90.   ❑

The prime factorization method for finding the LCM is suggested by the next example.

EXAMPLE 6   Use the prime factorization method to find the following.
(a) LCM(30, 45)

(b) LCM(252, 420)

Solution   (a) Factor 30 and 45 into products of primes:

$$30 = 2 \cdot 3 \cdot 5$$
$$45 = 3 \cdot 3 \cdot 5$$

Observe that any multiple of 30 must have a 2, a 3, and a 5 among its prime factors; and any multiple of 45 must have two 3s and a 5 among its prime factors. The smallest number that satisfies these two conditions is

$$2 \cdot 3 \cdot 3 \cdot 5$$

If we use exponential notation, the pattern is clearer:

$$30 = 2^1 \cdot 3^1 \cdot 5^1$$
$$45 = 2^0 \cdot 3^2 \cdot 5^1$$
$$\text{LCM}(30, 45) = 2^1 \cdot 3^2 \cdot 5^1$$

We got the LCM by multiplying the highest powers of distinct primes.

(b) As we did earlier, we express both 252 and 420 as products of powers of the same set of distinct primes:

$$252 = 2^2 \cdot 3^2 \cdot 5^0 \cdot 7^1$$
$$420 = 2^2 \cdot 3^1 \cdot 5^1 \cdot 7^1$$

Now multiply the highest powers:

$$\text{LCM}(252, 420) = 2^2 \cdot 3^2 \cdot 5^1 \cdot 7^1 = 1260$$ ❑

The generalization from the examples is this:

Prime Factorization Method for Finding the LCM

1. Express a and b as products of powers of primes. Include zero exponents, if necessary, so that the same primes appear in the representations of both a and b.

2. The product of the *highest* powers of all the distinct primes is the LCM.

The close connection between the prime factorization methods for finding the GCF and the LCM leads to an important relationship between the GCF and the LCM, which in turn provides us with a third method of finding the LCM. Consider the two numbers 420 and 990, which have these factored forms:

$$420 = 2^2 \cdot 3^1 \cdot 5^1 \cdot 7^1 \cdot 11^0$$
$$990 = 2^1 \cdot 3^2 \cdot 5^1 \cdot 7^0 \cdot 11^1$$

To find the LCM, we select the highest power of each prime:

$$\text{LCM} = 2^2 \cdot 3^2 \cdot 5^1 \cdot 7^1 \cdot 11^1$$

To find the GCF, we select the lowest power of each prime:

$$\text{GCF} = 2^1 \cdot 3^1 \cdot 5^1 \cdot 7^0 \cdot 11^0$$

If we now multiply the LCM times the GCF,

$$\text{LCM} \cdot \text{GCF} = (2^2 \cdot 3^2 \cdot 5^1 \cdot 7^1 \cdot 11^1) \cdot (2^1 \cdot 3^1 \cdot 5^1 \cdot 7^0 \cdot 11^0)$$

and rearrange and regroup factors,

$$\text{LCM} \cdot \text{GCF} = (2^2 \cdot 3^1 \cdot 5^1 \cdot 7^1 \cdot 11^0) \cdot (2^1 \cdot 3^2 \cdot 5^1 \cdot 7^0 \cdot 11^1)$$

we see that

$$\text{LCM} \cdot \text{GCF} = \text{the product of the original two numbers}$$

In general:

$$\text{LCM}(a, b) \cdot \text{GCF}(a, b) = a \cdot b$$

The practical significance of this relationship between the LCM and the GCF is that it allows us to consider the problem of computing the LCM as a problem of computing the GCF, for which we have the powerful Euclidean algorithm. This, then, is our third method of finding the LCM.

EXAMPLE 7   Use the formula

$$\text{LCM}(a, b) = \frac{a \cdot b}{\text{GCF}(a, b)}$$

to find the following.
(a) LCM(252, 420)
(b) LCM(6050, 12,199)

Solution   (a) Earlier, we found that GCF(252, 420) = 84. Thus

$$\text{LCM}(252, 420) = \frac{252 \cdot 420}{84} = 252 \cdot 5 = 1260$$

(b) Earlier, we found that GCF(6050, 12,199) = 11. Thus

$$\text{LCM}(6050, 12{,}199) = \frac{6050 \cdot 12{,}199}{11} = 550 \cdot 12{,}199 = 6{,}709{,}450$$

❑

EXERCISE SET 5.2

1. Fill in the Venn diagram of Figure 5.5 as completely as you can, and then locate in it the GCF of 18 and 30.

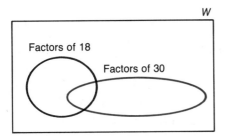

Figure 5.5

2. Begin filling in the Venn diagram of Figure 5.6, and then locate in it the LCM of 18 and 30.

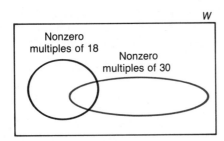

Figure 5.6

3. Refer to the factor lattice in Exercise 21, Section 5.1, and imagine that it includes all the natural numbers. Given a pair of natural numbers, say 28 and 40, how would you locate their LCM on the lattice? How would you locate their GCF?

4. Find the GCF of each pair of numbers. (Leave it in factored form.)
   (a) $2 \cdot 2 \cdot 3 \cdot 7 \cdot 11$ and $2 \cdot 3 \cdot 3 \cdot 5 \cdot 7$
   (b) $2 \cdot 3 \cdot 3 \cdot 7 \cdot 11$ and $3 \cdot 5 \cdot 11 \cdot 11$
   (c) $5 \cdot 7 \cdot 11$ and $2 \cdot 3 \cdot 3 \cdot 13$
   (d) $2^2 \cdot 3^4 \cdot 5^1 \cdot 7^0 \cdot 11^1$ and
       $2^1 \cdot 3^3 \cdot 5^4 \cdot 7^2 \cdot 11^0$

5. Find the LCM of each pair of numbers in Exercise 4. (Leave it in factored form.)

6. Given $a = 2 \cdot 3 \cdot 4 \cdot 5 \cdot 6 \cdot 7 \cdot 8$ and $b = 5 \cdot 6 \cdot 7 \cdot 8 \cdot 9 \cdot 10$
   (a) Find the GCF of a and b.
   (b) Find the LCM of a and b.

7. The GCF of 630 and 1716 is 6. What is their LCM?

8. The GCF of 66 and x is 11; the LCM of 66 and x is 858. Find x.

9. Use the Euclidean algorithm to find the GCF of each pair of numbers.
   (a) 286 and 92   (b) 2650 and 1855
   (c) 92 and 94   (d) n and $n + 1$

10. Find the LCM of each pair of numbers in Exercise 8. 9.

11. Reduce to lowest terms.
    (a) $\dfrac{92}{286}$ (b) $\dfrac{1855}{2650}$

    (c) $\dfrac{92}{94}$ (d) $\dfrac{n}{n + 1}$

12. Compute the sums.
    (a) $\dfrac{5}{286} + \dfrac{1}{92}$ (b) $\dfrac{12}{1855} + \dfrac{77}{2650}$

13. Mr. Wurst has donated 217 hot dogs and Ms. Fizz has donated 126 bottles of pop for a children's picnic. But they have stipulated that each child is to receive the same amount of refreshments, and all of the refreshments are to be used up.

   (a) How many children (at most) can be invited to the picnic? How many hot dogs will each have to eat?

   (b) If Mr. Wurst's dog eats one of the hot dogs, then how many children can be invited?

   (c) If Wurst's dog eats seven of the hot dogs, then how many children can be invited?

14. How many teeth should there be on gear A in Figure 5.7 if each turn of the shaft attached to A is to produce a whole number of turns of the shafts attached to gears B and C? (There is not room for more than 50 teeth on gear A.) If shaft A spins at 480 revolutions per minute (rpm), how fast will shaft B spin? If Shaft C spins at 500 rpm, how fast will shaft B spin? *Hint:* Count teeth.

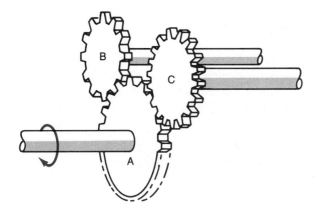

Figure 5.7

15. A child has a large supply of dominoes that measure 32 mm by 52 mm. She wants to lay them out to form a solid square, and she wants them all to be laid out horizontally. What will be the dimensions of the square, and how many dominoes will it require?

16. The swimming pool is open from 9:00 A.M. until 12:00 noon, and again from 1:00 P.M. until 5:12 P.M. Two lifeguards want to alternate shifts throughout the day. The shifts are all to be of the same length, and one is to end at noon. How long should each shift be?

17. Jack and Jill dive into the deep end of a pool simultaneously, and begin swimming lengths. Jack swims at the steady rate of 1 length every 84 seconds; Jill swims at the steady rate of 1 length every 78 seconds. How many lengths will Jill have swum at the moment when she and Jack first reach the same end of the pool (either deep or shallow) simultaneously?

18. Suppose you have a morning kindergarten class of 32 children and an afternoon class of 24. A room mother has promised to supply jelly beans for one of the classes, and you are to supply the other. The problem is that you've forgotten which class is yours. How many jelly beans should you bring if you want to be sure that every child gets the same number and that all of them are used up?

19. Seventeen-year locusts, known to biologists as periodical cicadas, spend the first 17 years of their lives underground, emerge briefly to reproduce, and then die. Biologist Monte Lloyd of the University of Chicago believes that this peculiar life span is actually a sophisticated strategy for survival. According to his theory, "If a predator had a life cycle of six years, for example, it would not encounter cicadas above-ground more than once a century." Explain, assuming that the predators have a subterranean lifestyle similar to that of the cicadas.

20. How frequently could a predator with a life cycle of 6 years encounter cicadas with the following life spans?

   (a) 15 years   (b) 16 years   (c) 18 years

21. Decide what is meant by the LCM of *three* numbers and then find the following.

   (a) LCM(10, 12, 14)
   (b) LCM($2^2 \cdot 3 \cdot 5, 2 \cdot 5^2 \cdot 11, 2 \cdot 3^2 \cdot 5 \cdot 7$)

22. Decide what is meant by the GCF of *three* numbers and then find the following.
    (a) GCF(10, 12, 14)
    (b) GCF($2^2 \cdot 3 \cdot 5, 2 \cdot 5^2 \cdot 11, 2 \cdot 3^2 \cdot 5 \cdot 7$)

23. Does GCF(a, b, c) × LCM (a, b, c) = a × b × c?

24. Find three consecutive positive integers having both of these properties: (i) none of the three is a prime number, (ii) their LCM is their product.

25. The breakfast cereal your factory produces is packaged in 4-in by 6-in by 10-in boxes. You are to design a cubical crate for shipping these boxes. The crate is to hold no more than 1000 boxes and there is to be no wasted space inside.
    (a) What will be the (inside) dimensions of the crate?
    (b) How many boxes of cereal will each crate hold?
    (c) What advantage does a cubical crate have over an ordinary oblong one?

26. Your new car needs a lube every 6000 miles, a tune-up every 9000 miles, and a brake inspection every 15,000 miles. When will you first have it in to get all three things done?

27. Gloria has three pieces of two-by-four lumber of lengths 60 in, 72 in, and 90 in. She wants to saw them up into building blocks, all of the same length, for use as playthings at the nursery school. If she wants to waste no wood, how long could she make the blocks, and how many (total) would there be?

28. It takes Frank 42 hr to paint a house, and it takes Joe 56 hr.
    (a) Estimate how long it would take them working together.
    (b) Now determine exactly how long it would take them working together, assuming that neither one of them is speeded up or slowed down by the collaboration.

Computer Vignette D

Figure 5.8 is a program that uses the Euclidean algorithm to compute the greatest common factor of any two positive integers you wish to input. Figure 5.9 is a typical run. Lines 60 and 70 carry out the switch "old divisor becomes new dividend and old remainder becomes new divisor."

Figure 5.8

```
10    PRINT "TYPE IN THE TWO POSITIVE INTEGERS WHOSE GCF
      YOU WANT. SEPARATE THEM BY A COMMA."
20    INPUT X, Y
30    LET Q = INT(X/Y)
40    LET R = X - Q * Y
50    IF R = 0 THEN 90
60    LET X = Y
70    LET Y = R
80    GOTO 30
90    LET G = Y
100   PRINT "THEIR GCF IS ";G
110   PRINT
120   PRINT "WANT TO STOP?"
```

```
130    PRINT "TYPE 1 FOR YES, 0 FOR NO"
140    INPUT A
150    IF A = 0 THEN 10
160    END
```

Figure 5.9

```
]RUN
TYPE IN THE TWO POSITIVE INTEGERS WHOSE GCF YOU WANT.
SEPARATE THEM BY A COMMA.
?120,48
THEIR GCF IS 24

WANT TO STOP?
TYPE 1 FOR YES, 0 FOR NO
?0
TYPE IN THE TWO POSITIVE INTEGERS WHOSE GCF YOU WANT.
SEPARATE THEM BY A COMMA.
?360,5280
THEIR GCF IS 120

WANT TO STOP?
TYPE 1 FOR YES, 0 FOR NO
?0
TYPE IN THE TWO POSITIVE INTEGERS WHOSE GCF YOU WANT.
SEPARATE THEM BY A COMMA.
?36742,40280
THEIR GCF IS 2

WANT TO STOP?
TYPE 1 FOR YES, 0 FOR NO
?1
```

5.3   *Divisibility*

In the previous sections we saw how important it is to be able to factor a number. In this section we give techniques for identifying certain small factors. These **divisibility tests** are useful tools to have at one's disposal. To explain the tests, we need to recall the basic definition and derive two simple theorems.

Definition.   We say that a is **divisible** by d (or that d divides a) if there is a whole number $\overline{a}$ such that

$$a = d \cdot \overline{a}$$

Theorem 1   Divisibility is transitive. That is, if a is divisible by b and b is divisible by c, then a is divisible by c.

Proof.

$$a \text{ divisible by } b \Rightarrow a = b \cdot \bar{a} \quad \text{ for some whole number } \bar{a}$$
$$b \text{ divisible by } c \Rightarrow b = c \cdot \bar{b} \quad \text{ for some whole number } \bar{b}$$

Substituting $c \cdot \bar{b}$ for b in the first equation yields

$$a = (c \cdot \bar{b}) \cdot \bar{a}$$

That is, by the associative property of multiplication,

$$a = c \cdot (\bar{b} \cdot \bar{a})$$

from which it follows that a is divisible by c.   ❏

EXAMPLE 1   Since 62,500 is divisible by 100 and since 100 is divisible by 4, it follows that 62,500 is divisible by 4. If we retrace the steps of the preceding proof, we get added verification:

$$62{,}500 = 100 \cdot 625$$

and

$$100 = 4 \cdot 25$$

so

$$62{,}500 = 4 \cdot 25 \cdot 625$$ ❏

Theorem 2   If two numbers are divisible by d, then so are their sum and their difference.

Proof.   Suppose both a and b are divisible by d. Then there are whole numbers $\bar{a}$ and $\bar{b}$ so that

$$a = d \cdot \bar{a} \quad \text{and} \quad b = d \cdot \bar{b}$$

Thus

$$a + b = d \cdot \bar{a} + d \cdot \bar{b} = d \cdot (\bar{a} + \bar{b})$$

from which it follows that $a + b$ is divisible by d.

To see that the difference between a and b is divisible by d, suppose for the sake of argument that $a \geq b$. From the equations

$$a - b = d \cdot \bar{a} - d \cdot \bar{b} = d \cdot (\bar{a} - \bar{b})$$

it follows that $a - b$ is divisible by d.   Q.E.D.

EXAMPLE 2 Since 100 is divisible by 4 and since 44 is divisible by 4, it follows that $100 + 44 = 144$ is divisible by 4 and $100 - 44 = 56$ is divisible by 4. Again, retracing the steps of the preceding proof in this specific numerical case makes it clear that the theorem is true:

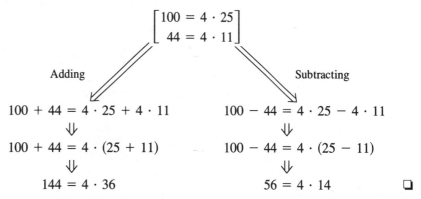

$$\begin{bmatrix} 100 = 4 \cdot 25 \\ 44 = 4 \cdot 11 \end{bmatrix}$$

Adding   Subtracting

$100 + 44 = 4 \cdot 25 + 4 \cdot 11$ $100 - 44 = 4 \cdot 25 - 4 \cdot 11$

$100 + 44 = 4 \cdot (25 + 11)$ $100 - 44 = 4 \cdot (25 - 11)$

$144 = 4 \cdot 36$ $56 = 4 \cdot 14$ ❏

Now we can go on to establish the standard divisibility tests. A word of warning, though: These tests refer specifically to the usual base-ten numerals for whole numbers. If you work in some other numeration system, you will need a whole new battery of tests.

Test for Divisibility by 2

A number is divisible by 2 if and only if its units digit is divisible by 2.

The phrase "if and only if" indicates that this test is a two-edged sword: If the units digit of a number *is* divisible by 2, then the number *is* divisible by 2. If the units digit of a number is *not* divisible by 2, then the number is *not* divisible by 2. All of the divisibility tests of this section are two-edged swords.

To see why the test for divisibility by 2 works, let us first consider the case of a number, say 5386, whose units digit is divisible by 2. Begin by breaking down 5386 as follows:

$$5386 = 5380 + 6 = 538 \cdot 10 + 6$$

Now, observe that $538 \cdot 10$ is divisible by 10 and 10 is divisible by 2, and so by transitivity (Theorem 1) $538 \cdot 10$ is divisible by 2. Furthermore, 6 is divisible by 2, so by Theorem 2 the sum $538 \cdot 10 + 6$ is also. That is, 5386 is divisible by 2.

Now, let us consider the case of a number, say 4873, whose units digit is *not* divisible by 2. Break it down as follows:

$$4873 = 487 \cdot 10 + 3$$

Thus

$$3 = 4873 - 487 \cdot 10$$

As before, $487 \cdot 10$ is divisible by 2. If the original number 4873 were divisible by 2, then by Theorem 2 the difference $4873 - 487 \cdot 10$ would also be divisible by 2. But 3 is not divisible by 2. Thus 4873 could not be divisible by 2.

Test for Divisibility by 5

A number is divisible by 5 if and only if its units digit is divisible by 5.

The explanation of why this test works is just like the explanation of the 2s test. Both tests stem ultimately from the fact that the base 10 of our numeration system is a multiple of 2 and of 5. The key step in showing why 7835 is divisible by 5 is:

$$7835 = 783 \cdot 10 + 5$$

Do you see why the right-hand side, and thus the left also, is divisible by 5?

Test for Divisibility by 3

A number is divisible by 3 if and only if the sum of its digits is divisible by 3.

For example, 4785 is divisible by 3 since

$$4 + 7 + 8 + 5 = 24$$

and 24 is divisible by 3. To see why the test works, observe that

$$
\begin{aligned}
4785 &= 4 \cdot 1000 + 7 \cdot 100 + 8 \cdot 10 + 5 \\
&= 4(999 + 1) + 7(99 + 1) + 8(9 + 1) + 5 \\
&= \underbrace{(4 \cdot 999 + 7 \cdot 99 + 8 \cdot 9)}_{\text{A number divisible by 9 and hence by 3}} + \underbrace{(4 + 7 + 8 + 5)}_{\text{The sum of the digits}}
\end{aligned}
$$

Since each of the two groupings on the right is divisible by 3, it follows that their sum 4785 is also divisible by 3.

As a second example, consider a number like 625, the sum of whose digits is *not* divisible by 3. Expand as we just did:

$$
\begin{aligned}
625 &= 6 \cdot 100 + 2 \cdot 10 + 5 \\
&= 6(99 + 1) + 2(9 + 1) + 5 \\
&= \underbrace{(6 \cdot 99 + 2 \cdot 9)}_{\text{A number divisible by 9 and hence by 3}} + \underbrace{(6 + 2 + 5)}_{\text{The sum of the digits}}
\end{aligned}
$$

Thus

$$(6 + 2 + 5) = 625 - (6 \cdot 99 + 2 \cdot 9)$$

If the original number were divisible by 3, then $(6 + 2 + 5)$ would be the difference of two numbers divisible by 3 and hence would itself be divisible by 3. But it is not.

Similar reasoning leads immediately to a test for divisibility by 9.

Test for Divisibility by 9

A number is divisible by 9 if and only if the sum of its digits is divisible by 9.

For the sake of completeness we shall catalog the divisibility tests for the rest of the natural numbers from 2 through 12. The easiest one of all is the 10s test.

Test for Divisibility by 10

A number is divisible by 10 if and only if its units digit is 0.

The explanation was given in Chapter 4: The effect of multiplying a whole number by 10 is to append a 0 to its (base-ten) numeral.

Test for Divisibility by 4

A number is divisible by 4 if and only if the number represented by its last *two* digits is divisible by 4.

For example, 9736 is divisible by 4 since 36 is, and 2715 is not divisible by 4 since 15 is not. The explanation is similar to the ones for the 2s and 5s tests and is based on the fact that 100, the square of the base of our numeration system, is divisible by 4. Specifically, write

$$9736 = 97 \cdot 100 + 36$$

to see that 9736 is the sum of two numbers that are divisible by 4. And write

$$2715 = 27 \cdot 100 + 15$$

that is,

$$15 = 2715 - 27 \cdot 100$$

to see that 2715 could not be divisible by 4.

> ### Test for Divisibility by 8
>
> A number is divisible by 8 if and only if the number represented by its last three digits is divisible by 8.

For example, 39,168 is divisible by 8 since 168 is. The explanation depends on the decomposition

$$39,168 = 39 \cdot 1000 + 168$$

and the fact that 1000, the cube of our base, is divisible by 8.

The tests for divisibility by 6 and by 12 depend on tests already developed and on the fundamental theorem of arithmetic.

> ### Test for Divisibility by 6
>
> A number is divisible by 6 if and only if it is divisible by both 2 and 3.

Explanation: A number will be divisible by 6 if and only if it has both a 2 and a 3 in its prime factorization.

> ### Test for Divisibility by 12
>
> A number is divisible by 12 if and only if it is divisible by both 4 and 3.

Explanation: A number is divisible by 12 if and only if it has two 2s and a 3 in its prime factorization.

The last two divisibility tests on our list are those for the prime numbers 7 and 11. These tests are rather technical algorithms, and we shall not take the time to justify them.

> ### Test for Divisibility by 11
>
> Sum alternate digits. Sum the remaining digits. Subtract one of these sums from the other. The original number is divisible by 11 if and only if this difference is.

EXAMPLE 3   Test 8,273,958 for divisibility by 11.

Solution

$$
\begin{array}{c}
8\quad 2\quad 7\quad 3\quad 9\quad 5\quad 8 \qquad \overset{\text{Add}}{\longrightarrow} \;\; 32 \\
\text{Add} \nearrow \; \dfrac{10}{22} \;\; \text{Subtract}
\end{array}
$$

Since 22 is divisible by 11, so is 8,273,958.   ❏

> **Test for Divisibility by 7**
>
> Double the units digit of the original number. Subtract this product from the number obtained by dropping the units digit from the original number. The original number is divisible by 7 if and only if this difference is.

EXAMPLE 4   Test these numbers for divisibility by 7

(a) 462
(b) 5269

Solution   (a)   4   6 ⎪ 2
                       4 ↙
                  ———————
                  4   2

and 42 is divisible by 7, so 462 is too.

(b)   5   2   6 ⎪ 9
          1   8 ↙
      ———————————
      5   0   8

To see whether 508 is divisible by 7, run the "double, drop, and subtract" algorithm again:

                5   0 ⎪ 8
                1   6 ↙
            ———————————
            3   4

Now 34 is not divisible by 7, so 508 is not divisible by 7, so 5269 is not divisible by 7. ❑

We conclude this section by using our two simple theorems about divisibility to prove some important results stated earlier. First we prove, as Euclid did, that there are infinitely many prime numbers.

1. Suppose, on the contrary, that there are only finitely many primes. Label them $p_1, p_2, \ldots, p_n$.

2. Now consider the number k given by

$$k = p_1 \cdot p_2 \cdot p_3 \cdot \cdots \cdot p_n + 1$$

3. Rewrite the equation as

$$1 = k - p_1 \cdot p_2 \cdot p_3 \cdot \cdots \cdot p_n$$

4. Now none of the primes $p_1, p_2, \ldots, p_n$ could be a divisor of k, for if it were, it would be a divisor of both terms on the right-hand side of the equation in step 3 and hence a divisor of their difference, 1. But no prime number is a divisor of 1.

5. Thus the prime factorization of k must consist of prime numbers not on the list $p_1, p_2, \ldots, p_n$. That is, the list was incomplete. The number of primes is infinite.   Q.E.D.

Second, let us see *why* the Euclidean algorithm produces the GCF of its two input numbers. To be specific, suppose the input numbers are 70 and 252. The schematic description of the algorithm,

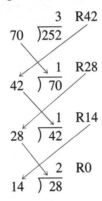

can be restated as a sequence of equations:

$$252 = 3 \cdot 70 + 42$$
$$70 = 1 \cdot 42 + 28$$
$$42 = 1 \cdot 28 + 14$$
$$28 = 2 \cdot 14$$

The claim to be justified is that the last divisor, 14, is the GCF of 70 and 252.

To see that 14 is a *common* factor of 70 and 252, look at the equations from the bottom up. The fourth equation shows that 28 is divisible by 14. Now, consider the third equation. On the right-hand side are two terms, each divisible by 14. Thus by Theorem 2 their sum, 42, is divisible by 14. Now, consider the second equation. Again, both terms on the right-hand side are divisible by 14, and thus their sum, 70, is also. Finally, in the top equation 14 is a divisor of both 70 and 42, hence of 252. Thus 14 is a common divisor of 70 and 252.

To see that 14 is the *greatest* common factor, suppose d is any common factor of 70 and 252 and work from the top down. Since d is a factor of 70, and 70 is a factor of $3 \cdot 70$, by Theorem 1, d is also a factor of $3 \cdot 70$. But d is a factor of 252 as well. Hence, by Theorem 2, d is a factor of the difference $252 - 3 \cdot 70 = 42$. Now, using the fact that d is a factor of both 70 and 42, deduce from the second equation that d is a factor of 28. Finally, move to the third equation and infer similarly that d is a factor of 14. What we have shown, then, is that any common factor of 70 and 252 is also a factor of 14. Thus 14 is the greatest common factor.

EXERCISE SET 5.3

1. If a number is *not* divisible by 2, could it be divisible by 4, 6, 8, 10, or 12?

2. If a number is *not* divisible by 3, could it be divisible by 6, 9, or 12?

In Exercises 3–10 test each number for divisibility by each of 2, 3, 4, 5, 6, 7, 8, 9, 10, 11, 12.

3. 295   4. 3215   5. 2358   6. 8325

7. 52,829   8. 95,712   9. 391,963   10. 123,456

11. Find the missing digit d so that the following statements are true.
    (a) 250,4d8 is divisible by 9.
    (b) 25d,408 is divisible by 11.
    (c) d4,173 is divisible by 7.
    (d) 22,9d6 is divisible by 12.
    (e) $7777 \cdot d + d5$ is divisible by 7.

12. Use divisibility tests to factor each of the following into primes.
    (a) 205   (b) 341   (c) 153   (d) 828

13. List all the prime numbers between 390 and 400.

14. Determine whether each statement is true or false.
    (a) If n is divisible by 4 and by 5, then n is divisible by 20.
    (b) If n is divisible by 6 and by 10, then n is divisible by 60.
    (c) If n is divisible by 5, 6, and 7, then n is divisible by $5 \cdot 6 \cdot 7$.
    (d) If n is divisible by 6, 7, and 8, then n is divisible by $6 \cdot 7 \cdot 8$.

15. What is the smallest natural number that is divisible by all of the numbers 1 through 10?

16. Invent a test for divisibility by 25, explain why it works, and apply it to the numbers 7375 and 9240.

17. A club with 105 members is to be partitioned into as many committees as possible, subject to the conditions that all committees be of the same size, that each committee have at least two members, and that everyone be on exactly one committee. How many committees should there be?

18. One of the tasks of the 12-member mathematics department is to read 253 applications for fellowships. Is it possible to choose a fellowship committee from the department (having more than one member) so that each application is read by just one member of that committee, and so that each member reads the same number of applications?

19. The divisibility test for 9 works because 9 is one less than the base of our numeration system. Invent a procedure for testing whether a number, expressed in base-seven notation, is divisible by 6. Try out your test on the following numbers:
    345_{seven} 5102_{seven} $10,221_{seven}$
    Then check your results by converting to base ten.

20. In base seven, what is the test for divisibility by seven?

21. In base twelve, what is the test for divisibility by three?

22. Invent a procedure for testing whether a number, expressed in base-seven notation, is divisible by eight. Try out your test on the numbers 50421_{seven} and 1264_{seven}. Check your answers by converting to base ten.

23. In the list of all natural numbers there are very long chains of consecutive composite numbers.
    (a) There is a chain of five consecutive composite numbers all less than 30. What are they?
    (b) Explain why the number
    $(100 \cdot 99 \cdot 98 \cdot \cdots \cdot 4 \cdot 3 \cdot 2) + 2$
    is composite.
    (c) Beginning with the number in (b), at least how many consecutive numbers will be composite?

24. Here is a theorem that militates against long chains of consecutive composite numbers: For every natural number n greater than 1, there is a prime number between n and $2n$. Verify this property for $n = 2, 5, 10, 100$.

25. Is every six-digit palindrome divisible by 11? Generalize.

26. A "repunit" prime is a prime whose digits are  all 1s. The first repunit prime is 11. Some very large ones are known. In 1978 an undergraduate student and a faculty member at the University of Manitoba showed that the number represented by 317 consecutive 1s is prime. It was the first new repunit prime found in 50 years.

    (a) Explain why the number represented by 316 consecutive 1s is not prime.

    (b) Explain why the number represented by 315 consecutive 1s is not prime.

The formal definitions of even and odd are as follows: A whole number n is even if there exists a whole number k such that $n = 2k$. A whole number n is odd if there exists a whole number r such that $n = 2r + 1$. Use these definitions to prove the statements in Exercises 27–30.

27. Even plus even is even.

28. Even minus even is even.

29. Odd plus even is odd.

30. Odd minus even is odd.

31. Five pennies are arranged in a row so that the pattern of heads and tails is H T H H T. The only move permitted is turning over two adjacent pennies.

    (a) Can you make all heads by using permissible moves?

    (b) Can you make all tails?

32. Repeat Exercise 31 for the arrangement H T T H T H H H.

33. Kevin lives at street corner K and his school is at S in Figure 5.10.

    (a) One day Kevin tells his mother that he had to go out of his way so that he walked a distance of 12 blocks to school. His mother responds that either he retraced some of his steps, or he didn't stay on the sidewalk, or he miscounted. Is she right?

    (b) The next day he claims that his roundtrip, home-school-home, covered a distance of 23 blocks. His mother's response is the same as before. Is she right again?

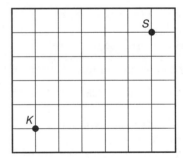

Figure 5.10

5.4 *Number Patterns (Optional)*

Some of the earliest work in number theory was done on *figurate numbers* by members of the Pythagorean brotherhood, a secret society formed in Crotona, Italy, around 500 B.C. We will look at some figurate numbers in the more general context of *sequences*, and we will describe a formal technique that is sometimes useful for discovering patterns in sequences. This technique is a particularly useful tool when you are carrying out the problem-solving strategy of looking for a pattern.

A **sequence** of numbers is an unending, ordered list. There is a first **term,** a second term, a third term, and so on. For example, in the sequence

   1, 2, 4, 7, 11, 16, 22, . . .

the first term is 1, the second is 2, the third is 4, and so forth. Can you guess a reasonable eighth term? The terms of a sequence need not, of course, follow a regular pattern, but for many important sequences they do.

Sequences from Geometry

Geometric considerations often lead to sequences of numbers. Consider, for example, the successively larger square arrays of dots in Figure 5.11.

Figure 5.11

The sequence of numbers suggested is the sequence of so-called **square numbers:**

   1, 4, 9, 16, . . .

The pattern here should be clear. What is the fifth term of this sequence? The tenth? The hundredth?

Now, suppose that instead of considering squares, we consider equilateral triangles, as in Figure 5.12. In this case the sequence of numbers suggested is the sequence of so-called **triangular numbers:**

Figure 5.12

   1, 3, 6, 10, . . .

What is the fifth term of this sequence? The tenth? How about the hundredth? We shall look further into square, triangular, and other figurate numbers in the exercises.

Another interesting sequence arises when we count diagonals in polygons (see Figure 5.13). What is the fifth term in this sequence?

   0, 2, 5, 9, . . .

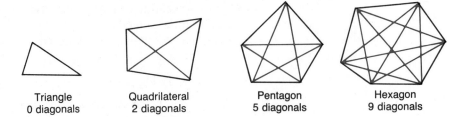

Figure 5.13

Triangle	Quadrilateral	Pentagon	Hexagon
0 diagonals	2 diagonals	5 diagonals	9 diagonals

Check your guess by drawing a heptagon and counting diagonals. What is the tenth term? How about the hundredth?

Difference Sequences

What is a reasonable eighth term for sequence A?

> A: 5, 6, 14, 32, 64, 115, 191, . . .

If you are like most people you probably consider this a hard question. But the same question about sequence B

> B: 7, 10, 14, 19, 25, 32, 40, . . .

you probably consider easy: The differences between successive terms in sequence B are

> 3, 4, 5, 6, 7, 8

Thus it would be reasonable to suppose that the next term in sequence B differs from 40 by 9 and hence is 49.

The same technique of differencing can be applied to sequence A to expose its pattern. For sequence A, however, more than one **difference sequence** probably needs to be computed:

Sequence:		5	6	14	32	64	115	191
First differences:			1	8	18	32	51	76
Second differences:				7	10	14	19	25
Third differences:					3	4	5	6
Fourth differences:						1	1	1
Fifth differences							0	0

It does no harm to carry out this differencing until a sequence of zeros is obtained, as here, but we can stop as soon as a pattern becomes obvious. For example, after the third differences

> 3, 4, 5, 6

have been computed, it is clear that the next difference should be 7. Thus in the sequence of second differences, the number following 25 should be 32.

(Why?) And hence in the sequence of first differences, the number following 76 should be 108. (Why?) Finally, then, the number following 191 in the original sequence should be 299. (Why?)

EXAMPLE 1   What is a reasonable ninth term for this sequence?

$$7, 7, 11, 20, 37, 69, 129, 238, \ldots$$

Solution   Form successive difference sequences until one is reached for which the pattern is obvious:

$$
\begin{array}{ccccccccccccccc}
7 && 7 && 11 && 20 && 37 && 69 && 129 && 238 \\
& 0 && 4 && 9 && 17 && 32 && 60 && 109 & \\
&& 4 && 5 && 8 && 15 && 28 && 49 && \\
&&& 1 && 3 && 7 && 13 && 21 &&& \\
&&&& 2 && 4 && 6 && 8 &&&& \\
\end{array}
$$

Then extend that obvious pattern by another term and work from the bottom up; see Figure 5.14. Thus a reasonable ninth term is 427. ❏

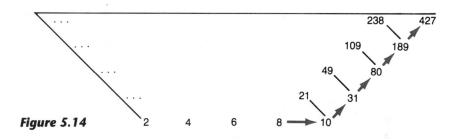

Figure 5.14

EXERCISE SET 5.4

In Exercises 1–4, use the notation illustrated in Figure 5.15 for square and triangular numbers.

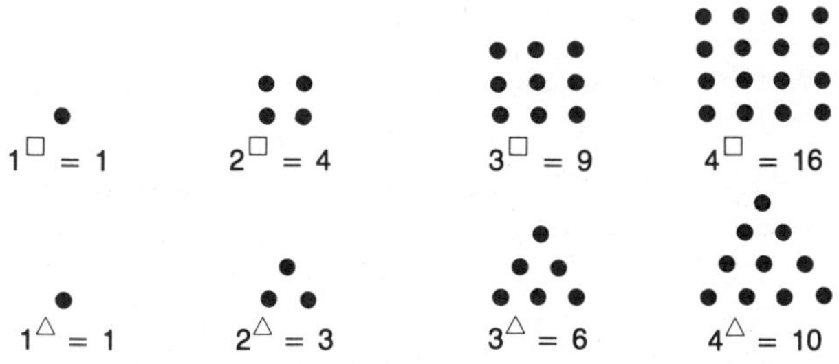

Figure 5.15

1. Figure 5.16 suggests how each square number can be expressed in terms of triangular numbers. Express $n^\square$ in terms of triangular numbers.

$$1^\square = 1^\triangle \qquad 2^\square = 2^\triangle + 1^\triangle \qquad 3^\square = 3^\triangle + 2^\triangle \qquad 4^\square = 4^\triangle + 3^\triangle$$

Figure 5.16

2. Compute each of the following sums.
   (a) $(1 + 2) + 1$
   (b) $(1 + 2 + 3) + (2 + 1)$
   (c) $(1 + 2 + 3 + 4) + (3 + 2 + 1)$
   (d) $1 + 2 + \cdots + 99 + 100 + 99 + \cdots$
   $$+ 2 + 1$$

★ 3. An interesting fact about numbers is that the square of the sum of the first n natural numbers is the sum of their cubes. For example,
   $$(1 + 2)^2 = 1^3 + 2^3$$
   $$(1 + 2 + 3)^2 = 1^3 + 2^3 + 3^3$$
   and in general
   $$(1 + 2 + \cdots + n)^2 = 1^3 + 2^3 + \cdots + n^3$$
   The calculations in Exercise 2 play a key role in a very elegant proof of this result, which we shall sketch in the case $n = 4$.
   (a) Explain why the sum of all the numbers in the square of Figure 5.17 is $1^2 + 2^2 + 3^2 + 4^2$. (The red lines should be helpful.)

1	1	1	1
1	2	2	2
1	2	3	3
1	2	3	4

Figure 5.17

   (b) Explain why the sum of all the numbers in the square of Figure 5.18 is $1^3 + 2^3 + 3^3 + 4^3$.

1	2	3	4
2	4	6	8
3	6	9	12
4	8	12	16

Figure 5.18

   (c) Now ignore the red lines in the square of Figure 5.18 and explain why the sum of its entries is $(1 + 2 + 3 + 4)^2$. *Hint:* Think of applying the distributive principle to the product $(1 + 2 + 3 + 4) \cdot (1 + 2 + 3 + 4)$.

4. Figure 5.19 suggests a way of calculating any triangular number.
   (a) What is the hundredth triangular number?
   (b) Complete this general formula: $n^\triangle = ?$

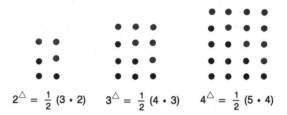

$2^\triangle = \frac{1}{2}(3 \cdot 2)$ $3^\triangle = \frac{1}{2}(4 \cdot 3)$ $4^\triangle = \frac{1}{2}(5 \cdot 4)$

Figure 5.19

★ 5. Three-dimensional analogs of square numbers are cube numbers, as illustrated in Figure 5.20. Decide what the three-dimensional analogs of triangular numbers should be, write the first five, and look for a pattern.

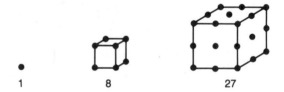

1   8   27

Figure 5.20

6. Copy each of the following sequences and write the sequences of first differences, second differences, . . . , until a sequence of zeros is obtained.
   (a) 0, 12, 25, 41, 62, 90, 127, . . .
   (b) 5, 6, 14, 29, 51, 80, 116, . . .
   (c) ⁻8, ⁻4, 1, 10, 26, 52, 91, . . .
   (d) 10, 8, 3, 0, 4, 20, 53, . . .

7. Give a reasonable eighth term for each sequence in Exercise 6.

8. The fourth through eighth terms of a sequence are 10, 9, 12, 19, and 30 in that order. Give a plausible value for the first term of that sequence.

9. The first four pentagonal numbers are shown in Figure 5.21. Find the tenth pentagonal number.

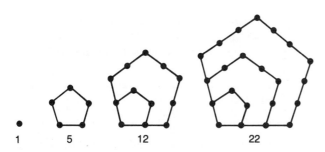

1   5   12   22

Figure 5.21

10. Fill in all missing numbers.
- (a) Sequence: 0 — — — — — —

    First
    differences: 6 — — — — —
    Second
    differences: 2 — — — —
    Third
    differences: 0   0   0   0

- (b) Sequence: —   5 — — — — —

    First
    differences: — — — — 36 44
    Second
    differences: — — — — —
    Third
    differences: 0   0   0   0

- (c) Sequence: 2 — — —

    First
    differences: 1 — —
    Second
    differences: 5 —
    Third
    differences: 3

- (d) Sequence: — — — 20 32 47 —

    First
    differences: — — — — — —
    Second
    differences: — — — — —
    Third
    differences: 0   0   0   0

11. Here are the enrollments in a school district:

Year	1950	1960	1970	1980
Enrollment	3529	3506	3843	3460

Predict the enrollment in the year 2000.

12. During its first six years in business the profits of a company (in millions of dollars) have been ⁻5, ⁻10, ⁻5, 10, 35, and 70. Predict the company's profits in years 7, 8, 9, and 10.

13. A physics student lets a ball roll down a ramp and observes the following:

Time (sec)	0	1	2	3	4	5
Distance traveled (cm)	0	3.2	12.8	28.8	51.2	80

- (a) How far will the ball travel in 10 sec?
- (b) In theory, how could you find how far it would roll in 100 sec?

14. Given the function
$$f(x) = x^2 + 2x + 3$$
- (a) Write the first six terms of the sequence
$$f(0), f(1), f(2), f(3), \ldots$$
This sequence is called the sequence **determined** by f.
- (b) Now write the sequences of first, second, and third differences.

15. For each function, write the first seven terms of the sequence it determines, and then write successive difference sequences until you get a sequence of zeros.
- (a) $f(x) = 3x + 5$ (b) $g(x) = x - 4$
- (c) $h(x) = x^2 + 1$ (d) $k(x) = 2x^2 - x$
- (e) $s(x) = x^2 - 5x + 1$ (f) $t(x) = x^3 + x^2$

Do you see any connection between the degree of a polynomial function (that is, the greatest exponent appearing in its formula) and the sequence and successive difference sequences that it determines?

16. Find two numbers a and b so that the function
$$f(x) = a \cdot x + b$$
determines the sequence
4, 7, 10, 13, . . .
Hint: The numbers a and b satisfy the equations
$$4 = f(0) = a \cdot 0 + b$$
$$7 = f(1) = a \cdot 1 + b$$

★ 17. Find three numbers a, b, and c so that the function
$$g(x) = ax^2 + bx + c$$
determines the sequence of Exercise 13. How far would the ball in Exercise 13 roll in 100 sec?

18. Figure 5.22 shows into how many pieces a disk is partitioned by joining randomly placed points on its boundary.
   (a) By drawing a figure, fill in the entry below the 5 in this table:

Number of points	2	3	4	5	6	7	8
Number of pieces	2	4	8				

   (b) On the basis of the entries below 2, 3, 4, and 5, predict arithmetically how many pieces will result when 6 randomly placed points are joined.
   (c) Test your prediction of part (b) geometrically; that is, actually draw a figure and count pieces.
   (d) By drawing a figure, fill in the entry that goes below 7 in the table.
   (e) On the basis of the entries below 2, 3, 4, 5, 6, and 7, predict arithmetically how many pieces will result when 8 randomly placed points are joined.
   (f) Test your prediction of part (e) geometrically.

★ 19. Lines drawn randomly in a plane (that is, no two parallel and no three concurrent) partition it into pieces. The first few entries in this table are obvious:

Number of lines	0	1	2				
Number of pieces	1	2	4				

   Gather some more data and then try to devise a function, $p(x) = ?$ that predicts the number of pieces that will arise when x lines are drawn. Test your formula geometrically in the case $x = 5$.

★ 20. Figure 5.23 shows another kind of number pattern.
   (a) What number will appear 7 squares to the right and 7 squares up from the number 1?
   (b) Where will the number 400 appear?

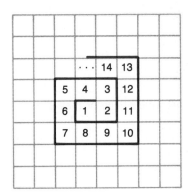

Figure 5.23

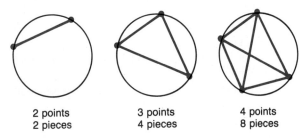

2 points	3 points	4 points
2 pieces	4 pieces	8 pieces

Figure 5.22

Key Concepts in Chapter 5

Factor
Multiple
Prime
Composite
Fundamental theorem of arithmetic
Greatest common factor
Least common multiple
Euclidean algorithm
Divisibility tests
*Sequence
*Difference sequences

Chapter 5 Review Exercises

1. One of the factors of 1222 is 47.
   (a) Express 1222 as a product of primes.
   (b) List all of the factors (not just the prime factors) of 1222.

2. What is the smallest composite number that is divisible by none of the primes 2, 3, 5, 7, 11, and 13?

3. What can you conclude about a whole number if:
   (a) It has exactly one factor?
   (b) It has exactly two factors?
   (c) It has exactly three factors?

4. You want to sweep the sieve of Eratosthenes through the numbers 2 through 400 just enough times so that only prime numbers survive. How many sweeps of the sieve are necessary?

5. Find the LCM of 220 and 700.

6. The GCF of two numbers m and n is 12, their LCM is 600, and $m < n < 500$. Find m and n.

7. Use the Euclidean algorithm to find the GCF of 1739 and 5291. Show your work.

8. Given $a = 12 \cdot 13 \cdot 14$ and $b = 15 \cdot 16 \cdot 17$
   (a) Find the GCF of a and b and express it as a product of primes.

   (b) Find the LCM of a and b and express it as a product of primes.

9. Complete each sentence with "odd" or "even."
   (a) The GCF of two odd numbers is _____ .
   (b) The GCF of two even numbers is _____ .
   (c) The LCM of two odd numbers is _____ .
   (d) The LCM of two even numbers is _____ .
   (e) The GCF of an odd and an even number is

   _____ .

   (f) The LCM of an odd and an even number is

   _____ .

10. True or false
    (a) If a is a factor of b, then b is the LCM of a and b.
    (b) If g is the GCF of a and b, then g^2 is the GCF of a^2 and b^2.
    (c) If m is the LCM of a and b, then m^2 is the LCM of a^2 and b^2.
    (d) The number $(100 \cdot 99 \cdot 98 \cdot \cdots \cdot 3 \cdot 2 \cdot 1) - 1$ is divisible by no prime number less than 100.

11. A rectangular sheet of cardboard 420 mm long and 378 mm wide is to be cut up into many

squares, all of the same size. There is to be no waste. How large could these squares be, and how many of them would be produced?

12. Find the smallest natural number that is divisible (without remainder) by all of the *even* numbers 10 through 20 (inclusive).

13. Two artificial satellites are in orbits that pass directly over Baltimore. One makes one revolution around the Earth every 20 hr; the other makes one revolution around the Earth every 21 hr. At 8:00 A.M. on December 3 they were both directly over Baltimore. When (date and time) will they next be directly over Baltimore?

14. Explain briefly but clearly why $177 \cdot (98^7 - 17 \cdot 7)$ is divisible by 7.

15. Try to find a subset of $\{3, 9, 15, 18, 21, 30\}$ that sums to 50. If you think the task is impossible, explain why.

16. If n is divisible by 9 and also by 6, does it follow that n is divisible by 54? Why or why not?

17. Find the largest prime number less than 96.

18. Find the missing digit d so that the following statements are true.
    (a) $517,3d4$ is divisible by 9.
    (b) $5d7,384$ is divisible by 11.
    (c) $d12,287$ is divisible by 21.

19. Find digits a and b so that the six-digit number $ab7254$ is divisible by 99.

20. Devise and state a simple test for divisibility by four in the base-twelve numeration system.

* 21. Determine a reasonable eighth term for this sequence: 3, 3, 8, 20, 41, 73, 118, ——— .

* 22. What is the eighth term of a sequence whose first three terms are 7, 5, 3 and whose sequence of second differences is the sequence of multiples of 3: 0, 3, 6, 9, 12, 15, . . . ?

* 23. Figure 5.24 shows the first four heptagonal numbers: 1, 7, 18, 34. Find the eighth heptagonal number.

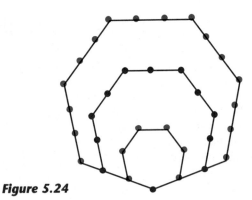

Figure 5.24

* 24. The odd triangular numbers exhibit an interesting geometric-arithmetic pattern, as shown in Figure 5.25.
    (a) Make a drawing and write the corresponding equation for $9^{\triangle}$.
    (b) Do not make a drawing, but do write an equation, like the ones in Figure 5.25 for $97^{\triangle}$.

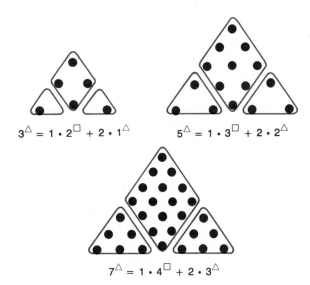

$$3^{\triangle} = 1 \cdot 2^{\square} + 2 \cdot 1^{\triangle}$$

$$5^{\triangle} = 1 \cdot 3^{\square} + 2 \cdot 2^{\triangle}$$

$$7^{\triangle} = 1 \cdot 4^{\square} + 2 \cdot 3^{\triangle}$$

Figure 5.25

* 25. In 1665 Pascal conjectured and in 1796 Gauss proved that every natural number can be expressed as the sum of three or less triangular numbers. Express 30 as such a sum in as many ways as you can.

References

Bezuszka, S. and M. Kenney. *Number Theory: A Sourcebook of Problems for Calculators and Computers*. Palo Alto, Calif.: Dale Seymour, 1982.

Burton, D. *The History of Mathematics*. Boston: Allyn and Bacon, 1985.

Long, C. *Elementary Introduction to Number Theory*. 3rd ed. Englewood Cliffs, N.J.: Prentice-Hall, 1987.

Ore, O. *Invitation to Number Theory*. New York: Random House, 1967.

Readings from *Scientific American*. *Mathematics, An Introduction to Its Spirit and Use*. San Francisco: Freeman, 1979.

6 THE INTEGERS

The nineteenth-century mathematician Leopold Kronecker remarked that "God made the whole numbers. Everything else is man's work." For many of man's purposes the set of whole numbers $W = \{0, 1, 2, 3, \ldots\}$ is inadequate. It became necessary to invent negative numbers and extend the set of whole numbers to the set of integers

$$I = \{\ldots, {}^-3, {}^-2, {}^-1, 0, 1, 2, 3, \ldots\}$$

In this chapter we study this larger set of numbers and the operations and order relation on it.

Our approach to the integers parallels our approach to the whole numbers. We begin informally in the first two sections by looking at interpretations or models for the integers and the operations on them. These models lead to definitions of the operations, to real-world applications, to identification of some general properties, and to computational algorithms. In the third section we describe the integers formally as a mathematical system. The abstract properties of this system are seen to be nearly the same as they were for the whole numbers. In the brief, optional fourth section we look again at the system of seven-clock arithmetic, and see how closely its structure resembles that of the integers. The chapter concludes with a short section on the order relation for integers.

6.1 Addition and Subtraction

Our first task is to see what sort of meanings are commonly associated with the integers themselves

$$\ldots, {}^-3, {}^-2, {}^-1, 0, {}^+1, {}^+2, {}^+3, \ldots$$

Then we will look for meanings for the addition and subtraction operations on them.

Perhaps one's first encounter with integers is in connection with temperatures. When the temperature is reported to be ${}^-8$ degrees, the whole number 8 counts how many **units** (degrees) the temperature is away from some **refer-**

ence point (zero). The minus sign indicates in what **direction.** In this case temperatures warmer than zero are called **positive,** while temperatures colder than zero are called **negative.**

When the elevation at a point in Death Valley is given as ⁻276 ft, the 276 tells by how many units (feet) the elevation differs from a reference point (sea level), and the minus sign tells in what direction. Elevations above sea level are considered positive; those below, negative.

When the net worth of Joe's Clothing Store is listed as ⁺2500 dollars, the whole number 2500 tells how many units (dollars) this net worth is from a reference point (no net worth). The plus sign gives the direction: Assets are considered positive; liabilities, negative. Frequently, raised plus signs are omitted ("Paul Smith is worth $30,000"). The reader is to assume that the integer is positive unless indicated otherwise. We shall use the raised plus signs for a while for emphasis.

Number Line Models

All three of the preceding examples illustrate the use of integer symbols to specify **states**—that is, to tell where things stand with respect to a reference point. Besides having a reference point, one also needs to know the unit and which direction is positive. *Points* on a number line serve as an accurate representation of the integers thought of as states. See Figure 6.1.

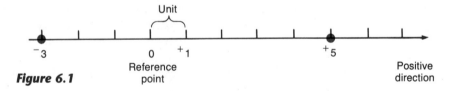

Figure 6.1

This number line model of the integers is useful for showing their relative sizes (smaller integers lie to the left of larger integers) and for illustrating that the nonnegative integers can be identified with the whole numbers. But it is not adequate for representing operations on the integers. How, for example, does one add the point ⁻3 to the point ⁺5?

To arrive at a more useful number line model, we investigate another way of thinking about integers: as **operators** (or actions). Consider these statements:

> The change in temperature was ⁻14 degrees.
> The change in the plane's elevation was ⁺500 feet.
> The change in Joe's net worth was ⁻225 dollars.

Now the integer symbols ⁻14, ⁺500, ⁻225 tell what has happened. A unit and a direction are still associated with each report, but now there is no reference point. We don't know the state of the temperature; we only know that it dropped by 14 degrees. When integers are thought of as operators, we represent them by **vectors** (or arrows) anywhere on a number line. Some vectors are illustrated in Figure 6.2.

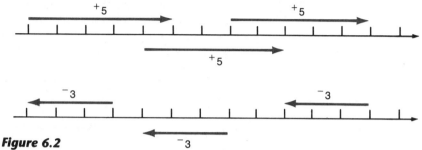

Figure 6.2

In problems the two views of integers (thought of as states and represented by points; thought of as operators and represented by vectors) are often mixed.*

EXAMPLE 1   The temperature was ⁺5 this morning, and since then it has fallen 12 degrees. What is the temperature now?

Solution   See Figure 6.3. By simply counting, we arrive at the final state, ⁻7.   ❏

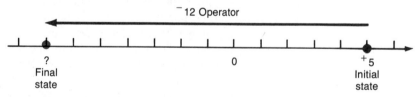

Figure 6.3

EXAMPLE 2   A year ago Joe's Clothing Store had a net worth of ⁻3000 dollars. Now the net worth is ⁺2500 dollars. What happened during the year?

Solution   See Figure 6.4. Again, by counting, we see that the operator (change) was ⁺5500 dollars.   ❏

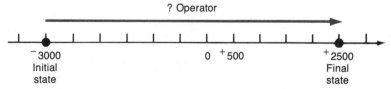

Figure 6.4

*The state-operator terminology that we are using is borrowed from Z. P. Dienes. The ideas, however, derive from a connection between states and operators made by Arthur Cayley (1821–1895) in his theorem on the (isomorphic) representation of a group by a group of permutations of its own elements.

EXAMPLE 3   In the past three months the monthly changes in hamburger prices have been (in cents) $^+2$, $^-3$, $^+5$. What has been the cumulative price change?

Solution   Here there is just one interpretation: All of the integers are thought of as operators. See Figure 6.5. By counting, we arrive at the answer of $^+4$. ❏

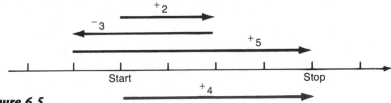

Figure 6.5

Most adults would not have solved Examples 1–3 geometrically as we did. Instead, they might have set up equations, as follows, and then used their computational skills with integers to solve them:

Example 1: $^+5 + {^-12} = \square$
Example 2: $^-3000 + \square = {^+2500}$
Example 3: $^+2 + {^-3} + {^+5} = \square$

When people write such equations, they must surely have in mind some meaning for the (large) plus signs. Yet this meaning is not the meaning "union" that we identified for addition of whole numbers, since no sets are being united. If we refer to the number line representations of the examples, we can see two distinct meanings for the plus sign.

In Examples 1 and 2, + means "feed in." In Example 1 the state $^+5$ is fed into the operator $^-12$ and comes out as the state $^-7$, as illustrated in Figure 6.6. In Example 2 the state $^-3000$ is fed into an unknown operator and the state $^+2500$ comes out, as indicated in Figure 6.7.

In Example 3 the meaning of + is quite different. It clearly means "hook up," as illustrated in Figure 6.8.

The hookup view of addition is called *vector addition* in higher mathematics, and it is used in solving real-world problems like the one in the next example.

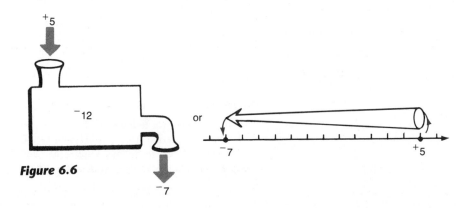

Figure 6.6

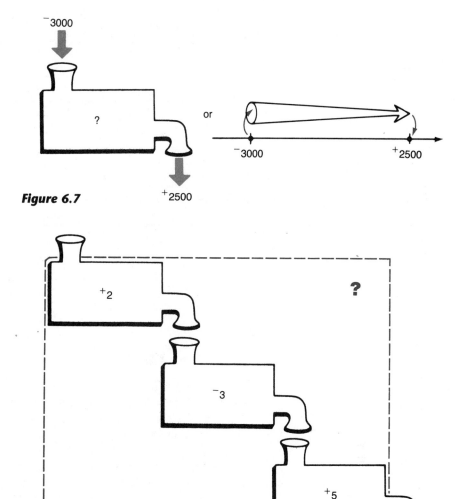

Figure 6.7

Figure 6.8

EXAMPLE 4   The current in a river is 4 mi/hr. A motorboat that has a top speed of 9 mi/hr in still water is traveling upstream at top speed. How fast is it going relative to an observer on the bank?

Solution   Imagine laying a number line along the bank of the river, with 0 where the observer stands with unit length 1 mi, and with positive integers heading upstream. See Figure 6.9. Imagine also the observer throwing a cork in the water as the boat passes by. Then 1 hr later the cork will be 4 mi downstream from the observer, and the boat will be 9 mi upstream from the cork. Thus the boat will be 5 mi upstream from the observer. Its speed relative to the observer is 5 mi/hr. One can find this *resultant velocity* by vector addition, as shown in Figure 6.10. ❏

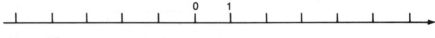

Figure 6.9

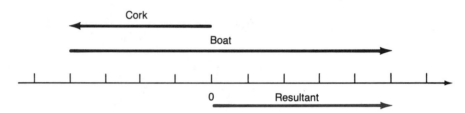

Figure 6.10

The Poker Chip Model

While the number line models of the integers with the "feed in" and "hook up" interpretations for addition fit a variety of real-world situations, they are not as concrete as the sets-and-union model was for the whole numbers under addition. There is another model for the integers that has several pedagogical advantages: Each integer corresponds to a tangible set, and the operation of addition continues to correspond to union. The model employs two colors of poker chips to represent integers—say red and black, where red will signify negative.

Each integer has many different representations in poker chips. For example, each of the arrays of chips in Figure 6.11 represents the negative integer ⁻5 because in each there is a preponderance of five reds over blacks. Notice

Figure 6.11

that each of the first three arrays can be reduced to the simplest array at the far right by pairing up a red with a black and then discarding the pair. One can think of the blacks as little pieces of matter and the reds as little pieces of anti-matter that come together and disappear in a puff of smoke. Or one can think of the blacks as positive charges and the reds as negative charges that exactly nullify each other. Some arrays of chips representing ⁺2 are shown in Figure 6.12.

Figure 6.12

Addition of integers in this model is viewed as the union of arrays. For example, to find the sum ⁻5 + ⁺2, push together any representation for ⁻5 and any representation for ⁺2; see Figure 6.13. Then pair off reds and blacks to simplify the representation so that the sum is obvious, as in Figure 6.14. *Answer:* ⁻5 + ⁺2 = ⁻3.

Figure 6.13

Certain real-world situations, particularly financial ones, are represented rather naturally by the poker-chip model. For example, a net worth of $2500 for Joe's Clothing Store can be thought of as a stack of 6500 black chips (assets) and 4000 red ones (liabilities).

Figure 6.14

Addition

The number line and poker-chip models suggest how we should define addition of integers. They also suggest a number of properties that will be fundamental in our formal description of the system of integers in Section 6.3. But before defining addition, let us review some basic terminology.

The set of numbers

$$I = \{\ldots, \,^-3, \,^-2, \,^-1, 0, 1, 2, 3, \ldots\}$$

is called the set of **integers.** Notice that here we have dropped the raised plus signs so that the whole numbers are an actual subset of the integers. The subset $\{\ldots, \,^-3, \,^-2, \,^-1\}$ is referred to as the set of **negative integers,** and the subset of natural numbers $\{1, 2, 3, \ldots\}$ is often called the set of **positive integers** and is sometimes written $\{^+1, \,^+2, \,^+3, \ldots\}$. The integers ⁻3 and 3 (or ⁻3 and ⁺3) are referred to as **opposites** of each other, perhaps because of their relative positions on the number line; see Figure 6.15. The integer 0 is its own opposite.

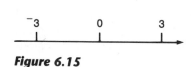

Figure 6.15

To see how addition of integers should be defined, we can refer to either the number line model or the poker-chip model.

EXAMPLE 5   Find each sum by referring to the models.
(a) ⁻5 + 8
(b) ⁻5 + 3
(c) ⁻5 + ⁻2
(d) 4 + 2

Solution   (a) ⁻5 + 8: In the poker-chip model, unite 5 red chips with 8 black ones. Then pair 5 of the black chips with the red, leaving 3 blacks, as shown in Figure 6.16. Symbolically, ⁻5 + 8 = 3. In the number line model (state-operator); start at the point ⁻5 and slide right 8 units. In Figure 6.17 we see that 5 units of the slide are consumed in getting back to zero. The slide stops 3 units to the right of zero. Symbolically, ⁻5 + 8 = 3.

In general, if m and n are whole numbers with $m \leq n$, then the sum of integers $^-m + n$ can be found by subtracting whole numbers: $^-m + n = n - m$.

Figure 6.16

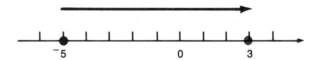

Figure 6.17

(b) ⁻5 + 3: In the poker-chip model, unite 5 red chips with 3 black ones. Here 3 reds are paired with the 3 blacks, as in Figure 6.18, leaving 2 reds. Symbolically, ⁻5 + 3 = ⁻2. In the number line model (all operators), slide left 5 units, then right 3, as shown in Figure 6.19. Since the left slide is longer, the resulting slide is to the left, and its length is 5 − 3, or 2. Symbolically, ⁻5 + 3 = ⁻2.

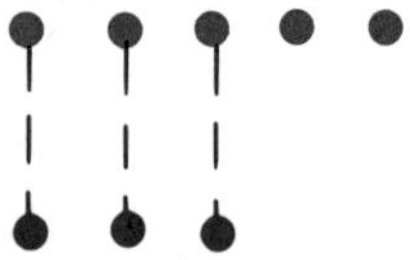

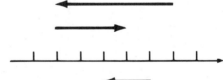

Figure 6.18

Figure 6.19

In general, if m and n are whole numbers with $m > n$, then the sum $^-m + n$ can be found by subtracting whole numbers and then attaching a minus sign: $^-m + n = ^-(m - n)$.

(c) ⁻5 + ⁻2: In the poker-chip model, uniting 5 red and 2 red chips yields 7 red chips. Symbolically, ⁻5 + ⁻2 = ⁻7. In the number line model (state-operator), starting at ⁻5 and sliding left 2 units leaves us at ⁻7. Symbolically, ⁻5 + ⁻2 = ⁻7.

In general, for any whole numbers m and n, $^-m + ^-n = ^-(m + n)$, where the plus sign on the left side of the equation denotes addition of integers and the plus sign on the right denotes usual addition of whole numbers.

(d) $4 + 2$: In the poker-chip model, uniting 4 black and 2 black chips yields 6 black chips. Symbolically, $4 + 2 = 6$. In the number line model (all operators), sliding right 4 units and then right 2 more amounts to sliding right $4 + 2 = 6$ units.

In general, addition of two whole numbers viewed as nonnegative integers is the same as usual whole number addition. ❏

The general definition of addition of integers is the untidy case-by-case one suggested by Example 5. In its statement we use red plus signs to indicate the newly defined addition of integers, and we use black plus and minus signs to indicate the familiar addition and subtraction operations on whole numbers. Hereafter, though, we will follow the standard practice of making no distinction between the two. (This is justified by the first case of the following definition, which tells us that integer addition is an extension of whole number addition.)

Definition of Addition (+) of Integers

For all whole numbers m and n:

$$m + n = m + n$$
$$\bar{}m + n = n + \bar{}m = n - m \quad \text{if} \quad m \leq n$$
$$\bar{}m + n = n + \bar{}m = \bar{}(m - n) \quad \text{if} \quad m > n$$
$$\bar{}m + \bar{}n = \bar{}(m + n)$$

Addition of integers shares the following general properties with addition of whole numbers: It is associative, it is commutative, and it has an additive identity element (zero).

Using the preceding definition to prove that the associative property holds for an arbitrary triple (a, b, c) of integers is a formidable task because of the large number of cases that need to be investigated. For any specific triple, however, it is routine.

EXAMPLE 6 Explain why $5 + (\bar{}7 + 8) = (5 + \bar{}7) + 8$.

Solution

$$5 + (\bar{}7 + 8) = 5 + (8 - 7) \qquad \text{case 2 of definition}$$
$$= 5 + 1 \qquad \text{subtracting whole numbers}$$
$$= 6 \qquad \text{adding whole numbers}$$

$$(5 + \bar{}7) + 8 = \bar{}(7 - 5) + 8 \qquad \text{case 3 of definition}$$
$$= \bar{}2 + 8 \qquad \text{subtracting whole numbers}$$
$$= 8 - 2 \qquad \text{case 2 of definition}$$
$$= 6 \qquad \text{subtracting whole numbers} \quad ❏$$

Simple and convincing arguments for associativity in general refer to the models. Here is one: The formal four-case definition of addition was devised so that addition of integers would reflect union of sets of poker chips. But union of sets is an associative operation. Hence addition of integers must also be associative. We could also use the all-operators number-line model and argue that addition of integers is associative because composition of functions is.

The poker-chip model shows clearly that addition should be commutative. In fact, that is what justified building commutativity into cases 2 and 3 of the definition. (Commutativity is already present in cases 1 and 4 because addition of whole numbers is commutative.)

That zero is the additive identity element is immediate from the general definition or from either model.

The one new property of addition that is true in the integers but was not true in the whole numbers is this:

> Every integer has an opposite, or **additive inverse;** that is, corresponding to each integer is another integer that adds to it to give zero.

In our formal development of the integers in Section 6.3 we shall turn the tables and show how this and the other abstract properties force addition to satisfy the equations that were used to define it here.

Subtraction

Figure 6.20

Figure 6.21

Figure 6.22

Our definition of subtraction in the whole number system was fairly complicated. We defined $m - n$ to be the missing addend in the equation $n + \square = m$. To ensure existence of such an addend, we had to impose the condition $n \leq m$; and to demonstrate its uniqueness, we had to invoke the cancellation property of addition. In the system of integers all these complications fall away and one simple definition emerges. We shall motivate that definition by returning to the poker-chip model.

Think of subtraction of integers as corresponding to a take-away procedure in the poker-chip model. For example, to find $^-3 - {}^+2$, begin by displaying an array for $^-3$, but be sure this array has enough blacks so that 2 of them can be taken away. See Figure 6.20. Now, remove two black chips and simplify the resulting array, as in Figure 6.21, to find the difference. Thus $^-3 - {}^+2 = {}^-5$.

There is another way, though, of removing two blacks: Simply throw in two extra reds to neutralize them, as indicated in Figure 6.22. Symbolically,

$$\underset{\substack{\nearrow \\ \text{Take} \\ \text{away}}}{^-3} \; \underset{}{-} \; \underset{\substack{\uparrow \\ \text{Two} \\ \text{blacks}}}{^+2} \; = \; \underset{}{^-3} \; \underset{\substack{\uparrow \\ \text{Add}}}{+} \; \underset{\substack{\uparrow \\ \text{Two} \\ \text{reds}}}{^-2}$$

In words: "to subtract two integers, change the sign of the subtrahend and add."

EXAMPLE 7   Find $^-2 - {}^-5$ by interpreting subtraction as a take-away operation in the poker-chip model.

Solution   Begin with an array for $^-2$; see Figure 6.23. Insert enough red-black pairs, as in Figure 6.24, so that five reds can be removed. Now, take away and simplify, as in Figure 6.25. *Answer:* $^-2 - {}^-5 = {}^+3$. Notice that the deletion of five reds could have been accomplished by the insertion of five blacks: $^-2 - {}^-5 = {}^-2 + {}^+5 = {}^+3$. ❏

Figure 6.23   **Figure 6.24**   **Figure 6.25**

Here is the formal definition:

Definition of Subtraction of Integers

For all integers a and b,

$$a - b = a + {}^-b$$

In words: "to subtract, change the sign of the subtrahend and add."

Three things should be noted about this definition of subtraction. First, $a - b$ as defined is the missing addend in the equation $b + \square = a$. For if we put $a + {}^-b$ in the box, we get

$b + (a + {}^-b) = b + ({}^-b + a)$	commutativity of addition
$= (b + {}^-b) + a$	associativity of addition
$= 0 + a$	b and ^-b are opposites
$= a$	0 is the additive identity

Thus our new definition of subtraction of integers agrees with our former missing-addend definition in the event where both integers are whole numbers.

Second, *any* two integers can be subtracted. Subtraction is a binary operation on I.

Third, in the formal definition we attached a raised minus sign to a symbol b for an arbitrary integer. Up to this point we had attached raised minus signs only to numerals for whole numbers. It is time to sort out the uses of the minus sign. There are three, two of which we have seen already:

1. The raised minus sign in $^-4$ tells us we are dealing with a *negative* integer. In the number-line models it indicates a point to the left of zero or a slide to the left. In the poker-chip model it denotes red chips.

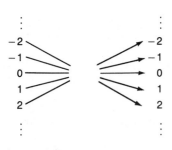

Figure 6.26

2. The centered minus sign in $^+5 - {}^-8$ represents *subtraction,* a binary operation on I.

The third meaning of the minus sign is to denote the *opposite-of* function, a one-to-one correspondence from I to I that matches each integer with its opposite. See Figure 6.26. For example, $^{--}3$ denotes the opposite of negative 3, namely 3, and $^{-+}3$ denotes the opposite of $^+3$, namely $^-3$. It is this third meaning that the raised minus sign carries in the definition of subtraction, $a - b = a + {}^-b$.

Caution: When a raised minus sign, used in this third sense, is attached to a symbol for an arbitrary integer, no conclusion can be drawn about positivity or negativity. For example:

$$^-b \text{ is negative if } b = 4$$

$$^-b \text{ is positive if } b = {}^-5$$

To clarify the multiple meanings of the minus sign, most elementary textbooks follow this convention: When the minus sign is used to mean subtraction, it is centered; when it is used to indicate negativity, it is raised. When the minus sign is used to indicate opposite-of, some texts center it, while others raise it. We have chosen to raise it.

Calculators usually have a special key $\boxed{+/-}$ for the opposite-of function. The key $\boxed{-}$ is reserved for the binary operation of subtraction. Thus if you want to display $^-5$ on your calculator, you will need to press $\boxed{5}$ $\boxed{+/-}$; pressing $\boxed{-}\boxed{5}$ or $\boxed{5}\boxed{-}$ will not work. (Try pressing $\boxed{+/-}$ $\boxed{5}$ on your calculator and see what you get.)

Accountants have their own special convention that cuts down on the number of meanings for the overworked minus sign. They use parentheses to indicate negative numbers. Thus if your accountant reports that last month your net worth changed by (540.00), you have lost money.

Algorithms

When we studied the whole numbers, we spent a considerable amount of time and effort on algorithms. For integers no such major effort will be required. The algorithms for integers are short because they are built on powerful subroutines. The addition algorithm uses whole number addition and subtraction as subroutines; the subtraction algorithm uses integer addition as a subroutine. As a matter of fact, you have already met both the addition and the subtraction algorithm in shorthand algebraic notation. It is not far from the truth to say that for integers the definitions of the operations *are* the algorithms.

EXAMPLE 8   Compute each of the following.
(a) $^-134 + 58$
(b) $^-288 + {}^-117$

(c) ⁻37 − ⁻264
(d) 325 − 468

Solution   (a) ⁻134 + 58 = ⁻(134 − 58)   definition of addition, case 3
                     = ⁻76   whole number subtraction algorithm
            (b) ⁻288 + ⁻117 = ⁻(288 + 117)   definition of addition, case 4
                     = ⁻405   whole number addition algorithm
            (c) ⁻37 − ⁻264 = ⁻37 + 264   definition of subtraction
                     = 264 − 37   definition of addition, case 2
                     = 227   whole number subtraction algorithm
            (d) 325 − 468 = 325 + ⁻468   definition of subtraction
                     = ⁻(468 − 325)   definition of addition, case 3
                     = ⁻143   whole number subtraction algorithm

❏

In the exercises you will get a chance to flowchart the addition and subtraction algorithms for integers.

EXERCISE SET 6.1

1. In scientific work temperatures are often reported on the *Kelvin* scale. On the Kelvin scale 0 is assigned to the lowest temperature that is theoretically possible ("absolute zero"). Temperatures range upward from 0, with the freezing point of water being (approximately) 273°K and the boiling point being (approximately) 373° K. Thus by using the Kelvin scale, one can avoid negative numbers in reporting temperatures.
   (a) Is there a natural "absolute-zero elevation" so that all elevations can be reported using nonnegative numbers?
   (b) Is there a natural "absolute-zero net worth" so that all net worths can be reported using nonnegative numbers?

2. The illuminated sign in front of a brokerage office flashes the following wordless message about the Dow-Jones industrial average: "2825, ⁻7." Which number indicates the *state* of the average? What does the other number represent?

3. Write the integer represented by each array of poker chips.

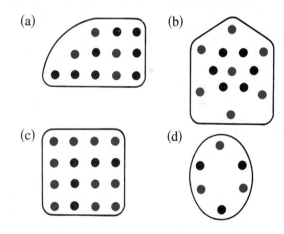

4. Draw an array for the following.
   (a) 10 chips that represent ⁻4
   (b) 6 chips that represent ⁺4
   (c) 11 chips that represent ⁻3
   (d) 5 chips that represent ⁺2

5. Generalize your observation in Exercise 4(d).

6. Write the addition problem, and answer, suggested by the following diagrams.

(a)

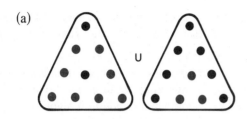

(b)

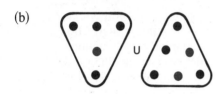

7. Write the subtraction problem, and answer, suggested by the following diagrams.

(a)   (b)

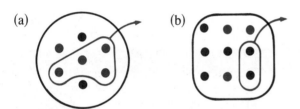

8. Find each sum or difference by drawing an appropriate poker-chip diagram.
   (a) $^+3 + {}^-7$ (b) $^+6 + {}^-4$
   (c) $^-2 - {}^+3$ (d) $^-1 - {}^-4$

9. Mark and label points on the number line in Figure 6.27 for each of the following integers (thought of as states): $^+3, {}^-3, {}^+5, {}^-5$

Figure 6.27

10. Sketch arrows above or below the line in Figure 6.28, which is scaled in units but has no origin specified, for each of the following integers (thought of as operators): $^-4, {}^+4, {}^+2, {}^-7$

Figure 6.28

11. Each of the following sketches suggests an addition statement relating three integers, just one of which is thought of as an operator. Write the addition statement and circle the operator as in the example in Figure 6.29.

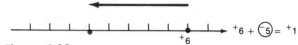

Figure 6.29

(a)

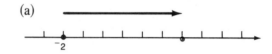

(b)

(c)

(d)

12. Each of the following sketches suggests an addition statement relating three integers, all three of which are thought of as operators. Write the statement as in the example in Figure 6.30.

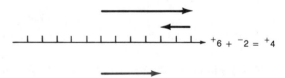

Figure 6.30

(a)

(b)

(c)

(d)

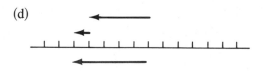

13. Find each sum in a graphical way in the style of Exercise 11 or Exercise 12.
    (a) $^+2 + ^-6$ (b) $^+5 + ^-3$
    (c) $^-8 + ^-4$ (d) $^-2 + ^+7$
    (e) $^+3 + ^-4 + ^+6 + ^-1$ (f) $^-2 + ^-4 + ^+3$

14. Write a symbolic expression (like $^-5 + ^+3$) corresponding to each of the following stories. Describe the unit and the positive direction in each case.
    (a) She earned 4 dollars and then spent 7 dollars.
    (b) He walked 8 blocks north and then 5 blocks south.
    (c) She rode up 5 floors in the elevator, then down 3, and then up 7.
    (d) During the past five days the noontime temperature cooled 3 degrees, cooled 2 degrees, warmed 1 degree, cooled 6 degrees, and warmed 8 degrees.
    (e) In four downs the team gained 3 yd, gained 2 yd, gained 0 yd, and lost 8 yd.

15. For each part of Exercise 14, write a single integer symbol that represents the resultant event.

Solve the word problems of Exercises 16–23. Illustrate your solution techniques on a number line.

16. It is now 12 min after blastoff. What time was it 30 min ago?

17. A missile is fired from 30 ft underwater, and 5 sec later it is 90 ft in the air. How many feet did it travel in those 5 sec?

18. The temperature was $^-4$ degrees this noon, and since then it has fallen 9 degrees. What is the temperature now?

19. Three years ago a pound of sugar cost 42 cents. Since then, its yearly price changes have been $^-3$, $^+21$, $^-9$. How much does it cost now?

20. Mr. Stout's record at his diet workshop for the past 6 weeks is as follows: $^-4$, $^-2$, 0, $^+1$, $^-2$, $^+3$. What has been his net gain or loss?

21. The daily changes in the Dow-Jones industrial average last week were $^+6$, $^-3$, $^-10$, $^-2$, $^+4$. What was the change for the week?

22. In still water the boat can go 16 mph. How fast can it go downstream in a river with a current of 5 mph?

23. Flying into the wind, the plane can go 190 mph. Flying with the wind, it can go 220 mph. What is the wind's speed? How fast can the plane go in still air?

24. Identify each use of the minus sign in these expressions as subtraction, opposite-of, or negative.
    (a) $^-(^+5 - ^-4)$
    (b) $^-4 - ^-^+3$

25. Put the following into appropriately shaped boxes and arrange them into a flowchart for the subtraction algorithm for integers. Identify the most sophisticated subroutine used.
    (a) Add.
    (b) A pair of integers: a (minuend) and b (subtrahend)
    (c) Change the sign on b.
    (d) The difference, $a - b$
    (e) Start.
    (f) Stop.

26. Before asking you to flowchart the algorithm for adding two integers, we review the idea of absolute value. The *absolute value* of an integer can be thought of as its distance from the origin on

the number line. For example, the absolute value of ⁻3 is 3; the absolute value of 5 is 5. Give the absolute value of each of these integers.

(a) ⁻7   (b) ⁻4
(c) ⁺4   (d) 13
(e) 0

27. Put parts (a)–(o) into appropriately shaped boxes and arrange them into a flowchart for adding integers. Test your flowchart with the inputs shown in Figure 6.31. On what subroutines does this algorithm depend? (As complicated as your flowchart may appear, it probably reflects how your mind operates when presented with an addition-of-integers problem.)

(a) Start.
(b) Two integers
(c) Is one of them zero?
(d) Write the other.
(e) The sum
(f) Stop.
(g) Do they have the same sign?
(h) Are they both positive?
(i) Add them.
(j) Add their absolute values.
(k) Attach a minus sign.
(l) Are they additive inverses?
(m) Write zero.
(n) Subtract their absolute values, smaller from larger.

(o) Attach the sign of the (original) integer having the larger absolute value.

First estimate, then compute the exact value of each of the following sums or differences.

28. ⁻212 + 157

29. ⁻156 + ⁻229

30. 403 + ⁻278

31. 231 + ⁻377

32. ⁻328 + ⁻285

33. ⁻451 + 614

34. 235 − 421

35. ⁻163 − ⁻89

36. ⁻158 − 327

37. 472 − ⁻472

38. 829 − ⁻383

39. 375 − 227

40. ⁻175 + 227 + ⁻318

41. 125 − 276 + ⁻84

42. 137 − 288 − ⁻165

43. 714 + ⁻435 − 714

44. Get acquainted with the use of the $\boxed{+/-}$ key by using your calculator to work some of Exercises 28–43.

Figure 6.31

6.2 *Multiplication and Division*

The definitions and algorithms for multiplication and division of integers are simpler than the corresponding rules for addition and subtraction. The imprecise mnemonics

"Minus times (divided by) plus is minus."

"Minus times (divided by) minus is plus."

pretty much tell the whole story.

To motivate these rules, however, requires some thought. Two general approaches are possible. One can look inward and see what is required for mathematical harmony within the system of integers, or one can look outward and see what is suggested by schematic or realistic external models for the integers. We begin with the internal approach.

Internal Algebraic Motivation

It would be mathematically pleasing if the system of integers satisfied the distributive property. If it did, we would be able to argue as follows:

$$0 = 2 \cdot 0 \qquad \text{multiplicative property of zero in } W$$
$$= 2 \cdot (3 + {}^-3) \qquad 3 \text{ and } {}^-3 \text{ are opposites}$$
$$= 2 \cdot 3 + 2 \cdot {}^-3 \qquad \text{assumed distributive property in } I$$
$$= 6 + 2 \cdot {}^-3 \qquad \text{multiplication fact in } W$$

Thus, $2 \cdot {}^-3$ adds to 6 to give 0; that is, $2 \cdot {}^-3$ is the opposite of 6. Symbolically, $2 \cdot {}^-3 = {}^-6$. If we ask also that multiplication be commutative in I, then ${}^-3 \cdot 2 = {}^-6$ as well.

Having thus motivated the minus-times-plus-is-minus rule, we could go on to motivate the minus-times-minus-is-plus rule:

$$0 = {}^-2 \cdot 0 \qquad \text{assumed multiplicative property of zero in } I$$
$$= {}^-2 \cdot (3 + {}^-3) \qquad 3 \text{ and } {}^-3 \text{ are opposites}$$
$$= {}^-2 \cdot 3 + {}^-2 \cdot {}^-3 \qquad \text{assumed distributive property in } I$$
$$= {}^-6 + {}^-2 \cdot {}^-3 \qquad \text{minus-times-plus-is-minus rule}$$

Thus ${}^-2 \cdot {}^-3$ adds to ${}^-6$ to give 0; that is, ${}^-2 \cdot {}^-3$ is the opposite of ${}^-6$. Symbolically, ${}^-2 \cdot {}^-3 = 6$.

We shall investigate the internal algebraic approach thoroughly in Section 6.3. We turn now to an external model.

The Poker-Chip Model

When we studied the whole numbers, we saw that one way of introducing multiplication is as repeated addition. This point of view extends to the poker-chip model, where calculating the product $3 \cdot {}^-2$ can be thought of as follows: Begin with a representation for zero, such as the empty set of chips, and 3 times *add* 2 red chips to it, as indicated in Figure 6.32. Symbolically, $3 \cdot {}^-2 = {}^-6$.

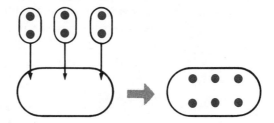

Figure 6.32

Without a prior assumption of commutativity we need to attach a different meaning to a product of the form ⁻2 · 3. Here is one: Begin with a representation for zero having 6 red and 6 black chips, and twice *take away* 3 black chips from it, as indicated in Figure 6.33. Symbolically, ⁻2 · 3 = ⁻6.

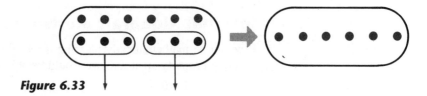

Figure 6.33

When we apply this second interpretation to a product of two negative factors, a positive integer results. For example, to compute ⁻2 · ⁻3, begin with a 12-chip representation for zero, and twice take away 3 reds, as illustrated in Figure 6.34. Symbolically, ⁻2 · ⁻3 = 6.

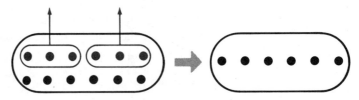

Figure 6.34

Figure 6.35 (p. 303) shows how a variant of the poker-chip model is used to motivate the rules for multiplying integers in a seventh-grade textbook.

We will look at multiplication in the number-line model when we study order in Section 6.5.

Realistic Models

The poker-chip model, while pedagogically attractive, is more schematic than realistic. Real-world models of multiplication of integers also exist, although they might be too complicated to present to children. We will look at two.

The first is a **velocity-time-position model.** Imagine a straight east-west railroad track, with positions (in miles) west of an observer given by negative integers and positions (in miles) east of the observer given by positive integers. The observer's position is given by 0. See Figure 6.36. Times (in hours) be-

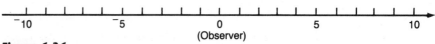

Figure 6.36

Multiplying integers

To understand multiplication of integers, think of multiplying by $^+2$ as putting in two sets of charges and think of multiplying by $^-2$ as taking out two sets of charges.

EXAMPLE 1. $^+\mathbf{2} \times {}^+\mathbf{3} = \mathbf{?}$

Put in two sets of $^+3$ charges.

EXAMPLE 2. $^+\mathbf{2} \times {}^-\mathbf{3} = \mathbf{?}$

Put in two sets of $^-3$ charges.

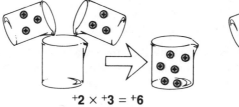

$$^+\mathbf{2} \times {}^+\mathbf{3} = {}^+\mathbf{6}$$

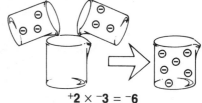

$$^+\mathbf{2} \times {}^-\mathbf{3} = {}^-\mathbf{6}$$

EXAMPLE 3. $^-\mathbf{2} \times {}^+\mathbf{3} = \mathbf{?}$

We need to take out two sets of $^+3$ charges. So, draw at least 6 ⊕⊖ pairs.

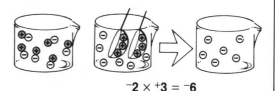

$$^-\mathbf{2} \times {}^+\mathbf{3} = {}^-\mathbf{6}$$

EXAMPLE 4. $^-\mathbf{2} \times {}^-\mathbf{3} = \mathbf{?}$

We need to take out two sets of $^-3$ charges. So, draw at least 6 ⊕⊖ pairs.

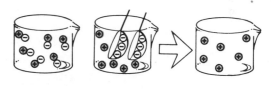

$$^-\mathbf{2} \times {}^-\mathbf{3} = {}^+\mathbf{6}$$

These examples give us a way to multiply.

> The product of two integers with the *same* sign is *positive*.
> The product of two integers with *different* signs is *negative*.
> The product of any integer and 0 is 0.

338

Figure 6.35 Multiplying integers in a seventh-grade textbook.

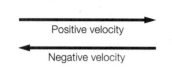

Positive velocity

Negative velocity

Figure 6.37

fore a train passes the observer are given by negative integers, and times (in hours) after it passes the observer are given by positive integers. Velocities of trains (in miles per hour) are given by negative integers for trains traveling east to west and by positive integers for trains traveling west to east. See Figure 6.37. For this model, under the assumption that velocities remain constant, position is found by multiplying velocity by time.

EXAMPLE 1   Find the position of each train.
(a) Velocity is 5; time is 3.
(b) Velocity is ⁻4; time is 2.
(c) Velocity is 6; time is ⁻2.
(d) Velocity is ⁻5; time is ⁻4.

Solution   (a) Since velocity is 5, the train is traveling west to east at 5 mph. Since time is 3, it has been 3 hr since the train passed the observer. Thus the train is 15 mi east of the observer. That is, its position is 15:

$$5 \cdot 3 = 15 \qquad \text{(velocity} \cdot \text{time} = \text{position)}$$

(b) This time the train is traveling east to west at 4 mph, and it has been 2 hr since it passed the observer. Thus it is 8 mi west of the observer at position ⁻8:

$$^{-}4 \cdot 2 = {}^{-}8 \qquad \text{(velocity} \cdot \text{time} = \text{position)}$$

(c) The train is traveling 6 mph from west to east. It is still 2 hr before it will pass the observer. Thus it is 12 mi west of the observer at position ⁻12:

$$6 \cdot {}^{-}2 = {}^{-}12 \qquad \text{(velocity} \cdot \text{time} = \text{position)}$$

(d) The train is traveling 5 mph from east to west. It is still 4 hr before it will pass the observer. Thus it is 20 mi east of the observer at position 20:

$$^{-}5 \cdot {}^{-}4 = 20 \qquad \text{(velocity} \cdot \text{time} = \text{position)} \qquad ❏$$

The second real-world model of integer multiplication is a **weight-position-moment model.** Consider a teeter-totter as shown in Figure 6.38. The positions on this teeter-totter are assigned integers in the usual way, with the positive direction to the right. (The unit of length here is the centimeter.) Suppose also that we have a collection of blocks (say each weighs a gram) and a collection of helium balloons, each balloon just able to balance each block. We assign integer symbols to these *weights* as shown in Figure 6.39.

Figure 6.38

Figure 6.39

If a weight is attached to the teeter-totter, it will tend to pivot. This tendency to pivot is called the (first) **moment** of the system. The moment of the system depends on how much weight is put on and where. For example, the moment of system B in Figure 6.40 is twice that of system A, and the moment of system C is three times that of system A. The moment of system D is the same as that of A but is oppositely directed. We agree to call clockwise moments positive and counterclockwise moments negative. With this agreement the moment of a (simple) system can be computed by multiplying the weight times the position at which it is applied.

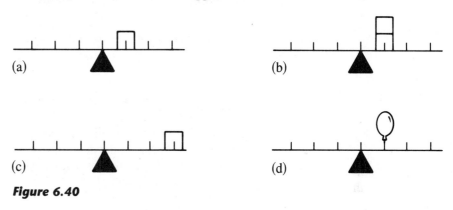

Figure 6.40

EXAMPLE 2   Find the moment of each system.

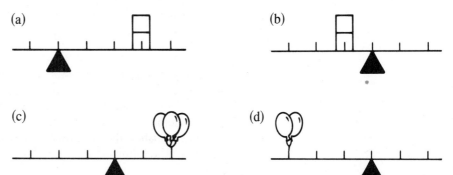

Solution   (a) Moment = weight · position = 2 · 3 = 6
(b) Moment = weight · position = 2 · ⁻1 = ⁻2
(c) Moment = weight · position = ⁻3 · 2 = ⁻6
(d) Moment = weight · position = ⁻2 · ⁻3 = 6
(Do you agree that the moment is clockwise?)   ❏

Computing the moment of a complicated system involves adding as well as multiplying.

EXAMPLE 3   Find the moment of the system shown in Figure 6.41.

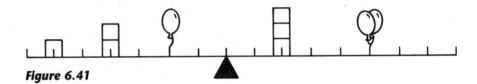

Figure 6.41

Solution
$$\text{Moment} = 1 \cdot {}^-6 + 2 \cdot {}^-4 + {}^-1 \cdot {}^-2 + 3 \cdot 2 + {}^-2 \cdot 5$$
$$= {}^-6 + {}^-8 + 2 + 6 + {}^-10 = {}^-16 \qquad ❏$$

Multiplication

The definition of multiplication of integers, like the one for addition, involves several cases. Again, in the definition only, we use red multiplication dots for the newly defined operation of multiplication of integers and black ones for the familiar operation of multiplication of whole numbers.

> **Definition of Multiplication (·) of Integers**
>
> For all whole numbers m and n:
>
> $$m \cdot n = m \cdot n$$
> $${}^-m \cdot n = n \cdot {}^-m = {}^-(m \cdot n)$$
> $${}^-m \cdot {}^-n = m \cdot n$$

Multiplication of integers has the same general properties as does multiplication of whole numbers. It is associative, is commutative, has 1 as an identity element, and satisfies the cancellation property. Furthermore, it distributes over addition. The following instances of these properties suggest their truth in general.

EXAMPLE 4 Use the definition of multiplication to show the following.

(a) $(4 \cdot {}^-5) \cdot {}^-3 = 4 \cdot ({}^-5 \cdot {}^-3)$
(b) $6 \cdot {}^-2 = {}^-2 \cdot 6$
(c) $1 \cdot {}^-17 = {}^-17$
(d) If ${}^-3 \cdot x = {}^-3 \cdot 5$, then $x = 5$.
(e) $3 \cdot (1 + {}^-5) = 3 \cdot 1 + 3 \cdot {}^-5$

Solution

(a) $(4 \cdot {}^-5) \cdot {}^-3 = {}^-(4 \cdot 5) \cdot {}^-3$ definition, case 2
$= {}^-20 \cdot {}^-3$ multiplication of whole numbers
$= 20 \cdot 3$ definition, case 3
$= 60$ multiplication of whole numbers
$4 \cdot ({}^-5 \cdot {}^-3) = 4 \cdot (5 \cdot 3)$ definition, case 3
$= 4 \cdot 15$ multiplication of whole numbers
$= 60$ multiplication of whole numbers

(b) $6 \cdot {}^-2 = {}^-(6 \cdot 2)$ definition, case 2
$= {}^-(2 \cdot 6)$ commutativity of whole number multiplication
$= {}^-2 \cdot 6$ definition, case 2

(c) $1 \cdot {}^-17 = {}^-(1 \cdot 17)$ definition, case 2
$= {}^-17$ multiplicative property of 1 in W

(d) Here x must be a positive integer; otherwise, ${}^-3 \cdot x$ would not equal the negative integer ${}^-3 \cdot 5$. Thus we can treat x just like the m and the n in the general definition of multiplication. By that definition

$${}^-3 \cdot x = {}^-(3 \cdot x) \qquad \text{and} \qquad {}^-3 \cdot 5 = {}^-(3 \cdot 5)$$

Thus the equation

$${}^-3 \cdot x = {}^-3 \cdot 5$$

can be written as

$${}^-(3 \cdot x) = {}^-(3 \cdot 5)$$

Adding $3 \cdot x$ and then $3 \cdot 5$ to both sides yields

$$3 \cdot 5 = 3 \cdot x$$

from which, by the cancellation property of multiplication in W,

$$5 = x$$

(e) $3 \cdot (1 + {}^-5) = 3 \cdot {}^-4$ addition of integers
$= {}^-(3 \cdot 4)$ definition, case 2
$= {}^-12$ multiplication of whole numbers
$3 \cdot 1 + 3 \cdot {}^-5 = 3 \cdot 1 + {}^-(3 \cdot 5)$ definition, cases 1 and 2
$= 3 + {}^-15$ multiplication of whole numbers
$= {}^-12$ addition of integers   ❑

Division

Exact division of integers can be defined just as it was for whole numbers.

> **Definition of Exact Division of Integers**
>
> If $a \neq 0$, then b/a is the solution to the equation $a \cdot \square = b$, if there is one.

To guarantee the existence of a solution to $a \cdot \square = b$, we need to impose the condition $|a|$ divides $|b|$. And to prove its uniqueness, we invoke the cancellation property of multiplication:

> If d_1 and d_2 both satisfy $a \cdot \square = b$, then $a \cdot d_1 = b$ and $a \cdot d_2 = b$.
> Thus $a \cdot d_1 = a \cdot d_2$
> But $a \neq 0$, so it can be canceled, leaving $d_1 = d_2$.

EXAMPLE 5   Use the definition of division to find the following.
(a) $^-12/4$
(b) $10/^-2$
(c) $^-8/^-4$

Solution   (a) Look for a solution of $4 \cdot \square = {}^-12$. If we were to ignore all signs, 3 would work. To make the signs work out properly, we use $^-3$.
(b) Consider the equation $^-2 \cdot \square = 10$. Again, two candidates, 5 and $^-5$, stand out, but only $^-5$ works.
(c) Consider the equation $^-4 \cdot \square = {}^-8$. Of the two candidates, 2 and $^-2$, 2 works.   ❑

Algorithms

An algorithm for division of integers is suggested by the preceding examples.

> To divide two integers, drop all signs and compute their whole number quotient. If the original integers had opposite signs, attach a minus sign to this quotient. Otherwise, leave it alone.

For multiplication the three-case definition itself serves as an algorithm.

EXAMPLE 6   Compute each of the following.
(a) $^-145 \cdot 82$
(b) $63 \cdot {}^-92$
(c) $^-243/^-9$
(d) $^-825/11$

Solution   (a) ⁻145 · 82 = ⁻(145 · 82)   definition of multiplication, case 2
                     = ⁻11,890   whole number multiplication algorithm
          (b) 63 · ⁻92 = ⁻(63 · 92)   definition of multiplication, case 2
                     = ⁻5796   whole number multiplication algorithm
          (c) ⁻243/⁻9 = 243/9   integer division algorithm
                     = 27   whole number division algorithm
          (d) ⁻825/11 = ⁻(825/11)   integer division algorithm
                     = ⁻75   whole number division algorithm   ❏

   In the exercises you will get a chance to flowchart the multiplication and division algorithms for integers.

EXERCISE SET 6.2

1. Write the multiplication of integers problem, and answer, suggested by each poker-chip diagram.

   (a)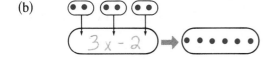

   (b)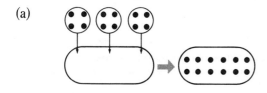

   (c)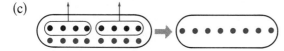

   (d)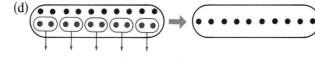

   (e)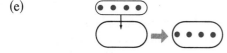

   (f)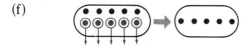

2. Draw a poker-chip diagram representing each of the following products.
   (a) 2 · ⁻5
   (b) ⁻2 · ⁻5
   (c) ⁻2 · 3
   (d) 2 · 3

3. Write the multiplication equation, and solution, suggested by each velocity-time-position question. Use the sign conventions that positions to the east of the observer, velocities toward the east, and times after observation are all positive.
   (a) A train is traveling from west to east at 10 mph, and it will reach the observer in 3 hr. Where is it now?
   (b) A train passed the observer 2 hr ago traveling east to west at 18 mph. Where is it now?
   (c) A train traveling from east to west at 27 mph will reach the observer in 4 hr. Where is it now?
   (d) A train traveling from west to east at 13 mph passed the observer 5 hr ago. Where is it now?
   (e) A train 60 mi east of the observer will pass her in 3 hr. What is its velocity?
   (f) A train 24 mi east of the observer is traveling from east to west at 8 mph. How many hours ago (from now) did (will) it pass the observer?

(g) A train 42 mi west of the observer is traveling west at 14 mph. How many hours ago (from now) did (will) it pass the observer?

(h) A train passed the observer 2 hr ago and is now 36 mi west of her. What is its velocity?

4. Calculate the moment of each system.

(a)

(b)

(c)

(d)

(e)

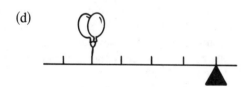

(f)

(g)

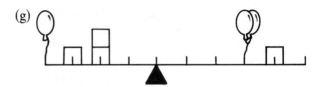

(h)

5. Sketch a teeter-totter system whose moment is as follows:
   (a) $3 \cdot 2$ (b) $3 \cdot {}^{-}2$
   (c) ${}^{-}2 \cdot 4$ (d) ${}^{-}2 \cdot {}^{-}4$

6. Where should you place a two-gram weight ⊟ to balance this teeter-totter?

7. Here is a standard teaching device for motivating the plus-times-minus-is-minus rule. Fill in the boxes so that the pattern continues.

$$3 \cdot 3 = 9$$
$$3 \cdot 2 = 6$$
$$3 \cdot 1 = 3$$
$$3 \cdot 0 = 0$$
$$3 \cdot {}^{-}1 = \Box$$
$$3 \cdot {}^{-}2 = \Box$$
$$\cdots$$

8. Assuming the minus-times-plus-is-minus rule, the same sort of device can be used to motivate the minus-times-minus-is-plus rule. Fill in the boxes so that the pattern continues.

$${}^{-}3 \cdot 3 = {}^{-}9$$
$${}^{-}3 \cdot 2 = {}^{-}6$$

$$-3 \cdot 1 = -3$$
$$-3 \cdot 0 = 0$$
$$-3 \cdot -1 = \square$$
$$-3 \cdot -2 = \square$$

. . .

9. Here is another way of getting at the ideas in Exercises 7 and 8.
   (a) Using W as input set, graph the multiply-by-three function, M_3, in the coordinate plane. Now, enlarge the input set to I and extend your graph in the most natural way.
   (b) Using W as input set, graph the multiply-by-negative-three function, M_{-3}, in the coordinate plane. Now, enlarge the input set to I and extend your graph in the most natural way.

10. Put the following phrases into appropriately shaped boxes, and arrange them into a flowchart for the multiplication algorithm for integers. Identify the most sophisticated subroutine.
    (a) A pair of integers
    (b) Attach a minus sign.
    (c) Is one positive and one negative?
    (d) Multiply their absolute values.
    (e) Multiply their absolute values.
    (f) Start.
    (g) Stop.
    (h) The product

11. Adjust your flowchart in Exercise 10 so that it becomes a flowchart for the division algorithm for integers (in the case where the quotient is an integer).

Simplify the expressions in Exercises 12–27. Check your work by using a calculator, particularly the $\boxed{+/-}$ key.

12. $-14 \cdot 7$

13. $-12 \cdot -13$

14. $-6 \cdot 5 \cdot -4 \cdot 3 \cdot -2 \cdot 1$

15. $(-2)^4$

16. $90/-5$

17. $-90/5$

18. $-72/-4$

19. $0/-6$

20. $-3 \cdot (5 - -2)$

21. $12/(3 - 3^2)$

22. $\dfrac{-(3 \cdot -4) + 8}{6 + -2}$

23. $(-5)^2 - 8 \cdot 2 - 7$

24. $-3 \cdot [15 - (8 - 2)]$

25. $15 - (3 - |-20|)$

26. $5 \cdot |6 - 8| - 12$

27. $(9 - 44)/(3 - |-10|)$

28. Estimate the value of each expression.
    (a) $-47 \cdot -81$
    (b) $-17 \cdot 9 \cdot 11$
    (c) $-4543/77$
    (d) $\dfrac{-57 \cdot 64}{-12}$

29. If x represents an arbitrary nonzero integer, which of the following are sure to be negative?
    (a) $-x$ (b) $-(-x)$
    (c) $(-x)^2$ (d) $-(x^2)$
    (e) x^3 (f) $(-x)^3$
    (g) $|x|$ (h) $-|x|$

30. Celsius temperatures are related to Fahrenheit temperatures by the equation

    $$C = \frac{5 \cdot (F - 32)}{9}$$

    Find the Celsius temperature corresponding to these Fahrenheit temperatures.
    (a) 104°F   (b) 212°F
    (c) 14°F   (d) 32°F
    (e) -4°F   (f) -40°F

31. In the course of one day's trading a speculator bought and sold shares in companies A, B, and C in the amounts and at the prices shown in the table. Her expenses (brokerage fees and so on) amounted to $210. What was her net gain or loss for the day?

Company	Number of shares	Bought at	Sold at
A	150	67	64
B	200	31	33
C	100	45	46

32. The owner of an 8-player semipro basketball team has expenses of $30 per player per game and $25 per game for the coach. Costs for renting the arena and paying the custodian, ticket seller, and so on come to $150 per game. The team plays a 20-game schedule before an average crowd of 175 fans. The owner receives $2 for each ticket sold. How much can he expect to profit (or lose) during the season?

6.3 *The System of Integers: A Formal Approach*

In the previous two sections we used a variety of external models—number-line, poker-chip, velocity-time-position, and weight-position-moment—to associate meanings with the integers and to motivate definitions of the arithmetic operations on them. From these interpretations and definitions we were able to deduce familiar structural properties such as associativity and commutativity.

In this section our point of view is entirely different. We divest the integers of all external connotations and view them simply as elements of an abstract set. We dissociate the operations of addition and multiplication from any particular interpretations and think of them only as undefined binary operations. We accept a small body of structural properties as axioms, and then we deduce from them all of the usual rules of integer arithmetic. The theorems of the previous section become axioms in this section, and the definitions of the previous section become theorems here.

The principal reason for presenting the integers as an abstract mathematical system is to give you a clear mental picture of its fundamental features. From the abstract point of view the system of integers is simple, differing from the system of whole numbers in just one essential way. Thus we can build an understanding of the integers on our prior knowledge of the whole numbers. And we can trace all of the rules for signed numbers to this single new property. Quoting again from the 5–8 *Standards:* "Instruction that facilitates students' understanding of the underlying structure of arithmetic should . . . emphasize . . . relationships between number systems."

The same warning that we gave in the introduction to Chapter 4 applies again: This stark abstract approach is for you; for children it would be strong medicine.

Basic Assumptions and Definitions

We begin by assuming that there is a set I, which includes the subset W of whole numbers, and that there are two binary operations, $+$ and $\cdot$, on I. As in any mathematical system, we have the usual logical properties: the RST properties of equality, and substitution. The structural properties for the integers are exactly the same as those for the whole numbers, with one exception: The cancellation property of addition is replaced by the new property that each integer has a unique opposite (additive inverse).

STRUCTURAL PROPERTIES FOR THE INTEGERS

Associative property of addition	Associative property of multiplication
Commutative property of addition	Commutative property of multiplication
Additive property of 0	Multiplicative property of 1
Each integer has a unique opposite.	Cancellation property of multiplication

Distributive property

Three comments: First, remember that when we say addition and multiplication are binary operations on I, we mean, among other things, that I is *closed* under these operations; that is, sums and products of integers are again integers. Second, when we write "commutative property of addition," we now mean that addition is a commutative operation on the *entire* set of integers, not just on the subset of whole numbers. This comment applies to the other properties that seem to repeat what we already know about W. Third, we need a definition of *opposite* for the one new property to have meaning.

Definition.   The **opposite,** or **additive inverse,** of a is the integer that adds to a to give 0. We denote this integer by ^-a. Thus

$$^-a + a = 0 \quad \text{and} \quad a + {}^-a = 0$$

The second (and last) new assumption about the system of integers is a limiting property that distinguishes the integers from the larger systems of rationals and reals, which satisfy the same nine basic structural properties as do the integers.

Every integer is either a whole number or the opposite of a whole number.

Thus

$$I = \{ \ldots, {}^-3, {}^-2, {}^-1, 0, 1, 2, 3, \ldots \}$$

Emmy Noether

David Hilbert

۶ **EMMY NOETHER (1882–1935)** did pioneering research on mathematical systems called *rings* (systems that have very nearly the same structural properties as the system of integers), and she earned the reputation as the greatest woman mathematician up to her time. Her life story is one of perseverance in the face of discrimination. The daughter of a mathematics professor in the small South German university town of Erlangen, she began auditing courses at the all-male university in 1900. Shortly thereafter, women were allowed to register officially, and in 1907 she completed her thesis and passed the doctoral examination summa cum laude. She remained at home in Erlangen until 1916, when David Hilbert invited her to Göttingen.

Despite Hilbert's pleas that she be hired ("After all, we are a university and not a bathhouse"), Göttingen was not yet ready for a woman faculty member. Three years later she was given a low-level, nonpaying appointment, but it was 1922 before she finally began to receive a small salary for her teaching and research. During the 1920s she was the leader of an active group of young algebraists, one of whom, B. L. van der Waerden, subsequently brought her discoveries to the attention of the world in his classic textbook *Moderne Algebra*.

In 1933 she was summarily dismissed from Göttingen, over Hilbert's protests, because of her Jewish ancestry. The last 18 months of her life were spent in the United States at Bryn Mawr College and the Institute for Advanced Study at Princeton. She died suddenly, at the height of her career, following what had seemed to be a successful operation.

Perhaps you are wondering why we deleted the cancellation property of addition from the list of assumed structural properties. The reason is that using our new assumption about opposites, we can now *prove* the cancellation property as a theorem.

Theorem   Cancellation property of addition: If $a + b = a + c$, then $b = c$.

Proof.   Since this theorem is an if-then theorem, we temporarily assume that $a + b = a + c$ and we try to deduce that $b = c$:

$a + b = a + c$	given
$^-a + (a + b) = {}^-a + (a + c)$	existence of opposites, addition property of equality
$(^-a + a) + b = (^-a + a) + c$	associative property of addition
$0 + b = 0 + c$	definition of opposite
$b = c$	additive property of zero Q.E.D.

Since the cancellation property of addition has been shown to be true for the system of integers, we now know that all nine of the basic structural properties of the whole numbers remain true in the larger system of integers. Hence all of the logical consequences of those nine properties must also be true for the integers. In particular, the multiplicative properties of zero must be true. (Do you remember how carefully we *deduced* those properties of zero from the nine structural properties of the whole number system?) So we have another theorem.

Theorem   Multiplicative properties of zero:

1. $0 \cdot a = 0$ for any integer a.
2. If $a \cdot b = 0$, where a and b are integers, then $a = 0$ or $b = 0$.   ❑

Before we can deduce other arithmetic properties of the integers, we need a definition of the secondary operation, subtraction. The following definition was suggested by our earlier work with models.

Definition of Subtraction

$$a - b = a + \bar{b}$$

Notice that subtraction is a binary operation on the set of integers:

$$(a, b) \rightarrow a + \bar{b}$$

Rules of Arithmetic of Integers

The groundwork has now been laid. We have identified the basic properties of the system of integers and have made two key definitions: definition of opposite and definition of subtraction. Everything else there is to know about the arithmetic of the integers can now be deduced. Perhaps surprisingly, all of the various rules for minus signs are *forced* on us once we accept a single alteration in the structural properties of the whole numbers and make two natural definitions. We have collected a number of common properties of minus signs into a single theorem.

Theorem   Rules for minus signs: For all integers a and b,

1. $\bar{(\bar{a})} = a$ "the opposite of the opposite of a is a"
2. $\bar{a} + \bar{b} = \bar{(a + b)}$ for example, $\bar{5} + \bar{9} = \bar{(5 + 9)}$
3. $a - b = \bar{(b - a)}$ for example, $5 - 12 = \bar{(12 - 5)}$

4. $^-a = ^-1 \cdot a$

5. $^-a \cdot b = ^-(a \cdot b)$

6. $^-a \cdot ^-b = a \cdot b$

Proof of 1.   The integer (^-a) has just one opposite, and it is denoted by $^-(^-a)$. Thus if we can show that a behaves like an opposite of (^-a), then we can conclude that it *is* $^-(^-a)$, that is, $a = ^-(^-a)$. To behave like an opposite of (^-a), a would have to add to (^-a) to give 0. But, of course, it does: $a + ^-a = 0$ because ^-a is the opposite of a.

Proof of 2.   The sum $(a + b)$ has just one opposite, and it is denoted by $^-(a + b)$. Thus if we can show that $^-a + ^-b$ behaves like an opposite of $(a + b)$, then we can conclude that $^-a + ^-b = ^-(a + b)$. That is, it suffices to show that $^-a + ^-b + (a + b) = 0$.

$$^-a + ^-b + (a + b) = (^-a + a) + (^-b + b) \qquad \text{associative and commutative properties of addition}$$

$$= 0 + 0 \qquad \text{definition of opposites}$$

$$= 0 \qquad \text{additive property of 0}$$

Proof of 3.   As in the proofs of 1 and 2, it suffices to show that $a - b$ adds to $b - a$ to give 0:

$$a - b + b - a = a + ^-b + b + ^-a \qquad \text{definition of subtraction}$$

$$= (a + ^-a) + (b + ^-b) \qquad \text{associative and commutative properties of addition}$$

$$= 0 + 0 \qquad \text{definition of opposites}$$

$$= 0 \qquad \text{additive property of 0}$$

Proof of 4.   It suffices to prove that $^-1 \cdot a + a = 0$ (why?):

$$^-1 \cdot a + a = ^-1 \cdot a + 1 \cdot a \qquad \text{multiplicative property of 1}$$

$$= (^-1 + 1) \cdot a \qquad \text{distributive property}$$

$$= 0 \cdot a \qquad \text{definition of opposites}$$

$$= 0 \qquad \text{multiplicative property of 0} \qquad ❑$$

The proofs of 5 and 6 are left as exercises.

Integers and Equations

A thorough, self-contained discussion of equations and their solution is given in Section 15.1. In this subsection, without going into all of the details, we illustrate the key roles played by the addition property of equality and the property that every integer has an additive inverse.

EXAMPLE 1   Solve each equation.
(a) $x + 7 = 4$
(b) $2x + 3(x + 6) = 8$
(c) $2x + 5 = x - 4$

Solution   (a) $x + 7 = 4 \Rightarrow x + 7 + {}^-7 = 4 + {}^-7 \Rightarrow x + 0 = {}^-3 \Rightarrow x = {}^-3$
Check: ${}^-3 + 7 \overset{?}{=} 4$; yes.
(b) $2x + 3(x + 6) = 8 \Rightarrow 2x + 3x + 18 = 8 \Rightarrow 5x + 18 + {}^-18 = 8 + {}^-18$
$\Rightarrow 5x = {}^-10 \Rightarrow x = {}^-2$ Check: $2({}^-2) + 3({}^-2 + 6) \overset{?}{=} 8$; yes, since
${}^-4 + 12 = 8$.
(c) $2x + 5 = x - 4 \Rightarrow 2x + 5 + {}^-5 = x - 4 + {}^-5 \Rightarrow 2x = x - 9 \Rightarrow 2x$
$+ {}^-x = x - 9 + {}^-x \Rightarrow x = {}^-9$ Check: $2({}^-9) + 5 \overset{?}{=} {}^-9 - 4$; yes, since
${}^-18 + 5 = {}^-13$.   ❑

Words and Symbols

How should one pronounce the expression ${}^-3 - {}^-x$? The quickest way is to simply pronounce every minus sign in sight as "minus." The locution

"minus three minus minus x"

is decipherable, although the burden of sorting out the different uses of the minus sign is left to the listener. To assist the listener one might say

"negative three minus the opposite of x"

or

"the opposite of three minus the opposite of x"

However, one probably should *not* pronounce ${}^-x$ as "negative x" because this could suggest to the listener that ${}^-x$ is a negative integer, which it may or may not be, depending on the value of x.

EXERCISE SET 6.3

1. Write the simplest symbol you can for each of the following elements of I.
   (a) The additive inverse of 3
   (b) The opposite of 5
   (c) Negative six
   (d) The number that adds to 4 to give 0
   (e) The solution to the equation $2 + \square = 0$
2. In the system of whole numbers, subtraction was defined implicitly as follows: $a - b$ is the solution to the equation $b + \square = a$, if there is one. In the system of integers a different, and explicit, definition of subtraction was given.
   (a) Write out that explicit definition of $a - b$.
   (b) Show that the two definitions of subtraction are consistent by showing that $a - b$, as you just defined it, is a solution to $b + \square = a$.

3. Assuming that the $\boxed{-}$ button on your calculator is broken, but the $\boxed{+/-}$ button works, how could you compute $2074 - 1887$?

Exercises 4–7 refer to the theorem on p. 315.

4. Prove rule 5 of the rules for minus signs by using the method we used for rules 1–4.

5. Prove rule 5 of the rules for minus signs by using rule 4 and the associative property of multiplication.

6. Supply the missing reasons in this proof of rule 6:

$$^-a \cdot {}^-b = {}^-(a \cdot {}^-b)$$? _prop 6 opposites_

$$= {}^-({}^-b \cdot a)$$? _commutative prop._

$$= {}^-[{}^-(b \cdot a)]$$? _prop. of opposites_

$$= b \cdot a$$? _ll_

$$= a \cdot b$$?

7. Supply reasons in this completely symbolic proof of rule 1:

$$a = 0 + a$$? _add. prop of 0_

$$= [{}^-({}^-a) + ({}^-a)] + a$$? _def. of opposites_

$$= {}^-({}^-a) + [({}^-a) + a]$$? _assoc. prop of addition_

$$= {}^-({}^-a) + 0$$? _def. of opposites_

$$= {}^-({}^-a)$$? _add. prop. of zero_

8. Supply one main reason at steps (a)–(h) in this proof that

$$(x + y)(x - y) = x^2 - y^2 \qquad \text{(where } x \text{ and } y \text{ are integers).}$$

$$(x + y)(x - y) = x(x - y) + y(x - y) \quad \text{(a)}$$

$$= x(x + {}^-y) + y(x + {}^-y) \quad \text{(b)}$$

$$= x \cdot x + x \cdot {}^-y + y \cdot x + y \cdot {}^-y \quad \text{(c)}$$

$$= x \cdot x + {}^-(x \cdot y) + (y \cdot x) + {}^-(y \cdot y)$$

a property of minus signs

$$= x \cdot x + {}^-(x \cdot y) + (x \cdot y) + {}^-(y \cdot y) \quad \text{(d)}$$

$$= x \cdot x + 0 + {}^-(y \cdot y) \quad \text{(e)}$$

$$= x \cdot x + {}^-(y \cdot y) \quad \text{(f)}$$

$$= x^2 + {}^-(y^2) \quad \text{(g)}$$

$$= x^2 - y^2 \quad \text{(h)}$$

9. Using any of the results in this section as reasons, prove that multiplication distributes over subtraction; that is,

$$a \cdot (b - c) = a \cdot b - a \cdot c$$

where a, b, and c can be any integers. *Hint:* Use the definition of subtraction, and the problem-solving strategy of working from both ends toward the middle.

10. Our one new structural assumption about the integers was an existence-uniqueness assumption. We assumed that for any integer a the equation $a + \square = 0$ has precisely one solution. It turns out that uniqueness need not be assumed; it can be proved from existence and the other structural properties. The plan of the proof is to assume that b and c are solutions to $a + \square = 0$, and then to show that $b = c$. Supply a reason at each equal sign in the following proof:

$$c = 0 + c = (a + b) + c = (b + a) + c$$
$$= b + (a + c) = b + 0 = b$$

11. Solve each equation. Remember to check your solutions.
    (a) $10 + x = 4$
    (b) $3x + 7 = {}^-8$
    (c) $5 + 2(x + 3) = 3$
    (d) $13 - 2(4 - x) = 31$
    (e) $23 - 2x = 5$
    (f) $6x + 10 = 3x - 11$
    (g) $x + 4(x + 3) = 2(x - 3)$
    (h) $(x + 1)(x + 2) = 0$
    (i) $2x^2 - 5x = x(3 + 2x) + 32$
    (j) $6x + 7 = 5 - 2(4 - 3x)$
    (k) $^-3x^2 + 10 = {}^-17$
    (l) $x(2 - x) = 2x + 1$

6.4 *Seven-Clock Arithmetic (Optional)*

To tighten our grasp on the abstract mathematical structure of the system of integers, we consider again the mathematical system of seven-clock arithmetic. Recall that this sytem consists of a set

$$I_7 = \{0, 1, 2, 3, 4, 5, 6\}$$

and two binary operations, which we used to write as $+_7$ and $\cdot_7$, but which we shall now write as simply $+$ and $\cdot$ to keep the notation manageable. Remember that this system enjoys the same nine basic structural properties as the system of whole numbers. In addition, it also satisfies the extra property of the system of integers:

> Every seven-clock number has an opposite.

For example, the opposite of 4 is 3 since 3 adds to 4 to give 0, and the opposite of 2 is 5 since $5 + 2 = 0$.

Let us explore what happens if we make the same two definitions that we did for the integers.

Definition (of Opposite). ^-a denotes the opposite of a in seven-clock arithmetic. For example, $^-4 = 3$ and $^-2 = 5$.

Definition (of Subtraction).

$$a - b = a + {}^-b$$

For example, $4 - 5 = 4 + {}^-5 = 4 + 2 = 6$.

Since all of the basic structural properties of the integers are true in seven-clock arithmetic and since the definitions of opposite and subtraction are unchanged, all strictly logical consequences of these properties and definitions must also be true. In particular, the six common rules for minus signs that we just proved for integers must also be true in seven-clock arithmetic. If any of them fail to be true, then there must be a flaw in our logic. Seven-clock arithmetic, then, provides a finite context in which we can verify our theoretical results.

Before considering some examples, we need to extend our convention about the order of operations. Namely, in the absence of parentheses the opposite-of function takes precedence over all of addition, subtraction, multiplication, and division. Thus

$$^-2 \cdot 3 + {}^-6 = 5 \cdot 3 + 1 = 1 + 1 = 2$$

Now to the examples that test our theoretical results.

EXAMPLE 1   Theory says that $2 - 5 = {}^-(5 - 2)$. This is rule 3 for minus signs.

Testing   By the definitions of subtraction and opposite:

$$2 - 5 = 2 + {}^-5 = 2 + 2 = 4$$
$${}^-(5 - 2) = {}^-(5 + {}^-2) = {}^-(5 + 5) = {}^-3 = 4$$

Theory is corroborated.   ❏

EXAMPLE 2   Theory says that ${}^-3 + {}^-6 = {}^-(3 + 6)$. This is rule 2 for minus signs.

Testing $${}^-3 + {}^-6 = 4 + 1 = 5$$
$${}^-(3 + 6) = {}^-2 = 5$$

Theory is corroborated.   ❏

EXAMPLE 3   Theory says that ${}^-3 \cdot {}^-5 = 3 \cdot 5$. This is rule 6 for minus signs.

Testing $${}^-3 \cdot {}^-5 = 4 \cdot 2 = 1$$
$$3 \cdot 5 = 1$$

Theory is corroborated.   ❏

One of the many other facts about minus signs that we know to be true of the integers is this distributive property:

$$a \cdot (b - c) = a \cdot b - a \cdot c$$

Let us test this fact in seven-clock arithmetic with $a = 5$, $b = 3$, and $c = 4$:

$$\begin{cases} 5 \cdot (3 - 4) = 5 \cdot (3 + {}^-4) = 5 \cdot (3 + 3) = 5 \cdot 6 = 2 \\ 5 \cdot 3 - 5 \cdot 4 = 1 - 6 = 1 + {}^-6 = 1 + 1 = 2 \end{cases}$$

Again, we have corroborating evidence for our general assertion that all of the manipulative rules for minus signs are inevitable logical consequences of the basic structural properties and the definitions of opposite and subtraction.

EXERCISE SET 6.4

1. Write the simplest symbol you can for each of the following elements of I_7.
   (a) $5 + 6$ (b) $5 \cdot 6$ (c) ${}^-5$
   (d) ${}^-2$ (e) $6 - 2$ (f) $3 - 4$

2. In integer arithmetic the minus sign can mean three different things: negative, opposite-of, or subtraction. What are its possible meanings in seven-clock arithmetic?

3. Verify, by simplifying both sides, that each of the following statements is true in I_7.
   (a) $^-(^-2) = 2$
   (b) $1 - 5 = {^-}(5 - 1)$
   (c) $^-4 + {^-}6 = {^-}(4 + 6)$
   (d) $^-5 = {^-}1 \cdot 5$
   (e) $^-4 \cdot 5 = {^-}(4 \cdot 5)$
   (f) $^-3 \cdot {^-}6 = 3 \cdot 6$
   (g) $4 \cdot (2 - 5) = 4 \cdot 2 - 4 \cdot 5$
   (h) $3 - (2 - 6) = 3 - 2 + 6$

4. Solve each of the I_7 equations by adding an appropriate number to both sides. Check your solutions.
   Example
   $x + 6 = 4 \Rightarrow x + 6 + 1 = 4 + 1 \Rightarrow$
   $x + 0 = 5 \Rightarrow x = 5.$ *Check:* $5 + 6 = 4.$
   (a) $x + 2 = 1$ (b) $4 + x = 2$
   (c) $0 = x + 5$ (d) $x + 1 = 6$
   (e) $x - 4 = 5$ (f) $x - 3 = 4$
   (g) $2 - x = 1$ (h) $6 - x = 2$

5. Think about what division might mean in seven-clock arithmetic, and then assign values to each of the following.
   (a) $3/5$ (b) $5/3$ (c) $6/2$ (d) $2\frac{3}{4}$

6. There is something sensible and something nonsensical about this statement: "When 4 is divided by 5 in seven-clock arithmetic, the quotient is 2 and the remainder is 1."
   (a) What is sensible?
   (b) What is nonsensical?

★ 7. There is an interesting connection between the seven clock and music. Instead of numbering the points of the clock, assign them letters from the piano keyboard, as shown in Figure 6.42. We have put C in the 0 position because the key of C has 0 sharps. To find what (major) key has 1 sharp, move 4 spaces clockwise from C (the key of G). To find what that 1 sharp is, move 1 space counterclockwise from G (the sharped note is F). To find what key has 2 sharps, move 4 spaces clockwise from G (the key of D). To find what the second sharp is, move 1 space counterclockwise from D (the second sharped note is C).
   (a) What key has 3 sharps, and what are they?
   (b) What key has 5 sharps, and what are they?
   (c) Determine a scheme for finding out about flats.

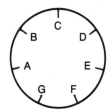

Figure 6.42

6.5 *Order in the System of Integers*

To complete our description of the system of integers, we need to discuss the less-than relation, $<$. As in the system of whole numbers, both algebraic and geometric definitions are available.

Algebraic Definition of Less Than

$a < b$ means there is a natural number solution to the equation $a + \square = b$; that is, $b - a \in N$.

> ### Geometric Definition of Less Than
>
> $a < b$ means a is left of b on the number line.

EXAMPLE 1   Show that $^-6 < 3$.

Algebraic Solution   The equation $^-6 + \square = 3$ has a natural number solution, namely 9. Equivalently, $3 - {}^-6$ is a natural number, namely 9.

Geometric Solution   The integer $^-6$ stands to the left of 3 on the number line, as shown in Figure 6.43.   ❏

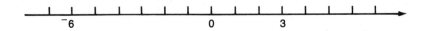

Figure 6.43

Since these definitions are identical to the ones we gave for the system of whole numbers, it is not surprising that essentially the same basic order properties remain true in the system of integers. Trichotomy, transitivity, and the addition property of less than all remain literally true for the larger system of integers. (Can you state these properties?) The multiplication property of less than, however, must be modified as follows, where, as usual, $x > y$ is alternate notation for $y < x$.

> ### Multiplication Property of Less Than
>
> 1. If $a < b$ and $c > 0$, then $a \cdot c < b \cdot c$.
> 2. If $a < b$ and $c < 0$, then $a \cdot c > b \cdot c$.

That is, an inequality is left unchanged when both sides are multiplied by the same positive integer, but it is *reversed* when both sides are multiplied by the same negative integer.

EXAMPLE 2

$5 < 8$ but $^-2 \cdot 5 > {}^-2 \cdot 8$ because $^-10 > {}^-16$.

$^-8 < 3$ but $^-4 \cdot {}^-8 > {}^-4 \cdot 3$ because $32 > {}^-12$.

$^-6 < {}^-4$ but $^-3 \cdot {}^-6 > {}^-3 \cdot {}^-4$ because $18 > 12$.   ❏

Let us prove statement 2 to see why the order reversal occurs. In our proof we shall use statement 1 and the addition property of less than. As usual in proving an if-then statement, we begin by assuming the if clause

$$a < b \qquad \text{and} \qquad c < 0$$

and we try to deduce the then clause

$$a \cdot c > b \cdot c$$

The proof is as follows:

$a < b$ and $c < 0$	given
$a < b$ and $c + \bar{}c < 0 + \bar{}c$	addition property of less than
$a < b$ and $0 < \bar{}c$	definition of opposite, additive property of 0
$a \cdot \bar{}c < b \cdot \bar{}c$	statement 1 of the multiplication property of less than
$\bar{}(a \cdot c) < \bar{}(b \cdot c)$	property of minus signs
$(a \cdot c + b \cdot c) + \bar{}(a \cdot c) < (a \cdot c + b \cdot c) + \bar{}(b \cdot c)$	addition property of less than
$b \cdot c < a \cdot c$	associative and commutative properties of addition, definition of opposite, additive property of zero
$a \cdot c > b \cdot c$	rewriting using $>$ instead of $<$ Q.E.D.

The two parts of the multiplication property of less than can be explained geometrically as well if we extend our number line model for the integers to include an interpretation for multiplication. Let us begin by agreeing to represent each integer by a vector with tail at the origin, as in Figure 6.44. And let us restrict our attention, for the time being, to the case of a positive multiplier. Multiplication by a *positive* integer can be interpreted as a *stretch,* just as it was in our study of the whole numbers (see Section 4.6).

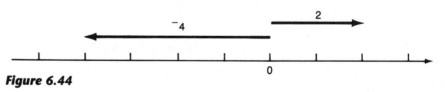

Figure 6.44

EXAMPLE 3

To find $3 \cdot 2$ geometrically, start with the vector from 0 to 2 and stretch it to three times its original length, as shown in Figure 6.45. Similarly, to find $2 \cdot \bar{}4$ geometrically, start with the vector from 0 to $\bar{}4$ and stretch it to two

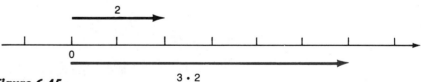

Figure 6.45

times it original length, as shown in Figure 6.46. *Caution:* For the remainder of this section, black and red indicate input and output, respectively, *not* positive and negative. ❏

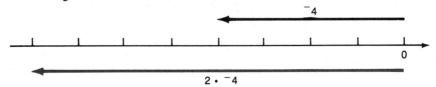

Figure 6.46

As in the case of whole numbers, stretching two vectors preserves their left-right relationship. That is:

> If a is left of b and if c is positive, then $c \cdot a$ is left of $c \cdot b$.

In the diagrams that follow, we have taken $c = 2$ for the sake of concreteness.

CASE 1. For $a < b$ and both positive, see Figure 6.47.

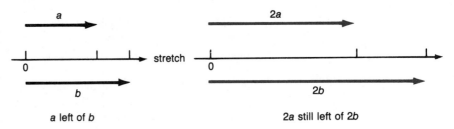

Figure 6.47

CASE 2. For $a < b$, one positive, and one negative, see Figure 6.48.

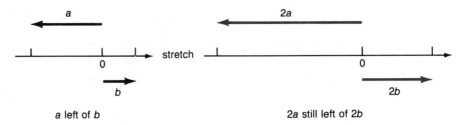

Figure 6.48

CASE 3. For $a < b$ and both negative, see Figure 6.49.

 To give multiplication by a negative integer a geometric interpretation in our number line model, we need to bring in the idea of a *flip*.

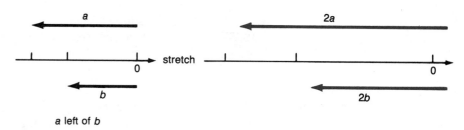

a left of b

Figure 6.49

EXAMPLE 4   To find ⁻1 · 5 geometrically, start with the vector from 0 to 5 and flip it across the origin. See Figure 6.50. To find ⁻3 · 2, begin with the vector from 0 to 2, stretch it to three times its length, and then flip it. See Figure 6.51.

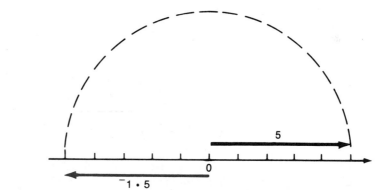

Figure 6.50

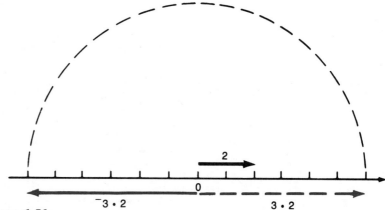

Figure 6.51

Would it have made any difference if we had done the flip first and then the 3 stretch?   ❑

The flip interpretation of multiplication by a negative integer is reasonable, of course, because it is consistent with the algebraic rules for multiplying integers.

EXAMPLE 5   To find $^-2 \cdot \, ^-3$, begin with the vector from 0 to $^-3$, give it a 2 stretch, and then flip it. Clearly, $^-2 \cdot \, ^-3 = 6$. See Figure 6.52.   ❏

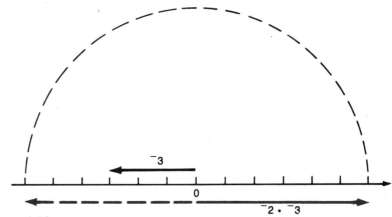

Figure 6.52

Our purpose in discussing flips here is that they provide a geometric explanation for the order-reversal phenomenon when both sides of an inequality are multiplied by a negative number. Simply put, flipping two vectors reverses their left-right relationship. That is:

> If a is left of b, then ^-a is right of ^-b.

Again, there are three cases to consider.
CASE 1. For $a < b$ and both positive, see Figure 6.53.

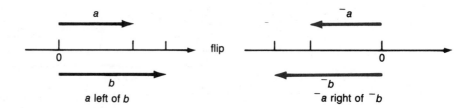

Figure 6.53

CASE 2. For $a < b$, one positive, and one negative, see Figure 6.54.

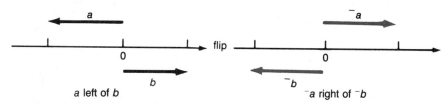

flip

a left of *b*

^-a right of ^-b

Figure 6.54

CASE 3. For $a < b$ and both negative, see Figure 6.55.

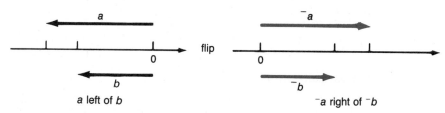

flip

a left of *b*

^-a right of ^-b

Figure 6.55

EXERCISE SET 6.5

1. Each diagram suggests a multiplication problem involving integers. Write the problem and answer as in the example.

   Example See Figure 6.56.

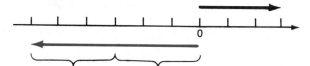

Figure 6.56

Solution: The input (multiplicand) is 3. The operator (multiplier) is a 2 stretch with a flip; that is $^-2$. The output (product) is $^-6$. *Answer:* $^-2 \cdot 3 = {}^-6$.

(a)

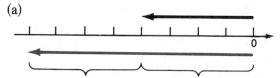

(b)

(c)

(d)

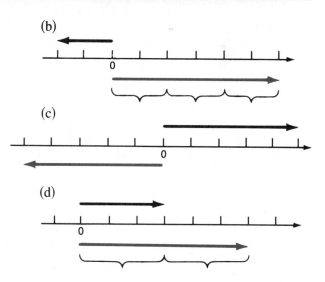

2. Locate each product geometrically as in the example.

   Example Find $^-2 \cdot {}^-3$.

(i) Start with a vector from 0 to ⁻3.

(ii) Flip it over the origin.

(iii) Stretch it to twice its original length. The product is 6.

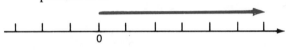

(a) ⁻2 · 3　　　　　　　(b) 2 · ⁻3
(c) 2 · 3　　　　　　　(d) ⁻4 · ⁻1

3. Show geometrically that $3 < 5$ and $⁻2 · 3 > ⁻2 · 5$.

4. Show geometrically that $⁻2 < 3$ and $⁻3 · ⁻2 > ⁻3 · 3$.

5. Fill in a reason at each implication arrow in the proof illustrated in Figure 6.57 that the inequality $x + 4 < 2$ is equivalent to (has the same solution set as) the inequality $x < ⁻2$.

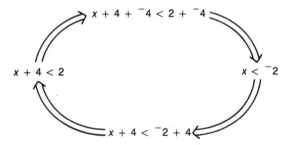

Figure 6.57

6. Solve each of the following inequalities by replacing it by an equivalent inequality whose solution set is obvious.
   (a) $x + 5 < 1$　　　　(b) $x + 2 < ⁻3$
   (c) $x - 3 < 1$　　　　(d) $x - 5 < ⁻7$
   (e) $4 - x < 1$　　　　(f) $2x - 4 < 3 + x$
   (g) $2 · x < 0$　　　　(h) $2x - 3 < 5$

★ 7. Prove that if $2a < 2b$, then $a < b$. *Hint:* By trichotomy either $a < b$, $a = b$, or $a > b$.

8. Fill in the appropriate order symbol.
   (a) If $a · c < b · c$ and $c > 0$, then a ◯ b.
   (b) If $a · c < b · c$ and $c < 0$, then a ◯ b.

9. What can be said about the relative sizes of a and b under the following conditions?
   (a) $a = b + c$ where $c \in N$
   (b) $a + c = b$ where $c \in N$
   (c) $a + c = b$ where $c \in W$
   (d) $a + c = b$ where $c \in I$
   (e) $a + c = b$ where $⁻c \in N$

10. True or false, for all integers a and b:
    (a) If $a < b$, then $a - b$ is a negative integer.
    (b) If $a < b$, then $2 - a < 2 - b$.
    (c) If $a < b$, then $a^2 < b^2$.
    (d) If $a < b$, then $ab < b^2$.
    (e) If $a + b = 0$, then $ab \le 0$.

★ 11. Use the algebraic definition of less than to prove the following:
    If $a < b$ and $c > 0$, then $c · a < c · b$

12. Find the solution set in I of each of these inequalities.
    (a) $(x + 3)(x - 2) > 0$　*Hint:* Under what conditions can a product of two integers $a · b$ be positive?
    (b) $(x - 1)(5 - x) > 0$

Key Concepts in Chapter 6

State
Operator
Vector
Number-line models
Poker-chip model

Addition of integers
Additive inverse
Subtraction of integers
Velocity-time-position model
Weight-position-moment model

Multiplication of integers
Division of integers

Structural properties
Properties of less than

❧ *Chapter 6 Review Exercises* ❧

1. Each diagram represents an arithmetic problem involving integers. Write the problem and the answer.

(a)

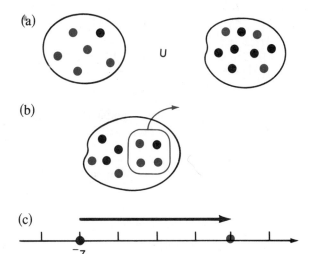

(b)

(c)

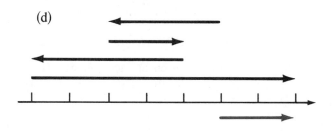

(d)

(e)

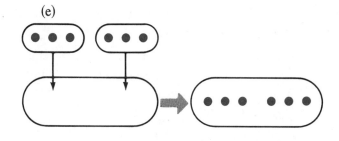

(f)

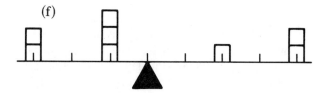

(g)

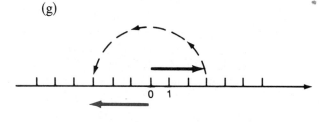

(h)

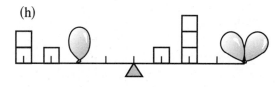

2. Draw a state-operator-state, number-line diagram that represents $2 + {}^-5$.

3. Draw a poker-chip diagram that represents $3 - {}^-2$. Use ○ for red and ● for black.

4. Draw a poker-chip diagram that represents ${}^-2 \cdot 3$.

5. Draw a balance-beam diagram that represents $4 \cdot {}^-2 + 1 \cdot 3$.

6. At what point could you attach a single balloon to balance this teeter-totter?

7. A train traveling from east to west at 12 mph passed the station 4 hr ago. Where is it now?

8. Three hours ago a train, moving at a constant speed, was 125 miles west of the Kansas-Colorado border. The track runs straight east and west. Four hours from now it will be 253 miles east of the border. Find the train's velocity.

9. I began with a left-pointing vector of length 3 with its tail at the origin. First I flipped it over the origin and doubled its length. Then I quadrupled the length of the resulting vector. Finally, I flipped it across the origin again.
   (a) Write down a product of integers that tells this same story.
   (b) Calculate the product in part (a).

10. Frank's Diner has been losing 12 dollars per day for the past 30 days and has a net worth right now of ⁻150 dollars. What was its net worth 30 days ago?

11. A Reno blackjack dealer reports that one evening she had 20 customers. Eight of them lost $15 apiece, three lost $18 apiece, six won $4 apiece, one won $50, and the other two broke even.
   (a) What was the dealer's net gain (or loss)?
   (b) What was the average gain (or loss) to the dealer per customer?

12. A passenger train is speeding northward at 70 mph. The conductor, walking from the front to the rear of the train at a rate of 4 mph, accidentally kicks a child's toy car down the aisle ahead of him. If the toy car is moving away from the conductor at a rate of 8 mph, what is its speed and direction relative to the railroad track?

13. An investor owns 200 shares of stock in company A, 150 in company B, and 60 in company C. The opening and closing prices for those stocks on a certain day are given in the following chart:

	Open	Close
A	76	78
B	29	25
C	18	18

Express, with an integer, the net change in the value of her holdings that day.

14. Simplify.
   (a) $^-5 + {}^+9 + {}^-7 + {}^-4$
   (b) $^+5 - {}^-7 - {}^+4$
   (c) $76 - 131$
   (d) $^-283 - 177$
   (e) $^-4 \cdot {}^-3 \cdot {}^-2$
   (f) $^-36 \div {}^-4$
   (g) $^-223 + 75 - {}^-82$
   (h) $(^-2)^5 \cdot {}^-9 \div {}^-6$
   (i) $3 - (^-|^-3|)$
   (j) The solution x to $39 - 2(3 - 2x) = 5$
   (k) $\dfrac{|^-19 - 4 \cdot {}^-2| + (^-2)^2}{1 - |^-4|}$

15. In the coordinate plane, graph the multiply-by-minus-two function, M_{-2}, with the input set being the set I of integers.

16. Supply a reason at each step in this proof that $^-a \cdot b = {}^-(a \cdot b)$:

$^-(a \cdot b) = 0 + {}^-(a \cdot b)$	?
$= 0 \cdot b + {}^-(a \cdot b)$	?
$= [^-a + a] \cdot b + {}^-(a \cdot b)$	?
$= [^-a \cdot b + a \cdot b] + {}^-(a \cdot b)$	?
$= {}^-a \cdot b + [a \cdot b + {}^-(a \cdot b)]$	?
$= {}^-a \cdot b + 0$	?
$= {}^-a \cdot b$	?

17. Supply one main reason at each step (a)–(f) in this proof that in the system of integers, $^-x + {}^-y = {}^-(x + y)$.

$^-x + {}^-y$

$= (^-x + {}^-y) + 0$	(a)
$= (^-x + {}^-y) + [(x + y) + {}^-(x + y)]$	(b)
$= [(^-x + {}^-y) + (x + y)] + {}^-(x + y)$	(c)
$= [(^-x + x) + (^-y + y)] + {}^-(x + y)$	generalized associative-commutative property of addition
$= [0 + 0] + {}^-(x + y)$	(d)
$= 0 + {}^-(x + y)$	(e)
$= {}^-(x + y)$	(f)

18. State carefully the one structural property that distinguishes the system of integers from the system of whole numbers.

19. Write an algebraic equation (all symbols, no words) that conveys this message: "To subtract two integers, change the sign of the subtrahend and add."

20. In your equation in Exercise 19, classify each use of the symbol − as "subtraction," "negative," or "opposite of."

21. Using addition of whole numbers as a subroutine, make a flowchart for adding two negative integers.

22. Here are three algorithms for integers.
    A: Addition of integers based on the subroutines of addition and subtraction of whole numbers
    S: Subtraction of integers based on the subroutine of addition of integers
    M: Multiplication of integers based on the subroutine of multiplication of whole numbers.
    (a) Which has the most complicated flowchart?
    (b) Which does not involve calculation of absolute values?
    (c) Which has a flowchart with no decision box?
    (d) Which requires one to compare two whole numbers for size?

23. Find all integer solutions.
    (a) $2x + 3 = 11$
    (b) $5 - 2x < x + 14$

(c) $(x + 4)(x - 1) = 0$
(d) $^-3(5 - 2x) = 6x - 7$

24. Refer to the number line shown in Figure 6.58, and classify each statement as true or false

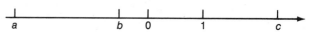

Figure 6.58

(a) $a < c$
(b) $a < a + b$
(c) $a \cdot c < b \cdot c$
(d) $b - a < 0$
(e) $-\frac{1}{2} \cdot a < c$
(f) $a/b < c$

25. Suppose that a and b are integers with $|a| < |b|$ and $a < 0 < b$. Classify each of the following integers as positive or negative.
    (a) $a + b$
    (b) $a - b$
    (c) $a \cdot b$
    (d) $a^2 \cdot b$
    (e) $a \cdot |b|$

★ 26. In seven-clock arithmetic, find the following.
    (a) The opposite (additive inverse) of 5
    (b) $^-(3 - ^-5)$

* 27. In seven-clock arithmetic, verify the following equation by simplifying both sides.
    $(4 - 6)^2 = 4^2 - 2(4 \cdot 6) + 6^2$

References

Gilbert, J. and L. Gilbert. *Elements of Modern Algebra*. Boston: Prindle, Weber, and Schmidt, 1984.

Kelly, J., and D. Richert. *Elementary Mathematics for Teachers*. San Francisco: Holden-Day, 1970.

National Council of Teachers of Mathematics. *30th Yearbook: More Topics in Mathematics for Elementary School Teachers*. Reston, Va.: NCTM, 1969.

Perl, T. *Math Equals*. Menlo Park, Calif.: Addison-Wesley, 1978.

Ward, M., and C. Hardgrove. *Modern Elementary Mathematics*. Reading, Mass.: Addison-Wesley, 1964.

CHAPTER

7

THE RATIONAL NUMBERS: FRACTIONS

We begin our study of the rational numbers, as we began our study of the integers, by looking at models or external referents. Models for fractions suggest the fundamental relation of equivalence of fractions—and hence the concept of rational number. The models also lead to definitions for the operations on rational numbers, to computational algorithms, to identification of general properties, and to real-world applications.

Because applying rational arithmetic to word problems is possibly the most difficult task in the elementary curriculum, we devote an unusual amount of time to that topic. Word problems are considered throughout the first three sections (those in which the concept of rational number and the operations on rationals are developed). Then two more sections are devoted exclusively to their solution. Section 7.4 uses fraction language and notation in developing a variety of approaches to word problems. Section 7.5 uses the language of ratio and proportion.

Our feelings about the importance of being able to attack a problem from several different directions are expressed colorfully in the 5–8 *Standards:* "Different representations of problems serve as different lenses through which students interpret the problems and solutions. If students are to become mathematically powerful, they must be flexible enough to approach situations in a variety of ways and recognize the relationships among different points of view."

In Section 7.6 we look at the skeletal structure of the rational number system in the cold, bright light of axiomatic, deductive mathematics. The simplicity of the system and its similarity to the system of integers stand out sharply. The abstract "field" structure is further illuminated by a brief, optional reexamination of seven-clock arithmetic. We agree wholeheartedly with this precept from the 5–8 *Standards:* "Students should understand how analogies among structures can give a clearer picture of mathematics."

The chapter concludes with an examination of the order relation on the rational numbers.

7.1 *Fractions and Rational Numbers*

A **common fraction** is ultimately an ordered pair of whole numbers whose second component is nonzero. For reasons that will be made clear shortly, the symbol $\frac{3}{4}$ is more appropriate than the conventional ordered-pair symbol (3, 4). When referring to the common fraction $\frac{3}{4}$, we call 3 the **numerator,** rather than the first component, and 4 the **denominator,** rather than the second component. Unless we indicate otherwise, the word *fraction* will be used to mean "common fraction."

Our first task in this section is to see what sort of meanings are ordinarily associated with fractions. The following examples illustrate that whereas whole numbers arise when we want to describe the size (numerosity, or cardinality) of a *single* set, fractions arise when we want to compare *two* sets for size. In fact, if you think about how fractions are used in everyday conversation, they are always used to make such comparisons.

EXAMPLE 1   "The class is two-thirds girls." A set of students is being compared for size (numerosity) with a subset of girls. A helpful schematic representation of this size comparison is shown in Figure 7.1.

From this representation a variety of questions can be answered by using only simple, whole number computational skills:

1. If there are 14 girls in the class, how many boys are there?

2. If there are 8 more girls than boys, how many students are in the class? ❏

EXAMPLE 2   "Tom will be home in three-fourths of an hour." The time interval between now and when Tom gets home is being compared for size (duration) with a standard time interval known as an hour. Again, a simple schematic like the one in Figure 7.2 is helpful for solving problems of the following kind:

1. If Tom is cycling at the rate of 8 mph, how far is he from home?

2. If Tom is 12 mi from home, how fast will he have to cycle?   ❏

EXAMPLE 3   "George planted five-eighths of an acre in tomatoes." A portion of land is being compared for size (area) with a standard portion known as an acre. This time a schematic of the kind shown in Figure 7.3 is useful for answering such questions as these:

1. If an acre of tomatoes brings in a profit of $400, how much can George expect to clear?

2. This year George spent 80 hr tending his tomatoes. Next year he plans to grow only a quarter of an acre of tomatoes. How much time should that require?   ❏

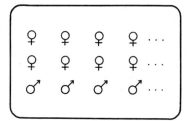

Figure 7.1 The class is two-thirds girls.

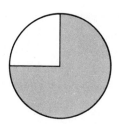

Figure 7.2 Three-fourths of an hour.

Figure 7.3 Five-eighths of an acre.

For your information, the answers to the preceding six questions are 7 boys, 24 students, 6 mi, 16 mph, $250, and 32 hr. The point of the examples is that the key to solving simple fraction problems is to be able to look at a fraction and see a clear picture of the size comparison it conveys.

The schematics we drew may actually have been too realistic. To emphasize their essential similarity, we could have represented all three situations using a square for the unit (the class, the hour, the acre). See Figure 7.4. We refer to such a uniform representation for fractions as an **area model.**

Figure 7.4 $\frac{2}{3}$ of the class $\frac{3}{4}$ of an hour $\frac{5}{8}$ of an acre

Area Models

Area models for fractions can be based on a variety of figures—squares, circles, rectangles, triangles—but no matter what figure is chosen, the basic principles are the same. A *unit* figure is chosen once and for all, and then all other regions are compared to it. To represent a fraction such as $\frac{2}{3}$, we partition the unit into 3 same-size pieces and then we unite 2 of them. That is, the denominator of the fraction describes the partition of the unit region, and the numerator counts how many pieces of the partition are to be united. Figure 7.5 gives examples based on a unit circle; Figure 7.6 shows examples for a unit square.

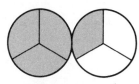

Figure 7.5   Unit circle   Representation of $\frac{2}{3}$ Representation of $\frac{4}{3}$

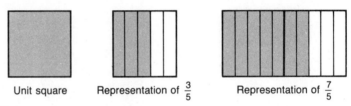

Unit square   Representation of $\frac{3}{5}$ Representation of $\frac{7}{5}$

Figure 7.6

EXAMPLE 4   What is wrong with each representation?
(a)

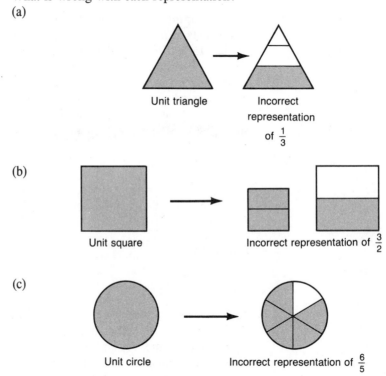

Unit triangle   Incorrect
                                representation
                                  of $\frac{1}{3}$

(b)

Unit square   Incorrect representation of $\frac{3}{2}$

(c)

Unit circle   Incorrect representation of $\frac{6}{5}$

Solution   (a) The unit triangle is not partitioned into three *same-size* pieces.
(b) The size of the unit square varies; the three pieces are not all of the same size.
(c) The roles of denominator and numerator are confused.   ❏

   We shall usually use a square as unit. Our area model could be extended easily to represent negative fractions, too, by simply mimicking the pattern of the poker-chip model for integers: Let a red square represent ⁻1 and then represent ⁻($\frac{2}{3}$) by the obvious subregion of the red unit. We shall have little need, however, to discuss negative numbers in this chapter until Section 7.6.

Equivalent Fractions

Different fractions (ordered pairs) can be represented by the same region in our area model, as illustrated in Figure 7.7. Such fractions are said to be **equivalent.** Arithmetically, we can produce an infinite collection of fractions equivalent to a given fraction by simply multiplying both numerator and denominator by the same (arbitrary) natural number:

$$\frac{2}{3} \qquad \frac{2 \cdot 2}{3 \cdot 2} \qquad \frac{2 \cdot 3}{3 \cdot 3} \qquad \frac{2 \cdot 4}{3 \cdot 4} \qquad \dots$$

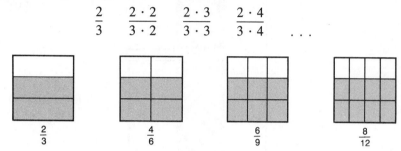

Figure 7.7 Equivalent fractions.

Later in this section we will formulate a precise algebraic definition of equivalence.

Figure 7.8 shows how a fourth-grade textbook uses a paper-folding activity to introduce the idea of equivalence of fractions to children.

The relation of equivalence among fractions is important because in most situations equivalent fractions can be used interchangeably ($\frac{2}{3}$ of a ton of sand is precisely the same amount of sand as $\frac{4}{6}$ of a ton), although on a few occasions misleading connotations can result when such a substitution is made. (Replace $\frac{4}{5}$ by $\frac{8}{10}$ in the statement "$\frac{4}{5}$ of the Great Lakes touch Michigan" and consider the nuances.) When we study addition and subtraction in the next section, we will see how important it is to be able to replace a fraction by an equivalent fraction.

The essential sameness and interchangeability of the fractions

$$\frac{2}{3} \qquad \frac{4}{6} \qquad \frac{6}{9} \qquad \frac{8}{12} \qquad \dots$$

suggests that underlying all of them is a single "abstract magnitude" called a **rational number.** The description of a rational number as the single abstract magnitude represented by all of the diagrams in Figure 7.7 is a bit vague, but no more so than the description of a whole number. After all, what is the whole number 3 except the single abstract magnitude represented by the different sets of peanuts, marbles, golf tees, and jacks shown in Figure 7.9?

The idea of rational number will come into sharper focus as we study first a geometric representation by points on a number line and then an arithmetic representation by lowest-terms fractions. Bear in mind in what follows that throughout this section *rational number* means *nonnegative* rational number.

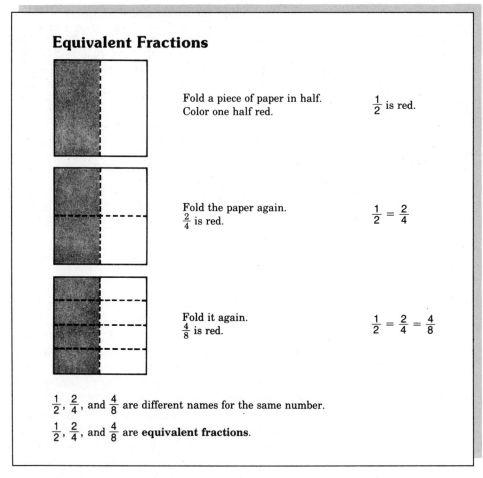

Figure 7.8 Equivalent fractions in a fourth-grade textbook.

Figure 7.9

Number Line Models

One way of thinking about a number line model for fractions is as a one-dimensional analog of an area model, that is, as a length model. Choose the vector from 0 to 1 on the whole number line as unit, and represent a fraction such as $\frac{2}{3}$ as before: Partition the unit vector into 3 same-size (and similarly di-

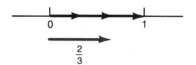

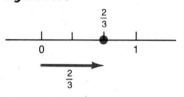

Figure 7.10

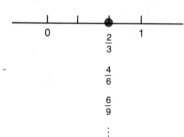

Figure 7.11 Representation of $\frac{2}{3}$ as a point and as a vector on the number line.

Figure 7.12

rected) subvectors, and join 2 of them end to end. The fraction $\frac{2}{3}$ is represented by the resulting vector, as shown in Figure 7.10. Notice again how easy it would be to represent $^-(\frac{2}{3})$ in this model by a left-pointing vector.

As you recall, each whole number (in fact, each integer) has a *dual* interpretation on the number line. It can be thought of either as a vector or as a point, namely, the point where the vector terminates if its tail is at the origin. This same dual interpretation applies to fractions. See Figure 7.11.

A concrete geometric representation of the abstract rational numbers is provided by this point representation of fractions. Here we have one specific geometric object associated with the entire *equivalence class* of fractions $\{\frac{2}{3}, \frac{4}{6}, \frac{6}{9}, \frac{8}{12}, \ldots\}$, namely, the single point that represents them all. See Figure 7.12.

Thus *there is a one-to-one correspondence between the set of all rational numbers and a set of points on a line.* We will see in Chapter 8 that this set of points does not fill up the line; there are points of the line that correspond to "irrational" numbers.

The number line, point representation of the rational numbers leads to several other observations. First, the symbols $\frac{2}{3}$, $\frac{4}{6}$, $\frac{6}{9}$, . . . can be thought of not only as labels for an infinite set of fractions but also as labels for a single rational number. From the latter point of view it is consistent with our agreement on the use of the equal sign, to write

$$\frac{2}{3} = \frac{4}{6} = \frac{6}{9} = \cdots$$

Thus the use of the fraction symbols involves some ambiguity. You must decide from the context whether the symbols $\frac{2}{3}$ and $\frac{4}{6}$ represent fractions (ordered pairs), in which case $\frac{2}{3} \neq \frac{4}{6}$ (two ordered pairs are equal if and only if their first components are equal and their second components are equal), or whether they represent rational numbers, in which case $\frac{2}{3} = \frac{4}{6}$.

As fractions, $\frac{2}{3}$ and $\frac{4}{6}$ are *equivalent*. As rational numbers, $\frac{2}{3}$ and $\frac{4}{6}$ are *equal*.

Second, since $\frac{6}{2}$ and 3 are represented by the same point on the number line, as shown in Figure 7.13, the whole number 3 is also a rational number. More generally, the whole number n and the rational number $n/1$ correspond to the same point on the number line. That is:

Figure 7.13

The whole numbers are a subset of the rational numbers.

Note, in particular, the various ways of expressing the two key whole numbers, 0 and 1:

$$0 = \frac{0}{1} = \frac{0}{2} = \frac{0}{3} = \cdots$$

$$1 = \frac{1}{1} = \frac{2}{2} = \frac{3}{3} = \cdots$$

Third, the symbol $\frac{6}{2}$ had a meaning different from either fraction or rational number. Recall that we used this symbol in Chapter 3 to represent the quotient in an exact-division problem, namely, the missing factor (3) in the equation $2 \cdot \square = 6$. We can see now that the present usage is consistent with the earlier one. There was a good reason for writing the fraction six-halves as $\frac{6}{2}$ rather than as (6, 2). In general:

If a and b are whole numbers and b divides a exactly ($b \mid a$), then the rational number a/b is the whole number quotient obtained by dividing a by b.

Lowest-Terms Fractions

A reasonably concrete *arithmetic* representation of the abstract rational numbers is based on the concept of lowest-terms fractions and an algebraic definition of equivalence.

Definition. A fraction is in **lowest terms** if the greatest common factor of numerator and denominator is 1.

EXAMPLE 5   Which of the following are in lowest terms?
(a) $\frac{10}{21}$

(b) $\frac{15}{24}$

(c) $\frac{220}{1617}$

Solution   We will use the methods that we developed in the number theory chapter.
(a) If we factor both numerator and denominator into primes, we see that their GCF is 1:

$$\frac{10}{21} = \frac{2 \cdot 5}{3 \cdot 7} \quad \text{No common factor greater than 1}$$

Thus the fraction $\frac{10}{21}$ is in lowest terms.
(b) Since

$$\frac{15}{24} = \frac{3 \cdot 5}{2 \cdot 2 \cdot 2 \cdot 3}$$

the GCF is 3 and the fraction $\frac{15}{24}$ is *not* in lowest terms.

(c) This time, factoring into primes is tiresome:

$$\frac{220}{1617} = \frac{2^2 \cdot 5 \cdot 11}{3 \cdot 7^2 \cdot 11} \qquad \text{GCF is 11}$$

It would have been quicker to apply the mental test for divisibility by 11 to both numerator and denominator. Either way, the fraction $\frac{220}{1617}$ is *not* in lowest terms. ❏

Note: The property of being or not being in lowest terms is a property of fractions, not of rational numbers, since the same rational number is named by both the fraction $\frac{2}{3}$, which is in lowest terms, and the fraction $\frac{4}{6}$, which is not.

The algebraic definition of equivalence of fractions is motivated by both geometric and formal consideration. The geometric diagrams in Figure 7.14 convince us that any fraction of the form $(2 \cdot n)/(3 \cdot n)$ should qualify as being equivalent to $\frac{2}{3}$. For example,

$$\frac{70}{105} = \frac{2 \cdot 35}{3 \cdot 35} \qquad \text{and} \qquad \frac{100}{150} = \frac{2 \cdot 50}{3 \cdot 50}$$

should both be equivalent to $\frac{2}{3}$. But if they are equivalent to $\frac{2}{3}$, and if equivalence of fractions is to be a symmetric and transitive relation (a formal consideration), then they must be equivalent to each other. Close examination of the fractions

$$\frac{2 \cdot 35}{3 \cdot 35} \qquad \text{and} \qquad \frac{2 \cdot 50}{3 \cdot 50}$$

reveals an algebraic pattern that generalizes to the definition we seek: The numerator of the first $(2 \cdot 35)$ times the denominator of the second $(3 \cdot 50)$ is equal to the denominator of the first $(3 \cdot 35)$ times the numerator of the second $(2 \cdot 50)$.

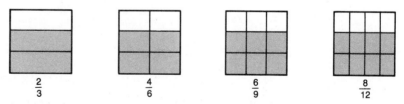

$$\frac{2}{3} \qquad\qquad \frac{4}{6} \qquad\qquad \frac{6}{9} \qquad\qquad \frac{8}{12}$$

Figure 7.14

Definition. Fraction a/b is **equivalent** to fraction c/d if and only if $a \cdot d = b \cdot c$. In terms of rational numbers, rational number a/b is *equal* to rational number c/d if and only if $a \cdot d = b \cdot c$.

Symbolically:

$$\frac{a}{b} = \frac{c}{d} \iff a \cdot d = b \cdot c$$

This definition is sometimes referred to as the **crisscross equality criterion** because of the schematic arrangement of the products that must be equal:

$$\frac{a}{b} \bowtie \frac{c}{d}$$

EXAMPLE 6   Does $\frac{12}{30} = \frac{26}{65}$?

Solution   Yes, it does, since $12 \cdot 65 = 780 = 30 \cdot 26$.   ❏

An immediate consequence of this definition is the familiar rule (theorem) for reducing to lower terms or raising to higher terms:

For every nonzero whole number n,

fraction $\dfrac{n \cdot a}{n \cdot b}$ is equivalent to fraction $\dfrac{a}{b}$.

In terms of rational numbers, we get this **rule for reducing** (read the equation from left to right) **and raising** (read the equation from right to left):

$$\frac{n \cdot a}{n \cdot b} = \frac{a}{b} \qquad (n \neq 0, b \neq 0)$$

A quick and easy proof is based on the crisscross equality criterion: $na/nb = a/b$ because $(na)b = (nb)a$, by the associative and commutative properties of whole number multiplication.

EXAMPLE 7   Reduce each fraction to lowest terms. That is, find a lowest-terms fraction that labels the same rational number.

(a) $\dfrac{84}{180}$

(b) $\dfrac{2^3 \cdot 3 \cdot 7^2 \cdot 13}{2^2 \cdot 3 \cdot 5 \cdot 7 \cdot 11^2}$

Solution   (a) Factor common primes from numerator and denominator, and use the rule for reducing:

$$\frac{84}{180} = \frac{\not{2} \cdot 42}{\not{2} \cdot 90} = \frac{\not{2} \cdot 21}{\not{2} \cdot 45} = \frac{\not{3} \cdot 7}{\not{3} \cdot 15} = \frac{7}{15}$$

(b) $\dfrac{2^3 \cdot 3 \cdot 7^2 \cdot 13}{2^2 \cdot 3 \cdot 5 \cdot 7 \cdot 11^2} = \dfrac{\not{2} \cdot \not{2} \cdot 2 \cdot \not{3} \cdot \not{7} \cdot 7 \cdot 13}{\not{2} \cdot \not{2} \cdot \not{3} \cdot 5 \cdot \not{7} \cdot 11 \cdot 11} = \dfrac{2 \cdot 7 \cdot 13}{5 \cdot 11^2}$ ❏

From the fundamental theorem of arithmetic every fraction is equivalent to exactly one fraction in lowest terms. Thus *the set of (abstract) rational num-*

bers is in one-to-one correspondence with the set of (reasonably concrete) lowest-terms fractions.

EXAMPLE 8 Again, does $\frac{12}{30} = \frac{26}{65}$?

Solution Yes, it does, since both $\frac{12}{30}$ and $\frac{26}{65}$ reduce to the same lowest-terms fraction, $\frac{2}{5}$. ❏

A skill that will important when we add, subtract, and compare rational numbers is raising two fractions to higher terms so that a common denominator results.

EXAMPLE 9 Raise both $\frac{5}{12}$ and $\frac{13}{30}$ to higher terms so that the resulting fractions have a common denominator.

Solution One can *always* use the product of the two original denominators as a common denominator. By the rule for raising,

$$\frac{5}{12} = \frac{5 \cdot 30}{12 \cdot 30} = \frac{150}{360} \quad \text{and} \quad \frac{13}{30} = \frac{12 \cdot 13}{12 \cdot 30} = \frac{156}{360}$$

Thus a pair of fractions having a common denominator and equivalent to the original pair is $\frac{150}{360}$ and $\frac{156}{360}$.

This answer is not unique; infinitely many other pairs also satisfy the requirements of the example. Here, for instance, are two:

$$\frac{1500}{3600} \quad \text{and} \quad \frac{1560}{3600} \qquad \frac{75}{180} \quad \text{and} \quad \frac{78}{180} \qquad ❏$$

For some purposes it is desirable to find a pair of fractions (equivalent to the original pair) having the *least* common denominator.

> The **least common denominator** of two fractions is the least common multiple of their denominators.

For the fractions $\frac{5}{12}$ and $\frac{13}{30}$ the least common denominator is

$$\text{LCM}(12, 30) = \text{LCM}(2^2 \cdot 3, 2 \cdot 3 \cdot 5) = 2^2 \cdot 3 \cdot 5 = 60$$

By the rule for raising

$$\frac{5}{12} = \frac{5 \cdot 5}{12 \cdot 5} = \frac{25}{60} \quad \text{and} \quad \frac{13}{30} = \frac{13 \cdot 2}{30 \cdot 2} = \frac{26}{60}$$

Thus the pair of fractions equivalent to $\frac{5}{12}$ and $\frac{13}{30}$ and having the least common denominator is $\frac{25}{60}$ and $\frac{26}{60}$.

We have seen that the (nonnegative) rational numbers are in one-to-one correspondence with a set of points on a line and with a set of lowest-terms fractions. We have also described them as "abstract magnitudes," which you might like to think of now as lengths of vectors on the number line. But we have not formally defined them. A formal definition that is common in college abstract algebra courses is this: A rational number is an equivalence class of ordered pairs of whole numbers (with second component nonzero), where the equivalence relation is the one (crisscross) that we defined on page 342. That is, in fraction rather than ordered-pair notation, the entire set of fractions

$$\left\{\tfrac{2}{3}, \tfrac{4}{6}, \tfrac{6}{9}, \tfrac{8}{12}, \ldots\right\}$$

is one rational number, and the entire set of fractions

$$\left\{\tfrac{1}{2}, \tfrac{2}{4}, \tfrac{3}{6}, \tfrac{4}{8}, \ldots\right\}$$

is another. It is not clear at what age a person becomes capable of conceiving of sets like these as entities.

EXERCISE SET 7.1

1. What fraction is represented by each shaded region? In each case the unit is the square.

(a)

(b)

(c)

(d)

(e)

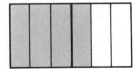

(f)

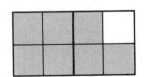

(g)

(h)

2. What fraction is represented by each shaded region? In each case the unit is the circle.

(a)

(b)

(c)

(d)

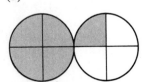

3. If the large triangle is the unit, what fraction does the shaded region represent?
   (a)   (b)

4. In Figure 7.15, what fraction does the shaded region represent for the following choices of the unit?
   (a) The unit is the square.
   (b) The unit is the large rectangle.

Figure 7.15

5. Using a square as unit, represent each of the following fractions in the area model.
   (a) $\frac{3}{4}$ (b) $\frac{3}{8}$
   (c) $\frac{4}{3}$ (d) $\frac{6}{3}$
   (e) $\frac{5}{2}$ (f) $\frac{0}{2}$

6. Repeat Exercise 5, using a circle as unit.

7. In each of the following sentences, a fraction is used to make a size comparison. Draw a unit square and state what real quantity it represents. Then shade a region for the fraction, and state what real quantity the shaded region represents.
   (a) $\frac{3}{5}$ of her salary is take-home pay.
   (b) The recipe calls for $\frac{5}{4}$ cups of sugar.
   (c) There are $\frac{5}{6}$ as many cats as dogs.
   (d) A Celsius degree is $\frac{9}{5}$ of a Fahrenheit degree.

8. We said that a fraction like $\frac{3}{4}$ can be thought of as follows: Partition a unit into 4 same-size pieces and unite 3 of them. But we never tried to define *same-size*. What is the unit, and what does *same-size* mean in each of the following contexts?
   (a) $\frac{3}{4}$ of a mile
   (b) $\frac{3}{4}$ of an acre

(c) $\frac{3}{4}$ of a gallon
(d) $\frac{3}{4}$ of an hour
(e) $\frac{3}{4}$ of a ton
(f) $\frac{3}{4}$ of the sixth-grade class
(g) $\frac{3}{4}$ of Uncle Waldo's estate

In Exercises 9–16, solve the word problems by using an area-model representation and whole number skills.

9. In a can of mixed nuts $\frac{3}{4}$ of the nuts are peanuts. There are 280 nuts in the can. How many are peanuts?

10. There are 240 people at a play. The audience is $\frac{5}{6}$ children. How many adults are present?

11. The 28 sixth graders make up $\frac{1}{7}$ of the student population at the elementary school. What is the total student population?

12. There are 180 pets at a pet show, $\frac{2}{9}$ of which are dogs. There are three times as many cats as dogs. How many pets are neither cats nor dogs?

13. The class is $\frac{2}{3}$ girls, and there are 12 boys in the class. What is the total enrollment?

14. An ore sample is $\frac{2}{9}$ iron, and the rest waste. How much waste must be removed from this ore to produce 100 kg of iron?

15. A box of firecrackers is $\frac{1}{8}$ duds. There are 120 more good firecrackers than duds. How many duds are in the box?

16. The school chorus is $\frac{5}{8}$ girls. Twelve more boys must be added to equalize the sexes. How many students are presently in the chorus?

17. In Donna's library, $\frac{5}{8}$ of the books are fiction and $\frac{1}{3}$ of the nonfiction books are biographies. If there are 180 more fiction books than biographies, how many biographies are there?

18. The Democratic candidate got $\frac{7}{12}$ of the votes and the Republican got the rest. If the Republican lost by 650 votes, how many votes did the Democrat get?

19. By selectively ignoring certain lines in Figure 7.16, you should be able to see four equivalent

fractions represented by the shaded portion of the (large) unit square. What are they?

Figure 7.16

20. By selectively ignoring certain lines in Figure 7.17, you should be able to see several equivalent fractions represented by the shaded portion of the (large) unit hexagon. What are they?

Figure 7.17

21. Draw area model diagrams to show the following geometrically.
    (a) $\frac{3}{5}$ is equivalent to $\frac{6}{10}$.
    (b) $\frac{1}{4}$ is equivalent to $\frac{3}{12}$.

22. A young girl wants to jump rope. Her father finds 16 ft of clothesline in the garage, and he asks her if she wants half of it or two-fourths. How do you suppose she would answer? Why?

23. Sketch a number line, and on it plot and label points corresponding to each fraction.
    (a) $\frac{3}{4}$ (b) $\frac{5}{4}$
    (c) $\frac{8}{4}$ (d) $\frac{1}{8}$
    (e) $\frac{6}{8}$ (f) $\frac{0}{8}$

24. Sketch a number line, and on it draw and label vectors corresponding to each fraction.
    (a) $\frac{1}{2}$ (b) $\frac{3}{2}$
    (b) $\frac{9}{4}$ (d) $\frac{3}{3}$

25. Write five different fractions that correspond to point A in Figure 7.18.

Figure 7.18

26. Write five different fractions that correspond to vector V in Figure 7.19.

Figure 7.19

27. Write three fraction symbols for each whole number.
    (a) 4   (b) 17
    (c) 1   (d) 0

28. Write a standard Hindu-Arabic numeral for each of the following.
    (a) $\frac{28}{4}$ (b) $\frac{324}{27}$
    (c) $\frac{0}{4}$ (d) $\frac{12}{12}$

29. Reduce to lowest terms, first by hand, then using a Math Explorer calculator if you have access to one.
    (a) $\dfrac{12}{15}$ (b) $\dfrac{91}{21}$
    (c) $\dfrac{2 \cdot 3 \cdot 5^2 \cdot 7}{2 \cdot 5 \cdot 11}$ (d) $\dfrac{85}{5}$
    (e) $\dfrac{33}{100}$ (f) $\dfrac{625}{1000}$
    (g) $\dfrac{9 \cdot 28}{12}$ (h) $\dfrac{15 \cdot 12}{9 \cdot 70}$
    (i) $\dfrac{15}{4} \cdot \dfrac{12}{21} \cdot \dfrac{7}{10}$ (j) $\dfrac{5}{8} \cdot \dfrac{14}{3} \cdot \dfrac{36}{35}$
    (k) $\dfrac{1547}{2023}$ (l) $\dfrac{1987}{1988}$

30. Decide whether or not the fractions in each pair are equivalent.
    (a) $\frac{3}{8}$ and $\frac{11}{30}$
    (b) $\frac{12}{15}$ and $\frac{8}{10}$
    (c) $\dfrac{2^2 \cdot 3 \cdot 7^3}{5 \cdot 11}$ and $\dfrac{2^3 \cdot 3 \cdot 7^5}{2 \cdot 5 \cdot 7^2 \cdot 11}$
    (d) $\frac{246}{437}$ and $\frac{221}{391}$
    (e) $\frac{221}{299}$ and $\frac{323}{437}$
    (f) $\frac{145}{155}$ and $\frac{201}{217}$

31. Explain why no common fraction that is equivalent to $\frac{5}{12}$ can have an odd denominator.

32. Decide whether or not the rational numbers in each pair are equal.

    (a) $\dfrac{9}{14}$ and $\dfrac{7}{11}$

    (b) $\dfrac{a \cdot c}{b \cdot c}$ and $\dfrac{a}{b}$

    (c) $\dfrac{0}{2}$ and $\dfrac{0}{7}$

    (d) $\dfrac{n}{n + 1}$ and $\dfrac{n + 1}{n + 2}$

33. I am thinking of a common fraction. It is equivalent to $\frac{9}{15}$, and the sum of its numerator and denominator is 136. What is the fraction?

34. Raise both fractions to higher terms so that the resulting fractions have a common denominator.

    (a) $\dfrac{5}{6}$ and $\dfrac{3}{8}$

    (b) $\dfrac{5}{18}$ and $\dfrac{7}{30}$

    (c) $\dfrac{2 \cdot 5}{2^2 \cdot 3 \cdot 7^2}$ and $\dfrac{7 \cdot 11^2}{2^2 \cdot 5 \cdot 11}$

    (d) $\dfrac{20}{3 \cdot 11}$ and $\dfrac{28}{5 \cdot 7}$

35. First, reduce the fractions to lowest terms; then identify the least common denominator; and finally, raise them to higher terms so that each has that denominator.

    (a) $\dfrac{5}{8}$ and $\dfrac{3}{10}$

    (b) $\dfrac{3}{16}$ and $\dfrac{1}{20}$

    (c) $\dfrac{2 \cdot 3 \cdot 7}{3^2 \cdot 5}$ and $\dfrac{2 \cdot 7}{2^3 \cdot 3 \cdot 5^2}$

    (d) $\dfrac{52}{2^2 \cdot 5 \cdot 11}$ and $\dfrac{189}{2 \cdot 3^2 \cdot 7}$

36. Write three more fractions equivalent to the given fractions.

    (a) $\frac{1}{3}, \frac{2}{6}, \frac{3}{9}$ (b) $\frac{2}{5}, \frac{4}{10}$

    (c) $\frac{6}{10}, \frac{12}{20}$ (d) $\frac{8}{12}$

37. Can every fraction that is equivalent to $\frac{8}{12}$ be written in the form $(8 \cdot n)/(12 \cdot n)$ for some natural number n? Answer the question for $\frac{2}{3}$.

38. List the first eight fractions in the equivalence class of the following.

    (a) $\frac{3}{4}$ (b) $\frac{6}{9}$

39. If we consider the set of equivalent fractions
    $\{\frac{1}{2}, \frac{2}{4}, \frac{3}{6}, \frac{4}{8}, \ldots\}$
    to be a set of ordered pairs
    $\{(1, 2), (2, 4), (3, 6), (4, 8), \ldots\}$
    and if we graph these pairs in the coordinate plane, then they will lie on a ray from the origin, as shown in Figure 7.20.

    (a) Sketch, similarly, the points and ray for this set of equivalent fractions: $\{\frac{2}{3}, \frac{4}{6}, \frac{6}{9}, \frac{8}{12}, \ldots\}$.

    (b) Repeat for the equivalence class containing $\frac{2}{6}$.

    (c) Where does the lowest-terms fraction appear on each ray?

    (d) The ray from the origin through point (84, 70) passes through many lattice points (street corners) in the coordinate plane. Which one is nearest the origin?

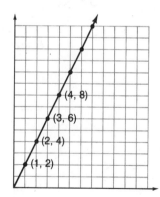

(4, 8)
(3, 6)
(2, 4)
(1, 2)

Figure 7.20

★ 40. Use the algebraic definition of equivalence of fractions,
$$\frac{a}{b} \sim \frac{c}{d} \iff ad = bc$$
to prove that this relation is reflexive, symmetric, and transitive.

7.2 *Addition and Subtraction*

Addition and subtraction have natural interpretations in both the area and number line models. As usual, both problem-solving methods and formal algebraic definitions of the operations are based on these interpretations.

Area Models

When rational numbers are represented in an area model, the addition operation is interpreted once again as union of (disjoint) sets.

EXAMPLE 1   At a picnic $\frac{3}{10}$ of the people are men and $\frac{4}{10}$ are women. What fraction of the picnickers are adults?

Solution   Let a unit square represent the total number of picnickers. Then schematically, we have the representation in Figure 7.21. By simply counting regions in the figure on the right, we conclude that its shaded portion represents $\frac{7}{10}$. *Answer:* $\frac{7}{10}$ of the picnickers are adults.

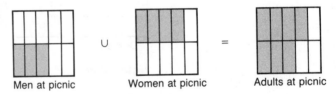

Men at picnic   Women at picnic   Adults at picnic

Figure 7.21   ❏

The preceding solution is the kind that might be presented to children. Adults would solve this problem in a purely symbolic fashion based on their understanding of the connection between union and addition and on their computational skills with fractions:

$$\frac{3}{10} + \frac{4}{10} = \frac{3 + 4}{10} = \frac{7}{10}$$

In an area model subtraction has the same meanings (take away, compare, missing addend) that it had in the set model for whole numbers.

EXAMPLE 2   A bowl of pineapple-grapefruit punch contains $\frac{14}{10}$ qt of fruit juice. If it contains $\frac{5}{10}$ qt of pineapple juice, how much grapefruit juice does it contain?

Solution   Let a unit square represent a quart, as in Figure 7.22. Then the total amount of fruit juice is represented by the rectangle in Figure 7.23, which can in turn be viewed as the union of regions representing the $\frac{5}{10}$ qt of pineapple juice and the

Figure 7.22

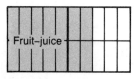

Figure 7.23

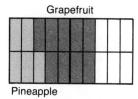

Figure 7.24

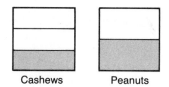

Figure 7.25

unknown amount of grapefruit juice. See Figure 7.24. By counting subrectangles, we see that the amount of grapefruit juice is $\frac{9}{10}$ qt. Symbolically,

$$\frac{14}{10} - \frac{5}{10} = \frac{14 - 5}{10} = \frac{9}{10}$$ ❏

Consider now the following question: How many pounds of mixed nuts result when you combine $\frac{1}{3}$ lb of cashews with $\frac{1}{2}$ lb of peanuts? If we let our unit square represent a pound, then we are led to the natural representations in Figure 7.25 and a temporary impasse. We can count the shaded regions all right (2), but they are not of the same size. The quantity of mixed nuts is neither $\frac{2}{3}$ nor $\frac{2}{2}$.

A geometric way of extricating ourselves from the impasse is as follows: Represent the cashews as in Figure 7.25 by partitioning the unit square with horizontal lines, but represent the peanuts by partitioning the unit square vertically, as in Figure 7.26. Next, superimpose the horizontal lines onto the peanut representation and the vertical lines onto the cashew representation, as in Figure 7.27.

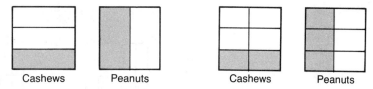

Figure 7.26   **Figure 7.27**

Now all of the little subrectangles have the same size. The unit square is partitioned into 6 of them, 5 of which are shaded. The quantity of mixed nuts is $\frac{5}{6}$ lb. Symbolically,

$$\frac{1}{3} + \frac{1}{2} = \frac{2}{6} + \frac{3}{6} = \frac{2 + 3}{6} = \frac{5}{6}$$

Arithmetically, our superposition of partition lines amounted to replacing the given fractions by fractions having a common denominator.

EXAMPLE 3   Illustrate the calculation of the following sum and difference by using an area model.
(a) $\frac{2}{3} + \frac{3}{5}$
(b) $\frac{4}{5} - \frac{3}{4}$

Solution   (a) See Figure 7.28.
(b) See Figure 7.29. Or if you prefer, subtraction can be thought of as it was for integers. Replace "take away" by "union" in Figure 7.29, and represent $\frac{3}{4}$ (and then $\frac{15}{20}$) by a red (antimatter) region.   ❏

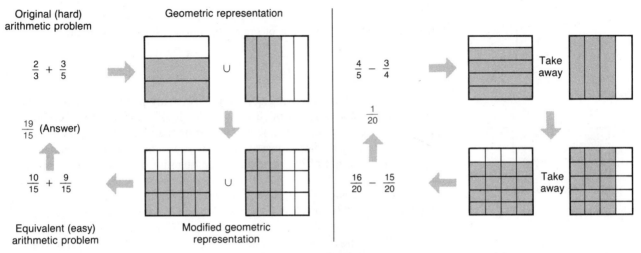

Figure 7.28   **Figure 7.29**

Number Line Models

The operations of addition and subtraction of rational numbers are represented on the number line in the same ways that addition and subtraction of whole numbers were.

EXAMPLE 4   Illustrate the calculation of the following sum and difference by using a number line model.
(a) $\frac{4}{5} + \frac{2}{5}$ (b) $\frac{7}{8} - \frac{5}{8}$

Solution   (a) If we think solely in terms of vectors (operators), we get the representation in Figure 7.30. If we think in terms of points and vectors (states and operators), we get the representation in Figure 7.31.

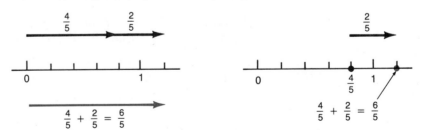

Figure 7.30   **Figure 7.31**

(b) We can think of $\frac{7}{8} - \frac{5}{8}$ as the missing addend in the equation $\frac{5}{8} + \square = \frac{7}{8}$. Then we can draw the vector-vector-vector diagram in Figure 7.32. Or we can draw the point-vector-point diagram in Figure 7.33.   ❏

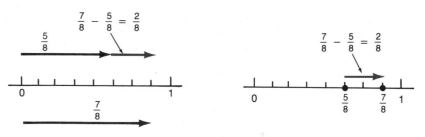

Figure 7.32   **Figure 7.33**

Definitions

The models we have just considered leave no doubt about how addition and subtraction of rational numbers should be defined. There is one question that merits discussion, though, before we state the definitions. Why do we define addition and subtraction of *rational* numbers rather than of fractions?

The difficulty with fractions is as follows: Suppose you and I are asked to find the sum of the fractions $\frac{3}{4}$ and $\frac{1}{6}$. Let's say that I proceed methodically, superimposing vertical and horizontal partition lines onto a unit square and counting shaded regions, as in Figure 7.34. And let's say that you also think about the area model, but you partition the unit more creatively so that you get larger same-size pieces and hence a fraction with a smaller denominator, as in Figure 7.35.

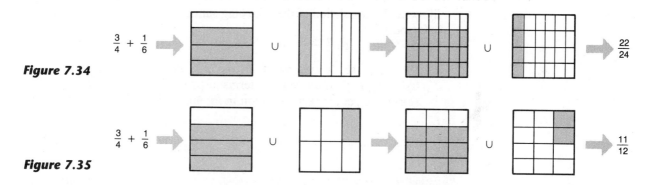

Figure 7.34

Figure 7.35

We both started out with the same pair of fractions, $\frac{3}{4}$ and $\frac{1}{6}$, and we both were guided by the area model; but we ended up with different fractions, $\frac{22}{24}$ and $\frac{11}{12}$, as the sum. To be sure, $\frac{22}{24}$ and $\frac{11}{12}$ are *equivalent* fractions, but they are not the *same* fraction. (One has an even numerator and the other has an odd one.) If you are as stubborn as I am, then we will both demand that, however addition is defined, both $\frac{11}{12}$ and $\frac{22}{24}$ must be correct values for the sum of $\frac{3}{4}$ and $\frac{1}{6}$. The problem is to reconcile the disparity of our sums with the requirement that a binary operation yield unique outputs. The resolution lies in viewing all inputs and outputs as rational numbers. From that point of view, sums are always unique. (See Exercise 28.)

The definition of addition of rational numbers that is suggested by our models is an algorithmic one. A flowchart is given in Figure 7.36. The "yes" path through this chart is usually summarized in a simple algebraic definition:

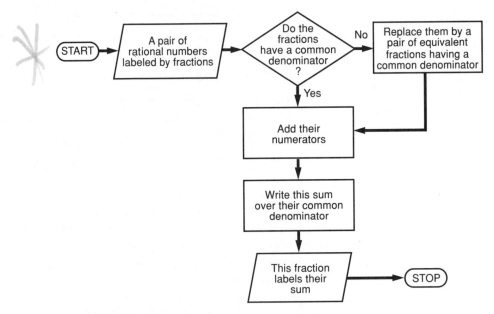

Figure 7.36 Algorithmic definition of addition of rational numbers.

Definition of Addition (+) of Rational Numbers

If a/c and b/c are rational numbers, then

$$\frac{a}{c} + \frac{b}{c} = \frac{a+b}{c}$$

Note that the plus sign on the right represents the operation of whole number addition, while the plus sign on the left denotes the operation that we are defining, addition of rational numbers.

The "no" path can also be summarized algebraically if we first recall that a pair of common-denominator fractions equivalent to a/b and c/d is ad/bd and bc/bd.

If a/b and c/d are rational numbers, then

$$\frac{a}{b} + \frac{c}{d} = \frac{ad + bc}{bd}$$

The situation for subtraction is nearly the same as for addition, with one exception. We have restricted our attention to nonnegative rational numbers. Until we lift the restriction and consider the full set of rational numbers, including negatives, certain ordered pairs such as $\left(\frac{3}{10}, \frac{7}{10}\right)$ cannot be subtracted. Again, the area and number line models suggest an algorithmic definition. A flowchart for it is asked for in Exercise 11. The algebraic formulation for the case of common denominators follows.

Definition of Subtraction ($-$) of Rational Numbers

If a/c and b/c are rational numbers, with $a \geq b$, then

$$\frac{a}{c} - \frac{b}{c} = \frac{a - b}{c}$$

For the general (arbitrary denominators) case the definition of subtraction is the following:

If a/b and c/d are rational numbers, with $ad \geq bc$, then

$$\frac{a}{b} - \frac{c}{d} = \frac{ad - bc}{bd}$$

Note that subtraction continues to supply a missing addend (when one exists). For example, $\frac{7}{10} - \frac{3}{10}$ is the missing addend in the equation $\frac{3}{10} + \square = \frac{7}{10}$, because

$$\frac{3}{10} + \left(\frac{7}{10} - \frac{3}{10}\right) = \frac{3}{10} + \left(\frac{7 - 3}{10}\right) \qquad \text{definition of subtraction}$$

$$= \frac{3 + (7 - 3)}{10} \qquad \text{definition of addition}$$

$$= \frac{7}{10} \qquad \text{whole number arithmetic}$$

The general argument is similar and is considered in the exercises.

Algorithms

In adding and subtracting rational numbers represented by fractions, one has a choice of following a flowchart or using one of the algebraic rules.

EXAMPLE 5   Calculate these sums and differences.

(a) $\frac{2}{7} + \frac{3}{7}$ (b) $\frac{7}{36} + \frac{5}{24}$ (c) $\frac{1789}{1755} - \frac{1492}{1755}$

Solution   (a) By following the flowchart or by using the algebraic rule for the common-denominator case, we get

$$\frac{2}{7} + \frac{3}{7} = \frac{2 + 3}{7} = \frac{5}{7}$$

If we ignore the flowchart and use the algebraic rule for the *general* case,

$$\frac{a}{b} + \frac{c}{d} = \frac{ad + bc}{bd}$$

no real harm is done. We just have to work a little harder:

$$\frac{2}{7} + \frac{3}{7} = \frac{2 \cdot 7 + 7 \cdot 3}{7 \cdot 7} = \frac{14 + 21}{49} = \frac{35}{49}$$

Notice that this answer reduces to the first one:

$$\frac{35}{49} = \frac{5 \cdot \cancel{7}}{7 \cdot \cancel{7}} = \frac{5}{7}$$

(b) Again, the general algebraic rule can be used:

$$\frac{7}{36} + \frac{5}{24} = \frac{7 \cdot 24 + 36 \cdot 5}{36 \cdot 24} = \frac{168 + 180}{864} = \frac{348}{864}$$

But unless one is using a calculator, it is more convenient to follow the flowchart and find a smaller common denominator than $36 \cdot 24$. In this case the least common denominator is 72:

$$\frac{7}{36} + \frac{5}{24} = \frac{7 \cdot 2}{36 \cdot 2} + \frac{5 \cdot 3}{24 \cdot 3} = \frac{14}{72} + \frac{15}{72} = \frac{29}{72}$$

(c) The common-denominator rule applies:

$$\frac{1789}{1755} - \frac{1492}{1755} = \frac{1789 - 1492}{1755} = \frac{297}{1755}$$

While it is difficult to visualize the fraction $\frac{297}{1755}$ in an area or number line model, its size can be estimated by doing some rounding:

$$\frac{297}{1755} \approx \frac{300}{1800} = \frac{1}{6}$$

The general rule would entail more difficult computations.   ❏

Mixed Numerals

A common fraction, you recall, is one whose numerator and denominator are whole numbers (and the denominator is nonzero). If the numerator is less than the denominator ($\frac{3}{4}$), then the fraction is said to be **proper.** If the numerator is greater than or equal to the denominator ($\frac{5}{3}$), then the fraction is called **improper.** Clearly, then, any (nonnegative) rational number is named by either a proper or an improper fraction. On the number line rationals left of 1 have proper-fraction labels; those at or to the right of 1 have improper-fraction labels. See Figure 7.37. In particular, all of the nonzero whole numbers are found among the rationals with improper-fraction labels.

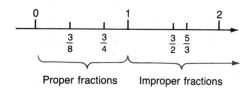

Figure 7.37

Mixed-numeral notation is based on the fact that every (nonnegative) rational number is expressible as the sum of a whole number and a rational less than 1. This fact can be seen geometrically, as in Figure 7.38; every rational

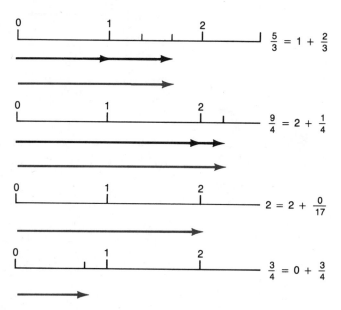

Figure 7.38

that is not a whole number lies between two whole numbers. **Mixed-numeral notation** displays the *whole number part* and the *proper-fraction part* of a rational number but omits the plus sign:

$$1\tfrac{2}{3} \text{ means } 1 + \tfrac{2}{3}. \qquad 2\tfrac{1}{4} \text{ means } 2 + \tfrac{1}{4}.$$

It is less common, but not incorrect, to write

$$2\tfrac{0}{17} \quad \text{for} \quad 2 \qquad 0\tfrac{3}{4} \quad \text{for} \quad \tfrac{3}{4}$$

Mixed-numeral notation is particularly helpful for displaying the approximate size of a rational number. While it may be difficult to glance at $\frac{228}{13}$ and get a feeling for its magnitude, the mixed numeral $17\frac{7}{13}$ for the same number shows its magnitude clearly. Being able to convert back and forth between common-fraction and mixed-numeral notation is a useful skill.

EXAMPLE 6   Convert $\frac{35}{8}$ to a mixed numeral.

Solution   To count off 35 eighths on the number line is impractical. Instead, proceed algebraically and divide 35 by 8 as whole numbers to find quotient 4 and remainder 3. From the relationship

$$\text{Dividend} = \text{quotient} \cdot \text{divisor} + \text{remainder}$$

conclude that

$$35 = 4 \cdot 8 + 3$$

and hence

$$\frac{35}{8} = \frac{4 \cdot 8 + 3}{8} \qquad \text{substitution}$$

$$= \frac{4 \cdot 8}{8} + \frac{3}{8} \qquad \text{definition of addition}$$

$$= 4 + \frac{3}{8} \qquad \begin{array}{l}\text{interpretation of fraction}\\ \quad \text{bar as exact division}\end{array}$$

$$= 4\tfrac{3}{8} \qquad \text{definition of mixed numerals} \qquad ❏$$

EXAMPLE 7   Convert $5\frac{3}{4}$ to an improper common fraction.

Solution

$$5\frac{3}{4} = 5 + \frac{3}{4} \qquad \text{definition of mixed numerals}$$

$$= \frac{5 \cdot 4}{4} + \frac{3}{4} \qquad \begin{array}{l}\text{interpretation of fraction}\\ \quad \text{bar as exact division}\end{array}$$

$$= \frac{5 \cdot 4 + 3}{4} \qquad \text{definition of addition}$$

$$= \frac{23}{4} \qquad \text{whole number arithmetic} \qquad ❏$$

Calculating sums and differences in mixed-numeral notation involves the same sort of regrouping understandings that underlie the corresponding whole number algorithms.

EXAMPLE 8 Express each sum and difference as a mixed numeral.
(a) $9\frac{3}{4} + 10\frac{5}{6}$
(b) $5\frac{1}{6} - 3\frac{5}{6}$

Solution We could, of course, convert all mixed numerals to common fractions, use our fraction algorithms, and then convert the answers to mixed numerals. But let us, instead, use a vertical arrangement of calculations and think of regrouping as we did for whole numbers.

(a)
$$
\begin{array}{r}
9\frac{3}{4} \\
+\ 10\frac{5}{6} \\
\hline
\end{array}
\quad \rightarrow \quad
\begin{array}{r}
9\frac{9}{12} \\
+\ 10\frac{10}{12} \\
\hline
19\frac{19}{12}
\end{array}
\quad \rightarrow \quad 19 + 1\frac{7}{12} = 20\frac{7}{12}
$$

(b)
$$
\begin{array}{r}
5\frac{1}{6} \\
-\ 3\frac{5}{6} \\
\hline
\end{array}
\quad \rightarrow \quad
\begin{array}{r}
4\frac{7}{6} \\
-\ 3\frac{5}{6} \\
\hline
1\frac{2}{6} = 1\frac{1}{3}
\end{array}
$$
❏

A note on terminology: We have used the term *mixed numeral,* rather than the more common term *mixed number,* to emphasize that $2\frac{3}{4}$ is not some new kind of number but, rather, just new notation for a familiar old rational number. As long as you understand this fact, there is no harm in using the common term.

Abstract Properties

Addition of rational numbers satisfies the expected abstract structural properties: It is a binary operation on the set of rational numbers; it is associative and commutative; and it has a rational identity element, namely, zero. All of these properties are clear if you think of the connection between addition of rational numbers and union of regions in the area model. All of these properties can also be derived algebraically, and you will be given a chance to do that in the exercises. The significance of these properties in the mathematical system of rational numbers will be explored in Section 7.6.

EXERCISE SET 7.2

1. Write the addition problem suggested by each area diagram. Then calculate the sum, and express it by a fraction in lowest terms. (The unit is the square.)

(a)

(b)

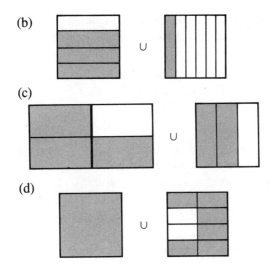

(c)

(d)

2. Write the subtraction problem suggested by each area diagram. Then calculate the difference, and express it by a fraction in lowest terms.

(a)

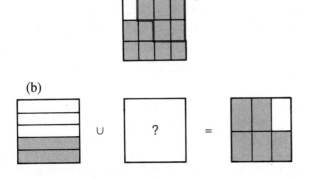

(b)

Visualize area diagrams to solve the word problems in Exercises 3–8.

3. If income taxes take $\frac{2}{9}$ of your income, and other taxes (Social Security, sales, excise, and so on) take $\frac{1}{6}$, what fraction of your income goes for taxes?

4. How much succotash do you get when you mix $\frac{2}{3}$ lb of beans with $\frac{3}{2}$ lb of corn?

5. A class is $\frac{1}{4}$ freshmen, $\frac{1}{3}$ sophomores, $\frac{1}{8}$ juniors, and $\frac{1}{10}$ seniors. The rest are graduate students. What fraction of the class is undergraduate?

6. According to a spokesman (Orson Bean) for the U.S. Postal Service, $\frac{2}{3}$ of all first-class letters are delivered the next day, and $\frac{9}{10}$ are delivered within two days. What fraction of first-class letters take two days for delivery?

7. Sally planted $\frac{3}{4}$ acre in corn and $\frac{3}{5}$ acre in potatoes. How much more land did she devote to corn than to potatoes?

8. One-fourth of the expected tomato crop was destroyed by drought and $\frac{1}{5}$ by insect pests. What fraction of the expected crop survived?

9. Illustrate the calculation of each sum and difference by using a geometric and then a modified geometric representation as in Example 3.
   (a) $\frac{2}{3} + \frac{1}{4}$ (b) $\frac{3}{4} + \frac{1}{3}$
   (c) $\frac{1}{2} - \frac{1}{3}$ (d) $\frac{4}{3} - \frac{1}{2}$

10. Write the addition or subtraction problem, and answer, suggested by each number line diagram.

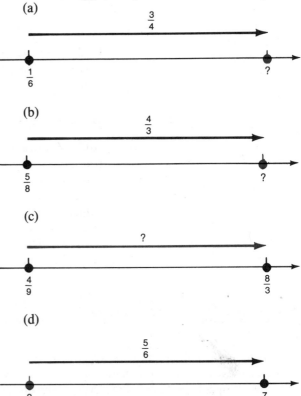

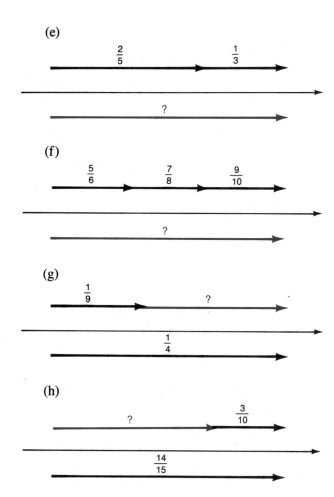

(e)

$\frac{2}{5}$ $\frac{1}{3}$

?

(f)

$\frac{5}{6}$ $\frac{7}{8}$ $\frac{9}{10}$

?

(g)

$\frac{1}{9}$?

$\frac{1}{4}$

(h)

? $\frac{3}{10}$

$\frac{14}{15}$

11. Put the following phrases into appropriately shaped boxes and arrange them into a flowchart for subtracting rational numbers.

(a) An ordered pair of rational numbers labeled by fractions.

(b) Do the fractions have a common denominator?

(c) Is numerator of first fraction $\geq$ numerator of second?

(d) Replace them by an equivalent pair of fractions having a common denominator.

(e) Start.

(f) Stop.

(g) Subtract second numerator from first numerator.

(h) Their difference is undefined at present.

(i) This fraction labels their difference.

(j) Write this difference over their common denominator.

12. In the flowchart for Exercise 11, what is the most sophisticated subroutine?

13. Calculate these sums and differences by following the flowcharts. Check your work using a Math Explorer calculator if you have one.

(a) $\frac{11}{20} + \frac{7}{20}$ (b) $\frac{13}{8} - \frac{7}{8}$

(c) $\frac{49}{90} - \frac{8}{15}$ (d) $\frac{5}{6} + \frac{11}{84}$

(e) $\frac{14}{45} + \frac{7}{30}$ (f) $\frac{19}{20} - \frac{8}{15}$

(g) $\dfrac{5}{2^2 \cdot 3 \cdot 7} + \dfrac{7}{2 \cdot 3^2 \cdot 5}$

(h) $\dfrac{10}{3 \cdot 7} - \dfrac{41}{2^3 \cdot 3 \cdot 5}$

14. Estimate each of the following with a fraction having single-digit numerator and denominator.

(a) $\frac{39}{117}$ (b) $\frac{913}{1548}$

(c) $\frac{29}{74}$ (d) $\frac{247}{440}$

In Exercises 15–17 check your work using a Math Explorer calculator if you have one.

15. Convert each improper fraction to a mixed numeral.

(a) $\frac{20}{3}$ (b) $\frac{22}{7}$

(c) $\frac{100}{12}$ (d) $\frac{365}{7}$

(e) $\frac{7628}{137}$ (f) $\frac{4546}{109}$

16. Convert each mixed numeral to an improper fraction.

(a) $6\frac{3}{4}$ (b) $2\frac{2}{3}$

(c) $14\frac{7}{8}$ (d) $7\frac{3}{16}$

17. Express each sum and difference as a mixed numeral.

(a) $8\frac{7}{8} + 3\frac{5}{8}$ (b) $12\frac{1}{4} - 5\frac{3}{4}$

(c) $6\frac{1}{2} + 2\frac{2}{3}$ (d) $3\frac{3}{10} - 2\frac{1}{3}$

18. Estimate each sum and difference to the nearest whole number.

(a) $12\frac{1}{5} + 10\frac{1}{4} + 8\frac{1}{3}$ (b) $2\frac{1}{10} + 7\frac{1}{9} + 4\frac{1}{8}$

(c) $12\frac{7}{8} - 2\frac{1}{4}$ (d) $6\frac{1}{2} - 4\frac{3}{5}$

Solve the following word problems. Express your answers in mixed-numeral notation.

19. How many gallons of blood are collected by the Red Cross during a blood drive in which 227 donors each gives a pint? (There are 8 pints in a gallon.)

20. A worker who smokes spends 2 min per hour in getting a cigarette, lighting it, flicking ashes, and so on. How many (work) hours per year does he spend on his habit if he works 40 hr per week for 50 weeks of the year?

21. The price of a share of Amalgamated Widget rose from $30\frac{3}{4}$ to $32\frac{1}{8}$. What was the change in price?

22. Three pieces of ribbon—of lengths $15\frac{1}{2}$ in, $12\frac{3}{4}$ in, and $10\frac{7}{8}$ in—are cut from a 48-in piece. How much remains?

Use the general algebraic definition of addition, $a/b + c/d = (ad + bc)/bd$, to verify the properties in Exercises 23–25.

23. Addition of rational numbers is commutative.

24. Addition of rational numbers is associative.

25. The rational number zero is the additive identity.

26. Use the general algebraic definitions of addition and subtraction and the rule for reducing (pp. 352–353) to prove that $a/b - c/d$ is the missing addend in the equation

$$\frac{c}{d} + \Box = \frac{a}{b}$$

27. Prove that the general rule $a/b + c/d = (ad + bc)/bd$ gives the same sum as the special rule $a/b + c/b = (a + c)/b$ when $b = d$.

★ 28. Before the flowchart in Figure 7.36 can be accepted as a definition of addition (or even as a rule for computing sums), one must show that when one follows the "no" branch, the output sum does not depend on the choice of equivalent fractions. That is, if I replace the pair of fractions a/b and c/d by the equivalent pair e/g and f/g and thus arrive at the sum $(e + f)/g$, and you replace a/b and c/d by the equivalent pair m/k and n/k and thus arrive at the sum $(m + n)/k$, then our sums are equal. That is, our fractions $(e + f)/g$ and $(m + n)/k$ are equivalent. Fill in missing statements and reasons in the following algebraic proof of that fact.

1. e/g is equivalent to a/b, and f/g is equivalent to c/d 1. Given

2. m/k is equivalent to a/b, and n/k is equivalent to c/d 2. Given

3. e/g is equivalent to m/k, and f/g is equivalent to n/k 3. Steps 1 and 2 and the fact that equivalence of fractions is symmetric and transitive; see Exercise 40, Section 7.1

4. $ek = gm$ and $fk = gn$ 4. _____

5. _____   5. _____

6. _____   6. _____

7. $(e + f)/g$ is equivalent to $(m + n)/k$ 7. Definition of equivalence of fractions

 ## 7.3 *Multiplication and Division*

At one time we all were taught how to multiply and divide fractions:

$$\frac{3}{5} \cdot \frac{4}{7} = \frac{3 \cdot 4}{5 \cdot 7} \qquad \frac{3}{5} \div \frac{4}{7} = \frac{3}{5} \cdot \frac{7}{4} = \cdots$$

The purposes of this section are to motivate and analyze these rules, to explore their consequences, and to brush up on some computational skills. We shall also look at a few applications. Sections 7.4 and 7.5 are devoted entirely to further applications.

Area Model

Figure 7.39 $\frac{2}{3}$ of the picnickers are adults.

Consider the statement

"$\frac{2}{3}$ of the picnickers are adults."

We have been representing size comparisons like this one between the set of all picnickers and the subset of adult picnickers as follows. First, we choose a region, say a square, to represent the set of all picnickers. Then we partition it into 3 same-size pieces and shade 2 of them, as in Figure 7.39.

Using this diagram, we are able to answer questions such as this one:

"If there are 24 picnickers, how many are adults?"

Figure 7.40 $\frac{2}{3}$ of the picnickers are adults; $\frac{3}{4}$ of the adults are men.

In this context *same size* means "same number." Thus each of the three pieces represents 8 people, and so the two shaded pieces represent 16 adults. Arithmetically, we found $\frac{2}{3}$ of 24 by dividing 24 by 3 and multiplying by 2:

$$\tfrac{2}{3} \text{ of } 24 = 2 \cdot \tfrac{24}{3}$$

Suppose now that we are given the added information that

"$\frac{3}{4}$ of the adults are men."

To represent this size comparison, we should again begin with a region that represents these adults. But now there is no question about how to choose the region; we already have a rectangle, the shaded rectangle in Figure 7.39, that represents the adults. Thus we move on to the next step, partitioning the rectangular region of adults into 4 same-size regions and shading 3 of them, as in Figure 7.40.

Figure 7.41 Men, women, and children at a picnic.

If we extend the vertical partition lines to the top of the unit square, the diagram becomes even more informative: White represents children, lightly shaded represents women, and heavily shaded represents men. Furthermore, each little subrectangle represents the same number of people. See Figure 7.41.

Here is a sample of some of the questions we can answer by referring to Figure 7.41.

EXAMPLE 1   (a) If there are 12 children at the picnic, how many women are there?
(b) If there are 20 more men than women, how many children are there?
(c) Men make up what fraction of the picnickers?

Solution   (a) Divide 12 by 4 to get the number of people (3) represented by each little rectangle. Multiply by 2 to get the number of women. *Answer:* 6. Or we could also infer from the diagram that there are half as many women as children. *Answer:* 6.

(b) The excess of men over women is represented by four little rectangles, but so is the number of children. *Answer:* 20.

(c) By simply counting total rectangles and heavily shaded rectangles, we get the answer: $\frac{6}{12}$.   ❏

Let us look at question (c) a little more closely. On the one hand, men make up $\frac{3}{4}$ of the adults, and the adults are $\frac{2}{3}$ of the total picnickers. Thus men make up $\frac{3}{4}$ of $\frac{2}{3}$ of the picnickers. On the other hand, by simply counting, we find that men make up $\frac{6}{12}$ of the picnickers. Thus

$$\frac{3}{4} \text{ of } \frac{2}{3} = \frac{6}{12}$$

The origins of the 6 and the 12 on the right-hand side of this equation can also be traced. The number 12 is the total number of little rectangles, a number that can be found by multiplying the number of segments into which the bottom edge of the unit square was partitioned (4) by the number of segments into which the left edge was partitioned (3). The number 6 represents the number of segments along the bottom edge of the heavily shaded rectangle (3) multiplied by the number along its left edge (2). Thus the preceding equation becomes

$$\frac{3}{4} \text{ of } \frac{2}{3} = \frac{3 \cdot 2}{4 \cdot 3}$$

The two equations that have arisen from questions about the picnickers,

$$\frac{2}{3} \text{ of } 24 = 2 \cdot \frac{24}{3} \qquad \frac{3}{4} \text{ of } \frac{2}{3} = \frac{3 \cdot 2}{4 \cdot 3}$$

suggest strongly that we should define multiplication of fractions (think of 24 as $\frac{24}{1}$) by the rule "numerator times numerator over denominator times denominator" and then use "of" as the referent of multiplication in the area model.

To give multiplication of fractions a more tangible geometric interpretation, we revise Figure 7.41 to emphasize lengths. See Figure 7.42. The area of the men's region is found by multiplying $\frac{3}{4}$ times $\frac{2}{3}$. Similarly, the area of the women's region is $\frac{1}{4} \cdot \frac{2}{3}$ (women make up $\frac{2}{12}$ of the picnickers), and the area of the children's region is $\frac{1}{3} \cdot 1$ (children make up $\frac{1}{3}$ of the picnickers). In general:

Multiplying two fractions corresponds to finding the area of a rectangle.

That is, the area-of-a-rectangle interpretation that holds for multiplication of whole numbers extends to fractions as well.

Here is a more precise formulation of the area interpretation.

If length and width of a rectangle are given in the same unit (inch, centimeter, . . .) by fractions, then the product of these fractions gives the area of the rectangle in the corresponding square unit (square inch, square centimeter, . . .).

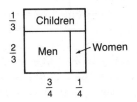

Figure 7.42

EXAMPLE 2   Write the multiplication problem, and answer, suggested by each diagram.

(a) 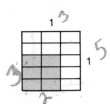   (b)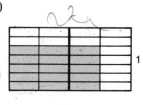

Solution   (a) $\frac{2}{3} \cdot \frac{3}{5} = \frac{6}{15}$

(b) $\frac{3}{2} \cdot \frac{5}{7} = \frac{15}{14}$ ❑

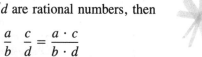

Definition and Properties of Multiplication

As we did for addition and subtraction, we define multiplication of rational numbers rather than of fractions.

> **Definition of Multiplication (·) of Rational Numbers**
>
> If a/b and c/d are rational numbers, then
>
> $$\frac{a}{b} \cdot \frac{c}{d} = \frac{a \cdot c}{b \cdot d}$$

The two black multiplication dots on the right signify whole number multiplication; the red one on the left denotes the operation we are defining, multiplication of rational numbers. The same question that came up for addition comes up again: Is our definition unambiguous? That is, is the product of two rational numbers independent of the fraction labels that were used to compute it? Geometrically, using the area-of-a-rectangle interpretation, the answer is, "Obviously, yes." To prove the same result algebraically takes a little effort.

The strategy is to suppose that a_1/b_1 is equivalent to a_2/b_2 and that c_1/d_1 is equivalent to c_2/d_2 and then to show that a_1c_1/b_1d_1 is equivalent to a_2c_2/b_2d_2. The tactics are to work from both ends toward the middle:

1. a_1/b_1 is equivalent to a_2/b_2, and   given
   c_1/d_1 is equivalent to c_2/d_2

2. $a_1b_2 = b_1a_2$ and $c_1d_2 = d_1c_2$ definition of equivalence

3. $(a_1b_2)(c_1d_2) = (b_1a_2)(d_1c_2)$ multiplication property of equality

4. $(a_1c_1)(b_2d_2) = (b_1d_1)(a_2c_2)$ commutativity and associativity
                                                                                  of whole number multiplication

5. a_1c_1/b_1d_1 is equivalent to a_2c_2/b_2d_2 definition of equivalence

EXAMPLE 3   Compute the following products.
                  (a) $\frac{2}{3} \cdot \frac{1}{4}$ (b) $\frac{8}{12} \cdot \frac{3}{12}$

Solution   (a) $\dfrac{2}{3} \cdot \dfrac{1}{4} = \dfrac{2 \cdot 1}{3 \cdot 4}$ definition of (rational) multiplication

                          $= \dfrac{2}{12}$ whole number arithmetic

                  (b) $\dfrac{8}{12} \cdot \dfrac{3}{12} = \dfrac{8 \cdot 3}{12 \cdot 12}$ definition of (rational) multiplication

                          $= \dfrac{24}{144}$ whole number arithmetic

Notice that this product is the same product as in part (a), since $\frac{8}{12} = \frac{2}{3}$ and $\frac{3}{12} = \frac{1}{4}$ (as rational numbers). The computed values $\frac{2}{12}$ and $\frac{24}{144}$ are also the same (as they must be), since both reduce to the same lowest-terms fraction, $\frac{1}{6}$, or since they satisfy the crisscross criterion, $2 \cdot 144 = 12 \cdot 24$. Notice too that the presence of common denominators was no help at all in part (b). When you compute a product, the fractions that are easiest to work with are lowest-terms fractions.   ❏

All of the familiar structural properties are immediate consequences of the definition: Multiplication is a binary operation on the set of rational numbers; it is associative and commutative; and the rational number 1 is its identity element. Furthermore, multiplication distributes over addition. You are asked to verify all of these properties in the exercises. The one new property of multiplication that is true for the rational numbers, but was not true for the whole numbers or the integers, is this:

> Every nonzero rational number has a **reciprocal** or **multiplicative inverse.** That is, corresponding to each nonzero rational number is another nonzero rational number that multiplies it to give 1.

For example, the nonzero rational number $\frac{3}{4}$ has $\frac{4}{3}$ as its multiplicative inverse:

$$\frac{3}{4} \cdot \frac{4}{3} = \frac{3 \cdot 4}{4 \cdot 3}$$ definition of (rational) multiplication

$$= \frac{12}{12}$$ whole number multiplication

$$= 1$$ interpretation of fraction bar as exact division

In general, if $a/b \neq 0$ (and hence $a \neq 0$), then b/a is its multiplicative inverse, because

$$\frac{a}{b} \cdot \frac{b}{a} = \frac{a \cdot b}{b \cdot a} = \frac{a \cdot b}{a \cdot b} = 1$$

The restriction of the reciprocals property to nonzero rational numbers is clearly necessary. For example, there is no rational number a/b such that

$$\frac{a}{b} \cdot \frac{0}{7} = 1$$

since

$$\frac{a}{b} \cdot 0 = \frac{a}{b} \cdot \frac{0}{1} = \frac{a \cdot 0}{b \cdot 1} = \frac{0}{b} = 0$$

Division

We want to define division of rational numbers in a way that is consistent with our missing-factor definition of (exact) division of whole numbers. Consider the equation

$$\frac{c}{d} \cdot \square = \frac{a}{b}$$

where, as usual, $b \neq 0$ and $d \neq 0$; and consider the associated pair of questions: Is there a solution, and is it unique? Without the further restriction that $c \neq 0$, there would be no hope of showing existence because the equation

$$\frac{0}{7} \cdot \square = \frac{3}{4}$$

for example, has no solution. Under the assumption $c \neq 0$, though, both existence and uniquences are provable.

Existence   The idea is to fill in the box so that the left-hand side of

$$\frac{c}{d} \cdot \square = \frac{a}{b}$$

assumes the same value as the right-hand side. Think of first putting a/b in the box, since that's the target value, and then putting in d/c, to rid the left-hand side of c/d. The formal verification that $a/b \cdot d/c$ is a solution follows.

$$\frac{c}{d} \cdot \left(\frac{a}{b} \cdot \frac{d}{c} \right) = \frac{c}{d} \cdot \left(\frac{d}{c} \cdot \frac{a}{b} \right) \qquad \text{commutativity of multiplication}$$

$$= \left(\frac{c}{d} \cdot \frac{d}{c} \right) \cdot \frac{a}{b} \qquad \text{associativity of multiplication}$$

$$= 1 \cdot \frac{a}{b} \qquad \text{reciprocals property}$$

$$= \frac{a}{b} \qquad \text{multiplicative property of 1} \qquad \square$$

Uniqueness Suppose x_1/y_1 and x_2/y_2 are rational numbers such that

$$\frac{c}{d} \cdot \frac{x_1}{y_1} = \frac{a}{b} \qquad \text{and} \qquad \frac{c}{d} \cdot \frac{x_2}{y_2} = \frac{a}{b}$$

Our task is to show that $x_1/y_1 = x_2/y_2$. By substitution (or the symmetric and transitive properties of equality),

$$\frac{c}{d} \cdot \frac{x_1}{y_1} = \frac{c}{d} \cdot \frac{x_2}{y_2}$$

Now, multiply both sides of this equation by d/c, the reciprocal of c/d, to arrive at

$$\frac{x_1}{y_1} = \frac{x_2}{y_2} \qquad\qquad\qquad ❑$$

In view of the existence-uniqueness property we *could* define a/b divided by c/d to be the unique solution to the equation

$$\frac{c}{d} \cdot \square = \frac{a}{b}$$

We can do better, though. In the existence proof we saw that this solution can be described explicitly as the product $a/b \cdot d/c$, and an explicit definition is usually easier to use than an implicit one.

Definition of Division (——, ÷) of Rational Numbers

If a/b and c/d are rational numbers such that $c \neq 0$, then the quotient of a/b divided by c/d, written

$$\frac{a/b}{c/d} \qquad \text{or} \qquad a/b \div c/d$$

is defined as follows:

$$\frac{a/b}{c/d} = \frac{a}{b} \cdot \frac{d}{c} \qquad \text{or} \qquad \frac{a}{b} \div \frac{c}{d} = \frac{a}{b} \cdot \frac{d}{c}$$

The standard verbalization is "Invert the divisor and multiply."

EXAMPLE 4   Express each quotient as a common fraction.

(a) $\dfrac{\frac{5}{8}}{\frac{2}{3}}$

(b) $\dfrac{3}{5} \div \dfrac{5}{7}$

Solution (a) $\dfrac{\frac{5}{8}}{\frac{2}{3}} = \dfrac{5}{8} \cdot \dfrac{3}{2}$ definition of division

$= \dfrac{5 \cdot 3}{8 \cdot 2}$ definition of multiplication

$= \dfrac{15}{16}$ whole number arithmetic

(b) $\dfrac{3}{5} \div \dfrac{5}{7} = \dfrac{3}{5} \cdot \dfrac{7}{5}$ definition of division

$= \dfrac{3 \cdot 7}{5 \cdot 5}$ definition of multiplication

$= \dfrac{21}{25}$ whole number arithmetic   ❏

Algorithms

The algebraic definition $a/b \cdot c/d = ac/bd$ provides complete instructions for multiplying rational numbers when they are labeled by common fractions. By combining it with some judicious factoring and the rule for reducing, $ac/bc = a/b$, we can often simplify calculations.

EXAMPLE 5 Calculate the product $\frac{12}{17} \cdot \frac{17}{18}$.

Solution $\dfrac{12}{17} \cdot \dfrac{17}{18} = \dfrac{12 \cdot 17}{17 \cdot 18}$ definition of multiplication

$= \dfrac{2 \cdot 6 \cdot 17}{17 \cdot 6 \cdot 3}$ factoring (multiplication facts in W)

$= \dfrac{2}{3}$ rule for reducing   ❏

If one or both of the rational numbers is represented by a mixed numeral or by an ordinary Hindu-Arabic numeral, then conversion to (and from) fraction notation can be used.

EXAMPLE 6 Calculate the following products.
  (a) $\frac{3}{16} \cdot 4$ (b) $2\frac{3}{4} \cdot 3\frac{1}{5}$
  (c) $5 \cdot 2\frac{3}{8}$ (d) $\frac{2}{3} \cdot 3\frac{3}{8}$

Solution (a) $\dfrac{3}{16} \cdot 4 = \dfrac{3}{16} \cdot \dfrac{4}{1} = \dfrac{3 \cdot 4}{16 \cdot 1} = \dfrac{3 \cdot 4}{4 \cdot 4} = \dfrac{3}{4}$

(b) $2\frac{3}{4} \cdot 3\frac{1}{5} = \dfrac{11}{4} \cdot \dfrac{16}{5} = \dfrac{11 \cdot 4 \cdot 4}{4 \cdot 5} = \dfrac{44}{5} = 8\frac{4}{5}$

(c) A methodical way of finding this product is to begin by converting both factors to common fractions:

$$5 \cdot 2\tfrac{3}{8} = \frac{5}{1} \cdot \frac{19}{8} = \frac{5 \cdot 19}{1 \cdot 8} = \frac{95}{8} = 11\tfrac{7}{8}$$

Another approach, which can be carried out mentally, uses the definition of mixed numerals and the distributive property:

$$5 \cdot 2\tfrac{3}{8} = 5(2 + \tfrac{3}{8}) = 5 \cdot 2 + 5 \cdot \tfrac{3}{8} = 10 + \tfrac{15}{8} = 11\tfrac{7}{8}$$

(d) Converting to fractions:

$$\frac{2}{3} \cdot 3\tfrac{3}{8} = \frac{2}{3} \cdot \frac{27}{8} = \frac{2 \cdot 3 \cdot 9}{3 \cdot 2 \cdot 4} = \frac{9}{4} = 2\tfrac{1}{4}$$

Using the distributive property:

$$\tfrac{2}{3} \cdot 3\tfrac{3}{8} = \tfrac{2}{3}(3 + \tfrac{3}{8}) = \tfrac{2}{3} \cdot 3 + \tfrac{2}{3} \cdot \tfrac{3}{8} = 2 + \tfrac{2}{8} = 2\tfrac{1}{4} \qquad \square$$

The algorithm situation for division is much like that for multiplication. The invert-and-multiply definition is the basis, but factoring, reducing, and converting to and from mixed-numeral or standard whole number notation can enter in.

EXAMPLE 7   Calculate the following quotients.

(a) $\dfrac{5}{12} \div \dfrac{3}{8}$ (b) $\dfrac{8/3}{10}$

(c) $\dfrac{6}{3/8}$ (d) $3\tfrac{3}{4} \div 2\tfrac{1}{2}$

Solution   (a) $\dfrac{5}{12} \div \dfrac{3}{8} = \dfrac{5}{12} \cdot \dfrac{8}{3} = \dfrac{5 \cdot 4 \cdot 2}{4 \cdot 3 \cdot 3} = \dfrac{10}{9}$

(b) $\dfrac{8/3}{10} = \dfrac{8/3}{10/1} = \dfrac{8}{3} \cdot \dfrac{1}{10} = \dfrac{2 \cdot 4}{3 \cdot 2 \cdot 5} = \dfrac{4}{15}$

(c) $\dfrac{6}{3/8} = \dfrac{6/1}{3/8} = \dfrac{6}{1} \cdot \dfrac{8}{3} = \dfrac{3 \cdot 2 \cdot 8}{1 \cdot 3} = \dfrac{16}{1} = 16$

(d) $3\tfrac{3}{4} \div 2\tfrac{1}{2} = \dfrac{15}{4} \div \dfrac{5}{2} = \dfrac{15}{4} \cdot \dfrac{2}{5} = \dfrac{5 \cdot 3 \cdot 2}{2 \cdot 2 \cdot 5} = \dfrac{3}{2} = 1\tfrac{1}{2} \qquad \square$

EXERCISE SET 7.3

1. Write the multiplication problem suggested by each area diagram. Then calculate the product, and express it by a fraction in lowest terms. (The unit is the same square throughout.)

(a)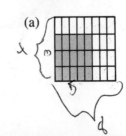

(b)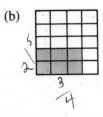

(c)

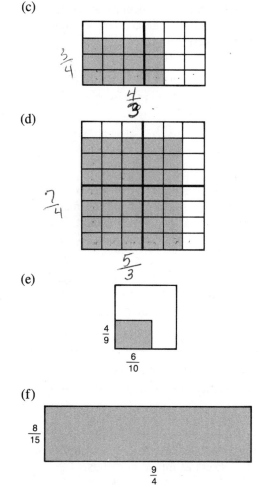

(d)

(e)

(b)

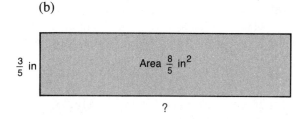

Use area diagrams to solve these word problems.

3. Three-fifths of the students live in dormitories. There are 1500 students in all. How many live in the dorms?

4. Four out of every seven registered voters in Salem are Republicans. Registered Republicans outnumber all other registered voters by 1250. How many registered Republicans are there in Salem?

5. Three-fourths of the land in Green County is tillable, and $\frac{7}{10}$ of the tillable land is under cultivation. What fraction of the land in Green County is under cultivation?

6. If $\frac{2}{5}$ of the retail price of an item is markup, and $\frac{1}{4}$ of the wholesale price represents the cost of raw materials, what fraction of the retail price represents the cost of materials?

7. If $\frac{1}{4}$ of the tomato crop was destroyed by drought, and $\frac{1}{3}$ of the surviving crop was lost to an early frost, what fraction of the crop survived?

8. If $\frac{1}{12}$ of the labor force is unemployed, and $\frac{2}{9}$ of the employed are less than fully employed, what fraction of the labor force is fully employed?

9. The audience at a play is $\frac{2}{5}$ adults, and $\frac{2}{3}$ of the adults are women.
   (a) Women make up what fraction of the audience?
   (b) Men make up what fraction of the audience?
   (c) If there are 75 more children than women, how many men are there?
   (d) If there are 60 more children than adults, how many more women are there than men?

10. Suppose that $\frac{1}{3}$ of your income goes for taxes, and that $\frac{5}{8}$ of your taxes are federal, $\frac{1}{8}$ are state, and the rest are local.

(f)

2. Write the division problem suggested by each diagram. Then calculate the quotient, and express it by a fraction in lowest terms.
   (a)

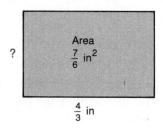

(a) What fraction of your income goes for federal taxes?

(b) What fraction of your income goes for state taxes?

(c) If your local tax bill is $1200, what is your after-tax income?

(d) If your after-tax income is $16,000, how much federal tax do you pay?

We have seen that "of" *usually* translates into multiplication. Use that fact to solve Exercises 11–14.

11. If $\frac{9}{11}$ of the people are eligible to vote, and $\frac{2}{3}$ of those eligible to vote actually do vote, and the winner in the election gets $\frac{11}{20}$ of the vote, what fraction of the people put the winner in office?

12. One-sixth of the students were absent, and $\frac{1}{5}$ of those present were tardy. What fraction of the students were present and on time?

13. If $\frac{5}{8}$ of all criminals are apprehended, $\frac{2}{3}$ of those apprehended are brought to trial, $\frac{1}{2}$ of those brought to trial are convicted, $\frac{2}{3}$ of those convicted are incarcerated, and $\frac{3}{10}$ of those incarcerated serve their full sentences, what fraction of criminals pay for their crimes with a full sentence?

14. Sue weighed 70 kg before a loss of 5 kg. How much does she weigh now?

15. Illustrate the calculation of each product by a diagram of the kind in Example 2 of this section.
    (a) $\frac{3}{4} \cdot \frac{2}{3}$

    (b) $\frac{4}{3} \cdot \frac{5}{6}$

16. Using Figure 7.36 as a model, make a flowchart for multiplying rational numbers labeled by fractions.

17. Using the multiplication algorithm of Exercise 16 as a subroutine, make a flowchart for dividing rational numbers labeled by fractions.

18. Make a flowchart for multiplying rational numbers labeled by mixed numerals.

19. Make a flowchart for dividing rational numbers labeled by mixed numerals.

20. First estimate, then calculate these products and quotients. Write your answers as common fractions in lowest terms.
    (a) $\frac{5}{12} \cdot \frac{4}{10}$ (b) $\frac{28}{15} \cdot \frac{5}{12}$

    (c) $\frac{3}{4} \cdot \frac{8}{9} \cdot \frac{15}{16}$ (d) $\frac{5}{6} \cdot \frac{6}{7} \cdot \frac{7}{8} \cdot \frac{8}{9} \cdot \frac{9}{10}$

    (e) $\frac{3}{8} \cdot 12$ (f) $15 \cdot \frac{5}{6} \cdot \frac{3}{20}$

    (g) $\frac{7}{10} \div \frac{4}{5}$ (h) $\dfrac{\frac{15}{16}}{\frac{3}{4}}$

    (i) $\dfrac{30}{\frac{4}{5}}$ (j) $\frac{7}{8} \div 4$

21. Five rational numbers *A–E* are expressed below by "complex fractions." By estimation, decide which is greatest and which is least. Verify by paper-and-pencil or machine calculation.

    $$A = \dfrac{\frac{7}{10}}{\frac{4}{5}} \qquad B = \dfrac{\frac{7}{10}}{\frac{4}{5}} \qquad C = \dfrac{\frac{7}{\frac{10}{4}}}{5}$$

    $$D = \dfrac{\frac{7}{\frac{10}{4}}}{5} \qquad E = \dfrac{\frac{\frac{7}{10}}{4}}{5}$$

22. Write the complex fraction that is evaluated by this sequence of keystrokes on an AOS calculator.

    | 8 | ÷ | 4 | ÷ | 2 | ÷ | 2 | = |

23. Calculate these products and quotients. Write your answers as mixed numerals.
    (a) $7\frac{1}{2} \cdot 2\frac{3}{5}$ (b) $6\frac{2}{3} \cdot 1\frac{7}{10}$

    (c) $5\frac{1}{4} \div 1\frac{3}{4}$ (d) $12 \div 2\frac{2}{3}$

24. Find $4\frac{2}{3} \cdot 6\frac{1}{4}$ by applying the distributive property to $(4 + \frac{2}{3})(6 + \frac{1}{4})$.

25. Give a whole number estimate for each product and quotient.
    (a) $4\frac{1}{4} \cdot 2\frac{3}{4}$ (b) $\frac{2}{3} \cdot 8\frac{5}{8}$

    (c) $\frac{1}{4} \cdot 8\frac{5}{8}$ (d) $3\frac{1}{2} \cdot 8\frac{1}{16}$

    (e) $\dfrac{7\frac{1}{2}}{1\frac{7}{8}}$ (f) $\dfrac{9\frac{1}{8}}{2\frac{7}{8}}$

For the word problems in Exercises 26–29, first estimate the answers, then express the precise values in mixed-numeral notation.

26. Find the area and the perimeter of a square of side length $1\frac{3}{8}$ in.

27. What is the weight (in ounces) of an $8\frac{1}{2}$-in by 11-in rectangle of sheet metal, if one square inch weighs $\frac{1}{8}$ oz?

28. How long, to the nearest minute, do you have to walk at the steady rate of $3\frac{1}{2}$ mph to cover a distance of $12\frac{1}{2}$ mi?

29. You have a 48-in coil of wire. How many $3\frac{3}{4}$-in lengths can you cut, and how much wire will be wasted?

30. What is the greatest number of $8\frac{1}{2}$-by-11 sheets that can be cut from a $12\frac{1}{2}$-by-26 piece of paper (all dimensions in inches), and how many square inches of paper will be wasted?

31. The whole numbers 6 and 2 are also rational numbers and can be labeled by the common fractions $\frac{6}{1}$ and $\frac{2}{1}$. Show that the sum, difference, product, and quotient of these rational numbers agree with the whole number sum, difference, product, and quotient.

32. Simplify each expression. Write your answer as a fraction in lowest terms.

    (a) $\dfrac{\frac{9}{2}(\frac{3}{8} - \frac{1}{3})}{\frac{1}{8}}$ (b) $\dfrac{\frac{7}{8} + \frac{2}{3} \cdot \frac{5}{6}}{\frac{5}{2}}$

33. In the following squares you are to multiply across and divide down. Fill in the missing entries.

    (a)   (b)

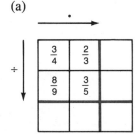
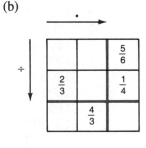

34. In the general square in Figure 7.43, why do the two different routes to the lower right-hand corner lead to the same value?

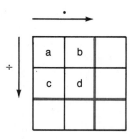

Figure 7.43

35. Repeat Exercise 34 with $\cdot$ and $\div$ replaced by $+$ and $-$, respectively.

Use the definition of multiplication of rational numbers to verify Exercises 36–39.

36. Multiplication is associative.

37. Multiplication is commutative.

38. One is the multiplicative identity.

39. Multiplication distributes over addition.

40. Determine the next three terms a_5, a_6, a_7 in the sequence that begins as follows. *Hint:* Look for a recursion formula that expresses a_{n+1} in terms of a_n.

$a_1 = 1$

$a_2 = 1 + \frac{1}{1} = 2$

$a_3 = 1 + \dfrac{1}{1 + \frac{1}{1}} = \dfrac{3}{2}$

$a_4 = 1 + \dfrac{1}{1 + \dfrac{1}{1 + \frac{1}{1}}} = \dfrac{5}{3}$

Do you see any pattern in the numerators and denominators of the simplified fractional forms?

Computer Vignette E

Figure 7.44 is a BASIC computer program that prints out (in decimal notation) the first 20 terms of the sequence of *continued fractions* described in Exercise 40, Section 7.3. Figure 7.45 shows a run of the program.

Figure 7.44

```
10    PRINT "TERM NUMBER", "VALUE"
20    PRINT
30    LET N = 1
40    LET A = 1
50    PRINT N,A
60    FOR N = 2 TO 20
70    LET A = 1 + 1 / A
80    PRINT N,A
90    NEXT N
100   END
```

Figure 7.45

```
]RUN
TERM NUMBER              VALUE

1                        1
2                        2
3                        1.5
4                        1.66666667
5                        1.6
6                        1.625
7                        1.61538461
8                        1.61904762
9                        1.61764706
10                       1.61818182
11                       1.61797753
12                       1.61805556
13                       1.61802575
14                       1.61803714
15                       1.61803279
16                       1.61803445
17                       1.61803381
18                       1.61803406
19                       1.61803396
20                       1.618034
```

Apparently, this sequence approaches some limiting number, call it a_∞. What equation do you suppose a_∞ satisfies? If you remember how to solve such an equation, do so.

7.4 *Solving Fraction Problems*

Word problems involving fractions present some of the toughest mathematical challenges that children ever face. In the previous sections we looked at some relatively simple problems, and we introduced some helpful techniques and ways of thinking:

1. *Geometric diagrams* that represent size comparisons are useful, particularly diagrams based on unit squares and unit segments. Adding fractions corresponds to finding the total area of a union of (disjoint) rectangular regions having prescribed areas. Multiplying fractions corresponds to finding the area of a rectangular region having prescribed length and width.

2. The *linguistic clue* that "of" usually corresponds to multiplication is a powerful tool for translating word problems into symbolic ones.

In this section we consider a sampling of some harder problems involving fractions, and we add arithmetic and algebraic methods and a schematic device called a tree diagram to our list of techniques for solving such problems. There is no single best way. For any problem there are usually several different approaches that will work. You are encouraged to familiarize yourself with a variety of techniques. Remember that, as a teacher, your being able to get an answer will not be enough. You will also have to choose a method that is appropriate for your students. As you read the examples that follow, think about which method you prefer personally and which you consider most comprehensible to youngsters.

EXAMPLE 1　　There are $\frac{2}{3}$ as many girls as boys, and there are 24 boys. How many girls are there?

Discussion: This problem is similar to ones we solved previously, but now we will look a bit more closely at both our geometric and linguistic methods. (In ensuing examples we will not go into as much detail.)

Solution 1　　*Geometric:* If we let the unit square represent the *set* of boys, then the *set* of girls will be represented not by a subrectangle of that square but by a rectangle disjoint from it. See Figure 7.46. If, however, we let our unit square represent the *number* of boys, then the *number* of girls can be represented by a subrectangle. See Figure 7.47. From either diagram, since there are 24 boys, there will be 16 girls.

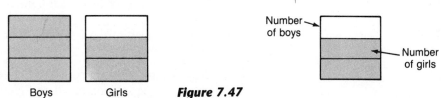

Figure 7.46　　Boys　　Girls　　**Figure 7.47**

Solution 2   *Linguistic/arithmetic:* While it is nonsense to say

(!)   "$\frac{2}{3}$ of the boys are girls."   (!)

it is perfectly correct to say

"The number of girls is $\frac{2}{3}$ of the number of boys."

This latter sentence can now be translated partially into symbols, using the given information that there are 24 boys and the correspondence between "of" and $\cdot$.

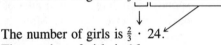

The number of girls is $\frac{2}{3}$ of the number of boys.

The number of girls is $\frac{2}{3} \cdot 24$.
The number of girls is 16.

Solution 3   *Linguistic/algebraic:* To completely symbolize this problem, we introduce variables, or unknowns, being very careful to identify them precisely:

Let b = number of boys (not "let b = boys").
Let g = number of girls (not "let g = girls").

Then we translate the verbal size comparison between the sets of boys and girls into symbols to get one equation:

There are $\frac{2}{3}$ as many boys as girls.

↓

The number of girls is $\frac{2}{3}$ of the number of boys.

$g \quad = \quad \frac{2}{3} \quad \cdot \quad b$

We translate the given information about the size of the set of boys into symbols to get another equation:

There are 24 boys

↓

The number of boys is 24

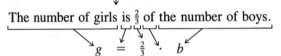

$b \quad = \quad 24$

Substituting from the second of the equations

$$\begin{cases} g = \frac{2}{3}b \\ b = 24 \end{cases}$$

into the first, we get $g = 16$, which translates into English as "The number of girls is 16."

  Discussion: Which of the following four solutions do you think would be most clear for youngsters?

The geometric solution based on Figure 7.46
The geometric solution based on Figure 7.47

The linguistic/arithmetic solution
The linguistic/algebraic solution

Which of the four solutions do you prefer at your own mathematical level? ❏

EXAMPLE 2   A chili recipe calls for (by weight) $\frac{3}{4}$ as much tomatoes as beans and $\frac{2}{5}$ as much meat as beans. Compare the amounts of tomatoes and meat.

Solution 1   *Arithmetic:* To make the problem numerical, we choose a specific quantity of beans, say 20 oz. Then we must use

$$\frac{3}{4} \cdot 20 = 15 \text{ oz tomatoes}$$
$$\frac{2}{5} \cdot 20 = 8 \text{ oz meat}$$

Thus there is $\frac{8}{15}$ as much meat as tomatoes. You can see now why we chose 20 oz as the quantity of beans: 20 is divisible by both 4 and 5.

Solution 2   *Algebraic:* Let t, m, b be the number of ounces of tomatoes, meat, and beans, respectively. Then

$$t = \tfrac{3}{4} \cdot b \qquad \text{and} \qquad m = \tfrac{2}{5} \cdot b$$

We want to relate t and m, so we solve one of these equations (say the first) for b and substitute into the other:

$$b = \tfrac{4}{3} \cdot t \;\; \Rightarrow \;\; m = \tfrac{2}{5}\big(\tfrac{4}{3}t\big) = \tfrac{8}{15}t$$

Thus there is $\frac{8}{15}$ as much meat as tomatoes.

Solution 3   *Geometric:* Let the unit square represent the weight of beans. Then the weights (T, B, M) of the ingredients (tomatoes, beans, and meat) are represented as in Figure 7.48. Since we want to compare T with M, we superimpose the horizontal and vertical partition lines, as in Figure 7.49. There is $\frac{8}{15}$ as much meat as tomatoes. ❏

T   B   M

Figure 7.48

T   M

Figure 7.49

EXAMPLE 3   The population of a certain state is $\frac{5}{8}$ urban and $\frac{3}{8}$ rural. If $\frac{1}{4}$ of the urban and $\frac{1}{6}$ of the rural population is under 18, what fraction of the state's population is under 18?

Solution 1 *Arithmetic:* Let's suppose that the total population is 192 (an absurdly low number, but convenient for our purposes—it is the product of the three denominators appearing in the problem). Then the urban population is

$$\tfrac{5}{8} \cdot 192 = 5 \cdot 24 = 120$$

of whom

$$\tfrac{1}{4} \cdot 120 = 30$$

are under 18. The rural population is

$$\tfrac{3}{8} \cdot 192 = 3 \cdot 24 = 72$$

of whom

$$\tfrac{1}{6} \cdot 72 = 12$$

are under 18. Thus the total number of people under 18 is $30 + 12 = 42$. *Answer:* $\frac{42}{192}$, or $\frac{7}{32}$, of the population is under 18.

Solution 2 *Algebraic:* Let n be the total population. Then

Urban: $$\dfrac{5n}{8}$$

Urban under 18: $$\dfrac{1}{4} \cdot \dfrac{5n}{8} = \dfrac{5n}{32}$$

Rural: $$\dfrac{3n}{8}$$

Rural under 18: $$\dfrac{1}{6} \cdot \dfrac{3n}{8} = \dfrac{3n}{48}$$

Total under 18: $$\dfrac{5n}{32} + \dfrac{3n}{48} = \left(\dfrac{5}{32} + \dfrac{3}{48}\right)n = \dfrac{7}{32}n$$

Interpretation: $\frac{7}{32}$ of the population is under 18.

Solution 3 *Geometric:* Let a unit square represent population. Partition it (vertically) to show the urban-rural split, as in Figure 7.50. Now, partition each piece horizontally to show the young-old split, as in Figure 7.51. The fraction of young people is just the sum of the areas of the two rectangles YU and YR, namely,

$$\frac{1}{4} \cdot \frac{5}{8} + \frac{1}{6} \cdot \frac{3}{8} = \frac{5}{32} + \frac{3}{48} = \frac{5}{32} + \frac{1}{16} = \frac{7}{32}$$

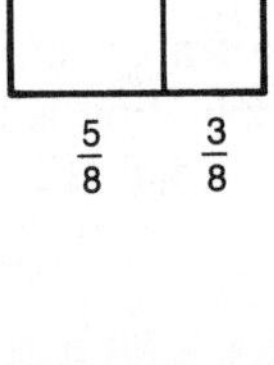

Figure 7.50

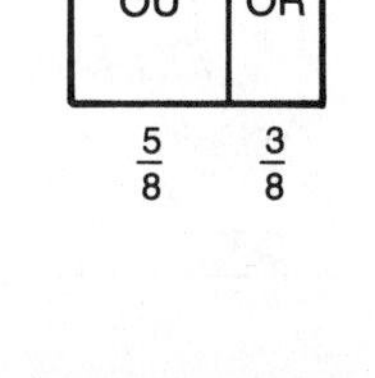

Figure 7.51

Solution 4

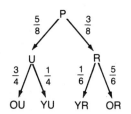

Figure 7.52

Tree diagram: The size comparisons between the various populations and sub-populations in this problem can be represented schematically by a so-called **tree diagram,** as in Figure 7.52. The main rule for using a tree diagram is *multiply down the branches*. For example, to find what fraction of the total population (P) is young rural people (YR), simply multiply down the branches leading from P to YR: $\frac{3}{8} \cdot \frac{1}{6} = \frac{1}{16}$. The rule can be justified by referring to Figure 7.51 or by going back to the connection between multiplication and "of":

$$\text{Number of young rural} = \tfrac{1}{6} \text{ of number of rural}$$

but

$$\text{Number of rural} = \tfrac{3}{8} \text{ of population}$$

Thus

$$\text{Number of young rural} = \tfrac{1}{6} \text{ of } \tfrac{3}{8} \text{ of population}$$

and

$$\tfrac{1}{6} \text{ of } \tfrac{3}{8} = \tfrac{1}{6} \cdot \tfrac{3}{8}$$

To answer the original question (What fraction of the population is young?), multiply down the branches leading to YU and to YR and add:

$$\tfrac{5}{8} \cdot \tfrac{1}{4} + \tfrac{3}{8} \cdot \tfrac{1}{6} = \tfrac{7}{32} \qquad \square$$

The tree diagram in Solution 4 probably seems like a rather sophisticated symbolic device to use, and chances are you preferred one of the other methods. When we study probability, though, tree diagrams will be virtually indispensable. Even now, if we complicate our problem just a bit, the virtues of the method emerge.

EXAMPLE 4

Suppose the population is $\frac{5}{8}$ urban and $\frac{3}{8}$ rural, that $\frac{1}{4}$ of the urban population is young and $\frac{1}{6}$ of the rural population is young, and that $\frac{2}{9}$ of the urban young and $\frac{3}{10}$ of the rural young are enrolled in high school. What fraction of the population is enrolled in high school?

Solution 1

Arithmetic: This method is still possible, but choosing a convenient number for the total population is becoming troublesome.

Solution 2

Algebraic: This method still works.

	Population:	n		
Urban:	$\frac{5}{8}n$		Rural:	$\frac{3}{8}n$
Young urban:	$\frac{1}{4} \cdot \frac{5}{8}n$		Young rural:	$\frac{1}{6} \cdot \frac{3}{8}n$
Young urban HS:	$\frac{2}{9} \cdot \frac{1}{4} \cdot \frac{5}{8}n$		Young rural HS:	$\frac{3}{10} \cdot \frac{1}{6} \cdot \frac{3}{8}n$
Total HS:	$\left(\frac{2}{9} \cdot \frac{1}{4} \cdot \frac{5}{8} + \frac{3}{10} \cdot \frac{1}{6} \cdot \frac{3}{8}\right)n = \cdots$			

Solution 3   *Geometric:* This method is inconvenient. One would probably want to begin with a unit *cube* to represent the population, and then partition it by planes to form various rectangular boxes whose volumes would have to be computed.

Solution 4   *Tree diagram:* See Figure 7.53. *Answer:*

$$\frac{5}{8} \cdot \frac{1}{4} \cdot \frac{2}{9} + \frac{3}{8} \cdot \frac{1}{6} \cdot \frac{3}{10} = \frac{10}{2^5 \cdot 3^2} + \frac{9}{2^5 \cdot 3 \cdot 5} = \frac{50}{2^5 \cdot 3^2 \cdot 5} + \frac{27}{2^5 \cdot 3^2 \cdot 5}$$

$$= \frac{77}{1440} \qquad \square$$

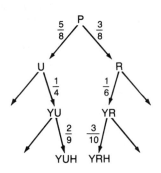

Figure 7.53

Note: Of course, few people nowadays would do the arithmetic we just did with pencil and paper. Use of a calculator would produce a decimal approximation, 0.05347, to the answer. And this decimal would probably be transformed, in turn, into a percent, 5⁺%, to give more meaningful information than our precise answer $\frac{77}{1440}$. It is surely much easier to visualize 5 people among 100 than 77 among 1440.

EXAMPLE 5   The electorate is $\frac{1}{3}$ Democrats, $\frac{1}{4}$ Republicans, $\frac{3}{8}$ Independents, and the rest minor parties. A Democratic candidate figures she can capture $\frac{3}{5}$ of the Independent votes, $\frac{7}{10}$ of the Democrat votes, and none of the minor party votes. What fraction of Republican votes will have to cross over to her if she is to get $\frac{1}{2}$ of the total vote?

Solution   Let x be the unknown fraction. See Figure 7.54.

$$\frac{1}{3} \cdot \frac{7}{10} + \frac{1}{4} \cdot x + \frac{3}{8} \cdot \frac{3}{5} = \frac{1}{2} \quad \Longleftrightarrow$$

$$\frac{x}{4} = \frac{1}{2} - \frac{7}{30} - \frac{9}{40} \quad \Longleftrightarrow$$

$$x = 2 - \frac{28}{30} - \frac{36}{40} = \frac{240 - 112 - 108}{120} = \frac{20}{120} = \frac{1}{6}$$

She will need a crossover vote of $\frac{1}{6}$ of the Republicans. $\qquad \square$

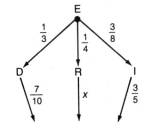

Figure 7.54

Rational Numbers as Operators (Optional)

Attaching rational numbers to arrows as in Figure 7.54 suggests that it might be possible to think of rational numbers as functions. In fact, it is. Rational numbers, like integers, can be viewed as operators as well as states. The rational number $\frac{3}{8}$ in Figure 7.54, for example, can be thought of as an operator (machine, function) that shrinks the input set E to $\frac{3}{8}$ of its original size (see Figure 7.55). The operator labeled $\frac{3}{5}$ then shrinks I to $\frac{3}{5}$ of its size. The composition of the two operators corresponds to the product of their rational number labels. Mathematicians who feel uneasy about having a *word* ("of ") correspond to a mathematical operation (multiplication) are comfortable with this model, which provides a more substantial referent, namely, composition of functions.

In certain kinds of problems it can also be helpful to think of a rational less than 1 as a shrinker and a rational number greater than 1 as a stretcher.

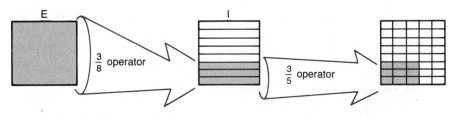

Figure 7.55

EXAMPLE 6   The middleman marks up the wholesale price by $\frac{1}{4}$. The retailer marks up the middleman's price by $\frac{1}{3}$. The salesman marks down the retail price by $\frac{1}{10}$. How does the price the customer pays compare with the original wholesale price?

Solution   Another way of saying that the middleman marks the wholesale price up by $\frac{1}{4}$ is to say that he stretches the wholesale price by a factor of $\frac{5}{4}$. The retailer subjects the middleman's price to a further stretch, this time by a factor of $\frac{4}{3}$. Finally, the salesman shrinks the retail price by a factor of $\frac{9}{10}$. Thus, letting W be wholesale price and C be customer's price, we have

$$W \xrightarrow{\frac{5}{4}} \xrightarrow{\frac{4}{3}} \xrightarrow{\frac{9}{10}} C$$

Since composition of operators corresponds to multiplication of their rational number labels, the diagram telescopes to

$$W \xrightarrow{\frac{5 \cdot 4 \cdot 9}{4 \cdot 3 \cdot 10}} C \quad \text{or} \quad W \xrightarrow{\frac{3}{2}} C$$

Decoding the arrow diagram produces the answer: The customer's price is $1\frac{1}{2}$ times the wholesale price.   ❏

The National Council of Supervisors of Mathematics (NCSM) has enumerated the twelve components of mathematics that they view as essential for the twenty-first century. Under the component "problem solving" they state: "Students should see alternate solutions to problems; they should experience problems with more than a single solution." In the exercises that follow, try to expand your mathematical powers by using a variety of methods.

EXERCISE SET 7.4

1. John is $\frac{4}{5}$ as heavy as his father. His father weighs 180 lb. How much does John weigh?

2. John says he is $\frac{2}{3}$ as tall as his father. If John is 54 in tall, how tall must his father be?

3. If $\frac{3}{4}$ of the strawberry plants from a certain nursery will survive, and if you want 120 good plants, how many should you order?

4. If $\frac{3}{5}$ of the population is eligible to vote, and $\frac{2}{5}$ of the eligible voters actually voted, what fraction of the population actually voted?

5. The class is $\frac{3}{5}$ in-state students and $\frac{2}{5}$ out-of-state students. One-fourth of the in-state students and $\frac{1}{3}$ of the out-of-state students are freshmen.
   (a) Partition and label a unit square to show the four categories of students: in-state freshmen (IF), in-state nonfreshmen (IN), out-of-state freshmen (OF), and out-of-state nonfreshmen (ON).
   (b) In-state nonfreshmen make up what fraction of the class?
   (c) Freshmen make up what fraction of the class?
   (d) What fraction of the freshmen are from out of state?

6. One-fifth of the population is too young to work, and $\frac{1}{4}$ is too old. Of those who are of working age, $\frac{1}{10}$ are unemployed. What fraction of the population is employed?

7. On a cruise ship $\frac{4}{7}$ of the passengers are female, $\frac{1}{6}$ of the males are rich, and $\frac{3}{10}$ of the rich males are young. What fraction of the passengers are old, rich males?

8. Suppose that $\frac{9}{10}$ of all mistakes in a manuscript are corrected in each proofreading. Suppose that a manuscript was proofread twice in succession, but 23 mistakes still escaped notice. How many mistakes were in the manuscript before the first proofreading?

9. At a picnic there are $\frac{2}{3}$ as many boys as adults and $\frac{4}{5}$ as many boys as girls. Compare the number of adults with the number of children.

10. A dealer sells $\frac{2}{5}$ as many trucks as new cars and $\frac{4}{3}$ as many used cars as new cars.
    (a) Compare truck sales with used-car sales.
    (b) Compare truck sales with total car sales.

11. To say that the annual inflation rate is 10% means that everything will cost $\frac{11}{10}$ as much a year from now as it does now. If inflation proceeds at a 10% rate, how much will it cost 3 years from now to buy goods that presently cost $1000? How long do you think it will take before costs double? Check with a calculator.

12. If $\frac{2}{5}$ of the fish in the lake are out of season, and $\frac{3}{4}$ of the fish that are in season are under the legal size limit, what fraction of the fish in the lake are legal to catch?

13. Seven-tenths of the farmers in Cobb County raise only corn; the rest raise only soybeans. Three-fifths of the corn farmers and $\frac{4}{5}$ of the soybean farmers own their own land. What fraction of the farmers in Cobb County own their own land?

14. A sewage treatment plant treats sewage in three stages. At the first stage $\frac{9}{10}$ of the phosphates are removed. At the second stage $\frac{3}{4}$ of the remaining phosphates are removed. At the third stage $\frac{1}{2}$ of the remaining phosphates are removed. What fraction of the phosphates are removed by this three-stage plant?

15. Three-fourths of the students walk to school, and $\frac{2}{3}$ of the rest ride their bikes. What fraction of the students get to school by some way other than walking or biking?

16. Suppose that 3 out of every 10 smokers have a certain disease, while only 1 out of 8 nonsmokers has the disease. If smokers make up $\frac{1}{5}$ of the population, what fraction of the population has the disease?

17. Suppose that gin is $\frac{2}{3}$ alcohol, vermouth is $\frac{1}{6}$ alcohol, and a martini is made with 5 parts of gin and 1 part of vermouth. Alcohol makes up what fraction of a martini?

18. If $\frac{5}{8}$ of the children in Norway are blue-eyed blonds, and $\frac{9}{10}$ of the blond children in Norway have blue eyes, what fraction of the children in Norway are blond?

19. For a pass play to succeed, the quarterback has to have time to throw, the pass has to be accurate, and the receiver has to make the catch. Suppose the quarterback gets sacked on 2 out of every 15 pass plays, that he throws wildly 3 out of 8 throws, and that the receiver drops 2 of every 5 balls thrown to him. What fraction of pass plays succeed?

20. The first stage of a 3-stage rocket fails 1 time in 10. The second stage fails 1 time in 8 (when tested separately). The third stage fails 1 time in 5 (when tested separately). For a successful launching all 3 stages must function properly. What fraction of launchings of this 3-stage rocket are unsuccessful?

21. Suppose that of the adult population $\frac{1}{8}$ are habitual drinkers, $\frac{1}{2}$ are occasional drinkers, and the rest are nondrinkers. Suppose also that $\frac{4}{5}$ of the habitual drinkers, $\frac{3}{8}$ of the occasional drinkers, and $\frac{1}{4}$ of the nondrinkers will eventually be arrested for a traffic violation. What fraction of the adult population will eventually be arrested for a traffic violation?

22. Suppose that $\frac{2}{9}$ of your salary is withheld for taxes, insurance, etc. Suppose further that $\frac{3}{8}$ of your take-home pay is budgeted for food, and that $\frac{1}{6}$ of your food money is spent on junk food. What fraction of your salary goes for wholesome (not junk) food?

23. A farmer raises chickens, ducks, and skunks. There are $\frac{2}{3}$ as many chickens as ducks and $\frac{4}{5}$ as many chickens as skunks. How does the number of skunks compare with the number of fowl?

★ 24. Four out of five criminal cases are misdemeanors. The rest are felonies. Two-thirds of the felony cases are solved, while $\frac{2}{3}$ of all criminal cases go unsolved. What fraction of misdemeanor cases are solved?

25. One-ninth of the people with a certain disease show visible symptoms. One in a hundred people without the disease shows (false) symptoms. One-twenty-fifth of the population shows symptoms. What fraction of the population has the disease?

★ 26. It is estimated that $\frac{1}{1000}$ of the U.S. population is infected with tuberculosis. About $\frac{95}{100}$ of the infected people will test positive on the standard diagnostic test, and about $\frac{2}{100}$ of the uninfected people will also test positive ("false positive"). If everyone were subjected to a tuberculosis test, what fraction of those who tested positive would actually be infected?

7.5 *Ratio and Proportion*

Many of the most common problems involving fractions are expressed in the language of ratio and proportion. The idea behind the word *ratio* is one we have worked with already; we will only need to learn some new terminology. *Proportion*, though, is a new and rather subtle idea that will require some careful analysis.

Ratio

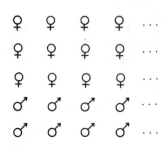

Figure 7.56

There are many different ways of verbalizing size comparisons. About Figure 7.56 we might say the following:

"The number of boys is $\frac{2}{3}$ the number of girls."
"There are $\frac{2}{3}$ as many boys as girls."

"There are 2 boys for every 3 girls."
"The *ratio* of boys to girls is 2 to 3."

All four sentences give exactly the same information, although the images they call to mind are slightly different. The first two, perhaps, suggest viewing the boys and girls as partitioned in Figure 7.57. The last two probably suggest the kind of partitioning shown in Figure 7.58.

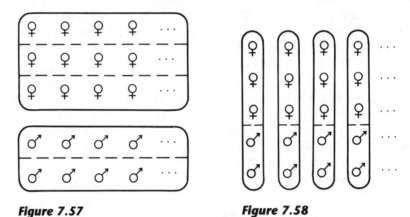

Figure 7.57   **Figure 7.58**

An ancient notation that still survives uses a colon to express a ratio, as in

"The ratio of boys to girls is 2 : 3"

Many modern texts use fractions instead, as in

"The ratio of boys to girls is $\frac{2}{3}$"

to emphasize that ultimately ratios behave like fractions. Mathematically, there is no distinction: a ratio is a fraction. Be warned, though, that the equivocal use of the word *fraction* to mean both ordered pair and rational number is reflected in the use of the word *ratio*. In some contexts the ratios 2 : 3 and 4 : 6 will be viewed as "equivalent" but not really the same, and in others they will be viewed as "equal." The important thing to bear in mind is that what we have are two different *languages,* ratio language and fraction language, for describing size comparisons.

As we noted before, the word *size* in *size comparison* can mean many things: numerosity, length, area, weight, volume, duration, and so on. Usually, one is left to decide from context what meaning is intended. In the following example it is numerosity.

EXAMPLE 1   Refer to Figure 7.59 and give the ratio of the following:
(a) Circles to triangles
(b) Triangles to circles

(c) Circles to squares
(d) Squares to triangles
(e) Circles to polygons

Solution

(a) There are three correct answers: 8 to 4, 4 to 2, 2 to 1. In symbols, $\frac{8}{4}$, $\frac{4}{2}$, or $\frac{2}{1}$ (8 : 4, 4 : 2, or 2 : 1). In this context one does *not* view the ratios 4 : 2 and 6 : 3 as interchangeable.
(b) Again three answers: $\frac{4}{8}$, $\frac{2}{4}$, or $\frac{1}{2}$ (4 : 8, 2 : 4, or 1 : 2).
(c) Two answers: $\frac{8}{6}$ or $\frac{4}{3}$ (8 : 6 or 4 : 3).
(d) Two answers: $\frac{6}{4}$ or $\frac{3}{2}$ (6 : 4 or 3 : 2).
(e) Two answers: $\frac{8}{10}$ or $\frac{4}{5}$ (8 : 10 or 4 : 5).

Many of the size comparisons that we cited in previous sections can be rephrased by using the word *ratio*. The ability to make the translation is prerequisite to using the powerful ratio-proportion problem-solving format that we will study shortly. ❏

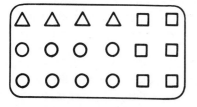

Figure 7.59

EXAMPLE 2

Translate into ratio language:
(a) In an ore sample there is $\frac{3}{8}$ as much iron as waste (by weight).
(b) In a choir there are $\frac{4}{5}$ as many girls as boys.
(c) John is $\frac{2}{3}$ as tall as his father.
(d) Three-fourths of the strawberry plants will survive.
(e) A martini is 5 parts gin and 1 part vermouth (by volume).

Solution

(a) The ratio of iron to waste is 3 to 8 (by weight).
(b) The ratio of girls to boys is 4 to 5.
(c) The ratio of John's height to his father's is 2 to 3.
(d) The ratio of surviving plants to total plants is 3 to 4.
(e) The ratio of gin to vermouth is 5 to 1 (by volume).

Comment: "Success ratios" or "survival ratios," like the one in part (d), are referred to frequently in a variety of everyday contexts. They serve as counterexamples to the often repeated assertion that a ratio must always compare two disjoint sets. ❏

Proportion

The usual definition of proportion that appears in elementary textbooks is the following.

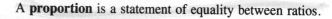

A **proportion** is a statement of equality between ratios.

By this definition

$$\tfrac{6}{21} = \tfrac{8}{28}$$

is an example of a proportion. Alternatively, one might say, then, that a proportion is a statement of equivalence between fractions (or a statement of equality between rational numbers). In practice, one of the fractions will generally involve an unknown numerator or denominator.

EXAMPLE 3   The ratio of moose to wolves is 9 to 2. If there are 40 wolves, how many moose are there?

Solution   Since there are 9 moose for each 2 wolves, there will be 18 moose for each 4 wolves, 27 moose for each 6 wolves, and so forth. That is, the equivalent fractions

$$\tfrac{9}{2}, \tfrac{18}{4}, \tfrac{27}{6}, \ldots$$

compare the same two sets. We are looking for the fraction on this list having 40 as its denominator. Let x be its numerator. The fraction $x/40$ gets on the list if and only if it is equivalent to $\tfrac{9}{2}$. Thus we need to solve the equation

$$\frac{x}{40} = \frac{9}{2}$$

for the unknown x. Multiplying both sides by 40 yields $x = 180$. Or one can think of crisscross multiplying to get $x \cdot 2 = 40 \cdot 9$, and then dividing both sides by 2 to get $x = 180$.   ❏

The formal, stylized procedure for solving a simple ratio-proportion problem like the one in Example 3 consists of four steps:

1. Introduce a variable to represent the unknown quantity:

    Let x equal the number of moose

2. Formulate a statement of equality between ratios:

    9 (moose) is to 2 (wolves) as x (moose) is to 40 (wolves)

    Carrying along the labels, as we have done, makes it less likely that we will mistakenly invert one of the fractions at the next step.

3. Recast the statement into an equation involving fractions:

    $$\frac{9}{2} = \frac{x}{40} \qquad \text{(the constant moose-to-wolves ratio)}$$

4. Solve for the variable. The first step usually employs the crisscross equality criterion for rational numbers, $a/b = c/d$ if and only if $ad = bc$.

    $$\frac{9}{2} = \frac{x}{40}$$
    $$9 \cdot 40 = x \cdot 2$$
    $$x = 180$$

EXAMPLE 4 The ratio of boys to girls is 2 to 3. If there are 12 boys, how many girls are there?

Solution **Step 1** Let x = number of girls.

Step 2 2 (boys) is to 3 (girls) as 12 (boys) is to x (girls)

Step 3 $\dfrac{2}{3} = \dfrac{12}{x}$

Step 4 $2 \cdot x = 3 \cdot 12$

$x = 18$ ❏

Let us analyze Example 4 mathematically to see what further ideas underlie proportion. When we say that there are 2 boys for every 3 girls, we are asserting that this is true no matter how many girls (or boys) there are: if 6 girls, then 4 boys; if 9 girls, then 6 boys; and so on. We can display this numerical relationship in a table, as in Table 7.1, which certainly has all the characteristics of an input-output table for a function.

Table 7.1

Number of Girls	Number of Boys
3	2
6	4
9	6
⋮	⋮

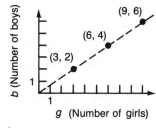

Figure 7.60

When we graph this function in the usual way (Figure 7.60), we see that its points lie on a straight line through the origin.

Deducing a formula that expresses b in terms of g is a simple matter of examining Table 7.1 and observing that each output (b value) is $\frac{2}{3}$ of the corresponding input (g value). Thus a formula for the function is

$$b = \tfrac{2}{3}g$$

This discussion suggests an alternative definition of proportion.

A **proportion** is a function given by a formula of the form $y = mx$, where m is a constant called the *constant of proportionality*.

If we solve for m, we see that it is just the constant ratio of output to input.

Sometimes, functions of the form $y = mx$ are called **direct-variation functions,** and we say that "y varies directly with x." What we have observed here is that the basic idea underlying proportion is precisely that of direct variation. The next example illustrates that there is practical value in thinking about a proportion as a function.

EXAMPLE 5   John can run a mile in 4 min. How far can he run in an hour?

Solution   *Incorrect:*

Let x = number of miles
1 (mile) is to 4 (minutes) as x (miles) is to 60 (minutes)

$$\frac{1}{4} = \frac{x}{60}$$
$$60 = 4 \cdot x$$
$$x = 15$$

Solution   *Correct:* The question cannot be answered. We know enough about human physiology to be certain that no one runs at a constant (high) rate for very long. The graph of distance as a function of time is not a straight line. The problem is not a proportion problem. See Figure 7.61.   ❏

Here are some test questions you can ask to determine whether the function you are dealing with is a proportion (direct variation):

If the input is doubled, does the output double?
If the input is halved, is the output also halved?

EXAMPLE 6   A car traveling along a freeway at a constant speed covers 5 mi in 6 min. At that rate, how far will it go in 2 hr?

Solution   The key phrases here are "at a constant speed" and "at that rate." They assure us that if we double the travel time, the distance traveled will also double. From a function point of view the graph of this distance function is a straight line, like the black one in Figure 7.61. The problem really is a proportion problem and can be solved in a mechanical fashion:

Let x = number of miles
5 (miles) is to 6 (minutes) as x (miles) is to 120 (minutes)

$$\frac{5}{6} = \frac{x}{120}$$
$$5 \cdot 120 = 6 \cdot x$$
$$x = 100$$ ❏

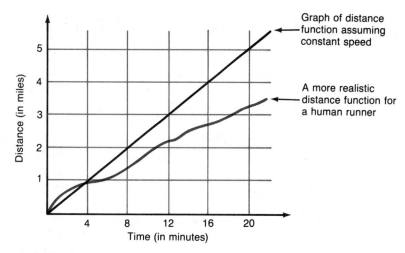

Figure 7.61

EXAMPLE 7   Under a pure flat-rate tax system, one's tax is proportional to one's earnings. Suppose that under this system earnings of $16,000 are assessed a tax of $1760. How much tax is assessed on earnings of $20,000?

Solution 1   *Equating ratios:*

Let x = unknown tax
x (tax) is to 20,000 (earnings) as 1760 (tax) is to 16,000 (earnings)

$$\frac{x}{20,000} = \frac{1760}{16,000}$$
$$16,000x = 20,000 \cdot 1760$$
$$x = 2200$$

Solution 2   *Functional:* We know that tax T varies directly with earnings E; that is, $T = mE$.

Plan:

1. Use the data—when E is $16,000, T is $1760—to find the value of m.
2. Having found m, substitute the value 20,000 for E and compute T.

Details:

1. $T = mE \;\Rightarrow\; m = \dfrac{T}{E} = \dfrac{1760}{16,000} = \dfrac{11}{100}$

2. $T = mE \;\Rightarrow\;$ tax on 20,000 = $\dfrac{11}{100} \cdot 20,000 = 2200$ ❏

1. See if you can add to this list of everyday occurrences of the word *ratio:* white cell–to–red cell ratio in blood, price-to-earnings ratio for a common stock, kill ratio in volleyball (ratio of successful slams to attempted slams).

2. Write the following ratios using both fraction and colon notation.
   (a) The ratio of consonants to vowels in the word *euphoria*
   (b) The ratio of primes to perfect squares among the first ten counting numbers
   (c) The ratio of edges to vertices in a square
   (d) The ratio of edges to vertices in a cube

3. Translate these phrases into ratio language.
   (a) For every 10 pet cats there are 3 homeless ones.
   (b) Ben is $2\frac{1}{2}$ times as heavy as Debbie.
   (c) Jane hits $\frac{2}{3}$ as many home runs as doubles.
   (d) Soda A has $\frac{1}{3}$ less calories than soda B.
   (e) Brand X is half again as expensive as brand Y.
   (f) For every person who cheats on taxes there are 4 who do not.

4. At Johnson Elementary School the ratio of boys to adults is 15 to 2, and the ratio of girls to adults is 20 to 3.
   (a) Are there more boys or more girls? (Decide mentally!)
   (b) What is the ratio of boys to girls?
   (c) What is the ratio of children to adults?

5. If the ratio of men to women is 5 to 6 and the ratio of adults to children is 3 to 2, what is the ratio of children to women?

6. Solve each proportion for x.
   (a) x is to 42 as 3 is to 2
   (b) 120 is to x as 30 is to 28
   (c) $\dfrac{7}{36} = \dfrac{x}{180}$ (d) $\dfrac{15}{40} = \dfrac{9}{x}$
   (e) $\dfrac{9}{x} = \dfrac{x}{25}$ (f) $\dfrac{x}{x+5} = \dfrac{9}{10}$

7. Some of the following problems are proportion problems and some are not. Solve the ones you can.
   (a) If cornflakes are sold at 3 boxes for $1.88. how much will 12 boxes cost?
   (b) In his first 65 official times at bat a baseball player hits 4 home runs. If he can expect to maintain this hitting pace and come to bat officially 585 times during the season, how many home runs can he expect to hit?
   (c) If a puppy weighs 5 lb at 3 months, how much will it weigh at 1 year?
   (d) If 1 in on a map represents 200 mi, how far apart are two cities that are 2 in apart on the map?
   (e) A cookie recipe calls for 2 cups of sugar and $1\frac{1}{4}$ cups of shortening. Sue finds that she has only $1\frac{1}{3}$ cups of sugar and decides to use it all to make a smaller batch. How much shortening should she use?
   (f) If Ed can type 600 words in 15 min, how many can he type in 3 hr?
   (g) Six boys can pick 50 qt of strawberries in a day. A farmer gets an order for 175 qt of strawberries for the next day. How many boys should he hire?
   (h) Annual interest on $5000 in a savings account amounts to $425. How much annual interest would $6000 earn in the same kind of account?
   (i) Tom can eat 2 pancakes in 5 min. How long will it take him to eat 12?
   (j) If 5 girls drink 3 qt of lemonade, how much lemonade can 30 girls be expected to drink?
   (k) If, on the average, your car uses $3\frac{1}{2}$ gal of gas to go 100 mi, how far can you expect to get on a full tank of 13 gal?
   (l) For every $4 that Joe saves, his brother saves $11. How much will Joe have to save if the two boys want to pool their savings to buy a $60 bicycle?

8. In 1988, a Japanese businessman, Hideaki To- moyori, recited from memory the first 40 thou- sand digits of pi. It took him 17 hr and 21 min. In 1989, two mathematicians from Columbia University, David and Gregory Chudnovsky, announced that they had calculated pi to 480 mil- lion decimal places. At Tomoyori's rate, how long would it take (to the nearest year) to recite the Chudnovskys' digits?

9. The initials ERA have different meanings for sports fans and for feminists. A pitcher's ERA (earned-run average) is the number of earned runs he yields per nine innings. What is the ERA of a pitcher who has yielded 32 earned runs in 120 innings? (ERAs are normally stated in deci- mal notation.)

10. If 8 men can chop 9 cords of wood in 6 hr, how many hours will it take 4 men to chop 3 cords? (Assume that the 4 men work at the same steady rate as the 8.)

11. In a simple electric circuit with fixed resistance, the current varies directly with the electromotive force. If an electromotive force of 6 volts (V) in- duces a current of 3 amperes (A), what current will be induced by an electromotive force of 9 V?

12. A spring scale operates on the principle (Hooke's law) that within its elastic limits the amount that a spring is compressed varies directly with the amount of weight placed on it. If a 5-kg weight compresses the spring in Figure 7.62 by 8 cm, how much does an object weigh that compresses it 14 cm?

Figure 7.62

13. On the Instant Cream of Wheat box is this recipe for two servings: $\frac{1}{3}$ cup cereal, $1\frac{1}{2}$ cups milk, $\frac{1}{4}$ tsp salt. No recipe is given for three servings. Write one.

14. The cereal box described in Exercise 13 gives this recipe for four servings: $\frac{2}{3}$ cup cereal, $3\frac{1}{4}$ cup milk, $\frac{1}{2}$ tsp salt. Are the recipes for two and four servings proportional?

15. The mayor wants to hold the cops-to-robbers ra- tio constant at 2 to 25. If an additional 225 rob- bers come to town, how many more cops will have to be hired?

16. In a school system of 2520 students the student- to-teacher ratio is 28 to 1. How many new teach- ers need to be hired to reduce this ratio to 24 to 1?

17. Assume that the number of pheasants p in a county is proportional to the number of acres c planted in corn in that county.
    (a) Fill in the missing entries in Table 7.2.

Table 7.2

c	p
0	☐
90	☐
180	14
☐	21
☐	28

(b) Graph p as a function of c. Use Figure 7.63.

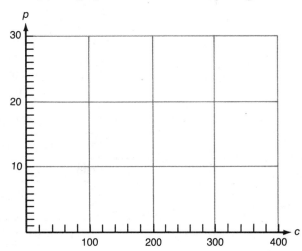

Figure 7.63

18. Why is the function shown in Figure 7.64 not a direct-variation function?

 19. In a pack of less than 50 hounds, the ratio of fleas to hounds is 20 to 3. Another hound joins the pack, and the ratio jumps to 100 to 11. How many fleas did the new hound bring along?

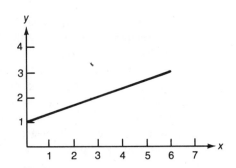

Figure 7.64

7.6 *The System of Rational Numbers: A Formal Approach*

In this section we change our point of view from concrete to abstract. We consciously ignore all area model and number line representations, and we think of the rational numbers as simply elements of an abstract set on which two undefined binary operations, addition and multiplication, act. As in our formal study of whole numbers and integers, we accept a small body of basic properties as axioms, and then we deduce from them all of the usual rules of rational arithmetic. The parallels between this section and the corresponding section (Section 6.3) about integers are striking. You may wish to skim over that section before reading this one.

Basic Assumptions and Definitions

We begin by assuming that there is a set Q, which includes the integers as a subset, and there are two binary operations, $+$ and $\cdot$, on Q. As in any mathematical system, we have the usual logical properties: substitution and the RST properties of equality. The structural properties for the rational numbers are exactly the same as those for integers, with one exception: The cancellation property of multiplication is replaced by the property that each nonzero rational number has a unique reciprocal (multiplicative inverse).

STRUCTURAL PROPERTIES FOR THE RATIONALS

Associative property of addition	Associative property of multiplication
Commutative property of addition	Commutative property of multiplication
Additive property of 0	Multiplicative property of 1
Each rational number has a unique opposite (additive inverse).	Each nonzero rational number has a unique reciprocal (multiplicative inverse).

Distributive property

Four comments are in order. First, remember that when we say addition and multiplication are <u>binary operations</u> we mean, among other things, that Q is *closed* under these operations; that is, sums and products of rational numbers are again rational numbers. Second, when we write "<u>associative property</u> of multiplication" now, we mean that multiplication is an <u>associative operation</u> on the *entire* set of rational numbers, not just on the subset of integers. The same comment applies to the other properties that seem to repeat what we already know about the integers. In particular, every rational number is assumed to have <u>an additive inverse,</u> a plausible assumption if one thinks about antimatter area diagrams or left-pointing vectors. Thus in this section we are studying the *full* set of rationals, including negatives. Third, we need a definition of *reciprocal* for the one new property to have meaning.

Definition. The **reciprocal,** or multiplicative inverse, of r $(r \neq 0)$ is the rational number that multiplies r to give 1. We denote this rational number by $1/r$. Thus

$$\frac{1}{r} \cdot r = 1 \quad \text{and} \quad r \cdot \frac{1}{r} = 1$$

Fourth, observe that the new existence-of-reciprocals property is restricted to nonzero rationals. That is, <u>0 has no multiplicative inverse.</u> The reason for this is rather subtle. To begin with, as we shall soon see, the multiplicative properties of zero remain true in the system of rational numbers. Thus 0 times any rational number is 0. But if 0 had a multiplicative inverse, then 0 times that number would be 1. So it would follow that $0 = 1$. This is absurd. Thus 0 has no multiplicative inverse and the symbol "1/0" is undefined; it represents no number. (*Note:* In a completely rigorous formal description of the rational number system the "obvious fact," $0 \neq 1$, has to be assumed; it cannot be deduced from the nine structural properties we have listed.)

We begin our deductions about the rational number system by establishing, as a theorem, the cancellation property of multiplication that was replaced on the list of structural properties by the new reciprocals property.

Theorem Cancellation property of multiplication: If $r \cdot s = r \cdot t$ and $r \neq 0$, then $s = t$.

Proof Since this is an if-then theorem, we temporarily assume that $r \cdot s = r \cdot t$ and $r \neq 0$. Our goal is to deduce that $s = t$.

1. $r \cdot s = r \cdot t$	assumed
2. $\frac{1}{r} \cdot (r \cdot s) = \frac{1}{r} \cdot (r \cdot t)$	existence of reciprocals, multiplication property of equality
3. $\left(\frac{1}{r} \cdot r\right) \cdot s = \left(\frac{1}{r} \cdot r\right) \cdot t$	associative property of multiplication

4. $1 \cdot s = 1 \cdot t$ definition of reciprocal

5. $s = t$ multiplicative property of 1   Q.E.D.

Since the cancellation property of multiplication has been shown to be true for the system of rational numbers, we now know that all nine of the basic structural properties of the integers remain true in the larger system of rationals. Hence all of the logical consequences of those nine properties must also be true for the rational numbers. In particular, the multiplicative properties of zero mentioned earlier must be true. So we get another theorem without having to prove it.

Theorem

Multiplicative properties of zero:

1. $0 \cdot r = 0$ for any rational number r.
2. If $r \cdot s = 0$,   where r and s are rational numbers, then $r = 0$ or $s = 0$. ❏

Corresponding to the definition of subtraction in I is the definition of **division** in Q.

> If r and s are rational numbers and $s \neq 0$, $r/s = r \cdot 1/s$.

We shall refer to this definition as "definition of division." Notice that division is not quite a binary operation on Q. Only those ordered pairs whose second components are nonzero can be used as inputs:

$$(r, s) \xrightarrow{\div} r \cdot \frac{1}{s} = \frac{r}{s}$$

The output of this division function is generally referred to as a **quotient.** We use the word *quotient* in stating the final limiting assumption that distinguishes the system of rational numbers from the larger system of real numbers.

> Every rational number is a quotient of integers. That is, each rational number can be expressed in the form a/b, where a and b are integers and $b \neq 0$.

Rules of Arithmetic of Fractions

With our now complete list of assumptions and the two key definitions, definition of reciprocal and definition of division, we are in a position to deduce nearly all of the usual rules governing the arithmetic of fractions. We have collected the most common ones into a single theorem. You might find it interesting to compare the first three properties listed in this theorem with the first three listed in the theorem on page 391. These first three properties are the basic ones on which the more familiar last five rest.

Theorem In the following properties r, s, t, and u represent arbitrary rational numbers except that all denominators are assumed to be nonzero.

1. $\dfrac{1}{1/r} = r$ (The reciprocal of the reciprocal of r is r.)

2. $\dfrac{1}{r \cdot s} = \dfrac{1}{r} \cdot \dfrac{1}{s}$ for example, $\dfrac{1}{3 \cdot 2} = \dfrac{1}{3} \cdot \dfrac{1}{2}$

3. $\dfrac{1}{s/r} = \dfrac{r}{s}$ for example, $\dfrac{1}{2/3} = \dfrac{3}{2}$

4. $\dfrac{r \cdot t}{r \cdot s} = \dfrac{t}{s}$ (rule for reducing to lower or raising to higher terms)

5. $\dfrac{r}{s} \cdot \dfrac{t}{u} = \dfrac{r \cdot t}{s \cdot u}$ (rule for multiplying)

6. $\dfrac{r/s}{t/u} = \dfrac{r}{s} \cdot \dfrac{u}{t}$ (rule for dividing)

7. $\left. \begin{aligned} \dfrac{r}{t} + \dfrac{s}{t} &= \dfrac{r + s}{t} \\[2mm] \dfrac{r}{s} + \dfrac{t}{u} &= \dfrac{r \cdot u + s \cdot t}{s \cdot u} \end{aligned} \right\}$ (rules for adding)

8. $\dfrac{r}{s} = \dfrac{t}{u} \iff r \cdot u = s \cdot t$ (crisscross equality criterion)

Proof of 1 $1/r$ has just one reciprocal, and it is denoted by $1/(1/r)$. Thus if we can show that r behaves like a reciprocal of $1/r$, then it *is* $1/(1/r)$. To behave like a reciprocal of $1/r$, r would have to multiply $1/r$ to give 1. But, of course, that is the case: $r \cdot 1/r = 1$, because $1/r$ is the reciprocal of r.

Proof of 2 As in the proof of 1, it suffices to show that $1/r \cdot 1/s$ behaves like a reciprocal of $r \cdot s$. But

$$\dfrac{1}{r} \cdot \dfrac{1}{s} \cdot r \cdot s = \left(\dfrac{1}{r} \cdot r \right) \cdot \left(\dfrac{1}{s} \cdot s \right) \qquad \text{associative and commutative properties of multiplication}$$

$$= 1 \cdot 1 \qquad \text{definition of reciprocals}$$

$$= 1 \qquad \text{multiplicative property of 1}$$

Proofs of 3–7 Proofs of rules 3–7 are outlined in the exercises.

Proof 8 The circle of implications that follows shows that

$$\dfrac{r}{s} = \dfrac{t}{u} \implies r \cdot u = s \cdot t \qquad \text{and} \qquad r \cdot u = s \cdot t \implies \dfrac{r}{s} = \dfrac{t}{u}$$

For the first implication start at 9 o'clock; for the second implication start at 3 o'clock.

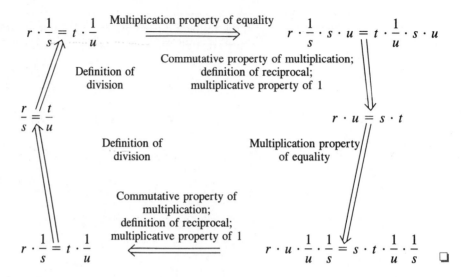

$$r \cdot \frac{1}{s} = t \cdot \frac{1}{u} \xrightarrow{\text{Multiplication property of equality}} r \cdot \frac{1}{s} \cdot s \cdot u = t \cdot \frac{1}{u} \cdot s \cdot u$$

Definition of division

Commutative property of multiplication; definition of reciprocal; multiplicative property of 1

$$\frac{r}{s} = \frac{t}{u}$$

$$r \cdot u = s \cdot t$$

Definition of division

Multiplication property of equality

Commutative property of multiplication; definition of reciprocal; multiplicative property of 1

$$r \cdot \frac{1}{s} = t \cdot \frac{1}{u} \Longleftarrow r \cdot u \cdot \frac{1}{u} \cdot \frac{1}{s} = s \cdot t \cdot \frac{1}{u} \cdot \frac{1}{s}$$

The one common rule that we omitted from the previous theorem was the rule for subtracting. The reason for this omission is that although we defined subtraction in the integers, we have not as yet defined subtraction in the system of rational numbers. That is easy to remedy. We simply define opposites and subtraction for rational numbers exactly as we did for integers.

Definition of Opposites $-r$ is the rational number that adds to r to give 0.

Definition of Subtraction $r - s = r + -s$

Now since all of the structural properties we assumed for I are also true for Q, and since the definitions of opposite and subtraction are identical, we can claim, without having to prove them, all of the rules for minus signs that appear in the theorem on page 315. For example,

$$(-\tfrac{3}{4}) + (-\tfrac{2}{3}) = -(\tfrac{3}{4} + \tfrac{2}{3}) \qquad \text{by part 2 of that theorem}$$
$$(-\tfrac{5}{8}) \cdot (-\tfrac{2}{3}) = \tfrac{5}{8} \cdot \tfrac{2}{3} \qquad \text{by part 6 of that theorem}$$

There are, however, some further properties of minus signs that need to be proved for the rational numbers since they do not correspond to any properties of the integers.

Theorem   1. $-\left(\dfrac{r}{s}\right) = \dfrac{-r}{s} = \dfrac{r}{-s}$ (rule for moving a minus sign in a fraction)

2. $\dfrac{r}{t} - \dfrac{s}{t} = \dfrac{r - s}{t}$

$\dfrac{r}{s} - \dfrac{t}{u} = \dfrac{r \cdot u - s \cdot t}{s \cdot u}$ } (rules for subtracting)

Proof of 1   First we prove that $-r/s = -(r/s)$ by showing that $-r/s$ acts like an additive inverse of r/s and, hence, is $-(r/s)$:

$$\frac{-r}{s} + \frac{r}{s} = \frac{-r + r}{s} \qquad \text{rule for adding fractions}$$

$$= \frac{0}{s} \qquad \text{definition of opposite}$$

$$= 0 \cdot \frac{1}{s} \qquad \text{definition of division}$$

$$= 0 \qquad \text{multiplicative property of 0}$$

Then we prove that $^{-}r/s = r/^{-}s$ by invoking the crisscross equality criterion and the minus-times-minus-is-plus rule.

Proof of 2   We consider first the case of common denominators:

$$\frac{r}{t} - \frac{s}{t} = \frac{r}{t} + -\left(\frac{s}{t}\right) \qquad \text{definition of subtraction}$$

$$= \frac{r}{t} + \frac{-s}{t} \qquad \text{part 1 of this theorem}$$

$$= \frac{r + -s}{t} \qquad \text{rule for adding}$$

$$= \frac{r - s}{t} \qquad \text{definition of subtraction}$$

The case of arbitrary denominators is simple:

$$\frac{r}{s} - \frac{t}{u} = \frac{r \cdot u}{s \cdot u} - \frac{s \cdot t}{s \cdot u} \qquad \text{rule for raising to higher terms}$$

$$= \frac{r \cdot u - s \cdot t}{s \cdot u} \qquad \text{case of common denominators} \qquad \text{Q.E.D.}$$

Rational Numbers and Equations

The following example suggests how the addition and multiplication properties of equality can be combined with the additive and multiplicative inverse properties of rational numbers to solve certain equations. (For a thorough discussion of equations, see Chapter 15.)

EXAMPLE 1   Solve each equation.
(a) $3x - 8 = 19$
(b) $15 + 2x = 1$
(c) $3(7 - 2x) = 1 - x$

Solution   (a) $3x - 8 = 19 \Rightarrow 3x - 8 + 8 = 19 + 8 \overset{?}{\Rightarrow} 3x = 27 \Rightarrow$
$\frac{1}{3}(3x) = \frac{1}{3}(27) \Rightarrow x = 9$ *Check:* $3(9) - 8 \overset{?}{=} 19$ Yes, since
$27 - 8 = 19.$

(b) $15 + 2x = 1 \Rightarrow 2x = {}^-14 \Rightarrow \frac{1}{2}(2x) = \frac{1}{2}({}^-14) \Rightarrow x = {}^-7$
Check: $15 + 2({}^-7) \overset{?}{=} 1$ Yes, since $15 + {}^-14 = 1.$

(c) $3(7 - 2x) = 1 - x \Rightarrow 21 - 6x = 1 - x \Rightarrow 20 = 5x \Rightarrow$
$x = 4$ *Check:* $3(7 - 2 \cdot 4) \overset{?}{=} 1 - 4$ Yes, since $3({}^-1) = {}^-3.$ ❏

EXERCISE SET 7.6

1. Write a fraction to represent each of the following elements of Q.
   (a) The multiplicative inverse of 7
   (b) The number that multiplies 10 to give 1
   (c) The reciprocal of 12
   (d) The solution to the equation $5 \cdot x = 1$
   (e) The product of 3 with the multiplicative inverse of 4
   (f) 8 times the reciprocal of 4

2. Write each of these fractions as the product of a whole number with the reciprocal of a natural number.
   (a) $\frac{2}{3}$ (b) $\frac{8}{5}$ (c) $\frac{6}{3}$
   (d) $\frac{1}{6}$ (e) $\frac{5}{1}$ (f) $\frac{0}{3}$

3. In the system of whole numbers division was defined implicitly as follows: a/b is the solution to the equation $b \cdot \square = a$, if there is one. In the system of rationals, a different, and explicit, definition of division was given.
   (a) Write out that explicit definition of a/b.
   (b) Show that the two definitions of division are consistent by showing that a/b, as you just defined it, is a solution to $b \cdot \square = a$.

4. Use the explicit definition to prove each of the following.
   (a) $\dfrac{0}{b} = 0$
   (b) If $a \neq 0$, then $\dfrac{a}{b} \neq 0$.
   (c) $\dfrac{12}{12} = 1$

5. Assuming that the division button $\boxed{\div}$ on your calculator is broken but that the reciprocal button $\boxed{1/x}$ works, how could you compute 6552 $\div$ 28?

The next five exercises will constitute proofs of rules 3–7 of the major theorem on page 393 once you have supplied the missing reasons.

6. Proof of rule 3: $\dfrac{1}{s/r} = \dfrac{r}{s}$.

$$\frac{1}{s/r} = \frac{1}{s \cdot 1/r} \qquad \rule{3cm}{0.4pt}$$

$$= \frac{1}{s} \cdot \frac{1}{1/r} \qquad \text{rule 2 of the major theorem}$$

$$= \frac{1}{s} \cdot r \qquad \text{rule 1 of the major theorem}$$

$$= r \cdot \frac{1}{s} \qquad \rule{3cm}{0.4pt}$$

$$= \frac{r}{s} \qquad \rule{3cm}{0.4pt}$$

7. Proof of rule 4: rule for reducing or raising.

$$\frac{r \cdot t}{r \cdot s} = r \cdot t \cdot \frac{1}{r \cdot s} \qquad \rule{2.5cm}{0.4pt}$$

$$= r \cdot t \cdot \frac{1}{r} \cdot \frac{1}{s} \qquad \rule{2.5cm}{0.4pt}$$

$$= \left(r \cdot \frac{1}{r}\right) \cdot \left(t \cdot \frac{1}{s}\right) \qquad \rule{2.5cm}{0.4pt}$$

$$= 1 \cdot \left(t \cdot \frac{1}{s} \right)$$ _____

$$= 1 \cdot \frac{t}{s}$$ _____

$$= \frac{t}{s}$$ _____

8. Proof of rule 5: rule for multiplying.

$$\frac{r}{s} \cdot \frac{t}{u} = r \cdot \frac{1}{s} \cdot t \cdot \frac{1}{u}$$ _____

$$= r \cdot t \cdot \frac{1}{s} \cdot \frac{1}{u}$$ _____

$$= r \cdot t \cdot \frac{1}{s \cdot u}$$ _____

$$= \frac{r \cdot t}{s \cdot u}$$ _____

9. Proof of rule 6: rule for dividing.

$$\frac{r/s}{t/u} = \frac{r}{s} \cdot \frac{1}{t/u}$$ _____

$$= \frac{r}{s} \cdot \frac{u}{t}$$ _____

10. Proof of rule 7: rule for adding. First case: common denominators.

$$\frac{r}{t} + \frac{s}{t} = r \cdot \frac{1}{t} + s \cdot \frac{1}{t}$$ _____

$$= (r + s) \cdot \frac{1}{t}$$ _____

$$= \frac{r + s}{t}$$ _____

Second case: arbitrary denominators.

$$\frac{r}{s} + \frac{t}{u} = \frac{r \cdot u}{s \cdot u} + \frac{s \cdot t}{s \cdot u}$$ _____

$$= \frac{r \cdot u + s \cdot t}{s \cdot u}$$ case of common denominators

11. Prove this cancellation rule: $\frac{a}{b} \cdot \frac{b}{c} = \frac{a}{c}$.

12. Write a fraction symbol that translates each of the following as literally as possible.
    (a) The reciprocal of $^-5$
    (b) 3 times the reciprocal of $^-5$
    (c) $^-3$ times the reciprocal of 5
    (d) The additive inverse of (3 times the reciprocal of 5)

13. Replace each expression by a fraction that has a positive integer denominator and is in lowest terms. (Each rational number is represented by exactly one such fraction.)
    (a) $\dfrac{3}{^-4}$
    (b) $\dfrac{^-6}{10}$
    (c) $\dfrac{8}{^-12}$
    (d) $\dfrac{^-15}{^-24}$
    (e) $-\left(\dfrac{9}{30} \right)$
    (f) $-\left(\dfrac{4}{^-14} \right)$
    (g) $-\left(\dfrac{^-10}{35} \right)$
    (h) $-\left(\dfrac{^-6}{^-20} \right)$
    (i) $^-6$

14. Compute.
    (a) $\dfrac{3}{8} - \dfrac{5}{6}$
    (b) $\dfrac{2}{5} + \dfrac{4}{^-3}$
    (c) $\dfrac{^-3}{8} - \dfrac{1}{4}$
    (d) $\dfrac{^-2}{3} \cdot -\left(\dfrac{4}{5} \right)$
    (e) $\dfrac{5}{8} \div \dfrac{^-3}{10}$
    (f) $\dfrac{^-7}{8} \div {}^-2$

15. Solve each equation. Remember to check your solutions.
    (a) $3x + 4 = 25$
    (b) $\frac{1}{4}x + 7 = 10$
    (c) $3 - 2x = 15$
    (d) $4(5 + \frac{1}{3}x) = 12$
    (e) $x - 2 = 5 + \frac{1}{3}x$
    (f) $\dfrac{3}{x} + 6 = 1$
    (g) $7 - \frac{1}{2}(5 - 3x) = x - 2$
    (h) $\frac{1}{2}x - \frac{3}{4} = \frac{5}{6}$
    (i) $\dfrac{x}{x + 1} + 3 = 7$
    (j) $\dfrac{12}{x} = \dfrac{x}{75}$

16. Calculate the moment of the system shown in Figure 7.65. As usual, the unit of weight is the small square.

Figure 7.65

17. The analogy between the integers and the (nonzero) rational numbers is made explicit in the following table, which shows corresponding concepts.

	Integers	**Rationals**
Operation	$+$	$\cdot$
Identity element	0	1
Inverse of element	$-a$ (additive inverse of a)	$\dfrac{1}{a}$ (multiplicative inverse of a)
Inverse operation	$a - b$	$\dfrac{a}{b}$

Beginning with a property of the integers and making replacements from this table, we arrive at a property of the rational numbers.

Example

Property of integers $\quad -(a + b) = -a + -b$

Replacements from table $\qquad\downarrow\qquad\quad\downarrow$

Property of rationals $\quad \dfrac{1}{a \cdot b} = \dfrac{1}{a} \cdot \dfrac{1}{b}$

Conversely, given a property of rational numbers we can make replacements from the table to get a property of integers.

Example

Property of rationals $\qquad \dfrac{a \cdot c}{b \cdot c} = \dfrac{a}{b}$

Replacements from table $\qquad\quad\downarrow\qquad\quad\downarrow$

Property of integers $(a + c) - (b + c) = a - b$

Fill in corresponding properties in this chart.

Property of Integers	Property of Rationals
(a) $a - b = -(b - a)$	
(b) $-(-a) = a$	
(c)	$\dfrac{a}{b} \cdot \dfrac{c}{d} = \dfrac{a \cdot c}{b \cdot d}$
(d)	$\dfrac{a}{b} = \dfrac{c}{d} \Leftrightarrow a \cdot d = b \cdot c$
(e)	$\dfrac{a/b}{c/d} = \dfrac{a}{b} \cdot \dfrac{d}{c}$

18. Our one new structural assumption about the rationals was an existence-uniqueness assumption. We assumed that for any nonzero rational number r, the equation $r \cdot \square = 1$ has precisely one solution. It turns out that uniqueness need not be assumed; it can be proved from existence and the other structural properties. The plan of the proof is to assume that s and t are solutions to $r \cdot \square = 1$ and then to show that $s = t$. Supply a reason at each equal sign in the following proof.
$t = 1 \cdot t = (r \cdot s) \cdot t = (s \cdot r) \cdot t = s \cdot (r \cdot t)$
$= s \cdot 1 = s$

7.7 *Seven-Clock Arithmetic Again (Optional)*

The one strong impression that should remain with you after the details of the preceding careful deductive section have faded from memory is the following.

All of the usual rules for fractions and minus signs are *forced* on us once we make a few (reasonable) assumptions and (natural) definitions.

To clinch this impression, let us return to seven-clock arithmetic.

What should the symbol $\frac{1}{3}$ represent in seven-clock arithmetic? The only reasonable answer is that it should represent the multiplicative inverse of 3. But $5 \cdot 3 = 1$ in seven-clock arithmetic; that is, 5 is the multiplicative inverse of 3. In symbols, $5 = \frac{1}{3}$. Similarly,

$$\frac{1}{2} = 4 \qquad \frac{1}{4} = 2 \qquad \frac{1}{5} = 3 \qquad \frac{1}{6} = 6 \qquad \frac{1}{1} = 1$$

Do you see why? Thus every nonzero seven-clock number has a multiplicative inverse.

The next question is, what should a symbol like $\frac{2}{5}$ represent in seven-clock arithmetic? Again, there is only one reasonable answer: Division ought to be defined in seven-clock arithmetic in the same way that it is defined in rational arithmetic. That is,

$$\frac{2}{5} = 2 \cdot \frac{1}{5}$$

But $\frac{1}{5} = 3$, so

$$\frac{2}{5} = 2 \cdot \frac{1}{5} = 2 \cdot 3 = 6$$

Consider now the situation in seven-clock arithmetic. We have a mathematical system I_7 consisting of a set, $\{0, 1, 2, 3, 4, 5, 6\}$, and two binary operations, addition and multiplication. This system satisfies the same nine structural properties as the rational number system. Furthermore, we have imposed on I_7 verbatim definitions of opposite, subtraction, reciprocal, and division. Thus, if it is true that all of the manipulative rules for fractions and minus signs are inevitable logical consequences of the structural properties and definitions, then it must follow that all of these rules apply equally well to seven-clock arithmetic as they do to rational arithmetic. Consequently, we can use I_7 as a check on our deductions.

EXAMPLE 1

Theory says that $\dfrac{2}{3} \cdot \dfrac{5}{4} = \dfrac{2 \cdot 5}{3 \cdot 4}$.

Testing

$$\frac{2}{3} \cdot \frac{5}{4} = 2 \cdot \frac{1}{3} \cdot 5 \cdot \frac{1}{4} = 2 \cdot 5 \cdot 5 \cdot 2 = 3 \cdot 5 \cdot 2 = 1 \cdot 2 = 2$$

$$\frac{2 \cdot 5}{3 \cdot 4} = \frac{3}{5} = 3 \cdot \frac{1}{5} = 3 \cdot 3 = 2$$

Theory is corroborated. ❏

EXAMPLE 2

Theory says that $-\left(\dfrac{5}{3}\right) = \dfrac{5}{-3}$.

Testing

$$-\left(\frac{5}{3}\right) = -\left(5 \cdot \frac{1}{3}\right) = {}^-(5 \cdot 5) = {}^-4 = 3$$

$$\frac{5}{-3} = \frac{5}{4} = 5 \cdot \frac{1}{4} = 5 \cdot 2 = 3$$

Theory is corroborated. ❏

It would seem then that our deductions were sound.

Any mathematical system satisfying the nine structural properties displayed on page 390 (with $0 \neq 1$) is called a **field.** Thus the system of rational numbers and the system of seven-clock numbers are both fields. The key difference between them is that the system of rationals is an *ordered* field, while the system of seven-clock numbers is not ordered. It is interesting that the common rules of arithmetic that describe the behavior of minus signs and fractions are consequences of the field axioms alone and do not depend on the order-related concepts of negativity or size.

EXERCISE SET 7.7

1. In seven-clock arithmetic, is it most useful to pronounce 1/5 as "one over five," "one-fifth," or "the multiplicative inverse of five"?

2. Write the simplest symbol you can for each of these elements of seven-clock arithmetic.

   (a) $\dfrac{1}{5}$ (b) $\dfrac{1}{2}$ (c) $\dfrac{5}{2}$

   (d) $\dfrac{3}{5}$ (e) $\dfrac{^-2}{3}$ (f) $\dfrac{1}{^-4}$

3. Simplify each of these mixed numerals of seven-clock arithmetic.

   (a) $2\frac{3}{4}$ (b) $1\frac{4}{5}$
   (c) $3\frac{1}{2}$ (d) $^-4\frac{5}{6}$

4. Verify, by simplifying both sides, that each of the following statements is true in seven-clock arithmetic.

   (a) $\dfrac{4 \cdot 5}{4 \cdot 3} = \dfrac{5}{3}$ (b) $\dfrac{3}{4} \cdot \dfrac{2}{5} = \dfrac{3 \cdot 2}{4 \cdot 5}$

   (c) $\dfrac{3/4}{2/5} = \dfrac{3}{4} \cdot \dfrac{5}{2}$ (d) $\dfrac{3}{4} + \dfrac{6}{4} = \dfrac{3 + 6}{4}$

   (e) $\dfrac{2}{3} + \dfrac{1}{5} = \dfrac{2 \cdot 5 + 3 \cdot 1}{3 \cdot 5}$ (f) $\dfrac{^-4}{5} = \dfrac{4}{^-5}$

(g) $-\left(\dfrac{5}{6}\right) = \dfrac{5}{^-6}$ (h) $\dfrac{1}{5} - \dfrac{4}{5} = \dfrac{1 - 4}{5}$

5. Solve each of these I_7 equations by adding the same number to both sides or multiplying both sides by the same number. Check your solution.

   Example

   $2x + 3 = 6 \quad \Rightarrow \quad 2x + 3 + 4 = 6 + 4$
   $\Rightarrow \quad 2x = 3$
   $\Rightarrow \quad 4 \cdot 2x = 4 \cdot 3$
   $\Rightarrow \quad x = 5$

   Check: $2 \cdot 5 + 3 = 3 + 3 = 6$

   (a) $5x + 1 = 4$ (b) $4x - 2 = 3$
   (c) $-5x + 6 = 0$ (d) $3 \cdot (2x + 5) = 4$

6. Solve the equation $3\frac{2}{5} \cdot x = \frac{1}{3}$ in seven-clock arithmetic.

7. Which numbers of ten-clock arithmetic have reciprocals (multiplicative inverses)? Make a Cayley table, using the set of invertible ten-clock numbers and the operation of (ten-clock) multiplication.

7.8 *Order in the System of Rational Numbers*

To complete our description of the rational number system, we must describe the less-than relation, $<$. As in the case of integers, both algebraic and geometric approaches are possible, but now each approach presents some new difficulties.

Algebraic Approach to Order

As soon as one writes down the straightforward definition:

Algebraic Definition of Less-than

$$a < b \quad \text{means} \quad b - a \text{ is positive}$$

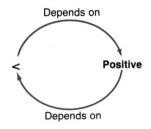

Depends on

Positive

Depends on

Figure 7.66

it is clear that a prior definition of positiveness for rational numbers is needed. And, of course, that prior definition cannot involve the relation $<$ or we would have circularity, as indicated in Figure 7.66. Thus it would not be sufficient to say that a rational number is positive if it is greater than zero.

The way out of this trap is to recall that every rational number can be expressed as a quotient of integers, and to define positiveness for such quotients as follows:

$$\frac{m}{n} \text{ is \textbf{positive}} \quad \text{means} \quad m \cdot n \in N.$$

EXAMPLE 1

$\dfrac{3}{5}$ is positive since $3 \cdot 5 \in N$.

$\dfrac{^-5}{8}$ is not positive since $^-5 \cdot 8 \notin N$.

$\dfrac{^-11}{^-3}$ is positive since $^-11 \cdot {}^-3 \in N$. ❑

EXAMPLE 2   Prove that $\frac{3}{8} < \frac{5}{8}$.

Solution   The following proof was devised by working backwards.

1. $5 - 3 \in N$ arithmetic fact about N
2. $(5 - 3) \cdot 8 \in N$ N is closed under multiplication
3. $\dfrac{5 - 3}{8}$ is positive   definition of positive in Q
4. $\dfrac{5}{8} - \dfrac{3}{8}$ is positive   subtraction rule in Q
5. $\dfrac{3}{8} < \dfrac{5}{8}$ definition of $<$ in Q ❑

The generalization from this example is what you would expect.

> **Numerator Less-than Test for Fractions with Common Positive Denominator**
>
> If a, b, c are integers and c is *positive,* then
>
> $$\frac{a}{c} < \frac{b}{c}$$
>
> if and only if $a < b$.

And the proof of this general result parallels the steps of the proof in Example 2.

EXAMPLE 3   Fill in each circle with $<$ or $>$.

(a) $\dfrac{^{-}5}{9} \bigcirc \dfrac{2}{9}$

(b) $\dfrac{1}{^{-}4} \bigcirc \dfrac{3}{^{-}4}$

(c) $\dfrac{4}{11} \bigcirc \dfrac{3}{8}$

Solution   (a) The two fractions have a positive common denominator, 9. Thus

$$^{-}5 < 2 \quad \Rightarrow \quad \frac{^{-}5}{9} < \frac{2}{9}$$

(b) Replace the given fractions by equivalent ones having a positive common denominator:

$$\frac{1}{^{-}4} = \frac{^{-}1}{4} \quad \text{and} \quad \frac{3}{^{-}4} = \frac{^{-}3}{4}$$

Now

$$^{-}3 < {^{-}1} \quad \Rightarrow \quad \frac{^{-}3}{4} < \frac{^{-}1}{4}$$

Thus

$$\frac{1}{^{-}4} > \frac{3}{^{-}4}$$

(c) Replace the given fractions by equivalent ones having a positive common denominator:

$$\frac{4}{11} = \frac{4 \cdot 8}{11 \cdot 8} \quad \text{and} \quad \frac{3}{8} = \frac{11 \cdot 3}{11 \cdot 8}$$

Now

$$4 \cdot 8 \ (= 32) < 11 \cdot 3 \ (= 33) \quad \Rightarrow \quad \frac{4 \cdot 8}{11 \cdot 8} < \frac{11 \cdot 3}{11 \cdot 8}$$

Thus

$$\frac{4}{11} < \frac{3}{8} \qquad \qquad ❏$$

The generalization of part (c) of the solution is this analog of the crisscross equality criterion.

Crisscross Less-than Criterion for Fractions with Positive Denominators

If a, b, c, d are integers and b and d are *positive*, then

$$\frac{a}{b} < \frac{c}{d}$$

if and only if $a \cdot d < b \cdot c$.

A proof is sketched in the exercises.

It can be shown, though we shall not take the time to do so, that all of the following familiar general order properties are consequences of the algebraic definitions of positivity and less than and the fact that the positive rational numbers are closed under addition and multiplication.

Trichotomy. If r and s are rational numbers, then exactly one of $r < s$, $r = s$, $r > s$ is true.

Transitivity. For rational numbers r, s, and t, if $r < s$ and $s < t$, then $r < t$.

Addition Property of Less Than. For rational numbers r, s, and t: if $r < s$, then $r + t < s + t$.

Multiplication Properties of Less Than. For rational numbers r, s, and t:

1. If $r < s$ and $t > 0$, then $t \cdot r < t \cdot s$.
2. If $r < s$ and $t < 0$, then $t \cdot r > t \cdot s$.

The last two of these properties play major roles in the solution of inequalities, a subject that will be discussed in Chapter 15. The following example gives a flavor of the method.

EXAMPLE 4 Solve the inequality $^-2x - \frac{2}{3} < \frac{4}{5}$. That is, replace it by an equivalent inequality whose solution set is obvious.

Solution 1 The goal is to isolate x on one side:

$$^-2x - \frac{2}{3} < \frac{4}{5}$$

$\Updownarrow$ addition property of less than

$$^-2x - \frac{2}{3} + \frac{2}{3} < \frac{4}{5} + \frac{2}{3}$$

$\Updownarrow$ rational arithmetic

$$^-2x < \frac{22}{15}$$

$\Updownarrow$ multiplication property of less than

$$\frac{^-1}{2}(^-2x) > \frac{^-1}{2}\left(\frac{22}{15}\right)$$

$\Updownarrow$ rational arithmetic

$$x > \frac{^-11}{15}$$

The graph of the solution set is shown in Figure 7.67.

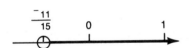

Figure 7.67

Solution 2 If we first multiply both sides of the original inequality by a common multiple of the denominators that appear there, we can clear of fractions and perhaps simplify the arithmetic:

$$^-2x - \frac{2}{3} < \frac{4}{5}$$

$\Updownarrow$ multiplication property of less than

$$15\left(^-2x - \frac{2}{3}\right) < 15 \cdot \frac{4}{5}$$

$\Updownarrow$ distributive property and rational arithmetic

$$^-30x - 10 < 12$$

$\Updownarrow$ addition property of less than

$$^-30x - 10 + 10 < 12 + 10$$

$\Updownarrow$ rational arithmetic

$$^-30x < 22$$

$\Updownarrow$ multiplication property of less than

$$\left(\frac{^-1}{30}\right)(^-30x) > \left(\frac{^-1}{30}\right)(22)$$

$\Updownarrow$ rational arithmetic

$$x > \frac{^-11}{15}$$

❑

Density

The rational numbers do have one new order property that is *not* true of the whole numbers or the integers. In the system of integers 5 and 6 are "right next to each other"; there is no integer strictly between them. In the system of rational numbers there *never* are two adjacent numbers; no matter how close together two rational numbers are, there are *always* more rational numbers strictly between them. We say that the rational numbers are **dense.**

EXAMPLE 5   Find at least one rational number between $\frac{5}{6}$ and $\frac{7}{8}$.

Solution 1   Their average,

$$\frac{\frac{5}{6} + \frac{7}{8}}{2} = \frac{41}{48}$$

is between them.

Solution 2 $\frac{5}{6} \cdot \frac{8}{8} = \frac{40}{48} = \frac{400}{480}$ and $\frac{7}{8} \cdot \frac{6}{6} = \frac{42}{48} = \frac{420}{480}$

All of the 19 numbers $\frac{401}{480}, \frac{402}{480}, \ldots, \frac{419}{480}$ are between them.

Solution 3   By Calculator:

$$\frac{5}{6} = 0.833333 \ldots \qquad \text{and} \qquad \frac{7}{8} = 0.875$$

Each of the 4 numbers 0.84, 0.85, 0.86, and 0.87 is between them. So is each of the 41 numbers 0.834, 0.835, 0.836, . . . , 0.874. You are to accept on faith, for the moment, that these decimals do label rational numbers.   ❏

Geometric Approach to Order

Just as the straightforward algebraic definition of less than didn't quite work, the straightforward geometric definition also presents problems.

> **Geometric Definition of Less Than**
>
> $a < b$ means a is left of b on the number line.

For any pair of *integers* we can easily see which one stands further to the left, but this decision is by no means always obvious for rational numbers. We can see that $\frac{2}{3}$ is left of $\frac{3}{4}$ from the diagram in Figure 7.68. But consider the problem of deciding which of $\frac{7}{8}$ or $\frac{22}{25}$ is further to the left. No amount of careful plotting of points on a line will give a convincing answer to this question. In fact, if an infallible person were to plot points for $\frac{7}{8}$ and $\frac{22}{25}$ using an infinitely sharp compass, the points would be only $\frac{1}{200}$ of a unit apart on the line.

$$0 \qquad \frac{1}{3} \qquad \frac{2}{3} \qquad 1$$

$$\frac{1}{4} \qquad \frac{2}{4} \qquad \frac{3}{4}$$

Figure 7.68

To compare two rational numbers like $\frac{7}{8}$ and $\frac{22}{25}$, one is forced to resort to some sort of algebraic technique. One way is to employ the crisscross less-than criterion:

$$\tfrac{7}{8} < \tfrac{22}{25} \qquad \text{because} \qquad 7 \cdot 25 = 175 < 176 = 8 \cdot 22$$

A second algebraic solution, and the one most people would probably think of first, is to convert both fractions to decimals, either by hand or by calculator:

$$\tfrac{7}{8} = 0.875 \qquad \text{and} \qquad \tfrac{22}{25} = 0.88$$

From the decimal equivalents it is obvious that $\frac{7}{8}$ is the lesser. This solution brings us to the topic of the next chapter, decimals, which is of great practical value and even of some theoretical interest.

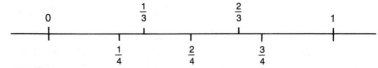

EXERCISE SET 7.8

1. Fill in the correct order symbol for each of the following. Use any technique you please.

   (a) $\dfrac{3}{4} \bigcirc \dfrac{5}{8}$ (b) $\dfrac{2}{9} \bigcirc \dfrac{11}{50}$

   (c) $\dfrac{1}{12} \bigcirc \dfrac{2}{13}$ (d) $\dfrac{1}{75} \bigcirc \dfrac{1}{76}$

   (e) $\dfrac{^-2}{3} \bigcirc \dfrac{1}{10}$ (f) $\dfrac{^-3}{5} \bigcirc \dfrac{7}{^-8}$

   (g) $\dfrac{^-1}{99} \bigcirc \dfrac{^-1}{100}$ (h) $\dfrac{18}{24} \bigcirc \dfrac{^-39}{^-52}$

   (i) $(^-5)^{200} \bigcirc (^-6)^{200}$

   (j) $\left(\dfrac{^-1}{10}\right)^{201} \bigcirc \left(\dfrac{^-1}{11}\right)^{201}$

2. Use the addition and multiplication properties of inequality in solving these inequalities. Graph each solution set on a number line.

   (a) $3x - 2 < 2$ (b) $\frac{2}{3}x + 1 < 6$
   (c) $\frac{3}{8}x + \frac{5}{8} > \frac{7}{8}$ (d) $4 - \frac{2}{3}x < 10$
   (e) $3(4 - \frac{1}{2}x) < 2$ (f) $5 + x < 1 - 2x$
   (g) $^-2 - x \leq 2x$ (h) $^-4 < 3 + 2x < 0$

3. A child writes "$\frac{3}{4} + \frac{2}{3} = \frac{5}{7}$." Explain, using estimation, why the answer $\frac{5}{7}$ does not make sense.

4. Find a rational number strictly between each two rationals given.

   (a) $\dfrac{4}{9}$ and $\dfrac{5}{9}$ (b) $\dfrac{4}{5}$ and $\dfrac{7}{9}$

   (c) $\dfrac{1}{13}$ and $\dfrac{1}{15}$ (d) $\dfrac{^-3}{17}$ and $\dfrac{2}{41}$

   (e) $\dfrac{3}{^-7}$ and $\dfrac{^-7}{17}$

   (f) $\dfrac{a}{b}$ and $\dfrac{c}{d}$, where a, b, c, d are integers

   with $b \neq 0$, $d \neq 0$, and $\dfrac{a}{b} \neq \dfrac{c}{d}$.

5. Supply the missing reason (the name of a familiar order property) in this proof of half of the crisscross criterion for less than: If $a/b < c/d$, where a, b, c, d are integers and b, d are positive, then $ad < bc$.

i. bd is positive since the positive integers are closed under multiplication.

ii. $a/b < c/d \Rightarrow bd(a/b) < bd(c/d)$ by _____ .

iii. But $bd(a/b) = ad$ and $bd(c/d) = bc$ by arithmetic of fractions.

6. Supply missing reasons in this proof of the other half of the crisscross criterion: If a, b, c, d are integers with b and d positive and $ad < bc$, then $a/b < c/d$.

i. Either $a/b < c/d$ or $a/b = c/d$ or $c/d < a/b$ by __(a)__ .

ii. If $a/b = c/d$ then $ad = bc$ by __(b)__ , which would contradict $ad < bc$ by __(c)__ .

iii. If $c/d < a/b$ then $bc < ad$ by __(d)__ , which would contradict $ad < bc$ by __(e)__ .

iv. Thus the only remaining possibility from step (i) is that $a/b < c/d$.

7. Supply missing reasons in the following proof that if

$$\frac{a_1}{b_1} < \frac{a_2}{b_2} \quad \text{and} \quad \frac{c_1}{d_1} < \frac{c_2}{d_2}$$

then $\dfrac{a_1}{b_1} + \dfrac{c_1}{d_1} < \dfrac{a_2}{b_2} + \dfrac{c_2}{d_2}$

i. $\dfrac{a_1}{b_1} < \dfrac{a_2}{b_2} \Rightarrow \dfrac{a_1}{b_1} + \dfrac{c_1}{d_1} < \dfrac{a_2}{b_2} + \dfrac{c_1}{d_1}$ by __(a)__ .

ii. $\dfrac{c_1}{d_1} < \dfrac{c_2}{d_2} \Rightarrow \dfrac{a_2}{b_2} + \dfrac{c_1}{d_1} < \dfrac{a_2}{b_2} + \dfrac{c_2}{d_2}$ by __(b)__ .

iii. Thus $\dfrac{a_1}{b_1} + \dfrac{c_1}{d_1} < \dfrac{a_2}{b_2} + \dfrac{c_2}{d_2}$ by __(c)__ .

8. There are two kinds of blood cholesterol, HDL (high-density lipoprotein) and LDL (low-density lipoprotein). HDL is desirable; LDL is undesirable. One school of medical thought holds that a person is safe as long as the ratio of total cholesterol to HDL is 9 to 2 or less. Is a person safe or at risk for the following ratios?
(a) The ratio of total cholesterol to HDL is 15 to 4.
(b) The ratio of HDL to LDL is 1 to 3.
(c) The ratio of LDL to total cholesterol is 4 to 5.

9. Restate the safety condition in Exercise 8 in terms of the ratio of HDL to LDL.

10. A second school of medical thought contends that the ratio of total cholesterol to HDL must be at most 9 to 2 *and* total cholesterol must be at most 250 mg/ml. What is the greatest amount of LDL one could possibly have and still satisfy these medical guidelines?

11. Joan has been flipping coins and keeping score. Right now the number of heads H exceeds the number of tails T. Will the head-to-tail ratio H/T decline, stay the same, or increase if on the next two flips she gets one more head and one more tail? Generalize.

12. Table 7.3 shows the batting averages of two players versus right-hand pitching and versus left-hand pitching.

Table 7.3

	vs. Right	vs. Left
Casey	.400	.200
Jones	.500	.250

(a) Who do you suppose has the better average overall (versus all kinds of pitching)?
(b) The actual data on Casey and Jones are given in Table 7.4. Verify that these data do yield the four decimals given in Table 7.3.

Table 7.4

	vs. Right		vs. Left	
	at Bats	Hits	at Bats	Hits
Casey	30	12	20	4
Jones	10	5	40	10

(c) Using the data from the table in part (b), compute the batting averages of Casey and Jones versus all kinds of pitching. Who has the better overall average?

(d) Do parts (b) and (c) contradict the order property of rational numbers that

if $\dfrac{a_1}{b_1} < \dfrac{a_2}{b_2}$ and $\dfrac{c_1}{d_1} < \dfrac{c_2}{d_2}$

then $\dfrac{a_1}{b_1} + \dfrac{c_1}{d_1} < \dfrac{a_2}{b_2} + \dfrac{c_2}{d_2}$?

(e) If you were the manager and you knew that you would be facing a left-handed pitcher, which of Casey and Jones would you put in the lineup? What if you knew that the oppos-ing pitcher was right-handed? What if you didn't know which hand he pitched with?

★ 13. This exercise asks for a proof that our definition of positivity does not depend on the particular fraction chosen to represent a given rational number. Suppose that m, n, p, q are integers, that $m/n = p/q$, and that $m \cdot n$ is a positive integer. Prove that $p \cdot q$ must also be positive. Use the fact that a product of two integers is positive if and only if both factors have the same sign.

Key Concepts in Chapter 7

Common fraction
Area model
Equivalent fractions
Rational number
Number line models
Mixed numeral
Algorithms for fractions and mixed numerals
Multiplicative inverse
Tree diagram

Operator
Ratio
Proportion
Direct variation
Structural properties
Field
Order, algebraically
Order, geometrically

❧ *Chapter 7 Review Exercises* ❧

1. Draw an area-model diagram that shows $\frac{2}{3}$ is equivalent to $\frac{6}{9}$.

2. At a certain college there are 7 men for every 5 women. If there are 420 more men than women, what is the total enrollment?

3. At another college there are $\frac{5}{8}$ as many nonresi-dent students as resident students. If residents outnumber nonresidents by 120, what is the total enrollment?

4. Give the measure in square inches of the shaded region in Figure 7.69.

Figure 7.69

5. If the heavy triangle is the unit, what fraction does the shaded region represent? (The dotted line segments trisect the sides of the triangle.)

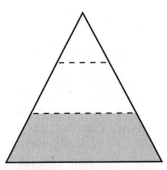

6. Find positive integers a, b, and c so that all three fractions represent the same positive rational number

$\dfrac{a}{25} \quad \dfrac{4}{a} \quad \dfrac{b}{c}$ (lowest terms)

7. Write the arithmetic problem, and answer, suggested by each diagram. The units in both cases are the inch and the square inch.

(a)   (b)

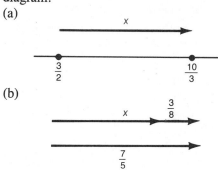

8. On the number line shown, mark the point corresponding to $\frac{5}{2}$. Be as precise as possible.

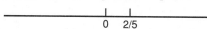

        0 2/5

9. Write, then solve, the equation suggested by each diagram.

(a)

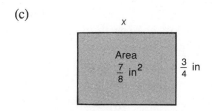

(b)

(c)

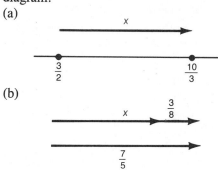

        Area
        $\frac{7}{8}$ in² $\frac{3}{4}$ in

10. If $\frac{4}{7}$ of the class is girls, and if half of the boys and one-third of the girls are absent, what fraction of the class is absent?

11. Calculate each of the following and express your answer as a fraction in lowest terms.

(a) $\frac{9}{10} - \frac{3}{4}$

(b) $\frac{9}{10} \div \frac{3}{4}$

(c) $180 \div 105$

(d) The coordinate of the point $\frac{2}{3}$ of the way from point 2 to point 4 on the number line.

12. Calculate each of the following and express your answer as a mixed numeral.

(a) $2\frac{3}{4} + 3\frac{5}{6}$ (b) $6\frac{1}{3} - 2\frac{7}{8}$

(c) The multiplicative inverse of $\frac{3}{16}$

(d) $1\frac{3}{4} \cdot 1\frac{3}{5}$ (e) $6 \div 2\frac{1}{4}$

13. The distributive property has been used in calculating the product of two mixed numbers:

$$A\tfrac{2}{3} \times B\tfrac{3}{4} = 72 + 4 + 9 + \tfrac{6}{12} = 85\tfrac{1}{2}$$

Find the whole numbers A and B.

14. A strip of paper 12 in wide and 200 ft long is fed through a machine that cuts it into $9\frac{5}{6}$ in (by 12 in) sheets.

(a) How many sheets are produced?

(b) What are the dimensions of the rectangular piece of waste paper at the end of the strip?

15. Suppose that 40% of the registered voters in the United States live in the eastern time zone, that 55% of these easterners are registered Democrats, and that (nationwide) 46% of all registered voters are registered Democrats. What fraction of the registered voters outside the eastern time zone are registered Democrats?

16. An ice cream vendor sells $2\frac{1}{2}$ times as many chocolate cones as vanilla, and $\frac{3}{4}$ as many strawberry cones as chocolate. Compare strawberry and vanilla cone sales.

17. If 3 out of every 100 cars are Ford Mustangs, and if 1 out of every 6 cars is a Ford, what fraction of the Ford cars are Ford Mustangs?

18. The work force at Badger Industries is 24% temporaries and 76% permanent employees. Eighty percent of the permanent employees are considered blue collar and the rest are considered managerial. If 60% of the temporaries, 30% of the permanent blue-collar employees, and 40% of the permanent managerial workers are women, what percent of the work force at Badger is women?

19. Inspectors are to be hired to stand side by side next to a conveyor belt carrying widgets from the

factory to the shipping department. Is it more economical to hire 2 excellent inspectors, each of whom will spot 9 out of every 10 defective widgets, at $9.00 per hour apiece, or 3 average inspectors, each of whom will spot 4 out of every 5 defective widgets, at $6 per hour apiece?

20. The IRS plans to sort tax returns into two categories, "plausible" and "suspicious." Then, in a random way, they will audit 1 of every 20 "plausible" returns and 1 of every 3 "suspicious" returns. If they have sufficient staff to audit only 10% of all returns, what fraction should they sort into the "suspicious" category?

21. If profit is proportional to sales, and if sales of $12,000 resulted in profits of $1500, how much profit will result from sales of $20,000?

22. Suppose that the duration of a meeting varies directly with the number of people in attendance. Last week 15 people were at the meeting. This week 18 people were at the meeting and it ran 10 min longer than last week's meeting. How long did last week's meeting run?

23. Does the area of a square vary directly with side length?

24. At 7:30 the hour hand is ahead of the minute hand; at 7:45 the minute hand is ahead of the hour hand. Which hand is ahead at 7:38?

25. State the one structural property that distinguishes the system of rational numbers from the system of integers.

26. Write the lowest terms fraction for this number: "The reciprocal of the opposite of the product of $\frac{3}{4}$ with the multiplicative inverse of the additive inverse of $\frac{1}{2}$."

27. Supply one main reason for each step in this proof that $\frac{x}{y} \cdot \frac{y}{z} = \frac{x}{z}$ where $x, y, z \in Q$ and $y, z \neq 0$.

$$\frac{x}{y} \cdot \frac{y}{z} = \left(x \cdot \frac{1}{y} \right) \cdot \left(y \cdot \frac{1}{z} \right) \qquad \underline{\hspace{2cm}} \text{(a)}$$

$$= x \cdot \left(\frac{1}{y} \cdot y \right) \cdot \frac{1}{z} \qquad \underline{\hspace{2cm}} \text{(b)}$$

$$= x \cdot 1 \cdot \frac{1}{z} \qquad \underline{\hspace{2cm}} \text{(c)}$$

$$= x \cdot \frac{1}{z} \qquad \underline{\hspace{2cm}} \text{(d)}$$

$$= \frac{x}{z} \qquad \underline{\hspace{2cm}} \text{(e)}$$

28. State the property of integers under addition that "corresponds" to the multiplication property of rational numbers stated in Exercise 27 above.

29. Assuming the basic structural properties of the rational number system and the extra property

$$(*) \qquad \frac{1}{u} \cdot \frac{1}{v} = \frac{1}{u \cdot v}$$

write a proof, with reasons, of the multiplication rule

$$\frac{a}{b} \cdot \frac{c}{d} = \frac{a \cdot c}{b \cdot d}$$

* 30. In seven-clock arithmetic, find the additive inverse of the multiplicative inverse of 4.

* 31. Write each of these expressions from seven-clock arithmetic in simplest form.
(a) $\frac{1}{3}$ (b) $\frac{3}{4}$ (c) $4\frac{2}{3}$

* 32. Solve the equation

$$\frac{4(x + 2)}{5} = 3$$

in the following fields:
(a) The field Q of rational numbers
(b) The field of seven-clock numbers

33. In the past three weeks the price of a certain stock fell $2\frac{5}{8}$, rose $1\frac{3}{4}$, then fell $3\frac{1}{2}$. Over that time period it lost one-fourth of its value. What was its price three weeks ago?

34. Fill in the correct order symbol.
(a) $\frac{13}{14} \bigcirc \frac{15}{16}$ (b) $\frac{-3}{7} \bigcirc \frac{-3}{8}$
(c) $\left(\frac{3}{4}\right)^{800} \bigcirc \left(\frac{3}{4}\right)^{801}$ (d) $\left(\frac{-22}{10}\right)^{801} \bigcirc \left(\frac{-23}{10}\right)^{801}$

35. Find integers a, b, c, and d for which $\frac{a}{b} < \frac{c}{d}$ but $a \cdot d \not< b \cdot c$.

36. Find a rational number between $\frac{7}{8}$ and $\frac{8}{9}$.

37. Find the solution set in Q of the inequality

$$2\left(3 - \frac{3x}{4} \right) < 6$$

References

Arithmetic Teacher. Focus Issue—"Rational Numbers." vol. 31, no. 6, February 1984.

Arithmetic Teacher. Focus Issue—"Number Sense." vol. 36, no. 6, February 1989.

Fehr, H., and T. Hill. *Contemporary Mathematics for Elementary Teachers*. Boston: Heath, 1966.

National Council of Teachers of Mathematics. *37th Yearbook: Mathematics Learning in Early Childhood*. Reston, Va.: NCTM, 1975.

————. *1978 Yearbook: Developing Computational Skills*. Reston, Va.: NCTM, 1978.

Williams, E., and H. Shuard. *Elementary Mathematics Today: A Resource for Teachers, Grades 1–8*. Menlo Park, Calif.: Addison-Wesley, 1970.

DECIMALS AND REAL NUMBERS

Decimal notation is of enormous practical importance. Virtually all of the numerical information we encounter is expressed in the language of decimals or in the closely allied languages of percent and scientific notation. The data in the social and medical sciences, the physical constants that appear in engineering and the natural sciences, the various price indices reported in business and finance, even the batting averages on the sports page—all are in decimal notation. To function in our society, one must understand decimals.

Two modern developments promise to give even greater importance to decimal and scientific notation in the future. One is the increasing use of the metric system. The other is the emergence of calculators, which receive their input in these notations and, with a few exceptions, do not give output in any other form. Decimals also have theoretical and pedagogical value as a bridge from the relatively concrete rational numbers to the more abstract real numbers.

The simplest kind of decimals (terminating decimals) are just new symbols for certain familiar rational numbers, namely, those that can be expressed by fractions with denominators 1, 10, 100, 1000, ... In the first section of this chapter we take that elementary-school point of view and use it to develop the basic algorithms for terminating decimals. In the second section we investigate the two close relatives of decimal notation, percent and scientific notation, which are so common in applications. In the third (optional) section, one area of applications, simple and compound interest, is studied in detail. In the fourth section we explore the connection between rational numbers and terminating and repeating infinite decimals. Real numbers are introduced in the final section as the numbers represented by all decimals—terminating, repeating infinite, and nonrepeating infinite. Examples of commonly occurring irrational numbers are presented, with special emphasis on square roots. Algorithms for approximating square roots by terminating decimals are also described.

8.1 *Terminating Decimals*

Howard Eves, an eminent contemporary mathematics historian, lists the four great laborsaving inventions in mathematics as the Hindu-Arabic numeration system, decimals, logarithms, and computing machines. While no one person is given credit for inventing decimals, Simon Stevin (1548–1620) is usually considered to be the chief expositor of the new idea. In this section we will see why decimals are so important, but first we need some definitions.

Definitions

To arrive at a precise meaning for the word *decimal,* let us begin by considering how it is commonly used. Everyone agrees that ".75" is a decimal, but scarcely anyone would state that "$\frac{3}{4}$" is a decimal. Yet ".75" and "$\frac{3}{4}$" name the same number. Thus the word *decimal* must refer to a symbol for a number, not the number itself.

Now, what about these symbols?

.274274274 . . .　　　and　　　1.011011101111011111 . . .

They are like .75 because they have a decimal point, but they are unlike .75 because they do not terminate. The ellipsis marks indicate that there is no end to the digits. Such symbols are referred to as **infinite decimals.** We shall study them thoroughly in Section 8.4. In this section we restrict the discussion to terminating decimals, the first kind of decimals that youngsters encounter.

An important fact to keep in mind is that terminating decimals are *not* some new kind of numbers. They are just new numerals for familiar numbers, namely those rational numbers that can be expressed by fractions with numerators that are integers and denominators that are whole number powers of ten, the **decimal fractions.**

> **Decimal Fraction Definition of Terminating Decimals**
>
> Given a decimal fraction, the equivalent terminating decimal numeral is just the numerator of that fraction, except that it contains a dot called a **decimal point.** The number of digits to the right of that decimal point, referred to as the number of **decimal places,** corresponds to the exponent of 10 in the denominator of the decimal fraction.

EXAMPLE 1　　Write each decimal fraction as a (terminating) decimal.

(a) $\dfrac{475}{10^2}$　　　　(b) $\dfrac{208}{1000}$

(c) $\dfrac{12}{10,000}$　　　　(d) $\dfrac{17}{10^0}$

Solution   (a) In the denominator the exponent on 10 is 2. Thus after copying the numerator, we should position the decimal point so that there are 2 decimal places:

$$\frac{475}{10^2} = 4.75$$

(b) If we write the denominator as a power of ten, $1000 = 10^3$, we see that the corresponding decimal must have 3 decimal places:

$$\frac{208}{1000} = \frac{208}{10^3} = .208$$

Children arrive at the same conclusion by counting zeros in the denominator rather than converting to exponential notation. A completely mechanical technique that accomplishes the same thing involves lining up the digits of the numerator and the denominator from right to left and then positioning the decimal point so that all digits that stand over zeros appear to its right:

$$\frac{208}{1000} = \frac{208}{1 \, | \, 000} = .208$$

(c) Since $12/10{,}000 = 12/10^4$, we need four decimal places in the corresponding decimal numeral. The way to get them is to rewrite the numerator as 0012. Mechanically,

$$\frac{12}{10{,}000} = \frac{0012}{1 \, | \, 0{,}000} = .0012$$

(d) We have

$$\frac{17}{10^0} = \frac{17}{1} = 17$$

which could be written "17." but almost never is.   ❏

EXAMPLE 2   Write each decimal as a decimal fraction.
(a) 128.63   (b) .0005

Solution   (a) 128.63 has two decimal places. Thus the corresponding decimal fraction is $12{,}863/10^2$. Mechanically,

$$128.63 = \frac{128 \, | \, 63}{1 \, | \, 00} = \frac{12{,}863}{100}$$

(b) .0005 has four decimal places. Thus the corresponding decimal fraction is $0005/10^4 = 5/10^4$. Mechanically,

$$.0005 = \frac{0005}{1 \, | \, 0000} = \frac{5}{10{,}000}$$ ❏

Notice that the property, number of decimal places, is a property of numerals, not of numbers, since a given number can be represented by decimals showing various numbers of decimal places:

$$29.1 = 29.10 = 29.100 = \ldots$$

The corresponding decimal fractions are

$$\frac{291}{10} = \frac{2910}{100} = \frac{29100}{1000} = \ldots$$

A second definition of (terminating) decimals, equivalent to the decimal fraction definition, is a natural extension of the expanded-form definition of base-ten whole number numerals. All of the following are instances of this second definition, which we shall call the **expanded-form definition** of decimals:

$$37.842 = 3 \cdot 10 + 7 + 8 \cdot \frac{1}{10} + 4 \cdot \frac{1}{10^2} + 2 \cdot \frac{1}{10^3}$$

$$= 3 \cdot 10 + 7 + \frac{8}{10} + \frac{4}{100} + \frac{2}{1000}$$

$$507.08 = 5 \cdot 10^2 + 0 \cdot 10 + 7 + 0 \cdot \frac{1}{10} + 8 \cdot \frac{1}{10^2}$$

$$= 5 \cdot 100 + 0 \cdot 10 + 7 + \frac{0}{10} + \frac{8}{100}$$

$$.0049 = 0 \cdot \frac{1}{10} + 0 \cdot \frac{1}{10^2} + 4 \cdot \frac{1}{10^3} + 9 \cdot \frac{1}{10^4}$$

$$= \frac{0}{10} + \frac{0}{100} + \frac{4}{1000} + \frac{9}{10,000}$$

The expanded-form definition underlies the usual method of introducing young children to decimals (see Figure 8.1). The following example illustrates the equivalence of the two definitions.

EXAMPLE 3   (a) Write $\frac{5307}{100}$ in expanded form.
(b) Write $8 \cdot 10^2 + 0 \cdot 10 + 6 + \frac{5}{10}$ as a decimal fraction.

Solution   (a) $\dfrac{5307}{100} = \dfrac{5 \cdot 10^3 + 3 \cdot 10^2 + 0 \cdot 10 + 7}{10^2}$ expanded form (of numerator)

$$= \frac{5 \cdot 10^3}{10^2} + \frac{3 \cdot 10^2}{10^2} + \frac{0 \cdot 10}{10^2} + \frac{7}{10^2} \quad \begin{array}{l}\text{rule for adding fractions with}\\ \text{a common denominator}\end{array}$$

$$= \frac{5 \cdot 10 \cdot 10^2}{10^2} + \frac{3 \cdot 10^2}{10^2} + \frac{0 \cdot 10}{10 \cdot 10} + \frac{7}{10^2} \quad \text{exponents}$$

$$= 5 \cdot 10 + 3 + \frac{0}{10} + \frac{7}{10^2} \quad \text{rule for reducing fractions}$$

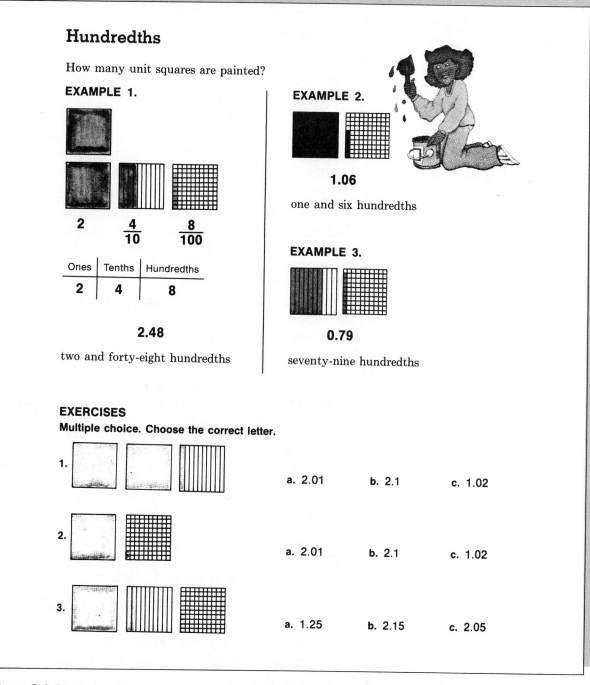

Hundredths

How many unit squares are painted?

EXAMPLE 1.

2 $\dfrac{4}{10}$ $\dfrac{8}{100}$

Ones	Tenths	Hundredths
2	4	8

2.48

two and forty-eight hundredths

EXAMPLE 2.

1.06

one and six hundredths

EXAMPLE 3.

0.79

seventy-nine hundredths

EXERCISES
Multiple choice. Choose the correct letter.

1.

a. 2.01   b. 2.1   c. 1.02

2.

a. 2.01   b. 2.1   c. 1.02

3.

a. 1.25   b. 2.15   c. 2.05

Figure 8.1 Representation of decimals in a fourth-grade textbook.

(b) $8 \cdot 10^2 + 0 \cdot 10 + 6 + \dfrac{5}{10}$

$$= \frac{8 \cdot 10^2 \cdot 10}{10} + \frac{0 \cdot 10 \cdot 10}{10} + \frac{6 \cdot 10}{10} + \frac{5}{10} \qquad \begin{array}{l} \text{rule for raising} \\ \text{fractions to higher} \\ \text{terms} \end{array}$$

$$= \frac{8 \cdot 10^3}{10} + \frac{0 \cdot 10^2}{10} + \frac{6 \cdot 10}{10} + \frac{5}{10} \qquad \text{exponents}$$

$$= \frac{8 \cdot 10^3 + 0 \cdot 10^2 + 6 \cdot 10 + 5}{10} \qquad \begin{array}{l} \text{rule for adding fractions with} \\ \text{a common denominator} \end{array}$$

$$= \frac{8065}{10} \qquad \begin{array}{l} \text{expanded form} \\ \text{(of numerator)} \end{array} \qquad ❏$$

When we *talk* about decimals we tend to adhere to neither definition but, rather, to take a mixed-numeral point of view. Thus we read "27.635" as "twenty-seven *and* six hundred thirty-five thousandths" rather than as either "twenty-seven thousand six hundred thirty-five thousandths" or "two tens plus seven units plus six-tenths plus three-hundredths plus five-thousandths." The decimal point is pronounced as *and* or as *point*.

EXAMPLE 4   (a) Pronounce 500.03.
(b) Symbolize "twelve and seventeen thousandths."

Solution   (a) "Five hundred and three hundredths" or "five zero zero point zero three."
(b) 12.017   ❏

As you worked through the preceding definitions and examples, the following question might have crossed your mind: Since decimals are just new labels on certain special rational numbers, and since we already have a set of labels (lowest-terms fractions with positive denominators) in one-to-one correspondence with all of the rational numbers, why were decimals invented? The answer goes back to Professor Eves's view of decimals as an ingenious labor-saving device: Decimals are important because they are so much easier to work with than fractions.

We caught a glimpse of their computational virtue in Section 7.8, where the order relation on the rational numbers was examined. There we noted that to answer the question

Which is greater, $\frac{7}{8}$ or $\frac{22}{25}$?

requires some calculation. But the same question phrased in terms of decimal equivalents,

Which is greater, .875 or .88?

can be answered by inspection, because the transition to common denominators can be carried out mentally:

$$.88 = .880 = \tfrac{880}{1000} > \tfrac{875}{1000} = .875$$

We also noted that decimal notation is very convenient for finding a rational number between any two given rationals. Using the same example, we see that .876 is obviously between $\frac{7}{8}$ and $\frac{22}{25}$ since $\frac{7}{8} = .875$ and $\frac{22}{25} = .880$.

While decimal notation is convenient in questions of order, its laborsaving qualities really stand out when we investigate the arithmetic operations. The addition, subtraction, multiplication, and division algorithms for decimals turn out to be nearly as easy to perform as the corresponding algorithms for whole numbers, and they are much easier than the corresponding algorithms for fractions.

Algorithms

The algorithm for adding decimals can be thought of as a three-step process:

1. Line up decimal points. (Append zeros if necessary.)
2. Add, ignoring decimal points.
3. Insert a decimal point in the sum directly below those in the summands.

EXAMPLE 5

$$3.175 + 21.4 \rightarrow \begin{array}{r} 3.175 \\ + 21.400 \\ \hline \downarrow \\ 24.575 \end{array}$$

Observe that the first and third steps of the algorithm are trivial, and the second is a whole number subroutine. Thus it is just about as easy to add decimals as it is to add whole numbers.

An explanation of *why* the algorithm works can be given in statement-reason form. The small numbers over the equal signs correspond to the steps in the algorithm.

$$3.175 + 21.4 = \frac{3175}{1000} + \frac{214}{10} \qquad \text{decimal fraction definition of decimals}$$

$$\overset{1}{=} \frac{3175}{1000} + \frac{21400}{1000} \qquad \text{raising a fraction to higher terms} \left(\frac{a}{b} = \frac{a \cdot 100}{b \cdot 100} \right)$$

$$= \frac{3175 + 21400}{1000} \qquad \text{adding fractions with a common denominator}$$

$$\overset{2}{=} \frac{24575}{1000} \qquad \text{adding whole numbers}$$

$$\overset{3}{=} 24.575 \qquad \text{decimal fraction definition of decimals}$$

The algorithm can also be justified by using the expanded-form definition of decimals:

$$3.175 + 21.4 = (3 + \tfrac{1}{10} + \tfrac{7}{100} + \tfrac{5}{1000}) + (2 \cdot 10 + 1 + \tfrac{4}{10})$$

expanded-form definition of decimals

$$= 2 \cdot 10 + (3 + 1) + (\tfrac{1}{10} + \tfrac{4}{10}) + \tfrac{7}{100} + \tfrac{5}{1000}$$

commutative and associative properties of addition

$$= 2 \cdot 10 + 4 + \tfrac{5}{10} + \tfrac{7}{100} + \tfrac{5}{1000}$$ addition of whole numbers and of fractions with a common denominator

$$= 24.575$$ expanded-form definition of decimals ❏

The algorithm for subtracting decimals is essentially the same as the addition algorithm:

1. Line up decimal points, appending zeros if necessary.
2. Subtract, ignoring decimal points.
3. Insert a decimal point in the difference directly below those in the minuend and subtrahend.

EXAMPLE 6

$$15.4 - 6.73 \rightarrow \quad \begin{array}{r} 15.40 \\ -\ \ 6.73 \\ \hline \downarrow \\ 8.67 \end{array}$$

The explanation of *why* this algorithm works is also essentially the same as the explanation for addition and is left to the exercises.   ❏

Before moving on to multiplication and division, we reemphasize two obvious facts. First, when introducing decimals, one reverts to fractions to show why the decimals behave as they do. This is the standard problem-solving strategy of translating a new problem into a familiar one that we already know how to solve and then translating the answer back:

Second, once the computational virtues of decimals have been recognized, the correspondence between decimals and fractions is exploited in the reverse direction:

The multiplication algorithm for decimals likewise involves three steps:

1. Multiply, ignoring decimal points.
2. Add up the number of decimal places in the factors.
3. Insert a decimal point in the product so that

$$
\begin{bmatrix} \text{Number of} \\ \text{decimal places} \\ \text{in product} \end{bmatrix} = \begin{bmatrix} \text{number of} \\ \text{decimal places} \\ \text{in first factor} \end{bmatrix} + \begin{bmatrix} \text{number of} \\ \text{decimal places} \\ \text{in second factor} \end{bmatrix}
$$

Notice, again, that two of these steps are trivial. Only step 1 involves any effort. That is, multiplying two decimals is just about as easy as multiplying two whole numbers. For example,

$$
\begin{array}{r}
1.751 \\
\times\ 2.34 \\
\hline
7004 \\
5253 \\
3502 \\
\hline
4.09734
\end{array}
$$

$\quad$ (3 decimal places)
$\quad$ (2 decimal places)

$\quad$ (5 decimal places)

An explanation of why the algorithm works relies on properties of fractions. As before, the small numbers over the equal signs refer to the steps in the algorithm:

$$
1.751 \times 2.34 = \frac{1751}{1000} \times \frac{234}{100} \qquad \text{decimal fraction definition of decimals}
$$

$$
= \frac{1751 \times 234}{1000 \times 100} \qquad \text{rule for multiplying fractions}
$$

$$
\overset{1,2}{=} \frac{409{,}734}{100{,}000} \qquad \text{multiplying whole numbers}
$$

$$
\overset{3}{=} 4.09734 \qquad \text{decimal fraction definition of decimals}
$$

For certain special products a fourth step is included in the algorithm:

4. Drop terminal zeros to the right of the decimal point.

For example,
$$
.5 \times .4 \x;\overset{\text{steps 1, 2, 3}}{=\!=\!=\!=}\; .20 \;\overset{\text{step 4}}{=\!=\!=\!=}\; .2
$$

Division of decimals is more difficult to describe, for the following reason: Dividing one decimal fraction by another doesn't always result in another decimal fraction. For example,

$$
\tfrac{2}{10} \div \tfrac{3}{10} = \tfrac{2}{10} \cdot \tfrac{10}{3} = \tfrac{2}{3}
$$

and $\tfrac{2}{3}$ is not equal to any decimal fraction (as we shall soon see). In careful mathematical language: Even though the set of all nonzero rational numbers is closed with respect to division, the subset of nonzero rational numbers that can be expressed by decimal fractions is not.

We begin our investigation of the division algorithm for decimals with a simple problem for which the quotient *is* a decimal: Find $10.92595 \div 2.65$. The usual algorithm is as follows. Set up the calculation in the usual whole number format.

$$2.65\overline{)10.92595}$$

Move the decimal point in the divisor just enough places to the right so that the new divisor is a whole number, and move the decimal point in the dividend the same number of places to the right:

$$2.65\ \overline{)10.92\ 595}$$

Divide as usual, and insert the decimal point in the quotient directly above the decimal point in the (new) dividend:

$$
\begin{array}{r}
4.123 \\
265\overline{)1092.595} \\
1060 \\
\hline
325 \\
265 \\
\hline
609 \\
530 \\
\hline
795 \\
795 \\
\hline
0
\end{array}
$$

To see why this algorithm works, we note that the answer has to check. That is, we must have

$$\text{Quotient} \times \text{divisor} = \text{dividend}$$

By what we know about multiplication of decimals, (and because no terminal zeros occur) this equation implies that

$$\begin{bmatrix}\text{Number of decimal} \\ \text{places in quotient}\end{bmatrix} + \begin{bmatrix}\text{number of decimal} \\ \text{places in divisor}\end{bmatrix} = \begin{bmatrix}\text{number of decimal} \\ \text{places in dividend}\end{bmatrix}$$

That is,

$$\begin{bmatrix}\text{Number of decimal} \\ \text{places in quotient}\end{bmatrix} = \begin{bmatrix}\text{number of decimal} \\ \text{places in dividend}\end{bmatrix} - \begin{bmatrix}\text{number of decimal} \\ \text{places in divisor}\end{bmatrix}$$

In other words, to find the number of decimal places in the quotient, one must diminish the number of decimal places in the dividend by the number in the divisor. But this is exactly what is accomplished by sliding decimal points over and up:

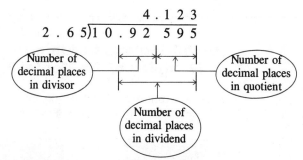

In some other problems, one may have to append zeros to the dividend to make the division come out even.

EXAMPLE 7   Find $1 \div 62.5$

Solution

$$
\begin{array}{r}
.016 \\
62.5\,\overline{)1.0000} \\
625 \\
\hline
3750 \\
3750 \\
\hline
0
\end{array}
$$

□

In general, however, it may be impossible to append enough zeros because the quotient can fail to be a terminating decimal.

EXAMPLE 8   Find $2 \div 3$.

Attempt at a Solution

$$
\begin{array}{r}
.666\ldots \\
3\,\overline{)2.000\ldots} \\
1\;8 \\
\hline
20 \\
18 \\
\hline
20 \\
18 \\
\hline
2 \\
\vdots
\end{array}
$$

We shall return to the theoretical questions raised by this kind of division problem in Section 8.4.   □

Figure 8.2, a page from a fifth-grade text, shows how estimation can be used to arrive at the usual shortcut rules for multiplying and dividing decimals by powers of ten. We will establish the same results more formally in Exercises 15 and 16.

Multiplying and Dividing
by Multiples of 10: Mental Math

Jack multiplied 3.142 by 10, 100, and 1,000 on a calculator. Do the products seem reasonable?

3.142 × 10   **3.142 × 100**   **3.142 × 1,000**
↓   ↓   ↓
3 × 10 = 30   **3 × 100 = 300**   **3 × 1,000 = 3,000**

About 30. Seems   About 300. Seems   About 3,000. Seems
reasonable.   reasonable.   reasonable.

The products above suggest these short cuts:

To **multiply** by $\begin{cases}10\\100\\1{,}000\end{cases}$ move the decimal point $\begin{cases}\text{1 place right}\\\text{2 places right}\\\text{3 places right}\end{cases}$

Megan divided 5,978.6 by 10, 100, and 1,000 on a calculator. Do the quotients seem reasonable?

5,978.6 ÷ 10   **5,978.6 ÷ 100**   **5,978.6 ÷ 1,000**
↓   ↓   ↓
6,000 ÷ 10 = 600   **6,000 ÷ 100 = 60**   **6,000 ÷ 1,000 = 6**

About 600. Seems   About 60. Seems   About 6. Seems
reasonable.   reasonable.   reasonable.

The quotients above suggest these short cuts:

To **divide** by $\begin{cases}10\\100\\1{,}000\end{cases}$ move the decimal point $\begin{cases}\text{1 place left}\\\text{2 places left}\\\text{3 places left}\end{cases}$

Multiply or divide.

1. 7.623 × 10   **2.** 7.623 × 100   **3.** 7.623 × 1,000   **4.** 100 × 4.38

5. 3,842.3 ÷ 10   **6.** 3,842.3 ÷ 100   **7.** 3,842.3 ÷ 1,000   **8.** 5.7 ÷ 10

Figure 8.2 Multiplying and dividing by powers of ten in a fifth-grade textbook.

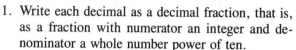

EXERCISE SET 8.1

1. Write each decimal as a decimal fraction, that is, as a fraction with numerator an integer and denominator a whole number power of ten.
   (a) 5.74
   (b) 3.14159
   (c) 0.5
   (d) .0007
   (e) 6
   (f) 22.875
   (g) ⁻40.5
   (h) ⁻117.83
   (i) .000000017
   (j) 3.50

2. Write each fraction as a decimal.
   (a) $\dfrac{2575}{10^2}$
   (b) $\dfrac{37}{10^3}$
   (c) $\dfrac{528}{1000}$
   (d) $\dfrac{463}{10}$
   (e) $\dfrac{3}{10,000}$
   (f) $\dfrac{5}{10^7}$
   (g) $\dfrac{4}{5}$
   (h) $\dfrac{17}{2 \cdot 5 \cdot 5}$ (*Hint:* Multiply numerator and denominator by 2.)
   (i) $\dfrac{3}{2 \cdot 2 \cdot 2 \cdot 5}$
   (j) $\dfrac{135}{2^3 \cdot 5^4}$

3. Write each decimal in expanded form.
   (a) 37.5
   (b) 501.64
   (c) 8.003
   (d) .0000065

4. Write a decimal for each of the following.
   (a) $2 \cdot 10^2 + 4 \cdot 10 + 0 + \dfrac{6}{10} + \dfrac{2}{10^2} + \dfrac{5}{10^3}$
   (b) $3 \cdot 100 + 8 + \dfrac{5}{10} + \dfrac{9}{1000}$
   (c) $100 + 7 + \dfrac{53}{10} + \dfrac{1}{100}$
   (d) $78\dfrac{43}{1000}$
   (e) Ten and twenty-three hundredths
   (f) Four hundred thirty-nine and eight hundredths
   (g) Two hundred seven thousandths
   (h) Two hundred and seven thousandths

5. Tell what is wrong with the following deduction: .5 is a one-place decimal; .5 = .500; therefore by the substitution principle, .500 is a one-place decimal.

6. Which of each two decimals is the lesser?
   (a) .4 or .28
   (b) 8.19543 or 8.196
   (c) .0002 or ⁻27.44
   (d) 1.05 or 1.499

7. Use a calculator to find a decimal between each two rational numbers.
   (a) $\dfrac{4}{7}$ and $\dfrac{21}{37}$
   (b) $\dfrac{2}{3}$ and $\dfrac{37}{53}$
   (It is a fact that between *any* two distinct rational numbers is a third one that can be expressed by a terminating decimal. Notice that this property says *more* than just that the rational numbers are dense.)

8. Supply reasons in this justification of the usual subtraction algorithm for decimals. As before, the small numbers over the equal signs correspond to the steps of the algorithm.

$$15.4 - 6.73 = \dfrac{154}{10} - \dfrac{673}{100} \qquad \text{(a)}$$
$$\overset{1}{=} \dfrac{1540}{100} - \dfrac{673}{100} \qquad \text{(b)}$$
$$= \dfrac{1540 - 673}{100} \qquad \text{(c)}$$
$$\overset{2}{=} \dfrac{867}{100} \qquad \text{(d)}$$
$$\overset{3}{=} 8.67 \qquad \text{(e)}$$

9. Find each sum or difference first by introducing fractions, as in the example, and then by following the mechanical three-step algorithm.

Example

$$9.3 + .24 \rightarrow \dfrac{93}{10} + \dfrac{24}{100} = \dfrac{930}{100} + \dfrac{24}{100} =$$
$$\dfrac{930 + 24}{100} = \dfrac{954}{100} = 9.54$$

(a) $15.034 + .98$ (b) $3.75 + 12.1 + .249$
(c) $9.6 - .381$ (d) $4.85 - 10.7$

10. Find each product first by introducing fractions, as in the example, and then by following the mechanical three-step algorithm.

Example

$$.056 \times 12.3 \rightarrow \frac{56}{1000} \times \frac{123}{10} = \frac{56 \times 123}{1000 \times 10}$$

$$= \frac{6888}{10,000} = .6888$$

(a) 39.9×1.75 (b) $.0074 \times .035$

11. Find each quotient first by introducing fractions and then by the mechanical algorithm.

(a) $\dfrac{7.2}{.0012}$ (b) $\dfrac{.5882}{17.3}$ (c) $\dfrac{300}{.003}$

12. Find the following sums by converting all fractions and then by the mechanical algorithm.

(a) $\dfrac{3}{4} + \dfrac{3}{5}$ (b) $\dfrac{5}{8} + \dfrac{12}{25} + \dfrac{7}{10}$

13. Find each of the following.
    (a) $17.382 - (152.6 + 29.85)$
    (b) $7.41 \times (36.6 - 40.5)$
    (c) $(^-2.1)^3$
    (d) $\dfrac{21.94 - (3.2)^2}{4.5}$

14. Estimate each of the following with a whole number.
    (a) $2.376 + 3.095 + 6.577$
    (b) $22.847 - 6.135$
    (c) 6×3.689
    (d) $\dfrac{22}{3.487}$

15. The following calculation suggests the general rule that multiplying a decimal by 10^n, where n is a natural number, moves the decimal point n places to the right. Supply one main reason at each step.

$$2.076 \times 10^2 = \frac{2076}{10^3} \times 10^2 \qquad \underline{\quad\text{(a)}\quad}$$

$$= \frac{2076}{10^3} \times \frac{10^2}{1} \qquad \underline{\quad\text{(b)}\quad}$$

$$= \frac{2076 \times 10^2}{10^3 \times 1} \qquad \underline{\quad\text{(c)}\quad}$$

$$= \frac{2076 \times 10^2}{10^3} \qquad \underline{\quad\text{(d)}\quad}$$

$$= \frac{2076 \times 10^2}{10^1 \times 10^2} \qquad \underline{\quad\text{(e)}\quad}$$

$$= \frac{2076}{10^1} \qquad \underline{\quad\text{(f)}\quad}$$

$$= 207.6 \qquad \underline{\quad\text{(g)}\quad}$$

16. The following calculation suggests the general rule that dividing a decimal by 10^n, where n is a natural number, moves the decimal point n places to the left. Supply one main reason at each step.

$$\frac{2561.7}{10^2} = \frac{\dfrac{25617}{10^1}}{10^2} \qquad \underline{\quad\text{(a)}\quad}$$

$$= \frac{\dfrac{25617}{10^1}}{\dfrac{10^2}{1}} \qquad \underline{\quad\text{(b)}\quad}$$

$$= \frac{25617}{10^1} \times \frac{1}{10^2} \qquad \underline{\quad\text{(c)}\quad}$$

$$= \frac{25617 \times 1}{10^1 \times 10^2} \qquad \underline{\quad\text{(d)}\quad}$$

$$= \frac{25617}{10^1 \times 10^2} \qquad \underline{\quad\text{(e)}\quad}$$

$$= \frac{25617}{10^3} \qquad \underline{\quad\text{(f)}\quad}$$

$$= 25.617 \qquad \underline{\quad\text{(g)}\quad}$$

17. Express each of the following as a decimal.
    (a) 75.46821×100 (b) 2.637×10^5
    (c) $\dfrac{175.4}{100}$ (d) $\dfrac{3.62}{10^5}$

18. Solve each equation. In some cases you may want to begin by multiplying both sides by a power of ten that will "clear decimals."

(a) $.03x + 1.5 = 3.75$

(b) $.4 - .12x = 1$

(c) $.3(x - .5) = .1x + .55$

(d) $.4(.7 - .2x) = .01(x + 1)$

19. In the base-twelve numeration system, there are symbols called **duodecimals**. The duodecimal 6.4_{twelve} represents six and four-twelfths. Fill in missing equivalents in Table 8.1.

Table 8.1

Ordinary symbol	$6\frac{4}{12}$	$2\frac{2}{3}$	$5\frac{95}{144}$	$.5$	
Duodecimal symbol	6.4_{twelve}			$.4_{\text{twelve}}$	$T.9_{\text{twelve}}$

20. Express 3.24_{five} as an ordinary (base-ten) decimal.

21. According to a radio advertisement, a cellular car telephone can be yours for only $1.89 per day. Estimate the annual cost to the nearest hundred dollars.

22. Estimate the area of a 4.3-cm by 2.7-cm rectangle. Now compute it exactly.

23. A map bears the caption "1 inch = 31.6 miles." First estimate, then calculate the actual distance between two cities that are $2\frac{1}{4}$ in apart on the map.

24. There are 2.54 centimeters in 1 inch. What is the area in square centimeters of an $8\frac{1}{2}$-in by 11-in sheet of paper?

25. When gold is stamped ".997 fine," it means that out of every 1 g (1 gram), .997 g is pure gold and .003 g is impurities, usually silver or copper. How much pure gold is there in a .997 fine brick weighing 7.8 kg?

26. The last time Jenny stopped at a gas station, her odometer read 25843.8 (miles), and she filled up the tank. Now her odometer reads 26041.2 and she fills up again with 8.4 gal. How many miles per gallon did she get?

27. If gasoline costs $1.25 per gallon, how many gallons will you get for $12.25?

28. The chemical formula H_2O indicates that each molecule of this particular compound (water) consists of 2 atoms of hydrogen (H) and 1 atom of oxygen (O). Using the atomic weights given in Table 8.2, we find its molecular weight to be 18.016. Find the molecular weights of the following compounds.

(a) C_8H_{18} (octane)

(b) $C_6H_5NO_2$ (nitrobenzene)

(c) $(CH_3)_2CO$ (acetone)

(d) $C_6H_2CH_3(NO_2)_3$ (trinitrotoluene)

Table 8.2

Element	H	O	C	N
Atomic weight	1.008	16.000	12.011	14.007

29. Ed has a rule of thumb for relating annual earnings to hourly wages. According to his rule, a person earning $6.00 per hour will earn about $12,000 in a year, and a person earning $7.50 per hour will earn about $15,000 in a year.

(a) By Ed's rule, a person earning $4.75 per hour will earn about how much in a year?

(b) By Ed's rule, a worker with an annual salary of $28,000 earns about how much per hour?

(c) Express Ed's rule in full generality: If a worker earns X per hour, then . . . .

(d) Explain why Ed's rule makes sense by stating explicitly his assumption about what constitutes a "work year."

30. On March 23, 1989, an asteroid of diameter perhaps one-half mile had a near miss (450,000 miles) with the earth. The asteroid and the earth are in orbits around the sun that (nearly) meet at just one point. It takes the earth about 365.24 days (1 year) to orbit the sun. It takes the asteroid about 379.86 days. In what year will we have our next close encounter with that asteroid? *Hint:* How many days away from the rendezvous point is the asteroid one year after the near miss? Two years? Three years? . . .

31. Why didn't we discuss associativity, commutativity, and so on, for addition and multiplication of (terminating) decimals?

Computer Vignette F

The following problem is ideally suited to solution by computer because of the repetitive nature of the calculations.

PROBLEM   After long years of observation a naturalist has concluded that the following relationships hold between the populations of lemmings and snowy owls. If the ratio of snowy owls to lemmings exceeds .001 one year, then the following year the lemming population contracts by a factor of .89, while the snowy owl population contracts by a factor of .60. If the ratio of snowy owls to lemmings is less than or equal to .001 one year, then the following year the lemming population expands by a factor of 1.1, while the snowy owl population expands by a factor of 1.5. Suppose that in 1990 there are 100,000 lemmings and 80 snowy owls on an isolated Arctic island. What will the two populations be in each of the next 10 years.?

Solution   A program incorporating these relationships is shown in Figure 8.3. Its printout is shown in Figure 8.4. If you have access to a computer, type in this program, but make one small revision so that it will give the populations for the next 100 years instead of just 10. Then run it. If you do not have access to a computer, use a calculator to find the numbers of lemmings and owls in each of the three years 1991, 1992, 1993. Check your answers against Figure 8.4. ❏

Figure 8.3

```
10    PRINT "YEAR", "LEMMING", "OWL"
20    PRINT
30    PRINT 1990, 100000, 80
40    LET S = 80
50    LET L = 100000
60    LET D = 1990
70    FOR I = 1 TO 10
80    LET R = S / L
90    IF R > .001 THEN 130
100   LET L = 1.1 * L
110   LET S = 1.5 * S
120   GOTO 150
130   LET L = .89 * L
140   LET S = .6 * S
150   PRINT D + I, INT(L), INT(S)
160   NEXT I
170   END
```

Figure 8.4

```
]RUN
YEAR                    LEMMING              OWL
1990                    100000               80
1991                    110000               120
1992                    97900                72
1993                    107690               108
1994                    95844                64
1995                    105428               97
1996                    115971               145
1997                    103214               87
1998                    113535               131
1999                    101047               78
2000                    111151               118
```

8.2 *Percent and Scientific Notation*

In this section we consider briefly two close relatives of decimal notation. The first, percent, is used in a wide variety of common, everyday situations. It is almost impossible to read a newspaper without running across percents. The second, scientific notation, is used, as its name suggests, in scientific contexts. It is a particularly convenient notation to use when you are dealing with very large or very small numbers. It is also the notation that calculators revert to when a number gets too large or too small to fit in the display. The *Standards* recommend that scientific notation be part of the curriculum at the 5–8 levels.

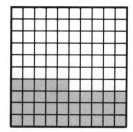

Figure 8.5 Thirty-five percent of the square is shaded.

Percent

Percent literally means "out of (per) a hundred (cent)." Thus thirty-five percent means "thirty-five out of a hundred." See Figure 8.5.

If we use the usual symbol % for **percent,** the formal definition is as follows:

$$x\% = \frac{x}{100}$$

For example,

$$7\% = \frac{7}{100} \qquad 5\tfrac{1}{3}\% = \frac{5\tfrac{1}{3}}{100} \qquad 132.7\% = \frac{132.7}{100} = 1.327$$

Converting back and forth between decimal and percent notation is easy to do; we will see that it is also a very important ability to have when solving problems involving percent.

EXAMPLE 1 Convert each decimal to a percent.
(a) .15   (b) .123   (c) 6.4

Solution The idea is to produce a denominator of 100, so in each case we simply divide and multiply by 100.

(a) $.15 = \dfrac{.15 \times 100}{100} = \dfrac{15}{100} = 15\%$

(b) $.123 = \dfrac{.123 \times 100}{100} = \dfrac{12.3}{100} = 12.3\%$

(c) $6.4 = \dfrac{6.4 \times 100}{100} = \dfrac{640}{100} = 640\%$ ❏

The rule of thumb that emerges from the example is that to convert a decimal to a percent, one should move the decimal point two places to the right (that multiplies the original number by 100) and then append the percent symbol % (that divides by 100). In the exercises you are asked to assemble a flowchart for this algorithm.

The reverse conversion, from percent to decimal notation, involves moving the decimal point two places to the left.

EXAMPLE 2 Change each percent to a decimal.
(a) 37.5%   (b) 250%   (c) 1.3%   (d) $8\frac{1}{4}\%$

Solution

(a) $37.5\% = \dfrac{37.5}{100} = .375$

(b) $250\% = \dfrac{250}{100} = 2.5$

(c) $1.3\% = \dfrac{1.3}{100} = \dfrac{01.3}{100} = .013$

(d) $8\frac{1}{4}\% = 8.25\% = \dfrac{8.25}{100} = .0825$ ❏

The following percent word problems illustrate the importance of being able to convert to and from decimal notation.

EXAMPLE 3 How much is 12% of $225?

Solution The word *of* is the clue that the rational number 12% (or $\frac{12}{100}$, or .12) is acting as a multiplier of the input number, or **base** as it is often called in percent problems, $225:

$$12\% \text{ of } \$225 = 0.12 \times \$225 = \$27$$ ❏

EXAMPLE 4   Out of a group of 80 candidates for the Marine Corps, 24 failed the physical exam. What percent failed the physical?

Solution 1   We are being asked to express the ratio $\frac{24}{80}$ as a percent. We get there by passing through decimal notation:

$$\tfrac{24}{80} = \tfrac{3}{10} = .3 = 30\%$$

Solution 2   Some people prefer to avoid passing through decimal notation by thinking in terms of ratio and proportion. The task is to find x so that $\frac{24}{80} = x\%$; that is,

$$\frac{24}{80} = \frac{x}{100} \qquad \text{(``24 is to 80 as x is to 100'')}$$

Cross multiplying yields

$$80x = 2400$$

or

$$x = 30$$

Answer: 30%.

Solution 3   The problem can also be solved by formally translating words into mathematical symbols, as follows:

$$24 \text{ is what percent of } 80?$$
$$24 = x\% \times 80$$
$$24 = \frac{x}{100} \times 80$$
$$\frac{240}{8} = x \qquad \text{or} \qquad x = 30$$

Answer: 30%.

The method of Solution 1 seems to be simple, direct, and admirably suited to the use of a calculator.   ❏

The next examples point out a fact that is true to some degree of all word problems, but is strikingly evident for many percent problems: The real difficulty is understanding the English.

EXAMPLE 5   A television set with a list price of $380 is on sale at 20% off. How much does it cost?

Solution 1   The amount taken *off* the list price (the base) is

$$20\% \text{ of } \$380 = .20 \times \$380 = \$76$$

Thus the sale price is

$$\$380 - \$76 = \$304$$

Solution 2   On sale at 20% off means one pays only 80% of the list price:

$$80\% \text{ of } \$380 = .8 \times \$380 = \$304 \qquad \square$$

EXAMPLE 6   The population of Richland experienced a 20% increase between 1900 and 1910. If the population was 250 in 1900, what was it in 1910?

Solution 1   The amount of increase was

$$20\% \text{ of } 250 = .2 \times 250 = 50$$

Thus the 1910 population was

$$250 + 50 = 300$$

Solution 2   The population in 1910 was 120% of the population in 1900:

$$120\% \text{ of } 250 = 1.2 \times 250 = 300 \qquad \square$$

EXAMPLE 7   The population of Richland fell by 20% from 1910 to 1920. What was the population in 1920?

Solution 1   The amount of decrease was 20% of the base; that is,

$$20\% \text{ of } 300 = 60$$

Thus the 1920 population was

$$300 - 60 = 240$$

Solution 2   The population in 1920 was 80% of what it was in 1910:

$$80\% \text{ of } 300 = .8 \times 300 = 240 \qquad \square$$

Note: A 20% increase followed by a 20% decrease did *not* leave the population unchanged:

$$80\% \text{ of } 120\% \text{ of } 250 = .8 \times 1.2 \times 250 = .96 \times 250 \neq 250$$

EXAMPLE 8   Women made up 52% of the voters. The Liberal candidate captured 60% of the women's vote and 45% of the men's vote. What percent of the total vote did the Liberal candidate get?

Solution   This is the type of problem we solved earlier by using a unit square or a tree diagram as a visual aid. See Figure 8.6. The answer is

$$.6 \times .52 + .45 \times .48 = .312 + .216 = .528 = 52.8\% \qquad \square$$

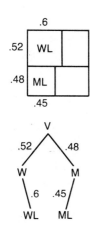

Figure 8.6

Scientific Notation

Before we can introduce this close relative of decimal notation, we must extend the concept of exponent from positive integers to all integers. That is, we must decide on a meaning for expressions like these:

$$10^0 \qquad 10^{-3} \qquad 2^{-4} \qquad (^-3)^{-2}$$

Here are the definitions for **zero and negative exponents:**

For any nonzero real number b,

$$b^0 = 1$$

$$b^{-n} = \frac{1}{b^n} \qquad (n \text{ a positive integer})$$

Thus

$$10^0 = 1 \qquad\qquad 10^{-3} = \frac{1}{10^3} = \frac{1}{1000} = .001$$

$$2^{-4} = \frac{1}{2^4} = \frac{1}{16} \qquad (^-3)^{-2} = \frac{1}{(^-3)^2} = \frac{1}{9}$$

The following discussion is motivation for the definitions. Let b be an arbitrary nonzero number (b for "base"). We know that the following **exponent addition property** is true for all *positive* integers m and n.

$$b^m \cdot b^n = b^{m+n}$$

We would like this property to remain true when $m = 0$. That is, we want

$$b^0 \cdot b^n = b^{0+n}$$

that is,

$$b^0 \cdot b^n = b^n$$

Clearly, then, we *must* define b^0 to be 1.

Now suppose we want the exponent addition property to be true for *all* integer exponents m and n. In particular, then, it must be true when $m = {}^-3$ and $n = 3$; that is, we must have

$$b^{-3} \cdot b^3 = b^{-3+3} = b^0 = 1$$

Thus we *must* define b^{-3} to be $1/b^3$. Similarly, we must define b^{-7} to be $1/b^7$, b^{-20} to be $1/b^{20}$, and so on. Under the definitions we have made, the exponent addition property is true for all integers m and n.

We can now describe what is meant by scientific notation. It is based on the observation that any (positive) decimal can be expressed as the product of a decimal between 1 and 10 and an integral power of 10. Such a product is referred to as **scientific notation.**

EXAMPLE 9   Express each of the following numbers in scientific notation.
(a) 2305   (b) .0321   (c) 7.4

Solution   The idea is to produce a decimal between 1 and 10. In some cases the given number needs to be divided by a power of ten, and then we must compensate by multiplying by that same power of ten. In other cases we must multiply the given number by a power of ten and compensate by dividing.

(a) $2305 = \dfrac{2305}{1000} \times 1000 = 2.305 \times 10^3$

(b) $.0321 = \dfrac{.0321 \times 100}{100} = \dfrac{3.21}{10^2} = 3.21 \times 10^{-2}$

(c) 7.4 is already between 1 and 10: $7.4 = 7.4 \times 10^0$.   ❏

Computation with numbers expressed in scientific notation uses the exponent addition property.

EXAMPLE 10   Express each product or quotient in scientific notation.
(a) $(3.5 \times 10^7) \times (5.1 \times 10^{-3})$

(b) $\dfrac{3 \times 10^4}{4 \times 10^5}$

(c) $\dfrac{1.3 \times 10^{-2}}{2 \times 10^{-10}}$

Solution   (a) $(3.5 \times 10^7) \times (5.1 \times 10^{-3}) = (3.5 \times 5.1) \times (10^7 \times 10^{-3})$
$$= 17.85 \times 10^4 = 1.785 \times 10^1 \times 10^4$$
$$= 1.785 \times 10^5$$

(b) $\dfrac{3 \times 10^4}{4 \times 10^5} = \dfrac{3}{4} \times 10^4 \times 10^{-5} = .75 \times 10^{-1}$
$$= 7.5 \times 10^{-1} \times 10^{-1} = 7.5 \times 10^{-2}$$

(c) $\dfrac{1.3 \times 10^{-2}}{2 \times 10^{-10}} = \dfrac{1.3}{2} \times 10^{-2} \times 10^{10} = .65 \times 10^8$
$$= 6.5 \times 10^{-1} \times 10^8 = 6.5 \times 10^7$$ ❏

As we mentioned earlier, scientific notation is particularly convenient for representing very large and very small numbers. The mass of an electron is about 9.1×10^{-28} g; the mass of the earth is about 6.0×10^{27} g. If you use your calculator for a very large number such as 2^{100}, by punching in $\boxed{2}$ $\boxed{y^x}$ $\boxed{100}$, it will display something like

1.2676506   30

which you are to interpret as

$$1.2676506 \times 10^{30}$$

(a good approximation to 2^{100}, though not its exact value). If you then hit the reciprocal button $\boxed{1/x}$ to produce a very small number, the display will look something like

$$7.8886091 \quad {}^-31$$

which stands for

$$7.8886091 \times 10^{-31}$$

EXERCISE SET 8.2

1. Express each percent as a decimal
   (a) 23.7%
   (b) 4%
   (c) 156%
   (d) .1%
   (e) 9.35%
   (f) 90%
   (g) $5\frac{1}{2}\%$
   (h) $7\frac{3}{4}\%$

2. Express each of the following as a percent.
   (a) .75
   (b) .034
   (c) 2.1
   (d) 5
   (e) .009
   (f) $\frac{1}{4}$
   (g) $\frac{1}{8}$
   (h) $\frac{5}{8}$

3. Put these instructions into appropriately shaped boxes and arrange them into a flowchart for converting from decimal to percent notation.
   (a) Start.
   (b) Stop.
   (c) Append a zero.
   (d) Append the symbol %.
   (e) A decimal
   (f) The equivalent percent
   (g) Move the decimal point 2 places to the right
   (h) Does it have at least 2 digits to the right of the decimal point?

4. Estimate to the nearest whole number.
   (a) 1% of 123
   (b) 2% of 85
   (c) 10% of 79
   (d) 5% of 46
   (e) 46% of 12
   (f) 35% of 12
   (g) 65% of 8.83
   (h) 27% of 7.9
   (i) 153% of 3.94
   (j) 400% of 5.04

5. Many people feel that 15% of the restaurant bill is a reasonable amount to tip the waitperson. Estimate the tip for each of these bills. Explain your thinking.
   (a) $12.60
   (b) $27.95

Exercises 6, 7, and 8 give practice with the three categories into which simple percent problems have traditionally been sorted.

6. Compute.
   (a) 14% of 65
   (b) 200% of 45
   (c) 1% of $7500
   (d) 6% of 30% of $400
   (e) 20% of 90%
   (f) 10% of 40% of 25%

7. Write your answer in percent notation.
   (a) 1 is what percent of 20?
   (b) 16 is what percent of 40?
   (c) 8 is what percent of 5?
   (d) 50 is what percent of 40?
   (e) 2 is what percent of 500?
   (f) 165 is what percent of 1,000,000?

8. Find the missing number.
   (a) 17 is 1% of what number?
   (b) 17 is 2% of what number?
   (c) 60 is 30% of what number?
   (d) 33.6 is 8% of what number?
   (e) 180 is 225% of what number?
   (f) $\frac{1}{4}$ is 150% of what number?

A calculator would be very helpful for Exercises 9–24.

9. If the sales tax rate is 4%, how much will it cost you for an item priced at $14.50?

10. Sixty-five chickens walked out of their minimum-security coop. Fifty-two were recaptured. What percent escaped?

11. Fixed expenses claim $258.40 from Joan's paycheck of $340. What percent of her pay is discretionary income?

★ 12. The temperature of a metal rod was 450°C. After 15 min its temperature has fallen by 10%. What is its temperature now? *Hint 1:* The answer is *not* 405°C. *Hint 2:* Absolute zero, the lowest possible temperature, occurs at about −273°C.

13. Ollie's Appliance Store reported 12% more customers this year than last. Last year Ollie had 7500 customers. How many did Ollie have this year?

14. Big Al's Appliance Store reported 10% less customers this year than last. This year Al had 6400 customers. How many did Al have last year?

15. Linda wants to unload a $250 white elephant at a price of $150. What percent off should she advertise?

16. In the past two weeks the price of an item was first marked down 30% and then marked up 20%. Compare its present price with its price two weeks ago. Would the result have been the same if the markup had preceded the markdown?

17. A meat loaf recipe calls for 30% pork, 70% beef, and negligible spices. If the pork is 25% fat, and the beef is 20% fat, what percent of the meat loaf is fat?

18. Ida has diversified her savings as follows: 45% into savings certificates yielding 10%, 30% into bonds yielding 8%, and the rest into stocks yielding 6%. What overall rate of return is she earning on her savings?

19. The value of a painting increased from $8400 to $9000 in the course of one year. What was the percent of increase in its value?

20. The population of Springdale fell by 50 to a low of 200 people last year. What was the percent of decrease?

21. A proposal is made to raise the state's sales tax from 4% to 5%. Supporters say it is only a 1% increase; opponents say it is a 25% increase. Identify the base each group is using.

22. The label on a package of turkey kielbasa contains the following message: "This product contains 15% fat, which is 45% less fat than USDA data for beef and pork kielbasa." Beef and pork kielbasa is what percent fat?

23. In 1980, 50% of Harding High School graduates went on to college. By 1990 the percentage had risen to 70%. At Buchanan High the corresponding figures were 20% in 1980 and 30% in 1990. Make an argument to show the following:
(a) Harding improved more than Buchanan.
(b) Buchanan improved more than Harding.
Which argument is more convincing to you?

24. In 1980 Tyler Prep sent 90% of its graduates to college. By 1990 that figure had risen to 95%. Use the data in Exercise 23 and give arguments to show the following.

(a) Tyler's improvement was worse than both Harding's and Buchanan's.
(b) Tyler's improvement was better than both Harding's and Buchanan's.

★ 25. Recently, the growth rate of the population of Mexico has been 2.8% per year. If that rate holds steady, in how many years will Mexico's population double?

26. There is a rule of thumb called the *Rule of 72* that gives the approximate doubling time for populations: 100 × growth rate × doubling time ≈ 72 For example, Kenya's population is growing at an annual rate of 4%, so its doubling time d satisfies $4 \times d \approx 72$; that is, $d \approx 18$ years.

(a) Use the Rule of 72 to estimate the doubling time for Mexico's population. Compare your answer with what you found in Exercise 25.
(b) The population of the continent of Africa in 1989 was 625 million. If it continues to grow

at its current annual rate of 3.1%, estimate the year in which it will reach 2.5 billion.

(c) Kenya's population in 1989 was 25 million. If its current rate of growth continues, estimate its population in the year 2043.

27. A new employee starts out at an annual salary of $20,000 and the promise of 10% raises annually. An older employee earns $40,000 annually and receives 5% raises annually. How many years will it be before the new employee's salary overtakes the older employee's salary?

28. Ms. Merrill is in the 28% tax bracket. Thus if she buys a $1000 bond that pays 8% annual interest, she will get to keep only 72% of the $80 that it earns in a year. That is, she will get to keep $57.60, thus earning an after-tax yield of 5.76% on her $1000 investment.

   (a) What will be her after-tax yield on a bond that pays 10% interest?

   (b) What rate of interest will she have to earn on a bond in order to realize an after-tax yield of 8%?

   (c) The interest on municipal bonds is not subject to Federal tax. Assuming that both bonds are equally safe, which is the better investment for Ms. Merrill, a municipal bond yielding 9.3% or a taxable bond yielding 13%?

29. Express in the form 10^n, where n is an integer.

   (a) $\dfrac{1}{10^4}$ (b) $\dfrac{1}{10^{-3}}$

   (c) $10^3 \times 10^4$ (d) $10^5 \times 10^{-2}$

   (e) $10^{-5} \times 10^2$ (f) $10^{-7} \times 10^{-6}$

   (g) $\dfrac{10^6}{10^2}$ (h) $\dfrac{10}{10^4}$

   (i) $\dfrac{10^5}{10^{-2}}$ (j) $\dfrac{10^{-3}}{10}$

30. Express the scientific notation in ordinary decimal notation.

   (a) 5.716×10^2 (b) 9.3×10^4

   (c) 7.54×10^{-3} (d) 1.005×10^{-5}

31. Express in scientific notation.

   (a) 5280   (b) .237

   (c) 16,000,000   (d) .00016

   (e) $(4.0 \times 10^4) \times (3.2 \times 10^{-8})$

   (f) $(7.5 \times 10^{-2}) \times (3.2 \times 10^{-3})$

   (g) $\dfrac{1.6 \times 10^4}{4 \times 10^7}$ (h) $\dfrac{8.4 \times 10^{-10}}{2.0 \times 10^3}$

   (i) $.000004 \times 140{,}000{,}000{,}000{,}000$

   (j) $\dfrac{28{,}000{,}000{,}000{,}000{,}000{,}000}{.000008}$

32. Use your calculator to put these numbers in scientific notation.

   (a) 3^{100} (b) 5^{-20}

33. By trial and error, determine the greatest (integral) power of 3 that your calculator can handle before it flashes an error message. Now find the least (integral) power of 3 for which your calculator displays a nonzero value.

34. Light travels about 3.0×10^8 meters per second (m/sec). The average distance from the sun to the earth is about 1.5×10^{11} m. How long does it take light from the sun to reach us?

35. Using the speed of light from Exercise 34 and the fact that the diameter of a hydrogen atom is about 10^{-10} m, determine how long it takes light to travel the diameter of a hydrogen atom.

36. In the previous section we wrote the expanded form of a decimal such as 423.965 using positive exponents and fraction notation:

$$4 \cdot 10^2 + 2 \cdot 10 + 3 + \frac{9}{10} + \frac{6}{10^2} + \frac{5}{10^3}$$

Use zero and negative exponents to rewrite this expression so that the pattern of decreasing powers of ten is emphasized.

8.3 *Interest (Optional)*

The basic assumption in interest theory is that money earns money. Suppose, for example, that you lend a merchant $1000. He uses it to buy a batch of blue jeans, which he then sells for $1700. After paying expenses of $400 he has $1300 left. It would not be fair for him to simply return your $1000 and keep $300 as profit. After all, without the use of your money he would not have been able to buy the jeans. He should share the profit with you. Perhaps he gives you $120 and keeps $180 for himself. Your loan of $1000 earned you $120. The money loaned ($1000) is called the **original principal,** or simply the principal, and the money it earns for the lender ($120) is called the **interest.**

The interest earned is, of course, important to you, but of equal importance is the **term** of the loan: the length of time from when you made the loan until the principal plus interest, the **amount,** was returned to you. If the term of the loan to the merchant were six months, you would have your money back and could lend it a second time in the same year to earn additional interest, perhaps another $120 for a total of $240 in that year, or maybe even more than $120, because after repayment of the first loan, you would have $1120 to lend. If, on the other hand, the term of the original loan had been two years, you would receive an average of only $60 interest each year.

Interest Rates

There are several ways of describing the *rate* at which money earns money. We will look at two, "effective" and "nominal" rates of interest. Consider again the situation in which you loaned a principal of $1000 and were repaid an amount $1000 + $120 = $1120. If the term of the loan were six months, then we would say that you earned an effective *semiannual* rate of interest of $120/1000 = 12\%$. If the term of the loan were a year, then we would say that you earned an effective *annual* rate of interest of 12%. And if the term of the loan were two years, then we would say that you earned an effective *biennial* rate of interest of 12%.

> If a principal of P earns an interest of I in a given term, then the **effective rate** of interest for that term is I/P.

EXAMPLE 1   Describe the interest rate in each of the following situations:
(a) You deposit $1000 in a savings account, and one year later the bank reports that the amount of your balance is $1060.
(b) You lend me $10 and a month later I repay you $10.25.
(c) You lend me $25 and three months later I repay you $27.

Solution   (a) The (original) principal is $1000, the interest earned is $1060 − $1000 = $60, and the term is one year. Thus interest was paid (and earned) at an effective annual rate of $60/$1000 = .06 = 6%. ⌃
(b) The principal is $10.00, the interest is $.25, and the term is one month.

Thus interest was earned at an effective monthly rate of $.25/10 = .025 = 2.5\%$.

(c) The principal is \$25, the interest is \$2, and the term is one-quarter of a year. Thus interest was earned at an effective *quarterly* rate of $2/25 = .08 = 8\%$. ❏

EXAMPLE 2

A bank advertises that it pays interest at an effective rate of $6\frac{3}{4}\%$. You deposit \$500. What will be the amount in your account one year from now?

Solution

The first thing to notice about this example is that, technically, the advertisement is ambiguous, because no term is mentioned. This imprecision is common practice. The convention is the following: *when no term is mentioned, the phrase "effective rate" is understood to mean effective annual rate.* Thus your balance one year from now will be

$$500 + .0675 \times 500 = 500 + 33.75 = \$533.75 \qquad ❏$$

Because it is often desirable to be able to compare the rates of interest on loans having different terms, we agree on a common unit of time, namely a year, and express rates as "nominal" rates. "Annualized" might be a better word than "nominal", but the latter is widely used and understood. For Example 1(b), where the effective monthly rate of interest is 2.5%, the nominal rate is found by multiplying by 12:

$$12 \times 2.5\% = 30\% \qquad \text{nominal rate}$$

In Example 1(c), for an effective quarterly rate of interest of 8%, the nominal rate of interest is found by multiplying by 4:

$$4 \times 8\% = 32\% \qquad \text{nominal rate}$$

You as lender should prefer the loan in Example 1(c); I as borrower should prefer the loan in Example 1(b).

The general definition of nominal rate is this:

> If a loan earns an effective rate of interest r for a term of $1/m$ of a year, then its **nominal rate** of interest is $m \times r$.

EXAMPLE 3

Find the nominal rate of interest for each of the following loans:
(a) A loan of \$200 that earns interest of \$1 in one week
(b) A loan of \$1000 that earns \$120 in six months
(c) A loan of \$1000 that earns \$120 in two years
(d) A savings account that grows from \$1000 to \$1060 in one year

Solution

(a) One week is $\frac{1}{52}$ of a year. Thus the nominal rate of interest is 52 times the effective weekly rate of $\frac{1}{200}$.

$$52 \times \tfrac{1}{200} = \tfrac{26}{100} = 26\%$$

(b) Six months is $\frac{1}{2}$ of a year. Thus the nominal rate of interest is

$$2 \times \frac{120}{1000} = \frac{24}{100} = 24\%$$

(c) Two years is $\dfrac{1}{\frac{1}{2}}$ of a year. Thus the nominal rate of interest is

$$\tfrac{1}{2} \times \frac{120}{1000} = \frac{60}{1000} = 6\%$$

(d) Nominal rate = effective annual rate = $\frac{60}{1000} = 6\%$ ❏

EXAMPLE 4   Find the effective quarterly rate of interest on a three-month loan that bears a nominal rate of interest of 7%.

Solution   Let r be that effective quarterly rate. Then $4 \times r = .07$ and hence $r = .07/4 = .0175 = 1\frac{3}{4}\%$.   ❏

Simple Interest

When the principal (the money that earns interest) does not change during the term of a loan, we say that the loan earns **simple interest.** In the case of simple interest, the phrase "effective annual rate" is abbreviated to "annual rate."

EXAMPLE 5   To finance your education you borrow $10,000 for five years from a company that charges you simple interest at an annual rate of 10%. What amount (principal plus interest) will you owe after five years?

Solution   The loan earns *simple* interest, so the principal remains at $10,000 for the full five years. In the first year, it earns interest of 10% × $10,000 = $1000. In the second year, it earns $1000 in interest again—similarly for years three, four, and five. Thus after five years you will owe

$15,000 (amount) = $10,000 (principal) + 5 × $1000 (interest)   ❏

Here is a generalization of Example 5:

> **Simple Interest**
>
> The interest I earned in t years by a simple interest loan of principal P and annual interest rate r is given by
>
> $$I = Prt$$
>
> The amount repayable after t years is given by
>
> $$A = P + I = P + Prt = P(1 + rt)$$

Figure 8.7 shows graphs of the two functions: principal (a constant function), and amount (a linear function). The straight-line shapes of these two graphs are characteristic of simple interest. We shall soon see that in the case of "compound interest" neither the principal function, nor the amount function has a straight-line graph.

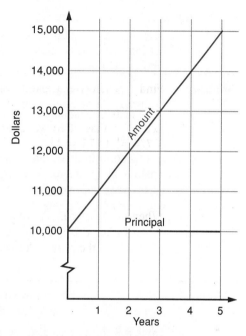

Figure 8.7 A simple interest loan of $10,000 at an annual rate of 10%.

EXAMPLE 6   A deposit of $1000 is made in an account that earns simple interest at an annual rate of 8%.

(a) What is the amount in the account after 3 years?

(b) What is the amount in the account after 41 months?

Solution   (a) $A = P + Prt = 1000 + 1000 \times (.08) \times 3 = \$1240$

(b) We would like to use the formula $A = P + Prt$ again. We still have $P = 1000$, and $r = .08$, but now the term is given in months instead of years. So we simply convert to years, $t = \frac{41}{12}$, and go right ahead and use the formula

$$A = 1000 + 1000 \times (.08) \times \tfrac{41}{12} \doteq \$1273.33$$

The "linearity" of the amount graph in Figure 8.7 is based on the convention that simple interest is "prorated" between periods; that is, the value of the amount function continues to be given by the formula $A = P(1 + rt)$ even for nonintegral values of t.   ❑

Compound Interest

When the principal (money that earns interest) does not change during the term of a loan, we say that the loan earns simple interest. When the principal does change during the term of a loan because interest earned is added to it, we say that the loan earns **compound interest.**

EXAMPLE 7   You borrow $10,000 for college at an effective annual rate of interest of 10%, but interest is to be *compounded* (i.e., converted to principal) annually. What amount will you owe after five years?

Solution   After one year the amount you will owe is

$$11,000 \text{ (amount)} = 10,000 \text{ (principal)} + (.10) \times 10,000 \text{ (interest)}$$
$$= 1.10 \times 10,000$$

At this point in time, the total amount that you owe (11,000) is viewed as principal on which interest is charged during the second year. The amount of interest in the second year is $(.10) \times 11,000 = 1100$ and thus the total amount you will owe after two years is

$$12,100 = 11,000 + 1100$$
$$= 11,000 + (.10) \times 11,000$$
$$= 1.10 \times 11,000$$
$$= 1.10 \times 1.10 \times 10,000$$
$$= 1.10^2 \times 10,000$$

Table 8.3 shows changing values of principal and interest at the ends of years 0 through 5. Notice how at the end of each year the principal gets "stretched" by a factor of 1.10. Figure 8.8 shows clearly that the principal function is a "step function," and suggests that the amount function is not linear, but "exponential." Returning to the original question, at the end of five years you will owe $16,105.10, which is $1105.10 more than you would have owed had the interest been simple rather than compound.   ❏

Table 8.3

Year	Interest Charged that Year	Principal at End of that Year
0	0	10,000
1	1000	$11,000 = 1.10 \times 10,000$
2	1100	$12,100 = 1.10^2 \times 10,000$
3	1210	$13,310 = 1.10^3 \times 10,000$
4	1331	$14,641 = 1.10^4 \times 10,000$
5	1464.10	$16,105.10 = 1.10^5 \times 10,000$

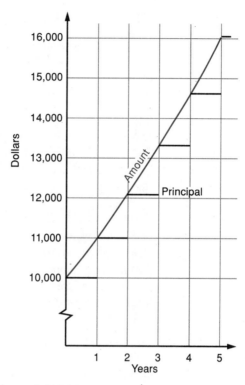

Figure 8.8 A loan of $10,000 at an effective annual rate of 10% compounded annually.

Here is a generalization of Example 7:

Compound Interest

If an original principal P earns an effective rate of interest r per time period, and if interest is compounded (converted to principal) at the end of each period, then at the end of t time periods the amount (or accumulated value) is given by

$$A = P(1 + r)^t$$

EXAMPLE 8   Suppose that $3000 is deposited in an account that pays a nominal rate of interest of 6.8% compounded quarterly.
(a) What will its accumulated value be at the end of five years?
(b) What will its accumulated value be after 29 months?

Solution   (a) The original principal is 3000, the time period is the quarter-year, the effective quarterly rate of interest is $.068/4 = .017$, and the number of periods is $5 \times 4 = 20$. Thus the accumulated value is

$$A = P(1 + r)^t$$
$$= 3000(1 + .017)^{20}$$
$$\doteq \$4202.82$$

(b) We would like to use the formula $A = P(1 + r)^t$ again. We still have $P = 3000$ and $r = .017$, but now t is the number of quarter-years in 29 months, that is $t = 29/3 = 9\frac{2}{3}$ quarters. Thus our formula yields

$$A \doteq 3000 \times (1.017)^{9.6667}$$

The mathematical theory of nonintegral exponents is too deep for this course, but an exponent like 9.6667 will not faze your calculator. Punching in the expression above using the $\boxed{y^x}$ key yields $A \doteq \$3530.96$.
Note: The smoothness of the amount graph in Figure 8.8 is based on the convention that, for compound interest, the value of the amount function for nonintegral values of t continues to be given by the formula $A = P(1 + r)^t$.   ❏

EXAMPLE 9   A savings account is advertised as paying a nominal rate of interest of 7.2% compounded monthly. What is the equivalent effective annual rate of interest?

Solution   Imagine depositing an initial principal of $100, and use the compound interest formula to see what it grows to in one year. Because the time period is the month, the effective monthly rate of interest is $.072/12 = .006$, and the number of periods is 12, it follows that the amount at the end of one year is

$$A = 100(1 + .006)^{12} \doteq \$107.44$$

Interest of $7.44 was earned on an initial principal of $100.00, so the equivalent effective annual rate of interest is

$$\frac{I}{P} = \frac{7.44}{100} = 7.44\%$$ ❏

EXERCISE SET 8.3

1. You deposit $500 in a savings account and make no further transactions. Six months later your balance is reported to be $522.50.
   (a) What effective semiannual rate of interest did your account earn?

   (b) What nominal rate of interest did your account earn?

2. Interest of $5 is charged on a three-month loan of $200.

(a) What is the effective quarterly rate of interest?

(b) What is the nominal rate of interest?

3. You deposit $10,000 into a money market account. For opening the account (and for promising not to close it within a year) your account is immediately credited with a bonus of $25. At the end of the next four quarters, dividends of $185, $188, $201, $193 are credited to your account. After the third quarter your account is debited $10 for the "annual maintenance fee."
   (a) What effective annual rate of interest did your account earn?
   (b) What nominal rate of interest did your account earn?

4. A credit card company charges its customers an effective monthly rate of interest of 1.5% on any unpaid balance.
   (a) If your present (unpaid) balance is $100 and you make no further payments or charges, what will your balance be one year from now?
   (b) What nominal rate of interest is this company charging?

5. How much interest is earned in a year by a deposit of $6500 in an account that pays an effective rate of interest of 9%?

6. How much money should you put into an account paying 8% effective if you want to have $1000 in the account one year from now?

7. Your uncle lends you $20,000 for college, and charges simple interest at an annual rate of 6%. Assuming you make no repayments, calculate how much you will owe him after
   (a) 1 year   (b) 4 years
   (c) $2\frac{1}{2}$ years   (d) 5 years, 5 months

8. On January 1, 1992, a principal of $4000 is deposited into an account that pays simple interest at an annual rate of 8%. Calculate the amount in the account on
   (a) January 1, 1993
   (b) January 1, 1999
   (c) June 1, 1994
   (d) September 1, 1997

9. Sketch graphs of both the principal and the amount functions from Exercise 8, letting the horizontal axis be the time axis and the vertical axis be the money axis.

10. A principal of $3000 is deposited in an account that compounds interest annually at an effective rate of 12%. Make a table that shows the balance in the account (to the nearest cent) at the end of years 0, 1, 2, . . . , 10.

11. Sketch graphs of both the principal and the amount functions from Exercise 10, letting the horizontal axis be the time axis and the vertical axis be the money axis.

12. If $6500 is placed in an account that compounds interest annually at an effective rate of 7%, what will the accumulated value be
    (a) After 5 years
    (b) After 7 years, 4 months

13. About how long will it take for the balance in the account in Exercise 12 to reach $20,000?

14. If $5000 is placed in an account that pays a nominal rate of interest of 6.8% compounded quarterly, what will the value of the account be after ten years?

15. About how long will it take for the balance in the account in Exercise 14 to reach $20,000?

16. A savings account pays a nominal rate of 4.8% compounded monthly. If $3000 is deposited in that account, how much interest will be earned in five years?

17. What effective annual rate of interest is equivalent to a nominal rate of 4.8% converted monthly?

18. Fill in the chart that follows to show the growth of an initial principal of $100 in accounts that pay the same nominal rate of interest (12%) but that are compounded with different frequency. Round all amounts to the nearest cent.

Number n of Compoundings per Year	Amount at the End of One Year, $A = 100\left(1 + \dfrac{0.12}{n}\right)^n$
1 (annually)	
2 (semiannually)	
4 (quarterly)	
12 (monthly)	
52 (weekly)	
365 (daily)	
8760 (hourly)	

What do you think would be the year-end amount if interest were compounded "continuously"?

19. On July 1, 1987, $4000 was deposited in a savings account that compounds interest annually at an effective rate of 8%. How much interest did the account earn in 1990?

20. You would like to make a lump-sum payment at age 21 into a savings account paying interest at a nominal rate of 7.6% compounded quarterly so that at age 65 the account will be worth $100,000. What must the lump sum be?

21. What price should you pay for a bond, redeemable for $10,000 ten years from now, if you want to earn 7.5% effective on your investment?

★ 22. You vow to deposit $1000 every January 1st from January 1, 1995 through January 1, 2004 into an account that compounds interest annually at an effective rate of 8%. What will be the value of the account immediately after your final payment on January 1, 2004?

8.4 *The Family of Decimals*

In Section 8.1 we mentioned that the family of decimals is divided into two major classes: terminating and infinite (nonterminating). In this section we will further split the class of infinite decimals into two subclasses, repeating and nonrepeating (see Figure 8.9), and examine the relationship between the three types of decimals and the set of rational numbers. We begin by investigating the terminating branch of the family.

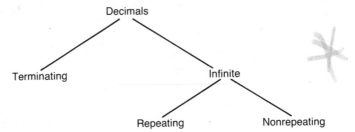

Figure 8.9 The family of decimals.

Terminating Decimals

In working Exercise 2, Section 8.1, you might have observed the following:

Every common fraction having only 2s and 5s as factors of its denominator is equal to a terminating decimal.

Thus

$$\frac{7}{2 \cdot 2 \cdot 5} = \frac{7 \cdot 5}{2 \cdot 5 \cdot 2 \cdot 5} = \frac{35}{10 \cdot 10} = \frac{35}{100} = .35$$

$$\frac{11}{5 \cdot 5 \cdot 5} = \frac{2 \cdot 2 \cdot 2 \cdot 11}{2 \cdot 5 \cdot 2 \cdot 5 \cdot 2 \cdot 5} = \frac{88}{10 \cdot 10 \cdot 10} = \frac{88}{1000} = .088$$

$$\frac{3}{2^4 \cdot 5^7} = \frac{2^3 \cdot 3}{2^3 \cdot 2^4 \cdot 5^7} = \frac{8 \cdot 3}{2^7 \cdot 5^7} = \frac{24}{10^7} = .0000024$$

The converse is also true.

> The *only* fractions that are equal to terminating decimals are those that, when written in lowest terms, have only 2s and 5s as factors in their denominators.

The following example should serve as evidence of the truth of this statement.

EXAMPLE 1   The number $\frac{2}{3}$ cannot be expressed as a terminating decimal.

Proof   Suppose, on the contrary, that $\frac{2}{3}$ could be expressed as a terminating decimal. Then $\frac{2}{3}$ would be equal to some decimal fraction. Let's say

$$\frac{2}{3} = \frac{X}{10^n}$$

Then, factoring 10^n into primes, we have

$$\frac{2}{3} = \frac{X}{2^n \cdot 5^n}$$

which, by the crisscross equality criterion, yields

$$2^{n+1} \cdot 5^n = 3 \cdot X$$

But this result contradicts the unique factorization theorem (the fundamental theorem of arithmetic), because the prime factor 3 appears on the right-hand side but not on the left. Thus we are forced to reject our original assumption that $\frac{2}{3}$ is expressible as a terminating decimal.   Q.E.D.

Thus the terminating-decimal branch of the decimal family corresponds to a very special subset of rational numbers, namely, those whose lowest-terms fraction labels have only 2s and 5s as factors in their denominators. It turns out that all of the other rational numbers have repeating-infinite-decimal labels. Let's see why.

Repeating Decimals

Consider the rational number $\frac{5}{27}$, which, in view of the denominator, does *not* correspond to a terminating decimal. Long division of 5 by 27 reveals a very interesting pattern:

$$
\begin{array}{r}
.185185\ldots \\
27\overline{)5.000000\ldots} \\
\underline{2\ 7} \\
2\ 30 \\
\underline{2\ 16} \\
140 \\
\underline{135} \\
50 \\
\underline{27} \\
230 \\
\underline{216} \\
140 \\
\underline{135} \\
5 \\
\vdots
\end{array}
$$

The digits 1, 8, and 5 occur in repeating blocks. If you try the same thing with other nondecimal fractions, like $\frac{4}{11}$ or $\frac{3}{7}$, sooner or later a similar pattern appears:

$$
\begin{array}{r}
.36\overline{36}\ldots \\
11\overline{)4.0000\ldots} \\
\underline{3\ 3} \\
70 \\
\underline{66} \\
40 \\
\underline{33} \\
70 \\
\underline{66} \\
4 \\
\vdots
\end{array}
\qquad
\begin{array}{r}
.42857142\ldots \\
7\overline{)3.00000000\ldots} \\
\underline{2\ 8} \\
20 \\
\underline{14} \\
60 \\
\underline{56} \\
40 \\
\underline{35} \\
50 \\
\underline{49} \\
10 \\
\underline{7} \\
30 \\
\underline{28} \\
20 \\
\underline{14} \\
6 \\
\vdots
\end{array}
$$

(The repeating blocks of digits are indicated by bars.) It is not hard to see that this repetition is inevitable. Consider, for example, the division of 7 into 3. During the performance of the algorithm many remainders appear:

$$30 - 28 = 2 \qquad 20 - 14 = 6 \qquad 60 - 56 = 4 \qquad 40 - 35 = 5 \qquad . \ . \ .$$

Since all remainders must be less than the divisor 7 and greater than zero (because the decimal for $\frac{3}{7}$ does not terminate), they are forced to assume one of the six values

$$\underline{\quad}\ 1 \qquad \underline{\quad}\ 2 \qquad \underline{\quad}\ 3 \qquad \underline{\quad}\ 4 \qquad \underline{\quad}\ 5 \qquad \underline{\quad}\ 6$$

If we continue dividing until we have generated more than six remainders, then by the pigeonhole principle, a remainder that appeared earlier will have to appear again; and as soon as that happens, the computations will repeat. In the case of $\frac{3}{7}$ the computations began to repeat as soon as the remainder 3 occurred, because that remainder duplicated the original dividend.

Symbols such as

$$.185185\overline{185} . \ . \ . \qquad .428571\overline{428571} . \ . \ . \qquad .3636\overline{36} . \ . \ .$$

are referred to as **repeating decimals.** The repeating block of digits is called the **repetend.** For purposes of emphasis we will usually write each block more than once and use the bar and an ellipsis, as in the preceding display. A more abbreviated notation uses the bar alone:

$$.\overline{185} \qquad .\overline{428571} \qquad .\overline{36}$$

We can now state the general result suggested by the preceding examples.

> Every common fraction is equal to a terminating or a repeating decimal.

The converse of this result is also true.

> Every terminating and every repeating decimal is equal to a common fraction.

For terminating decimals this result is trivial:

$$5.174 = \frac{5174}{1000} \qquad \text{(by definition)}$$

$$.00013 = \frac{13}{100,000} \qquad \text{(by definition)}$$

For repeating decimals it is far from obvious.

EXAMPLE 2   Write a fraction for $.397397\overline{397}$ . . . .

Solution   The technique here is tricky. Let

$$x = .397\overline{397} \ldots$$

Then

$$1000x = 397.\overline{397} \ldots$$

So (and now it becomes clear why we multiplied both sides by 1000)

$$
\begin{array}{r}
1000x = 397.397\overline{397} \ldots \\
-x = -.397397 \ldots \\
\hline
999x = 397
\end{array}
$$

Thus

$$x = \frac{397}{999}$$

That is,

$$.397\overline{397} \ldots = \frac{397}{999}$$ ❏

EXAMPLE 3   Write a common fraction for $12.743\overline{43}$ . . . .

Solution   We begin as before. Let $x = 12.743\overline{43}$ . . . . In the previous example the repetend had 3 digits, and multiplying by 10^3 was successful. This time the repetend has 2 digits, so we try multiplying by 10^2:

$$
\begin{array}{r}
100x = 1274.34\overline{43} \ldots \\
-x = -12.743\overline{43} \ldots \\
\hline
99x = 1261.6
\end{array}
$$

Thus

$$x = \frac{1261.6}{99}$$

To produce a common fraction for x, multiply numerator and denominator by 10:

$$x = \frac{12{,}616}{990}$$ ❏

Decimals and Rational Numbers

Our displayed results relating decimals to common fractions can be restated to relate decimals to rational numbers.

> Every rational number is labeled by a terminating decimal or a repeating decimal; every terminating decimal and every repeating decimal labels a rational number.

Thus our family tree for decimals can be embellished as shown in Figure 8.10.

Two questions are suggested by Figure 8.10. A specific one is, What do the nonrepeating infinite decimals label? We will answer that question in the next section. A broader question is, How good a system of labels is the collection of terminating and repeating decimals? There are both theoretical and practical answers to this question.

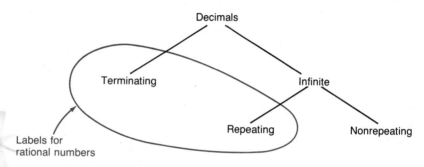

Figure 8.10

From a purely theoretical point of view the system of decimals is *not* as good as the system of lowest-terms fraction labels because decimals are *not* in one-to-one correspondence with rational numbers. In fact, every rational number that has a terminating-decimal label also has a repeating-decimal label.

EXAMPLE 4   Show that $2.6 = 2.599\overline{9}$ . . . .

Solution   Let $x = 2.599\overline{9}$ . . . . Then

$$
\begin{array}{rl}
10x = & 25.99\overline{9} \ldots \\
- \quad x = - & 2.59\overline{9} \ldots \\
\hline
9x = & 23.4
\end{array}
$$

from which it follows that

$$
x = \frac{23.4}{9} = 2.6
$$
❑

Rational numbers that do not have terminating-decimal labels, however, have unique decimal labels. For example, the only decimal label for $\frac{3}{7}$ is $.428571\overline{428571}$ . . . .

To arrive at a practical answer to the question "How good a system of labels is the set of decimals?" let us retrace our steps in this chapter. We began by observing that terminating decimals are excellent for computations because their algorithms are nearly the same as the corresponding whole number algorithms. Thus from a computational point of view, terminating decimals are very good labels. Unfortunately, many rational numbers do not have terminating-decimal labels, and computation with repeating decimals is not particularly easy.

EXAMPLE 5   Compute the difference $1.5353\overline{53}\ldots - 0.716\overline{716}\ldots$.

Solution   The left-to-right subtraction algorithm seems the most natural one to use, but some effort is required:

$$
\begin{array}{r}
1.5353535353535353\ldots \\
-\ .716716716716716\ldots \\
\hline
.8296478296478\ldots
\end{array}
$$

$$\underset{18\quad36\quad18\quad36}{}$$

The difference is $.818636\overline{818636}\ldots$.   ❏

Computing products and quotients of infinite decimals is even more daunting. Thus the full set of decimals, terminating and repeating, is *not* a computationally desirable set of labels for the rationals. From a practical point of view, however, we can always avoid infinite decimals and do all of our computations with terminating-decimal approximations, because of the following property.

> There is a terminating decimal as close as one pleases to any number.

EXAMPLE 6   Find a two-place terminating decimal within $\frac{1}{100}$ of $\frac{1}{3}$.

Solution   Since $\frac{1}{3} = .3333\ldots$, a terminating decimal within $\frac{1}{100}$ of $\frac{1}{3}$ is .33. Verification:

$$
\begin{array}{r}
.3333\ldots \\
-\ .33 \\
\hline
.0033\ldots
\end{array}
$$

and this difference is less than .01. The terminating decimal .34 is also within .01 of $\frac{1}{3}$.   ❏

EXAMPLE 7   Find a three-place terminating decimal within $\frac{1}{1000}$ of $\frac{15}{7}$.

Solution   Since $\frac{15}{7} = 2.142857\overline{142857}\ldots$, we can choose either 2.142 and 2.143.   ❏

Rounding

Reconsider the two preceding examples. In the first one .33 and .34 are both within .01 of .333 . . . , but .33 is the closer of the two. We say that .333 . . . rounded to the nearest hundredth is .33. That is:

> Rounding to the nearest hundredth means finding the closest two-place decimal.

In the second example, 2.142 and 2.143 are both within .001 of 2.142857142857 . . . , but 2.143 is the closer of the two. We say that 2.142857142857 . . . rounded to the nearest thousandth is 2.143. That is:

> Rounding to the nearest thousandth means finding the closest three-place decimal.

An algorithm for rounding to the nearest hundredth is suggested by the following example.

EXAMPLE 8 Round each number to the nearest hundredth.
(a) 2.71828   (b) 35.6347
(c) 1.92503   (d) 14.625

Solution (a) Draw a line after the hundredths place:

$$2.71|828$$

Examine the first digit to the right of that line. Since it is greater than 5, add .01 to the number to the left of the line:

$$2.71 + .01 = 2.72$$

Answer: 2.72.
(b) Draw a line after the hundredths place:

$$35.63|47$$

Since the first digit to the right of the line is less than 5, leave the number to the left of the line alone. *Answer:* 35.63.
(c) Draw a line after the hundredths place:

$$1.92|503$$

Since the first digit to the right of the line *is* 5, look further to the right. Since there is a nonzero digit to the right of the 5, add .01 to the number to the left of the line. *Answer:* 1.93.

(d) Draw a line after the hundredths place:

$$14.62|5$$

Since there is a 5 to the right of the line, we are to look further right. No nonzero digit is visible. At this point we are stymied. There are two two-place decimals that are precisely equidistant from 14.625, namely, 14.62 and 14.63. In this ambiguous case three conventions are possible:

1. When in doubt, round up. *Answer:* 14.63.
2. When in doubt, round down. *Answer:* 14.62.
3. When in doubt, round to the candidate that has an even digit in the hundredths place. *Answer:* 14.62.

The virtue of the third convention is that about half the time you will be rounding up and the other half down. Your calculations will not have a consistent inflationary or deflationary bias.   ❏

Rounding to positions other than hundredths is done similarly.

EXAMPLE 9   Round each number as indicated.
(a) 4.18237 to the nearest thousandth
(b) 75.351 to the nearest tenth
(c) 268.79 to the nearest ten
(d) $14.374\overline{374}$ . . . to the nearest 5-place decimal

Solution   (a) $4.182|37 \rightarrow 4.18\overset{\cdot}{2}$ (b) $75.3|51 \rightarrow 75.4$
(c) $26|8.79 \rightarrow 270$ (d) $14.37437|4374$ . . . $\rightarrow 14.37437$ ❏

EXERCISE SET 8.4

1. Express each of the following rational numbers as a terminating decimal if possible, and otherwise as a repeating infinite decimal.

   (a) $\dfrac{27}{2 \cdot 5^3}$ (b) $\dfrac{7}{625}$

   (c) $\dfrac{5}{11}$ (d) $\dfrac{5}{3}$

   (e) $\dfrac{124}{33}$ (f) $\dfrac{4}{7}$

   (g) $6\frac{1}{3}\%$ (h) $\dfrac{569}{5500}$

2. Concluding from a calculator display that a decimal is repeating, as in Exercise 1(h), is risky. If your calculator displays ten digits, then a display like 0.103454545 is fairly convincing evidence that the decimal repeats. But when you punch in $\boxed{5}\ \boxed{\div}\ \boxed{7}$ and get 0.714285714, there is less of a pattern from which to predict succeeding digits. It might not be absolutely clear that the next digit after the last 4 is a 2. Here is a way to uncover that next digit, which the calculator holds internally but does not display. Subtract 0.7, producing a new display of 0.014285714; now multi-

ply by 10 and the display will be 0.142857142. Sure enough, the next digit after the 4 is a 2.

(a) Find the digit that follows the 2 by subtracting 0.1 and then multiplying by 10.

(b) Try to find additional digits beyond the digit found in part (a).

(c) Clear your calculator and punch these keys $\boxed{1}$ $\boxed{e^x}$. Predict what digit follows the last digit in the display.

(d) Uncover that next digit by the technique described above. Was your prediction in part (c) correct?

(e) Do you think that the number $e^1 = e$ (Euler's number) from part (c) is rational?

3. When we factor numerator and denominator of the fraction $\frac{12}{30}$ we get

$$\frac{2 \cdot 2 \cdot 3}{2 \cdot 3 \cdot 5}$$

Notice that a factor besides 2 and 5, namely 3, appears in the denominator. How is it possible, then, that $\frac{12}{30}$ can be expressed as the terminating decimal .4?

4. Write a fraction for each of these repeating infinite decimals.

(a) $.27\overline{27} \ldots$ (b) $.528\overline{528} \ldots$

(c) $4.3295\overline{3295} \ldots$ (d) $47.3288\overline{8} \ldots$

(e) $5.072\overline{72} \ldots$ (f) $1.03652\overline{652} \ldots$

(g) $.99\overline{9} \ldots$ (h) $13.76199\overline{9} \ldots$

5. Look for a pattern in the repeating decimals for $\frac{1}{9}$, $\frac{2}{9}$, $\frac{3}{9}$; for $\frac{19}{99}$, $\frac{20}{99}$, $\frac{21}{99}$. Generalize.

6. Use Exercise 5 to explain why $.99\overline{9} \ldots = 1$.

7. Use the concept of density to explain why $.99\overline{9} \ldots$ could not be less than 1.

8. Write a repeating decimal equal to 7.001.

9. Suppose we define a *proper* repeating decimal to be one whose repetend is not 9 (or 0).

(a) Is any rational number represented by *both* a terminating decimal and a proper repeating decimal?

(b) Is any rational number represented by *neither* a terminating decimal nor a proper repeating decimal?

(c) Is any rational number represented by two proper repeating decimals?

10. Compute each of the following, using a left-to-right technique.

(a) $.475\overline{475} \ldots$
    $+ .93\overline{93} \ldots$

(b) $.93\overline{93} \ldots$
    $- .475\overline{475} \ldots$

★ 11. Compute each of the following by any method you wish.

(a) $(.93\overline{93} \ldots) \times (.4)$

(b) $(.495\overline{495} \ldots) \times (.74\overline{74} \ldots)$

(c) $(.407\overline{407} \ldots) \div (.02\overline{02} \ldots)$

12. Find two three-place decimals within $\frac{1}{1000}$ of each of the following numbers.

(a) $.547\overline{547} \ldots$ (b) $\frac{5}{6}$

(c) $\frac{14}{3}$ (d) $.717117111711117 \ldots$

(e) 3.75 (f) π

13. Does $.717117111711117 \ldots$ represent a rational number?

14. Put the following into appropriately shaped boxes and arrange them into a flowchart for rounding a (positive, terminating) decimal to the nearest hundredth. Use the convention "When in doubt, round up."

(a) Add .01 to the number left of the line.

(b) Discard digits to the right of the line.

(c) A decimal with three or more decimal places

(d) The best two-place decimal approximation

(e) Is the digit to the right of the line ≥ 5?

(f) Stop.

(g) Draw a line after the hundredths place.

(h) Start.

15. In the BASIC computer language there is a function INT that rounds every nonintegral input number *down* to the immediately preceding integer, leaving integers alone. For example: $INT(7.635) = 7$, $INT(^-2.13) = ^-3$, $INT(3) = 3$. Decide what the flowchart in Figure 8.11 accomplishes by tracing a variety of inputs through it.

16. Round each number to the specified place.

(a) 37.058 to the nearest hundredth

(b) 283.046 to the nearest tenth

(c) 6.799 to the nearest hundredth

(d) .03999 to the nearest thousandth

(e) ⁻83.875 to the nearest unit

(f) ⁻1.2345 to the nearest hundredth

(g) $\frac{7}{8}$ to the nearest tenth

(h) $\frac{22}{7}$ to the nearest thousandth

★ 17. Express the repeating duodecimal .T7T7$\overline{\text{T}7}$ . . . as an ordinary fraction.

★ 18. Express $\frac{1}{5}$ as a repeating duodecimal.

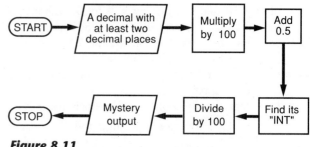

Figure 8.11

8.5 *Real Numbers, Pi, and Square Roots*

In the previous section we made several implicit assumptions about infinite decimals. Without ever stating precisely what was meant by such symbols as .397$\overline{397}$ . . . and 1.53$\overline{53}$ . . . , we assumed that they behaved like ordinary terminating decimals. For example, we assumed that multiplying .397$\overline{397}$ . . . by 1000 had the effect of sliding the decimal point three places to the right. And when we wanted to subtract .716$\overline{716}$ . . . from 1.53$\overline{53}$ . . . , we just went ahead and applied a conventional subtraction algorithm.

Fortunately, our assumptions about these infinite decimals are well founded. Not only repeating decimals like those just mentioned but also nonrepeating infinite decimals like

.717117111711117 . . .   and   .12345678910111213 . . .

can be given a specific meaning. They represent numbers that are called *real numbers,* and except for a few mild surprises such as .99$\overline{9}$ . . . equaling 1, they behave just like ordinary terminating decimals.

Real Numbers

The mathematical theory of real numbers and their representation by infinite decimals is considerably more difficult than the theory behind the integers or the rational numbers, which we explored previously. We won't be able to fill in all the details. The main ideas of the theory, however, are fairly simple to outline.

Consider an infinite decimal such as

.717117111711117 . . .

If this symbol is to represent a number, then that number should be greater than .7, a little greater than .71, a tiny bit greater than .717, ... Thus we are led to consider the steadily increasing sequence of rational numbers:

.7 < .71 < .717 < .7171 < .71711 < . . .

And we suppose that this sequence "approaches some limit." This limiting number is the meaning assigned to the infinite decimal

$$.717117111711117 \ldots$$

Thus any axiomatic description of the real number system has to guarantee the existence of such limits. Here is a somewhat loose, but straightforward, set of assumptions.

Assumptions About the Real Numbers

1. There is a set R of numbers called *real numbers* that includes the set Q of rationals as a subset.

2. There are binary operations $+$ and $\cdot$ and an order relation $<$ on R that extend those on Q.

3. All the structural and order properties that were true for Q remain true for R.

4. Any steadily increasing sequence of real numbers that is bounded above approaches a real number.

The third assumption on this list guarantees that the real numbers obey the same computational rules that the rationals and the integers obey.

EXAMPLE 1   Simplify.
   (a) $(^-\pi)(^-\sqrt{2})$
   (b) $\dfrac{\pi}{3} \div \dfrac{\sqrt{2}}{7}$

Solution   (a) $(^-\pi)(^-\sqrt{2}) = \pi\sqrt{2}$
   (b) $\dfrac{\pi}{3} \div \dfrac{\sqrt{2}}{7} = \dfrac{\pi}{3} \cdot \dfrac{7}{\sqrt{2}} = \dfrac{7\pi}{3\sqrt{2}}$ ❑

The fourth assumption on the list, the **completeness property** that sets the system of reals apart from the system of rationals, needs illustration.

EXAMPLE 2   Determine whether each of the following sequences approaches a limit.
   (a) $\dfrac{1}{2}, \dfrac{2}{3}, \dfrac{3}{4}, \dfrac{4}{5}, \ldots$
   (b) .2, .25, .252, .2525, .25252, .252525, . . .
   (c) .7, .71, .717, .7171, .71711, .717117, .7171171, .71711711, .717117111, .7171171117, . . .
   (d) $\dfrac{1}{8}, \dfrac{1}{4}, \dfrac{1}{2}, 1, 2, 4, 8, 16, \ldots$

(e) $\dfrac{1}{2}, \dfrac{^-3}{4}, \dfrac{7}{8}, \dfrac{^-15}{16}, \dfrac{31}{32}, \dfrac{^-63}{64}, \cdots$

Solution

(a) The sequence of rational numbers $\frac{1}{2}, \frac{2}{3}, \frac{3}{4}, \frac{4}{5}, \ldots$ is steadily increasing and is clearly bounded above since each term is less than 1. Thus by assumption 4, it approaches some real number. A glance at the number line in Figure 8.12 suggests that the real number being approached is 1. Arithmetically, the differences

$$1 - \tfrac{1}{2} \qquad 1 - \tfrac{2}{3} \qquad 1 - \tfrac{3}{4} \qquad 1 - \tfrac{4}{5} \qquad 1 - \tfrac{5}{6} \qquad \cdots$$

get exceedingly small as you move far out in the sequence.

(b) The sequence of rational numbers .2, 25, .252, .2525, . . . is also steadily increasing and is clearly bounded above by 1, or by .3, or by .26, ... Its limiting number is $\frac{25}{99}$. (Let $x = .25\overline{25}$ . . . and consider $100x - x$.)

(c) The sequence of rational numbers .7, .71, .717, . . . is steadily increasing and is bounded above (by all of .8, .72, .718, . . .). Thus by assumption 4, it approaches some limiting real number.

(d) The sequence of rational numbers $\frac{1}{8}, \frac{1}{4}, \frac{1}{2}, 1, \ldots$ is steadily increasing, but it is *not* bounded above. It does not approach a real number. "Infinity" is not a real number.

(e) The sequence of rational numbers $1/2, {}^-3/4, 7/8, {}^-15/16, \ldots$ is bounded above, by 1, but it is not steadily increasing. It does not approach *a* real number. ❏

Figure 8.12

Irrational Numbers

In this section and the previous one we have made two main points:

1. Every decimal, terminating or infinite, represents some real number.

2. The terminating and the repeating infinite decimals represent all of the rational numbers.

Thus all of the nonrepeating infinite decimals, such as the limiting number .717117111711117 . . . in part (c) of Example 2, represent real numbers that are not rational. Such numbers are called **irrational numbers.** Irrational numbers, it would seem, are very common. If fact, it should appear extremely unlikely that an infinite decimal, chosen at random, would exhibit a repeating pattern. Perhaps this point of view makes more plausible the bewildering result

Karl Weierstrass

Sonya Kovalesky

⚓ **KARL WEIERSTRASS** (1815–1897) was a towering figure in nineteenth-century mathematics, the genius who provided a rigorous logical foundation for the real number system and the mathematics built on it. He is known as the father of modern analysis. His life presents an interesting contrast to the lives of most other mathematicians. Born in Ostenfelde, Prussia, young Weierstrass showed brilliance in his high school work, but apparently devoted his four years at the University of Bonn to fencing and drinking. He dropped out after four years, with no degree, and enrolled in a teachers' college near his home, where he earned a teaching certificate. For the next 14 years he taught high school classes ranging from calligraphy to gymnastics.

During these years he also worked on mathematics, on his own and without benefit of a mathematics library or a colleague to talk to. When he finally published his research results in 1854, they created tremendous excitement. Still, the path to a professorship was not an easy one. It was 1864 before he was finally appointed full professor at the University of Berlin. Thus, at an age when many mathematicians have stopped doing creative work, Weierstrass was finally free to begin. His career at Berlin was a brilliant one. His lectures were prepared with painstaking care and were considered models of clarity. Students, including Hilbert and Cantor (with whom Weierstrass sided against his colleague Kronecker), flocked to his courses. One in particular deserves special mention.

Sonya Kovalesky (1850–1891), considered to be the greatest woman mathematician before 1900, was born in Moscow and, as one might expect, was barred from Russian universities because of her sex. The University of Berlin also barred women, and even the eminent Weierstrass could not obtain permission for her to attend his lectures. Thus began four years of private tutoring and mathematical discussions between Weierstrass and Kovalesky. In 1874 the University of Göttingen awarded her a doctorate, in absentia without examination. Nine years of nonmathematical jobs followed before the newly formed University of Stockholm broke with tradition and appointed this talented woman to an academic position. She rose to full professor by 1889. Less than two years later she died of influenza. Six years later her mentor, Weierstrass, succumbed to the same disease.

of page 76, which (in combination with Exercise 8 of Section 2.5) says, in essence, that the infinite set of irrational numbers is "larger" than the infinite set of rational numbers:

Real Numbers

Rationals

(Represented by terminating and repeating infinite decimals)

Irrationals

(Represented by nonrepeating infinite decimals)

Granted that, in theory, irrational numbers are plentiful, one question still remains. In practice, particularly in the elementary school, how common are irrational numbers? The honest answer to this question is that they are quite rare.

The Irrational Number Pi

The first irrational number that elementary school children encounter is the number pi (π), and this doesn't occur until, in the upper elementary grades, they begin to calculate the circumference and area of circles.

Circumference = $\pi \cdot$ diameter

Area = $\pi \cdot$ square of radius

(The first of these equations is usually taken as a definition of π. The second is a theorem that we will derive in Chapter 12.)

The infinite-decimal representation for π begins as follows:

$$\pi = 3.141592653 \ldots$$

A classroom activity for finding a terminating-decimal approximation to π is to find some large circle, like the top of a wastebasket or the wheel of a bicycle; wrap a string around it and measure the string to find the circumference; then measure its diameter; and finally, divide the circumference by the diameter.

The *proof* that π is irrational (that the preceding infinite decimal is not a repeating decimal) is, however, very difficult. In fact, the first proof of the irrationality of π was given only as recently as 1767 by Johann Heinrich Lambert (1728–1777). Fortunately, there are other commonly occurring irrational numbers for which proofs of irrationality are simple. Square roots provide perhaps the best example.

Square Roots

About the same time that children encounter the irrational number pi (π), they also meet the square root of two ($\sqrt{2}$), that is, the positive number whose square is 2. One can picture $\sqrt{2}$ geometrically as the side length of a square of area 2; see Figure 8.13.

A proof that $\sqrt{2}$ is irrational can be based on this simple observation, which we display for future reference:

The square of a whole number has an even number of factors in its prime factorization.

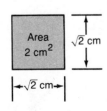

Figure 8.13

EXAMPLE 3   Show that each of these perfect squares has an even number of prime factors.
(a) 12^2
(b) 90^2

Solution   (a) 12 has an odd number (3) of prime factors, $12 = 2 \cdot 2 \cdot 3$; 12^2 has exactly twice as many, an even number, $12^2 = 2 \cdot 2 \cdot 3 \cdot 2 \cdot 2 \cdot 3$.
(b) 90 has an even number (4) of prime factors, $90 = 2 \cdot 3 \cdot 3 \cdot 5$; 90^2 has exactly twice as many, still an even number, $90^2 = 2 \cdot 3 \cdot 3 \cdot 5 \cdot 2 \cdot 3 \cdot 3 \cdot 5$. ❑

Now we proceed to the proof that $\sqrt{2}$ is irrational. Suppose, on the contrary, that $\sqrt{2}$ is rational; that is, suppose that $\sqrt{2}$ can be expressed by a common fraction, say

$$\sqrt{2} = \frac{m}{n}$$

Then squaring yields

$$2 = \frac{m^2}{n^2}$$

and hence

$$2 \cdot n^2 = m^2$$

Now, imagine factoring both the left- and the right-hand members of this equation into products of primes. On the right side there would be an even number of factors (by our simple observation); on the left side there would be an odd number of factors (n^2 has an even number of prime factors, but then there is the extra factor 2). This disparity is impossible by the fundamental theorem of arithmetic. Thus we are forced to reject our supposition that $\sqrt{2}$ is rational. That is:

$\sqrt{2}$ is irrational.

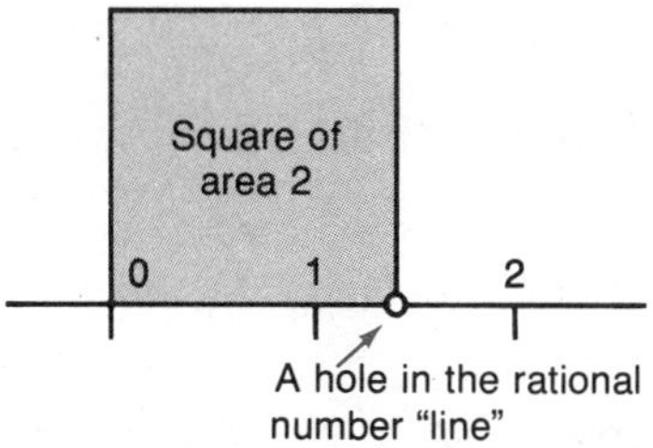

The fact the $\sqrt{2}$ is irrational reminds us that the "rational number line," like the "integer number line" before it, is not really a line. It is full of holes, as indicated in Figure 8.14. The *real* number line, however, is a bona fide line. It has no holes in it. For this reason one sometimes refers to the *continuum* of real numbers.

The real numbers are in one-to-one correspondence with *all* of the points on a line.

Square of area 2

0   1   2

A hole in the rational number "line"

Figure 8.14

If we accept the fact that there are no holes (a consequence of the completeness property), then it follows that many other square roots appear in R. See Figure 8.15. In fact, the following property can be deduced rigorously, using techniques that are well beyond the scope of this book.

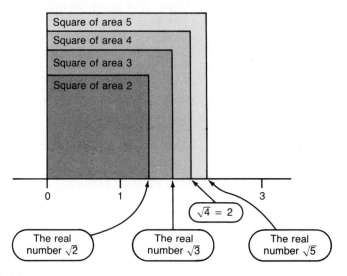

Figure 8.15

> Every nonnegative real number has exactly one (nonnegative) square root.

On this existence-uniqueness theorem one can base a definition of the *square root function.*

> If a is any nonnegative real number, then the **square root** of a, written $\sqrt{a}$, is *the* nonnegative real number whose square is a.

The symbol $\sqrt{}$ for the square root function is called a **radical.** A number that appears inside a radical is called a **radicand:**

$$\sqrt{49} \;=\; 7$$

Radical   Radicand   Value

Caution: Many people have the mistaken impression that $\sqrt{4} = \pm 2$. To see that this is *not* the case, punch in $\boxed{4}$ $\boxed{\sqrt{}}$ on your calculator and look at the display! Here is a precept worth remembering when working with real numbers: *The square root function* $\sqrt{}$ *neither accepts nor produces negative numbers*. (How does your calculator respond when you punch in $\boxed{4}$ $\boxed{+/-}$ $\boxed{\sqrt{}}$?)

For certain whole numbers n (the perfect squares 0, 1, 4, 9, . . .) $\sqrt{n}$ is again a whole number. For all other whole numbers n, $\sqrt{n}$ is irrational. Thus any algorithm for assigning decimal values to square roots will, in general, provide only approximations. Up until about thirty years ago every algebra student was taught an algorithm for finding such approximations with pencil and paper. This hand algorithm is quite complicated to carry out and even more difficult to explain. It is rarely taught nowadays because of the availability of calculators. Most calculators have a square root button that instantly gives a ten-digit decimal approximation, but even cheap ones that can only add, subtract, multiply, and divide can be used to approximate square roots. Here are two techniques.

First Technique (Bracket by Decimals).   Suppose you want decimal approximations to $\sqrt{2}$. First try whole numbers.

$$1^2 = 1 \qquad \text{is too small}$$
$$2^2 = 4 \qquad \text{is too large}$$

Therefore

$$1 < \sqrt{2} < 2$$

Now, try various one-place decimals (square them using the calculator) to narrow it down further:

$$1.4^2 = 1.96 \qquad \text{is too small}$$
$$1.5^2 = 2.25 \qquad \text{is too large}$$

Therefore

$$1.4 < \sqrt{2} < 1.5$$

Now, try two-place decimals to get still closer:

$$1.41^2 = 1.9881 \qquad \text{is too small}$$
$$1.42^2 = 2.0164 \qquad \text{is too large}$$

Therefore

$$1.41 < \sqrt{2} < 1.42$$

Continue this process until you have accuracy to as many decimal places as you desire.

Second Technique (Divide and Average).   Suppose you want decimal approximations to $\sqrt{2}$. Take a guess, say 1.5, and divide it into 2 on the calculator:

$$\frac{2}{1.5} \doteq 1.333333333$$

That is,

$$1.5 \times 1.333333333 \doteq 2$$

Note that the larger factor must exceed $\sqrt{2}$,

$$1.5 > \sqrt{2}$$

while the smaller factor must be less than $\sqrt{2}$,

$$1.333333333 < \sqrt{2}$$

So it is reasonable to average them (on the calculator),

$$\frac{1.5 + 1.333333333}{2} \doteq 1.416666667$$

and use this new number as a second approximation.

Divide it into 2 (on the calculator):

$$\frac{2}{1.416666667} \doteq 1.411764706$$

That is,

$$1.416666667 \times 1.411764706 \doteq 2$$

Again, the larger factor must exceed $\sqrt{2}$,

$$1.416666667 > \sqrt{2}$$

and the smaller factor must be less than $\sqrt{2}$,

$$1.411764706 < \sqrt{2}$$

So it is reasonable to average them (on the calculator),

$$\frac{1.416666667 + 1.411764706}{2} \doteq 1.414215686$$

and use this new number as a third approximation.

If you were to continue this process two more times, you would obtain the following record of approximations to $\sqrt{2}$:

First approximation: 1.5
Second approximation: 1.416666667
Third approximation: 1.414215686

Fourth approximation: 1.414213562
Fifth approximation: 1.414213562

From this record it is clear that the best nine-place decimal approximation to $\sqrt{2}$ is 1.414213562.

The divide-and-average technique, known already to Heron of Alexandria (ca. A.D. 100), is a special case of a much more general algorithm, known as Newton's method, that can be used to approximate a large class of roots including square roots, cube roots, fourth roots, and all higher roots.

EXERCISE SET 8.5

1. Simplify.
   (a) $\dfrac{(5 + \pi) - (3 - 5\pi)}{2} - 1$

   (b) $\dfrac{-3\pi/\sqrt{2}}{\pi/{}^-12\sqrt{2}}$

   (c) $\dfrac{1/\pi - 5/(3\pi)}{2}$

   (d) $\dfrac{\pi^3 + ({}^-\pi)^3}{\sqrt{2}}$

2. For each of the following sequences, specify an upper bound, if one exists. Then try to determine the real number approached by the sequence, if such a number exists. For some parts of this problem a calculator would be useful.
   (a) $\dfrac{1}{2}, \dfrac{3}{4}, \dfrac{5}{6}, \dfrac{7}{8}, \dfrac{9}{10}, \cdots$

   (b) .7, .74, .742, .7427, .74274, .742742, .7427427, . . .

   (c) $\dfrac{^-1}{1}, \dfrac{^-1}{2}, \dfrac{^-1}{3}, \dfrac{^-1}{4}, \dfrac{^-1}{5}, \cdots$

   (d) $\dfrac{1 + 2}{3 + 4}, \dfrac{5 + 6}{7 + 8}, \dfrac{9 + 10}{11 + 12}, \dfrac{13 + 14}{15 + 16}, \cdots$

   (e) $\dfrac{1 \cdot 2}{3 \cdot 4}, \dfrac{5 \cdot 6}{7 \cdot 8}, \dfrac{9 \cdot 10}{11 \cdot 12}, \dfrac{13 \cdot 14}{15 \cdot 16}, \cdots$

   (f) $\dfrac{1}{2}, \dfrac{1}{2} + \dfrac{1}{4}, \dfrac{1}{2} + \dfrac{1}{4} + \dfrac{1}{8}, \dfrac{1}{2} + \dfrac{1}{4} + \dfrac{1}{8} + \dfrac{1}{16}, \cdots$

   ★ (g) $\dfrac{1}{2}, \dfrac{1}{2} + \dfrac{1}{3}, \dfrac{1}{2} + \dfrac{1}{3} + \dfrac{1}{4}, \dfrac{1}{2} + \dfrac{1}{3} + \dfrac{1}{4} + \dfrac{1}{5}, \cdots$

   (h) $.99^1, .99^2, .99^3, .99^4, \cdots$
   (i) $1.01^1, 1.01^2, 1.01^3, 1.01^4, \cdots$

3. Give an example of a steadily increasing sequence of rational numbers that is bounded above but does not approach a *rational* limit. (Thus the rational number system does not satisfy all of the properties of the real number system; the rational number system is not *complete*.)

4. Classify each of the following numbers as rational or irrational.
   (a) .1232123212321 . . .
   (b) .121232123432123454321 . . .
   (c) $\frac{22}{7}$ (d) 3.14159
   (e) π (f) 2π
   (g) $\dfrac{3\pi + 17}{37}$ (h) 0
   (i) $-\pi$ (j) $\pi - \left(\dfrac{\pi^2 - 1}{\pi - 1}\right)$

5. Is the set of irrational numbers closed under these operations?
   (a) Addition   (b) Subtraction
   (c) Multiplication   (d) Division

6. Between any two (distinct) real numbers is a terminating-decimal rational number. This statement is stronger than the statement that the real numbers are dense. Use a guess-and-check method to find a terminating decimal between the following.
   (a) π and $\sqrt{10}$ (b) $\sqrt{99}$ and $\sqrt{100}$

7. Between what two whole numbers does each of the following lie?
   (a) $\sqrt{60}$ (b) $\sqrt{85}$ (c) $\sqrt{3.5}$ (d) $\sqrt{200}$

8. Find a two-place decimal approximation to $\sqrt{3}$ by the bracket-by-decimals technique.

9. Find a four-place decimal approximation to $\sqrt{5}$ by the divide-and-average technique.

★ 10. A sequence of numbers is defined recursively as follows:

   1. The first term is 1.

   2. Every term of the sequence beyond the first is obtained by squaring the previous one, adding 2, and dividing this sum by twice the previous term.

      (a) Find the second, third, and fourth terms of the sequence.

      (b) What number does the sequence seem to be approaching?

11. Find the following without using a calculator.
    (a) $\sqrt{36}$
    (b) $\sqrt{3600}$
    (c) $\sqrt{360000}$
    (d) $\sqrt{.36}$
    (e) $\sqrt{.0036}$
    (f) $\sqrt{1/4}$
    (g) $\sqrt{9/4}$
    (h) $\sqrt{0}$

12. Solve each equation
    (a) $\sqrt{\dfrac{x}{3}} = 4$

    (b) $\sqrt{2x - 1} = 5$

    (c) $5 = 2\sqrt{\dfrac{75}{x}}$

    (d) $\sqrt{\dfrac{x + 1}{x - 1}} = 3$

13. Prove that each of the following numbers is irrational.
    (a) $\sqrt{3}$
    (b) $\sqrt{5}$
    ★ (c) $\sqrt{6}$

★ (d) $\sqrt[3]{2}$ (This symbol, read "the cube root of 2," represents the positive number whose third power is equal to 2.)

★ (e) $\log_{10}(2)$

14. Is it true that $\sqrt{11} = 3.31666\ldots$? Explain why or why not.

15. How can you use Figure 8.16 to prove that the diagonal of the unit square has length $\sqrt{2}$, *without* invoking the Pythagorean theorem?

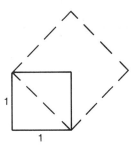

Figure 8.16

16. Justify each statement in this four-step proof that $\sqrt{2} \cdot \sqrt{5} = \sqrt{10}$.
    (a) $\sqrt{10}$ is the unique positive number whose square is 10.
    (b) $\sqrt{2} \cdot \sqrt{5}$ is a positive number.
    (c) $(\sqrt{2} \cdot \sqrt{5})^2 = 10$.
    (d) $\sqrt{2} \cdot \sqrt{5} = \sqrt{10}$.

17. Prove each of the following rules in which a and b represent arbitrary positive real numbers.

    (a) $\sqrt{a \cdot b} = \sqrt{a} \cdot \sqrt{b}$ (b) $\sqrt{\dfrac{a}{b}} = \dfrac{\sqrt{a}}{\sqrt{b}}$

18. Decide whether each of the following statements is true or false.
    (a) $(^-2)^2 = 4$
    (b) $\sqrt{4} = {}^-2$
    (c) $\sqrt{4} = \pm 2$
    (d) The only solution to $x^2 = 2$ is $x = \sqrt{2}$
    (e) $\sqrt{(^-2)^2} = {}^-2$
    (f) $\sqrt{x^2} = x$ for every real number x
    (g) $\sqrt{^-4} = -\sqrt{4}$
    (h) $\sqrt{a + b} = \sqrt{a} + \sqrt{b}$ for all positive real numbers a and b

19. Megan claims that the equation $x^2 = 4$ has two solutions, 2 and $^-2$. Esther disagrees and gives the "proof" below that there is just one. Find the flaw in her argument.

$$x^2 = 4 \Rightarrow \sqrt{x^2} = \sqrt{4} \Rightarrow x = 2$$

20. We have studied the chain of number systems

$$W \subset I \subset Q \subset R$$

For each equation, name the *first* number system in the chain in which that equation has a solution.

(a) $\frac{3}{8}x = 5$
(b) $9 - 2x = 1$
(c) $x\left(\dfrac{5x}{17} - \dfrac{2}{3}\right) = 0$
(d) $x \cdot 2 = 1$
(e) $x + 2 = 1$
(f) $x^2 = 1$
(g) $x^2 = 2$
(h) $x^2 = {}^-2$

21. Galileo discovered that the speed v of a falling object is proportional to the square root of the distance d it has fallen. Specifically,

$$v = \sqrt{2gd}$$

where g is the gravitational constant, 980 cm/sec², d is measured in centimeters, and v is given in centimeters per second (cm/sec). (The formula does not apply to objects like parachutes that encounter significant air resistance.)

(a) A marble is dropped from a height of 10 cm above a desk. How fast is it traveling when it hits the desk?

(b) If the marble is dropped from a height of 90 cm above the desk, how fast is it traveling when it hits?

(c) Do you think the formula is valid for large values of d like $d = 10^{12}$?

22. For a simple pendulum as shown in Figure 8.17, the time T that it takes the bob to make one round-trip (the *period* of the pendulum) does not depend on either the angle of displacement θ (as long as θ is fairly small) or the mass of the bob. It depends only on the length l and the gravitational constant g. The formula is

$$T = 2\pi\sqrt{\dfrac{l}{g}}$$

where $g = 980$ cm/sec², l is given in centimeters, and T is given in seconds.

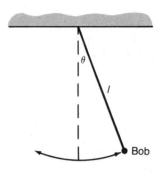

Figure 8.17

(a) What is the period of a simple pendulum of length 20 cm?

(b) What is the period of a simple pendulum of length 80 cm?

(c) Find the length, to the nearest tenth of a centimeter, of a simple pendulum of period 1 sec.

(d) Find the length, to the nearest centimeter, of a simple pendulum that takes 1 sec to swing from its far left to its far right positon.

★ 23. According to Einstein's theory, the mass of an object increases as its velocity increases. The formula involves a radical,

$$m = \dfrac{m_0}{\sqrt{1 - v^2/c^2}}$$

where m_0 is the object's mass when at rest, c is the speed of light, v is the object's velocity, and m is the object's mass at velocity v.

(a) Suppose that an object of rest mass 100 kg is traveling at 60% of the speed of light. What is its mass?

(b) What is the object's mass when it is traveling at 80% of the speed of light?

(c) What happens to the object's mass as its velocity approaches the speed of light?

★ 24. In seven-clock arithmetic, what meaning would you assign to each of the following symbols?

(a) $\sqrt{2}$ (b) $\sqrt{3}$ (c) $\sqrt[3]{1}$ (d) $\sqrt[6]{1}$

★ 25. You may recall that in ordinary algebra the solutions to a *quadratic equation*

$$ax^2 + bx + c = 0$$

are given by the *quadratic formula*,

$$x = \frac{-b \pm \sqrt{b^2 - 4ac}}{2a}$$

Use this formula to solve the following quadratic equations in the algebra of seven-clock numbers.
(a) $3x^2 + x + 4 = 0$ (b) $x^2 + 6x + 3 = 0$

Key Concepts in Chapter 8

Decimal fraction
Terminating decimal
Expanded form
Algorithms for decimals
Percent
Percent of increase and decrease
Scientific notation
*Principal
*Interest
*Term

*Amount
*Effective rate
*Nominal rate
*Simple interest
*Compound interest
Repeating decimal
Completeness
Irrational number
Square root

✍ Chapter 8 Review Exercises ✍

1. Express each of the following as directed.
   (a) .073 as a fraction with denominator a power of ten
   (b) 294/1,000,000 as a decimal
   (c) 275.36 in expanded form
   (d) Sixty and five-hundredths as a decimal
   (e) $7.65/10^4$ as a decimal
   (f) 6% as a decimal
   (g) .9 as a percent
   (h) $12\frac{1}{2}$ as a percent
   (i) 1947 in scientific notation
   (j) 3.6×10^{-3} as a decimal

2. Compute.
   (a) $19.4 + 136 + 4.825$
   (b) $2500 \times .018$
   (c) $65 \div 3.125$
   (d) 15% of 15
   (e) $(3.2 \times 10^5) \times (1.5 \times 10^{-2})$
   (f) $\dfrac{1.5 \times 10^2}{6.0 \times 10^5}$

3. Give a reason at each step in this calculation of a product of decimals via fractions.

$$.028 \times 6.4 = \frac{28}{1000} \times \frac{64}{10} \qquad \text{(a)} \underline{\hspace{2cm}}$$

$$= \frac{28 \times 64}{1000 \times 10} \qquad \text{(b)} \underline{\hspace{2cm}}$$

$$= \frac{1792}{10,000} \qquad \text{(c)} \underline{\hspace{2cm}}$$

$$= .1792 \qquad \text{(d)} \underline{\hspace{2cm}}$$

4. Calculate the difference $21.254 - 5.4$ by converting to fraction notation, subtracting the fractions, and then converting the answer to a decimal. Show the main steps of your work.

5. Which is greater, $-(\frac{4}{7})$ or $-.572$?

6. A medicinal compound costs $2.65 per gram. How much does 3.4 g cost?

7. Maria leaves on a trip with a full tank of gas. After driving 300 miles she refills the tank for $6.75 at a station that charges 89.9 cents per gallon. How many miles per gallon did she get?

8. Last year the price of a kilogram of cashews rose $.75 to a new high of $8.25. What was the percent of increase?

9. If the price of oil rose 40% between 1970 and 1980 and fell 30% between 1980 and 1990, what was the percent of increase or decrease from 1970 to 1990?

10. Al's Discount Store normally sells an item at 25% off retail price. By what percent must Al mark down his already low price in order to bring the item's price down to half of the retail price?

11. On January 1, 1980 the population of a resort town was 4000. For the next ten years the population increased 10% in June and decreased 10% in September. What was the population on January 1, 1990?

12. A machine is 65% energy-efficient if 65% of the energy supplied to it is converted into useful work. A generator that is 65% energy-efficient supplies energy to a mill that is 55% energy-efficient. If 8400 joules (J) of energy are supplied to the generator, how many joules of useful work are done by the mill?

★ 13. An original principal of $800 is deposited in a savings account that pays a nominal rate of interest of 7.8% and compounds monthly.
   (a) Find the effective monthly rate of interest.
   (b) Find the amount in the account after one year.
   (c) What effective annual rate of interest does this account pay?
   (d) If you close the account after $7\frac{1}{2}$ months, what amount will you be paid?
   (e) How much principal is in this account during the third month, and how much interest does it earn during that month?

14. (a) If a number can be expressed as a terminating decimal, then what can be said about its lowest-terms fraction label?
   (b) If a number can be expressed by neither a terminating nor a repeating decimal, then what can be said about that number?

15. Express each as directed.
   (a) $\frac{2}{13}$ as a repeating decimal
   (b) $.247\overline{47}$ . . . as a common fraction
   (c) $.123\overline{123}$ . . . as a fraction in lowest terms.

16. Express the sum $5.72\overline{72}$ . . . $+ .856\overline{856}$ . . . as a repeating decimal.

17. Show that $.99\overline{9}$ . . . $= 1$ by computing $1 - .99\overline{9}$ . . . left to right.

18. Write a terminating decimal equal to $3.189\overline{99}$ . . . .

19. Round each number as indicated.
   (a) 5.7961 to the nearest hundredth
   (b) 13.451 to the nearest tenth
   (c) π to the nearest hundredth

20. Classify as rational or irrational.
   (a) .12112211122211112222111112222 . . .
   (b) .27972
   (c) $\dfrac{4(5 - 3\pi) + 6(2\pi + 5)}{10}$
   (d) $\dfrac{7\pi}{22} + 3$
   (e) $\sqrt{64}$

21. True or false?
   (a) The sum of two terminating decimals is a terminating decimal.
   (b) The product of a rational and an irrational number is irrational.
   (c) Every steadily increasing sequence of negative real numbers approaches zero.
   (d) For every real number x, $\sqrt{x^4} = x^2$.
   (e) The sum of two *proper repeating decimals* (that is, decimals in which the repetend is neither 0 nor 9) is again a proper repeating decimal.
   (f) Every proper common fraction with denominator 21 (except 0/21) is equal to a proper repeating decimal.

22. Is 2 an upper bound on the following sequence?
   $\frac{1}{2}, \frac{1}{2} + \frac{1}{3}, \frac{1}{2} + \frac{1}{3} + \frac{1}{4}, \frac{1}{2} + \frac{1}{3} + \frac{1}{4} + \frac{1}{5}, \ldots$

23. Write a symbol for the positive number which when multiplied by itself yields the circumference of a circle having diameter 1.

24. Solve the equation $\sqrt{\dfrac{80}{x - 3}} = 4$.

25. Express $\sqrt{1.44 \times 10^{100}}$ in scientific notation.

26. Write a proof that $\sqrt{7}$ is irrational.

27. Find $\sqrt{.00000144}$

28. Suppose you are trying to find $\sqrt{75}$ by the divide-and-average process, and your first approximation (guess) is 5. What will be the second and third approximations?

References

Chinn, W., R. Dean, and T. Tracewell. *Arithmetic and Calculators*. San Francisco: Freeman, 1978.

National Council of Teachers of Mathematics. *30th Yearbook: More Topics in Mathematics for Elementary School Teachers*. Reston, Va.: NCTM, 1969.

———— *1982 Yearbook: Mathematics for the Middle Grades*. Reston, Va.: NCTM, 1982.

Niven, I. *Numbers: Rational and Irrational*. New York: Random House, 1961.

PROBABILITY

One of the most stable trends in mathematics education in recent years has been the increasing emphasis on the related fields of probability and statistics. Both have become established as standard topics in the junior high school curriculum, and both are receiving some attention at the elementary level as well. Here is what the *Standards* have to say: "In grades K–4 the mathematics curriculum should include experiences with data analysis and probability so that students can collect, organize, and describe data; construct, read, and interpret displays of data; formulate and solve problems that involve collecting and analyzing data; explore concepts of chance." Figure 9.1 shows how experiences in probability and statistics are treated in a fifth-grade textbook. In this chapter we begin with a survey of some of the basic concepts of probability; in the next chapter we will go on to statistics.

The earliest published works concerning mathematical probability were inspired by problems from gambling and appeared in Italy at about the time of Columbus's voyages to America. Later an Italian, Girolamo Cardano (1501–1576), wrote a gambler's manual that touched on the subject. But two French mathematicians, Blaise Pascal (1623–1662) and Pierre Fermat (1601?–1665), laid the real foundations for probability. They did so in response to a gambling problem posed to Pascal by the Chevalier de Méré in 1654.

From its origins as a method for studying games of chance, probability has evolved into a powerful and widely applicable branch of mathematics. The uses of probability range from the determination of life insurance premiums, to the prediction of election outcomes, to the description of the behavior of molecules in a gas. Its utility is one good reason why the study of probability has found its way into junior high and even elementary textbooks.

Another reason the study of probability continues to move down in the grades is its simplicity. The only real prerequisite for solving simple probability problems is a familiarity with positive rational numbers. Before commencing a careful study, let us take a quick look at a few problems from a completely intuitive viewpoint to get a preview of the connection between rational numbers and probability.

11. Toss a penny 40 times and complete this record of your experiment.

Possible outcomes	● Heads	● Tails
Tally of outcomes		
Fraction of all outcomes		

Andrew tossed a paper cup and recorded the outcomes on a bar graph.

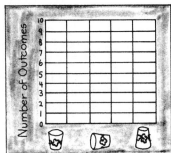

12. How many possible outcomes?

13. How many times did he toss the cup?

14. What fraction of the outcomes were right side up?

15. If you were to toss the cup one time, how do you think it would land?

EXPERIMENT: Tossing a Thumbtack		
Possible outcomes	⌄	●
Tally of outcomes	⅏⅏ ⅏ ⅏ III	⅏ II
Fraction of all outcomes	?	?

7. How many possible outcomes?

8. How many times did the thumbtack land "point down"? "point up"?

9. What fraction of the outcomes were "point up"?

10. If you were to toss the thumbtack once, how do you think it would land?

Figure 9.1 Probability and statistics in a fifth-grade textbook.

PROBLEM 1	A class consists of 12 boys and 15 girls. If a student is picked at random, what is the probability that it will be a girl?
Solution	Girls make up $\frac{15}{27}$ of the class. The probability that a girl will be picked is $\frac{15}{27}$. ❑

Figure 9.2

PROBLEM 2	A single die (Figure 9.2) is to be rolled. What is the probability that a 5 will turn up?
Solution	If the die were rolled a large number of times, one would expect each of the 6 numbers to come up about the same fraction of the time; that is, about $\frac{1}{6}$ of the time. The probability that a 5 will turn up is $\frac{1}{6}$. ❑

PROBLEM 3	A number is chosen at random from among the whole numbers 1, 2, 3, . . ., 20. What is the probability that it will be a prime?
Solution	The prime number from 1 to 20 are 2, 3, 5, 7, 11, 13, 17, and 19. That is, $\frac{8}{20}$ of the numbers are prime. The probability of drawing a prime is $\frac{8}{20}$. ❑

9.1 *Outcomes and Their Probabilities*

Although applications of probability can be found in a wide variety of practical fields, the study of simple games of chance remains an ideal vehicle for presenting the basic concepts and terminology of the subject.

Consider the **random experiment** of spinning the spinner shown in Figure 9.3. Each spin is called a **trial.** On each trial there are four possible **outcomes.** The point can stop on red, white, blue, or green. (If it stops on a dividing line, we agree to ignore that spin and try again.) The set of all possible outcomes {R, W, B, G} is called the **outcome set** or **sample space** for the experiment.

If the experiment is repeated many times, it is reasonable to expect, from the sizes of the sectors on the dial, that green should come up about $\frac{1}{2}$ the time, red $\frac{1}{4}$ the time, and white and blue $\frac{1}{8}$ of the time each. Thus we have an assignment of rational numbers to outcomes. We refer to this assignment as the **probability function** p for the experiment. An arrow diagram (Figure 9.4) for p is called a **probability diagram** for the experiment.

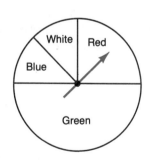

Figure 9.3

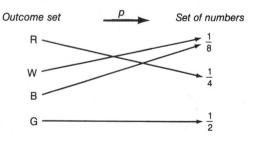

Figure 9.4

We read the symbols

$$p(\text{R}) = \tfrac{1}{4}$$

as "the probability of red is $\tfrac{1}{4}$."

Two important observations can be made from the probability diagram in Figure 9.4:

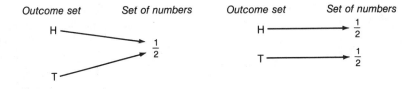

Each outcome has probability between 0 and 1.

The sum of the probabilities of all of the outcomes is 1.

In this case

$$p(\text{R}) + p(\text{W}) + p(\text{B}) + p(\text{G}) = \tfrac{1}{4} + \tfrac{1}{8} + \tfrac{1}{8} + \tfrac{1}{2} = 1$$

To emphasize the fact that the probabilities add to 1, we often draw the probability diagram as in Figure 9.5, even though, technically, the listing of $\tfrac{1}{8}$ twice in the second set is superfluous.

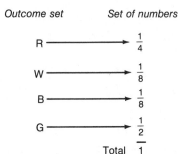

Figure 9.5

EXAMPLE 1   Decide on an outcome set and draw a probability diagram for the experiment of flipping a coin.

Solution   The natural outcome set to consider is {H, T}. Assuming the coin is "honest," the probability diagram should be drawn as in Figure 9.6 or Figure 9.7.

Outcome set	Set of numbers		Outcome set	Set of numbers
H			H ⟶	$\tfrac{1}{2}$
	$\tfrac{1}{2}$			
T			T ⟶	$\tfrac{1}{2}$

Figure 9.6   **Figure 9.7**   ❏

A classroom activity for verifying that $\tfrac{1}{2}$ is indeed a reasonable probability to assign to both H and T would be to have each student flip a coin 10 times and keep track of the number of heads. While only about one-fourth of the students might flip exactly 5 heads and 5 tails, still the ratio of heads to total tosses in the *entire* class should be close to $\tfrac{1}{2}$. Table 9.1 shows an actual record of 100 coin tosses. Notice how the ratio of heads to total tosses approaches .50 as the number of tosses increases.

EXAMPLE 2   Suppose that the student body at a certain college consists of 1400 freshmen, 1000 sophomores, 800 juniors, and 700 seniors. The experiment consists of

Table 9.1 100 Tosses of a Coin

	Number of Heads	Ratio of Heads to Tosses	Cumulative Ratio of Heads to Tosses
First 10 tosses	7	$\frac{7}{10} = .70$	$\frac{7}{10} = .70$
Second 10 tosses	6	$\frac{6}{10} = .60$	$\frac{13}{20} = .65$
Third 10 tosses	7	$\frac{7}{10} = .70$	$\frac{20}{30} \doteq .67$
Fourth 10 tosses	4	$\frac{4}{10} = .40$	$\frac{24}{40} = .60$
Fifth 10 tosses	4	$\frac{4}{10} = .40$	$\frac{28}{50} = .56$
Sixth 10 tosses	5	$\frac{5}{10} = .50$	$\frac{33}{60} = .55$
Seventh 10 tosses	2	$\frac{2}{10} = .20$	$\frac{35}{70} = .50$
Eighth 10 tosses	3	$\frac{3}{10} = .30$	$\frac{38}{80} \doteq .48$
Ninth 10 tosses	7	$\frac{7}{10} = .70$	$\frac{45}{90} = .50$
Tenth 10 tosses	6	$\frac{6}{10} = .60$	$\frac{51}{100} = .51$

Outcome set   Set of numbers

Fr ⟶ $\frac{1400}{3900} \doteq .36$

So ⟶ $\frac{1000}{3900} \doteq .26$

Jr ⟶ $\frac{800}{3900} \doteq .21$

Sr ⟶ $\frac{700}{3900} \doteq .18$

Figure 9.8

going to the records office and selecting a student file at random. Decide on an outcome set and draw a probability diagram.

Solution   See Figure 9.8. ❑

EXAMPLE 3   Medical records indicate that of the 7325 patients treated at the student infirmary last year, 6420 were discharged the same day. What is the probability that a patient, chosen at random, will not be discharged on the day of admission?

Solution   See Figure 9.9. The probability is about .12.

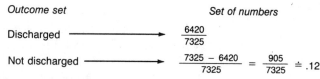

Outcome set   Set of numbers

Discharged ⟶ $\frac{6420}{7325}$

Not discharged ⟶ $\frac{7325 - 6420}{7325} = \frac{905}{7325} \doteq .12$

Figure 9.9 ❑

In each of the experiments that we have considered so far one natural outcome set has suggested itself. This is not always the case. Different people may observe the same experiment and decide on quite different outcome sets. The only criterion that a set of "happenings" must satisfy to qualify as an outcome set is this:

On each trial, exactly one of the happenings must take place.

EXAMPLE 4 An experiment consists of drawing one marble from an urn containing 5 red glass marbles, 3 red plastic marbles, 4 blue glass marbles, and 1 blue plastic marble. Draw three different probability diagrams.

Solution See Figure 9.10.   ❏

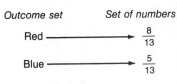

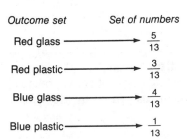

Figure 9.10

The examples we have considered suggest two different ways in which one can assign probabilities to outcomes of a random experiment. One way is to make an *a priori* judgment about a random device: The probability of heads on a flip of an honest coin ought to be $\frac{1}{2}$; the probability of a 5 on a roll of an honest die ought to be $\frac{1}{6}$; the probability of a 17 on an honest roulette wheel with 38 equally large sectors ought to be $\frac{1}{38}$. In general:

> In an experiment with n equally likely outcomes, the probability of each outcome is $1/n$.

For a spinner experiment, of course, the assumption is that each of the infinitely many directions that the needle might point is equally likely. The probabilities of the outcomes red, blue, . . . depend on the sizes of the sectors of those colors.

Another way of assigning probabilities to outcomes of an experiment is to make an *a posteriori* judgment based on statistical data from past performances. By flipping a coin a large number of times and observing the behavior of the ratio of heads to tosses, one can assign a probability to heads. This method will work as well for a biased coin (or a loaded die, or a nonrandom roulette wheel), as it will for an honest device. It also works in situations, such as the infirmary example, where there is no physical device to analyze. In general:

> If F is the number of occurrences of a particular outcome in n trials, and if F/n approaches a limit as n gets large, then this limiting number is the probability of the outcome in question.

See Exercise 12 following for an example of statistical estimation of probabilities.

You probably noticed that we did not try to formally define the term *random*. Your intuition will have to guide you. Drawing a marble out of a fishbowl with your eyes wide open is not a random experiment; drawing with your eyes closed is. Choosing the last student back from recess is not a random selection from your class; putting each student's name on a slip of paper and drawing one (blindly) from a hat is. In the exercises you will be asked to devise other methods of random selection.

EXERCISE SET 9.1

1. The experiment consists of spinning the spinner in Figure 9.11.

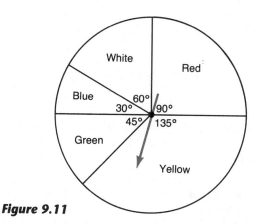

Figure 9.11

(a) Complete the probability diagram in Figure 9.12.

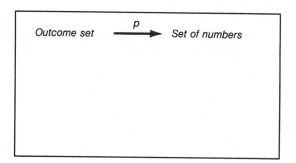

Figure 9.12

(b) Check that the sum of the probabilities of all of the outcomes is 1.

2. The experiment consists of spinning the spinner in Figure 9.13. Draw a probability diagram and check that the probabilities add to 1.

3. In an urn are 7 red, 4 white, and 4 blue marbles. The experiment consists of drawing 1 marble at random from the urn. Sketch a probability diagram for this experiment.

4. An urn is known to contain ten or less colored marbles. A marble is drawn, its color recorded, and the marble is then returned to the urn. One thousand repetitions of this experiment yield the data: red—430, white—139, blue—287, yellow—144. How many marbles of each color would you estimate are in the urn?

5. The experiment consists of rolling a single die and observing what number turns up. Sketch a probability diagram.

6. The experiment consists of drawing one card from a well-shuffled standard deck. The outcome set is
{2C, 2D, 2H, 2S, 3C, 3D, 3H, 3S, . . . , AC,
AD, AH, AS}
How many outcomes are there, and what probability would you assign to each?

7. When Ohio State's former football coach Woody Hayes was asked why his teams passed so infrequently, he replied that when you throw the ball three things can happen (completion, incompletion, interception) and two of them are bad.
(a) Do you think the three outcomes are equally likely?
(b) How would one go about assigning probabilities to the three outcomes?

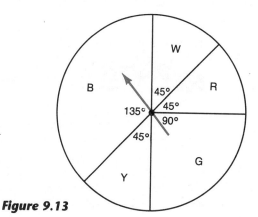

Figure 9.13

8. For the experiment of drawing one card from a standard deck of cards, which of the following qualify as outcome sets? For each legitimate outcome set, draw a probability diagram.
   (a) {red, black}
   (b) {even, odd}
   (c) {face card, not a face card}
   (d) {club, diamond, heart, spade}

9. How would you go about randomly selecting a number from among the integers 1 through 20?

10. An interviewer at a busy shopping center asked 100 people about their smoking habits and obtained these data: 81 never smoke, 7 smoke occasionally, and 12 smoke habitually. What is the (approximate) probability that a shopper chosen at random will be a habitual smoker? Describe a procedure for choosing a shopper in an essentially random way.

11. Describe an essentially random technique for selecting, from this text, a letter from our alphabet. If the outcome set for this experiment is {vowel, consonant}, how would you go about assigning a probability to each outcome?

12. One way to arrive at the probabilities asked for in the previous exercise is as follows. Consider a representative piece of the text, such as this exercise, and do some counting. The first sentence here has 72 letters, of which 32 are vowels. We won't count y and w as vowels. We say that the relative frequency of vowels in the first sentence

Table 9.2 Relative Frequency of Vowels, Rounded to the Nearest Hundredth

in the first sentence	$\frac{32}{72} \doteq .44$
in the first 2 sentences	_____
in the first 3 sentences	_____
in the first 4 sentences	_____
in the first 5 sentences	_____
in the first 6 sentences	_____
in all 7 sentences	_____

is $\frac{32}{72}$ or about .44. Complete Table 9.2. Then estimate reasonable probabilities for vowel and consonant.

13. *Class project:* Approximate the relative frequency of vowels in the surnames of the students in your college by using your math class as a representative sample and filling in a table like Table 9.3. If the relative frequency of vowels stabilizes at a value different from that in Table 9.2, suggest reasons why.

★ 14. A favorite classroom activity for the statistical determination of probabilities involves dropping an ordinary thumbtack. The outcome set for this

Figure 9.14   {Point up, point down}

Table 9.3 Relative Frequency of Vowels in Surnames.

Students	Number of Letters	Number of Vowels	Relative Frequency of Vowels
First 1			
First 2			
First 3			
First 4			
⋮			

experiment is shown in Figure 9.14. If 20 people each drop 15 tacks and pool their results, a fairly reliable probability (relative frequency) can be assigned to the 2 outcomes. Try this as a class project.

★ 15. A famous experiment known as Buffon's needle experiment, after Georges Louis Leclerc, Comte de Buffon (1707–1788), is set up as follows: Take an ordinary needle and measure its length *l* as precisely as you can. Now, take a large sheet of unlined paper and carefully draw parallel lines on it 2*l* units apart. The experiment consists of dropping the needle onto the paper. The outcome set is

{Crosses a line, does not cross a line}

Perform this experiment 10 times and assign a probability to the two outcomes. Now, perform the experiment 90 more times, and assign revised probabilities. The *reciprocal* of the probability that it crosses a line approximates an important number in mathematics. What do you suppose it is?

★ 16. Most everyone agrees that when you flip a coin, the probability of heads is $\frac{1}{2}$. Do you suppose, then, that if you toss 6 coins you will be quite certain to get 3 heads? Test your conjecture by performing the following experiment. Put 6 pennies in a paper cup, shake them up, pour them out on a table, and count the number of heads. The outcome set for this experiment is

{0 heads, 1 head, 2 heads, 3 heads, 4 heads,

5 heads, 6 heads}

Perform this experiment 100 times, and on the basis of your data, assign approximate probabilities to each of the 7 outcomes. (This experiment could also be carried out as a classroom activity with each of 20 students performing the experiment 5 times.)

★ 17. *Class project:* Have each student in the class roll a pair of dice 10 times and report the 10 resulting sums. Do the data suggest that all of the sums 2 through 12 are equally likely?

9.2 *Events and Their Probabilities: Simulation*

The experiment consists of spinning the spinner in Figure 9.15. The natural outcome set is indicated in the probability diagram of Figure 9.16.

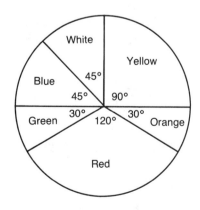

Figure 9.15

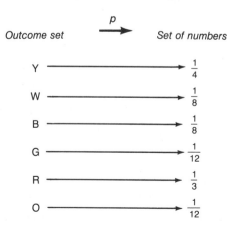

Figure 9.16

From this probability diagram we can read off answers to easy questions like these:

What is the probability of blue?
What is the probability of orange?

But we can also answer tougher questions like this one:

What is the probability of a primary color?

Since red comes up $\frac{1}{3}$ of the time, blue $\frac{1}{8}$ of the time, and yellow $\frac{1}{4}$ of the time, we conclude that a primary color comes up $\frac{1}{3} + \frac{1}{8} + \frac{1}{4}$ of the time. That is, the probability of a primary color is $\frac{1}{3} + \frac{1}{8} + \frac{1}{4} = \frac{17}{24}$.

In this way we can assign a probability to any *subset* of the original outcome set. For example,

$$P(\{R, Y, B\}) = p(R) + p(Y) + p(B) = \frac{1}{3} + \frac{1}{4} + \frac{1}{8} = \frac{17}{24}$$
$$P(\{B, G\}) = p(B) + p(G) = \frac{1}{8} + \frac{1}{12} = \frac{5}{24}$$

In the terminology of probability theory:

> Any subset of the outcome set is called an **event.**

Thus we are able to assign a probability to every event according to the following general principle.

> The **probability of an event** is the sum of the probabilities of the outcomes making up that event.

More often than not, events are described in words rather than in roster notation, such as "primary color" rather than as {R, Y, B}. In such cases one needs to translate before calculating.

EXAMPLE 1   For the preceding experiment, what is the probability of spinning an American-flag color?

Solution   · American-flag color → {R, W, B}

$$P(\{R, W, B\}) = p(R) + p(W) + p(B) = \frac{1}{3} + \frac{1}{8} + \frac{1}{8} = \frac{7}{12} \qquad ❏$$

EXAMPLE 2   For the preceding experiment, what is the probability of spinning a color *not* in the American flag?

Solution   Color not in American flag → {Y, G, O}

$$P(\{Y, G, O\}) = p(Y) + p(G) + p(O) = \frac{1}{4} + \frac{1}{12} + \frac{1}{12} = \frac{5}{12} \qquad ❏$$

The events {R, W, B} and {Y, G, O} of the preceding examples are called **complementary events** because each subset is the complement of the other in the outcome set. Since the probabilities of all of the outcomes add to 1, the following generalization is clear.

If A is any event, then the complementary event A' has probability $P(A') = 1 - P(A)$.

Another (stronger) generalization is the following.

If A and M are *mutually exclusive* (disjoint) events, then $P(A \cup M) = P(A) + P(M)$.

EXAMPLE 3   For the preceding experiment, what is the probability of an American-flag color or a Mauritanian-flag color?

Solution   Let A be the event of an American-flag color and let M be the event of a Mauritanian-flag color: $M = \{Y, G\}$. Then the probability of spinning an American or a Mauritanian color is

$$P(A \cup M) = P(A) + P(M) = \tfrac{7}{12} + [p(Y) + p(G)]$$
$$= \tfrac{7}{12} + (\tfrac{1}{4} + \tfrac{1}{12}) = \tfrac{11}{12}$$

A quicker solution is based on the property of complementary events and the observation that the only color not in either flag is orange:

$$P(A \cup M) = 1 - P(\{O\}) = 1 - \tfrac{1}{12} = \tfrac{11}{12} \qquad \square$$

The use of both P and p to designate *probability* in the preceding discussion is not due to carelessness. It reminds us that we actually have two probability functions associated with our experiment. The original one, p, assigns a number to each of the 6 outcomes of the experiment: R, W, B, G, Y, O. The new function, P, assigns a number to each event, that is to each of the $2^6 = 64$ subsets of the outcome set:

$$\varnothing, \{Y\}, \{W\}, \{B\}, \{G\}, \{R\}, \{O\}, \{Y, W\}, \ldots, \{Y, W, B, G, R, O\}$$

The first event on this list, $\varnothing$, is called the **impossible event,** and its probability is 0. (The probability of spinning no color at all is 0.) The last event on this list, {Y, W, B, G, R, O}, is called the **certain event,** and its probability is 1:

$$P(\{Y, W, B, G, R, O\}) = p(Y) + p(W) + p(B) + p(G) + p(R) + p(O)$$
$$= \tfrac{1}{4} + \tfrac{1}{8} + \tfrac{1}{8} + \tfrac{1}{12} + \tfrac{1}{3} + \tfrac{1}{12} = 1$$

EXAMPLE 4   The experiment consists of spinning the spinner in Figure 9.17. Draw arrow diagrams for both p and P.

Solution   See Figure 9.18.

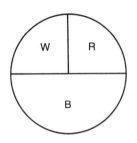

Figure 9.17

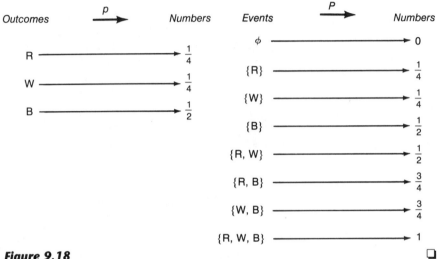

Figure 9.18   ❑

In the spinner experiment that we have been considering, the outcomes are not equally likely. In probability experiments where the outcomes *are* equally likely, there is a simple formula for the probability of an event.

> In an experiment with equally likely outcomes the probability of an event is just F/n, where F is the number of outcomes making up the event in question (the *favorable* outcomes) and n is the total number of outcomes.

EXAMPLE 5   The whole numbers 1 through 100 are printed on slips of paper, put in a hat, and mixed thoroughly. The experiment consists of drawing out one slip.
(a) What is the probability of drawing a multiple of 15?
(b) What is the probability of drawing a two-digit number?
(c) What is the probability of drawing a number having at least one 7 among its digits?

Solution   There are 100 equally likely outcomes.
(a) There are 6 favorable outcomes: 15, 30, 45, 60, 75, 90. The probability of drawing a multiple of 15 is $\frac{6}{100}$.
(b) There are 90 favorable outcomes: 10, 11, 12, . . . , 99. The probability of drawing a two-digit number is $\frac{90}{100}$.
(c) There are 10 numbers with tens digit 7, and there are 9 *other* numbers

with units digit 7. Thus the probability of drawing a number with at least one digit 7 is $\frac{19}{100}$. ❏

Simulation

Physical experiments such as flipping a coin, rolling a die, drawing a slip of paper out of a hat, or spinning a spinner can be time-consuming even when all the necessary devices are available in the classroom. An efficient alternative is to **simulate** such experiments by using a table of random digits. When implemented on a high-speed computer, the technique of simulation by random digits is an extremely practical and powerful tool for solving complex real-world probability problems. Even by hand, simulation by random digits can be valuable. We illustrate by using the brief table of 1000 random digits shown in Table 9.4. (Imagine that some patient being created this table by methodically spinning, 1000 times, a perfectly unbiased spinner having 10 same-size sectors numbered 0 through 9.)

Table 9.4 One Thousand Random Digits

36422	93239	76046	81114	77412	86557	19549	98473	15221	87856
78496	47197	37961	67568	14861	61077	85210	51264	49975	71785
95384	59596	05081	39968	80495	00192	94679	18307	16265	48888
37957	89199	10816	24260	52302	69592	55019	94127	71721	70673
31422	27529	95051	83157	96377	33723	52902	51302	86370	50452
07443	15346	40653	84238	24430	88834	77318	07486	33950	61598
41348	86255	92715	96656	49693	99286	83447	20215	16040	41085
12398	95111	45663	55020	57159	58010	43162	98878	73337	35571
77229	92095	44305	09285	73256	02968	31129	66588	48126	52700
61175	53014	60304	13976	96312	42442	96713	43940	92516	81421
16825	27482	97858	05642	88047	68960	52991	67703	29805	42701
84656	03089	05166	67571	25545	26603	40243	55482	38341	97782
03872	31767	23729	89523	73654	24626	78393	77172	41328	95633
40488	70426	04034	46618	55102	93408	10965	69744	80766	14889
98322	25528	43808	05935	78338	77881	90139	72375	50624	91385
13366	52764	02407	14202	74172	58770	65348	24115	44277	96735
86711	27764	86789	43800	87582	09298	17880	75507	35217	08352
53886	50358	62738	91783	71944	90221	79403	75139	09102	77826
99348	21186	42266	01531	44325	61042	13453	61917	90426	12437
49985	08787	59448	82680	52929	19077	98518	06251	58451	91140

EXAMPLE 6   Explain how the table of random digits can be used to simulate repeated trials of the following experiments.

(a) Flipping a coin

(b) Rolling a die

(c) Drawing numbers from a hat containing slips numbered 1 through 100

(d) Spinning the spinner in Figure 9.19

Solution (a) Let even numbers represent heads and odd numbers represent tails. Then the first row of the table becomes a record of fifty trials:

THHHH TTHTT THHHH HTTTH TTHTH HHTTT TTTHT
                                                        THHTT TTHHT HTHTH

In this row the relative frequency of heads is $\frac{23}{50} = .46$.

(b) Ignore the digits 0, 7, 8, 9. Then the sixth row of the table gives this record:

443 15346 4653 423 2443 34 31 46 335 615

The relative frequencies given by this row are

1s: $\frac{3}{31}$ 2s: $\frac{2}{31}$ 3s: $\frac{9}{31}$ 4s: $\frac{9}{31}$ 5s: $\frac{4}{31}$ 6s: $\frac{4}{31}$

If we used the entire table of random digits, we would expect each of these frequencies to tend toward $\frac{1}{6}$.

(c) Take the digits in blocks of two and let 00 represent 100. Then the ninth line of the table gives this record:

77 22 99 20 95 44 30 50 92 . . . 65 27 100

(d) Ignore the digits 0 and 9. Let 1, 2, and 3 correspond to red, 4 to yellow, 5 and 6 to blue, and 7 and 8 to green. Then line 11 of the table gives this record:

RBGRB RGYGR GGBG BBYR GGYG . . .   ❏

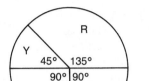

Figure 9.19

EXAMPLE 7 The experiment consists of flipping a coin 5 times in succession. Use simulation to determine the approximate probability of getting exactly 2 heads.

Solution Treat even digits as heads and odd digits as tails, and consider each block of five digits in the table as one performance of the experiment. In the first row the first block has 4 heads and 1 tail; the second, 1 head and 4 tails; the third, 4 heads and 1 tail; the fourth, 2 heads and 3 tails; . . . . Table 9.5 gives the record for the first ten rows.

The probability suggested by 100 performances of the experiment is .28. It turns out that the theoretical probability of getting exactly 2 heads is .3125. The reason for the discrepancy is that 100 is not really a very large number. If we could perform the experiment 1000 times, the empirical probability would almost certainly be closer to the theoretical one. Perhaps you can see now why the practicality of simulation is so closely tied to modern computers, which can easily run simulations of several thousand trials of experiments similar to this one.

Table 9.5

	Relative Frequency of 2 Heads	Cumulative Relative Frequency of 2 Heads
First row	$\frac{5}{10}$	$\frac{5}{10} = .50$
Second row	$\frac{2}{10}$	$\frac{7}{20} \doteq .35$
Third row	$\frac{4}{10}$	$\frac{11}{30} \doteq .37$
Fourth row	$\frac{4}{10}$	$\frac{15}{40} \doteq .38$
Fifth row	$\frac{2}{10}$	$\frac{17}{50} = .34$
Sixth row	$\frac{2}{10}$	$\frac{19}{60} \doteq .32$
Seventh row	$\frac{2}{10}$	$\frac{21}{70} = .30$
Eighth row	$\frac{1}{10}$	$\frac{22}{80} \doteq .28$
Ninth row	$\frac{3}{10}$	$\frac{25}{90} \doteq .28$
Tenth row	$\frac{3}{10}$	$\frac{28}{100} = .28$

Mathematical Models

Simulation, using a table of random digits, can be used to test which of two mathematical models better describes a physical experiment. Consider, for example, the random experiment of dropping two pennies on the floor. How should we choose an outcome set and an assignment of probabilities? One plausible answer was suggested by Rebecca (Figure 9.20):

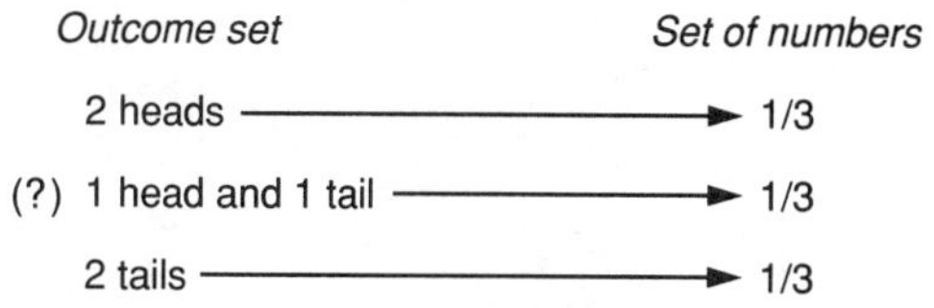

Outcome set   Set of numbers

2 heads ⟶ 1/3

(?) 1 head and 1 tail ⟶ 1/3

Figure 9.20 Rebecca's model.   2 tails ⟶ 1/3

A second model arose from Leslie's contention that one of the two pennies always comes to rest first, and thus it is reasonable to say that the outcomes of the experiment are actually ordered pairs. See Figure 9.21.

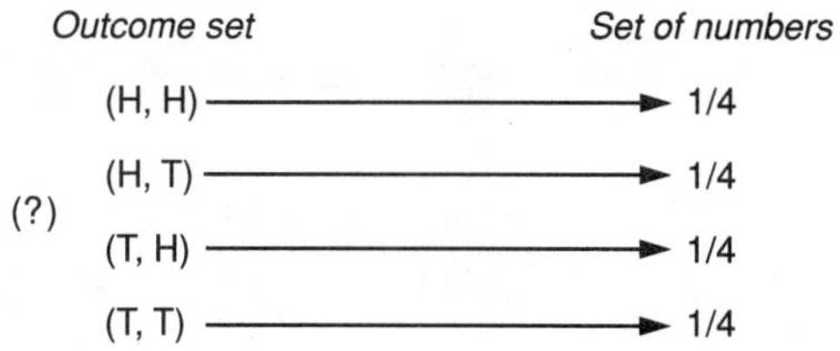

Outcome set   Set of numbers

(H, H) ⟶ 1/4

(H, T) ⟶ 1/4

(?) (T, H) ⟶ 1/4

Figure 9.21 Leslie's model.   (T, T) ⟶ 1/4

Using Leslie's model the event of getting exactly 1 head has probability $\frac{1}{2}$. Which model do you think more closely matches the coin-drop experiment?

In the absence of experience we simply cannot say which model is a better fit. To get the experience we ought to perform the actual physical experiment over and over again. For example, each person in the class could drop two coins and someone could tally up the number of occurrences of 2 heads, 1 head, and 0 heads. By repeating this activity several times, a fairly large amount of data could be accumulated. Then the ratios

$$\frac{\text{number of 2 heads}}{\text{number of trials}}, \qquad \frac{\text{number of 1 heads}}{\text{number of trials}}, \qquad \frac{\text{number of 0 heads}}{\text{number of trials}}$$

could be compared with the competing theoretical values from the two models: $\frac{1}{3}, \frac{1}{3}, \frac{1}{3}$ and $\frac{1}{4}, \frac{1}{2}, \frac{1}{4}$ respectively.

A quicker (and quieter) way to collect the data is to use the table of random digits. Let even digits represent heads and odd digits represent tails; then block off the digits by twos. Thus the first row of the table begins

36   42   29   32   39   76   04   68   11   14   . . .

which corresponds to

TH   HH   HT   TH   TT   TH   HH   HH   TT   TH   . . .

For these first ten trials the relative frequencies are

2 heads: $\frac{3}{10} = .30,$ 1 head: $\frac{5}{10} = .50,$ 0 heads: $\frac{2}{10} = .20$

If we use the first four rows of the table of random digits (perform the experiment 100 times), the relative frequencies are

2 heads: .21,   1 head: .48,   0 heads: .31

It appears that the probability of 1 head is $\frac{1}{2}$ rather than $\frac{1}{3}$; Leslie's model is a better fit to the coin-drop experiment than is Rebecca's.

We conclude that, for the coin-drop experiment, Rebecca is "wrong." There are, however, other contexts in which Rebecca's model is "right." Theoretical physicists were surprised to learn that the analog of Rebecca's model (known as the Bose–Einstein model) is a better decriber of the behavior of certain particles than is the analog of Leslie's model (known as the Maxwell–Boltzmann model).

EXERCISE SET 9.2

1. The experiment consists of spinning the spinner in Figure 9.22. Draw arrow diagrams for both p and P.

2. The experiment consists of rolling a regular dodecahedron with the numbers 1 through 12 on its faces. See Figure 9.23. The outcome set is {1, 2, 3, 4, 5, 6, 7, 8, 9, 10, 11, 12} What probability would you assign to each out-

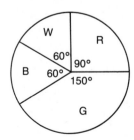

Figure 9.22

come? List, in roster notation, each event that is described in words here. Then find its probability.

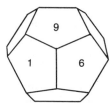

Figure 9.23

(a) An even number turns up.
(b) A prime number turns up.
(c) A divisor of 12 turns up.
(d) A multiple of 1 turns up.
(e) A multiple of 8 turns up.
(f) The square of 4 turns up.

3. In a hat are 10 poker chips bearing the numbers 1 through 10, respectively. The experiment consists of drawing one chip out of the hat. This time the outcome set S is indicated in a Venn diagram rather than in roster notation. See Figure 9.24.

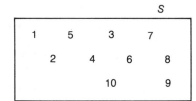

Figure 9.24

(a) Loop and label with a D the event of drawing a divisor of 10.
(b) Loop and label with an E the event of drawing an even number. Now, calculate the following probabilities

(c) $p(7)$
(d) $P(D)$
(e) $P(D \cap E)$
(f) $P(D \cup E)$
(g) $P(D')$
(h) $P(\emptyset)$
(i) $P(\{7\})$
(j) $P(\{7\}')$

4. The experiment consists of flipping a coin three times in succession and recording H each time a head comes up and T each time a tail comes up.
(a) Complete the listing of the outcome set begun here:

{HHH, HHT, HTH, . . .}

(b) How many outcomes are there?
(c) What is the probability of each outcome?
(d) What is the probability of exactly two heads coming up?
(e) What is the probability of getting more heads than tails?
(f) What is the probability of getting equally many heads and tails?

5. The experiment consists of rolling an ordinary die twice in succession. The outcome set S consists of 36 ordered pairs of numbers,

{(1, 1), (1, 2), (1, 3), . . . , (6, 5), (6, 6)}

that we represent as usual by a rectangular array of dots in the coordinate plane. See Figure 9.25.

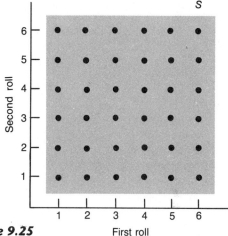

Figure 9.25   First roll

(a) Locate the dot for the pair (3, 5) that represents a 3 on the first roll and a 5 on the second.
(b) What probability would you assign to the outcome (3, 5)?
(c) List, in roster notation, the event "a sum of 8 results from the two rolls."
(d) In Figure 9.25, draw a loop around the event of (c).
(e) What is the probability of rolling a sum of 8 on two rolls?

6. In the game of craps two dice are tossed simultaneously and the sum of the two numbers is com-

puted. What is the probability of each of these events?

(a) The sum is 8. (b) The sum is 7.
(c) The sum is 11. (d) The sum is 12.

Compare these theoretical probabilities with the empirical ones of Exercise 17, Section 9.1.

7. Which is more probable, rolling a 9 by using the regular dodecahedron of Exercise 2 or the pair of dice of Exercise 6? Answer the same question for rolling a 10.

8. When an experiment has a large number of outcomes, you have to be able to think about various events without actually listing them. Consider the experiment of drawing one card from a standard deck. Give the probability of drawing the following.

(a) The queen of spades
(b) An ace
(c) A club
(d) A face card (jack, queen, or king)
(e) A red card
(f) Anything but a jack
(g) A multiple of five
(h) A multiple of five or a face card
(i) A card that is not a multiple of five and not a face card
(j) A green queen

★ 9. The experiment consists of drawing two cards simultaneously from a standard deck. Some typical outcomes are the following:

2 of spades and queen of hearts
7 of clubs and 9 of diamonds
jack of diamonds and 5 of hearts

(a) How many such outcomes are there?
(b) What is the probability of drawing a pair of aces?
(c) What is the probability of drawing any pair (two 2s, or two 3s, or . . .)?

★ 10. A basic property of the probability function p is that the sum of the p probabilities of all outcomes is 1. Try to determine what can be said about the sum of the P probabilities of all events. (Example

4 and Exercise 1 of this set are good places to gather some data.)

11. We have paid a lot of attention to spinner experiments for two reasons. One is that they illustrate nicely the basic concepts of probability. The other is that any probability experiment can be simulated by a spinner. For example, the experiments of flipping a coin, rolling a die, and surviving from birth to age 70 can be simulated by the respective spinners in Figure 9.26.

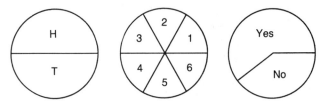

Figure 9.26

(a) Draw a spinner to simulate the experiment of Exercise 3, Section 9.1.
(b) Describe a spinner that would simulate the experiment of Exercise 6, Section 9.1.
(c) Describe a spinner that would simulate the experiment of Exercise 10, Section 9.1.
(d) Describe a spinner that would simulate the experiment of Exercise 14, Section 9.1.
★ (e) Draw a spinner with 11 sectors labeled 2 through 12 that could be used to simulate the game of craps (Exercise 6). Be precise in measuring the sizes of the angles at the center of the spinner.

12. Turn the tables and simulate the spinner experiment of Exercise 1 of this section by an experiment involving colored marbles in an urn.

13. How would you use the table of random digits to simulate repeated trials of each of these experiments?

(a) Drawing one marble out of an urn containing 5 red, 3 white, and 2 blue marbles
(b) Spinning the spinner in Figure 9.27
(c) Rolling a pair of dice

(d) Simultaneously drawing two digits out of a hat containing the digits 0 through 9

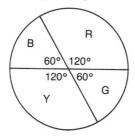

Figure 9.27

Exercises 14–23 can be done as class projects as follows. Each of the 20 rows of random digits in Table 9.4 is assigned to a different student or two-student team. Each student, or team, carries out the simulation in question and reports the data obtained to a person acting as recorder, who compiles it in a chart on the blackboard in a style similar to that of Exercise 15. If, in Exercises 18–21, a play of the game runs off the end of a row of random digits, wrap around and work backwards along the next row to complete the play.

14. The experiment consists of simultaneously drawing two digits out of a hat containing the ten digits 0 through 9. Your task is to estimate the probability of drawing two *consecutive* digits by simulating the experiment and conducting 100 trials.

15. In Exercise 16, Section 9.1, we described a classroom activity for estimating, experimentally, the probabilities of getting 0, 1, 2, 3, 4, 5, and 6 heads when 6 coins are tossed. Simulate this experiment by using the table of random digits, and conduct 100 trials. Keep track of the 100 outcomes by making tally marks on the chart in Figure 9.28.

0 heads _____

1 head _____

2 heads _____

3 heads _____

4 heads _____

5 heads _____

6 heads _____

Figure 9.28

16. Four people are asked to write a digit from among 1 through 9 on slips of paper. Assuming that their choices are random, estimate, by simulation, the probability that no two write down the same digit.

17. A bull rider estimates that every time he rides a bull, the probability of breaking a bone is $\frac{1}{8}$. Use simulation to estimate the probability that he will make it through 5 rides without breaking a bone.

18. The experiment consists of rolling a die until a 6 comes up. Use simulation to estimate the number of rolls you should expect to make. You will need to keep a list of each of the number-of-rolls-until-a-six and then average these numbers.

19. Suppose the probability of getting through a semester at State U. without getting food poisoning is .7. Use simulation to estimate how many semesters one should expect to survive up to and including the first semester in which food poisoning strikes.

20. The experiment consists of flipping a coin repeatedly until the number of heads exceeds the number of tails by 2, or the number of tails exceeds the number of heads by 2. Then you write down how many flips were needed. Simulate this experiment by using the table of random digits, keep score in a systematic way, and then assign estimated probabilities to the outcomes: 2 flips, 4 flips, 6 flips, ... Study the empirical estimates and then conjecture what the exact theoretical probabilities might be.

21. Each box of Krunchy breakfast cereal contains a picture of one of five famous rock stars (but you can't tell which one from the outside). Assume that each star appears in the same number of boxes, and that the boxes are thoroughly mixed up. Use simulation by random digits to estimate how many boxes you will have to buy to get a complete set of pictures.

22. How would you revise your simulation in Exercise 21 if one of the rock stars appeared in only half as many boxes as each of the other rock stars?

23. An interesting experiment for approximating the value of pi is based on simulation by random digits. Consider a circle of radius 1 unit and a square of side length 2 units, each of which has its center at the origin in the coordinate plane, and consider in particular the upper right-hand quarter of each. See Figure 9.29. If points were chosen at random in the upper right-hand square, then it would seem that the ratio of the number of those points that fell inside the circle to the total number of points chosen should be the same as the ratio of the area of the quarter circle to the area of the small square. That is,

$$\frac{\text{Number of points inside}}{\text{Total number of points}} \doteq \frac{\frac{1}{4}\pi \cdot 1^2}{1 \cdot 1}$$

or

$$\pi \doteq 4 \cdot \frac{\text{number of points inside}}{\text{total number of points}}$$

Thus if we had a way to select, say, 100 points at random in the small square, and a way to decide which ones were inside the circle, we could get an approximate value for π:

$$\pi \doteq 4\left(\frac{\text{number of points inside}}{100}\right)$$

Here is a way to select the points. Choose digits in blocks of four from the table of random digits. Suppose the first block is 6449. Then consider that the first randomly chosen point is the one with coordinates (.64, .49). To decide whether that point is inside the circle, calculate its distance from (0, 0), using the Pythagorean theorem:

$.64^2 + .49^2 = .4096 + .2401 = .6497$

Since $.6497 < 1$, it follows that $\sqrt{.6497} < 1$, so that the point (.64, .49) is inside the circle. Obviously, selecting and testing 100 points is an enor-

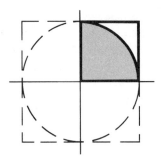

Figure 9.29

mous job, but if 20 people in a class each do 5 and then pool their results, the task is manageable, especially if calculators are used.

24. A student asserts that a natural outcome set for the experiment of rolling two dice is the one shown in Figure 9.30

1&6	2&6	3&6	4&6	5&6	6&6
1&5	2&5	3&5	4&5	5&5	
1&4	2&4	3&4	4&4		
1&3	2&3	3&3			
1&2	2&2				
1&1					

Figure 9.30

She further declares that these outcomes seem to be equally likely so that each should be assigned probability $\frac{1}{21}$.

(a) Using her outcome set and probabilities, find the probability of rolling a sum of 7. A sum of 11. A sum of 12.

(b) How could you decide which mathematical model, the one in Exercise 5 or the one described here, best fits the physical experiment of rolling a real pair of dice?

Computer Vignette G

Random numbers need not be copied laboriously from a table; computers have the capacity to generate them. The interactive program in Figure 9.31 uses the random number generator RND (lines 80 and 90) to simulate the rolling of a pair of dice. (You get to choose how many rolls.) Besides showing you the ac-

Figure 9.31

```
10   PRINT
20   PRINT "HOW MANY TIMES DO YOU WANT TO ROLL A PAIR OF
     DICE?"
30   INPUT N
40   LET C = 0
50   PRINT
60   PRINT "HERE ARE THE RESULTS"
70   FOR I = 1 TO 2 * N STEP 2
80   LET F = INT(6 * RND(I) + 1)
90   LET S = INT(6 * RND(I + 1) + 1)
100  PRINT F; ",";S;" ";
110  IF F + S <> 7 THEN 130
120  LET C = C + 1
130  NEXT I
140  PRINT
150  PRINT "THERE WERE ";C;" SEVENS OUT OF ";N;" ROLLS.
     THAT IS A FREQUENCY OF ";C/N
160  PRINT "CARE TO ROLL AGAIN? 1 = YES, 0 = NO"
170  INPUT A
180  IF A = 1 THEN 10
190  END
```

Figure 9.32

```
] RUN
HOW MANY TIMES DO YOU WANT TO ROLL A PAIR OF DICE?
?10

HERE ARE THE RESULTS
6,1 1,5 4,4 6,4 5,5 1,5 6,6 4,2 3,6 3,1
THERE WERE 1 SEVENS OUT OF 10 ROLLS. THAT IS A
FREQUENCY OF .1
CARE TO ROLL AGAIN? 1 = YES, 0 = NO
?1

HOW MANY TIMES DO YOU WANT TO ROLL A PAIR OF DICE?
?50

HERE ARE THE RESULTS
2,6 1,5 4,6 3,1 1,6 1,6 5,6 5,2 5,5 1,6 5,1 2,5 6,5
2,4 3,2 1,1 4,5 4,4 1,2 1,2 5,4 4,5 3,2 5,3 3,3 2,1
4,6 3,3 5,5 2,5 2,4 3,5 1,4 5,3 6,5 6,4 6,2 4,6 2,5
2,3 2,3 6,4 3,2 6,5 2,5 4,2 5,5 3,2 6,1 6,2
THERE WERE 9 SEVENS OUT OF 50 ROLLS. THAT IS A
FREQUENCY OF .18
CARE TO ROLL AGAIN? 1 = YES, 0 = NO
?0
```

tual outcomes, this program also reports how frequently a sum of 7 appeared. Theoretically, this frequency should be near $\frac{1}{6} \doteq .1667$ if the number of rolls is large. Figure 9.32 shows two runs. You might like to see how close you come to the theoretical frequency when you request, say, 300 rolls.

9.3 *Probability Trees*

Most of the experiments we have considered so far have been single-stage experiments: flipping a coin, spinning a spinner, rolling a die, drawing a marble from an urn. We did, however, consider two multistage experiments: flipping a coin three times in succession, and rolling a die twice in succession. In this section we shall study multistage experiments more carefully, and we shall describe a useful device, the probability tree, for calculating probabilities in such experiments.

Consider the two-stage experiment of spinning the spinner of Figure 9.33 twice in succession. The outcomes are nine ordered pairs,

(R, R), (R, W), (R, B), (W, R), (W, W), (W, B), (B, R), (B, W), (B, B)

that can be represented by paths down a tree, as in Figure 9.34. Can you trace the path corresponding to (R, W)? to (W, R)?

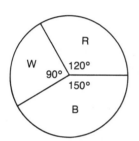

Figure 9.33

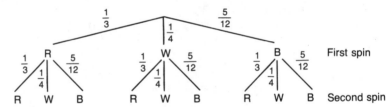

Figure 9.34

Once we have determined the outcomes, the next task is to assign a probability to each one. Here is where the fractions on the tree come in. The various occurrences of the fraction $\frac{1}{3}$ on the tree tell us that the probability of spinning a red is $\frac{1}{3}$ regardless of whether it is the first or the second spin and, in the latter case, regardless of what color came up on the first spin. Similarly, the occurrences of the fractions $\frac{1}{4}$ and $\frac{5}{12}$ give the probabilities of white and blue, respectively, under all circumstances.

Consider now the outcome (R, W), that is, the outcome of red on the first spin followed by white on the second. If the two-spin experiment were repeated many times, red would come up on the first spin about $\frac{1}{3}$ of the time. And out of all the times that red came up first, white would come up second about $\frac{1}{4}$ of the time. Thus the outcome (R, W) would occur about $\frac{1}{4}$ of $\frac{1}{3}$ of the time. That is,

$$p((R, W)) = \tfrac{1}{4} \cdot \tfrac{1}{3} = \tfrac{1}{12}$$

Mechanically, one finds the probability of (R, W) by multiplying the fractions along its path on the tree.

By multiplying along each of the nine paths, we arrive at the assignment of probabilities to each of the nine outcomes shown in Figure 9.35. Check these calculations to see whether the nine probabilities sum to 1.

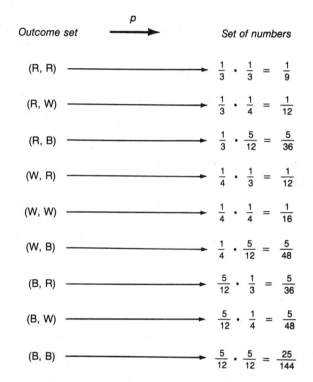

Outcome set p *Set of numbers*

(R, R) $\longrightarrow$ $\frac{1}{3} \cdot \frac{1}{3} = \frac{1}{9}$

(R, W) $\longrightarrow$ $\frac{1}{3} \cdot \frac{1}{4} = \frac{1}{12}$

(R, B) $\longrightarrow$ $\frac{1}{3} \cdot \frac{5}{12} = \frac{5}{36}$

(W, R) $\longrightarrow$ $\frac{1}{4} \cdot \frac{1}{3} = \frac{1}{12}$

(W, W) $\longrightarrow$ $\frac{1}{4} \cdot \frac{1}{4} = \frac{1}{16}$

(W, B) $\longrightarrow$ $\frac{1}{4} \cdot \frac{5}{12} = \frac{5}{48}$

(B, R) $\longrightarrow$ $\frac{5}{12} \cdot \frac{1}{3} = \frac{5}{36}$

(B, W) $\longrightarrow$ $\frac{5}{12} \cdot \frac{1}{4} = \frac{5}{48}$

(B, B) $\longrightarrow$ $\frac{5}{12} \cdot \frac{5}{12} = \frac{25}{144}$

Figure 9.35

Once probabilities have been assigned to the outcomes, we can compute the probabilities of various events in the usual way:

$$P(\text{same color twice}) = P(\{(R, R), (W, W), (B, B)\})$$
$$= \tfrac{1}{9} + \tfrac{1}{16} + \tfrac{25}{144} = \tfrac{50}{144} = \tfrac{25}{72}$$
$$P(\text{no red}) = P(\{(W, W), (W, B), (B, W), (B, B)\})$$
$$= \tfrac{1}{16} + \tfrac{5}{48} + \tfrac{5}{48} + \tfrac{25}{144} = \tfrac{64}{144} = \tfrac{4}{9}$$
$$P(\text{more red than white}) = P(\{(R, R), (R, B), (B, R)\})$$
$$= \tfrac{1}{9} + \tfrac{5}{36} + \tfrac{5}{36} = \tfrac{14}{36} = \tfrac{7}{18}$$

The principle of multiplying along a path on a tree can be stated in a general way as follows.

> **Multiplication Rule for Probabilities**
>
> Suppose an event A has probability a, and suppose the probability of event B occurring after A has occurred is b. Then the probability of the event "first A, then B" is $a \cdot b$.

EXAMPLE 1   Suppose in a certain city the probability of being apprehended for any particular burglary is .3, and that, if one is apprehended, the probability of being sent to jail is .6. As a burglar sets out on a job, what is his probability of winding up in jail?

Solution   Probability of being caught and then jailed
= probability of being caught × probability of being jailed once caught
= .3 × .6 = .18   ❏

EXAMPLE 2   Every working day Ann either drives to work or rides her bicycle. If Ann oversleeps, the probability of her driving is .9. If she does not oversleep, the probability of her driving is .3. Suppose that the probability of Ann's oversleeping is .2. What is the probability that on a given workday she will drive to work?

Solution   Draw the tree, as in Figure 9.36, and observe that there are two circumstances in which she might drive. Now, use the multiplication rule along those two paths:

$$.2 \times .9 + .8 \times .3 = .18 + .24 = .42$$

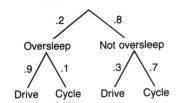

Figure 9.36

The products, .2 × .9 and .8 × .3, give the probabilities of the outcomes, "oversleep, then drive" and "not oversleep, then drive," respectively. Their sum gives the probability of the event consisting of those two outcomes.   ❏

The multiplication rule for probabilities applies to trees with more than just two levels.

EXAMPLE 3   An urn contains 4 red and 2 green marbles. The experiment consists of drawing a marble, recording its color, replacing it in the urn, drawing a second marble, recording its color, replacing it in the urn, drawing a third marble, and recording its color. Sketch a probability tree for this experiment, and calculate the probabilities of the following events.
(a) 3 reds
(b) 3 greens
(c) 2 reds and 1 green (in any order)
(d) 1 red and 2 greens (in any order)

Solution   This three-stage experiment is represented by a three-level tree. See Figure 9.37.

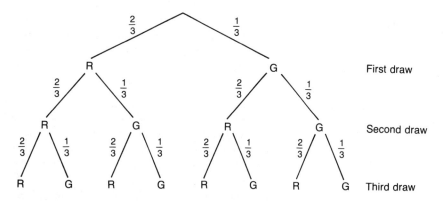

Figure 9.37

(a) There is just one path, the leftmost one, that yields 3 reds:

$$\text{Probability of 3 reds} = \tfrac{2}{3} \cdot \tfrac{2}{3} \cdot \tfrac{2}{3} = \tfrac{8}{27}$$

(b) There is just one path, the rightmost one, that yields 3 greens:

$$\text{Probability of 3 greens} = \tfrac{1}{3} \cdot \tfrac{1}{3} \cdot \tfrac{1}{3} = \tfrac{1}{27}$$

(c) There are three paths that yield 2 reds and 1 green: RRG, RGR, and GRR. The probability of the event "2 reds and 1 green" is thus the sum of the probabilities of these three outcomes. Multiplying along the branches yields

$$\text{Probability of 2 reds and 1 green} = \tfrac{2}{3} \cdot \tfrac{2}{3} \cdot \tfrac{1}{3} + \tfrac{2}{3} \cdot \tfrac{1}{3} \cdot \tfrac{2}{3} + \tfrac{1}{3} \cdot \tfrac{2}{3} \cdot \tfrac{2}{3}$$
$$= \tfrac{4}{27} + \tfrac{4}{27} + \tfrac{4}{27} = \tfrac{12}{27}$$

(d) One could trace paths down the tree or simply add the three probabilities already obtained $(\tfrac{8}{27} + \tfrac{1}{27} + \tfrac{12}{27} = \tfrac{21}{27})$ and subtract from $1(1 - \tfrac{21}{27} = \tfrac{6}{27})$, since the four events in parts (a) through (d) are mutually exclusive (pairwise disjoint) and exhaustive (their union is the outcome set). ❑

EXAMPLE 4 Again, we have an urn containing 4 red and 2 green marbles, and again we are to draw three in succession and record their colors. But this time we are *not* to replace a marble once it has been drawn. Draw a probability tree for this experiment, and calculate the probabilities of the following events.
(a) 3 reds
(b) 3 greens
(c) 2 reds and 1 green (in any order)
(d) 1 red and 2 greens (in any order)

Solution This time the probabilities of red and green change as one moves down the tree, because the contents of the urn changes with each draw. Originally, 4 of the 6 marbles were red, so on the first draw the probability of red is $\tfrac{4}{6}$. The probability of red on the second draw, however, depends on what marble was removed on the first draw. If a red was removed on the first draw, then 3 of the 5 remaining marbles are red; so the probability of red on the second draw is $\frac{3}{5}$. If a green was removed on the first draw, then 4 of the 5 remaining marbles are red; so the probability of red on the second draw is $\frac{4}{5}$. (In more advanced treatments you will encounter the term *conditional probability* applied to probabilities such as that of red on the second draw given [on the "condition"] that a green marble is drawn first.) Probabilities for the third draw depend on what happened on the first two draws. The complete tree is shown in Figure 9.38. Notice how the denominators decrease as one moves down the tree, and how the numerators indicate how many marbles of each color still remain in the urn. Probabilities of events are calculated, as before, by following paths down the tree.

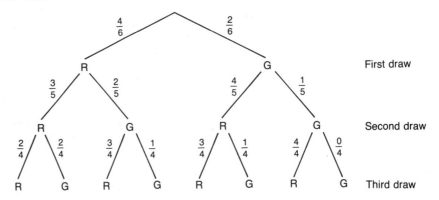

Figure 9.38

(a) $P(3 \text{ reds}) = \frac{4}{6} \cdot \frac{3}{5} \cdot \frac{2}{4} = \frac{1}{5}$
(b) $P(3 \text{ greens}) = \frac{2}{6} \cdot \frac{1}{5} \cdot \frac{0}{4} = 0$
(c) $P(2 \text{ reds and 1 green}) = \frac{4}{6} \cdot \frac{3}{5} \cdot \frac{2}{4} + \frac{4}{6} \cdot \frac{2}{5} \cdot \frac{3}{4} + \frac{2}{6} \cdot \frac{4}{5} \cdot \frac{3}{4}$
$= \frac{1}{5} + \frac{1}{5} + \frac{1}{5} = \frac{3}{5}$
(d) $P(1 \text{ red and 2 greens}) = 1 - (\frac{1}{5} + 0 + \frac{3}{5}) = \frac{1}{5}$ ❑

EXERCISE SET 9.3

1. The experiment consists of spinning the spinner in Figure 9.39 twice in succession.
   (a) On any trial, what is the probability of red on the first spin?
   (b) On any trial, what is the probability of white on the second spin?
   (c) Attach a fraction to each segment on the probability tree in Figure 9.40.
   (d) What is the probability of spinning first a red and then a white?
   (e) Complete the probability diagram begun in Figure 9.41.

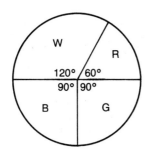

Figure 9.39

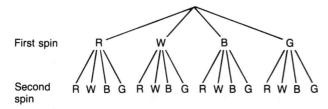

First spin

Second spin

Figure 9.40

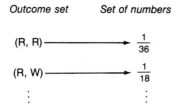

Outcome set   Set of numbers

(R, R) ⟶ $\frac{1}{36}$

(R, W) ⟶ $\frac{1}{18}$

Figure 9.41

(f) P(the same color twice) = ?

(g) P(at least one blue) = ?

(h) P(no reds or greens) = ?

2. The experiment consists of spinning the spinner in Figure 9.42 three times in succession.

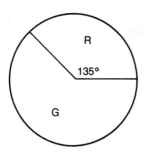

Figure 9.42

(a) Draw a probability tree for this experiment, and attach fractions to its segments.

(b) $p((R, G, R))$ = ?

(c) $p((G, R, G))$ = ?

(d) P(more reds than greens) = ?

(e) P(the same color three times in succession) = ?

(f) P(the same number of reds as greens) = ?

3. In an urn are 5 red, 3 yellow, and 2 blue marbles. The experiment consists of drawing a marble, recording its color, replacing the marble in the urn, drawing again, and again recording the color.

(a) Draw a probability tree for this experiment with fractions attached to its segments.

(b) $p((R, Y))$ = ?

(c) $p((Y, B))$ = ?

(d) P(at least one yellow) = ?

(e) P(two different colors) = ?

4. In an urn are 5 red, 3 yellow, and 2 blue marbles. The experiment consists of drawing a marble and recording its color, and then—without replacing the first marble—drawing a second marble and recording its color. Suppose that on the first draw a red marble was chosen.

(a) How many marbles remain in the urn?

(b) How many of these are red?

(c) What is the probability that the second marble drawn will also be red?

(d) What is the probability that the second marble drawn will be yellow?

5. Draw a probability tree, with fractions, for the experiment of Exercise 4. Then use it to compute the following.

(a) $p((Y, B))$ (b) $p((B, B))$

(c) P(no reds)   (d) P(at least one yellow)

6. An urn contains 5 red and 2 green marbles. The experiment consists of drawing 3 marbles in succession, without replacement.

(a) Draw a probability tree for this experiment.

(b) What is the probability of drawing 3 red marbles?

(c) What is the probability of drawing exactly 2 reds?

(d) What is the probability of drawing more greens than reds?

7. In an urn are 3 red and 2 green marbles. The experiment consists of drawing a marble from the urn three times in succession. If a green marble is drawn it is returned to the urn before the next draw; if a red marble is drawn it is not returned. What is the probability of drawing more greens than reds?

★ 8. An experiment consists of flipping a coin ten times in succession. Answer the following questions by thinking about a probability tree but not drawing it completely.
   (a) How many outcomes are there? (One typical outcome is HTHHTHTTTT.)
   (b) What is the probability of each outcome?
   (c) What is the probability of getting exactly one head?
   (d) What is the probability of getting exactly two heads?

9. If it snows, the probability that schools will close is .15. One day the weather report indicates a snow probability of .32. What is the probability that schools will close for snow that day?

10. The probability of buying a winning ticket in a certain state lottery is .1, but of all the winners only 1 in 2000 wins a big prize. What is the probability of buying a ticket that will win a big prize?

11. An auto insurance company groups it drivers into three categories, young, middle-aged, and old. These three groups constitute 30%, 50%, and 20% of its policyholders, respectively. Suppose the probabilities that drivers in these categories will be involved in accidents (in a year) are .12, .05, and .06, respectively. What is the probability that a randomly chosen policyholder will be involved in an accident (in a year)?

12. The probability that a smoker will contract a certain disease is .3. The probability for a nonsmoker is .04. If the population is 15% smokers and 85% nonsmokers, what is the probability that a person chosen at random will contract the disease?

★ 13. A nursery is having a closeout sale on year-old tulip bulbs. Suppose the probability that such a bulb will produce a flower is $\frac{1}{2}$. How many bulbs should you buy to be "95% certain" of having at least one flower?

14. Use a probability tree to determine the probability asked for in Exercise 16, Section 9.2. Compare the theoretical probability of this exercise with the empirical estimate of the former one.

15. Use a probability tree to determine the probability asked for in Exercise 17, Section 9.2. Compare the theoretical probability of this exercise with the empirical estimate of the former one.

16. Use a probability tree to determine the probabilities asked for in Exercise 20, Section 9.2. Compare the theoretical probabilities of this exercise with the empirical estimates of the former one.

★ 17. How likely do you think it is that if five people are chosen at random, then at least two of them will have been born in the same month? Suppose, for the sake of this problem, that births are equally distributed among the 12 months of the year. Thus, if a person is chosen at random, the probability that that person was born in any particular month, such as April, is $\frac{1}{12}$.
   (a) Find the probability that two randomly chosen people have two different birth months.
   (b) Find the probability that three randomly chosen people have three different birth months.
   (c) Fill in a complete table like Table 9.6.

Table 9.6

Number of People	Probability that at Least Two of Them Share a Birth Month
1	_____
2	_____
3	_____
⋮	⋮
12	_____
13	_____

 9.4 *Experiments with Many Equally Likely Outcomes (Optional)*

Recall that for an experiment with equally likely outcomes the probability of an event is the fraction

$$\frac{\text{Number of favorable outcomes}}{\text{Total number of outcomes}}$$

where an outcome is considered *favorable* if it belongs to the event in question. For example, if the experiment consists of drawing one card from a standard deck and the event in question is the event of drawing a king, then there are four favorable outcomes (king of clubs, king of diamonds, king of hearts, king of spades), and the probability of drawing a king is $\frac{4}{52}$. When an experiment involves a large number of equally likely outcomes, counting them and counting the favorable ones become nontrivial tasks. In Chapter 3 we developed some powerful "counting" techniques that will help us. The *choice principle* of Section 3.4 (often called the **fundamental principle of counting** in the context of probability) will be crucial in what follows:

> If there are F choices for how to perform a first act and S choices for how to perform a second act, then there are $F \cdot S$ choices for how to perform the two acts in succession.

So will the formulas of optional Section 3.7 that count permutations and combinations (which is why this section is labeled *optional*):

$$P_k^n = n(n - 1)(n - 2) \cdots (n - k + 1) \qquad (k \text{ factors})$$

$$C_k^n = \frac{P_k^n}{k!} = \frac{n(n - 1)(n - 2) \cdots (n - k + 1)}{k(k - 1)(k - 2) \cdots 3 \cdot 2 \cdot 1}$$

A calculator is strongly recommended for this section.

EXAMPLE 1   The names of the 50 states are printed on slips of paper and put in a hat. Three slips are drawn. Determine the following probabilities.
(a) All 3 states drawn touch the Mississippi River.
(b) Exactly 2 of the 3 states touch the Mississippi.
(c) Exactly 1 of the 3 states touches the Mississippi.
(d) None of the 3 states touches the Mississippi.
As a point of information, 10 of the 50 states touch the Mississippi River.

Solution   The outcomes of this experiment are all the 3-element subsets of the original 50-element set. For example,

$$\{\text{Arizona, Delaware, Iowa}\}$$

is one outcome. The total number of outcomes is just the number of combinations of 50 things taken 3 at a time:

$$C_3^{50} = \frac{50 \cdot 49 \cdot 48}{3 \cdot 2 \cdot 1} = 19{,}600$$

If the drawing is indeed random, then each outcome has the same probability, namely 1/19,600. Now we proceed to the questions.

(a) The task here is one of counting how many 3-element subsets (the favorable outcomes) can be made up from the 10 river states. That number is just the number of combinations of 10 things taken 3 at a time:

$$C_3^{10} = \frac{10 \cdot 9 \cdot 8}{3 \cdot 2 \cdot 1} = 120$$

Thus the probability of drawing 3 river states is

$$\frac{C_3^{10}}{C_3^{50}} = \frac{120}{19{,}600} \doteq .006$$

less than 1 in 160.

(b) The task here is to determine how many 3-element subsets consist of 2 river states and 1 nonriver state. We use the choice principle. The number of ways of choosing the 2 river states out of the 10 available is $C_2^{10} = 45$; the number of ways of choosing the 1 nonriver state out of the 40 available is $C_1^{40} = 40$. Thus the number of favorable outcomes is

$$C_2^{10} \cdot C_1^{40} = 45 \cdot 40 = 1800$$

and the probability of drawing exactly 2 river states is

$$\frac{1800}{19{,}600} \doteq .092$$

about 1 in 11.

(c) Since there are $C_1^{10} = 10$ ways of choosing the 1 river state and $C_2^{40} = 780$ ways of choosing the 2 nonriver states, the probability of drawing exactly 1 river state is

$$\frac{10 \times 780}{19{,}600} \doteq .398$$

nearly 2 chances in 5.

(d) Since there are $C_3^{40} = 9880$ ways of choosing 3 nonriver states, the probability of drawing zero river states is

$$\frac{9880}{19{,}600} \doteq .504$$

just a bit more than $\frac{1}{2}$.

As a check, notice that the events described in (a), (b), (c), and (d) are mutually exclusive (pairwise disjoint) and exhaustive (their union is the entire outcome set). Thus the sum of the probabilities should be 1:

$$.006 + .092 + .398 + .504 = 1.000 \qquad \square$$

EXAMPLE 2

You are dealt 5 cards from a well-shuffled standard deck of 52 cards. What is the probability that you hold a full house? (A full house consists of 3 cards of one value and 2 of another, such as 3 kings and 2 sevens.)

Solution

Let's begin by asking an easier question. What is the probability of getting 3 kings and 2 sevens? The outcomes of this experiment are all possible 5-element subsets of the original 52-element set. Some of the outcomes are favorable,

$$\{7C,\ 7S,\ KC,\ KD,\ KH\}$$

but most are not,

$$\{AH,\ 4D,\ 4S,\ 10C,\ JC\}$$

Since all outcomes are equally likely (that is the significance of the well-shuffled hypothesis), the probability we seek is just the fraction

$$\frac{\text{Number of favorable outcomes}}{\text{Total number of outcomes}}$$

Finding the denominator is straightforward. It is the number of combinations of 52 things taken 5 at a time:

$$C_5^{52} = \frac{52 \cdot 51 \cdot 50 \cdot 49 \cdot 48}{5 \cdot 4 \cdot 3 \cdot 2 \cdot 1} = 2{,}598{,}960$$

To find the numerator, we use the choice principle. The number of ways of choosing 3 kings out of the 4 available is $C_3^4 = 4$; the number of ways of choosing 2 sevens out of the 4 available is $C_2^4 = 6$. Thus the number of favorable outcomes is $4 \cdot 6 = 24$, and the probability of 3 kings and 2 sevens is

$$\frac{24}{2{,}598{,}960}$$

Now, return to the original question: What is the probability of any kind of a full house? Again, the choice principle comes into play. There are 13 choices for the card value in which to get 3 of a kind, and 12 choices for the card value in which to get a pair (picture a tree). Thus the probability of a full house is

$$\frac{13 \cdot 12 \cdot 24}{2{,}598{,}960} = \frac{3744}{2{,}598{,}960} \doteq .00144$$

roughly 1 in 700. $\qquad \square$

1. An experiment consists of drawing 3 numbers (at once) from a hat containing the numbers 1, 2, 3, 4, 5, 6, 7, 8, 9, 10.
   (a) List two more outcomes in the outcome set $\{\{1, 2, 3\}, \{1, 2, 4\}, \{1, 2, 5\}, \ldots\}$
   (b) How many outcomes in this outcome set?
   (c) What is the probability of each outcome?
   (d) How many outcomes consist of 3 even numbers?
   (e) What is the probability of drawing 3 even numbers?
   (f) What is the probability of drawing 3 numbers over 6?
   (g) What is the probability of drawing 3 numbers under 7?
   (h) What is the probability of drawing 3 numbers with sum 10?

2. An experiment consists of drawing 2 numbers (at once) from a hat containing the numbers 1, 2, 3, 4, 5, 6, 7.
   (a) Decide on an outcome set and list several outcomes.
   (b) What is the probability of drawing 2 odd numbers?
   (c) What is the probability of drawing 2 even numbers?
   (d) What is the probability of drawing a sum of 8?
   (e) What is the probability of drawing a sum greater than 7?

3. An experiment consists of randomly choosing 4 different letters of the alphabet. Express each probability in terms of symbols of the type C_k^n. Do not simplify.
   (a) P (all four are vowels)
   (b) P (all four are consonants)
   (c) P (none follow j in the alphabet)
   (d) P (all precede e in the alphabet)
   (e) P (at least one is a vowel)

4. The experiment consists of drawing 2 balls (without replacement) from an urn containing 5 red and 3 green balls.
   (a) View this experiment as a two-stage experiment and draw a probability tree.
   (b) What is the probability of drawing 2 red balls?
   (c) In how many ways can 2 balls be chosen from among 8?
   (d) In how many ways can 2 balls be chosen from among 5?
   (e) Use your answers to (c) and (d) to check your answer to (b).

5. Write an expression for the probability that the first 2 entrants are both among the 100 lucky winners in a sweepstakes with 1 million entrants.

6. The principal randomly chooses 5 students from your class of 12 boys and 13 girls. What is the probability that she chooses 1 boy and 4 girls?

In Exercises 7–12 you are to find the probabilities of various poker hands when 5 cards are chosen randomly from a standard 52-card deck.

7. A royal flush (10, jack, queen, king, ace, all of the same suit)

8. A straight flush (5 consecutive values, all in the same suit, but not a royal flush)

9. Four of a kind (4 cards of the same value)

10. A flush (5 cards all of the same suit, but not consecutive)

11. A straight (5 consecutive values, but not all of the same suit)

12. Three of a kind (3 cards of the same value, but not a full house)

In Exercises 13 and 14, leave the probabilities in combination number notation.

13. If 10 of the 50 states are chosen at random, what are the following probabilities?

(a) Not 1 of them will touch the Pacific Ocean.

(b) Exactly 2 of them will touch the Pacific Ocean.

14. What is the probability that a bridge hand (13 cards) will contain the following?

(a) No card higher than a 10 (aces are high in bridge)

(b) Exactly 3 face cards (jacks, queens, or kings)

15. Calculate the theoretical probability called for in Exercise 14, Section 9.2, and compare it with the empirical estimate obtained there.

★ 16. Calculate the theoretical probabilities called for in Exercise 15, Section 9.2, and compare them with the empirical estimates obtained there.

🐚 17. A roulette wheel has 38 same-sized sectors: 18 red, 18 black, and 2 green. The house matches your bet if you bet on red or black. Suppose that you decide to always bet $1 on red. What is the probability that you will walk away with a profit if you quit after 1 play? 3 plays? 5 plays? 7 plays? Look at your data and offer a generalization.

 ## 9.5 *Expected Value and Odds*

We have considered a number of gambling devices, but so far we have been playing for fun. Now it's time to study games that have a payoff. The average payoff per play will be called the *expected value* of the game.

Consider, for example, the game of spinning the spinner in Figure 9.43, where the payoffs are as shown. Observe that

$$p(\text{B}) = \tfrac{1}{2} \qquad p(\text{G}) = \tfrac{1}{4} \qquad p(\text{R}) = \tfrac{1}{8} \qquad p(\text{Y}) = \tfrac{1}{8}$$

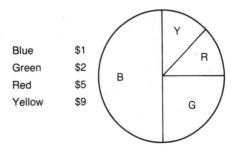

Blue	$1
Green	$2
Red	$5
Yellow	$9

Figure 9.43

Suppose you were to play this game a large number of times, say 800 times. Then you would expect the following results:

Spin blue about 400 times, and thus win about 400 × $1.
Spin green about 200 times, and thus win about 200 × $2.
Spin red about 100 times, and thus win about 100 × $5.
Spin yellow about 100 times, and thus win about 100 × $9.

In dollars your total winnings in 800 plays would be about

$$400 \times 1 + 200 \times 2 + 100 \times 5 + 100 \times 9$$

and thus the average payoff per play would be

$$\tfrac{1}{800}(400 \times 1 + 200 \times 2 + 100 \times 5 + 100 \times 9)$$
$$= \tfrac{400}{800} \times 1 + \tfrac{200}{800} \times 2 + \tfrac{100}{800} \times 5 + \tfrac{100}{800} \times 9$$
$$\text{(*)} \qquad = \tfrac{1}{2} \times 1 + \tfrac{1}{4} \times 2 + \tfrac{1}{8} \times 5 + \tfrac{1}{8} \times 9$$
$$= \tfrac{4}{8} + \tfrac{4}{8} + \tfrac{5}{8} + \tfrac{9}{8} = \tfrac{22}{8} = 2.75$$

That is, the expected value (average payoff) of this game is $2.75.

If the casino charges you less than $2.75 to spin the spinner, then you should play, because in the long run you will come out ahead. If they charge you more than $2.75 to play, then stay away. If they charge you exactly $2.75 to play, then we call it a **fair game.**

Before we leave this example, two more observations are in order. First, notice that the expected value of the game, $2.75, is a *long-run* average. On any one play it is impossible to win $2.75. Second, reconsider the equation we labeled with a star,

$$\text{(*)} \qquad \text{Expected value} = \tfrac{1}{2} \times 1 + \tfrac{1}{4} \times 2 + \tfrac{1}{8} \times 5 + \tfrac{1}{8} \times 9$$

On the right-hand side we have a **weighted average** of payoffs: the payoff on blue, 1, is weighted by its probability $\tfrac{1}{2}$; the payoff on green, 2, is weighted by its probability $\tfrac{1}{4}$; the payoff on red, 5, is weighted by its probability $\tfrac{1}{8}$; and the payoff on yellow, 9, is weighted by its probability $\tfrac{1}{8}$. Equation (*) can be generalized as follows to give us a formal definition of **expected value.**

> If an experiment has outcomes $O_1, O_2, O_3, \ldots$ with respective probabilities $p_1, p_2, p_3, \ldots$ and respective payoffs $D_1, D_2, D_3, \ldots$, then the expected value of the experiment is
>
> $$E = p_1 \times D_1 + p_2 \times D_2 + p_3 \times D_3 + \ldots$$

EXAMPLE 1 The game consists of spinning the spinner in Figure 9.44. The payoffs are as shown. What is the expected value?

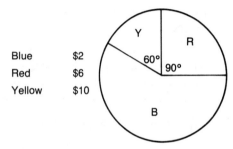

Blue $2
Red $6
Yellow $10

Figure 9.44

Table 9.7

Outcomes	R	Y	B
Probabilities	$\frac{1}{4}$	$\frac{1}{6}$	$\frac{7}{12}$
Payoffs	6	10	2

Solution   We begin by filling in Table 9.7. Then

$$\text{Expected value} = \tfrac{1}{4} \times 6 + \tfrac{1}{6} \times 10 + \tfrac{7}{12} \times 2$$
$$= \tfrac{6}{4} + \tfrac{10}{6} + \tfrac{14}{12} = \tfrac{52}{12} \doteq \$4.33 \qquad \square$$

EXAMPLE 2   The game consists of rolling two dice. If you roll a pair, you are paid $1.00 for each spot showing. If you don't roll a pair, you pay the casino $1.50. What is the expected value?

Solution   See Table 9.8. Then

$$\text{Expected value} = \tfrac{1}{36} \times 2 + \tfrac{1}{36} \times 4 + \tfrac{1}{36} \times 6 + \tfrac{1}{36} \times 8 + \tfrac{1}{36} \times 10 + \tfrac{1}{36} \times 12$$
$$+ \tfrac{30}{36} \times (-1.5)$$
$$= \tfrac{42}{36} - \tfrac{45}{36} = \tfrac{-3}{36} = -8\tfrac{1}{3}\cent$$

Table 9.8

Outcomes	(1, 1)	(2, 2)	(3, 3)	(4, 4)	(5, 5)	(6, 6)	nonpair
Probabilities	$\frac{1}{36}$	$\frac{1}{36}$	$\frac{1}{36}$	$\frac{1}{36}$	$\frac{1}{36}$	$\frac{1}{36}$	$\frac{30}{36}$
Payoffs	2	4	6	8	10	12	−1.5

This game is not a fair game; to be fair, the expected value should be 0. Here the advantage is to the casino. In the long run you can expect to lose about $8\tfrac{1}{3}\cent$ per play. $\qquad \square$

The next two examples show that the payoff in an expected-value problem need not be a monetary one.

EXAMPLE 3   A math instructor gave a six-question quiz to 100 students. The distribution of scores is given in Table 9.9. If a paper is chosen at random, how many correct answers should you expect it to have?

Table 9.9

Number correct	6	5	4	3	2	1	0
Number of students	8	20	36	18	10	6	2

Solution   A standard problem-solving strategy is to relate a new problem to a type of problem solved earlier, so think of choosing a paper as a gambling game in which you are paid $1 for each correct answer. See Table 9.10. Then

$$\text{Expected value} = 6 \times .08 + 5 \times .20 + 4 \times .36 + 3 \times .18 + 2 \times .10$$
$$+ 1 \times .06 + 0 \times .02$$
$$= .48 + 1.00 + 1.44 + .54 + .20 + .06 = 3.72$$

Table 9.10

Outcomes	6 correct	5 correct	4 correct	3 correct	2 correct	1 correct	0 correct
Probabilities	.08	.20	.36	.18	.10	.06	.02
Payoffs	6	5	4	3	2	1	0

In terms of the gambling game you expect to win about $3.72 per play. In terms of the original problem you expect to find about 3.72 correct answers. ❏

EXAMPLE 4 In Exercise 18, Section 9.2, we described an experiment consisting of rolling a die until a 6 comes up, and you were to estimate, by simulation, how many rolls to expect. Could we put this problem into a gambling context to determine the expected number of rolls?

Solution Think of rolling the die as a gambling game. You get to keep rolling until you have rolled a 6. Then you are paid $1 per roll. From the tree in Figure 9.45 we can calculate the probabilities to attach to games of length (payoff) 1, 2, 3, 4, . . . The expected value of the game is the sum of the weighted payoffs:

$$E = \tfrac{1}{6} \cdot 1 + \tfrac{5}{6} \cdot \tfrac{1}{6} \cdot 2 + \tfrac{5}{6} \cdot \tfrac{5}{6} \cdot \tfrac{1}{6} \cdot 3 + \tfrac{5}{6} \cdot \tfrac{5}{6} \cdot \tfrac{5}{6} \cdot \tfrac{1}{6} \cdot 4 + \cdots$$
$$= \tfrac{1}{6}[1 + 2(\tfrac{5}{6}) + 3(\tfrac{5}{6})^2 + 4(\tfrac{5}{6})^3 + \cdots]$$

The pattern of terms should be clear. Assigning a numerical value to this *infinite series,* however, is not easy. It turns out that it *converges* to 6, but it does so rather slowly. (In fact, one has to add 18 terms of the series before its value passes 5.) Thus the expected number of rolls is 6.   ❏

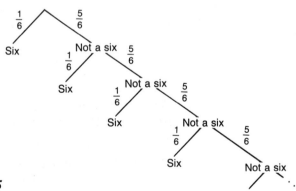

Figure 9.45

Odds

Consider the experiment of spinning the spinner in Figure 9.46. The probability of red is $\tfrac{5}{8}$, the probability of blue is $\tfrac{1}{8}$, and the probability of green is $\tfrac{2}{8}$. The ratio of the probability of red to the probability of not red,

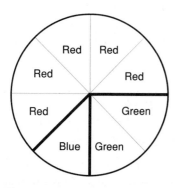

Figure 9.46

$$\frac{5/8}{3/8} = \frac{5}{3}$$

is referred to as the *odds* in favor of red. We say:

> "The odds in favor of red are 5 to 3."

or

> "Red is a 5 to 3 favorite to win."

In general:

> If an event A has probability p, then the **odds in favor** of that event are
>
> $$\frac{P(A)}{P(A')} = \frac{p}{1 - p}$$
>
> (p to $1 - p$).

In the preceding example the odds in favor of green are

$$\frac{\frac{2}{8}}{1 - \frac{2}{8}} = \frac{\frac{2}{8}}{\frac{6}{8}} = \frac{2}{6} = \frac{1}{3} \qquad \text{or} \qquad 1 \text{ to } 3$$

Sometimes, we also say that the odds *against* green are 3 to 1 to emphasize the fact that green is unlikely to occur.

> If an event A has probability p, then the **odds against** that event are
>
> $$\frac{P(A')}{P(A)} = \frac{1 - p}{p}$$
>
> ($1 - p$ to p).

EXAMPLE 5

The probability that the Dodgers will beat the Cubs is $\frac{5}{9}$. What are the odds in favor of the Dodgers winning? What are the odds against the Dodgers winning?

Solution

The odds in favor of the Dodgers winning are

$$\frac{\frac{5}{9}}{1 - \frac{5}{9}} = \frac{\frac{5}{9}}{\frac{4}{9}} = \frac{5}{4} \qquad \text{or} \qquad 5 \text{ to } 4$$

The odds against the Dodgers winning are the same as the odds in favor of the Cubs winning:

$$\frac{1 - \frac{5}{9}}{\frac{5}{9}} = \frac{\frac{4}{9}}{\frac{5}{9}} = \frac{4}{5} \qquad \text{or} \qquad 4 \text{ to } 5 \qquad \square$$

EXAMPLE 6   The odds in favor of the Celtics beating the Lakers are 7 to 5. What is the probability that the Celtics will win?

Solution   Let p be the probability that the Celtics will win. Then

$$\frac{p}{1 - p} = \frac{7}{5} \Rightarrow 5p = 7(1 - p) \Rightarrow$$

$$5p = 7 - 7p \Rightarrow 12p = 7 \Rightarrow p = \frac{7}{12}$$ ❏

There is a close connection between odds and expected value. Suppose that the odds in favor of the Celtics beating the Lakers are 7 to 5, and suppose we decide to bet on the game. If I bet $5 on the Celtics against your $5 on the Lakers, is it a fair game in the sense of expected value? From my point of view the outcomes, probabilities, and payoffs are as given in Table 9.11. And the expected value of the game is

$$\tfrac{7}{12}(+5) + \tfrac{5}{12}(-7) = 0$$

From your point of view the outcomes, probabilities, and payoffs are as given in Table 9.12. And the expected value of the game is again 0:

$$\tfrac{7}{12}(-5) + \tfrac{5}{12}(+7) = 0$$

In general, if the odds in favor of event A are a to b, then an $a bet on A matched with a $b bet against A constitutes a fair game (a game with expected value 0).

Table 9.11

Outcomes	Celtics win	Celtics lose
Probabilities	$\frac{7}{12}$	$\frac{5}{12}$
Payoffs	$+5$	-7

Table 9.12

Outcomes	Celtics win	Celtics lose
Probabilities	$\frac{7}{12}$	$\frac{5}{12}$
Payoffs	-5	$+7$

EXERCISE SET 9.5

1. The game consists of spinning the spinner in Figure 9.47. The payoffs are as shown.
   (a) What is the expected value?
   (b) If it costs $4 to play the game, is it a fair game?

R $15
B $5
Y $3
G $2

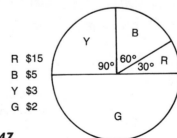

Figure 9.47

2. The game consists of drawing one card from a well-shuffled standard deck. The payoffs are as follows:

Ace:	$5
Face card:	$2
Anything else:	−$1

(a) What is the expected value?
(b) How much should it cost to play if the game is to be fair?

3. A charitable organization sells 10,000 raffle tickets. The first prize is a $5000 automobile; there are two second prizes, each a $500 television set; and there are ten third prizes, each a $35 portable radio. What is the expected value of a raffle ticket?

4. Suppose the probability that a 40-year-old man will live for at least one more year is .99, and suppose that an insurance company sells him a $10,000 one-year term policy for $125. What is the expected value (gain) for the insurance company? *Hint:* The outcome set is {live, die}.

5. Frank and Ernest each flip a penny. If they match (both heads or both tails), then Frank gets both pennies. If they do not match, Ernest wins both pennies. Is this game a fair game?

6. An investor has to decide whether to put her $1000 savings into a safe stock or a risky one. The profits and probabilities are shown in Tables 9.13 and 9.14. Which stock should she buy?

Table 9.13 Safe Stock

Estimated annual profits	−100	0	+100	+300
Estimated probabilities	.10	.25	.45	.20

Table 9.14 Risky Stock

Estimated annual profits	−500	−100	0	+100	+500
Estimated probabilities	.10	.20	.25	.20	.25

★ 7. Carla has to park her car for an hour while she is shopping. She decides it is cheaper to feed the meter 25¢ for an hour of time than it is to risk a $5 parking ticket. What can you say about the probability she assigns to having a police officer look at her meter within an hour? *Hint:* Let p be that probability. Now compare the expected values of the two courses of action (safe and risky) open to Carla.

8. The probability of event A is $\frac{7}{10}$.
   (a) What is the probability of A'?
   (b) What are the odds in favor of A?
   (c) What are the odds against A?

9. The odds in favor of event B are 6 to 5.
   (a) What are the odds against B?
   (b) What is the probability of B?
   (c) What is the probability of B'?

10. An urn contains 7 red marbles and 3 green ones. What are the following odds?
    (a) In favor of drawing a red
    (b) In favor of drawing a green
    (c) In favor of drawing 2 reds in a row (without replacement)
    (d) In favor of drawing 3 reds in a row (without replacement)
    (e) In favor of drawing 2 reds in a row (with replacement)
    (f) In favor of drawing 2 greens in a row (with replacement)

11. For the spinner of Exercise 1, what are the following odds?
    (a) In favor of spinning a yellow
    (b) In favor of spinning either a yellow or a green
    (c) Against spinning a red
    (d) Against spinning three greens in a row
    (e) Against spinning any color twice in a row

12. The Wildcats are 9 to 5 favorites to beat the Tamedogs. You decide to place a $45 bet on the Tamedogs. How much should your bookie put up to cover your bet if it is to be a fair game?

13. The experts tell the coach that the odds in favor of beating each of the six teams on his baseball

schedule are 5 to 3, 3 to 2, 1 to 1, 1 to 9, 2 to 3, and 2 to 1, respectively. What odds do the experts give against his going through the season undefeated?

★ 14. An urn contains 4 red and 3 green marbles. Three marbles are drawn in succession without replacement. What is the expected number of red marbles? *Hint:* Think of this as a gambling game in which you are paid $1 for each red marble you draw.

★ 15. In a hat are five slips numbered 1 through 5. The game consists of drawing them out, one at a time without replacement, and keeping a running total of the numbers drawn. As soon as the running total becomes even, the game is over. Find the expected number of draws. *Note:* If the first number drawn is even, the game is finished in one draw.

★ 16. An apple vendor has a large barrel of apples, $\frac{1}{4}$ of which are rotten, from which he chooses in a random way. He sells apples at one location until he sells 5 or until he sells a rotten one, whichever happens first. Then he moves to a new location. How many apples can he expect to sell at each location? *Hint:* Since it is a *large* barrel the probability of drawing a rotten apple remains very nearly $\frac{1}{4}$ at each draw.

17. A common gambling game at carnivals consists of tossing a dime onto a board, a portion of which is

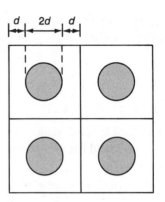

Figure 9.48

shown in Figure 9.48. If the dime stays entirely within a black circle, you win a kewpie doll (worth $1.50) but lose the dime. If it touches white, you lose the dime. Ignoring any effects of aiming, what is the expected value of this game? In Figure 9.48 d represents the diameter of a dime. *Hint:* If a dime is to be a winner, in what region must its center point fall?

★ 18. Make a probability tree for Exercise 19, Section 9.2, and write an infinite series for the expected number of semesters up to and including the first semester in which food poisoning strikes.

Key Concepts in Chapter 9

Random experiment
Outcome
Outcome set
Probability function
Event
Complementary events
Mutually exclusive events
Favorable outcome
Simulation
Random digits

Tree for multistage experiment
Multiplication rule for probabilities
*Fundamental principle of counting
*Permutations
*Combinations
 Expected value
 Odds in favor (against)

❧ *Chapter 9 Review Exercises* ❧

1. The experiment consists of spinning the spinner shown in Figure 9.49. Draw a probability diagram for the experiment, showing what probability is assigned to each outcome.

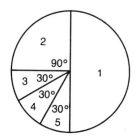

Figure 9.49

2. Suppose that spinning the spinner in Figure 9.49 is a gambling game, and the payoff (in dollars) for each sector is the number appearing on that sector. What is the expected value of the game?

3. The experiment consists of drawing one marble from an urn containing a *total* of no more than 100 red, yellow, blue, and green marbles. The probability diagram is given in Figure 9.50.

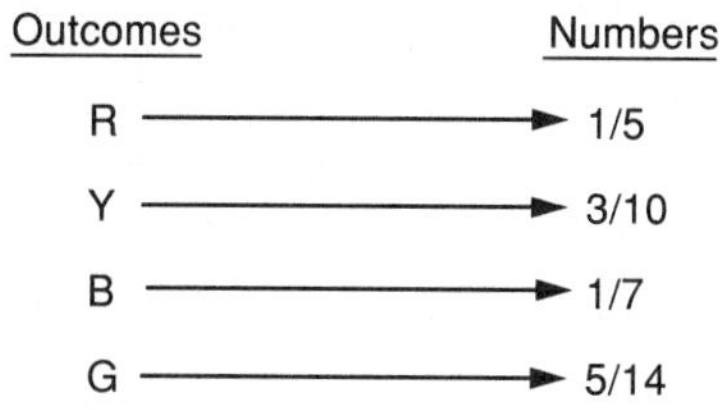

Outcomes	Numbers
R ⟶	1/5
Y ⟶	3/10
B ⟶	1/7
G ⟶	5/14

Figure 9.50

   (a) Which is the most likely outcome?
   (b) How many yellow marbles are in the urn?
   (c) What are the odds against drawing a red?
   (d) How many events are there that do not involve green?

4. A favorite children's game is to find out where one will live by picking a point on a globe in a random way. The usual procedure is to close one's eyes, spin the globe, and then put a finger on the globe. Describe how this game could be used to find (approximately) what portion of the earth's surface is covered by water.

5. The whole numbers 1–100 are marked on tags and put in a hat. The experiment consists of drawing out one tag at random and observing its number. Find the probability of drawing:
   (a) A multiple of 3 between 20 and 40
   (b) A number that is a multiple of 3 or is strictly between 20 and 40
   (c) A number that is not a multiple of 3

6. Suppose you have 6 nickels, 4 dimes, 3 quarters, and 2 half-dollars in your pocket, and suppose it is possible to randomly pull out two coins. What is the probability of pulling out exactly 50¢?

7. The probability diagram for a spinner experiment is given in Figure 9.51. Find x.

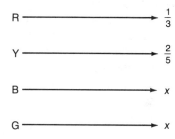

Figure 9.51

8. Refer to the experiment of Exercise 7.
   (a) How many events are there?
   (b) What are the odds in favor of spinning a yellow?

9. The experiment consists of spinning the spinner shown in Figure 9.52 three times in succession.
   (a) What is the probability of spinning three yellows?
   (b) What is the probability of spinning each color once?

512

9 ✷ Probability

(c) What is the probability of spinning more blues than any other color?

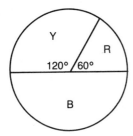

Figure 9.52

10. How many times must the spinner of Figure 9.52 be spun if you want to be 99% certain of spinning at least one blue?

11. Describe how a table of random digits could be used to simulate the experiment of Exercise 9.

12. A dreidel (Figure 9.53) is a random device in the shape of a four-sided top. Its four faces bear Hebrew letters, which we will write as N, G, H, and S.
    (a) Describe how to use a table of random digits to simulate the experiment of spinning a dreidel.
    (b) Describe in step-by-step detail how to approximate the number of spins you should expect to make until all four letters have come up.

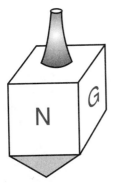

Figure 9.53

13. The experiment consists of rolling an ordinary pair of dice. The outcomes are ordered pairs of numbers.

(a) How many outcomes has this experiment?
(b) List the event "a sum less than 5 results."
(c) What is the probability that a sum less than 5 results?

14. A box of outwardly indistinguishable chocolates consists of 12 creams, 10 mints, 8 jellies, and 6 butters.
    (a) Draw a spinner that simulates the experiment of choosing a chocolate to eat from this box.
    (b) Does spinning this spinner three times in succession simulate the experiment of choosing three chocolates to eat?

15. Two cards are drawn (without replacement) from a standard deck. What is the probability that their sum is 6? (Treat aces as 1s and face cards as 10s.)

16. In this experiment a coin is tossed. If it comes up heads, a die is rolled and the number on the die is recorded; if it comes up tails, a card is drawn from a standard deck and the number (or letter) on that card is recorded. What is the probability that on one trial of this experiment the number 5 will be recorded?

17. Suppose the probability that an uninsured motorist will be involved in an auto accident in a given year is .12, while the probability for an insured motorist is .05. Suppose further that 7% of all motorists are uninsured. What is the probability that a motorist, chosen at random, will be involved in an accident that year?

* 18. The 26 alphabet letters are printed on individual tags. The tags are placed in a hat, and then 4 of them are chosen at random. Use combination symbols C_k^n to express each of these probabilities.
    (a) The probability that all 4 are vowels
    (b) The probability that all 4 come from the first half of the alphabet
    (c) The probability that at least one is a vowel

19. In Michigan's "zinger" lottery game, six digits are drawn *in order*. If a player's ordered 6-tuple matches all six digits in order, then he wins $100,000. If he matches only the first five, the prize is $5000; the first four, $500; the first three,

$100; the first two, $20. If the player does not match the first two, he wins nothing. It costs $1 to buy an ordered 6-tuple.

(a) What is the probability of winning $20 or more?

(b) What is the probability of winning exactly $100?

(c) What is the expected value of the game?

20. A quality control expert at a fruit cannery selects 100 cans of cherries, at random, and goes through each one counting cherry pits. Her data are given in Table 9.15. How many pits should a consumer expect to find in a can of these cherries?

Table 9.15

Number of pits	0	1	2	3	4	5	6
Number of cans	27	24	39	7	0	2	1

21. This is how the game is played: Each of us spins the spinner in Figure 9.54. If your number matches mine, then I pay you $3. If the difference between your number and mine is 1, then I pay

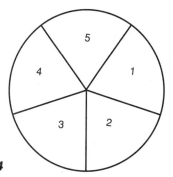

Figure 9.54

you $1. In all other cases, you pay me $2. What is the expected value of this game from your point of view?

22. On the basis of past experience a shoe salesman has found that (1) he makes a sale to 70% of all females who walk in and to 80% of all males who walk in; (2) the average sale to a female buyer is $25, while the average sale to a male buyer is $20; (3) 40% of the people who come in the store are males. While shelving shoes in the back room, he hears someone come in. How large a sale should he expect to make to that person?

References

Blakeslee, D. and W. Chinn. *Introductory Statistics and Probability*. Boston: Houghton Mifflin, 1971.

Gnanadesikan, M., R. Scheaffer, and J. Swift. *The Art and Techniques of Simulation*. Palo Alto, Calif.: Dale Seymour Publications, 1986.

Kemeny, J., J. Snell, and G. Thompson. *Introduction to Finite Mathematics*. 3rd ed. Englewood Cliffs, N.J.: Prentice-Hall, 1974.

National Council of Teachers of Mathematics. *1981 Yearbook: Teaching Statistics and Probability*. Reston, Va.: NCTM, 1981.

Newman, C., T. Obremski, and R. Scheaffer. *Exploring Probability*. Palo Alto, Calif.: Dale Seymour Publications, 1986.

Phillips, E., G. Lappan, M. Winter, and W. Fitzgerald. *Probability*. Menlo Park, Calif.: Addison Wesley, 1986.

Shulte, A., and S. Choate. *What Are My Chances? Books A and B*. Palo Alto, Calif.: Creative Publications, 1977.

10

STATISTICS

At about the same time that Pascal and Fermat were developing probability theory, John Graunt of London published (in 1662) what is considered to be the first statistics book, a thin volume entitled *Natural and Political Observations Made upon the Bills of Mortality*. In it he classified, tabulated, and drew conclusions from the data obtained from the weekly birth and death notices. From that humble beginning statistics has grown to the point where today thousands of people earn a living as statisticians in many fields. And everyone who reads magazines or newspapers, listens to the radio, or watches television is bombarded with statistics. An understanding of the basic ideas of statistics has become a requirement for today's educated citizen. This is perhaps the main reason for the strong trend toward including more statistics in the elementary and junior high school mathematics curriculum. In the words of the *Standards* for grades 5–8: "A knowledge of statistics is necessary if students are to become intelligent consumers who can make critical and informed decisions."

10.1 *Graphs*

At its most basic level, statistics has to do with organizing, summarizing, displaying, and interpreting data. This aspect of the subject is often referred to as **descriptive statistics.** Various graphical displays of data are in everday use. We will investigate four of the most common types: bar graphs, broken-line graphs, circle graphs, and pictographs.

Graphical Displays

One familiar device is the **bar graph,** which can illustrate vividly certain size comparisons. For example, the six highest waterfalls in the world and their heights in meters are tabulated in Table 10.1. A bar graph of these data shows us the relative heights at a glance (Figure 10.1). Clearly, the bar graph is a close relative of the ordinary sort of graph we draw for functions.

A second close relative of our customary function graph is the **broken-line graph** or polygonal graph. Graphs of this type are often used to show changes

Table 10.1

Waterfall	Height
Angel (Venezuela)	1000 m
Tugela (South Africa)	914 m
Cuquenan (Venezuela)	610 m
Sutherland (New Zealand)	580 m
Takkakaw (British Columbia)	503 m
Ribbon (California)	491 m

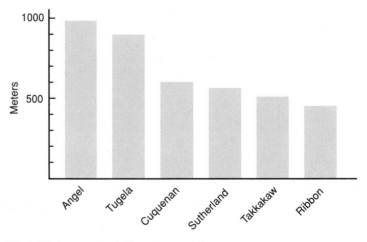

Figure 10.1 Highest waterfalls.

in a quantity over time. For example, Figure 10.2 shows the population of the United States between 1880 and 1940. The graph has sharp corners because population is estimated only every ten years. If it were possible to calculate population on a daily basis, the graph would appear to be smooth.

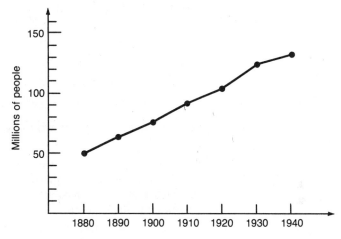

Figure 10.2 U.S. population.

A third very common graphical device is the **circle graph** or pie chart. This type of representation is generally used to show how some whole is partitioned. Figure 10.3 is typical. The whole is actually the total amount of the

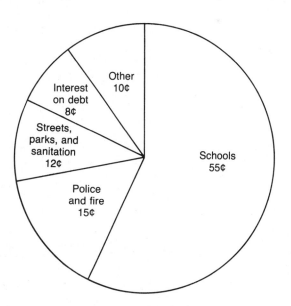

Figure 10.3 How the city spends your tax dollar.

city's tax revenues, of which schools receive 55%, police and fire 15%, and so on. In the figure, for the purpose of making a personal impact on the reader, all expenditures have been shrunken proportionately so that the whole is $1.

To draw a circle graph like Figure 10.3, begin by drawing a circle with a compass. Then calculate the measures of the central angles as follows:

Schools: 55% of 360° = .55 × 360° = 198°

Police: 15% of 360° = .15 × 360° = 54°

Streets: 12% of 360° = .12 × 360° = 43.2°

Interest: 8% of 360° = .08 × 360° = 28.8°

Other: 10% of 360° = .10 × 360° = 36°

Finally, draw the sectors with a protractor and a straightedge.

EXAMPLE 1   Figure 10.4 is a bar graph, with partitioned bars, showing how the eight major blood groups are distributed in the U.S. population. Draw a circle graph representing the distribution.

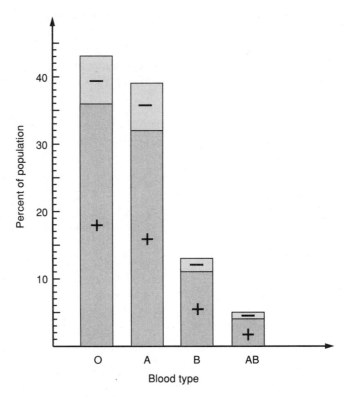

Figure 10.4 Distribution of blood types.

Solution   From the bar graph, about 36% of the population has blood type O^+. Thus the sector for O^+ in the circle graph should have central angle of measure

$$36\% \text{ of } 360° = .36 \times 360° \doteq 130°$$

Other sector sizes are found similarly. The circle graph is shown in Figure 10.5. Which graph do you prefer, bar or circle? Would a broken-line graph be a good representation for the distribution of blood types?

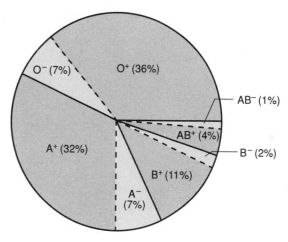

Figure 10.5 Distribution of blood types.   ❏

A fourth, rather amorphous category of displays is the class of **pictographs.** Many pictographs are just artistic versions of bar graphs, drawn either vertically or horizontally. By their very nature, pictographs provide only crude estimates of data.

EXAMPLE 2   The pictograph in Figure 10.6 shows automobile production of three companies in 1990.
(a) About how many cars did Company A produce?
(b) Company C produced about how many more cars than Company B?

Figure 10.6 Automobile production in 1990.

Solution   (a) About 150,000
                (b) About 175,000   ❏

Frequency Diagrams

Suppose one of your colleagues gave a 10-point quiz to her class of 20 students, showed you the numbers in her grade book (Figure 10.7), and asked you what you thought about the results. You might remark that there was one perfect paper, that quite a few people seemed to get 7s, and that no one got less than a 3. Beyond those observations nothing is very obvious. The difficulty is that the data have not been organized and presented in a helpful way.

6 7 3 8 5 7 4 7 6 3 8 6 7 9 4 4 8 10 7 5

Figure 10.7 Quiz scores.

Quiz scores	Tally	Frequency
3	‖	2
4	‖‖	3
5	‖	2
6	‖‖	3
7	‖‖‖‖	5
8	‖‖	3
9			1
10			1

Figure 10.8

A first step toward organizing the data might be to make a **frequency distribution,** as in Figure 10.8. The **dot frequency graph** (reminiscent of a bar graph) in Figure 10.9 is even more revealing From this figure, the "average" score appears to be around 6 or 7. By simply counting dots, we can see that 25% of the class got scores of 4 or less, 50% got scores of 6 or less, and 75% got scores of 7 or less.

Often dot frequency graphs are replaced by a special kind of bar graph called a **histogram.** The histogram corresponding to Figure 10.9 is shown in Figure 10.10. Notice that the bars are touching and are centered over the scores, and notice that the *area* covered by the histogram is precisely the same as the number of pieces of data (in this case 20). This connection between area and frequency will be important when we look at "normal curves."

Histograms are useful for indicating the distribution of **grouped data.** Suppose, for example, that one wanted to show a distribution of these 20 test scores:

49 52 58 60 61 65 69 72 75 75
76 78 81 81 83 84 88 90 91 96

An ordinary dot frequency graph or histogram of the ungrouped data would not be particularly revealing, since there are 18 distinct scores among the 20. A clearer picture would be provided by compiling a **grouped frequency distribution,** as in Figure 10.11, and then drawing the histogram shown in Figure 10.12.

If we draw line segments joining the midpoints of the upper edges of the bars in a histogram, and then join the left and right end points to points on the horizontal axis one-half an interval to the left and to the right, respectively, we get what is called a **frequency polygon.** Figure 10.13 shows the frequency polygon associated with the grouped test scores of Figures 10.11 and 10.12.

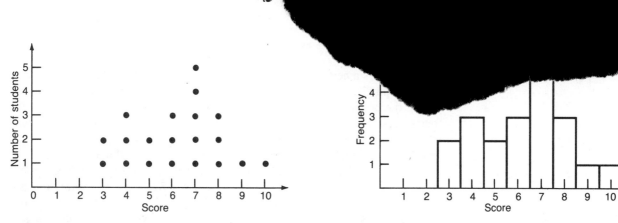

Figure 10.9 Dot frequency graph of quiz scores.

Figure 10.10 Histogram of quiz scores.

Interval of scores	Tally	Frequency
40–49	|	1
50–59	||	2
60–69	||||	4
70–79	~~||||~~	5
80–89	~~||||~~	5
90–99	|||	3

Figure 10.11

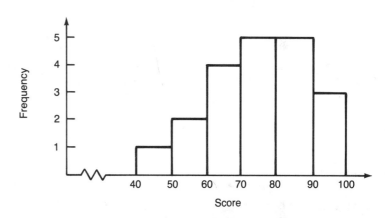

Figure 10.12 Histogram of grouped test scores.

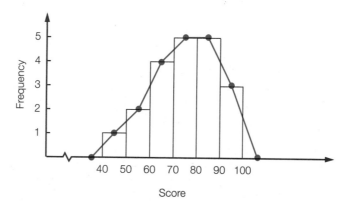

Figure 10.13 Frequency polygon of grouped test scores.

f Plots

s a new way of grouping and displaying data, the so-called **stem-
plot,** has been gaining popularity. Figure 10.14 is a stem-and-leaf
of the previous set of test scores. The third line 6 | 0 1 5 9 represents the
four scores 60, 61, 65, and 69. Notice that if the stem-and-leaf plot is turned
90° counterclockwise, it looks a lot like a dot frequency graph.

For certain kinds of data a **two-sided stem-and-leaf plot** is helpful. Consider, for example, the data in Table 10.2 on suicide rates (per 100,000 population) for men and women in selected countries. We begin by making a stem-
and-leaf plot for the men, using the tens digits 0–4 as stem. Then we record
the units digits as leaves. Since these data are not arranged in order, the leaf
digits will also be out of order. See Figure 10.15. Now we use the same stem
but plot the women's leaves on the left, as in Figure 10.16. Finally, we rearrange the leaves so that they increase as one moves away from the stem; see
Figure 10.17.

The finished two-sided stem-and-leaf plot shows graphically the difference
by sex in suicide rates. Examination of the leaves reveals that the suicide rate
for men in 9 of the countries exceeds the highest suicide rate for women in the
entire sample of 16 countries.

```
6 | 0      5   6
7 | 2 5 5 6
8 | 1 1 3 4 8
9 | 0 1 6
```

Stem. The digits represent tens.   Leaves. The digits represent units.

Figure 10.14

Men
```
0 | 6 8
1 | 6 2 9 1 9
2 | 2 5 2 2 8
3 | 9 0 7
4 | 0
```

Figure 10.15

Table 10.2 Suicide Rates for Men and Women per 100,000 Population

Country	Men	Women
Australia	16	6
Austria	40	15
Canada	22	7
Denmark	39	21
France	25	10
W. Germany	30	14
Ireland	6	4
Israel	8	4
Japan	22	13
Netherlands	12	8
Norway	19	7
Poland	22	4
Sweden	28	11
Switzerland	37	15
United Kingdom	11	7
United States	19	6

```
           Women                         Men
6  7  4  7  8  4  4  7  6 | 0 | 6  8
         5  1  3  4  0  5 | 1 | 6  2  9  1  9
                        1 | 2 | 2  5  2  2  8
                          | 3 | 9  0  7
                          | 4 | 0
```

Figure 10.16

```
           Women                         Men
8  7  7  7  6  6  4  4  4 | 0 | 6  8
            5  5  4  3  1  0 | 1 | 1  2  6  9  9
                        1 | 2 | 2  2  2  5  8
                          | 3 | 0  7  9
                          | 4 | 0
```

Figure 10.17

EXERCISE SET 10.1

1. The chart maker inadvertently omitted the vertical axis from the bar graph in Figure 10.18, which compares the surface areas of the five Great Lakes: Superior, Huron, Michigan, Erie, and Ontario.
   (a) Lake Superior has an area of about 32,000 square miles (mi^2). What is the approximate area of Lake Huron?
   (b) Lake Erie's area is about what percent of Lake Michigan's?

2. In 1966 the leading salt-producing states and their production in millions of tons were Louisiana, 8.7; Texas, 7.7; Ohio, 5.1; New York, 5.0; Michigan, 4.5; and California, 1.7. Make a bar graph to display these data.

3. Figure 10.19 appeared in a football report in the *Ann Arbor News* (November 13, 1988) with the caption, "Game at a Glance." Comment on the bar graphs and the caption.

4. The pictograph in Figure 10.20 supposedly portrays the data in Table 10.3. What is misleading about the pictograph?

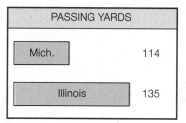

Figure 10.19

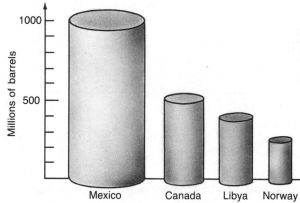

Figure 10.20 Oil production.

Table 10.3 Estimated 1984 Crude Oil Production (in Millions of Barrels)

Canada	500
Libya	400
Mexico	1000
Norway	250

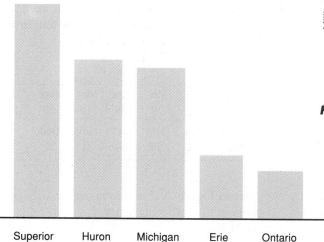

Figure 10.18 Surface areas of the Great Lakes.

5. One of Michigan's legislators published the bar graph of Figure 10.21 in his newsletter to constituents.
   (a) Does U.S. spending seem dwarfed by the others?
   (b) What would the visual effect have been if the percent axis had been numbered from 0 to 44 rather than from 29 to 44?
   (c) Is this legislator for or against greater U.S. government spending?

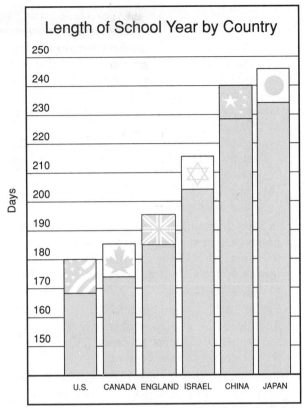

Figure 10.22

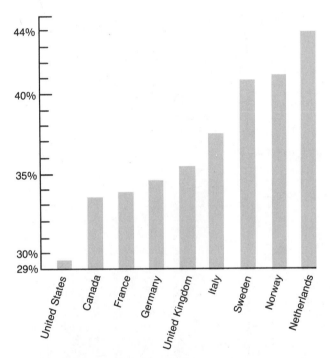

Figure 10.21 Government spending as a percent of gross domestic product.

6. Figure 10.22 is a bar graph prepared by the Center for Education Statistics and published in the magazine *Learning 89* (vol. 17, no. 9, p. 5). Comment on it.

7. Figure 10.23 shows the annual earnings per share of common stock of Amalgamated Widget for each year since 1975. What impression might a stockholder get if the annual report showed only the last four dots on the graph?

8. Draw a broken-line graph to represent the data in Table 10.4 on the average daily low temperature (Fahrenheit), by month, in Chicago.

Table 10.4

Month	Jan	Feb	Mar	Apr	May	June
Temp.	17	20	29	39	49	59

Month	July	Aug	Sept	Oct	Nov	Dec
Temp.	64	62	55	44	31	21

9. Refer to Figure 10.2 and estimate the U.S. population in the following years.
   (a) 1885
   (b) 1870
   (c) 1960

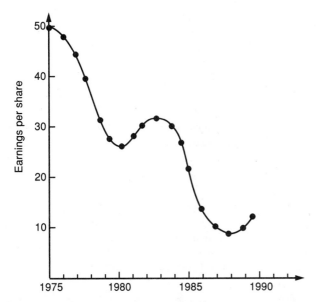

Figure 10.23 Earnings per share.

10. Table 10.5 was prepared by the Bureau of Justice Statistics; all populations are as of December 31. Draw a broken-line graph. (How will you round the data before plotting points?) Use your graph to predict plausible lower and upper limits on the prison population in the year 2000.

11. The city budget described by Figure 10.3 (p. 517) actually allots $2 million for police and fire protection. What actual dollar amount does it allot for streets, parks, and sanitation?

12. Draw a circle graph to represent these data on production in the state of New Mexico: mineral products, 64%; agricultural products, 25%; man-

ufactured products, 11%. What are the measures of the three central angles of your graph?

13. Table 10.6 was prepared by the National Center for Health Statistics. Draw two circle graphs, one for 1970 and one for 1987.

14. *Class project:* Let each student report the number of hours of class she or he has on a typical Monday. Display the data in a dot frequency graph on the blackboard. Here is a typical data set to practice on:

4 3 4   2 5 3   4 5 5   3 6 4   8 2 4   4 5 6   3 4

Similar class projects can be carried out in an elementary classroom using data supplied by the students: the number of blocks from school the student lives, the age of the youngest member of the student's family, and so forth.

Table 10.5 State and Federal Prison Populations

Year	Number of Inmates
1980	329,821
1981	369,930
1982	413,806
1983	437,248
1984	464,567
1985	502,502
1986	544,972
1987	584,435
1988	627,402

Table 10.6 First Births and Mothers' Ages

Age of Mother at Birth of First Child	Percent of First-Time Mothers in 1970	Percent of First-Time Mothers in 1987
under 20	35.6%	23.3%
20–24 years	45.6%	33.0%
25–29 years	14.8%	27.8%
30–34 years	3.0%	12.4%
35 and over	1.0%	3.5%

15. *Class project:* Let everyone look at her or his watch. When a signal is given, everyone write down the time, to the nearest minute. Represent the data obtained by a dot frequency graph on the blackboard.

16. The 1985 *Information Please Almanac* gives the figures in Table 10.7 for burglaries per 1000 population in selected U.S. cities. Using the intervals 2–3, 3–4, 4–5, 5–6, 6–7, 7–8, 8–9, make a grouped frequency distribution and a histogram for these data. Finally, use your histogram to make a frequency polygon.

17. Round each piece of data in Table 10.7 to the nearest tenth and then make a stem-and-leaf plot, using units digits for the stem and tenths digits for the leaves.

18. Using tens digits as stem and units digits as leaves, make a two-sided stem-and-leaf plot of the scores in Table 10.8 on the first two exams given to a class of 20 students. Comment on the exams or the students.

Table 10.7

Dallas	6.13
Phoenix	3.07
Detroit	5.10
San Francisco	5.30
New York	6.03
Washington, D.C.	5.78
Los Angeles	6.57
Baltimore	8.22
San Diego	2.39
Memphis	3.59
San Antonio	3.67
Chicago	2.76
Philadelphia	3.40
Indianapolis	4.09

Table 10.8

Exam 1	34	37	39	44	46	46	49	51	57	70
	74	74	79	80	80	82	85	88	91	96
Exam 2	45	49	52	58	58	60	64	67	67	68
	70	71	73	73	74	78	82	84	88	93

10.2 *Measures of Central Tendency*

In the previous section our approach to data was purely graphical. In this section we take our first steps toward quantification, that is, the assignment of numbers to sets of data.

Mean, Median, and Mode

Consider again the 20 quiz scores that we studied earlier. For ease of reference, the dot frequency graph is reproduced in Figure 10.24. Notice that the scores seem to be "centered" around 6 or 7. The three common measures of central tendency are the mean, the median, and the mode.

The **mean,** or more precisely the **arithmetic mean,** is what we usually call the average. It is found by adding all of the numbers and then dividing by the number of summands. For example:

$$\text{The mean of 7 and 10 is } \frac{7 + 10}{2} = 8.5.$$

$$\text{The mean of 6, 7, and 11 is } \frac{6 + 7 + 11}{3} = 8.$$

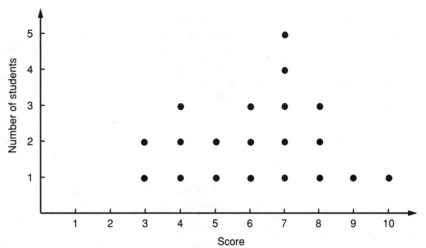

Figure 10.24

In general:

The mean $\bar{x}$ of a set of numbers x_1, x_2, x_3, . . . x_n is given by the formula

$$\bar{x} = \frac{x_1 + x_2 + x_3 + \cdots + x_n}{n}$$

Calculating the mean of the quiz scores given in Figure 10.24 can be a tedious task unless one is adept at mental arithmetic or has a calculator:

$$\frac{2 \cdot 3 + 3 \cdot 4 + 2 \cdot 5 + 3 \cdot 6 + 5 \cdot 7 + 3 \cdot 8 + 9 + 10}{20} = \frac{124}{20} = 6.2$$

If we rewrite this equation in the form

$$\tfrac{2}{20} \cdot 3 + \tfrac{3}{20} \cdot 4 + \tfrac{2}{20} \cdot 5 + \tfrac{3}{20} \cdot 6 + \tfrac{5}{20} \cdot 7 + \tfrac{3}{20} \cdot 8 + \tfrac{1}{20} \cdot 9 + \tfrac{1}{20} \cdot 10 = 6.2$$

we see that the mean can be thought of as the weighted average of the distinct scores 3 through 10, the weights being their relative frequencies. Thus the mean of our set of 20 scores is the expected value for the experiment of drawing 1 of the 20 scores out of a hat.

Calculating the median is simpler. Once the scores have been arranged in order from small to large, the **median** is just the middle score, if there is one. If not, it is the average of the two contenders. For example:

The median of 2, 3, 7, 12, 20 is 7.
The median of 3, 3, 3, 4, 6, is 3.
The median of 4, 6, 7, 10 is 6.5.

For the set of 20 quiz scores that we have been looking at, there are 10 at or below 6 and 10 at or above 7. Thus the median is 6.5.

The median 6.5 divides the scores into an upper half and a lower half. (In the case of an odd number of pieces of data, the middle one is discarded in defining the upper and lower halves.) The scores can be partitioned into quarters by calculating the medians of the two halves. The median of the lower half (in this case 4.5) is called the **lower quartile;** the median of the upper half (in this case 7.5) is called the **upper quartile:**

$$3\ 3\ 4\ 4\ 4\ |\ 5\ 5\ 6\ 6\ 6\ |\ 7\ 7\ 7\ 7\ 7\ |\ 8\ 8\ 8\ 9\ 10$$

| Lower quartile 4.5 | Median 6.5 | Upper quartile 7.5 |

The third measure of central tendency, the mode, is less useful than the other two. The **mode** of a set of data is the most common number (or numbers). For example:

The mode of 1, 3, 4, 4, 5, 6, 6, 6, 9 is 6.
The mode of 2, 2, 3, 5, 6, 8, 9, is 2.
The modes of 1, 3, 3, 5, 6, 7, 7, are 3 and 7.

For our set of quiz scores the mode is 7. Notice that no student actually received either the mean score (6.2) or the median score (6.5). The most fashionable (modish) score was 7.

EXAMPLE 1   A radio talk show receives telephone calls from ten cities as shown in Table 10.9. Find the mean, median, and mode for the numbers of calls.

Solution   Begin by putting the numbers in order from small to large

$$2\quad 3\quad 4\quad 4\quad 6\quad 6\quad 6\quad 7\quad 8$$

Now it is easy to see that the mode is 6 and the median is 5. Even the mean can be found mentally to be $\frac{49}{10} = 4.9$.   ❏

Table 10.9 Telephone Calls and Their Sources

City	Calls
Belmont	2
Boston	8
Cambridge	7
Dedham	4
Needham	3
Newton	4
Quincy	6
Somerville	6
South Boston	6
Watertown	3

Box-and-Whisker Plots

Of the three averages—mean, median, and mode—the mean has played by far the largest role in the development of mathematical statistics. In just the past few years, though, the median and the upper and lower quartiles have begun to be used in a format known as a **box-and-whisker plot.** We illustrate the construction of a box-and-whisker plot by using the lengths (in hundreds of miles) of the 21 longest rivers in the world. (The longest is the Nile.)

42	39	37	36	35	29	28
28	28	27	27	27	26	26
25	23	23	23	20	20	20

The first step is to find the median, the quartiles, and the extreme values:

Median = 11th number = 27
Upper quartile = average of 5th and 6th largest numbers = 32
Lower quartile = average of 5th and 6th smallest numbers = 23
Upper extreme value = 42
Lower extreme value = 20

The next step is to plot these numbers on a number line, as in Figure 10.25. The last step is to draw a box between the two quartiles, mark the median with a line across the box, and draw two "whiskers" out to the extreme values, as in Figure 10.26. From the length of the whiskers and the location of the median, it is clear that there are a few very long rivers, but most are clustered near the short end of the range.

Box-and-whisker plots have their greatest utility when two or more sets of data are being compared.

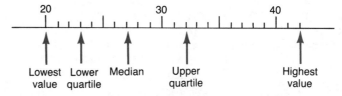

Figure 10.25

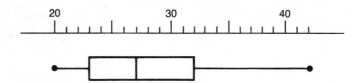

Figure 10.26 A box-and-whisker plot.

EXAMPLE 2   Table 10.10 gives the birth rates (per 1000 population) of 15 selected countries in 1970 and in 1980. Make a double box-and-whisker plot and draw some conclusions.

Solution   Begin by arranging each list in increasing order and circling the quartiles and the medians. See Table 10.11. Now, draw two box-and-whisker plots under a single number line, as in Figure 10.27. The double plot shows clearly an overall decline in birth rates. The shortening of the box (1980) suggests tighter packing about the median. The persistent long whisker to the right indicates a continued unusually high rate in at least one country.

Table 10.10 Birth Rates per 1000 Population

Country	1970	1980
Australia	20.6	15.3
Belgium	14.7	12.7
Canada	17.4	15.4
Denmark	14.4	11.2
El Salvador	40.0	34.7
France	16.8	14.8
W. Germany	11.4	10.0
Hungary	14.7	13.9
Israel	26.9	24.1
Japan	18.9	13.7
Netherlands	18.3	12.8
Panama	37.2	26.8
Portugal	20.0	16.4
Singapore	23.0	17.3
United States	18.3	16.2

Table 10.11

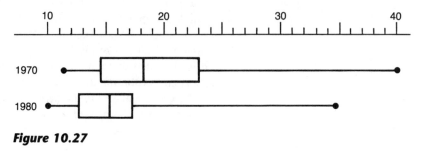

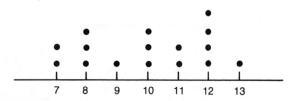

Figure 10.27

EXERCISE SET 10.2

1. Find the mean, the median, and the mode of the data represented by the dot frequency graph of Figure 10.28.

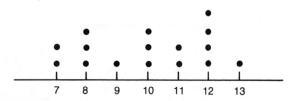

Figure 10.28

2. Table 10.12 gives the number of years of compulsory education in fifteen selected countries in 1980.
   (a) Make a dot frequency graph representing these data.
   (b) Find the median number of years.
   (c) Find the mean.
   (d) Find the mode.

Table 10.12

Country	Years of Compulsory Education
Brazil	8
Chile	8
Egypt	6
France	10
W. Germany	9
India	5
Indonesia	6
Japan	9
Netherlands	10
Nigeria	6
Poland	8
Sweden	9
U.K.	11
U.S.A	10
U.S.S.R.	10

3. Lori's scores on her first six math tests were

   82, 75, 88, 80, 78, 86

   She computes her mean score *mentally* by choosing a convenient number somewhere near the middle, say, 80. Then she moves along her list of scores and says

   "2 over, 3 under, 5 over, 5 over, 3 over, 9 over"

   from which she concludes that her mean score is
   $$80 + \tfrac{9}{6} = 81.5$$
   Explain her method.

4. For each set of data, calculate the mean, median, and mode.
   (a) 1, 7, 9, 2, 1, 7, 7, 6
   (b) 5, −2, 3, 3, −1, 4, 4, −1, 3
   (c) 3.4, 2.9, 2.8, 2.4, 3.0, 2.9
   (d) 2412, 2403, 2394, 2409, 2397, 2409

5. To get an A in the class, a student needs a mean score of 90 (or more) on the four exams. Sue's scores on the first three were 85, 96, and 92. What (minimum) score does she need on the fourth exam to earn an A?

6. On the three tests Lucy took, her median score was 88, her mean score was 90, and her range (the difference between her high and low score) was 8. What were her three test scores?

7. The following numbers are the years of teaching experience of the staff at Fillmore Elementary School: 0, 1, 2, 4, 4, 36, 44. The principal boasts that her staff has an average of 13 years of teaching experience.
   (a) What does she mean by *average?*
   (b) Suppose each teacher has a class of 25 students, and suppose a student is chosen at random. What is the probability that he will have a teacher with 13 or more years of experience?

8. The mean age of the 175 students at Fillmore Elementary is 8. The mean age of the 12 adults (teachers, administrators, clericals, custodians)

there is 40. What is the mean age of all persons at Fillmore?

9. Determine the numerical values of the lower and upper quartiles of the data in Exercise 2, and make a box-and-whisker plot.

10. Under a single number line, make box-and-whisker plots for each of these sets of data.
    (a) 1, 2, 3, 4, 5, 6, 7
    (b) 0, 2, 3, 4, 5, 6, 8
    (c) 1, 3, 3, 4, 5, 5, 7
    (d) 3, 3, 4, 4, 4, 5, 5
    (e) 1, 1, 2, 2, 3, 4, 7
    (f) 1, 2, 3, 5, 6, 7, 7
    (g) 0, 2, 2, 3, 4, 5, 7, 7
    (h) 2, 2, 2, 3, 4, 4, 8, 8

11. Box-and-whisker plots of the IQ scores in two fourth-grade classes are shown in Figure 10.29. Which class would probably be easier to teach?

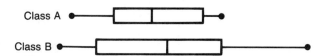

Figure 10.29

12. Make a double box-and-whisker plot of the test scores in Exercise 18 of Section 10.1. Comment again on the exams or the students.

13. In Exercise 12 the mean of the scores on test 2 is 68.7 and the median is 69. Suppose an additional score of 0 is included in the data (the teacher flunked the test).
    (a) What is the new mean?
    (b) What is the new median?

14. Repeat Exercise 13 supposing that the additional score had been 68 instead of 0. Now comment on the relative sensitivities of the mean and the median to "outliers" (extreme data).

15. In simulation Exercises 18, 19, and 21 in Section 9.2, did you use the mean or the median of the data you generated?

 **10.3** *Measures of Dispersion*

Suppose you and a colleague both gave the same 10-point quiz to your classes of 20 students, and the scores are those in Table 10.13. Computation of the three measures of central tendency yields identical values for both sets of data:

$$\text{Mean} = \tfrac{124}{20} = 6.2 \qquad \text{Median} = 6.5 \qquad \text{Mode} = 7$$

Table 10.13 Quiz Scores in Two Classes

Your class	4	4	5	5	5	5	6	6	6	6	7	7	7	7	7	7	7	7	8	8
Colleague's	3	3	4	4	4	5	5	6	6	6	7	7	7	7	7	8	8	8	9	10

Still, there is something different about the data. Your scores seem to be more clustered together, your colleague's more dispersed. A double box-and-whisker plot (Figure 10.30) illustrates the difference graphically.

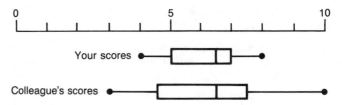

Figure 10.30

There are three common numerical measures of the degree of dispersion. The simplest one is the **range,** which is just the difference between the highest and the lowest scores. (Look at the whiskers.) Your range is $8 - 4 = 4$; your colleague's is $10 - 3 = 7$. One suspects, though, that range cannot be a particularly useful measure because its value depends on only 2 of the 20 scores.

A measure of dispersion that takes all scores into account is the variance. Calculating variance takes several steps. We illustrate each step by using the scores for your class.

1. Compute the mean. For your scores it is 6.2.
2. Subtract the mean from each score and square the difference:

$$2 \times (4 - 6.2)^2 = 2 \times (-2.2)^2 = 2 \times 4.84 = 9.68$$
$$4 \times (5 - 6.2)^2 = 4 \times (-1.2)^2 = 4 \times 1.44 = 5.76$$
$$4 \times (6 - 6.2)^2 = 4 \times (-0.2)^2 = 4 \times 0.04 = 0.16$$
$$8 \times (7 - 6.2)^2 = 8 \times (0.8)^2 = 8 \times 0.64 = 5.12$$
$$2 \times (8 - 6.2)^2 = 2 \times (1.8)^2 = 2 \times 3.24 = 6.48$$

3. Sum the numbers from step 2 and divide by the number of scores (pieces of data):

$$\frac{9.68 + 5.76 + 0.16 + 5.12 + 6.48}{20} = \frac{27.20}{20} = 1.36$$

Clearly, computation of variance would be easier with a calculator or a computer. Carrying out the same three steps on your colleague's scores (with a calculator) yields a variance of 2.876. Your colleague's variance is more than twice yours.

Here is a formal definition of **variance.**

Given a collection numbers $x_1, x_2, \ldots, x_n$ with mean $\bar{x}$, the variance v is given by the formula

$$v = \frac{(x_1 - \bar{x})^2 + (x_2 - \bar{x})^2 + \cdots + (x_n - \bar{x})^2}{n}$$

Note: This definition of variance is not universally accepted. Some statisticians use $n - 1$ rather than n as the denominator in certain contexts.

One point in our description of variance may have troubled you. Why is it that at step 2 the differences are squared? One reason is that some of the differences are positive and some are negative, and we do not want cancellation to take place; that is, we want every difference to contribute to the variance. Squaring differences makes everything positive. Because this squaring operation is a somewhat artificial mathematical contrivance, a third measure of dispersion that partially compensates for the squaring is more widely used than variance. This third measure is called **standard deviation,** and, by definition, it is just the square root of the variance.

The standard deviation s of a collection of numbers is given by the formula $s = \sqrt{v}$, where v is the variance.

Thus in the two examples we have been following:

The standard deviation for your scores is $\sqrt{1.36} \doteq 1.17$.
The standard deviation for your colleague's scores is $\sqrt{2.876} \doteq 1.70$.

The more widely dispersed the data, the larger the standard deviation.

EXAMPLE 1   Find the mean height and the standard deviation for these data on heights of basketball players: Alice, 6 ft 1 in; Barb, 5 ft 9 in; Connie, 5 ft 7 in; Dawn, 5 ft 11 in; Elena, 5 ft 10 in.

Solution   To keep the numbers manageable by hand, we will just keep track of the number of inches over 5 ft. After finding their mean, we can add 5 ft.

>   Mean of 13, 9, 7, 11, 10 is 10.
>   Mean height = 5 ft 10 in = 70 in

To compute variance we first express all heights in inches.

>   Variance = $\frac{1}{5}[(73 - 70)^2 + (69 - 70)^2 + (67 - 70)^2 + (71 - 70)^2$
> $+ (70 - 70)^2]$
> $= \frac{1}{5}[9 + 1 + 9 + 1 + 0] = 4$
>   Standard deviation = $\sqrt{4}$ = 2 in   ❏

Note: Had we carried units along in our calculation of variance, we would have ended up with a variance of 4 *square* inches—another good reason for preferring standard deviation.

EXAMPLE 2   Find the standard deviation for {13, 9, 7, 11, 10}.

Solution
>   Mean of 13, 9, 7, 11, 10 is 10.
>   Variance = $\frac{1}{5}[(13 - 10)^2 + (9 - 10)^2 + (7 - 10)^2 + (11 - 10)^2$
> $+ (10 - 10)^2]$
> $= \frac{1}{5}[9 + 1 + 9 + 1 + 0] = 4$
>   Standard deviation = $\sqrt{4}$ = 2   ❏

Some general conclusions can be drawn by comparing Examples 1 and 2. In Example 1 we simplified the calculation of the mean by subtracting the same number, 60, from each of the heights (73, 69, 67, 71, 70). After finding the mean (10) of the reduced numbers (13, 9, 7, 11, 10), we then added the 60 back in to get the mean (70) of the original set of numbers. Thinking geometrically: we took five points on the number line (73, 69, 67, 71, 70), translated (slid) them left 60 units, calculated the mean of the new set of points (13, 9, 7, 11, 10), and finally translated that mean (slid right) 60 units. In general notation:

> The mean of $x_1 + k, x_2 + k, \ldots, x_n + k$ is k plus the mean of $x_1, x_2, \ldots, x_n$.

From Example 2 it is evident that we could also have found the standard deviation of the original numbers (73, 69, 67, 71, 70) by calculating (more easily) the standard deviation of the reduced numbers (13, 9, 7, 11, 10). In fact, we could just as well have subtracted 70 from each original number and then calculated the standard deviation of the even further reduced numbers 3, ⁻1, ⁻3, 1, 0—a task that could be performed mentally. We generalize our observation by saying that standard deviation is *translation invariant*; that is,

> The standard deviation of $x_1 + k, x_2 + k, \ldots, x_n + k$ is the same as the standard deviation of $x_1, x_2, \ldots, x_n$.

EXERCISE SET 10.3

1. For each set of data, find the mean, the variance, and the standard deviation.
   (a) 5, 5, 7, 7
   (b) 1, 2, 3, 4, 5
   (c) 3, 3, 3, 3, 3
   (d) 4.0, 5.2, 7.6, 8.4, 10.8

2. For each set of data, find the mean and the standard deviation. Verbalize any observations you make.
   (a) 0, 2, 3, 4, 6
   (b) $k, k + 2, k + 3, k + 4, k + 6$
   (c) $0, 2k, 3k, 4k, 6k$

3. Use the formal definition of mean to prove that the mean of $x_1 + k, x_2 + k, \ldots, x_n + k$ is just k plus the mean of $x_1, x_2, \ldots, x_n$.

★ 4. Use the result of Exercise 3 and the formal definitions of variance and standard deviation to prove that the standard deviation of $x_1 + k$, $x_2 + k, \ldots, x_n + k$ is the same as the standard deviation of $x_1, x_2, \ldots, x_n$.

5. Find the mean and standard deviation for these weights (in pounds) of football players: 247, 260, 255, 230, 273.

6. Use the formal definition of mean to prove that the mean of $kx_1, kx_2, \ldots, kx_n$ is just k times the mean of $x_1, x_2, \ldots, x_n$.

★ 7. Use the result of Exercise 6 and the formal definitions of variance and standard deviation to prove that the standard deviation of $kx_1, kx_2, \ldots, kx_n$ is $|k|$ times the standard deviation of $x_1, x_2, \ldots, x_n$.

8. Find the mean and the standard deviation for these data: 0, 0.002, 0.003, 0.004, 0.006. *Hint:* Use the results of Exercises 6, 7, and 2(a).

9. Table 10.14 gives the birth rates per thousand in eight selected states in 1976. Compute the mean and the standard deviation.

Table 10.14

California	15.4	Pennsylvania	12.5
Connecticut	11.4	New York	13.0
Iowa	14.5	Texas	17.5
Mississippi	18.2	Utah	28.7

10. Table 10.15 gives the per capita personal incomes (in thousands of dollars) in eight Midwestern states in 1983. Compute the mean and the standard deviation.

Table 10.15

Illinois	12.4	Minnesota	11.9
Indiana	10.5	Missouri	11.0
Iowa	10.7	Ohio	11.2
Michigan	11.5	Wisconsin	11.4

★ 11. Suppose $\bar{x}$ is the mean of the numbers $x_1, x_2, \ldots, x_n$ and $\bar{y}$ is the mean of the numbers $y_1, y_2, \ldots, y_r$. Find a formula, in terms of $\bar{x}$ and $\bar{y}$, for the mean z of the combined set of numbers $x_1, x_2, \ldots, x_n, y_1, y_2, \ldots, y_r$.

12. Ten students took a quiz: one got 0, one got 100, and eight got 50s. The next day they took another and five got 20s and five got 80s. Calculate and compare the means, ranges, and standard deviations on the two quizzes.

13. What can you say about a class's performance on a test if the distribution of scores has the following?

(a) A standard deviation of zero
(b) A large range but a small standard deviation
(c) A small range but a large standard deviation

Computer Vignette H

The desire to simplify statistical calculations was a motivating force in the invention and development of computers (see Chapter 16). Not surprisingly, one of the most impressive areas of application of today's computing technology is statistics. If you found the means, variances, and standard deviations called for in the previous section with pencil and paper or with a calculator, then you should appreciate the program of Figure 10.31, which directs a computer to find them for you. All you need to do is type in the data, remembering to press the RETURN button after each datum. The only lines of the program that contain unfamiliar mathematics are lines 160 and 170, which make use of the fact that the variance of a collection of data is the mean of the squares minus the square of the mean. (Proving this fact from the formal definition of variance is an interesting algebraic exercise.)

Figure 10.32 shows two runs, one for the data of Exercise 1(b), Section 10.3, and one for the data of Exercise 9, Section 10.3.

Figure 10.31

```
10    PRINT "THIS PROGRAM FINDS THE MEAN,"
20    PRINT "VARIANCE, AND THE STANDARD"
30    PRINT "DEVIATION FOR ANY SET OF"
40    PRINT "DATA. INPUT A DATUM EACH"
50    PRINT "TIME THE MACHINE ASKS FOR"
60    PRINT "ONE UNTIL YOU HAVE NO MORE."
70    PRINT "THEN TYPE IN THE NUMBER"
80    PRINT "111111 TO INDICATE THE"
90    PRINT "END OF THE DATA."
100   PRINT "DATA?"
110   INPUT X
120   IF X = 111111 THEN 200
130   LET N = N + 1
140   LET S = S + X
150   LET M = S / N
160   LET Q = Q + X ∧ 2
170   LET V = Q / N - M ∧ 2
180   LET D = SQR (V)
190   GOTO 100
200   PRINT "MEAN = ";M
210   PRINT "VARIANCE = "; V
220   PRINT "STANDARD DEVIATION = ";D
230   END
```

Figure 10.32

```
]RUN
THIS PROGRAM FINDS THE MEAN,
VARIANCE, AND THE STANDARD
DEVIATION FOR ANY SET OF
DATA. INPUT A DATUM EACH
TIME THE MACHINE ASKS FOR
ONE UNTIL YOU HAVE NO MORE.
THEN TYPE IN THE NUMBER
111111 TO INDICATE THE
END OF THE DATA.
DATA?
?1
DATA?
?2
DATA?
?3
DATA?
?4
DATA?
?5
DATA?
?111111
MEAN = 3
VARIANCE = 2
STANDARD DEVIATION = 1.41421356

]RUN
THIS PROGRAM FINDS THE MEAN,
VARIANCE, AND THE STANDARD
DEVIATION FOR ANY SET OF
DATA. INPUT A DATUM EACH
TIME THE MACHINE ASKS FOR
ONE UNTIL YOU HAVE NO MORE.
THEN TYPE IN THE NUMBER
111111 TO INDICATE THE
END OF THE DATA.
DATA?
?15.4
DATA?
?11.4
DATA?
?14.5
DATA?
?18.2
DATA?
```

```
?12.5
DATA?
?13.0
DATA?
?17.5
DATA?
?28.7
DATA?
?111111
MEAN = 16.4
VARIANCE = 26.515
STANDARD DEVIATION = 5.1492718
```

10.4 *Normally Distributed Data*

Let us return to quizzes and scores. Suppose you administered a 10-question, true-false quiz to 1000 kindergartners on the subject of thermodynamics. What do you think would be the mean score? The median? The mode? (Do you agree that this experiment is essentially the same as 1000 repetitions of the experiment of flipping a coin 10 times in a row and counting the heads?) The mean would be very close to 5 but probably not exactly 5. The median and mode would very likely both equal 5. A histogram giving the relative frequency of the scores would have the shape of the one in Figure 10.33. (What is the probability of guessing correctly on all 10 true-false questions—or, equivalently, of flipping 10 heads in a row?)

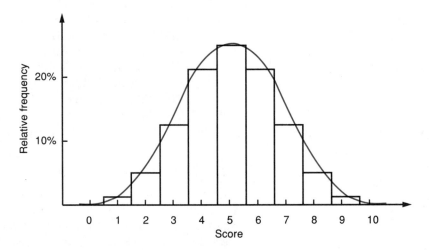

Figure 10.33 Scores on kindergarten thermodynamics quiz.

Normal Curves

In Figure 10.33 we have approximated the histogram with a smooth *bell-shaped* curve. Such curves arise in a variety of contexts and are fundamental in the theory of statistics. An ideal bell-shaped curve is called a **normal curve** and has the properties that mean, median, and mode have a common value, call it $\bar{x}$ (see Figure 10.34); that the curve is symmetric about the vertical line through $\bar{x}$; and that the standard deviation, call it s, has the following properties:

About 50% of the data lies within $\frac{2}{3}s$ of $\bar{x}$.
About 68% of the data lies within s of $\bar{x}$.
About 95% of the data lies within $2s$ of $\bar{x}$.
Nearly 100% of the data lies within $3s$ of $\bar{x}$.

In geometrical terms, half of the area under the normal curve is contained in the vertical strip of width $\frac{4}{3}s$ centered about the mean $\bar{x}$. Data whose dot frequency graph (or histogram or frequency polygon) has the shape of a normal curve are called **normally distributed data.**

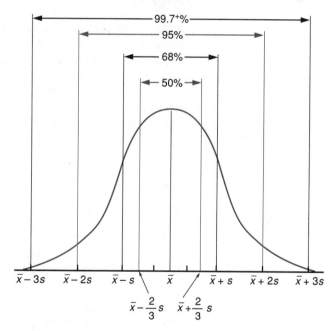

Figure 10.34 Normal curve.

EXAMPLE 1   The life of a light bulb is defined to be the number of hours it stays lit before burning out. Suppose that the distribution of lives for a batch of light bulbs is normal with $\bar{x} = 500$ (hours) and $s = 50$ (hours). What is the probability that the bulb you buy will give less than 400 hr of service?

Solution   Label the (horizontal) axis in Figure 10.34 "Light Bulb Life in Hours" and set $\bar{x} = 500$ and $s = 50$. Then about 95% of all bulbs have lives between 400 and 600. The remaining 5% of the bulbs are evenly divided between those with lives greater than 600 hr and those with lives less than 400 hr. Thus about $2\frac{1}{2}\%$ of the bulbs will give less than 400 hr of service. In other words, the probability of getting a bulb that gives less than 400 hr of service is about .025. ❏

EXAMPLE 2   Suppose that the distribution of weights of children entering kindergarten is normal with $\bar{x} = 50$ (pounds) and $s = 5$ (pounds). What is the probability that all 15 children in your kindergarten class will weigh between 45 and 55 lb?

Solution   Attach the label "Weight in pounds" to the axis in Figure 10.34 and set $\bar{x} = 50$ and $s = 5$. Then about 68% of all entering kindergartners weigh between 45 and 55 lb; that is, the probability that a child chosen at random weighs between 45 and 55 lb is about .68. The probability that 15 children in a row have weights in that range is $(.68)^{15}$, which, by calculator, is about .003. ❏

z-scores

In order to compare performances on two different tests (having normally distributed "raw scores"), it is necessary to adjust the raw scores so that both sets of adjusted test scores have the same mean and the same standard deviation. The convention is to make the common mean 0 and the common standard deviation 1. A normally distributed set of scores with mean 0 and standard deviation 1 is called a set of *z-scores*.

We illustrate the process of producing z-scores using the (not quite normal) set of raw scores

$$74, 76, 77, 78, 80$$

which has mean

$$\bar{x} = \tfrac{1}{5}(74 + 76 + 77 + 78 + 80) = 77$$

and standard deviation

$$s = \sqrt{\tfrac{1}{5}[(74 - 77)^2 + (76 - 77)^2 + (77 - 77)^2 + (78 - 77)^2 + (80 - 77)^2]}$$
$$= 2$$

The first adjustment is to subtract the mean, $\bar{x} = 77$, from each raw score to produce a new set of scores with mean 0:

$$^-3, \ ^-1, 0, 1, 3$$

The second adjustment is to divide each of these new scores by the standard deviation, $s = 2$:

$$^-1.5, \ ^-0.5, 0, 0.5, 1.5$$

These final scores are the z-scores. Notice that the set of z-scores has mean 0 and standard deviation 1:

$$s = \sqrt{\tfrac{1}{5}[(^-1.5)^2 + (^-0.5)^2 + (0.5)^2 + (1.5)^2]} = \sqrt{1} = 1$$

We can summarize the process of producing z-scores with a single equation:

Given a normally distributed set of raw scores with mean $\bar{x}$ and standard deviation s, the **z-score** corresponding to the raw score x is given by

$$z = \frac{x - \bar{x}}{s}$$

The set of z-scores has mean 0 and standard deviation 1.

EXAMPLE 3

On her first math test Tracy got a 76; the mean was 70 and the standard deviation was 3. On the second math test the mean was 76, the standard deviation was 8, and Tracy got an 84. Relative to her classmates, did Tracy's performance improve or decline from the first to the second test?

Solution

On the first test Tracy's z-score was

$$z = \frac{x - \bar{x}}{s} = \frac{76 - 70}{3} = 2$$

On the second test Tracy's z-score was lower:

$$z = \frac{x - \bar{x}}{s} = \frac{84 - 76}{8} = 1$$

Because Tracy's z-score declined, her performance relative to her classmates' declined. Let's see why.

When we solve the equation

$$z = \frac{x - \bar{x}}{s}$$

for x we get

$$x = \bar{x} + z \cdot s$$

Thus, on the first test Tracy's raw score was

$$x = \bar{x} + 2s \qquad (z = 2)$$

That is, she was 2 standard deviations above the mean. Referring to Figure 10.34, p. 539, we see that this puts her above 97.5% of the class:

$$97.5\% = 95\% + \tfrac{1}{2}(100\% - 95\%)$$

On the second test Tracy's raw score was

$$x = \bar{x} + 1s \qquad (z = 1)$$

That is, she was 1 standard deviation above the mean, which put her above only 84% of the class:

$$84\% = 68\% + \tfrac{1}{2}(100\% - 68\%) \qquad ❏$$

EXAMPLE 4   On a test with mean 76 and standard deviation 8, Jason's z-score was $^-0.75$. What was his raw score?

Solution   Solving the basic equation

$$z = \frac{x - \bar{x}}{s}$$

for x yields

$$x = \bar{x} + z \cdot s = 76 + (^-0.75) \times 8 = 76 - 6 = 70 \qquad ❏$$

Examples 3 and 4 illustrate this important point:

> The z-score tells how many standard deviations the corresponding raw score is above (if z positive) or below (if z negative) the mean of the raw scores.

In many cases z-scores can be computed mentally by thinking of them as counting standard deviations.

EXAMPLE 5   The scores on an examination are normally distributed with mean 81 and standard deviation 6.
(a) What z-score corresponds to a raw score of 90?
(b) What raw score corresponds to a z-score of $^-2.5$?

Solution   (a) Since 90 is $1\tfrac{1}{2}$ standard deviations above the mean, the corresponding z-score is 1.5.
(b) Since the raw score is $2\tfrac{1}{2}$ standard deviations below the mean, it must be $81 - 15 = 66$. ❏

The next example gives a geometric interpretation of the connection between z-scores, raw scores, and the standard deviation.

EXAMPLE 6   The scores on a test are distributed normally with mean 73 and standard deviation 6. Sketch a normal curve showing the correspondence between raw scores and z-scores. Now estimate the percent of scores that fall below a z-score of 1.5.

Solution   See Figure 10.35. We have already seen that about 84% of the scores fall below $z = 1$ and about 97.5% fall below $z = 2$. So a reasonable estimate of the
percent of scores below $z = 1.5$ might be about 91%. In fact, as Table 10.16
shows, a better estimate is about 93%.

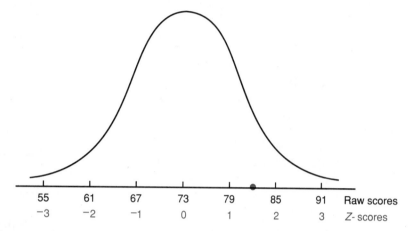

55	61	67	73	79	85	91	Raw scores
⁻3	⁻2	⁻1	0	1	2	3	Z- scores

Figure 10.35

Table 10.16 The Percent P of Scores That
Fall Below a Given z-score

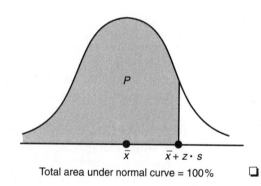

z	P	z	P
0.0	50.0%	1.6	94.5%
0.2	57.9%	1.8	96.4%
0.4	65.5%	2.0	97.7%
0.6	72.6%	2.2	98.6%
0.8	78.8%	2.4	99.2%
1.0	84.1%	2.6	99.5%
1.2	88.5%	2.8	99.7%
1.4	91.9%	3.0	99.9%

Total area under normal curve = 100%

EXAMPLE 7   Use Table 10.16 to determine the percent of scores that fall below each of
these z-scores.
   (a) $z = 1$ (b) $z = 1.8$
   (c) $z = 0$ (d) $z = {}^{-}1.2$

Solution   (a) 84.1%
   (b) 96.4%
   (c) 50%
   (d) By symmetry of the normal curve in the vertical line through $\bar{x}$, the percent of scores below $z = {}^{-}1.2$ is the same as the percent of scores above
$z = 1.2$, which, by Table 10.16, is $100\% - 88.5\%$ or 11.5%.

EXERCISE SET 10.4

1. An exam is given to 1000 students, and the distribution of scores has the shape of a normal curve with mean 62 and standard deviation 12.
   (a) About how many students have scores between 50 and 74?
   (b) About how many students have scores between 38 and 86?
   (c) About how many students have scores between 26 and 98?
   (d) What are the upper and lower quartiles?
   (e) What is the probability that a randomly selected student has a score between 54 and 74?
   (f) What is the probability that a randomly selected student has a score below 50?

2. The distribution of scores on a test administered to every student in the district is normal with $\bar{x} = 170$ and $s = 30$.
   (a) If a student is chosen at random, what is the probability that his score exceeds 200?
   (b) What is the probability that four randomly chosen students will all have scores between 150 and 190?
   (c) What is the probability that three randomly chosen students will all have scores over 150?

3. An exam is given to a large number of students, and the distribution of scores has the shape of a normal curve with mean 70. Suppose that about 16% of the students scored above 79.
   (a) About what percent of the students scored between 70 and 79?
   (b) What (approximately) is the standard deviation?
   (c) If one-quarter of all those who took the test failed, what was the lowest passing grade?

4. A box-and-whisker plot is made of data that are normally distributed with standard deviation s. How long is the box?

5. A normal curve, like the one in Figure 10.34, has "inflection points" above $\bar{x} - s$ and $\bar{x} + s$. That is, if you drive along the curve from left to right,

you will be turning left until you are above $\bar{x} - s$. Then you will begin turning right and continue doing so until you are above $\bar{x} + s$, where you will again begin to turn left. Use this geometric fact to estimate the standard deviation for each of these normal curves.

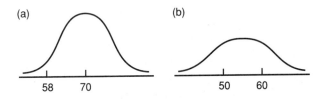

6. A math specialist gives the same mathematics assessment examination to all sixth graders in the school district, first in September and again in June. The distributions of scores for September and June are normal and are plotted in Figure 10.36.
   (a) Which curve is probably the September curve and which the June curve? (Don't be cynical.)
   (b) Estimate the September mean and standard deviation.
   (c) Estimate the June mean and standard deviation.

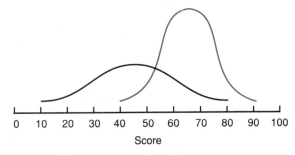

Figure 10.36

7. A professor gave a 50-point quiz to her large class. The distribution of scores was approximately normal, with mean 30 and standard devia-

tion 5. By mental computation find the z-scores corresponding to these raw scores.

(a) 37   (b) 20   (c) 30
(d) 49   (e) 27   (f) 0

8. For the quiz of Exercise 7, find the raw scores corresponding to these z-scores. Again compute mentally.

(a) 2   (b) $^-$1.8
(c) 2.2   (d) 0

9. For each score in Exercise 7, find the percent of scores in the class that were lower than it. Use Table 10.16.

10. If the mean of a set of scores is 63 and a raw score of 53 corresponds to a z-score of $^-$1.25, what is the standard deviation?

11. If the standard deviation of a set of scores is 12 and a raw score of 114 corresponds to a z-score of 0.75, what is the mean?

12. On her math test (mean 76, standard deviation 7) Jodie got 73. On her science test (mean 150, standard deviation 15) she got 140. Did Jodie do better in math or in science?

13. Pam has kept meticulous records of her performance in math (Table 10.17). Calculate her z-scores and make a broken-line graph of them. Is a trend evident?

14. Use Table 10.16 to decide what percent of the z-scores on a test fall between these values:
(a) $z = 1$ and $z = 2$

(b) $z = 0$ and $z = 1.6$
(c) $z = ^-0.8$ and $z = 2.2$
(d) $z = ^-2.4$ and $z = ^-1.4$

15. Use Table 10.16 and estimate the z-score that exceeds
(a) 58% of all other z-scores
(b) 82% of all other z-scores
(c) 8% of all other z-scores
(d) 14% of all other z-scores

16. Suppose that the heights (in centimeters) of the women at Siena College are normally distributed with mean 168 and standard deviation 9.
(a) What height separates the tallest 10% of these women from the other 90%? (This height is called the *90th percentile*.) *Hint:* If Table 10.16 were more detailed, it would show that $P = 90\%$ when $z = 1.282$.
(b) What is the 10th percentile for heights? That is, what height separates the shortest 10% from the rest?

Table 10.17

Test number	1	2	3	4	5	6
Mean	64	70	52	64	60	70
Standard deviation	9	7	5	8	6	10
My score	67	75	56	70	64	77

10.5 *Sampling (Optional)*

"Sampling" is one of the four major components of the Quantitative Literacy Project, a joint curriculum development effort of the American Statistical Association and the National Council of Teachers of Mathematics. It has also been described in the 5–8 *Standards* as "a critical issue in data collection." In this section we investigate some of the basic ideas associated with sampling.

Sampling is concerned with questions of the following sort: Suppose you drew a "random sample" of four marbles from a very large urn and found that two were red and two were black. How "confident" would you be about predicting that the urn contained "about" half red and half black marbles? Would you be astonished to learn that, in fact, three-fourths of the marbles in the urn were red and one-fourth black? Suppose next that you drew a random sample of 4000 marbles from the urn and found that 2000 were red and 2000 black. Would you feel more confident in predicting that about half the marbles in the urn were red and half black? Would you believe it if someone told you that, actually, three-fourths of the marbles in the urn were red?

To develop the theory of sampling we will look at an example in detail.

Sampling Distributions

Suppose we want to determine what fraction of the voters in this country favor capital punishment. It would take too long and be too expensive to poll every registered voter, so we decide instead to survey just some of the voters and then infer from their responses the mood of all of the voters. The (large) group whose opinion we want to ascertain, namely the set of all registered voters, is called the "target population" or simply the **population.** The subset whose members we will actually poll is called the **sample.**

We will first illustrate why a large sample is a better predictor than a small sample. For the sake of argument let us suppose that, in fact, 60% of the population favors capital punishment. And suppose that we randomly select a sample of just two people. This is equivalent to drawing two marbles from a very large urn containing 60% red marbles (favor capital punishment) and 40% black (oppose). The possible outcomes of the draw are the four ordered pairs: BB, BR, RB, RR. The events and their (approximate) probabilities are given in Table 10.18.

Table 10.18

Event	Probability
0% red = {BB}	$.4 \times .4 = .16$
50% red = {BR, RB}	$.4 \times .6 + .6 \times .4 = .48$
100% red = {RR}	$.6 \times .6 = .36$

We can interpret the probabilities in Table 10.18 this way: if a large number of 2-person random samples were surveyed, about 16% of those samples would be unanimously opposed to capital punishment (both black), another 36% would be unanimously in favor of capital punishment (both red), and 48% would be split on the question (one red, one black). Thus not quite half of the 2-person samples (.48) would give a reasonable indication of the sentiment of the population (a 60–40 split in favor of capital punishment).

Figure 10.37 presents the data from Table 10.18 graphically in the style of a histogram. Such a graph is called a "sampling distribution." The 48% of samples that serve as reasonable predictors are represented by the red portion of the histogram in Figure 10.37.

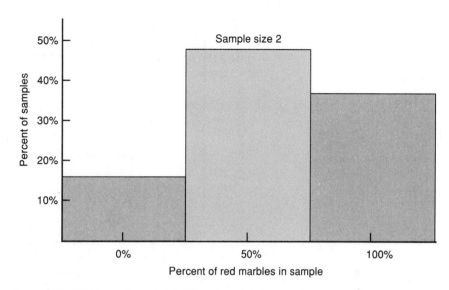

Figure 10.37 Sampling distribution for sample size 2.

If the sample size were four rather than two, the outcomes would be ordered 4-tuples of B's and R's, the events and probabilities would be as in Table 10.19, and the sampling distribution would be as in Figure 10.38. Notice that about two-thirds (2 × .3456) of the samples of size 4 (the red portion of the histogram in Figure 10.38) give a ballpark estimate of the percent of red marbles in the urn.

Table 10.19

Event	Probability
0% red = {BBBB}	$(.4)^4 = .0256$
25% red = {RBBB, BRBB, BBRB, BBBR}	$4(.4)^3(.6) = .1536$
50% red = {RRBB, RBRB, RBBR, BRRB, BRBR, BBRR}	$6(.4)^2(.6)^2 = .3456$
75% red = {RRRB, RRBR, RBRR, BRRR}	$4(.4)(.6)^3 = .3456$
100% red = {RRRR}	$(.6)^4 = .1296$

If we now jump to a sample size of 20, computation of probabilities becomes a major chore (Table 10.20), but the sampling distribution (Figure 10.39) begins to assume a familiar shape. It is beginning to look a lot like a normal curve centered at 60%. Moreover, about three-fourths (12% + 16% + 18% + 17% + 12%) of all samples of size 20 (the red portion of the histogram in Figure 10.39) now show a percent of red marbles between 50% and

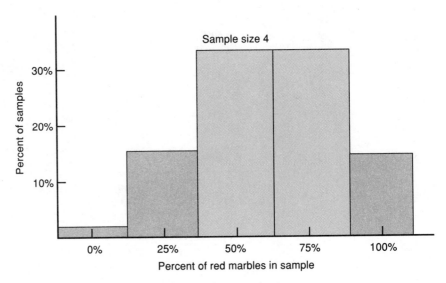

Figure 10.38 Sampling distribution for sample size 4.

70%; that is, three-fourths of the samples of size 20 are reasonable estimators of the actual percent of the population (60%) that favors capital punishment.

The predictive ability of samples continues to improve as sample size increases. In fact, we shall soon see that about 95% of all samples of size 100 will show a percent of red marbles between 50% and 70%.

Table 10.20

Event	Probability (to Nearest Whole Percent)
0%–30% red	0%
35% red	2%
40% red	4%
45% red	7%
50% red	12%
55% red	16%
60% red	18%
65% red	17%
70% red	12%
75% red	7%
80% red	3%
85% red	1%
90%–100% red	0%

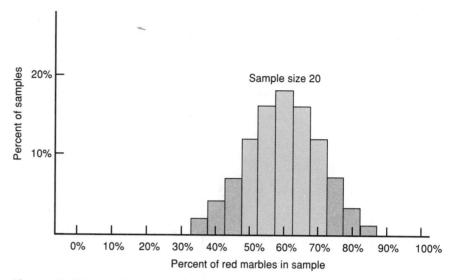

Figure 10.39 Sampling distribution for sample size 20.

The Central Limit Theorem

A fundamental theorem of probability, the central limit theorem, generalizes and quantifies the observations we have been making. To understand what it says, we need some further terminology and notation.

Our goal has been to estimate the fraction F of the population that favors capital punishment. A number like F that refers to the population is called a **parameter.** Our method has been to choose a random sample of size n and determine the fraction $\hat{F}$ of the sample that favors capital punishment. A number like $\hat{F}$ that is extracted from a sample is called a **statistic.** We have imagined repeating, over and over again, the process of choosing a sample of size n, finding its fraction $\hat{F}$, and then making a histogram of these values for $\hat{F}$ which we called the **sampling distribution** of $\hat{F}$ for samples of size n.

The **central limit theorem** tells us the following.

When the sample size n is large, the sampling distribution of $\hat{F}$ is approximately a normal curve with mean F and standard deviation

$$\sqrt{\frac{F(1-F)}{n}}.$$

When we combine this new information with what we already know about normal curves (the 68–95–99.7 facts), we can draw some specific quantitative conclusions about sampling. For example, in our capital punishment survey with sample size $n = 100$, the sampling distribution looks like the normal curve in Figure 10.40 with mean 60% and standard deviation

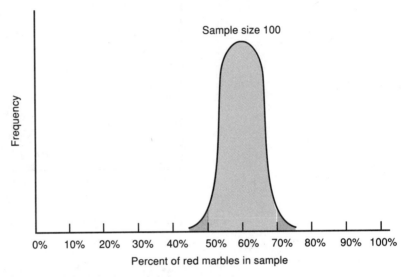

Figure 10.40 Sampling distribution for sample size 100.

$$\sqrt{\frac{.6 \times .4}{100}} \doteq .05 = 5\%$$

That is, of all the random samples of size 100, approximately

68% will have fraction of red marbles between 55% and 65%
95% will have fraction of red marbles between 50% and 70%
99.7% will have fraction of red marbles between 45% and 75%

The red portion of the region in Figure 10.40 represents the 95% of all samples for which the fraction of red marbles is between 50% and 70%.

Inference from a Sample

So far we have been deducing information about samples from known information about the population. The payoff from our efforts, however, comes from reversing the process—drawing conclusions about the population on the basis of observations of a sample. That is, we now try to deduce approximately what fraction F of the population favors capital punishment from the results of polling one specific sample.

Let's say that in our sample of 100 people, 56 favored capital punishment. Thus our value of $\hat{F}$ is .56. If our sample is one of the 95% of all samples whose $\hat{F}$ lies within 2 standard deviations of F, then, of course, F lies within 2 standard deviations of $\hat{F}$. That is (assuming our sample is among the 95%)

$$\hat{F} - (2 \text{ standard deviations}) \leq F \leq \hat{F} + (2 \text{ standard deviations})$$

We want to assign numerical values to those lower and upper bounds on F. We know $\hat{F} = 56\%$; all that is left to do is to calculate the value of the standard deviation. But here we encounter a problem. The central limit theorem tells us that the standard deviation is given by

$$\sqrt{\frac{F(1 - F)}{100}}$$

an expression whose value depends on the very fraction F that we are trying to find! The way around the difficulty is to simply use $\hat{F}$ as an approximation to the unknown F in this formula. The substitution is justified because the values of

$$\sqrt{\frac{\hat{F}(1 - \hat{F})}{100}} \qquad \text{and} \qquad \sqrt{\frac{F(1 - F)}{100}}$$

are very close together. In our example

$$\sqrt{\frac{\hat{F}(1 - \hat{F})}{100}} = \sqrt{\frac{.56 \times .44}{100}} \doteq 0496$$

and

$$\sqrt{\frac{F(1 - F)}{100}} = \sqrt{\frac{.60 \times .40}{100}} \doteq .0490$$

a difference of only about six ten-thousandths! Thus our inequality bracketing F is

$$56\% - 2 \times 5\% \leq F \leq 56\% + 2 \times 5\%$$

that is

$$46\% \leq F \leq 66\%$$

We can summarize the conclusion about the population that we deduced from our sample in several different ways. Here are three common ones:

1. "We are 95% confident that the percent of voters favoring capital punishment is between 46% and 66%."

2. "At the 95% *confidence level,* the percent of voters favoring capital punishment is 56%, with a *margin of error* of ±10%."

3. "The 95% *confidence interval* for the percent of voters favoring capital punishment is 56% ± 10%."

All mean the same thing, namely: assuming that our sample is one of the 95% whose fractions lie closest to the population fraction, that population fraction lies between 46% and 66%. From a negative perspective, 5% of the time when we select a sample of size 100 and calculate an interval we will be dead wrong: the population fraction will not lie in our interval. But 95% of the time it will, as 60% fell in the interval from 46% to 66%.

Before going on to further examples we summarize the discussion up to this point as follows:

Steps in Making an Inference from a Sample

1. Choose a random sample of size n from the population.
2. Find the fraction $\hat{F}$ of the sample that answers "yes" to your survey question.
3. Compute the value of $\sqrt{\dfrac{\hat{F}(1 - \hat{F})}{n}}$ (This "standard error" is a good approximation to the standard deviation of the sampling distribution of $\hat{F}$.)
4. Conclude that the fraction F of the population that would answer "yes" to your survey question lies between

   (a) $\hat{F} - 2\sqrt{\dfrac{\hat{F}(1 - \hat{F})}{n}}$ and $\hat{F} + 2\sqrt{\dfrac{\hat{F}(1 - \hat{F})}{n}}$ at the 95% confidence level

   (b) $\hat{F} - 3\sqrt{\dfrac{\hat{F}(1 - \hat{F})}{n}}$ and $\hat{F} + 3\sqrt{\dfrac{\hat{F}(1 - \hat{F})}{n}}$ at the 99.7% confidence level

---

EXAMPLE 1   A random sample of 1000 college students voted 740 to 260 in favor of proctored examinations. What can you infer about the sentiments of all college students on that issue?

Solution   Here $n = 1000$ and $\hat{F} = .74 = 74\%$. Because

$$\sqrt{\frac{.74 \times .26}{1000}} \doteq .014 = 1.4\%$$

we can infer, with 95% confidence, that between

$$74\% - 2(1.4)\% = 71.2\% \quad \text{and} \quad 74\% + 2(1.4\%) = 76.8\%$$

of all college students favor proctored examinations. The 99.7% confidence interval ranges from

$$74\% - 3(1.4\%) = 69.8\% \quad \text{to} \quad 74\% + 3(1.4\%) = 78.2\%. \quad ❑$$

The previous example illustrates a general principle—for a fixed sample size, higher levels of confidence go with wider confidence intervals (cruder estimates of the population parameter). The next example illustrates a second general principle: for a fixed confidence level, larger samples lead to narrower confidence intervals (sharper estimates of the population parameter).

EXAMPLE 2   Two different survey organizations study the public's opinion toward compulsory retirement at age 70. Organization A surveys 500 people and finds that 395 of them are in favor. Organization B surveys 2000 people and finds that 1560 are in favor. Find 95% confidence intervals for each survey.

Solution   For organization A, $\hat{F} = \frac{395}{500} = .79$ and

$$\sqrt{\frac{\hat{F}(1 - \hat{F})}{n}} = \sqrt{\frac{.79 \times .21}{500}} \doteq .018 = 1.8\%$$

Thus their 95% confidence interval is 79% ± 3.6%; that is, between 75.4% and 82.6%. For organization B, $\hat{F} = 1560/2000 = .78$ and

$$\sqrt{\frac{\hat{F}(1 - \hat{F})}{n}} = \sqrt{\frac{.78 \times .22}{2000}} \doteq .009\% = .9\%$$

So their 95% confidence interval is 78% ± 1.8%; that is, between 76.2% and 79.8%.   ❏

In Example 2, multiplying the sample size by 4 (from 500 to 2000) divided the standard deviation by 2 (from .018 to .009). In general, in order to divide the standard deviation by r, the sample size needs to be multiplied by r^2.

EXAMPLE 3   The Gallup organization uses a sample size of about 1500.
(a) What is their 95% confidence interval for a survey on which they received a 35% "yes" response?
(b) How many people would they have to survey in order to get the margin of error down to 1%, still at the 95% confidence level?

Solution   (a) Since $\hat{F} = .35$, the standard deviation is

$$\sqrt{\frac{.35 \times .65}{1500}} \doteq 1.2\%$$

and the 95% confidence interval is 35% ± 2.4%.
(b) To get the 95% confidence interval down to 35% ± 1%, the researchers would need to choose n so that

$$\sqrt{\frac{.35 \times .65}{n}} = .5\% = .005$$

Squaring both sides and isolating n yields

$$n = \frac{.35 \times .65}{(.005)^2} = 9100$$

They would have to survey 9100 people.   ❏

EXERCISE SET 10.5

1. Random samples of size 400 are drawn from a very large adult population, 55% of whom are women. For each sample, the fraction $\hat{F}$ of women is calculated.
   (a) Find the mean and the standard deviation of the normal curve that approximates the sampling distribution of $\hat{F}$.
   (b) What percent of the samples will have their $\hat{F}$ between 50% and 60%?
   (c) About 99.7% of the samples will have their $\hat{F}$ between _____ and _____ .

2. Repeat Exercise 1 for samples of size 100.

3. *Class project:* Suppose that 60% of the population favors capital punishment. Each of 20 students simulates the experiment of polling a sample of size 50 by using a row of the table of random digits (p. 483), where digits 0–5 represent votes in favor of capital punishment and digits 6–9 represent votes opposed. Each student also calculates the value of $\hat{F}$ for her/his row. Now compile these statistics in the first two columns of Table 10.21. Sketch a histogram for the resulting grouped frequency distribution. Theoretically, the distribution of values of $\hat{F}$ should be close to normal, with mean 0.60 and standard deviation

$$\sqrt{\frac{.6 \times .4}{50}} \doteq 7\%$$

Fill in the third column of Table 10.21 and compare columns two and three.

4. Suppose that the Internal Revenue Service randomly selects 600 tax returns and finds that 240 of them contain errors. At the 95% confidence level, what percent of all tax returns contain errors?

5. When random sample of 2400 baseball fans is surveyed, 60% of them say they favor the designated-hitter rule. Find the 95% confidence interval for the percent of all baseball fans who favor the designated-hitter rule.

6. For a given population, which is wider: the 95% confidence interval deduced from a random sample of size 200 with $\hat{F} = .32$, or the 99.7% confidence interval deduced from a random sample of size 600 with $\hat{F} = .31$?

7. What is missing from each report?
   (a) "We are 95% confident that 39% of all television sets in America were tuned in to the telecast of Super Bowl XXIII."
   (b) On the basis of a telephone survey using randomly generated telephone numbers, a market research company reports that between 35% and 40% of all telephone owners also use answering machines.

8. At the beginning of this section you were presented with the following situation. You had just drawn 4000 marbles from an urn, 2000 of which had turned out to be red and 2000 black. Then

Table 10.21

Interval of values for $\hat{F}$	Number of values of $\hat{F}$ in interval	Percent of values of $\hat{F}$ in interval	Theoretical percent of values of $\hat{F}$ in interval
.39 to .46⁻			
.46 to .53⁻			
.53 to .60⁻			
.60 to .67⁻			
.67 to .74⁻			
.74 to .81⁻			

someone told you that, actually, the urn contained three-fourths red marbles and only one-fourth black. You were asked if you believed that. Answer the question in terms of confidence intervals.

9. Three hundred malted milk balls are removed at random from a conveyor at a candy factory. The quality control expert determines that 15 of them are defective.
   (a) Find the 95% confidence interval for the fraction of defective malted milk balls in the entire production run.
   (b) A person who buys a box of 250 of these malted milk balls should expect, with 95% confidence, to find between _____ and _____ defective balls.

10. A news report indicates that an exit poll of a random sample of voters shows, at the 95% confidence level, that candidate Baxter will capture between 51% and 59% of the vote.
   (a) What percent of the voters in the sample said that they voted for Baxter?
   (b) Is Baxter certain to win the election?
   (c) Find the 99.7% confidence interval for Baxter's percent of the vote.
   (d) About how many voters were in the sample?

★ 11. In order to estimate the number of trout in a lake, 1000 tagged trout are released; fishermen are then required to release all trout they catch and to report their data to a warden. Their reports show a total of 240 tagged and 1260 untagged trout were caught. Assuming that these 1500 trout constitute a random sample from the entire trout population, find the 95% confidence interval for the number (not the percent) of trout, both tagged and untagged, in the lake.

★ 12. The April 1989 issue of the *National Geographic* magazine (vol. 175, no. 4, p. 420) reported the following surprising statistics relating to chromosome damage in Japanese children:

1. In a sample of 8000 children born to parents affected by the Hiroshima atomic bomb, 40 showed chromosome damage.

2. In a sample of 8000 children born to parents *not* affected by an atomic bomb, 48 showed chromosome damage.

Clearly these statistics cannot be used to show that people's exposure to an atomic bomb is harmful to their future children's chromosomes. Let us see if, on the contrary, these statistics show that such exposure is actually beneficial!
   (a) Using statistic 2, find the 95% confidence interval for the fraction of the population of Japanese children, born to parents who were alive during World War II, that shows chromosome damage.
   (b) Does the percentage of children of bomb-affected parents in sample 1 fall in the 95% confidence interval from part (a)?
   (c) Interpret your answer in (b).

13. Suppose, as in the discussion in this section, that a very large urn contains 60% red and 40% black marbles. The central limit theorem asserts that for *large n*, about 68% of all random samples of size *n* will have a fraction of red marbles between

$$.60 - \sqrt{\frac{(.6)(.4)}{n}} \quad \text{and} \quad .60 + \sqrt{\frac{(.6)(.4)}{n}}$$

Even though 20 is not a very large value for *n*, still the numbers in Table 10.20 agree reasonably well with this theoretical prediction.
   (a) How well?
   (b) How closely do the numbers in Table 10.20 agree with the 95% prediction of the central limit theorem?
   (c) Repeat part (b) for the 99.7% prediction.

Key Concepts in Chapter 10

Bar graph
Broken-line graph

Circle graph
Frequency distribution

Dot frequency graph
Grouped frequency distribution
Histogram
Frequency polygon
Stem-and-leaf plot
Mean
Median
Quartiles (lower and upper)
Box-and-whisker plot
Range
Variance

Standard deviation
Normal curve
z-score
*Population
*Parameter
*Sample
*Statistic
*Sampling distribution
*Central limit theorem
*Confidence interval
*Margin of error

⮲ *Chapter 10 Review Exercises* ⮲

1. Figure 10.41 is a dot frequency graph of quiz scores.
   (a) What is the mean?
   (b) What is the mode?
   (c) What is the median?
   (d) What are the lower and upper quartiles?
   (e) What is the range?
   (f) Directly below the dot frequency graph, draw a box-and-whisker plot.

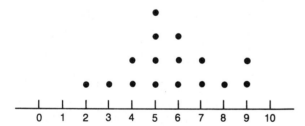

Figure 10.41

2. Add three more data to those in Exercise 1 so that the median rises, the mean falls, and the mode stays the same.

3. The heights of the members of a basketball squad are: 5 ft 10 in, 5 ft 11 in, 6 ft 3 in, 6 ft 4 in, 6 ft 6 in, 6 ft 6 in, 6 ft 10 in, 7 ft 0 in, 7 ft 1 in, 7 ft 4 in.

   (a) Make a stem-and-leaf plot with feet as stem and inches as leaves.
   (b) Find the upper quartile of the heights.

4. Eight students took a test and made these scores: 62, 68, 71, 71, 73, 78, 80, 97.
   (a) Find the mean score.
   (b) Find the median score.
   (c) A ninth student takes the test late. When his score is included in the data, the new mean and new median are equal. What was his score?

5. For the data {70, 72, 73, 74, 76}, calculate the following.
   (a) The mean
   (b) The variance
   (c) The standard deviation

6. Suppose the distribution of heights of a group of 400 children is normal with mean 150 cm and standard deviation 12 cm.
   (a) About how many of these children are taller than 162 cm?
   (b) About how many of these children are shorter than 126 cm?

7. An intelligence test is administered to a large number of people. The distribution of scores is approximately normal, with mean 100 and standard deviation 20.

(a) About what percent of scores fall between 120 and 140?

(b) About what percent of scores fall below 120?

(c) To the nearest whole number, what is the lower quartile score?

(d) If 100 is subtracted from each test score, what is the new mean and the new standard deviation?

(e) If each of the scores from part (d) is multiplied by .05, what is the new mean and new standard deviation?

8. The scores on an examination are distributed normally, with mean 140 and standard deviation 18.

(a) Jan's raw score is 167. What is her z-score?

(b) Beth's z-score is $^-1.33$. What is her raw score?

(c) To the nearest whole percent, what percent of the z-scores fall between $z = {}^-1$ and $z = 3$?

* 9. A random sample of 2500 voters splits 1600 to 900 in favor of an increase in the state sales tax. What can you say, with 95% confidence, about the percent of all voters who favor the increase?

* 10. On the basis of a random sample a statistician asserts, with 99.7% certainty, that between 46% and 64% of all college graduates took at least one psychology course.

(a) What could she assert with 68% certainty?

(b) How large was her sample?

References

Curcio, F. *Developing Graph Comprehension: Elementary and Middle School Activities*. Reston, Va.: NCTM, 1989.

Landwehr, J., J. Swift, and A. Watkins. *Exploring Surveys and Information from Samples*. Palo Alto, Calif.: Dale Seymour Publications, 1986.

Landwehr, J. and A. Watkins. *Exploring Data*. Palo Alto, Calif.: Dale Seymour Publications, 1986.

Mathematics Teacher. Minifocus Issue—"Data Analysis" vol. 83, no. 2, February 1990.

Moses, Lincoln E. *Think and Explain with Statistics*. Reading, Mass.: Addison-Wesley, 1986.

Mosteller, F., W. Kruskal, R. Link, R. Pieters, and G. Rising, eds. *Statistics by Example*. Reading, Mass.: Addison-Wesley, 1973.

National Council of Teachers of Mathematics. *Organizing Data and Dealing with Uncertainty*. Reston, Va.: NCTM, 1979.

Nuffield Mathematics Project: *Probability and Statistics*. New York: John Wiley, 1969.

11

GEOMETRIC FIGURES

Geometry is well established as a theme that runs through the entire K–12 mathematics curriculum. One need only riffle through any up-to-date textbook series to see its pervasiveness. The writers of the *Standards* reiterate the importance attached to geometry by listing it as a curriculum strand at both the K–4 and 5–8 grade levels. Although we all recognize geometry when we see it, the following loose definition of the term might still be useful.

Geometry can be thought of as the mathematical study of idealized shapes, or geometric figures. Some of the simpler shapes appear in the real world. Stars in the night sky suggest points, the full moon a circle, the horizon between sea and sky a line. In elementary school, children begin to get acquainted with these figures. They learn to recognize and name them; they begin to sketch and classify them. In the middle school years, the range of figures is widened, definitions and classifications are refined, and—with the introduction of drawing tools—sketches become more precise. Properties of geometric figures are extracted from the improved drawings.

In high school, further properties are added, and the task of arranging the body of properties into a logical structure is undertaken. Interrelationships are observed among the properties: some of them can be deduced from others. This observation suggests that the properties be separated into two categories, assumed ones (axioms) and derived ones (theorems). The axioms make up the skeleton of the structure; the theorems flesh it out.

In this book we will stop short of axiomatization. We will occupy ourselves almost exclusively with studying geometric phenomena. What little logical deduction we do will be local rather than global. For example, we will point out dependencies among the properties of angles and parallel lines—and later do the same for properties of congruent triangles—but we will not attempt to describe an axiomatic framework. For us, as for elementary and middle school students, there will be no axioms and theorems, only properties.

In this first of four chapters on geometry we survey the subject from a nonmetric point of view. That is, we do not use the familiar and powerful concepts of congruence and measurement. The next two geometry chapters, Chapter 12 and 13, will be devoted to them.

Many of the ideas in this first chapter will be familiar from precollege encounters with geometry. While we are bringing them into sharper focus and reviewing the associated terminology and notation, you will be given many opportunities to exercise your problem-solving skills. At all levels, geometry remains a rich source of problems that lend themselves to exploration and creative inquiry. The eminent contemporary French mathematician, René Thom, has gone so far as to declare that "While there are geometry problems there are no algebra problems . . . any question in algebra is either trivial or impossible to solve. By contrast, the classic problems of geometry present a wide range of challenges."

A few of the later ideas in this chapter will probably be unfamiliar. They are included not so much for their own sake as to deepen and strengthen your understanding of the more common ideas of elementary geometry.

Van Hiele Levels

A theoretical model of the stages through which children pass as they learn geometry was postulated by a Dutch couple, Pierre van Hiele and Dina van Hiele-Geldof, in the late 1950s. The five stages that they described are now known as the "van Hiele levels" and have become part of the vocabulary with which you, as a professional mathematics educator, should be acquainted.

At level 0 ("visualization") children recognize a figure by its shape as a whole, not by its parts or properties. For example, a child at this level might describe a picture frame as a rectangle because, in some vague sense, it looks like other things that have been called rectangles. At level 1 ("analysis") the child recognizes a figure by its parts. Now the picture frame is a rectangle because it has four straight sides and four square corners. At level 2 ("informal deduction") the child begins to perceive relationships both within figures (opposite sides of a rectangle are parallel and of equal length) and among classes of figures (a rectangle is a parallelogram because it has all of the properties of a parallelogram).

Level 3 ("deduction") is the level at which the traditional rigorous tenth-grade course has operated. Students come to understand the relationships among undefined terms, axioms, defined terms, and theorems. They learn about proof and the principles of logical deductive reasoning. Level 4 ("rigor") is the level of a college geometry course. Here the student engages in the study of several axiom systems, perhaps looking at different axiomatizations of Euclidean geometry, or comparing and contrasting Euclidean geometry with one or more non-Euclidean geometries.

In the language of the van Hieles, children in elementary and middle school operate at levels 0–2, and we will also largely restrict our study of geometry to those levels. Only in optional sections will we sample the atmosphere at level 3.

11.1 *Points, Lines, Planes, and Space*

We read and hear about **physical space** almost every day. Scientists at the Houston Space Center plan and calculate with great care to ensure that two manned vehicles will rendezvous at a point in space. To guarantee that a rocket and the planet Venus will arrive at the same location in space at the same time is a similar problem. These problems cannot be solved by trial and error. Scientists solve these real problems about physical space by first posing and solving corresponding theoretical problems about **abstract space.** Abstract space is an idealized model of physical space that exists only in people's minds, but it is enough like physical space so that studying it leads to useful information about our real environment.

At various times in history various people have devised different abstract models for physical space. In this book we shall study the one that was first described by Euclid. This abstract space is often called **Euclidean space,** and its study is known as **Euclidean geometry.** Euclid's abstract space is an excellent model for the portion of physical space that we see around us, and for this reason Euclidean geometry has been an important and useful school subject for over two thousand years. Euclidean space, which we shall refer to simply as *space* from now on, is a mathematical idea, and so we describe it in mathematical terms. We describe it as the set of all points.

> **Space** is the set of all points.

Of course, this definition of space is incomplete without some clarification of the notion of **point.**

A point can be thought of as an *exact location*. If you are asked to find where you are on a globe, you might begin by pointing with your finger. But your finger is too big. It probably only picks out the correct state. By using a pencil, you might be able to indicate the city. With a sharp needle you might even be able to suggest which part of the city. But there is no hope of your *making* a mark so small that it describes your exact location: state, city, street, building, room, desk. You can *think* about this location, though, and the idea of a dot so small that no smaller dot can be drawn inside it is the idea of a point (see Figure 11.1). Euclid described a point as "that which has no part."

Many things in the real world suggest the idea of point: grains of sand on a beach, specks of algae in a lake, particles of dust in the air. Entire *sets of points* are suggested by other things in the real world. A beam of light passing through a small hole in a window shade into a darkened room illuminates many dust particles. We refer to the set of points suggested as a *line segment* (see Figure 11.2). The smoke cloud from a factory chimney is made up of many tiny smoke particles. The set of points suggested, on a calm day, is

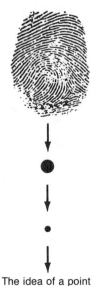

The idea of a point

Figure 11.1

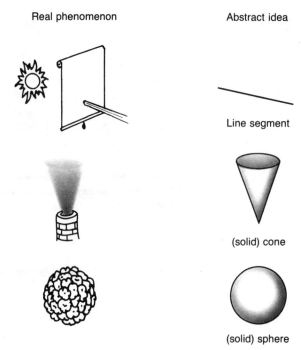

Real phenomenon   Abstract idea

Line segment

(solid) cone

(solid) sphere

Figure 11.2

called a (solid) *cone*. A popcorn ball suggests a set of points called a (solid) *sphere*.

Line segments, cones, and spheres are all examples of geometric figures. There are many other configurations of points in space that we shall want to study and refer to as geometric figures, and so we want a definition that is broad enough to include all of them. We define a geometric figure to be any set of points, or using the term *subset:*

> Any subset of space is called a **geometric figure.**

All of our work in geometry can be thought of in terms of describing, classifying, and studying geometric figures.

We have introduced the ideas of abstract space, point, and geometric figure very much as you might introduce them to a child—by relating them to physical reality. From a purely mathematical point of view, however, there is no need to relate these ideas to reality. Mathematicians are content to say: "I am thinking about a set which I will call space. Its elements I will call points. Its subsets I will call geometric figures."

Lines

After points, the next most basic geometric figures are lines. Euclid described a line as "length without breadth." We can think of a line as the geometric figure suggested by the horizon between sky and ocean, a telephone wire, or the juncture of the ceiling with one wall. None of these physical objects is a perfect model of the abstract idea of a line, however, because each is too short. We should think of lines as stretching endlessly far in both directions. We should also think of them as being straight rather than curved or having any corners. Finally, we should think of them as having no breadth. Another way of expressing this last property is as follows:

The removal of any point from a line separates the line into two "pieces."

Here is another way of stating the first two properties—that lines are long and straight.

Through any two points there is exactly one line.

Before going on, we need to say something about rigor. Without ever stating precisely what it means, we used the word *pieces* in stating the first property of points and lines, and we will use the same word several more times in this and the next section before defining it in Section 11.3. There are two reasons why we took this unrigorous approach. First, the intuitive idea of what pieces are is clear to anyone who has ever dropped a dish on the floor. Even young children have no difficulty in understanding what is meant. Second, the careful mathematical definition of a piece as a "maximal connected subset" is quite technical and depends on a prior definition of *connected*. In Section 11.3 we will define *connected* in terms of the concept of *curve*, but we will stop short of formally defining *curve* because even though this concept can be described ultimately in terms of functions and real numbers, the ideas involved are definitely not elementary ones. Absolute rigor, like the grapes of Tantalus, seems to always remain just beyond one's grasp.

To work with the abstract ideas of point and line, we need to attach symbols to them and agree on schematic drawings to represent them. Points are usually denoted by capital letters $(A, B, C, \ldots)$ and represented by dots. Lines are represented by straight strokes, with or without arrows as reminders that the line extends endlessly in both directions. Figure 11.3 shows two ways in which lines are symbolized. The first is with lowercase script letters $(\ell, m, n, \ldots)$. The second needs a little more explanation. Since there is just one line through two given points, it is reasonable to incorporate the symbols for those points

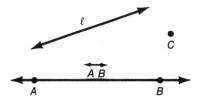

Figure 11.3 Some points and lines.

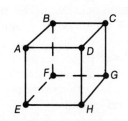

Figure 11.4 A cube.

into the symbol for the line. The accepted notation for the line through A and B is $\overleftrightarrow{AB}$ or $\overleftrightarrow{BA}$.

Certain so-called incidence relationships among points and lines are fundamental in geometry.* These relationships and the terminology that goes with them are probably familiar to you. Two points are said to **determine** a line because there is just one line through them. The "dual" statement is false: Two lines do not necessarily determine a point since there need not be a point common to them. Two lines with a point in common, such as $\overleftrightarrow{AB}$ and $\overleftrightarrow{AD}$ in Figure 11.4, are called **intersecting lines.** Two lines without a point in common, such as $\overleftrightarrow{AB}$ and $\overleftrightarrow{EH}$, are called **nonintersecting.**

These ideas are simple ones, but we need to be careful not to be misled by a (necessarily) incomplete sketch like the one in Figure 11.4. Even though it has not been emphasized in the sketch, there still is a line through points A and G. Can you see that $\overleftrightarrow{AG}$ and $\overleftrightarrow{BH}$ are intersecting lines, whereas $\overleftrightarrow{AG}$ and $\overleftrightarrow{BD}$ are not?

If three or more points lie on a line, we say they are **collinear;** otherwise, we call them **noncollinear.** Points A, B, C in Figure 11.4 are noncollinear. If three or more lines have a point in common, we say they are **concurrent;** otherwise, we call them **nonconcurrent.** In Figure 11.4 lines $\overleftrightarrow{AG}$, $\overleftrightarrow{AC}$, and $\overleftrightarrow{AE}$ are concurrent (at A), while lines $\overleftrightarrow{AB}$, $\overleftrightarrow{BC}$, and $\overleftrightarrow{CD}$ are nonconcurrent.

Planes

The third basic geometric figure is a plane. *Plane,* like *point* and *line,* is an undefined term, and we have to rely on our ideas about physical space to give it meaning. Physical objects that suggest the idea of plane are the surface of a pond on a calm day, the ceiling of a room, and a flat sheet of paper. Each of these objects is too small, however, to represent a plane accurately. We should think of a plane as stretching endlessly far in all directions, being flat, and having no thickness. Here are two mathematical expressions of these properties.

The line determined by any two points in a plane lies entirely in that plane (see Figure 11.5).

The removal of any line from a plane separates it into two pieces (see Figure 11.6).

Planes are usually denoted by capital script letters ($\mathscr{P}$, $\mathscr{L}$, $\mathscr{E}$, . . .) and represented by *perspective drawings* (Figure 11.7), with or without arrows.

---

* The word *incidence* comes from a Latin word meaning "to fall upon." One might say, for example, that given two points, there is one line that falls upon them.

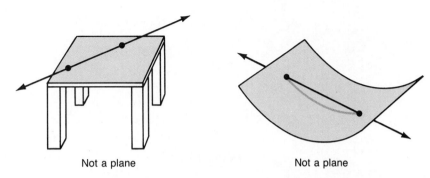

Not a plane   Not a plane

Figure 11.5

Figure 11.6

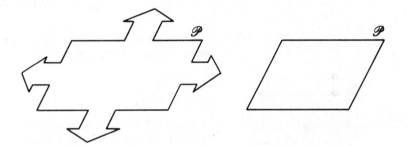

Figure 11.7 Planes.

The listing of incidence relationships that we began with points and lines can be extended to points, lines, and planes. For instance, through a single point there are infinitely many lines. How many planes do you think there are through a given line? How many planes do you think there are through a given point? Among all of the planes through the given line ℓ in Figure 11.8, how many do you think will also pass through the point A? A fundamental property of Euclidean geometry says there is precisely one.

> Through any line and any point not on the line there is exactly one plane.

This plane is sometimes called the plane "determined" by ℓ and A.

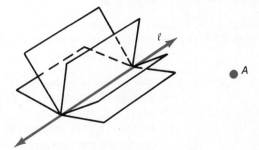

Figure 11.8

Figure 11.9

How many planes do you think there are through three given points? See Figure 11.9. If the points are collinear, there will be infinitely many. But:

> Through any three noncollinear points there is exactly one plane.

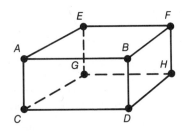

Figure 11.10

Do two lines "determine" a plane? The situation now is more complicated. See Figure 11.10.

Lines $\overleftrightarrow{AB}$ and $\overleftrightarrow{BF}$ lie in a plane and intersect.
Lines $\overleftrightarrow{AB}$ and $\overleftrightarrow{CD}$ lie in a plane and do not intersect.
Lines $\overleftrightarrow{AB}$ and $\overleftrightarrow{CG}$ do not lie in a plane and do not intersect.

We can say the following for certain.

> Two intersecting lines determine a plane.

That is, if two lines intersect, then there is exactly one plane in which they both lie. If two or more lines lie in a single plane, they are said to be **coplanar lines.**

   If two lines do not intersect, they may or not lie in a plane. Nonintersecting lines that lie in a plane are called **parallel lines.** We write $\ell \parallel m$ as shorthand for "ℓ is parallel to m." In Figure 11.10, $\overleftrightarrow{AB} \parallel \overleftrightarrow{CD}$. Can you find some other pairs of parallel lines? Two lines that do not lie in a plane are called **skew lines.** In Figure 11.10, $\overleftrightarrow{AB}$ and $\overleftrightarrow{CG}$ are skew. Can you find some other pairs of skew lines?

EXAMPLE 1   What are the possible numbers of crossing points that can be formed when three lines are drawn in a plane?

Solution   We will use the ideas of parallelism and concurrence and the problem-solving strategy of exhausting all possibilities. Either all three lines are parallel (Figure 11.11(a)), or they are not. If not, then either some of two them are parallel (Figure 11.11(b)), or no two are parallel. If no two are parallel, then either the three lines are concurrent (Figure 11.11(c)), or they are not (Figure 11.11(d)).

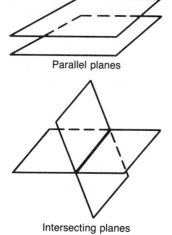

Parallel planes

Intersecting planes

Figure 11.12

(a) 0 crossing points (b) 2 crossing points (c) 1 crossing point (d) 3 crossing points

Figure 11.11

From Figure 11.11 we conclude that the possible numbers of crossing points are 0, 1, 2, and 3. ❏

There is a notion of parallelism for planes as well as for lines. It is based on this property of planes in space: The intersection of two planes is either a line or is empty (see Figure 11.12). If two planes have empty intersection, we say that they are **parallel** or nonintersecting. Thus:

> Two planes are either parallel or intersect in a line.

Again we write $\mathcal{P} \parallel \mathcal{R}$ as shorthand for "plane $\mathcal{P}$ is parallel to plane $\mathcal{R}$."

EXAMPLE 2 The tent-shaped solid in Figure 11.13 is called a right triangular prism. In one word, how are the following figures related?

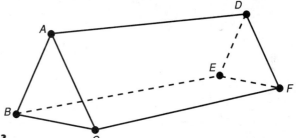

Figure 11.13

(a) $\overleftrightarrow{AD}$ and $\overleftrightarrow{CF}$
(b) $\overleftrightarrow{AD}$ and $\overleftrightarrow{BC}$
(c) $\overleftrightarrow{AC}$, $\overleftrightarrow{BC}$, and $\overleftrightarrow{CF}$
(d) Plane ABC and plane DEF
(e) Plane ABD and plane EFC

Solution

(a) Parallel
(b) Skew
(c) Concurrent
(d) Parallel
(e) Intersecting ❏

EXERCISE SET 11.1

Exercises 1–3 concern the connection between geometry and the physical world. They are designed to let you check how many geometric figures you remember from your school days. Don't worry if some of the terminology is unfamiliar; all of these figures will be studied in more detail later.

1. What geometric figure is suggested by the following?
   (a) The ripples in a pond shortly after a pebble has been dropped in the middle; see Figure 11.14
   (b) The ripples in a pond formed by a duck swimming across it
   (c) The surface of the pond on a perfectly calm day
   (d) A flock of geese in flight; see Figure 11.15
   (e) A log; see Figure 11.16
   (f) The growth rings visible on the end of the log

Figure 11.14

Figure 11.15

Figure 11.16

2. Name a physical object, either natural or man-made, that suggests each of the following geometric figures.

(a) Square   (b) Cube
(c) Sphere   (d) Hemisphere
(e) Parallel lines (f) Perpendicular lines
(g) Triangle   (h) Rectangle
(i) Hexagon

3. Look for geometric figures in your room. Name both the physical object and the abstract geometric figure that it suggests.

4. What occurs when the sun, the earth, and the moon are collinear and
   (a) the Earth is between the sun and the moon?
   (b) the moon is between the Earth and the sun?
   Which configuration, (a) or (b), is associated with higher tides?

5. In aiming a rifle at a target, the goal is to establish collinearity among three points. Name them.

★ 6. A hiker walks 5 mi south, 5 mi east, and 5 mi north, and ends up right where she began. Where is she? (There is more than one correct answer.)

7. Try to draw four lines (in a plane) that have the following number of crossing points.
   (a) 0   (b) 1   (c) 2   (d) 3   (e) 4
   (f) 5   (g) 6   (h) 7

8. How many crossing points are formed by the eight (coplanar) lines shown in Figure 11.17?

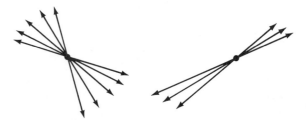

Figure 11.17

9. We say that two points determine a line because there is just one line containing them. The word *determine* is used in a slightly different sense when we say that three noncollinear points determine three lines.

(a) Make a sketch to illustrate three noncollinear points determining three lines.

(b) How many lines are determined by four points, no three of which are collinear?

(c) How many lines are determined by five points, no three of which are collinear?

(d) Look for a pattern and decide how many lines are determined by 100 points, no three of which are collinear.

★ 10. Complete the following precise definition: A line ℓ is said to be determined by a set S of points if. . . .

11. State conditions under which:
(a) Three points determine a plane
(b) Three planes determine a point

12. Make a sketch to show that four points need not all lie in a single plane. (Points that do lie in a single plane are said to be **coplanar.**)

13. Which is easier to build, a three-legged stool that does not teeter or an ordinary four-legged chair that does not teeter? Why?

14. Can two skew lines ever meet? Are there such things as skew planes?

15. Drawing three-dimensional figures on a two-dimensional surface is not easy. As a teacher, you will have to do it often. Here are some practice exercises. Using dotted lines and perspective, make drawings that suggest each.
(a) A quarter pound of butter
(b) A doghouse
(c) One of the great pyramids of Egypt
(d) A cube
(e) A slice of pie
(f) Two parallel planes
(g) Two intersecting planes
(h) A line and a plane intersecting in a point
(i) A line and a plane that are parallel (have empty intersection).
(j) A plane intersecting two other planes that are parallel to each other

16. How many points would have to be removed to separate (disconnect, break in two) the following figures?

(a) A circle   (b) A figure eight

17. Into how many pieces is a line separated by the removal of 1000 points?

18. Into how many pieces is a plane separated by the removal of the following?
(a) Two parallel lines
(b) Two intersecting lines
(c) Three parallel lines
(d) Three lines, two of which are parallel
(e) Three concurrent lines
(f) Three nonconcurrent lines, no two of which are parallel

19. Can a plane be separated into five parts by the removal of the following?
(a) Three lines
(b) Four lines

★ 20. Is it possible to draw four lines in a plane in such a way that they separate it into 11 pieces? Into 7 pieces?

★ 21. What is the maximum number of pieces into which a plane can be partitioned by 7 lines? (Which problem-solving strategy seems natural here?)

★ 22. Suppose L lines are drawn in a plane so that no three are concurrent. Suppose they form C crossing points and partition the plane into P pieces. Find a relationship among L, C, and P. *Hint*: Example 1 and Exercise 18 provide some data in the case of $L = 3$; Exercises 7 and 20 might be helpful in the case of $L = 4$.

23. Into how many pieces is space separated by the removal of the following?
(a) Two parallel planes
(b) Two intersecting planes
(c) Three parallel planes
(d) Three planes, two of which are parallel
(e) Three planes that have one line in common
(f) Three planes that have only a point in common
(g) Three planes that cross in three parallel lines

24. Set notation can be used to describe many of the geometric relationships we have discussed. For example, the property "If two points lie in a

plane, then so does their line" becomes, in set notation,

"If $A \in \mathcal{P}$ and $B \in \mathcal{P}$, then $\overleftrightarrow{AB} \subset \mathcal{P}$."

Explain why $\in$ was used where it was and why $\subset$ was used where it was.

25. Mark each statement true or false. Refer to Figure 11.18.

(a) $C \in \overleftrightarrow{AB}$
(b) $B \in \mathcal{P}$
(c) $\ell = \overleftrightarrow{AB}$
(d) $\overleftrightarrow{AC} = \overleftrightarrow{CA}$
(e) $\overrightarrow{AD} = \overrightarrow{BD}$
(f) $\overrightarrow{CA} = \overrightarrow{BA}$
(g) $\{A, B, C\} \subset \ell$
(h) $\ell \in \mathcal{P}$
(i) $\overleftrightarrow{CD} \subset \mathcal{P}$
(j) $\overleftrightarrow{BC} \subseteq \overleftrightarrow{AC}$

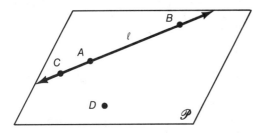

Figure 11.18

26. The points in the Venn diagram of Figure 11.19 represent (schematically) all possible pairs of lines in space. Shade all regions that must necessarily be empty.

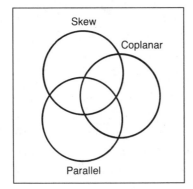

Figure 11.19

27. Mark each statement true or false.
(a) Two different lines cannot cross at more than one point.

(b) Removing a point from a line breaks it in two.
(c) If two lines intersect, then they lie in the same plane.
(d) If three lines are concurrent, then they lie in the same plane.
(e) Two lines either are parallel or they intersect.
(f) Through any three points there is at least one plane.
(g) Through any four points there is a plane.
(h) Removing a line from a plane breaks it in two.
(i) Two different planes have as their intersection either the empty set or a line.
(j) Three different planes can have at most one point in common.
(k) Removing a plane from space breaks it in two.

28. In this section we have listed many properties of points, lines, and planes. None of these properties was new or surprising, because all of them were suggested by our intuition about physical space. But we noted earlier that from a purely mathematical point of view there is no need to base geometry on physical space. For this exercise *space* consists of just four *points—A, B, C, D*—which you may want to visualize as the vertices of a tetrahedron; see Figure 11.20. The *lines*

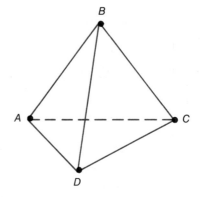

Figure 11.20

are all possible two-element subsets of space. The *planes* are all possible three-element subsets of space.

(a) List all the lines in this geometry.

(b) List all the planes in this geometry.

(c) Eight properties of points, lines, and planes have been underlined in the text. Which of these eight properties are *not* true of the four-point geometry?

11.2 *Rays, Segments, and Angles*

We have studied the three basic geometric figures: points, lines, and planes. These figures will now be used as raw materials from which we will build more geometric figures. The tools we will use are the operations of set theory: complementation, union, and intersection. In mathematical language, while points, lines, and planes are *undefined* figures, the figures we are about to study are *defined*.

Half Lines, Rays, and Segments

The first new figures we build are half lines. See Figure 11.21.

Figure 11.21 Two half lines.

> If a point is removed from a line, each of the two remaining pieces is called a **half line.**

Figure 11.22 The half line $\overset{\circ}{AB}$ from *A* through *B*.

In the language of set theory, the complement of a point in a line—a disconnected set—is the union of two connected sets, each of which is called a half line. If *A* and *B* are two points, then the half line determined by *A* that contains *B*, also called the half line from *A* through *B*, is denoted by $\overset{\circ}{AB}$. See Figure 11.22. The hollow circle at the tail of the arrow is used to remind us that *A* does *not* belong to this half line.

Figure 11.23 The ray $\overrightarrow{AB}$ from *A* through *B*.

If we unite *A* with this half line, the resulting figure is called the ray from *A* through *B* and is denoted by $\overset{\bullet}{AB}$, or more commonly by $\overrightarrow{AB}$. See Figure 11.23. The solid circle at *A* reminds us that *A* *does* belong to the ray.

> The **ray** from *A* through *B* is the union of {*A*} with the half line from *A* through *B*.

The arrow in the symbols $\overrightarrow{AB}$ and $\overset{\circ}{AB}$ is always directed from left to right, no matter which way the actual ray or half line from *A* through *B* points; see Figure 11.24. This is a notational convention. Of course, the symbol $\overset{\leftarrow}{BA}$ would suggest the ray from *A* through *B* as surely as $\overrightarrow{AB}$ does.

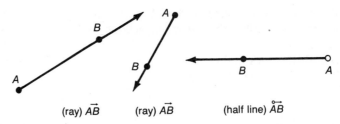

Figure 11.24

By intersecting rays and half lines in different combinations, we can manufacture a variety of segments. The terminology, notation, and definitions are as follows (see Figure 11.25):

Closed segment: $\overline{AB} = \overset{\circ\!\!\rightarrow}{AB} \cap \overset{\circ\!\!\rightarrow}{BA}$ A •——————————• B

Open segment: $\underset{\circ}{\overline{AB}} = \overset{\circ\!\!\rightarrow}{AB} \cap \overset{\circ\!\!\rightarrow}{BA}$ A ○——————————○ B

Half-open segment: $\underset{\circ}{\overline{AB}} = \overset{\circ\!\!\rightarrow}{AB} \cap \overrightarrow{BA}$ A ○——————————• B

Half-open segment: $\overline{AB} = \overrightarrow{AB} \cap \overset{\circ\!\!\rightarrow}{BA}$ A •——————————○ B

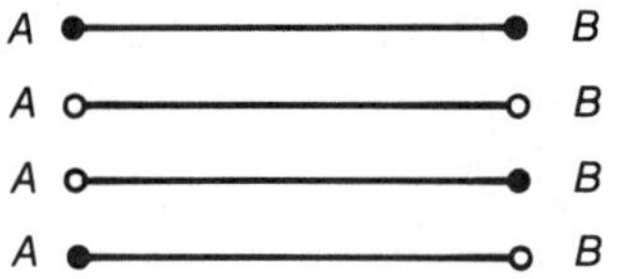

Figure 11.25

When the word *segment* is used without a qualifying adjective, you can assume that *closed segment* is meant.

Inequalities and the Number Line

As we noted earlier, there is a special one-to-one correspondence between the set of real numbers and the set of points making up a line. This specially matched pair of sets is known as the (real) number line; it is shown in Figure 11.26. Under the matching, the less-than relation among real numbers corresponds to the left-of relation among points; that is, point A is to the left of point B if and only if the number matched with A is less than the number matched with B. Thus the number line allows us to represent geometrically some rather intangible algebraic concepts.

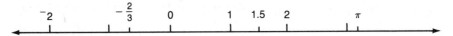

Figure 11.26 The number line.

For example, the range of legal speeds (in miles per hour) on a certain freeway is given algebraically by an inequality

$$40 \le x \le 55$$

Geometrically, the legal speeds make up the closed segment $\overline{AB}$ in Figure 11.27. Illegally high speeds, $x > 55$, constitute the half line $\overset{\circ\!\!\rightarrow}{BC}$, and illegally

Figure 11.27

low speeds, $0 < x < 40$, constitute the open segment $\overset{\circ\!\!-\!\!\circ}{OA}$. Speeds outlawed by no-stopping/no-backing laws, $x \leq 0$, make up the ray $\overrightarrow{OD}$. One of the main reasons for studying the derived figures of this section is their close connection with inequalities.

EXAMPLE 1   Graph the solutions to the inequality

$$3 \leq 5 - 2x < 7$$

on a number line and name the graph, using standard geometric terminology.

Solution   By properties of the less-than relation

$$3 \leq 5 - 2x < 7 \qquad \Longleftrightarrow$$
$$3 - 5 \leq {}^-2x < 7 - 5 \qquad \Longleftrightarrow$$
$${}^-2 \leq {}^-2x < 2 \qquad \Longleftrightarrow$$
$$1 \geq x > {}^-1$$

Thus the solution set is the half-open segment from $^-1$ to 1, excluding $^-1$. See Figure 11.28.

Figure 11.28

                -1   0   1   ❏

Perhaps you have been wondering why we concern ourselves with the presence or absence of endpoints of a segment. A common misconception goes something like this:

(?) "There is no need to even consider open segments. If you want to talk about the segment from O to A with the endpoints excluded, simply consider the point O_1 right next to O and the point A_1 right next to A, and talk about $\overline{O_1 A_1}$."

A quick glance at Figure 11.27 reveals the fallacy. Point O corresponds to the number 0. If there were a point O_1 next to O, on the right, then there would be a smallest positive real number. But, of course, given any positive real number, we can get a smaller one by simply dividing it by 2. Likewise, there is no point right next to A, on the left, because there is no largest real number less than 40. In fact, between any two real numbers, no matter how close together, there is another real number, for example, their average. This property is the density property of rational and real numbers that we studied in Chapters 7 and 8. The corresponding property of points is also known as the **density property.**

> Between any two points is another point.

Half Planes and Half Spaces

Removing a point from a line separates it into two pieces each called a half line. Removing a line from a plane separates it into two pieces each called an **open half plane.** See Figure 11.29. The union of an open half plane with the line that determined it is called a **closed half plane.** See Figure 11.30. Closed half planes are analogous to rays. In fact, purists would probably prefer the term *closed half line* to the word *ray*. The word *ray* is well established historically, however, and is used uniformly in elementary school textbooks.

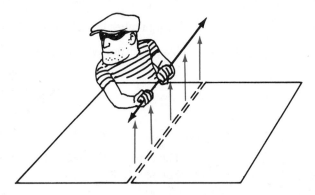

Figure 11.29

Figure 11.30

EXAMPLE 2   Name all possible geometric figures that could arise when a ray is intersected with a closed half plane.

Solution   Figure 11.31 exhausts the possibilities.   ❏

In space there are corresponding concepts, but now the pictures are harder to draw. Removing a plane from space separates it into two pieces, each of which is called an **open half space.** See Figure 11.32. The union of an open half space with the plane that determined it is called a **closed half space.** See Figure 11.33.

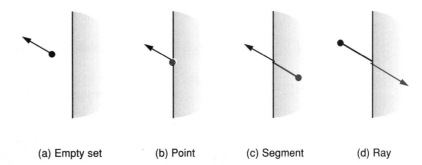

(a) Empty set   (b) Point   (c) Segment   (d) Ray

Figure 11.31

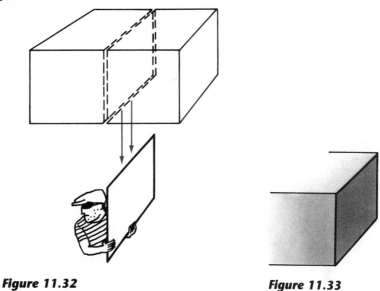

Figure 11.32   *Figure 11.33*

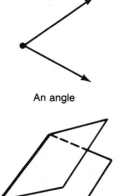

An angle

A dihedral angle

Figure 11.34

One reason for studying half planes and half spaces is that they occur as graphs of the simplest kinds of inequalities involving two and three variables (Chapter 15). Another reason is that various common geometric figures can be described in terms of them, as we see in the following discussion of angles.

Angles

There are two kinds of figures that are called angles. One is suggested by the hands on a clock. This figure is referred to simply as an angle. See Figure 11.34. The other is suggested by a partly opened book. This figure is called a dihedral angle. Definitions can be formulated in terms of rays and half planes.

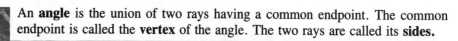

An **angle** is the union of two rays having a common endpoint. The common endpoint is called the **vertex** of the angle. The two rays are called its **sides.**

> A **dihedral angle** is the union of two closed half planes having a common edge.

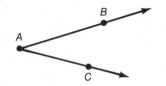

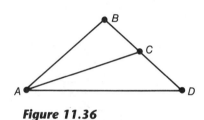

Figure 11.35

Dihedral angles will not be of much use to us in our future work, and so we restrict our attention to (ordinary) angles. Two observations should be made about the definition. First, when we say "two rays" we really mean *two*. We do not recognize a "zero angle." Second, if the two rays are oppositely directed, then their union is a line and is called a **straight angle.**

Since an angle is the union of two rays, we could name it accordingly. For example, we could refer to the angle in Figure 11.35 as $\overrightarrow{AB} \cup \overrightarrow{AC}$. That is not the usual way of naming angles, however. The usual way is first to make a little mark that looks like an angle ($\angle$) and then write, in order, the names of a point on one side of the angle, the vertex, and a point on the other side of the angle. Thus the previous angle is named

$$\angle BAC \qquad \text{or} \qquad \angle CAB$$

The symbol $\angle BAC$ is read "angle B, A, C."

Sometimes, one can simply make the angle symbol and name the vertex. The previous angle would be named $\angle A$. At other times, this abbreviated notation is ambiguous and inappropriate. In Figure 11.36, what angle does $\angle A$ name? We cannot decide. If the largest angle with vertex A is intended, it must be named $\angle BAD$ or $\angle DAB$. One of the smaller angles with vertex A could be named $\angle CAD$ or $\angle DAC$. Do you see why the symbol $\angle C$ is ambiguous, while the symbols $\angle B$ and $\angle D$ are not?

Removing an angle from a plane separates the plane into two pieces. (Notice that this property would be false if we recognized a zero angle, or if we defined an angle as the union of two segments with a common endpoint.) If the angle is not a straight angle, then there is a "smaller" piece called the interior of the angle and a "larger" piece called the exterior. See Figure 11.37.

Figure 11.36

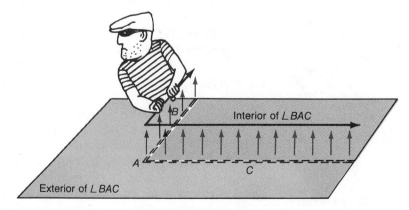

Figure 11.37

The interior and the exterior of an angle need not be defined in such vague terms as *smaller* and *larger*. Precise set-theoretic definitions are possible (providing *A*, *B*, and *C* are noncollinear).

> The **interior** of ∠*BAC* is the intersection of the two open half planes: *B*'s side of $\overleftrightarrow{AC}$ and *C*'s side of $\overleftrightarrow{AB}$. The **exterior** is the union of the two open half planes: the side of $\overleftrightarrow{AC}$ opposite *B* and the side of $\overleftrightarrow{AB}$ opposite *C*.

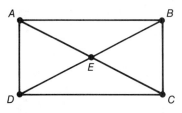

Figure 11.38

Certain pairs of angles have been given special names. Two angles are said to be **adjacent angles** if (1) they lie in the same plane, (2) they share a common side, (3) their interiors do not intersect. In Figure 11.38, ∠*BAE* and ∠*CAD* are adjacent. Two angles are said to be a **linear pair** if (1) they are adjacent and (2) their noncommon sides form a line. In Figure 11.38, ∠*AED* and ∠*DEC* are a linear pair. Finally, two angles are said to be **vertical angles** if (1) they are not adjacent and (2) they are formed by two intersecting lines. In Figure 11.38, ∠*AED* and ∠*BEC* are vertical angles.

By now we have built up a fairly extensive vocabulary of geometric terms, and the list will be even longer by the end of the chapter. What value is there is learning so many technical words? Surely, geometry for elementary school *children* should be more than just the learning of vocabulary. The reason we are looking at terminology so carefully is that correct geometric usage, like correct English usage, is best taught by example. If the *teacher* knows and uses the correct language, the children will learn it by imitation. On the other hand, a teacher who repeatedly refers to rays as lines is doing the students the same sort of disservice as the one who greets them in the morning with a cheery, "Ain't it a nice day today?"

EXERCISE SET 11.2

1. Name a physical object that suggests the idea of ray.

2. What does it mean to say that two points determine two rays? (Here is another meaning for the multipurpose word *determine*.)

3. Draw three noncollinear points *A*, *B*, *C*. Now sketch and name all of the rays they determine.

4. Repeat Exercise 3 for collinear points *A*, *B*, *C*. How many rays are determined?

5. Sketch figures and count how many rays are determined by four points.
   (a) If the four points are collinear

   (b) If exactly three of the points are collinear
   (c) If no three of the points are collinear

6. Two segments are said to be *parallel* if they lie on parallel lines, *skew* if they lie on skew lines, and *collinear* if they lie on a single line. Refer to Figure 11.39.

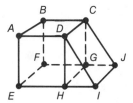

Figure 11.39

(a) Name a pair of parallel segments.

(b) Name a pair of skew segments.

(c) Name a pair of collinear segments.

(d) Name a pair of segments that are neither parallel, nor skew, nor collinear.

7. Mark each statement true or false (for Figure 11.39).

(a) $\overset{\circ\circ}{JG} \cap \overset{\circ}{EF} = \{F\}$

(b) $\overline{FG} = \overline{AD}$

(c) $\overline{HI} \subset \overset{\circ}{IE}$

(d) $\overline{GI} \parallel \overset{\circ\!-\!\circ}{FH}$

8. Draw three noncollinear points A, B, and C, and join them by segments in all possible ways. Excluding their endpoints, how many crossing points were formed by the segments?

9. Repeat Exercise 8 for four (coplanar) points A, B, C, D, no three of which are collinear.

10. If in your drawing for Exercise 9 there was one crossing point, rearrange the original four points so that there will be no crossing points.

11. Repeat Exercise 8 for five (coplanar) points no three of which are collinear, and arrange them so that the connecting segments cross as few times as possible.

12. Try to draw six (coplanar) points, no three of which are collinear, so that the segments joining them will form only three crossing points. (You are an electrician and you want to arrange six terminals on a board in such a way that the wires joining them will cross each other a minimum number of times.)

13. Graph each inequality on the number line and name the graph, using standard geometric terminology.

(a) $x < 1$ (b) $-2 \le x$

(c) $0 < x < 2$ (d) $x^2 \ge 0$

(e) $x^2 \le 1$ (f) $2 < x \le 3$

(g) $x \not> 2$ (h) $x + 1 < x$

14. Find a real number between the following.

(a) $\frac{1}{11}$ and $\frac{1}{10}$

(b) 0.749 and 0.75

(c) π and $\frac{22}{7}$

15. True or false? Between any two points there are infinitely many points. Explain.

16. Figure 11.40 suggests several open half planes that could be described by phrases like "C's side of $\overleftrightarrow{AB}$," "the side of $\overleftrightarrow{AC}$ opposite B," and so on.

(a) Describe the *interior* of the triangle as an intersection of open half planes.

(b) Describe its *boundary* as a union of segments.

(c) Describe its *exterior* as a union of open half planes.

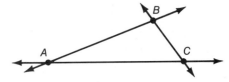

Figure 11.40

17. Try to describe the interior of the polygon in Figure 11.41 as an intersection of open half planes.

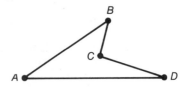

Figure 11.41

18. Describe the interior of the tetrahedron in Figure 11.42 as an intersection of open half spaces.

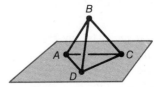

Figure 11.42

★ 19. Removal of one plane from space separates it into two pieces. Into how many pieces (maximum) can space be separated by the removal of two planes? Three planes? Four planes? Five planes? Six planes? Seven planes? (Unless a person has remarkable spatial perception, these questions become very difficult very quickly. *Hint:* Your solution to Exercise 21, Section 11.1, should be helpful.)

20. By the "size" of an angle we mean the "amount of opening." In Figure 11.43, which angle is "larger"? Why do you suppose that an angle is defined as the union of two rays rather than as the union of two segments?

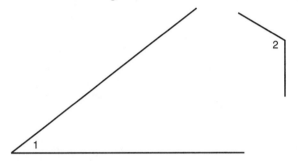

Figure 11.43

21. How do you know that all points of an angle lie in the same plane?

22. Do three noncollinear points determine *an* angle?

23. Do two lines determine *an* angle?

24. How many (nonstraight) angles are determined by seven points, no three of which are collinear?

25. Decide whether each pair of angles drawn on the cube of Figure 11.44 is a pair of adjacent angles. If not, tell which of the three conditions of the definition (coplanar, share a side, nonintersecting interiors) is not satisfied.

(a) ∠BAC and ∠CAD   (b) ∠CDA and ∠ADF
(c) ∠EFD and ∠DFG   (d) ∠AEF and ∠FED
(e) ∠CAD and ∠DEF   (f) ∠FDE and ∠ADC
(g) ∠BAC and ∠DAF   (h) ∠DBA and ∠BAF
(i) ∠BCA and ∠ACD   (j) ∠BAC and ∠BAD

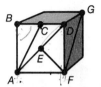

Figure 11.44

26. In the plane figure of Figure 11.45, which of the following pairs of angles are linear pairs?
(a) ∠BEA and ∠AEF   (b) ∠BDC and ∠BDA
(c) ∠GEA and ∠AEB   (d) ∠CEF and ∠FEG
(e) ∠BEA and ∠GEF   (f) ∠DEC and ∠GED
(g) ∠EDC and ∠ADB

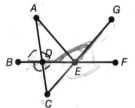

Figure 11.45

27. Find four pairs of vertical angles in Figure 11.45.

28. How many different pairs of vertical angles are formed by three concurrent lines?

29. How many different linear pairs are formed by three concurrent lines?

11.3 *Curves, Polygons, and Connectivity*

The figures we have studied so far have all been *rectilinear;* that is, none of them were curved. In this section we add some curved figures, as well as some more rectilinear ones, to our catalog.

Curves

If you drop a length of string onto a table, the geometric figure suggested is called a **planar curve.** See Figure 11.46. There are also figures called **space**

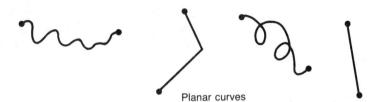

Planar curves

Figure 11.46

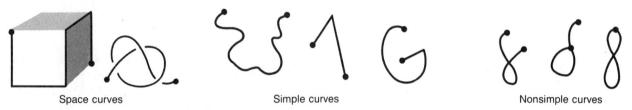

Space curves

Figure 11.47

Simple curves   Nonsimple curves

Figure 11.48

curves, as shown in Figure 11.47. The single word *curve* (or *path*) will be used to describe both planar and space curves. Notice that a curve need not have any smooth bends in it.

Here is another way of thinking: planar curves are those figures you can draw without lifting your pencil from the paper. Curves have a beginning and an endpoint. Thus (closed) segments are curves, but lines, half lines, rays, half-open segments, open segments, and angles are not.* Curves that never intersect themselves are called **simple curves;** see Figure 11.48.

Closed Curves

If the beginning and endpoints of a curve coincide, then the curve is called a **closed curve.** Closed curves, like ordinary curves, may or may not lie in a plane, as indicated in Figure 11.49.

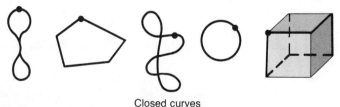

Closed curves

Figure 11.49

*Unfortunately, there is some disagreement among mathematicians as to what type of figures should be called curves. We have accepted the definition that requires a curve to have a beginning and an endpoint. Another definition does not make that demand, so that, to some mathematicians, lines, rays, open segments, and so on, qualify as curves.

Technically, no closed curve is simple, since every closed curve intersects itself at its common beginning-end point. Nevertheless, certain closed curves are called simple. A closed curve is called a **simple closed curve** if, when you draw it, no intersections are made until the endpoint is drawn. See Figure 11.50. In Figure 11.49, the second, fourth, and fifth curves are simple closed curves; the first and third are nonsimple closed curves.

Many of the geometric figures that are most familiar to us are examples of simple closed curves: triangles, squares, rectangles, trapezoids, pentagons, hexagons, circles, ovals. It is exactly because there are so many useful special examples that we study the general class of figures called simple closed curves.

Figure 11.50 A simple closed curve.

Polygons

A simple curve that is made up of segments joined at their endpoints is called a **polygonal curve,** a broken-line, or a piecewise linear curve. A simple closed curve made up of segments joined at their endpoints is called a **polygon.** See Figure 11.51. The segments of which a polygon is constructed are called its **sides;** the endpoints of these segments are called its **vertices.**

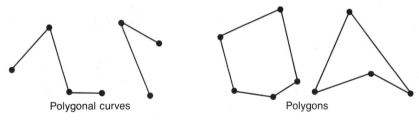

Polygonal curves   Polygons

Figure 11.51

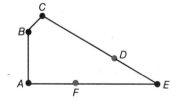

Figure 11.52

Several details deserve mention. First, the polygon in Figure 11.52 is considered to have just four sides, not six, because four is the minimum number of segments from which it can be constructed. Second, we refer to ∠E in Figure 11.52, as an angle—or more precisely an *interior angle*—of the polygon, even though it is not a subset of the polygon. (Remember that the sides of an angle are rays, not segments.) Furthermore, we consider the polygon to have just four angles, not six, and four vertices, not six.

The polygonal Figures 11.51 and 11.52 are all planar. There are, of course, polygonal space curves and polygonal closed space curves, but we shall have little to do with them. Unless specified otherwise, you can assume that all polygonal curves in this text are planar.

One source of difficulty in studying polygons is the language. Over the many centuries during which polygons have been investigated, special names have arisen. See Table 11.1. These names refer to the number of sides of the polygon. Etymologically, most of them refer to the number of angles, not sides, but this distinction is not important. A polygon has exactly as many sides as angles.

Table 11.1

Polygon	poly- (Gk., *many*)	+ gon (Gk., *angle*)
Triangle	tri- (L., *three*)	+ angle
Quadrilateral	quadri- (L., *four*)	+ laterus (L., *side*)
Pentagon	penta- (Gk., *five*)	+ gon
Hexagon	hexa- (Gk., *six*)	+ gon
Heptagon	hepta- (Gk., *seven*)	+ gon
Octagon	octa- (Gk., *eight*)	+ gon
Nonagon	nona- (L., *nine*)	+ gon
Decagon	deca- (Gk., *ten*)	+ gon

Occasionally, mathematicians find themselves studying polygons having a large number of sides. For example, the great mathematician Gauss proved a remarkable theorem about polygons that have 3, 5, 17, 257, and 65,537 sides (that "regular" polygons having these Fermat-numbers of sides are "constructible" with straightedge and compass). If a mathematician needs to talk about a 17-sided polygon, he will not look for an appropriate Greek prefix but will call it simply a 17-gon. In general, an *n*-sided polygon is called an *n*-gon.

EXAMPLE 1 How many different pentagons are there having A, B, C, D, and E as vertices, where A, B, C, D, and E are the points in
(a) Figure 11.53(a)?
(b) Figure 11.53(b)?
(c) Figure 11.53(c), in which E, D, and C are collinear?

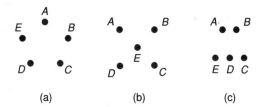

Figure 11.53   (a)   (b)   (c)

Solution   (a) One.

(b) Four. One is obtained by starting at *A* and joining the vertices in the order *AEBCDA*. The other three are like this one, but have their "dent" in a different side.

(c) Zero.   ❏

Connected Figures

In our discussion of half lines, half planes, and half spaces, we used the idea of connectivity without formal explanation. Intuitively, a figure is connected if it is just one piece, that is, if a bug, say, can walk from any point in the figure to any other point in the figure without stepping out of the figure. See Figure 11.54. The path of the bug will be a curve, which suggests defining connectivity in terms of curves.

Connected figures   Disconnected figures

Figure 11.54

> A geometric figure is **connected** if any two points in it can be joined by a simple curve that lies entirely in it.

A figure that is not connected is said to be **disconnected** or **separated.**

The concept of connectedness plays an important role in geometry. It makes possible a definition of the term *piece* that we have been using intuitively up to now. (Mathematicians call a piece of a geometric figure a *connected component* of the figure.)

> A **connected** component (piece) of a geometric figure is a maximal connected subset.

For example, each of the disconnected figures in Figure 11.54 is the union of two disjoint pieces.

As a reminder, two of the fundamental axioms on which Euclidean plane geometry is based involve the concept of piece (connected component). They are:

1. *The removal of any point from a line separates the line into two pieces.* That is, the complement of a point in a line is a disconnected set that is the union of two connected components.

2. *The removal of any line from a plane separates the plane into two pieces.* That is, the complement of a line in a plane is a disconnected set that is the union of two connected components.

The concept of connectedness also makes possible a precise statement of a famous result known as the **Jordan curve theorem** (see Figure 11.55):

> The complement of a simple closed curve in a plane is a disconnected set that is the union of two connected components (called the interior and the exterior of the curve).

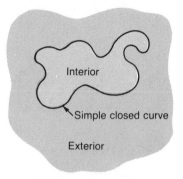

Interior

Simple closed curve

Exterior

Figure 11.55

Convex Figures

An ordinary bug can walk from any point in a connected figure to any other point in that figure without leaving the figure. Suppose now that the bug is not ordinary. Suppose he refuses to walk along anything but a straight line to his goal. Then in some connected figures he can still get around, but in others he cannot, as indicated in Figure 11.56. Figures in which this stubborn bug can get from any point to any other point are called convex figures. In mathematical language:

> A figure is **convex** if, whenever two points are in it, then so is the segment joining them.

Convex figures, then, are very special kinds of connected figures. If a figure is convex it must be connected; but if it is connected, it may or may not be convex.

The definition of convexity applies as well as to figures in space as to figures in a plane. See Figure 11.57.

Convex figure

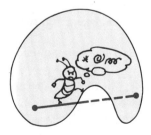

Nonconvex figure

Figure 11.56

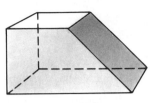

Convex solid figure   Nonconvex solid figure

Figure 11.57

EXAMPLE 2   Which of these pieces of sports equipment are convex: baseball bat, bowling ball, hockey puck, tennis ball?

Solution   Only the hockey puck is convex. The tennis ball fails because it is hollow, the baseball bat fails because of the knob on the end of the handle, and the bowling ball fails because of the finger holes.   ❏

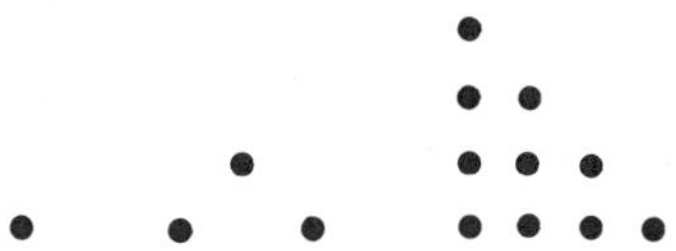

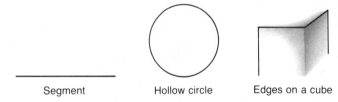

Figure 11.58 Zero-dimensional figures.

Dimension

The concept of the *dimension* of a figure turns out to be a very difficult one to describe mathematically. Still the idea is important enough that you should have at least an intuitive feeling for it.

A point or any set of isolated points should be thought of as being **zero-dimensional.** See Figure 11.58.

Intuitively, a figure should be thought of as being **one-dimensional** if it could be made of fine wire. See Figure 11.59. Familiar examples of one-dimensional figures include lines, half-lines, rays, and angles.

Segment   Hollow circle   Edges on a cube

Figure 11.59 One-dimensional figures.

Intuitively, a figure is **two-dimensional** if it could be made of paper. See Figure 11.60. Familiar examples of two-dimensional figures include planes, half-planes, dihedral angles, and interiors and exteriors of ordinary angles.

Intuitively, a figure is **three-dimensional** if it could be made of modeling clay. See Figure 11.61. Familiar three-dimensional figures include space itself, half-spaces, and interiors and exteriors of dihedral angles.

Sometimes, the dimension of a figure seems to depend on what part of it you happen to be looking at, as indicated in Figure 11.62. In such cases we

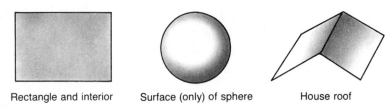

Figure 11.60 Two-dimensional figures.

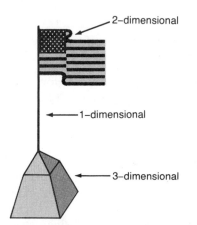

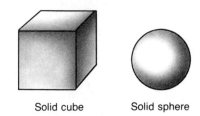

Figure 11.61 Three-dimensional figures.

Figure 11.62

agree to choose the largest dimension. Thus we would say that the figure in Figure 11.62 is three-dimensional. Ambiguous figures like this one will not turn up very often in our work with geometry.

Recently researchers in the field of "fractal geometry" have described figures that seem to have dimension intermediate (!) between 1 and 2, and between 2 and 3.

EXERCISE SET 11.3

From each set of four figures in Exercises 1–9, pick out one that does not belong. Use correct geometric terminology to defend your choice. Many of the problems have more than one right answer.

1.

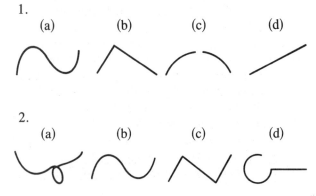

2.

3. (a)   (b)   (c)   (d)

4. (a)   (b)   (c)   (d)

5. (a)   (b)   (c)   (d)

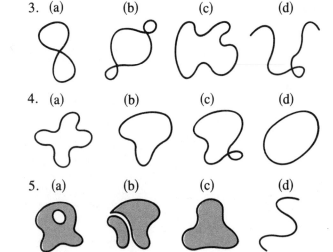

6. (a)   (b)   (c)   (d)

7. (a)   (b)   (c)   (d)

8. (a)   (b)   (c)   (d)

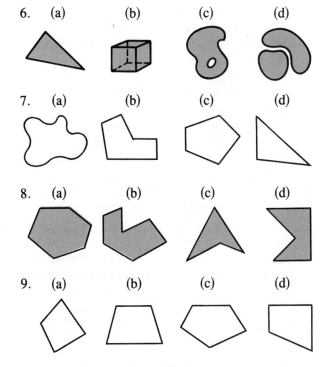

9. (a)   (b)   (c)   (d)

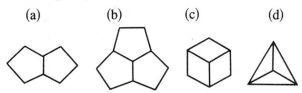

10. Beginning outside each figure, draw a simple curve as in part (a) that cuts each side exactly once.

    (a)   (b)   (c)   (d)

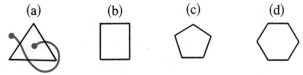

11. Try to draw a simple curve that cuts across each segment in these figures exactly once. (Do not go through any corners.)

    (a)   (b)   (c)   (d)

★ 12. If a figure, such as those in Exercise 10, has an odd number of sides, and if you begin outside and draw a simple curve cutting each side once, will you finish up inside or outside? Use your observa-

tion to explain why Exercises 11(b) and 11(d) are impossible to do.

13. Try to draw a simple *closed* curve that cuts each side of each figure exactly once.

    (a)   (b)   (c)   (d)

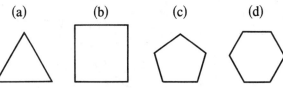

14. You are driving a car, as shown in Figure 11.63, along a simple closed curve. On which side of the road is the interior of the simple closed curve?

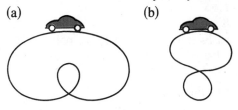

Figure 11.63

15. Now you are driving along nonsimple closed curves. Is the interior always on your left?

    (a)   (b)

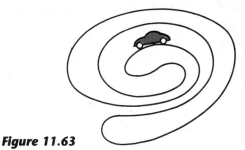

16. According to the Jordan curve theorem, removing a simple closed curve from a plane separates the plane into two pieces. Draw a closed curve that is not simple whose removal separates the plane as follows:

    (a) Into three pieces (Ignoring endpoints, how many times did your curve intersect itself?)

    (b) Into four pieces (same question)

    (c) Into five pieces (same question)

17. Is the point *P* an interior point or an exterior point of the simple closed curve in Figure 11.64? Try to devise a quick test for deciding whether a

point is in the interior or the exterior of a simple closed curve.

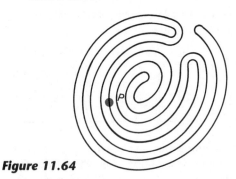

Figure 11.64

18. Refer to Figure 11.65. Draw as many polygonal curves as you can, beginning at *A*, ending at *E*, and using all of the other points (*B*, *C*, *D*) as vertices. Remember the agreement that a polygonal curve is simple. Use the problem-solving strategy of making a systematic list.

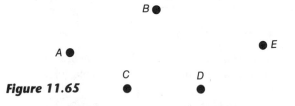

Figure 11.65

19. Repeat Exercise 18, but relocate points *B*, *C*, and *D* so that you get *more* polygonal curves than before.

20. Refer to Figure 11.66.

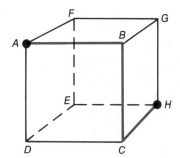

Figure 11.66

(a) How many polygonal space curves are there from *A* to *H* that consist of three edges of the

cube? (One, *ABCH*, is emphasized in the figure.)

(b) Repeat (a) for four edges instead of three.
(c) Repeat (a) for five edges.
(d) Repeat (a) for six edges.
(e) Repeat (a) for seven edges.

★ 21. Refer to Figure 11.66 and explain.
(a) Why every edge path from *A* to *B* must consist of an odd number of edges
(b) Why every edge path from *A* to *C* must consist of an even number of edges
(c) Why every edge path from *A* to *H* must consist of an odd number of edges

22. Polygons can be named by naming their vertices in the order in which they are to be traced. It is understood that the last vertex named is to be joined to the first vertex named. For each polygon named, first sketch a copy of the set of points in Figure 11.67, and then sketch the polygon.
(a) *AFCB*   (b) *ABCDE*
(c) *ABCFDE*   (d) *DEABCF*

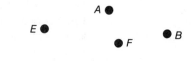

Figure 11.67

23. Name each polygon in Exercise 22 with a different name. How many different names are there for a polygon with *n* vertices?

24. How many polygons can you draw having all four of the points in Figure 11.68 as vertices?

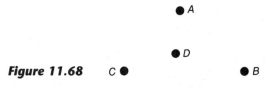

Figure 11.68

25. A quadrilateral can be *triangulated* by drawing one segment, as in Figure 11.69.
(a) Draw a pentagon and triangulate it. How many segments did you have to draw to triangulate it?

(b) Repeat (a) for a hexagon, a heptagon, a nonagon, a decagon, an *n*-gon.

Figure 11.69

(In Chapter 12 we shall review the procedure for finding the area of a triangle. The technique of triangulation will then allow us to find the area of any kind of polygon.)

26. A multipurpose teaching device known as the *geoboard* is particularly useful in connection with the study of polygons. A four-by-four geoboard is made from a piece of wood and 25 nails, as shown in Figure 11.70. Rubber bands can then be stretched over the nails to form a variety of polygons. How many squares could you make on this geoboard? Ask another question about geoboards suggested by this problem.

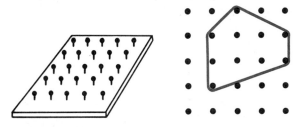

Figure 11.70

★ 27. In Figure 11.71 a light source has been placed inside a polygon. Notice that two sides of the

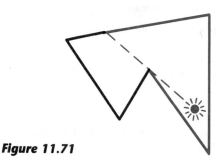

Figure 11.71

polygon are completely in the shade and another is partially shaded. Try to draw a polygon and place a light source in it so that *every* side is either completely or partially shaded.

★ 28. An inner tube can be disconnected (separated) by the removal of a bent circle, as shown in Figure 11.72.
    (a) Can it be disconnected by the removal of a flat (planar) circle?
    (b) Can it be disconnected by the removal of two flat circles?
    (c) Can you find two flat circles whose simultaneous removal will *not* disconnect the inner tube?

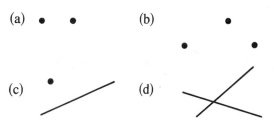

Figure 11.72

29. Sketch the smallest convex set that includes the given set.

★ 30. Draw pictures to illustrate your answers to the following questions.
    (a) Must the intersection of two connected sets be a connected set?
    (b) Must the intersection of two convex sets be a convex set?

31. A convex polygon includes all of its diagonals (segments joining its nonadjacent vertices). Is the converse true? That is, if it is true that a polygon includes all of its diagonals, can you conclude that it is convex?

32. A farmer wants to fence in a yard for his chickens by using a wall of the barn as one side and 20 ft of flexible chicken wire for the rest of the boundary. He would like the enclosure to have as large an area as possible. Show that the maximal region must be convex by showing that an enclosure (like the one in Figure 11.73) that is not convex can always be enlarged. *Hint:* Line ℓ should be useful in your explanation. What do you suppose is the optimal shape for the enclosure?

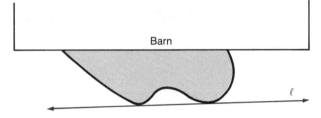

Barn

ℓ

Figure 11.73

33. What is the dimension of the goemetric figure suggested by the following?
(a) A square of chicken wire
(b) A basketball

(c) A baseball
(d) The highways on a map
(e) The towns on a map
(f) The map
(g) An empty milk carton
(h) A yo-yo on a string
(i) A single dip ice cream cone
(j) A balloon on a string

34. Draw two two-dimensional figures whose intersection is as follows:
(a) A two-dimensional figure
(b) A one-dimensional figure
(c) A zero-dimensional figure
(d) The empty set

35. Sketch a cube. It has _____ faces, _____ edges, and _____ vertices. Each face is a _____ dimensional figure, each edge is a _____ dimensional figure, each vertex is a _____ dimensional figure, and the solid cube itself is a _____ dimensional figure.

36. Sketch a connected, nonconvex, two-dimensional region whose boundary is a simple closed polygonal curve.

11.4 *Graph Theory (Optional)*

You worked with graphs throughout your high school years, and we reviewed the concept in Chapter 2. In this section the word *graph* has an altogether different meaning. The things we are about to investigate are sometimes called networks but are more often called graphs. We will follow this common usage, and trust that you will not be confused by the new meaning for the old word.

A **graph** is a finite collection of points, called **vertices,** joined by simple curves, called **edges,** having the following three properties:

1. Every edge joins two vertices.
2. Wherever two edges meet, there must be a vertex.
3. The graph is a connected set.

For example, Figure 11.74 is a graph with seven vertices and six edges, but none of the three figures in Figure 11.75 is a graph. Can you explain why?

Figure 11.74

Figure 11.75

The beginnings of graph theory as a mathematical field can be traced back to 1736 when Euler solved the problem of the Seven Bridges of Königsberg. The East Prussian city of Königsberg was built on two islands and the two banks of the river Weser. There were seven bridges, as shown in Figure 11.76. Citizens out for a Sunday stroll would try to discover a path that would take them over each of the seven bridges exactly once. The task seemed to be impossible. Euler provided the first mathematical proof that there could be no such path.

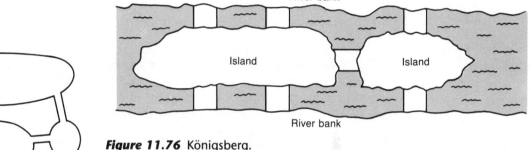

Figure 11.76 Königsberg.

Figure 11.77 Stylized Königsberg.

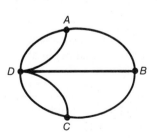

Figure 11.78 Graph Königsberg.

His reasoning proceeded along these lines: First, he probably stylized the map to look something like Figure 11.77. Then he abstracted the essential features (four bodies, seven connections) by drawing what we now call a graph, as in Figure 11.78. The citizens' problem could thus be rephrased as follows: Is it possible to begin at a vertex and traverse each edge exactly once without lifting your pencil from the paper? (Such a tour is called **a tracing** of a graph.)

Euler continued his argument by supposing the graph could be traced and making these key observations. If you begin the tour *away* from A, then after traversing one of the three edges touching A, you are *at* A. After traversing the second of these edges, you are again *away* from A. Finally, after traversing the third edge, you are back *at* A. But now you are stuck there. You cannot leave A because all edges touching it have been traveled. Thus if you begin the tour away from A, you must conclude the tour at A. Schematically,

$$\text{away} \xrightarrow{\ 1\ } \text{at} \xrightarrow{\ 2\ } \text{away} \xrightarrow{\ 3\ } \text{at}$$

with *Start* over "away" and *Finish* over the final "at".

The reason this chain ends with *at* rather than *away* is that A is an *odd vertex;* that is, A has an odd number of edges touching it.

The argument just made for vertex *A* can be repeated for each of the other vertices *B*, *C*, *D*, because all of them are also odd. Thus the situation is as follows:

If you start *away* from *A*, you must end *at A*.
If you start *away* from *B*, you must end *at B*.
If you start *away* from *C*, you must end *at C*.
If you start *away* from *D*, you must end *at D*.

But no matter where you start, you will be away from three of the vertices. Thus if you could trace the graph, you would have to end at those three vertices. And, of course, no one can be in three places at the same time. Thus it is impossible to trace the graph.

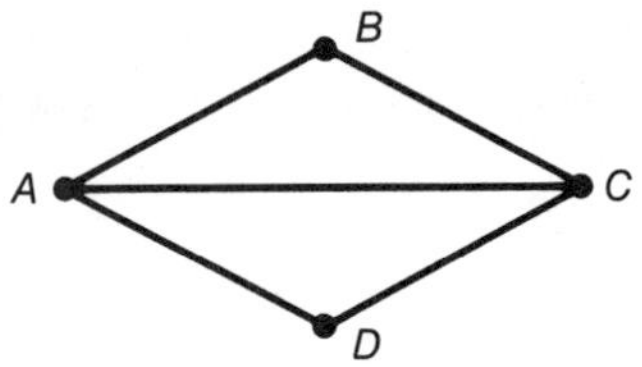

Figure 11.79

Before reading on, try your hand at tracing the graph in Figure 11.79. Where did you start, and where did you finish? Can you explain why, in terms of odd vertices, you cannot trace it starting at *B* or *D*? Can you explain why any tracing that starts at *C* must end at *A*?

Euler proved the following results about graphs and their traceability:

1. A graph always has an even number of odd vertices.

2. A graph with 0 odd vertices is traceable.

3. A graph with 2 odd vertices is traceable, but one has to begin at one of the odd vertices and end at the other.

4. A graph with more than 2 odd vertices cannot be traced.

We have gone through the proof of 4 only. A proof of 1 is outlined in Exercise 8.

EXAMPLE 1   Is the graph in Figure 11.80 traceable?

Solution   Yes, because it has just two odd vertices, *A* and *B*. There are two tracings that begin at *A* and end at *B* (*AECDEB* and *AEDCEB*), and two that begin at *B* and end at *A*.   ❏

EXAMPLE 2   Can a night watchman walk through each door in the 11-office building in Figure 11.81 exactly once? If so, in which room should he start?

Solution   Represent each room by a vertex and each door by an edge. The resulting graph is shown in Figure 11.82. Since it has just two odd vertices, *B* and *J*, the

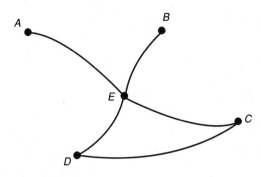

Figure 11.80

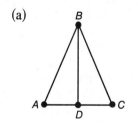

Figure 11.82

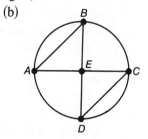

Figure 11.81

watchman can make the tour starting at B and ending at J, or vice versa. One route is

B C D H K F H G F B A E F E I J F J　　　　❑

EXERCISE SET 11.4

1. Can you trace these graphs beginning at vertex A? B? C? D?

(a)　　　　(b)

(c)　　　　(d)

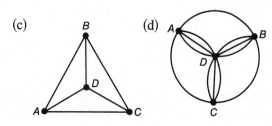

2. Can you trace these graphs? (You get to choose the vertex at which to begin.)

(a)　　　　(b)

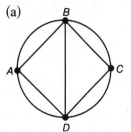

(c)　　　　(d)

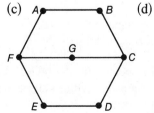
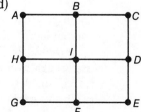

3. A cloud has settled over part of the traceable graph in Figure 11.83. If you start your tracing at *A*, will you finish behind the cloud or out in the sun?

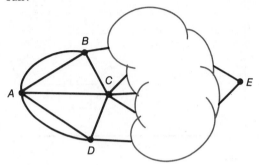

Figure 11.83

★ 4. Two clouds have settled over the graph in Figure 11.84. Explain why that graph must have some odd vertices.

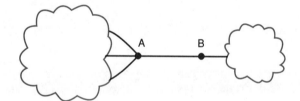

Figure 11.84

5. After World War II, the seven bridges of Königsberg became the eight bridges of Kaliningrad. Two different travelers have brought back two different versions of the place where the new bridge stands. Does each version give a traceable graph? (You do not need their diagrams to answer the question.)

6. Can a rat walk through each doorway in the up-scale four-room cages of Figure 11.85 exactly once?

7. Draw a graph with eight vertices (use O for the great outdoors) corresponding to the floor plan for the house in Figure 11.86. Is it possible to pass through every doorway in the house exactly once? If so, describe a path with a string of letters. If not, explain why not.

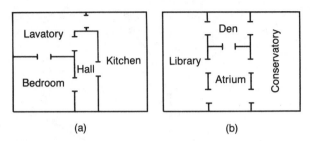

(a)   (b)

Figure 11.85

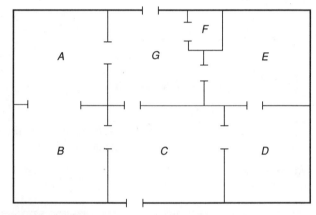

Figure 11.86

8. Here is an outline of a proof that in any graph the number of odd vertices is even. Define the *degree* of a vertex to be the number of edges touching it. Let *S* be the sum of the degrees of all the vertices.

   (a) Why is *S* equal to 2 times the number of edges? (Hence *S* in an even number.)

   Let S_e be the sum of the degrees of all the even vertices, and let S_o be the sum of the degrees of all the odd vertices.

   (b) Why does $S = S_e + S_o$?

   (c) Why is S_e an even number?

   (d) Why must S_o be an even number?

   (e) Why can't S_o consist of an odd number of addends?

9. Explain why the following two problems are equivalent. (In Figure 11.87 the letters label regions; in Figure 11.88 they label vertices.)

(a) Draw a simple curve that cuts each segment in the figure in Figure 11.87 exactly once.

(b) Trace the graph in Figure 11.88.

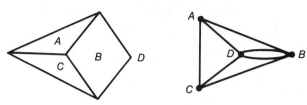

Figure 11.87   **Figure 11.88**

10. Reconsider Exercise 11, Section 11.3, in light of the preceding exercise.

11. Reconsider Exercise 13, Section 11.3.

12. The graph in Figure 11.89 has 6 vertices ($V = 6$), 7 edges ($E = 7$), and partitions the plane into 3 pieces ($P = 3$). We have entered those values in the first line of the accompanying chart. Enter corresponding values from each of the graphs in Exercises 1 and 2. Now, try to discover a general relationship among V, E, and P.

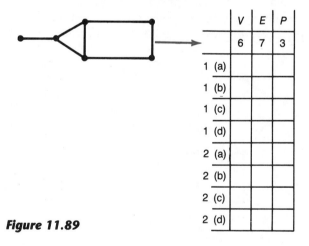

	V	E	P
	6	7	3
1 (a)			
1 (b)			
1 (c)			
1 (d)			
2 (a)			
2 (b)			
2 (c)			
2 (d)			

Figure 11.89

13. In Exercise 12 you probably inferred from the arithmetic data that the following relationship holds for all (planar) graphs:

$$V - E + P = 2$$

Here V is the number of vertices, E is the number of edges, and P is the number of pieces. Let us try to establish that same result now, using geometric reasoning. For the sake of concreteness, consider the graph in Figure 11.90. We shall perform two operations on this graph, a *pruning* operation that removes a protruding edge (and vertex) and an *opening* operation that removes a boundary between two pieces. Figure 11.91 shows how we can reduce this graph to the trivial one-vertex graph by successive prunings and openings.

Figure 11.90

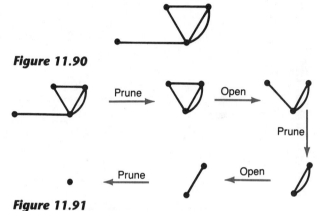

Figure 11.91

(a) Prune and open the graph in Figure 11.92 until you have reduced it to the trivial one-vertex graph.

Figure 11.92

(b) What is the effect of a pruning operation on the number V? On E? On P? On $V - E + P$?

(c) What is the effect of an opening operation on the number V? On E? On P? On $V - E + P$?

(d) What is the effect of a sequence of prunings and openings on the number $V - E + P$?

(e) What is the numerical value of $V - E + P$ for the trivial one-vertex graph?

(f) Why does $V - E + P = 2$ for every planar graph?

14. Does Euler's formula, $V - E + P = 2$, remain true for the following graphs?
    (a) A graph drawn on the surface of a sphere
    (b) A graph drawn on an inner tube

15. We are at a party counting handshakes again. Explain why the number of people who report shaking hands an odd number of times must be even.

16. The five regular polyhedra are shown in Figure 13.42 (page 669). View each one as a graph. Which are traceable?

Computer Vignette I

If your machine has high-resolution graphics capability, type in the program of Figure 11.93. When you run it, a facsimile of Figure 11.94 should appear on your screen.

Figure 11.93

```
10   HGR
20   HCOLOR = 3
30   HPLOT 130,90 TO 100,50 TO 140,20 TO 170,60 TO
     200,60 TO 200,90 TO 170,90 TO 170,130 TO 130,130
     TO 130,90 TO 170,90 TO 170,60 TO 130,90
40   END
```

If you think of Figure 11.94 as a (traceable) graph, then you can slow down the plotting process and actually watch the graph being traced by using the laborious program in Figure 11.95. To slow things down even further, replace 400 by, say, 800 in line 500.

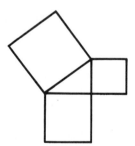

Figure 11.94

Figure 11.95

```
10   HGR
20   HCOLOR = 3
30   HPLOT 130,90 TO 100,50
40   GOSUB 500
50   HPLOT 100,50 TO 140,20
60   GOSUB 500
70   HPLOT 140,20 TO 170,60
80   GOSUB 500
```

```
90  HPLOT 170,60 TO 200,60
100 GOSUB 500
110 HPLOT 200,60 TO 200,90
120 GOSUB 500
130 HPLOT 200,90 TO 170,90
140 GOSUB 500
150 HPLOT 170,90 TO 170,130
160 GOSUB 500
170 HPLOT 170,130 TO 130,130
180 GOSUB 500
190 HPLOT 130,130 TO 130,90
200 GOSUB 500
210 HPLOT 130,90 TO 170,90
220 GOSUB 500
230 HPLOT 170,90 TO 170,60
240 GOSUB 500
250 HPLOT 170,60 TO 130,90
260 GOTO 999
500 FOR I = 1 TO 400
510 NEXT I
520 RETURN
999 END
```

The previous graphics programs, like all of our programs up to this point, were written in BASIC. Another computer language that is better suited to geometric tasks is Logo. (Logo and BASIC are both covered in Chapter 16.) Figure 11.96 shows two Logo programs. The short one teaches the computer how to draw squares of arbitrary (variable) side length S. The long one uses that capability as a subroutine in drawing the same kind of diagram that our BASIC program produced.

Figure 11.96

```
TO VSQUARE :S
  REPEAT 4 [FORWARD :S RIGHT 90]
END

TO PYTHAGORAS
  LEFT 37
  VSQUARE 50
  RIGHT 127
  VSQUARE 40
  FORWARD 40 LEFT 90
  VSQUARE 30
  HIDETURTLE
END
```

Key Concepts in Chapter 11

Geometric figure
Collinear points
Concurrent lines
Parallel lines
Skew lines
Parallel planes
Half line
Ray
Segment
Density
Half plane
Half space
Angle

Dihedral angle
Adjacent angles
Linear pair of angles
Vertical angles
Curve
Simple curve
Simple closed curve
Polygon
Connected figure
Convex figure
Dimension of a figure
*Graph
*Tracing of a graph

✿ *Chapter 11 Review Exercises* ✿

1. Refer to the cube shown in Figure 11.97 and use symbols such as $\overleftrightarrow{AB}$ to name the following.
   (a) Two parallel lines
   (b) Two skew lines
   (c) Two intersecting lines
   (d) Three concurrent lines that do not lie in a single plane
   (e) Three concurrent lines that do lie in a single plane
   (f) Three nonconcurrent lines that lie in a single plane
   (g) Six lines that lie in a single plane

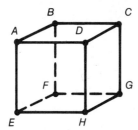

Figure 11.97

2. Into how many pieces is a plane separated by the removal of the following?
   (a) Three parallel lines

   (b) Three lines, exactly two of which are parallel
   (c) Three concurrent lines
   (d) Three nonconcurrent lines, no two of which are parallel

3. How many planes are determined by 10 points, no 4 of which are coplanar?

4. How many pairs of skew lines are determined by the four vertices of a tetrahedron (pyramid with triangular base)?

5. Three planes $\mathcal{P}_1$, $\mathcal{P}_2$, $\mathcal{P}_3$ are arranged so that $\mathcal{P}_1 \cap \mathcal{P}_2$, $\mathcal{P}_1 \cap \mathcal{P}_3$, $\mathcal{P}_2 \cap \mathcal{P}_3$ are three parallel lines. Into how many pieces do these planes partition space?

6. Refer to Figure 11.98, and decide whether each of the following is true or false.
   (a) $C \in \overleftrightarrow{AB}$
   (b) $\overline{BD} \subseteq \overleftrightarrow{DF}$
   (c) $\overline{EG} \cap \overleftrightarrow{FC} = \varnothing$
   (d) $\overline{BD} = \overline{FG}$
   (e) $\{A, B, C, F, G\} \subseteq \angle FCB$
   (f) $\overset{\circ}{GF} \cup \overset{\circ}{FC} = \overline{GC}$

7. Given three noncollinear points A, B, and C, write a simpler symbol for each of the following.

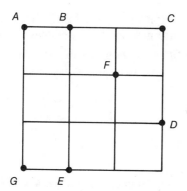

Figure 11.98

(a) $\overrightarrow{AC} \cup \overrightarrow{AB}$
(b) $\overrightarrow{BC} \cap \overrightarrow{CB}$
(c) $\overrightarrow{AC} \cup \overrightarrow{CA}$
(d) $\overset{\leftrightarrow}{BA} \cap \overrightarrow{BC}$

8. Given three noncollinear points *A*, *B*, and *C*, what kind of geometric figure—give a *name*, not a symbol—is each of the following?
   (a) *B*'s side of $\overleftrightarrow{AC}$
   (b) The intersection of *B*'s side of $\overleftrightarrow{AC}$ with *C*'s side of $\overleftrightarrow{AB}$
   (c) The intersection of $\overleftrightarrow{BC}$ with *C*'s side of $\overleftrightarrow{AB}$

9. Draw two angles that intersect in exactly three points. The union of those two angles separates their plane into how many pieces?

10. In Figure 11.99 points *A*, *O*, and *D* are collinear, as are points *B*, *O*, and *E*.
    (a) Find an angle that is adjacent to both $\angle COE$ and $\angle AOE$.
    (b) Find two angles, each of which forms a linear pair with $\angle AOB$.
    (c) Find all pairs of vertical angles.

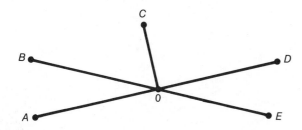

Figure 11.99

11. I am thinking of two angles in Figure 11.100 that form a linear pair. One of them and $\angle FOE$ are vertical angles. The other and $\angle AOC$ are adjacent angles. Name my two angles.

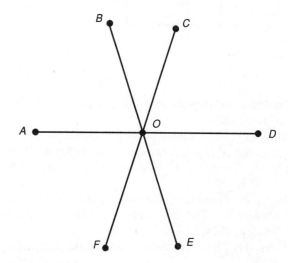

Figure 11.100

12. Sketch a closed curve that is not a simple closed curve.

13. Write all terms from the following list that apply to each plane figure: closed curve, connected, convex, hexagon, octagon, one-dimensional, polygon, simple closed curve, three-dimensional, two-dimensional, zero-dimensional.

(a)   (b)

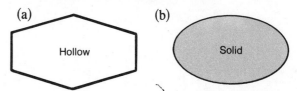

14. Sketch a nonconvex (solid) pentagon having three collinear vertices.

15. As you do this exercise keep in mind that going through a corner is not allowed.
    (a) Sketch a simple curve that cuts each of the nine segments in this diagram exactly once.
    (b) Explain why no simple closed curve could cut each of the nine segments exactly once.

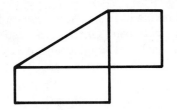

* 16. A (planar) graph has 50 vertices and 80 edges. Into how many pieces does it partition the plane?

* 17. Sketch a nontraceable (planar) graph that has as few vertices and as few edges as possible.

References

Chartrand, G. *Introductory Graph Theory*. New York: Dover, 1985.

Greenberg, M. *Euclidean and non-Euclidean Geometry*, 2nd ed. San Francisco: W. H. Freeman, 1980.

Hill, J. *Geometry for Grades K–6*. Reston, Va.: NCTM, 1987.

Moise, E. *Elementary Geometry from an Advanced Standpoint*. 2nd ed. Reading, Mass.: Addison-Wesley, 1974.

Myers, N. *The Math Book*. New York: Macmillan, 1975.

National Council of Teachers of Mathematics. *36th Yearbook: Geometry in the Mathematics Classroom*. Reston, Va.: NCTM, 1973.

―――――――――――――――――――――. *1987 Yearbook: Learning and Teaching Geometry, K–12*. Reston, Va.: NCTM, 1987.

Peressini, A., and D. Sherbert. *Topics in Modern Mathematics for Teachers*. New York: Holt, Rinehart and Winston, 1971.

12

Figure 12.1

MEASUREMENT

In the previous chapter we reviewed a variety of geometric figures and classified them on the basis of nonmetric properties, some of which—connectedness, dimension, and convexity—might have been unfamiliar. Nowhere did we use the ordinary metric concepts of length, area, volume, or angle measure. We actually had no way of distinguishing between the two figures in Figure 12.1. In this and the next chapter we remedy the deficiency by developing concepts that allow us to classify figures by size.

The *Standards* affirm the centrality of metric ideas in the middle school mathematics curriculum in these words: "As students progress through grades 5–8, they should develop more efficient procedures and, ultimately, formulas for finding measures. Length, area, and volume of one-, two-, and three-dimensional figures are especially important over these grade levels."

12.1 *Congruence and Rigid Motions*

The relationship between the ideas of congruence and measurement is a tricky one. On the one hand, congruence seems to be the more fundamental and intuitively accessible notion, and thus it makes a good foundation on which to build a theory of measurement. On the other hand, when a precise definition of congruence is required, resort is usually made to length and angle measurement concepts. In this section we content ourselves with an intuitive description of congruence. We use it as a basis for ensuing work on measurement. In the next chapter we will define congruence more rigorously.

Congruence of Plane Figures

Here is a first approximation to a definition of congruence.

Two figures are **congruent** if they have the same size and shape.

601

Figure 12.2

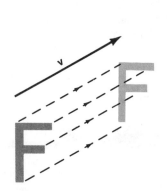

Figure 12.4 Congruent figures.

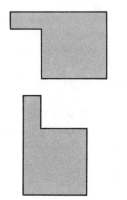

Figure 12.7 A translation along vector **v.**

The trouble with this definition is that the ideas of size and shape are fuzzy. For instance, do the two figures in Figure 12.2 have the same shape? Do the two figures in Figure 12.3 have the same size?

A second approximation, and one that is adequate for young children, is as follows:

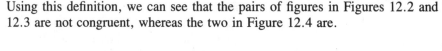

Two (plane) figures are **congruent** if one can be moved so that it coincides with the other.

Using this definition, we can see that the pairs of figures in Figures 12.2 and 12.3 are not congruent, whereas the two in Figure 12.4 are.

Figure 12.3

This second definition, while clearer, is still somewhat ambiguous. The trouble now is the slippery word *moved*. For example, in Figure 12.5 the wind could very well move cloud A so that it coincides with figure B, yet we would not call them congruent. Moving a stack of papers from one table to another usually changes the shape of the stack, too, as indicated in Figure 12.6. To tighten up the definition a bit more, we need to specify what moves are legal.

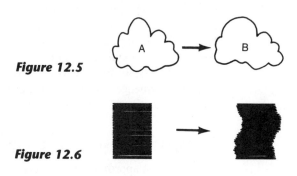

Figure 12.5

Figure 12.6

Rigid Motions

The first type of legal move is a slide, or a **translation.** See Figure 12.7. Notice that there is no twist or turn in a translation. The second type of legal move is a turn, or a **rotation.** See Figure 12.8. The third type of legal move is a flip, or a **reflection,** across a line. See Figure 12.9.

Figure 12.8 A rotation about point *P*.

Figure 12.9 A reflection across line ℓ.

Any translation, rotation, reflection, or composition (sequence, or hookup) of such moves is called a **rigid motion.** Thus our third approximation to a definition reads as follows:

> Two (plane) figures are **congruent** if one can be made to coincide with the other by means of a rigid motion.

EXAMPLE 1

The figures in Figure 12.10 are congruent because the black figure can be made to coincide with the red figure by this rigid motion: a translation 5 units to the right and 2 units up, followed by a 90° clockwise rotation about *P*. ❏

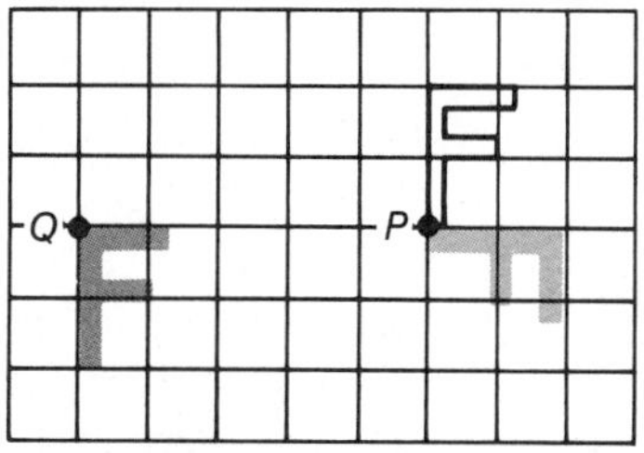

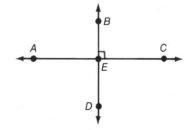

Figure 12.10

Two things should be noted about this example. First, there is nothing unique about the description of the rigid motion used. The two figures could also be made to coincide by first rotating the black figure 90° clockwise about *Q* and then translating 7 units right. (Try it.) Second, as you probably noticed, we used measurement concepts to specify moves: *5 units right, 2 units up, 90° clockwise*. So even our third definition is still imperfect. We will have to describe more precisely what is meant by each of the terms *translation*, *rotation*, and *reflection* before we can say that the concept of congruence has been defined. We will describe these terms in Section 13.5.

Figure 12.11 (p. 604) shows how composition of slides, flips, and turns is presented in a fifth-grade text. Do you see that region **a** could be superimposed on region **b** in just one simple move?

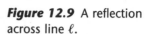

Figure 12.12   ❏

EXAMPLE 2

The symbol ⌐ in Figure 12.12 indicates that the two lines $\overleftrightarrow{AC}$ and $\overleftrightarrow{BD}$ are **perpendicular,** or meet at **right angles;** that is, they intersect so that adjacent angles are congruent. Describe two different rigid motions that will make ∠*AEB* coincide with ∠*CEB*.

Combining slides, flips, and turns

To fit region **a** below over region **b** we can combine slides, flips, and turns. Three moves are used to go from start to stop.

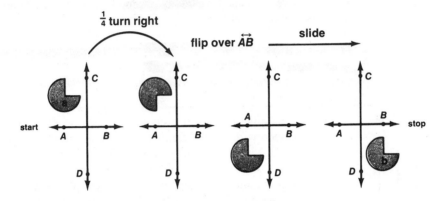

There is more than one way to fit region **a** over region **b**. We can go from start to stop in two moves, as shown below.

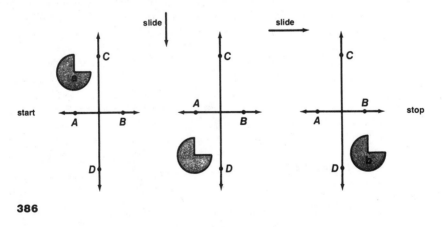

386

Figure 12.11 Rigid motions in a fifth-grade textbook.

Solution   One rigid motion is a reflection in the line $\overleftrightarrow{BD}$. A second rigid motion is a 90° clockwise rotation about E.

A useful classroom device for working with reflections of plane figures is a *Mira®,* a plastic transparent mirror that allows one to see simultaneously the original figure, its reflection image, and anything behind the mirror. See Figure 12.13. The lower edge of the Mira acts as the line of reflection.

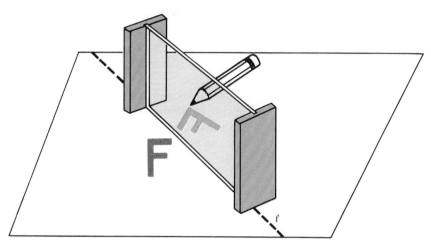

Figure 12.13 A Mira.   ❑

Congruence of Space Figures

For figures in space the problem of checking for congruence is more difficult. It is not possible to move two wooden blocks until they coincide. How would you decide if the two blocks in Figure 12.14 are congruent?

Here is one way. Since they are both cubes, they have the same shape. To conclude that they are congruent, you need only check that they have the same size as well. Probably the easiest way to do this is to push them together, as in Figure 12.15, and see if an edge of one is congruent to an edge of the other. A more complicated way would be to make a plaster cast of one (Figure 12.16) and see if the other fits into it exactly. This amounts to checking that they both can be made to occupy the same set of points in space.

The second method reminds us that figures in space are really sets of points or locations in space. They are not made of wood. There is no reason why we cannot think of these figures as being moved through each other to coincide, as in Figure 12.17. Thus it is reasonable to write a definition similar to the one for plane figures.

Figure 12.14

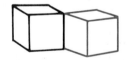

Figure 12.16

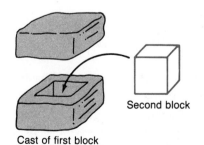

Cast of first block

Second block

Figure 12.15

Figure 12.17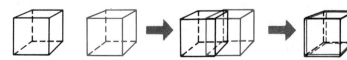

> Two space figures are **congruent** if they can be made to coincide by a sequence of translations, rotations, and reflections.

There is one striking difference between the situations in the plane and in space, however. Pictures of congruent figures in a plane can actually be moved around by a sequence of slides, turns, and flips until they coincide. This is *not* the case in space. Consider the block figure in Figure 12.18 and its reflection. (Notice that in space we reflect in a *plane,* whereas in the plane we reflected in a line.) According to our definition, these two figures are congruent. But if you think of picking them up and trying to make them coincide, you will soon discover that it cannot be done, even if you suppose that they can be slid through one another.

An application of reflecting solid figures, which would be particularly interesting to children, occurs in paleontology. To reconstruct a complete skeleton of a dinosaur from an incomplete set of fossilized bones it is frequently necessary to build mirror images of various body parts.

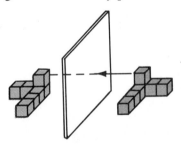

Figure 12.18

EXERCISE SET 12.1

1. Trace figure A of Figure 12.19 onto a sheet of translucent paper, and use the tracing to determine which of the figures B through F are congruent to A.

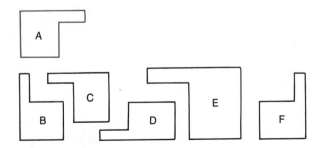

Figure 12.19

2. Print the 26 capital letters, and beside each one sketch its mirror image in a vertical line. See Figure 12.20. Which letters are indistinguishable from their mirror images? Use a Mira if one is available.

Figure 12.20   A⏐A   B⏐B   . . .

3. Print a three-letter word that is indistinguishable from its mirror image in a vertical line.

4. Sketch the image of figure A in Figure 12.21 under the translation specified by the vector **v**. Begin by sketching lines parallel to **v** through the vertices of *A*.

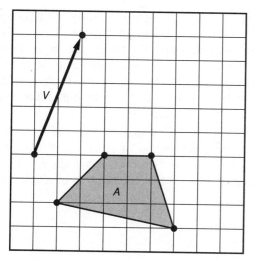

Figure 12.21

5. Sketch the image of figure A in Figure 12.22 under a 90° counterclockwise rotation about *P*. Use a translucent overlay and a pin.

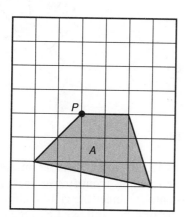

Figure 12.22

6. Sketch the image of figure A in Figure 12.23 under a reflection in line ℓ. Use a Mira if you have one.

7. Sketch the image of figure A in Figure 12.24 under this rigid motion: first translation by **v**, then clockwise rotation through 90° about *P*. Can you invent a different sequence of translations and rotations that will send *A* to the same position?

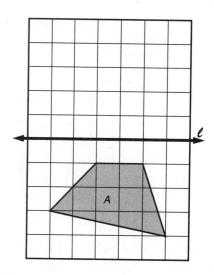

Figure 12.23

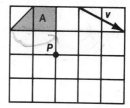

Figure 12.24

8. In Figure 12.25, sketch the image of △*ABC* under the following rigid motion: a 90° rotation clockwise about *B*, followed by a reflection in $\overleftrightarrow{EF}$, followed by the translation specified by the vector from *E* to *G*. In a word, how are △*ABC* and the image you just sketched related?

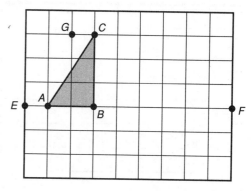

Figure 12.25

9. For Figure 12.26, describe a rigid motion of A that will make it coincide with B. Are figures A and B congruent?

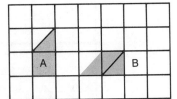

Figure 12.26

A Mira would be helpful in Exercises 10–13.

10. In Figure 12.27, sketch the image of figure A under the rigid motion of reflection in ℓ_1 followed by reflection in ℓ_2. Describe a single translation that is equivalent to this composition of reflections.

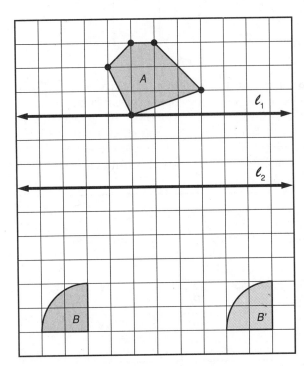

Figure 12.27

11. In Figure 12.27, figure B′ is the image of figure B under a translation. Identify two lines so that B is mapped onto B′ under the rigid motion, reflection in the first line followed by reflection in the second. Do you suppose that every translation can be accomplished by composing reflections in two parallel lines?

12. In Figure 12.28, sketch the image of figure A under the rigid motion of reflection in ℓ_1 followed by reflection in ℓ_2. Describe a single rotation that is equivalent to this composition of reflections.

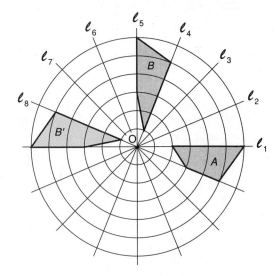

Figure 12.28

13. In Figure 12.28, figure B′ is the image of figure B under a rotation. Identify two lines so that B is mapped onto B′ under the rigid motion of reflection in the first line followed by reflection in the second. Do you suppose that every rotation can be accomplished by composing reflections in two intersecting lines?

14. Do you think that every rigid motion can be accomplished by composing sufficiently many reflections?

15. How would you go about deciding whether the geometric figures suggested by the pairs of real objects shown in Figure 12.29 are congruent?

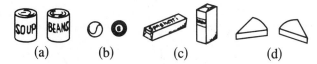

Figure 12.29

16. Refer to Figure 12.30 to answer each of the following questions.

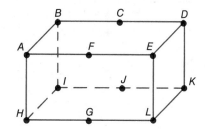

Figure 12.30

(a) Where does point *B* go under reflection in plane *FCJG*?

(b) Where does triangle *AHG* go under reflection in plane *FCJG*?

(c) Where does tetrahedron *AHGI* go under reflection in plane *FCJG*?

(d) Where does point *H* go under reflection in plane *BIGF*?

(e) Where does point *C* go under reflection in plane *AEKI*?

(f) Where does point *F* go under reflection in plane *AEKI*?

17. On a table are two sheets of translucent paper with geometric figures drawn on them, as shown in Figure 12.31.

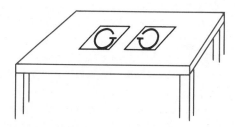

Figure 12.31

(a) You are asked to make the figures coincide, but you are forbidden to lift either piece of paper off the tabletop. That is, you are allowed to slide and turn but not to flip. Could you do it?

(b) If you were allowed to escape the two-dimensional tabletop and move the paper freely in three-dimensional space, could you make the figures coincide?

(c) Can you make the two wire figures in Figure 12.32 coincide? (Now you are allowed to slide and turn in space but not to reflect.)

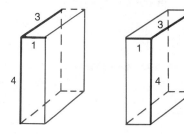

Figure 12.32

(d) Mathematicians study spaces of dimension greater than three. Do you think that if you could somehow escape three-dimensional space and work in four-dimensional space, you could then make the wire figures coincide?

18. For each of the pairs of figures in Figure 12.33, decide (i) whether they are congruent and if so (ii) whether a reflection is *required* to make them coincide.

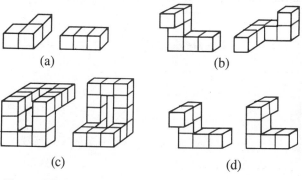

Figure 12.33

19. Two lines ℓ and m intersect in such a way that m coincides with its reflection image in ℓ. How are lines ℓ and m related?

20. Figure 12.34 shows two lines intersecting a plane. Line $\overleftrightarrow{AB}$ is said to be **perpendicular** to $\mathcal{E}$ because it is perpendicular to *every* line in $\mathcal{E}$ that passes through O. Line $\overleftrightarrow{CD}$ is not perpendicular to $\mathcal{E}$ because some lines in $\mathcal{E}$ passing through P are not perpendicular to $\overleftrightarrow{CD}$.

(a) How is $\overleftrightarrow{AB}$ related to its reflection image in $\mathcal{E}$?

(b) Are $\overleftrightarrow{CD}$ and its reflection image in $\mathcal{E}$ related in the same way?

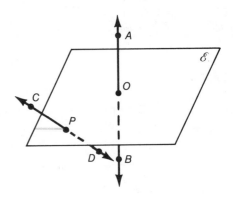

Figure 12.34

Computer Vignette J

Figures and their images under reflections, rotations, and translations can be drawn by using Logo. Figure 12.35 shows six Logo procedures (programs); the figures they produce are shown in Figure 12.36. Notice that the procedure TRIANGLE2 is just like the procedure TRIANGLE1 except that every right turn has been replaced by a left turn of the same degree measure. The procedure ARROWHEAD shows TRIANGLE1 and TRIANGLE2 as reflections of each other in a vertical line. The procedure TRANSLATION draws ARROW-HEAD and its image under a translation of length 60 units in the direction 70° right of straight up. The procedure ROTATION draws TRIANGLE1 and its image under a 60° clockwise rotation about its sharpest corner. Finally, the procedure FLOWER, which shows TRIANGLE1 and its images under successive rotations, gives a preview of some of the designs that are possible by using Logo. See Chapter 16 for other creations.

Figure 12.35

```
TO TRIANGLE1
    FORWARD 50
    RIGHT 60
    FORWARD 30
    RIGHT 141.8
    FORWARD 70
    RIGHT 158.2
END
```

Figure 12.36

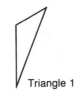

Triangle 1

**Figure 12.35
(continued)**

```
TO TRIANGLE2
   FORWARD 50
   LEFT 60
   FORWARD 30
   LEFT 141.8
   FORWARD 70
   LEFT 158.2
END

TO ARROWHEAD
   TRIANGLE1
   TRIANGLE2
END

TO TRANSLATION
   ARROWHEAD
   PENUP
   RT 70 FD 60 LT 70
   PENDOWN
   ARROWHEAD
END

TO ROTATION
   TRIANGLE1
   RIGHT 60
   TRIANGLE1
END

TO FLOWER
   REPEAT 6 [TRIANGLE1 RT 60]
END
```

Figure 12.36 (continued)

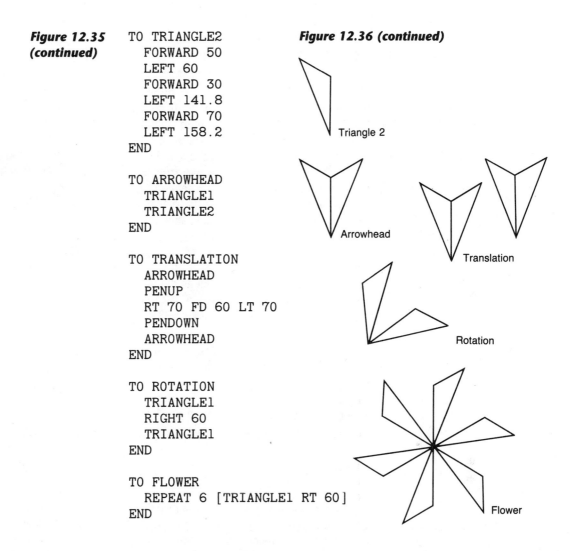

Triangle 2

Arrowhead

Translation

Rotation

Flower

12.2 *Measurement*

The variety of measurements that are made in the modern world is staggering. Time is measured in minutes, temperature in degrees Celsius, weight in grams, intelligence in IQ points, electric charge in coulombs, net worth in dollars, loudness in decibels, and so on. In this chapter we restrict ourselves to the measurement of geometric figures. The goal in geometric measurement is always the same: to describe the size of a given figure by comparing it with a standard figure of familiar size.

For example, if your mother were asked to measure the following segment, she might use her ruler and report that it is 4 in long:

If you were asked to do the same thing, you might report that it is about 10 centimeters (cm) long. Both of your replies would involve two things: a number (4 or 10) and a standard figure (inch or centimeter). These are the two essential ingredients in any measurement situation.

One obvious condition on the standard figure, or **unit of measure,** as it is called, is that it have the same dimension as the figure to be measured. Thus a farmer measures the *length* of a fence in *feet,* the *area* of a field in *acres,* and the *volume* of a corncrib in *bushels.* It would be absurd for him to try to measure the length of the fence in bushels, the area of the field in feet, or the volume of the corncrib in acres.

Having chosen a unit of measure, the next thing to do is to count how many copies of this unit are required to fill up the figure. For example, suppose triangle U in Figure 12.37 is chosen as the unit of measure, and figure A is the object to be measured. We cover A with congruent copies of U and count how many are required, as in Figure 12.38.

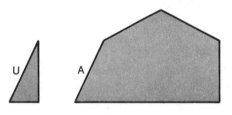

Figure 12.37

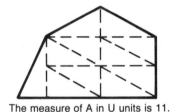

The measure of A in U units is 11.

Figure 12.38

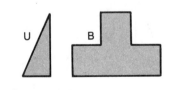

Figure 12.39

The process is complicated somewhat when the figure to be measured cannot be filled by copies of U. Consider, for example, figure B in Figure 12.39. In such cases we make the assumption that the size of a figure is unchanged if it is cut up and reassembled.* See Figure 12.40.

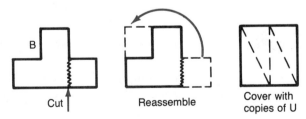

Cut   Reassemble   Cover with copies of U

The measure of B in U units is 4.

Figure 12.40

Figure 12.41

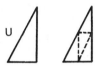

Figure 12.42

Another problem is posed by figure C in Figure 12.41. No amount of cutting and pasting will help here. So now we make a further reasonable assumption: Congruent figures have the same measure (in U units for any choice of U). We produce a lot of congruent copies of C and glue some, as shown in Figure 12.42. Thus four copies of C have U measure 1, so it is reasonable to say that

The measure of C in U units is $\frac{1}{4}$.

We can summarize our work so far with an arrow diagram, using m_U for the measure-in-U-units function:

$$A \xrightarrow{m_U} 11$$
$$B \xrightarrow{m_U} 4$$
$$C \xrightarrow{m_U} \tfrac{1}{4}$$

Soon we shall be looking at functions that measure length, area, and volume in a variety of units. All such functions share the following properties with the function m_U that we've just been studying.

> **Properties of Any Measure Function m**
>
> 1. The input set is a set of geometric figures.
> 2. The output set is a set of nonnegative numbers.
> 3. If A is congruent to B, then $m(A) = m(B)$.
> 4. If A and B have, at most, boundary points in common, then $m(A \cup B) = m(A) + m(B)$.

Property 3 (the **congruence** property) and property 4 (the **additivity** property) formalize our assumption that area is unchanged by cutting and pasting. We used both implicitly when we found the measure of B in Figure 12.40. Let's see how:

EXAMPLE 1 Refer to Figure 12.43 and use the properties of a measure function to explain why the measure of figure B is the same as the measure of figure S.

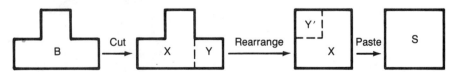

Figure 12.43

* This assumption is intuitively reasonable but difficult to justify mathematically. In fact, mathematicians have described techniques for cutting and reassembling figures that *do* change the sizes of the figures.

Solution $m(\text{B}) = m(\text{X} \cup \text{Y})$ substitution

$\quad = m(\text{X}) + m(\text{Y})$ property 4

$\quad = m(\text{X}) + m(\text{Y}')$ property 3 (and substitution)

$\quad = m(\text{X} \cup \text{Y}')$ property 4

$\quad = m(\text{S})$ substitution   ❏

In the next example we again use a nonstandard unit of measure, in accordance with a recommendation from the *Standards:* "If children's initial explorations use nonstandard units, they will develop some understanding about units and come to recognize the necessity of standard units in order to communicate."

EXAMPLE 2   In Figure 12.44 find the measure of $\triangle ABC$ in U units.

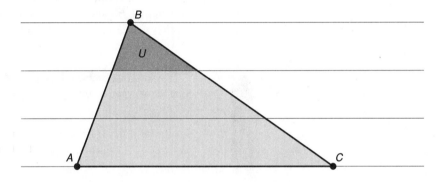

Figure 12.44

Solution   Draw two line segments parallel to $\overline{AB}$ and two parallel to $\overline{BC}$, as shown in Figure 12.45. The resulting partition of $\triangle ABC$ shows that its measure in U units is 9.

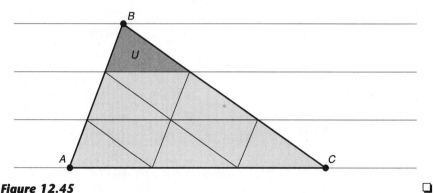

Figure 12.45   ❏

EXERCISE SET 12.2

1. Using U as unit of measure, find the measure of each of the figures A through E in Figure 12.46 by covering and counting.

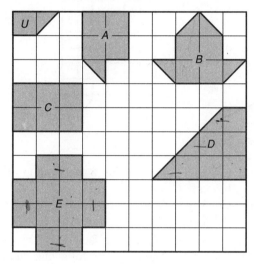

Figure 12.46

2. Let m_U stand for the measure-with-respect-to-U function of Exercise 1. Complete this arrow diagram for m_U:

Input Set	Set Including Output Set
A	1
B	2
C	3
D	4
E	5
U	6
	7
	8
	9

3. Find the U measure of each figure in Figure 12.47. If a figure needs to be cut and reassembled or replicated before it can be filled with copies of U, show how it could be done.

4. Find the U measure of each of the figures in Figure 12.47 by covering them with $\frac{1}{4}$ U units:

5. Counting can be thought of as a function n that accepts finite sets as inputs and produces whole numbers as outputs. Complete these statements of properties of the counting function that are analogous to properties 3 and 4 of measure functions.
   (a) If sets A and B are _____, then $n(A) = n(B)$.
   (b) If sets A and B are _____, then $n(A \cup B) = n(A) + n(B)$.

6. In one word, what property of measure functions underlies the statement that the surface area of a tin can is the sum of its curved surface area and the areas of its bases?

★ 7. Supply reasons in this argument that if m is a measure function and $A \subset B$, then $m(A) \leq m(B)$. For simplicity we denote $B \cap A'$ by $B - A$.
   (a) $m(B) = m[A \cup (B - A)]$ Why?

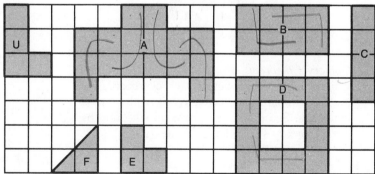

Figure 12.47

(b) $m[A \cup (B - A)] = m(A) + m(B - A)$
    Why?

(c) $m(B - A) \geq 0$ Why?

(d) $m(A) + m(B - A) \geq m(A) + 0$ Why?

(e) $m(B) \geq m(A)$ Why?

8. In the early years, before rulers are introduced, measuring is a process of covering and counting. A favorite classroom unit of length measure is the paper clip. Explain how paper clips can be used to illustrate the transition from covering and counting to using a ruler.

9. Two diagonally opposite corner squares have been removed from a checkerboard with 1-in by 1-in squares. You are given a large supply of 1-in by 2-in dominoes.

   (a) What is the measure of the mutilated board in domino units?

   (b) It is impossible to cover the mutilated board with dominoes. Can you prove it? (*Hint:* The squares in Figure 12.48 weren't given two colors for purely artistic reasons!)

Figure 12.48

★ 10. *Gomory's theorem:* If any black square and any white square are cut out of a checkerboard, the mutilated board can be covered with 1-by-2 dominoes. See if you can prove this theorem by using Gomory's diagram in Figure 12.49.

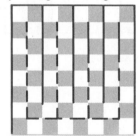

Figure 12.49

11. For measuring purposes one covering is as good as another. For other purposes that's not always the case. Figure 12.50 shows a 6-by-6 wall built from 1-by-2 bricks. Unfortunately, the wall has two fault lines.

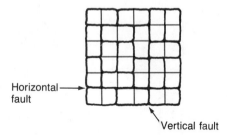

Horizontal fault

Vertical fault

Figure 12.50

(a) Build a fault-free 5-by-6 wall, using 1-by-2 bricks.

(b) Could you build a 5-by-5 wall, with or without faults, using 1-by-2 bricks?

12. It is impossible to build a fault-free 6-by-6 wall by using 1-by-2 bricks. The following questions suggest a proof.

   (a) How many potential fault lines are there in all?

   (b) What pattern do you discern in the number of bricks that span each of the potential fault lines in Figure 12.50?

   (c) Can any brick span more than one potential fault line?

   (d) How many bricks would be required to span all potential fault lines?

13. A knight can move on a chessboard as follows: either two squares horizontally followed by one vertically or two vertically followed by one horizontally. A "knight's tour" is a sequence of 63 moves that takes a knight to each of the 64 squares on the board. Prove that there is no knight's tour that begins at one corner of the board and ends at the diagonally opposite corner.

12.3 *Linear Measurement*

The first figures that we measure for length are *segments*. We begin by choosing a unit segment U. In Figure 12.51 we have chosen a centimeter for U. To measure a segment like $\overline{AB}$, we lay off copies of U, end-to-end, and count. We read $m_U(\overline{AB}) = 5$ as "the measure with respect to U of $\overline{AB}$ is 5." (To simplify our task, we usually use devices on which congruent copies of a unit are already stuck end-to-end and numbered. We call such devices *rulers*.)

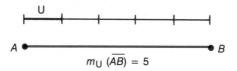

Figure 12.51

To measure a segment such as $\overline{CD}$ in Figure 12.52, we lay off copies of both $\overline{CD}$ and U until congruent segments result. Then we reason as follows:

$$3 = m_U(\overline{CE}) = m_U(\overline{CD} \cup \overline{DE}) \qquad \text{substitution}$$
$$= m_U(\overline{CD}) + m_U(\overline{DE}) \qquad \text{property 4 (additivity)}$$
$$= m_U(\overline{CD}) + m_U(\overline{CD}) \qquad \text{property 3 (congruence)}$$

Hence

$$3 = 2 \times m_U(\overline{CD}) \qquad \text{or} \qquad m_U(\overline{CD}) = \tfrac{3}{2}$$

Figure 12.52

The natural question suggested by our approach to measuring $\overline{CD}$ is: Could it be that there are segments U and V so that no matter how many copies of U and V are pasted together, the hash marks never line up? See Figure 12.53. The answer to this question is yes. There are such pairs of *incommensurable segments*. The classic examples follow.

Figure 12.53

EXAMPLE 1　The diameter and circumference of any circle are incommensurable segments, for if a whole number n copies of the diameter exactly coincided with a whole number m copies of the circumference (see Figure 12.54), we would have

$$n \cdot \text{diameter} = m \cdot \text{circumference}$$

that is
$$\text{Circumference} = \frac{n}{m} \cdot \text{diameter}$$

But
$$\text{Circumference} = \pi \cdot \text{diameter}$$

and π is an irrational number.

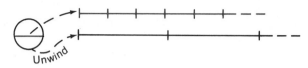

Figure 12.54　　　　　　　　　　　　　　　　　　　　　　　　　　❑

EXAMPLE 2　The diagonal and edge of a square are incommensurable segments. See Figure 12.55. Again, the reason is that the ratio of diagonal to edge is an irrational number, namely $\sqrt{2}$.

Figure 12.55　　　　　　　　　　　　　　　　　　　　　　　　　　❑

Since we now have at our disposal the full set of real numbers, irrational as well as rational, we can assert that no matter what unit is used (centimeter, inch, and so on), *every* segment has a length.

Segments are not the only figures to which lengths are assigned. **Polygonal curves** are assigned lengths in the obvious way, as shown in Figure 12.56.

When a length is assigned to a simple closed polygonal curve (a polygon), it is usually referred to as **perimeter.** (The prefix *peri-* means "around" and *-meter* comes from the Greek *metron,* meaning "measure.") Some perimeters are given in Figure 12.57.

Arc Length

Certain nonpolygonal curves are also assigned lengths. In the elementary and middle schools the only such curves that are considered are circles and arcs (connected subsets) of circles. (Lengths are assigned to a larger class of smooth curves in calculus, but the mathematical problems involved are very

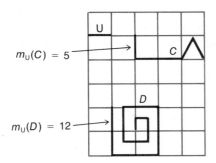

$m_U(C) = 5$

$m_U(D) = 12$

Figure 12.56

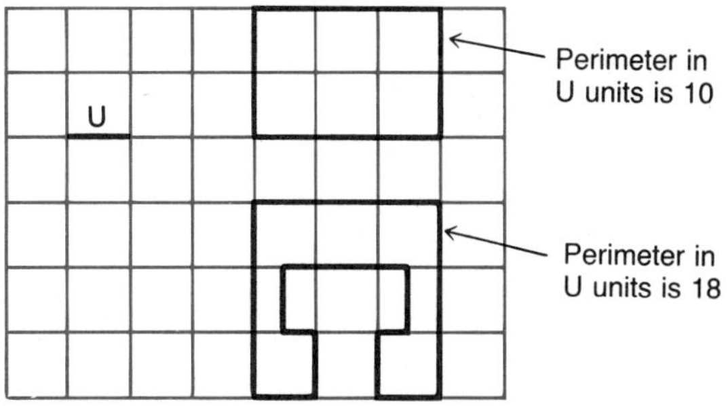

Perimeter in U units is 10

Perimeter in U units is 18

Figure 12.57

difficult.) We have mentioned before that the circumference (perimeter) of any circle (Figure 12.58) is just a constant multiple of its diameter, the constant being $\pi \doteq 3.14 \doteq \frac{22}{7}$. In symbols,

$$C = \pi d = 2\pi r$$

To calculate the length of an arc (Figure 12.58), we need to know what fraction it is of the whole circle and what the circumference (or diameter, or radius) of the full circle is. When the arc's fraction of the circle is not obvious, we have to work with the measure of its *central angle,* an idea that we haven't formally reviewed yet, but one that you might recall.

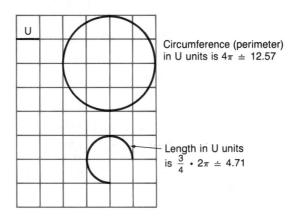

Circumference (perimeter) in U units is $4\pi \doteq 12.57$

Length in U units is $\frac{3}{4} \cdot 2\pi \doteq 4.71$

Figure 12.58

EXAMPLE 3   Find the length a of the circular arc shown in Figure 12.59.

Solution 1   Since there are 360° in a full circle, the arc shown is $\frac{40}{360}$ ths of the circle. Thus its length is

$$a = \frac{40}{360} \cdot 2\pi \cdot (3) = \frac{2\pi}{3} \doteq 2.09 \text{ cm}$$

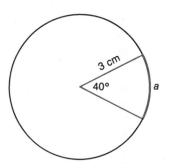

Figure 12.59

Solution 2   The first part of the preceding equation can be written as a proportion:

$$\frac{a}{2\pi \cdot 3} = \frac{40}{360}$$

It is read: "arc length is to circumference as central angle measure (in degrees) is to 360." Many people find the language of proportion a convenient guide for solving arc-length problems.   ❏

The Pythagorean Theorem

The Pythagorean theorem is probably the most famous and most important result in all of elementary geometry. Its consequences and generalizations are fundamental in trigonometry and in such higher mathematical fields as linear algebra, analysis, and topology. We introduce it here because it is a useful tool for the indirect measurement of length. We will examine it more fully in subsequent chapters.

EXAMPLE 4   A ramp is to be built from street level to a loading dock 7 ft above street level. The distance from the foot of the ramp to the base of the loading dock is to be 24 ft. See Figure 12.60. How long will the ramp be?

Solution   The Pythagorean theorem gives us a way of computing the unknown length in terms of the given dimensions. It tells us to square each of those dimensions,

$$7^2 = 49 \qquad 24^2 = 576$$

add,

$$49 + 576 = 625$$

and then take the square root,

$$\sqrt{625} = 25$$

The ramp will be 25 ft long.   ❏

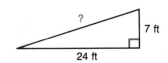

Figure 12.60

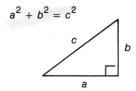

$$a^2 + b^2 = c^2$$

Figure 12.61 Pythagorean theorem.

Here is the general statement of the **Pythagorean theorem** (see also Figure 12.61).

> Given a *right triangle* (a triangle having one right angle), the square of the length of the *hypotenuse* (the side opposite the right angle) is equal to the sum of the squares of the lengths of the *legs* (the sides that form the right angle). That is,

An informal proof of this result is suggested by the diagrams in Figure 12.62. It makes use of the fact that the area of a square of side length s is s^2.

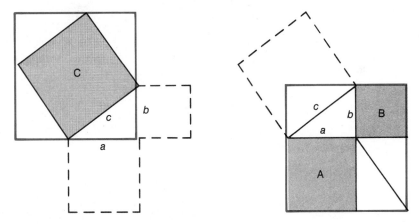

Figure 12.62

Since the two red squares shown in Figure 12.62 have the same areas, it follows that

Area of C + 4 · area of triangle =

area of A + area of B + 4 · area of triangle

Hence   Area of C = area of A + area of B

That is, $c^2 = a^2 + b^2$

EXERCISE SET 12.3

1. If you want to measure the length of the page you are reading with a 6-in ruler, which property of a measure function will you have to use?

2. Fill in missing outputs in the arrow diagram of Figure 12.63 for the measure-in-centimeters function m_{cm}. Use the additivity and congruence properties of a measure function whenever they are helpful. Assume that each grid square is 1 cm by 1 cm.

Input Set: Geometric Figures   Output Set: Numbers

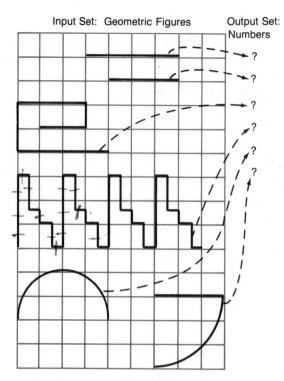

Figure 12.63

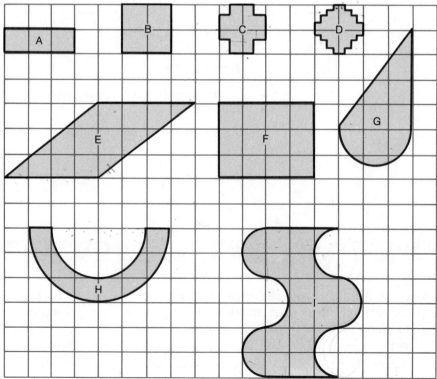

Figure 12.64

3. Find the perimeter (in centimeters) of each of the figures in Figure 12.64. Assume that each grid square is 1 cm by 1 cm.

4. First estimate, then find all missing dimensions.

(a)   (b)   (c)

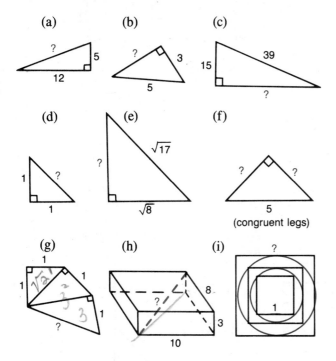

(d)   (e)   (f)

(congruent legs)

(g)   (h)   (i)

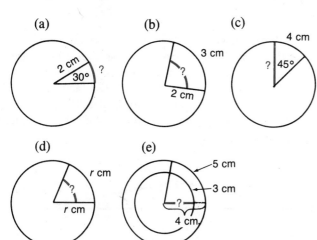

5. Fill in missing arc lengths, angle measures, or segment lengths.

(a)   (b)   (c)

(d)   (e)

6. Quito, Ecuador, and Kisumu, Kenya, both lie on the equator, Quito at 78° West Longitude and Kisumu at 35° East Longitude. What is the length of the shortest route from Quito to Kisumu? *Note:* The equatorial radius of the Earth is 6378.14 km.

7. A *paper-and-scissors activity illustrating the Pythagorean theorem:* In Figure 12.65, N is the center of square $AGIK$, $\overline{LH}$ is parallel to $\overline{AD}$, and $\overline{MJ}$ is perpendicular to $\overline{LH}$. Trace this pattern onto a piece of paper. Then, cut out square $DEFG$ and the four quadrilaterals $LAMN$, $NMGH$, $NHIJ$, and $NJKL$. Now, try to arrange these five cutouts so that they exactly cover square $ABCD$. How will this procedure illustrate the Pythagorean theorem?

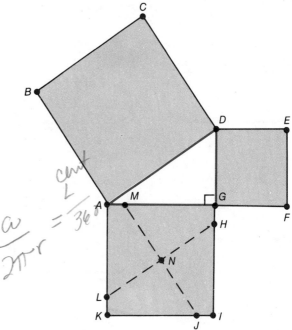

Figure 12.65

8. *An old standard:* A bug that cannot fly is sitting in one corner of the ceiling of a 9-ft by 12-ft room with a 7-ft ceiling. In the extreme opposite corner of the floor is a crumb. Describe the shortest path from the bug to the crumb. How long is it?

★ 9. Two electric toy cars race around these tracks along slots that are always 1 in apart. How much further must the car in the red slot travel during a one-lap race than the car in the black slot? (You may assume that all curves are either full circles, semicircles, or quarter circles.)

(h)

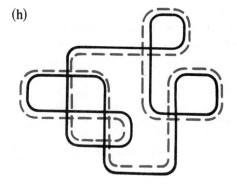

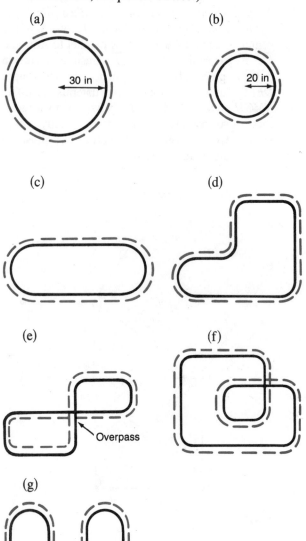

(a)

(b)

30 in

20 in

(c)

(d)

(e)

(f)

Overpass

(g)

★ 10. A Little Leaguer asks his mother to make him a home plate. According to her encyclopedia, an official plate is made from a square by making two 12-in cuts as shown in Figure 12.66 (p. 624). (The slanting sides lie along the first- and third-base lines.) What size square of plywood should she buy?

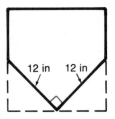

12 in   12 in

Figure 12.66

11. Two steel beams, each 100 ft long, are lying on the ground butted end to end, as shown in Figure 12.67. Their far ends are fixed so that they cannot move. Then the beams are heated, and each expands 1 in. in length, forcing the abutting ends to buckle and rise above the ground. How high would they rise?

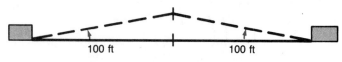

100 ft   100 ft

Figure 12.67

12. Suppose a tire of radius 1 ft picks up a piece of gravel at point A in Figure 12.68. As the wheel rolls along, the piece of gravel traces out a path called a *cycloid*. One arch of the cycloid is shown in red. Using techniques from calculus, it has been shown that the length of that arch is exactly eight times the radius of the circle. Thus, in our case, the red curve from A to B has length 8 ft. As the wheel rolls 1 mi down the road, how far does the piece of gravel travel?

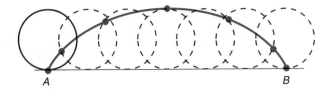

Figure 12.68 One arch of a cycloid.

12.4 *Area Measurement*

In theory, the basic ideas underlying the measuring of area are the same as those for length. One chooses a unit (square centimeter, square inch, and so on), covers the figure to be measured with congruent copies of that unit, and counts. In practice, however, measuring area in this way is much more tedious than measuring length. Consider, for example, the task of determining how many square feet of wall-to-wall carpeting are needed for a rectangular room. In theory, one would cover the floor with (paper?) copies of a square foot and count how many it took. In practice, no one does this. Instead one measures the length and the width of the room in feet, using a measuring tape (an easy task), and then multiplies the resulting numbers (also easy). That is, area *formulas* permit one to replace the tedious covering-and-counting process by the easy tasks of linear measurement and arithmetic.

Area Formulas

We have already had experience with the basic area formula for **rectangles** (see Figure 12.69). Remember that this formula applies only if both base and height are measured using the same linear unit, and then area will be given in the square of that unit. That is, the unit for area is a square with sides of length 1 linear unit.

$A = b \cdot h$

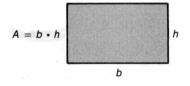

Figure 12.69

EXAMPLE 1   The area of a 4-cm by 3-cm rectangle is 12 square centimeters. See Figure 12.70.

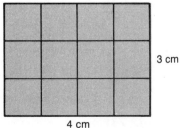

3 cm

Figure 12.70   4 cm   ☐

$A = b \cdot h$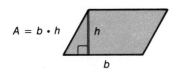

Figure 12.71

From the basic area formula for rectangles we can derive formulas for the areas of other common figures. The **area formula for parallelograms** is the same as for rectangles. See Figure 12.71.

$$A = b \cdot h$$

In using this formula, keep in mind that h refers to the *vertical* height of the parallelogram, *not* the length of one of its sides. The derivation of this formula is sketched in Figure 12.72. Notice the use of the assumption that area is not changed by cutting and pasting.

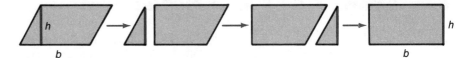

Figure 12.72

From the area formula for parallelograms we can derive, in turn, the **area formula for triangles** (Figure 12.74).

$$A = \tfrac{1}{2}b \cdot h$$

By the congruence property of measure functions and the area formula for parallelograms,

$$2 \cdot \text{area of T} = b \cdot h$$

so

$$\text{Area of T} = \tfrac{1}{2} \cdot b \cdot h$$

Again, in the area formula for triangles, the h refers to vertical height and a consistent set of units needs to be used for b, h, and A.

In Figures 12.73 and 12.74 we followed the usual practice of calling the "bottom" edge of the triangle the base. Any edge, though, can be called the base. The corresponding height, then, is measured to the opposite vertex. The following example illustrates the value of being able to choose a base at will.

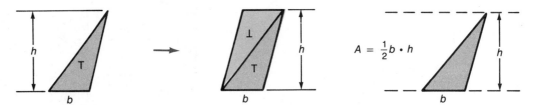

Figure 12.73　　　　　　　　　　　　　　　　**Figure 12.74**

EXAMPLE 2 In Figure 12.75 find the length x of $\overline{AC}$.

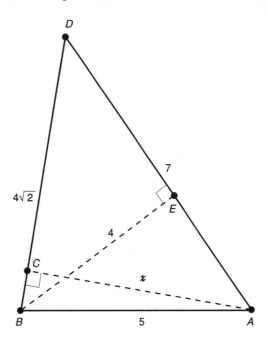

Figure 12.75

Solution Using $\overline{AD}$ as base and $\overline{EB}$ as height, we find that the area of $\triangle ABD$ is $\frac{1}{2}(7)(4) = 14$. Of course, we must get the same area if we use $\overline{BD}$ as base and $\overline{CA}$ as height. Thus

$$\tfrac{1}{2}(4\sqrt{2})(x) = 14$$

so

$$x = 7/\sqrt{2} \doteq 4.95 \qquad \square$$

Using the area formula for triangles, we can calculate the area of any **polygonal region** by triangulation, linear measurement, and arithmetic. See Figure 12.76.

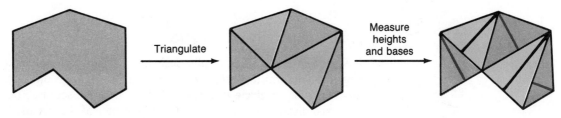

Figure 12.76

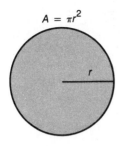

$$A = \pi r^2$$

Figure 12.77

The area formula for triangles can also be used to give a plausible derivation of the formula for the **area of a circle** (see Figure 12.77).

$$A = \pi r^2$$

We begin the derivation by chopping up the circle into a great number of very thin sectors $S_1, S_2, S_3, \ldots$ and letting $b_1, b_2, b_3, \ldots$ be the lengths of their (nearly straight) arcs, as in Figure 12.78. Now we observe that each of these sectors is very nearly a triangle of height r. Thus

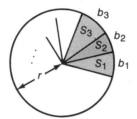

Figure 12.78

$$\text{Area of circle} = \text{area of } S_1 + \text{area of } S_2 + \text{area of } S_3 + \cdots$$
$$\doteq \tfrac{1}{2}b_1 r + \tfrac{1}{2}b_2 r + \tfrac{1}{2}b_3 r + \cdots$$
$$= \tfrac{1}{2}r(b_1 + b_2 + b_3 + \cdots)$$
$$= \tfrac{1}{2}r(2\pi r) = \pi r^2$$

The area of a **sector** of a circle can be found by a proportion technique similar to the one we used to determine the length of an arc.

EXAMPLE 3   Find the area of the sector shown in Figure 12.79.

Solution   The area of S is to the area of the entire circle as the measure (in degrees) of the central angle of S is to 360°. That is,

$$\frac{\text{Area of S}}{\pi \cdot 6^2} = \frac{40}{360}$$

$$\text{Area of S} = \frac{\pi \cdot 6 \cdot 6 \cdot 40}{360} = 4\pi \text{ (square centimeters)} \qquad \square$$

A Word About Language

Precision in language is usually desirable in mathematics, but sometimes it is better to conform to everyday usage. That is what we did in this section on area formulas. A **circle** is formally defined to be the set of all points in a plane at a fixed distance from a given point (the center of the circle). Thus a circle is a one-dimensional figure and has zero area. When we spoke of the "area of

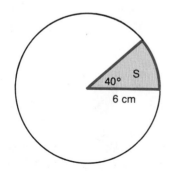

Figure 12.79

a circle" we meant the area of the two-dimensional region bounded by the circle, a region that is sometimes called a **disk.** Similar comments apply to the phrases "area of a rectangle," "area of a parallelogram," and so on.

Surface Area

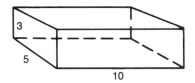

Figure 12.80

So far our discussion of area has been limited to planar figures. Certain other figures can be assigned *surface areas* in a natural way. For example, the surface area of a 3-in by 5-in by 10-in tissue box (Figure 12.80) is found by computing the areas of its two ends (15 square inches each), its front and back (30 square inches each), and its top and bottom (50 square inches each), and then calculating the sum: total surface area is 190 square inches.

When the figure under consideration has curved surfaces, the problems are more complicated.

EXAMPLE 4   Find the area of the curved surface of an auto muffler (Figure 12.81) of girth 20 in and length 30 in.

Figure 12.81

Solution   Imagine cutting the muffler along the dotted line and rolling it out flat. The resulting figure would be a 20-in by 30-in rectangle. Thus the curved surface has area 600 square inches.   ❑

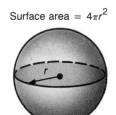
Surface area = $4\pi r^2$

Figure 12.82

For some very special surfaces, area formulas exist. In the exercises you are asked to derive a few. A rather surprising one, which we will accept without proof, is the formula for the **surface area of a sphere** (see Figure 12.82):

$$SA = 4\pi r^2$$

That is, the surface area of a sphere is exactly four times the area of a cross section formed by a plane through its center.

EXERCISE SET 12.4

1. Using the longest edge of a dollar bill as the unit, measure the length and the width of a sheet of your notebook paper to the nearest half-dollar.

Using the face of the dollar bill as the unit, measure the area of the notebook paper. Does length times width equal area? Why?

2. Find the area in square centimeters of each figure.

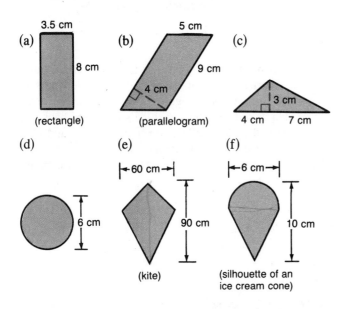

(a)

3.5 cm

8 cm

(rectangle)

(b)

5 cm

9 cm

4 cm

(parallelogram)

(c)

3 cm

4 cm   7 cm

(d)

6 cm

(e)

|← 60 cm →|

90 cm

(kite)

(f)

|← 6 cm →|

10 cm

(silhouette of an
ice cream cone)

3. Find the area in square centimeters of each of the figures in Exercise 3, Section 12.3.

4. Determine the missing dimension x in Figure 12.83.

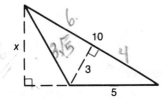

6.

3.5

10

x

3

4

5

Figure 12.83

5. Find the area in square centimeters of each of these sectors.

(a)

72°

5 cm

(b)

6 cm

160°

(c)

10 cm

6 cm

6. Find the area of the region shown in Figure 12.84.

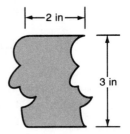

|← 2 in →|

3 in

Figure 12.84

7. You plan to re-roof your house and need to know how many shingles to order. How many square feet of roof does the house shown in Figure 12.85 have? Two feet of roof overhang all four sides of the house.

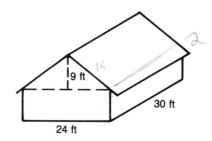

9 ft

15

2

30 ft

24 ft

Figure 12.85

8. Find the area of the shaded region in Figure 12.86.

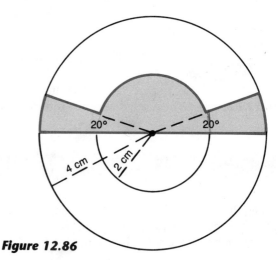

20°   20°

4 cm   2 cm

Figure 12.86

9. Derive a formula for the area of the **trapezoid** shown in Figure 12.87. (The top and bottom edges are parallel.)

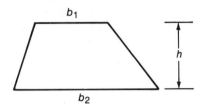

Figure 12.87

10. There is a remarkable formula known as **Heron's formula** that expresses the area of a triangle in terms of the lengths of its three sides. It is particularly useful when finding a height for a triangle would be inconvenient. The formula is

$$A = \sqrt{s(s-a)(s-b)(s-c)}$$

where A is the area; a, b, and c are the side lengths; and s is the *semiperimeter:* $s = \frac{1}{2}(a+b+c)$. Calculate the areas of the following triangles.

(a)

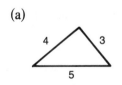

(b)

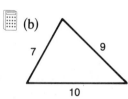

(c)

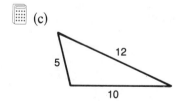

(d)

11. Use your answer to Exercise 10(d) to find the height of that equilateral triangle.

12. The tax assessor needs to know the acreage of Ms. Fields' farm. He has measured its four sides and one diagonal and has arrived at the dimensions (in yards) shown in Figure 12.88. What is its area in acres? (1 acre = 4840 yd^2)

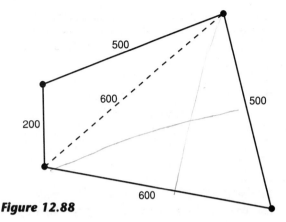

Figure 12.88

13. First estimate, then use a ruler and triangulation to find the area of the polygonal region shown in Figure 12.89. Use Heron's formula if you want to avoid measuring heights.

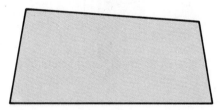

Figure 12.89

★ 14. *L. Kolnowski's theorem:* "For every $n(n > 3)$ there is an n-gon that can be completely triangulated by drawing just one segment." Draw polygons to show that this is true.

15. How many 2-in by 3-in by 8-in bricks will you need to build a (uniformly wide) brick walk with the shape shown in Figure 12.90? (Lay them so that the largest face is up.)

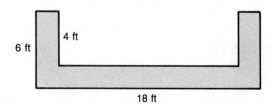

Figure 12.90

16. How many square centimeters of construction paper are required to make a tube like the one in Figure 12.91? Make no allowance for overlap.

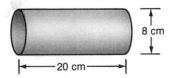

Figure 12.91

17. Figure 12.92 shows a *right circular cylinder*.
    (a) Write a formula for its lateral (side) surface area.
    (b) Write a formula for its total surface area.

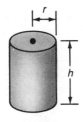

Figure 12.92

★ 18. How many square centimeters of construction paper are required to make a paper cup like the one shown in Figure 12.93? Make no allowance for overlap. *Hint:* Consider the pattern you would cut out to roll up into the cup.

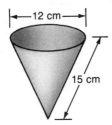

Figure 12.93

19. Write a formula for the lateral surface area of a *right circular cone* (Figure 12.94) of radius r and slant height s.

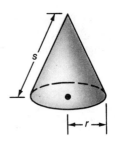

Figure 12.94

20. Find the total surface area of the wooden toadstool with a hemispherical cap shown in Figure 12.95. The problem-solving strategy of establishing subgoals should be useful here.

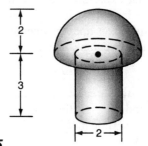

Figure 12.95

21. The diameter of the moon is about one-fourth that of the Earth. How do the surface areas compare?

22. You just finished painting your garage (see Figure 12.96), and it took exactly 2 quarts (qt) of paint. How much paint should you buy to paint your house (ignore windows)?

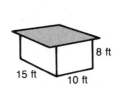
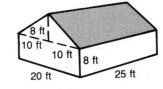

Figure 12.96

23. *A paper-and-scissors activity for deducing the formula for the area of a circle:* Cut out a large paper circle and cut it into many thin sectors. Now, arrange those sectors into a figure that is

nearly a parallelogram, as shown in Figure 12.97. Find the base, height, and area of that "parallelogram" in terms of the radius r of the original circle.

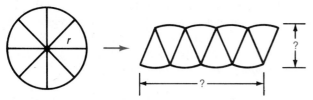

Figure 12.97

24. Complete the following proof of the Pythagorean theorem (use Figure 12.98):
Area of large square
= area of small square + 4 · area of triangle
$$(a + b)^2 = \underline{\quad?\quad} + \underline{\quad?\quad}$$
:
:

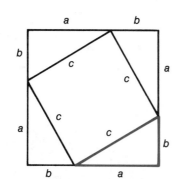

Figure 12.98

★ 25. Pennies are arranged on a table as shown in Figure 12.99. The table is so large that what happens

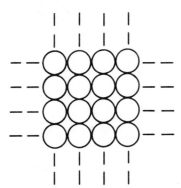

Figure 12.99

at the edges is insignificant. What percent of the table is covered by pennies?

26. Repeat Exercise 25 for the arrangement shown in Figure 12.100.

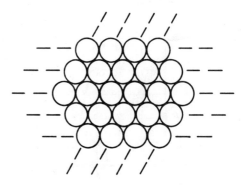

Figure 12.100

27. Explain why regions A (shaded red) and B (unshaded) in Figure 12.101 have the same area. (Regions C and D are semicircles.)

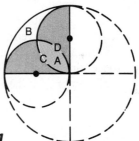

Figure 12.101

★ 28. Figure 12.102 shows a grid of unit squares and a polygon having all of its vertices at lattice points of the grid. About a hundred years ago the German mathematician Georg Pick discovered a beautiful formula for calculating the area A of such a *lattice polygon* from just two easily determined numbers: I, the number of lattice points in the interior of the polygon, and B, the number of lattice points on its boundary. Your task is to rediscover the relationship among A, I, and B. For the polygon shown, $B = 7$ and $I = 10$ by inspection. To find A takes a little work. Cut the poly-

gon up into convenient pieces—perhaps two triangles *PQN* and *RLM* and one rectangle *QRMN*—
and sum their areas: $5 + 2\frac{1}{2} + 5 = 12\frac{1}{2}$. Draw
some more lattice polygons, record B, I, and A,
and look for a pattern.

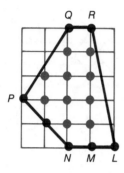

Figure 12.102

★ 29. A perhaps surprising fact is that the surface area
of a spherical *zone* (see Figure 12.103) depends
only on its (vertical) height h and the radius r of
the sphere, *not* on how near or far it is from the
equator. Thus, for example, if a spherical tomato
of diameter 8 cm is cut into eight slices, each
1 cm thick, each slice will have the same amount
of peel. Use this fact and the formula for the surface area of the entire sphere to deduce a formula, in terms of r and h, for the surface area of
a zone.

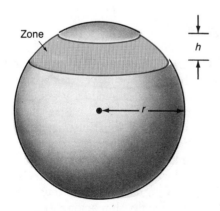

Figure 12.103

★ 30. Refer to Figure 12.104 and explain why the
square of the length of a segment R in a plane is
equal to the sum of the squares of the lengths of
its "shadows" (S_1 and S_2) on two perpendicular
lines in that plane. What do you suppose is the relationship between the area of a plane region R in
space and the areas of its "shadows" (S_1, S_2, and
S_3) on three perpendicular planes in space? (See
Figure 12.105.)

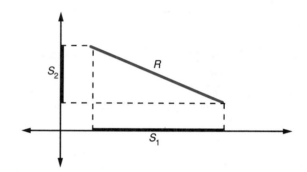

Figure 12.104

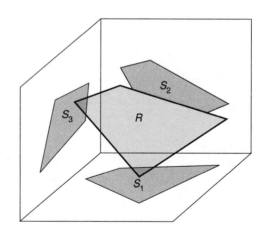

Figure 12.105

12.5   *Volume Measurement*

To determine what size window air conditioner to buy for a room, one must know how many cubic feet of space it will have to cool. In theory, one could fill the room with (styrofoam?) copies of a cubic foot and count how many are required. In practice, volumes are rarely determined by filling and counting. As in the case of area measurement, formulas are available that reduce this problem, and many other problems of volume measurement, to the simpler tasks of linear measurement and arithmetic.

Some Definitions

Before we give the volume formulas for common figures in space, we review some definitions.

A (closed, hollow) **cylinder** is the union of (1) two congruent simple closed curves that lie in parallel planes and are oriented so that all the line segments joining corresponding points are parallel to each other; (2) all those line segments; and (3) the interiors of the simple closed curves. The two simple closed curves and their interiors make up the **bases**; the line segments make up the **lateral surface**. The cylinder is called a **right cylinder** if the line segments are perpendicular to the bases. The shape of the base is often included in the name of the cylinder. For example, when we call the usual tin can a **right circular cylinder,** the word *circular* gives the shape of the base. See Figure 12.106. If the bases are **polygons**, then the cylinder is called a **prism.** See Figure 12.107.

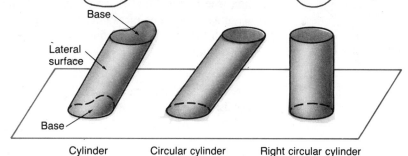

Figure 12.106 Cylinders.

Cylinder   Circular cylinder   Right circular cylinder

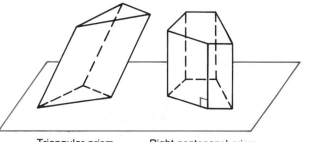

Figure 12.107 Prisms.

Triangular prism   Right pentagonal prism

A (closed, hollow) cone is the union of (1) a simple closed curve in a plane, (2) a point not in that plane, (3) all line segments joining that point to points of the simple closed curve, and (4) the interior of the simple closed curve. The simple closed curve and its interior constitute the base of the cone; the line segments, its lateral surface. The common endpoint of the line segments is called the apex (or vertex) of the cone. The most familiar cone is the **right circular cone**, which has a circular base and has its apex directly over the center of that circle. In Figure 12.108, $\overleftrightarrow{AO}$ is perpendicular to the base. If the base is a polygon, the cone is called a **pyramid.**

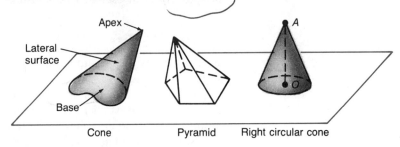

Figure 12.108 Cones and a pyramid.

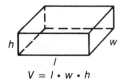

$V = l \cdot w \cdot h$

Figure 12.109

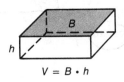

$V = B \cdot h$

Figure 12.110

Volume Formulas

The basic volume formula is the formula $V = l \cdot w \cdot h$ for a **right rectangular prism**, or box, (Figure 12.109). Since $l \cdot w$ gives the area B of the base of the box (see Figure 12.110), an equivalent formula is $V = B \cdot h$. Again, all of l, w, and h need to be measured in the same unit, and then V will be given in the cube of that unit. That is, the unit for volume is a cube with edges of length 1 linear unit.

EXAMPLE 1   The volume of a 3-cm by 4-cm by 6-cm box is 72 cubic centimeters. See Figure 12.111.

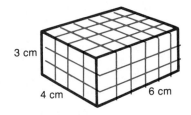

Figure 12.111   ❏

EXAMPLE 2   The volume of a box of height 3 cm and base 10 square centimeters is 30 cubic centimeters. See Figure 12.112.   ❏

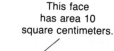

This face
has area 10
square centimeters.

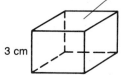

3 cm

Figure 12.112

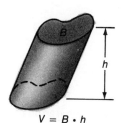

$V = B \cdot h$

Figure 12.114

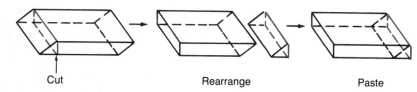

Cut   Rearrange   Paste

Figure 12.113

The same formula $V = B \cdot h$ holds for an *arbitrary*—not necessarily right—rectangular prism, as Figure 12.113 shows. (This reconstruction should be very reminiscent of the one we did for parallelograms.) In fact, the formula applies to arbitrary cylinders, such as the one shown in Figure 12.114. In summary, the **volume of any cylinder** is given by the formula.

$$V = B \cdot h \qquad \ast$$

where B is the area of its base and h is its height.

The spatial analog of a triangle is a tetrahedron (Figure 12.115), or, more generally, a pyramid, or, still more generally, a cone (Figure 12.116).

Figure 12.115

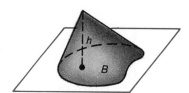

Figure 12.116

The formula for the **volume of any cone** is

$$V = \tfrac{1}{3}B \cdot h$$

where B is the area of the base and h is the vertical height of the apex above the base. (A proof of this result in the case of a special tetrahedron is asked for in Exercise 16.) You might remember this formula $\tfrac{1}{3}Bh$ as the 3-dimensional analog of the formula $\tfrac{1}{2}bh$ for (2-dimensional) triangles.

A sphere is the set of all points in space at a fixed distance from a given point called its center. It is interesting to do for spheres what we did for circles. For circles we assumed the circumference formula $C = \pi \cdot d$, chopped the circle into many pieces that looked like triangles, and derived the area formula $A = \pi r^2$. For spheres we shall assume the surface area formula,

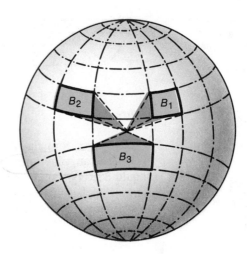

Figure 12.117

$SA = 4\pi r^2$, chop the sphere into many pieces that look like pyramids (Figure 12.117), and derive the **volume formula for a sphere**

$$V = \tfrac{4}{3}\pi r^3$$

as follows:

Volume of sphere = volume of "pyramid" 1 + volume of "pyramid" 2
                          + volume of "pyramid" 3 + · · ·

$$\doteq \tfrac{1}{3}B_1 h + \tfrac{1}{3}B_2 h + \tfrac{1}{3}B_3 h + \cdots$$
$$= \tfrac{1}{3}h(B_1 + B_2 + B_3 + \cdots)$$
$$= \tfrac{1}{3}r(4\pi r^2) = \tfrac{4}{3}\pi r^3$$

Pappus's Theorem (Optional)

Over 1600 years ago the Greek mathematician Pappus stated a remarkable formula for the volume of doughnutlike figures like the one in Figure 12.119. The formula involves the idea of "center of gravity" of a planar region. Imagine that the planar region A is made from a thin piece of cardboard. Its center of gravity is the point at which it would balance on a sharp nail. See Figure 12.118.

For nice figures the center of gravity is obvious. For example, the center of gravity of a circle is its ordinary center, and the center of gravity of a rectangle is the point where its diagonals cross. Imagine now that the region A is revolved about a line ℓ that lies in its plane but does not cut across it. A doughnutlike solid called a *torus* is swept out, as shown in Figure 12.119. Pappus's formula states the following.

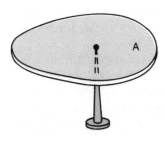

Figure 12.118

> The **volume of a torus** is the product of the area of cross-sectional region A and the distance traveled by its center of gravity.

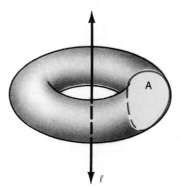

Figure 12.119

EXAMPLE 3   A circle of radius 3 cm is revolved about a line in its plane and 5 cm from its center. Find the volume of the torus (doughnut) generated.

Solution   Make a sketch (Figure 12.120) and use Pappus's formula:

$$\text{Volume} = \text{area of cross section} \times \text{distance traveled by center of gravity}$$
$$= (\pi \cdot 3^2) \times (2 \cdot \pi \cdot 5) = 90\pi^2 \text{ cubic centimeters} \quad \square$$

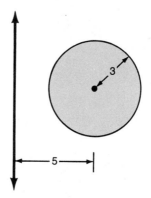

Figure 12.120

EXERCISE SET 12.5

A calculator is strongly recommended for this exercise set.

1. Fill in each blank with one of the words *cone, cylinder, prism, pyramid.*

(a) Every pyramid is a _____ .
(b) A _____ is a special kind of cylinder.
(c) A _____ with a polygonal base is a prism.
(d) A cone with a polygonal base is a _____ .

2. Determine the capacity of each figure.
   (a) The box shown in Figure 12.121

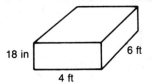

Figure 12.121

   (b) The watering trough shown in Figure 12.122

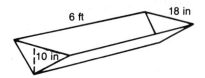

Figure 12.122

   (c) The house shown in Figure 12.123

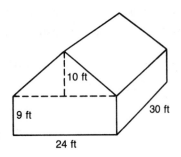

Figure 12.123

3. Find the volume of each figure.
   (a) The pyramid in Figure 12.124

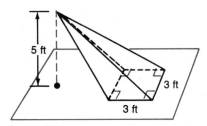

Figure 12.124

   (b) The truncated pyramid shown in Figure 12.125. (The missing apex stands directly over the centers of the square bases.)

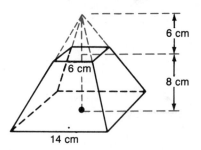

Figure 12.125

4. Find the volume of the truncated right circular cylinder in Figure 12.126.

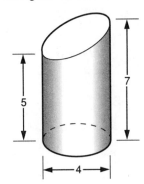

Figure 12.126

5. The planes in Figure 12.127 are parallel. Which pyramid has the greater volume, *ABCD* or *EBCD*? Which has the greater surface area?

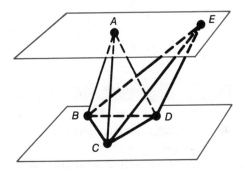

Figure 12.127

Pappus

Hypatia

❧ **PAPPUS OF ALEXANDRIA** (ca. A.D. 350) was the last of the major Greek mathematicians who studied, taught, and wrote at the great library in Alexandria, Egypt. Alexandria was founded by Alexander the Great in 332 B.C., and soon afterwards Ptolemy I began the construction of a university there. The great library was developed by Ptolemy II and Ptolemy III in the 200s B.C., and it eventually housed over 600,000 scrolls. Euclid (ca. 300 B.C.) was probably the first professor of mathematics and established Alexandria as the mathematical center of the ancient world. Archimedes (ca. 287–212 B.C.), the greatest mathematician of antiquity, undoubtedly spent some time at Alexandria, since he counted Eratosthenes, the chief librarian, among his friends. Other notable mathematicians and astronomers who worked at Alexandria were Apollonius (ca. 262–200 B.C.), Hipparchus (ca. 140 B.C.), Menelaus (ca. A.D. 100), Claudius Ptolemy (ca A.D. 150), and Diophantus (possibly ca. A.D. 300).

By the time Pappus arrived in Alexandria, creative work in geometry had been in steady decline for many years. Pappus strove unsuccessfully to rekindle the flame. His comprehensive treatise *Mathematical Collection,* a summary of large portions of the mathematics of antiquity including many of his own discoveries, is the source of much of our knowledge of Greek geometry. Howard Eves refers to it as "the requiem of Greek geometry." After Pappus, mathematics was perpetuated at Alexandria by lesser figures. One, Theon of Alexandria, wrote a minor revision of Euclid's *Elements,* which is the surviving version on which modern translations are based.

The story of Theon's daughter, Hypatia (370–415), provides the first historical mention of a woman mathematician. In addition to being a mathematician, Hypatia was also a philosopher and a defender of the old culture against Christianity, which had gained momentum with the conversion of the fourth-century Roman emperors. Bent on eradicating "pagan science," Christian mobs destroyed 300,000 scrolls at Alexandria and then turned to murdering the scholars as well. Hypatia was seized on her way from classes, slashed with oyster shells, and finally dismembered and burned.

In 529 Emperor Justinian permanently closed the university at Alexandria. In 641 the Moslems captured Alexandria from the Christians and completed the destruction of the library, the remaining scrolls being parceled out for use as fuel at public baths.

6. The previous exercise asked questions about figures in space. Pose (and answer) corresponding questions about figures in a plane by deciding what planar concepts are analogous to: parallel planes, pyramids that share a base, volume of a pyramid, and surface area of a pyramid.

7. A guest at your party claims that his paper cup (the righthand one in Figure 12.128) is only half full. What *should* he say?

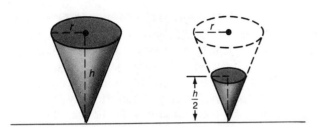

Figure 12.128

8. Pose (and answer) a question about planar figures that is analogous to the question in Exercise 7.

★ 9. Find the volume of the pyramid (with square base) shown in Figure 12.129; each of the eight edges is 5 ft long. Here D is the center of the base, and A stands directly over D.

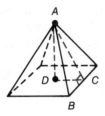

Figure 12.129

10. Finding the volume or surface area of a complicated figure provides excellent experience in the problem-solving strategy of breaking a tough problem down into several more manageable ones. Find the volume, in cubic centimeters, and the total surface area, in square centimeters, of each of the following figures. All dimensions are in centimeters. Leave your answers in terms of π.

(a)

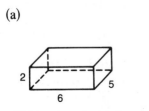

Right rectangular prism   Solid hemisphere

(c)

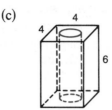

Block of wood (4 by 4 by 6) with a hole of diameter 2 bored through it as shown.

(d)

Pyramid with square base and apex directly over its left rear corner.

★ (e)

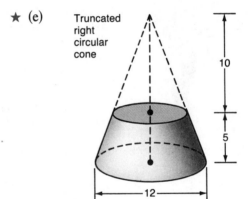

Truncated right circular cone

(f)

Note: In this instance volume refers to the amount of rind, not to its capacity to hold orange juice.

Hemispherical orange rind 0.5 thick

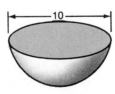

11. If you were to step on the orange rind in Exercise 10 (f), the result would be roughly a cylinder of height 0.5 cm and base perhaps the average of the

areas of the formerly inner and outer hemispherical surfaces. See Figure 12.130. Calculate the volume of that cylinder and compare your result with the volume you computed in Exercise 10 part (f).

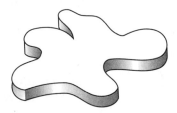

Figure 12.130

12. A jeweler wishes to plate completely a thin hemispherical bowl of diameter 14 cm with a layer of gold 0.1 cm thick. If 1 cubic centimeter of gold weighs 19.3 g and gold costs $1.10 per gram, about how many dollars worth of gold will he use?

13. After sharpening a (right circular cylindrical) pencil in sharpener A, you decide to sharpen it again in sharpener B. See Figure 12.131. What volume of wood and lead is ground away by sharpener B?

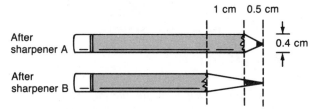

Figure 12.131

14. How many gallons of paint are needed to paint the silo shown in Figure 12.132, with hemispherical cap, if 1 gal covers 500 square feet?

15. The circumference of the earth is about 25,000 mi. The area of the United States is about 3,600,000 square miles.
   (a) What is the approximate surface area of the earth?

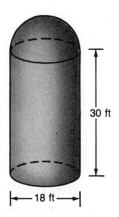

Figure 12.132

   (b) The United States covers about what percent of the earth's surface?

16. *A paper-and-scissors activity for showing that the volume of one particular cone is given by formula $V = \frac{1}{3}B \cdot h$.* Make three copies of the pattern shown in Figure 12.133. Then cut, fold, and tape each one into a tetrahedron. Now, arrange these three tetrahedra into a cube. Conclude that for this particular tetrahedron
   Volume $= \frac{1}{3} \cdot$ volume of cube $= \frac{1}{3} \cdot$ base $\cdot$ height

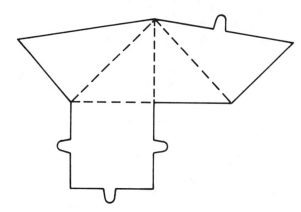

Figure 12.133

17. Use Pappus's formula to find the volume of a doughnut with inner radius 2 cm, outer radius 5 cm, and circular cross section.

18. A piece of heavy lead pipe has inner diameter 4 cm, outer diameter 6 cm, and length 5 cm. Find its volume.
    (a) By Pappus's formula
    (b) By the volume formula for cylinders

19. Think of rotating a segment of length r through 360° about one of its endpoints. Formulate a Pappus-like theorem about the area of the region swept out, and validate it by using a known area formula.

★ 20. Find the center of gravity of a semicircular region of radius r. (*Hint:* Revolve the region about its diameter, and use the known formula for the volume of a sphere.)

21. There is also a Pappus formula for the surface area of doughnutlike figures. It depends on the idea of center of gravity of a simple closed curve. Think of a simple closed curve as being made of wire and bounding a weightless membrane. The center of gravity of the simple closed curve is the point at which this tambourine would balance. See Figure 12.134. Perhaps surprisingly, this center of gravity of the boundary does not always coincide with the center of gravity of the region itself, although for the nicest kinds of figures, like circles and rectangles, it does. Pappus's formula states that when a planar region with simple closed boundary is revolved about a line in its plane (that does not cross it), the surface area of the figure generated is the product of the perimeter of the region and the distance traveled by the

Figure 12.134

center of gravity of its boundary. Use this formula to find the (total) surface areas of the following solids.
    (a) The doughnut in Exercise 17.
    (b) The lead pipe in Exercise 18.

★ 22. Pappus's surface area formula applies to nonclosed simple curves as well as to closed ones: "*If a simple planar curve is revolved about a line that lies in its plane, but does not cross it, then the area of the surface generated is the product of the length of the curve and the distance traveled by its center of gravity.*" Use this result to find the (outside) lateral surface area of the water tumbler shown in Figure 12.135.

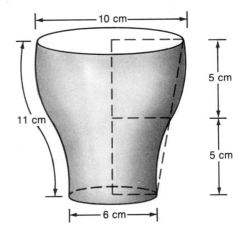

Figure 12.135

23. *A plausibility argument for the Pappus theorems:* Figure 12.136 shows an ideal doughnut. Figure 12.137 shows the same doughnut after it has been cut into wedges and reassembled into a solid that closely resembles a right circular cylinder.
    (a) Write an expression for the approximate volume of the reassembled doughnut. Does it agree with the volume of the pristine doughnut as given by Pappus's formula?
    (b) Write an expression for the approximate lateral surface area of the reassembled doughnut. Does it agree with the surface area of the

pristine doughnut as given by Pappus's formula?

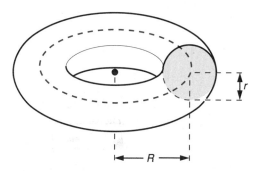

Figure 12.136 Pristine doughnut.

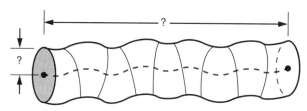

Figure 12.137 Reassembled doughnut.

*24. The volume of a *cap* of a sphere (Figure 12.138) is given by
$$V = \tfrac{1}{3}\pi h^2(3r - h)$$

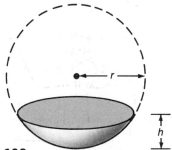

Figure 12.138

A spherical tomato of diameter 8 cm is cut into 8 slices, each 1 cm thick. Find the volume of each slice.

★ 25. *For students who have had some calculus:* The volume V of a sphere is a function of the radius r. Express V in terms of r, calculate $\dfrac{dV}{dr}$, and identify the resulting formula. Now carry out analogous calculations in the two-dimensional case.

Key Concepts in Chapter 12

Congruent figures
Translation
Rotation
Reflection
Rigid motion
Perpendicular lines
Right angle
Unit of measure
Measure function
Length
Perimeter
Arc length

Pythagorean theorem
Area
Sector
Surface area
Heron's formula
Volume
Cylinder
Prism
Cone
Pyramid
*Pappus's theorems

❧ *Chapter 12 Review Exercises* ❧

1. In Figure 12.139, sketch the image of triangle T
   under each of these three rigid motions:
   (a) Translation by the vector **v**
   (b) Rotation through 180° about P
   (c) Reflection in the line $\overleftrightarrow{QR}$

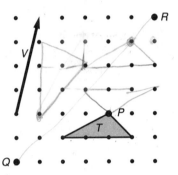

Figure 12.139

2. In Exercise 1, what one word describes the relation among figure T and its three images?

3. For Figure 12.140, describe a rigid motion of
   figure A that will make it coincide with figure B.
   Label any points or lines in the figure that will
   help in your description.

turn about pt
slide over 1 block to rt.
Flip over CD

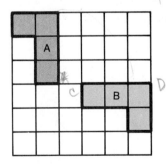

Figure 12.140

4. In Figure 12.141, polygon A is subjected to the
   following rigid motion: reflection in $\overleftrightarrow{PQ}$ followed
   by reflection in $\overleftrightarrow{PR}$.

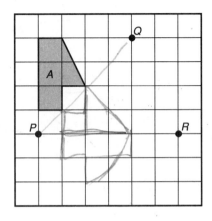

Figure 12.141

(a) Draw the image A′ of A under that rigid mo-
    tion.
(b) Describe a single rotation that sends A onto
    A′.   *reflect'n*

5. Using U in Figure 12.142 as unit of measure, calculate the measure of region C. Show your covering.   6

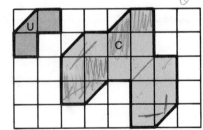

Figure 12.142

6. In Figure 12.143,
   (a) What is the measure of figure A in U-units?
   (b) What is the measure of figure B in U-units?

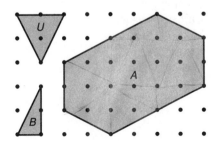

Figure 12.143

7. Suppose that region A in Figure 12.144 has area 7 cm² and region B has area 7 cm². What is the area of the unshaded border region (A ∪ B)'?

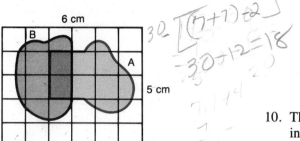

6 cm

B

A

5 cm

Figure 12.144

8. In this problem, all capital letters denote geometric figures.
   (a) If the measure of B in A units is 6 and the measure of C in B units is 5, what is the measure of C in A units?
   (b) If the measure of E in F units is 4, what is the measure of F in E units?
   (c) If the measure of G in J units is 9 and the measure of H in J units is 15, what is the measure of G in H units?

9. Supply the missing dimension in each of the following diagrams.

   (a)

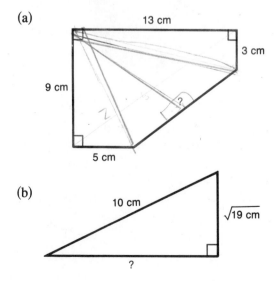

   13 cm

   3 cm

   9 cm

   ?

   5 cm

   (b)

   10 cm

   √19 cm

   ?

(c)

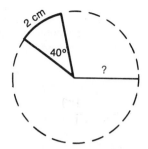

2 cm

40°

?

10. The curved portion of the boundary of the region in Figure 12.145 is a semicircle. Calculate the perimeter of the region.

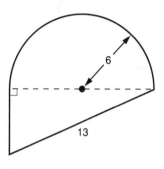

6

13

Figure 12.145

11. A bug that cannot fly is sitting at position B on the right circular cylinder of height 4 cm and circumference 6 cm shown in Figure 12.146. A crumb is at position C. How long is the shortest path from bug to crumb?

B

C

Figure 12.146

12. Find the perimeter and the area of the figure in Figure 12.147. Leave your answers in terms of square roots and π. Assume each small square is 1 cm by 1 cm.

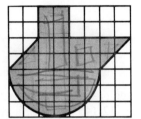

Figure 12.147

13. Find the area of each shaded region. (All circles are of radius 1.)

(a)   (b)

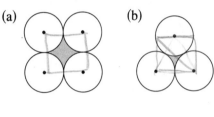

(c)

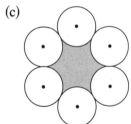

14. Assuming that the circumference of a circle is given by the formula $C = 2\pi r$, present a plausibility argument for the area formula $A = \pi r^2$ based on Figure 12.148.

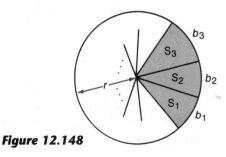

Figure 12.148

15. Find the area of a triangle with sides of lengths 9, 10, and 11.

16. The right rectangular prism in Figure 12.149 has volume 78 cm³. What is the volume of the tetrahedron with vertices A, B, C, D?

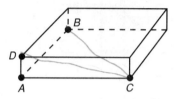

Figure 12.149

17. Archimedes' tomb bore an engraving of a sphere inscribed in a right circular cylinder (Figure 12.150) to commemorate a discovery of which he was particularly proud. The discovery concerned the ratio of the volume of the sphere to the volume of the cylinder, and the ratio of the surface area of the sphere to the (total) surface area of the cylinder. Find and simplify those two ratios.

Figure 12.150

18. Figure 12.151 is the silhouette of a turnip-shaped solid. Calculate its volume.

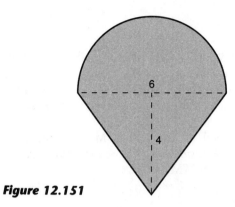

Figure 12.151

19. Calculate the volume of the nut in Figure 12.152. Ignore the threads. The hole through the nut has diameter 1 cm.

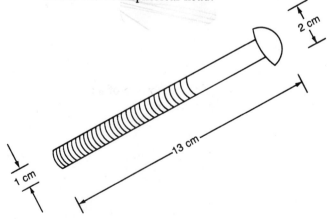

Figure 12.152

20. Calculate the total surface area of the nut in Figure 12.152. Again, ignore the threads.

21. Calculate the volume of the bolt in Figure 12.153. Ignore the threads and the screwdriver slot in the hemispherical head.

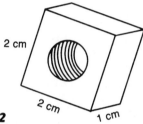

Figure 12.153

* 22. Imagine revolving the square in Figure 12.154 about the line ℓ to sweep out a solid figure. Find the volume and surface area of that solid.

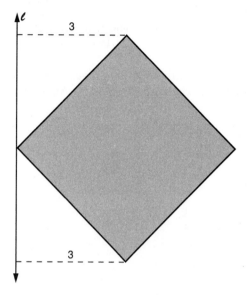

Figure 12.154

★ 23. Use Pappus's theorem to find the coordinates $\bar{x}$ and $\bar{y}$ of the center of mass of the triangular region in Figure 12.155. Remember that the volume of a right circular cone of radius r and height h is $\frac{1}{3}\pi r^2 h$.

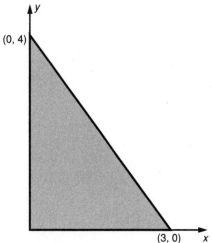

Figure 12.155

References

Arithmetic Teacher. Focus Issue—"Spatial Sense." vol. 37, no. 6, February 1990.

Beaumont, V., R. Curtis, and J. Smart. *How to Teach Perimeter, Area, and Volume*. Reston, Va.: NCTM, 1986.

Eccles, F. *An Introduction to Transformational Geometry*. Menlo Park, Calif.: Addison-Wesley, 1971.

Groza, V. *A Survey of Mathematics*. New York: Holt, Rinehart and Winston, 1968.

Mira Math Company. *Mira Math for Elementary School*. Palo Alto, Calif.: Creative Publications, 1973.

National Council of Teachers of Mathematics. *1976 Yearbook: Measurement in School Mathematics*. Reston, Va.: NCTM, 1976.

13

FURTHER TOPICS IN MEASUREMENT

We begin this chapter by extending to angle measurement most, but not all, of the metric concepts from Chapter 12. Then, after applying angle measurement ideas to the classification of polygons and to tessellations of a plane, we go on to look at some of the practical aspects of measurement: systems of units (in particular, the metric system), dimensional analysis in problem solving, and the quantification of the concepts of precision and accuracy in approximate measurement. We conclude the chapter by reexamining rigid motions in the light of metric ideas, and then using rigid motions as a basis for an analysis of the concept of symmetry. The material in this chapter supports the contention made in the 5–8 *Standards,* that "measurement clearly shows the usefulness of mathematics in everyday life."

13.1 *Angle Measurement*

An angle, you remember, is the union of two rays that share a common endpoint. So an angle is a one-dimensional figure. But an angle is not measured as other one-dimensional figures are. It would be foolish to try to measure the length of an angle since all angles have sides of infinite length. It would also be pointless to measure the area of the interior of an angle, since all such interiors are infinite.

The unit of measure for measuring angles is another angle. The one we commonly use is called a **degree.** See Figure 13.1. To measure an angle is to determine how many degrees, laid side by side (adjacent to each other), are

A degree

Figure 13.1

needed to fill up the interior of the angle being measured. The degree was chosen of such a size that 360 of them, laid side by side, fill up a plane. As before, the assignment of numbers to angles can be described as a function. Its domain is a set of angles; its range is the set of all real numbers x such that $0 < x \leq 180$. See Figure 13.2.

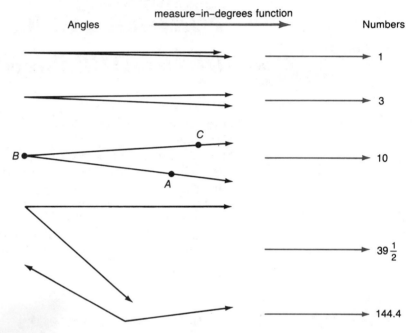

Figure 13.2

There is a standard abbreviation for reporting angle measure. Instead of writing

The measure in degrees of $\angle ABC$ is 10

we write

$$m \angle ABC = 10°$$

Often we simply write

$$m \angle ABC = 10$$

in which case the degree is understood to be the unit of measure.

The instrument for measuring angles is the **protractor.** See Figure 13.3. It is quite similar to a ruler. The protractor has many copies (180) of the unit of angle measure (the degree) already arranged side by side, just as the ruler has many copies (perhaps 30) of the unit of linear measure (the centimeter) already arranged end to end.

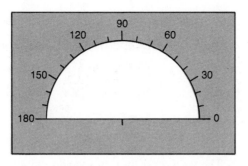
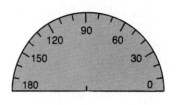

Two kinds of protractors

Figure 13.3

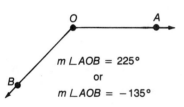

$m \angle AOB = 225°$

or

$m \angle AOB = -135°$

Figure 13.4

One difficulty you might face in teaching angle measurement to children is that you know too much about angles. In high school trigonometry you may have worked with *ordered angles,* angles having an initial side and a terminal side. When working with such angles in a "counterclockwise-oriented plane," it makes good sense to assign measures as we have in Figure 13.4. But in the elementary school an angle is simply a set of points. There is no preferred initial side. Also, no orientation is given to the plane. In the elementary school every angle has positive degree measure less than or equal to 180. For Figure 13.4

$$m \angle AOB = 135° = m \angle BOA$$

A consequence of this fact is that the measure-in-degrees function falls a little short of being a true measure function. It is still true that its domain is a set of geometric figures, its range is a set of positive real numbers, and congruent angles are assigned the same number; but the additivity property occasionally fails. Angle measures do not always "add up." For instance, for Figure 13.5

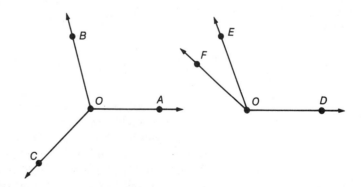

Figure 13.5

the measures of $\angle DOE$ and $\angle EOF$ do add up,

$$m\angle DOE + m\angle EOF = 110 + 30 = 140 = m\angle DOF$$

but the measures of $\angle AOB$ and $\angle BOC$ do not,

$$m\angle AOB + m\angle BOC = 105 + 120 = 225 \neq m\angle AOC$$

In fact,

$$m\angle AOC = 135°$$

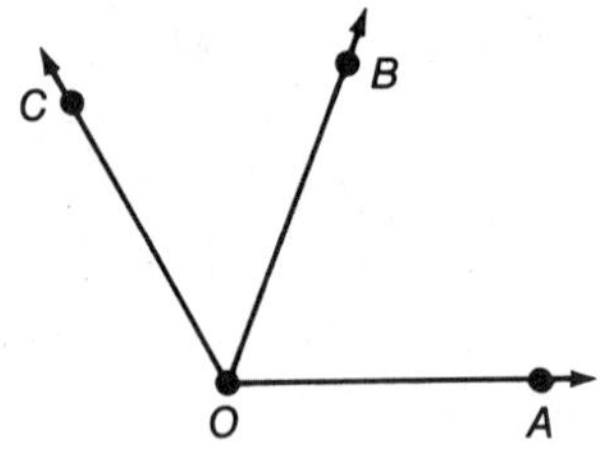

The weakened form of the additivity property can be stated in two cases.

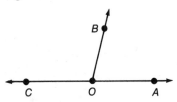

Figure 13.6

If point B lies in the interior of $\angle AOC$, then $m\angle AOB + m\angle BOC = m\angle AOC$. See Figure 13.6.

If $\angle AOC$ is a straight angle (and thus has no interior) and if B is any point not on $\overleftrightarrow{AC}$, then $m\angle AOB + m\angle BOC = 180$. See Figure 13.7.

Figure 13.7

In most contemporary high school geometry texts, the first half of this property is referred to as the **angle addition postulate,** and the second half is referred to as the **angle supplement postulate.** Any two angles whose degree measures add to 180 are called **supplementary angles.** The angle supplement postulate states that any two angles that form a linear pair are supplementary. Of course, the converse is false: Supplementary angles need not be adjacent.

Three other fundamental properties of angle measure deserve mention. The first is the **equal-measures congruence criterion.** See Figure 13.8.

Figure 13.8

$$\angle 1 \cong \angle 2 \qquad \text{if and only if} \qquad m\angle 1 = m\angle 2.$$

In high school geometry courses this criterion is taken as the definition of congruence of angles. In the elementary school we simply accept as an empirical fact that angles can be made to coincide if and only if they have the same measure. Notice the two notational abbreviations that were used in the statement of this property: angles were named by numbers rather than by triples of points, and the symbol $\cong$ was used for the phrase "is congruent to."

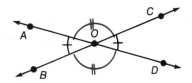

Figure 13.9

The second fundamental property of angle measure is that vertical angles are congruent (see Figure 13.9). Or in view of the first criterion:

> Vertical angles have the same measure.

One rigid motion that will make ∠*AOB* coincide with ∠*COD* is a 180° rotation of ∠*AOB* about the point *O*. Can you describe a rigid motion other than a rotation that will make the two coincide? Notice that another notational convention is introduced in Figure 13.9: One pair of congruent angles is indicated by arcs with a single hash mark; a second pair of congruent angles, different in size from the first pair, is indicated by arcs with a double hash mark.

Here is the third basic property of angle measure.

> The sum of the (degree) measures of the three angles of a triangle is 180.

One can demonstrate this fact convincingly to children by cutting out a large paper triangle, tearing it into three pieces, and rearranging the pieces as shown in Figure 13.10. The observation that the bottom edge of the right-hand figure is a straight line, together with the angle supplement property, leads one to conclude that $m\angle 1 + m\angle 2 + m\angle 3 = 180$.

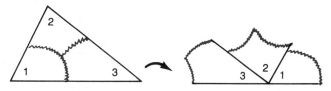

Figure 13.10

In the following example, a somewhat more sophisticated derivation of this 180-sum property is illustrated. In Chapter 14 the same property will be deduced carefully from other properties of angles.

EXAMPLE 1   Figure 13.11 shows the triangular path followed by a ladybug. When the bug reached point A it turned left $\alpha°$, when it reached B it turned left $\beta°$, and when it reached C it turned left $\gamma°$. By the time it got back to its original position it had turned completely around (360°). Thus $\alpha + \beta + \gamma = 360$. Conclude that $a + b + c = 180$.

Solution   By the angle supplement property,

$$\alpha + a = 180, \qquad \beta + b = 180, \qquad \gamma + c = 180$$

Thus

$$\alpha + \beta + \gamma + a + b + c = 3 \cdot 180$$

But

$$\alpha + \beta + \gamma = 2 \cdot 180$$

Thus

$$a + b + c = 180$$

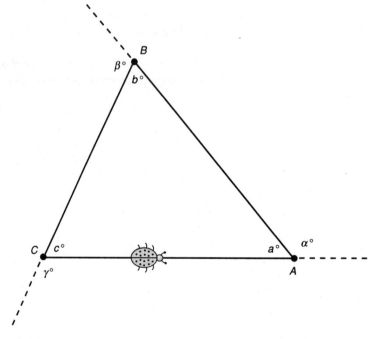

Figure 13.11   ❏

EXAMPLE 2   In Figure 13.12 points A, O, and D are collinear, as are points E, O, and C. Without using a protractor, find the measure of $\angle AOB$.

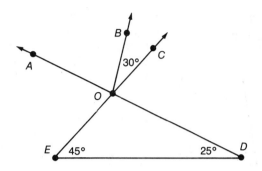

Figure 13.12

Solution   We find the measure of ∠*AOB* in five steps.

Step 1 $m\angle EOD = 110$, since the sum of the measures of the three angles in △*EOD* is 180.

Step 2 $m\angle AOC = 110$, since ∠*AOC* and ∠*EOD* are vertical angles and hence have the same measure.

Step 3 $m\angle AOB + m\angle BOC = m\angle AOC$, by the angle addition postulate.

Step 4 $m\angle AOB + 30 = 110$, by substitution of known values into Step 3.

Step 5 $m\angle AOB = 80$, by Step 4.   ❏

In Example 2, ∠*BOC* is called **acute** (sharp) because its measure is less than 90°, and ∠*EOD* is called **obtuse** (dull) because its measure is more than 90°. An angle of measure exactly 90° is a **right angle.**

EXERCISE SET 13.1

1. Estimate the measure of the angle in Figure 13.13. Now describe how you could find its measure using the given battered protractor. On what property of the angle-measure function does your method depend?

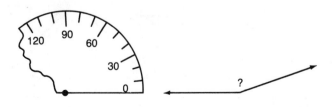

Figure 13.13

2. The additivity property for angle measure was stated in terms of *pairs* of angles. Give arguments based on the additivity property for pairs of angles to show the following.
   (a) $m\angle AOB + m\angle BOC + m\angle COD = m\angle AOD$ for the angles in Figure 13.14.

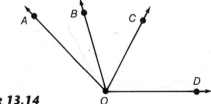

Figure 13.14

(b) $m\angle AOB + m\angle BOC + m\angle COD = 180$ for the angles in Figure 13.15.

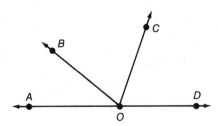

Figure 13.15

Is it clear that the additivity properties of angle measure apply to suitable *triples, quadruples,* . . . , of angles?

3. Refer to Figure 13.16. Without using a protractor, find the measure of $\angle AOB$. (Everything that looks like a straight line is intended to be one.)

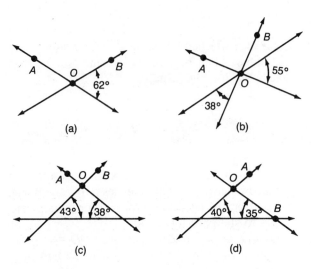

Figure 13.16

4. Figure 13.17 shows three concurrent lines. Find the sum of the measures of angles 1, 3, and 5.

5. Generalize your observation in Exercise 4 to the case of *n* concurrent lines.

6. Use the method of Example 1 to determine the sum of the measures of the interior angles of any convex quadrilateral. (See Figure 13.18.)

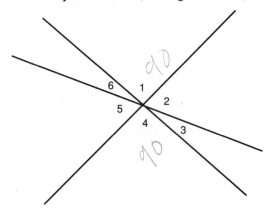

Figure 13.17

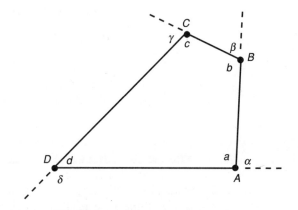

Figure 13.18

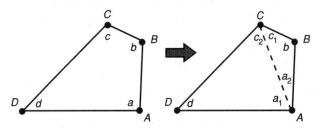

Figure 13.19

7. Verify the conclusion you drew in Exercise 6 by referring to Figure 13.19, which shows a triangulation of the quadrilateral of Figure 13.18.

8. Discover a general formula for the sum of the measures of the interior angles of any convex *n*-gon.

9. A student refers to Figure 13.20 and presents you with the following paradox: "Since $\angle 1 = \angle 3$ and since $\angle 1$ and $\angle 2$ are vertical angles, it follows, by the substitution principle, that $\angle 3$ and $\angle 2$ are vertical angles." Find the flaw in his argument.

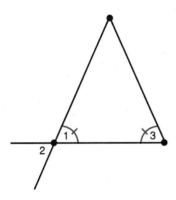

Figure 13.20

10. The task is to define what is meant by "the measure of the angle" between a line and a plane. Figure 13.21 shows a line ℓ piercing a plane $\mathscr{P}$ at a point O. The (unique) line m perpendicular to $\mathscr{P}$ at O is also shown; you should find it helpful as you try to define the measure of the angle between ℓ and $\mathscr{P}$.

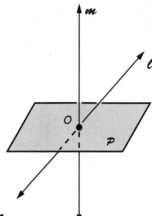

Figure 13.21

11. Formulate a definition of the measure of the angle between two planes. Refer to Figure 13.22.

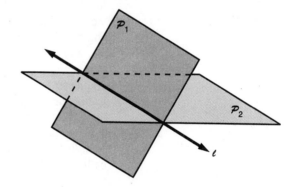

Figure 13.22

12. The 0° longitude semicircle (the "prime meridian") passes through Greenwich, England. The 90° West longitude semicircle passes through Memphis, Tennessee. Consider a "spherical triangle" formed by those two semicircles and some circle of latitude, say, the 30° North latitude circle. What are the measures of the three angles of that triangle?

13.2 *Polygons, Tessellations, and Polyhedra*

In the discussion of polygons that follows, we use a simple but basic property of segments that corresponds to the equal-measures congruence criterion for angles, namely, the **equal-measures congruence criterion for segments.**

Two segments are congruent if and only if they have the same measure (length).

In high school geometry courses this criterion is taken as the definition of congruence of segments. In the elementary school it is taken as an empirical fact that segments can be made to coincide if and only if they have the same length.

Classification of Polygons

Polygons can be classified in many different ways. Perhaps the simplest classification is by number of sides (or vertices or angles). Under this classification we could imagine all polygons with three sides going into a drawer marked triangles, all polygons with four sides into a different drawer marked quadrilaterals, and so forth. Another classification is based on the property of convexity. For example, the drawer full of quadrilaterals could be partitioned into two compartments, one labeled convex and the other nonconvex. (Would this be a useful partition of the drawer full of triangles?) Now that we have discussed the concepts of length and angle measure, still finer classifications are possible.

Triangles can be classified according to the relative lengths of their sides. A triangle having all three sides of the same length (all three sides congruent) is called **equilateral.** A triangle having *at least* two sides of the same length (congruent) is called **isosceles.** And a triangle having all three sides of different lengths (no two congruent) is called **scalene.**

Caution: There are two widely accepted definitions of *isosceles*. The one that we have chosen includes equilateral triangles as a special kind of isosceles triangle. The other definition requires that an isosceles triangle have *exactly* two congruent sides. Under this latter definition equilateral triangles are *not* isosceles. A case can be made for either definition, but keep in mind that neither one is wrong. A definition is simply an agreement on the meaning of a word; it is not a proposition that can be considered correct or incorrect. As a teacher, you will have to be alert to which definition is used in your text. And be especially wary if your text offers the ambiguous description, "An isosceles triangle is one with two congruent sides."

Triangles can also be classified according to the measures of their angles. A triangle having three acute angles is called an **acute triangle;** a triangle having a right angle is called a **right triangle;** and a triangle having an obtuse angle is called an **obtuse triangle.** Since the sum of the angle measures in a triangle is

180°, a triangle cannot have more than one angle of measure greater than or equal to 90°. Thus these three categories are mutually exclusive (and exhaustive).

The usual classification of quadrilaterals involves concepts of parallelism, side length, and angle measure. Again, there is some lack of unanimity on definitions, and as a teacher, you will want to fall in step with the text you happen to be using. Here are our choices (see Figure 13.23.).

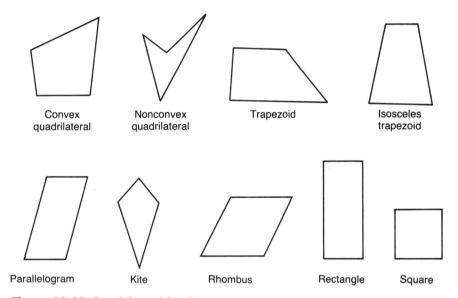

Figure 13.23 Quadrilateral family portrait.

Quadrilateral: Any four-sided polygon (some books implicitly restrict attention to convex ones)

Trapezoid: A quadrilateral with precisely one pair of parallel sides

Isosceles trapezoid: A trapezoid whose nonparallel sides are congruent

Parallelogram: A quadrilateral with two pairs of parallel sides

Kite: A quadrilateral with two pairs of congruent sides and no pair of parallel sides. (Some books implicitly require kites to be convex.)

Rhombus: A quadrilateral with four congruent sides. [It turns out (see Exercise 5, Section 14.5) that a rhombus is a parallelogram. Some authors define a rhombus to be a parallelogram with four congruent sides.]

Rectangle: A parallelogram with four right angles. (It turns out that if a parallelogram has one right angle, then it has four. Thus you might see a rectangle defined to be a parallelogram having one right angle.)

Square: A rectangle with four congruent sides; equivalently, a rhombus with one right angle (and hence four)

The lattice in Figure 13.24 shows the special-case relation. For example, the fact that a rectangle is a special case of a parallelogram is indicated by putting *rectangle* below *parallelogram* in the hierarchy and joining them with a line segment.

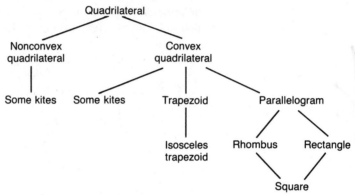

Figure 13.24 Quadrilateral family tree.

When the number of sides of a polygon exceeds four, only a few classifications are used. General *n*-gons can still be classified as convex or nonconvex. An *n*-gon is said to be **equilateral** if all of its sides are congruent and **equiangular** if all of its angles are congruent. If it is both equilateral and equiangular, then it is called **regular.** See Figure 13.25.

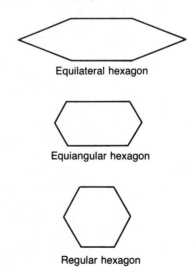

Figure 13.25

Regular polygons occur so often in mathematics, science, art, and design that they deserve closer study.

Regular Polygons and Tessellations

The word *tessellation* comes from the Latin word *tessellatus,* meaning mosaic, or tiling. Figure 13.26 shows a portion of a **general tessellation** of the plane by polygons, that is, a covering of the plane by nonoverlapping polygons. General tessellations are so easy to draw (and so aesthetically unsatisfying) that extra restrictions are usually placed on the tessellations that people study.

One common restriction is the requirement that all of the polygons in the tessellation be congruent to each other. But, as Figure 13.27 shows, that restriction alone still allows infinitely many different-looking tessellations, most of which are not very pleasing. The single rectangle used to build a tessellation like any of those in Figure 13.27 is called a **prototile** for the tessellation.

A second restriction that eliminates many of the uninteresting general tessellations is the requirement that any two polygons in the tessellation intersect in either the empty set, or a vertex of both, or an entire edge of both. Such tessellations are called **edge-to-edge tessellations.** In Figure 13.27 only tessellation (b) is edge-to-edge.

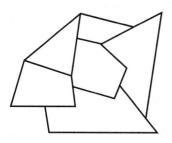

Figure 13.26 A general tessellation.

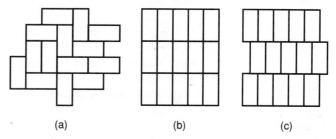

(a) (b) (c)

Figure 13.27 Three general tessellations using a 1 by 2 rectangle as prototile.

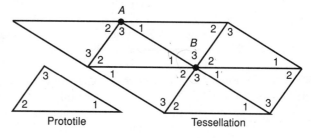

Prototile Tessellation

Figure 13.28 Edge-to-edge tessellation by a single triangle.

Figure 13.28 shows that

Any triangle can be used as the prototile for an edge-to-edge tessellation of the plane.

The key property of triangles that makes this possible is the 180-sum property. That is why angles 1, 2, and 3 fit together at point *A* to form a straight line, and why two copies of each of angles 1, 2, and 3 fit together to surround point *B*. In the exercises you are asked to demonstrate the following.

> Any quadrilateral can be used as the prototile for an edge-to-edge tessellation of the plane.

It is not true, however, that an arbitrary pentagon can be used as a prototile for an edge-to-edge tessellation of the plane. Figure 13.29 shows one *particular* pentagon that does the job, but we shall soon see that the regular pentagon fails.

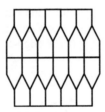

Figure 13.29 Edge-to-edge tessellation by a particular pentagon.

By a **regular tessellation** we mean an edge-to-edge tessellation using a single *regular* polygon as prototile. In order to catalog the regular tessellations, and later the "semi-regular" tessellations, we need to recall what is meant by an interior angle of a regular polygon and what the measure of each interior angle is. Figure 13.30 shows two types of angles in a regular *n*-gon and also suggests another explanation of the following important property.

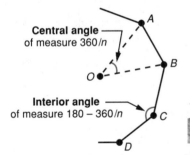

Central angle of measure 360/*n*

Interior angle of measure 180 − 360/*n*

Figure 13.30 A regular *n*-gon and two of its angles.

> Each interior angle of a regular *n*-gon has measure $180 - 360/n$.

(You were asked to give one explanation in Exercise 8 of Section 13.1.) The argument goes like this: since there are *n* central angles arranged around *O* and since each has the same measure, that common measure must be $360/n$. Now obviously

$$m\angle BCD = m\angle OAB + m\angle OBA$$

But

$$m\angle OAB + m\angle OBA = 180 - m\angle AOB$$

Thus

$$m\angle BCD = 180 - 360/n$$

Table 13.1 evaluates the expression $180 - 360/n$ for some small values of n to give the interior angle measures of a few of the most common regular polygons.

Table 13.1

Value of n	Name of regular n-gon	Interior angle measure
3	Equilateral triangle	60
4	Square	90
5	Regular pentagon	108
6	Regular hexagon	120
8	Regular octagon	135
10	Regular decagon	144
12	Regular dodecagon	150

By combining the angle measures in Table 13.1 to make 360, we can find various arrangements of regular polygons that surround a point. Some of these arrangements will be extendable to tessellations of the plane; others will not.

EXAMPLE 1   Is it possible to arrange equilateral triangles to surround a vertex, and, if so, can that arrangement be extended to tessellate the plane?

Solution   Since $6 \cdot 60 = 360$ it is possible to arrange six equilateral triangles around a point. See Figure 13.31. Furthermore, this arrangement can be extended to tessellate the plane. See Figure 13.32.

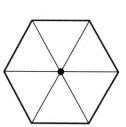

Figure 13.31

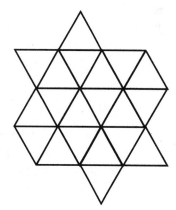

Figure 13.32 The regular tessellation by equilateral triangles.   ❏

EXAMPLE 2   Describe all the regular tessellations of the plane.

Solution   One is the tessellation by equilateral triangles given above. A second is found by looking at Table 13.1, noting arithmetically that $360/90 = 4$, and observing that the arrangement of four squares about a point can be extended to cover the plane. See Figure 13.33. The next entry in Table 13.1, the regular pentagon, does *not* tessellate the plane; we cannot surround a point with regular pentagons because 108 does not divide exactly into 360. See Figure 13.34. The next entry in Table 13.1, the regular hexagon, gives the third and final regular tessellation. See Figure 13.35. There are no other regular tessellations, because if $n > 6$, the interior angles of the n-gon have measure greater than 120 (so three are too many to fit around a point) and less than 180 (so two are not enough).

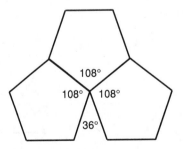

Figure 13.33 The regular tessellation by squares.

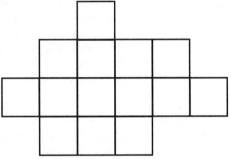

Figure 13.34 Regular pentagons fail to tessellate.

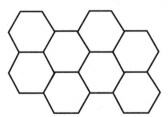

Figure 13.35 The regular tessellation by hexagons.   ❏

Regular tessellations are the simplest tiling patterns. You have probably seen tile floors in at least one of the three regular tessellation patterns. A second category of tessellations that includes more complicated, but also very beautiful designs, is the category of "semiregular" tessellations. A **semiregular tessellation** is an edge-to-edge tessellation that uses at least two different regular polygons as prototiles. Furthermore, in a semiregular tessellation every vertex is required to have the same arrangement of polygons around it. Figure 13.36 shows a semiregular tessellation of hexagons and triangles. Notice that around each vertex we have (in cyclic order) a triangle, a hexagon, another triangle, and then another hexagon. We say that each vertex is of **type** 3,6,3,6 and also that the semiregular tessellation is of type 3,6,3,6. We could as well say that it is of type 6,3,6,3. (The vertex types for the three regular tessellations mentioned earlier are 3,3,3,3,3,3, and 4,4,4,4 and 6,6,6.)

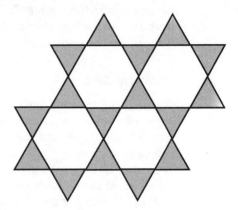

Figure 13.36 The semiregular tessellation of type 3,6,3,6.

EXAMPLE 3   Draw the semiregular tessellation of type 3,3,3,4,4.

Solution   Begin with one vertex (vertex *A* in Figure 13.37) and arrange three triangles and two squares around it in the order 3,3,3,4,4. It is possible to do this because 60 + 60 + 60 + 90 + 90 = 360. Next move to one of the newly created vertices (vertex *B* in Figure 13.37) and repeat the process. Proceeding to other vertices we eventually arrive at the semiregular tessellation shown in Figure 13.38.

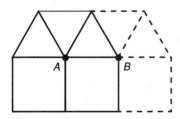

Figure 13.37

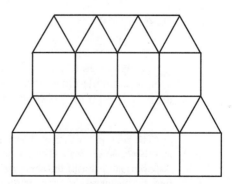

Figure 13.38 The semiregular tessellation of type 3,3,3,4,4.   ❑

EXAMPLE 4   Show that there is no semiregular tessellation of type 3,4,4,6.

Solution   In Figure 13.39 we began at vertex *A* and drew the surrounding polygons so that *A* would be of type 3,4,4,6. Then we moved to vertex *B*, where we had no choice but to draw two squares below it. But that forced vertex *C* to be of type 4,3,4,6 rather than 3,4,4,6.   ❑

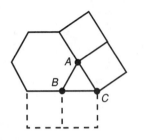

Figure 13.39

It was Johann Kepler (1571–1630) who first exhibited the complete family of semiregular tessellations.* There are exactly eight of them, of which we have seen two so far (Figure 13.36 and 13.38). Table 13.2 lists them all by type. In the exercises you are asked to draw some of them.

Polyhedra

We observed that regular pentagons fail to tessellate the plane because they leave gaps at the vertices. See Figure 13.40. Now imagine cutting out the pattern in Figure 13.40 and folding along edges $\overline{AB}$ and $\overline{BC}$ until points *D* and *E* coincide. In *space* it *is* possible to fit three pentagons around a vertex so there is no gap. In fact, something even better is possible in space. The pattern in Figure 13.41 can be folded along the dotted segments to form a regular dodecahedron (see also Figure 13.42), which is a very special kind of figure called a *polyhedron*.

Table 13.2 The Eight Semiregular Tessellations

3,3,3,3,6	3,4,6,4
3,3,3,4,4	3,12,12
3,3,4,3,4	4,6,12
3,6,3,6	4,8,8

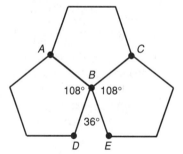

Figure 13.40

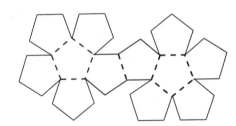

Figure 13.41 Pattern for regular dodecahedron.

A polyhedron is the spatial analog of a polygon. You can think of a polyhedron as a simple closed surface in space whose faces are polygons. A polyhedron is a **regular polyhedron** if (1) all of its faces are congruent regular

---

*The book in which Kepler published his findings, *Harmonice Mundi,* appeared in 1619 and then was ignored and forgotten for about 300 years. Mathematicians continued to rediscover (and publish) the same results, ignorant of Kepler's and each other's work, right into this century—the last four "discoveries" occurring in 1887, 1905, 1907, and 1931.

polygons, and (2) the same number of faces meet at each vertex. In striking contrast to the situation in the plane, where there are regular polygons with any number of sides, in space there are just five types of regular polyhedra (Figure 13.42).

The regular tetrahedron: The 4 faces are equilateral triangles, and 3 faces meet at each vertex.

The regular dodecahedron: The 12 faces are regular pentagons, and 3 faces meet at each vertex.

The regular hexahedron (cube): The 6 faces are squares, and 3 faces meet at each vertex.

The regular icosahedron: The 20 faces are equilateral triangles, and 5 faces meet at each vertex.

The regular octahedron: The 8 faces are equilateral triangles, and 4 faces meet at each vertex.

Figure 13.42 The five regular polyhedra.

EXERCISE SET 13.2

1. Classify the triangles in Figure 13.43 as acute, right, or obtuse.

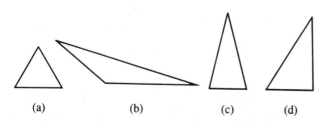

(a)   (b)   (c)   (d)

Figure 13.43

2. Classify the triangles in Figure 13.43 as scalene, isosceles, or equilateral.

3. Either make a sketch or declare that no such figure exists.
   (a) An isosceles acute triangle
   (b) An isosceles right triangle
   (c) An isosceles obtuse triangle
   (d) An equilateral right triangle

4. Give the briefest and most informative description you can of each quadrilateral in Figure 13.44.

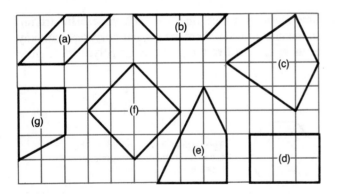

Figure 13.44

5. Draw an arbitrary quadrilateral. Connect the mid-points of adjacent sides with line segments. Is there anything special about this second quadrilateral?

6. Make a carboard cut-out of the quadrilateral in Figure 13.45 and use it as your prototile. By tracing around it with a pencil, show an edge-to-edge tessellation of the plane. What do you notice about the angles that surround each vertex of your tessellation?

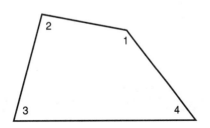

Figure 13.45

7. Repeat Exercise 6 for the nonconvex quadrilateral shown in Figure 13.46.

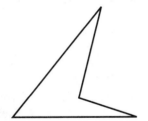

Figure 13.46

8. Use a ruler, a protractor, and the known value of the measure of its interior angles to draw a regular pentagon having edges of length 1 in.

9. What is the usual name given to the following?
   (a) A regular 3-gon
   (b) A regular 4-gon

10. You will need some tools to carry out this activity.
    (a) Use a compass and a straightedge to draw an equilateral triangle. Check with a protractor to see whether it is also equiangular.
    (b) Use a protractor and a straightedge to sketch an equiangular triangle. Check with a ruler (or compass) to see whether it is also equilateral.
    (c) Sketch a quadrilateral that is equilateral but not regular. What do you call such a figure?
    (d) Sketch a quadrilateral that is equiangular but not regular. What do you call such a figure?

11. Must an equilateral pentagon be equiangular? Must an equiangular pentagon be equilateral?

12. Generalize your observations from Exercises 10 and 11.

13. Figure 13.47 suggests how a regular hexagon can be constructed by using only a compass and a straightedge. Why is it that after swinging the third arc, you are exactly halfway around the circle?

Figure 13.47

14. *Pascal's mystic hexagram:* Inscribe an irregular hexagon in a circle so that no two "opposite" sides are parallel. Extend pairs of opposite sides until they intersect. What appears to be true of the three points of intersection thus obtained?

15. Find the common measure of the interior angles of each regular polygon below.
    (a) Regular 9-gon
    (b) Regular 18-gon
    (c) Regular 42-gon
    (d) Regular 7-gon

16. Find the number of sides of the regular polygon whose interior angles have the following measures.
    (a) 168°　　　　(b) 170°
    (c) $163\frac{7}{11}°$　　(d) 179°

17. Refer to Table 13.1 and decide how many of each of the following regular polygons could be arranged to surround a vertex.
    (a) Pentagons and decagons
    (b) Triangles and dodecagons
    (c) Triangles, squares, and dodecagons
    (d) Triangles and hexagons

★ 18. Which regular n-gon can be used, along with an equilateral triangle and a regular 7-gon, to surround a vertex?

19. What regular polygon do bees use in designing their honeycombs?

20. Figure 13.48 shows an edge-to-edge tessellation by triangles and hexagons. Why is it not semiregular?

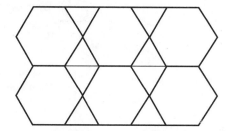

Figure 13.48

21. Draw the semiregular tessellation of each of the following types.
    (a) 4,8,8　　　　(b) 3,4,6,4

22. Figure 13.49 shows how regular pentagons can be arranged tightly around a regular decagon.

Try to extend Figure 13.49 and then explain why there is no semiregular tessellation of type 5,5,10.

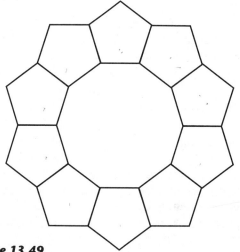

Figure 13.49

23. Trace the pattern in Figure 13.41, cut it out, and fold and tape it to make a regular dodecahedron.

24. Draw a pattern, in the style of Figure 13.41, for each of the following polyhedra.
    (a) Regular tetrahedron
    (b) Regular hexahedron
    (c) Regular octahedron

25. Refer to Figure 13.42 and fill in Table 13.3, where V stands for the number of vertices, E for the number of edges, and F for the number of faces.

Table 13.3

	V	E	F
Regular tetrahedrona			
Regular hexahedron			
Regular octahedron			
Regular dodecahedron			
Regular icosahedron			

26. Refer to Figure 13.42 and try to guess what sort of polyhedron would have its vertices at the centers of the faces of the following. *Hint:* Use Table 13.3.
    (a) A regular tetrahedron
    (b) A regular hexahedron
    (c) A regular octahedron
    (d) A regular dodecahedron
    (e) A regular icosahedron

27. Calculate $V - E + F$ for each of the five regular polyhedra.

28. The similarity between the formula that you just observed, $V - E + F = 2$, and Euler's formula for planar graphs, $V - E + P = 2$, can hardly be accidental! Figure 13.50 shows how the regular hexahedron can be deformed into a planar graph. Be prepared to explain how each face of the original polyhedron becomes a piece of the new planar graph. Conclude that $V - E + F$ must equal 2. (*Note:* This argument can be applied to more polyhedra than just the regular ones. In fact, any polyhedron with the property that a rubber replica could be inflated to be a sphere will satisfy Euler's formula.)

29. Verify Euler's formula for these polyhedra.

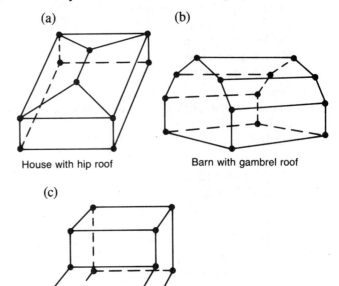

(a) House with hip roof

(b) Barn with gambrel roof

(c) Factory

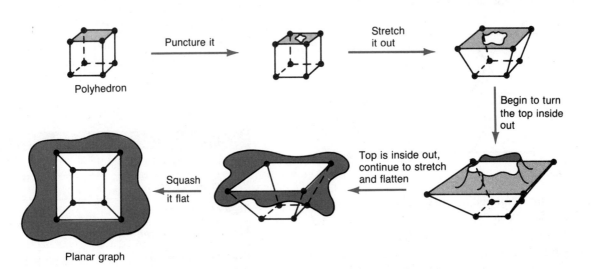

Figure 13.50

★ 30. By the *apothem* of a regular polygon we mean the common length of the segments joining the center to the midpoints of the sides. It is a fact that these segments are perpendicular to the sides. Express the area of the regular hexagon in Figure 13.51 in terms of its apothem a and its perimeter p.

31. Generalize the result of Exercise 30 to an arbitrary regular n-gon.

32. How does the result of Exercise 31 suggest the formula for area of a circle?

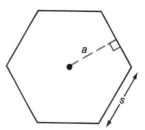

Figure 13.51 Regular hexagon.

13.3 *Systems of Units; The Metric System*

In Chapter 12 and Section 13.1 we discussed the theory of measuring ideal geometric figures. In this section and the next we will consider some of the practical problems associated with measuring real things.

One problem of practical measurement is the Babel of units. Records dating back to 3000 B.C. indicate that the Egyptians used the following units of linear measurement:

Cubit: Length of a forearm from the elbow to the tip of the ·middle finger
Palm: The width of a hand excluding the thumb; one-seventh of a cubit
Digit: The width of one finger; one-fourth of a palm

The advantage of this system of units is obvious: Everyone had these units of measure on his person at all times. The disadvantage is also clear: Different people carried around cubits of different lengths.

The Customary System

The Romans are responsible for introducing a *standard* cubit into some of the lands they conquered. Their cubit (about 26.6 modern inches) was divided into 2 **feet,** and each foot consisted of 12 *unciae*. According to legend, in the time of King Henry I of England (ca. 1100) the **yard** was defined to be the distance from the tip of Henry's nose to the end of his thumb. A yard consisted of 3 feet, and each foot of 12 **inches.** The other "customary" (English, British-American) unit of length, the **mile,** can also be traced back to the Romans. The word *mile* comes from the Latin *mille passuum,* meaning "one thousand paces." A Roman pace consisted of 2 steps and was about 5 feet long. Now, of course, a mile has been standardized as 5280 feet. Many other units of linear measurement appeared in the customary system in the past but are now fading from the scene. Here are a few that have not yet vanished completely.

Barleycorn: Originally, the length of a kernel of barley; later standardized as $\frac{1}{3}$ inch; still the basis for shoe sizing, each size differing from the next by $\frac{1}{3}$ inch

Rod: Originally, the length of the left feet of 16 men chosen at random; now standardized as $16\frac{1}{2}$ feet

Furlong: 40 rods or $\frac{1}{8}$ mile; still used in horse racing

So far we have discussed only units of *linear* measurement in the customary system. There are, of course, units of *area* and *volume* as well. As units of area, besides square inches, square feet, square yards, and square miles, we also have **acres** and **townships.** Originally, an acre was the amount of land that a man could plow in one day with a yoke (pair) of oxen. It has now been standardized as $\frac{1}{640}$ square mile. A township is 36 square miles. As units of volume measure, besides cubic inches, cubic feet, and cubic yards, we have

teaspoon $= \frac{1}{3}$ tablespoon	pint $= \frac{1}{2}$ quart
tablespoon $= \frac{1}{16}$ cup	quart
gill $= \frac{1}{2}$ cup	gallon $= 4$ quarts
cup $= \frac{1}{2}$ pint	barrel $= 31\frac{1}{2}$ quarts

The avoirdupois system of weights is equally complicated.

grain	stone $= 14$ pounds
dram $= 27\frac{11}{32}$ grains	hundredweight $= 100$ pounds
ounce $= 16$ drams	ton $= 2000$ pounds
pound $= 16$ ounces	long ton $= 2240$ pounds

The Metric System

Napoleon I appointed a commission of French scientists to devise a sensible and coherent system of weights and measures. Their response (1799) has come to be known as the **metric system.**

The basic unit of linear measure in the metric system is the **meter,** which was defined originally to be one ten-millionth of the distance from equator to North Pole measured along the meridian through Paris. Since then, it has been redefined more precisely as 1,650,763.73 wavelengths of orange-red light from the isotope krypton 86. For people familiar with the customary system, the meter is slightly longer than a yard:

$$1 \text{ meter} \doteq 39.37 \text{ inches}$$

If you are a golfer, think of a meter as the approximate length of a two iron.

The other units of length in the metric system (Table 13.4) are defined in terms of the meter (m) and powers of ten. Figure 13.52 shows the actual sizes of the three short metric units. Of the seven units in the table only four are commonly used—millimeter, centimeter, meter, and kilometer—although it seems likely that the decimeter will get quite a bit of use because of its convenient size.

Table 13.4 Metric Units of Length

$$1 \text{ millimeter (mm)} = \tfrac{1}{1000} \text{ m} = 10^{-3} \text{ m}$$
$$1 \text{ centimeter (cm)} = \tfrac{1}{100} \text{ m} = 10^{-2} \text{ m}$$
$$1 \text{ decimeter (dm)} = \tfrac{1}{10} \text{ m} = 10^{-1} \text{ m}$$
$$1 \text{ meter (m)}$$
$$1 \text{ dekameter (dam)} = 10 \text{ m} = 10^{1} \text{ m}$$
$$1 \text{ hectometer (hm)} = 100 \text{ m} = 10^{2} \text{ m}$$
$$1 \text{ kilometer (km)} = 1000 \text{ m} = 10^{3} \text{ m}$$

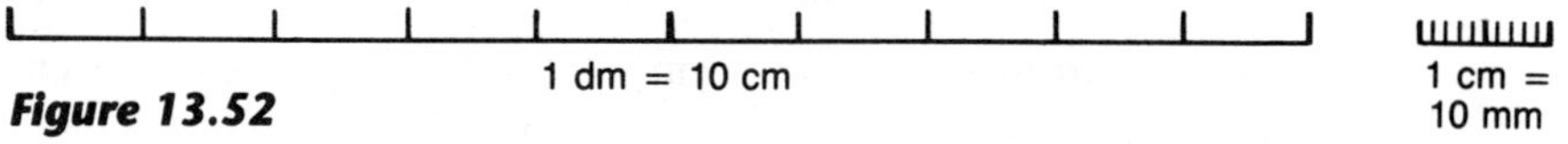

1 dm = 10 cm

1 cm = 10 mm

Figure 13.52

Converting between units within the metric system is straightforward, as the following examples show, since multiplication and division by powers of ten can be done mentally.

EXAMPLE 1   Use Table 13.4 only if necessary.
(a) Convert 2.7 m to centimeters.
(b) Convert 15.9 m to kilometers.

Solution   (a) $2.7 \text{ m} = 2.7 \times 1 \text{ m} = 2.7 \times 100 \text{ cm} = 270 \text{ cm}$
(b) $15.9 \text{ m} = 15.9 \times 1 \text{ m} = 15.9 \times \tfrac{1}{1000} \text{ km} = .0159 \text{ km}$ ❏

Conversions within the customary system are not so simple. Compare, for example, this conversion of 100 in to miles:

$$100 \text{ in} = 100 \times 1 \text{ in} = 100 \times \tfrac{1}{12} \text{ ft} = \tfrac{100}{12} \times 1 \text{ ft} = \tfrac{100}{12} \times \tfrac{1}{5280} \text{ mi} = \tfrac{10}{6336} \text{ mi}$$

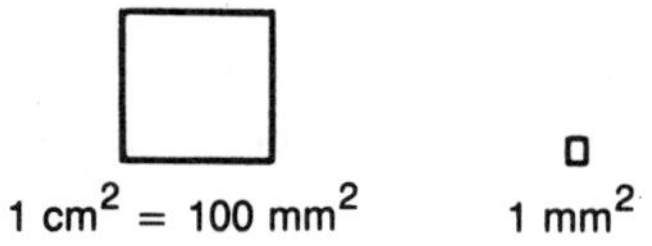

The common metric units of area measure are given in Table 13.5 in terms of the square meter (m^2). Figure 13.53 shows the size of two metric units of area measure. For measurements of land areas the **are** (100 m^2) and **hectare** ($100 \text{ are} = 10{,}000 \text{ m}^2$) are used. A hectare is about $2\tfrac{1}{2}$ acres.

The use of exponential notation for square units makes possible a simple mechanical technique for solving area problems. We illustrate it with examples.

$1 \text{ cm}^2 = 100 \text{ mm}^2$ 1 mm^2

Figure 13.53

Table 13.5 Metric Units of Area

$$1 \text{ square millimeter (mm}^2) = \frac{1}{1{,}000{,}000} \text{ m}^2 = 10^{-6} \text{ m}^2$$

$$1 \text{ square centimeter (cm}^2) = \frac{1}{10{,}000} \text{ m}^2 = 10^{-4} \text{ m}^2$$

$$1 \text{ square meter (m}^2)$$
$$1 \text{ square kilometer (km}^2) = 1{,}000{,}000 \text{ m}^2 = 10^{6} \text{ m}^2$$

EXAMPLE 2   Find the area of each region.
(a) A 12-cm by 8-cm rectangle   (b) A circle of radius 7 cm

Solution   (a) $A = b \times h = 12 \text{ cm} \times 8 \text{ cm} = 12 \times 8 \times \text{cm} \times \text{cm} = 96 \text{ cm}^2$
(b) $A = \pi r^2 = \pi \times (7 \text{ cm})^2 = \pi \times 7 \times \text{cm} \times 7 \times \text{cm} = 49\pi \text{ cm}^2$ ❏

This technique can also be used to determine the conversion factors given in Table 13.5.

EXAMPLE 3   Express 1 square centimeter in terms of square meters.

Solution $1 \text{ cm}^2 = 1 \times 1 \times \text{cm} \times \text{cm} = 1 \text{ cm} \times 1 \text{ cm}$

$$= \frac{1}{100} \text{ m} \times \frac{1}{100} \text{ m} = \frac{1}{100} \times \frac{1}{100} \times \text{m} \times \text{m} = \frac{1}{10,000} \text{ m}^2$$ ❏

$1 \text{ cm}^3 = 1000 \text{ mm}^3$ 1 mm^3

Figure 13.54

The common metric units of volume measure are given in Table 13.6 in terms of the cubic centimeter (cm³). Figure 13.54 shows two of them. A cubic centimeter is also referred to as a milliliter (mL), particularly when describing the volume of a liquid. Again, the use of exponential notation simplifies the solution of certain problems.

Table 13.6 Metric Units of Volume

1 cubic millimeter (mm³) =	$\frac{1}{1000}$ cm³ = 10^{-3} cm³
1 cubic centimeter (cm³)	
1 liter (L) = 1 dm³ =	1000 cm³ = 10^3 cm³
1 cubic meter (m³) =	1,000,000 cm³ = 10^6 cm³

EXAMPLE 4   Find the volume of a box that is 4 cm deep, 12 cm wide, and 26 cm long.

Solution $V = l \times w \times h = 26 \text{ cm} \times 12 \text{ cm} \times 4 \text{ cm}$

$$= 26 \times 12 \times 4 \times \text{cm} \times \text{cm} \times \text{cm} = 1248 \text{ cm}^3$$ ❏

The basic metric unit of weight is the gram (g), which is defined to be the weight of 1 cm³ of water under standard conditions of temperature (0°C) and pressure (sea level). The other common metric units of weight are defined in Table 13.7 in terms of the gram, using the familiar prefixes.

Table 13.7 Metric Units of Weight

1 milligram (mg) =	$\frac{1}{1000}$ g = 10^{-3} g
1 gram (g)	
1 kilogram (kg) =	1000 g = 10^3 g
1 metric ton = 1000 kg =	1,000,000 g = 10^6 g

EXAMPLE 5   Find the weight in kilograms of 1 m^3 of water.

Solution   Since
$$1 \text{ m}^3 = 10^6 \text{ cm}^3$$
and since 1 cm^3 of water weighs 1 g, then 1 m^3 of water weighs 10^6 g. Now
$$10^6 \text{ g} = 10^3 \cdot 10^3 \text{ g} = 10^3 \text{ kg}$$
Answer: 1000 kg, or 1 metric ton.   ❑

Teaching the Metric System

The metric system is a simpler system than the customary system once one has learned a few Latin and Greek prefixes. Almost from the time the metric system was devised, there have been pressures to adopt it in the United States. In 1821 John Quincy Adams recommended to Congress that it be adopted officially. It was not, but that did not end the matter. Scientists and technicians went ahead and used the metric system because it was simpler and because it was used elsewhere. The schools even made gestures at teaching it. An old classic from 1889, Wentworth's *Grammar School Arithmetic,* included a chapter on the metric system. As time went on, more and more nations adopted the metric system, until the United States found itself as one of the last holdouts. (At this writing the only other nonmetric countries are Burma and Liberia.) We are now in the process of switching over.

Most elementary schools now teach the metric system, either exclusively or alongside the customary system. Many educators favor the former approach to the switchover. The feeling is that children should grow up with the metric system as the one that they feel in their bones. Only after they are completely at home with metric units should they be exposed to the customary system as some sort of historical relic. Yardsticks are to be hidden away; metersticks should be the rule. Objects should be measured in metric units and then used as mnemonics. For example, the thickness of a worn dime is about 1 mm; the width of one's small fingernail is about 1 cm; the width of one's hand, including the thumb, is about 1 dm; two paper clips weigh about 1 g.

During this transitional period, which is sure to last for many years, there may be times when a student will need to convert a measurement from customary units to metric units, or vice versa. If such a need arises, a table of conversion factors, like Table 13.8, will have to be consulted. We repeat, though, that children are not supposed to think of metric units in terms of their relationships to customary units.

Table 13.8 Approximate Conversion Factors

1 in = 2.54 cm (exactly)	1 cm $\doteq$ 0.4 in
1 yd $\doteq$ 0.9 m	1 m $\doteq$ 1.1 yd
1 mi $\doteq$ 1.6 km	1 km $\doteq$ 0.6 mi
1 lb $\doteq$ 0.45 kg	1 kg $\doteq$ 2.2 lb
1 qt $\doteq$ 0.95 L	1 L $\doteq$ 1.06 qt

EXAMPLE 6 Convert.
(a) 12 in to centimeters
(b) 15 m to feet
(c) 8 lb 6 oz to kilograms

Solution (a) 12 in = 12 × 1 in = 12 × 2.54 cm = 30.48 cm
(b) 15 m = 15 × 1 m $\doteq$ 15 × 1.1 yd $\doteq$ 15 × 1.1 × 1 yd $\doteq$
15 × 1.1 × 3 ft $\doteq$ 49.5 ft
(c) 8 lb 6 oz = $8\frac{6}{16}$ lb = $8\frac{6}{16}$ × 1 lb $\doteq$ 8.375 × 0.45 kg $\doteq$ 3.8 kg   ❑

Units of Angle Measurement

Two systems of units for angle measurement are in common use. One is based on the degree, the other on the radian. A **degree,** you recall, is an angle of such a size that 360 of them, when placed adjacent to each other, fill up a plane. Equivalently, there are 180° in a straight angle, or 90° in a right angle. The degree itself can be thought of as being composed of 60 smaller (congruent) angles called **minutes.** Each minute, in turn, can be thought of as being composed of 60 still smaller (congruent) angles called **seconds.** See Table 13.9.

Table 13.9

1 right angle	= 90 degrees (90°)
1 degree	= 60 minutes (60′)
1 minute	= 60 seconds (60″)

EXAMPLE 7 Refer to Figure 13.55.
(a) If $m\angle BOA = 47°28'53''$ and $m\angle COB = 35°41'10''$, what is $m\angle COA$?
(b) If $m\angle BOA = 51°43'45''$ and $m\angle COA = 82°37'30''$, what is $m\angle COB$?

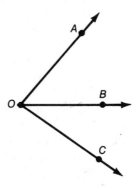

Figure 13.55

Solution (a) $m\angle COA = 47°28'53'' + 35°41'10'' = 82°69'63'' = 82°69'(60 + 3)''$
$= 82°70'3'' = 82°(60 + 10)'3'' = 83°10'3''$
(b) $m\angle COB = m\angle COA - m\angle BOA = 82°37'30'' - 51°43'45''$
$= 82°36'90'' - 51°43'45''$ (regrouped minutes and second)
$= 81°96'90'' - 51°43'45''$ (regrouped degrees and minutes)
$= 30°53'45''$ ❑

EXAMPLE 8   What size angle has the property that 1000 of them fill up a plane?

Solution   If 1000 are to fill up a plane, then the angle must be $\frac{1}{250}$th of a right angle.

$$\tfrac{1}{250} \times 90° = \tfrac{9}{25}° = \tfrac{9}{25} \times 60'$$
$$= 21\tfrac{3}{5}' = 21' + \tfrac{3}{5} \times 60'' = 21'36'' \qquad \square$$

The second common system of angle measure employs the *radian* (rad) as unit of measure. See Figure 13.56.

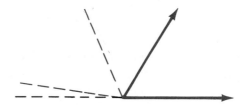

Figure 13.56 A radian.

A **radian** is an angle of such a size that there are π of them in a straight angle.

Since there are $\pi \doteq 3.1416$ radians in 180 degrees,

$$1 \text{ rad} \doteq \frac{180°}{3.1416} \doteq 57.30° \doteq 57°18'$$

$$1° \doteq \frac{3.1416}{180} \text{ rad} \doteq 0.017 \text{ rad}$$

The radian system of angle measure is used extensively in high school and college mathematics and physics courses, where it greatly simplifies many formulas. Since it is not used in the elementary grades, we will give just one example to illustrate the convenience of the system.

EXAMPLE 9   Express the area A of a sector of a circle in terms of the radius r and the measure θ of the central angle in two cases:
(a) When θ is given in degrees
(b) When θ is given in radians

Solution   See Figure 13.57.
(a) We noted in our work with area that A is proportional to θ; that is, if θ is given in degrees, then

$$\frac{A}{\text{Area of entire circle}} = \frac{\theta}{360}$$

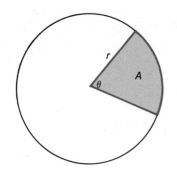

Figure 13.57

So

$$\frac{A}{\pi r^2} = \frac{\theta}{360}$$

which yields the formula

$$A = \frac{\pi r^2 \theta}{360}$$

(b) If θ is given in radians, then the proportion becomes

$$\frac{A}{\pi r^2} = \frac{\theta}{2\pi}$$

which yields the simpler formula

$$A = \frac{r^2 \theta}{2}$$ ❑

Units in Problem Solving

Most real-world problems involve units of various kinds. Symbols such as cm and ft are called *dimension symbols*. We have already seen examples of how helpful it is to manipulate these dimension symbols just as though they were numerals or variables. Often this formal *dimensional analysis* is a valuable tool in problem solving.

EXAMPLE 10   Gasoline costs $1.20 per gallon. What is the cost of gasoline for a 500-mi trip in a car that gets 20 miles per gallon?

Solution   The answer must bear the dimension symbol $. What can we do to the expressions

$$1.20 \text{ \$/gal} \qquad 20 \text{ mi/gal} \qquad 500 \text{ mi}$$

to get an answer in dollars? Since

$$\$ = \frac{\$}{\text{gal}} \times \frac{\text{gal}}{\text{mi}} \times \text{mi} \qquad \text{(cancel the gal and mi)}$$

the answer is

$$1.20 \frac{\$}{\text{gal}} \times \frac{1}{20} \frac{\text{gal}}{\text{mi}} \times 500 \text{ mi} = \frac{1.20 \times 500}{20} \$ = \$30$$ ❑

EXAMPLE 11   A car is traveling at the rate of 88 ft/sec. Its tires have radius 14 in. At how many revolutions (rev) per minute (min) are the wheels turning?

Solution By the circumference formula $C = 2\pi r$, with $r = 14$, each wheel moves 28π in/rev. So our task is to somehow combine ft/sec with in/rev and get rev/min. By dimensional analysis

$$\frac{rev}{min} = \frac{rev}{in} \times \frac{in}{ft} \times \frac{ft}{sec} \times \frac{sec}{min}$$

Thus the answer is

$$\frac{1}{28\pi} \frac{rev}{in} \times 12 \frac{in}{ft} \times 88 \frac{ft}{sec} \times 60 \frac{sec}{min} = \frac{12 \times 88 \times 60}{28\pi} \frac{rev}{min} \doteq 720 \text{ rpm}$$

Note: Since 1 ft = 12 in, we can view multiplication by $12 \frac{in}{ft}$ as multiplication by 1. Likewise, $60 \frac{sec}{min}$ and $\frac{1}{28\pi} \frac{rev}{in}$ both equal 1, so the product we computed is equal to $88 \frac{ft}{sec}$. ❏

EXERCISE SET 13.3

1. How many of *your* palms are there in *your* cubit?

2. There are some common English words that might help you keep straight the meanings of the prefixes *milli-, centi-, deci,* and *deka-*. If you don't already know them, look up the meanings of these words.
   (a) Mill (as used in expressing tax rates)
   (b) Cent
   (c) Decimate (original meaning)
   (d) Decade

3. Perhaps you noticed that *Latin* prefixes (*milli-, centi-, deci-*) go with units *less* than a meter, while *Greek* prefixes (*deka, hecto-, kilo-*) go with units *greater* than a meter. Have you noticed any other pattern that will help you to remember the order of size among metric units?

4. List the following units in order of increasing length: centimeter, decimeter, dekameter, hectometer, kilometer, meter, millimeter.

5. Which metric unit (mm, cm, m, or km) would you probably use in expressing the following?
   (a) The width of a basketball court

   (b) The thickness of a magazine
   (c) The length of a new pencil
   (d) The distance from St. Louis to New Orleans
   (e) The circumference of a hockey puck
   (f) The distance you drive between oil changes

6. Which metric unit (mm^2, cm^2, m^2, or km^2) would you probably use in expressing the following?
   (a) The area of Wyoming
   (b) The area of a rectangular television screen
   (c) The area of the head of a thumbtack
   (d) The area of a soccer field
   (e) The surface area of a can of soda
   (f) The surface area of a pearl

7. Which metric unit (mm^3, cm^3, or m^3) would you probably use in expressing the following?
   (a) The volume of a shoe box
   (b) The volume of a classroom
   (c) The volume of a nickel

8. Estimate each of the following in centimeters; then check your estimate with a ruler.
   (a) The length of your thumbnail
   (b) The length of a pencil

(c) The width of a dollar bill

(d) The length of a dollar bill

9. Fill in missing numbers.
    (a) 1 cm = _____ m
    (b) 1 mm = _____ m
    (c) 1 km = _____ m
    (d) 1 cm = _____ km
    (e) 1 kg = _____ g
    (f) 5374 cm = _____ m
    (g) 1027 mm = _____ m
    (h) 88 mm = _____ m
    (i) 716 mm = _____ cm
    (j) 3.5 m = _____ cm
    (k) 0.0052 m = _____ mm
    (l) 15 km = _____ m
    (m) 72 km = _____ cm
    (n) 72 mi = _____ in
    (o) 1 barrel = _____ teaspoons
    (p) 1 ton = _____ drams

10. Solve this pair of problems. (Which involves simpler calculations?)
    (a) The highway department is planning to build a $2\frac{1}{2}$ mi stretch of highway. It is to be 32 ft wide, and the concrete is to be 8 in thick. How many cubic yards of concrete will be required?
    (b) The highway department is planning to build another stretch of highway. It is to be 4.1 km long, 9 m wide, and 20 cm thick. How many cubic meters of concrete will be required?

11. Is there any simple relation between the following?
    (a) An ounce and an inch
    (b) A gram and a centimeter

12. Which is more?
    (a) A kilometer or a mile
    (b) 1500 m or a mile
    (c) A gram or an ounce
    (d) An inch or a centimeter
    (e) A quart or a liter
    (f) A pound or a kilogram

13. Use the fact that 1 in = 2.54 cm (exactly) to calculate *exactly* how many meters there are in

1 yd. Now, comment on this question that was put to track star Rick Wohlhuter by a television sports reporter: "Do you train differently for the 800 meters than you do for the 880 yards?"

14. *A true story:* While trying to loosen a nut on his foreign car, a home handyman discovers that his $\frac{3}{8}$-in socket wrench is just a bit too small and his $\frac{7}{16}$-in socket wrench is too large. What size metric wrench should he probably buy?

15. Express your height and weight in metric units.

16. What is the area, in square centimeters, of a triangle with base 0.8 m and height 31 cm?

17. What is the total surface area, in square centimeters, of a meterstick that is 4 mm thick and 2.5 cm wide?

18. A single yellow stripe 6 cm wide is to be painted down the center of a highway for a distance of 12 km. If 1 L of paint covers 9 m², how many liters of paint will be needed?

A calculator would be helpful for the next six exercises.

19. What is the approximate volume, in liters, of a (right circular) cylindrical garbage can of height 1.2 m and diameter 46 cm?

20. Find the approximate volume of the earth in cubic meters. *Hint:* Assume that the earth is a sphere, and use the original definition of a meter.

21. Water weighs about 62.4 lb per cubic foot. How much weight is a flat supermarket roof, with dimensions 80 ft by 60 ft, supporting after a 16-in snowfall? (You may assume that 10 in of snow is equivalent to 1 in of rain. Round your answer to the nearest 1000 lb.)

22. A floating object is known to displace its own weight of water. A 6 in by 8 in by 6 ft railroad tie is floating in a pond with its largest face up so that only 2 in of it shows above the surface of the water. How heavy is the railroad tie, to the nearest pound? (Use the density of water given in the previous exercise.)

23. The deodorant stick in Figure 13.58 has a hemispherical top and weighs 50 g. Will it float in water?

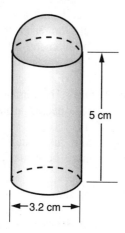

Figure 13.58

24. A nurse is given a cylindrical glass container with inside diameter 1.4 cm and is asked to calibrate it to show its capacity in cubic centimeters (milliliters). How far apart should the calibration marks be?

25. Find $m\angle AOC$ in Figure 13.59 under the following assumptions.
    (a) $m\angle AOB = 42°55'18''$
       and $m\angle BOC = 35°8'35''$
    (b) $m\angle AOB = 40°27'5''$
       and $m\angle BOC = 36°38'57''$
    (c) $m\angle AOB = 41°27''$
       and $m\angle BOC = 37°10'40''$
    (d) $m\angle AOB = 40°28'17''$
       and $m\angle BOC = 39°31'43''$

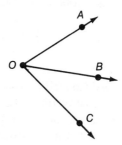

Figure 13.59

26. Find $m\angle A$ in the triangles shown in Figure 13.60. Do not try to use a protractor.

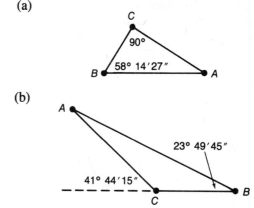

Figure 13.60

27. Find $m\angle AOF$ in Figure 13.61 if $m\angle AOB = 16°39'47''$ and all of the angles, $\angle AOB$, $\angle BOC$, $\angle COD$, $\angle DOE$, $\angle EOF$, are congruent.

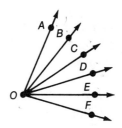

Figure 13.61

28. A distant ratio tower appears to be 27°15′ east of north, and a mountain peak appears to be 19°50′ north of west. What size angle does the observer perceive between the radio tower and the mountain peak?

29. One pie is to be shared equally by seven people. What size central angle should each piece have (to the nearest minute)?

30. If the minute hand on a clock moves steadily rather than in jerks, how long does it take to rotate through the following?
    (a) An angle of 1°
    (b) An angle of 1′

★ 31. For Figure 13.62, express arc length *a* in terms of radius *r* and central angle *θ*.
   (a) When *θ* is given in degrees
   (b) When *θ* is given in radians

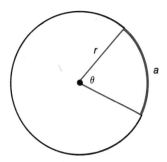

Figure 13.62

32. Engineers sometimes use a unit of angle measure called a *grad*. There are 100 grads in a right angle. What is the sum of the measures in grads of the three angles of any triangle?

33. Simplify.
   (a) 14 mi/hr × 6 ¢/mi × 3 hr
   (b) $\dfrac{24 \text{ mi/gal}}{6 \text{ mi/hr}}$

34. Convert.
   (a) 22 cm/sec to km/hr
   (b) 7.20 $/hr to ¢/min

35. To estimate the heights of primitive people on the basis of a few fosssil fragments, anthropologists use a rule of thumb that the ratio of the length of one's foot to one's height is about $\frac{15}{100}$. Measure your own foot length and height, and compute your ratio. Does it matter whether you make your measurement in inches or in centimeters?

The problem-solving strategy of dimensional analysis should be helpful in Exercises 36–38.

★ 36. Joe has a single-speed bicycle with a front sprocket with 30 teeth and a rear sprocket with 18 teeth. The teeth on each sprocket are $\frac{3}{4}$ in apart. The outside diameter of his rear tire is 28 in. The outside diameter of his front tire is 20 in.
   (a) If he never coasts, how many times will Joe have to push the pedals around to go 1 mi? (Use $\pi \doteq \frac{22}{7}$.)
   (b) If he can make his pedals go around 100 times per minute, how many miles per hour can he go?

★ 37. The distance from the center to the outermost groove on a certain long-playing record is $5\frac{3}{4}$ in. The distance from the center to the innermost groove is $2\frac{1}{8}$ in. The playing time, at $33\frac{1}{3}$ rpm, is 24 min.
   (a) How far apart are the grooves on the record?
   (b) What (approximately) is the total length of the groove?
   (*Hint:* Make the simplifying assumption that there is not one groove but many concentric circular grooves all the same distance apart).

38. It was one of those pronouncements that make politics so fascinating. On February 7, 1984, a prominent legislator made the following two statements about a $1.9 billion defense appropriation: (1) "It's enough money to give every single American $7000." (2) "A $1.9 billion stack of 1000 dollar bills would reach 134 miles high." Assuming this politician is correct:
   (a) How many Americans are there?
   (b) How thick is a 1000 dollar bill?

Computer Vignette K

According to the 5–8 *Standards* of the National Council of Teachers of Mathematics, children are not supposed to spend time converting measurements from metric to customary and vice versa. Machines can be easily programmed to carry out such tasks if the need arises. Here is a straightforward BASIC program (Figure 13.63) that converts a measurement made in meters into miles, yards, feet, and inches. Notice that the third sample run (Figure 13.64) sheds light on Exercise 13 of the previous section.

Figure 13.63

```
10    PRINT
20    PRINT "TYPE IN THE NUMBER OF METERS"
30    INPUT M
40    LET I(1) = M * 39.37
50    LET F(1) = INT(I(1)/12)
60    LET Y(1) = INT(F(1)/3)
70    LET M(1) = INT(Y(1)/1760)
80    LET I = I(1) - 12 * F(1)
90    LET F = F(1) - 3 * Y(1)
100   LET Y = Y(1) - 1760 * M(1)
110   PRINT M;" METERS EQUALS ";M(1);" MILES,
      ";Y;" YARDS, ";F; " FEET, ";I;" INCHES"
120   PRINT "WANT TO STOP? 1 = YES, 0 = NO"
130   INPUT A
140   IF A = 0 THEN 10
150   END
```

Figure 13.64

```
]RUN

TYPE IN THE NUMBER OF METERS
?10
10 METERS EQUALS 0 MILES, 10 YARDS, 2 FEET,
 9.70000005 INCHES
WANT TO STOP? 1 = YES, 0 = NO
?0

TYPE IN THE NUMBER OF METERS
?10000
10000 METERS EQUALS 6 MILES, 376 YARDS, 0 FEET,
 4 INCHES
WANT TO STOP? 1 = YES, 0 = NO
?0

TYPE IN THE NUMBER OF METERS
?800
800 METERS EQUALS 0 MILES, 874 YARDS, 2 FEET,
 8.00000763 INCHES
WANT TO STOP? 1 = YES, 0 = NO
?1
```

 **13.4   *Approximation and Error***

When we studied the *theory* of measurement, we considered *ideal* segments of length exactly 5 units, ideal rectangles with dimensions exactly 4 units by 3 units, ideal spheres, and so on. When we deal with the practical matter of measuring *real* things, however, nothing is ever exact. If you measure an ordinary sheet of $8\frac{1}{2}$-by-11 notebook paper, you will find that it is not *exactly* 11 in long. Probably it is closer to being $10\frac{63}{64}$ in or $11\frac{1}{64}$ in long. In any real situation we always deal with approximations, and each situation dictates how "good" an approximation is required. When you fill in your weight on a driver's license application form, for example, an approximation to the nearest pound is good enough, and even an approximation within 10 lb of the truth is tolerable. When you bring a small parcel to the post office, however, an approximation to the nearest pound is not good enough.

Precision and Accuracy

The word *good* is rather vague. In measurement situations we use language more carefully. We talk about the **precision** and the **accuracy** of a measurement. Both of these words refer to the "goodness" of an approximation but in quite different ways. The exact meanings of these two words will be made clear by the following examples.

EXAMPLE 1   Suppose Arthur is handed this segment,

---

and is asked to give its length to the nearest centimeter. He will, of course, report that it is 10 cm long if it is anywhere between $9\frac{1}{2}$ and $10\frac{1}{2}$ cm long. The unit in which he reports its length, the centimeter, is called the precision unit for that measurement. Since the actual length of the segment can differ from Arthur's report by $\frac{1}{2}$ cm, we say that the greatest possible error (GPE) in his report is $\frac{1}{2}$ cm.   ❏

> The **precision unit** of a measurement is the smallest unit used in reporting the measurement.

> **Greatest possible error** (GPE) = $\frac{1}{2}$ of precision unit

---

EXAMPLE 2   If Beulah reports her height as 5 ft 7 in. Her precision unit is the inch. The GPE in her reported measurement is $\frac{1}{2}$ in. One can infer from her report that her true height (whatever that means) is between 5 ft $6\frac{1}{2}$ in and 5 ft $7\frac{1}{2}$ in.   ❏

Arthur's measurement is **more precise** than Beulah's because his precision unit (centimeter) is smaller than hers (inch).

> A first measurement is said to be more precise than a second if the precision unit of the first is smaller than the precision unit of the second.

It is not, however, more accurate. The GPE in Arthur's report, $\frac{1}{2}$ cm, represents about $\frac{1}{20}$ of the length of the segment ($\frac{1}{19}$ if the segment is $9\frac{1}{2}$ cm long, and $\frac{1}{21}$ if it is $10\frac{1}{2}$ cm long). We say that the **relative error** in Arthur's report is $\frac{1}{20}$, or 5%.

> $$\text{Relative error} = \frac{\text{GPE}}{\text{reported measurement}}$$

In Beulah's report the relative error is

$$\frac{\frac{1}{2} \text{ in}}{5 \text{ ft } 7 \text{ in}} = \frac{\frac{1}{2}}{67} = \frac{1}{134} < 1\%$$

Although her GPE is larger than his, hers is *relatively* less serious when compared with the size of the object measured. We say that Beulah's measurement is **more accurate** than Arthur's because its relative error is smaller.

> A first measurement is said to be more accurate than a second if the relative error in the first is smaller than the relative error in the second.

EXAMPLE 3

Compare these two reported measurements for precision and accuracy:
(a) Cora is $19\frac{1}{2}$ years old, to the nearest half year.
(b) Dan can run the 100 yd dash in 9.8 sec, to the nearest tenth of a second.

Solution

The precision unit in Cora's age measurement is a half year. Thus her GPE is $\frac{1}{4}$ year. (Her true age is between $19\frac{1}{4}$ and $19\frac{3}{4}$ years.) The relative error in her report is

$$\frac{\frac{1}{4}}{19\frac{1}{2}} = \frac{\frac{1}{4}}{\frac{39}{2}} = \frac{1}{78} \doteq 1.3\%$$

The precision unit in Dan's speed measurement is a tenth of a second. Thus his GPE is $\frac{1}{20}$ sec, and his relative error is

$$\frac{\frac{1}{20}}{9.8} = \frac{1}{196} \doteq 0.5\%$$

Hence Dan's speed measurement is both more precise ($\frac{1}{10}$ sec is less than $\frac{1}{2}$ year) and more accurate (0.5% is less than 1.3%) than Cora's age measurement. ❏

EXAMPLE 4   A farmer has 400 ft³ of fertilizer (to the nearest cubic foot) to spread on a 20-acre field (to the nearest acre). Compare these two measurements for precision and accuracy.

Solution   They cannot be compared for precision since the precision units, cubic foot and acre, are incomparable, one being a unit of volume and the other of area. They can, however, be compared for accuracy. The relative error in the fertilizer measurement is

$$\frac{\frac{1}{2}}{400} = \frac{1}{800}$$

The relative error in the land measurement is

$$\frac{\frac{1}{2}}{20} = \frac{1}{40}$$

Thus the fertilizer measurement is much more accurate.   ❏

Error Buildup

When approximations are used in arithmetic calculations, one is often misled to unwarranted conclusions. Consider again Example 6(b) of Section 13.3: Convert 15 m to feet. Our solution was based on the *approximate* relation, 1 m $\doteq$ 1.1 yd, and proceeded as follows:

$$15 \text{ m} = 15 \times 1 \text{ m}$$
$$\doteq 15 \times 1.1 \text{ yd}$$
$$\doteq 15 \times 1.1 \times 1 \text{ yd}$$
$$\doteq 15 \times 1.1 \times 3 \text{ ft}$$
$$\doteq 49.5 \text{ ft}$$

One might suppose that the answer 49.5 ft would be correct to the nearest tenth of a foot. That, however, is not the case. In fact, the conversion factor between meters and yards is not exactly 1.1; it is just slightly more than 1.09. Using the exact conversion factor, one would find

$$15 \text{ m} \doteq 49.1 \text{ ft} \qquad \text{(to the nearest tenth of a foot)}$$

Even more dramatic examples arise when two or more approximations are used in a single calculation. Suppose we are told that a parking lot is 48 ft wide (to the nearest foot) and 76 ft long (to the nearest foot), and we are asked for its area in square feet. If we simply multiply, we get

$$48 \text{ ft} \times 76 \text{ ft} = 3648 \text{ ft}^2$$

Now the question is, How reliable is this product? The only way to decide for certain is to keep careful track, as follows, of the greatest lower and least upper bounds on each measurement.

Since the width is 48 ft to the nearest foot, the lot could be as narrow as 47.5 ft or as wide as 48.5 ft. Since the length is 76 ft to the nearest foot, the lot could be as short as 75.5 ft or as long as 76.5 ft. Thus the area of the lot could be as small as

$$47.5 \text{ ft} \times 75.5 \text{ ft} = 3586.25 \text{ ft}^2$$

or as large as

$$48.5 \text{ ft} \times 76.5 \text{ ft} = 3710.25 \text{ ft}^2$$

Thus the true area of the lot lies somewhere between 3586.25 ft² and 3710.25 ft². Our calculated product, 3648 ft², lies very near the middle of that interval, but the greatest possible error associated with 3648 ft² is *not* $\frac{1}{2}$ ft² but, rather, 62.25 ft², the difference between 3710.25 ft² and 3648 ft². That is, the area of the lot is not necessarily 3648 ft² to the nearest square foot, nor 3650 ft² to the nearest 10 ft², nor even 3600 ft² to the nearest 100 ft². If we round off to thousands it is true that the area of the lot is 4000 ft to the nearest 1000 ft², but the best answer we can give is the interval answer

$$3586.25 \text{ ft}^2 \le \text{area} \le 3710.25 \text{ ft}^2$$

EXERCISE SET 13.4

1. Measure the length of the following segment, using $\frac{1}{8}$ in as your precision unit.

   ———————————————

   (a) Now report that length, accordingly, to the nearest eighth of an inch.
   (b) Your report implies that the actual length of the segment lies between what two numbers?
   (c) What is the GPE (greatest possible error) in your report?
   (d) Give the relative error of your measurement to the nearest tenth of a percent.

2. Give the GPE and relative error (to the nearest tenth of a percent) for each of the following reported measurements.
   (a) 16 m, to the nearest meter
   (b) 6 ft 2 in, to the nearest inch
   (c) 4200 lb, to the nearest hundred pounds
   (d) 6 mm, to the nearest millimeter
   (e) 45°, to the nearest degree
   (f) 3 days, 5 hours, and 24 minutes, to the nearest minute

   (g) 100 in², to the nearest 10 square inches
   (h) 274 light-years, to the nearest light-year

3. Arrange the reported measurements of Exercise 2 in order of increasing accuracy.

4. Can you arrange the measurements of Exercise 2 in order of increasing precision?

5. Arrange the linear measurements of Exercise 2 in order of increasing precision.

6. The distance between two airports is reported to be 254 mi, to the nearest mile. The length of an airplane is reported to be 35 ft, to the nearest foot. Which measurement is more precise? Which is more accurate?

7. To the nearest centimeter the length and width of a dollar bill are 16 cm and 7 cm, respectively.
   (a) What is the precision unit in each measurement?
   (b) What is the GPE in each measurement?
   (c) What is the relative error in each measurement?

(d) Find greatest lower and least upper bounds for the area of the dollar bill in square centimeters.

8. The dimensions of a right rectangular prism are given, to the nearest centimeter, as 15 cm by 11 cm by 6 cm.
   (a) Give least upper and greatest lower bounds on its volume.
   (b) By how much could its volume differ from the product $15 \times 11 \times 6$ cm³?

9. The diameter of a solid right circular cylinder is reported to be d units, with a relative error of 1%. The height is reported to be h units, with a relative error of 3%. To the nearest whole percent, what is the relative error in reporting its volume as $\pi (d/2)^2 h$ square units?

10. Several notational conventions are in use for reporting how good an approximate measurement is. For each report, express the possible values for M in interval notation:
    $? \leq M \leq ?$
    (a) $M = 19 \pm 0.2$ m   (plus-or-minus notation)
    (b) $|M - 45| \leq 0.01°$ (absolute value notation)
    (c) $M = 2.75 \times 10^8$ kg (significant digits/scientific notation)

 **13.5 *Symmetry***

At the beginning of Chapter 12 we defined a rigid motion to be any sequence of translations, rotations, and reflections. These three basic moves were described rather loosely, and a promise was made that better descriptions would be given once we had developed the key measurement concepts of distance and angle measure. In this section we make good on that promise, and then we use the (now more precise) notion of rigid motion to clarify the idea of symmetry.

Rigid Motions Revisited

Under a **translation** (slide) every point of a figure moves the same distance and in the same direction. Thus a translation can be specified by an arrow or vector. The length of the vector tells how far each point moves. The ray determined by the vector gives the direction of motion; that is, all points of the figure move along rays parallel to and pointing the same way as the vector. In Figure 13.65 the original figure is shown black, the image red. Notice that when the original figure is a polygon, one need only determine where the vertices go in order to sketch the image. A ruler is a useful tool.

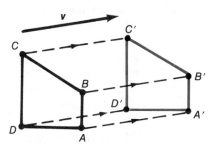

Figure 13.65 Translation.

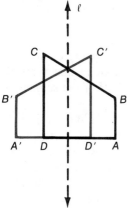

Figure 13.66 Rotation.

Under a **rotation** (turn) one point, the center of rotation C, is fixed. All other points remain at their original distances from C but turn through the same angle. For example, in Figure 13.66 all points turn through a 90° counterclockwise angle. Thus to specify a rotation, one needs to give three things: a center point, an angle measure, and a direction (clockwise or counterclockwise). Notice that in contrast to a translation, where all points move along parallel rays, for a rotation all points move along concentric circles. Apparently, a compass and a protractor will be useful tools for sketching images under a rotation. Again, observe that in the case of a polygonal original, it is enough to locate the images of the vertices.

Under a **reflection** (flip) all points move along parallel lines, namely, lines perpendicular to the line of reflection, but they need not all move in the same direction and they need not all move the same distance. Notice that in Figure 13.67 points to the left of ℓ move to the right, and points to the right of ℓ move left. Points close to ℓ move a short distance, points far from ℓ move a greater distance, and points on ℓ remain stationary. For points off ℓ the precise connection between the original point P and its image P' is that ℓ is the perpendicular bisector of $\overline{PP'}$. To specify a reflection, we need give only one thing, the line of reflection ℓ. Any object with a square corner, for example, a draftsman's triangle, will be useful for drawing perpendiculars to ℓ (see Figure 13.68), as would the Mira described earlier.

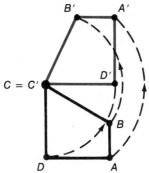

Figure 13.67 Reflection.

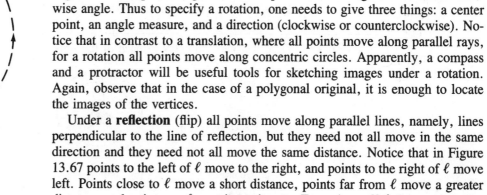

Figure 13.68

Symmetry

We all have at least a vague idea of what is meant by symmetry. Certainly figure A in Figure 13.69 is "more symmetric" than figure B. We will try to clarify that phrase in what follows.

Here is the formal definition.

Figure 13.69

A **symmetry** of a (plane) figure is a rigid motion of the figure onto itself.

If the rigid motion is a reflection, then the symmetry is called a reflectional symmetry or, more commonly, a **line symmetry.** If the rigid motion is a rotation or a translation, then the symmetry is called, respectively, a **rotational symmetry** or a **translational symmetry.**

EXAMPLE 1   Describe one symmetry of each of the figures in Figure 13.70.

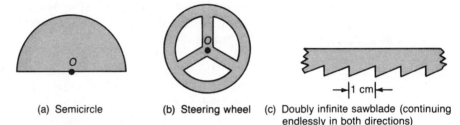

(a) Semicircle   (b) Steering wheel   (c) Doubly infinite sawblade (continuing
                                                    endlessly in both directions)

Figure 13.70

Solution   (a) Reflection in the vertical line through O is a *line symmetry* of the semicircle. This result can be verified by placing a Mira along that vertical line and observing that the reflected image of the left half of the semicircle coincides exactly with the (original) right half.

(b) Imagine cutting out a cardboard steering wheel, placing it on a sheet of paper, and tracing its outline onto the paper. Now stick a pin through O, and rotate the cardboard 120° clockwise. The cardboard would again coincide with the tracing. That is, the figure would be sent onto itself. Thus clockwise rotation about O through 120° is a *rotational symmetry* of the steering wheel. Do you see that a 90° clockwise rotation about O does *not* send the steering wheel onto itself, and thus is not a symmetry?

(c) Imagine cutting out a cardboard copy of the doubly infinite sawblade, placing it on a doubly infinite strip of paper, and tracing its outline. If you now slide the sawblade 1 cm to the right, it will come into coincidence with the tracing. Thus translation 1 cm to the right is a *translational symmetry* of the sawblade. Do you see that a translation 1.5 cm to the right does *not* send the sawblade onto itself, and thus is not a symmetry?   ❏

You probably thought of other symmetries as you read the previous example: a 120° counterclockwise rotation of the steering wheel, a translation of the sawblade 1 cm to the left, a translation of the sawblade 2 cm to the right, and so on. To describe all the symmetries of a given figure, we look at rigid motions from a functional point of view.

Symmetry Groups (Optional)

Consider the isosceles triangle shown in Figure 13.71. It has two symmetries. One obvious one is the flip (reflection) across line ℓ, which we shall designate

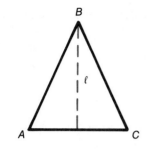

Figure 13.71

by F_ℓ. Under this motion, vertices A and C trade places, while vertex B remains unmoved. Thus F_ℓ can be thought of as a function on the vertices and described by a table or an arrow diagram.

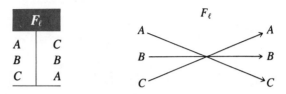

The other symmetry is so obvious that it is hard to see. We know that hooking up (composing) two flips produces a rigid motion, so, in particular, if we hook up F_ℓ with itself, we should get another symmetry of $\triangle ABC$. That hookup has the following effect on the vertices:

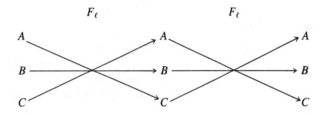

That is, ultimately $A \to A$, $B \to B$, and $C \to C$. It is reasonable to call this function the **identity function** and denote it by I. Its table is

A natural question to ask is, If we could generate one new symmetry of $\triangle ABC$ by hooking up two flips F_ℓ, why not hook up three flips F_ℓ and get still another symmetry? Let's try it. Hooking up three flips F_ℓ produces a symmetry, all right, and finding its effect on the vertices is easy enough:

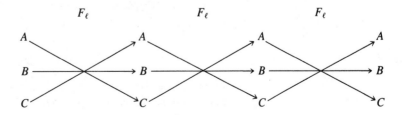

But now we note that the ultimate effect of this symmetry on vertices is exactly the same as that of F_ℓ alone:

$$
\begin{array}{lcl}
A & \longrightarrow & C \\
B & \longrightarrow & B \\
C & \longrightarrow & A
\end{array}
$$

Thus we have not generated a new symmetry. We have simply come back to our original one.

By observing where the various vertices go, we can verify the following equations, where the symbol Ⓣ denotes the hookup (composition) operation and can be read "then":

$$F_\ell \; ⓉEfmt \; F_\ell = I$$
$$F_\ell \; Ⓣ \; I = F_\ell$$
$$I \; Ⓣ \; F_\ell = F_\ell$$
$$I \; Ⓣ \; I = I$$

Table 13.10

Ⓣ	I	F_ℓ
I	I	F_ℓ
F_ℓ	F_ℓ	I

From these equations we conclude that no new symmetries of $\triangle ABC$ can be generated by hooking up any combination of the two symmetries F_ℓ and I. The hookup operation Ⓣ is a binary operation of $\{F_\ell, I\}$. The Cayley table for this **group of symmetries** of the isosceles triangle is given in Table 13.10.

EXAMPLE 2 Find all symmetries of the equilateral triangle in Figure 13.72.

Solution Three symmetries are immediately obvious: F_{ℓ_1}, F_{ℓ_2}, and F_{ℓ_3}. By hooking up any one of these with itself, we get the identity symmetry I. Suppose now that we hook up two different flips, say F_{ℓ_1}, then F_{ℓ_2}. The effect on the vertices is as follows:

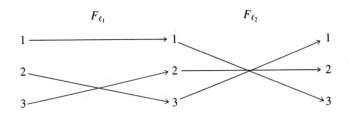

That is, F_{ℓ_1} Ⓣ F_{ℓ_2} has the effect

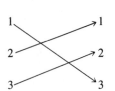

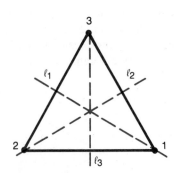

Figure 13.72

Table 13.11

$R_{120}^{\curvearrowright}$	
1	2
2	3
3	1

If we refer to Figure 13.72, we see that this moving of vertex 1 to position 3, vertex 3 to position 2, and vertex 2 to position 1 is just a 120° counterclockwise rotation about the point where ℓ_1, ℓ_2, and ℓ_3 concur. Thus we have a fifth symmetry, $R_{120}^{\curvearrowleft}$. This symmetry immediately suggests a sixth symmetry, $R_{120}^{\curvearrowright}$ (Table 13.11), clockwise rotation through 120° about that same point.

It turns out that there are no others in the group of symmetries of the equilateral triangle. In the exercises you are asked to make a Cayley table for the binary operation Ⓣ on the set

$$\{I,\ R_{120}^{\curvearrowleft},\ R_{120}^{\curvearrowright},\ F_{\ell_1},\ F_{\ell_2},\ F_{\ell_3}\} \qquad ❑$$

EXERCISE SET 13.5

1. Draw three copies of the rectangle of Figure 13.73 on a clean sheet of paper, and then draw the images under the three given rigid motions. Be as precise as you can.

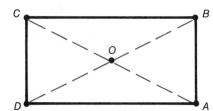

Figure 13.73

(a) Translation given by the vector from C to O
(b) Rotation 90° clockwise about O
(c) Reflection in the line $\overleftrightarrow{AC}$

Is any one of these three rigid motions a symmetry of the rectangle?

2. Describe all symmetries of each of the following figures.

(a)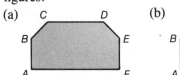

(b)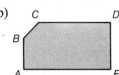

(c)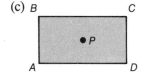

(d)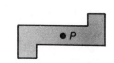

(e)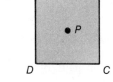

(f)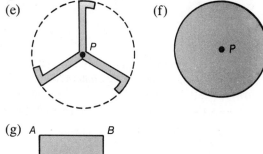

(g)

(h) The moon in Figure 13.69
(i) The moon in Figure 13.69 if its eye, nose, and mouth are removed
(j) The star in Figure 13.69

(k)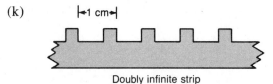

|←1 cm→|

Doubly infinite strip

★ (l)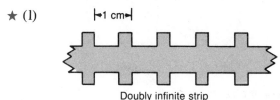

|←1 cm→|

Doubly infinite strip

3. A line ℓ is called an **axis of symmetry** of a figure A if reflection in ℓ is a symmetry of A. Locate axes of symmetry in the following figures. Use a Mira if you have one.

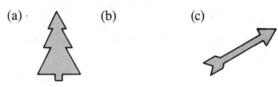

(a)   (b)   (c)

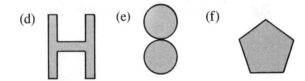

(d)   (e)   (f)

4. Refer to the quadrilateral family portrait in Figure 13.23. Which of these quadrilaterals have the following as their only axis (axes) of symmetry?
   (a) Exactly one line through a pair of opposite (nonadjacent) vertices
   (b) Exactly two lines through pairs of opposite vertices
   (c) Exactly one line through the midpoints of a pair of opposite (nonadjacent) sides
   (d) Exactly two lines through pairs of midpoints of opposite sides

5. A 180° rotational symmetry with center O is sometimes called a **point symmetry** about O because O is the midpoint of each segment that joins an original point to its image. For example, the oval of Figure 13.74 has point symmetry in

the center point O. One can think of each point on the oval as being sent to its diametrically opposite point.
   (a) Which of the quadrilaterals in Figure 13.23 have point symmetry?
   (b) Does the star in Figure 13.69 have point symmetry?

6. The spatial analog of a line of symmetry is a **plane of symmetry.** One plane of symmetry for a right rectangular prism is shown in Figure 13.75. Describe some others.

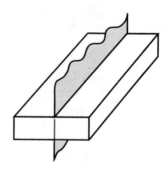

Figure 13.75 Plane of symmetry.

7. Refer to Figure 13.42 and determine how many planes of symmetry there are for the following.
   (a) The regular tetrahedron
   (b) The regular hexahedron
   (c) The regular octahedron

8. The spatial analog of a (point) center of rotation is an **axis of rotation.** Describe all the rotational symmetries of the cube in Figure 13.76 about the axis shown.

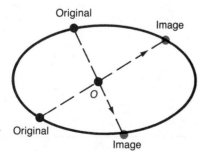

Figure 13.74 Point symmetry.

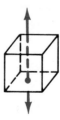

Figure 13.76 Axis of rotation.

9. For the cube in Figure 13.76, find as many axes as you can about which there will be a nontrivial rotational symmetry, that is, one for which the angle of rotation is not 0°.

10. Ultimately a symmetry of a polygon is a function on the vertices. Make an input-output table for the 180°-clockwise rotation, about O, of the square in Figure 13.77. Do the same for the 180°-*counter*clockwise rotation about O. Are these two rotations one and the same symmetry of the square?

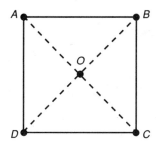

Figure 13.77

11. "Two wrongs don't make a right, but three lefts do." Explain this statement in terms of rigid motions. What do 73 lefts make? What do 82 lefts make?

★ 12. Fill in the Cayley table (Table 13.12) for the group of symmetries of the equilateral triangle.

★ 13. Think of the set $\{I, R_{120}\curvearrowright, R_{120}\curvearrowleft, F_{\ell_1}, F_{\ell_2}, F_{\ell_3}\}$ and the binary operation ⓣ of Exercise 12 as a mathematical system.
    (a) Is it commutative?
    (b) Does it have an identity element?
    (c) Does every element have an inverse?
    (d) Find all of the proper subsets that are closed under the operation ⓣ.

★ 14. Make a Cayley table for the group of symmetries of the rectangle in Figure 13.78.

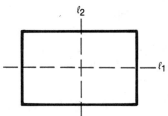

Figure 13.78

15. Towns A and B are situated on the same side of a straight river as shown in Figure 13.79. They agree to split the total cost of building a pumping station P and laying water pipes from P to A and P to B. Your problem is to locate P to minimize the amount of water pipe needed, that is, to minimize the length of polygonal path APB. The location of P in Figure 13.79 is *not* optimal. *Hint:* Consider the reflection B' of B in the north bank of the river.

Table 13.12

ⓣ	I	$R_{120})$	R_{120}↲	F_{ℓ_1}	F_{ℓ_2}	F_{ℓ_3}
I						
$R_{120})$						
R_{120}↲						
F_{ℓ_1}						
F_{ℓ_2}						
F_{ℓ_3}						

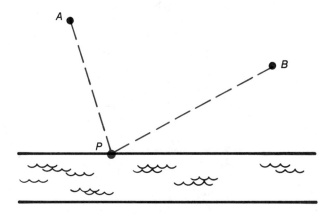

Figure 13.79

Key Concepts in Chapter 13

Angle addition property
Angle supplement property
Equal measures congruence criteria
   for angles
   for segments
Triangle family
Quadrilateral family
Regular polygon
General tessellation
Edge-to-edge tessellation
Prototile
Regular tessellation
Interior angle of a polygon

Central angle of a regular polygon
Semiregular tessellation
Type, of a vertex
Polyhedron
Regular polyhedron
Metric system
Dimensional analysis
Precision unit
Greatest possible error
Relative error
Symmetry
*Group of symmetries

❧ Chapter 13 Review Exercises ❧

1. In each figure find the measure of $\angle AOB$. Everything that looks like a straight line is one.

(a)

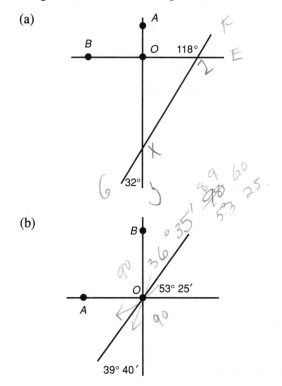

(b)

(c)

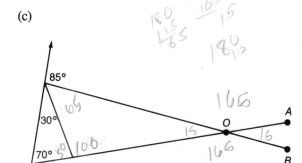

2. Draw each figure as carefully as you can.
   (a) A nonsquare rhombus
   (b) An obtuse scalene triangle
   (c) An equiangular quadrilateral that is not equilateral
   (d) A regular hexahedron

3. The triangle, quadrilateral, and pentagon in Figure 13.80 are all regular. Find the measure of $\angle ABC$.

4. A regular polygon with sides of length 5 cm has interior angles of measure 150°. Find its perimeter.

5. Sketch what is meant by a vertex of type 3,3,4,3,4 in a semiregular tessellation.

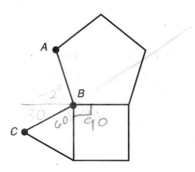

Figure 13.80

6. Twelve angles appear in Figure 13.81. Find the sum of their measures.

Figure 13.81

7. Fill in the missing numbers.
   (a) 27 cm = _____ m
   (b) 12 km = _____ mm
   (c) 4 m² = _____ cm²
   (d) 1 L = _____ cm³

8. A metric fanatic decides to partition the day into time periods called "decidays." How long, in hours and minutes, is a deciday?

9. How many cubic inches are there in 1 L?

10. Suppose that licorice sticks cost $5 per kilogram, and that a single 25 cm licorice stick weighs 60 g. Express the cost of licorice sticks in cents per centimeter.

11. Karen leaves home with a full tank of gas and drives for a hr and b min at the steady rate of c mph. Then she stops and spends d dollars and e cents to refill the tank with gasoline costing f cents per gallon. How many miles per gallon did she get?

12. Ethel reports her height to the nearest half inch as 5 ft $5\frac{1}{2}$ in, and her weight to the nearest pound as 115 lb.
    (a) What is the GPE in her reported height?
    (b) What is the relative error in her reported weight?
    (c) Which measurement is more accurate?
    (d) How do the two measurements compare in precision?

13. Give (best possible) lower and upper bounds on the actual area of a triangle whose base was reported as 15 cm to the nearest centimeter and whose height was reported as 7.4 cm to the nearest millimeter.

14. Sketch an isosceles trapezoid and describe all of its symmetries.

15. Describe all symmetries of the simple closed curve in Figure 13.82.

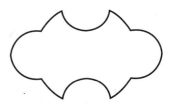

Figure 13.82

16. How many axes of symmetry has a regular n-gon?

17. Which regular n-gons have point symmetry?

18. Complete the drawing in Figure 13.83 so that it will be symmetric in line ℓ and also in line m.

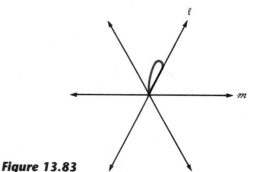

Figure 13.83

References

Bezuszka, S., M. Kenny, and L. Silvey. *Tessellations: The Geometry of Patterns*. Palo Alto, Calif.: Creative Publications, 1979.

Grünbaum, B. and G. C. Shephard. *Tilings and Patterns*. New York: W. H. Freeman and Company, 1987.

Martin, George E. *Transformation Geometry*. New York: Springer Verlag, 1982.

O'Daffer, P. and S. R. Clemens. *Geometry: An Investigative Approach*. Menlo Park, Calif.: Addison-Wesley, 1976.

Seymour, D. and J. Britton. *Introduction to Tessellations*. Palo Alto, Calif.: Dale Seymour Publications.

14

CONSTRUCTIONS, TRANSFORMATIONS, CONGRUENCE, AND SIMILARITY

Geometric figures, we know, are ideals that exist only in our minds. Nevertheless, to study them, most of us need to look at facsimiles on paper or a blackboard. And the more realistic the representation is, the more likely we are to discover properties. In Figure 14.1, for instance, triangle A, produced with a straightedge and compass or a ruler, is more likely to suggest the property "Base angles of an isosceles triangle are congruent" than is the crudely sketched triangle B.

In this chapter we first review the fundamental geometric constructions. These constructions lead very naturally to the classical congruence criteria for triangles, criteria that are seen to be intimately associated with the transformations known as rigid motions. After this *specialization* (to triangles) of the congruence concept, a new nonrigid transformation, dilation, leads us to a *generalization* of the congruence concept, namely, similarity. Similarity is studied in the context first of arbitrary figures, then of triangles. The crucial connections between similarity and measurement are investigated, as the 5–8 *Standards* request: "Students should explore the relationships among the lengths, areas, and volumes of similar solids. . . . The different growth rates for linear measures, areas, and volumes of similar figures . . . are fundamental to measurement and critical to scientific applications."

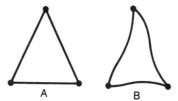

Figure 14.1

701

14.1   *Basic Constructions*

The ancient Greeks were the first people to organize geometric information into a unified subject of study. Literal translations of Euclid's *Elements* have been used as texts for 2000 years. Even today's texts still bear a strong imprint of the Greek tradition. One enduring aspect of that tradition is the construction of geometric figures with straightedge and compass.

Constructions and Drawings

A **straightedge** is a device for drawing line segments. Think of it as a ruler flipped over so that none of the markings show. A **compass** (Figure 14.2) is a device for drawing circles. A "Euclidean compass," like the straightedge, has no markings on it. Your compass may have a scale on it that indicates the distance from tip to tip. You should ignore that scale when doing a construction.

A picture of a geometric figure produced with straightedge and compass alone is called a **construction.**

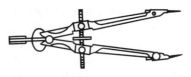

Figure 14.2   Compass

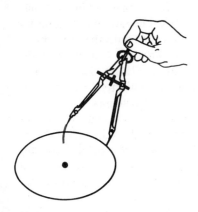

Figure 14.3

Rulers and protractors played no role in Greek geometry. If we use either one of these instruments, we will call the resulting picture a **drawing** to distinguish it from a construction. To illustrate the difference between a construction and a drawing, consider the task of picturing a regular hexagon.

A procedure for *constructing* a regular hexagon was suggested in Exercise 13, Section 13.2. It is based on the fact that equilateral triangles are equiangular and hence all of their angles have measure 60°. The algorithm is as follows:

1. Draw a circle with a *compass*.
2. Without changing the opening of the compass, put the metal tip on the circle and swing an arc to cut the circle (Figure 14.3).
3. Move the compass so that the metal tip is at the point of intersection of the circle and the arc. Swing another arc.
4. Move the compass to the new intersection point and swing another arc, and so on.
5. When you have gone completely around the circle, join the six points with line segments by using the *straightedge* (See Figure 14.4).

Figure 14.4

Figure 14.5

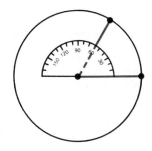

Figure 14.6

A procedure for *drawing* a regular hexagon by using a protractor (and compass and straightedge) is based on the observation that if a hexagon were inscribed in a circle and if each of its six vertices were joined to the center of the circle, then six congruent angles would be arranged around the center of the circle (see Figure 14.5). Each, then, would have measure $360°/6 = 60°$. The algorithm is clear.

1. Draw a circle with a compass.

2. Draw a radius with the straightedge.

3. Use protractor and straightedge to draw a 60° angle having the original radius as one of its sides (Figure 14.6).

4. Move the protractor to the second radius drawn, draw another 60° angle, and so on.

5. Finally, join the six points on the circle with segments.

Constructibility

Most people consider the construction of the hexagon to be more elegant than the drawing. It is quicker, easier, more exact, and somehow more satisfying. Unfortunately, instances in which construction has the advantage over drawing are rare. In the case of the regular pentagon, for example, drawing remains routine (we now need 5 angles, each of measure 72°, arranged around the center of the circle), but constructing becomes quite complicated (see Exercise 14). The case of the regular nonagon is even more dramatic. Drawing one is still a triviality; simply arrange 9 angles, each of measure 40°, around the center of a circle. Constructing one, however, turns out to be impossible.

Proofs that certain constructions are impossible involve some rather sophisticated algebraic techniques—techniques that go well beyond the level of this text. In fact, it was not until the nineteenth century that the "three classical problems of antiquity" were finally proved to be unsolvable. Those problems—known familiarly as "trisecting an angle," "duplicating a cube," and "squaring a circle"—were all questions about constructibility. Can one construct two rays in the interior of an arbitrary angle that partition it into three congruent regions? Can one construct a cube whose volume is twice that of a given cube? Can one construct a square whose area is equal to that of a given circle? It is now known that the answer to all three questions is no. It is also known exactly which regular polygons can and cannot be constructed (see Exercise 15). Even though many geometric figures cannot be constructed, a good number of the simplest and most important ones can. We will describe the basic constructions in this and the next section.

One final remark before we present the constructions. What we are discussing here are *algorithms*—step-by-step procedures for producing various figures. Six basic algorithms are described in this section in words and pictures. The first two, Figures 14.7, and 14.8, produce (congruent) copies of segments and angles.

Original

Step 1. Use a straightedge to produce a long segment.

Step 2. Open compass so that it exactly spans the original segment $\overline{AB}$.

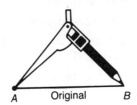
A   Original   B

Step 3. Without changing the compass opening, put its point at a point A' of the long segment and swing an arc to cross that segment at a point B': $\overline{A'B'}$ will be congruent to $\overline{AB}$.

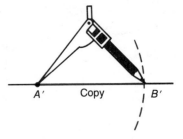
A'   Copy   B'

Figure 14.7 Copying a segment.

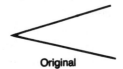
Original

Step 1. Use a straightedge to produce a long segment.

Step 2. Put point of compass at vertex A of original angle and swing an arc that crosses its sides at say B and C.

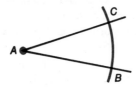
C
A
B

Step 3. Mark a point A' on the long segment. With the compass opening unchanged from step 2, put the point at A' and swing an arc that cuts the long segment at a point B'.

A'   B'

Figure 14.8 Copying an angle.

Step 4. Put the compass point at *B* and reset the opening so it will produce an arc through *C*.

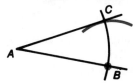

Step 5. Without changing the compass opening from step 4, put the point at *B'* and swing an arc that crosses the arc from step 3 at a point *C'*.

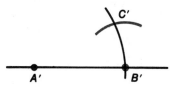

Step 6. Use straightedge to produce ray $\overline{A'C'}$: $\angle C'A'B'$ will be congruent to original $\angle CAB$.

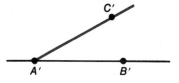

Figure 14.8 (continued).

The next pair of constructions produce bisectors. The formal definitions are as follows (see Figure 14.9).

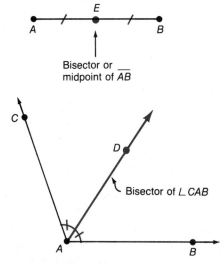

Figure 14.9 Two kinds of bisectors.

The **bisector** or **midpoint** of a segment $\overline{AB}$ is the point E on $\overleftrightarrow{AB}$ such that $\overline{AE} \cong \overline{EB}$.

The **bisector** of an angle $\angle CAB$ is the ray $\overrightarrow{AD}$, where D is in the interior of $\angle CAB$, such that $\angle CAD \cong \angle DAB$.

The two bisector constructions are described in Figures 14.10 and 14.11. Further discussion of why these algorithms work can be found in Section 14.5.

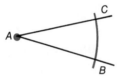

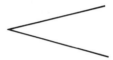

Step 1.   With point of compass at vertex A, swing an arc that crosses the sides of the angle at B and C.

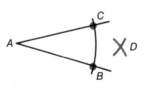

Step 2.   Using a single compass opening swing arcs centered at B and C that cross at say D in the interior of $\angle CAB$.

Step 3.   Use straightedge to produce $\overrightarrow{AD}$: $\angle CAD$ will be congruent to $\angle DAB$. That is, $\overrightarrow{AD}$ will besect $\angle CAB$.

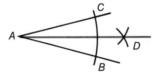

Figure 14.10 Bisecting an angle.

The construction described in Figure 14.11 actually does more than just locate the midpoint of a given segment; it produces the **perpendicular bisector,** that is, the line passing through that midpoint that is *perpendicular* to the original segment. Remember the formal definition (see Figure 14.12).

Two lines are **perpendicular** if they cross to form congruent adjacent angles.

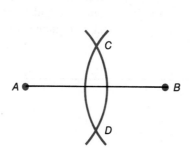

Step 1. Using a single compass opening swing arcs centered at the endpoints *A* and *B* of the original segment. Let *C* and *D* be the points where they cross.

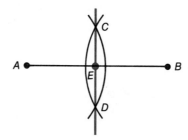

Step 2. Use straightedge to produce $\overleftrightarrow{CD}$. The point *E* where $\overleftrightarrow{CD}$ meets $\overline{AB}$ is the midpoint of $\overline{AB}$. That is, $\overline{AE} \cong \overline{EB}$.

Figure 14.11 Bisecting a segment.

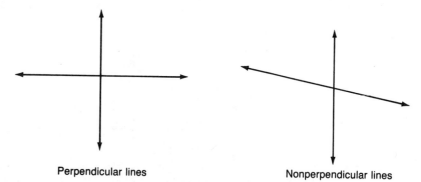

Perpendicular lines   Nonperpendicular lines

Figure 14.12

The next two constructions that we describe, in Figures 14.13 and 14.14, also involve perpendiculars.

The algorithms we have just reviewed can be used to construct circles *inscribed* in and *circumscribed* about any triangle. A circle is said to be **inscribed** in a triangle if it lies inside the triangle and just touches each of the triangle's three sides. A circle is said to be **circumscribed** about a triangle if it encloses the triangle and just touches the triangle's three vertices.

Step 1. Using the given point *A* as center, swing an arc that crosses the given line ℓ at points *B* and *C*.

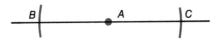

Step 2. Using points *B* and *C* as centers and using a single compass opening, swing arcs that cross at a point *D*.

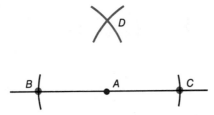

Step 3. Use a straightedge to produce $\overleftrightarrow{AD}$: $\overleftrightarrow{AD}$ will be perpendicular to ℓ at *A*.

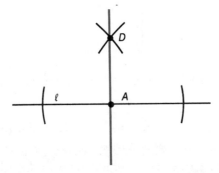

Figure 14.13 Erecting a perpendicular to a line at a point on the line.

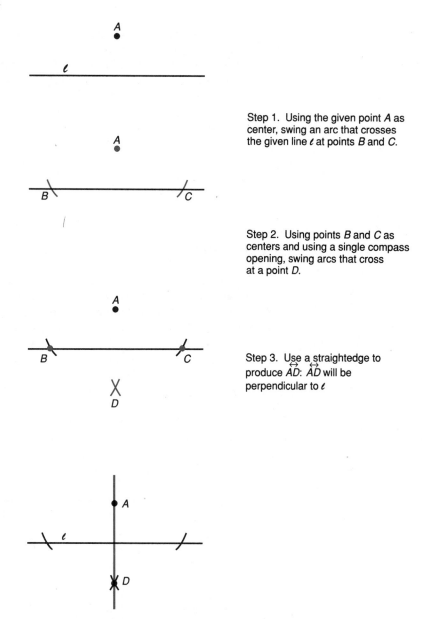

Step 1. Using the given point *A* as center, swing an arc that crosses the given line *ℓ* at points *B* and *C*.

Step 2. Using points *B* and *C* as centers and using a single compass opening, swing arcs that cross at a point *D*.

Step 3. Use a straightedge to produce $\overleftrightarrow{AD}$: $\overleftrightarrow{AD}$ will be perpendicular to *ℓ*

Figure 14.14 Dropping a perpendicular to a line from a point off it.

EXAMPLE 1 Circumscribe a circle about △*ABC* in Figure 14.15.

Solution The task is, of course, to locate the center *O* about which to swing the circumscribing circle. We work backwards. If a circle centered at *O* is to pass through both *B* and *C*, then *O* must be equidistant from *B* and *C*. But the points

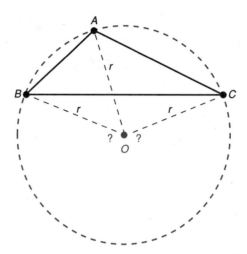

Figure 14.15

equidistant from B and C make up the perpendicular bisector of $\overline{BC}$. (This fact about perpendicular bisectors should be obvious, but we will also deduce it in Section 14.5.) Thus O must lie on the perpendicular bisector of $\overline{BC}$. Similarily, O must be equidistant from A and C and hence lie on the perpendicular bisector of $\overline{AC}$. So, to locate O we construct the perpendicular bisectors of $\overline{BC}$ and $\overline{AC}$ and let O be their point of intersection. See Figure 14.16. The last step is to place the point of the compass at O, open it until the pencil point is at B (or A or C), and swing the circle.   ❏

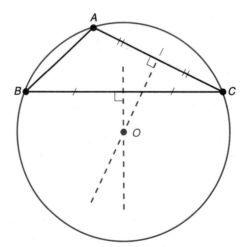

Figure 14.16

EXAMPLE 2   Inscribe a circle in $\triangle ABC$ in Figure 14.17.

Solution   Again the first task is to locate the center O about which to swing the inscribing circle. This time the "obvious" fact we need is that the points equidistant from the rays $\overrightarrow{BA}$ and $\overrightarrow{BC}$ make up the bisector of $\angle ABC$. (This property will also be deduced in Section 14.5.) Since O is to be equidistant from $\overrightarrow{BA}$ and $\overrightarrow{BC}$, it must lie on the bisector of $\angle ABC$. Similarly, since O is to be equidistant from $\overrightarrow{CB}$ and $\overrightarrow{CA}$, it must lie on the bisector of $\angle ACB$. So, to locate O, construct the bisectors of $\angle ABC$ and $\angle ACB$ and let O be their point of intersection. See Figure 14.18. The next step is to locate one of the three points at which the inscribed circle touches the triangle. In Figure 14.18 we have located D by dropping a perpendicular from O to $\overline{BC}$. Finally, put the point of the compass at O, open it until the pencil is at D, and swing the circle.   ❑

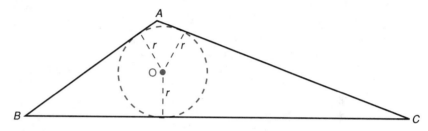

Figure 14.18

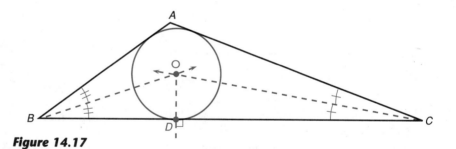

Figure 14.17

EXERCISE SET 14.1

1. Sketch an angle.
   (a) Use straightedge and compass to construct a copy of it.
   (b) Use straightedge and protractor to draw a copy of it.
2. Sketch two angles that form a linear pair.
   (a) Use straightedge and compass to construct the bisector of one of the angles.
   (b) Use straightedge and protractor to draw the bisector of the other angle.

   (c) What do you notice about the two rays you just produced?
3. Sketch two segments.
   (a) Use straightedge and compass to construct the perpendicular bisector of one.
   (b) Use ruler and protractor to draw the perpendicular bisector of the other.
4. Sketch a line.
   (a) Mark a point on it, and use straightedge and

compass to construct the perpendicular to the line at the point.

(b) Mark another point on it, and use straight-edge and protractor to draw the perpendicular to the line at this point.

5. Sketch a line. Mark a point that is not on the line. Use straightedge and compass to construct a line through the point and perpendicular to the original line.

6. Construct these angles.

   (a) A 45° angle   (b) A 135° angle

7. By copying segments and angles, construct a copy of the quadrilateral shown in Figure 14.19.

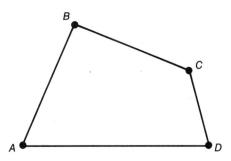

Figure 14.19

8. Draw a triangle on a sheet of paper and construct its inscribed circle.

9. Draw an acute triangle, a right triangle, and an obtuse triangle on a sheet of paper. Construct the circumscribing circle of each. Do you notice anything about the locations of the "circumcenters"?

10. How do you think the inscribed and circumscribed circles of a (single) equilateral triangle are related?

11. Construct the image of △ABC of Figure 14.20 under reflection in the line ℓ.

12. Construct the image of △ABC of Figure 14.21 under the given rotation about A.

13. Use compass and straightedge to construct each of the following. *Hint:* Begin each construction with a circle.

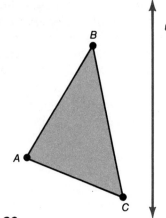

Figure 14.20

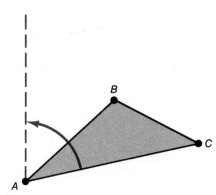

Figure 14.21

(a) A regular hexagon
(b) An equilateral triangle
(c) A square
(d) A regular octagon
(e) A 75° angle

14. See if you can follow this recipe for constructing a regular pentagon. Construct a circle; let O be its center. Construct a diameter of that circle; let A and B be its endpoints. Construct the midpoint of $\overline{OB}$; call it C. Construct a perpendicular to $\overleftrightarrow{AB}$ at O; let D be one of the points where it meets the circle. With the point of the compass at C and the pencil end at D, swing an arc to cut $\overline{AO}$ at E. Now, move the compass point to D, and set the opening so that the pencil end is at E. Using this

compass opening, proceed, as in the hexagon construction, to cut off successive arcs around the circle. If your work has been accurate, this should divide the circle into five arcs all of the same size. Joining their endpoints results in a regular pentagon.

15. A deep theorem, usually credited to Gauss, states that a regular n-gon is constructible (with straight-edge and compass) if and only if n is either a power of 2 (greater than 2^1) or the product of a nonnegative power of 2 and one or more distinct Fermat primes, that is, primes of the form $2^{(2^k)} + 1$ for $k = 0, 1, 2, \ldots$. For example, some values of n for which regular n-gons are constructible are
$2^3, 2 \cdot 3 \cdot 5, 2^0 \cdot 17, 2^7 \cdot 257 \cdot 65{,}537$
(It was Gauss who, at the age of eighteen, startled the mathematical world with the announcement that he had constructed the regular 17-gon—a task that had been considered impossible for over 2000 years.) Calculate the first three Fermat primes, and then list all values of n up through 25 for which a regular n-gon is constructible.

16. It has been proved that one cannot construct a 20° angle.
    (a) Construct an angle whose trisectors cannot be constructed.
    (b) Explain why a 40° angle cannot be constructed.
    (c) Which of the following angles cannot be constructed?
    $90°$ $11\frac{1}{4}°$ $10°$ $100°$ $105°$

17. *A practical application of angle bisection:* If you are ever lost (in the Northern Hemisphere), but you have a wristwatch and the sun is shining, here is a way to find approximate directions. Hold the watch so that the face is up and parallel to the ground. Point the hour hand in the direction of the sun. The bisector of the angle between the hour hand and the 12 on your watch will point south. For this method to work, in what direction should the sun be at 12 noon? At 9 A.M.? At 6 A.M.? At 3 P.M.? At 6 P.M.?

18. Figure 14.22 shows a portion of a flat, partly wooded tract of land. Construct line-segment mirrors at points B and C so that a signal light flashed at point A will be seen at point D. *Hint:* A beam of light bounces off a mirror so that the angle of incidence is congruent to the angle of reflection.

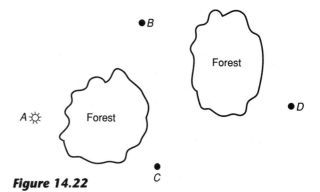

Figure 14.22

19. Two pebbles are dropped simultaneously, but several feet apart, into a still pond. See Figure 14.23.

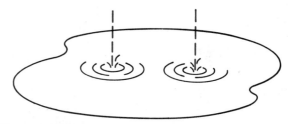

Figure 14.23

    (a) Describe the point at which their first rings will first meet.
    (b) Describe the set of *all* points in which the first rings will meet as they travel across the pond.

20. Describe the shortest path from a point to a line.

21. Use the Pythagorean theorem and Figure 14.24 to explain algebraically why the shortest segment joining a point to a line is the segment perpendicular to the line.

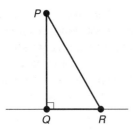

Figure 14.24

22. Draw an angle on a sheet of paper. Discover how to find its bisector by folding the paper. (Wax paper is particularly convenient for paper-folding activities because it is easy to see through and creases in it become white.)

23. On a sheet of paper, draw a line ℓ and a point A on ℓ. Locate the perpendicular to ℓ through A by paper folding.

24. Repeat Exercise 23 with the point A off ℓ.

25. Draw a segment on a sheet of paper, and locate its perpendicular bisector by paper folding.

26. If you have a Mira, explore and discover how to use it to locate the figures called for in Exercises 22–25.

27. In Figure 14.25 points A' and B' are the images of points A and B, respectively, under a rotation with center P. Find P.

Figure 14.25

14.2 *Constructing Parallel Lines*

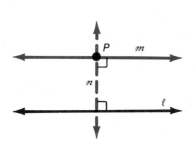

Figure 14.26

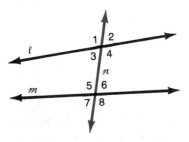

Figure 14.27

A famous property in Euclidean geometry, known as the **parallel postulate,** states that given a line ℓ and a point P not on ℓ, there is exactly one line m through P parallel to ℓ. We already have a method for constructing the line m. Begin by constructing a perpendicular to ℓ from P; call it n. See Figure 14.26. Now, construct a perpendicular to n at P; call it m. Lines ℓ and m must be parallel because (1) they are coplanar (all of our constructions were carried out in the plane of ℓ and P) and (2) they do not intersect—for if they did, a triangle would be formed in which the sum of the measures of the three angles exceeds 180°. (Why?)

Simpler constructions of the line through P parallel to ℓ will be described shortly, but first we need to generalize Figure 14.26 and introduce some terminology. When two coplanar lines ℓ and m are cut by a third line n, that third line is referred to as a **transversal** of the first two. See Figure 14.27.

The angles that appear in such a configuration are given special names. Angles 3, 4, 5, and 6 are referred to as **interior angles;** angles 1, 2, 7, and 8 are **exterior angles.** Various pairs of these angles are also given special names.

> **Alternate interior angles:** $\angle 3$ and $\angle 6$, $\angle 4$ and $\angle 5$
> **Alternate exterior angles:** $\angle 1$ and $\angle 8$, $\angle 2$ and $\angle 7$
> **Corresponding angles:** $\angle 1$ and $\angle 5$, $\angle 2$ and $\angle 6$, $\angle 3$ and $\angle 7$, $\angle 4$ and $\angle 8$.

The question of whether or not lines ℓ and m are parallel can be settled by measuring any pair of these angles. The facts are as follows.

In Figure 14.27: (1) if ℓ is parallel to m, then any pair of alternate interior angles will be a congruent pair, any pair of alternate exterior angles will be a congruent pair, and any pair of corresponding angles will be a congruent pair; (2) if ℓ is *not* parallel to m, then no pair of alternate interior, no pair of alternate exterior, and no pair of corresponding angles will be a congruent pair.

It is a simple matter to base a construction of a parallel to ℓ through P on these facts. Here is one based on the congruence of corresponding angles. Begin with straightedge and produce any line n through P that crosses ℓ. See Figure 14.28. Say n crosses ℓ at Q, and one of the angles formed is called $\angle 1$. Mark a point R on $\overrightarrow{QP}$ beyond P. Now, use straightedge and compass to construct a (congruent) copy of $\angle 1$ on the same side of n but having vertex at P and $\overrightarrow{PR}$ as one of its sides. Call it $\angle 2$. See Figure 14.29. The other side of $\angle 2$ will lie on a line parallel to ℓ, since $\angle 1$ and $\angle 2$ are congruent corresponding angles. Extend that side with straightedge.

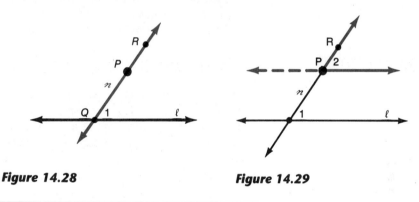

Figure 14.28   **Figure 14.29**

EXAMPLE 1   Construct a parallelogram having the points A, B, and C of Figure 14.30 as three of its vertices.

●B

A●   ●C

Figure 14.30

Solution   Construct segments $\overline{AC}$ and $\overline{BC}$. Through A construct a line parallel to $\overline{BC}$, and through B construct a line parallel to $\overline{AC}$. Let D be the point of intersection of these two lines. Construct segments $\overline{AD}$ and $\overline{BD}$. See Figure 14.31.

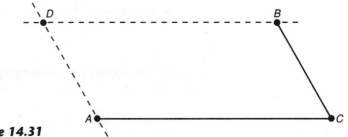

Figure 14.31

EXAMPLE 2   How many different parallelograms are there that have points *A*, *B*, and *C* of Figure 14.30 as vertices?

Solution   There are three, as we see by exhausting all possibilities. For the final parallelogram *ABCD*, there are three possibilities. Either *A* is opposite *B*, in which case we get the parallelogram of Example 1. Or *A* is opposite *C*, in which case we get the parallelogram having $\overline{AB}$ and $\overline{BC}$ as two sides (and $\overline{AC}$ as a diagonal). Or *A* is opposite *D*, in which case we get the parallelogram having $\overline{BA}$ and $\overline{AC}$ as two sides (and $\overline{BC}$ as a diagonal). ❏

Partitioning a Segment

We noted that trisecting an angle, with straightedge and compass, is usually impossible; only a few very special angles can be trisected with those tools. Constructing the trisectors of a segment, however, is always possible. In fact, there is a construction for partitioning a given segment into any number of congruent parts. It is based on the construction of parallel lines and the following fact about parallels and transversals.

> If a family of (coplanar) parallel lines cuts off congruent segments on one transversal, then it cuts off congruent segments on any transversal.

In Figure 14.32, for example, if $\overline{AB} \cong \overline{BC} \cong \overline{CD}$, then $\overline{EF} \cong \overline{FG} \cong \overline{GH}$.

We illustrate the algorithm for the case of trisection. See Figure 14.33. In Exercise 6 you are asked to modify the algorithm to partition a segment into five congruent parts.

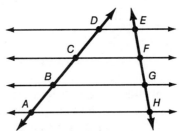

Figure 14.32

Step 1. Use a straightedge to produce any ray from O.

Step 2. Use compass to swing 3 congruent segments $\overline{OA}$, $\overline{AB}$, and $\overline{BC}$ on this ray. Their length is immaterial.

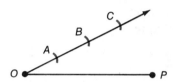

Step 3. Use straightedge to produce $\overline{CP}$.

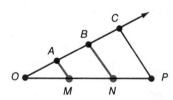

Step 4. Construct parallels to $\overline{CP}$ through A and B. Say they cut $\overline{OP}$ at M and N, respectively. The points M and N trisect $\overline{OP}$ because the parallel lines $\overleftrightarrow{AM}$, $\overleftrightarrow{BN}$, and $\overleftrightarrow{CP}$ cut off congruent segments on $\overline{OC}$ and hence they must also cut off congruent segments on $\overline{OP}$. That is $\overline{OM} \cong \overline{MN} \cong \overline{NP}$.

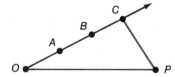

Figure 14.33 Trisecting a segment.

EXERCISE SET 14.2

1. For Figure 14.34, construct a line m through P parallel to ℓ, using our algorithm that is based on the congruence of corresponding angles.
2. Repeat Exercise 1, using a construction based on the congruence of alternate interior angles.
3. Repeat Exercise 1, using a construction based on the congruence of alternate exterior angles.

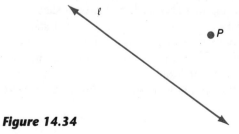

Figure 14.34

4. Draw a 6-cm segment, construct its trisectors, and check your work with your ruler.

5. Refer to Figure 14.33, and explain how you could get by with constructing just one parallel. That is, suppose you have constructed $\overline{AM}$ parallel to $\overline{CP}$, and now you want to locate point N without going through another parallel construction.

6. Draw a 10-cm segment, construct points that partition it into five congruent segments, and check with a ruler.

7. Explain how, in principle, you could construct points on the number line of Figure 14.35 corresponding to the following numbers.
   (a) $\frac{1}{5}$ (b) $\frac{1}{10}$ (c) $\frac{7}{10}$ (d) $-\frac{13}{10}$
   (e) m/n, where m and n are any natural numbers

Figure 14.35

8. Two parallel lines are cut by a transversal. Eight angles are formed, one of which has measure 50°. What are the measures of the other seven?

9. Construct the image of $\triangle ABC$ of Figure 14.36 under the translation specified by the vector **v**.

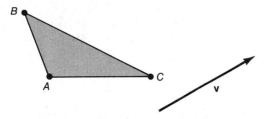

Figure 14.36

10. Draw a segment about 7 cm long on a sheet of translucent paper. Position it over a sheet of lined notebook paper in such a way that you can mark the points that trisect it. Repeat, finding points that partition it into 5 congruent parts. How could you now partition it into 15 congruent parts?

11. Draw a line ℓ and a point P off it on a sheet of paper. Discover how to locate the line through P parallel to ℓ by paper folding.

12. Consider two numbers r and s on the number line, and let b be the number corresponding to their midpoint (Figure 14.37). Then
$$b - r = s - b$$

so that
$$2b = r + s$$

or
$$b = \tfrac{1}{2}r + \tfrac{1}{2}s$$

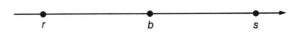

Figure 14.37

(a) Suppose now that t_1 and t_2 are the trisectors of the segment from r to s (Figure 14.38). Prove that
$$t_1 = \tfrac{2}{3}r + \tfrac{1}{3}s \quad \text{and} \quad t_2 = \tfrac{1}{3}r + \tfrac{2}{3}s$$

Figure 14.38

(b) Suppose next that q_1, q_2, and q_3 divide the segment from r to s into four congruent parts (Figure 14.39). Express each of q_1, q_2, and q_3 in terms of r and s.

Figure 14.39

13. One of the most famous pieces of indirect measurement in history is based on the congruence of corresponding angles. Eratosthenes (ca. 230 B.C.) calculated the circumference of the earth by observing that at noon on the summer solstice the sun stood directly over Syene, while about 500 mi to the north, at Alexandria, the sun's rays made

an angle of 7.2° with the vertical. Use (exaggerated) Figure 14.40 to calculate the circumference of the earth.

★ 14. Is the parallel postulate true in the four-point geometry of Exercise 28, p. 570?

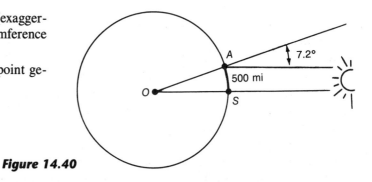

Figure 14.40

14.3 *Properties of Angles; Deduction (Optional)*

In the previous section we encountered a number of properties relating congruence of angles to parallelism of lines. When we combine these new properties of angles with the earlier ones from Section 13.1, we get quite a list—a longer one than most people like to remember. One of the goals of high school geometry is to separate a long list of properties into two categories, postulates (or axioms) and theorems. The postulates should be few in number and fundamental or obvious. The theorems must all be logical consequences of the postulates. That is, one assumes some of the properties and calls them postulates, and one proves the others and calls them theorems.

Prior to high school there is no such separation of properties into postulates and theorems. Still, there are times when the existence of logical relationships among properties is so evident that some deduction seems to be appropriate. We list here some of the properties of angles that have been encountered so far. In the exercises you are asked to prove some things about them.

Property 1   Equal-measures congruence criterion: In Figure 14.41, $\angle 1 \cong \angle 2 \iff m\angle 1 = m\angle 2$.

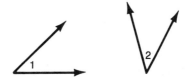

Figure 14.41

Property 2   Additivity property of angle measure: In Figure 14.42, $m\angle AOB + m\angle BOC = m\angle AOC$, which is 180 in the case of collinear points A, O, C.

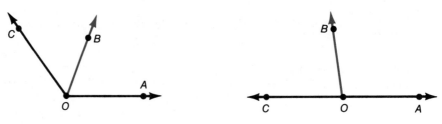

Figure 14.42

Property 3   Vertical angles are congruent: In Figure 14.43 $\angle 1 \cong \angle 2$.

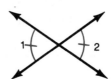

Figure 14.43

Property 4   Sum of measures of angles of triangle is 180: In Figure 14.44 $m\angle A + m\angle B + m\angle C = 180$.

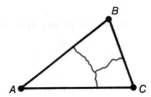

Figure 14.44

Property 5   Congruent alternate interior angles imply parallel lines: In Figure 14.45 if $\angle 1 \cong \angle 2$, then $n \parallel \ell$.

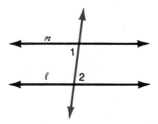

Figure 14.45

Property 6 Parallel lines imply congruent alternate interior angles: In Figure 14.45, if $n \parallel \ell$, then $\angle 1 \cong \angle 2$.

EXAMPLE 1 Use Properties 1–4 and any general properties of equality to prove that the measure of an exterior angle of a triangle ($\angle BCD$ in Figure 14.46) is equal to the sum of the measures of the two remote interior angles ($\angle A$ and $\angle B$ in Figure 14.46).

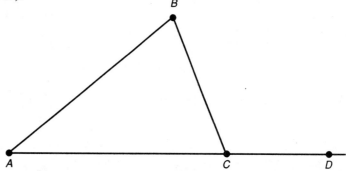

Figure 14.46

Solution
1. $m\angle A + m\angle B + m\angle ACB = 180$ Property 4
2. $m\angle BCD + m\angle ACB = 180$ Property 2
3. $m\angle A + m\angle B + m\angle ACB = m\angle BCD + m\angle ACB$ Substitution
4. $m\angle A + m\angle B = m\angle BCD$ Addition property of equality
     [adding $-(m\angle ACB)$ to both sides] ❑

EXAMPLE 2 Use Properties 1–6 and any general properties of equality to prove that when parallel lines are cut by a transversal (lines ℓ, n, p in Figure 14.47), alternate exterior angles ($\angle 2$ and $\angle 7$ in Figure 14.47) are congruent.

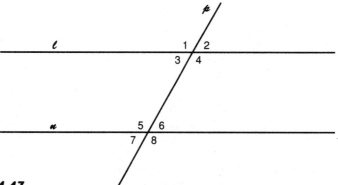

Figure 14.47

Solution   1. $\angle 2 \cong \angle 3$ Property 3

2. $m\angle 2 = m\angle 3$ Property 1

3. $\angle 3 \cong \angle 6$ Property 6

4. $m\angle 3 = m\angle 6$ Property 1

5. $\angle 6 \cong \angle 7$ Property 3

6. $m\angle 6 = m\angle 7$ Property 1

7. $m\angle 2 = m\angle 7$ Transitivity of equality
(steps 2, 4, 6)

8. $\angle 2 \cong \angle 7$ Property 1

Note: The solution would have been much shorter had we been willing to use the "transitive property of congruence." But the ground rules restricted us to Properties 1–6 and the properties of equality.   ❑

EXERCISE SET 14.3

1. Use Properties 1 and 2 and Figure 14.48 to complete the following proof of Property 3: $\angle 1 \cong \angle 3$. (Common properties of equality and inequality such as the addition properties, the transitive properties, and substitution can also be used as reasons.)

   (a) $m\angle 1 + m\angle 2 = 180$ Why?
   (b) $m\angle 3 + m\angle 2 = 180$ Why?
   (c) $m\angle 1 + m\angle 2 = m\angle 3 + m\angle 2$ Why?
   (d) $m\angle 1 = m\angle 3$ Why?
   (e) $\angle 1 \cong \angle 3$ Why?

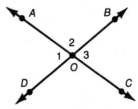

Figure 14.48

Given: A, O, C collinear
            B, O, D collinear

2. Use Properties 1, 2, and 6 and Figure 14.49 to complete the following proof of Property 4: $m\angle 1 + m\angle 3 + m\angle 5 = 180$.

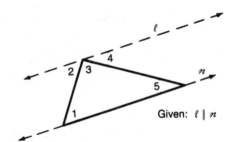

Given: $\ell \parallel n$

Figure 14.49

   (a) $\angle 4 \cong \angle 5$ Why?
   (b) $m\angle 4 = m\angle 5$ Why?
   (c) $\angle 1 \cong \angle 2$ Why?
   (d) $m\angle 1 = m\angle 2$ Why?
   (e) $m\angle 1 + m\angle 3 + m\angle 5 = m\angle 2 + m\angle 3 + m\angle 4$ Why?
   (f) $m\angle 2 + m\angle 3 + m\angle 4 = 180$ Why?
   (g) $m\angle 1 + m\angle 3 + m\angle 5 = 180$ Why?

3. We shall use Properties 1, 2, and 4 and Figure 14.50 to prove Property 5: If $\angle 1 \cong \angle 2$, then $n \parallel \ell$. Our plan will be to suppose $n \not\parallel \ell$ and to show that then $\angle 1 \not\cong \angle 2$. (Does this plan sound logical?)

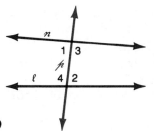

Figure 14.50

(a) We suppose that $n \not\parallel \ell$.
(b) n and ℓ intersect.   Why?
(c) Let us say they intersect to the right of p.
(d) $m\angle 2 + m\angle 3 < 180$ Why?
(e) $m\angle 1 + m\angle 3 = 180$ Why?
(f) $m\angle 2 + m\angle 3 < m\angle 1 + m\angle 3$ Why?
(g) $m\angle 2 < m\angle 1$ Why?
(h) $\angle 2 \not\cong \angle 1$ Why?

4. Replace step (c) of Exercise 3 by "Let us say they intersect to the left of p." Rewrite steps (d), (e), (f), (g), and (h).

5. Write a statement-reason proof of this property:

> If parallel lines are cut by a transversal, then corresponding angles are congruent.

In your proof, use any of the six properties as reasons. Refer to Figure 14.51, assume that $\ell \parallel n$, and first prove that $\angle 1 \cong \angle 5$. Then prove that $\angle 4 \cong \angle 8$, $\angle 2 \cong \angle 6$, and $\angle 3 \cong \angle 7$.

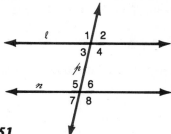

Figure 14.51

6. Write a statement-reason proof of this property:

> If corresponding angles are congruent when two lines are cut by a transversal, then the two lines are parallel.

In your proof, refer to Figure 14.51, assume that $\angle 1 \cong \angle 5$, and deduce that $\ell \parallel n$. Use any of the first six properties as reasons. The strategy of working from both ends toward the middle should be helpful.

7. Write a statement-reason proof of this property:

> If parallel lines are cut by a transversal, then interior angles on the same side of the transversal have measure sum 180.

Use any previous properties as reasons. Refer to Figure 14.51, assume that $\ell \parallel n$, and show that $m\angle 4 + m\angle 6 = 180$.

8. Write a statement-reason proof of this property:

> If when two lines are cut by a transversal the interior angles on one side of the transversal have measure sum 180, then the two lines are parallel.

Use any previous properties as reasons. Refer to Figure 14.51, assume that $m\angle 4 + m\angle 6 = 180$, and show that $\ell \parallel n$.

9. Write a statement-reason proof of this property:

> Opposite angles of a parallelogram are congruent.

Use any previous properties as reasons. Refer to Figure 14.52, assume $\ell \parallel n$ and $p \parallel m$, and show that $\angle 1 \cong \angle 3$. (A similar argument would show that $\angle 2 \cong \angle 4$.)

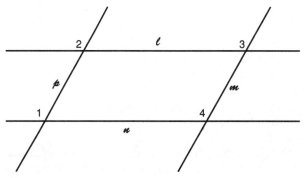

Figure 14.52

10. For Figure 14.53, assume that lines ℓ and n are parallel, $m\angle 2 = 55°$, and $m\angle 10 = 50°$. Fill in the blanks and give, in a few words, a reason for your answer.

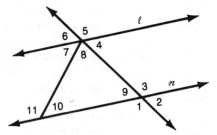

Figure 14.53

  (a) $m\angle 9 =$ _____ because _____
  (b) $m\angle 8 =$ _____ because _____

  (c) $m\angle 7 =$ _____ because _____
  (d) $m\angle 11 =$ _____ because _____

11. Refer to Figure 14.54.
  (a) Which two rays are collinear: $\overrightarrow{OA}$ and $\overrightarrow{OC}$, or $\overrightarrow{OB}$ and $\overrightarrow{OD}$?
  (b) What is the measure of $\angle AOD$?

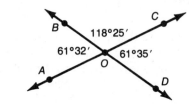

Figure 14.54

14.4 *Congruent Triangles*

The last straightedge-compass constructions we shall work on are those for copying triangles. If you are given a triangle (Figure 14.55) and asked to construct a (congruent) copy of it, there are several ways you can do it. One algorithm is shown in Figure 14.56.

    To copy a triangle, then, you need only copy (any) two sides and the angle they determine—the *included angle*. This property of triangles is known as the **side-angle-side** (SAS) condition for congruence (Figure 14.57).

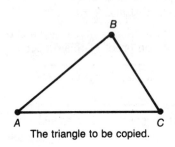

The triangle to be copied.

Figure 14.55

SAS: If two sides and the included angle of one triangle are congruent respectively to two sides and the included angle of another triangle, then the triangles are congruent.

Step 1. Construct a copy of $\overline{AC}$.

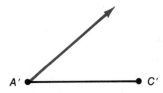

Step 2. Construct a copy of $\angle A$, using A' as vertex and $\overline{A'C'}$ as one side.

Figure 14.56

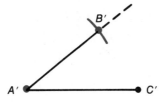

Step 3. Construct a copy of $\overline{AB}$ as shown. There is no need to copy $\angle C$, $\angle B$, or $\overline{BC}$. By simply joining B' to C' you will get a congruent copy of $\triangle ABC$. The other corresponding parts will automatically be congruent:

Figure 14.56 (continued)

$\overline{B'C'} \cong \overline{BC}$ $\angle B' \cong \angle B$ $\angle C' \cong \angle C$

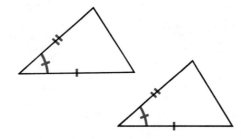

Figure 14.57   Triangles congruent by SAS condition.

Another way to construct a copy of $\triangle ABC$ is shown in Figure 14.58.

To copy a triangle, then, you need only copy (any) two angles and the side they share—the *included side*. This property of triangles is known as the **angle-side-angle** (ASA) condition for congruence (Figure 14.59).

ASA: If two angles and the included side of one triangle are congruent respectively to two angles and the included side of another triangle, then the triangles are congruent.

Step 1. Construct a copy of $\overline{AC}$.

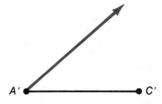

Step 2. Swing an arc of radius AB from A'.

Figure 14.58

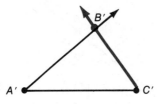

Step 3. Swing an arc of radius *CB* from *C'*. The arcs will intersect at a point for which $\overline{A'B'} \cong \overline{AB}$ and $\overline{C'B'} \cong \overline{CB}$, and $\triangle A'B'C'$ will be congruent to $\triangle ABC$. The corresponding angles will automatically be congruent:

$$\angle A' \cong \angle A \quad \angle B' \cong \angle B \quad \angle C' \cong \angle C$$

Figure 14.58 (continued).

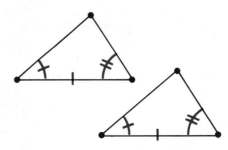

Figure 14.59   Triangles congruent by ASA condition.

Figure 14.60 shows a third way to construct a copy of $\triangle ABC$.

To copy a triangle, then, you need only copy all three sides. This property of triangles is known as the **side-side-side** (SSS) condition for congruence (Figure 14.61).

SSS: If three sides of one triangle are congruent respectively to three sides of another triangle, then the two triangles are congruent.

Step 1. Construct a copy of $\overline{AC}$.

Step 2. Swing an arc of radius *AB* from *A'*.

Figure 14.60

❧ 14.4 Congruent Triangles **727**

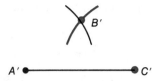

Step 3. Swing an arc of radius CB from C'. The arcs will intersect at a point for which $\overline{A'B'} \cong \overline{AB}$ and $\overline{C'B'} \cong \overline{CB}$, and $\triangle A'B'C'$ will be congruent to $\triangle ABC$. The corresponding angles will automatically be congruent:

$$\angle A' \cong \angle A \quad \angle B' \cong \angle B \quad \angle C' \cong \angle C$$

Figure 14.60 (continued)

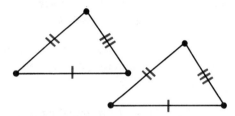

Triangles congruent by SSS condition.

Figure 14.61

To sharpen the concept of *corresponding parts*, let us look at congruence of triangles in terms of rigid motions. Consider Figure 14.62. To say that triangle T is congruent to triangle S is to say that there is a rigid motion—some sequence of slides, turns, flips—that will make triangle T coincide with triangle S. In the figure a 90° clockwise turn about C followed by a slide 4.5 cm right will work. Under this rigid motion the vertices A, B, C of triangle T and the vertices D, E, F of triangle S will be matched up as follows:

$$A \leftrightarrow E \qquad B \leftrightarrow F \qquad C \leftrightarrow D$$

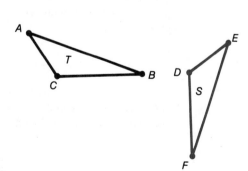

Figure 14.62

Any one of these matched pairs of vertices is called a pair of **corresponding vertices** with respect to this particular rigid motion.

The match-up of vertices induces a match-up of angles and sides as well:

$$\angle A \leftrightarrow \angle E \qquad \angle B \leftrightarrow \angle F \qquad \angle C \leftrightarrow \angle D$$
$$\overline{AB} \leftrightarrow \overline{EF} \qquad \overline{BC} \leftrightarrow \overline{FD} \qquad \overline{CA} \leftrightarrow \overline{DE}$$

Any one of these six pairs is said to be a pair of **corresponding parts** with respect to the rigid motion. In summary:

Corresponding vertices (sides, angles) of congruent triangles are those pairs of vertices (sides, angles) that will be matched up by a rigid motion that makes the triangles coincide.

If two triangles are congruent, then, of course, there are six pairs of congruent corresponding parts, three pairs of angles and three pairs of sides (Figure 14.63).

Corresponding parts of congruent triangles are congruent: CPCTC.

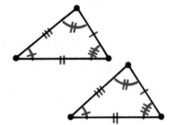

Figure 14.63

The SAS, ASA, and SSS congruence conditions tell us that if in two triangles we can find three strategically located pairs of congruent parts, then the triangles must be congruent, and so all the other parts must also match up in congruent pairs.

Notational Convention

There are acceptable and unacceptable ways to report that two triangles are congruent. We illustrate the notational convention by using the pair of congruent triangles in Figure 14.64.

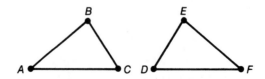

Figure 14.64

Acceptable report: $\triangle ABC \cong \triangle FED$ (because vertices *A, B, C* correspond to vertices *F, E, D* in that order).

Unacceptable report: $\triangle ABC \cong \triangle DEF$ (because there is no rigid motion matching *A* with *D*, *B* with *E*, and *C* with *F*).

Acceptable report: $\triangle CAB \cong \triangle DFE$.

Unacceptable report: $\triangle CAB \cong \triangle FED$.

EXAMPLE 1   Explain why the two triangles in Figure 14.65 are congruent, report the congruence using the notational convention, and describe a rigid motion that would put one triangle on the other.

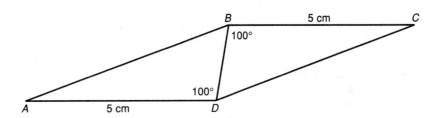

Figure 14.65

Solution   The triangles are congruent by the SAS condition ($\overline{AD} \cong \overline{BC}$, $\angle ADB \cong \angle CBD$, $\overline{DB} \cong \overline{DB}$). In symbols, $\triangle ADB \cong \triangle CBD$. A 180° rotation about the midpoint of $\overline{BD}$ would put $\triangle ADB$ on $\triangle CBD$.   ❏

EXAMPLE 2   Explain why $\overleftrightarrow{AB}$ is parallel to $\overleftrightarrow{CD}$ in Figure 14.65.

Solution   View $\overleftrightarrow{BD}$ as a transversal of $\overleftrightarrow{AB}$ and $\overleftrightarrow{CD}$. Then $\angle DBA$ and $\angle BDC$ are alternate interior angles, so if we knew that these angles were congruent, we could conclude that $\overleftrightarrow{AB}$ and $\overleftrightarrow{CD}$ are parallel. But $\angle DBA \cong \angle BDC$ because, by Example 1, they are corresponding parts of congruent triangles.   ❏

EXERCISE SET 14.4

1. Construct copies of the triangle in Figure 14.66 by using the following. Check that all of your copies can be made to coincide with the original.

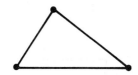

Figure 14.66

(a) The SAS procedure
(b) The ASA procedure
(c) The SSS procedure

2. Refer to Figure 14.67.
   (a) Why are the two triangles congruent?
   (b) What side corresponds to $\overline{AC}$? What is true of the sides opposite corresponding angles?
   (c) Complete: $\triangle ABC \cong \triangle$ _ _ _

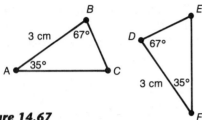

Figure 14.67

3. In Figure 14.68 points B, C, E are collinear, as are points A, C, D.
   (a) Why are the two triangles congruent?
   (b) What angle corresponds to $\angle D$? What is true of the angles opposite corresponding sides?
   (c) Complete: $\triangle BCA \cong \triangle$ ____
   (d) Describe a rigid motion that would make the left triangle coincide with the right one.

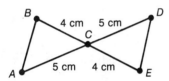

Figure 14.68

4. In Figure 14.69, B and D are the centers of congruent circles.
   (a) Why are the two triangles congruent?
   (b) Describe a reflection that will make the right-hand triangle coincide with the left-hand triangle.
   (c) Complete: $\triangle ABC \cong \triangle A$___
   (d) Describe a rotation that will make the right-hand triangle coincide with the left-hand one.
   (e) Complete: $\triangle ABC \cong \triangle C$___

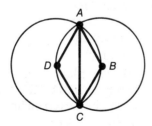

Figure 14.69

5. Complete, in all possible ways, the following report of congruence between the two triangles in Figure 14.70: $\triangle ABC \cong \triangle$ ____

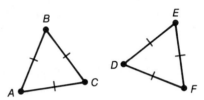

Figure 14.70

6. For each of the following pairs of triangles, state why the two triangles are congruent, report the congruence according to the notational convention, and be prepared to describe (roughly) a rigid motion that would put one triangle on the other.

   (a)

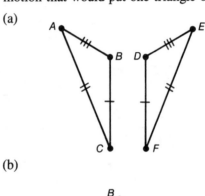

   (b)

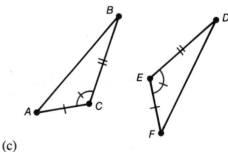

   (c)

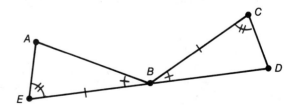

(d)

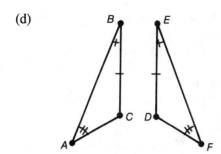

(c)

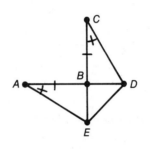

(d)

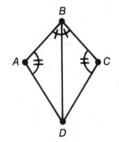

7. Write out an SAA congruence condition for triangles.

8. Explain how Figure 14.71 shows that there is *no* SSA congruence condition.

(e)

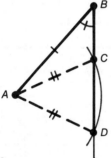

(f)

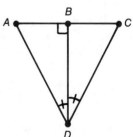

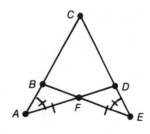

Figure 14.71

9. Sketch a diagram that shows there is *no* AAA congruence condition.

10. In each figure, find a pair of congruent triangles, cite the congruence condition that assures you they are congruent, and report the congruence by using the notational convention. (Any time three points appear to be collinear, you may assume that they are.)

(g)

(h)

(a)

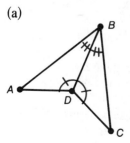

(b)

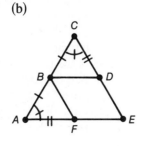

(i)

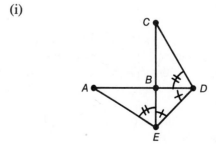

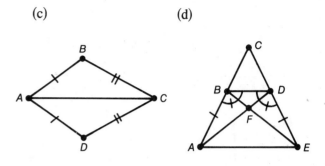

(j)

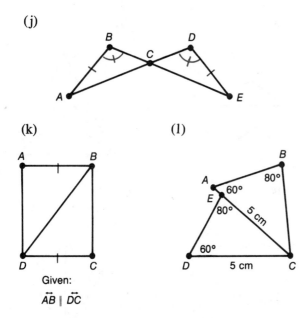

(k)

(l)

Given:

$\overleftrightarrow{AB} \parallel \overleftrightarrow{DC}$

11. Refer to Figure 14.72. Without measuring, fill in the blanks. (The dimensions are approximate.)
    (a) $EF =$ _____   (b) $m\angle F =$ _____
    (c) $m\angle C =$ _____   (d) $m\angle B =$ _____

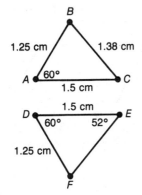

Figure 14.72

12. Locations on a map are assigned coordinates (ordered pairs) according to the "first right, then up" convention. For example, the approximate coordinates of forest ranger A in Figure 14.73 are (44.4, 66.3).
    (a) What are the approximate coordinates of forest ranger B?

(b) Forest ranger A sees a flash of lightning 40° east of north. Forest ranger B sees the same flash 15° west of north. Find the approximate coordinates of the lightning strike, using your protractor.

(c) Lightning strikes again somewhere to the north, but this time neither ranger is able to read an angle. By counting the elapsed time between flash and thunder, ranger A computes the distance to the strike as 3 mi. Ranger B computes a distance of 2 mi. Find approximate coordinates of the strike. (Each square on the map is 1 mi by 1 mi.)

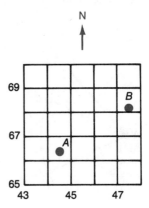

Figure 14.73

13. Describe where to aim the billiard ball A so it will bounce off the rail, as shown in Figure 14.74, and go to position B. Use the physical fact that, in the absence of "English," the moving ball behaves like a reflecting beam of light: $\angle AED \cong \angle BEC$. How far does the ball travel along polygonal path AEB?

★ 14. Figure 14.75 shows a tetrahedron $ACFH$ determined by four vertices of a 3-by-4-by-5 right rectangular prism.
    (a) Calculate the lengths of the six edges of the tetrahedron.
    (b) Is the tetrahedron regular?
    (c) Are the four faces of the tetrahedron all congruent to each other?
    (d) Find the sum of the measures of the three face angles at each vertex.

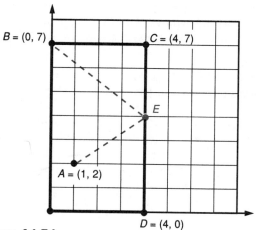

Figure 14.74

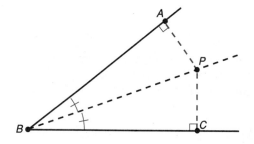

Figure 14.75

14.5 *Congruent Triangles and Deduction (Optional)*

The congruence conditions for triangles can be used to explain *why* various straightedge-compass constructions work and *why* a number of other geometric properties should be true. A good deal of time is spent on this sort of deduction in conventional high school geometry courses. The exercise set that concludes this section contains only a sampling. It is not clear how much of this work at van Hiele level 3 is appropriate below the high school level.

EXAMPLE 1   Explain why every point on the bisector of an angle is equidistant from the sides of the angle. That is, explain why $\overline{AP} \cong \overline{CP}$ in Figure 14.76.

Solution   By the SAA condition, $\triangle PBA \cong \triangle PBC$. (The common side $\overline{PB}$ is the S in SAA.) Thus $\overline{AP} \cong \overline{CP}$ because these two segments are corresponding parts of congruent triangles.

Figure 14.76   ❑

EXAMPLE 2   Explain why every point on the perpendicular bisector of a segment is equidistant from the endpoints of the segment. That is, explain why $\overline{AP} \cong \overline{CP}$ in Figure 14.77.

Solution   By the SAS condition, $\triangle ABP \cong \triangle CBP$. Thus $\overline{AP} \cong \overline{CP}$ because these two segments are corresponding parts of congruent triangles.

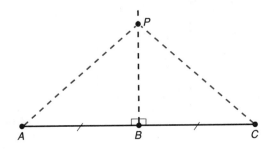

Figure 14.77   ❏

EXERCISE SET 14.5

1. Figure 14.78 suggests how compass and straightedge were used to bisect an angle.
   (a) Why is $\overline{AB} \cong \overline{AC}$?
   (b) Why is $\overline{BD} \cong \overline{CD}$?
   (c) Why is $\triangle ABD \cong \triangle ACD$?
   (d) Why is $\angle BAD \cong \angle CAD$?

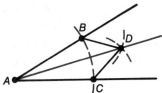

Figure 14.78

2. In the construction of the perpendicular bisector of $\overline{AB}$ in Figure 14.79, the compass opening is left fixed so that $\overline{AC} \cong \overline{BC} \cong \overline{BD} \cong \overline{AD}$.
   (a) Why is $\triangle ACD \cong \triangle BCD$?
   (b) Why is $\angle ACD \cong \angle BCD$?
   (c) Why is $\triangle ACE \cong \triangle BCE$?
   (d) Why is $\overline{AE} \cong \overline{EB}$?

(e) Why is $\overline{CD} \perp \overline{AB}$? (Recall the definition: Two lines are perpendicular if they meet to form congruent adjacent angles.)

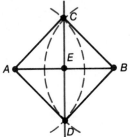

Figure 14.79

3. Recall that an isosceles triangle is one with at least two congruent sides. The angles opposite the congruent sides in an isosceles triangle are called its **base angles** and have the following property:

> The base angles of an isosceles triangle are congruent.

To show this is so, let D be the midpoint of $\overline{CB}$ in Figure 14.80 and draw $\overline{AD}$.
(a) Why is $\triangle ACD \cong \triangle ABD$?
(b) Why is $\angle C \cong \angle B$?

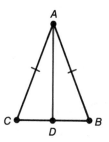

Figure 14.80

4. Recall that a parallelogram is a quadrilateral whose opposite sides are parallel. For parallelogram $ABCD$ in Figure 14.81, answer the following.

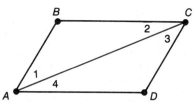

Figure 14.81

(a) Why is $\angle 1 \cong \angle 3$?
(b) Why is $\angle 2 \cong \angle 4$?
(c) Why is $\triangle ABC \cong \triangle CDA$.
(d) Why is $\overline{AB} \cong \overline{CD}$?
(e) Why is $\overline{BC} \cong \overline{AD}$?
(f) Why is $\angle B \cong \angle D$?
(g) Why is $\angle BAD \cong \angle DCB$?

Parts (d) and (e) suggest the following general statement:

> Opposite sides of a parallelogram are congruent.

(h) What general statement is suggested by parts (f) and (g)?

5. Use Figure 14.82 and show:

> If opposite sides of a quadrilateral are congruent, then the quadrilateral is a parallelogram.

The problem-solving strategy of working backwards will suggest the steps of the proof.

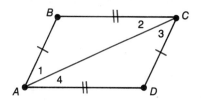

Figure 14.82

6. Use Figure 14.83 and show:

> The diagonals of a parallelogram bisect each other.

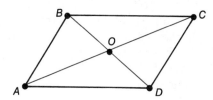

Figure 14.83

7. Figure 14.84 suggests the construction of a perpendicular to line ℓ at point A. Show that $\overleftrightarrow{DA} \perp \overleftrightarrow{BC}$.

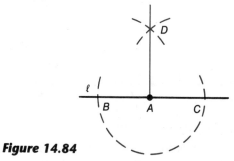

Figure 14.84

8. The bisector of an angle is ultimately a set of points. Let us call it $\mathcal{B}$. And let us denote by $\mathcal{E}$ the set of all points that are equidistant from the sides of the same angle. In Example 1 we proved that for any point P, if $P \in \mathcal{B}$, then $P \in \mathcal{E}$.
   (a) Use Figure 14.85 to prove the converse: if $P \in \mathcal{E}$, then $P \in \mathcal{B}$. Use the problem-solving strategy of working backwards.
   (b) How do Example 1 and part (a) show that $\mathcal{B} = \mathcal{E}$?

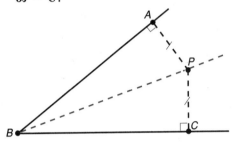

Figure 14.85

9. The perpendicular bisector of a segment is ultimately a set of points. Let us call it $\mathcal{B}$. And let us denote by $\mathcal{E}$ the set of all points that are equidistant from the ends of the same segment. In Example 2 we proved that for any point P, if $P \in \mathcal{B}$, then $P \in \mathcal{E}$.
   (a) Use Figure 14.86 to prove the converse: if $P \in \mathcal{E}$, then $P \in \mathcal{B}$.
   (b) How do Example 2 and part (a) show that $\mathcal{B} = \mathcal{E}$?

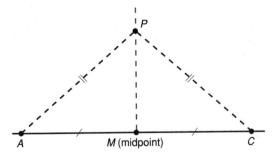

Figure 14.86

10. Using the fact that the perpendicular bisector of a segment $\overline{AB}$ is the set of all points P such that

$AP = PB$, prove that the perpendicular bisectors of the three sides of a triangle are concurrent. (*Hint:* Use Figure 14.87. Let the perpendicular bisectors of $\overline{BC}$ and $\overline{AC}$ meet at, say, P. Show that P is on the perpendicular bisector of $\overline{AB}$.)

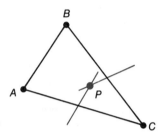

Figure 14.87

11. Show that the bisectors of the three angles of a triangle are concurrent.

12. Figure 14.88 suggests the construction of the trisectors G and F of the original segment $\overline{AB}$. In the figure,
$\overline{AC} \cong \overline{CD} \cong \overline{DE}$ and $\overline{CG} \parallel \overline{DF} \parallel \overline{EB}$
The problem is to show that $\overline{AG} \cong \overline{GF} \cong \overline{FB}$. Begin by sketching a line through C parallel to $\overline{AB}$. Let it meet $\overline{DF}$ at H and $\overline{EB}$ at I. Also sketch a line through D parallel to $\overline{AB}$. Let it meet $\overline{EB}$ at J. Use the general property stated in Exercise 4.

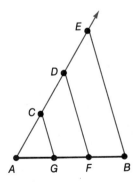

Figure 14.88

13. Draw a figure and show:

> If two opposite sides of a quadrilateral are both congruent and parallel, then the quadrilateral is a parallelogram.

★ 14. Towns *A* and *B* are situated on opposite sides of a river, as shown in Figure 14.89. A bridge $\overline{MN}$ is to be built perpendicular to the banks of the river, and then straight roads $\overline{AM}$ and $\overline{NB}$ are to be constructed. Your problem is to locate the bridge so that the polygonal path *AMNB* will be as short as possible. The location of the bridge shown in Figure 14.89 is *not* optimal. *Hint:* Complete the parallelogram having *A*, *M*, and *N* as three of its vertices.

 15. Figure 14.90 shows a triangle $\triangle ABC$ on a grid. Imagine that the grid lines are streets and you are a cab driver. Mark all the street intersections that are equidistant (by cab) from points *A* and *B*. Using a second color, mark all the street intersections that are equidistant (by cab) from points *B* and *C*. Using a third color, mark all the street intersections that are equidistant (by cab) from points *A* and *C*. Are the three sets of points that you drew concurrent? Compare with Exercise 10.

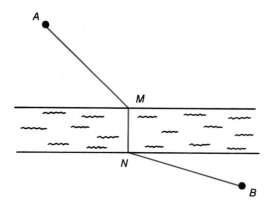

Figure 14.89

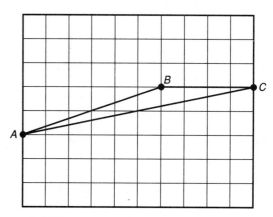

Figure 14.90

 ## 14.6 *Similar Figures*

The concept of similarity is a generalization of the concept of congruence. In this and the next section we investigate similarity in a discussion that parallels the one for congruence. Recall that we began our discussion of congruence with a somewhat informal definition: Two figures are congruent if they have the same shape *and* size. For similarity the informal definition is as follows (see Figure 14.91):

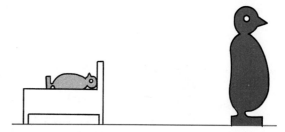

Figure 14.91 Similar figures.

> Two figures are **similar** if they have the same shape but not necessarily the same size.

According to these definitions, then, any two figures that are congruent are also similar—but similar figures need not be congruent. That is exactly what we mean when we say that similarity is a generalization of congruence.

To formalize the definition of congruence, we introduced three basic transformations: translations (slides), rotations (turns), and reflections (flips). Our formal definition was this: Two figures are congruent if one can be made to coincide with the other by a sequence of translations, rotations, and reflections, that is, by a rigid motion. To formalize the definition of similarity, we have to introduce a fourth class of transformations, the so-called *dilations*.

Dilations

Dilations are transformations that stretch or shrink figures in a uniform way. A dilation is specified by a **projection point** and a **scale factor.** For example, Figure 14.92 shows an original triangle, $\triangle ABC$, and its image $\triangle A'B'C'$ under the dilation having projection point P and scale factor 2. We call such a dilation a 2-stretch. If, as usual, we let PA denote the distance from P to A, PA' denote the distance from P to A', and so forth, then the scale factor 2 occurs in three equations:

$$PA' = 2 \cdot PA \qquad PB' = 2 \cdot PB \qquad PC' = 2 \cdot PC$$

We sometimes say that $\triangle A'B'C'$ is a scale drawing of $\triangle ABC$ drawn to the scale 2 to 1.

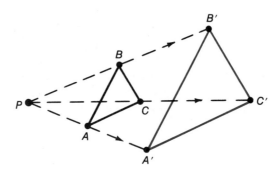

Figure 14.92 A 2-stretch.

Figure 14.93 shows an original quadrilateral $ABCD$ and its image $A'B'C'D'$ under the dilation with projection point P and scale factor 3. Notice that this time, for variety, we chose the projection point inside the figure. Points A', B', C', D' are determined by these conditions:

$$PA' = 3 \cdot PA \qquad \text{and} \qquad A' \in \overrightarrow{PA}$$
$$PB' = 3 \cdot PB \qquad \text{and} \qquad B' \in \overrightarrow{PB}$$
$$PC' = 3 \cdot PC \qquad \text{and} \qquad C' \in \overrightarrow{PC}$$
$$PD' = 3 \cdot PD \qquad \text{and} \qquad D' \in \overrightarrow{PD}$$

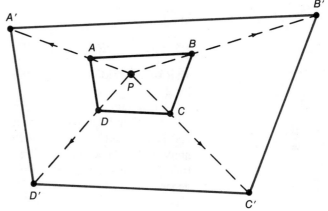

Figure 14.93 A 3-stretch.

Dilations can shrink figures as well as stretch them. Figure 14.94 shows a large original triangle, $\triangle ABC$, and its shrunken image $\triangle A'B'C'$. This time the scale factor is $\frac{1}{4}$, and the projection point was chosen to be a point on the figure, namely the vertex A. Notice that

$$PC' = \tfrac{1}{4} \cdot PC$$
$$PB' = \tfrac{1}{4} \cdot PB$$
$$PA' = \tfrac{1}{4} \cdot PA \qquad \text{(since both } PA \text{ and } PA' \text{ are 0)}$$

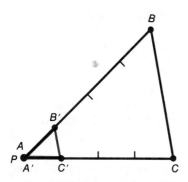

Figure 14.94 A $\frac{1}{4}$-shrink.

So far we have worked only with polygons. Figure 14.95 shows how one can use a dilation to stretch (or shrink) an *arbitrary* figure by using enough points.

Figure 14.95 A $\frac{3}{2}$-stretch.

Effect of Dilations on Length, Area, Volume, and Angle Measure

By studying the preceding diagrams, we can draw some definite quantitative conclusions about what happens to the size of a figure under a dilation. Consider Figure 14.92. If you were to measure and compare the corresponding segments $\overline{AB}$ and $\overline{A'B'}$, you would find that

$$A'B' = 2 \cdot AB$$

Similarly,

$$B'C' = 2 \cdot BC \qquad \text{and} \qquad C'A' = 2 \cdot CA$$

That is, each side of the original triangle is stretched by the original scale factor 2.

If, in Figure 14.93 you were to measure the side lengths of quadrilaterals $A'B'C'D'$ and $ABCD$, you would find that each side of the original quadrilateral is stretched by the original scale factor 3. Even in Figure 14.95 this phenomenon could be verified: The distance from top of head to tip of nose is multiplied by the scale factor $\frac{3}{2}$. So is the distance from eye to corner of mouth. In general:

> When a figure is subjected to a dilation with scale factor r, the length of every segment in that figure is multiplied by r.

EXAMPLE 1   The perimeter of the black triangle in Figure 14.94 is 24 cm. What is the perimeter of the red triangle?

Solution   The scale factor is $\frac{1}{4}$, so each side of the red triangle is only $\frac{1}{4}$ as long as the corresponding side of the black triangle. Thus the perimeter of the red triangle is also just $\frac{1}{4}$ that of the black triangle. *Answer:* $\frac{1}{4} \cdot 24$ cm $= 6$ cm   ❏

The effect of a dilation on the area of a figure is not quite as simple. Consider again the triangles of Figure 14.92. Apparently, $\triangle A'B'C'$ can be covered by exactly 4 copies of $\triangle ABC$, as shown in Figure 14.96. That is, the area of $\triangle ABC$ is multiplied by 4, the *square* of the scale factor 2.

In Figure 14.93 this simple covering and counting argument doesn't work, but the conclusion is the same. To see why the area of the red quadrilateral in Figure 14.97 is 9 times the area of the black one, consider what the dilation does to a square centimeter of area inside the black figure. Since every segment's length is multiplied by 3, the red square is 3 cm by 3 cm and thus has area 9 cm². From this result it should be clear that the area of the entire red quadrilateral is 9 times the area of the original black quadrilateral. In general:

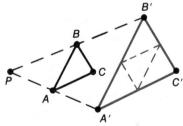

Figure 14.96

When a figure is subjected to a dilation with scale factor r, its area is multiplied by r^2.

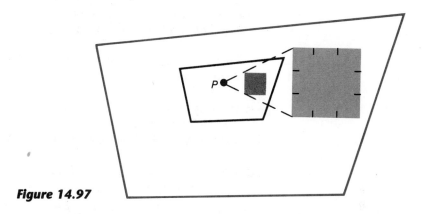

Figure 14.97

EXAMPLE 2   If the area of the black face in Figure 14.95 is 6.48 cm², what is the area of the red face?

Solution   The scale factor is $\frac{3}{2}$, so the area of the red face is

$$(\tfrac{3}{2})^2 \times 6.48 \text{ cm}^2 = \tfrac{9}{4} \times 6.48 \text{ cm}^2 = 14.58 \text{ cm}^2 \qquad \square$$

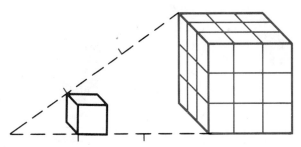

Figure 14.98

To see what the effect of a dilation is on volume, consider the perspective drawing in Figure 14.98 of a cube being stretched, in space, with scale factor 3. Clearly, we would need 27 of the small cubes to fill up the large one. That is, the volume of the small cube is multiplied by 27, the third power of the scale factor 3. In general:

When a figure is subjected to a dilation with scale factor r, its volume is multiplied by r^3.

EXAMPLE 3　The diameter of the earth is about 3.67 times that of the moon. How do their volumes compare?

Solution　We can think of creating the earth by subjecting the moon to a dilation with scale factor 3.67. Thus the volume of the earth is about 3.67^3, or approximately 49 times that of the moon.　❏

　　Figures 14.92, 14.93, and 14.94 all indicate very clearly one final property of dilations and size.

> When a figure is subjected to a dilation, the measure of every angle in that figure is left unchanged.

In other words, each angle is congruent to its image under a dilation. For instance, in Figure 14.93

$$\angle A \cong \angle A' \qquad \angle B \cong \angle B' \qquad \angle C \cong \angle C' \qquad \angle D \cong \angle D'$$

Similarity

We now have all the pieces necessary for putting together a formal definition of similarity. The idea is this: Given two similar figures like the birds on page

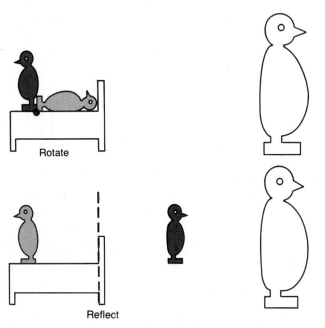

Rotate

Reflect

Figure 14.99

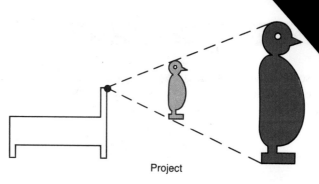

Project

Figure 14.99 (continued).

737, move one of the figures into position, by rigid motions, and then project it onto the other by a dilation (Figure 14.99). Here is the formal definition.

> Two figures are **similar** if one can be made to coincide with the other by subjecting it to a rigid motion followed by a dilation.

EXAMPLE 4   Explain why $\triangle ABC$ in Figure 14.100 is similar to $\triangle DEC$.

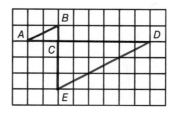

Figure 14.100

Solution   First, rotate $\triangle ABC$ through 180° about C. Then, using C as projection point, subject the dotted figure in Figure 14.101 to a stretch with scale factor 3. Thus $\triangle ABC$ can be made to coincide with $\triangle DEC$ by the composition of a rigid motion (the 180° rotation) and a dilation (the 3-stretch).

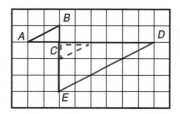

Figure 14.101   ❏

EXERCISE SET 14.6

following figures, us-
and the scale factor

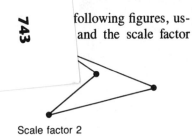

Scale factor 2

(a)

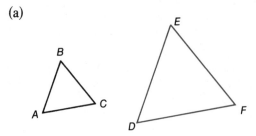

(b)

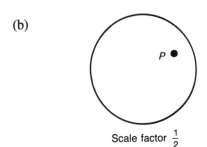

P ●

Scale factor $\frac{1}{2}$

(b)

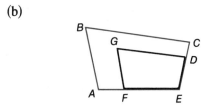

(c)

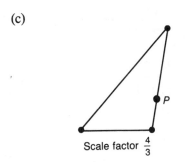

P

Scale factor $\frac{4}{3}$

(c)

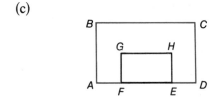

3. The incomplete diagram in Figure 14.102 suggests a technique used by Michelangelo and other fresco painters to enlarge a small drawing to a full-scale pattern, or *cartoon,* for the fresco. Complete the enlargement. What problem-solving strategy does this technique employ?

(d)

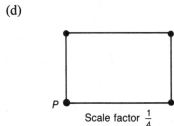

P

Scale factor $\frac{1}{4}$

2. Locate the projection point P and estimate the scale factor for a dilation that will map the black figure onto the red one.

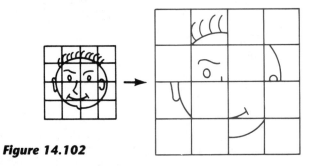

Figure 14.102

4. Suppose that the perimeter of the circle in Exercise 1(b) is 10 cm. What is the perimeter of the scale drawing?

5. Suppose that the area of the triangle in Exercise 1(c) is 5 cm². What is the area of the scale drawing?

6. In this exercise, assume that the figures in each pair are similar. Fill in the missing numbers. A calculator is recommended.

(a)

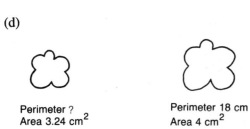

(b)

(c)

Perimeter 10 cm
Area 3 cm²

Perimeter 7 cm
Area?

(d)

Perimeter ?
Area 3.24 cm²

Perimeter 18 cm
Area 4 cm²

(e)

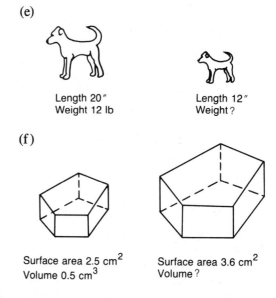

Length 20″
Weight 12 lb

Length 12″
Weight?

(f)

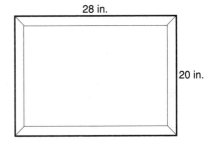

Surface area 2.5 cm²
Volume 0.5 cm³

Surface area 3.6 cm²
Volume?

7. Figure 14.103 shows a picture frame that is 2 in wide. Is its rectangular outer border similar to its rectangular inner border?

28 in.

20 in.

Figure 14.103

8. Suppose that a large egg is $2\frac{1}{2}$ in long and a small one is 2 in long. Assuming that all eggs have the same shape, which is the better buy, a dozen large eggs for $1.00 or a dozen small eggs for 65¢.

9. The triangles in each pair in Figure 14.104 are similar. Describe a composition (hookup) of a rigid motion and a dilation that will bring the black one into coincidence with the red one. Remember that to describe a dilation, you need to specify a projection point and a scale factor.

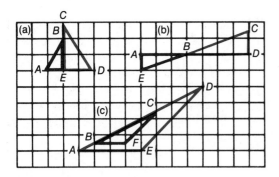

Figure 14.104

★ 10. The strength of a cylindrical rod is a constant times its cross-sectional area, where the constant depends on the material of which it is made. An engineer builds a model water tower consisting of a tank supported by a cylindrical rod. When he fills the tank with water, the model holds up admirably. When the real thing is constructed (on a scale of 50 to 1) and filled with water, however, the rod buckles. Explain (See Figure 14.105.)

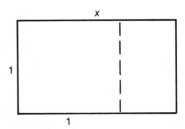

Figure 14.105

11. *Why wedding cakes use scaffolding:* Pam's favorite cake is a three-layer chocolate cake, 8 in in diameter and 3 in high, weighing $1\frac{1}{2}$ lb. She really wanted to have a 4 to 1 scale enlargement as her wedding cake, but her friends said that although it would be all right to quadruple the diameter, she should probably only triple the height. So she settled for a nine-layer version of the cake, 32 in in diameter and 9 in high.

(a) For the small cake, how many pounds-per-square-inch of pressure do the top two layers exert on the bottom layer?

(b) For the large cake, how many pounds-per-square-inch of pressure do the top eight layers exert on the bottom layer? Compare your answer to the answer to part (a).

★ 12. A cubical box with edge length 12 in is filled to the top with 27 (congruent) apples, arranged in 3 layers of 9 each. A second cubical box of the same size is filled to the top with 64 (congruent) apples, similar to but smaller than the first apples, arranged in 4 layers of 16 each. See Figure 14.106. Compare the volume of apples in the two boxes.

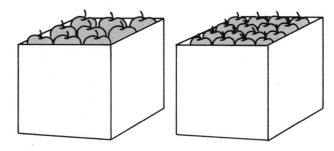

Figure 14.106

★ 13. The ancient Greeks considered the most beautifully proportioned rectangle (a "golden rectangle") to be one with the property that removal of a square from one end would leave a rectangle similar to the original one. Find the length x of the golden rectangle of height 1 (see Figure 14.107).

Figure 14.107

14. The stringed portion of an old-fashioned tennis racket is an oval 27 cm long. On a modern over-sized racket the oval is similar but 34 cm long. The "sweet spot" on each racket is an oval similar to but 12 cm shorter than the entire stringed portion.
    (a) Compare the areas of the sweet spots on the two rackets.

(b) Salesmen tout the area of the sweet spot. Is it more useful to a player to know the area of the sweet spot or its linear dimensions (maximum length and width)?

15. Suppose that the peeling on a lemon is 0.5 cm thick and that the (unpeeled) lemon is 10 cm long. By volume, approximately what percent of the lemon is peeling?

Computer Vignette L

Similar figures can be produced by incorporating a variable into a Logo procedure. For example, the procedure TRAPEZOID in Figure 14.108 uses a variable S to represent the length of the two nonparallel sides and the upper base in an isosceles trapezoid. When the variable is replaced by specific numbers, similar trapezoids of various sizes are drawn. Two are shown in Figure 14.109.

Figure 14.108

```
TO TRAPEZOID :S
  RIGHT 30
  FORWARD :S
  RIGHT 60
  FORWARD :S
  RIGHT 60
  FORWARD :S
  RIGHT 120
  FORWARD 2 * :S
  RIGHT 90
END
```

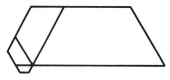

TRAPEZOID 40

TRAPEZOID 60

Figure 14.109

Figure 14.110 lists the *recursive* Logo procedure TRAPEZOIDAL, which again involves a variable S. What makes this program recursive is that it uses *itself* as a subroutine. (It also uses TRAPEZOID as a subroutine.) When TRAPEZOIDAL is run with the variable replaced by a specific number, a whole family of similar trapezoids is assembled into a design. The design TRAPEZOIDAL 64 is shown in Figure 14.111. The more ornate designs in Chapter 16 are drawn by recursive procedures.

Figure 14.110

```
TO TRAPEZOIDAL :S
  IF :S < 8 THEN STOP
  TRAPEZOID :S
  LEFT 60
  TRAPEZOIDAL :S/2
  HIDETURTLE
END
```

Figure 14.111

TRAPEZOIDAL 64

14.7   *Similar Triangles*

Our development of congruence proceeded from general to special. We began by defining what it means to say that two arbitrary figures are congruent (one can be superimposed on the other by a rigid motion). Then we specialized the discussion to triangles. It turned out that for triangles the question of superimposability could be decided by making three pairs of strategic measurements with ruler and protractor or by making three congruence checks with compass. These superimposability criteria, or congruence conditions, bore the initials SAS, ASA, SAA, and SSS.

Our development of the topic of similarity also began with the general case (two arbitrary figures are similar if one can be superimposed on the other by the composition of a rigid motion and a dilation). Now we specialize the discussion to triangles. We will see shortly that the question of whether two triangles are similar (superimposable in this new sense) can again be decided by making some well-chosen measurements or by checking the congruence of just two pairs of angles.

Corresponding Parts

Consider the similar triangles in Figure 14.112. To superimpose the smaller on the larger, reflect it in the perpendicular bisector of $\overline{CD}$; then project from D with scale factor 2. See Figure 14.113.

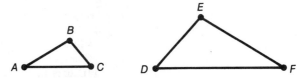

Figure 14.112 Similar triangles.

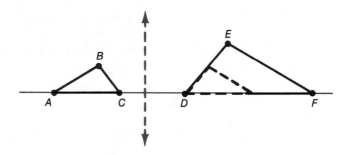

Figure 14.113

Under this composition of transformations, vertex A is ultimately mapped to F, vertex B to E, and vertex C to D. We refer to these pairs of vertices as *corresponding vertices:*

$$A \leftrightarrow F \qquad B \leftrightarrow E \qquad C \leftrightarrow D$$

And we define *corresponding sides* and *corresponding angles* in terms of them just as we did in the case of congruence. For example,

$\angle BAC$ and $\angle EFD$ are corresponding angles.

$\overline{CB}$ and $\overline{DE}$ are corresponding sides.

As before, corresponding sides are located opposite corresponding angles. The notational convention for reporting the similarity is the same as for congruence except that $\cong$ is replaced by $\sim$ (read $\sim$ as "is similar to"). For example,

"$\triangle ABC \sim \triangle FED$" is an acceptable report

but

"$\triangle ABC \sim \triangle DEF$" is not acceptable

since it is impossible to superimpose A on D, B on E, and C on F by a rigid motion and then a dilation.

We observed in the general case that under a dilation every segment in a figure is stretched (or shrunk) by the same factor, namely, the scale factor of the dilation. In particular, in Figure 14.113 every side of $\triangle ABC$ is stretched by the factor 2:

$$EF = 2 \cdot AB \qquad FD = 2 \cdot CA \qquad DE = 2 \cdot CB$$

Thus all three ratios of corresponding sides (really, side lengths) are equal (to 2):

$$\frac{EF}{AB} = \frac{FD}{CA} = \frac{DE}{CB}$$

A common way of expressing this fact is as follows:

Corresponding sides of similar triangles are proportional.

More generally, corresponding sides of similar polygons are proportional.

The companion property of angles was likewise noted in greater generality in the previous section.

Corresponding angles of similar triangles are congruent.

EXAMPLE 1   Given that $\triangle ABC \sim \triangle DEF$ in Figure 14.114, calculate the side lengths BC and ED.

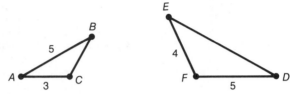

Figure 14.114

Solution   The triangles are similar, so corresponding sides—determined from the report that $\triangle ABC \sim \triangle DEF$ must be proportional:

$$\frac{AB}{DE} = \frac{BC}{EF} = \frac{CA}{FD}$$

Substituting the given side lengths into the proportion

$$\frac{5}{DE} = \frac{BC}{4} = \frac{3}{5}$$

leads to two equations:

$$\frac{5}{DE} = \frac{3}{5} \Leftrightarrow 3 \cdot DE = 25 \Leftrightarrow DE = 8\tfrac{1}{3}$$

$$\frac{BC}{4} = \frac{3}{5} \Leftrightarrow 5 \cdot BC = 12 \Leftrightarrow BC = 2\tfrac{2}{5}$$

Figure 14.115 shows how similar triangles are illustrated in a seventh-grade textbook. It also indicates that the properties of corresponding sides and angles are true for similar rectangles—and in general for similar polygons—not just for similar triangles. ❏

Similarity Criteria

There are three simple tests for similarity of triangles, and they closely resemble the tests for congruence. We will put their initials in quotation marks as a reminder that they are not exactly the same. The first is a side-angle-side criterion.

"SAS": If two sides of one triangle are *proportional* to two sides of another, and if the included angles are congruent, then the triangles are similar.

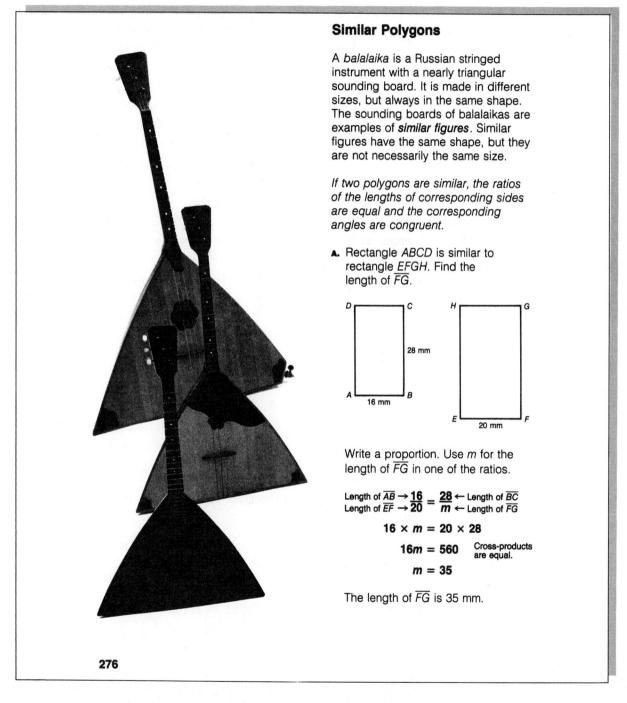

Similar Polygons

A *balalaika* is a Russian stringed instrument with a nearly triangular sounding board. It is made in different sizes, but always in the same shape. The sounding boards of balalaikas are examples of ***similar figures***. Similar figures have the same shape, but they are not necessarily the same size.

If two polygons are similar, the ratios of the lengths of corresponding sides are equal and the corresponding angles are congruent.

A. Rectangle *ABCD* is similar to rectangle *EFGH*. Find the length of $\overline{FG}$.

Write a proportion. Use *m* for the length of $\overline{FG}$ in one of the ratios.

$$\text{Length of } \overline{AB} \to \frac{16}{20} = \frac{28}{m} \leftarrow \text{Length of } \overline{BC}$$
$$\text{Length of } \overline{EF} \to \qquad \qquad \leftarrow \text{Length of } \overline{FG}$$

$$16 \times m = 20 \times 28$$

$$16m = 560 \qquad \text{Cross-products are equal.}$$

$$m = 35$$

The length of $\overline{FG}$ is 35 mm.

276

Figure 14.115 Similar figures in a seventh-grade textbook.

For example, the triangles in Figure 14.116 are similar by the "SAS" condition (since 3.6/3 = 4.8/4), and the correspondence between vertices is given by $\triangle BAC \sim \triangle EDF$. The scale factor, or *constant of proportionality*, is 1.2.

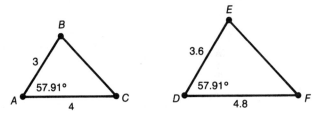

Figure 14.116 Triangles similar by "SAS."

EXAMPLE 2   Suppose, in Figure 14.116, that $BC = 3.5$ and $m\angle C = 46.57°$. Find missing side lengths and angle measures in $\triangle DEF$.

Solution   The triangles are similar, so the angles of $\triangle DEF$ will have the same measures as the corresponding angles in $\triangle ABC$. Since two of the angle measures in $\triangle ABC$ are given, the third can be found by using the 180° sum property:

$$m\angle B = 180° - 57.91° - 46.57° = 75.52°$$

Thus

$$m\angle E = m\angle B = 75.52°$$
$$m\angle F = m\angle C = 46.57°$$

To find EF, simply apply the scale (stretch) factor 1.2 to the length of the corresponding side BC:

$$EF = 1.2 \times 3.5 = 4.2 \qquad \square$$

A second similarity criterion corresponds to the side-side-side congruence condition.

"SSS": If three sides of one triangle are *proportional* to three sides of another, then the two triangles are similar.

For example, the triangles in Figure 14.117 are similar since

$$\frac{9.6}{12} = \frac{8}{10} = \frac{6}{7.5}$$

EXAMPLE 3   Give an acceptable report of the similarity in Figure 14.117, find the scale factor, and compare the areas of the triangles.

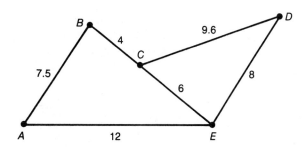

Figure 14.117 Triangles similar by "SSS."

Solution   If one traces both triangles so that the long side is traveled first, the medium side second, and the short side third, then the vertices will be paired up correctly:

$$\triangle AEB \sim \triangle CDE$$

The scale factor is the common ratio of corresponding sides, namely, $\frac{8}{10} = 0.8$, or $\frac{10}{8} = 1.25$, depending on which triangle is thought of as a scale drawing of the other. Then

$$\text{Area of } \triangle CDE = (0.8)^2 \times \text{area of } \triangle AEB \qquad \square$$

The last, but perhaps the most useful, similarity criterion corresponds to the ASA and SAA congruence conditions.

"AA": If two angles of one triangle are congruent to two angles of another, then the triangles are similar.

For example, suppose that in Figure 14.118 the points A, B, and D are collinear as are the points E, B, and C. Then the triangles are similar because $\angle A \cong \angle D$ (same measure) and $\angle ABE \cong \angle DBC$ (vertical angles).

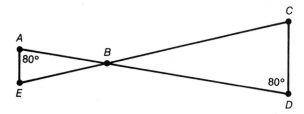

Figure 14.118 Triangles similar by "AA."

EXAMPLE 4   Explain why "$\triangle ABE \sim \triangle CBD$" is *not* an acceptable report of the similarity in Figure 14.118, correct it, and describe a rigid motion that would put $\triangle ABE$ in position for dilation onto $\triangle CBD$.

Solution   The report "$\triangle ABE \sim \triangle CBD$" implies that $\angle EAB$ corresponds to $\angle DCB$. But $m\angle EAB = 80°$, and we have no reason to assume that $m\angle DCB = 80°$. A correct report is "$\triangle ABE \sim \triangle DBC$." A 180° rotation of $\triangle ABE$ about point B would set the stage for dilation.   ❏

EXERCISE SET 14.7

1. Using only a protractor, can one decide the following?
   (a) Whether two triangles are similar
   (b) Whether two triangles are congruent

2. Using only a ruler, can one decide the following?
   (a) Whether two triangles are similar
   (b) Whether two triangles are congruent

3. Using only a compass, can one decide the following?
   (a) Whether two triangles are similar
   (b) Whether two triangles are congruent

4. Construct, by an "SAS" procedure, a triangle similar to $\triangle ABC$ (Figure 14.119) but having twice the perimeter.

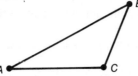

Figure 14.119

5. Repeat Exercise 4, using an "SSS" procedure.

6. Explain why each two triangles are similar, report the similarity using the notational convention, and, using a ruler only when necessary, find the scale factor relating the two. (Anytime three points appear to be collinear, you may assume that they are.)
   (a)

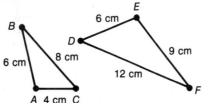

(b)

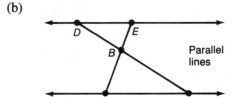

(c)

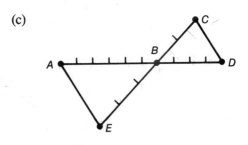

(d)

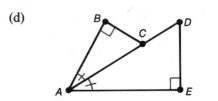

(e)

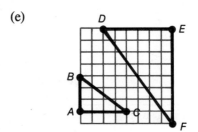

(f)

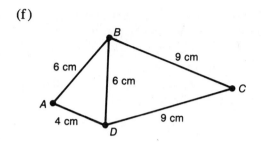

In Exercises 7–11, explain why the triangles are similar, and then fill in the blanks.

7. Use Figure 14.120.
   (a) $BC =$ _____
   (b) $EF =$ _____

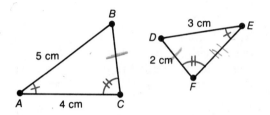

Figure 14.120

8. Use Figure 14.121
   (a) $m \angle C =$ _____
   (b) $m \angle A =$ _____

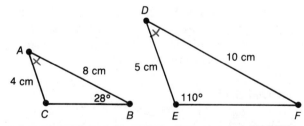

Figure 14.121

9. Use Figure 14.122. Angle measures are approximate.
   (a) $m \angle B =$ _____
   (b) $m \angle E =$ _____

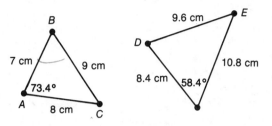

Figure 14.122

10. In Figure 14.123, points A, B, and D are collinear as are points E, B, and C.
    (a) $AE =$ _____
    (b) $BC =$ _____

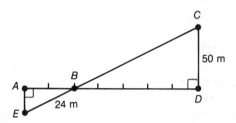

Figure 14.123

11. In Figure 14.124, points A, C, and D are collinear as are points D, E, and F.
    (a) $m \angle F =$ _____   (b) $m \angle ACB =$ _____
    (c) $m \angle B =$ _____   (d) $AF =$ _____

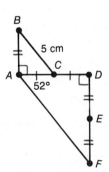

Figure 14.124

12. Find the missing numbers in Figure 14.125.

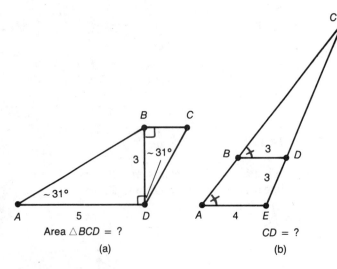

Area △BCD = ?

(a)

CD = ?

(b)

Figure 14.125

13. Refer to Figure 14.126.
   (a) Why is △ABC ~ △DEF?
   (b) What assumption did you make about the sun's rays?
   (c) Did you make any other assumptions?
   (d) If the man is 6 ft tall and casts a 7 ft shadow, and the tree casts a 42 ft shadow, how tall is the tree?

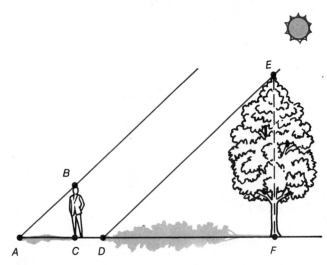

Figure 14.126

In Exercises 14–16, use the similarity criteria for triangles as the basis for your explanations.

14. Refer to Figure 14.127 and show that the segment joining the midpoints of two sides of a triangle must be parallel to the third side. (How is BD related to AE?)

Given $BC = \frac{1}{2}AC$, $DC = \frac{1}{2}EC$
Show $\overleftrightarrow{BD} \parallel \overleftrightarrow{AE}$

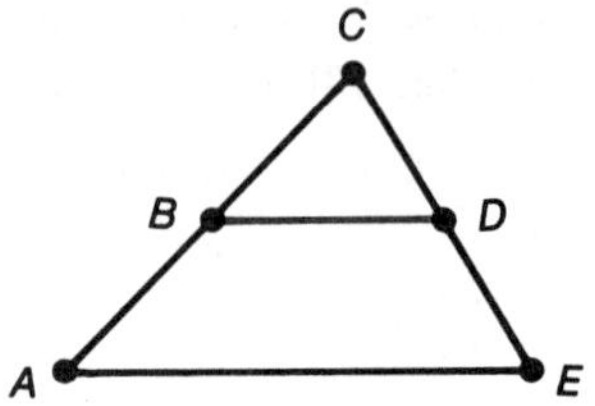

Figure 14.127

15. Refer to Figure 14.128 and show that a segment that "divides two sides of a triangle proportionally" must be parallel to the third side. (How is BD related to AE?)

Given $\dfrac{BC}{AC} = \dfrac{DC}{EC}$
Show $\overleftrightarrow{BD} \parallel \overleftrightarrow{AE}$

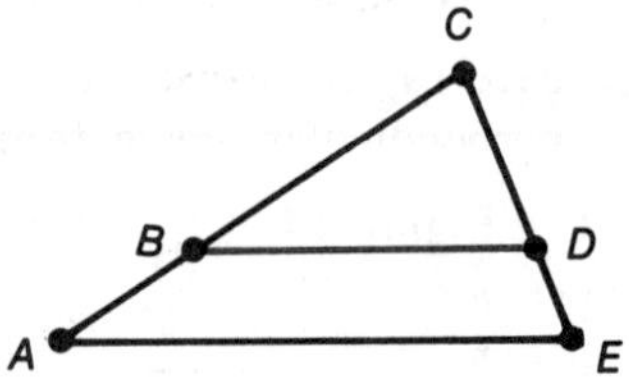

Figure 14.129

16. Refer to Figure 14.129 and show that a line drawn through two sides of a triangle parallel to the third side divides those two sides proportionally. (How is BD related to AE?)

Given $\overleftrightarrow{BD} \parallel \overleftrightarrow{AE}$
Show $\dfrac{BC}{AC} = \dfrac{DC}{EC}$

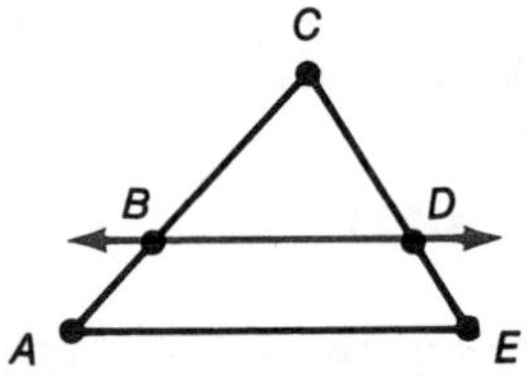

Figure 14.128

★ 17. A rain gauge has the shape shown in Figure 14.130. The top is an open 1-in by 1-in square.
   (a) How many cubic inches of water can it hold?
   (b) How high up from the bottom should the

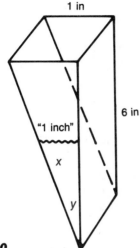

1 in

6 in

"1 inch"

x

y

Figure 14.130

mark for "1 inch of rain" be drawn? (That is, find y.)

(c) How high up should the "$\frac{1}{2}$-inch" mark be drawn?

(d) Can you see any reason why this shape is better than an ordinary right square prism?

★ 18. Figure 14.131 shows a right triangle, $\triangle ABC$, and a perpendicular drawn from the right angle vertex, C, to the hypotenuse, $\overline{AB}$.

(a) Explain why $\triangle BDC \sim \triangle BCA$.

(b) What is the shrink factor you would have to apply to $\triangle BCA$ to get a congruent copy of $\triangle BDC$?

(c) Explain why $\triangle CDA \sim \triangle BCA$.

(d) What is the shrink factor you would have to apply to $\triangle BCA$ to get a congruent copy of $\triangle CDA$?

(e) Use parts (a)–(d) and the fact that area $\triangle BCA$ = area $\triangle BDC$ + area $\triangle CDA$ to deduce the Pythagorean theorem, $a^2 + b^2 = c^2$.

🐚 19. Geometrically, the Pythagorean theorem says that if one draws squares on the sides of a right triangle, then the area of the large square is equal to the sum of the areas of the two smaller squares. See Figure 14.132. This result remains

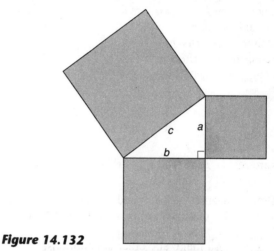

Figure 14.132

true for *any* three similar figures on the sides of a right triangle. For example, in Figure 14.133 the area of figure L (large) is equal to the sum of the areas of figure M (medium) and figure S (small). Use the Pythagorean theorem to prove this.

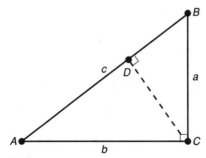

Figure 14.131

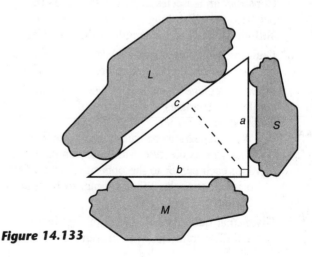

Figure 14.133

Key Concepts in Chapter 14

Construction
Bisector of an angle
Perpendicular lines
Perpendicular bisector of a segment
Parallel postulate
Transversal of two lines
Alternate interior (exterior) angles
Corresponding angles
SAS congruence criterion
ASA congruence criterion
SSS congruence criterion

SAA congruence criterion
Corresponding parts of congruent figures
Similar figures
Dilation
Scale factor
Projection point
Corresponding parts of similar figures
Similar triangles
"SAS" similarity criterion
"SSS" similarity criterion
"AA" similarity criterion

❧ Chapter 14 Review Exercises ❧

In Exercises 1–7, use only a straightedge and compass.

1. Draw a triangle △ABC, and construct its image under a 90° clockwise rotation about C.

2. Draw a triangle △DEF, and construct its image under a reflection in the bisector of ∠DEF.

3. Draw a triangle △GHI, and construct its image under a translation that takes the midpoint of $\overline{GI}$ to the original location of H.

4. Construct a regular 12-gon.

5. Construct an isosceles trapezoid for which the upper base is half as long as the lower base and the altitude is equal to the length of the upper base.

6. Draw an isosceles triangle △JKL and construct both its inscribed and its circumscribed circles.

7. Draw a scalene triangle △MNO and construct equilateral triangles on each of its sides. Also construct their centers.
   (a) What appears to be true of the three centers? Test your conjecture with your compass.
   (b) Join each center to the opposite vertex of the original triangle. What appears to be true of these three segments?

* 8. Given that quadrilateral ABCD of Figure 14.134 is a parallelogram, find the measure of ∠E, and

cite the properties of angles that led you to your answer.

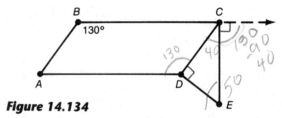

Figure 14.134

* 9. Figure 14.135 shows two lines $\overleftrightarrow{AC}$ and $\overleftrightarrow{BD}$ intersecting to form congruent adjacent angles. Supply reasons in this proof that $m\angle AOB = 90$ and $m\angle BOC = 90$.

   $m\angle AOB + m\angle BOC = 180$ _____(a)_____
   $m\angle AOB = m\angle BOC$ _____(b)_____

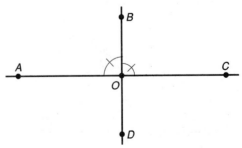

Figure 14.135

$2 \cdot m\angle AOB = 180$ (c) _____

$m\angle AOB = 90$ (d) _____

$90 = m\angle BOC$ (e) _____

10. Figure 14.136 shows a triangle $\triangle ABC$ "inscribed in a semicircle" with center O. You are to show that $\angle ABC$ has measure 90. To get you started we have drawn in segment $\overline{OB}$, which created two isosceles triangles, and we have symbolized the measures of the (congruent) base angles of these isosceles triangles as well as their third angles.

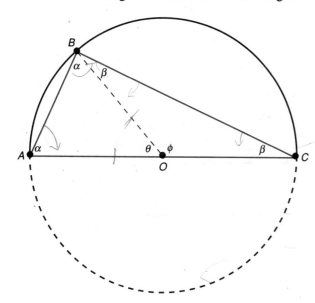

Figure 14.136

11. Refer to the triangles of Figure 14.137.
    (a) Cite the congruence condition that assures you they are congruent. _SAS_

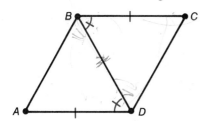

Figure 14.137

(b) Report the congruence using the notational convention. △ $ABC \cong BDA$

(c) Describe a rigid motion that would put one triangle on the other. turn flip

12. Repeat Exercise 11 for the triangles of Figure 14.138. (Points A, E, C are collinear, as are D, E, and B.)

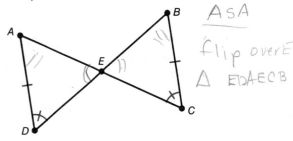

ASA

flip over E

△ EDAECB

Figure 14.138

13. Suppose $\triangle DPT \cong \triangle BOQ$. Which of the following statements are *certain* to be true?
    (a) $\angle PTD \cong \angle OQB$
    (b) $\overline{TD} \cong \overline{BQ}$
    (c) $\overline{TP} \cong \overline{OB}$
    (d) $\angle DTP \cong \angle OQB$
    (e) $\triangle PDT \cong \triangle OQB$
    (f) $\triangle TDP \cong \triangle QBO$

* 14. Write a statement-reason proof that a radius of a circle drawn through the midpoint of a chord (Figure 14.139) is perpendicular to the chord. That is,

    Given (1) B is the midpoint of AC.

            (2) O is the center of the circle.

    Prove $\overline{OB} \perp \overline{AC}$; that is, $\angle ABO \cong \angle CBO$

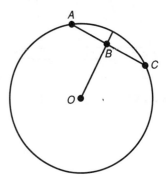

Figure 14.139

15. Use only a compass and a straightedge to construct the image of $\triangle ABC$ in Figure 14.140 under a dilation with center P and scale factor $\frac{3}{2}$.

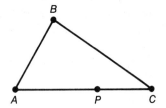

Figure 14.140

16. A large triangle is similar to a small triangle, but has four times the perimeter. How do their areas compare?

17. Suppose that a mother and daughter are "similar" in the precise mathematical sense of the word. If the mother is 5 ft 5 in tall, the daughter is 4 ft 4 in tall, and the daughter weighs 64 lb, how much does the mother weigh?

18. A large sphere has twice the surface area of a small sphere.
    (a) Find the ratio of their radii (large to small).
    (b) Find the ratio of their volumes (large to small).

19. Figure 14.141 shows an avant-garde scalene picture frame that is 2 in wide. Is its triangular outer border similar to its triangular inner border?

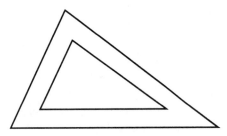

Figure 14.141

20. Refer to the triangles in Figure 14.142.
    (a) Cite a similarity criterion that guarantees that the two triangles are similar.
    (b) Report the similarity using the notational convention.
    (c) Find the length of $\overline{CD}$.

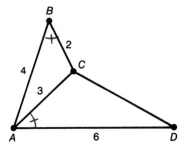

Figure 14.142

21. If the area of $\triangle ABE$ in Figure 14.143 is 30 m², how long is $\overline{BD}$? (Points A, B, and D are collinear, as are points C, B, and E.)

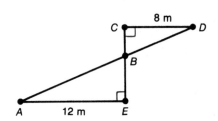

Figure 14.143

References

Bunt, L., P. Jones, and J. Bedient. *The Historical Roots of Elementary Mathematics,* Englewood Cliffs, N.J.: Prentice Hall, 1976.

Eves, H. *A Survey of Geometry*. Boston: Allyn and Bacon, 1963.

Garfunkel, S. et al. *For All Practical Purposes*. New York: W. H. Freeman, 1988.

Heath, T. *The Thirteen Books of Euclid's Elements*. vols. I, II, III. New York: Dover, 1956.

Mathematics Teacher. Special Issue—"Geometry." vol. 78, no. 6, September 1985.

O'Daffer, P., and S. Clemens. *Geometry: An Investigative Approach*. Reading, Mass.: Addison-Wesley, 1976.

Smart, J. *Modern Geometries*. 2nd ed. Monterey, Calif.: Brooks/Cole, 1978.

15

ALGEBRA AND GEOMETRY

It is probably impossible to write a definition of algebra that is broad enough to encompass all of the mathematics that goes by that name. For our purposes we can think of algebra as generalized arithmetic. The objects of investigation are the same in both subjects: numbers, operations on numbers, and relations between numbers. The differences between algebra and arithmetic are differences in generality. In arithmetic one deals with specific numbers represented either by standard numerals

$$14, \quad ^-5, \quad \tfrac{13}{4}, \quad 3\tfrac{1}{4}, \quad 3.25, \quad \sqrt{2}$$

or by numerical expressions

$$79 \times 64, \qquad \frac{65 + 3(35 - 18)}{4}, \qquad (12 - 6 \cdot 5)^3$$

In algebra one deals with unspecified numbers (unknowns, variables) represented by letters

$$x, \qquad t, \qquad a$$

or by variable expressions

$$3t - 5, \qquad x^2 + x - 4, \qquad (x + 2)(x - 3), \qquad 3rs + 3r + s + 1$$

Clearly, then, we have been doing algebra throughout this book. We used variables in our earliest work with problem solving. See, for example, Problem 8, p. 9 where we used the strategies of selecting appropriate notation and writing an open sentence to reduce the word problem to the algebraic task of solving the equation

$$b + \tfrac{3}{2}b = 60$$

We used variables in stating structural and order properties of the number systems. For example, we expressed the commutative property of addition by stating that for all numbers a and b

$$a + b = b + a$$

We used variables to abbreviate computational rules, such as the rule for dividing fractions

$$\frac{a/b}{c/d} = \frac{a}{b} \cdot \frac{d}{c}$$

We used variables to summarize geometric relationships, as in this formula for the volume of a cone:

$$V = \tfrac{1}{3}Bh$$

In fact, any time that a generalization was called for, the symbolism of algebra was used.

We have several purposes in returning to algebra in this chapter. We want to organize and formalize what we have been doing informally up to now. We want to bring algebra and geometry together for mutual support. We want to develop further our ability to use algebra in problem solving—to hone what Polya considered the single most important skill in all of high school mathematics. We want to point the way to generalizations from the simple algebra of our course to the more powerful techniques of junior high and high school algebra.

Much of the content of this chapter goes beyond the bounds of the elementary school curriculum. But since the teaching of algebra is commonplace at the eighth-grade level, and prealgebra is not unusual in the seventh grade, an elementary school teacher should be familiar with this material so that she can prepare her students. And, of course, a middle school teacher needs a solid foundation in algebra. For example, the 5–8 *Standards* specify that students at that level should come to "understand the concepts of variable, expression, and equation"; solve linear equations; and "apply algebraic methods to solve a variety of real-world and mathematical problems."

 ## 15.1 *Equations and Inequalities in One Variable; The Number Line*

To put our study of algebra on a firm foundation, we will define a few technical terms.

Statements and Open Sentences

In algebra and in everyday life we deal with statements constantly. A **statement** is a declarative sentence that is either true or false, not neither and not both.

EXAMPLE 1   Which of the following are statements?
(a) The capital of Texas is Austin.

(b) The population of California is less than one million.
(c) What state is known as the Empire State?
(d) $\sqrt{49} = 7$
(e) $8 \cdot 7 = 63$
(f) $5(4 + 2^2)$
(g) $\sqrt{55} < 8$
(h) $2x + 9 = 3$

Solution (a) A (true) statement
(b) A (false) statement
(c) Not a statement (cannot be classified as true or false)
(d) A (true) statement
(e) A (false) statement
(f) Not a statement; not even a sentence (no verb)
(g) A (true) statement
(h) Not a statement (cannot be classified as true or false) ❑

Although a question—like sentence (c) in Example 1—is obviously not a statement, it can be made to look more like one by means of a blank:

_____ is known as the Empire State.

This is essentially how the mathematical question "What number when doubled and then increased by nine yields three?" was camouflaged in sentence (h). Sentence (h) could just as well have been written as

$$2 \cdot \underline{} + 9 = 3$$

For more involved mathematical sentences, however, blanks tend to get confused with fraction bars and minus signs, so letters or **variables** like x are used instead.

Sentences that involve blanks or variables are called **open sentences.** Notice how an open sentence becomes a statement as soon as the blank is filled:

Alabama is known as the Empire State. (A false statement.)
Alaska is known as the Empire State. (A false statement.)
New York is known as the Empire State. (A true statement.)

and

$$2 \cdot \underline{1} + 9 = 3 \qquad \text{(a false statement)}$$
$$2 \cdot \underline{{}^-3} + 9 = 3 \qquad \text{(a true statement)}$$

The fill-ins that yield true statements are called the **solutions** of the open sentences. Thus New York is the solution to the open sentence

_____ is known as the Empire State.

while $^-3$ is the solution to the open sentence

$$2x + 9 = 3$$

The set of all possible fill-ins is called the **replacement set** for the blank or variable. For instance, we used the set of 50 states in the United States as the replacement set because the original question asked, "What *state* is known as the Empire State?" The mathematical open sentence, however, offered few clues for how to choose the replacement set. Obviously, it had to be some set of numbers, but which one was not indicated.

We shall always take the set of all real numbers as our replacement set unless there is specific indication to the contrary.

Note that it is very important to agree on the replacement set. A young child who knows only about positive integers would say that $2x + 9 = 3$ has *no* solutions—and for his replacement set he would be right.

Each of the two open sentences that we considered turned out to have exactly one solution. This need not always be the case. Consider, for example, these open sentences for which the replacement set is the set of 50 states of the United States.

> The population of _____ is more than ten million.
> The capital of _____ is Chicago.

The first has seven solutions: California, New York, Texas, Pennsylvania, Illinois, Florida, and Ohio. The second has no solutions at all. The same situations arise for mathematical open sentences. The open sentence $x^2 = {}^-1$ has no solution (in the replacement set we agreed on), the open sentence $x^2 = 4$ has two solutions, and the open sentence $x < 4$ has infinitely many solutions.

Designating Solution Sets

The set of all replacements that make an open sentence true is called the **solution set,** or **truth set,** of the open sentence. Finding the solution set is called *solving* the open sentence. In mathematical contexts there is further special terminology. If the verb of a mathematical sentence is $=$, the sentence is called an **equation.** If the verb is any one of $\neq$, $<$, $\leq$, $>$, $\geq$, it is called an **inequality.**

Consider the task of solving the equations

$$2x + 9 = 3 \qquad x^2 = {}^-1 \qquad x^2 = 4$$

There are two slightly different ways of thinking about these problems. Although both lead to the same solutions, there are psychological and notational differences that you should be aware of. Each approach has its virtues and you should feel comfortable switching back and forth between them.

One can think of x as a *blank* to be filled by numbers. People who think this way indicate the solution sets by using braces:

Solution set of $2x + 9 = 3$ is $\{^-3\}$
Solution set of $x^2 = {}^-1$ is $\{\ \}$ or $\varnothing$ (the empty set).
Solution set of $x^2 = 4$ is $\{^-2, 2\}$.

This approach has been stressed in many modern math programs.

An older point of view is to think of x as an *unknown*. From this viewpoint $2x + 9 = 3$ is not a question but a statement about a masked number. One's task is to remove that mask—that is, to determine a standard numeral for x. One indicates completion of the task by writing the equation $x = {}^-3$. (From the first point of view this looks like answering one question with another, although admittedly the second question is much easier to answer.)

For the equation $x^2 = {}^-1$, people who think in terms of unknowns should write "No such x." A common mistake is to write "$x = \varnothing$." Not only is this mathematically incorrect, but it reflects a fundamental confusion of the two interpretations of x. For the equation $x^2 = 4$, people who think in terms of unknowns should write "$x = {}^-2$ or $x = 2$," although some write "$x = {}^-2$ and $x = 2$" or "$x = {}^-2, 2$." Again, it is incorrect to write "$x = \{^-2, 2\}$." The older "unknown" approach (and notation) usually seems more natural in cases where there is exactly one solution. In cases of no or several solutions the "blank" approach, with its set notation, is probably preferable.

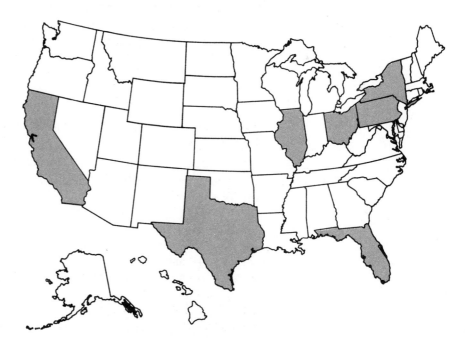

Figure 15.1 A graph of the states with population more than ten million.

How should one indicate a solution set when it has too many members to list? Let's go back and look at the open sentence

The population of _____ is more than ten million.

where the replacement set is the 50 states. To represent the solution set in a schematic way, begin with a geometric representation of the entire replacement set, such as a map of the United States, and then color in those members that are solutions (Figure 15.1). The resulting picture is called a **graph** of the (solution set of the) original open sentence, and the act of producing the picture is called *graphing*.

For a mathematical open sentence such as the inequality $x < 4$, one begins with the familiar geometric representation of the replacement set of real numbers, namely the number line, and then darkens all the solutions (Figure 15.2). The hollow circle at 4 indicates that 4 is not part of the solution set. The graph of this *strict* inequality is a half line, not a ray. By contrast, the graph of the inequality $2 \leq x$, shown in Figure 15.3, is a ray.

Figure 15.2 Graph of $x < 4$.

Figure 15.3 Graph of $2 \leq x$.

Solving Equations

Two open sentences are said to be **equivalent** if they have exactly the same solution set.

EXAMPLE 2 Are these pairs of equations equivalent?
(a) $3x - 11 = 10$ and $3x = 21$
(b) $3(x - 11) = 10$ and $3x = 21$
(c) $2(x - 5) = 18$ and $x - 5 = 9$
(d) $2(x - 5) = 18$ and $2x = 28$
(e) $x^2 = 4$ and $x = 2$
(f) $x^3 = 8$ and $\sqrt{31 - 3x} = 5$

Solution (a) Yes; both have the unique solution $x = 7$.
(b) No; the first equation has solution $x = \frac{43}{3}$; the second, $x = 7$.
(c) Yes; both have solution $x = 14$.
(d) Yes; both have solution $x = 14$.

(e) No; the first equation has solution set $\{^-2, 2\}$; the second has solution set $\{2\}$.

(f) Yes; both have the unique solution $x = 2$. ❏

There is a qualitative difference among the solutions to Example 2. In part (f), it appears to be a matter of sheer coincidence that the equations $x^3 = 8$ and $\sqrt{31 - 3x} = 5$ have the same solution. For parts (a), (c), and (d) the equivalence does not seem to depend on luck. In part (a) we can imagine adding 11 to both sides of the equation $3x - 11 = 10$ to arrive at the equation $3x = 21$. In part (c) we can think of multiplying both sides of the equation $2(x - 5) = 18$ by $\frac{1}{2}$ to arrive at the equation $x - 5 = 9$. And in part (d) perhaps we see a two-step transition:

$$2(x - 5) = 18 \quad \rightarrow \quad 2x - 10 = 18 \quad \rightarrow \quad 2x = 28$$

Apparently, then, there are certain operations one can perform on equations that will always yield equivalent equations. Such operations are called **equivalence transformations.** There are three basic types, all of which we encountered in Section 4.2 in our work with substitution.

Equivalence Transformations for Equations

1. The addition property of equality (APE): Adding the same number to both sides of an equation yields an equivalent equation.

2. The multiplication property of equality (MPE): Multiplying both sides of an equation by the same nonzero number yields an equivalent equation.

3. Simplification: Replacing either side of an equation by an equivalent expression yields an equivalent equation.

Only transformation 3 needs further explanation.

A **side** of an equation is an expression which may or may not involve a variable. For example, the sides of the equation

$$5(x + 3) = 10 - (x - 11)$$

are the variable expressions

$$5(x + 3) \quad \text{and} \quad 10 - (x - 11)$$

By the distributive property and a multiplication fact, the first expression $5(x + 3)$ is **equivalent** to the expression $5x + 15$ in the sense that, for any value of x, they represent the same number. [In function language, $5(x + 3)$ and $5x + 15$ are equal functions—they produce the same output when given the same input.] Likewise, by properties of subtraction and addition, the second expression $10 - (x - 11)$ is equivalent to the expression $21 - x$. Thus by simplification,

$$5(x + 3) = 10 - (x - 11) \quad \text{is equivalent to} \quad 5x + 15 = 21 - x$$

To complete the solution of the original equation

$$5(x + 3) = 10 - (x - 11)$$

note that the second (equivalent) equation

$$5x + 15 = 21 - x$$

is equivalent in turn to a third

$$5x + 15 + (x - 15) = 21 - x + (x - 15)$$

by the addition property of equality. But by simplification, this third equation is equivalent to a fourth,

$$6x = 6$$

Then by the multiplication property of equality, this fourth equation is equivalent to a fifth,

$$\tfrac{1}{6}(6x) = \tfrac{1}{6}(6)$$

which, finally, by simplification, is equivalent to a sixth,

$$x = 1$$

Thus by judicious choices of equivalence transformations, we have produced a chain of equivalent equations, stretching from the original complicated equation

$$5(x + 3) = 10 - (x - 11)$$

to the final trivial equation

$$x = 1$$

We conclude that the original equation (and every equation in between) has the unique solution $x = 1$.

A careful way of summarizing the solution process uses double implication arrows, as follows:

$$5(x + 3) = 10 - (x - 11)$$
$$\Longleftrightarrow \qquad 5x + 15 = 21 - x \qquad \text{simplification}$$
$$\Longleftrightarrow \quad 5x + 15 + (x - 15) = 21 - x + (x - 15) \qquad \text{addition property}$$
$$\text{of equality}$$
$$\Longleftrightarrow \qquad 6x = 6 \qquad \text{simplification}$$
$$\Longleftrightarrow \qquad \tfrac{1}{6}(6x) = \tfrac{1}{6}(6) \qquad \text{multiplication property of equality}$$
$$\Longleftrightarrow \qquad x = 1 \qquad \text{simplification}$$

People who think of x as an unknown pronounce the double arrow "if and only if"; those who think of x as a blank pronounce it "is equivalent to." In practice, many people omit the double arrows entirely and let the vertical listing of the equations imply tacitly that each is equivalent to its predecessor (and successor).

EXAMPLE 3   Solve the equation $x^2 - 3x + 6 = (x + 2)(x - 7)$.

Solution 1   Here is a solution with one reason per step.

$$x^2 - 3x + 6 = (x + 2)(x - 7)$$

$\Longleftrightarrow \quad x^2 - 3x + 6 = x^2 - 5x - 14$ \hfill simplification

$\Longleftrightarrow \quad x^2 - 3x + 6 + (-x^2 + 5x - 6)$ \hfill addition
$$= x^2 - 5x - 14 + (-x^2 + 5x - 6)$$ \hfill property
\hfill of equality

$\Longleftrightarrow \qquad\qquad 2x = -20$ \hfill simplification

$\Longleftrightarrow \qquad\quad \frac{1}{2}(2x) = \frac{1}{2}(^-20)$ \hfill multiplication
\hfill property
\hfill of equality

$\Longleftrightarrow \qquad\qquad\quad x = {}^-10$ \hfill simplification

Solution 2   In this solution the steps are more natural, but their justifications are more complicated. Double arrows are omitted this time.

$$x^2 - 3x + 6 = (x + 2)(x - 7)$$

$x^2 - 3x + 6 = x^2 - 5x - 14$	simplification
$^-3x + 6 = {}^-5x - 14$	APE (add $-x^2$ to both sides) and simplification
$2x + 6 = {}^-14$	APE (add $5x$ to both sides) and simplification
$2x = {}^-20$	APE (add $^-6$ to both sides) and simplification
$x = {}^-10$	MPE (multiply both sides by $\frac{1}{2}$) and simplification ❑

Solving Inequalities

Inequalities are just special kinds of open sentences, so the definition of equivalence given before still applies: Two inequalities are equivalent if they have the same solution set. Once again the strategy for solving an inequality is to replace it by simpler and simpler equivalent inequalities until one is reached whose solution set is obvious. The equivalence transformations (legal moves) for inequalities are just like those for equations, except for the multiplication transformation.

> ### *Equivalence Transformations for Inequalities*
>
> 1. Addition property of inequality (API): Adding the same number to both sides of an inequality yields an equivalent inequality.
> 2. Multiplication property of inequality (MPI): Multiplying both sides of an inequality by the same *positive* number yields an equivalent inequality; multiplying both sides of an inequality by the same *negative* number *and reversing the inequality sign* yields an equivalent inequality.
> 3. Simplification: Replacing either side of an inequality by an equivalent expression yields an equivalent inequality.

We first encountered transformations 1 and 2 in our work with the order relation on whole numbers (Section 4.6) and on integers (Section 6.5).

EXAMPLE 4   Solve these inequalities and graph each solution set.

(a) $2(3x - 4) < 19$ (b) $8 - (2x + 3) \leq 1$

Solution   (a) Here is a careful solution using double arrows.

$$2(3x - 4) < 19$$
$$\Longleftrightarrow \qquad 6x - 8 < 19 \qquad \text{simplification}$$
$$\Longleftrightarrow \qquad 6x < 27 \qquad \text{API and simplification}$$
$$\text{(What was added?)}$$
$$\Longleftrightarrow \qquad x < 4\tfrac{1}{2} \qquad \text{MPI and simplification}$$
$$\text{(What was multiplied?)}$$

The graph is shown in Figure 15.4.

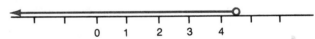

Figure 15.4

(b) In this solution we omit the double arrows.

$$8 - (2x + 3) \leq 9$$
$$5 - 2x \leq 9 \qquad \text{simplification}$$
$$^-2x \leq 4 \qquad \text{API and simplification (What was added?)}$$
$$x \geq {}^-2 \qquad \text{MPI and simplification (What was multiplied?)}$$

The graph is shown in Figure 15.5.

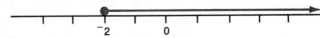

Figure 15.5   ❏

Compound Open Sentences

Technically, the inequality $x \geq {}^-2$ is a compound open sentence formed by joining the equation $x = {}^-2$ to the strict inequality $x > {}^-2$ with the logical connective *or:*

$$x \geq {}^-2 \quad \Longleftrightarrow \quad x = {}^-2 \text{ or } x > {}^-2$$

To graph this compound open sentence, we graph the two simple open sentences first, as in Figure 15.6. Then we form the *union* (Figure 15.7). (Remember how the union operation was defined in terms of the word *or*.)

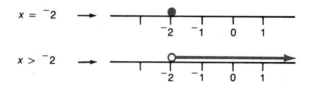

Figure 15.6

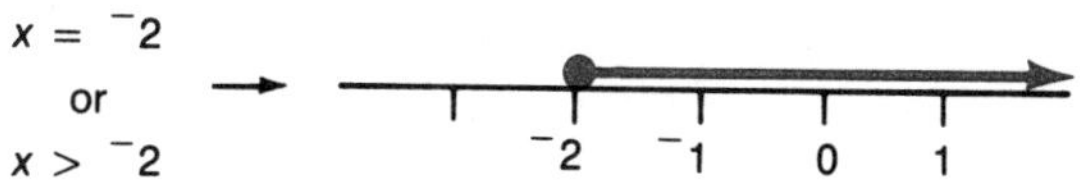

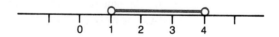

Figure 15.7

When the logical connective is *and*, the set operation is *intersection*. For example, the graph of $1 < x$ and $x < 4$ is the intersection of the right-directed half line from 1 with the left-directed half line from 4 (Figure 15.8). Frequently, this compound inequality is written in the form $1 < x < 4$.

Figure 15.8

EXAMPLE 5   Graph each compound open sentence.
(a) $x < 0$ or $x > 2$
(b) $x > 0$ or $x < 2$
(c) $x < 0$ or $x < 2$
(d) $x = 0$ or $x > 2$
(e) $x > 0$ and $x < 2$
(f) $x > 0$ and $x > 2$
(g) $x < 0$ and $x > 2$
(h) $0 < x < 2$

Solution   (a)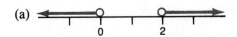

0   2

(b) The graph is the entire number line.

(c)

0   2

(d)

0   2

(e)

0   2

(f)

0   2

(g) The graph is the empty set.
(h) Same as (e).   ❏

Absolute Value

The usual definition of **absolute value** involves two cases:

$$|x| = \begin{cases} x, & \text{if } x \geq 0 \\ {}^{-}x, & \text{if } x < 0 \end{cases}$$

A convenient equivalent algebraic definition is that $|x|$ is the larger of x and ${}^{-}x$. For example:

$$|3| = \text{the larger of 3 and } {}^{-}3 = 3$$
$$|{}^{-}2| = \text{the larger of } {}^{-}2 \text{ and } {}^{-}({}^{-}2) = 2$$
$$|0| = \text{the larger of 0 and } {}^{-}0 = 0$$

Geometrically, $|x|$ is the distance between x and 0 on the number line. See Figure 15.9.

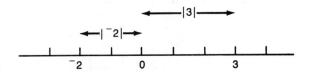

Figure 15.9

More generally:

> If a and b are any two points on the number line, then $|a - b|$ represents the **distance** between them.

The reason is simple: distance between two points is preserved if both are translated the same amount in the same direction. Thus

$$\text{Distance between } a \text{ and } b = \text{distance between } a - b \text{ and } b - b$$
$$= \text{distance between } a - b \text{ and } 0$$
$$= |a - b|$$

One consequence of this property is the following:

> The **midpoint** of the segment with endpoints at a and b is $(a + b)/2$.

That is, to find the midpoint of a segment on the number line, simply average its endpoints. Here is a proof:

$$\text{Distance between } a \text{ and } \frac{a + b}{2} = \left| a - \frac{a + b}{2} \right| = \left| \frac{a - b}{2} \right|$$

$$\text{Distance between } b \text{ and } \frac{a + b}{2} = \left| b - \frac{a + b}{2} \right| = \left| \frac{b - a}{2} \right|$$

But

$$\left| \frac{a - b}{2} \right| = \left| \frac{b - a}{2} \right| \qquad \text{(Why?)}$$

Thus $(a + b)/2$ is equidistant from a and b.

EXAMPLE 6 (a) Find the midpoint of the segment with endpoints $^-11$ and 8.
(b) One endpoint of a segment is at $^-3.21$. The midpoint is at 2.76. Where is the other endpoint?

Solution (a) Midpoint is at $(^-11 + 8)/2 = {}^-3/2 = {}^-1.5$.
(b) Let x be the coordinate of the other endpoint. Then

$$\frac{x + {}^-3.21}{2} = 2.76$$

$$\Longleftrightarrow \qquad x - 3.21 = 5.52$$

$$\Longleftrightarrow \qquad x = 8.73 \qquad \qquad \square$$

A dual algebraic-geometric understanding of absolute value often gives one a choice of methods for solving open sentences involving absolute value.

EXAMPLE 7   Solve and graph the inequality $|x - 3| < 5$.

Geometric Solution

$$|x - 3| < 5$$

⟺   distance between x and 3 is less than 5

⟺ $x > {}^-2$ and $x < 8$ (look at the number line)

⟺ ${}^-2 < x < 8$

The graph is shown in Figure 15.10.

Figure 15.10

Algebraic Solution

$$|x - 3| < 5$$

⟺   the larger of $x - 3$ and $-(x - 3)$ is less than 5

⟺ $x - 3 < 5$ *and* $-(x - 3) < 5$

⟺ $x < 8$ *and* $x > {}^-2$

⟺ ${}^-2 < x < 8$

Do you understand why the connective *and*, rather than *or*, was used?   ❏

EXAMPLE 8   Solve and graph the inequality $|x + 2| > 3$.

Geometric Solution

$$|x + 2| > 3$$

⟺ $|x - ({}^-2)| > 3$

⟺   distance between x and ${}^-2$ is greater than 3

⟺ $x < {}^-5$ or $x > 1$ (look at the number line)

The graph is shown in Figure 15.11.

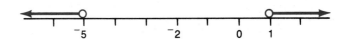

Figure 15.11

Algebraic Solution

$$|x + 2| > 3$$

⟺   the larger of $x + 2$ and $-(x + 2)$ is greater than 3

⟺ $x + 2 > 3$ *or* $-(x + 2) > 3$

⟺ $x > 1$ or $x < {}^-5$

Do you understand why the connective *or*, rather than *and*, was used?   ❏

Caution: A common notational error is to try to abbreviate the solution $x > 1$ or $x < {}^-5$ as $1 < x < {}^-5$. This notation is, of course, incorrect since $1 < x < {}^-5$ would mean that $1 < x$ *and* (simultaneously) $x < {}^-5$.

EXERCISE SET 15.1

For Exercises 1–10, classify each as a statement, an open sentence, or neither.

1. C. F. Gauss was born in 1777.
2. What a year that was!
3. $9 - 2^2$
4. $2x^2 = 50$
5. $180 = 2^2 \cdot 3^2 \cdot 5$
6. $87\frac{1}{2}\% = \frac{5}{6}$
7. $2x < x$
8. $|2x - 5|$
9. $3(x - 4) = 3x - 12$
10. $x^2 < 0$
11. Which of the open sentences in Exercises 1–10 are inequalities?
12. Which of the open sentences in Exercises 1–10 are equations?

The replacement set for the next two open sentences is the set of the 50 states of the United States. For each open sentence, (a) list the solution set in braces, and (b) graph it on the map in Figure 15.1.

13. _____ touches Lake Michigan.
14. _____ has a direction (compass point) as part of its name.

Describe a plausible replacement set for each open sentence in Exercises 15–18; then list a few solutions.

15. x is a prime number.
16. x is divisible by both $^-3$ and 4.
17. _____ has perimeter 12.
18. _____ is equilateral.

19. List the solution set of the open sentence "_____ has a common boundary with Mexico," when the replacement set is the following.
    (a) The 50 states of the United States
    (b) The nations of the world
20. List the solution set of the open sentence $x^2 = 9$, when the replacement set is the following.
    (a) The whole numbers W
    (b) The integers I
    (c) The real numbers R

In Exercises 21–22 a replacement set and an open sentence are given. Draw a loop around each solution set.

21.

'cello	clarinet
piccolo	oboe
piano	violin

_____ is a stringed instrument.

22.

baseball		chess
golf	hockey	tennis
	horseshoes	

_____ is played with a ball.

23. Use this replacement set.

sea turtle	shark	dolphin
robin	shrimp	whale	cow

(a) Loop in red the truth set of "_____ is a mammal."
(b) Loop in black the truth set of "_____ lives in the sea."

(c) The *intersection* of the two truth sets you looped is the truth set of what open sentence?

(d) The *union* of the two truth sets you looped is the truth set of what open sentence?

(e) The *complement* of the truth set you looped in red is the truth set of what open sentence?

(f) The complement of the truth set you looped in black is the truth set of what open sentence?

24. Fill in the blanks.

(a) When two open sentences are joined by the word *and*, the set operation _____ is applied to their truth sets.

(b) When two open sentences are joined by the word *or*, the set operation _____ is applied to their truth sets.

(c) When an open sentence is denied by means of the word *not*, the set operation _____ is applied to its truth set.

Graph the solution set of each inequality, and name the figure.

25. $x > {}^-1$

26. $x \leq 4$

27. ${}^-1 \leq x \leq 3$

28. $2 < x \leq 5$

29. $0 < x \leq 1$

30. ${}^-3 < x < 0$

31. $x < 1$ or $x > 3$

32. $x \leq 0$ or $4 < x$

33. $x \not< 3$

34. $x \neq 2$

Write an inequality whose solution set is given by each graph.

35.

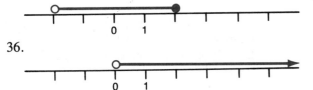

36.

37.

38.

39.

40.

Solve each equation. Identify the equivalence transformations that you use.

41. $\frac{2}{3}x - 5 = 7$

42. $\frac{1}{4}x + 9 = 3$

43. $3(5 + 2x) = x + 5$

44. $3(6 - x) = 2^4$

45. $x(x + 5) = 5(x + 5)$

46. $x(3x - 6) = {}^-2(3x - 6)$

Solve each inequality, and graph the solution set on the number line. Identify the equivalence transformations that you use.

47. $5x + 7 \leq {}^-8$

48. $3x - 1.6 \geq 8$

49. $6 - (x + 2) < 1$

50. $5(6x + 3) \leq 3$

51. $x(3 + x) > x^2 + 5x - 12$

52. $(x + 2)^2 < x^2 + 2^2$

Solve and graph each compound inequality on the number line.

53. ${}^-1 \leq 3x - 7 \leq 5$

54. $0 \leq \dfrac{5 + 2x}{3} < 1$

55. $1 < \dfrac{4 - 5x}{3} < 2$

56. $^{-}2 \le \dfrac{2 - 3x}{5} < 0$

Translate into a (symbolic) open sentence involving absolute value.

57. The distance from x to 4 is less than 5.

58. The distance from x to 2 exceeds 4.

59. The distance from 1 to x is at least 3.

60. The distance from $^{-}2$ to x is at most 3.

61. x is nearer to 1 than to 5.

62. x is half as far from 4 as from 0.

Solve and graph on the number line. Think geometrically.

63. $|x - 3| = 4$

64. $|x + 4| = 3$

65. $|x + 1| < 3$

66. $|x - 3| \le 3$

67. $|x - 2| > 5$

68. $|x + 5| > 2$

69. $|3 - x| \le 1$

70. $|1 - x| \ge 3$

71. $|x - 2| = |x - 5|$

72. $|x - 3| = 2|x - 6|$

73. $|x + 1| < |x - 3|$

74. $|x - 1| > 2|x - 4|$

Write an absolute value inequality whose graph is shown.

75.

$^{-}2$ ⟷ 6

76.

$^{-}7$ ⟷ $^{-}1$

77.

0   10

78.

1   5

Solve algebraically, and graph on the number line.

79. $|x - 2| > 4$

80. $|x + 5| < 3$

81. $|2x - 5| < 1$

82. $|1 + 2x| > 5$

83. $|x - 2| < 2x + 5$

★ 84. $|x + 5| > 3x - 4$

In Exercises 85–88, find the midpoint of the segment with the given endpoints.

85. Endpoints 7 and 13

86. Endpoints $^{-}5$ and 6

87. Endpoints 1 and $5\frac{1}{2}$

88. Endpoints $^{-}2.3$ and 4.7

89. In this exercise $a = 10$ and $b = 22$.
    (a) Plot the three points a, $\frac{1}{2}a + \frac{1}{2}b$, and b on a number line.
    (b) On another number line, plot the four points a, $\frac{2}{3}a + \frac{1}{3}b$, $\frac{1}{3}a + \frac{2}{3}b$, and b.
    (c) On another number line, plot the five points a, $\frac{3}{4}a + \frac{1}{4}b$, $\frac{2}{4}a + \frac{2}{4}b$, $\frac{1}{4}a + \frac{3}{4}b$, and b.
    (d) Generalize the pattern in parts (a)–(c).

★ 90. Given two points a and b on the number line, describe, in geometric terms, each of the following sets of points:
    (a) $\{ta + (1 - t)b \mid 0 \le t \le 1\}$
    (b) $\{ta + (1 - t)b \mid 0 \le t\}$
    (c) $\{ta + (1 - t)b \mid t \le 1\}$
    (d) $\{ta + (1 - t)b\}$ (t an arbitrary real number)

15.2 *Solving Word Problems Using One Variable*

"Write an open sentence" is one of the most powerful and widely applicable problem-solving strategies in all of mathematics, and it is also one of the most difficult to master. Weeks and weeks of junior high and high school algebra and precalculus courses are devoted to elaborating, inculcating, and exercising the open-sentence strategy; and the project continues in college calculus and beyond. Polya stated his opinion in his 1962 book *Mathematical Discovery:* ". . . the most important single task of mathematical instruction in the secondary schools is to teach the setting up of equations to solve word problems."

In your algebra courses you were undoubtedly presented with a loose algorithm, along the lines of the one that follows, that breaks the open-sentence process into smaller, more manageable steps. Such algorithms can be useful for organizing one's thinking, but they should not be followed slavishly. No one has yet invented a machine for the automatic solution of word problems.

Possible Steps in the Algebraic Solution of a Word Problem

1. Determine what it is you are asked to find, and introduce a variable to represent that unknown quantity. Certain key words like *what, how many,* and *find* often point to the unknown. Identify the variable carefully. For example, write a precise definition, "Let J = Jack's height in centimeters," not a careless abbreviation, "Let J = Jack."

2. Look for mathematical connections between known and unknown quantities. Do the units in the problem suggest operations? For example, multiplying hr by mi/hr yields mi. Are there linguistic clues? The word *of* often can be translated as "times"; words like *is* and *was* can sometimes be translated as "equals." Write algebraic expressions that show the connections.

3. Try to describe some quantity in two different ways. If you can say, "On the one hand, it is . . . , but on the other, it is . . . ," then you have an equation within your grasp.

4. Solve the equation or inequality by using formal techniques of the kind reviewed in the previous section.

5. Translate your mathematical solution back into the original language of the problem. Did you find what was asked for? Does your answer make sense? For example, if the problem was to find the length of a rectangle, an answer of ⁻4 would be absurd. Estimation rather than exact calculation is often appropriate at this checking step.

EXAMPLE 1   Ann is half as old as Bob. In 5 more years she will be $\frac{2}{3}$ as old as Bob. How old is Ann now?

Solution   1. Let a = Ann's present age (in years).

2. Then Bob's present age is $2a$, and so in 5 years Bob's age will be $2a + 5$.

3. On the one hand, in 5 years Ann's age will be $a + 5$; but on the other, it will be $\frac{2}{3}(2a + 5)$.

4. $a + 5 = \frac{2}{3}(2a + 5)$
$3a + 15 = 4a + 10$
$5 = a$

5. Ann is presently 5 years old. *Check:* That means Bob is now 10. In 5 years Ann and Bob will be 10 and 15, respectively, and 10 is $\frac{2}{3}$ of 15.   ❏

The previous example is a typical artificial "textbook" problem, exactly like the ones your great-grandparents solved in their beginning algebra courses. (And the problem-solving procedure we are reviewing here is precisely the one they followed!) The next example is somewhat more practical.

EXAMPLE 2   Jane's home is 180 mi from her college. She plans to set out from home at 9:00 A.M. and drive at a speed of 50 mph. When can she expect to arrive at school?

Solution   1. Let t = driving time (in hours).

2. Distance (mi) = rate (mi/hr) × time (hr).

3. On the one hand, distance = $50 \cdot t$; on the other, it is 180.

4. $50t = 180$
$t = \frac{180}{50} = 3.6$ (hr)

5. It takes her 3.6 hr to drive. But that is not what was asked for. If she sets out at 9:00 A.M. and drives for 3.6 hr, that is, for 3 hr 36 min, then she should arrive around 12:36 P.M.   ❏

Certain aspects of the preceding solution are worth emphasizing. First, note that we did not simplistically let x = time of arrival. That would have complicated the remaining steps considerably. A little extra thought at step 1 paid dividends later. Second, notice that at step 2 we expressed one quantity, distance, as a *function* of another, time. Third, but most importantly, observe how we used a "mathematical model" of the real situation.

In building our mathematical model, we simplified and idealized the problem. We ignored questions of how long it takes Jane to get from her home to the highway, whether traffic and road conditions will permit a speed of 50 mph, and how long it might take her to find a parking place once she arrives. The model we had in mind was that of a particle springing into motion at 50 mph, maintaining that constant speed for exactly 180 mi, and then stopping abruptly. For such an ideal situation distance, rate, and time are related by the simple formula $d = r \cdot t$, on which our solution was based.

EXAMPLE 3   A few feet below its surface the temperature of the earth remains at about 20°C winter and summer. As one goes deeper, the temperature rises steadily, about 10°C for each kilometer. How deep a shaft would a geothermal energy company have to sink in order to reach a point at which the temperature is 55°C?

Solution   1. Let x be the depth of the shaft (in kilometers).

2. The temperature *rise* from the top to the bottom of the shaft is a function of depth:

$$10 \ (°C)/km \cdot x \ (km) = 10x \ (°C)$$

Thus the *temperature* (in °C) at the bottom of the shaft is also a function of depth:

$$20 + 10x$$

3. We want to choose x so that this temperature is 55.

4. $20 + 10x = 55$
   $10x = 35$
   $x = 3.5$

5. The shaft must be about 3.5 km deep. *Check:* At 3.5 km the temperature will be about $20 + 10 \times 3.5 = 55$.   ❏

The next example is chosen from a large class of problems known as mixture problems. Mixture problems have been standard fare in algebra texts for a long, long time. Example 4 was taken verbatim from an 1881 text.

EXAMPLE 4   A wine merchant has two kinds of wine which cost 72 cents and 40 cents a quart respectively. How much of each must he take to make a mixture of 50 quarts worth 60 cents a quart?

Solution 1   1. Let x = the number of quarts of 72-cent wine in the mixture.

2. Then $50 - x$ is the number of quarts of 40-cent wine in the mixture. The value of the expensive wine in the mixture is

$$x \, (\text{qt}) \cdot 72 \left(\frac{\text{cents}}{\text{qt}} \right)$$

and the value of the cheap wine in the mixture is

$$(50 - x)(\text{qt}) \cdot 40 \left(\frac{\text{cents}}{\text{qt}} \right)$$

3. On the one hand, the value of the mixture is

$$\left[x \, (\text{qt}) \cdot 72 \left(\frac{\text{cents}}{\text{qt}} \right) \right] + \left[(50 - x)(\text{qt}) \cdot 40 \left(\frac{\text{cents}}{\text{qt}} \right) \right]$$

On the other hand, it is to be

$$50 (\text{qt}) \cdot 60 \left(\frac{\text{cents}}{\text{qt}} \right)$$

4. $72x + 40(50 - x) = 50 \cdot 60$
$72x + 2000 - 40x = 3000$
$32x = 1000$
$x = \frac{1000}{32} = 31\frac{1}{4}$ qt

5. He should mix $31\frac{1}{4}$ qt of 72-cent wine with $18\frac{3}{4}$ qt of 40-cent wine. This answer is plausible because an even mix of 25 qt of each wine would be worth the average of 72 and 40, namely, 56 cents per quart. To push its value up to 60 cents per quart, the merchant must use more of the 72-cent wine.

Solution 2   Mixture problems can often be solved by filling in a chart. (Recall that we used a similar technique in Section 3.3) In Table 15.1 black print indicates given information, red print indicates inferred information, the red line signifies multiplication, and the double lines signify addition. Notice how two different routes to the lower right-hand corner lead to the desired equation.

Table 15.1

	# Units	Unit Cost	Total Cost
Expensive Wine	x	72	$72x$
Cheap Wine	$50 - x$	40	$40(50 - x)$
Mixture	50	60	

$72x + 40(50 - x)$ on the one hand; $60 \cdot 50$ on the other

Equation: $72x + 40(50 - x) = 60 \cdot 50$ ❑

The most difficult spot in the five-step process, as you have probably decided, is at step 2 where one has to express, mathematically, connections between quantities that may be given verbally. In beginning algebra courses a good deal of time is spent on developing this skill with examples of the following sort.

EXAMPLE 5   Write an algebraic expression for the following.
(a) Lisa's age, if Megan is m years old and Lisa is 3 years older than Megan
(b) Jenny's savings, if Jenny is $3 short of having twice as much as the k dollars Kelly has saved
(c) The amount of alcohol in x liters of a solution that is 40% alcohol
(d) The interest in one year on an investment of x dollars in bonds that yield 8% annually
(e) The average speed of a car, in miles per hour, during an x-hour trip covering 212 mi

Solution   (a) $m + 3$
(b) $2k - 3$
(c) 40% *of* the solution *is* alcohol $\rightarrow$ $.4x$
(d) Interest = rate · principal $\rightarrow$ $.08x$
(e) Here is a case where keeping an eye on the units is helpful. The average speed will be expressed in mi/hr. Thus the expression is

$$\frac{212 \text{ (mi)}}{x \text{ (hr)}} = \frac{212}{x}\left(\frac{\text{mi}}{\text{hr}}\right)$$ ❏

Note that every one of these solutions can be viewed as the expression of one variable as a function of another: Lisa's age as a function of Megan's, Jenny's savings as a function of Kelly's, alcohol content as a function of total volume, interest as a function of principal, speed as a function of time.

EXERCISE SET 15.2

Each phrase suggests two quantities and a connection between them. You are to do two things: (a) define (carefully) a variable representing one of the quantities, and (b) write an algebraic expression involving that variable for the other.

1. Dean's weight, if Dean weighs 5 kg less than Jerry

2. Bob's IQ, if the combined IQ of Bob and Ray is 250

3. Lou's age, if in 5 months he will be $\frac{3}{4}$ as old as Bud

4. Wally's age, if 3 years ago he was twice as old as Beaver

5. The annual interest earned by a deposit in an account that pays interest at an annual rate of 7%

6. The amount of alcohol in a tank of solution that is 15% alcohol by volume

Write an algebraic expression involving x that represents each of the following. Note that you are actually being asked to describe a function by means of a formula.

7. The sum of the four consecutive integers beginning with x

8. The average (mean) of 7, 12, 20, and x

9. The value in cents of x nickels

10. The value in dollars of 20 coins, if x are nickels and the rest are dimes

11. Mario's average speed, if it takes him x hours to drive 500 mi

12. Pancho's average speed, if it takes him x hr and 20 min to drive 500 mi

13. The revenue generated by selling 200 widgets at x dollars apiece

14. The revenue generated by selling 150 pencils at x for a dollar

15. The cost of producing x widgets, if fixed costs are $125 and unit cost is $1.50

16. The cost of producing 100 pencils, if fixed costs are $125 and unit cost is x cents

17. The amount of water in a dish x hours after 100 grams (g) were poured in, if evaporation takes place at the steady rate of 8 g/hr

18. The amount of farmland in the United States in the year x ($x > 1980$), if there were 400 million acres in 1980 and urbanization gobbles up 3 million acres per year (Sadly, these data are essentially correct.)

19. The gross weight of a truck carrying x castings, each weighing 60 lb, if the truck weighs 2500 lb empty

20. The cost of having a repairman spend x hours working on the stove in your home, if the basic charge for a house call is $25 and the labor charge is $20 per hour

Solve the following word problems algebraically; that is, begin by introducing a variable.

21. If 65% of the population of a certain town is eligible to vote and 2800 people in the town are ineligible, what is the population of the town?

22. How much money would you need to put in bonds that yield 8% annually in order to earn $364 per year?

23. In a state with a 4% sales tax a pair of shoes costs $25.48. How much would it cost without the tax?

24. A worker earns $6.40 per hour for the first 40 hours per week and time and a half for overtime. How many hours of overtime must she work to earn $352 in one week?

25. The ratio of women to men at a certain college is 6 to 5. If there are 6600 men, how many students are there in all?

26. Out of every 20 students 3 are on the dean's list. If 120 are on the dean's list, how many are not?

27. In a family of 4 the older child weighs 20 lb more than the younger, the mother weighs 40 lb more than the older child, and the father weighs 3 times as much as the younger child. The average (mean) weight in the family is 102.5 lb. How much does each member weigh?

28. First estimate, then find four consecutive integers whose sum is 322.

29. Find two consecutive integers whose squares differ by 101.

30. Find two consecutive even integers whose squares differ by 100.

31. Every day Tracy swims the same number of lengths of the pool. As she touches an end of the pool she thinks to herself: "I am three-quarters finished. Only six more lengths and I will be five-sixths finished." How many lengths does she still have to swim?

★ 32. Last year 35% of Kim's gross pay was deducted for taxes, insurance, etc. This year she received a 6% raise in gross pay, but her deductions rose to 37%. By what percent did her take-home pay rise?

Solve the following mixture problems by filling in each chart and extracting an equation from the lower right-hand box.

33. Solution A is 20% alcohol, and solution B is 60% alcohol. How much of each solution should be mixed to make 10 L of solution that is 50% alcohol? Use Table 15.2.

34. An investor with $10,000 wants to put some of it in risky bonds that yield 18% annual interest and the rest into safe ones that yield 8%. She wants to earn a 10% return on her investments. How much should she put in each kind of bond? Use Table 15.3.

Table 15.2

	Volume of Solution	Concentration of Alcohol	Volume of Alcohol
Solution A			
Solution B			
Mixture			

Table 15.3

	Principal	Rate	Interest
Risky			
Safe			
Mixture			

Solve the next four mixture problems by any method you choose.

35. How much 30% alcohol solution and how much 70% alcohol solution should be mixed to produce 12 L of 40% alcohol solution?

36. Mr. Dodge has $6000 in bonds that yield 7%. How much additional money should he invest in bonds that yield 12% in order to bring the return on his total investment up to 10%?

37. How much maple syrup at $4.00 per pint should be mixed with corn syrup at $.30 per pint to make a pancake syrup to sell for $1.04 per pint?

38. A total of 38 dimes and quarters has a value of $5.45. How many quarters are there?

Try your hand at these four exercises taken verbatim from an 1865 algebra book.

39. An estate of $7500 is to be divided among a widow, two sons, and three daughters, so that each son shall receive twice as much as each daughter, and the widow herself $500 more than all the children: what was her share and what was the share of each child?

40. A person was desirous of giving 3 pence apiece to some beggars, but found he had not money enough in his pocket by 8 pence; he therefore gave them each 2 pence and had 3 pence remaining: required, the number of beggars.

41. Three regiments are to furnish 594 men, and each to furnish in proportion to its strength. Now, the strength of the first is to the second as 3 to 5; and that of the second to the third as 8 to 7. How many must each furnish?

42. A man and his wife usually drank out a cask of beer in 12 days; but when the man was from home, it lasted the woman 30 days: how many days would the man alone be in drinking it?

The last four exercises give some practice in the application of inequalities.

43. The interval of permissible speeds on a certain highway is described by the inequality $40 \leq x \leq 55$, where x represents speed in miles per hour. Your imported sports car has a speedometer that gives speed in kilometers per hour. Describe your legal interval by an inequality using a variable that represents speed in kilometers per hour. Recall that 1 mi $\doteq$ 1.6 km.

44. The inequality $32 \leq F \leq 212$ describes the interval of Fahrenheit temperatures at which water remains in a liquid state (under standard pressure). Kelvin temperature K is related to Fahrenheit temperature F by the equation
$F = \frac{9}{5}(K - 273) + 32$
Give the interval of Kelvin temperatures at which water remains in a liquid state.

45. The cost of producing and selling x widgets is $85 + 1.5x$ (dollars). The revenue from the sale of x widgets is $2.95x$ (dollars). Describe, by an

inequality, the levels of production (and sales) that yield a profit.

 46. Using the cost and revenue functions from Exercise 45, describe, by an inequality, the levels of production (and sales) that yield profits of between 10% and 20% of cost.

15.3 *Equations and Inequalities in Two Variables; The Cartesian Coordinate Plane*

In this section we return to the discussion of algebra, logic, and geometry that was begun in Section 15.1.

Open Sentences in Two Variables

In the period 1953–1973 the United States had four presidents: Eisenhower, Kennedy, Johnson, and Nixon. Using this set P as replacement set, we can list the solution sets for various open sentences:

_____ was a Democrat $\rightarrow$ {Kennedy, Johnson}
_____ was a vice president $\rightarrow$ {Johnson, Nixon}

And we can graph these solution sets with Venn diagrams, as in Figure 15.12.

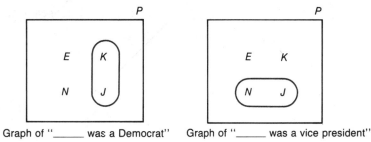

Graph of "_____ was a Democrat"   Graph of "_____ was a vice president"

Figure 15.12

Consider next the open sentence

_____ served as vice president under _____

Now two blanks need to be filled before this sentence becomes a statement; an *ordered pair* of presidents must be inserted in the ordered pair of blanks. For example, the ordered pair (Johnson, Kennedy) yields a true statement,

Johnson served as vice president under Kennedy   (true)

while the ordered pair (Kennedy, Johnson) yields a false statement,

Kennedy served as vice president under Johnson   (false)

The new replacement set consists of the 16 ordered pairs of U.S. presidents, 1953–1973. In the standard terminology and notation developed in Chapter 2, if

$$P = \{\text{Eisenhower, Kennedy, Johnson, Nixon}\}$$

then the new replacement set is the Cartesian product of P with itself, written $P \times P$.

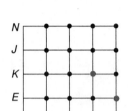

Figure 15.13 Graph of "_____ served as vice president under _____."

Two geometric representations of Cartesian products, trees and rectangular arrays of dots, were introduced in Chapter 2. In this chapter rectangular arrays will be used exclusively. The sixteen dots in Figure 15.13 make up the rectangular array for $P \times P$. The two red dots constitute the graph of the solution set

$$\{(\text{Johnson, Kennedy}), (\text{Nixon, Eisenhower})\}$$

of the open sentence "_____ served as vice president under _____" in the replacement set $P \times P$. Recall the "right-up" convention used in representing ordered pairs by dots in a rectangular array: To locate (Johnson, Kennedy) in the array, *first* go *right* to Johnson, *then up* to Kennedy.

EXAMPLE 1   Graph these open sentences in $P \times P$.
(a) _____ immediately preceded _____ in office.
(b) _____ preceded _____ in office.
(c) _____ lost to _____ in a presidential election.
(d) _____ and _____ belonged to the same political party.

Solution   See Figure 15.14.

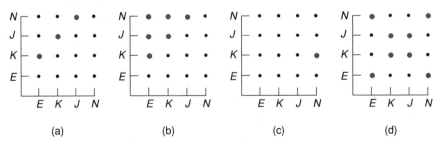

(a)   (b)   (c)   (d)

Figure 15.14   ❏

Open sentences involving two blanks are very important in mathematics; the rest of this chapter will give you some idea of just how important. Let us

begin with a simple example,

$$\underline{} \cdot \underline{\underline{}} = 6$$

where the replacement set is all ordered pairs that can be formed from numbers in the set $S = \{1, 2, 3, 4, 5, 6\}$; that is, the replacement set is $S \times S$. Figure 15.15 shows the four ordered pairs out of thirty-six—(1, 6), (2, 3), (3, 2), (6, 1)—that yield true statements.

Before looking at any further examples, we need to standardize notation. As we noted in Section 15.1, blanks are rarely used in mathematical open sentences; variables are used instead. When two variables are needed, as in our example, x is generally used for the first and y for the second. Thus the open sentence

$$\underline{} \cdot \underline{\underline{}} = 6$$

is written

$$x \cdot y = 6$$

and the solution set in $S \times S$ consists of those ordered pairs (x, y) for which $x \cdot y = 6$.

Figure 15.15 Graph of "$\underline{} \cdot \underline{\underline{}} = 6$."

EXAMPLE 2   Graph these open sentences in $S \times S$, where $S = \{1, 2, 3, 4, 5, 6\}$.
(a) $x + y = 8$
(b) $x = 2y$
(c) $x + y \leq 4$
(d) $x^y < 9$

Solution   In each case one can resort to testing all 36 ordered pairs to see which ones work. The graphs are shown in Figure 15.16. ❏

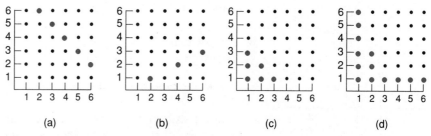

Figure 15.16

Open sentences (a) and (b) in Example 2 are called equations in two variables; (c) and (d) are called inequalities in two variables.

For most purposes the replacement set for a mathematical open sentence in two variables is the set $R \times R$ of all ordered pairs of real numbers. The fact

Table 15.4

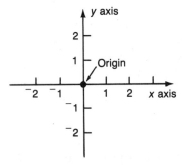

x	$\dfrac{6}{x} = y$
1	$\dfrac{6}{1} = 6$
2	$\dfrac{6}{2} = 3$
3	$\dfrac{6}{3} = 2$
4	$\dfrac{6}{4} = 1.5$
$^-1$	$\dfrac{6}{^-1} = {}^-6$
$\frac{2}{3}$	$\dfrac{6}{\frac{2}{3}} = 9$
$\vdots$	$\vdots$

that this replacement set is infinite presents some new problems. For one thing it is no longer possible to try out, one at a time, every ordered pair from the replacement set to see which ones yield true statements. For another, open sentences will ordinarily have infinite solution sets.

Consider again the open sentence $x \cdot y = 6$. We can generate as many solution pairs as we please by simply choosing any (nonzero) value for x and then determining what the corresponding value for y must be. For example, choose $x = 5$. Then to make $x \cdot y = 6$, we need to choose y so that $5y = 6$; that is, $y = \frac{6}{5}$. Or choose $x = 13$. Then to make $xy = 6$, we need to find y so that $13y = 6$; that is, $y = \frac{6}{13}$. Proceeding in this way, we can produce as many solution pairs as we please. A shortcut is to solve the original equation for y in terms of x. That is, isolate y on one side of the equation and get everything else not involving y on the other side:

$$xy = 6 \iff y = \frac{6}{x}$$

Now solution pairs (x, y) can be listed almost as fast as one can write. In Table 15.4 we use the traditional columnar form. In ordered-pair notation the solutions listed are $(1, 6)$, $(2, 3)$, $(3, 2)$, $(4, 1.5)$, $(^-1, {}^-6)$, $(\frac{2}{3}, 9)$.

Listing six solution pairs is still a long way, though, from describing the entire infinite solution set. To do that, we will need to return to the idea of graphing and to a geometric representation of the replacement set $R \times R$.

The Cartesian Coordinate Plane

The Cartesian coordinate plane is the two-dimensional analog of the number line. The number line consists of a set of algebraic objects (the real numbers), a set of geometric objects (the points of a line), and a reasonably transparent convention for matching up the two sets. Here is a precise description of the convention.

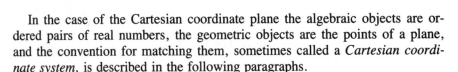

The matching of numbers with points on the number line is a one-to-one correspondence f from R to the line such that the distance from $f(a)$ to $f(b) = |a - b|$.

In the case of the Cartesian coordinate plane the algebraic objects are ordered pairs of real numbers, the geometric objects are the points of a plane, and the convention for matching them, sometimes called a *Cartesian coordinate system*, is described in the following paragraphs.

Begin with a number line in the usual horizontal position. Now, impose a second number line vertically so that (1) its numbers increase from the bottom up and (2) the two number lines cross at their respective origins. See Figure

Figure 15.17 Cartesian coordinate plane.

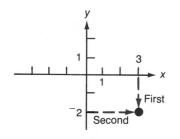

Figure 15.18 The point corresponding to (3, ⁻2).

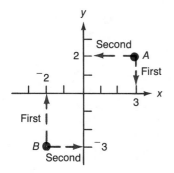

Figure 15.19 Coordinates corresponding to points.

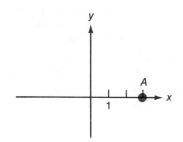

Figure 15.20

15.17. The horizontal number line is called the first axis, or **x axis,** the vertical one is called the second axis, or **y axis,** and their crossing point is called the **origin.** Ordinarily, the same unit of distance is used on both number lines, although sometimes they differ.

Given an ordered pair of numbers, say (a, b), the corresponding point is located as follows. Locate the point a on the x axis, and draw a vertical line through it. Locate the point b on the y axis, and draw a horizontal line through it. The point where those lines cross corresponds to the ordered pair (a, b). Figure 15.18 shows how the point corresponding to (3, ⁻2) is found.

Conversely, given a point, one determines the corresponding ordered pair as follows. Look straight down (or up) at the x axis, and read the number you see. That will be the first coordinate (or component) of the ordered pair. Now look straight across at the y axis, and read the number you see. That will be the second coordinate of the ordered pair. Figure 15.19 shows how the ordered pairs (3, 2) and (⁻2, ⁻3) are assigned to the points A and B, respectively.

Much of the terminology associated with the coordinate plane closely parallels that for the number line. The point matched with an ordered pair is called the graph of the ordered pair. For example, in Figure 15.19, A is the graph of (3, 2). The coordinates of the ordered pair matched with a point are also called the coordinates of the point. For example, in Figure 15.19 the first coordinate (or x coordinate, or *abscissa*) of B is ⁻2, and the second coordinate (or y coordinate, or *ordinate*) of B is ⁻3. To keep the language simple, we shall identify algebraic objects (ordered pairs of real numbers) with geometric objects (points). That is, we shall treat them as synonymous. Thus we shall not hesitate to refer to "the point (2, 3)" rather than to "the point corresponding to (2, 3)," or to "the distance from (2, 3) to (5, ⁻1)" instead of to "the distance from the graph of (2, 3) to the graph (5, ⁻1)."

Points that lie on the coordinate axes raise an interesting question. As a point of the horizontal number line, the point A in Figure 15.20 has a real number coordinate, namely 3. As a point of the coordinate plane, A has an ordered pair of coordinates (3, 0). Which address should we use for A? Usually, we will use the second, but sometimes we will use the first. This ambiguity is common and should not disturb you. For instance, to her fellow residents of Lincoln Dormitory, Jane's address is room number 203. To students in the larger college community, her address is the ordered pair (203, Lincoln). Jane uses whichever address is appropriate for the occasion.

EXAMPLE 3 Plot the following points in a coordinate plane:

$$A = (3, 5) \qquad B = (^-2, 4) \qquad C = (0, 3)$$
$$D = (^-2, ^-3) \qquad E = (1, ^-4) \qquad F = (4, 0)$$

Solution The points are plotted in Figure 15.21. ❏

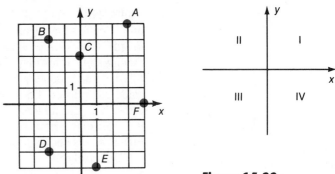

Figure 15.21   **Figure 15.22**

The axes partition the coordinate plane into four regions called the first through the fourth **quadrants.** These quadrants are located as shown in Figure 15.22, and they are generally designated by Roman numerals, as we have done.

EXAMPLE 4

In what quadrant does a point lie under the following conditions?
(a) Its first coordinate is positive.
(b) Its second coordinate is negative.
(c) Its first coordinate is negative and its second coordinate is positive.

Solution

(a) I or IV   (b) III or IV   (c) II   ❏

One of the key features of the number line is that it depicts the order relation that exists among real numbers. This feature is *absent* for the coordinate plane. There is no apparent algebraic reason why the pair (1, 4) should precede (or follow) the pair ($^-$2, 1), and there seems to be no convincing geometric argument why one point in Figure 15.23 should lead and the other follow. While it is possible to set up various order relations on the set of ordered pairs, none stands out as particularly natural or important. Thus it is not misleading to say that "there is no order relation among ordered pairs of reals."

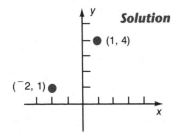

Figure 15.23

Distance

A feature of the number line that *is* present in the coordinate plane is distance. Corresponding to any two points in the coordinate plane is a positive number, their distance apart, where the unit of distance measure is the segment from (0, 0) to (1, 0). We shall consider how this number can be computed, algebraically, from the coordinates of the points.

If both points lie on the same horizontal line, then by what we know about number lines, the distance between them is just the absolute value of the difference of their first coordinates. In Figure 15.24 the distance from A to B is $|^-1 - 3| = |^-4| = 4$. Similarly, if they lie on the same vertical line, then the

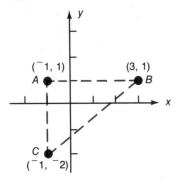

Figure 15.24

distance between them is the absolute value of the difference of their second coordinates. In Figure 15.24 the distance from A to C is $|1 - {}^{-}2| = |3| = 3$.

Figure 15.24 also suggests how to compute the distance between two points when they lie on neither the same horizontal nor the same vertical line. To find the distance from B to C, we observe that $\triangle BAC$ is a right triangle with legs AB and AC and hypotenuse BC. By the Pythagorean theorem, $(AB)^2 + (AC)^2 = (BC)^2$. That is, the distance from B to C is $\sqrt{4^2 + 3^2} = \sqrt{25} = 5$.

In general, suppose we have two points, P_1 with coordinates (x_1, y_1) and P_2 with coordinates (x_2, y_2). Then in Figure 15.25 a third point Q with coordi-

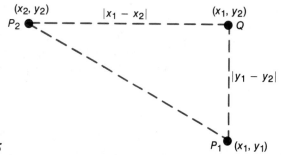

Figure 15.25

nates (x_1, y_2) will complete a right triangle with horizontal leg of length $|x_1 - x_2|$ and vertical leg of length $|y_1 - y_2|$. Thus, by the Pythagorean theorem, the distance from P_1 to P_2 is

$$\sqrt{|x_1 - x_2|^2 + |y_1 - y_2|^2}$$

But the absolute value signs can be omitted since $|a|^2 = a^2$. We summarize the result using the standard abbreviation P_1P_2 for "the distance from P_1 to P_2."

If $P_1 = (x_1, y_1)$ and $P_2 = (x_2, y_2)$, then the **distance** from P_1 to P_2 is

$$P_1P_2 = \sqrt{(x_1 - x_2)^2 + (y_1 - y_2)^2}$$

In words: to calculate the distance between two points, square the difference of the first coordinates, square the difference of the second coordinates, add, and take the square root.

EXAMPLE 5   For $A = (2, {}^{-}3)$, $B = ({}^{-}5, {}^{-}4)$, and $C = (6, {}^{-}3)$, find AB, BA, BC, and AC.

Solution $$AB = \sqrt{(2 - {}^{-}5)^2 + ({}^{-}3 - {}^{-}4)^2} = \sqrt{7^2 + 1^2} = \sqrt{50}$$

Note: Beware the common error of equating $\sqrt{7^2 + 1^2}$ with $\sqrt{7^2} + \sqrt{1^2}$; they are *not* equal!

$$BA = \sqrt{({}^{-}5 - 2)^2 + ({}^{-}4 - {}^{-}3)^2} = \sqrt{({}^{-}7)^2 + ({}^{-}1)^2} = \sqrt{50}$$

$$BC = \sqrt{(^-5 - 6)^2 + (^-4 - {}^-3)^2} = \sqrt{(^-11)^2 + (^-1)^2} = \sqrt{122}$$

$$AC = \sqrt{(2 - 6)^2 + (^-3 - {}^-3)^2} = \sqrt{(^-4)^2 + 0^2} = \sqrt{16} = 4 \qquad \Box$$

Notice that the general distance formula works even when the points P_1 and P_2 lie on the same horizontal or vertical line. If, for example, they lie on the same horizontal line, then $y_1 = y_2$ and the formula reduces to

$$P_1 P_2 = \sqrt{(x_1 - x_2)^2} = |x_1 - x_2|$$

since $\sqrt{a^2} = |a|$. Similarly, if P_1 and P_2 lie on the same vertical line,

$$P_1 P_2 = |y_1 - y_2|$$

The distance formula can be used to establish an algebraic formula for the midpoint of a given segment in terms of the coordinates of the endpoints. Figure 15.26 shows two points, P_1 and P_2, and the midpoint M of their segment.

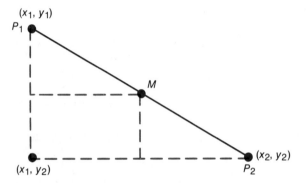

Figure 15.26

The dotted lines *suggest* that the first coordinate of M is midway between x_1 and x_2, and that the second coordinate is midway between y_1 and y_2. Thus by what we learned about the midpoint of a segment on the number line, it is *plausible* that

$$M = \left(\frac{x_1 + x_2}{2}, \frac{y_1 + y_2}{2} \right)$$

To *prove* that this M is the midpoint of segment $\overline{P_1 P_2}$, we need to show two things:

(1) $P_1 M = MP_2$ (2) M lies on line $\overleftrightarrow{P_1 P_2}$

The first is straightforward:

$$P_1 M = \sqrt{\left[x_1 - \left(\frac{x_1 + x_2}{2} \right) \right]^2 + \left[y_1 - \left(\frac{y_1 + y_2}{2} \right) \right]^2}$$

$$= \sqrt{\left[\frac{x_1 - x_2}{2} \right]^2 + \left[\frac{y_1 - y_2}{2} \right]^2}$$

and also

$$MP_2 = \sqrt{\left[\left(\frac{x_1 + x_2}{2}\right) - x_2\right]^2 + \left[\left(\frac{y_1 + y_2}{2}\right) - y_2\right]^2}$$

$$= \sqrt{\left[\frac{x_1 - x_2}{2}\right]^2 + \left[\frac{y_1 - y_2}{2}\right]^2}$$

Thus

$$P_1 M = MP_2$$

To show that M lies on line $\overleftrightarrow{P_1 P_2}$, it suffices to show that

$$P_1 M + MP_2 = P_1 P_2$$

For if M were *off* the line, then the sum of the distances from M to P_1 and P_2 would exceed the distance from P_1 to P_2. (If you do not see why, make a sketch.) By the preceding calculations,

$$P_1 M + MP_2 = 2\sqrt{\left(\frac{x_1 - x_2}{2}\right)^2 + \left(\frac{y_1 - y_2}{2}\right)^2} = 2\sqrt{\frac{(x_1 - x_2)^2 + (y_1 - y_2)^2}{4}}$$

$$= \sqrt{(x_1 - x_2)^2 + (y_1 - y_2)^2} = P_1 P_2$$

Our result has been established.

If $P_1 = (x_1, y_1)$ and $P_2 = (x_2, y_2)$, then the **midpoint** M of segment $\overline{P_1 P_2}$ is given by

$$M = \left(\frac{x_1 + x_2}{2}, \frac{y_1 + y_2}{2}\right)$$

In words: to find the midpoint, simply average the coordinates of the endpoints.

EXAMPLE 6   Find the midpoint of the segment joining $(^-3, 4)$ to $(5, ^-4)$.

Solution
$$\text{Midpoint} = \left(\frac{^-3 + 5}{2}, \frac{4 + ^-4}{2}\right) = \left(\frac{2}{2}, \frac{0}{2}\right) = (1, 0) \qquad ❏$$

For future reference we display the **collinearity test** that was used in establishing the midpoint formula.

Points A, B, and C are collinear (with B between A and C) if and only if $AB + BC = AC$.

EXAMPLE 7   Show that $(^-1, ^-1)$ lies on the line through the points $(^-3, ^-2)$ and $(3, 1)$ and is between them.

Solution   We apply the collinearity test:

$$\text{Distance } (^-3, ^-2) \text{ to } (^-1, ^-1) = \sqrt{(^-3 - ^-1)^2 + (^-2 - ^-1)^2} = \sqrt{5}$$
$$\text{Distance } (^-1, ^-1) \text{ to } (3, 1) = \sqrt{(^-1 - 3)^2 + (^-1 - 1)^2} = \sqrt{20}$$
$$\text{Distance } (^-3, ^-2) \text{ to } (3, 1) = \sqrt{(^-3 - 3)^2 + (^-2 - 1)^2} = \sqrt{45}$$

And $\sqrt{5} + \sqrt{20} = \sqrt{45}$ because $\sqrt{20} = 2\sqrt{5}$ and $\sqrt{45} = 3\sqrt{5}$.   ❏

We have just seen how the (algebraic) distance formula can be used to test for (geometric) collinearity of points. Other geometric information can be derived from it as well. For example, the *converse* of the Pythagorean theorem asserts the following.

> If A, B, and C are distinct points and $(AB)^2 + (BC)^2 = (AC)^2$, then A, B, C are vertices of a right triangle having its right angle at B.

Thus we can establish that the three points

$$A = (^-1, 5) \qquad B = (^-3, 2) \qquad C = (3, ^-2)$$

are vertices of a right triangle with right angle at B by checking that the distances behave properly:

$$(AB)^2 = (^-1 - ^-3)^2 + (5 - 2)^2 = 2^2 + 3^2 = 13$$
$$(BC)^2 = (^-3 - 3)^2 + (2 - ^-2)^2 = (^-6)^2 + 4^2 = 52$$
$$(AC)^2 = (^-1 - 3)^2 + (5 - ^-2)^2 = (^-4)^2 + 7^2 = 65$$

Since $13 + 52 = 65$, we have a right triangle.

Finally, we can test whether a given point lies inside, on, or outside a given circle by checking whether its distance from the center is less than, equal to, or greater than the radius.

EXAMPLE 8   Determine the position of the point $P = (5, 6)$ relative to the circle with center $C = (0, 3)$ and radius $r = 6$.

Solution
$$PC = \sqrt{(5 - 0)^2 + (6 - 3)^2} = \sqrt{5^2 + 3^2} = \sqrt{34}$$

Since $\sqrt{34} < 6$, P lies inside the circle.   ❏

Generalization of the example leads to the equation of an arbitrary circle.

> A point (x, y) lies on the circle with center (a, b) and radius r if and only if $(x - a)^2 + (y - b)^2 = r^2$.

If $(x - a)^2 + (y - b)^2 < r^2$, then (x, y) is *inside* the circle. If $(x - a)^2 + (y - b)^2 > r^2$, then (x, y) is *outside* the circle.

EXERCISE SET 15.3

For the first four exercises $M = \{$July, August, September, October, November$\}$, and you are to graph, in $M \times M$, the solution set of each open sentence.

1. _____ immediately precedes _____ .

2. _____ precedes _____ .

3. _____ has less days than _____ .

4. _____ and _____ have different numbers of days.

For the next four exercises $S = \{1, 2, 3, 4, 5, 6\}$, and you are to graph, in $S \times S$, the solution set of each open sentence.

5. $xy < 10$

6. $y - x = 2$

7. y/x is an integer.

8. $10y/x$ is an integer.

Figure 15.27 shows a dog. For Exercises 9–16, give the coordinates of the feature described.

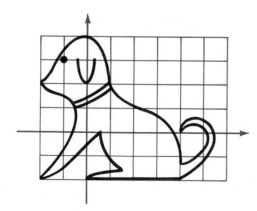

Figure 15.27

9. His front paw

10. His hind paw

11. The top of his collar

12. The tip of his tail

13. His nose

14. His eye

15. The top of his head

16. The bottom of his ear

17. Plot the following points in the coordinate plane. Then connect them in order, and connect P_{10} to P_1.

$P_1 = (4, 3)$ $P_2 = (^-2, 3)$ $P_3 = (^-2, 0)$

$P_4 = (^-4, ^-2)$ $P_5 = (^-2, ^-2)$ $P_6 = (^-2, ^-3)$

$P_7 = (0, ^-3)$ $P_8 = (^-2, ^-4)$ $P_9 = (^-2, ^-5)$

$P_{10} = (4, ^-5)$

18. Repeat Exercise 17, but first double all y coordinates and halve all x coordinates.

19. The point A has coordinates $(3, 2)$.
    (a) Plot A.
    (b) Plot B so that A and B are symmetric with respect to the y axis. What are the coordinates of B?
    (c) Give the coordinates of the midpoint of segment $\overline{AB}$.
    (d) Plot C so that A and C are symmetric with respect to the x axis. What are the coordinates of C?
    (e) Give the coordinates of the midpoint of segment $\overline{AC}$.

20. Repeat Exercise 19 beginning with the point $A = (^-4, 1)$.

21. If $A = (x, y)$ and A and B are symmetric with respect to the y axis, then $B = (?, ?)$.

22. If $A = (x, y)$ and A and B are symmetric with respect to the x axis, then $B = (?, ?)$.

In the coordinate plane, graph all points (x, y) satisfying the following conditions.

23. $x \geq 0$

24. $y \leq 0$

25. $x \leq 0$ and $y \leq 0$

26. $x \geq 0$ and $0 \leq y \leq 2$

27. $^-1 \leq x \leq 2$ and $^-5 \leq y \leq 3$

28. $x^2 > 0$ and $y^2 > 0$

29. $x = y$

30. $y = ^-x$

31. $x \cdot y = 0$

32. $x = 2$

33. $y = 3$

34. $0 \leq x \leq 4$ and $y = ^-2$

35. $x + y = 6$

36. $x - y = 2$

37. $x \cdot y = 6$

38. $x/y = 2$

39. $|x| \leq 1$

40. $|x| \geq 2$ and $|y| = 1$

For each pair of points A and B in Exercises 41–44, (a) find the midpoint M of segment $\overline{AB}$ by using the midpoint formula, and (b) verify that $AM = BM$ by using the distance formula.

41. $A = (6, 3)$, $B = (^-2, ^-3)$

42. $A = (^-3, 2)$, $B = (5, 2)$

43. $A = (^-1, 6)$, $B = (^-1, ^-3)$

44. $A = (3, ^-1)$, $B = (0, ^-7)$

45. First estimate, then find the point C that is $\frac{3}{8}$ of the way from $A = (^-2, ^-5)$ to $B = (2, ^-1)$.

46. If $A = (^-2, ^-5)$, $\underline{M} = (1, 2)$, and M is the midpoint of segment $\overline{AB}$, find B.

47. If $A = (0, 3)$, $\underline{M} = (4, ^-1)$, and M is the midpoint of segment $\overline{AB}$, find B.

48. Three vertices of a parallelogram are $(0, 0)$, $(3, 2)$, and $(1, 5)$. Find all possible coordinates for the fourth vertex. *Hint:* The diagonals of a parallelogram bisect each other.

In the next four exercises M is the midpoint of segment $\overline{AB}$, and quadrants are designated by Roman numerals. Sketch A, B, and M to satisfy the given conditions.

49. A is in I, B is in III, and M is in IV.

50. A is in I, B is in III, and M is in II.

51. A is in I, B is in III, and M is in I.

52. A is in I, B is in III, and M is in III.

53. If A is in quadrant I and B is in IV, in which quadrants could their midpoint M lie? Explain your answer algebraically.

54. Repeat Exercise 53 for A in III and B in IV.

Use the distance criterion to determine whether the following triples of points are collinear.

55. $A = (^-5, ^-3)$, $B = (^-1, 1)$, $C = (2, 3)$

56. $A = (6, ^-4)$, $B = (0, ^-1)$, $C = (^-2, 0)$

Use the Pythagorean theorem and its converse to determine whether the following triples of points determine right triangles.

57. $A = (^-2, 3)$, $B = (2, 4)$, $C = (4, ^-4)$

58. $A = (3, ^-2)$, $B = (^-2, ^-1)$, $C = (0, 5)$

Determine whether the given point lies inside, on, or outside the given circle.

59. Point $(10, 7)$; circle of radius 8 with center at $(4, 2)$

60. Point $(^-4, 2)$; circle of radius 13 with center at $(8, ^-3)$

61. Given $A = (^-2, 7)$, $B = (2, ^-1)$, $C = (2, 4)$ and $D = (^-6, 0)$.

(a) Is C equidistant from A and B?

(b) Is D equidistant from A and B?

(c) What geometric conclusion can you draw about line $\overleftrightarrow{CD}$ and segment $\overline{AB}$?

(d) Would you agree that points A and B are symmetric with respect to the line $\overleftrightarrow{CD}$?

62. Show that points (a, b) and (b, a) are symmetric in the line through $(0, 0)$ and $(1, 1)$ by showing that $(0, 0)$ is equidistant from (a, b) and (b, a) and $(1, 1)$ is equidistant from (a, b) and (b, a).

63. Show that (a, b) and $(^-b, ^-a)$ are symmetric in the line through $(0, 0)$ and $(^-1, 1)$.

64. Given $A = (5, 4)$, $B = (^-3, ^-8)$, $C = (4, ^-4)$, and $D = (^-2, 0)$.

(a) Do segments $\overline{AB}$ and $\overline{CD}$ bisect each other?

(b) What geometric conclusion can you draw about quadrilateral $ABCD$?

65. The vertices of a triangle are: $A = (4, 0)$, $B = (6, 5)$, $C = (0, 3)$.

(a) Find the area of $\triangle ABC$ using the distance formula and Heron's formula.

(b) Check your answer to part (a) by plotting $\triangle ABC$ on graph paper and using Pick's formula.

★ 66. Given a real number t and a point $P = (x, y)$, a multiplication operation, real number times point, is defined as follows:

$$tP = t(x, y) = (tx, ty)$$

For example, $\frac{1}{3}(^-2, 6) = (^-\frac{2}{3}, 2)$. Let $P = (^-2, 6)$. Plot several points and then describe each of these sets of points in geometric terms.

(a) $\{tP \mid 0 \le t \le 1\}$

(b) $\{tP \mid 0 \le t\}$

(c) $\{tP \mid t \le 0\}$

(d) $\{tP \mid t \le 1\}$

The distance we have discussed in this section is the usual "distance as the crow flies." In certain contexts other distances are more appropriate. If the lines on the coordinate plane in Figure 15.28 are viewed as streets in a city, then one is led to consider the "taxicab distance."

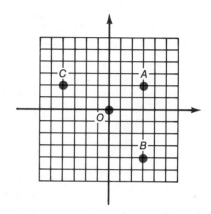

Figure 15.28

67. Determine the taxicab distance between O and A.

68. Determine the usual distance between O and A.

69. Plot a dozen points at taxicab distance 5 from O.

70. Plot all points at usual distance 5 from O.

71. Is B nearer to O or to A in taxicab distance?

72. Is B nearer to O or to A in usual distance?

73. Plot a dozen points equi-taxi-distant from O and C.

74. Plot all points equi-usual-distant from O and C.

Given points $A = (^-2, ^-0.7)$, $B = (0.9, 0.5)$, and $C = (3, 1.1)$, find the following and round your answers to three decimal places.

75. AB 76. AC

77. Midpoint of $\overline{AC}$ 78. Midpoint of $\overline{BC}$

For the points A, B, and C of Exercises 75–78:

79. Are A, B, and C collinear?

80. Does $\overleftrightarrow{AB}$ pass through the origin?

 ## 15.4   *Linearity*

Linearity is one of the most central concepts in all of mathematics; it is also one of the first ideas that a youngster encounters in a prealgebra or beginning algebra course. In this section we look at it briefly from both algebraic and geometric standpoints.

Linear Equations

A **linear equation in one variable** x is an equation of the **standard form**

$$ax + b = 0 \qquad \text{where} \qquad a \neq 0$$

or any equation that can be brought to that form by using the equivalence transformations that we reviewed in Section 15.1: addition property of equality, multiplication property of equality, simplification. The nonzero number a is called the **coefficient of** x; the number b is the **constant coefficient.** Most of the equations that we encountered in Sections 15.1 and 15.2 were linear.

EXAMPLE 1   Show that each of the following equations is linear in one variable.
(a) $2x + 3 = 10$
(b) $3x - 12 = 5 - x$

Solution   (a)

$$2x + 3 = 10$$
$$\Longleftrightarrow \quad 2x + 3 + {}^{-}10 = 10 + {}^{-}10 \qquad \text{addition property of equality}$$
$$\Longleftrightarrow \quad 2x + {}^{-}7 = 0 \qquad \text{simplification}$$

The third equation is the standard form with nonzero x coefficient. *Note:* We will also consider $2x - 7 = 0$ to be in standard form.

(b)

$$3x - 12 = 5 - x$$
$$\Longleftrightarrow \quad 3x - 12 + (x - 5) = 5 - x + (x - 5) \qquad \text{addition property of equality}$$
$$\Longleftrightarrow \quad 4x - 17 = 0 \qquad \text{simplification}$$

The third equation is the standard form with nonzero x coefficient.   ❑

Some sample equations in one variable that are *not* linear are

$$x^2 = 4 \qquad \sqrt{x} = 5 \qquad 4x + 3 = 2(5 + 2x)$$

Notice that when one tries to bring this third equation to standard form, it collapses to $0x - 7 = 0$, an equation with empty solution set.

The graph of a linear equation in one variable is just a point on the number line. See Figure 15.29.

Figure 15.29 Graph of the equation $2x + 10 = 3$.

A **linear equation in two variables** x and y is an equation of the **standard form**

$$ax + by + c = 0 \qquad \text{where at least one of } a \text{ and } b \text{ is nonzero}$$

or any equation that can be brought to that form by the equivalence transformations APE, MPE, and simplification.

EXAMPLE 2   Show that each of these equations is linear in two variables.
(a) $y = 6x + 2$ (b) $x + y - 3 = 5y - 4x$
(c) $v = 12 + 5t$ (d) $x = 3$

Solution   (a)
$$y = 6x + 2$$
$$\Longleftrightarrow \quad y + (^-6x - 2) = 6x + 2 + (^-6x - 2) \qquad \text{addition property of equality}$$
$$\Longleftrightarrow \quad 1y + (^-6)x + (^-2) = 0 \qquad \text{simplification}$$

The third equation is the standard form. *Note:* We will also consider $y - 6x - 2 = 0$ to be in standard form.

(b)
$$x + y - 3 = 5y - 4x$$
$$\Longleftrightarrow \quad x + y - 3 + (4x - 5y) = 5y - 4x + (4x - 5y)$$
$$\Longleftrightarrow \qquad\qquad 5x - 4y - 3 = 0$$

The third equation is in standard form.

(c) This time the two variables are t and v, and a standard form is $5t - v + 12 = 0$. Note that standard form is *not* unique: $10t - 2v + 24 = 0$ and $v - 5t - 12 = 0$ are two of infinitely many other standard forms for the same equation.
(d) $1x + 0y - 3 = 0$ qualifies as a standard form because even though the y coefficient is zero, the x coefficient is nonzero. ❏

Some typical nonlinear equations in two variables are

$$y = x^2 \qquad y = \sqrt{x} \qquad xy = 6$$

A linear equation is a very special kind of open sentence in two variables, and so the graphing procedure that we sketched in the previous section should apply: Solve for y in terms of x, choose values for x at will, compute corresponding y values, and plot the pairs (x, y) in the coordinate plane.

EXAMPLE 3   Graph the solution set of $x - y - 2 = y - 3x$.

Solution   **Step 1**   Solve for y in terms of x:

$$x - y - 2 = y - 3x$$
$$4x - 2 = 2y$$
$$y = 2x - 1$$

Step 2   Generate some solution pairs, as in Table 15.5.

Step 3   Plot those pairs in the coordinate plane. See Figure 15.30. As we look at these points in the coordinate plane, we see that they lie on a straight line and we would be greatly surprised if the graph of the complete solution set turned out to be anything other than the complete line. This is, in fact, the case. (See Figure 15.31.)

Table 15.5

x	y
$^-2$	$^-5$
$^-1$	$^-3$
0	$^-1$
1	1
2	3

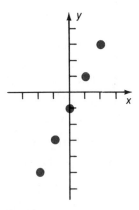

Figure 15.30

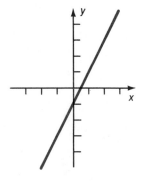

Figure 15.31 Graph of $x - y - 2 = y - 3x$.
❏

In general:

> The graph of a linear equation in two variables is a straight line in the Cartesian coordinate plane.

It is now clear why the adjective *linear* has been used. We shall sharpen this result and show why it is true shortly, but even in the unembellished form the theorem is extremely useful.

EXAMPLE 4   Graph the solution sets of these linear equations.
(a) $2x - 3y - 6 = 0$
(b) $x = 3$
(c) $y = ^-2$

Solution

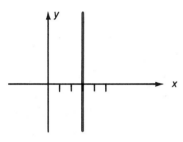

Figure 15.32 Graph of 2x − 3y − 6 = 0.

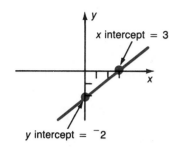

Figure 15.33 Graph of x = 3.

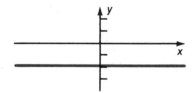

Figure 15.34 Graph of y = ⁻2.

(a) Since the equation is linear, the graph is a straight line. And since a line is determined by two points, it suffices to find two ordered pairs that satisfy the equation. The easiest ones to calculate are the points where the line crosses the x and y axes. Setting $x = 0$ in the equation $2x - 3y - 6 = 0$ yields $y = {}^-2$. Thus $(0, {}^-2)$ is a point of the graph. The y coordinate of the point where this line crosses the y axis is called its **y intercept.** Setting $y = 0$ in the same equation yields $x = 3$. Thus $(3, 0)$ is another point of the graph, namely, the point where it crosses the x axis. The x coordinate of this point is called the **x intercept** of the line. The complete graph is shown in Figure 15.32.

(b) If we think of the standard form $x + 0y - 3 = 0$, then no matter what value we assign to y, x always turns out to be 3. For example, $(3, {}^-2)$ and $(3, 4.7)$ both satisfy the equation. Thus the graph is the vertical line of all points with first coordinate 3. See Figure 15.33.

(c) If we think of the standard form $0x + y + 2 = 0$, then clearly y must be $^-2$, but x can be any number at all. Thus the graph is the horizontal line of all points with second coordinate $^-2$. See Figure 15.34. ❑

To clarify the connection between linear equations (algebraic objects) and lines (geometric objects), we need to investigate the concept of slope.

The Slope of a Line

Imagine hiking from left to right along the two trails shown in Figure 15.35. On the straight-line trail you ascend at a steady rate: For every 2 units you move horizontally (*run*), you move 1 unit vertically (*rise*). That is, the ratio of rise to run is always $\frac{1}{2}$, no matter where you start or stop. This constant ratio is called the **slope** of the line. (Notice that for a vertical line the run is zero, so the ratio of rise to run is undefined; that is, *a vertical line does not have slope*.)

On the other trail you do not ascend at a steady rate. Sometimes, the ratio of rise to run is small $(\frac{1}{3})$, and other times, it is large $(\frac{3}{2})$. The slope of this curve changes from point to point. One of the important tasks in calculus is to assign a precise meaning to the phrase "the slope of a curve at a point" and then to develop techniques for calculating such variable slopes.

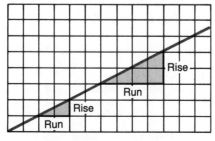

Similar triangles: Ratio of rise to run is always the same.

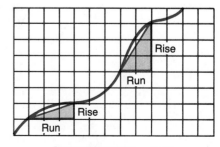

Dissimilar triangles: Ratio of rise to run varies.

Figure 15.35

We are now in a position to state, in precise language, a characteristic property of lines, that is, a property that distinguishes lines from all other continuous long curves. (Think of a continuous long curve as any figure you can make from a piece of string that extends infinitely in both directions.)

A continuous long curve L is a (nonvertical) straight line if and only if $(y_2 - y_1)/(x_2 - x_1)$ has the same value for *any* two points (x_1, y_1) and (x_2, y_2) on L. See Figure 15.36.

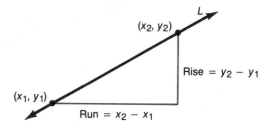

Figure 15.36 Slope of $L = \dfrac{\text{rise}}{\text{run}} = \dfrac{y_2 - y_1}{x_2 - x_1} = \text{constant.}$

If we accept this property as an axiom, we can deduce the following key result.

The graph of a linear equation in two variables is a straight line; in fact, the graph of the linear equation $y = mx + b$ is a line of slope m with y intercept b.

The main ideas of the proof are as follows: Suppose, to begin with, that the linear equation has been written in standard form

$$cx + dy + k = 0$$

If $d = 0$, then the equation is equivalent to $x = -k/c$, and the graph is a vertical line. If $d \neq 0$, then we can solve for y in terms of x, so the original equation is equivalent to one of the form

$$y = mx + b$$

Now suppose (x_1, y_1) and (x_2, y_2) are any two points on its graph L. Then these ordered pairs satisfy the equation; that is,

$$y_1 = mx_1 + b \qquad \text{and} \qquad y_2 = mx_2 + b$$

from which it follows, by subtraction, that

$$y_2 - y_1 = (mx_2 + b) - (mx_1 + b)$$

or

$$y_2 - y_1 = m(x_2 - x_1)$$

or

$$\frac{y_2 - y_1}{x_2 - x_1} = m$$

Thus the value of the quotient $(y_2 - y_1)/(x_2 - x_1)$ can be found by simply reading off the coefficient of x from the equation $y = mx + b$; it does not depend on where, on L, the points (x_1, y_1) and (x_2, y_2) happen to lie. Thus L is a straight line of slope m. Its y intercept is b; that is, it passes through $(0, b)$, since the ordered pair $(0, b)$ satisfies the equation $y = mx + b$.

Summary

Associated with each nonvertical straight line L is a number m called its slope.

1. If L is described pictorially by a straight stroke on a coordinate plane, then m can be found by moving along the stroke and recording rise/run.
2. If L is described as the line through points (x_1, y_1) and (x_2, y_2), then m can be found by computing $(y_2 - y_1)/(x_2 - x_1)$, which is often abbreviated $\Delta y/\Delta x$, the Greek letter delta (Δ) suggesting "difference."
3. If L is described as the graph of a linear equation, then m can be found by solving for y and reading off the coefficient of x.

EXAMPLE 5   Find the slope of each line.
(a) The line in Figure 15.37
(b) The line in Figure 15.38

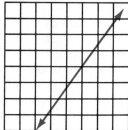

Figure 15.37   **Figure 15.38**

(c) The line through the points $(3, 0)$ and $(^-2, 4)$
(d) The line through the points $(3, ^-4)$ and $(3, 2)$
(e) The graph of $3x - 2y + 7 = 0$
(f) The graph of $x + y = 0$

Solution   (a) Slope $= \dfrac{\text{rise}}{\text{run}} = \dfrac{3}{2} = 1.5$

(b) Slope $= \dfrac{\text{rise}}{\text{run}} = \dfrac{0}{1} = 0$

(c) Slope $= \dfrac{\Delta y}{\Delta x} = \dfrac{4 - 0}{^-2 - 3} = \dfrac{^-4}{5}$

(d) Slope $= \dfrac{\Delta y}{\Delta x} = \dfrac{2 - {}^-4}{3 - 3} = \dfrac{6}{0}$ Slope is undefined; line is vertical.

(e) Solve for y, then read off the coefficient of x:

$$3x - 2y + 7 = 0 \iff 2y = 3x + 7 \iff y = \tfrac{3}{2}x + \tfrac{7}{2}$$

Slope is $\tfrac{3}{2}$.

(f) Proceed as in (e):

$$x + y = 0 \iff y = {}^-x$$

Slope is $^-1$.   ❏

Equations for a Line

Given an equation in x and y, there is precisely one solution set: the set of ordered pairs that satisfy the equation. The geometric representation of these pairs by points in the coordinate plane is called the graph of the equation. Each equation has a unique graph.

The converse, however, is not true. If we start with a collection of points, it certainly determines a unique set of ordered pairs, but this set of ordered pairs can be the solution set of many different-looking equations. For example, all of these equations

$$2x + 3y - 6 = 0 \qquad y = -\tfrac{2}{3}x + 2$$
$$(y - 4) = -\tfrac{2}{3}(x + 3) \qquad \frac{x}{3} + \frac{y}{2} = 1$$

have the same graph. Thus although we can speak of *the* graph of an equation, we can only refer to *an* equation of a graph. Our aim now is to learn how to write various equations for a given straight line.

If the line is vertical, writing an equation is a trivial matter. For example, an equation for the vertical line through $(7, 3)$ is $x = 7$, which, of course, is a linear equation. For nonvertical lines two general methods can be employed. One is based on the definition of slope (see Figure 15.39).

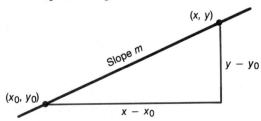

Figure 15.39

Point-Slope Method

There is exactly one line having a given slope m and passing through a given point (x_0, y_0). A point (x, y) lies on that line if and only if

$$\frac{y - y_0}{x - x_0} = m \qquad \text{or} \qquad (x, y) = (x_0, y_0)$$

that is $y - y_0 = m(x - x_0)$.

It is easy to see that the single equation

(A) $$y - y_0 = m(x - x_0)$$

is equivalent to the compound equation

(B) $$(x, y) = (x_0, y_0) \qquad \text{or} \qquad \frac{y - y_0}{x - x_0} = m$$

One need only check that each solution to (A) is a solution to (B) and vice versa. Equation (A) is called a **point-slope equation** of the line because it displays the slope m and both coordinates of a point (x_0, y_0) on the line.

EXAMPLE 6 Write an equation for the line of slope 3 through the point $(2, 4)$.

Solution By the point-slope method, (x, y) lies on this line if and only if

$$\frac{y - 4}{x - 2} = 3 \qquad \text{or} \qquad (x, y) = (2, 4)$$

This compound condition is equivalent to the single equation

$$y - 4 = 3(x - 2) \qquad\qquad ❑$$

Since the point-slope equation (A) is linear, its standard form being

$$-mx + y + (mx_0 - y_0) = 0$$

we have the converse to the key result proved earlier.

Every straight line is the graph of a linear equation; in fact, every nonvertical line has an equation of the form $y = mx + b$.

The equation $y = mx + b$ is called the **slope-intercept equation** of the line because m is its slope and b is its y intercept. Note that in this form the coefficients m and b *are* unique. This result suggests the second general method for writing an equation for a given straight line, the **method of undetermined coefficients.** We illustrate with examples.

EXAMPLE 7   Write the slope-intercept equation for each line.
(a) The line of slope 3 through the point (2, 4)
(b) The line through ($^-$2, 5) and (1, $^-$4)

Solution   (a) We know the equation has the form $y = mx + b$. Our problem is to determine the numerical values of m and b. The description of the line provides us with the slope $m = 3$. So we are half finished: $y = 3x + b$. To determine the value of b, we use the fact that (2, 4) lies on the line, that is, satisfies the equation:

$$4 = 3 \cdot 2 + b \iff b = {}^-2$$

Thus the final form of the equation is $y = 3x - 2$.

(b) We know the equation has the form $y = mx + b$. The problem is to determine numerical values for m and b. Applying the definition of slope to the two given points, we find m:

$$m = \frac{{}^-4 - 5}{1 - {}^-2} = \frac{{}^-9}{3} = {}^-3$$

So we are half done: $y = {}^-3x + b$. Now we can determine b by substituting either point into this equation. Using ($^-$2, 5), we get

$$5 = {}^-3 \cdot {}^-2 + b \iff b = {}^-1$$

Thus the slope-intercept equation is $y = {}^-3x - 1$.   ❏

Given a line, we have learned how to write equations for it in point-slope form and in slope-intercept form. Both of these forms, of course, can easily be transformed to standard form.

Parallel and Perpendicular Lines

There is a simple algebraic criterion for parallelism.

Two nonvertical lines are parallel if and only if they have the same slope.

(And, of course, any two vertical lines are parallel.)

EXAMPLE 8   Do the following linear equations describe parallel lines: $2x - 5y + 8 = 0$ and $9y - 4x + 1 = 0$?

Solution   If we write the equations in slope-intercept form, we can read off the slopes:

$$y = \tfrac{2}{5}x + \tfrac{8}{5} \qquad \text{slope } \tfrac{2}{5}$$
$$y = \tfrac{4}{9}x - \tfrac{1}{9} \qquad \text{slope } \tfrac{4}{9}$$

Since $\tfrac{2}{5} \neq \tfrac{4}{9}$, the lines are not parallel.   ❏

EXAMPLE 9   Line L passes through $(^-3, 1)$ and $(4, 5)$. Write an equation for the line G that is parallel to L but passes through $(2, 0)$.

Solution

$$\text{Slope of } L = \frac{5 - 1}{4 - (^-3)} = \frac{4}{7}$$

Thus the slope of G is $\frac{4}{7}$ also. By the method of undetermined coefficients, the *slope-intercept equation* of G is

$$y = \tfrac{4}{7}x + b$$

But $(2, 0)$ is on G, so

$$0 = \tfrac{4}{7}(2) + b \quad \Longleftrightarrow \quad b = -\tfrac{8}{7}$$

Thus

$$y = \tfrac{4}{7}x - \tfrac{8}{7} \qquad\qquad \square$$

The algebraic condition for *perpendicularity* is less obvious.

> Suppose line L_1 has slope m_1, and line L_2 has slope m_2. Then L_2 is perpendicular to L_1 if and only if $m_2 = ^-1/m_1$. That is, two (nonvertical, nonhorizontal) lines are perpendicular if and only if their slopes are negative reciprocals.

(And, of course, any horizontal line is perpendicular to any vertical line.)

Figure 15.40 suggests the reason for this condition. First, triangle T was attached to L_1. Then L_1 was rotated through a quarter turn about the origin to make it coincide with L_2. In this way the triangle T was brought to position T′.

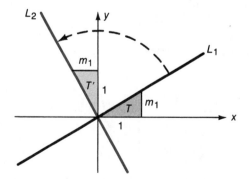

Figure 15.40

Thus for line L_2

$$\frac{\text{Rise}}{\text{Run}} = \frac{^-1}{m_1}$$

EXAMPLE 10   Line L has equation $y = \frac{2}{3}x + 5$. Write an equation for the line G that is perpendicular to L and passes through $(^-2, 6)$.

Solution   Line L has slope $\frac{2}{3}$, so G has slope

$$\frac{^-1}{\frac{2}{3}} = \frac{^-3}{2}$$

By the point-slope method, (x, y) is on G if and only if

$$\frac{y - 6}{x + 2} = \frac{^-3}{2} \quad \text{or} \quad (x, y) = (^-2, 6)$$

that is,

$$y - 6 = -\tfrac{3}{2}(x + 2) \qquad \square$$

EXERCISE SET 15.4

Write each of the linear equations in Exercises 1–6 in standard form.

1. $3x + 4 = x - 5$ 2. $5(y - 1) = 2y + 7$
3. $4y + x = 9 - x$ 4. $y = x$
5. $r + 3s = 4 - (3r + s)$
6. $5r + 2s = 2(r + s + 3)$
7. Which of the equations in Exercises 1–6 qualify as linear equations in one variable?
8. Which of the equations in Exercises 1–6 qualify as linear equations in two variables?

Give the slope of each of these lines, which are shown in Figure 15.41.

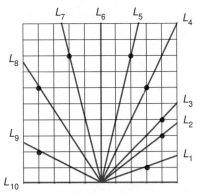

Figure 15.41

9. L_1 10. L_2 11. L_3
12. L_4 13. L_5 14. L_6
15. L_7 16. L_8 17. L_9
18. L_{10}

Sketch the following lines in a coordinate plane.

19. Slope 3 passing through $(2, ^-1)$
20. Slope $^-2/3$ passing through $(^-2, 0)$
21. Slope $^-1/3$ passing through $(2, ^-1)$
22. Slope $3/2$ passing through $(2, 6)$
23. Slope 0 passing through $(4, 5)$
24. Slope 0 passing through $(3, 0)$

Shade in the set of all lines that pass through $(0, 0)$ and have slope between the given values.

25. 0 and 1   26. 3 and 4
27. $^-3$ and $^-2$ 28. $^-1/2$ and $^-1/4$

Give the slope of the line that passes through the two points.

29. $(2, 3)$ and $(7, 5)$
30. $(0, 2)$ and $(12, 5)$
31. $(^-4, 13)$ and $(1, ^-2)$

32. ($^-$3, 2) and (1, 2)

33. (4.5, 71.3) and (9.1, 103.5)

34. ($^-$0.7, $^-$1.4) and (0, 0)

35. (*a*, *b*) and (*b*, *a*)

36. (0, $a^2 + b$) and (*a*, *b*)

Give the slope of the graph of each equation.

37. $y = 3x - 4$ 38. $y = 2.4x + 5$

39. $y = 9 - 2x$ 40. $y = {}^-3x$

41. $3x + 2y - 5 = 0$ 42. $5x - 8y + 1 = 0$

43. $y - 2 = 0$ 44. $x + 1 = 0$

45. $ax + by + c = 0$ 46. $x - ty + 5t = 0$

Write the slope-intercept equation for each of these lines, which are shown in Figure 15.42.

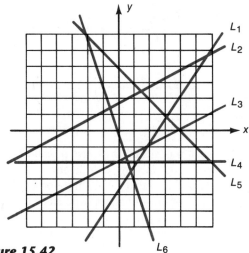

Figure 15.42

47. L_1 48. L_2 49. L_3

50. L_4 51. L_5 52. L_6

Write a point-slope equation for each of these lines.

53. Slope 2 passing through ($^-$3, 5)

54. Slope 1/3 passing through (4, 2)

55. Slope $^-$1/2 passing through (4, $^-$1)

56. Slope $^-$4 passing through ($^-$4, 0)

For each line, (a) write the slope-intercept equation, and (b) write an equation in standard form.

57. The line through ($^-$4, 1) and (1, $^-$2)

58. The line through ($^-$6, $^-$2) and (0, 1)

59. The line through (0, 0) and (3, 4)

60. The line through ($^-$2, 1) and (3, 1)

Graph each equation.

61. $y = \frac{2}{3}x + 1$ 62. $y = -\frac{1}{2}x + 4$

63. $x + 2y + 6 = 0$ 64. $x = \frac{1}{2}y + 3$

65. $x - y = 0$ 66. $x + y = 0$

67. $y - 3x = 3(1 - x)$

68. $3(x + y) = x - 4 + 3y$

69. Graph this family of linear equations in one coordinate plane: $y = 2x + 4$, $y = 2x + 3$, $y = 2x + 2$, $y = 2x + 1$, $y = 2x$, $y = 2x - 1$. How are the graphs related?

70. Graph this family of linear equations in one coordinate plane: $y = {}^-x + 3$, $y = {}^-x + 2$, $y = {}^-x + 1$, $y = {}^-x$, $y = {}^-x - 1$, $y = {}^-x - 2$.

71. Graph this family of linear equations in one coordinate plane: $y = x + 2$, $y = 2x + 2$, $y = 3x + 2$, $y = 0x + 2$, $y = {}^-1x + 2$, $y = {}^-2x + 2$. How are the graphs related?

72. Graph this family of linear equations in one coordinate plane: $y = x - 1$, $y = 2x - 1$, $y = 3x - 1$, $y = 0x - 1$, $y = {}^-x - 1$, $y = {}^-2x - 1$.

Give the slope of any one of the lines that is perpendicular to the following.

73. A line of slope 3

74. A line of slope 1/2

75. A line of slope $^-$2/3

76. A line of slope $^-$6.25

77. The graph of $5x + 2y = 10$

78. The graph of $x + y = 1$

79. The line through (2, 3) and ($^-$6, $^-$1)

80. The line through (0, 0) and (4, $^-$1)

In Exercises 81–86, write an equation for the line described.

81. The line through the origin parallel to the graph of $2y = 5 - x$

82. The line through (1, 2) parallel to the graph of $x + y = 0$

83. The line through (3, 0) perpendicular to the graph of $3y = x$

84. The line through (0, ⁻2) perpendicular to the graph of $y = x$

85. The perpendicular bisector of the segment joining (0, 3) and (2, ⁻5)

86. The perpendicular bisector of the segment joining (7, ⁻3) and (⁻5, 1)

87. Write an equation for the set of all points equidistant from (0, 3) and (2, ⁻5).

★ 88. Find the point on the graph of $4x + y = 12$ that is nearest to the origin.

89. In this exercise L_1, L_2, L_3 are lines in the Cartesian coordinate plane. Explain algebraically: if L_1 and L_2 are both perpendicular to L_3, then L_1 and L_2 are either equal or parallel.

90. A linear equation of the form

$$\frac{x}{a} + \frac{y}{b} = 1$$

is said to be in **two-intercept form.** Find the points where its graph crosses the axes.

Graph on the number line the solution sets of these linear inequalities in one variable. Name each graph, using proper geometric terminology.

91. $2x - 3 < 7$ 92. $4 - x \leq 2$

For Exercises 93–96, discover how to graph, in the Cartesian coordinate plane, the solution sets of the linear inequalities in two variables. Name each graph, using proper geometric terminology.

93. $x + 2y < 4$ 94. $x + y > 0$

95. $2x - 3y \leq 6$ 96. $y - 2x \geq {}^-2$

97. In the previous section we learned a criterion for collinearity based on distances. Formulate a collinearity criterion based on slopes: "Three points $A = (a_1, a_2)$, $B = (b_1, b_2)$, $C = (c_1, c_2)$ are collinear if and only if _____ ."

Use the collinearity criterion you formulated in Exercise 97 to test the triples in Exercises 98–100 for collinearity.

98. $A = ({}^-4, 14)$, $B = (36, 44)$, $C = (100, 92)$

99. $A = ({}^-4, {}^-16)$, $B = (36, 44)$, $C = (100, 142)$

★ 100. $A = (a_1, a_2)$, $B = (b_1, b_2)$, $M =$ midpoint of $\overline{AB}$

101. A nonrectangular parallelogram has been placed in the coordinate plane so that one vertex is at the origin, one edge is along the positive x axis, and the rest of the figure lies in the first quadrant. See Figure 15.43.

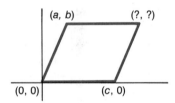

Figure 15.43

(a) Is such a positioning always possible?
(b) Express the missing coordinates in terms of a, b, and c so that the defining property of a parallelogram—that opposite sides be parallel—is satisfied.
(c) Prove algebraically that the diagonals of this parallelogram bisect each other.

★ 102. Refer to the parallelogram in Figure 15.43.
(a) Under what conditions on a, b, and c will it be a rhombus—that is, be equilateral?
(b) Prove algebraically that if it is a rhombus, then its diagonals are perpendicular.
(c) Prove algebraically that if its diagonals are perpendicular, then it is a rhombus.

103. Consider the four points $A = (2, {}^-4)$, $B = ({}^-14, 8)$, $C = (6, 20)$, $D = (22, 8)$.
(a) Do they determine a rectangle?

(b) Do they determine a parallelogram?

(c) Do they determine a rhombus?

★ 104. Sketch the circle of radius 1 with center at (0, 0), the line through (2, 0) that is tangent to (just touching) the circle in the first quadrant, and a radial segment from the center of the circle to the point of tangency.

(a) What appears to be the relationship between the segment and the line?

(b) Use your observation from part (a) to find the coordinates of the point of tangency.

Hint: We noted in Section 15.3 that a point (x, y) lies on the circle in question if and only if $x^2 + y^2 = 1$.

105. Think about a linear equation in three variables, such as $2x - 3y + 4z - 12 = 0$.

(a) Where could you graph its solution set?

(b) What sort of geometric figure do you think its graph would be?

(c) What sort of geometric figure do you think the graph of the inequality $2x - 3y + 4z - 12 > 0$ would be?

15.5 *Systems of Linear Equations*

When two linear equations in two variables are joined by the word *and,* the resulting compound open sentence is called a **system** of two linear equations in two variables. Frequently, the word *and* is replaced by special brace notation; that is, we write

$$\begin{cases} 2x - 3y = 8 \\ 3x + 4y = {}^-5 \end{cases}$$

to mean

$$2x - 3y = 8 \quad \textit{and} \quad 3x + 4y = {}^-5$$

By a solution to the linear system we mean, of course, an ordered pair of values for (x, y) that satisfies *both* of the individual linear equations. Later in this section we shall see how frequently and naturally such systems arise, but let us begin by learning ways to solve them.

Solving a Linear System

Sometimes, a linear system can be solved geometrically. The algebraic task of finding an ordered pair that satisfies both of the preceding linear equations is equivalent to the geometric task of finding a point that lies on both of their graphs. Figure 15.44 shows the graphs of the two linear equations and their point of intersection, which is the solution to the system.

Because of the inherent imprecision in drawing pictures, we check algebraically that $(1, {}^-2)$ does in fact satisfy both equations:

$$2(1) - 3({}^-2) = 8 \quad \text{and} \quad 3(1) + 4({}^-2) = {}^-5$$

The linear system we just solved was very special. Algebraically, its solution was an ordered pair of integers; geometrically, the two lines crossed at a lattice point of the coordinate plane. The more typical situation is for the lines

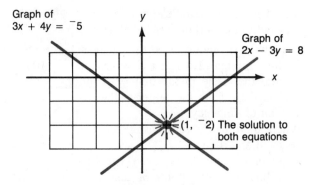

Figure 15.44 Graphical solution of a linear system.

to cross at a point whose coordinates are not geometrically obvious. In such cases it is essential to have an algebraic method for determining the ordered pair.

One algebraic method is the **substitution method,** which is illustrated in the following example.

EXAMPLE 1   Solve these linear systems.

(a) $\begin{cases} 5x + 6y = 10 \\ \phantom{5x + {}} 2y = 3 \end{cases}$ (b) $\begin{cases} x - 2y = 1 \\ 3x + y = {}^-1 \end{cases}$

Solution   (a) We begin by solving the (easy) second equation for y: $y = \frac{3}{2}$. Substituting this value for y in the first equation yields

$$5x + 6(\tfrac{3}{2}) = 10$$

a linear equation in one variable, which is easily solved for x:

$$5x + 9 = 10 \iff 5x = 1 \iff x = \tfrac{1}{5}$$

Thus the solution to the system is the ordered pair $(x, y) = (\frac{1}{5}, \frac{3}{2})$, a result that would have been difficult to read from the graphs of the two original equations.

The last step is to check that $(\frac{1}{5}, \frac{3}{2})$ satisfies both original equations:

$$5(\tfrac{1}{5}) + 6(\tfrac{3}{2}) \overset{?}{=} 10 \qquad \text{yes}$$
$$2(\tfrac{3}{2}) \overset{?}{=} 3 \qquad \text{yes}$$

(b) We follow the same pattern that worked in part (a): Solve the second equation for y,

$$y = {}^-1 - 3x$$

and substitute this value into the first equation,

$$x - 2({}^-1 - 3x) = 1$$

This substitution eliminates y from the first equation, and we again get a linear equation in one variable, which we can solve easily for x:

$$x + 2 + 6x = 1 \iff 7x = {}^-1 \iff x = \frac{{}^-1}{7}$$

Now we must make a second substitution, the substitution of $^-1/7$ for x in the equation $y = {}^-1 - 3x$ to determine the y coordinate:

$$y = {}^-1 - 3\left(\frac{{}^-1}{7}\right) = \frac{{}^-7}{7} + \frac{3}{7} = \frac{{}^-4}{7}$$

The solution to the system is $(x, y) = ({}^-1/7, {}^-4/7)$.
  Check:

$$\frac{{}^-1}{7} - 2\left(\frac{{}^-4}{7}\right) \overset{?}{=} 1 \qquad \text{yes}$$

$$3\left(\frac{{}^-1}{7}\right) + \left(\frac{{}^-4}{7}\right) \overset{?}{=} {}^-1 \qquad \text{yes} \qquad ❑$$

Clearly, this substitution method is based on the problem-solving strategy of reducing a new problem to problems of a type one already knows how to solve. In our example the task of solving linear systems in two variables was reduced to the easier task of solving linear equations in one variable. This same general problem-solving strategy motivates a second algebraic method, the so-called **elimination method.** The thinking goes like this: Example 1(a) was easier to solve than Example 1(b) because one of the equations involved just a single variable. Perhaps there is a way of transforming the system in (b) to a system in which one of the equations involves only a single variable. It turns out there is a way. We illustrate it first with examples; then we investigate it more carefully.

EXAMPLE 2   Solve each linear system by first eliminating one of the variables from one of the equations.

(a) $\begin{cases} 2x - 3y = 4 \\ 5x + 3y = 1 \end{cases}$ (b) $\begin{cases} x - 5y = {}^-2 \\ 3x + 2y = 11 \end{cases}$ (c) $\begin{cases} 2x + 3y = 5 \\ 3x + 4y = 6 \end{cases}$

Solution   (a) Since the coefficients of y are additive inverses, if we simply add the left- and right-hand sides of these equations, the y terms drop out and we are left with

$$7x = 5 \iff x = \tfrac{5}{7}$$

The new system

$$\begin{cases} 2x - 3y = 4 \\ x \qquad\quad = \tfrac{5}{7} \end{cases}$$

can now be solved by substitution:

$$2\left(\frac{5}{7}\right) - 3y = 4 \iff \frac{10}{7} - \frac{28}{7} = 3y \iff y = \frac{^-6}{7}$$

The solution is $(x, y) = (5/7, {}^-6/7)$.
   Check:

$$2\left(\frac{5}{7}\right) - 3\left(\frac{^-6}{7}\right) \overset{?}{=} 4 \qquad \text{yes}$$

$$5\left(\frac{5}{7}\right) + 3\left(\frac{^-6}{7}\right) \overset{?}{=} 1 \qquad \text{yes}$$

(b) This system is not as nice as system (a) because neither the x coefficients nor the y coefficients add to zero. But we can easily change it to the nicer form by multiplying both the left- and right-hand sides of the first equation by $^-3$:

$$\begin{cases} ^-3x + 15y = 6 \\ 3x + 2y = 11 \end{cases}$$

Now we add these equations, as in part (a), to arrive at the system

$$\begin{cases} ^-3x + 15y = 6 \\ 17y = 17 \end{cases}$$

which can be solved by substitution:

$$17y = 17 \iff y = 1$$
$$^-3x + 15(1) = 6 \iff 9 = 3x \iff x = 3$$

The solution is $(x, y) = (3, 1)$. You should check that this ordered pair satisfies both original equations.

(c) People with an aversion to fractions might multiply the first equation by 3 and the second by $^-2$ to arrive at a system

$$\begin{cases} 6x + 9y = 15 \\ ^-6x - 8y = {}^-12 \end{cases}$$

which is all set up for eliminating x terms by addition. If fractions don't bother you, simply multiply the original second equation by $^-2/3$ to arrive at

$$\begin{cases} 2x + 3y = 5 \\ ^-2x - \frac{8}{3}y = {}^-4 \end{cases}$$

Adding these equations yields

$$\tfrac{1}{3}y = 1 \iff y = 3$$

and substituting into the first equation yields

$$2x + 3(3) = 5 \iff 2x = {}^-4 \iff x = {}^-2$$

The solution is $(x, y) = ({}^-2, 3)$, which checks in the original system. ❑

To put these algebraic solution techniques on solid mathematical ground, we must again talk about equivalence transformations. Obviously, transforming a complicated looking linear system to a nice looking system is a fruitless exercise unless the new system is equivalent to the original one in the usual sense of having the same solution set. Only two types of equivalence transformations are needed to solve systems of the kind we have encountered. One is a **multiplication transformation.**

> Multiplying both sides of any equation in a linear system by a nonzero number yields an equivalent system.

For example,

$$\begin{cases} 2x + 3y = 5 \\ 3x + 4y = 6 \end{cases} \overset{M}{\iff} \begin{cases} 6x + 9y = 15 \\ 3x + 4y = 6 \end{cases} \overset{M}{\iff} \begin{cases} 6x + 9y = 15 \\ {}^-6x - 8y = {}^-12 \end{cases}$$

The first equation was multiplied by 3; then the second was multiplied by $^-2$. The "M" over the equivalence symbol $\iff$ indicates that a multiplication transformation was used at each step.

The other type of equivalence transformation is an **addition transformation.**

> Adding one equation to another equation (and discarding the old "other" equation) yields an equivalent system.

For example

$$\begin{cases} 6x + 9y = 15 \\ {}^-6x - 8y = {}^-12 \end{cases} \overset{A}{\iff} \begin{cases} 6x + 9y = 15 \\ y = 3 \end{cases}$$

The first equation was added to the second, and the old second equation was discarded. The "A" over the equivalence symbol indicates that an addition transformation was used.

Transformations M and A are the analogs of the familiar equivalence transformations MPE and APE that we applied to single equations.

So far every linear system we have considered has had a unique solution; geometrically, each pair of lines has had a unique point of intersection. But we know that there are other geometric possibilities: Lines may be parallel, or they may coincide so that we are actually dealing with one line, not two. Let us look at the algebra of these alternatives.

EXAMPLE 3   Solve the linear systems.

(a) $\begin{cases} x - 4y = 1 \\ {}^{-}3x + 12y = 2 \end{cases}$ (b) $\begin{cases} 2x - y = {}^{-}5 \\ {}^{-}4x + 2y = 10 \end{cases}$

Solution   (a) $\begin{cases} x - 4y = 1 \\ {}^{-}3x + 12y = 2 \end{cases} \overset{M}{\Longleftrightarrow} \begin{cases} 3x - 12y = 3 \\ {}^{-}3x + 12y = 2 \end{cases} \overset{A}{\Longleftrightarrow} \begin{cases} 3x - 12y = 3 \\ 0x + 0y = 5 \end{cases}$

Since there is clearly no solution (x, y) to the second equation of the third system, there can be *no solution* to the entire third system. (The intersection of the empty set with a line is the empty set.) But the third system is equivalent to the first, and thus the first system also has no solution. Geometrically, the equations of the original system have graphs that are parallel lines. See Figure 15.45. Note that both lines in Figure 15.45 have slope $\frac{1}{4}$.

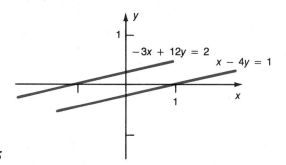

Figure 15.45

(b) $\begin{cases} 2x - y = {}^{-}5 \\ {}^{-}4x + 2y = 10 \end{cases} \overset{M}{\Longleftrightarrow} \begin{cases} 4x - 2y = {}^{-}10 \\ {}^{-}4x + 2y = 10 \end{cases} \overset{A}{\Longleftrightarrow} \begin{cases} 4x - 2y = {}^{-}10 \\ 0x + 0y = 0 \end{cases}$

This time, in the third system, every point of the coordinate plane satisfies the second equation. Thus the solution set of the third system is just the solution set of its equation, namely *a line*. (The intersection of a plane with a line in it is just the line.) Since the first system is equivalent to the third, its solution set is also that line. Had the equations in the original system been written in slope-intercept form, it would have been clear that we were talking about a single line.

$$\begin{matrix} 2x - y = {}^{-}5 \\ {}^{-}4x + 2y = 10 \end{matrix} \quad \rlap{\diagdown}{\diagup}\; y = 2x + 5 \qquad \square$$

In summary, these are the possibilities:

A system of two linear equations in two variables has either no solutions, one solution, or infinitely many solutions. Graphically these cases correspond to parallel lines, intersecting lines, coinciding lines.

Applications of Linear Systems

Many of the word problems that we solved by using one variable and one equation in Section 15.2 can also be solved by using two variables and two equations. Which approach to take is largely a matter of personal preference. The steps to a solution are quite similar, except that if we introduce two variables, we must write two equations.

EXAMPLE 4   Ann is half as old as Bob. In 5 more years she will be $\frac{2}{3}$ as old as Bob. How old is Ann now?

Solution

Let a = Ann's present age (in years)

Let b = Bob's present age (in years)

Since Ann is presently half as old as Bob, one equation is

$$a = \tfrac{1}{2}b$$

In 5 years Ann will be $a + 5$ and Bob will be $b + 5$, but Ann will also be $\frac{2}{3}$ as old as Bob. Thus a second equation relating a and b is

$$a + 5 = \tfrac{2}{3}(b + 5)$$

We can solve the system

$$\begin{cases} a \quad = \tfrac{1}{2}b \\ a + 5 = \tfrac{2}{3}(b + 5) \end{cases}$$

by substituting from the first equation into the second:

$$\tfrac{1}{2}b + 5 = \tfrac{2}{3}(b + 5) \iff \tfrac{1}{2}b + 5 = \tfrac{2}{3}b + \tfrac{10}{3} \iff \tfrac{5}{3} = \tfrac{1}{6}b \iff b = 10$$

But it is not Bob's age we are after; it is Ann's. So substitute $b = 10$ into the first equation:

$$a = \tfrac{1}{2}(10) = 5$$

Ann is presently 5 years old.   ❏

Mixture problems are often solved by introducing two variables and solving a linear system. Here is a third solution of the wine problem in Example 4, Section 15.2.

EXAMPLE 5   A wine merchant has two kinds of wine which cost 72 cents and 40 cents a quart respectively. How much of each must he take to make a mixture of 50 quarts worth 60 cents a quart?

Solution

Let x = number of quarts of expensive 72-cent wine

Let y = number of quarts of cheap 40-cent wine

Then since he is to mix a total of 50 qt, one equation is

$$x + y = 50$$

The cost of the expensive wine is

$$72 \left(\frac{\text{cents}}{\text{qt}} \right) \cdot x \text{ (qt)} = 72x \text{ (cents)}$$

The cost of the cheap wine is

$$40 \left(\frac{\text{cents}}{\text{qt}} \right) \cdot y \text{ (qt)} = 40y \text{ (cents)}$$

The cost of the mixture is

$$60 \left(\frac{\text{cents}}{\text{qt}} \right) \cdot 50 \text{ (qt)} = 3000 \text{ (cents)}$$

on the one hand, and $72x + 40y$, on the other. Thus a second equation relating x and y is

$$72x + 40y = 3000$$

We can solve the system

$$\begin{cases} x + y = 50 \\ 72x + 40y = 3000 \end{cases}$$

by multiplying the first equation by ⁻40 and adding it to the second,

$$\begin{cases} x + y = 50 \\ 32x = 1000 \end{cases}$$

then finally solving the new second equation for x,

$$x = \tfrac{1000}{32} = 31\tfrac{1}{4}$$

and substituting this value into the first equation:

$$31\tfrac{1}{4} + y = 50 \iff y = 18\tfrac{3}{4}$$

He should mix $31\tfrac{1}{4}$ qt of 72-cent wine with $18\tfrac{3}{4}$ qt of 40-cent wine.   ❏

The purpose of studying linear systems is not just to provide an alternative method for attacking problems that we already know how to solve by using one variable. In many contexts it is almost essential to introduce 2, 3, 4, or more variables and then to look for a like number of equations relating them. For instance, it is not unusual to encounter systems of 10 linear equations in 10 variables when analyzing an electric circuit, or 100 linear equations in 100 variables in a mathematical model of an economic system. The mathematical subfield of linear algebra is concerned with the uses and solutions of such systems.

Even in this book we had an encounter with larger linear systems. In (starred) Exercise 17 of Section 5.4 we were asked to find numbers a, b, and c so that the quadratic function $g(x) = ax^2 + bx + c$ would produce (among others) the input-output pairs $(0, 0)$ $(1, 3.2)$, and $(2, 12.8)$. We are now in a position to solve that problem systematically. On the one hand, input 0 yields output $a \cdot 0^2 + b \cdot 0 + c$; on the other it is to produce output 0. Thus one equation relating a, b, and c is

$$0 \cdot a + 0 \cdot b + 1 \cdot c = 0$$

On the one hand, input 1 yields output $a \cdot 1^2 + b \cdot 1 + c$; on the other, it is to produce output 3.2. Thus a second equation is

$$1 \cdot a + 1 \cdot b + 1 \cdot c = 3.2$$

Finally, input 2 yields output $a \cdot 2^2 + b \cdot 2 + c$ on the one hand, and 12.8 on the other. Thus a third equation is

$$4 \cdot a + 2 \cdot b + c = 12.8$$

The three displayed equations constitute a system of three linear equations in three variables. Fortunately, the first equation tells us immediately that $c = 0$, so our task becomes the simpler one of solving the linear system of two equations in two variables:

$$\begin{cases} a + b = 3.2 \\ 4a + 2b = 12.8 \end{cases}$$

Multiplying the first equation by $^-4$ and adding to the second produces the equivalent system

$$\begin{cases} a + b = 3.2 \\ \quad ^-2b = 0 \end{cases}$$

The second equation tells us that $b = 0$, and substitution of that value into the first equation yields $a = 3.2$. Thus the function $g(x) = ax^2 + bx + c$ that fits the input-output data is given by the formula

$$g(x) = 3.2x^2 + 0 \cdot x + 0 = 3.2x^2$$

EXERCISE SET 15.5

For each system, (a) graph both equations by finding x and y intercepts, and (b) estimate geometrically a solution to the system.

1. $\begin{cases} 2x - y = 6 \\ x + 4y = 4 \end{cases}$

2. $\begin{cases} 3x + 2y = 9 \\ y - 4x = 2 \end{cases}$

3. $\begin{cases} \dfrac{x}{2} + \dfrac{y}{3} = 1 \\ \dfrac{y}{4} - \dfrac{x}{5} = 1 \end{cases}$

4. $\begin{cases} \dfrac{x}{5} - \dfrac{y}{2} = 1 \\ \dfrac{x}{3} = 1 \end{cases}$

Solve each system by substitution. Be sure to check your solutions.

5. $\begin{cases} 2x - 5y = 4 \\ 2y = 7 \end{cases}$
6. $\begin{cases} 3r + 4s = {}^-2 \\ r + 2 = 0 \end{cases}$

7. $\begin{cases} 5x - y = {}^-13 \\ 2x + 3y = {}^-12 \end{cases}$
8. $\begin{cases} 2u + 3v = {}^-8 \\ 3u - 2 = 4 \end{cases}$

9. The system of Exercise 1

10. The system of Exercise 4

11. $\begin{cases} x - 2y = 7 \\ 4y - 2x = 15 \end{cases}$
12. $\begin{cases} 3z - y + 3 = 0 \\ 2y - 6z = 6 \end{cases}$

Solve each system by elimination. Check your solutions.

13. $\begin{cases} 6x - 2y = 5 \\ 3x + 2y = 13 \end{cases}$
14. $\begin{cases} 3t + 5w = 7 \\ {}^-3t - 2w = 5 \end{cases}$

15. $\begin{cases} 2r - 5t = 17 \\ 3t - 2r = {}^-5 \end{cases}$
16. $\begin{cases} 4x - 3y = 7 \\ 3y + x = 3 \end{cases}$

17. $\begin{cases} 4x - 3y = 27 \\ 3x + 2y = {}^-1 \end{cases}$
18. $\begin{cases} 2x + 5y = 7 \\ 3x + y = {}^-9 \end{cases}$

19. The system of Exercise 3

20. The system of Exercise 2

21. $\begin{cases} 12x - 39y = {}^-3 \\ 52y - 16x = 4 \end{cases}$
22. $\begin{cases} 4x + 6t = {}^-2 \\ 15t + 10x = 5 \end{cases}$

★ 23. $\begin{cases} 3\sqrt{x} - 2\sqrt{y} = {}^-4 \\ {}^-7\sqrt{x} + 3\sqrt{y} = 1 \end{cases}$
★ 24. $\begin{cases} \dfrac{1}{x} + 2|y| = 8 \\ \dfrac{5}{x} - 3|y| = 1 \end{cases}$

Solve by introducing two variables and setting up a system of two equations.

25. Exercise 35 of Section 15.2

26. Exercise 37 of Section 15.2

27. How many ounces of cashews at $4.00 per pound and how many ounces of peanuts at $.70 per pound should be used to make a pound of mixed nuts to sell for $1.69?

28. Here is the grading system in gym: You start the term with 100 points. Each time you are tardy, you lose some points and each time you are absent you lose even more; but the coach isn't saying how many points she takes off for each type of transgression. Linda was absent 5 times, tardy 4 times, and got a grade of 74. Sheila was absent 3 times, tardy 10 times, and got a 73. How many points did each absence cost?

29. A plane flying into the wind takes $2\frac{1}{2}$ hr to go 800 mi. The plane flying with the wind takes only 2 hr to return. What is the speed of the wind and the airspeed of the plane?

30. With the outboard motor running at full speed, it takes $3\frac{1}{2}$ hr to go 21 mi upstream. With the motor running at half speed, it takes 2 hr to make the return trip. Find the current of the river.

31. *From an 1881 textbook:* The cost of 12 horses and 14 cows is $1900; the cost of 5 horses and 3 cows is $650. What is the cost of a horse and cow respectively?

32. *From the same textbook:* The first of the two digits of a number is, when doubled, 3 more than the second, and the number itself is less by 6 than five times the sum of the digits. What is the number?

33. Find the coordinates of the circumcenter of the triangle with vertices $A = (1, 2)$, $B = (4, 5)$, $C = (7, 3)$.

Find a *linear function* $f(x) = ax + b$ that yields the given input-output pairs. Then, use your function to *interpolate* the output corresponding to input 2 and to *extrapolate* the output corresponding to input 6.

34. $(0, 8)$ and $(5, 3)$

35. $(0, {}^-2)$ and $(3, 4)$

36. $({}^-1, 5)$ and $(5, 1)$

37. $({}^-2, {}^-2)$ and $(4, 1)$

Find a *quadratic function* $f(x) = ax^2 + bx + c$ that yields the given input-output pairs. Then, use your function to interpolate the output corresponding to input 2 and to extrapolate the output corresponding to input 6.

38. $(0, 0)$, $(1, {}^-3)$, $(4, 12)$

39. $(0, {}^-1)$, $(1, 1)$, $(4, {}^-5)$

40. $(0, 4)$, $(1, 3)$, $(4, {}^-12)$

★ 41. (1, 2), (3, 6), (4, 11)

Refer to Exercises 93–96 of Section 15.4 and try to discover how to graph the solution set of each of these systems of linear inequalities.

42. $\begin{cases} 2x - 3y \leq 6 \\ 5x + 2y \leq 10 \end{cases}$ 43. $\begin{cases} x + 2y \leq 4 \\ y - 3x \leq 6 \end{cases}$

44. $\begin{cases} -x + 2y \leq 8 \\ 3x - y \leq 9 \\ x \geq 0 \end{cases}$ 45. $\begin{cases} x + y \leq 4 \\ 2x + y \leq 6 \\ x \geq 0 \\ y \geq 0 \end{cases}$

Write a system of linear inequalities having the given region as solution set.

46.
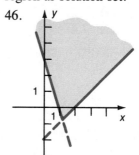

47.
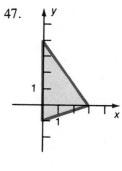

Key Concepts in Chapter 15

Statement
Variable
Open sentence
Replacement set
Solution set
Equation
Inequality
Equivalent open sentences
Equivalence transformations for equations
  (inequalities)
Equivalent expressions
Absolute value
Cartesian coordinate plane
Quadrants
Distance formula

Midpoint formula
Converse of Pythagorean theorem
Linear equation in one variable: standard form
Linear equation in two variables: standard form
Slope of a line
Point-slope equations of a line
Slope-intercept equation of a line
Undetermined coefficients method
Parallelism and slope
Perpendicularity and slope
System of linear equations
Substitution method
Elimination method
Equivalence tranformations for linear systems

éª Chapter 15 Review Exercises éª

1. Identify by name the type of equivalence transformation used at each step in the solutions of the equation.

$$5(x - 1) = 3 - (x - 10)$$
$$\Longleftrightarrow \qquad 5x - 5 = 3 - x + 10 \quad \underline{\text{(a)}}$$
$$\Longleftrightarrow \quad 5x - 5 + x + 5 = 3 - x + 10 + x + 5$$
$$\underline{\text{(b)}}$$
$$\Longleftrightarrow \qquad\qquad 6x = 18 \quad \underline{\text{(c)}}$$

$$\Longleftrightarrow \qquad \tfrac{1}{6}(6x) = \tfrac{1}{6}(18) \qquad \underline{\text{(d)}}$$
$$\Longleftrightarrow \qquad\qquad x = 3 \qquad \underline{\text{(e)}}$$

2. Describe the solution set of each equation in the given replacement set.
   (a) $x + 3 = 2$ in the replacement set W
   (b) $x + 3 = 2$ in the replacement set I
   (c) $3 \cdot x = 2$ in the replacement set I
   (d) $3 \cdot x = 2$ in the replacement set Q

(e) $x^2 = 3$ in the replacement set Q

(f) $x^2 = 3$ in the replacement set R

3. Solve the inequality $4(1 - 2x) < x - 41$, and graph its solution set on the number line.

4. Solve the absolute value inequality $|x - 3| + 4 \leq 5$, and graph its solution set on the number line.

5. Write an algebraic expression that represents the annual interest earned by a principal of x dollars if $\frac{1}{3}$ of it is in bonds paying 8% per year and the rest is in stocks paying 6% per year.

6. An item for sale at $19.88 bears a tag that reads "Price marked is 30% off the usual price." Find the "usual price."

7. Kelly just received a 6% raise, which amounts to an extra $100 per month. What is her new annual salary?

8. Niko is presented with the following problems: "A pile of dimes and quarters is worth $4.95. There are twice as many dimes as quarters. How many quarters are there?" He begins his solution by saying "Let D = dimes and Q = quarters. Then $Q = 2.5D$." Where did Niko go wrong? Now solve the problem.

9. A rectangle is $1\frac{1}{2}$ times as long as it is wide, and its perimeter is 60 cm. What is its area?

10. Suppose that in the latest sales period sales of domestically produced cars increased 4% compared with a year ago, while sales of imported cars increased 10%. If imports now account for 30% of sales, what percent of sales did imports account for one year ago?

11. Given $A = (^-5, 2)$ and $B = (3, ^-6)$. Does the midpoint of $\overline{AB}$ lie inside, on, or outside the circle of radius 4 with center at $(2, 1)$?

12. A quadrilateral has vertices $(0, 0)$, $(3, ^-2)$, $(6, 4)$, and $(^-1, 4)$.
    (a) Find its perimeter.
    (b) Are its diagonals congruent?

13. Given $C = (^-7, 12)$ and $D = (3, ^-4)$. Does the line $\overleftrightarrow{CD}$ pass through the origin?

14. Write an equation for the line with x-intercept $^-2$ that passes through $(3, ^-1)$.

15. Write an equation for the line with slope $^-2$ that passes through $(3, 4)$.

16. Write an equation for the line perpendicular to the line $2x + 3y = 6$ and passing through the origin.

17. Write an equation for the line passing through $(3, 0)$ that cuts off a triangle of area 6 from the fourth quadrant.

18. Graph the two equations
$$\begin{cases} 2x - 3y = ^-3 \\ 3x + \ y = 3 \end{cases}$$
and estimate the solution to the system from your graphs.

19. Solve the system in Exercise 18 algebraically.

20. The sum of the digits of a two-digit number is 11. When the digits are reversed, the new number is 27 less than the original. What is the original number?

21. I am thinking about a three-digit numeral. Its value in base ten is 184 more than its value in base eight and 328 more than its value in base six. What is its second digit?

References

Central Midwestern Regional Educational Laboratory. *Proceedings of the International Conference on the Teaching of Algebra at the Pre-College Level*. St. Louis: CEMREL, 1975.

Crawford, C. *Math Without Fear*. New York: Franklin Watts, 1980.

Davies, C. *New Elementary Algebra*. New York: Barnes & Burr, 1865.

Jacobs, H. *Elementary Algebra*. San Francisco: W. H. Freeman, 1979.

National Council of Teachers of Mathematics. *1988 Yearbook: The Ideas of Algebra, K–12*. Reston, Va.: NCTM, 1988.

16

COMPUTER PROGRAMMING

To a large degree the emergence and proliferation of calculators and computers are *responsible* for the restructuring of the mathematics curriculum as called for by the NCTM, first in the *Agenda* and now in the *Standards*. In the *Standards* we find the pleas that "a computer should be available in every classroom for demonstration purposes," and that "every student should have access to a computer for individual and group work." In the older *Agenda* we find a more explicit description of what students should be able to do with computers: "Beyond an acquaintance with the role of computers and calculators in society, most students must obtain a working knowledge of how to use them, including the ways in which one communicates with each and commands their services in problem solving."

The purpose of this chapter is to give a rudimentary description of how to communicate with and command computers in two languages, BASIC and Logo.

History

Any mechanical device used to assist in numerical calculations can be thought of as a computer. By this definition, the ancient abaci of the Chinese, Greeks, and Romans would qualify as early computers. A more complicated device appeared in 1642, when, at the age of 19, Blaise Pascal invented a mechanical adding-subtracting machine to assist his tax collector father in his bookkeeping. It employed wheels, cylinders, and gears. Pascal's machine was the ancestor of the four-operation desktop calculator patented in 1875 by the American, Frank Baldwin. If any one person could be called the father of the modern computer, however, it would probably have to be Charles Babbage, a mathematics professor at Cambridge. In 1812 he designed a *difference engine* to automatically perform simple computations needed for trigonometric and logarithmic tables. He further conceived of an *analytic engine* that would store both data and the instructions for a sequence of operations to be performed on the data. Unfortunately, manufacturing processes had not yet attained the degree of precision required for his machines.

The modern history of computers began in the 1930s when large mechanical computers were built by Vannevar Bush at the Massachusetts Institute of Technology and by Howard Aiken at Harvard University. Aiken's Mark I weighed 5 tons. The first electronic computer, ENIAC (electronic numerical integrator and calculator), was built at the University of Pennsylvania in 1945. It weighed 30 tons and filled a 30-ft by 50-ft room. The first commercial use of an electronic computer, UNIVAC I, was by the Bureau of the Census in 1951.

First-generation computers, those built before 1959, used vacuum tubes, were huge, required air-conditioning, and were relatively slow. Second-generation computers, built between 1959 and 1965, used transistors instead of vacuum tubes, were smaller, cheaper, required little power, and generated little heat. After 1965, integrated circuits—complete circuits formed by the controlled growth of a crystal structure—made possible further miniaturization in third-generation computers.

Personal computers, machines the size of a typewriter that can do what room-sized computers did only 30 years earlier, arrived on the scene in force in 1976 when two men in their early twenties, Steven Jobs and Stephen Wozniak, founded the Apple Computer Corporation. That date marks the beginning of the extensive use of computers in homes and schools.

Characteristics of a Modern Computing System

A modern computer has several characteristics. It has a large memory and recalls things flawlessly. It can perform mathematical calculations with split-second speed, and it almost never makes a mistake. It is able to make simple decisions, such as which of two numbers is smaller. Given an explicit list of instructions, it can carry them out in the prescribed order. It accepts data, processes it according to a prearranged plan, and outputs the results. Theoretically, human beings are able to do everything that computers do—but much more slowly and less accurately. The converse, of course, is false: computers are not yet able to match a human's ability to innovate, to adapt, to reason by analogy, or to deal with imprecision.

A modern **computing system** consists of a computer and one or more input and output devices. The **computer,** in turn, consists of three subunits. See Figure 16.1. The technical name for the computer is the *central processing unit,* or CPU.

The **input device** may be a machine that reads precompiled information from punched cards, magnetic tape, or magnetic disks; or it may be a typewriter keyboard by means of which an operator inputs data or instructions prior to or during the computing process. **Output devices** include television screens [also called cathode ray tubes (CRTs) or monitors] for immediate but temporary feedback to the operator, printers for a permanent human-readable transcript, and card punchers and magnetic recorders for permanent machine-readable records.

The heart of the system, the computer or CPU, has three components: the control unit, the memory, and the arithmetic-logic unit. The **control unit** does what its name implies: it controls. Think of it as a traffic cop, the quarterback

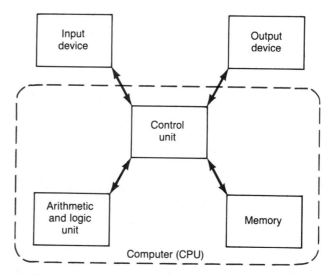

Figure 16.1 Schematic of a computing system.

on a football team, or the manager of an office. It accepts both data and instructions from input devices and channels them to the memory for filing. It calls data out of the memory and sends it to the arithmetic-logic unit for processing. It puts processed data back into the memory, and it sends information stored in the memory to output devices. The **memory** consists of a large number of locations at which numbers and words can be stored in binary code—that is, as sequences of 1s and 0s, as in the base-two numeration system. The **arithmetic-logic unit** functions as a calculator. It can perform arithmetic operations (addition, subtraction, multiplication, division, exponentiation), and it can evaluate a variety of functions (square root, absolute value, trigonometric, logarithmic and others). It also makes simple logical decisions, such as the larger-smaller decision mentioned earlier.

A personal computer system includes several input and output devices (Figure 16.2) all of which are connected to the computer by electric cables.

Figure 16.3 shows how the structure of a computing system is explained to children in a third-grade text. Notice how the function concept is implicit in the exercises.

Communicating with a Computer

Ultimately, the computer does all of its work in binary code, a system that is intelligible to only a relatively small number of computer specialists. The enormous success of computers, and their acceptance by nonspecialists, can be attributed to the development of **high-level languages** and the internal computer programs, called translators and interpreters, that convert them into machine language (the binary code). Programmers can learn these high-level languages fairly quickly, since they are closer to English than to binary code, and then

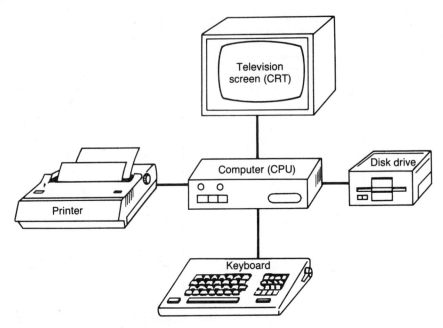

Figure 16.2 Components of a typical personal computer system.

use them to communicate with the computer. At present about 170 different high-level languages are in use. Some of the major ones are ALGOL, APL, BASIC, COBOL, FORTRAN, LISP, Logo, and Pascal.

By accident, Italian is better suited to opera than is English. By design, COBOL (common business-oriented language) is specially suited to business uses. The two languages that at the moment are most appropriate for elementary and middle school teachers are BASIC and Logo. BASIC (beginners' all-purpose symbolic instruction code) was developed in the 1960s at Dartmouth College for the express purpose of teaching students how to use a computer. It was designed to be easy to learn, and it has been the most common language for first courses in computer programming for two decades. Logo, a much newer language, was developed at the Massachusetts Institute of Technology, and is particularly suited to geometric and graphical activities. It was created with very young children in mind, and it has virtually exploded into elementary classrooms in the past few years. We will look at BASIC and then at Logo, but first we give a word of caution.

There are dialects of computer languages just as there are of natural languages. A Georgian and a New Yorker, both of whom speak English, will occasionally have some minor difficulties understanding each other. Various computer manufacturers have modified BASIC and Logo to conform to their own particular hardware. The differences in computer dialects are minor, but they do exist. The dialects we will use here are Applesoft BASIC and Terrapin Logo, both for the Apple IIe computer.

2 INPUT, PROCESS, OUTPUT

Robert uses the school computer. He gives words and numbers to the computer. They are called the **input**.

Then the computer uses rules. The rules tell it what to do with the input. This is called the **process**.

After the process, the results are shown. This is called the **output**.

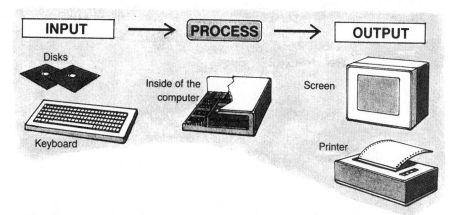

TRYOUT EXERCISES   Write the input or the output.

Input	Process	Output
8	Double the input.	1. ■
640	Print the digit in the tens place.	2. ■
Horse	Print the vowels.	3. ■
4. ■	Double and add 6.	30
5. ■	Multiply by 4.	40

Figure 16.3 Components of a computing system in a third-grade textbook.

16.1 *The Computer as a Calculator*

Before we discuss programming, we need to become familiar with some BASIC computer notation.

Operations

Table 16.1 shows that only the multiplication and exponentiation symbols are somewhat unusual. The symbol $*$ is used for multiplication since the common symbols, $\times$ and $\cdot$, could be confused with the letter X and with a decimal point, respectively. A symbol such as $\wedge$ for exponentiation, which we introduced in Section 4.1, is necessary because in ordinary notation there is no symbol at all for the exponentiation operation; the operation is implied by the relative positions of the operands, as in $2^3 = 8$. Some machines use the symbol $**$ or $\uparrow$ instead of $\wedge$ for exponentiation.

Table 16.1

BASIC symbol	Operation	Example
$\wedge$ (or $**$ or $\uparrow$)	exponentiation	$2 \wedge 3 = 8$
$*$	multiplication	$2 * 5 = 10$
$/$	division	$3 / 4 = .75$
$+$	addition	$2 + 3 = 5$
$-$	subtraction	$2 - 3 = -1$

Note: Even though many machines slash their zeros ($1\emptyset$ instead of 10) to distinguish them from the letter O, we will use the conventional symbol for zero in this book.

The top-to-bottom order of the operations in Table 16.1 corresponds to the usual precedence order. In the absence of parentheses, exponentiations are done first, then multiplications and divisions in left-to-right order, and finally addition and subtraction in left-to-right order.

EXAMPLE 1   Evaluate.
(a) $2 * 3 \wedge 4 - 5$
(b) $40 / 2 \wedge 3 * 4$
(c) $5 - 90 / 15 / 3 + (2 * 3) \wedge 2$

Solution (a) $2 * 3 \wedge 4 - 5 = 2 * 81 - 5$ exponentiation first
$\qquad\qquad\qquad = 162 - 5$ multiplication next
$\qquad\qquad\qquad = 157$ subtraction last
(b) $40 / 2 \wedge 3 * 4 = 40 / 8 * 4$ exponentiation first
$\qquad\qquad\qquad = 5 * 4 \rbrace$ $\lbrace$ multiplication and
$\qquad\qquad\qquad = 20 \rbrace$ $\quad$ division left to right

(c) $5 - 90 / 15 / 3 + (2 * 3) \wedge 2$

$\quad = 5 - 90 / 15 / 3 + 6 \wedge 2 \qquad$ parentheses say "do this first"

$\quad = 5 - 90 / 15 / 3 + 36 \qquad$ exponentiation

$\quad = 5 - 6 / 3 + 36$

$\quad = 5 - 2 + 36 \qquad$ {division left to right

$\quad = 3 + 36$

$\quad = 39 \qquad$ { addition and subtraction left to right ❏

As we have mentioned before, putting in some technically superfluous parentheses is harmless and can often clarify the meaning of an expression. For example, the left-hand member of this equation

$$(2 * (3 \wedge 4)) - 5 = 2 * 3 \wedge 4 - 5$$

leaves no doubt about the order in which the operations are to be performed. The right-hand member, while more streamlined, is perhaps less clear.

On a calculator there is one button $\boxed{-}$ for the binary operation of subtraction and another button $\boxed{+/-}$ for the negation function, "opposite of."

On a computer keyboard a single key serves for both. When the minus sign is used to indicate negation, it takes precedence over all binary operations. When it is used to indicate subtraction, it stands, with addition, at the bottom of the hierarchy.

EXAMPLE 2 Evaluate $- 3 \wedge 2 * 5 - 10$.

Solution

$\quad - 3 \wedge 2 * 5 - 10 = (-3) \wedge 2 * 5 - 10 \qquad$ negation first

$\qquad\qquad\qquad = 9 * 5 - 10 \qquad$ exponentiation next

$\qquad\qquad\qquad = 45 - 10 \qquad$ multiplication next

$\qquad\qquad\qquad = 35 \qquad$ subtraction last

Again, a few parentheses make the order of operations absolutely clear:

$$((-3) \wedge 2) * 5 - 10$$ ❏

Immediate-Execution Mode

A computer can be used in either immediate-execution mode or in deferred-execution mode. When it is used in immediate-execution mode, it behaves like a big (and very expensive) calculator. When it is used in deferred-execution mode, it does what it was created to do (and pays for itself). Using a computer in immediate-execution mode is a little like using an electronically controlled garage door to crack eggs. Still, there is some educational value in doing so. It allows one to familiarize oneself with the keyboard, particularly the locations of the new operation symbols and the RETURN key, to brush up on the order-of-operations conventions, to review some simple functions, and to learn the PRINT command, which is fundamental in programming.

Suppose you want the computer to calculate 2^{10} for you. You simply type the following line,

PRINT 2 $\wedge$ 10

then press the RETURN key. The computer will respond with the line

1024

Similarly, if you want the computer to calculate $2(12 - 4)/6$, you type the line

PRINT 2 * (12 − 4) / 6

And when you press RETURN, the machine will respond with the line

2.66666667

The machine cannot store (or print) an infinite decimal, so it displays the best approximation that it can.

If you type

PRINT 2 $\wedge$ 50

and then hit RETURN, the machine will respond with

1.12589991 E+15

which is the machine's way of giving the (approximate) value in scientific notation:

1.12589991 E+15   means $1.12589991 \times 10^{15}$

That is, the symbols E+15 tell you that the exponent on 10 is (positive) 15.

If you type

PRINT 2 $\wedge$ 200

and then press RETURN, the machine will display the message

? OVERFLOW ERROR

which indicates that the size of 2^{200} exceeds the limits of the computer.

Functions

So far we have dealt with only the arithmetic operations and a single function, the negation function. As we noted earlier, the computer has a variety of functions at its command. Some of the simpler ones are shown in Table 16.2. Again, you can verify each example in the table by using the computer in immediate-execution mode. For example, type

$$\text{PRINT SQR(81)}$$

and then press the RETURN key. The machine will respond with

$$9$$

Functions can be hooked up with arithmetic operations and with each other in useful ways.

EXAMPLE 3   Write an expression, using BASIC operations and functions, for the length of the hypotenuse of a right triangle whose legs have lengths 8 and 9.

Solution   By the Pythagorean theorem,

$$h = \sqrt{8^2 + 9^2}$$

Table 16.2

BASIC symbol	Function	Example
SQR(X)	Square root; produces (positive) square root of X	SQR(81) = 9
ABS(X)	Absolute value; produces absolute value of X	ABS(17 − 51) = 34
SGN(X)	Sign; produces −1 if X is negative, 0 if X is zero, and 1 if X is positive	SGN(2/3 − 3/4) = −1
INT(X)	Greatest integer; produces largest integer less than or equal to X	INT(22/7) = 3
RND(X)	Random number; input any positive integer for X and output will be a randomly chosen number between 0 and 1	RND(1) = .973136696 RND(1) = .103117626 RND(8) = .0177148333

So a BASIC expression is

$$\text{SQR}(8 \wedge 2 + 9 \wedge 2)$$

To evaluate this expression, we can use the computer in immediate-execution mode. We type

$$\text{PRINT } \text{SQR}(8 \wedge 2 + 9 \wedge 2)$$

Hitting the RETURN key brings the response

$$12.0415946 \qquad \square$$

EXAMPLE 4   Write an expression, using BASIC operations and functions, that gives the distance, on the number line between the divisor and the whole number quotient in this division problem: $217 \div 12$.

Solution   The whole number quotient is the greatest integer less than or equal to $\frac{217}{12}$. The distance between two numbers on the number line is the absolute value of their difference. Thus an expression that works is

$$\text{ABS}(12 - \text{INT}(217/12)) \qquad \square$$

EXAMPLE 5   Write an expression, using BASIC operations and functions, that simulates the flip of a coin.

Solution   Since flipping a coin is a random experiment, we should use the random number generator RND. This function essentially throws a dart at the interval from 0 to 1 on the number line. That is, it produces a randomly chosen number between 0 and 1. Let's agree that numbers between 0 and 0.5 will be viewed as tails, and numbers between 0.5 and 1 will be viewed as heads. If we subtract 0.5 from each number between 0 and 1, then the tails become negative and the heads remain positive. The sign function SGN would then assign -1 to each tail and 1 to each head. Thus an expression that does the job is

$$\text{SGN}(\text{RND}(1) - .5)$$

To try it out, we type

$$\text{PRINT } \text{SGN}(\text{RND}(1) - .5)$$

Hitting the RETURN key will produce either 1 or -1. To flip the coin a second time, we repeat the process of typing in the PRINT line and hitting RETURN. (We shall soon learn how to automate this process so that the machine will flip the coin for us as often as we please.) $\qquad \square$

EXERCISE SET 16.1

1. Fill in the missing entries in Table 16.3.

Table 16.3

BASIC notation	Scientific notation	Decimal notation
(a) 1.3 E + 10	_____	_____
(b) _____	2.5×10^{12}	_____
(c) _____		512,000,000,000
(d) 5 E - 10	_____	_____
(e) _____	9.7×10^{-9}	_____
(f) _____	_____	.000 000 000 012 345

2. How does your *calculator* respond when you try to find 2^{200}?

3. Fill in the missing entries in Table 16.4 in the next column.

4. Write the number that would result if you pressed the RETURN key after each of the following PRINT statements.
   (a) PRINT 5 - 3 ∧ 2 * 4 / 6
   (b) PRINT 2 ∧ (4 * 2 - 5)
   (c) PRINT -4 * (7 - 5 * 2) / 6 + 6
   (d) PRINT 6 * (14 - 3 ∧ 2) /
        -((6 + 2 * 12) / 3)

5. Fill in the missing entries in Table 16.5 in the next column.

6. What number results when you press the RETURN key after each of the following PRINT statements?
   (a) PRINT -54 * SGN(-54) 54
   (b) PRINT SGN(33 - SQR(10 ∧ 3))
   (c) PRINT INT(7.45) + SGN(7.45) 8
   (d) PRINT INT(3.7) + INT(-3.7)
   (e) PRINT INT(RND(1))
   (f) PRINT SGN(RND(1))

Table 16.4

BASIC notation	Ordinary notation	Value (in decimal notation)
(a) 1.3 * 6	_____	7.8
(b) _____	$7 \cdot 8 + 10$	66
(c) _____	$5(1.2 + 2.3)$	_____
(d) 8/5		_____
(e) _____	$108 \div 18$	_____
(f) _____	$4 + \dfrac{5}{2}$	_____
(g) _____	$\dfrac{4 + 5}{2}$	_____
(h) 4 ∧ 3	_____	_____
(i) _____	5^4	_____
(j) _____	$4 \cdot 5^2$	_____
(k) _____	$(4 \cdot 5)^2$	_____
(l) _____	2^{5-3}	_____
(m) _____	$\dfrac{2^5}{2^3}$	_____
(n) _____	$2^{2 \cdot 3}$	_____
(o) _____	$(2^2)^3$	_____
(p) _____	$2^{(2^3)}$	_____
(q) _____	$(-4)(-3)(-2)$	_____
(r) _____	$19 - {}^-12$	_____

Table 16.5

BASIC notation	Usual notation	Value
(a) _____	$\sqrt{144}$	12
(b) SQR(32 * 2)	_____	_____
(c) SQR((19 + 13) / 2)	_____	_____
(d) _____	$\sqrt{(-3)^2}$	_____
(e) ABS(-263)	_____	_____
(f) _____	$|9 \cdot 7 - 8^2|$	_____

7. Write an expression, using BASIC operations and functions.
   (a) That gives the age in years, at her last birthday, of a woman who has lived for 10,000 days
   (b) That simulates a spin of the spinner in Figure 16.4
   (c) That gives the perimeter of a square having area 50 cm^2
   (d) That gives the volume of a cube having surface area 50 cm^2

8. Which of the following are true for *every* value of X?
   (a) X * SGN(X) = ABS(X)
   (b) SQR(X ∧ 2) = ABS(X)
   (c) ABS(INT(X)) < ABS(X)
   (d) SGN(X - INT(X)) = 1

9. Determine the effect of the function X - 10 * INT(X/10) on an arbitrary whole number input X. *Hint:* Evaluate the function for several different specific whole number replacements for X and look for a pattern.

10. The INT function rounds every noninteger input down to the next lower integer. Devise a function (and express it in BASIC notation) that accepts real numbers (X) as inputs and rounds them to

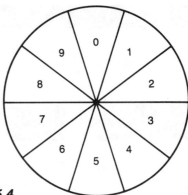

Figure 16.4

the *nearest* integer. In ambiguous cases, like 14.5, have it round up, to 15, rather than down. *Hint:* Consider what happens when 0.5 is added to various decimals.

11. In situations where money is involved it is often necessary to round amounts to the nearest cent. Devise a function that accepts real numbers as inputs and rounds them to the nearest hundredth. Use the when-in-doubt-round-up convention. *Hint:* Begin with a specific real number input like 47.38629 and try to make use of the function you found in Exercise 10, keeping in mind that you want the output to be 47.39.

16.2   *Introduction to Programming in BASIC*

We are now ready to begin using the computer in deferred-execution mode. Using the computer in immediate-execution mode is a little like standing up a domino with a PRINT statement

        PRINT 5 * 3

and then immediately knocking it over by pressing RETURN

               15

Using the computer in deferred-execution mode is more like setting up a whole pattern of dominoes and then, when you are good and ready, tipping over the first one to start the chain reaction.

In deferred-execution mode each statement is numbered. If you type

        10   PRINT   5 * 3

and press RETURN, nothing will happen. To run this one-line program, you need to type

                        RUN

Now when you press RETURN, the machine responds with

                        15

Suppose that you want to print the fifth powers of the integers 1, 2, 3. You can line up the dominoes by typing these lines (press RETURN after each line):

        10   PRINT 1 ∧ 5
        20   PRINT 2 ∧ 5
        30   PRINT 3 ∧ 5

Now when you type RUN and press RETURN, the machine will respond with the column of fifth powers:

                        1
                        32
                        243

Any numbered list of commands, like the preceding one, is called a **program.** The machine's response to it, like the column of numbers above, is called a **run** of the program.

Another program that would yield precisely the same run is this one:

        12   PRINT 2 ∧ 5
        17   PRINT 3 ∧ 5
        3   PRINT 1 ∧ 5

The computer carries out the commands in numerical order, no matter where they happen to appear in the program. This feature makes it very easy to insert extra steps into a program having lines numbered 10, 20, 30, ... To fit one in between steps 10 and 20, simply type a line numbered, say, 15. If we had numbered the lines of our program as 1, 2, 3, however, this insertion would not have been possible. The computer will not accept a line number like 1.5; line numbers must be positive integers.

Programming Commands

Recall that an algorithm is a step-by-step procedure. When the steps are represented schematically by variously shaped boxes and sequenced by chains of arrows, we call it a flowchart. When the steps are commands that a computer can carry out, we call it a program. In BASIC the sequencing of steps is accomplished by numbering the steps and by using certain signposts within the program itself. In other languages other sequencing conventions are used.

The only command we have encountered so far is the PRINT command. This command is an output command, and it corresponds roughly to our flowchart symbol

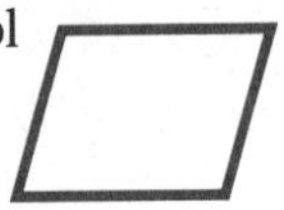

To write nontrivial programs, we need to learn some other commands. Perhaps the best way to learn is to look at some simple programs.

EXAMPLE 1   An instructor gave a 40-point quiz to six students. The scores were 27, 36, 33, 25, 31, and 28. She decides to convert these scores to equivalent scores based on 100 possible points by multiplying each by $\frac{100}{40}$. Figure 16.5 shows a program that does the job. A run of this program is shown in Figure 16.6.   ❏

```
10   READ R
20   LET S = R * 100/40
30   PRINT S
40   GOTO 10
50   DATA 27, 36, 33, 25, 31, 28
60   END
```

Figure 16.5

```
]RUN
67.5
90
82.5
62.5
77.5
70
```

Figure 16.6

The input command in the program of Figure 16.5, which corresponds roughly to our flowchart symbol

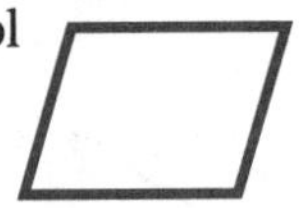

is the pair of statements READ, DATA. Clearly, the DATA statement supplies the computer with the six raw scores on the quiz. The statement

$$10 \quad READ \ R$$

is a little more complicated. It tells the computer to go to the list of data, remove the first piece, and store it in its memory at location R. Think of the memory of the computer as a collection of window envelopes labeled with letters of the alphabet. Think of the command READ R as causing a messenger to fetch from DATA the first scrap of paper, the one with 27 written on it, and to slip it into envelope R. (We could as well have used envelope A and the command READ A, but R is more suggestive of raw score.)

The next command

$$20 \quad \text{LET } S = R * 100/40$$

tells the messenger to read what is in envelope R (namely 27), multiply it by 100, divide by 40, write the result (67.5) on a slip of paper, and store it in envelope S (S for score). This computational step in the algorithm corresponds roughly to an operation box

in a flowchart.

The third command

$$30 \quad \text{PRINT } S$$

instructs the messenger to look through the window of envelope S, copy down its contents, and send it off to the TV screen or the printer.

The next command

$$40 \quad \text{GOTO } 10$$

is one of the internal signposts we mentioned earlier. It acts like a sequencing arrow in a flowchart, and it simply instructs the computer to go back to step 10 rather than to the next higher-numbered step, as it normally would.

Now back at the READ step, the situation is slightly different. The first surviving piece of data is 36. The messenger takes the old scrap of paper (bearing 27) out of envelope R, destroys it, and inserts the new scrap (bearing 36) into envelope R. This time, at the LET step, the calculation is

$$36 * 100/40 = 90$$

The new score 90 is inserted into envelope S in place of the previous one 67.5, which is destroyed. Finally, 90 gets sent to the TV screen or the printer at the PRINT step.

Once again the computer arrives at the line

$$40 \quad \text{GOTO } 10$$

and the process repeats with the third piece of data, 33. The procedure continues to go round and round, like a loop in a flowchart, until the last number in DATA, 28, has been processed and its equivalent score (70) printed. Again, the GOTO statement sends the computer back to the READ statement. This time there is no data remaining in line 50, so the computer moves to the next higher-numbered line to look for more data. Instead, it encounters

60   END

which simply tells the computer to stop. The END command corresponds to the stop button

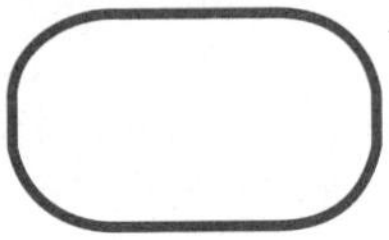

that we used in our flowcharts.

There is another input command that, unlike the READ . . . DATA statements, allows the person at the keyboard to input data *while the program is being run.* Programs that permit this are appropriately called **interactive programs,** and the crucial command is INPUT. Figure 16.7 shows an interactive program that performs the same score conversion as the previous program. But now when you type RUN, the computer responds with a question mark. It is your move, and you can reply with any number you please. The computer will put your number into envelope R, carry out the computation in line 20, respond with the equivalent score, and return to line 10. Thus if you type 27, the computer will print out its equivalent score, 67.5, and then flash another question mark. This tells you it is ready for a new piece of data.

```
10    INPUT R
20    LET S = R * 100/40
30    PRINT S
40    GOTO 10
```

Figure 16.7

Figure 16.8 shows a run of this program in which the keyboard operator fed in the same six raw scores that we used in our first program.

After you have processed all of your data, you can end a program like this one by simply turning off the machine. Of course, turning off the machine erases its memory. If you ever wanted to use the program in Figure 16.7 again, you would have to retype it line by line. A way of avoiding retyping is to exit the program without turning off the machine (by pressing control C on the Apple) and then to use appropriate system commands to copy the program onto an external memory device, typically a disk in the disk drive. The next section describes how to do it.

```
]RUN
?27
67.5
?36
90
?33
82.5
?25
62.5
?31
77.5
?28
70
?
```

Figure 16.8

System Commands*

While the machine is still on, and the program of Figure 16.7 is still in its memory, decide on a name for the program—let's say "score conversion." Then type the line

SAVE   SCORE CONVERSION

When RETURN is pressed, the disk drive will copy the program onto the disk under the name SCORE CONVERSION. The command SAVE is called a system command, as opposed to the programming commands such as PRINT and LET that we considered earlier.

Now suppose that a few months later you want to use the program again. After putting the disk in the disk drive, you type the system command CATALOG. When you press RETURN, the names of all programs stored on that disk are displayed on the TV screen. Among them you see SCORE CONVERSION. To put it into the computer's memory, you use another system command, LOAD. When you type

LOAD   SCORE CONVERSION

and press RETURN, the disk drive reverses what it did when it saved the program. It puts a copy of SCORE CONVERSION back into the computer (but keeps its own copy for future use).

---

*In this section we assume that disk operating system (DOS) programs were loaded into the computer's memory when it was turned on.

Before running the program, you probably want to remind yourself of what it does. The system command LIST is just what is needed. When you type LIST and press RETURN, the machine will respond by displaying the complete program as shown in Figure 16.7.

Dressing up a Program

Coming back to the program in Figure 16.7 after a few months away could be a disorienting experience. You might have forgotten just what it does or how to interact with it. A REM (reminder) statement at the beginning of the program can be helpful. The line

```
5   REM CONVERTS 40-POINT SCORES TO 100-POINT SCORES
```

has absolutely no effect on the running of the program, but it does appear at the top of the program each time you LIST it.

The PRINT command can be modified in a number of ways to improve the clarity of a program's run. You can print anything you want—numbers, letters, words, gibberish—by simply putting it in quotation marks after the word PRINT. For example, in immediate-execution mode, typing

```
PRINT "HE TOLD ME THAT 8 + 9 WAS 15, AND I
            BELIEVED HIM!@#*!"
```

and pressing RETURN will yield

```
HE TOLD ME THAT 8 + 9 WAS 15, AND I BELIEVED HIM!@#*!
```

Notice that the machine does *not* look at 8 + 9 and print 17 the way it did earlier. It prints things within quotation marks just as they are, symbol for symbol, including the extra spaces around the expression 8 + 9.

Suppose now that you want the machine to print the following:

```
FOR YOUR INFORMATION, 8 + 9 = 17.
```

The easy way to do it would be to type

```
PRINT "FOR YOUR INFORMATION, 8 + 9 = 17."
```

Another way to do it, which puts the burden of computation on the machine, is to type

```
PRINT "FOR YOUR INFORMATION, 8 + 9 = "; 8 + 9
```

When the machine sees the quotation marks, it faithfully reproduces everything between them, including the space following the equals sign. When it sees the semicolon, it does not space, but holds its position. When it sees 8 + 9 with *no* quotation marks, it calculates the sum (17) and prints it. If you insist on ending the sentence with a period, then type

```
PRINT "FOR YOUR INFORMATION, 8 + 9 =  "; 8 + 9; "."
```

Pressing RETURN will yield

```
FOR YOUR INFORMATION, 8 + 9 = 17.
```

Consider now the revision shown in Figure 16.9 of our interactive score conversion program. We have added two entirely new lines, the REM line 5 and the PRINT line 7. Line 7 explains to the user of the program what the input question mark is asking for. We also revised two old lines. Old line 30 was automatically deleted as soon as we typed in new line 30, which explains to the user the significance of the machine's response to the user's input. Notice that new line 30 has the machine print the number from envelope S after the word IS. New line 40 replaces old line 40. Its effect is to have the machine print the explanatory instructions in line 7 every time a new input is about to be called for. A three-input run of this improved program is shown in Figure 16.10.

Other modifications of the PRINT command are illustrated in the following example.

```
5    REM CONVERTS 40-POINT SCORES TO 100-POINT SCORES
7    PRINT "INPUT 40-POINT SCORE"
10   INPUT R
20   LET S = R * 100/40
30   PRINT "CORRESPONDING 100-POINT SCORE IS "; S
40   GOTO 7
```

Figure 16.9

```
INPUT 40-POINT SCORE
?27
CORRESPONDING 100-POINT SCORE IS 67.5
INPUT 40-POINT SCORE
?36
CORRESPONDING 100-POINT SCORE IS 90
INPUT 40-POINT SCORE
?33
CORRESPONDING 100-POINT SCORE IS 82.5
```

Figure 16.10

EXAMPLE 2   Suppose you are teaching a unit on the Pythagorean theorem, and you want
the computer to produce a short table of squares and square roots to distribute
to your class. Figure 16.11 shows a program that does the job, and Figure
16.12 shows the run.   ❏

```
10    REM TABLE OF SQUARES AND SQUARE ROOTS
20    PRINT "NUMBER", "SQUARE", "SQUARE ROOT"
30    PRINT
40    READ N
50    LET S = N * N
60    LET R = SQR(N)
70    PRINT N, S, R
80    GOTO 40
90    DATA 1, 2, 3, 4, 5, 6, 7, 8, 9, 10, 11,
         12, 13, 14, 15, 16, 17, 18, 19, 20
100   END
```

Figure 16.11

```
]RUN
```

NUMBER	SQUARE	SQUARE ROOT
1	1	1
2	4	1.41421356
3	9	1.73205081
4	16	2
5	25	2.23606798
6	36	2.44948974
7	49	2.64575131
8	64	2.82842713
9	81	3
10	100	3.16227766
11	121	3.31662479
12	144	3.46410162
13	169	3.60555128
14	196	3.74165739
15	225	3.87298335
16	256	4
17	289	4.12310563
18	324	4.24264069
19	361	4.35889894
20	400	4.47213595

Figure 16.12

To see how the neat 3-column display in Figure 16.12 was accomplished, look at the PRINT commands in the program. Notice the commas in line 20:

```
20   PRINT "NUMBER", "SQUARE", "SQUARE ROOT"
```

Commas in a PRINT statement act like a tab key on a typewriter. The display field is separated into three columns, as in Figure 16.12; a comma in a PRINT statement shifts the printing from one column to the next. That is why the three headings in Figure 16.12 are spaced out as they are. The commas in line 70

```
70   PRINT N, S, R
```

have the same effect: The contents of envelopes N, S, and R are printed in the first, second, and third columns, respectively.

The unembellished PRINT command in line 30,

```
30   PRINT
```

simply produces a line of empty space below the headings.

Illustrations of the use of quotation marks, semicolons, and commas in PRINT statements are given in Table 16.6. Table 16.7 summarizes all of the commands we have encountered so far. In the next section we will add two more powerful programming commands.

Table 16.6 Some PRINT Statements

Command	Display		
PRINT 5 ∧ 2	25		
PRINT "5 ∧ 2"	5 ∧ 2		
PRINT "BABBAGE"	BABBAGE		
PRINT "9 * 7 = "; 9 * 7	9 * 7 = 63		
PRINT 5 ∧ 2, 3, 8/4	25	3	2
PRINT			
PRINT 5 ∧ 2; 3, 8/4	253	2	

Table 16.7 Some BASIC Commands

Programming commands	System commands
PRINT (" " , ;)	SAVE
READ . . . DATA	CATALOG
LET	LOAD
GOTO	LIST
END	
INPUT	
REM	

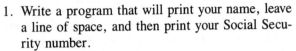

1. Write a program that will print your name, leave a line of space, and then print your Social Security number.

2. Revise the program of Exercise 1 so that it will print your street address and your city and state on two lines right below your name, then skip a line, and finally print your Social Security number.

3. Revise the program of Exercise 1 (again) so that it will print your zip code under your city and state and continue to skip a line above your Social Security number.

4. Here is a program that gets the computer to behave like the function machine $f(x) = 3x^2 - 5$ with input set $\{1, 2, 3, 4, 5\}$. That is, for each input, in turn, the computer will square, triple, subtract 5, and print the output.

```
10    READ X
20    LET Y = 3 * X ∧ 2 - 5
30    PRINT Y
40    GOTO 10
50    DATA 1, 2, 3, 4, 5
60    END
```

   (a) What numbers are in memory locations X and Y when the computer reaches line 30 for the first time?

   (b) What numbers are in memory locations X and Y immediately after the computer reads 4 from data?

5. Write a program that will send inputs from $\{1, 2, 3, 4, 5\}$ through the given function machine, and print the corresponding outputs.

   (a) $f(x) = 4 - 5x$

   (b) $g(x) = (x - 1)(x^2 + x + 1)$

   (c) $h(x) = \dfrac{x + 1}{5 - x}$ How does your machine respond to the input 5?

   (d) $r(x) = \sqrt{17 - x^2}$ How does your machine respond to the input 5?

6. Here is an interactive program that gets the computer to behave like the function machine $f(x) = 3x^2 - 5$:

```
10    INPUT X
20    LET Y = 3 * X ∧ 2 - 5
30    PRINT Y
40    GOTO 10
```

   (a) Suppose that the first time the machine flashed a question mark, you responded with the number 10. What numbers are in memory locations X and Y when the machine flashes the second question mark?

   (b) How is this interactive program more versatile than the program in Exercise 4?

7. Write interactive programs that get the computer to behave like each of these function machines.

   (a) $p(x) = x^2 + 5x - 14$

   (b) $a(x) = 2x - 19$

8. Suppose the computer is being used in immediate-execution mode. When RETURN is pressed after each of these PRINT commands, something will be displayed on the screen. Print exactly what will appear.

   (a) PRINT 8 ∧ 2; 64

   (b) PRINT 8 ∧ 2, 64

   (c) PRINT "8 ∧ 2 = 2 ∧ 6"

   (d) PRINT "8 ∧ 2 = "; 2 ∧ 6

9. Here is a program that lacks a PRINT command:

```
10    LET A = 5
20    LET B = SQR(A)
30    LET C = INT(B)
50    END
```

If it were run as it stands, nothing would be displayed on the screen or be printed by the printer. A variety of PRINT commands are given next. Insert each one, in turn, into the program; then, pretend you are the computer, and print what the machine would.

(a) 40 PRINT C
(b) 40 PRINT C; A
(c) 40 PRINT C, A, C + 1
(d) 40 PRINT "THE SQUARE ROOT OF A
         IS BETWEEN C AND C + 1"
(e) 40 PRINT "THE SQUARE ROOT OF ";
         A; "IS BETWEEN "; C; " AND ";
         C + 1
(f) 40 PRINT C $\wedge$ 2; " < "; A; " < ";
         (C + 1) $\wedge$ 2

10. Revise line 60 in the program in Figure 16.11 so that when the program is run (Figure 16.12), square roots will be displayed with only two digits to the right of the decimal point. *Hint:* To print a decimal with only two decimal places, multiply it by 100, eliminate all digits after the decimal point, and then divide it by 100. For example,
2.23606798 → 223.606798 → 223 → 2.23

11. Write a READ . . . DATA program that converts weights in pounds to weights in kilograms. Use the approximate conversion factor 1 pound $\doteq$ 0.45 kilogram. Use these weights in pounds as your data:

80, 92, 96, 109, 114, 125, 130, 160

Include a REM statement, and write your PRINT statements in such a way that the printout will list the corresponding weights in two columns under the headings POUNDS and KILOGRAMS.

12. Suppose that the 8 employees at your hamburger stand worked these hours last week,

32, 20, 24, 18, 30, 35, 28, 24

and that each earns $3.50 per hour. Write a READ . . . DATA program that lists hours and earnings in two columns. Include a REM statement and appropriate column headings.

13. Write an interactive program that accomplishes the weight conversion called for in Exercise 11. Include a REM statement and PRINT statements that tell the user what sort of input is expected from her and what the machine's response to it represents.

14. Write an interactive program that assigns earnings to hours at the hamburger stand in Exercise 12. Include a REM statement and PRINT statements that let the user know what is going on.

15. Write an interactive program that asks the user to input a whole number dividend (N) and a whole number divisor (D), and responds with the whole number quotient (Q) and remainder (R).

16. Complete this interactive program that asks the user to input the coordinates of (any) three points—(A1, A2), (B1, B2), (C1, C2)—in the Cartesian coordinate plane, and responds with the perimeter and the area of the triangle they determine. Validate your program by applying it to a triangle whose perimeter and area you can find by hand. *Hint:* Use Heron's formula. Note that symbols such as A1, A2, B1, . . . are perfectly acceptable variable names in BASIC.

```
10   REM FINDS PERIMETER AND AREA OF
     TRIANGLE IN COORDINATE PLANE
20   PRINT "ENTER COORDINATES OF
     ONE VERTEX"
30   INPUT A1
40   INPUT A2
50   PRINT "ENTER COORDINATES OF
     SECOND VERTEX"
60   INPUT B1
70   INPUT B2
80   PRINT "ENTER COORDINATES OF
     THIRD VERTEX"
90   INPUT C1
100  INPUT C2
```

16.3   *BASIC Commands for Looping and Branching*

In our early work with flowchart representation of algorithms, we observed that the most interesting flowcharts included loops and decision boxes (at which branching occurs). In BASIC, IF . . . THEN commands correspond to decision boxes, and FOR . . . NEXT commands correspond to loops.

FOR . . . NEXT Commands

Suppose you want the computer to print out the first 20 powers of 2. One program that does so is given in Figure 16.13. The tedious part of this program is typing all the data at line 50. By using FOR . . . NEXT commands, we can avoid that chore.

```
10   READ E
20   LET P = 2 ∧ E
30   PRINT P
40   GOTO 10
50   DATA 1, 2, 3, 4, 5, 6, 7, 8, 9, 10, 11,
          12, 13, 14, 15, 16, 17, 18, 19, 20
60   END
```

Figure 16.13

Figure 16.14 shows a program that produces precisely the same printout as the one in Figure 16.13.

```
10   FOR E = 1 TO 20
20   LET P = 2 ∧ E
30   PRINT P
40   NEXT E
50   END
```

Figure 16.14

The computer reacts to this program's **FOR . . . NEXT loop,** as lines 10–40 are known, as follows. When it sees FOR E = 1 in line 10, it puts the number 1 into envelope E and moves to line 20. At line 20 it looks through the window of envelope E, sees the 1, calculates $2 \wedge 1$, and puts that number (2) into envelope P. At line 30 it looks through the window of envelope P and prints what it sees there (2). Line 40 directs the machine to loop back to line 10 and use the *next* E, namely, 2. So now the machine puts 2 into envelope E (destroying the number, 1, that was there), calculates $2 \wedge 2$ and puts that number into envelope P (destroying the number, 2, that was there), prints the number

(4) that is now in P, and comes once more to line 40. Again the machine is sent back to line 10 with orders to use the *next* E, which this time is 3. On its third trip through the loop the machine prints $8 = 2 \wedge 3$. On its fourth trip it prints $16 = 2 \wedge 4$, and so on until on its twentieth trip it prints $1,048,576 = 2 \wedge 20$. Again, line 40 sends the machine back to line 10. But now there is no next E, because the phrase TO 20 in line 10 put a cap on the values that E could assume. The machine reacts by jumping to the line immediately following the FOR . . . NEXT loop, in this case line 50, which ends the program.

FOR . . . NEXT loops are very useful. They transfer much of the drudgery of repetitive tasks from the programmer to the machine.

EXAMPLE 1 Write a program, with a FOR . . . NEXT loop, that will print a table of squares and square roots of the first 20 positive integers, as in Figure 16.12.

Solution We need only amend the program in Figure 16.11 as follows: Replace old line 40 by

$$40 \quad \text{FOR } N = 1 \text{ TO } 20$$

replace old line 80 by

$$80 \quad \text{NEXT } N$$

and delete old line 90 entirely (by simply typing the line number with no subsequent command). ❏

EXAMPLE 2 Write a program that will print an input-output table for the function

$$f(x) = x^3 - 2x^2 - 45x + 120$$

with domain the set of all integers from -5 to 5.

Solution Figure 16.15 shows a program, and Figure 16.16 shows a run.

```
10   REM INPUT-OUTPUT TABLE FOR A THIRD-DEGREE
     POLYNOMIAL
20   PRINT "INPUT", "OUTPUT"
30   PRINT
40   FOR X = -5 TO 5
50   LET Y = X ∧ 3 - 2 * X ∧ 2 - 45 * X + 120
60   PRINT X, Y
70   NEXT X
80   END
```

Figure 16.15

```
]RUN
INPUT                      OUTPUT

-5                         170
-4                         204
-3                         210
-2                         194
-1                         162
0                          120
1                          74
2                          30
3                          -6
4                          -28
5                          -30
```

Figure 16.16   ❏

Suppose for the function of Example 2 that we wanted to find the input (a *real number* between −5 and 5) that leads to output 0. In the language of algebra suppose we wanted to solve the equation

$$x^3 - 2x^2 - 45x + 120 = 0$$

subject to the constraint $-5 \leq x \leq 5$. Inspection of the printout in Figure 16.16 tells us that as inputs increase from 2 to 3, outputs fall from positive (30) to negative (−6). Thus the input that produces output 0 must lie between 2 and 3.

A minor modification of the FOR command lets us take a closer look at what happens for X values between 2 and 3. When we replace old line 40 by

```
40   FOR X = 2 TO 3 STEP .1
```

and leave the rest of the program just as it is, the machine successively uses 2, 2.1, 2.2, . . . , 2.9, 3 for X, as shown in Figure 16.17. The printout of the revised program shows that the outputs Y drop from positive to negative as X increases from 2.8 to 2.9.

```
]RUN
INPUT                      OUTPUT

2                          30
2.1                        25.941
2.2                        21.968
2.3                        18.087
2.4                        14.3040001
2.5                        10.6250001
```

2.6	7.05600009
2.7	3.60300011
2.8	.272000104
2.9	−2.93099988
3	−5.99999988

Figure 16.17

To put a magnifying glass over this interval, revise line 40 again,

$$40 \quad \text{FOR X} = 2.8 \text{ TO } 2.9 \text{ STEP } .01$$

and the machine will compute Y values for each of X = 2.8, 2.81, 2.82, . . . , 2.89, 2.9 in turn, as shown in Figure 16.18. Now when we inspect the printout we see that Y drops from positive to negative as X increases from 2.8 to 2.81. Pacing off this interval in steps of .001 would place the X value we seek between 2.808 and 2.809. In this way we could approximate the desired X value to any reasonable number of decimal places. Recall that we used exactly this method to solve two practical problems in Section 1.2.

```
]RUN
INPUT                              OUTPUT

2.8                                .272000015
2.81                               −.0541589558
2.82                               −.379031956
2.83                               −.702612936
2.84                               −1.02489594
2.85                               −1.34587494
2.86                               −1.66554394
2.87                               −1.98389694
2.88                               −2.30092791
2.89                               −2.61663091
2.9                                −2.93099991
```

Figure 16.18

EXAMPLE 3   Write an interactive program that calculates factorials.

Solution   Recall that 5 factorial, written 5!, is defined by

$$5! = 5 \cdot 4 \cdot 3 \cdot 2 \cdot 1$$

and in general,

$$n! = n \cdot (n - 1) \cdot (n - 2) \cdot \quad \cdots \quad \cdot 3 \cdot 2 \cdot 1$$

We need a program that, when presented with a positive integer *n*, multiplies all positive integers up to and including *n*. Lines 30–70 of the program in Figure 16.19 accomplish this task. Let us see how.

```
10    REM CALCULATES FACTORIALS
20    PRINT "INPUT A POSITIVE INTEGER"
30    INPUT N
40    LET F = 1
50    FOR I = 1 TO N
60    LET F = I * F
70    NEXT I
80    PRINT N; "! = "; F
90    PRINT
100   GOTO 20
```

Figure 16.19

In line 30 the user inputs the number of his choice, say N = 4. In line 40 a 1 is placed into envelope F, in which 4! will ultimately appear. Figure 16.20 shows the changing contents of envelopes F and I, and the unchanging contents of envelope N, as the machine loops through lines 50–70 four times.

After four loops the machine exits to line 80, prints the contents of envelopes N and F in the format specified, and then goes back to line 20 and asks for another input. A sample run of the program is shown in Figure 16.21.

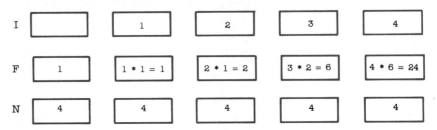

Figure 16.20

```
INPUT A POSITIVE INTEGER
?4
4! = 24

INPUT A POSITIVE INTEGER
?6
6! = 720

INPUT A POSITIVE INTEGER
?20
20! = 2.43290201E+18
```

Figure 16.21

IF . . . THEN Commands

An IF . . . THEN command in a computer program corresponds to a decision box in a flowchart. The kinds of decisions the computer is capable of making are simple ones concerning the relative sizes of two numbers. These size relations are given in Table 16.8.

Table 16.8

Standard notation	Relation	Computer notation
$=$	equal	$=$
$\neq$	not equal	$<>$
$<$	less than	$<$
$\leq$	less than or equal	$<=$
$>$	greater than	$>$
$\geq$	greater than or equal	$>=$

The IF clause of an IF . . . THEN command asks the computer a yes-no question about the sizes of two numbers. A yes answer by the computer sends it to the line number contained in the THEN clause; a no answer moves it to the line immediately following the IF . . . THEN statement.

Figure 16.22 shows a program that tests a number for divisibility by 7. A sample run is shown in Figure 16.23. The key steps in the program are lines 40 and 50. If N is divisible by 7, then the quotient $N/7 = Q$ will equal its integer part, and the machine will jump to line 90. If N is not divisible by 7, then the quotient will not equal its integer part, and the machine will go on to line 60.

The flowchart representation of lines 30, 40, 50, 60, and 90 shown in Figure 16.24 emphasizes the branching that the IF . . . THEN command effects.

The program in Figure 16.22, like several before it, has one annoying aspect—it keeps asking for more inputs. To stifle it we have to use a special keyboard control or else turn off the computer. In the next example we will see how to use an IF . . . THEN command to silence a garrulous program.

```
10    REM TESTS FOR DIVISIBILITY BY 7
20    PRINT "INPUT ANY INTEGER"
30    INPUT N
40    LET Q = N/7
50    IF Q = INT(Q) THEN 90
60    PRINT N; "IS NOT DIVISIBLE BY 7"
70    PRINT
80    GOTO 20
90    PRINT N; "IS DIVISIBLE BY 7"
100   PRINT
110   GOTO 20
```

Figure 16.22

```
]RUN
INPUT ANY INTEGER
?50
50 IS NOT DIVISIBLE BY 7

INPUT ANY INTEGER
?49
49 IS DIVISIBLE BY 7

INPUT ANY INTEGER
?13579
13579 IS NOT DIVISIBLE BY 7

INPUT ANY INTEGER
?97531
97531 IS DIVISIBLE BY 7
```

Figure 16.23

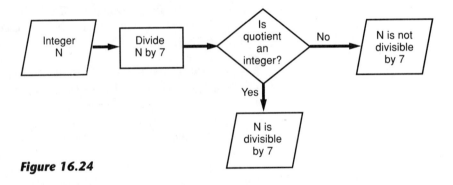

Figure 16.24

EXAMPLE 4   Write an interactive program that cubes numbers for the user until the user wishes to quit.

Solution   A program is shown in Figure 16.25. A sample run is shown in Figure 16.26. The branching in this program is arranged for in lines 20 and 30 and accomplished in line 40. The user is flashed the question in line 20 and decides whether to play or not. At line 30 the user signifies yes by placing the number 1 in envelope A ("A" for answer), and no by placing the number 0 there. At line 40 the machine looks through the window in envelope A. If it sees 0 there, it jumps to line 100, which ends the program. If it does not see 0, then it proceeds to the next line, 50, which initiates the cubing portion of the program. Do you see that typing a 7 for yes would work just as well as typing a 1?

```
10    REM POLITE NUMBER CUBER
20    PRINT "WOULD YOU LIKE TO HAVE A NUMBER CUBED?
      IF YES, TYPE IN 1.  IF NO, TYPE IN 0."
30    INPUT A
40    IF A = 0 THEN 100
50    PRINT "WHAT NUMBER WOULD YOU LIKE CUBED?"
60    INPUT N
70    PRINT "THE CUBE OF "; N; " IS "; N ∧ 3
80    PRINT
90    GOTO 20
100   END
```

Figure 16.25

```
]RUN
WOULD YOU LIKE TO HAVE A NUMBER CUBED? IF YES,
TYPE IN 1. IF NO, TYPE IN 0.
?1
WHAT NUMBER WOULD YOU LIKE CUBED?
?7
THE CUBE OF 7 IS 343

WOULD YOU LIKE TO HAVE A NUMBER CUBED? IF YES,
TYPE IN 1. IF NO, TYPE IN 0.
?0
```

Figure 16.26   ❑

EXAMPLE 5   Write a program that asks for a dividend and a divisor and responds with the quotient rounded to the nearest whole number.

Solution   Before we can work out a program, we need to resolve an ambiguity in the problem. What are we to do in a case where the quotient falls exactly between two whole numbers, as in $7 \div 2$? In such cases we might agree to always round down, always round up, flip a coin, always round to an even number, or always round to an odd number. Let's agree to always round up.

In the program in Figure 16.27 lines 60 and 70 calculate the integer part, I, of the quotient, and the rest of it, J. In line 80 the machine is asked if this other part is less than 0.5. If so, the nearest whole number to the quotient is just I. If not, then the nearest whole number to the quotient is $I + 1$.

The sample run in Figure 16.28 indicates that our program does what it is supposed to. In the exercises you are asked to make this program more polite by including interactive questions.   ❑

```
10    REM FINDS QUOTIENTS TO THE NEAREST WHOLE NUMBER
20    PRINT "WHAT IS THE DIVIDEND"
30    INPUT N
40    PRINT "WHAT IS THE DIVISOR"
50    INPUT D
60    LET I = INT(N/D)
70    LET J = N/D - I
80    IF J < .5 THEN 110
90    LET W = I + 1
100   GOTO 120
110   LET W = I
120   PRINT "THE QUOTIENT ROUNDED TO THE NEAREST WHOLE
      NUMBER IS "; W
130   GOTO 20
```

Figure 16.27

```
]RUN
WHAT IS THE DIVIDEND
?14
WHAT IS THE DIVISOR
?10
THE QUOTIENT ROUNDED TO THE NEAREST WHOLE NUMBER IS 1
WHAT IS THE DIVIDEND
?16
WHAT IS THE DIVISOR
?10
THE QUOTIENT ROUNDED TO THE NEAREST WHOLE NUMBER IS 2
WHAT IS THE DIVIDEND
?15
WHAT IS THE DIVISOR
?10
THE QUOTIENT ROUNDED TO THE NEAREST WHOLE NUMBER IS 2
WHAT IS THE DIVIDEND
?14.789
WHAT IS THE DIVISOR
?10.106
THE QUOTIENT ROUNDED TO THE NEAREST WHOLE NUMBER IS 1
WHAT IS THE DIVIDEND
?
```

Figure 16.28

Let us consider now a program that involves both of our new commands, FOR . . . NEXT and IF . . . THEN.

EXAMPLE 6   Write a program that accepts a positive integer as an input and responds with its smallest prime factor.

Solution   A program is shown in Figure 16.29, and a sample run is shown in Figure 16.30. To see how this program accomplishes its task, suppose the operator begins by inputting 55 for N at line 30. Then in lines 40–60 the machine divides 55 by 2, notices that the quotient 27.5 is not an integer (does not equal its integer part), and tries the next divisor, 3. Again, 55 divided by 3 is not an integer, so the machine tests the next divisor, 4, with the same result. When it tries the next divisor D = 5, it sees that $\frac{55}{5}$ is an integer, so it follows the instructions in the THEN clause of line 50: it jumps out of the loop to line 90. The divisor D = 5 is placed in envelope P and is subsequently printed. Line 110 starts the whole process over again.

```
10    REM FINDS SMALLEST PRIME FACTOR
20    PRINT "INPUT A POSITIVE INTEGER GREATER THAN 3"
30    INPUT N
40    FOR D = 2 TO INT(SQR(N))
50    IF N/D = INT(N/D) THEN 90
60    NEXT D
70    LET P = N
80    GOTO 100
90    LET P = D
100   PRINT P; " IS THE SMALLEST PRIME FACTOR OF "; N
110   GOTO 20
```

Figure 16.29

```
]RUN
INPUT A POSITIVE INTEGER GREATER THAN 3
?55
5 IS THE SMALLEST PRIME FACTOR OF 55
INPUT A POSITIVE INTEGER GREATER THAN 3
?59
59 IS THE SMALLEST PRIME FACTOR OF 59
INPUT A POSITIVE INTEGER GREATER THAN 3
?10007
10007 IS THE SMALLEST PRIME FACTOR OF 10007
```

Figure 16.30

Suppose that this time the operator inputs 59 for N at line 30. Now line 40 instructs the machine to test each of the integers from 2 to 7 in turn to see whether they divide into 59 without remainder. None do, so after six trips around the loop the computer moves on to line 70, where it places the original input 59 in envelope P. Then it jumps to line 100, where 59 is printed as the smallest prime factor of 59 (from which we conclude that 59 is a prime number).

The only fine point that we brought in from number theory is that to test a number for primeness, one need only try divisors up to its square root (see p. 249). Had we not known that fact, line 40 would have been

$$40 \quad \text{FOR } D = 2 \text{ TO } N$$

and the machine would have run around the loop 58 times before finally moving on to line 70 and subsequently declaring that 59 is prime.

For small numbers the preceding line 40 is not much worse than the original line 40. For large inputs, though, there is a difference. With the original line 40 my machine needed less than 2 seconds to decide that 10,007 is prime. With the new line 40 the same decision required 110 seconds. After all, even a speedy machine takes some time to run around a loop more than 10,000 times! The difference in efficiency between the two programs emphasizes that even in an age when machines do the computing, people still need to know some mathematics. ❏

EXERCISE SET 16.3

1. Trace through these programs, and print just what the computer would.

   (a) 10 FOR I = 1 TO 5
       20 PRINT 3 * I + 2
       30 NEXT I
       40 END

   (b) 10 FOR N = 1 TO 5
       20 LET M = N - 3
       30 PRINT SGN(M)
       40 NEXT N
       50 END

   (c) 10 FOR I = 1 TO 10 STEP 3
       20 PRINT I
       30 NEXT I
       40 END

   (d) 10 FOR I = 0 TO 2 STEP .5
       20 PRINT I, ABS(2 - 3 * I)
       30 NEXT I
       40 END

   (e) 10 FOR I = 5.5 TO 2.5 STEP -1
       20 PRINT 4 * I
       30 NEXT I
       40 END

   ★(f) 10 FOR I = 2 TO 4
       20 FOR J = 5 TO 6
       30 LET K = I * J
       40 PRINT I, J, K
       50 NEXT J
       60 NEXT I
       70 END

2. Write a program, with a FOR . . . NEXT loop, that does the following.
   (a) Prints a list of the first 20 odd numbers
   (b) Prints a table of first, second, and third powers of all positive integers from 1 to 50.

3. Write a program that prints an input-output table for each of the following functions.
   (a) $f(x) = (x - 2)^2$ with domain $\{0, 1, 2, 3, 4\}$

(b) $g(x) = \frac{1}{2}x + 3$ with domain $\{-4, -3, -2,$ $-1, 0, 1, 2, 3, 4\}$

(c) $h(x) = \sqrt{x^2 + 2x}$ with domain $\{0, .5, 1,$ $1.5, 2, 2.5, 3\}$

(d) $k(x) = |1 - x^2|$ with domain $\{0, .4, .8,$ $1.2, 1.6, 2\}$

4. The equation $x^2 + x - 1 = 0$ has a solution somewhere between $x = 0$ and $x = 1$.
   (a) Write a program that can be used to bracket the solution between successive tenths.
   (b) Revise the program in part (a) to bracket the solution between successive hundredths.

5. Write a program that simulates flipping a coin 50 times in succession, and prints the 50 outcomes. Represent heads by 1 and tails by 0.

6. Write a program that simulates rolling a die 50 times in succession, and prints the 50 outcomes. *Hint:* The range of the random number function, RND, is the interval of numbers between 0 and 1. Multiply each output of this function by 6, then add 1 to the integer part.

7. The following program calculates combination numbers. Recall that the number of combinations of 10 things taken 4 at a time is

$$C_4^{10} = \frac{10 \cdot 9 \cdot 8 \cdot 7}{4 \cdot 3 \cdot 2 \cdot 1}$$

and in general,

$$C_r^n = \frac{n(n - 1)(n - 2) \cdots (n - r + 1)}{r!}$$

```
10    PRINT "HOW MANY THINGS"
20    INPUT N
30    PRINT "TAKEN HOW MANY AT A
      TIME"
40    INPUT R
50    LET A = 1
60    LET B = 1
70    FOR I = 1 TO R
80    LET A = A * (N - I + 1)
90    LET B = B * I
100   NEXT I
110   LET C = A/B
```

```
120   PRINT "THE NUMBER OF
      COMBINATIONS IS "; C
130   GOTO 10
140   END
```

Trace through the program by hand. Then complete Table 16.9, the record of the contents of envelopes (memory locations) N, R, I, A, B, C when 7 is input for N and 3 for R.

Table 16.9

N	7	7	7	7
R	3	3	3	3
I		1	2	3
A	1	?	?	?
B	1	?	?	?
C				?

8. Revise the program of Exercise 7 so it calculates permutation numbers. Recall that the number of permutations of 10 things taken 4 at a time is
   $P_4^{10} = 10 \cdot 9 \cdot 8 \cdot 7$
   and in general,
   $P_r^n = n(n - 1)(n - 2) \cdots (n - r + 1)$

9. Trace through these programs, and print just what the computer would.
   (a)
   ```
   10 READ X
   20 IF X < 5 THEN 50
   30 LET Y = X + 1
   40 GOTO 60
   50 LET Y = X * 3
   60 PRINT Y
   70 DATA 1, 9, 4, 5
   80 GOTO 10
   90 END
   ```
   3, 10, 12, 6

   (b)
   ```
   10 READ X
   20 IF X >= 0 THEN 50
   30 LET Y = -X
   40 GOTO 60
   50 LET Y = X ∧ 2 + 1
   60 PRINT Y
   70 DATA 3, -4, 0
   80 GOTO 10
   90 END
   ```
   10, 4, 1

10. Write a "polite" interactive program that asks whether the user would like it to sum the first, second, and third powers of a number. If so, it should ask the user for a number, carry out the task, and then ask the user the opening question again. If not, it should turn itself off.

11. Amend these programs in the text to make them "polite."
    (a) The program of Figure 16.9
    (b) The program of Figure 16.19
    (c) The program of Figure 16.22
    (d) The program of Figure 16.27

12. Amend the program of Figure 16.27 so that it does the following in ambiguous cases.
    (a) It always rounds down.
    ★ (b) It always rounds to the nearest even number.

13. The *harmonic series* is the "infinite sum"
    $$1 + \tfrac{1}{2} + \tfrac{1}{3} + \tfrac{1}{4} + \tfrac{1}{5} + \cdots$$
    Its *partial sums* are the numbers
    $$1,\ 1 + \tfrac{1}{2} = \tfrac{3}{2},\ 1 + \tfrac{1}{2} + \tfrac{1}{3} = \tfrac{11}{6},$$
    $$1 + \tfrac{1}{2} + \tfrac{1}{3} + \tfrac{1}{4} = \tfrac{25}{12},\ \ldots$$
    Write a program that prints the first 100 partial sums of the harmonic series.

14. Repeat Exercise 13 for the *geometric series*
    $$1 + \tfrac{1}{2} + \tfrac{1}{4} + \tfrac{1}{8} + \tfrac{1}{16} + \cdots$$
    Inspect runs of the two programs for harmonic and geometric series. Do you notice any difference between the behavior of the partial sums of the harmonic series and the partial sums of the geometric series? What value would you assign to each infinite sum?

15. The total cost (in dollars) of producing X widgets in your shop is given by the cost function
    $$C(X) = \begin{cases} 4X + 50, & \text{if } X \leq 10 \\ 3X + 60, & \text{if } X > 10 \end{cases}$$
    Write an interactive program that prints the cost of filling an order for any number (X) of widgets.

16. Employees in your shop earn \$4 per hour for working up to 40 hours per week. For any hours over 40 they earn \$5.50. Write a program that prints the payroll for the eight employees who have worked the following numbers of hours:

    32, 40, 48, 36, 10, 18, 44, 28

The object of Exercises 17–19 is to determine the tens digit of 6^{789}, a problem similar to, but a bit harder than, Problem 2, page 837.

17. Replace P by a few different whole numbers and then describe, in general terms, the effect of the function $P - 100 * \text{INT}(P/100)$.

18. Describe what the run of this BASIC program will look like.

```
10    LET P  = 1
20    FOR E = 1 TO 4
30    LET P = P * 6
40    LET P = P - 100 * INT (P / 100)
50    PRINT E,P
60    NEXT E
70    END
```

19. Revise the program in Exercise 18 so that it prints out only the last two digits of 6^{789}.

20. Find the hundreds digit of 6^{543}.

 ## 16.4 *Introduction to Logo and Turtle Graphics*

The programming language Logo was created at the Massachusetts Institute of Technology in 1968. It shares with BASIC the ability to carry out arithmetic calculations and to evaluate a few simple functions. For example, in Logo, if one types

$$10 + 7 * (4 - 1)$$

and presses the RETURN key, the machine responds with

$$RESULT: 31$$

If one types

$$SQRT(18/2)$$

and presses RETURN, the machine responds with

$$RESULT: 3.$$

Beyond a few superficial similarities, though, Logo is fundamentally different from BASIC. The commands and conventions that we learned for BASIC will not apply in Logo. When we begin to write programs in Logo, we will see that the steps are not numbered, as they had to be in BASIC.* The most striking difference between the languages, though, is their graphics capabilities— that is, their capability to produce geometric figures and designs on the display screen.

To do graphics in BASIC, one needs to have some background in coordinate geometry. To do graphics in Logo requires only an intuitive feeling for distance and angles. Very young children are able to create impressive graphical displays by using Logo. In fact, special color codes have been devised to make Logo accessible to children who have not yet learned to read.

The Turtle

The device that does the drawing in Logo is known as a turtle. The original M.I.T. turtle was an actual robot that moved around on the floor and traced out figures with a pen protruding from its stomach. The turtle on the computer screen is a triangle that likewise can leave a trail as it moves under the programmer's command. We should think of the turtle as an intelligent creature. We should imagine that it has the innate ability to understand and carry out a short list of simple commands, called **primitives,** and is capable of learning a

---

*Structured BASICs that do not use line numbers have been developed recently.

large number of more complicated commands, called **procedures,** as long as the programmer defines these procedures (ultimately) in terms of the primitives. We begin with a look at some of the primitives, that is, the turtle's inborn vocabulary.

Driving the Turtle

After loading the Logo language into the computer, typing the word DRAW and pressing the RETURN key puts the system in **DRAW mode,** which corresponds to the immediate-execution mode we encountered in BASIC. The screen appears as shown in Figure 16.31. The turtle is poised for action, facing straight up, at its *home position* in the center of the screen. The question mark invites the programmer to issue a command to the turtle. The bottom four lines of the screen are reserved for displaying the commands. The rest of the screen is the turtle's canvas.

The primitive command FORWARD 50 moves the turtle 50 turtle steps in whatever direction it happens to be facing. (The dimensions of the screen are about 280 steps wide by 240 steps high.) Thus typing the command

FORWARD 50   or, in abbreviated form,   FD 50

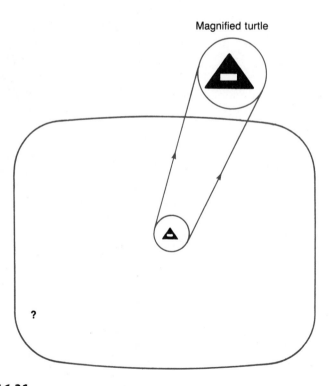

Figure 16.31

and pressing the RETURN key changes the screen display to the one shown in Figure 16.32. The primitive command RIGHT 90 turns the turtle, in place, 90° to the right. Thus typing

RIGHT 90   or, in abbreviated form,   RT 90

and pressing RETURN produces the screen display shown in Figure 16.33.

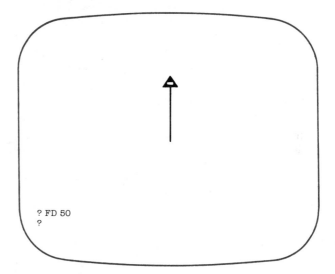

Figure 16.32

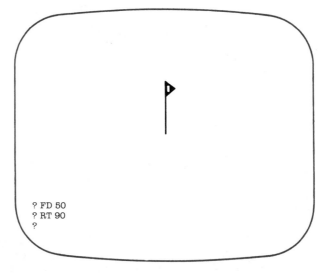

Figure 16.33

The turtle can also turn LEFT (abbreviation LT) and go BACK (abbreviation BK), and it can remember a whole sequence of instructions and then carry them out in order when asked to. Thus your next command might be

FD 40   LT 45   FD 40   RT 45   BK 100

The turtle sits motionless, memorizing the sequence of commands, until you press the RETURN key. Then it springs into action and leaves a trail as shown in Figure 16.34. The schematic diagram in Figure 16.35 should help you to understand why the turtle moved as it did.

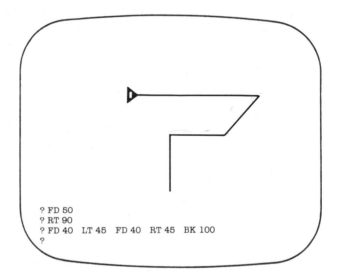

Figure 16.34

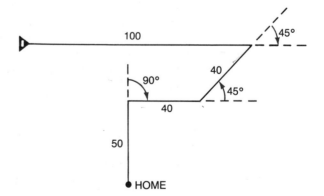

Figure 16.35

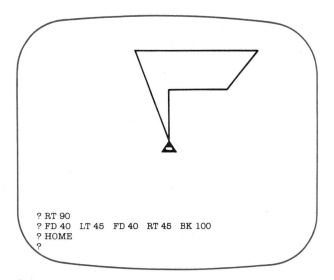

```
? RT 90
? FD 40   LT 45   FD 40   RT 45   BK 100
? HOME
?
```

Figure 16.36

To return the turtle to its starting position and heading (straight up), type the command

HOME

When you press RETURN, the screen changes as shown in Figure 16.36.
To erase the design and clear the screen for future work, simply type

DRAW

and press RETURN. This command also returns the turtle to its home position and heading if it is not already there.

Using only the primitives discussed so far, one can have some fun doodling and also explore Logo's responses to some unusual commands. For example, what do you suspect would be the effect of the command RT 270? Of the command FD −50? Of LT 900? These commands are equivalent to LT 90, BK 50, and LT 180 (or RT 180), respectively Suppose you have given the command

RT 38   FD 40   RT 29   BK 30   RT 46   FD 50

and now you want the turtle to turn straight north again. You could add up 38, 29, and 46 on a piece of scratch paper, and then issue the command

LT 113

Or you could have Logo do the arithmetic for you by simply typing in

$$LT \; 38 + 29 + 46$$

The effect would be the same.

You have probably wondered what happens if the turtle is sent off the screen. To see what happens, try typing

```
RT  30      (RETURN)
FD  200     (RETURN)
FD  200     (RETURN)
```

You will notice that the turtle "wraps around." When it comes to the top edge of the screen it wraps around (vertically) to the bottom of the screen and continue its path. When it comes to the right edge it wraps around horizontally and continues its path from the left edge. See Figure 16.37.

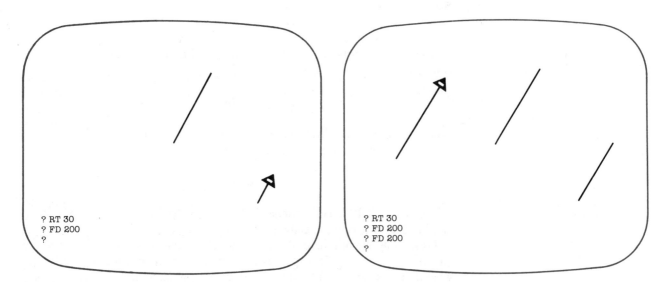

Figure 16.37 Wrapping turtle.

After a period of doodling and exploration you will want to begin drawing some *regular* geometric figures. How do you go about drawing a square of side length 40? Here is one sequence of instructions that will do the job:

```
FD 40   RT 90   FD 40   RT 90   FD 40   RT 90   FD 40   RT 90
```

When RETURN is pressed, the turtle will trace out a square as shown in Figure 16.38.

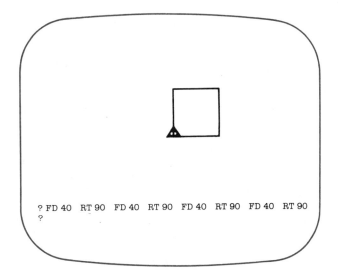

Figure 16.38

It is, of course, a chore to type in FD 40 RT 90 four times, and the task promises to become more tiresome if we try to draw octagons or decagons. What we need is some kind of repetition command, like the FOR . . . NEXT loop in BASIC, that shifts the drudgery to the machine. The Logo primitive that does the job is the **REPEAT** command. The instruction

REPEAT 4[FD 40 RT 90]

tells the turtle to repeat 4 times the movement, forward 40 (steps) then right 90 (degrees). Pressing RETURN displays precisely the square shown in Figure 16.38. Notice that the turtle has resumed its original heading after making a total (right) turn of 4 × 90 = 360°.

Now let's try drawing a regular octagon of side length 40. Again, the turtle ought to make a total turn of 360° to return to its original heading, so we have a choice of how to write the instructions. We can do some arithmetic on our own and decide that each of the eight turns should be through 45°, or we can turn the arithmetic over to Logo:

REPEAT 8[FD 40 RT 360/8]

The figure that results when RETURN is pressed is shown in Figure 16.39.

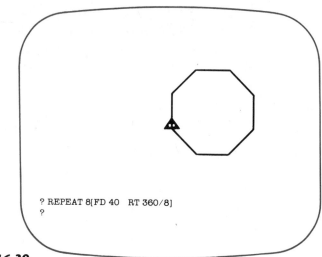

Figure 16.39

Procedures

The words (commands) that the turtle already understands when we first meet it are called primitives; so far we have used seven of them: DRAW, FORWARD, BACK, RIGHT, LEFT, HOME, REPEAT. The words (commands) that we teach it are called procedures. So far we have not taught the turtle any procedures; it is time that we did.

Let's begin with the word SQUARE. We would like to train the turtle to produce the diagram in Figure 16.38 every time we give the command SQUARE. To add SQUARE to the turtle's vocabulary is a simple matter. Just type

```
TO SQUARE
  REPEAT 4[FD 40   RT 90]
END
```

Typing the word TO takes the system out of DRAW mode and puts it in **EDIT mode,** which corresponds roughly to the deferred-execution mode that we encountered in BASIC. Following TO is the new word SQUARE that we want the turtle to learn. To put this new word in the turtle's memory, we press CONTROL–C (hold down the CONTROL key while pressing the C key). The turtle now knows the meaning of SQUARE—namely, repeat 4 times forward 40 right 90—and will draw one whenever we send the word. (Marvelously fast learner! Amazing retention! This turtle is a wonderful student!) Pressing CONTROL–C also takes us out of EDIT mode. If we now wish the turtle to draw a square, we simply type

SQUARE

and press the RETURN key; the square of Figure 16.38 appears on the screen.

The procedure SQUARE can now be used in exactly the same way that primitives such as FORWARD and RIGHT are used in drawing pictures on the screen. For example, the command

FD 50   SQUARE   LT 90   FD 50   SQUARE

produces the design in Figure 16.40.

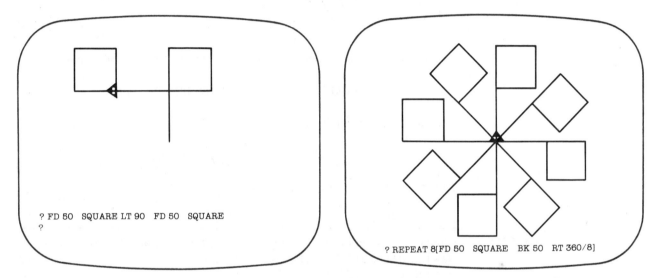

Figure 16.40   **Figure 16.41**

To draw another design, first type DRAW to wipe the screen clean and return the turtle to its starting attitude. Now the new command

REPEAT 8[FD 50 SQUARE BK 50 RT 360/8]

produces the design in Figure 16.41. Notice that the turtle performs the sequence of moves inside the brackets 8 times in succession. After the first performance it has drawn the upright flag in Figure 16.41, has rotated its nose $(\frac{360}{8})° = 45°$ to the right, and is about to draw the next flag.

Apparently, we can get the turtle to draw some nice designs if we take a little time to build up its vocabulary. The following programs define three new procedures, TRIANGLE, SEGMENT, and RHOMBUS, that are transferred to the turtle's memory by pressing CONTROL–C. Beside each one is the figure that the turtle learns to draw.

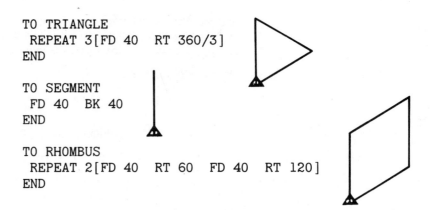

```
TO TRIANGLE
  REPEAT 3[FD 40  RT 360/3]
END

TO SEGMENT
  FD 40  BK 40
END

TO RHOMBUS
  REPEAT 2[FD 40  RT 60  FD 40  RT 120]
END
```

The range of figures one can draw by using the (learned) procedures

> SQUARE TRIANGLE SEGMENT RHOMBUS

and the (built-in) primitives

> FD BK RT LT REPEAT

is about as broad as one's imagination.

EXAMPLE 1   Predict what kind of figures will be produced by each of these commands.
(a) REPEAT 10[SEGMENT RT 360/10]
(b) REPEAT 6[TRIANGLE RT 60]
(c) REPEAT 12[RHOMBUS RT 360/12]

Solution   The designs are shown in Figure 16.42. If you find the turtle a distraction from the design, use the primitive **HIDETURTLE** (abbreviated HT) and the turtle becomes invisible. (It also moves faster when invisible.) To bring the turtle back into the picture, use the primitive **SHOWTURTLE** (abbreviated ST).

(a)   (b)   (c)

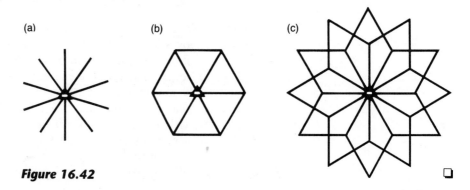

Figure 16.42   ❏

EXAMPLE 2 Write a procedure called DANDELION that will draw the flower shown in Figure 16.43, and teach the turtle the new word.

Solution Here is the procedure:

```
TO DANDELION
 HT
 BK 30   RT 60
 RHOMBUS
 RT 180
 RHOMBUS
 RT 120   FD 70
 REPEAT 20[SEGMENT   RT 360/20]
END
```

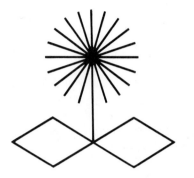

Figure 16.43 DANDELION.

Note: The command BK 30 was used so that the flower would not run off the top of the screen. ❑

Suppose now that we want to use the primitives TRIANGLE, SQUARE, and RHOMBUS to draw the house and doghouse as shown in Figure 16.44. A new problem presents itself. Drawing either building separately seems to be a manageable task, but how does one move the turtle from one to the other without leaving a trail? Fortunately, there are two primitives that provide for just such a contingency. The primitive PENUP (abbreviated PU) allows the turtle to move without leaving a trail. (Think of the robot turtle with its pen retracted.) To recommence drawing a trail, use the command PENDOWN (abbreviated PD).

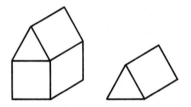

Figure 16.44 HOUSE.AND.
DOGHOUSE.

We break the task of drawing the house and doghouse into three subtasks. First, we define a procedure DOGHOUSE as follows:

```
TO DOGHOUSE
 RT 30
 TRIANGLE
 FD 40   RT 30
 SQUARE
END    (and CONTROL-C)
```

(Pretend you are the turtle, and make the moves listed in DOGHOUSE. Did you draw the picture in Figure 16.45?)

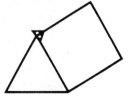

Figure 16.45 DOGHOUSE.

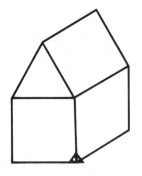

Figure 16.46 HOUSE.

Then we define a procedure HOUSE:

```
TO HOUSE
  SQUARE
  FD 40
  DOGHOUSE
  RT 90  FD 40  RT 30  FD 40  RT 180
  RHOMBUS
END     (and CONTROL-C)
```

(Again simulate, with paper and pencil, the turtle's moves. Did you draw the house as in Figure 16.46?)

Next, combining these procedures we get, HOUSE.AND.DOGHOUSE:

```
TO HOUSE.AND.DOGHOUSE
  PU
  LT 90  FD 60  RT 90
  PD
  HOUSE
  PU
  RT 90  FD 60  LT 90
  PD
  DOGHOUSE
  HT
END
```

Note: The first three lines of this procedure simply center the picture on the screen.

Finally, we press CONTROL-C to put this procedure in the turtle's memory and to leave the EDIT mode. Typing in the command HOUSE.AND.DOGHOUSE now produces the display of Figure 16.44.

The pyramiding of these geometric procedures, shown in Figure 16.47, should remind you of the pyramiding of arithmetic algorithms that we discussed earlier. It should also suggest similarities between how the turtle learns and how humans learn.

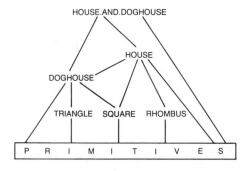

Figure 16.47 Lattice of subprocedures.

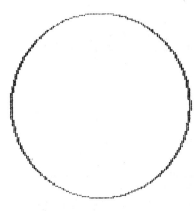

Figure 16.48 Computer's CIRCLE.

Circles

To conclude this section, we describe procedures for drawing circles and arcs of circles, since the ability to draw curves opens up a whole new range of possibilities for designs. Picture in your mind these regular polygons:

> A square of side length 90
> Then an octagon of side length 45
> Then a 20-gon of side length 18
> Then a 60-gon of side length 6

Can you see that each has perimeter 360 and that their silhouettes become more and more like circles as the number of sides increases?

Here is a procedure that causes the turtle to draw a regular 360-gon of side length 1, a figure that is close enough to being a circle for our purposes. (See Figure 16.48.)

```
TO CIRCLE
  HT
  REPEAT 360[FD 1  RT 1]
END   (and CONTROL-C)
```

The HIDETURTLE command is included to speed up the tracing of the circle.

EXAMPLE 3   Use the procedure CIRCLE and the procedure TRIANGLE to draw an ice cream cone.

Solution   Here is the procedure (see Figure 16.49):

```
DRAW
RT 90
TRIANGLE
FD 20   RT 180
CIRCLE
```

What would the picture have looked like if we had omitted the command RT 180 from the instructions?   ❑

Tables 16.10, 16.11, and 16.12 summarize the primitives that the turtle knew when we met it, the procedures we taught it in this section, and the steps one follows in teaching the turtle a new procedure.

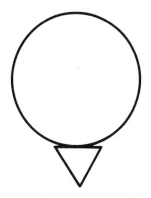

Figure 16.49

Table 16.10 Primitives

What you type	What computer does
DRAW	Erases screen, returns turtle to center facing north, puts system into DRAW mode
HOME	Returns turtle to center facing north
FORWARD (FD)	Moves turtle specified number of steps in the direction it is facing
BACK (BK)	Moves turtle specified number of steps in the opposite of the direction it is facing
RIGHT (RT)	Turns turtle specified number of degrees to the right
LEFT (LT)	Turns turtle specified number of degrees to the left
REPEAT	Repeats, specified number of times, whatever procedure is inside the brackets
HIDETURTLE (HT)	Makes turtle invisible, quickens its pace
SHOWTURTLE (ST)	Makes turtle visible
PENUP (PU)	Allows turtle to move without leaving a trail
PENDOWN (PD)	Makes turtle leave a trail

Table 16.11 Procedures

Name	Figure turtle produces
SQUARE	Figure 16.38
SEGMENT	See p. 872
TRIANGLE	See p. 872
RHOMBUS	See p. 872
DANDELION	Figure 16.43
DOGHOUSE	Figure 16.45
HOUSE	Figure 16.46
HOUSE.AND.DOGHOUSE	Figure 16.44
CIRCLE	Figure 16.48

Table 16.12 Teaching the Turtle

TO (Name of procedure)

    List of commands that make up the procedure

END
CONTROL—C

Saving Procedures

Suppose that we turn off the computer and call it a day. When we wake up the turtle tomorrow by turning on the machine and loading the Logo language, it will still *remember* the *primitives,* but it will have *forgotten* all of the *procedures.* To save ourselves the trouble of reteaching all these procedures, we can save them on a disk. The command

SAVE "SHAPES1

records all nine of today's procedures on the disk under the file name SHAPES1. Tomorrow all we have to do is insert the disk and give the command

READ "SHAPES1

and the nine procedures will be reimplanted in the turtle's memory. We used the file name SHAPES1 because tomorrow we might define a whole new collection of procedures that we want to save under a different file name, say SHAPES2.

EXERCISE SET 16.4

In each of the following exercises, assume that the turtle begins in its home position (center of screen, facing upwards). Predict, with pencil and paper, the trail it will leave in response to the command given. For your sketches, use the scale of turtle distances shown in Figure 16.50. Be sure to draw the final position and heading of the turtle. Check your work by using the computer.

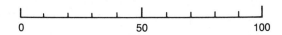

0   50   100

Figure 16.50

1. RT 90   FD 40   LT 90   FD 30   HOME
2. BK 20   LT 60   FD 40   RT 60   BK 20
3. FD 20   LT 60   BK 40   RT 60   FD 20

4. FD 20   RT 120   FD 40   LT 120
   FD 20
5. FD 60   RT 5 * 45   FD 50   RT 45
   BK 60
6. FD 18 + 22   RT 90   FD 200/5   RT 90
   PU   FD 40   PD   BK 20   RT 90   FD 20
7. REPEAT 2[FD 40   RT 90   FD 20
   RT 90]
8. REPEAT 4[FD 40   RT 90   FD 20
   RT 90   FD 20   RT 90]
9. REPEAT 6[FD 40   BK 40   RT 36]
10. REPEAT 3[RT 45   FD 40]

Write a list of commands that you would send the turtle to make it draw each figure. Here H denotes the turtle's home position. Check your work on the computer. Be sure to use REPEAT in Exercises 15–20.

11.    12.

13.   14.

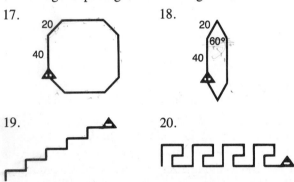

15. A regular hexagon of side length 20

16. A regular pentagon of side length 20

17.   18.

19.   20.

In each of the following exercises, assume that the turtle has been taught the procedures TRIANGLE, SEGMENT, and RHOMBUS that are defined on pages 871–872. Predict, with pencil and paper, what designs will be produced. Check your predictions on the computer.

21. RHOMBUS   RT 180   TRIANGLE

22. TRIANGLE
    FD 20   LT 90   FD 60
    RHOMBUS
    FD 40   LT 60   FD 40   RT 180
    RHOMBUS

23. REPEAT 10[SEGMENT   RT 90   FD 10
    LT 90]

24. REPEAT 6[RHOMBUS   RT 60]

25. REPEAT 4[FD 40   TRIANGLE   BK 40
    RT 90]

26. REPEAT 3[RHOMBUS   RT 90   SEGMENT
    RT 30]

In Exercises 27–32, use the procedures TRIANGLE, SEGMENT, and RHOMBUS and any primitives to write drawing instructions for each figure.

27.   28.

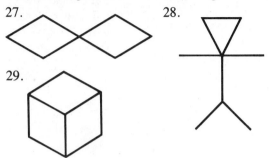

29.

30. Five-petaled flower with rhombus-shaped petals

31.

32.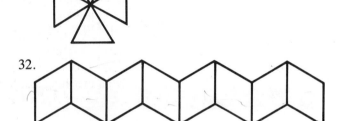

33. Your task is to produce the design in Figure 13.48 p. 671, where each segment is 20 turtle steps long. Begin by teaching the turtle the procedure PENTAGON of Exercise 16.

34. The procedure CIRCLE that we defined on page 875 produces a circle that is inconveniently large for many purposes.
    (a) What is its circumference (in turtle steps)?
    (b) What is its diameter (in turtle steps)
    Here is a procedure that produces a circle of manageable size.

```
TO CIRCLE1
 HT
 REPEAT 360[FD .5   RT 1]
END   (and CONTROL-C
```

    (c) What is its circumference?
    (d) What is its diameter?

35. Use the procedure CIRCLE1 in a procedure that draws three mutually tangent circles.

36. Use the step size .5 that we used for CIRCLE1.
    (a) Define a procedure RQC that produces a right-bending quarter circle as shown in Figure 16.51.
    (b) Define a procedure LQC that produces a left-bending quarter circle as shown in Figure 16.52.

Figure 16.51  **Figure 16.52**

(c) Use RQC and LQC to define a procedure ESS that causes the turtle to follow the S curve shown in Figure 16.53, retrace its path, and resume its original heading.

Figure 16.53

(d) Use ESS in a procedure that draws an octopus. Hide the turtle to speed up the drawing.

16.5 *Variable Procedures*

The procedures SQUARE, SEGMENT, TRIANGLE, and RHOMBUS that we defined in the previous section all had side length 40 (turtle steps). This common side length was convenient because it allowed us to fit the figures together with matching sides, but it also had a stifling effect on creativity. To produce a masterpiece like the one in Figure 16.54, we will have to be able to draw squares and triangles of several sizes.

Rather than define three new square procedures—one for side length 60, one for side length 12, and one for side length 6—we will define a procedure for a square of variable side length L. We preface its name with a V to distinguish it from our earlier procedure SQUARE and to remind ourselves of its variable nature. The commands follow. Notice especially how the colon is used. It warns Logo that what follows is a variable.

```
TO VSQUARE :L
  REPEAT 4[FD :L  RT 90]
END
```

[handwritten: can use word instead of letter]

[handwritten: make sure]

Pressing CONTROL–C adds this procedure to the turtle's vocabulary (and takes us out of EDIT mode). To have the turtle trace out a square of side length 60 now, we simply type

VSQUARE 60

and press RETURN. To get a square of side length 12, type

VSQUARE 12 (RETURN)

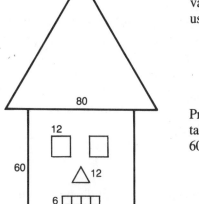

Figure 16.54 Masterpiece.

Notice that you do *not* prefix a value for the variable, like 60 or 12, with a colon. If you forget to assign a value to the variable—that is, if you simply type

VSQUARE (RETURN)

—the machine will send you an error message of the sort

VSQUARE NEEDS MORE INPUTS

We used a letter L to name the variable in the procedure VSQUARE since most people are accustomed to that convention from their work with x's and y's in algebra. In Logo, though, one can use an entire word as a variable. For example, we could have used the entire word LENGTH instead of L in defining the procedure VSQUARE:

```
TO VSQUARE :LENGTH
  REPEAT 4[FD :LENGTH  RT 90]
END
```

Using an entire word usually makes it easier to remember just what a procedure does.

EXAMPLE 1 Define these procedures, and run each one for some particular value of the variable.

(a) VTRIANGLE :LENGTH, a procedure for drawing equilateral triangles of arbitrary side length

(b) VCIRCLE :RADIUS, a procedure for drawing circles of arbitrary radius

(c) VPOLY20 :SIDES, a procedure for drawing regular polygons of side length 20 having an arbitrary number of sides

Solution (a) Here is the procedure (see Figure 16.55):

```
TO VTRIANGLE :LENGTH
  REPEAT 3[FD :LENGTH  RT 120]
END
```

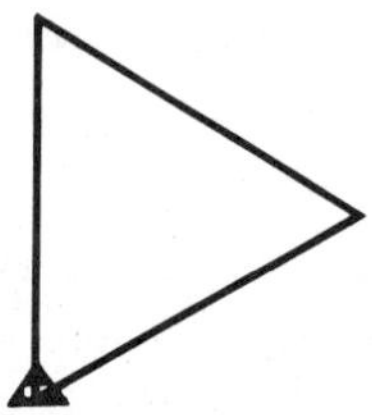

Figure 16.55 VTRIANGLE 80.

(b) This procedure requires a little more planning. We want the turtle to move forward a certain distance x and then turn right 1°, and to repeat this move 360 times. The question is: What distance x will produce a circle of given radius r? On the one hand, the circle will have circumference $360x$; on

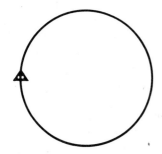

Figure 16.56 VCIRCLE 50.

Figure 16.57 VPOLY 20 6.

Figure 16.58 VPOLY 6 10.

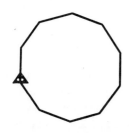

Figure 16.59 VPOLY 10 6.

the other hand, it will have circumference $2\pi r \doteq 6.28r$. Thus $x \doteq 6.28r/360$, and we define the procedure as follows:

```
TO VCIRCLE :RADIUS
  REPEAT 360[FD :RADIUS * 6.28/360  RT 1]
END
```

Notice how the variable name :RADIUS is used just like the letter r in the calculation of the distance x. A run of this procedure using radius 50 is shown in Figure 16.56.

(c) Here is the procedure:

```
TO VPOLY20 :SIDES
  REPEAT :SIDES[FD 20  RT 360/:SIDES]
END
```

To convince yourself that this program does define the desired procedure correctly, replace every occurrence of :SIDES in it by 6 and determine whether it will produce the regular hexagon of side length 20 shown in Figure 16.57. ❑

It is convenient to have one procedure that produces regular polygons of arbitrarily many sides, each of length 20. But it would be even more convenient if we had a procedure that would produce regular polygons having as many sides as we request *and* having whatever side length we want. We are talking about a procedure involving two variables, :SIDES and :LENGTH:

```
TO VPOLY :SIDES :LENGTH
  REPEAT :SIDES[FD :LENGTH  RT 360/:SIDES]
END  (and CONTROL-C)
```

When you run this program, keep in mind that :SIDES is the first variable and :LENGTH is the second. If you type

```
        VPOLY 6 10   (RETURN)
```

the turtle will trace out a regular hexagon of side length 10. See Figure 16.58. If you type

```
        VPOLY 10 6   (RETURN)
```

it will trace out a regular decagon of side length 6. See Figure 16.59. (The polygons in Figures 16.58 and 16.59 are greatly magnified.) Notice that the two-variable procedure VPOLY has made our earlier one-variable procedures—VSQUARE, VTRIANGLE, and VPOLY20—obsolete.

EXAMPLE 2   Define these procedures and run each one for some particular values of the two variables.
(a) VRECTANGLE :HEIGHT :BASE, a procedure for drawing rectangles with arbitrary height and arbitrary base
(b) VRARC :RADIUS :DEGREES, a procedure for drawing a right-bending arc of arbitrary radius and arbitrary degree measure. That is, VRARC 40 45 should produce an arc of a circle of radius 40 that subtends a central angle of 45°.

Solution   (a) Here is the two-variable procedure (see Figures 16.60 and 16.61 for specific runs):

```
TO VRECTANGLE :HEIGHT :BASE
 REPEAT 2[FD :HEIGHT  RT 90  FD :BASE  RT 90]
END
```

Figure 16.60 VRECTANGLE 40 20.

(b) The following two-variable procedure is a natural refinement of the one-variable procedure for VCIRCLE :RADIUS that we worked out earlier (see Figures 16.62 and 16.63 for specific runs):

```
TO VRARC :RADIUS :DEGREES
 REPEAT :DEGREES[FD :RADIUS * 6.28/360  RT 1]
END
```

Figure 16.61 VRECTANGLE 20 40.

Figure 16.62 VRARC 40 45.   **Figure 16.63** VRARC 20 270.   ❏

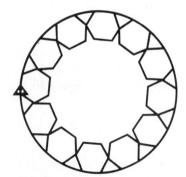

Figure 16.64 REPEAT 12 [VPOLY 6 11 VRARC 50 30].

Variable Subprocedures

Procedures involving variables can be used as subprocedures (building blocks for more complicated procedures) in the same way that procedures without variables were. By combining the procedures that we have defined so far,

```
VSQUARE  VTRIANGLE  VCIRCLE  VPOLY  VRECTANGLE  VRARC
```

a wide range of interesting figures and pictures can be created. The process of inventing original designs in this way is called **bottom-up** programming. It is exploratory and open-ended, and often begins with a query: "I wonder what would happen if . . ." For instance, the design in Figure 16.64 was created by fiddling with the VRARC and VPOLY procedures.

When one begins with a preconceived design, such as the masterpiece in Figure 16.54, and sets out to write a program to draw it, the thought process is quite different. Now the thinking is analytical and convergent. One must break down the design into its simple parts, write a (sub)procedure to draw each one, and then determine how to fit these subprocedures together to produce the final result. This way of thinking is often called **top-down** design.

Figure 16.65 is a program that will produce the masterpiece of 16.54. Note the general structure of the program: Drawing subprocedures alternate with (penup) moves of the turtle that position it for the next drawing. Figure 16.66 shows an actual computer printout of the procedure MASTERPIECE.

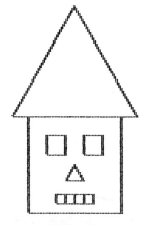

Figure 16.66 Computer's MASTERPIECE.

```
TO MASTERPIECE    (names the procedure)
 HT   RT 30
 VTRIANGLE 80    (draws hat, beginning at lower left corner)
 PU   RT 60   FD 10   PD
 VSQUARE 60   (draws head)
 PU   FD 12   RT 90   FD 12   LT 90   PD
 VSQUARE 12   (draws one eye)
 PU   FD 24   PD
 VSQUARE 12   (draws other eye)
 PU   RT 180   FD 6   LT 90   FD 18   LT 30   PD
 VTRIANGLE 12   (draws nose)
 PU   RT 30   FD 18   RT 90   FD 12   RT 180   PD
 REPEAT 4[VSQUARE 6   PU   FD 6 PD]   (draws teeth)
END
```

Figure 16.65

EXAMPLE 3

Write a procedure to draw the locomotive shown in Figure 16.67. No pen-up moves will be necessary.

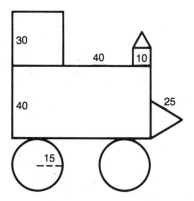

Figure 16.67 Locomotive.

Solution   Follow the steps of the program in Figure 16.68 by hand, beginning in the
                lower left-hand corner of the locomotive body. A computer rendition of
                LOCOMOTIVE is shown in Figure 16.69.

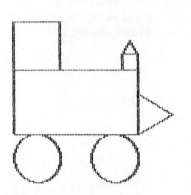

```
TO LOCOMOTIVE
 HT
 VRECTANGLE 40  80
 FD 40
 VSQUARE 30
 RT 90   FD 70   LT 90
 VSQUARE 10
 FD 10   RT 30
 VTRIANGLE 10
 RT 60   FD 10   RT 90   FD 50   RT 180
 VTRIANGLE 25
 LT 90   FD 15   RT 180
 VCIRCLE 15
 BK 50
 VCIRCLE 15
END
```

Figure 16.69 Computer's
LOCOMOTIVE.   ***Figure 16.68***   ❏

EXERCISE SET 16.5

1. Write a one-variable procedure VSEGMENT
   :LENGTH for drawing segments of arbitrary
   length (and returning the turtle to its original position and heading).

2. Write a one-variable procedure VPENTAGON
   :LENGTH for drawing regular pentagons of arbitrary side length.
   (a) Will all the pentagons produced by this pro-
       cedure be congruent?
   (b) Will they all be similar?

3. Write a one-variable procedure VRHOMBUS 40
   :ANGLE for drawing rhombi of side length 40
   with arbitrary angle.
   (a) Will all the rhombi produced by this proce-
       dure be congruent?
   (b) Will they all be similar?
   (c) Will VRHOMBUS 40 75 and VRHOMBUS
       40 105 be congruent? Generalize.

4. Write a two-variable procedure VLARC:RADIUS
   :DEGREES for drawing a left-bending arc of arbitrary radius and arbitrary degree measure.
   (a) Will VLARC 40 75 be congruent to VRARC
       40 75?
   (b) Will VLARC 40 75 be similar to VLARC 50
       75? Generalize.

5. Write a two-variable procedure VRHOMBUS
   :LENGTH :ANGLE for drawing a rhombus with
   arbitrary side length and angle.
   (a) What is a more familiar name for VRHOM-
       BUS 40 90?
   (b) Will VRHOMBUS 40 70 and VRHOMBUS
       40 110 be congruent? Generalize.
   (c) Will VRHOMBUS 40 70 and VRHOMBUS
       40 290 be congruent?

6. Write a three-variable procedure VPARALLEL-OGRAM :SIDE1 :ANGLE :SIDE2 for drawing a parallelogram with arbitrary side lengths and angle measure.
   (a) Will VPARALLELOGRAM 40 25 60 and VPARALLELOGRAM 40 155 60 be congruent?
   (b) Will VPARALLELOGRAM 40 25 60 and VPARALLELOGRAM 40 335 60 be congruent?
   (c) Choose x so that VPARALLELOGRAM 20 57 40 is similar to VPARALLELOGRAM 30 57 x.
   (d) Name three procedures from this section that are made obsolete by VPARALLELOGRAM.

7. Define one-variable procedures that will draw each of the following letters to any specified height. Use the procedures VRARC and VLARC as subprocedures.

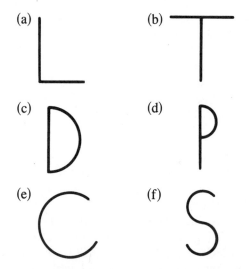

8. Will all the L's produced by your one-variable procedure in Exercise 7(a) be similar to each other? Will all L's produced by the following two-variable procedure be similar to each other?

```
TO VVL :HEIGHT :WIDTH
 BK :HEIGHT  RT 90  FD :WIDTH
END
```

9. What inputs would you give to VPOLY :SIDES :LENGTH if you wanted to draw the following?
   (a) A square of side length 50
   (b) A regular octagon of perimeter 200
   (c) A regular hexagon of maximum diameter 60
   (d) A (turtle) circle of diameter 100

10. Feel free to use any of the procedures VTRIANGLE, VSQUARE, VRECTANGLE, VCIRCLE, VSEGMENT, VRARC, or VLARC in programs for drawing the following figures.

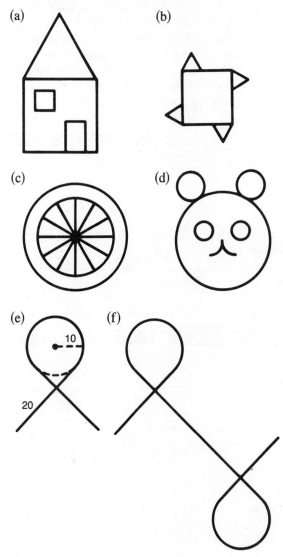

11. Write a procedure that produces the repeating design shown in Figure 16.70.

Figure 16.70

12. The task here is to write a two-variable procedure VFRAME :LENGTH :HEIGHT for drawing picture frames of the kind shown in Figure 16.71 (to use around your Logo creations). Here LENGTH and HEIGHT refer to the number of repetitions of the basic design element, whose dimensions in turtle steps are shown in Figure 16.72.

Figure 16.71
VFRAME 10 7.

13. The variable procedure VSQUARE behaves like a function: If you provide it with a suitable input, say 40, it will produce a square as an output. By trial and error on the machine, determine precisely what integers can be used as inputs to produce squares as outputs.

Figure 16.72
Design element.

14. Write a two-variable procedure VISOTRAP :BASE1 :BASE2 that will produce isosceles trapezoids with 45° base angles and lower and upper bases of variable lengths :BASE1 and :BASE2 respectively.

15. Run the procedure VISOTRAP for these values of :BASE1 and :BASE2.
    (a) 100, 80
    (b) 100, 50
    (c) 100, 0
    (d) 100, 100
    (e) 100, 120

16.6 *Recursion*

We have seen many examples where one procedure *calls* another. For example, our procedure LOCOMOTIVE (Figure 16.68) called all of the procedures VRECTANGLE, VSQUARE, VTRIANGLE, and VCIRCLE. An amazing feature of the Logo language is that a procedure can call itself. This phenomenon is referred to as **recursion.**

The simple procedure STAIRWAY illustrates how a recursive call is made. After defining the procedure,

```
TO STAIRWAY
FD 20   RT 90   FD 30   LT 90
STAIRWAY
END
```

and pressing CONTROL–C, we run it by typing STAIRWAY. The turtle behaves as follows: It performs the four moves of the first (indented) line, tracing out the first stair of the stairway, then looks at the next line of instructions. This line tells the turtle to loop back and carry out procedure STAIRWAY again. This line is the recursive call. So from its new position (20 units above and 30 right of home) it performs the four moves again, tracing out the second stair of the stairway, and looks at the next line. Again, the instructions are to go back and follow procedure STAIRWAY.

As you will see if you run this procedure, the turtle will never stop. It traces out a stairway leading up and to the right until it reaches the right edge of the screen. Then it wraps to the left and continues tracing until it reaches the top of the screen. Then it wraps to the bottom and continues tracing. . . . Unless the turtle is stopped, it will fill your screen with stairways and continue retracing them forever.

Fortunately, there are ways of stopping a runaway turtle short of turning off the computer. The easiest is to simply press CONTROL–G, which stops the turtle in its tracks. Figure 16.73 was produced by pressing CONTROL–G while the turtle was in the act of drawing the twelfth stair.

A second way of limiting the turtle's motion is to write the primitive NOWRAP into the program. The effect of this command is to prevent the turtle from wrapping, that is, to stop the turtle as soon as it reaches an edge of the screen. Figure 16.74 shows a run of the modified procedure STAIRWAY1, which follows:

```
TO STAIRWAY1
 NOWRAP
 FD 20  RT 90  FD 30  LT 90
 STAIRWAY1
END  (and CONTROL–C)
```

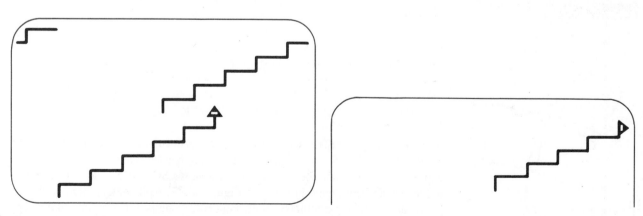

Figure 16.73 STAIRWAY, with CONTROL–G.   **Figure 16.74** STAIRWAY1.

Figure 16.75 SPINSQUARE20.

The recursive procedure STAIRWAY1 was defined completely in terms of primitives; that need not be the case. One may also use a previously defined procedure. Here is a recursive procedure SPINSQUARE20 that is defined in terms of the procedure SQUARE. (We repeat the definition of SQUARE in case you have forgotten it.)

```
TO SPINSQUARE20
  SQUARE   RT 20
  SPINSQUARE20
END

TO SQUARE
  REPEAT 4[FD 40   RT 90]
END
```

Notice that this time NOWRAP would be no help. The turtle keeps running around in squares and never gets near the edge of the screen. We used CONTROL–G to stop the turtle and HIDETURTLE to remove it before printing the drawing in Figure 16.75.

Figure 16.75 could also have been produced by the nonrecursive procedure

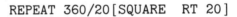

```
REPEAT 360/20[SQUARE   RT 20]
```

because the angle, 20°, through which the square was turned divides into 360° without remainder.

Suppose instead that we had chosen to turn the square through 80°. The recursive procedure

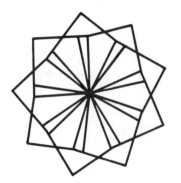

Figure 16.76 SPINSQUARE80.

```
TO SPINSQUARE80
  SQUARE   RT 80
  SPINSQUARE80
END
```

produces the lovely flower in Figure 16.76.

The nonrecursive procedure

```
REPEAT 360/80[SQUARE   RT 80]
```

in contrast is processed as follows: The computer divides 360 by 80, rounds off the quotient (4.5) to the nearest whole number (5; when in doubt, the machine rounds up), and repeats five times the move SQUARE   RT 80, producing the rather bedraggled blossom in Figure 16.77. Apparently, then, recursive procedures will be particularly convenient when one is not sure how many repetitions one wants.

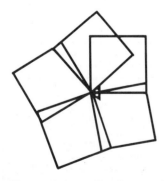

Figure 16.77 REPEAT 360/80[SQUARE   RT 80].

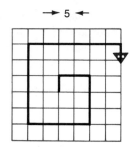

Figure 16.78

Recursion with Variables

By using variables in recursive procedures, one can create beautiful spiral designs. Consider the spiral in Figure 16.78. Apparently, we would like the turtle to make these moves:

```
FD  5    RT 90
FD 10    RT 90
FD 15    RT 90
FD 20    RT 90
            .
            .
            .
```

An efficient way of effecting these moves involves using a variable in a recursive procedure, which we will call SQUARAL.

```
TO SQUARAL :L
   FD :L  RT 90
   SQUARAL :L + 5
END  (and CONTROL-C)
```

When we type SQUARAL 5, we are assigning value 5 to the variable :L, and the turtle behaves as follows. It goes forward 5 steps, turns right 90°, and reads the next line of instructions (the recursive call). This line, with :L replaced by 5, is now SQUARAL 5 + 5, or SQUARAL 10. Thus the turtle is commanded to perform procedure SQUARAL 10; that is, it is to run through the SQUARAL procedure again, but this time with the value 10 for the variable. So the turtle moves forward 10 steps, turns right 90°, and comes again to the recursive call, which now commands it to do SQUARAL 10 + 5, or SQUARAL 15. So the turtle moves forward 15 steps, and so on. A run of SQUARAL 5 is shown in Figure 16.79 and of SQUARAL 17 in Figure 16.80.

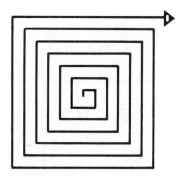

Figure 16.79 SQUARAL 5.

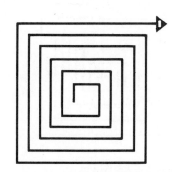

Figure 16.80 SQUARAL 17.

Suppose now that we decide to be a little ornery and have the turtle turn through 92° instead of 90° after each forwrd move. The new procedure follows, and a run is shown in Figure 16.81.

```
TO SQUARALTWIST :L
  FD :L RT 92
  SQUARALTWIST :L + 5
END
```

A different minor adjustment in the SQUARAL procedure causes the spiral to move in rather than out. Can you spot the change?

```
TO INSQUARAL :L
  FD :L  RT 90
  INSQUARAL :L − 5
END
```

Figure 16.82 shows INSQUARAL 100 halted by CONTROL–G after three spirals.

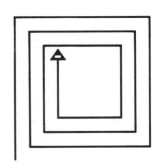

Figure 16.81 SQUARALTWIST 5.   **Figure 16.82** INSQUARAL 100.

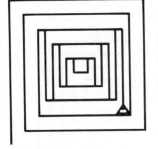

Figure 16.83 Runaway INSQUARAL 100.

If INSQUARAL 100 is allowed to run without interruption, the side lengths decrease, by 5s, from 100 to 0, then keep right on decreasing to −5, −10, −15, ... The moves FD :L actually become backward moves, and the design continues in the bizarre fashion suggested by Figure 16.83.

If we want the spiral to stop at this center, we can use an IF . . . THEN STOP primitive that is a lot like the IF . . . THEN statement in BASIC. The revised procedure we call INSQUARAL1.

```
TO INSQUARAL1 :L
  IF :L < 0 THEN STOP
  FD :L RT 90
  INSQUARAL1 :L − 5
END
```

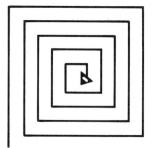

Figure 16.84 INSQUARAL1 100.

The effect of the IF . . . THEN STOP line is to act as a gatekeeper. As long as the value assigned to the variable :L remains nonnegative, the recursive procedure continues to run. As soon as this value becomes negative, the procedure is halted. Thus when we type in INSQUARAL1 100, we get an inward square spiral whose sides from the outside in have lengths 100, 95, 90, . . . , 15, 10, 5, 0. See Figure 16.84.

Any of the order relations <, =, or > can be used in an IF . . . THEN STOP command.

EXAMPLE 1   Write procedures for the following spirals. Include an IF . . . THEN STOP line, and run each one for some initial value of :L.

(a) Hexagonal outward spiral
(b) Twisted hexagonal outward spiral
(c) Hexagonal inward spiral

Solution   (a) Here is a recursive procedure. A run is shown in Figure 16.85.

```
TO OUTHEXAL :L
  IF :L > 50 THEN STOP
  FD :L  RT 60
  OUTHEXAL :L + 3
END
```

(b) Here is a recursive procedure. A computer run is shown in Figure 16.86.

```
TO OUTHEXALTWIST :L
  IF :L > 75 THEN STOP
  FD :L  RT 59
  OUTHEXALTWIST :L + 1
END
```

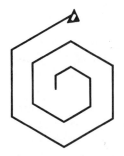

Figure 16.85 OUTHEXAL 10.

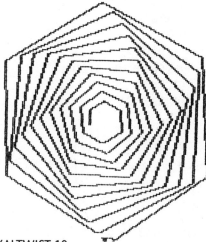

Figure 16.86 OUTHEXALTWIST 10.

Figure 16.87 INHEXAL 50.

(c) Here is a recursive procedure. A run is shown in Figure 16.87.

```
TO INHEXAL :L
  IF :L < 0 THEN STOP
  FD :L  RT 60
INHEXAL :L - 3
```

Do you see why the line IF :L = 0 THEN STOP would *fail* to stop INHEXAL 50? Try it.   ❏

EXERCISE SET 16.6

Predict the turtle's path with pencil and paper. Then, check your prediction by defining and running each procedure on the computer. Remember that CONTROL–G will stop a runaway turtle.

1. TO SERRATION
     RT 30   FD 20   LT 60   BK 20   RT 30
     SERRATION
   END

2. TO RAILING
     FD 40   RT 45   FD 20   LT 45   BK 40
     RAILING
   END

3. TO PARAPET
     REPEAT 3[FD 20   RT 90]
     BK 20   RT 90
     PARAPET
   END

4. TO PARAPET1
     REPEAT 5[FD 20   RT 45]
     RT 45   BK 20   RT 90
     PARAPET1
   END

For Exercises 5–8, write a recursive procedure to draw each pattern. Include a NOWRAP step.

5. LIGHTNING

6. MOLARS

7. SUBURBIA

8. RATTLESNAKE

9. Define a recursive procedure SPINSQUARE that spins (repeatedly) a square of side length 40 through 200° (clockwise). First, define the subprocedure SQUARE.

10. Define a recursive procedure SPINTRIANGLE that spins an equilateral triangle of side length 40 through 100°. First, define the subprocedure TRIANGLE.

11. Define a recursive procedure SPINRECTANGLE that spins a 60-by-20 rectangle through 160°. First, define the subprocedure RECTANGLE.

12. Define a recursive procedure SPINDECAGON that spins a regular decagon of side length 10 through 144°. First, define the subprocedure DECAGON.

13. A subprocedure FIGURE is used in a recursive procedure SPINFIGURE that spins the figure through 50°. How many copies of the figure will the turtle trace out before it begins retracing the first one?

14. The turtle traces the star in Figure 16.88 from the starting-ending position shown.

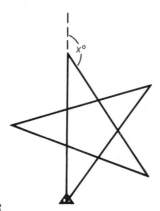

Figure 16.88

(a) How many complete (360°) right turns does the turtle make in tracing the star?
(b) How many turns of $x°$ each does it make?
(c) Find x.
(d) Write a nonrecursive procedure for drawing the star.
(e) Write a recursive procedure for drawing the star.

Write procedures for the spirals described in Exercises 15–18.

15. A triangular outward spiral OUTTRIAL whose side lengths increase by 5 turtle steps each time. Insert a step that will stop the procedure just before a side of length 100 or more appears. Check your program by running it with input 12.

16. A twisted triangular outward spiral OUTTRIAL-TWIST whose sides increase by 3 turtle steps each time. Put in a command that stops the turtle when it reaches any edge of the screen.

17. A triangular inward spiral INTRIAL, sides decreasing by 10 each time, that stops as soon as a side of length less than zero appears.

18. A twisted triangular inward spiral INTRIAL-TWIST, sides decreasing by 4 each time, that stops as soon as a side of length less than 20 appears.

Write procedures for the designs shown in Exercises 19 and 20.

19. SHRINKING.PARAPET of Figure 16.89; stop the design at the edge of the screen. What initial input will you give to your procedure?

Figure 16.89

20. GROWING.HOUSES of Figure 16.90. What initial input will you give to your procedure?

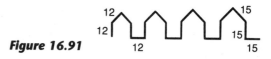

Figure 16.91

21. Write a recursive procedure NEWSQUARAL that will draw the spiral in Figure 16.91. Each square in the grid is 5 turtle steps by 5 turtle steps. Write your procedure in such a way that the spiral will stop as soon as a side of length 80 appears. What initial input will you give to your procedure?

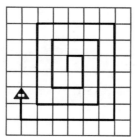

Figure 16.90

22. Repeat Exercise 21 for the TALLSPIRAL in Figure 16.92.

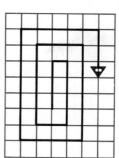

Figure 16.92

23. Write a recursive procedure NESTED.SQUARES that will draw the design in Figure 16.93. What initial input will you give your procedure?

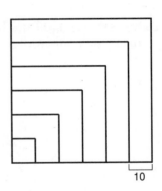

Figure 16.93

Key Concepts in Chapter 16

BASIC language
Immediate-execution mode
Deferred-execution mode
Programming commands
Interactive program
System commands
Looping command: FOR . . . NEXT
Branching command: IF . . . THEN
Logo language

Primitive
Procedure
Draw mode
Edit mode
Looping command: REPEAT
Variable procedure
Bottom-up programming
Top-down design
Recursion

❧ *Chapter 16 Review Exercises* ❧

1. Evaluate these BASIC expressions.
   (a) $- 3 + 4 * 6 \wedge 2 / 9 - 1$
   (b) SGN(10 − SQR(4 * 9))
   (c) ABS(INT(− 10 / 3))
   (d) INT(3 − RND(7))

2. Write an expression in BASIC that finds the remainder when 1000 is divided by 17.

3. Print just what the machine would when this BASIC program is run.
   ```
   10   LET A = 7
   20   LET B = 10
   30   LET B = A ∧ 2
   40   LET C = A + B
   50   PRINT "D = "; C/10
   60   END
   ```

4. Print just what the machine would when this BASIC program is run.
   ```
   10   LET Z = 10
   20   READ X
   30   LET Z = X + Z
   40   PRINT X, Z
   50   GOTO 20
   60   DATA 3, 5, 8
   70   END
   ```

5. Write a READ . . . DATA program that sends inputs from {1, 2, 4, 6, 7} through the function
   $$f(x) = \frac{x^3}{x + 1}$$
   and prints the corresponding outputs.

6. Show what would be printed if a user of this interactive BASIC program provided inputs 1, 4, 9 in that order.

```
10    INPUT X
20    LET Y = SQR(X) ∧ 3
30    PRINT Y
40    GOTO 10
```

7. Write an interactive BASIC program that accepts arbitrary inputs from the user, sends them through the function $f(x) = |5 - x^2|$, and prints the outputs.

8. Show what would be printed if a user of this interactive program provided inputs N = 14 and D = 3, then N = 17 and D = 7, then N = 30 and D = 4.

```
10    INPUT N
20    INPUT D
30    LET Q = INT (N / D + .5)
40    PRINT Q
50    GOTO 10
```

9. Describe what the run of this BASIC program will look like.

```
10    FOR N = 1 TO 100
20    PRINT N; ". I WILL NOT CHEW GUM
      IN COMPUTER CLASS."
30    NEXT N
40    END
```

10. Write a program with a FOR . . . NEXT loop that prints a two-column table showing the sixteen fractions $\frac{1}{16}$, $\frac{2}{16}$, . . . , $\frac{16}{16}$ opposite their decimal equivalents.

11. Revise the program in Exercise 10 so that the columns bear the headings FRACTION and DECIMAL EQUIVALENT followed by a line of space.

12. Print just what the machine would when this BASIC program is run.

```
10    FOR I = 1 TO 10
20    IF I/2 = INT(I/2) THEN 50
30    PRINT −I
40    GOTO 60
50    PRINT I
60    NEXT I
```

13. A triple of positive integers (A, B, C) is called a *Pythagorean triple* if $A^2 + B^2 = C^2$. For example, (3, 4, 5) is a Pythagorean triple because $3^2 + 4^2 = 5^2$. Write an interactive BASIC program that asks the user to input three positive integers (in order from smallest to largest) and then announces whether the user's triple is or is not a Pythagorean triple. *Hint:* Use N ∗ N rather than N ∧ 2 to avoid the difficulty noted at the end of Computer Vignette A, pp. 57–58.

14. Write a "polite" interactive BASIC program that lists all the divisors of any given whole number. *Hint:* D is a divisor of N if and only if N/D = INT(N/D).

15. Draw what the Logo turtle would draw. Exaggerate the size of the turtle step to 1 mm.
    (a) FD 40   RT 90   PU   FD 40   PD   LT 90   BK 40   LT 90   FD 40
    (b) REPEAT 3[FD 40   RT 45   FD 10 LT 45   BK 40   RT 45   BK 10]

16. Write a Logo procedure that draws the design shown in Figure 16.94.

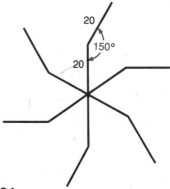

Figure 16.94

17. Write a Logo procedure that draws the semicircular design in Figure 16.95.

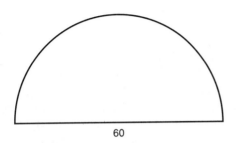

60

Figure 16.95

18. Write a one-variable Logo procedure VHEPTA-GON :LENGTH for drawing regular heptagons of arbitrary side length.

19. Figure 16.96 shows a run of VRECTANGLE 20 40. Sketch VRECTANGLE 60 20.

Figure 16.96　　

20. Write a recursive Logo procedure that draws the design in Figure 16.94.

21. Sketch the design that will be produced when WHATSIT 40 is run.

```
TO WHATSIT :L
  IF :L < 10 THEN STOP
  FD :L  RT 90
  WHATSIT :L - 10
END
```

References

Abelson, H., and A. diSessa. *Turtle Geometry: The Computer as a Medium for Exploring Mathematics.* Cambridge, Mass.: M.I.T. Press, 1979.

Arithmetic Teacher. Focus Issue—"Teaching with Microcomputers." vol. 30, no. 6, February 1983.

Johnson, J., and L. Malone. *Problems for BASIC Discoveries.* Palo Alto, Calif.: Creative Publications, 1983.

Kemeny, J., and T. Kurtz. *BASIC Programming.* 3rd ed. New York: Wiley, 1980.

Mathematics Teacher. Special Issue on Microcomputers. vol. 74, no. 8 November 1981.

Moore, M. *Logo Discoveries.* Palo Alto, Calif.: Creative Publications, 1984.

National Council of Teachers of Mathematics. *1984 Yearbook: Computers in Mathematics Education.* Reston, Va.: NCTM, 1984.

Shumway, R. *One Hundred and One BASIC Programs for Elementary School Mathematics.* Englewood Cliffs, N.J.: Prentice-Hall, 1987.

APPENDIX A: LOGIC

The great philosopher, logician, writer, and mathematician Bertrand Russell (1872–1970) once defined mathematics as "the subject in which we never know what we are talking about nor whether what we are saying is true." This oft-quoted definition will become more meaningful as we discuss the fundamental concept of *validity* and its relationship to *truth*.

A.1 Arguments, Validity, and Euler Diagrams

At its most basic level the purpose of logic is to codify common sense—to isolate and identify the patterns of reasoning that intelligent people find convincing. To achieve this end, logicians have subjected our thought patterns to the refining processes of generalization and symbolization. The resulting discipline gives us a clear picture of the accepted rules of reasoning, and provides us with specific procedures for deciding whether an argument is valid or invalid in complicated cases where our common sense might be confounded.

Before we can give examples of valid and invalid arguments, we need to define these terms. And in order to define them, we must explain the more primitive term *statement*. A **statement** is a declarative sentence that is unambiguously either true or false, not both.

EXAMPLE 1   Which of the following are statements?
(a) Thomas Jefferson was the third president of the United States.
(b) Who was the fourth president?
(c) Burt Reynolds was the fifth president.
(d) The first Republican president.

Solution   (a) Statement (true)
(b) Not a statement (not a declarative sentence)
(c) Statement (false)
(d) Not a statement (not a sentence)   ❏

A1

An **argument** is a set of statements, one of which—the **conclusion**—is viewed as "following" from the others—the **hypotheses,** or **premises.** The conclusion is listed last, and it is separated from the hypotheses by the word *therefore* or its three-dot symbolic abbreviation ∴.

An argument is called **valid** (or *logical*) if the assumption that all hypotheses are true *forces* the conclusion to be true.

An argument is called **invalid** (or *fallacious*) if all the hypotheses can be true and still the conclusion *can* be false.

Consider the following argument:

All spiders are animals.
All animals have four legs.
Therefore, all spiders have four legs.

The hypotheses are the two statements:

All spiders are animals.   (true)
All animals have four legs.   (false)

Their **truth values,** true and false, respectively, have been assigned by zoologists, not logicians. The conclusion is the statement:

All spiders have four legs.   (false)

Its truth value, false, has again been assigned by zoologists. The argument itself is classified as valid by logicians (and other reasonable people) because *if* both hypotheses were true, then the conclusion would also have to be true. It is the *form* of the argument, not the intrinsic meanings of its hypotheses and conclusion, that determines its validity.

A Venn diagram—or **Euler diagram,** as it is frequently called in the context of logic—can be used to illustrate the validity of the preceding argument.

Let S = set of all spiders.
Let A = set of all animals.
Let F = set of all four-legged things.

We begin by assuming that both hypotheses are true. The first, that all spiders are animals, translates into $S \subseteq A$, and the second, that all animals have four legs, translates into $A \subseteq F$. From the Euler diagram in Figure A.1 it follows that $S \subseteq F$; that is, all spiders have four legs. Notice that the same Euler diagram illustrates the validity of the following argument, all three statements of which are false:

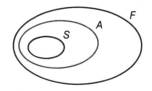

Figure A.1

All secretaries are athletic.
All athletic people are friendly.
Therefore, all secretaries are friendly.

The general valid argument form, of which the preceding examples were **substitution instances,** is this:

All S are A.
All A are F.
Therefore, all S are F.

The examples have illustrated a point worth remembering: the *validity* of an argument *does not guarantee* the *truth* of its conclusion. The next example will show that the *truth* of the conclusion *does not guarantee* the *validity* of the argument either. Thus truth and validity are two quite different concepts. Statements are true or false; arguments are valid or invalid. The connection between the two concepts is found in the definition of validity: a valid argument cannot have all true hypotheses and a false conclusion.

EXAMPLE 2   Analyze this argument.

Meryl Streep is a movie actress.
Some movie actresses have won Oscars.
Therefore, Meryl Streep has won an Oscar.

Solution   The hypotheses are the first two statements, both of which are true. The conclusion is the third statement, which is also true. The argument, however, is *invalid,* as your common sense probably tells you. (The two facts, that Meryl Streep is an actress and that some actresses have won Oscars, do not account for Meryl Streep's having won one.)

A more detailed explanation of why the argument is invalid involves looking at its general form. If the argument were valid, then it would remain so if *Meryl Streep* were replaced by any other name, because such a replacement would not alter the *form* of the argument. But if we insert *Brooke Shields,* we get two true hypotheses:

Brooke Shields is a movie actress.   (true)
Some movie actresses have won Oscars.   (true)

And we get a false conclusion:

Brooke Shields has won an Oscar.   (false)

That is, we get an invalid argument.

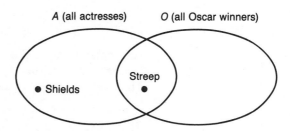

A (all actresses)   *O* (all Oscar winners)

Figure A.2

Again, an Euler diagram (Figure A.2) can be used to illuminate why the conclusion does not follow necessarily from the hypotheses. That is, just because a person is an actress and some actresses have won Oscars, it does not follow that that person has won an Oscar.   ❏

Since it is the form of an argument rather than the intrinsic contents of its hypotheses and conclusion that determines validity, we should be able to test for validity even when we don't understand the statements. In fact, it is often easier to analyze the structure of an argument without the distraction of having meanings attached to the statements.

EXAMPLE 3   Use an Euler diagram to test the validity of this argument.

> Some Toggies are Oompahs.
> Every Oompah is a Larp.
> Therefore, some Toggy is a Larp.

Solution   Let T, O, and L denote the sets of Toggies, Oompahs, and Larps respectively. If we can draw an Euler diagram in which the two hypotheses are true but the conclusion is false, then the argument is invalid. If no such diagram is possible—that is, if the truth of the hypotheses forces the truth of the conclusion— then the argument is valid. To guarantee that the first hypothesis is true we draw overlapping loops for T and O and put a dot in their intersection to indicate the existence of at least one member. (Figure A.3) To guarantee that the second hypothesis is true, the loop we draw for L must completely encircle the loop for O. (Figure A.4)

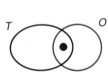

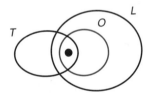

Figure A.3   **Figure A.4**

Now, since there is a dot in $T \cap L$ in Figure A.4, we are forced to conclude that some Toggy is a Larp. Thus the argument is valid.   ❏

EXAMPLE 4   Use an Euler diagram to test the validity of this argument.

> All professors are absentminded.
> No professors are rich.
> Therefore, no absentminded people are rich.

Solution   Let P, A, and R denote the sets of professors, absentminded people, and rich people, respectively. Again we set out to draw an Euler diagram in which the hypotheses are true but the conclusion is false. We represent the first hypothesis, $P \subseteq A$, as in Figure A.5. The second hypothesis, $P \cap R = \varnothing$, we represent by drawing the loop R as in Figure A.6.

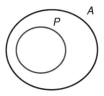

Figure A.5

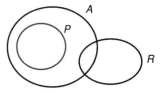

Figure A.6

Clearly, Figure A.6 allows the possibility that the set $A \cap R$ is nonempty; that is, that some absentminded people are rich. Thus the conclusion *can* be false, and the argument is invalid.   ❑

EXERCISE SET A.1

1. Pick out the statements from the following list, and classify them as true or false if you can.
   (a) $8 \cdot 7 = 54$
   (b) $\frac{3}{8} = 0.375$
   (c) $3x = 18$
   (d) $2x > x$
   (e) The population of Greenland at 12:00 noon, January 1, 1450, was 229.
   (f) This sentence is false.

2. Answer these four questions.
   (a) Can an invalid argument draw a true conclusion from true hypotheses?
   (b) Can an invalid argument draw a false conclusion from true hypotheses?
   (c) Can a valid argument draw a true conclusion from true hypotheses?
   (d) Can a valid argument draw a false conclusion from true hypotheses?

3. Answer these four questions.
   (a) Must an invalid argument draw a true conclusion from true hypotheses?
   (b) Must an invalid argument draw a false conclusion from true hypotheses?
   (c) Must a valid argument draw a true conclusion from true hypotheses?
   (d) Must a valid argument draw a false conclusion from true hypotheses?

4. Suppose the conclusion of an argument is false. With which of the following do you agree?
   (a) All the hypotheses are false.
   (b) Some hypothesis is false.
   (c) The argument is invalid.
   (d) Either the argument is invalid, or some hypothesis is false.

Match each of the statements in Exercises 5–12 with

the most appropriate diagram, (a), (b), (c), or (d), in Figure A.7.

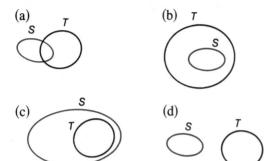

Figure A.7

5. Some toys are shiny.

6. All scientists are teetotalers.

7. No sculptors are typists.

8. Anyone who is thin is a suspect.

9. If one is timid, then one is shy.

10. At least one sailor is tall.

11. Only traitors are spies.

12. If one is studious, then one is not talkative.

Use Euler diagrams to test each of the arguments in Exercises 13–24 for validity.

13. Hypotheses: Blessed are the meek. Harvey is not blessed.
    Conclusion: Harvey is not meek.

14. Hypotheses: If one is healthy, then one is lucky. Bob is not healthy.
    Conclusion: Bob is not lucky.

15. If one is healthy, then one is lucky. Tom is lucky. Therefore, Tom is healthy.

16. All sculptors are anarchists. All anarchists enjoy broccoli. Therefore, all sculptors enjoy broccoli.

17. All joggers are happy. Some smokers are happy. Therefore, some smokers jog.

18. Only gourmets eat truffles. Some sows eat truffles. Therefore, some sows are gourmets.

19. Some blafustos are mundingas. Some arbochucks are mundingas. Therefore, some blafustos are arbochucks.

20. Some Wobbies are Looloos. Every Pimbolla is a Wobby. Therefore, some Pimbollas are Looloos.

21. No sensible person believes in flying saucers. Some physicists are not sensible. Therefore, some physicists believe in flying saucers.

22. Only fools fall in love. Fools are poor. Rock stars are rich. Therefore, rock stars do not fall in love.

23. All equilateral triangles are isosceles. All isosceles triangles have one obtuse angle. Therefore, all equilateral triangles have one obtuse angle.

24. Some parallelograms are rectangles. All squares are rectangles. Therefore, some squares are parallelograms.

For Exercises 25–28, sketch an Euler diagram. Then supply a conclusion that follows logically (validly) from the given hypotheses.

25. Any friend of yours is a friend of mine. All of my friends are good-natured.

26. Every parallelogram is a quadrilateral. Some parallelograms are equilateral.

27. If a decimal repeats, then it represents a rational number. Pi is not a rational number.

28. Every whole number is an integer. No integer is a solution to the equation $x^4 = \frac{1}{16}$.

 **A.2 Compound Statements**

Arguments are made up of statements—hypotheses and conclusions—and the validity of an argument is defined in terms of the truth values of those statements. Namely, the argument is invalid if the hypotheses can be true and the conclusion false. Our purpose in this section is to exhibit some rather formal techniques for assigning truth values to *compound* statements. Later we will use those techniques to test arguments for validity.

Fundamental Logical Connectives

Consider these statements:

Oranges contain vitamin C.	(T)
Silver conducts electricity.	(T)
Canaries hibernate.	(F)
$9 \cdot 7 = 64$.	(F)

These statements are called **simple** (or atomic) **statements** to indicate that they cannot be broken down into smaller statements. They are our indivisible building blocks; their truth values are assigned not by logicians but by biochemists, physicists, ornithologists, mathematicians, and so on. Statements that are built up from simple statements by means of the **logical connectives**—*and, or, not, if . . . then,* and *if and only if*—are called **compound** (or molecular) **statements.** Their truth values depend on the truth values of the component simple statements and on the particular connective used.

For example, the statement

Oranges contain vitamin C, and silver conducts electricity.

will be classified as true by a logician (or any reasonable person) because its component simple statements are both known to be true. The statement

Oranges contain vitamin C, and canaries hibernate.

is classified as false because of our understanding about the meaning of the word *and*. For an *and* statement to be true, both component statements must be true.

In the discussion that follows, a **truth table** will be very helpful for expressing this agreement about *and* symbolically. But before we consider truth tables, we need to introduce some standard notation and terminology. The logical connective *and* is referred to as the **conjunction operation,** and is denoted by the hat symbol ($\wedge$). Arbitrary statements are usually represented by lowercase letters (statement variables) $p, q, \ldots$ near the middle of the alphabet.

The truth table for conjunction (Table A.1) shows what truth values are assigned to the compound statement $p \wedge q$ for all possible pairs of truth values for its components p and q. *Note:* Sometimes, $p \wedge q$ is called a **statement form,** rather than a statement, to emphasize that it does not become a statement until the variables p and q are replaced by statements.

One way to remember this truth table is to notice the following property.

Table A.1 Truth Table for Conjunction (*and,* $\wedge$)

p	q	$p \wedge q$
T	T	T
T	F	F
F	T	F
F	F	F

An *and* statement (conjunction) is true in only one case—when both component statements are true.

The logical connective *or* is known as the **disjunction operation.** Its meaning is not quite as self-evident as that of *and;* in fact, there are two different meanings in common use. Suppose we are told that

The deciding vote was cast by a Democrat or a southerner.

You probably agree that we have not been lied to in all of the following cases.

A northern Democrat cast the deciding vote.
A southern Republican cast the deciding vote.
A southern Democrat cast the deciding vote.

That is, we classify the *or* statement as true in all cases except one—the case in which both component statements are false.

> An *or* statement (disjunction) is true if either or both component statements is true.

This meaning is the *inclusive* meaning of *or* that lawyers often express as *and/ or,* as in "It is illegal to sing and/or dance on Main Street on Sunday."

The other, *exclusive,* meaning of *or* disallows the conjunction. For example, when you read on a menu that "price of dinner includes soup or salad," *or* means that you cannot have both. The word *either* is often used as a signal that the exclusive meaning of *or* is intended.

For most logical and mathematical purposes the inclusive meaning is the more appropriate one. The vee symbol ($\lor$) for disjunction comes from the Latin word *vel,* meaning "inclusive or." (The Latin word for "exclusive or" is *aut.*) The truth table for disjunction is shown in Table A.2.

An easy way to remember this truth table is to notice the following property.

Table A.2 Truth Table for Disjunction (*or,* $\lor$)

p	*q*	*p* $\lor$ *q*
T	T	T
T	F	T
F	T	T
F	F	F

> An *or* statement (disjunction) is false in only one case—when both component statements are false.

The logical connective *not,* referred to as the **negation operation** and symbolized by a tilde ($\sim$), differs from *and* and *or* in that it is applied to a single statement rather than to a pair of statements. Usually, negating a simple statement is straightforward. The negation of

Oranges contain vitamin C.

is

Oranges do not contain vitamin C.

The negation of

> Canaries hibernate.

is

> Canaries do not hibernate.

Occasionally, though, one needs to be careful. The negation of

> Kenny is rich.

is

> Kenny is not rich.

The statement "Kenny is poor," while tempting, is incorrect. The difficulty is that "Kenny is rich" and "Kenny is poor" could both be false; and in all cases we want precisely one of a statement and its negation to be true.

A statement and its negation have opposite truth values.

Table A.3 Truth Table for Negation (*not,* ~)

p	~*p*
T	F
F	T

The truth table for negation (Table A.3) is only two lines long.

The logical connective *if . . , then* is another way of joining an ordered pair of statements to produce a third. The first statement is inserted after the word *if,* the second after *then*. For example, we can combine the two statements

> John is rich.
> John can afford to buy his own lunch.

into the new statement

> If John is rich, then John can afford to buy his own lunch.

The *if . . . then* connective is referred to as the **conditional operation,** and it is symbolized by an arrow (→). Thus the preceding conditional statement can be written

> John is rich → John can afford to buy his own lunch.

The truth table for the conditional (Table A.4) is reminiscent of our agreement about what constitutes an invalid argument.

The only time a conditional is false is when the first statement (the antecedent) is true and the second statement (the consequent) is false.

The four lines of this table are often justified by thinking of a conditional as a contract. If the contract is broken, the conditional is false; otherwise, it is true.

For example, suppose that a tenant and a landlord have agreed to the following:

Table A.4 Truth Table for
Conditional (*if . . . then,* →)

p	q	p → q
T	T	T
T	F	F
F	T	T
F	F	T

If the tenant shovels his own snow, then the landlord lowers the rent
   by $5.

Then:

Line 1 of the truth table corresponds to the situation in which the tenant
   shovels and the landlord lowers. The contract has been honored.

Line 2 of the truth table corresponds to the tenant shoveling and the
   landlord not lowering. The contract has been broken.

Line 3 corresponds to the tenant not shoveling and the landlord (gener-
   ously) lowering. The contract has not been broken.

Line 4 corresponds to neither party doing anything. The contract has not
   been broken.

The final logical connective is the **biconditional operation,** *if and only if,*
which is symbolized by a two-headed arrow (↔). For example, the statement

Tina will come along if and only if Sue's car will start.

Table A.5 Truth Table for
Biconditional (*if and only if,* ↔)

p	q	p ↔ q
T	T	T
T	F	F
F	T	F
F	F	T

is symbolized

Tina will come along ↔ Sue's car will start

There are just two situations in which we would consider this statement to be
false: Sue's car will start, and still Tina will not come along; Sue's car will not
start, and Tina will come along anyway. In the other two cases—when both
component statements have the same truth value, either true or false—the biconditional statement is true.

The truth table for the biconditional is shown in Table A.5.

A biconditional statement is true in just two cases: (1) when both components
are true and (2) when both components are false.

EXAMPLE 1   Let *A*, *B*, *C*, *D* stand for the following statements:

A: $2 + 2 = 5$ (F)
B: $2 < 5$ (T)
C: Cows fly.   (F)
D: 2 is an even number.   (T)

Translate each of the following symbolic expressions, and assign truth values.
(a) $B \wedge D$
(b) $B \vee C$
(c) $\sim A$
(d) $A \rightarrow C$
(e) $B \leftrightarrow A$

Solution   (a) $2 < 5$ and 2 is an even number.   (T)
(b) $2 < 5$ or cows fly.   (T)
(c) $2 + 2 \neq 5$ (T)
(d) If $2 + 2 = 5$, then cows fly.   (T)
(e) $2 < 5$ if and only if $2 + 2 = 5$.   (F)   ❏

Further Compounding

We have seen five different ways to make new statements out of old ones: conjunction, disjunction, negation, conditional, and biconditional. While we tended to think of p and q as representing simple statements from which we formed compound ones,

$$p \wedge q \quad p \vee q \quad \sim p \quad p \rightarrow q \quad p \leftrightarrow q$$

there is no reason why we cannot go on compounding compound statements, as long as we are careful to indicate the order in which the logical operations are to be performed. Aside from the usual "do this first" meaning of parentheses, we will adopt just one convention governing the order of operations:

In the absence of parentheses negation takes precedence over the other four operations.

EXAMPLE 2   What operation is performed first and what operation is performed last in producing these compound statements?
(a) $(p \vee q) \rightarrow r$
(b) $\sim((p \wedge q) \vee r)$
(c) $(q \rightarrow \sim p) \vee p$
(d) $p \vee q \wedge r$

Solution   (a) $\vee$ first; $\rightarrow$ last.
(b) $\wedge$ first; $\sim$ last.
(c) $\sim$ first; $\vee$ last.
(d) Without parentheses this expression is ambiguous. Does it mean $(p \vee q) \wedge r$ or does it mean $p \vee (q \wedge r)$?   ❏

EXAMPLE 3   Use these abbreviations for simple statements:

  A: Ann goes shopping.
  B: Beth stays home.
  C: Carol stays home.
  D: Diane takes the car.

Symbolize each of the following compound statements.

(a) If Diane takes the car, then Beth stays home and Ann does not go shopping.

(b) If Beth and Carol stay home, then Ann does not go shopping.

(c) If Beth stays home, but Carol does not, then Diane takes the car.

(d) Ann goes shopping; and if Diane does not take the car, then Beth does not stay home.

Solution   (a) $D \rightarrow (B \wedge \sim A)$.

(b) $(B \wedge C) \rightarrow \sim A$. Notice how in ordinary English we abbreviate the conjunction "Beth stays home and Carol stays home" as "Beth and Carol stay home."

(c) $(B \wedge \sim C) \rightarrow D$. Notice how in ordinary English *but* means *and*.

(d) $A \wedge (\sim D \rightarrow \sim B)$ ❑

Once one has translated an English statement into symbols, one can determine its truth or falsity in a purely mechanical way—assuming, of course, that the truth values of the simple statements are known.

EXAMPLE 4   Assuming that all four of the simple statements A, B, C, and D are true, determine the truth or falsity of the four compound statements of Example 3.

Solution   If you keep in mind the order of operations and the truth tables for the logical connectives, the following diagrams should be self-explanatory.

(a) $D \rightarrow (B \wedge \sim A)$

		T	(A is true)
	T	F	(B is true and $\sim A$ is false)
T		F	(D is true and $B \wedge \sim A$ is false)
	F		(the compound statement is false)

(b) $(B \wedge C) \rightarrow \sim A$

T T		T
T		F
	F	(the compound statement is false)

(c) $(B \wedge \sim C) \rightarrow D$

	T	
T F		
F		T
	T	(the compound statement is true)

(d) $A \wedge (\sim D \rightarrow \sim B)$

	T	T
	F	F
T	T	
T		(the compound statement is true) ❑

In the general case, where we want to allow the simple component statements to take on all possible truth values, a similar kind of mechanical procedure can be used to produce a complete truth table.

EXAMPLE 5   Make a truth table for the statement form $(p \wedge \sim q) \to q$.

Solution   Begin by thinking of all of the stages one passes through in building this statement. One begins with p and q, forms $\sim q$, then $p \wedge \sim q$, and finally, $(p \wedge \sim q) \to q$. Now, make a table that has all of those statements across the top (Table A.6). Start by filling in columns ① and ② with the four possible combinations of truth values for p and q. Next, fill in column ③ by looking at column ② and recalling the truth table for negation. Next, fill in column ④ by looking at columns ① and ③ and remembering the truth table for conjunction. Finally, fill in column ⑤ by looking at columns ④ and ② and using the truth table for the conditional. Columns ①, ②, and ⑤ constitute the finished truth table for the given statement.

Table A.6

p	q	$\sim q$	$p \wedge \sim q$	$(p \wedge \sim q) \to q$
T	T	F	F	T
T	F	T	T	F
F	T	F	F	T
F	F	T	F	T
①	②	③	④	⑤

EXERCISE SET A.2

In Exercises 1–6 statements have been symbolized by letters as follows:

　　A: Amy will drive.
　　B: Bruce will buy the gas.
　　C: Cathy will come along.

Translate each symbolic expression into words.

1. $A \to B$
2. $B \vee \sim C$
3. $A \wedge C$
4. $C \leftrightarrow (A \wedge B)$
5. $\sim B \to \sim A$
6. $(A \wedge \sim C) \to B$

Using the letters A, B, and C with the same meanings as in the previous exercises, translate each of the following sentences into symbols.

7. Bruce will not buy the gas.
8. Bruce will buy the gas, but Amy will not drive.
9. If Cathy will come along, Bruce will buy the gas.
10. Amy will drive if Bruce will buy the gas or Cathy will come along.

11. Cathy will come along if Amy will drive and Bruce will buy the gas.

12. Bruce will buy the gas if and only if Amy will not drive.

Suppose that A and B are true statements, and R and S are false statements. Classify each of these statements as true or false.

13. $A \wedge \sim R$

14. $\sim(A \vee S)$

15. $(A \vee R) \rightarrow S$

16. $(A \wedge (B \vee R)) \rightarrow \sim S$

17. $\sim(A \wedge B) \leftrightarrow (R \vee S)$

18. $((A \leftrightarrow R) \vee \sim S) \rightarrow (B \rightarrow S)$

Again, suppose A and B are true statements, and R and S are false. What (if any) truth value(s) for statement X will make each of the following true?

19. $(A \wedge \sim R) \rightarrow X$

20. $\sim(S \vee X)$

21. $R \vee (S \rightarrow X)$

22. $(\sim X \vee A) \rightarrow (S \wedge \sim B)$

23. $(X \wedge A) \leftrightarrow (\sim X \vee R)$

24. $\sim((X \vee R) \wedge S)$

In Exercises 25–30, make complete truth tables.

25. $p \rightarrow (p \wedge q)$

26. $(p \vee q) \rightarrow \sim q$

27. $((p \rightarrow q) \wedge q) \rightarrow p$

28. $((p \rightarrow q) \wedge \sim p) \rightarrow \sim q$

29. $((p \rightarrow q) \wedge p) \rightarrow q$

30. $((p \vee q) \wedge \sim p) \rightarrow q$

31. Make a truth table for $(p \wedge q) \rightarrow (r \vee \sim p)$. *Hint:* The table will have eight lines. A systematic way of obtaining all possible combinations of truth values for p, q, r is to assign p the values TTTTFFFF (in order), q the values TTFFTTFF (in order), and r the values TFTFTFTF (in order).

32. The truth table for $(p \rightarrow (q \vee \sim r)) \leftrightarrow (s \wedge t)$ would have how many lines? (Do *not* make the table.)

33. Each of the four operations $\wedge$, $\vee$, $\rightarrow$, $\leftrightarrow$ can be thought of as a binary operation on the two-element set $\{T, F\}$.
    (a) Make the Cayley table for each.
    (b) Why cannot $\sim$ be viewed as a binary operation on $\{T, F\}$? How can it be thought of?

A.3 *Truth Tables and Tautologies*

We are still working on the central problem of determining whether an argument is valid or invalid. In this section we describe a formal procedure for making that decision.

Validity and Invalidity via Truth Tables

✳Remember that an argument is valid if its general form is valid. And the general form is valid if every substitution instance of it that has true hypotheses must also have a true conclusion. Consider, for example, this argument:

If dysprosium is a rare-earth element, then its atomic number is less than 72.

Dysprosium is a rare-earth element.
Therefore, the atomic number of dysprosium is less than 72.

For many nonchemists assigning truth values to the three statements would be a difficult task. Ascertaining the validity of the argument, however, requires no knowledge of chemistry since validity depends only on the general form of the argument, not on whether the hypotheses actually are true.

Here is the general form of the argument:

$$r \rightarrow s$$
$$r$$
$$\therefore s$$

To re-create the instance that gave rise to this general form, replace r by "dysprosium is a *r*are-earth element" and s by "The atomic number of dysprosium is less than *s*eventy-two."

To see whether this argument form is valid, we need to check that if both $r \rightarrow s$ and r are true, then s must also be true. To do so, we make a truth table (Table A.7) that covers all possible substitution instances. We observe that there is only one line on which both hypotheses, $r \rightarrow s$ and r, have truth value T, namely, line 1. But on line 1 the conclusion s also has truth value T. Thus the argument form is valid, and thus the original argument (about dysprosium) is also valid. This particular valid argument form is often called the *law of detachment* because it allows one to detach a true antecedent (r) from a true conditional ($r \rightarrow s$) and be left with a true consequent (s).

An argument is invalid if its general form is invalid; that is, if some substitution instance of it has true hypotheses but a false conclusion. Consider this argument:

If Meg passes her chemistry course, then she will graduate.
Meg does not pass chemistry.
Therefore, Meg will not graduate.

Its general form is as follows:

$$c \rightarrow g$$
$$\sim c$$
$$\therefore \sim g$$

Again, we make a truth table (Table A.8) to cover all possible substitution instances.

This time, the hypotheses, $c \rightarrow g$ and $\sim c$, have truth value T on both lines 3 and 4. The conclusion, $\sim g$, has truth value F on line 3, however, which tells us that the argument form is invalid (fallacious). Supplying a substitution instance to highlight the fallacy completes the story.

Replace c by "Bruce Springsteen was born in California."
Replace g by "Bruce Springsteen was born in the U.S.A."

Table A.7

r	s	$r \rightarrow s$
T	T	T
T	F	F
F	T	T
F	F	T

Table A.8

c	g	$\sim c$	$\sim g$	$c \rightarrow g$
T	T	F	F	T
T	F	F	T	F
F	T	T	F	T
F	F	T	T	T

Then:

$c \rightarrow g$ is true (a geopolitical fact).
$\sim c$ is true (Bruce was born in New Jersey).
But $\sim g$ is false (another geopolitical fact).

This particular fallacy (incorrectly inferring $\sim g$ from $c \rightarrow g$ and $\sim c$) is so common that it has been honored with a name, the *fallacy of denying the antecedent*.

The truth table test for validity can be summarized in a flowchart, as in Figure A.8. (If you have not yet studied flowcharts, don't worry about the shapes of the boxes. Just follow the arrows.)

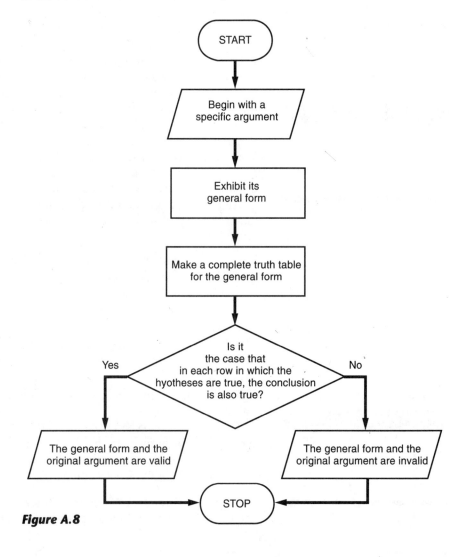

Figure A.8

EXAMPLE 1 Test the following argument for validity.

> If Ann is absent, then so is Carol.
> Ann or Betty is absent.
> Not both of Betty and Carol are absent.
> Therefore, Ann is absent.

Solution Let A, B, and C be the simple statements Ann is absent, Betty is absent, and Carol is absent. Then the argument becomes:

$$A \rightarrow C$$
$$A \vee B$$
$$\sim(B \wedge C)$$
$$\therefore A$$

A truth table (Table A.9) for the corresponding argument form requires eight lines. (Notice the pattern of T's and F's that we chose for the first three columns.)

Table A.9

	a	b	c	$a \rightarrow c$	$a \vee b$	$b \wedge c$	$\sim(b \wedge c)$
1	T	T	T	T	T	T	F
2	T	T	F	F	T	F	T
3	T	F	T	T	T	F	T
4	T	F	F	F	T	F	T
5	F	T	T	T	T	T	F
6	F	T	F	T	T	F	T
7	F	F	T	T	F	F	T
8	F	F	F	T	F	F	T
	①	②	③	④	⑤	⑥	⑦

Observe that the three hypotheses (columns ④, ⑤, ⑦) are all true in just two cases, line 3 and line 6. In line 3 the conclusion (column ①) is also true—so far, so good. But in line 6 the conclusion is false. Thus we conclude that the argument is invalid: it is possible for all three hypotheses to be true and the conclusion to be false. Perhaps you noticed a shortcut: lines 1–4 of the truth table were not really needed. The only lines in which invalidity could possibly appear are those lines in which the conclusion is false. ❑

Tautologies

A **tautology** is a statement form that is always true, no matter what truth values are assigned to its component statement variables.

EXAMPLE 2   Which of the following are tautologies?
(a) $p \lor \sim p$
(b) $(p \lor q) \to p$
(c) $(r \land (r \to s)) \to s$

Solution   Make truth tables.
(a) See Table A.10. Since the third column is all T's, $p \lor \sim p$ is a tautology.
(b) See Table A.11. Since the fourth column contains an F, $(p \lor q) \to p$ is not a tautology.

Table A.10

p	$\sim p$	$p \lor \sim p$
T	F	T
F	T	T

Table A.11

p	q	$p \lor q$	$(p \lor q) \to p$
T	T	T	T
T	F	T	T
F	T	T	F
F	F	F	T

(c) See Table A.12. Since the fifth column is all T's, $(r \land (r \to s)) \to s$ is a tautology.

Table A.12

r	s	$r \to s$	$r \land (r \to s)$	$(r \land (r \to s)) \to s$
T	T	T	T	T
T	F	F	F	T
F	T	T	F	T
F	F	T	F	T

❏

Example 2(c) suggests the connection between the concept of tautology and the fundamental problem of validity. The argument form

r
$r \to s$
$\therefore s$

is *valid* if and only if the conjunction of true hypotheses forces a true conclusion; the statement form $(r \land (r \to s)) \to s$ is a *tautology* if and only if assigning T's to both r and $r \to s$ results in a T for s as well. Thus one way to test an argument for validity is to check that the conditional having the conjunction of all the hypotheses as antecedent and the conclusion as consequent is a tautology. That is, the argument form

$$h_1$$
$$h_2$$
$$\vdots$$
$$h_n$$
$$\therefore c$$

is valid if and only if the statement form

$$(h_1 \wedge h_2 \wedge \cdots \wedge h_n) \to c$$

is a tautology. In practice, this test for validity is rarely used. To check that the argument in Example 1 is invalid, for example, would involve showing that the statement form

$$((a \to c) \wedge (a \vee b) \wedge \sim(b \wedge c)) \to a$$

is not a tautology, a task that would add at least two more columns to an already ungainly truth table, Table A.9.

Logical Equivalence

Two statement forms are said to be **logically equivalent** if they have identical truth tables. When r and s are logically equivalent, we write $r \Leftrightarrow s$.

EXAMPLE 3   Verify this rule for denying (negating) a conjunction (one of *DeMorgan's rules*): $\sim(p \wedge q) \Leftrightarrow \sim p \vee \sim q$

Solution   Fill in the truth table (Table A.13). Then compare columns ④ and ⑦. Since they are identical, the statement forms $\sim(p \wedge q)$ and $\sim p \vee \sim q$ are logically equivalent. In symbols, $\sim(p \wedge q) \Leftrightarrow \sim p \vee \sim q$.

Table A.13

p	q	$p \wedge q$	$\sim(p \wedge q)$	$\sim p$	$\sim q$	$\sim p \vee \sim q$
T	T	T	F	F	F	F
T	F	F	T	F	T	T
F	T	F	T	T	F	T
F	F	F	T	T	T	T
①	②	③	④	⑤	⑥	⑦

One reason for introducing the concept of logical equivalence here is that it allows us to explain, in careful terms, the connection between a conditional and various related statements.

Statements Related to a Conditional

With each conditional (*if . . . then* statement) are associated three other conditionals known as the converse, the contrapositive, and the inverse.

Let the conditional be $A \rightarrow C$. Then:
The **converse** is $C \rightarrow A$.
The **contrapositive** is $\sim C \rightarrow \sim A$.
The **inverse** is $\sim A \rightarrow \sim C$.

EXAMPLE 4   Write the converse, the contrapositive, and the inverse of the following conditional statement about a rectangle R. Also, decide on the truth or falsity of each.

If R is 5 by 3, then R has perimeter 16.

Solution   *Conditional* (given) is true.
Converse: If R has perimeter 16, then R is 5 by 3. The converse is false. Rectangle R could be 2 by 6, for example.
Contrapositive: If R does not have perimeter 16, then R is not 5 by 3. The contrapositive is true.
Inverse: If R is not 5 by 3, then R does not have perimeter 16. The inverse is false. Rectangle R could be 2 by 6, for example.   ❑

The generalizations from this example, which can be established via truth tables (see Exercise 24), follow.

A conditional and its contrapositive have the same truth values (are logically equivalent).

A conditional and its converse do *not* have the same truth values (they are *not* logically equivalent).

Since the inverse is the contrapositive of the converse, the inverse and the converse are logically equivalent.

EXERCISE SET A.3

Use truth tables to determine the validity or invalidity of each of the following argument forms.

1. p
   $\therefore p \vee q$

2. p
   $\therefore p \wedge q$

3. $p \rightarrow q$
   p
   $\therefore q \rightarrow p$

4. $p \rightarrow q$
   $p \vee q$
   $\therefore q$

5. $p \rightarrow q$
   $\sim q$
   $\therefore p$

6. $p \rightarrow q$
   $q \rightarrow p$
   $\therefore p \lor q$

7. $p \rightarrow q$
   $p \rightarrow r$
   p
   $\therefore q \land r$

8. $p \rightarrow (q \rightarrow r)$
   $p \rightarrow q$
   $\sim r$
   $\therefore p$

Use truth tables to determine the validity or invalidity of each of the following arguments.

9. If the doctor is right, then if Joan eats eggs, she gets sick. Joan does not get sick. Therefore, if Joan eats eggs, then the doctor is wrong. (Symbolize statements as follows: *D:* the doctor is right, *E:* Joan eats eggs, and *S:* Joan gets sick.)

10. If the bill passes, then employment rises, but so does the deficit. If the deficit rises, then employment does not rise. Therefore, if employment rises, then the bill does not pass. (Symbolize statements as follows: *B:* bill passes, *E:* employment rises, and *D:* deficit rises.)

11. If the Bluejays finish first, then the Red Sox or the Yankees finish second. If the Red Sox finish second, then the Bluejays do not finish first. Therefore if the Yankees finish second, then the Bluejays finish first.

12. Apartments become scarce if rent controls are imposed. Kelly gets elected, or rent controls are not imposed. Kelly does not get elected. Therefore apartments do not become scarce.

13. Collins resigns if Dickson or Baker is hired. Anderson or Baker is hired. Collins does not resign. Therefore Anderson is hired.

14. If the bass has a cold or the alto has an earache, then the quartet does not perform. If the soprano is in good voice, then the alto has an earache. Therefore the quartet performs if and only if the soprano is not in good voice.

Show, by making truth tables, that the statement forms in Exercises 15–22 are tautologies.

15. $p \rightarrow (p \lor q)$

16. $(p \land q) \rightarrow p$

17. $p \lor \sim p$

18. $\sim (p \land \sim p)$

19. $(p \lor q) \leftrightarrow (q \lor p)$

20. $(p \rightarrow (q \land \sim q)) \rightarrow \sim p$

21. $((p \rightarrow q) \land (q \rightarrow r)) \rightarrow (p \rightarrow r)$

22. $((p \land q) \rightarrow r) \leftrightarrow (p \rightarrow (q \rightarrow r))$

23. Show that $p \rightarrow q$ and $\sim p \lor q$ are logically equivalent. (Do the two statements "If Rose drives then I walk" and "Rose does not drive or I walk" convey the same message?)

24. Make one big truth table for all four of
    $$p \rightarrow q \qquad q \rightarrow p \qquad \sim q \rightarrow \sim p \qquad \sim p \rightarrow \sim q$$
    From it, pick out the logically equivalent pairs.

Write the contrapositive, the converse, and the inverse of each conditional in Exercises 25–26.

25. If you own a calculator, then you can convert fractions to decimals flawlessly.

26. If you do not endure pain, then you do not gain an athletic body. ("No pain, no gain.")

In Example 3 we established the rule for denying a conjunction, $\sim (p \land q) \Leftrightarrow \sim p \lor \sim q$, by filling in a truth table. To see how this rule is used in our everyday thought processes, consider the instance of it in which p is replaced by "Wendy is polite" and q by "Wendy is quiet." Then:

$\sim (p \land q)$ becomes "It is not the case that Wendy is polite and quiet."

$\sim p \lor \sim q$ becomes "Wendy is not polite or Wendy is not quiet."

Under the inclusive interpretation of *or* these two statements convey the same message (are logically equivalent). By filling in truth tables, establish these other negation rules. Also, illustrate each one by replacing p and q by the preceding specific statements.

27. $\sim (\sim p) \Leftrightarrow p$ (denying a negation)

28. $\sim (p \lor q) \Leftrightarrow \sim p \land \sim q$ (denying a disjunction; the other of *DeMorgan's rules*)

29. $\sim (p \rightarrow q) \Leftrightarrow p \land \sim q$ (denying a conditional)

30. $\sim(p \leftrightarrow q) \Leftrightarrow (\sim p \wedge q) \vee (p \wedge \sim q)$
(denying a biconditional)

Use the preceding negation rules to deny each of the following statements.

31. An appropriations bill will be passed, or Congress will remain in session.

32. Michael is a gentleman and a scholar.

33. If Claire will attend the meeting, she will be elected treasurer.

34. Debbie was either speeding or not paying attention.

35. Jim will get a raise if and only if he will marry the boss's daughter.

36. If Johnson will not pitch today, we will lose or forfeit.

Use the negation rules in writing the contrapositives of the statements in Exercises 37–38 about whole numbers.

37. If a is odd and b is odd, then $a \cdot b$ is odd.

38. If $a \cdot b = 0$, then $a = 0$ or $b = 0$.

39. A statement form that is always true is called a tautology; one that is always false is called a **contradiction.** (And one that has both T's and F's among its truth values is called a *contingency*.) Show that $p \wedge \sim p$ is a contradiction.

40. Fill in the truth table in Table A.14 and then explain why each of the following argument forms is invalid (fallacious).

Table A.14

a	c	$\sim a$	$\sim c$	$a \rightarrow c$
T	T			
T	F			
F	T			
F	F			

(a) $a \rightarrow c$ (the *fallacy of affirming the conse-*
    c *quent,* or the *converse fallacy*)
$\therefore a$

(b) $a \rightarrow c$ (the *fallacy of denying the an-*
    $\sim a$ *tecedent,* or the *inverse fallacy*)
$\therefore \sim c$

Certain advertisements seem designed to draw one into fallacious reasoning patterns. Identify the fallacy which the ads described in Exercises 41–44 tend to induce.

41. If you are convivial, then you drink a certain cola.

42. If you read a certain magazine, then you will not make foolish financial decisions.

43. If you do not rent a car from Ajax, then your vacation will not be carefree.

44. Beautiful women use a certain brand of soap.

45. When a novice complains that the computer is not doing what it should, an authority is likely to intone, "Garbage in, garbage out." Identify the logical fallacy that this reproof is intended to induce.

References

Bittinger, M. *Logic, Proof, and Sets*. Reading, Mass.: Addison-Wesley, 1982.

Copi, I. *Introduction to Logic*. 6th ed. New York: Macmillan, 1982.

Exner, R., and M. Rosskopf. *Logic in Elementary Mathematics*. New York: McGraw-Hill, 1959.

Stolyar, A. *Introduction to Elementary Mathematical Logic*. New York: Dover Publications, 1984.

Suppes, P., and S. Hill. *First Course in Mathematical Logic*. Waltham, Mass.: Blaisdell, 1964.

APPENDIX B: STANDARDS

In March, 1989, the National Council of Teachers of Mathematics published a 258-page book entitled *Curriculum and Evaluation Standards for School Mathematics*. These *Standards* represent a broad consensus on what mathematics should be included in the school curriculum of the 1990s. There are four main sections to the book: curriculum standards for grades K–4, curriculum standards for grades 5–8, curriculum standards for grades 9–12, and evaluation standards. For reasons of space we have chosen to reproduce only those curriculum standards that are most appropriate for users of this text, namely the K–4 and 5–8 standards. Again for reasons of space, we have listed each standard without the elaboration and illustrative examples that are found in the NCTM publication. The complete book can be purchased from NCTM, 1906 Association Drive, Reston, Virginia 22091.

 **B.1** *Curriculum Standards for Grades K–4*

1. *Mathematics as Problem Solving.* In grades K–4, the study of mathematics should emphasize problem solving so that students can

   - Use problem-solving approaches to investigate and understand mathematical content
   - Formulate problems from everyday and mathematical situations
   - Develop and apply strategies to solve a wide variety of problems
   - Verify and interpret results with respect to the original problem
   - Acquire confidence in using mathematics meaningfully

2. *Mathematics as Communication.* In grades K–4, the study of mathematics should include numerous opportunities for communication so that students can

   - Relate physical materials, pictures, and diagrams to mathematical ideas
   - Reflect on and clarify their thinking about mathematical ideas and situations
   - Relate their everyday language to mathematical language and symbols
   - Realize that representing, discussing, reading, writing, and listening to mathematics are a vital part of learning and using mathematics

A23

3. *Mathematics as Reasoning.* In grades K–4, the study of mathematics should emphasize reasoning so that students can

- Draw logical conclusions about mathematics
- Use models, known facts, properties, and relationships to explain their thinking
- Justify their answers and solution processes
- Use patterns and relationships to analyze mathematical situations
- Believe that mathematics makes sense

4. *Mathematical Connections.* In grades K–4, the study of mathematics should include opportunities to make connections so that students can

- Link conceptual and procedural knowledge
- Relate various representations of concepts or procedures to one another
- Recognize relationships among different topics in mathematics
- Use mathematics in other curriculum areas
- Use mathematics in their daily lives

5. *Estimation.* In grades K–4, the curriculum should include estimation so students can

- Explore estimation strategies
- Recognize when an estimate is appropriate
- Determine the reasonableness of results
- Apply estimation in working with quantities, measurement, computation, and problem solving

6. *Number Sense and Numeration.* In grades K–4, the mathematics curriculum should include whole number concepts and skills so that students can

- Construct number meanings through real-world experiences and use of physical materials
- Understand our numeration system by relating counting, grouping, and place-value concepts
- Develop number sense
- Interpret the multiple uses of numbers encountered in the real world

7. *Concepts of Whole Number Operations.* In grades K–4, the mathematics curriculum should include concepts of addition, subtraction, multiplication, and division of whole numbers so that students can

- Develop meaning for the operations by modeling and discussing a rich variety of problem situations
- Relate the mathematical language and symbolism of operations to problem situations and informal language
- Recognize that a wide variety of problem structures can be represented by a single operation
- Develop operation sense

8. *Whole Number Computation.* In grades K–4, the mathematics curriculum should develop whole number computation so that students can

- Model, explain, and develop reasonable proficiency with basic facts and algorithms
- Use a variety of mental computation and estimation techniques
- Use calculators in appropriate computational situations
- Select and use computation techniques appropriate to specific problems and determine whether the results are reasonable

9. *Geometry and Spatial Sense.* In grades K–4, the mathematics curriculum should include two- and three-dimensional geometry so that students can

- Describe, model, draw, and classify shapes
- Investigate and predict the results of combining, subdividing, and changing shapes
- Develop spatial sense
- Relate geometric ideas to number and measurement ideas
- Recognize and appreciate geometry in their world

10. *Measurement.* In grades K–4, the mathematics curriculum should include measurement so that students can

- Understand the attributes of length, capacity, weight, area, volume, time, temperature, and angle
- Develop the process of measuring and concepts related to units of measurement
- Make and use estimates of measurement
- Make and use measurements in problem and everyday situations

11. *Statistics and Probability.* In grades K–4, the mathematics curriculum should include experiences with data analysis and probability so that students can

- Collect, organize, and describe data
- Construct, read, and interpret displays of data
- Formulate and solve problems that involve collecting and analyzing data
- Explore concepts of chance

12. *Fractions and Decimals.* In grades K–4, the mathematics curriculum should include fractions and decimals so that students can

- Develop concepts of fractions, mixed numbers, and decimals
- Develop number sense for fractions and decimals
- Use models to relate fractions to decimals and to find equivalent fractions
- Use models to explore operations on fractions and decimals
- Apply fractions and decimals to problem situations

13. *Patterns and Relationships.* In grades K–4, the mathematics curriculum should include the study of patterns and relationships so that students can

- Recognize, describe, extend, and create a wide variety of patterns
- Represent and describe mathematical relationships
- Explore the use of variables and open sentences to express relationships

B.2 *Curriculum Standards for Grades 5–8*

1. *Mathematics as Problem Solving.* In grades 5–8, the mathematics curriculum should include numerous and varied experiences with problem solving as a method of inquiry and application so that students can

- Use problem-solving approaches to investigate and understand mathematical content
- Formulate problems from situations within and outside mathematics
- Develop and apply a variety of strategies to solve problems, with emphasis on multistep and nonroutine problems
- Verify and interpret results with respect to the original problem situation
- Generalize solutions and strategies to new problem situations
- Acquire confidence in using mathematics meaningfully

2. *Mathematics as Communication.* In grades 5–8, the study of mathematics should include opportunities to communicate so that students can

- Model situations using oral, written, concrete, pictorial, graphical, and algebraic methods
- Reflect on and clarify their own thinking about mathematical ideas and situations
- Develop common understandings of mathematical ideas, including the role of definitions
- Use the skills of reading, listening, and viewing to interpret and evaluate mathematical ideas
- Discuss mathematical ideas and make conjectures and convincing arguments
- Appreciate the value of mathematical notation and its role in the development of mathematical ideas

3. *Mathematics as Reasoning.* In grades 5–8, reasoning shall permeate the mathematics curriculum so that students can

- Recognize and apply deductive and inductive reasoning
- Understand and apply reasoning processes, with special attention to spatial reasoning and reasoning with proportions and graphs
- Make and evaluate mathematical conjectures and arguments
- Validate their own thinking
- Appreciate the pervasive use and power of reasoning as a part of mathematics

4. *Mathematical Connections.* In grades 5–8, the mathematics curriculum should include the investigation of mathematical connections so that students can

   - See mathematics as an integrated whole
   - Explore problems and describe results using graphical, numerical, physical, algebraic, and verbal mathematical models or representations
   - Use a mathematical idea to further their understanding of other mathematical ideas
   - Apply mathematical thinking and modeling to solve problems that arise in other disciplines such as art, music, psychology, science, and business
   - Value the role of mathematics in our culture and society

5. *Number and Number Relationships.* In grades 5–8, the mathematics curriculum should include the continued development of number and number relationships so that students can

   - Understand, represent, and use numbers in a variety of equivalent forms (integer, fraction, decimal, percent, exponential, and scientific notation) in real-world and mathematical problem situations
   - Develop number sense for whole numbers, fractions, decimals, integers, and rational numbers
   - Understand and apply ratios, proportions, and percents in a wide variety of situations
   - Investigate relationships among fractions, decimals, and percents
   - Represent numerical relationships in one- and two-dimensional graphs

6. *Number Systems and Number Theory.* In grades 5–8, the mathematics curriculum should include the study of number systems and number theory so that students can

   - Understand and appreciate the need for numbers beyond the whole numbers
   - Develop and use order relations for whole numbers, fractions, decimals, integers, and rational numbers
   - Extend their understanding of whole number operations to fractions, decimals, integers, and rational numbers
   - Understand how the basic arithmetic operations are related to one another
   - Develop and apply number theory concepts (e.g., primes, factors, and multiples) in real-world and mathematical problem situations

7. *Computation and Estimation.* In grades 5–8, the mathematics curriculum should develop the concepts underlying computation and estimation in various contexts so that students can

   - Compute with whole numbers, fractions, decimals, integers, and rational numbers

- Develop, analyze, and explain procedures for computation and techniques for estimation
- Develop, analyze, and explain methods for solving proportions
- Select and use an appropriate method for computing from among mental arithmetic, paper-and-pencil, calculator, and computer methods
- Use computation, estimation, and proportions to solve problems
- Use estimation to check the reasonableness of results

8. *Patterns and Functions.* In grades 5–8, the mathematics curriculum should include explorations of patterns and functions so that students can

- Describe, extend, analyze, and create a wide variety of patterns
- Describe and represent relationships with tables, graphs, and rules
- Analyze functional relationships to explain how a change in one quantity results in a change in another
- Use patterns and functions to represent and solve problems

9. *Algebra.* In grades 5–8, the mathematics curriculum should include explorations of algebraic concepts and processes so that students can

- Understand the concepts of variable, expression, and equation
- Represent situations and number patterns with tables, graphs, verbal rules, and equations and explore the interrelationships of these representations
- Analyze tables and graphs to identify properties and relationships
- Develop confidence in solving linear equations using concrete, informal, and formal methods
- Investigate inequalities and nonlinear equations informally
- Apply algebraic methods to solve a variety of real-world and mathematical problems

10. *Statistics.* In grades 5–8, the mathematics curriculum should include exploration of statistics in real-world situations so that students can

- Systematically collect, organize, and describe data
- Construct, read, and interpret tables, charts, and graphs
- Make inferences and convincing arguments that are based on data analysis
- Evaluate arguments that are based on data analysis
- Develop an appreciation for statistical methods as powerful means for decision making

11. *Probability.* In grades 5–8, the mathematics curriculum should include explorations of probability in real-world situations so that students can

- Model situations by devising and carrying out experiments or simulations to determine probabilities
- Model situations by constructing a sample space to determine probabilities

- Appreciate the power of using a probability model by comparing experimental results with mathematical expectations
- Make predictions that are based on experimental or theoretical probabilities
- Develop an appreciation for the pervasive use of probability in the real world

12. *Geometry.* In grades 5–8, the mathematics curriculum should include the study of geometry of one, two, and three dimensions in a variety of situations so that students can

- Identify, describe, compare, and classify geometric figures
- Visualize and represent geometric figures with special attention to developing spatial sense
- Explore transformations of geometric figures
- Represent and solve problems using geometric models
- Understand and apply geometric properties and relationships
- Develop an appreciation of geometry as a means of describing the physical world

13. *Measurement.* In grades 5–8, the mathematics curriculum should include extensive concrete experiences using measurement so that students can

- Extend their understanding of the process of measurement
- Estimate, make, and use measurements to describe and compare phenomena
- Select appropriate units and tools to measure to the degree of accuracy required in a particular situation
- Understand the structure and use of systems of measurement
- Extend their understanding of the concepts of perimeter, area, volume, angle measure, capacity, and weight and mass
- Develop the concepts of rates and other derived and indirect measurements
- Develop formulas and procedures for determining measures to solve problems

ANSWERS TO SELECTED EXERCISES

Chapter 2

SECTION 2.1

1. (b) $\{11, 13, 15, 17, 19\}$ (d) $\{Denver\}$ (f) $\{2, 4, 8\}$
3. Only (a), (b), (d), (e), and (j) are true.
4. (a) $\{10, 11, 12\}$ (c) $\{1, 2, 3, 4, 5, 6\}$
   (e) $\{1, 2, 3, 4, 5, 6, 7, 8, 9, 10, 11, 12\}$
   (g) $\{1, 2, 3, 11, 12\}$
5. (b) $\{x \in U \mid x/5 \in N\}$ (d) $\{x \in U \mid x = 7\}$
   (f) $\{x \in U \mid x \text{ is even and } x > 5\}$
   (h) $\{x \in U \mid x > 0\}$
7. Only (c) and (e) are true.
9. Only (a) and (d) are true.
11. and 12.

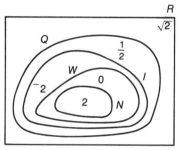

13. 4; listing a number twice does not make it two
    numbers.
16. $\varnothing$ $\{a\}$ $\{b\}$ $\{c\}$ $\{a, b\}$ $\{a, c\}$ $\{b, c\}$ $\{a, b, c\}$

SECTION 2.2

1. (a) $\{1, 3\}$ (c) $\{1, 2, 3, 4, 5, 7, 9\}$ (e) $\{6, 8, 10\}$
   (g) $\varnothing$
   (i) $\{(1, 1), (1, 2), (1, 3), (1, 4), (2, 1), (2, 2), (2, 3),$
   $(2, 4), (3, 1), (3, 2), (3, 3), (3, 4), (4, 1), (4, 2), (4, 3),$
   $(4, 4)\}$

2.

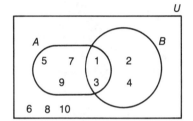

4. (a)

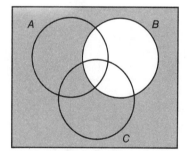

(c)

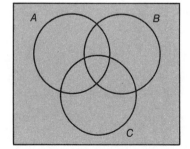

A31

(e)

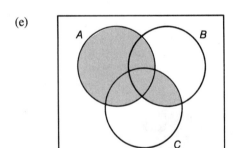

(g)

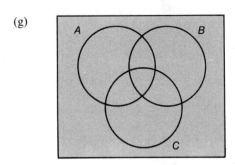

5. $S = \{a, b, c, d\}$, $T = \{r, b, s\}$
7. (a)

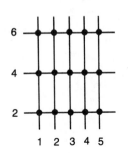

(c)

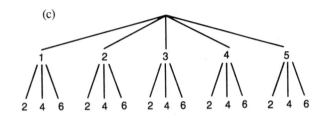

8. (c) $\{1, 2, 3, 4, 5, 6, 7, 8\}$ (e) No (g) No (i) 2
11. 50; $n(N \cup T) = n(N) + n(T) - n(N \cap T) \Rightarrow$
    $80 = 70 + 60 - n(N \cap T)$. Or $70 + 60 + 20 =$
    $150 \Rightarrow 50$ were counted twice.
14. (a) 20% (b) 55% See diagram.

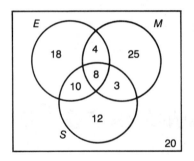

19. $A \cup \varnothing = A$ for any set A. Yes.

SECTION 2.3

1.

		$\{(0, 2), (1, 3), (2, 4), (3, 5), (4, 6), (5, 7)\}$
0	2	
1	3	
2	4	
3	5	$f(x) = x + 2$
4	6	
5	7	

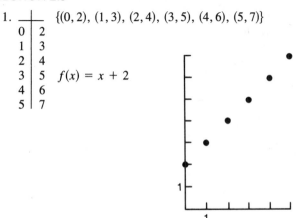

3. $f(x) = x^2$
7. $\{2, 4, 6\}$
11. (a) 7 (b) 19 (c) 9 (d) $c = \frac{1}{3}$. Solve the equation
    $4c - 1 = c$.
12. (a) 2 (b) $\frac{1}{2}$ (c) 6^- (d) 4^+
    (e) $f[f(7)] = f(4) = 3^+$ (f) 0 or $2\frac{1}{2}$
14. (b), (c), (e), (f)
17. (a) $4\frac{1}{2}$ lb (b) 4 weeks (c) 2 lb (d) 4 weeks
19. (a) $17 (b) $12 (c) Loss of $2 (d) Profit of $5
    (e) About 367 (f) 525 (g) $.04 (h) $2.00
    (i) $.01 (j) $.02

SECTION 2.4

1. (a) 10 (c) A circle of radius 3 cm (e) 8
2. Only (a), (c), (d), (e) and (g) make sense.
3. (a) 4, 8 (c) Circle of radius 1, 2π
    (e) 2π, circle of radius 2π

5. (a) $\xrightarrow{M_2}$ $\xrightarrow{S_3}$ $\xrightarrow{D_4}$

   (c) $\xrightarrow{D_4}$ $\xrightarrow{A_7}$ $\xrightarrow{M_3}$ $\xrightarrow{S_5}$

6. (a) 2639.25 (c) 3976

7. (a) and (d)

10. Only (b), (d), (e)

11. (b) S_2 (d) D_2

12. (a) 12 (c) 5

13. (a) $x \xrightarrow{M_2} \xrightarrow{S_1} 11$ becomes $x \xleftarrow{D_2} \xleftarrow{A_1} 11$; that is, $x = 6$. (c) 5

15. 36

18. (a) $20 \to 180 \to 36 \to 68$
    (b) Reverse arrows: $95 \xrightarrow{S_{32}} 63 \xrightarrow{M_5} 315 \xrightarrow{D_9} 35$

22. Yes

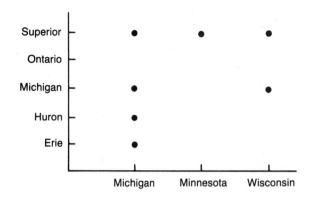

Reversing the arrows does not produce a function.

3. Not a function.

SECTION 2.5

2. (a) $0 \to 16$ $f(x) = x + 16$
   $1 \to 17$
   $2 \to 18$
   $3 \to 19$
   $4 \to 20$

9. The rays from point P constitute an arrow diagram for a one-to-one correspondence from the set of points making up the 2-cm segment to the set of points making up the 3-cm segment.

10. (a) $\sqrt{2}$ (b) Yes

14. There are 11 possible sums, 2 through 12. In the worst case each could come up 9 times during the first 99 rolls.

SECTION 2.6

1.

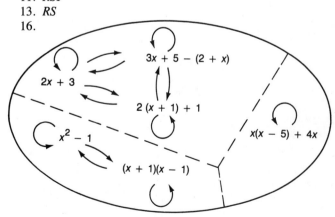

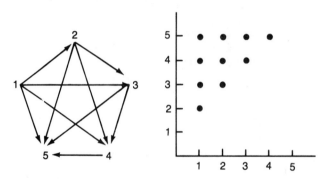

5. RST

7. T

9. RT

11. RST

13. RS

16.

18. $\{\{1, 2, 3\}, \{4, 7, 8\}, \{5, 6\}\}$

Chapter 3

SECTION 3.1

2. (a) Ordinal   (b) Naming
4. (a) Not a one-to-one correspondence; difference inputs yield a single output.   (c) Perfectly all right
9. (a) fum
10. (a) 326
11. (a)
13. (a)
15. (a)

SECTION 3.2

1. (a) 32_{four} (c) 130_{four}
2. (b)
3. (a)
4. (a) 121_{four} (c) 1232_{four}
5. 1 2 3 10 11 12 13 20 21 22 23 30 31 32 33 100 101 102 103 110 111 112 113 120 121
7. (a) 121_{three} (c) 104_{six}
9. (a)
10. (a) 1202_{six} (c) $10,000_{two}$
11. (a) 103_{four} (c) $30,200_{four}$ (e) 11_{twelve}
12. (a) 310_{four} (c) E_{twelve} (e) 10011_{two}
13. (a) $2_{four} \cdot 22_{four} = 110_{four}$
15. (a) 100
16. (a) $12,120_{three}$
18. (a) Eight
   (c) Nine
   (e) 100; $10_B \cdot 10_B \rightarrow (1B + 0) \cdot (1B + 0) = 1B^2 + 0B + 0 \rightarrow 100$.
20. (a) 1022_{seven} (c) $24,086_{nine}$
21. (a) Even
23. $\begin{array}{l} .2 \rightarrow \frac{2}{10} \\ \times \ .3 \rightarrow \frac{3}{10} \\ \hline .06 \leftarrow \frac{6}{100} \end{array}$
27. (a) 2400
28. (a)

SECTION 3.3

1.
3. 28
5. 17
9. $\frac{98}{110}$
11. 17
13. (a) And   (c) Set

SECTION 3.4

1. 12
3. $1,757,600,000 = 26 \cdot 26 \cdot 26 \cdot 10 \cdot 10 \cdot 10 \cdot 10 \cdot 10$
5. LRLR
7. 21
9. 220
11. 8
13. A: 24 cm^3, B: 7.2 cm^3 or 7200 mm^3
15. 1440
17. 600
19. 18
21. 12
24. (a) 26^4
25. 1024

SECTION 3.5

1. $10 - 7 = 3$
3. $12 - 12 = 0$
5. $9 - 5 = 4$
7. $5 - 3 = 2$
9. 23, take away
11. 59, missing addend
14. $k - g$, comparison

SECTION 3.6

1. $\frac{18}{6} = 3$
3. $\frac{17}{17} = 1$

5. $100 \div 17 = [5 \text{ (quotient)}, 15 \text{ (remainder)}]$
7. $7 \div 12 = [0 \text{ (quotient)}, 7 \text{ (remainder)}]$
9. $\frac{8}{2} = 4$, count subsets; $\frac{8}{4} = 2$, count elements
12. 3 do not get to play; 23 games are played
14. 1788, count subsets
16. 12 cm, missing factor
18. $\$(65,585/c)$, count elements
20. 58, count elements
22. 12 hr; $\frac{540}{3} = 180$, count elements; $\frac{180}{15} = 12$, either missing factor or count subsets
24. $a \cdot b + c \cdot d$
26. $\dfrac{a \cdot b - c}{d}$
28. $\dfrac{a \cdot b - c \cdot d - e}{f}$
30. $600 = \dfrac{3000}{5}$

SECTION 3.7

1. $5 \cdot 4 \cdot 3 \cdot 2 \cdot 1$
3. $9 \cdot 8 \cdot 7 \cdot 6 \cdot 5 \cdot 4 \cdot 3 \cdot 2 \cdot 1$
5. (a) 24 (b) 5040 (c) 362,880 (d) 1
7. $26 \cdot 25$
9. $50 \cdot 49 \cdot 48 \cdot 47 \cdot 46$
11. $5 \cdot 4 \cdot 3 \cdot 2 \cdot 1$
13. (a) $10 \cdot 9 \cdot 8$ (c) $100 \cdot 99 \cdot 98 \cdot 97$
    (e) 7 (g) $n(n-1)(n-2)(n-3)(n-4)$
14. (a) 5040 (b) 1560 (c) 1680 (d) 720
16. (a) $\dfrac{16 \cdot 15}{2 \cdot 1} = 120$
    (c) $\dfrac{12 \cdot 11 \cdot 10 \cdot 9 \cdot 8 \cdot 7}{6 \cdot 5 \cdot 4 \cdot 3 \cdot 2 \cdot 1} = 924$
    (e) $\dfrac{9 \cdot 8 \cdot 7 \cdot 6 \cdot 5 \cdot 4 \cdot 3}{7 \cdot 6 \cdot 5 \cdot 4 \cdot 3 \cdot 2 \cdot 1} = 36$
17. $C_2^{26} = 325$
19. $C_5^{52} = 2,598,960$
21. C_3^{12}
23. P_5^{200}
25. P_5^{70}
27. (a) $C_4^7 \cdot 3! = \dfrac{7!}{4!} = 210$
    (c) $C_3^8 \cdot C_2^5 \cdot 3! = \dfrac{8!}{3!2!} = 3360$
30. (a) 6 (b) 56 (c) 1 (d) 1
38. (a) Multiply numerator and denominator of $\dfrac{P_3^{10}}{3!}$ by 7!.

SECTION 3.8

1. (a) $\overset{\scriptscriptstyle 5}{5}\overset{\scriptscriptstyle 5}{5}4$
       66
2. (a)

	0	1
0	0	1
1	1	10

3. (a) 1014_{seven}
4. (a) $\overset{\scriptscriptstyle 7}{2}57,4 \rightarrow 357,000,000$
       3
   (c) $797,57 \rightarrow 798,000,000$
8. (a) 3465_{seven}
9. (a) $\overset{\scriptscriptstyle 4}{4}7,\overset{\scriptscriptstyle 5}{5}8 \rightarrow 37,000,000$
       3 4
11. (a) Seven
17. (a) $4(-5)(-3)(-1) \rightarrow 35(-3)(-1) \rightarrow 347(-1) \rightarrow 3469$

SECTION 3.9

3. (a)

	1	2	3	4	5	6
1	1	2	3	4	5	6
2	2	4	6	11	13	15
3	3	6	12	15	21	24
4	4	11	15	22	26	33
5	5	13	21	26	34	42
6	6	15	24	33	42	51

4. (a)

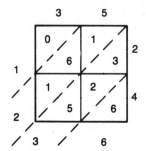

5. (a) $60 \times 50 = 3000$ (c) $200 \times 400 = 80,000$
6. (a) $350 \times 20 = 7000$ (c) $150 \times 80 = 12,000$

8. $3x^4 + 14x^3 + 31x^2 + 32x + 30$

11. (a) $1 \times 44 = 44$ $21 \times 44 = (16 + 4 + 1) \times 44$
      $2 \times 44 = 88$ $= 16 \times 44 + 4 \times 44 + 1 \times 44$
      $4 \times 44 = 176$ $= 704 + 176 + 44$
      $8 \times 44 = 352$ $= 924$
      $16 \times 44 = 704$

14. (c) Need to carry: 3 tens and 12 units → 42.
     (e) 3 tens and 10 units → 40

18. (a) $27\overline{)92\,|\,502} \rightarrow 3000$
           $\dfrac{81}{11}$

19. (a) 24_{seven}

20. $x = 13$ and $y = 7$

23. (a) Six

25. (a) By calculator, $400 \div 17 = 23.529\ldots$ Thus the quotient is 23. By calculator, $400 - 23 \cdot 17 = 9$. Thus the remainder is 9.
     (c) $Q = 46$, $R = 64$

SECTION 3.10

1. (a) Operation   (b) Start or stop   (c) Input or output
     (d) Decision

2.

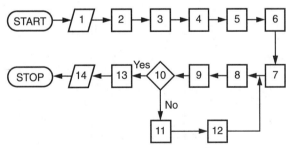

3.

5.

User must be able to use a ruler and to multiply positive rational numbers; $A = b \cdot h$

10. Same flowchart as in Exercise 9, except that the question in the decision box is now "Is it less than six?"

15. (a) 84

16. (a) 24, 26, 18, 27, 24

Chapter 4
SECTION 4.1

2. (a) 10, 6, 15   (b) Yes

3. (a) 7, $2\frac{1}{2}$, $\frac{11}{24}$ (b) No   (c) Yes

5. All

6. (a) Only (a) and (f)   (c) Only (b), (c), and (e)

7. Only (a), (c), and (d)

9. (a) No   (b) No

12. (a)

$^{+}7$	0	1	2	3	4	5	6
0	0	1	2	3	4	5	6
1	1	2	3	4	5	6	0
2	2	3	4	5	6	0	1
3	3	4	5	6	0	1	2
4	4	5	6	0	1	2	3
5	5	6	0	1	2	3	4
6	6	0	1	2	3	4	5

(b)

$^{\cdot}7$	0	1	2	3	4	5	6
0	0	0	0	0	0	0	0
1	0	1	2	3	4	5	6
2	0	2	4	6	1	3	5
3	0	3	6	2	5	1	4
4	0	4	1	5	2	6	3
5	0	5	3	1	6	4	2
6	0	6	5	4	3	2	1

15.

∪	∅	{a}	{b}	S
∅	∅	{a}	{b}	S
{a}	{a}	{a}	S	S
{b}	{b}	S	{b}	S
S	S	S	S	S

SECTION 4.2

1. (a) $y = 5 - 3t$ (c) $2 - x \neq x^2$
4. (a) "In lowest terms" is not a property of rational *numbers;* it is a property of fractions, which are *labels* for rational numbers.
6. (a) 11   (c) 24
   (f) $x +_7 5 = 4 \Rightarrow x +_7 5 +_7 2 = 4 +_7 2 \Rightarrow x = 6$
   (h) $2 \cdot_7 x = 5 \Rightarrow 4 \cdot_7 2 \cdot_7 x = 4 \cdot_7 5 \Rightarrow x = 6$ (j) 6
8. (a) Since $a = b$, we can substitute b for the first occurrence of a in the statement $a = a$.

SECTION 4.3

1. (a) Associative property of multiplication
   (c) Commutative property of multiplication
   (e) Associative property of addition
   (g) Multiplicative property of one
   (i) Commutative property of multiplication
   (k) Commutative property of addition
   (m) Associative property of multiplication
   (o) Additive property of zero
6. (a) 16, 24   (b) No   (c) 11, 10   (d) No
   (e) 5, 14   (f) No
7. (a) No   (c) No
8. All are true.
9. (a) 11   (c) 33   (e) 12   (g) 162
10. (a) 12
13. (b) No

SECTION 4.4

1. (a) 9   (c) 12
3. (a) 3   (c) 0   (e) 21
5. (a) {0}   (c) ∅
8. (a) $12 - 4$ is the solution to $x + 4 = 12$, namely, 8.

9. (a) $12/4$ is the solution to $4 \cdot x = 12$, namely, 3.
14. (a) 2
    (c) 6

SECTION 4.5

1. (a) Definition of 2, associative property of addition, definition of 3, definition of 4
2. (b) $3 + 3 = 3 + (2 + 1)$ definition of 3
       $= (3 + 2) + 1$ associative property of addition
       $= 5 + 1$ part (a)
       $= 6$ definition of 6
3. (d) $3 \cdot 24 = 3 \cdot (3 \cdot 8)$ elementary multiplication fact
       $= (3 \cdot 3) \cdot 8$ associative property of multiplication
       $= 9 \cdot 8$ elementary multiplication fact
       $= 72$ elementary multiplication fact
6. (a) $4 \cdot 10^3 + 1 \cdot 10^2 + 7 \cdot 10 + 5$
   (c) $1 \cdot 10^5 + 0 \cdot 10^4 + 0 \cdot 10^3 + 0 \cdot 10^2 + 9 \cdot 10 + 0$
7. (a) 468   (c) 700,208
8. (a) $6 \cdot 6 \cdot 6$ (c) $10 \cdot 10 \cdot 10$
9. (a) 10^4 (c) 4^3
10. (a) 7   (c) $m + 3$ (e) $m + n$ (g) 1
13. (a) 12   (c) $3n$
14. Expanded form, additive property of zero, multiplicative property of zero, additive property of zero, multiplicative property of one, exponents
17. Distributive property, distributive property, elementary multiplication fact, commutative property of multiplication, distributive property, elementary addition fact, exponents
19. Cancellation property of multiplication
20. Expanded form, commutative property of addition, addition fact, expanded form, distributive property, addition fact, addition fact, expanded form, distributive property, exponents, expanded form
22. Expanded form, distributive property, multiplication fact, expanded form, distributive property, multiplication fact, previously established result about sums, expanded form, distributive property, exponents, distributive property, multiplication fact, previously established result about sums, expanded form, distributive property, exponents, expanded form

24. Expanded form, distributive property, exponents, additive property of zero, multiplicative property of zero, additive property of zero, expanded form

SECTION 4.6

1. (a) $3 + \boxed{5} = 8$ and $5 \in N$

   (c) $n + \boxed{1} = n + 1$ and $1 \in N$
2. (a) Given (b) Definition of less than
   (c) Addition property of equality
   (d) Commutative property of addition (e) n
   (f) Definition of less than
4. (a) No. Consider $a = 2$ and $b = 3$, and also $a = 5$ and $b = 5$.
   (b) Yes
6. (a) $1 + 3 = 4$
7. (a) Right-directed arrow of length 3 with tail at 5
8. (a) $2 \cdot 4 = 8$
10. Only (a) and (b)
12. No. The whole numbers are well ordered by less than; the rationals are not.

Chapter 5

SECTION 5.1

1. (a) F (b) T (c) T (d) T (e) F (f) T (g) T
   (h) F (i) T (j) F
2. (a) 1, 18, 2, 9, 3, 6
   (c) 1, 2, 3, 5, 7, $2 \cdot 3$, $2 \cdot 5$, $2 \cdot 7$, $3 \cdot 5$, $3 \cdot 7$, $5 \cdot 7$,
   $2 \cdot 3 \cdot 5$, $2 \cdot 3 \cdot 7$, $2 \cdot 5 \cdot 7$, $3 \cdot 5 \cdot 7$, $2 \cdot 3 \cdot 5 \cdot 7$
   (one factor for each subset of $\{2, 3, 5, 7\}$)
8. 6
12. (a) $2 \cdot 3 \cdot 7$ (c) 2^6 (e) $2^3 \cdot 5^3$ (g) $2 \cdot 3^2 \cdot 7$
    (i) $2^4 \cdot 3 \cdot 5^2$ (k) $2^9 \cdot 3^3$
15. (a) 2, 3, 5, 7, 11, 13, 17, 19, 23, 29, 31, 37, 41, 43, 47, 53, 59, 61, 67, 71, 73, 79, 83, 89, 97
    (b) No (c) $11 \cdot 11 = 121$
16. 12 (the greatest integer $\leq \sqrt{167}$)
18. No
21. (a) Three is below 6 and joined to it by a segment. Six is not below 3. Three is below 12 and joined to it by a chain of segments. Three is not joined to 8.
    (e) Two is below both 8 and 12 and is joined to both by a chain of segments. The GCF is the highest number with those two properties, namely, 4.
22. (a) 41, 43, 47, 53, 61

SECTION 5.2

1. GCF is 6.

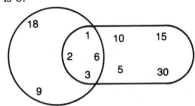

4. (a) $2 \cdot 3 \cdot 7$ (c) 1
5. (a) $2 \cdot 2 \cdot 3 \cdot 3 \cdot 5 \cdot 7 \cdot 11$
   (c) $2 \cdot 3 \cdot 3 \cdot 5 \cdot 7 \cdot 11 \cdot 13$
7. 180,180
9. (a) 2 (b) 265
10. (a) 13,156 (b) 18,550
11. (a) $\frac{46}{143}$ (b) $\frac{7}{10}$
12. (a) $373/13,156$ (b) $659/18,550$
13. (a) 7, 31 (b) 18 (c) 42
15. 416 mm × 416 mm square; 104 dominoes
18. 96
21. The smallest number that is a multiple of all three.
    (a) 420 (b) $2^2 \cdot 3^2 \cdot 5^2 \cdot 7 \cdot 11$
23. No
26. 90,000 miles

SECTION 5.3

1. No
3. 5
5. 2, 3, 6, 9
7. 7
9. 11
11. (a) 8 (c) 5 (e) 3
12. (a) $5 \cdot 41$ (c) $3 \cdot 3 \cdot 17$
14. (a) True (c) True
20. Last digit must be 0.
23. (a) 24, 25, 26, 27, 28
25. Yes
27. $2k + 2l = 2(k + l)$

SECTION 5.4

1. $n^\square = n^\triangle + (n - 1)^\triangle$
2. (a) 4 (b) 9 (c) 16
   (d) 10,000; this is $100^\triangle + 99^\triangle = 100^\square$.
4. (a) $100^\triangle = \frac{1}{2}(101 \cdot 100) = 5050$
7. (a) 175 (c) 146
10. (a) Work from the bottom up. Second differences are

all 2, so first differences are 6, 8, 10, 12, 14, 16; thus the original sequence is 0, 6, 14, 24, 36, 50, 66.

11. 3414
13. (a) 320 cm
14.

3   6   11   18   27   38
   3   5   7   9   11
     2   2   2   2
       0   0   0

15. (a) 5, 8, 11, 14, 17, 20, 23 (c) 1, 2, 5, 10, 17, 26, 37
(e) 1, −3, −1, 13, 45, 101, 187

Chapter 6

SECTION 6.1

3. (a) 4 (c) $^-6$
4. (a) 7 red, 3 black
6. (a) $^-6 + {^+4} = {^-2}$
7. (a) $^-3 - {^-4} = {^+1}$
11. (a) $^-2 + \boxed{^+6} = {^+4}$ (c) $0 + \boxed{^+4} = {^+4}$
12. (a) $^+3 + {^-5} = {^-2}$ (c) $^-2 + {^+5} = {^+3}$
14. (a) $^+4 + {^-7}$; unit: dollar; positive direction: earning
(c) $^+5 + {^-3} + {^+7}$; unit: floor; positive direction: up
(e) $^+3 + {^+2} + 0 + {^-8}$; unit: yard; positive direction: gain
15. (a) $^-3$ (c) $^+9$ (e) $^-3$
16. 18 minutes before blast-off
18. $^-13$ degrees
20. $^-4$
22. 21 mph
24. (a) Left to right: opposite of, subtraction, negative
26. (a) 7 (c) 4 (e) 0
28. $^-55$
30. 125
32. $^-613$
34. $^-186$
36. $^-485$
38. 1212
40. $^-266$
42. 14

SECTION 6.2

1. (a) $3 \cdot 4 = 12$ (c) $^-2 \cdot 4 = {^-8}$ (e) $1 \cdot {^-4} = {^-4}$
2. (a) Similar to 1(b) (c) Similar to 1(c)
3. (a) $10 \cdot {^-3} = \square$, $^-30$ (c) $^-27 \cdot {^-4} = \square$, 108
(e) $\square \cdot {^-3} = 60$, $^-20$ (g) $-14 \cdot \square = {^-42}$, 3
4. (a) $^+12$ (c) $^-8$ (e) $^-4$ (g) $^-5$

5. (a) 3 blocks at position 2 (c) 2 balloons at position 4
8. 3, 6
12. $^-98$
14. $^-720$
16. $^-18$
18. 18
20. $^-21$
22. 5
24. $^-27$
26. $^-2$

SECTION 6.3

1. (a) $^-3$ (c) $^-6$ (e) $^-2$
5. $^-a \cdot b = (^-1 \cdot a) \cdot b$ rule 4
       $= {^-1} \cdot (a \cdot b)$ associative property of multiplication
       $= {^-}(a \cdot b)$ rule 4
7. Additive property of zero, definition of opposites, associative property of addition, definition of opposites, additive property of zero
11. (a) $x = {^-6}$ (c) $x = {^-4}$ (e) $x = 9$ (g) $x = {^-6}$
(i) $x = {^-4}$

SECTION 6.4

1. (a) 4 (c) 2 (e) 4
3. (a) $^-(^-2) = {^-}(5) = 2$ (c) $^-4 + {^-6} = 3 + 1 = 4$; $^-(4 + 6) = {^-}(3) = 4$
(e) $^-4 \cdot 5 = 3 \cdot 5 = 1$; $^-(4 \cdot 5) = {^-}(6) = 1$
(g) $4 \cdot (2 - 5) = 4 \cdot (2 + {^-5}) = 4 \cdot (2 + 2) = 4 \cdot (4) = 2$; $4 \cdot 2 - 4 \cdot 5 = 1 - 6 = 1 + {^-6} = 1 + 1 = 2$
4. (a) $x + 2 = 1 \Rightarrow x + 2 + 5 = 1 + 5 \Rightarrow x = 6$
(c) $0 = x + 5 \Rightarrow 0 + 2 = x + 5 + 2 \Rightarrow 2 = x$
(e) $x - 4 = 5 \Rightarrow x - 4 + 4 = 5 + 4 \Rightarrow x = 2$
(g) $2 - x = 1 \Rightarrow 6 + 2 - x + x = 6 + 1 + x \Rightarrow 1 = x$
5. (b) 4

SECTION 6.5

1. (a) $2 \cdot {^-4} = {^-8}$ (c) $^-1 \cdot 5 = {^-5}$
2. (a) Start with the vector from 0 to 3, flip it over the origin, and stretch it to twice its original length; $^-6$.
3. Note what happens to the left-right relationship as you flip the vectors 3 and 5 across the origin.
5. Clockwise from the left: Addition property of less

than, arithmetic of integers, addition property of less than, arithmetic of integers

6. (a) $x < {}^-4$ (c) $x < 4$ (e) $3 < x$ (g) $x < 0$
8. (a) $<$
9. (a) $b < a$ (c) $a \le b$

Chapter 7

SECTION 7.1

1. (a) $\frac{3}{5}$ (c) $\frac{3}{8}$ (e) $\frac{4}{3}$
2. (a) $\frac{3}{8}$ (c) $\frac{3}{3}$
3. (a) $\frac{1}{4}$
4. (a) $\frac{3}{2}$
7. (a)

Unit square represents salary; shaded region represents take-home pay.

8. (a) Unit: mile, same size: same length
   (c) Unit: gallon, same size: same volume
   (e) Unit: ton, same size: same weight
9. 210

$$280 \xrightarrow{D_4} 70 \xrightarrow{M_3} 210$$

11. 196
13. 36
15. 20
17. 45
19. $\frac{1}{2}, \frac{2}{4}, \frac{4}{8}, \frac{8}{16}$
21. (a)

24. (a) Any right-directed arrow of length $\frac{1}{2}$
25. $\frac{4}{3}, \frac{8}{6}, \frac{12}{9}, \frac{16}{12}, \frac{20}{15}$
27. (a) $\frac{4}{1}, \frac{8}{2}, \frac{12}{3}$
28. (a) 7

29. (a) $\frac{4}{5}$ (c) $\dfrac{3 \cdot 5 \cdot 7}{11}$ (e) $\frac{33}{100}$ (g) $\frac{21}{1}$ (i) $\frac{3}{2}$
    (k) $\frac{13}{17}$; use Euclidean algorithm to find GCF, 119.
30. (a) No   (c) Yes   (e) Yes
32. (a) No   (c) Yes
34. (a) $\frac{20}{24}, \frac{9}{24},$ or $\frac{40}{48}, \frac{18}{48},$ or . . .
    (c) $\dfrac{2 \cdot 5^2 \cdot 11}{2^2 \cdot 3 \cdot 5 \cdot 7^2 \cdot 11}, \dfrac{3 \cdot 7^3 \cdot 11^2}{2^2 \cdot 3 \cdot 5 \cdot 7^2 \cdot 11}$
35. (a) $\frac{25}{40}, \frac{12}{40}$ (c) $\dfrac{2 \cdot 7}{3 \cdot 5}, \dfrac{7}{2^2 \cdot 3 \cdot 5^2} \rightarrow \dfrac{2^3 \cdot 5 \cdot 7}{2^2 \cdot 3 \cdot 5^2}, \dfrac{7}{2^2 \cdot 3 \cdot 5^2}$
36. (a) $\frac{4}{12}, \frac{5}{15}, \frac{6}{18}$
38. (a) $\frac{3}{4}, \frac{6}{8}, \frac{9}{12}, \frac{12}{16}, \frac{15}{20}, \frac{18}{24}, \frac{21}{28}, \frac{24}{32}$

SECTION 7.2

1. (a) $\frac{5}{12} + \frac{9}{12} = \frac{7}{6}$ (c) $\frac{3}{2} + \frac{2}{3} = \frac{13}{6}$
2. (a) $\frac{11}{12} - \frac{5}{12} = \frac{1}{2}$
3. $\frac{7}{18}$
5. $\frac{97}{120}$
7. $\frac{3}{20}$ acre
9. (a) $\frac{11}{12}$ (b) $\frac{13}{12}$ (c) $\frac{1}{6}$ (d) $\frac{5}{6}$
10. (a) $\frac{1}{6} + \frac{3}{4} = \frac{11}{12}$ (c) $\frac{8}{3} - \frac{4}{9} = \frac{20}{9}$ (e) $\frac{2}{5} + \frac{1}{3} = \frac{11}{15}$
    (g) $\frac{1}{4} - \frac{1}{9} = \frac{5}{36}$
13. (a) $\frac{18}{20}$ (c) $\frac{1}{90}$ (e) $\frac{49}{90}$ (g) $\dfrac{173}{2^2 \cdot 3^2 \cdot 5 \cdot 7}$
14. (a) $\frac{4}{12} = \frac{1}{3}$ (c) $\frac{2}{5}$ (or $\frac{3}{7}$ or $\frac{3}{8}$)
15. (a) $6\frac{2}{3}$ (c) $8\frac{1}{3}$ (e) $55\frac{93}{137}$
16. (a) $\frac{27}{4}$ (c) $\frac{119}{8}$
17. (a) $12\frac{1}{2}$ (c) $9\frac{1}{6}$
18. (a) 31 ($\frac{3}{5} <$ sum of fractional parts $< \frac{3}{3}$)   (c) 11
19. $28\frac{3}{8}$ gal
21. $1\frac{3}{8}$
23. $\dfrac{a}{b} + \dfrac{c}{d} = \dfrac{ad + bc}{bd} = \dfrac{cb + da}{db} = \dfrac{c}{d} + \dfrac{a}{b}$ (work from both ends toward the middle)

SECTION 7.3

1. (a) $\frac{5}{8} \cdot \frac{3}{4} = \frac{15}{32}$ (c) $\frac{4}{3} \cdot \frac{3}{4} = 1$ (e) $\frac{6}{10} \cdot \frac{4}{9} = \frac{4}{15}$
2. (a) $\frac{7}{6} \div \frac{4}{3} = \frac{7}{8}$
3. 900
5. $\frac{21}{40}$
7. $\frac{1}{2}$
9. (a) $\frac{4}{15}$ (c) 30
11. $\frac{11}{20} \cdot \frac{2}{3} \cdot \frac{9}{11} = \frac{3}{10}$
13. $\frac{1}{24}$

17.

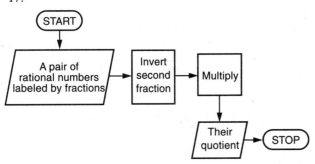

20. (a) $\frac{1}{6}$ (c) $\frac{5}{8}$ (e) $\frac{9}{2}$ (g) $\frac{7}{8}$ (i) $\frac{75}{2}$

23. (a) $19\frac{1}{2}$ (c) 3

25. (a) $4 \cdot 3 = 12$ (c) $\frac{1}{4} \cdot 8 = 2$ (e) $\frac{8}{2} = 4$

27. $11\frac{11}{16}$ oz

32. (a) $\frac{3}{2}$ (b) $\frac{103}{180}$

SECTION 7.4

1. 80 lb

3. 160

5. (b) $\frac{9}{20}$
   (d) $\frac{8}{17}$

7. $\frac{1}{20}$

9. $\frac{2}{3}$ as many adults as children (assume 4 boys)

11. $1331

13. $\frac{33}{50}$

$$\frac{3}{5} \cdot \frac{7}{10} + \frac{4}{5} \cdot \frac{3}{10}$$

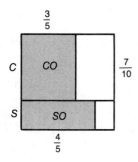

15. $\frac{1}{12}$; $\frac{1}{3}$ of $\frac{1}{4}$

17. $\frac{13}{36}$

19. $\frac{13}{40}$

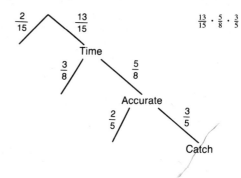

21. $\frac{7}{20}$

23. $\frac{1}{2}$ as many skunks as fowl

SECTION 7.5

2. (a) $\frac{3}{5}$, 3:5 (c) $\frac{4}{4}$, 4:4

3. (a) The ratio of strays to pets is 3 to 10.
   (c) The ratio of home runs to doubles is 2 to 3.
   (e) The ratio of X's to Y's price is 3 to 2.

4. (a) Boys (c) $\frac{85}{6}$

6. (a) 63 (c) 35 (e) 15 (or $^{-}15$)

7. (a) $7.52; $\frac{1.88}{3} = \frac{x}{12}$ (c) Not a proportion problem
   (e) $\frac{5}{6}$ cup; $\frac{1\frac{1}{4}}{2} = \frac{x}{1\frac{1}{3}}$ (g) 21; $\frac{6}{50} = \frac{x}{175}$
   (i) Not a proportion problem (k) About 371 miles

9. 2.4

11. 4.5 A

13. $\frac{1}{2}$ cup cereal, $2\frac{1}{4}$ cups milk, $\frac{3}{8}$ tsp salt

15. 18

17. (a) From top to bottom: 0, 7, 270, 360

SECTION 7.6

1. (a) $\frac{1}{7}$ (c) $\frac{1}{12}$ (e) $\frac{3}{4}$

2. (a) $2 \cdot \frac{1}{3}$ (c) $6 \cdot \frac{1}{3}$ (e) $5 \cdot \frac{1}{1}$

4. (a) $\frac{0}{b} = 0 \cdot \frac{1}{b}$ definition of division
   $= 0$ multiplicative property of zero:
      zero times anything is zero
   (c) $\frac{12}{12} = 12 \cdot \frac{1}{12}$ definition of division
   $= 1$ definition of reciprocal

6. Definition of division, commutative property of multiplication, definition of divison

8. Definition of division, commutative property of multiplication, rule 2, definition of division

10. Definition of division, distributive property, definition of division, rule 4

12. (a) $\dfrac{1}{-5}$ (b) $\dfrac{3}{-5}$ (c) $\dfrac{-3}{5}$ (d) $-\left(\dfrac{3}{5}\right)$

13. (a) $\dfrac{-3}{4}$ (c) $\dfrac{-2}{3}$ (e) $\dfrac{-3}{10}$ (g) $\dfrac{2}{7}$ (i) $\dfrac{-6}{1}$

14. (a) $\dfrac{-11}{24}$ (c) $\dfrac{-5}{8}$ (e) $\dfrac{-25}{12}$

15. (a) $x = 7$ (c) $x = {}^-6$ (e) $x = \frac{21}{2}$ (g) $x = {}^-13$

(i) $x = \dfrac{-4}{3}$

16. $\dfrac{{}^-1}{2}$

SECTION 7.7

2. (a) 3 (c) 6 (e) 4; $\dfrac{({}^-2)}{3} = ({}^-2) \cdot \dfrac{1}{3} = 5 \cdot 5 = 4$

3. (a) 1 (c) 0

4. (a) $\dfrac{4 \cdot 5}{4 \cdot 3} = \dfrac{6}{5} = 6 \cdot \dfrac{1}{5} = 6 \cdot 3 = 4; \dfrac{5}{3} = 5 \cdot \dfrac{1}{3} =$

$5 \cdot 5 = 4$

(g)$-\left(\dfrac{5}{6}\right) = -\left(5 \cdot \dfrac{1}{6}\right) = -(5 \cdot 6) = -(2) = 5;$

$\dfrac{5}{{}^-6} = \dfrac{5}{1} = 5 \cdot \dfrac{1}{1} = 5 \cdot 1 = 5$

5. (a) $5x + 1 = 4 \Rightarrow 5x + 1 + 6 = 4 + 6 \Rightarrow 5x =$
$3 \Rightarrow 3 \cdot 5x = 3 \cdot 3 \Rightarrow x = 2.$ *Check:* $5 \cdot 2 + 1 = 4.$
(c) 4

SECTION 7.8

1. (a) > (c) < (e) < (g) < (i) <
2. (a) $3x - 2 < 2 \Leftrightarrow 3x - 2 + 2 < 2 + 2 \Leftrightarrow 3x <$
$4 \Leftrightarrow \frac{1}{3} \cdot 3x < \frac{1}{3} \cdot 4 \Leftrightarrow x < \frac{4}{3}$

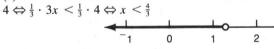

(c) $\frac{2}{3} < x$ (e) $\frac{20}{3} < x$ (g) $-\frac{2}{3} \le x$
4. (a) $\frac{1}{2}$ (c) $\frac{1}{14}$ (e) $-\frac{50}{119}$
8. (a) Safe
10. $194\frac{4}{9}$ mg

Chapter 8

SECTION 8.1

1. (a) $\dfrac{574}{100}$ (c) $\dfrac{5}{10}$ (e) $\dfrac{6}{1} = \dfrac{6}{10^0}$ (g) $\dfrac{{}^-405}{10}$ (i) $\dfrac{17}{10^9}$

2. (a) 25.75 (c) .528 (e) .0003 (g) .8 (i) .075

3. (a) $3 \times 10 + 7 + \dfrac{5}{10}$

(c) $8 + \dfrac{0}{10} + \dfrac{0}{10^2} + \dfrac{3}{10^3}$

4. (a) 240.625 (c) 112.31 (e) 10.23 (g) .207
6. (a) .28 (c) ${}^-27.44$
7. (a) .57
9. (a) 16.014 (c) 9.219
10. (a) 69.825
11. (a) 6000 (c) 100,000
12. (a) 1.35
13. (a) ${}^-165.068$ (c) ${}^-9.261$
14. (a) 12 (c) 22
17. (a) 7546.821 (c) 1.754
18. (a) 75 (c) 3.5
20. 3.56
22. 12 cm² (4 × 3), 11.61 cm²
24. 603.2246 cm²
26. 23.5 mpg
28. (a) 114.232 (c) 58.081

SECTION 8.2

1. .237 (c) 1.56 (e) .0935 (g) .055
2. (a) 75% (c) 210% (e) .9% (g) 12.5%
6. (a) 9.1 (c) $75 (e) 18%
7. (a) 5% (c) 160% (e) .4%
8. (a) 1700 (c) 200 (e) 80
9. $15.08
11. 24%
13. 8400
15. 40% off
17. 21.5%; 25% × 30% + 20% + 70%
19. About 7.14%
21. Supporters' base is total sales revenues; opponents' base is the existing sales tax.
28. (a) 7.2%
29. (a) 10^{-4} (c) 10^7 (e) 10^{-3} (g) 10^4 (i) 10^7
30. (a) 571.6 (c) .00754
31. (a) 5.28×10^3 (c) 1.6×10^7 (e) 1.28×10^{-3}
(g) 4×10^{-4} (i) 5.6×10^8; $4 \times 10^{-6} \times 1.4 \times 10^{14}$
32. (a) $5.15^+ \times 10^{47}$
35. About 3.3×10^{-19} sec

SECTION 8.3

1. (a) 4.5%
(b) 9%

3. (a) 7.82%
   (b) 7.82%
5. $585
7. (a) $21,200
   (c) $23,000
12. (a) $9116.59
    (b) $10,675.65
14. $9813.14
16. $811.92
19. $387.89
21. $4851.94

SECTION 8.4

1. (a) .108   (c) .45$\overline{45}$. . .   (e) 3.75$\overline{75}$. . .   (g) .06$\overline{33}$. .

4. (a) $\dfrac{3}{11}$ (c) $\dfrac{43{,}291}{9999}$ (e) $\dfrac{5022}{990}$ (g) $\dfrac{9}{9} = 1$
8. 7.000$\overline{99}$. . .
10. (a) 1.414869. . .
12. (a) .547, .548   (c) 4.666, 4.667
13. No
16. (a) 37.06   (c) 6.80   (e) $^-$84   (g) .9

SECTION 8.5

1. (a) 3π (c) $\dfrac{^-1}{3\pi}$
2. (a) 1   (c) 0   (e) 1
4. (a) Rational, 1232/9999   (c) Rational   (e) Irrational
   (g) Irrational   (i) Irrational
5. (a) No   (c) No
6. (a) 3.15 (first guess of 3.2 fails)
7. (a) 7, 8   (c) 1, 2
9. 2, 2.25, 2.236111111, 2.236067978, 2.236067978.
   Answer: 2.2361
11. (a) 6   (c) 600   (e) .06   (g) $\frac{3}{2}$
12. (a) 48
    (c) 12
13. (a) Suppose on the contrary that $\sqrt{3} = m/n$, where
    $m, n \in N$. Then $3 = m^2/n^2$, or $3 \cdot n^2 = m^2$. Now
    the right-hand side of this equation has an even num-
    ber of prime factors, while the left-hand side has an
    odd number.
14. No; $\sqrt{11}$ is irrational, but the repeating decimal
    3.31$\overline{66}$. . . is rational.
16. (a) Definition of radical symbol
    (b) The product of two positive numbers is positive.

(c) $(\sqrt{2} \cdot \sqrt{5})^2 = (\sqrt{2} \cdot \sqrt{5})(\sqrt{2} \cdot \sqrt{5}) =$
$(\sqrt{2} \cdot \sqrt{2}) \cdot (\sqrt{5} \cdot \sqrt{5}) = 2 \cdot 5 = 10$
(d) Steps (b) and (c) show that $\sqrt{2} \cdot \sqrt{5}$ satisfies the
defining conditions [given in step (a)] for $\sqrt{10}$.
18. (a) True   (c) False   (e) False   (g) False
20. (a) Q (c) W (e) I (g) R
21. (a) 140 cm/sec   (b) 420 cm/sec ($\sqrt{9} \times 140$)

Chapter 9

SECTION 9.1

1. $R \rightarrow \frac{90}{360}$ 3. $R \rightarrow \frac{7}{15}$
   $W \rightarrow \frac{60}{360}$ $W \rightarrow \frac{4}{15}$
   $B \rightarrow \frac{30}{360}$ $B \rightarrow \frac{4}{15}$
   $G \rightarrow \frac{45}{360}$
   $Y \rightarrow \frac{135}{360}$
6. 52 outcomes, each with probability $\frac{1}{52}$
8. (a) $R \rightarrow \frac{1}{2}$ (c) $F \rightarrow \frac{12}{52}$
   $B \rightarrow \frac{1}{2}$ $N \rightarrow \frac{40}{52}$
10. 0.12; however it is done, one's senses of sight and
    smell should play no role.
11. Close your eyes, open the book at random, and poke a
    pencil down on the page. Take the closest letter. If
    there is any doubt, start all over.

SECTION 9.2

2. $\frac{1}{12}$ (a) {2, 4, 6, 8, 10, 12}, $\frac{1}{2}$
   (c) {1, 2, 3, 4, 6, 12}, $\frac{1}{2}$ (e) {8}, $\frac{1}{12}$
3. (c) $\frac{1}{10}$ (e) $\frac{2}{10}$ (g) $\frac{6}{10}$ (i) $\frac{1}{10}$
4. (a) THH, HTT, THT, TTH, TTT   (c) $\frac{1}{8}$ (e) $\frac{4}{8}$
5. (c) {(2, 6), (3, 5), (4, 4), (5, 3), (6, 2)}   (e) $\frac{5}{36}$
6. (a) $\frac{5}{36}$ (c) $\frac{2}{36}$
8. (a) $\frac{1}{52}$ (c) $\frac{13}{52}$ (e) $\frac{26}{52}$ (g) $\frac{8}{52}$ (i) $\frac{32}{52}$
11. (a)

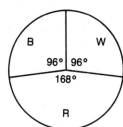

(c) Three sectors: *NS* of .81 × 360 = 291.6°, *SO* of
.07 × 360 = 25.2°, and *SH* of 43.2°
13. (a) Let 0, 1, 2, 3, 4 represent red; 5, 6, 7 represent
white; and 8, 9 represent blue.

(c) Ignore 0, 7, 8, 9; group the remaining digits into blocks of two; and treat each block as an outcome.

15. Simulate by taking digits in blocks of six and letting even digits represent heads.

17. Simulate by ignoring 0 and 9 and taking the remaining digits in blocks of five. Let 1 represent a broken bone and 2 through 8 no broken bone.

19. Simulate by letting 0, 1, 2 represent poisoning and counting how many digits up to (and including) the first appearance of a 0, 1, or 2. Repeat many times, then average the numbers you obtain.

21. Simulate by ignoring all digits except 1, 2, 3, 4, 5 and counting how long a string of these digits is needed before all five of them are represented. Repeat many times, then average the numbers you obtain.

SECTION 9.3

1. (a) $\frac{1}{6}$ (b) $\frac{1}{3}$
   (c) Any branch or twig terminating at an R gets $\frac{1}{6}$, at a W gets $\frac{1}{3}$, at a B gets $\frac{1}{4}$, and at a G gets $\frac{1}{4}$.
   (d) $\frac{1}{6} \cdot \frac{1}{3} = \frac{1}{18}$ (g) $\frac{7}{16}$

2. (a)

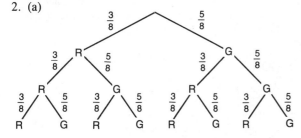

(c) $\frac{75}{512}$ (e) $\frac{152}{512}$

3. (b) $\frac{15}{100}$ (d) $\frac{51}{100}$

4. (a) 9   (b) 4   (c) $\frac{4}{9}$ (d) $\frac{3}{9}$

5.

(b) $\frac{2}{90}$ (d) $\frac{48}{90}$

6. (b) $\frac{60}{210} = \frac{5}{7} \cdot \frac{4}{6} \cdot \frac{3}{5}$ (d) $\frac{3}{21}$

10. $.00005 = .1 \times \dfrac{1}{2000}$

12. .079

14. .46

SECTION 9.4

1. (c) $\frac{1}{120}$ (e) $\frac{10}{120}$ (g) $\dfrac{C_3^6}{120} = \dfrac{20}{120}$

2. (b) $\dfrac{C_2^4}{C_2^7} = \dfrac{6}{21}$ (d) $\frac{3}{21}$

3. (b) $\dfrac{C_4^{21}}{C_4^{26}}$ (d) $\dfrac{C_4^4}{C_4^{26}}$

5. $\dfrac{C_{98}^{999,998}}{C_{100}^{1,000,000}}$

7. $\dfrac{4}{2,598,960}$

9. $\dfrac{624}{2,598,960}$

11. $\dfrac{10,200}{2,598,960}$

13. (a) $\dfrac{C_{10}^{45}}{C_{10}^{50}}$ (b) $\dfrac{C_2^5 C_8^{45}}{C_{10}^{50}}$

15. There are nine pairs of consecutive digits, so probability $= 9/C_2^{10} = .2$.

SECTION 9.5

1. (a) $\frac{1}{12} \times 15 + \frac{1}{6} \times 5 + \frac{1}{4} \times 3 + \frac{1}{2} \times 2 = \$3.83\frac{1}{3}$
   (b) No

2. (a) $\frac{4}{52} \times 15 + \frac{12}{52} \times 2 + \frac{36}{52} \times (-1) = \frac{8}{52} \doteq \$.15$
   (b) The expected value (about $.15)

4. $25

6. The safe stock

8. (a) $\frac{3}{10}$ (b) 7 to 3   (c) 3 to 7

10. (a) 7 to 3   (c) 7 to 8   (e) 49 to 51

11. (a) 1 to 3   (c) 11 to 1   (e) 47 to 25

12. $81

Chapter 10

SECTION 10.1

6. By cutting off the bottoms of the bars, the Center for Education Statistics produces a graph which, at a glance, misleads the reader into believing that China's school year is more than twice the United States's. In fact, China's school year is only $\frac{4}{3}$ as long as the United States's.

11. $1,600,000

SECTION 10.2

1. Mean, 10; median, 10; mode, 12

4. (a) Mean, 5; median, 6.5; mode, 7
   (c) Mean, 2.9; median, 2.9; mode, 2.9
5. 87
7. (a) Mean (b) $\frac{2}{7}$
9. Lower quartile, 6; upper quartile, 10

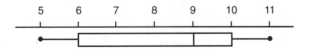

12. Quartiles on test 1: 46, 72, 81. Quartiles on test 2: 59, 69, 76.
13. (a) About 65.4 (b) 68

SECTION 10.3

1. (a) Mean, 6; variance, 1; standard deviation, 1
   (c) Mean, 3; variance, 0; standard deviation, 0
2. (a) Mean, 3; standard deviation, 2
5. Mean, 253; standard deviation, 14.27
8. Mean, 0.003; standard deviation, 0.002
10. Mean, 11.325; standard deviation, .58

SECTION 10.4

1. (a) 680 (c) 997 (e) .59
2. (a) .16 (c) $(\frac{3}{4})^3 = \frac{27}{64}$
3. (a) 34% (c) 64
7. (a) 1.4 (c) 0 (e) $^-0.6$
8. (a) 40 (c) 41
9. (a) 91.9% (c) 50% (e) 27.4%
12. Math
14. (a) 13.6% (c) 77.4%
15. (a) 0.2 (c) $^-1.4$

SECTION 10.5

1. (a) Mean, .55; standard deviation, .025 = 2.5%
   (b) 95% (c) 47.5%, 62.5%
4. Between 36% and 44%
6. The 95% confidence interval
9. (a) From 2.4% to 7.6% (b) 6, 19

Chapter 11

SECTION 11.1

1. (a) Concentric circles (c) Plane
   (e) Cylinder (technically, a right circular cylinder)

9. (b) 6 (c) 10
12. Use, for example, the four vertices of a tetrahedron.
14. No; not in ordinary three-dimensional space
16. (a) 2 (b) 1
18. (a) 3 (b) 4 (c) 4 (d) 6 (e) 6 (f) 7
23. (a) 3 (c) 4 (e) 6 (g) 7
25. (a) T (c) T (e) F (g) T (i) T
27. (a) T (c) T (e) F (g) F (i) T (k) T
28. (a) $\{A, B\}, \{A, C\}, \{A, D\}, \{B, C\}, \{B, D\}, \{C, D\}$

SECTION 11.2

3. Six rays: $\overrightarrow{AB}, \overrightarrow{AC}, \overrightarrow{BA}, \overrightarrow{BC}, \overrightarrow{CA}, \overrightarrow{CB}$
5. (a) 6 (c) 12
6. (a) $\overline{AE}$ and $\overline{DH}$ (many choices)
   (c) $\overline{EH}$ and $\overline{HI}$ (many choices)
7. (a) T (c) F
8. 0
13. (a) 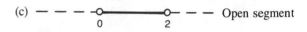 Half line

(c)  Open segment

(e)  Segment

(g) Ray

14. (b) .7493
16. (a) The intersection of A's side of $\overleftrightarrow{BC}$, B's side of $\overleftrightarrow{AC}$, and C's side of $\overleftrightarrow{AB}$
    (c) The union of the side of $\overleftrightarrow{BC}$ opposite A, the side of $\overleftrightarrow{AC}$ opposite B, and the side of $\overleftrightarrow{AB}$ opposite C
18. The intersection of A's side of plane BCD, B's side of plane ACD, C's side of plane ABD, and D's side of plane ABC
22. They determine three (nonstraight) angles.
24. 105
25. (a) Yes (c) No; not coplanar
    (e) No; do not share a side ($\overrightarrow{ED}$ is not a side of $\angle CAD$)
    (g) No; do not share a side (i) Yes
26. Only (a), (b), (d), and (f)
28. 6

SECTION 11.3

1. (c) is not a curve.

3. (d) is not closed.
5. (d) is not two-dimensional.
7. (a) is not a polygon.
9. (c) is not a quadrilateral.
14. Left
18. *ABCDE, ACBDE, ACDBE*
20. (a) 6   (b) 0
23. A polygon with *n* vertices can be named in 2*n* ways: *n* choices for which vertex to begin with, and 2 choices for which direction (clockwise or counterclockwise) to trace the polygon.
25. (a) 2
28. (a) No   (b) Yes   (c) Yes
29. (a) Segment having the two points as end points
(c) Two-dimensional triangle having the point and segment as vertex and opposite side
33. (a) 1   (c) 3   (e) 0   (g) 2   (i) 3; mixed 2 and 3

34. (a)   (c)

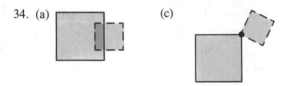

SECTION 11.4

1. (a) Traceable from *B, D*   (c) Not traceable
2. (a) Traceable from *B, D*   (c) Traceable from *F, C*
3. Behind the cloud
6. (a) Yes
9. Region *A* shares one segment with each of regions *B, C,* and *D* (the big region surrounding *A, B, C*); vertex *A* shares an edge with each of vertices *B, C, D.* Similar reasoning applies to *B, C, D.*
11. The task now is to tour a graph and finish at the same vertex at which you started. In part (a) the graph corresponding to

and while this graph is traceable, no tracing can begin and end at the same vertex.
13. (c) *V* is unchanged, *E* decreases by 1, and *P* decreases by 1; so *V − E + P* is unchanged.   (e) 1 − 0 + 1 = 2
14. (a) Yes.

Chapter 12

SECTION 12.1

8. Congruent
9. Rotate A 90° clockwise about its lower right-hand corner. Then reflect the image in the vertical line that passes through B's sharpest corner.
10. Translation straight down by 6 units
12. Counterclockwise, about 0, through 2/16 of a full turn
15. (a) Hold them together side by side to see whether their heights agree, then end to end to see whether their bases match.
(c) Try to match up three pairs of faces: the small ones, the long narrow ones, and the long broad ones.
16. (a) D   (c) Tetrahedron *ELGK*   (e) *G*
18. (a) Not congruent   (c) Yes; no

SECTION 12.2

1. $m_U(A) = 3, m_U(B) = 4, m_U(C) = 4, m_U(D) = 5, m_U(E) = 8$
7. (b) Property 4 of measure function
(d) Additive property of inequality [add $m(A)$ to both sides of (c)]
9. (a) $31 = 62 \div 2$

SECTION 12.3

2. 4, 3, 12, 32, $2\pi, \frac{3}{2}\pi + 3$
3. A, 8; C, 8; E, 18; G, $\frac{3}{2}\pi + 9$; I, $6\pi + 6$
4. (a) 13   (c) 36   (e) 3   (g) 2   (i) 2
5. (a) $\frac{1}{3}\pi$ cm   (c) $\dfrac{16}{\pi}$ cm   (e) 2.4 cm
9. (a) 2π in   (c) 2π in
(e) 0; award loops, one to each car.
(g) 2π in; black car is inside for 2 loops, red for 1.

SECTION 12.4

2. (a) 28 cm²   (c) 16.5 cm²   (e) 2700 cm²
3. A, 3; C, 3; E, 12; G, $\frac{9}{8}\pi + 6$; I, 18
5. (a) 5π cm²   (c) 30 cm²
7. 1156 ft²
9. $\frac{1}{2}(b_1 + b_2)h$
10. (a) 6   (c) 24.5 (approximately)
15. 312
17. (a) $2\pi rh$ (b) $2\pi rh + 2\pi r^2$
19. πrs

21. Moon surface area about one-sixteenth that of Earth
22. 4.4 qt

SECTION 12.5

2. (a) 36 ft³   (c) 10,080 ft³
3. (a) 15 ft³
7. His cup is only one-eighth full.
10. (a) 60 cm³, 104 cm²
    (c) $(96 - 6\pi)$ cm³ $\doteq$ 77.2 cm³; $(128 + 12\pi)$ cm² $\doteq$ 165.7 cm²
    (f) $V = \dfrac{61\pi}{12} \doteq 16.0$ cm³; $S = \dfrac{91\pi}{4} \doteq 71.5$ cm²
12. About $1300
14. $S = 702\pi$ ft² $\doteq$ 2200 ft², so about 4.4 gal
17. $\dfrac{63\pi^2}{4} \doteq 155$ cm³
21. (a) $21\pi^2$ cm²

Chapter 13

SECTION 13.1

2. (a) $m\angle AOD = m\angle AOC + m\angle COD$, but $m\angle AOC = m\angle AOB + m\angle BOC$. Now substitute.
3. (a) 118°   (c) 99°
4. 180°

SECTION 13.2

1. (a) Acute
2. (a) Equilateral
4. (a) Parallelogram   (c) Convex kite
   (e) Convex quadrilateral   (g) Trapezoid
9. (a) Equilateral triangle
15. (a) 140°   (c) $171\frac{3}{7}°$
16. (a) 30   (c) 22
17. (a) 2 pentagons and 1 decagon
    (c) 2 triangles, 1 square, and 1 dodecagon
24. (a)

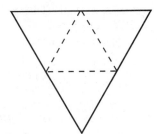

25. Dodecahedron has V = 20, E = 30, F = 12. Icosahedron has V = 12, E = 30, F = 20.
29. (b) V = 14, E = 21, F = 9

SECTION 13.3

2. (a) A thousandth of a dollar
   (c) To select by lot and kill every tenth man—a primitive form of discipline used by early military commanders
5. (a) m   (c) cm   (e) cm
6. (a) km²   (c) mm²   (e) cm²
7. (a) cm³   (c) mm³
9. (a) $\frac{1}{100}$ (c) 1000   (e) 1000   (g) 1.027   (i) 71.6
   (k) 5.2   (m) 7,200,000   (o) $31\frac{1}{2} \cdot 2 \cdot 2 \cdot 16 \cdot 3 =$ 6048
10. (a) About 10,430 yd³ (difficult calculation)
    (b) 7380 m³ (easy calculation)
11. (a) No
    (b) Yes; 1 cubic centimeter of water weighs 1 gram.
16. 1240 cm²
19. About 199 L
20. About 10.8×10^{20} m³
21. About 40,000 lb
24. About 6.5 mm
25. (a) 78°3′53″   (c) 78°11′7″
26. (a) 31°45′33″
28. 97°25′
30. (a) 10 sec   (b) $\frac{1}{6}$ sec
32. 200 grads
33. (a) 252¢
34. (a) 0.792 km/hr

SECTION 13.4

1. (c) $\frac{1}{16}$ in
2. (a) $\frac{1}{2}$ m, $\dfrac{\frac{1}{2}}{16} = \dfrac{1}{32} \doteq 3.1\%$ (c) 50 lb, $\dfrac{50}{4200} \doteq 1.2\%$
   (e) $\dfrac{1°}{2}$, $\dfrac{\frac{1}{2}}{45} = \dfrac{1}{90} \doteq 1.1\%$ (g) 5 in², $\dfrac{5}{100} = 5\%$
3. (d), (g), (a), (c), (e), (b), (h), (f)
5. (h), (a), (b), (d)
7. (a) cm   (b) $\frac{1}{2}$ cm   (c) $\frac{1}{32}$ for length, $\frac{1}{14}$ for width
   (d) Greatest lower bound on area = 15.5 × 6.5 = 100.75 cm². Least upper bound on area = 16.5 × 7.5 = 123.75 cm².
10. (a) 18.8 m $\leq M \leq$ 19.2 m   (b) 44.99° $\leq M \leq$ 45.01°
    (c) 2.745×10^8 kg $\leq M \leq 2.755 \times 10^8$ kg

SECTION 13.5

2. (b) Identity only   (d) Identity; 180° rotation about P
   (f) Identity; reflections in all diameters; rotations
   about P through all angles   (h) Identity only
   (j) Five rotations (including the trivial 0° rotation);
   five reflections
3. (a) Vertical line through center of tree
   (c) Line down center of shaft of arrow
   (e) One vertical and one horizontal line
5. (a) Parallelogram, rhombus, rectangle, square   (b) No
8. 0°, 90°, 180°, 270°
13. (a) No   (b) Yes   (c) Yes

Chapter 14

SECTION 14.1

2. (c) The rays are perpendicular.
11. From B, construct a perpendicular to ℓ; say it meets ℓ
    at B_0. On this perpendicular, on the other side of ℓ,
    locate B_1, with compass, so that $\overline{BB_0} \cong \overline{B_0B_1}$. In the
    same way, beginning at A and C, locate points A_1, and
    C_1 on the other side of ℓ. $\triangle A_1B_1C_1$ will be the image
    of $\triangle ABC$ under reflection in line ℓ.
13. (b) Equilateral triangle; connect alternate vertices of a
    regular hexagon.
    (d) Bisect one of the (right) angles in the previous
    construction. Now, swing arcs around the circle.
15. First three Fermat primes: 3, 5, 17. Constructible reg-
    ular n-gons: $n = 3, 4, 5, 6, 8, 10, 12, 15, 16, 17, 20,$
    24
16. (b) If it could, one could then bisect it and hence have
    constructed a 20° angle.
19. (a) The midpoint of the two points where the stones
    hit the water
20. The segment from the point perpendicular to the line

SECTION 14.2

5. Locate N by copying $\overline{OM}$, with a compass, on $\overrightarrow{MP}$.
9. Construct a ray from C parallel to V and pointing the
   same way. Locate C' on it by copying segment $\overrightarrow{V}$.
   Repeat this construction from points A and B. Finally,
   join A', B', C' with segments.
12. (a) $s - t_1 = 2(t_1 - r) \Rightarrow s + 2r = 3t_1 \Rightarrow t_1 =$
    $\frac{1}{3}s + \frac{2}{3}r$. Similarly, $t_2 - r = 2(s - t_2) \Rightarrow t_2 = \frac{1}{3}r + \frac{2}{3}s$

SECTION 14.3

1. (a) Property 2   (b) Property 2
   (c) Transitive property of equality
   (d) Addition property of equality   (e) Property 1
3. (b) Definition of parallel lines as (coplanar) lines that
   do not intersect   (d) Property 4   (e) Property 2
   (f) Substitution from (e) into (d)
   (g) Addition property of less than   (h) Property 1
10. (a) 55°; vertical angles   (c) 50°; alternate interior an-
    gles
11. (a) $\overrightarrow{OB}$ and $\overrightarrow{OD}$.

SECTION 14.4

2. (a) ASA
   (b) $\overline{EF}$; they are corresponding (hence congruent)
   sides.
   (c) $\triangle FDE$
6. (a) SSS, $\triangle ABC \cong \triangle EDF$, reflection in the line
   through the midpoints of $\overline{BD}$ and $\overline{CF}$
   (c) ASA, $\triangle ABE \cong \triangle DBC$, rotate $\triangle ABE$ about B
   until A coincides with D.
7. If a side, its opposite angle, and a second angle of one
   triangle are congruent respectively to a side, its opposite angle, and a second angle of another triangle,
   then the triangles are congruent.
10. (a) $\triangle ABD \cong \triangle CBD$ by ASA
    (d) $\triangle ABD \cong \triangle EDB$ by SAS
    (g) $\triangle ABF \cong \triangle EDF$ by ASA
    (j) $\triangle ABC \cong \triangle EDC$ by SAA
11. (a) 1.38 cm   (c) 52°

SECTION 14.5

1. (a) Same compass opening   (b) Same compass opening
   (c) SSS
   (d) CPCTC; in this case corresponding angles of congruent triangles are congruent.
4. (a) Alternate interior angles, $\overleftrightarrow{AC}$ being the transversal
   of parallel lines $\overleftrightarrow{AB}$ and $\overleftrightarrow{CD}$
   (b) Alternate interior angles, $\overleftrightarrow{AC}$ being the transversal
   of parallel lines $\overleftrightarrow{AD}$ and $\overleftrightarrow{BC}$ (c) ASA
   (d) CPCTC   (e) CPCTC   (f) CPCTC
   (g) $\angle 1 \cong \angle 3$ and $\angle 2 \cong \angle 4 \Rightarrow m\angle 1 = m\angle 3$ and
   $m\angle 2 = m\angle 4 \Rightarrow m\angle 1 + m\angle 4 = m\angle 2 + m\angle 3 \Rightarrow$
   $m\angle BAD = m\angle DCB \Rightarrow \angle BAD \cong \angle DCB$
   (h) Opposite angles of a parallelgram are congruent.

6. Working backwards suggests how to proceed. To show the diagonals bisect each other, we must show $\overline{OB} \cong \overline{OD}$ and $\overline{AO} \cong \overline{OC}$. A natural strategy for establishing these congruences is to show that $\overline{BO}$ and $\overline{DO}$ are corresponding parts of congruent triangles, as are $\overline{OA}$ and $\overline{OC}$. Thus it suffices to show that $\triangle BOA \cong \triangle DOC$. Since opposite sides of a parallelogram are congruent (Exercise 4), the ASA criterion will be met if $\angle ABO \cong \angle CDO$ and $\angle OAB \cong \angle OCD$. Both of these follow from the alternate interior angles property of parallel lines. The last step is to arrange this argument into a formal, forward-proceeding, statement-reason proof.

SECTION 14.6

2. (b) Projection point: E; scale factor: about $\frac{3}{2}$
4. 5 cm
6. (a) 12.5   (c) 1.47 cm² (e) 2.592 lb
9. (b) Rotate $\triangle ABE$ through 180° about B; then dilate by using projection point B and scale factor $\frac{4}{3}$.

SECTION 14.7

2. (a) Yes ("SSS")   (b) Yes (SSS)
4. Copy $\angle A$, double side $\overline{AC}$, copy $\angle C$.
6. (a) "SSS," $\triangle ABC \sim \triangle EFD$, scale factor $\frac{3}{2}$
   (c) "SAS," $\triangle ABE \sim \triangle DBC$, scale factor $\frac{2}{3}$
   (e) "SAS," $\triangle ABC \sim \triangle EDF$, scale factor 2
7. $\triangle ABC \sim \triangle EDF$ by "AA," scale factor $\frac{3}{5}$
   (a) $\frac{5}{3} \cdot 2 = \frac{10}{3}$ cm   (b) $EF = \frac{3}{5} \cdot 4 = \frac{12}{5}$ cm
9. $\triangle ABC \sim \triangle DFE$ by "SSS"   (a) 58.4°   (b) 48.2°
11. $\triangle CAB \sim \triangle ADF$ by "SAS," scale factor 2
   (a) 38°   (b) 52°   (c) 38°   (d) 10 cm
12. (a) 2.7   (b) 9
14. $\triangle BCD \sim \triangle ACE$ by "SAS" (scale factor $\frac{1}{2}$ and hence $BD = \frac{1}{2}AE$). Thus $\angle DBC \cong \angle EAC$, from which it follows, by the corresponding angles property, that $\overleftrightarrow{BD} \parallel \overleftrightarrow{AE}$.

Chapter 15

SECTION 15.1

1. Statement (true)
3. Neither
5. Statement (true)
7. Open sentence
9. Open sentence

11. 7 and 10
13. {Illinois, Indiana, Michigan, Wisconsin}
15. The natural numbers N; 2, 3, 5, 7
17. Polygons (perhaps); square of side length 3; 3–4–5 triangle
19. (a) {Texas, New Mexico, Arizona, California}
20. (a) {3}
23. (c) _____ is a mammal and lives in the sea.
24. (a) Intersection
25. Half line
27. Segment
29. Half-open segment
31. Union of two half lines
33. Ray
35. $^-2 < x \le 2$
37. $x < ^-1$
39. $x \le 1$ or $3 \le x$
41. $\frac{2}{3}x - 5 = 7$
   $\Leftrightarrow \frac{2}{3}x - 5 + 5 = 7 + 5$ APE
   $\Leftrightarrow \frac{2}{3}x = 12$ simplification
   $\Leftrightarrow \frac{3}{2}(\frac{2}{3}x) = \frac{3}{2}(12)$ MPE
   $\Leftrightarrow x = 18$ simplification
43. $x = ^-2$
45. Solution set = $\{^-5, 5\}$
47. $5x + 7 \le ^-8$
   $\Leftrightarrow 5x + 7 + ^-7 \le ^-8 + ^-7$ API
   $\Leftrightarrow 5x \le ^-15$ simplification
   $\Leftrightarrow \frac{1}{5}(5x) \le \frac{1}{5}(^-15)$ MPI
   $\Leftrightarrow x \le ^-3$ simplification
49. $3 < x$
51. $x < 6$
53. $2 \le x \le 4$
55. $^-\frac{2}{5} < x < \frac{1}{5}$
57. $|x - 4| < 5$
59. $|x - 1| \ge 3$
61. $|x - 1| < |x - 5|$
63. Solution set = $\{^-1, 7\}$, "distance from x to 3 is 4."
65. $^-4 < x < 2$
67. $x < ^-3$ or $7 < x$
69. $2 \le x \le 4$
71. $x = 3.5$
73. $x < 1$
75. $|x - 2| < 4$
77. $|x - 5| > 5$
79. The larger of $x - 2$ and $2 - x$ is more than $4 \Leftrightarrow x - 2 > 4$ or $2 - x > 4 \Leftrightarrow x > 6$ or $x < ^-2$.
81. $2 < x < 3$
85. 10
87. $3\frac{1}{4}$

SECTION 15.2

1. Let J = Jerry's weight (in kilograms); Dean's · weight = $J - 5$.
3. Let B = Bud's age (in years); Lou's age = $\frac{3}{4}(B + \frac{5}{12}) - \frac{5}{12}$.
5. Let D = amount of deposit (in dollars); interest = $.07 \times D$.
7. $x + (x + 1) + (x + 2) + (x + 3)$
9. $5x$
11. $\dfrac{500}{x}$ (miles per hour)
13. $200x$ (dollars)
15. $125 + 1.5x$ (dollars)
17. $100 - 8x$ (grams)
19. $2500 + 60x$ (pounds)
21. (i) Let P = population. (ii), (iii) Then on the one hand, the number of eligible voters is $.65P$, while on the other, it is $P - 2800$. (iv) $.65P = P - 2800 \Leftrightarrow 2800 = .35P \Leftrightarrow P = 2800/.35 = 8000$ (v) The population is 8000.
23. $24.50; $1.04x = 25.48$
25. $14{,}520; \dfrac{6}{5} = \dfrac{w}{6600} \Leftrightarrow w = 7920$
27. 55, 75, 115, 165
29. 50, 51 and $^-51$, $^-50$
31. 18
33. $.2x + .6(10 - x) = 5 \Rightarrow x = 2.5; 10 - x = 7.5$

x	$.2$	$.2x$
$10 - x$	$.6$	$.6(10 - x)$
10	$.5$	

35. 9 L of 30% solution and 3 L of 70% solution
37. .2 pint
39. $4000 to widow, $1000 to each son, and $500 to each daughter
41. First 144, second 240, third 210
43. Approximately $64 \le y \le 88$, where y represents speed in kilometers per hour
45. $x \ge 59$ or $x > 58$

SECTION 15.3

1.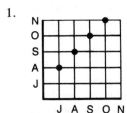
5.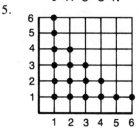
9. $(^-2, ^-2)$
11. $(1, 2)$
13. $(^-2, 2)$
15. $(0, 4)$
19. (b) $(^-3, 2)$ (c) $(0, 2)$ (d) $(3, ^-2)$ (e) $(3, 0)$
23. All points on or to the right of the y axis
25. Quadrant III and its boundary
27. Solid rectangle with vertices $(^-1, ^-5)$, $(^-1, 3)$, $(2, 3)$, $(2, ^-5)$
29. The line bisecting quadrant I (and quadrant III)
31. The union of the x and y axes
33. The horizontal line through $(0, 3)$
35. The line through the points $(6, 0)$ and $(0, 6)$
41. $(2, 0)$
43. $(^-1, 1.5)$
45. $(^-.5, ^-3.5)$
47. $(8, ^-5)$
49. For example, $A = (2, 1)$, $B = (^-1, ^-2)$
53. I or IV (or on the positive x axis) because since both A and B have positive first coordinate, so must M.
55. No; $AB + BC > AC$
57. Yes; $(AB)^2 + (BC)^2 = (AC)^2$
59. Inside; distance from $(10, 7)$ to $(4, 2)$ = $\sqrt{61} < 8$
67. 5
68. $\sqrt{13}$
71. A
72. O

SECTION 15.4

1. $2x + 9 = 0$
3. $2x + 4y - 9 = 0$
5. $4r + 4s - 4 = 0$ or $r + s - 1 = 0$
7. $1, 2, 6$
9. $\frac{1}{3}$
11. 1
13. 4
15. $^-4$
17. $-\frac{1}{2}$
29. $\frac{2}{3}$
31. $^-3$
33. 7
35. $^-1$
37. 3
39. $^-2$
41. $-\frac{3}{2}$
43. 0
45. $-\dfrac{a}{b}$ (assuming $b \neq 0$)
47. $y = \frac{3}{2}x - 4$
49. $y = \frac{1}{2}x - 2$
51. $y = -x + 4$
53. $y - 5 = 2(x + 3)$
55. $y + 1 = -\frac{1}{2}(x - 4)$
57. $y = -\frac{3}{5}x - \frac{7}{5}$, $3x + 5y + 7 = 0$
59. $y = \frac{4}{3}x + 0$, $4x - 3y + 0 = 0$
61. Line of slope $\frac{2}{3}$ through $(0, 1)$
73. $-\frac{1}{3}$
75. $\frac{3}{2}$
77. $\frac{2}{3}$
79. $^-2$
81. $y = -\frac{1}{2}x$
83. $y - 0 = ^-3(x - 3)$
85. $y + 1 = \frac{1}{4}(x - 1)$
91. Left pointing half line from 5
93. The open half plane below the line $x + 2y = 4$
99. Noncollinear

SECTION 15.5

5. $(x, y) = (\frac{43}{4}, \frac{7}{2})$
7. $(x, y) = (^-3, ^-2)$
11. No solution (parallel lines)
13. $(x, y) = (2, \frac{7}{2})$
15. $(r, t) = (-\frac{13}{2}, ^-6)$

17. $(x, y) = (3, ^-5)$
25. Let w = number of liters of weak (30%) solution. Let s = number of liters of strong (70%) solution. Solve the system
$$\begin{cases} w + s = 12 \\ .3\,w + .7\,s = .4(12) \end{cases}$$
29. Let w = speed of wind (in mph). Let a = airspeed of plane (in mph). Solve
$$\begin{cases} (a - w) \cdot 2\frac{1}{2} = 800 \\ (a + w) \cdot 2 = 800 \end{cases}$$
to get $w = 40$, $a = 360$.
31. \$100 for a horse and \$50 for a cow
34. $f(x) = -x + 8$, $f(2) = 6$, $f(6) = 2$
36. $f(x) = -\frac{2}{3}x + \frac{13}{3}$, $f(2) = 3$, $f(6) = \frac{1}{3}$
38. $f(x) = 2x^2 - 5x$, $f(2) = ^-2$, $f(6) = 42$
40. $f(x) = 4 - x^2$, $f(2) = 0$, $f(6) = ^-32$
42. The intersection of the closed half plane above the line $2x - 3y = 6$ and the closed half plane to the left of the line $5x + 2y = 10$

Chapter 16

SECTION 16.1

1. (a) 1.3×10^{10}; 13,000,000,000
   (c) 5.12 E $+ 11$; 5.12×10^{11}
   (e) 9.7 E $- 9$; .000 000 009 7
3. (a) 1.3×6
   (c) $5 * (1.2 + 2.3)$; 17.5
   (e) $108/18$; 6
   (g) $(4 + 5)/2$; 4.5
   (i) $5 \wedge 4$; 625
   (k) $(4 * 5) \wedge 2$; 400
   (m) $(2 \wedge 5)/(2 \wedge 3)$; 4
   (o) $2 \wedge 2 \wedge 3$; 64
   (q) $^-4 * ^-3 * ^-2$; -24
4. (a) $^-1$ (c) 8
5. (a) SQR(144)
   (c) $\sqrt{\dfrac{19 + 13}{2}}$; 4
   (e) $|^-263|$; 263
6. (a) 54 (c) 8 (e) 0

SECTION 16.2

4. (a) 1 is in X, $^-2$ is in Y.
   (b) 4 is in X, 22 is in Y.

5. (a) 10   READ X
       20   LET Y = 4 – 5 * X
       30   PRINT Y
       40   GOTO 10
       50   DATA 1,2,3,4,5
       60   END
6. (a) 10, 295
7. (a) 10   INPUT X
       20   LET Y = X ∧ 2 + 5 * X – 14
       30   PRINT Y
       40   GOTO 10
8. (a) 6464
   (c) 8 ∧ 2 = 2 ∧ 6
9. (a) 2   (c) 2   5   3
   (e) THE SQUARE ROOT OF 5 IS BETWEEN 2
       AND 3

SECTION 16.3

1. (a) 5   (c) 1
         8   4
        11   7
        14   10
        17
   (e) 22
       18
       14
       10
2. (a) 10   FOR I = 1 TO 20
       20   PRINT 2 * I – 1
       30   NEXT I
       40   END
3. (a) 10   PRINT "INPUT", "OUTPUT"
       20   FOR X = 0 TO 4
       30   LET Y = (X – 2) ∧ 2
       40   PRINT X,Y
       50   NEXT X
       60   END
9. (a) 3
        10
        12
         6
11. (a) 10   REM CONVERTS 40 POINT SCORES
              TO 100 POINT SCORES
        20   PRINT "DO YOU HAVE A 40 POINT
              SCORE YOU WOULD LIKE CONVERTED?
              TYPE 1 FOR YES AND 0 FOR NO."
        30   INPUT A

        40   IF A = 0 THEN 100
        50   PRINT "WHAT IS THE 40 POINT
              SCORE?"
        60   INPUT R
        70   LET S = R * 100/40
        80   PRINT "CORRESPONDING 100 POINT
              SCORE IS "; S
        90   GOTO 20
       100   END
13. 10   FOR I = 1 TO 100
    20   LET R = 1 / I
    30   LET S = S + R
    40   PRINT S
    50   NEXT I
    60   END

SECTION 16.4

1.   3.

11. LT 90   FD 40   RT 90   FD 20   RT 90
    FD 80
13. FD 40   LT 45   BK 20   RT 90   FD 20
    LT 45   BK 40
15. REPEAT 6[FD 20   RT 60]
17. REPEAT 4[FD 40   RT 45 FD 20 RT 45]
34. (a) 360   (b) 360/π ≐ 115

SECTION 16.5

1. TO VSEGMENT :LENGTH
     FD :LENGTH BK :LENGTH
   END
3. TO VRHOMBUS 40 :ANGLE
     REPEAT 2[FD 40   RT 180– :ANGLE   FD 40
     RT :ANGLE]
   END
   (a) No
   (b) No
   (c) Yes; VRHOMBUS θ is congruent to VRHOMBUS
       180 – θ.
7. (a) TO VL :HEIGHT
         BK :HEIGHT   RT 90   FD :HEIGHT * 2/3
       END

(c) TO VD :HEIGHT
    FD :HEIGHT RT 90 VRARC :HEIGHT/2
    180
END

(e) TO VC :HEIGHT
    PU VLARC :HEIGHT/2 45 PD VLARC
    :HEIGHT/2 270
END

9. (a) 4   50

SECTION 16.6

1.

(Allowed to wrap)

3.

5. TO LIGHTNING
     NOWRAP
     RT 30 FD 20 LT 30 BK 10
     LIGHTNING
   END

7. TO SUBURBIA
     NOWRAP
     FD 20 RT 45   FD 20   RT 90   FD 20   RT 45
     FD 20 LT 90   FD 20   LT 90
     SUBURBIA
   END

9. TO SQUARE
     REPEAT 4[FD 40   RT 90]
   END

TO SPINSQUARE
  SQUARE RT 200
  SPINSQUARE
END

15. TO OUTTRIAL :L
      IF :L > 99 THEN STOP
      FD :L RT 120
      OUTTRIAL :L + 5
    END

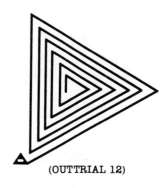

(OUTTRIAL 12)

Appendix A

SECTION A.1

1. (a) Statement, false
   (c) Not a statement
   (e) Statement
2. (a) Yes   (c) Yes
3. (a) No   (c) Yes
5. a
7. d
9. c
11. b
13. Valid

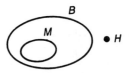

15. Invalid

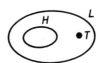

17. Invalid
19. Invalid
21. Invalid
23. Valid

25. All of your friends are good-natured.

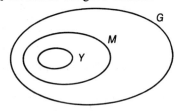

27. Pi is not a repeating decimal.

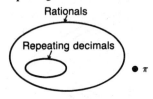

SECTION A.2

1. If Amy will drive, then Bruce will buy the gas.
3. Amy will drive and Cathy will come along.
5. If Bruce will not buy the gas, then Amy will not drive.
7. $\sim B$
9. $C \rightarrow B$
11. $(A \wedge B) \rightarrow C$
13. True
15. False
17. True
19. True
21. Either true or false
23. Neither true nor false
25.

p	q	$p \wedge q$	$p \rightarrow (p \wedge q)$
T	T	T	T
T	F	F	F
F	T	F	T
F	F	F	T

27.

p	q	$p \rightarrow q$	$(p \rightarrow q) \wedge q$	$((p \rightarrow q) \wedge q) \rightarrow p$
T	T	T	T	T
T	F	F	F	T
F	T	T	T	F
F	F	T	F	T

SECTION A.3

1. Valid; see lines 1 and 2.

p	q	$p \vee q$
T	T	T
T	F	T
F	T	T
F	F	F

3. Valid
5. Invalid
7. Valid
9. The specific argument is

$$D \rightarrow (E \rightarrow S)$$
$$-S$$
$$\therefore E \rightarrow \sim D$$

A truth table for the corresponding argument form is given on the next page. Lines 4, 6, and 8 show that the argument is valid.

d	e	s	$\sim d$	$\sim s$	$e \to s$	$d \to (e \to s)$	$e \to \sim d$
T	T	T	F	F	T	T	F
T	T	F	F	T	F	F	F
T	F	T	F	F	T	T	T
T	F	F	F	T	T	T	T
F	T	T	T	F	T	T	T
F	T	F	T	T	F	T	T
F	F	T	T	F	T	T	T
F	F	F	T	T	T	T	T

11. Let B, R, Y be the statements: Bluejays finish first, Red Sox finish second, Yankees finish second. The argument is invalid.

$B \to R \vee Y$
$R \to \sim B$
$\therefore Y \to B$

13. Let A, B, C, D be the statements: Anderson is hired, Baker is hired, Collins resigns, Dickson is hired. The argument is valid.

$D \vee B \to C$
$A \vee B$
$\sim C$
$\therefore A$

23. Fill in the truth table and observe that columns 4 and 5 are identical.

p	q	$\sim p$	$p \to q$	$\sim p \vee q$
:	:	:	:	:

25. Contrapositive: If you cannot convert fractions to decimals flawlessly, then you do not own a calculator.
Converse: If you can convert fractions to decimals flawlessly, then you own a calculator.
Inverse: If you do not own a calculator, then you cannot convert fractions to decimals flawlessly.

27. "It is not the case that Wendy is not polite." "Wendy is polite."

29. "It is not the case that if Wendy is polite, then she is quiet." "Wendy is polite and (but) not quiet."

31. An appropriations bill will not be passed and Congress will not remain in session.

33. Claire will attend the meeting and she will not be elected treasurer.

35. Jim will not get a raise and will marry the boss's daughter, or Jim will get a raise and will not marry the boss's daughter. More idiomatically, "Jim will marry the boss's daughter and still not get a raise, or Jim will get a raise even though he will not marry the boss's daughter."

37. If $a \cdot b$ is even, then a is even or b is even.

41. You are to infer (incorrectly) that if you drink the advertised cola, then you will be convivial. Fallacy of affirming the consequent.

43. You are to infer (incorrectly) that if you do rent a car from Ajax, then your vacation will be carefree. Fallacy of denying the antecedent.

INDEX